Beginning ASP.NET in VB .NET: From Novice to Professional

MATTHEW MACDONALD

APress Media, LLC

Beginning ASP.NET in VB .NET: From Novice to Professional

Originally published by Apress in 2004

ISBN 978-1-59059-278-6 ISBN 978-1-4302-0710-8 (eBook)
DOI 10.1007/978-1-4302-0710-8

Technical Reviewer: Tim Verycruysse

Assistant Publisher: Grace Wong

Project Manager: Tracy Brown Collins

Copy Editor: Mark Nigara

Production Manager: Kari Brooks

Senior Production Editor: Kelly Winquist

Proofreader: Lori Bring

Compositor: Susan Glinert

Indexer: John Collin

Artist: Christine Calderwood, Kinetic Publishing Services, LLC

Cover Designer: Kurt Krames

Manufacturing Manager: Tom Debolski

For my loving wife Faria

Contents at a Glance

Contents

Chapter 16 The DataList, DataGrid, and Repeater 457

Chapter 17 Files, Streams, and E-mail 501

Chapter 18 Using XML 529

Part Four Web Services 569

Chapter 19 Web Services Architecture 571

About the Author

Matthew MacDonald is an author, educator, and MCSD developer. He's a regular contributor to programming journals such as *Inside Visual Basic*, and the author of over a dozen books about .NET programming, including *The Book of VB .NET* (No Starch), *ASP.NET: The Complete Reference* (Osborne McGraw-Hill), *Microsoft Visual Basic .NET Programmer's Cookbook* (Microsoft Press), and *Microsoft .NET Distributed Applications* (Microsoft Press). In a dimly remembered past life he studied English literature and theoretical physics.

Acknowledgments

NO AUTHOR COULD COMPLETE a book without a small army of helpful individuals. I'm deeply indebted to the whole Apress team, including Kelly Winquist and Tracy Brown Collins, who helped everything move swiftly and smoothly, Mark Nigara, who performed the copy edit, and many other individuals who worked behind the scenes indexing pages, drawing figures, and proofreading the final copy. I owe a special thanks to Gary Cornell, who always offers invaluable advice about projects and the publishing world. He's helped to build a truly unique company with Apress.

I'd also like to thank those who were involved with the first edition of this book at Osborne McGraw-Hill. These include Emma Acker and Jane Brownlow, who saw the book through its many stages and occasional growing pains, and Tim Verycruysse, who provided valuable technical review. In addition, I'd like to thank Julian Skinner, who provided additional feedback on some of the early chapters, and all the readers who caught errors, including Mark Nicholson, Steven Mandel, Uli Horn, Jason Schmidt, Jim Storey, and many more who took time out to report problems and ask good questions. This list is by no means complete!

Finally, I'd never write *any* book without the support of my wife and these special individuals: Nora, Razia, Paul, and Hamid. Thanks everyone!

Introduction

ASP (Active Server Pages) is a relatively new technology that has already leapt through several stages of evolution. It was introduced about seven years ago as an easy way to add dynamic content to ordinary web pages. Since then, it has grown into something much more ambitious: a platform for creating advanced web applications, including e-commerce shops, data-driven portal sites, and just about anything else you can find on the Internet.

ASP.NET is the latest version of ASP, and it represents the most dramatic change yet. With ASP.NET, developers no longer need to paste together a jumble of HTML and script code in order to program the Web. Instead, you can create full-scale *web applications* using nothing but code and a design tool like Visual Studio .NET. The cost of all this innovation is the learning curve. In order to get up to speed with ASP.NET, you'll need to learn a whole new programming language (Visual Basic .NET) and an entirely new way to write web pages.

Beginning ASP.NET in VB .NET: Novice to Pro assumes that you want to master ASP.NET, starting from the basics. Using this book, you'll build your knowledge until you understand the concepts, techniques, and best practices for writing sophisticated web applications. The journey is long, but it's also satisfying. At the end of the day, you'll find that ASP.NET allows you to tackle challenges that are simply out of reach on many other platforms. You'll also become a part of the fast-growing ASP.NET developer community.

About This Book

This book explores ASP.NET, which is a core part of Microsoft's new *.NET Framework*. The .NET Framework isn't a single application—it's actually a collection of different technologies bundled into one marketing term. The .NET Framework includes new languages like C# and VB .NET (the successor to Visual Basic 6), an engine for hosting programmable web pages and web services (ASP.NET), a new model for interacting with databases (ADO.NET), and a class library stocked with tools for everything from sending e-mail to encrypting a password. In order to master ASP.NET, you need to learn about each of these ingredients.

This book covers all these topics from the ground up. As a side effect, you'll find yourself learning many techniques that will interest any .NET developer, even those who create Windows applications. For example, you'll learn about component-based programming, structured error handling, and how to access files, XML, and relational databases. You'll also learn the key topics that are required for web programming, like state management, web controls, and web services. By the end of this book, you'll be ready to create your own rich web applications, and make them available over the Internet.

NOTE This book has a single goal: to be as relentlessly practical as possible. I take special care not to leave you hanging in the places where other ASP.NET books abandon their readers. For example, when encountering a new technology, you'll not only learn how it works, but why (and when) you should use it. I also highlight common questions and best practices with tip boxes and sidebars at every step of the way. Finally, if a topic is covered in this book, it's covered *correctly*. This means that you won't learn how to perform a task without learning about potential drawbacks and the problems you might run into—and how you can safeguard yourself with real-world code.

Who Should Read This Book

This book is aimed at anyone who wants to create dynamic websites with ASP.NET. Ideally, you'll have experience with a previous version of the Visual Basic or VBScript programming language. If not, you should be familiar with basic programming concepts (loops, conditional structures, arrays, and so on), whether you've learned them in Java, C, Pascal, Turing, or a completely different programming language. This is the only requirement for reading this book.

Understanding HTML will help, but it isn't required. ASP.NET works at a higher level, allowing you to deal with full-featured web controls instead of raw HTML. You also won't need any knowledge of XML, because Chapter 18 covers it in detail.

NOTE .NET is an entirely new programming framework, which means even experienced developers will feel a little like beginners. For that reason, this book begins with the fundamentals: VB .NET and C# syntax, the basics of object-oriented programming, and the philosophy of the .NET Framework. If you've never worked with Visual Basic before, you can spend a little more time with the syntax review in Chapter 2 to pick up everything you need to know. If you aren't familiar with the ideas of object-oriented programming, Chapter 3 fills in the blanks with a quick, but comprehensive review of the subject. The rest of the book builds on this foundation, from ASP.NET basics to advanced examples that show the techniques you'll use in real-world web applications.

What You Need to Read This Book

If you're just starting with ASP.NET, you should check that you have all the necessary ingredients to create, test, and host web applications.

- To develop on the .NET Framework, your computer requires Windows 2000, Windows XP, or Windows 2003 Server. You'll also need to install the optional IIS (Internet Information Services) component, as described in Chapter 2. Windows XP Home Edition is *not* supported.
- The only software you need to create ASP.NET applications is the .NET Framework. You can download the .NET SDK (software development kit) from `http://www.asp.net`. You can also order it on CD from the Microsoft Evaluation and Resource Center at `http://microsoft.order-2.com/developertools`. Finally, if you're using Visual Studio .NET, you don't need to install the .NET Framework separately.
- For best results, you should use Visual Studio. NET, which comes complete with countless productivity enhancements and indispensable timesavers. You don't need Visual Studio .NET to read this book and create ASP.NET applications, but you will find that it simplifies your life a great deal. Visual Studio .NET is available in numerous editions, including cheaper fixed-language and academic versions (see `http://msdn.microsoft.com/vstudio/productinfo` for more information). Chapter 8 describes everything you need to know about using Visual Studio .NET.

TIP If you don't have a copy of Visual Studio .NET, you can use the freely downloadable Web Matrix tool (available at `http://www.asp.net/webmatrix`). Web Matrix is very similar to Visual Studio .NET, although it uses a slightly different coding style than the one used in this book. However, in order to use this book's sample code with a minimum of trouble, you should use Visual Studio .NET.

Code Samples

In order to master ASP.NET, you need to experiment with it. One of the best ways to learn ASP.NET is to try out the code samples for this book, examine them, and dive in with your own modifications. To obtain the sample code, surf to `http://www.prosetech.com`. You'll also find some links to additional resources, and any updates or errata that affect the book.

VB or C#?

ASP.NET applications can be designed with almost any .NET language, including Visual Basic .NET, C#, or J#. This book describes the syntax for Microsoft's most popular language, Visual Basic .NET. VB .NET represents the natural migration path for existing ASP developers who are familiar with VBScript or developers who have worked with a previous version of Visual Basic. But as you'll discover in first chapter, all .NET languages are created equal, and VB .NET and C# match features blow-for-blow, with only a few minor discrepancies.

ASP.NET 1.1

The .NET Framework is currently available in two versions: the original version 1.0 (released in 2002), and version 1.1 (released in 2003). There are very few noticeable differences between the two versions, because 1.1 mainly consists of minor bug fixes and performance enhancements. You can use this book to program with either version of .NET. Any differences are clearly highlighted in the text.

Visual Studio .NET, the professional design tool I recommend for creating ASP.NET websites, also exists in two versions. Visual Studio .NET 2002 is designed to work with .NET 1.0, while Visual Studio .NET 2003 supports .NET 1.1. Although VS .NET 2002 and VS .NET 2003 are very similar, they use a different format for project and solution files. The code samples for this book include VS .NET 2002 project files, which you can open in either version of Visual Studio .NET. For more information, consult the readme.txt file included with the code download.

TIP Before you can open a web project with Visual Studio .NET, you'll need to understand how to create virtual directories. For that reason, I recommend that you read Chapter 5 before you attempt to install the sample code.

Contents Overview

This book is divided into six parts. Unless you've already had experience with the .NET Framework, the most productive way to read this book is in order from start to finish. Chapters later in the book sometimes incorporate features that were introduced earlier in order to create more well-rounded and realistic examples. On the other hand, if you're already familiar with the .NET platform, the Visual Basic .NET language, and object-oriented programming, you'll be able to make short work of the first part of this book.

Part One: ASP.NET Introduction

You could start coding an ASP.NET application right away by following the examples in the second part of this book. But in order to really master ASP.NET, you need to understand a few fundamental concepts about the .NET Framework.

Chapter 1 sorts through the Microsoft jargon, and explains what the .NET Framework really does, and why we need it. Chapter 2 gets you started with ASP.NET and IIS (Internet Information Services), the web hosting software that's built into the Windows operating system. You'll learn the steps needed to install the software and create virtual directories. Next, Chapter 3 introduces you to VB .NET with a comprehensive language reference, and Chapter 4 explains the basics of modern object-oriented programming with VB .NET.

Part Two: Developing ASP.NET Applications

The second part of this book delves into the heart of ASP.NET programming, and introduces its new event-based model. In Chapter 5, you'll learn how to organize multiple web forms into an ASP.NET application. In Chapter 6 and Chapter 7, you'll learn how to program a web page's user interface through a layer of objects called *server controls*. You'll also see some of the most remarkable ASP.NET controls, like the full-featured Calendar and the new input validators in Chapter 9.

The second part also explores the fundamentals of ASP.NET programming. Chapter 8 introduces the Visual Studio .NET design environment. Chapter 10 describes different strategies for state management, and Chapter 11 presents different techniques for handling errors. Finally, Chapter 12 walks you through the steps for deploying your application to a web server. Taken together, these chapters contain all the core concepts you need to design web pages and create a basic ASP.NET website.

Part Three: Working with Data

Almost all software needs to work with data, and web applications are no exception. Chapter 13 begins your exploration into the world of data by considering ADO.NET—Microsoft's new technology for interacting with relational databases. Chapter 14 demonstrates practical ADO.NET code. Chapter 15 and Chapter 16 explain how to use data binding and the advanced ASP.NET data controls to create web pages that integrate attractive, customizable data displays with automatic support for paging, sorting, and editing.

Chapter 17 moves out of the database world and considers how to interact with files and send e-mail. Chapter 18 broadens the picture even further, and describes how ASP.NET applications can use the XML support that's built into the .NET Framework.

Part Four: Web Services

Web services are an entirely new introduction in ASP.NET, and one of Microsoft's most heavily promoted new technologies. Using web services, you can share pieces of functionality on your web server with other applications on other computers. Best of all, the whole process works with open standards like XML, thereby ensuring that applications written in different programming languages and running on different operating systems can interact without a hitch.

Chapter 19 presents an overview of web service technology. Chapter 20 shows how to create a basic web service, and then enhance it with caching, custom objects, and transactions. Chapter 21 shows how to use your web service in another web or Windows application, and presents a sample page that interacts with Microsoft's TerraService over the Internet.

Part Five: Advanced ASP.NET

This part includes the advanced topics you can use to take your web applications that extra step. Chapter 22 and Chapter 23 consider how you can create reusable components and web controls for ASP.NET applications. Chapter 24 demonstrates how a careful use of caching can boost the performance of almost any web application. Chapter 25 explains how to use different security models to safeguard your site or provide subscription services.

Chapter 26 shifts focus to the IBuySpy case studies. Microsoft provides these full-featured sample sites to demonstrate the best way to design an e-commerce application and web portal. Though they are incredibly useful examples, they're also hard to understand at first glance, and they provide little developer documentation. Chapter 26 dissects the IBuySpy samples, and shows how they use the concepts and features demonstrated throughout this book.

Part Six: ASP.NET Reference

The last part of this book provides a detailed reference for web controls and the configuration files. Chapter 27 and Chapter 28 list each web control with its picture, control tag, and list of properties. Chapter 29 dissects every setting in the ASP.NET configuration files. You can turn to these chapters once you've learned the ASP.NET basics for quick, at-a-glance information.

Feedback

This book has the ambitious goal of being the best tutorial and reference for ASP.NET. Toward that end, your comments and suggestions are extremely helpful. You can send complaints, adulation, and everything in between directly to `apress@prosetech.com`. I can't solve your ASP.NET problems or critique your own code, but I will benefit from information about what this book did right and wrong (and what it may have done in an utterly confusing way). You can also send comments about the website support for this book to the same address.

Part One

ASP.NET Introduction

CHAPTER 1

The .NET Framework

ONCE AGAIN, Microsoft is doing what it does best: creating innovative new technologies and wrapping them in marketing terms that cause widespread confusion. Just as developers are finally sorting out buzzwords like ActiveX and Windows DNA (Distributed interNet Architecture), Microsoft has created a whole new collection of jargon revolving around .NET. So exactly what does it all mean?

This chapter examines the technologies that underlie .NET. First, you'll take a quick look at the history of web development, and learn why the .NET Framework was created. Next, you'll get a high-level overview of the different parts of .NET, and see how ASP.NET fits into the wider world of development—and Microsoft's long-term plans.

The Evolution of Web Development

The Internet began in the late 1960s as an experiment. Its goal was to create a truly resilient information network—one that could withstand the loss of several computers without preventing the others from communicating. Driven by potential disaster scenarios (such as nuclear attack), the U.S. Department of Defense provided the initial funding.

The early Internet was mostly limited to educational institutions and defense contractors. It flourished as a tool for academic collaboration, allowing researchers across the globe to share information. In the early 1990s, modems were created that could work over existing phone lines, and the Internet began to open up to commercial users. In 1993, the first HTML browser was created, and the Internet revolution began.

HTML and HTML Forms

It would be difficult to describe early websites as web applications. Instead, the first generation of websites often looked more like brochures, consisting mostly of fixed HTML pages that needed to be updated by hand.

A basic HTML page is a little like a word-processing document—it contains formatted content that can be displayed on your computer, but it doesn't actually *do* anything. The following example shows HTML at its simplest, with a document that contains a heading and single line of text:

```
<html>
    <body>
        <h1>Sample Web Page Heading</h1>
        <p>This is a sample web page.</p>
    </body>
</html>
```

There are two types of content in an HTML document: your text, and the tags that tell the browser how to format it. The tags are easily recognizable, because they occur inside angled brackets (< >). The HTML language defines tags for different levels of headings, paragraphs, hyperlinks, italic and bold formatting, horizontal lines, and so on. For example, <h1>Some Text</h1> tells the browser to display "Some Text" in the Heading 1 style, which uses a large boldface font. Figure 1-1 shows the simple HTML page in a browser.

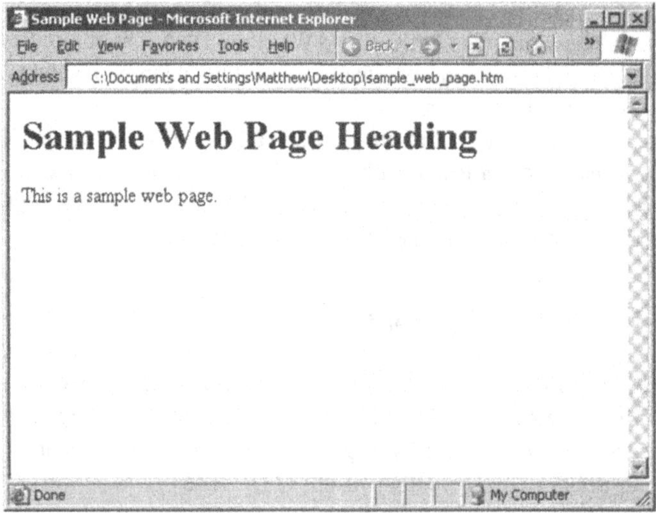

Figure 1-1. Static HTML: the "brochure" site

TIP You don't need to master HTML to program ASP.NET web pages, although it's often useful. For a quick introduction to HTML, refer to one of the excellent HTML tutorials on the Internet, such as `http://www.w3schools.com/html` or `http://archive.ncsa.uiuc.edu/General/Internet/WWW/HTMLPrimer.html`.

HTML 2.0 introduced the first seed of web programming with a technology called *HTML forms*. HTML forms expand the HTML language so that it includes not only formatting tags, but also tags for graphical widgets, or *controls*. These controls include common ingredients like drop-down lists, text boxes, and buttons. Here's a sample web page created with HTML form controls:

```
<html>
    <body>
        <form>
            <input type="checkbox">This is choice #1<br>
            <input type="checkbox">This is choice #2<br><br>
            <input type="submit" value="Submit">
        </form>
    </body>
</html>
```

In an HTML form, all the controls are placed between the <form> and </form> tags. The preceding example includes two check boxes (represented by the <input type="checkbox"> tag) and a button (represented by the <input type="submit"> tag). In a browser, this takes the appearance shown in Figure 1-2.

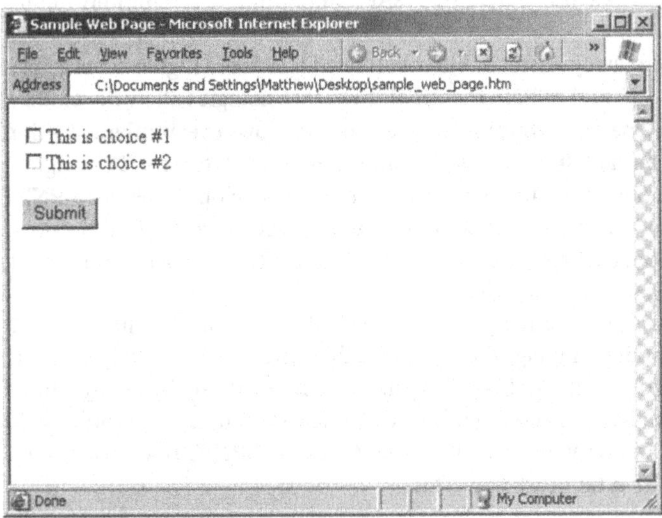

Figure 1-2. An HTML form

HTML forms allow web application developers to design standard input pages. When the user clicks the Submit button in the page shown in the previous example, all the data in the input controls (in this case, the two check boxes) is patched together into one long string and sent to the web server. On the server side, a custom application receives and processes the data. Amazingly enough, the controls that were created for HTML forms ten years ago are still the basic foundation that you'll use to build dynamic ASP.NET pages! The difference is the type of application that runs on the server side. In the past, when the user clicked a button on a form page, the information might have been emailed to a set account, or sent to an application on the server that used the challenging *CGI* (Common Gateway Interface) standard. Today, you'll work with the much more capable and elegant ASP.NET platform.

Server-Side Programming

In order to understand why ASP.NET was created, it helps to understand the problems of other web development technologies. CGI applications, for example, don't scale very well, which means they are hard pressed to support a large number of users. With a CGI application, the web server must launch a completely separate instance of the application for each web request. If the website is popular, the web server must struggle under the weight of hundreds of separate copies of the application, eventually becoming a victim of its own success. CGI applications also fare poorly when creating complex, integrated websites. Instead, CGI is best suited for "quick-and-dirty" website programming—in other words, when adding a couple of frills to a mostly static website.

To counter these problems, Microsoft developed *ISAPI* (Internet Server Application Programming Interface), a higher-level programming model. ISAPI solved the performance problem, but at the cost of significant complexity. Even after ISAPI developers master the tricky C++ programming language, they still lie awake at night worrying about confounding issues like multithreading. ISAPI programming is definitely not for the faint of heart.

ISAPI never really went away. Instead, Microsoft used it to build higher-level development platforms, like ASP and ASP.NET. Both of these technologies allow developers to program dynamic web pages without worrying about the low-level implementation details. For that reason, both platforms have become incredibly successful. The original ASP platform garnered a huge audience of nearly one million developers. When ASP.NET was released, it generated even more interest as the centerpiece of the .NET Framework. In fact, ASP.NET was enthusiastically put to work in dozens of large-scale commercial websites even when it was only in late beta.

Despite having similar underpinnings, ASP and ASP.NET are radically different. ASP is a script-based programming language that requires a thorough understanding of HTML, and a good deal of painful coding. ASP.NET, on the other hand, is an object-oriented programming model that lets you put together a web page as easily as you would build a Windows application. In many respects, it's easier to learn ASP.NET than to master ASP, even though ASP.NET is far more powerful.

Client-Side Programming

At the same time that server-side web development was moving through an alphabet soup of technologies, a new type of programming was gaining popularity. Developers began to experiment with the different ways they could enhance web pages by embedding multimedia and miniature applets built with JavaScript, DHTML (Dynamic HTML), and Java code. These client-side technologies don't involve any server processing. Instead, the complete application is downloaded to the client browser, which executes it locally.

The greatest problem with client-side technologies is that they aren't supported equally by all browsers and operating systems. One of the reasons that web development is so popular in the first place is because web applications don't require setup CDs, downloads, and other tedious (and error-prone) deployment steps. Instead, a web application can be used on any computer that has Internet access. But when developers use client-side technologies, they encounter a few familiar headaches. Suddenly, cross-browser compatibility becomes a problem. Developers are forced to test their websites with different operating systems and browsers, and they might even need to distribute browser updates to their clients. In other words, the client-side model sacrifices some of the most important benefits of web development.

For that reason, ASP.NET is designed as a server-side technology. All ASP.NET code executes on the server. When the code is finished executing, the user receives an ordinary HTML page, which can be viewed in any browser. Figure 1-3 shows the difference between the server-side and client-side model.

There are other reasons for avoiding client-side programming. These include the following:

- **Isolation.** Client-side code can't access server-side resources. For example, there's no easy way for a client-side application to read a file or interact with a database on the server.

- **Security.** Client-side code can be viewed by the end user. And once users understand how an application works, they can tamper with it.

- **Thin clients.** As the Internet continues to evolve, new web-enabled devices like mobile phones, palmtop computers, and PDAs are appearing. These devices can communicate with web servers, but they don't support all the features of a traditional browser. Thin clients can use server-based web applications, but they won't support client-side features like JavaScript.

In some cases, ASP.NET allows you to combine the best of client-side programming with server-side programming. For example, the best ASP.NET controls can intelligently detect the features of the client browser. If the browser supports JavaScript, these controls will return a web page that incorporates JavaScript for a richer, more responsive user interface. However, no matter what the capabilities of the browser, *your* code is always executed on the server.

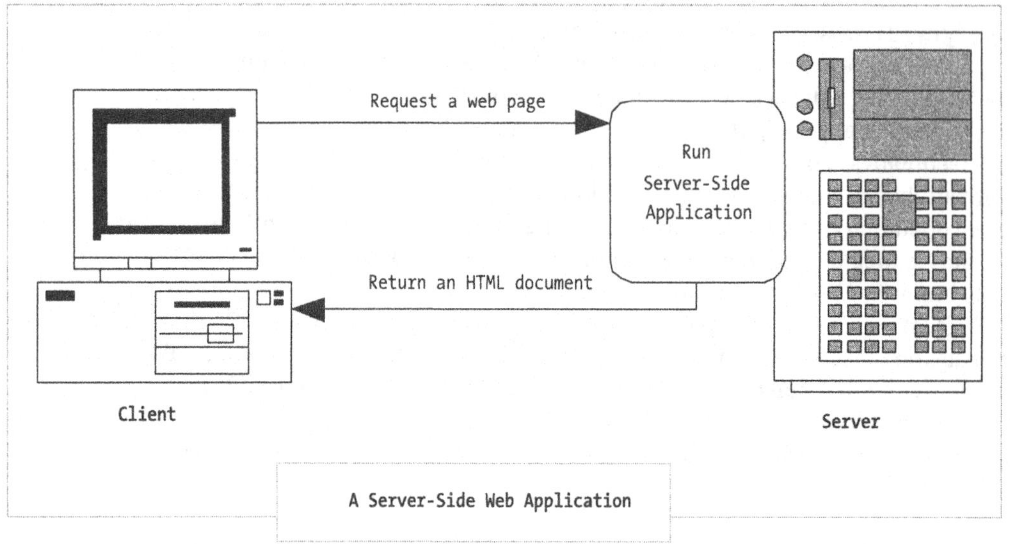

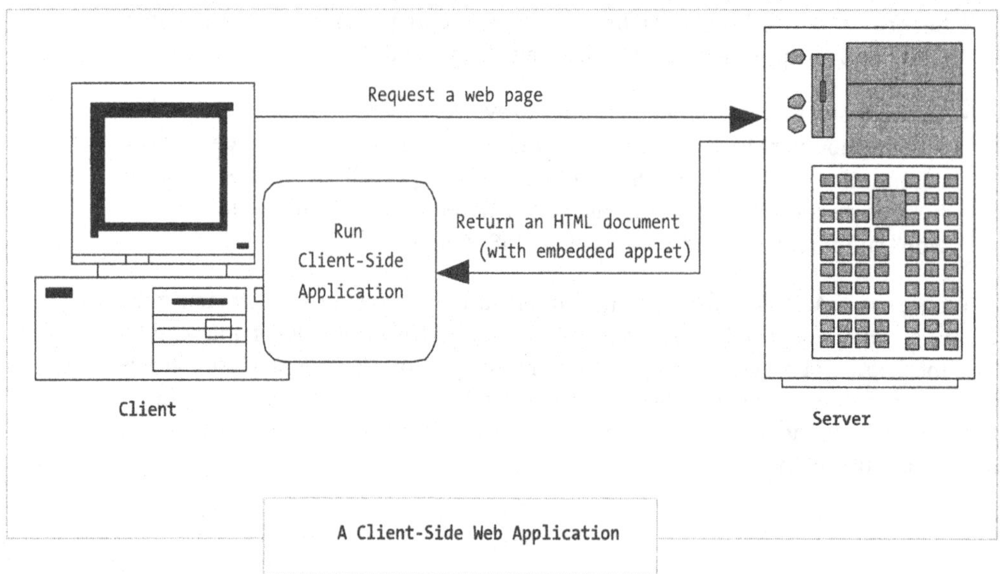

Figure 1-3. Server-side and client-side web applications

The Problems with ASP

The original ASP became more popular than even Microsoft had anticipated, and it wasn't long before it was being wedged into all sorts of unusual places, including mission-critical business applications and highly trafficked e-commerce sites. Because ASP hadn't been designed with these uses in mind, a number of problems began to appear. What began as a simple solution for creating interactive web pages became a complicated discipline that required knowledge in several fields as well as some painful experience.

If you've programmed with ASP before, you may already be familiar with some or all of these problems. They include the following:

- **Scripting limitations.** ASP applications rely on the VBScript language, which suffers from a number of limitations, including poor performance. To overcome these problems, developers usually need to add separately developed components, which add a new layer of complexity. In ASP.NET, web pages are designed in a modern .NET language, not a scripting language.

- **No application structure.** ASP code is inserted directly into a web page along with the HTML markup. The resulting tangle of code and HTML has nothing in common with today's modern, object-oriented languages. As a result, web form code can rarely be reused or modified without hours of effort.

- **Headaches with deployment and configuration.** Because of the way COM works, you can't easily update the components your website uses. Often, you need to manually stop and restart the server, which just isn't practical on a live website. Changing configuration options can be just as ugly. ASP.NET introduces a slew of new features to allow websites to be dynamically updated and reconfigured.

- **State limitations.** One of ASP's strongest features is its integrated session state facility, which allows you to retain temporary information about each client on the web server. However, session state is useless in scenarios where a website is hosted by several separate web servers. In this scenario, a client might access server B while its session information is trapped on server A and essentially abandoned. ASP.NET corrects this problem by allowing state to be stored in a central repository, such as a separate process or a database that all servers can access.

ASP.NET deals with these problems (and many more) by introducing a completely new model for web pages. This model is based on a remarkable new piece of technology called the .NET Framework.

The .NET Framework

The first thing that you should understand about the .NET Framework is that .NET is really a cluster of different technologies. These technologies include the following:

- **The .NET languages.** These include C# and Visual Basic .NET, the object-oriented and modernized successor to Visual Basic 6.0, as well as JScript .NET (a server-side version of JavaScript) and J# (a Java clone).
- **The CLR (Common Language Runtime).** The CLR is the engine that executes all .NET programs and provides automatic services for these applications, such as security checking, memory management, and optimization.
- **The .NET class library.** The class library collects thousands of pieces of prebuilt functionality that you can "snap in" to your applications. These features are sometimes organized into technology sets, such as ADO.NET (the technology for creating database applications) and Windows Forms (the technology for creating desktop user interfaces).
- **ASP.NET.** This is the engine that hosts web applications and web services, with almost any feature from the .NET class library. ASP.NET also includes a set of web-specific services.
- **Visual Studio .NET.** This optional development tool contains a rich set of productivity and debugging features. The Visual Studio .NET setup CD includes the complete .NET Framework.

The division between these components sometimes isn't clear. For example, ASP.NET is sometimes used in a very narrow sense to refer to the portion of the .NET class library used to design web pages. On the other hand, ASP.NET is also used to refer to the whole topic of .NET web applications, which includes .NET languages and many fundamental pieces of the class library that aren't web-specific. (That's generally the way that the term is used in this book. Our exhaustive examination of ASP.NET includes .NET basics, the VB .NET language, and topics that any .NET developer could use, such as component-based programming and database access.)

The .NET class library and CLR—the two fundamental parts of .NET—are shown in Figure 1-4.

The Confusion Behind .NET

Some developers have hesitated to embrace .NET because they believe they will be forced to subscribe to Microsoft's .NET Building Block Services (formerly called My Services and Hailstorm). These services, which are built on the .NET foundation, allow developers to use centralized user authentication, information, and notification services—for a cost. The debate over the validity of .NET Building Block Services is heated, but it really has little to do with ASP.NET development. You certainly won't need to use (or even understand) any part of the .NET Building Block Services product to create full-featured websites. In fact, at the time of this writing, version 1.1 of the .NET Framework is in widespread use, but the .NET Building Block Services still haven't been released, and their features still haven't been finalized.

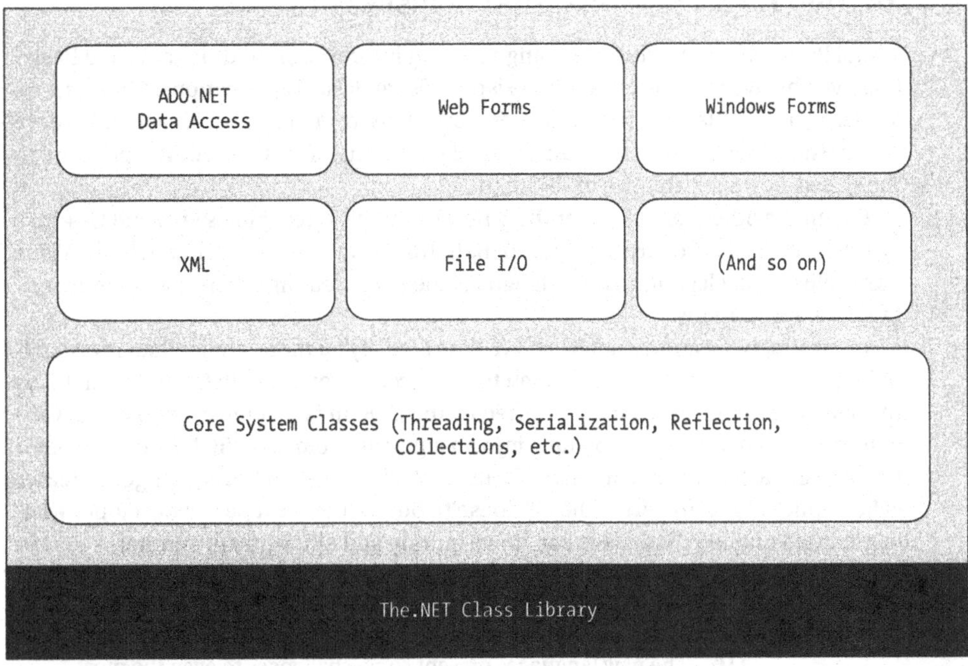

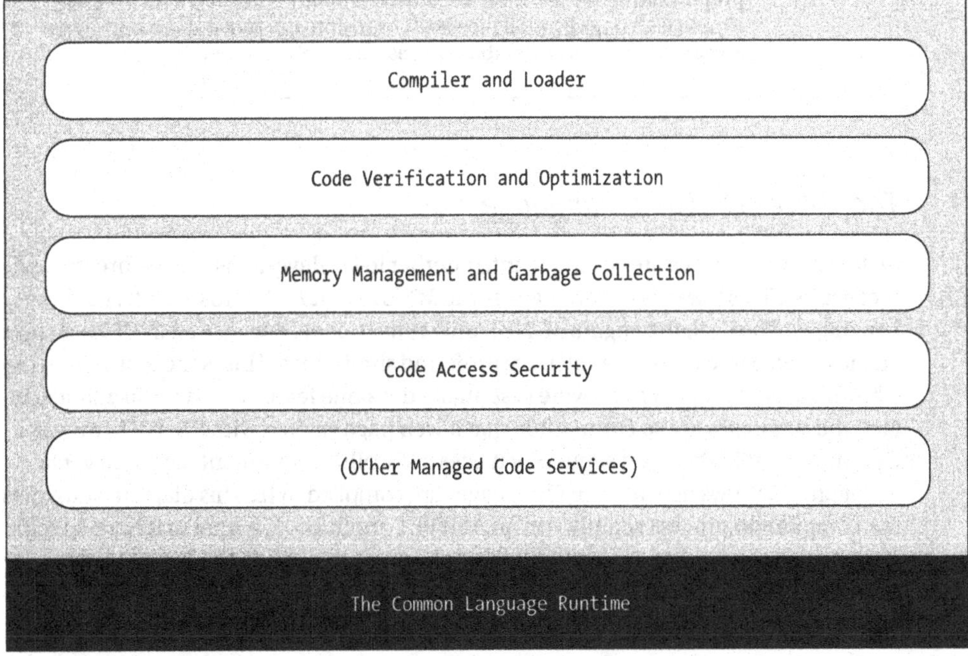

Figure 1-4. The .NET Framework

VB .NET, C#, and the .NET Languages

Visual Basic .NET is a redesigned language that improves on traditional Visual Basic, and even breaks compatibility with existing Visual Basic 6 applications. Migrating to Visual Basic .NET is a stretch—and a process of discovery for most seasoned VB developers. The change is even more dramatic if you're an ASP or Office developer used to the scaled-down capabilities of VBScript.

C#, on the other hand, is an entirely new language. It resembles Java and C++ in syntax, but there is no direct migration path from Java or C++. In short, C#, like Visual Basic .NET, is an elegant, modern language ideal for creating the next generation of business applications.

Interestingly, C# and Visual Basic .NET are actually far more similar than Java and C# or Visual Basic 6 and VB .NET. Though the syntax is different, both C# and VB .NET use the .NET class library and are supported by the CLR. In fact, almost any block of C# code can be translated, line-by-line, into an equivalent block of VB .NET code. There is the occasional language difference (for example, VB .NET supports a language feature called optional parameters while C# doesn't), but for the most part, a developer who has learned one .NET language can move quickly and efficiently to another.

TIP The new languages present some challenges to even the most experienced of developers. In Chapters 3 and 4, you'll sort through the new syntax of Visual Basic .NET and learn the basics of object-oriented programming. By learning the fundamentals before you start creating simple web pages, you'll face less confusion and move more rapidly to advanced topics like database access and web services.

The Intermediate Language

All the .NET languages are compiled into another lower-level language before the code is executed. This lower-level language is the *MSIL* or just *IL* (Microsoft Intermediate Language). The CLR, the engine of .NET, only runs IL code. Because all .NET languages are designed based on IL, they all have profound similarities. This is the reason that the C# and VB .NET languages provide essentially the same features and performance. In fact, the languages are so compatible that a web page written with VB .NET can use a C# component in the exact same way it uses a VB .NET component, and vice versa.

Figure 1-5 shows how the .NET languages are compiled to IL. This diagram simplifies the compilation process slightly—in an ASP.NET application, a final machine-specific executable is created and cached on the web server to provide the best possible performance.

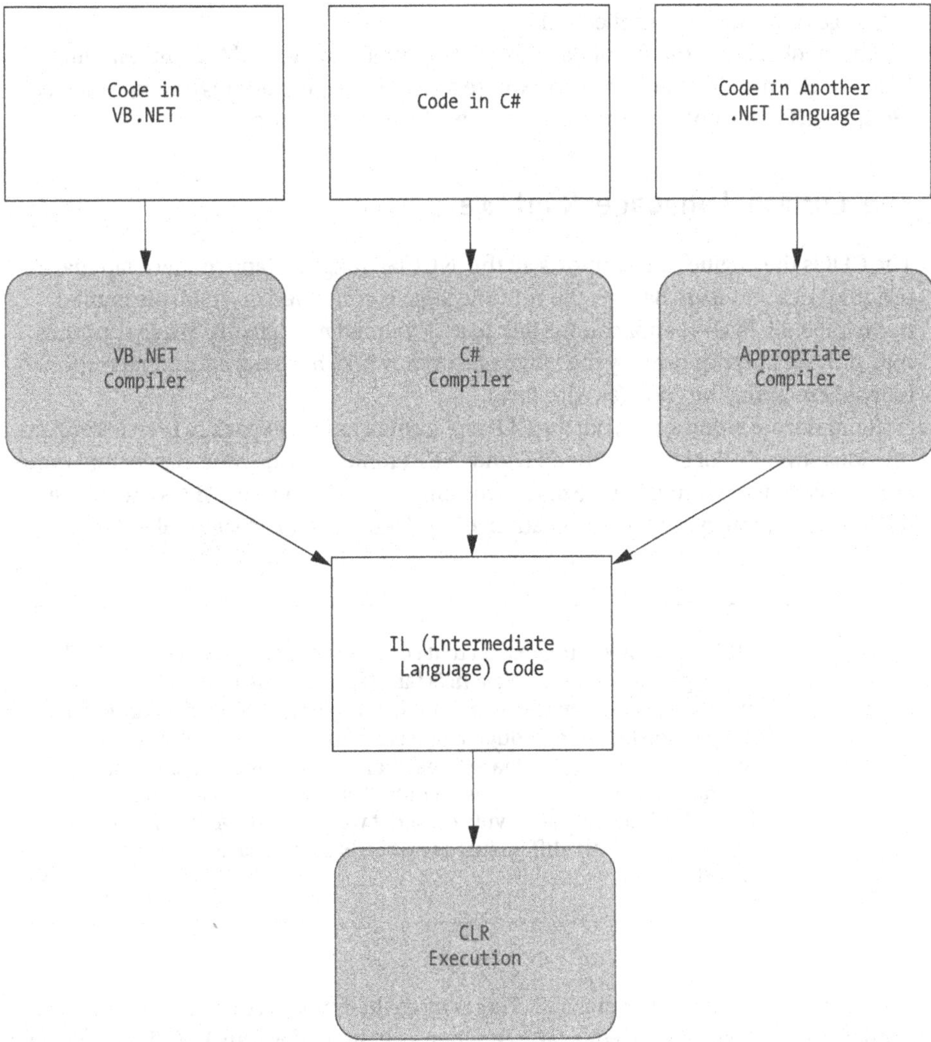

Figure 1-5. Language compilation in .NET

Other .NET Languages

C# and VB .NET aren't the only choices for ASP.NET development. Version 1.0 of the .NET Framework shipped with three languages: VB .NET, C#, and JScript .NET. In version 1.1, the .NET Framework added J#, a language with Java-like syntax. When creating an ASP.NET web application, you can use any of these languages. You can even use a .NET language provided by a third-party developer, such as a .NET version of Eiffel or Perl. This increasing range of language choices is possible because Microsoft has released a set of guidelines called the *CLS* (Common Language Specifications), which define basic requirements and standards that allow other companies to write languages that can be compiled to IL.

This book focuses on Visual Basic .NET. Once you understand the fundamentals of the .NET Framework, you're free to explore other languages, although some (such as JScript .NET) may not support the full range of possible features.

The Common Language Runtime

The CLR is the engine that supports all the .NET languages. Many modern languages use runtimes. In Visual Basic 6, the runtime logic is contained in a DLL file named msvbvm60.dll. In C++, applications link to a file named mscrt40.dll. These runtimes may provide libraries used by the language, or they may have the additional responsibility of executing the code (as with Java).

Runtimes are nothing new, but the CLR represents a radical departure from Microsoft's previous strategy. For starters, the CLR and .NET Framework are much larger and more ambitious than the Visual Basic 6 or C++ runtimes. The CLR also provides a whole set of related services such as code verification, optimization, and garbage collection.

NOTE The CLR is the reason that some developers have accused .NET of being a Java clone. The claim is fairly silly. It's true that .NET is quite similar to Java in key respects (both use a special managed environment and provide features through a rich class library), but it's also true that every programming language "steals" and improves from previous programming languages. This includes Java, which adopted parts of the C/C++ language and syntax when it was created. Of course, in many other aspects .NET differs just as radically from Java as it does from VBScript.

All .NET code runs inside the CLR. This is true whether you're running a Windows application or a web service. For example, when a client requests an ASP.NET web page, the ASP.NET service runs inside the CLR environment, executes your code, and creates a final HTML page to send to the client.

The implications of the CLR are wide-ranging:

- **Deep language integration.** C# and VB .NET, like all .NET languages, compile to a special language called IL. In other words, the CLR makes no distinction between different languages—in fact, it has no way of knowing what language was used to create an executable. This is far more than mere language compatibility; it's language *integration*.

- **Side-by-side execution.** The CLR also has the ability to load more than one version of a component at a time. In other words, you can update a component many times, and the correct version will be loaded and used for each application. As a side effect, multiple versions of the .NET Framework can be installed, meaning that you'll be able to upgrade to new versions of ASP.NET without replacing the current version or needing to rewrite your applications.
- **Fewer errors.** Whole categories of errors are impossible with the CLR. For example, the CLR prevents the wide variety of memory mistakes that are possible with lower-level languages like C++. For Visual Basic programmers, many of these advantages are nothing new—they're similar to features of the traditional VB environment.

Along with these truly revolutionary benefits, there are some other potential drawbacks. The following are three issues that are often raised by new developers, but aren't always answered:

- **Performance.** A typical ASP.NET application is much faster than a comparable ASP application, because ASP.NET code is compiled natively. However, other .NET applications probably won't match the blinding speed of well-written C++ code, because the CLR imposes some additional overhead. Generally, this is only a factor in a few performance-critical high-workload applications (like real-time games). With high-volume web applications, the potential bottlenecks are rarely processor-related, but are usually tied to the speed of an external resource such as a database or the web server's file system. With ASP.NET caching and some well-written database code, you can ensure excellent performance for any web application.
- **Code transparency.** The IL language is much easier to disassemble, meaning that if you distribute a compiled application or component, other programmers may have an easier time determining how your code works. This isn't much of an issue for ASP.NET applications, which aren't distributed, but are hosted on a secure web server.
- **Cross-platform support?** No one is entirely sure whether .NET will be adopted for use on other operating systems and platforms. Ambitious projects, like Mono (.NET on Linux) are currently underway (see `http://www.go-mono.com`). However, .NET will probably never have the wide reach of a language like Java because it incorporates too many different platform-specific and operating system–specific technologies and features.

The .NET Class Library

The .NET class library is a giant repository of classes that provide prefabricated functionality for everything from reading an XML file to sending an email message. If you've had any exposure to Java, you may already be familiar with the idea of a class library. However, the .NET class library is more ambitious and comprehensive than just about any other programming framework. Any .NET language can use the .NET class library's features by interacting with the right objects. This helps encourage consistency among different .NET languages and removes the need to install numerous separate components on your computer or web server.

Some parts of the class library include features you'll never need to use in web applications (such as the classes used to create desktop applications with the Windows interface). Other parts of the class library are targeted directly at web development, like those used for web services and web pages. Still more classes can be used in a number of different programming scenarios, and aren't specific to web or Windows development. These include the base set of classes that define common variable types, and the classes for data access, to name just a few.

You'll explore the .NET Framework throughout this book. In the meantime, here are some general characteristics of the .NET Framework:

- **Open standards.** Microsoft currently provides programming tools that allow you to work with many open standards, such as XML. In .NET, however, many of these standards are "baked in" to the framework. For example, ADO.NET (Microsoft's data access technology) uses XML natively, behind the scenes. Similarly, web services work automatically through XML and HTTP. This deep integration of open standards makes cross-platform work much easier.

- **Emphasis on infrastructure.** Microsoft's philosophy is that they will provide the tedious infrastructure so that application developers only need to write business-specific code. For example, the .NET Framework automatically handles files, databases, and transactions. You just add the logic needed for your specific application.

- **Disconnected model.** The .NET Framework emphasizes distributed and Internet applications. Technologies like ADO.NET are designed from the ground up to be scalable even when used by hundreds or thousands of simultaneous users.

Visual Studio .NET

The last part of .NET is the optional Visual Studio .NET editor, which provides a rich environment where you can rapidly create advanced applications. You don't need to use Visual Studio .NET to create web applications. In fact, you might be tempted to use the freely downloadable .NET Framework and a simple text editor to create ASP.NET web pages and web services. However, in doing so you'll multiply your work, and you'll have a much harder time debugging, organizing, and maintaining your code.

Some of the features of Visual Studio .NET include the following:

- **Page design.** You can create an attractive page with drag-and-drop ease using Visual Studio .NET's integrated web form designer. There's no need to understand HTML.

- **Automatic error detection.** You could save hours of work when Visual Studio .NET detects and reports an error before you run your application. Potential problems are underlined, just like the "spell-as-you-go" feature found in many word processors.
- **Debugging tools.** Visual Studio .NET retains its legendary debugging tools, which allow you to watch your code in action and track the contents of variables.
- **IntelliSense.** Visual Studio .NET provides statement completion for recognized objects, and automatically lists information such as function parameters in helpful tooltips.

I recommend Visual Studio .NET highly. However, in this book you'll start with the basics of ASP.NET, code behind, and web-control development using the Notepad text editor. This is the best way to get a real sense of what is happening behind the scenes. Once you understand how ASP.NET works, you can quickly master Visual Studio .NET, which is introduced in Chapter 8. I hope you'll use Visual Studio .NET for all the remaining examples, but if you prefer Notepad or a third-party tool like the freely downloadable Web Matrix, you can use that instead—with a little more typing required.

The Last Word

This chapter presented a high-level overview that gave you your first taste of some of the radical changes that will affect ASP.NET applications as well as some of the long-awaited improvements that are finally in place. But before you can get to work writing web pages, you need to continue with Chapter 2, which shows you how to prepare your computer with the Internet Information Services web hosting software.

CHAPTER 2

Setting Up Internet Information Services and ASP.NET

THE LAST CHAPTER GAVE a sweeping introduction to the .NET Framework. But before you start creating ASP.NET web pages and applications, you need to make sure that you have the correct environment on your computer.

In other words, before you dive into the theory and concepts of ASP.NET in any more detail, it's time to take care of a few easier tasks. In this chapter, you'll walk through the process of installing ASP.NET, configuring Internet Information Services (IIS), and creating virtual directories. These tasks are supported by wizards or graphical tools, so they don't require the same level of expertise as actual ASP.NET programming.

Web Servers and You

Web servers run special software to support mail exchange, FTP and HTTP access, and everything else clients need in order to access web content. In the Microsoft Windows operating system, the built-in IIS component plays this role, allowing any computer to become a web server.

In most cases, you won't be developing on the same computer that you use to host your website. If you were, you would hamper the performance of your web server by tying it up with development work. You would also frustrate clients if a buggy test application crashes the computer and leaves the website unavailable, or if you accidentally overwrite the deployed web application with a work in progress! Generally, you'll perfect your web application on another computer, and then copy all the files to the web server. This process of deployment is described in Chapter 12.

However, in order to use ASP.NET, your computer needs to *act* like a web server. In fact, while you're testing an ASP.NET application your development computer will work in exactly the same way as it would over an Internet connection to a remote client. When you test a page, you'll actually request it through IIS, and receive the rendered HTML over an HTTP channel. The only difference between the way your computer works while testing the website and the way a web server behaves when the application is deployed is that your computer won't be visible and accessible to remote clients on the Internet.

This configuration allows you to perfect your security model and perform realistic testing on your development computer. The drawback is that you need to have the IIS web hosting software on your computer in order to test an ASP.NET website. IIS is included with Windows 2000, Windows XP, and Windows 2003 Server, but it's an optional component and it isn't installed by default. To create ASP.NET programs successfully, you need to make sure IIS is installed before you install the .NET Framework or Visual Studio .NET.

Installing Internet Information Services

Installing IIS is easy. Here are the steps you follow on a Windows 2000 or Windows XP computer:

1. Click Start, and select Settings ➤ Control Panel.
2. Choose Add or Remove Programs.
3. Click Add/Remove Windows Components.
4. If Internet Information Services is checked (see Figure 2-1), you already have this component installed. Otherwise, click it and click Next to install the required IIS files. You'll probably need to have your Windows setup CD handy.

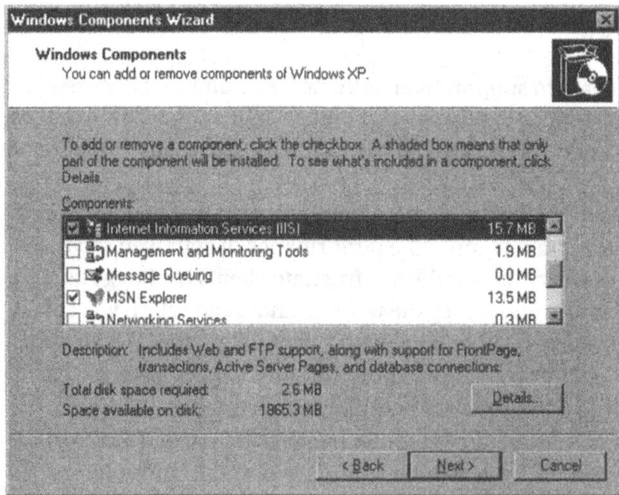

Figure 2-1. Installing Internet Information Services

If you're using Windows Server 2003, you can install IIS through the Add/Remove Windows Components dialog box, but it's more likely that you'll use the Manage Your Server wizard. Choose Add or Remove a Role when you start the wizard, and follow all the instructions. Choose the Web application server role to install IIS and the ASP.NET engine in one operation.

When IIS is installed, it automatically creates a directory named c:\Inetpub\wwwroot, which represents your website. Any files in this directory will appear as though they're in the root of your web server.

To test that IIS is installed correctly and running, browse to the c:\Inetpub\wwwroot directory and verify that it contains a file called localstart.asp. This is a simple ASP (not ASP.NET) file that is automatically installed with IIS. If you try to double-click this file to run it from the local directory, you'll receive an error message informing you that your computer doesn't know how to handle direct requests for ASP files (see Figure 2-2) or another program such as Microsoft FrontPage will try to open it for editing.

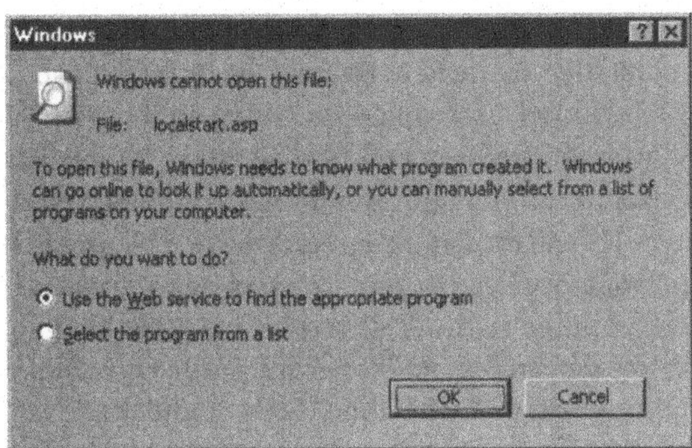

Figure 2-2. Attempting to open an ASP file through Windows Explorer

This limitation exists because of the way that ASP and ASP.NET files are processed. In a typical web scenario, IIS receives a request for a file. It then looks at the file extension and uses that to determine if the file should be allowed, and what program (if any) is required to handle it. Ordinary HTML files will be sent directly to your browser. ASP files, however, will be processed by the ASP service, which IIS will start automatically. The ASP service loads the requested file, runs the code it contains, and then creates the final HTML document, which it passes back to IIS. IIS then sends the HTML document to the client. The whole process, which is diagrammed in Figure 2-3, is quite similar to how ASP.NET files are processed, as you'll see later.

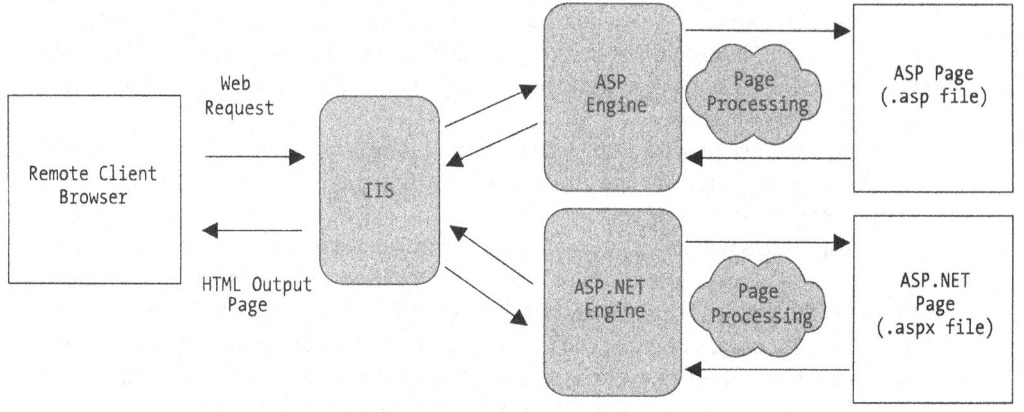

Figure 2-3. How IIS handles an ASP file request

In order to test that IIS is working correctly, you need to request the localstart.asp file through IIS, over the standard HTTP channel. You can do this using an Internet browser. Just open an application like Internet Explorer, and type a request for the file using the name of your computer. For example, if your computer's name is devtest, you would type http://devtest/localstart.asp. IIS will receive your request, ASP will process the file, and you'll receive a generic introductory page in your browser (see Figure 2-4).

If you don't know the name of your computer, right-click the My Computer icon either on your desktop or in Windows Explorer, and select Properties. Then, choose the Computer Name tab. The computer name is next to the heading "Full computer name." Alternatively, you can save some effort by using one of two presets that automatically refer to the local computer, whatever its name. These are the "loopback" address 127.0.0.1, and the alias localhost. That means you can try entering http://localhost/localstart.asp or http://127.0.0.1/localstart.asp on any computer to test if IIS is installed.

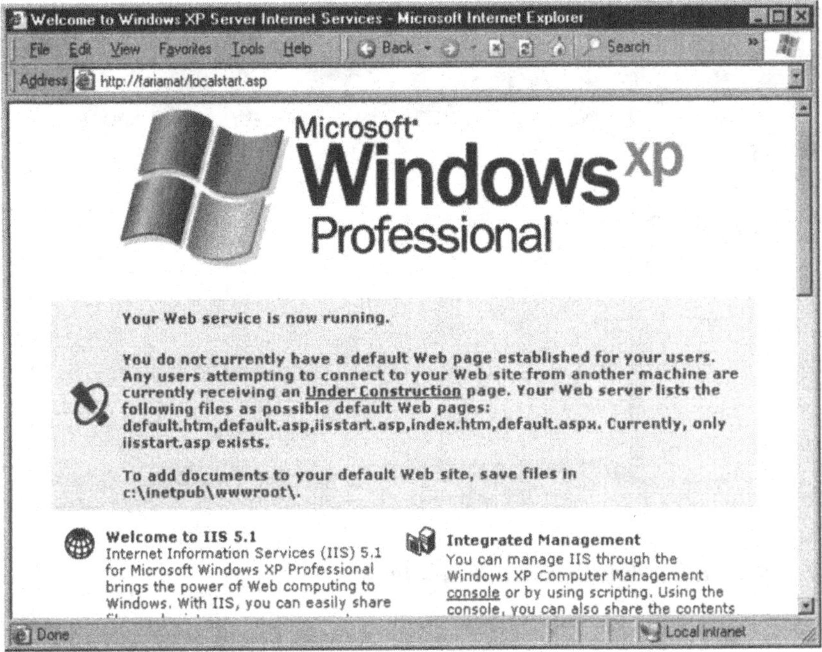

Figure 2-4. Requesting an ASP file through IIS

What If I Can't Connect?

If you try the previous steps, but receive an "Unable to connect" message, you may need to investigate further. Your first step is to check that IIS is installed correctly and enabled. To check this, you need to use a utility called IIS Manager by selecting Settings ➤ Control Panel ➤ Administrative Tools ➤ Internet Services Manager from the Start menu. You should see your computer listed under the Internet Information Services node in the tree. Expand this node, and click on the Websites folder. In the list on the right, it should indicate that your computer's default website is running, as shown in Figure 2-5. If not, try right-clicking the icon that represents your computer and choose to restart IIS.

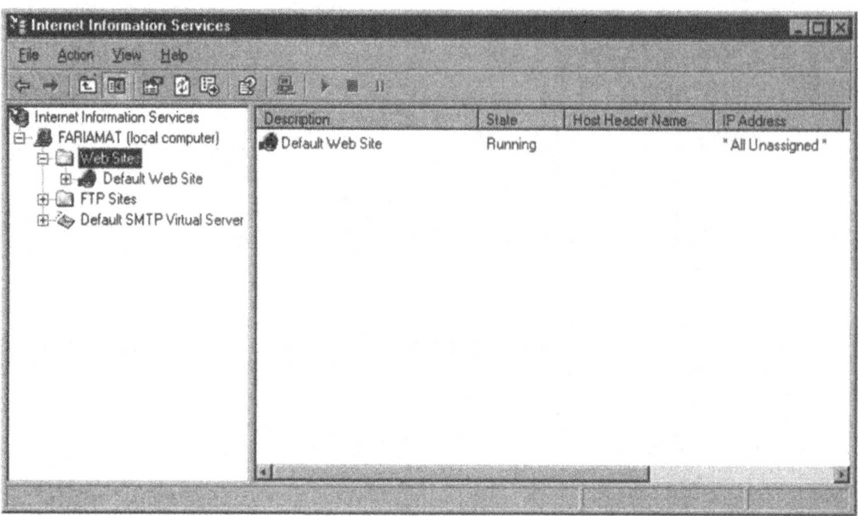

Figure 2-5. The default website is currently running

Lastly, you may need to tweak your Internet settings. For this task, choose Settings ➤ Control Panel ➤ Internet Options from the Start menu. Then choose the Connections tab. If you're working on a local network and have special proxy server settings applied, verify that they don't conflict with your computer by clicking the LAN Settings button.

If you connect to the Internet using a connection that isn't always present (such as a modem that connects over a telephone line), you may receive an error message that informs you that a local page cannot be loaded because you're currently working offline. In this case, just click Connect, and the page will appear successfully without you needing to actually connect to the Internet. To prevent this message from appearing, you can select Never Dial A Connection from the Connections tab, although this will not always stop the problem from reoccurring. If you're prevented from performing another operation (such as creating a web project in Visual Studio .NET) because the operating system believes you're offline, simply enter http://localhost/localstart.asp in a browser, and then click Connect when you're prompted to go online.

Managing Websites

To add more pages to your web server, you can copy HTML, ASP, or ASP.NET files directly to the c:\Intetpub\wwwroot directory. For example, if you add the file TestFile.html to this directory, you can request it in a browser through the URL http://localhost/TestFile.html. You can even create subdirectories to group together related resources. For example, the file c:\Intetpub\wwwroot\MySite\MyFile.html can be accessed through a browser using the URL http://localhost/MySite/MyFile.html. If you're using Visual Studio .NET to create new web projects, you'll find that it automatically generates new subdirectories in the wwwroot directory. So if you create a web application named WebApplication1, the files will be stored in c:\Inetpub\wwwroot\WebApplication1, and made available through http://localhost/WebApplication1.

Using the wwwroot directory is straightforward, but it makes for poor organization. To properly use ASP or ASP.NET, you need to make your own *virtual directory* for each web application you create. With a virtual directory, you can expose any physical directory (on any drive on your computer) on your web server, as though it were located in the c:\Inetpup\wwwroot directory.

To create virtual directories, you need to use the administrative Internet Information Services utility. To start it, select Settings ➤ Control Panel ➤ Administrative Tools ➤ Internet Services Manager from the Start menu on the taskbar. The next few sections walk you through the steps and explain the settings that you can configure.

NOTE This chapter is written with IIS 5 in mind. Both Windows 2000 and Windows XP use IIS 5. However, if you're programming on Windows 2003 Server, you'll be using IIS 6 instead. IIS 6 features a revamped request processing architecture, and a slightly tweaked user interface. You'll be able to use most of the instructions in this chapter with IIS 6, but you may want to supplement your knowledge with the online help for IIS 6 or a dedicated book about IIS 6 administration.

Creating a Virtual Directory

When you're ready to create a new website, the first step you'll usually take is to create the physical directory where the pages will be stored (for example, c:\MySite). The second step is to expose this physical directory as a virtual directory through IIS. This means that the website becomes publicly visible to other computers that are connected to your computer. Ordinarily, a remote computer won't be allowed to access your c:\MySite directory. However, if you map c:\MySite to a virtual directory, the remote user will be able to request the files in the directory through IIS.

To create a new virtual directory for an existing physical directory, right-click the Default Website item in the IIS tree, and choose New ➤ Virtual Directory from the context menu. A wizard will start to manage the process, as shown in Figure 2-6.

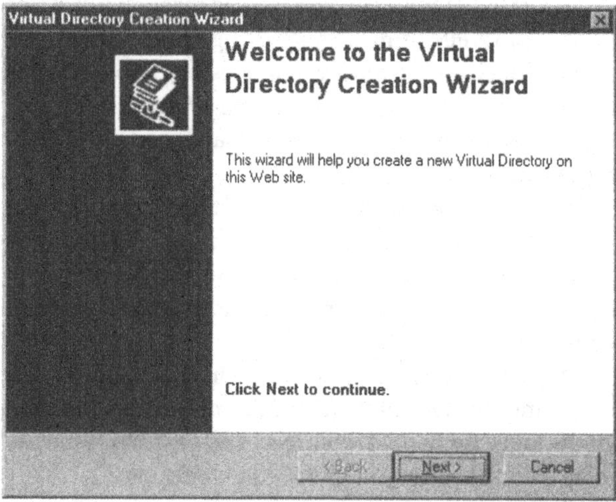

Figure 2-6. The Virtual Directory Creation wizard

As you step through the wizard, you'll need to provide three pieces of information: an alias, a directory, and a set of permissions. These settings are described in the following sections.

Alias

The alias is the name a remote client will use to access the files in this virtual directory. For example, if your alias is MyApp and your computer is named MyServer, you can request pages using URLs such as http://MyServer/MyApp/MyPage.aspx.

Directory

The directory is the physical directory on your hard drive that will be exposed as a virtual directory. For example, c:\Intetpub\wwwroot is the physical directory that is used for the root virtual directory of your web server. IIS will provide access to all the allowed file types in this directory.

Permissions

Finally, the wizard asks you to set permissions for your virtual directory, as shown in Figure 2-7. There are several permissions you can set:

- **Read.** This is the most basic permission—it's required in order for IIS to provide any requested files to the user. If this is disabled, the client will not be able to access ASP or ASP.NET pages, or static files like HTML and images. Note that even when you enable read permission, there are several other layers of possible security in IIS. For example, some file types (such as those that correspond to ASP.NET configuration files) are automatically restricted, even if they're in a directory that has read permission.

- **Run scripts.** This permission allows the user to request an ASP or ASP.NET page. If you enable read, but don't allow script permission, the user will be restricted to static file types such as HTML documents. ASP and ASP.NET pages require a higher permission because they could conceivably perform operations that would damage the web server or compromise security.
- **Execute.** This permission allows the user to run an ordinary executable file or CGI application. This is a possible security risk as well, and shouldn't be enabled unless you require it (which you won't for ordinary ASP or ASP.NET applications).
- **Write.** This permission allows the user to add, modify, or delete files on the web server. This permission should never be granted, because it could easily allow the computer to upload and then execute a dangerous script file (or at the least, use up all your available disk space). Instead, use an FTP site, or create an ASP.NET application that allows the user to upload specific types of information or files.
- **Browse.** This permission allows you to retrieve a full list of files in the virtual directory, even if the contents of those files are restricted. Browse is generally disabled, because it allows users to discover additional information about your website and its structure as well as exploit possible security holes. On the other hand, it's quite useful for testing, so you might want to enable it on a development computer.

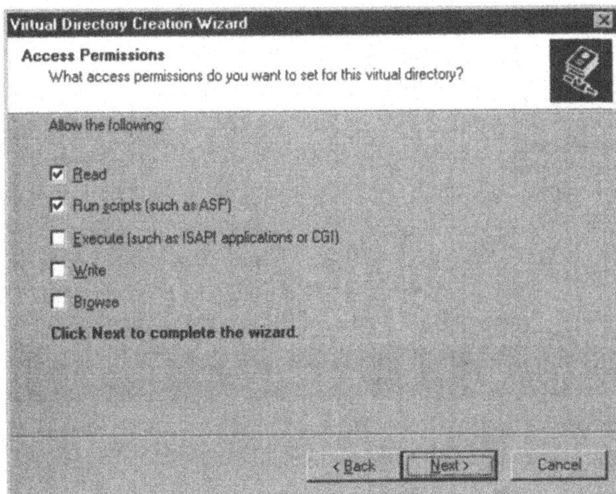

Figure 2-7. Virtual directory permissions

To host an ASP.NET application, you only need to enable the read and execute permissions (the first two check boxes). If you're using a development computer that will never act as a live web server, you can allow additional permissions. (Keep in mind, however, this could allow other users on a local network to access and modify files in the virtual directory.) You can also change the virtual directory permissions after you have created the virtual directory.

NOTE Remember, virtual directory permissions are only used when you're requesting a page through IIS. If you can directly access the computer's hard drive using Windows Explorer or some other tool, these permissions won't come into effect.

Virtual Directories and Web Applications

You can manage all the virtual directories on your computer in the Internet Information Service utility by expanding the tree under the Default Website item. You'll notice that items in the tree have three different types of icons, as shown in Figure 2-8.

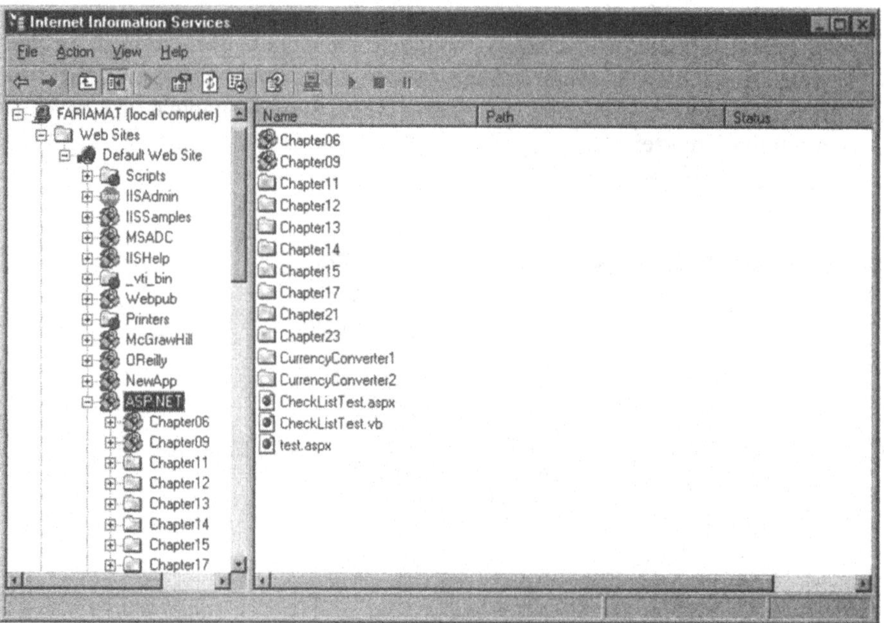

Figure 2-8. Web folders

Different icons have different meanings:

- **Ordinary folder.** This represents a subdirectory inside another virtual directory. For example, if you create a virtual directory and then add a subdirectory to the physical directory, it will be displayed here.

- **Folders with a globe.** This represents a virtual directory.
- **Package folders.** This represents a virtual directory that is also a web application. By default, when you use the wizard to create a virtual directory, it's also configured as a web application. This means that it will share a common set of resources and run in its own separate application domain. The topic of web applications is examined in more detail in Chapter 5.

When you create a virtual directory with the Virtual Directory Creation wizard, it's also configured as a web application. This is almost always what you want. If your virtual directory *isn't* a web application, you won't be able to control its ASP.NET configuration settings, and you won't be able to create a web application in it using Visual Studio .NET.

Virtual Directories Allow Access to Subdirectories

Imagine you create a virtual directory called MyApp on a computer called MyServer. The virtual directory corresponds to the physical directory c:\MyApp. If you add the subdirectory c:\MyApp\MoreFiles, this directory will automatically be included in the IIS tree as an ordinary folder. Clients will be able to access files in this folder by specifying the folder name, as in http://MyServer/MyApp/MoreFiles/SomeFile.html.

By default, the subdirectory will inherit all the permissions of the virtual directory. However, you can change these settings using the Internet Information Services utility. This is a common technique used to break a single application into different parts (for example, if some pages require heightened security settings).

Folder Settings

IIS makes it easy to configure virtual directories after you've created them. Simply right-click the virtual directory in the list and choose Properties. The Properties window will appear, as shown in Figure 2-9, with its information divided into several tabs.

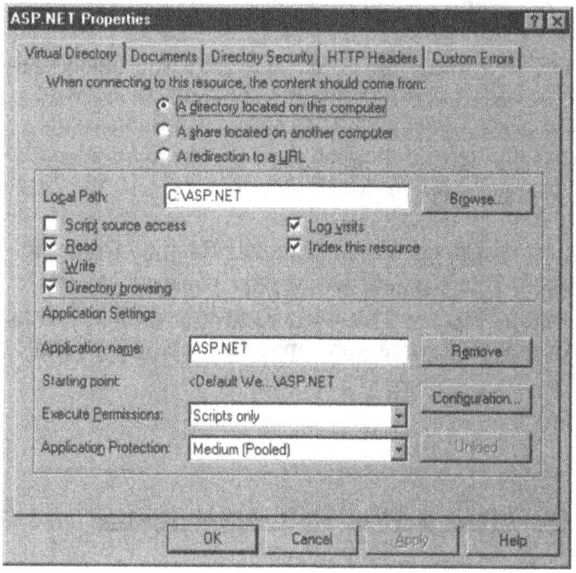

Figure 2-9. *Web directory properties*

The Virtual Directory tab contains the most important settings. These include options that allow you to change the permissions you set when creating the virtual directory with the wizard. You can also see the local path that corresponds to this virtual directory. If you're looking at the root of a virtual directory, you can set the local path to point to a different physical directory by clicking the Browse button. If you're looking at an ordinary subdirectory *inside* a virtual directory, the local path will be read-only.

Remember, when you create a virtual directory with the wizard, it's also configured as a web application. You can change this by clicking the Remove button next to the application name. Similarly, you can click the Create button to transform an ordinary virtual directory into a full-fledged application. Usually you won't need to perform these tasks, but it's nice to know they are available if you need to make a change. They can come in useful when transplanting an application from one computer to another (as discussed in Chapter 12).

Any changes that you make will be automatically applied to all subdirectories. If you want to make a change that will affect all the virtual directories on your server, right-click the Default Website item and choose Properties. The change will be cascaded down to all the contained virtual directories. If your change conflicts with the custom settings that you have set for a virtual directory, IIS will warn you. It will present a list of the directories that will be affected and give you the chance to specify exactly which ones you want to change and which ones you want to leave as is (as shown in Figure 2-10).

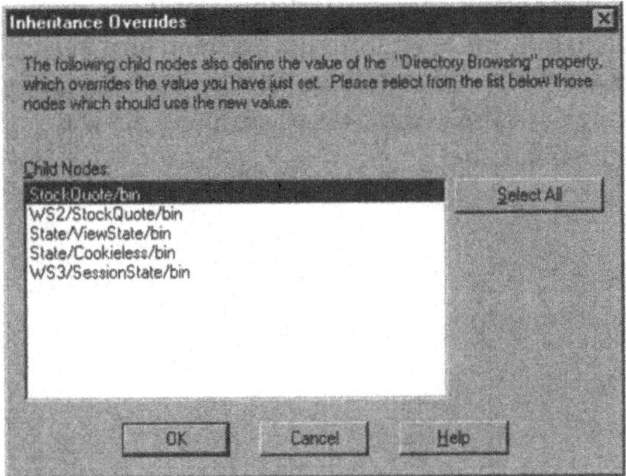

Figure 2-10. A change that affects several directories

If you explore the directory properties, you'll discover several other settings that affect ASP applications but don't have any effect on ASP.NET websites. These include the Application Protection (memory isolation) setting, and the options for session state, script timeout, and default language. These settings are all replaced by ASP.NET's new configuration file system, which you'll learn about in Chapter 5. Some other settings are designed for security, and these are examined in Chapter 25.

TIP Remember, IIS permissions are set on a directory-by-directory basis, which means that all the files in a directory need to share the same set of IIS permissions. As a consequence, the easiest way to apply different settings to different files is to create a virtual directory with more than one subdirectory, and set different options for each subdirectory.

The next two sections briefly explain two other types of IIS configuration: custom error pages and file mappings.

Documents

This tab allows you to specify the default documents for a virtual directory. For example, consider the virtual directory http://localhost/MySite. A user can request a specific page in this directory using a URL like http://localhost/MySite/MyPage1.aspx. But what happens if the user simply types http://localhost/MySite into a web browser?

In this case, IIS will examine the list of default documents defined for that virtual directory. It will scan the list from top to bottom, and return the first matching page. Using the list in Figure 2-11, IIS will check first for a Default.htm file, then for Default.asp, index.htm, iisstart.asp, and Default.aspx. If none of these pages are found, IIS will return the HTTP 404 (page not found) error.

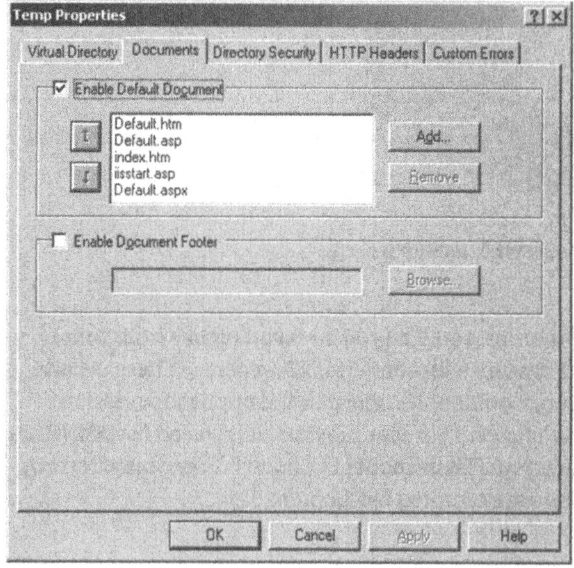

Figure 2-11. The default document list

You can configure the default document list by removing entries or adding new ones. Most ASP.NET applications simply use Default.aspx as their homepage.

Custom Errors

The Custom Errors tab (Figure 2-12) allows you to specify an error page that will be displayed for specific types of HTTP errors. As you'll discover in Chapter 11, you can use various ASP.NET features to replace HTTP errors or application errors with custom messages. However, these techniques won't work if the web request never makes it to the ASP.NET service (for example, if the user requests an HTML file that doesn't exist). In this case, you may want to supplement custom ASP.NET error handling with the appropriate IIS error pages for other generic error conditions.

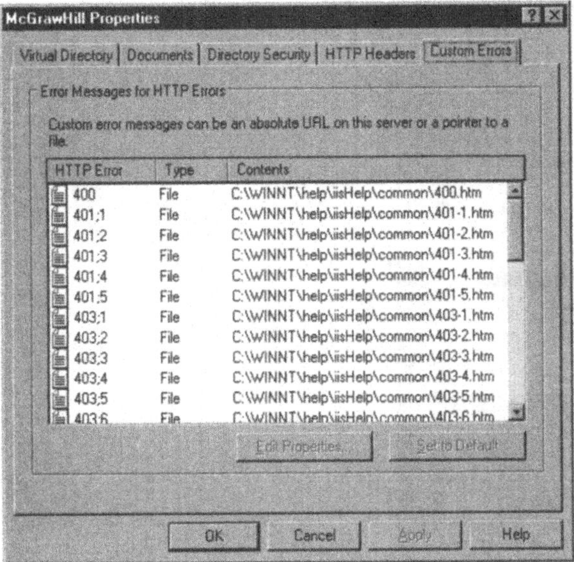

Figure 2-12. IIS custom errors

File Mappings

As explained earlier in this chapter, IIS hands off requests for ASP pages to the ASP service, and requests for ASP.NET pages to the ASP.NET service. However, both ASP and ASP.NET support a variety of file types. How does IIS know which files belong to ASP.NET and which ones belong to ASP?

The answer is found in the application file mappings. To view file mappings, click the Configuration button on the Virtual Directory tab. You'll see the window shown in Figure 2-13.

You'll notice that ASP files are mapped differently than ASP.NET files. For example, .asp requests are handled by C:\[WinDir]\System32\inetsrv\asp.dll, while .aspx requests are handled by C:\[WinDir]\Microsoft.NET\Framework\[Version]\aspnet_isapi.dll. In other words, ASP.NET doesn't replace ASP. Instead, it runs alongside it, allowing ASP requests to be handled by the existing asp.dll, and providing a new aspnet_isapi.dll for ASP.NET page requests. This design allows both types of applications to be hosted on the same web server with no potential conflict (and little possible integration). You could also use a similar approach to make sure that .aspx page requests in one virtual directory are handled by a different version of the ASP.NET service than requests in another virtual directory. If a file type isn't mapped (like .html), its contents are sent directly to the user as plain text, without any processing.

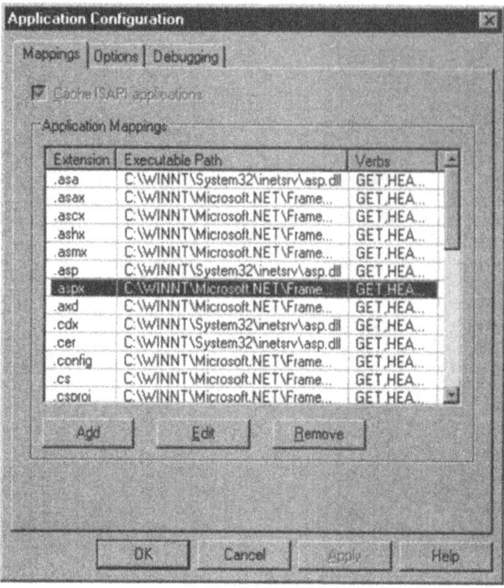

Figure 2-13. File mappings

If you're only working with a single version of ASP.NET, you probably won't need to worry about file mapping. One reason that you might want to work with file mapping is to explicitly remove file mappings you don't need or mappings that could be a security risk. In other cases, you might want to add a file mapping. For example, you could specify that the ASP.NET service will handle any requests for GIF images by adding a mapping for the .gif file type that points to the aspnet_isapi.dll file. This would allow you to use ASP.NET security services and logging for GIF file requests. (Note that this sort of change can slow down performance for GIF requests, because these requests will need to trickle through more layers on the server.) ASP.NET uses this technique to improve security with configuration and source code files. ASP.NET is registered to handle all requests for .config, .cs, and .vb files so that it can explicitly deny these requests, regardless of the IIS security settings.

CAUTION You should never remove any of the ASP.NET file type mappings! If you remove the .aspx or .asmx file types, web pages and web service won't work. Instead of being processed by the ASP.NET service, the raw file will be sent directly to the browser. If you remove other files types like .vb or .config, you'll compromise security. ASP.NET will no longer process requests for these types of files, which means that malicious users will be able to request them through IIS and inspect the code and configuration information for your web application.

Adding a Virtual Directory to Your Neighborhood

Working with a web application can sometimes be a little awkward. If you use Windows Explorer and look at the physical directory for the website, you can see the full list of files, but you can't execute any of them directly. On the other hand, if you use your browser and go through the virtual directory, you can run any page, but there's no way to browse through a directory listing because virtual directories almost always have directory browsing permission disabled.

While you're developing an application you may want to circumvent this limitation. That way you can examine exactly what comprises your web application and run several different pages easily, without needing to constantly type a full file name or dart back and forth between Internet Explorer and Windows Explorer. All you need to do is enable directory browsing for your virtual directory. You can easily enable or disable this setting from the Virtual Directory Properties window.

To make life even easier, you can add a virtual directory to the Network Neighborhood in Windows Explorer. First, open Windows Explorer. Then click Network, and double-click Add Network Place from the file list, as shown in Figure 2-14.

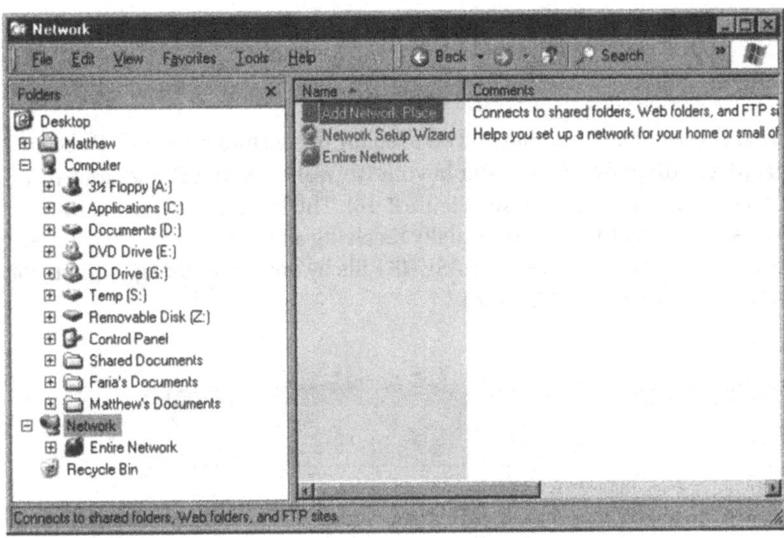

Figure 2-14. Select Add Network Place

The Add Network Place wizard will appear. This wizard allows you to create a network folder in Windows Explorer that represents your virtual directory (see Figure 2-15). The only important piece of information you need to specify is the address for your virtual directory (such as http://MyServer/MyFolder). Don't use the physical directory path.

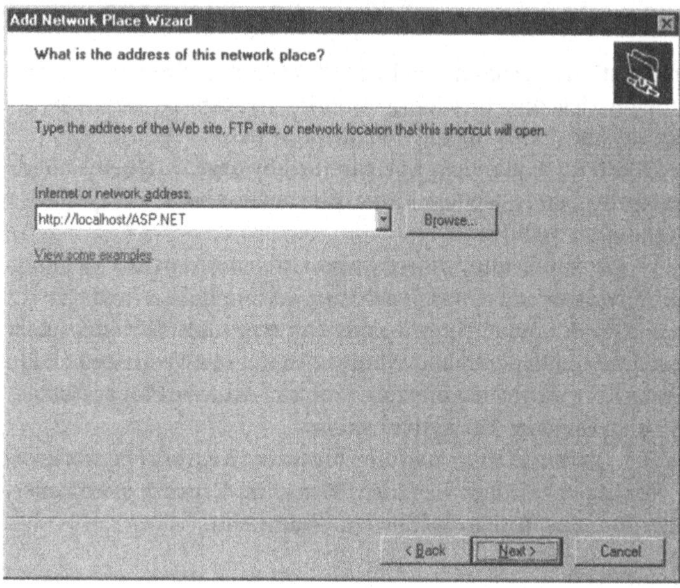

Figure 2-15. Specify the virtual directory

You can then choose the name that will be used for this virtual directory. Once you finish the wizard, the directory will appear in your Network Neighborhood, and you can browse through the remote files (see Figure 2-16). The interesting thing is that when you browse this directory, you're actually receiving all the information you need over HTTP. You can also execute an ASP or ASP.NET file by double-clicking—which you can't do directly from the physical directory.

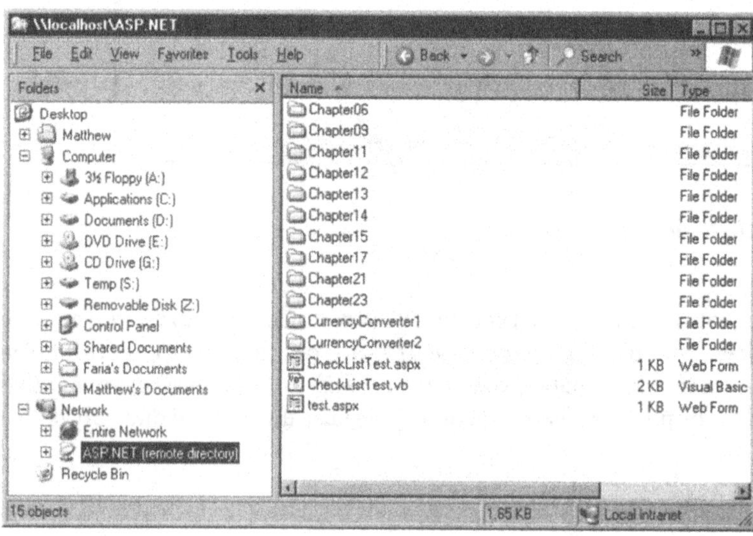

Figure 2-16. The mapped virtual directory

Installing ASP.NET

Once you've installed IIS, you can install ASP.NET. At the time of publication ASP.NET was available in two different packages:

- The free .NET runtime. You can download the installation files from `http://www.asp.net`, or you can order them on a CD at `http://microsoft.order-2.com/developertools`.
- The Visual Studio .NET application, which includes the .NET Framework and an IDE to design your applications.

Like most Microsoft setup applications, the process is quite straightforward. A graphical wizard (shown in Figure 2-17) takes you through every step of the lengthy process.

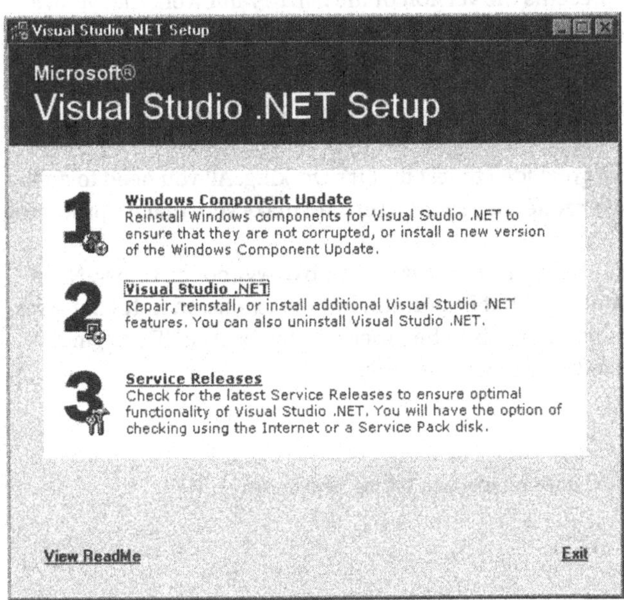

Figure 2-17. The Visual Studio .NET setup

After the setup is complete, you'll find several new directories on your computer. These include the following, among others:

- **C:\[WinDir]\Microsoft.NET\[Version]** contains the core .NET files. This includes the VB .NET, C#, JScript .NET, and J# language compilers, the ASP.NET service, and numerous utilities.

- **C:\[WinDir]\Assembly** contains the higher-level functionality of .NET—namely, it's where the shared .NET Framework assemblies are located. These assemblies contain all the types in .NET class library.
- **C:\[WinDir]\Microsoft.NET\[Version]\Config** contains computer-specific configuration files, the most important of which is the machine.config file.
- **C:\[WinDir]\Microsoft.NET\[Version]\Temporary ASP.NET Files** contains natively compiled ASP.NET web page code. The ASP.NET service uses this directory behind the scenes, compiling code and caching it for the best possible performance.
- **C:\Program Files\Microsoft Visual Studio .NET** is the default location for the Visual Studio .NET software, if you've installed it. The directory name varies slightly depending on the version of Visual Studio .NET that you've installed.

Note that [WinDir] represents your Windows directory (typically WINDOWS or WINNT), while [Version] represents the version of the .NET Framework that you've installed (such as v1.1.4322).

Verifying that ASP.NET Is Correctly Installed

After installing ASP.NET, it's a good idea to test that it's working. All you need to do is create a simple ASP.NET page, request it in a browser, and make sure that it's processed successfully.

To perform this test, create a text file in the c:\Inetpub\wwwroot directory. Name this file test.aspx. The filename isn't that important, but the extension *is*. It's the .aspx extension that tells IIS that this file needs to be processed by the ASP.NET engine.

Inside the test.aspx file, paste the following code:

```
<html>
<body>
<h1>The date is <% Response.Write(DateTime.Now.ToLongDateString()) %>
</h1>
</body>
</html>
```

When you request this file in a browser, ASP.NET will load the file, execute the embedded code statement (which retrieves the current date and inserts it into the page), and then return the final HTML page. This example isn't a full-fledged ASP.NET web page, because it doesn't use the web control model you'll be exploring in the second part of this book. However, it's still enough to test that ASP.NET is working properly. When you enter http://localhost/test.aspx in the browser, you should see a page that looks like the one shown in Figure 2-18.

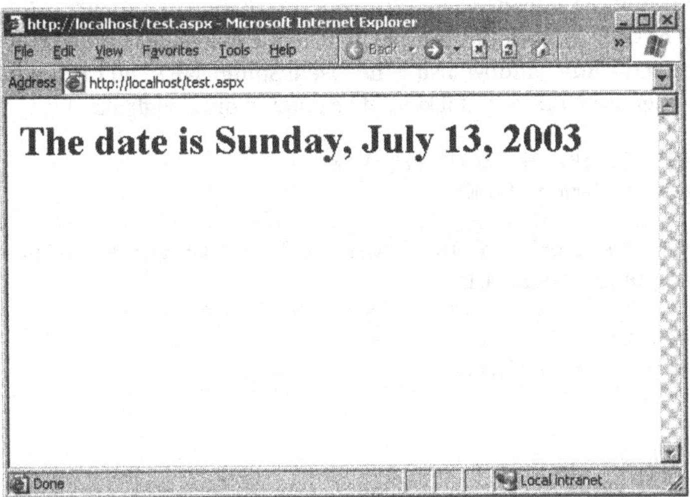

Figure 2-18. ASP.NET is correctly installed

If you see only the plain text, as in Figure 2-19, ASP.NET isn't installed correctly. This problem commonly occurs if ASP.NET is installed but the ASP.NET file types aren't registered in IIS. In this case, ASP.NET won't actually process the request. Instead, the raw page will be sent directly to the user, and the browser will only display the content that isn't inside a tag or script block.

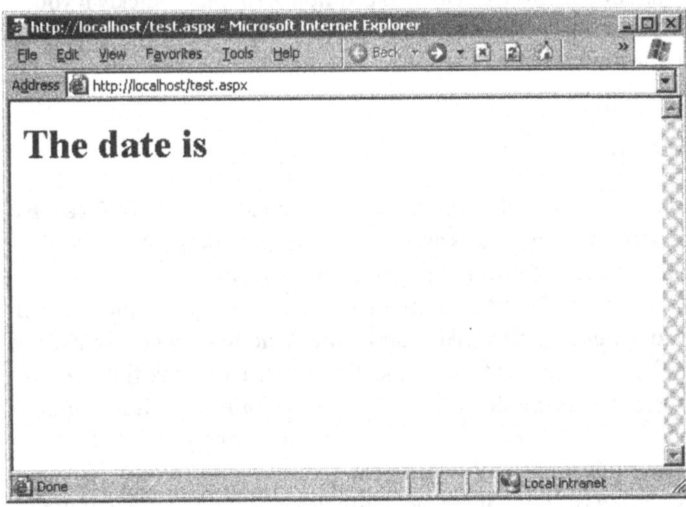

Figure 2-19. ASP.NET isn't installed or configured correctly

This problem can usually be solved by repairing your installation of ASP.NET using the original setup CD or DVD. To start this process, type in the following command at the command line (or in the Run window) using the Visual Studio .NET DVD. (It's split into two lines due to page constraints, but it should be entered on a single line.)

```
<DVD Drive>:\wcu\dotNetFramework\dotnetfx.exe /t:c:\temp
  /c:"msiexec.exe /fvecms c:\temp\netfx.msi"
```

If you're using the CD version of Visual Studio .NET, use the following command line with the Windows Component Update CD:

```
<CD Drive>:\dotNetFramework\ dotnetfx.exe /t:c:\temp
  /c:"msiexec.exe /fvecms c:\temp\netfx.msi"
```

Getting the Samples

This book includes a wide range of code examples that are available online at `http://www.prosetech.com`. These samples are downloadable as a single ZIP file, which you can extract onto your computer using a utility like WinZip. In order to run the files, you'll need to place them into a virtual directory of your choice.

Along with the sample files are the additional project and solution files that Visual Studio .NET creates automatically for web applications. In order to open these projects in Visual Studio .NET without any problem, you *must* use the exact same directory structure that I've used (which incorporates a C:\ASP.NET root directory). Generally, this directory structure will be created automatically when you unzip the file, but you'll need to make sure you use the same drive (C:) to match what Visual Studio .NET expects. After you've unzipped all the code files, you'll have to map the new directories to the appropriate virtual directories. This can be accomplished quite quickly if you follow the exact installation instructions described on the website or in the readme.txt file included with the code download.

The ASP.NET Account

When ASP.NET is installed, a new Windows user account is created called ASPNET. By default, the ASP.NET service runs under this account when it executes any ASP.NET code, including the code in your custom web pages and web services.

The ASPNET account has a set of carefully limited privileges. By default, the ASPNET account won't be allowed to perform tasks like reading the Windows registry, retrieving information from a database, or writing to most locations on the local hard drive. On the other hand, it will have the permissions that are essential for normal functioning. For example, the ASPNET account *is* allowed to access the Temporary ASP.NET Files directory, so that it can compile and cache web pages.

The limited security settings of the ASPNET account are designed to prevent malicious code from damaging your web server. However, you'll probably find that your applications require some additional permissions beyond those given to the ASPNET account. For example, your code might need to write data to a specific directory, use the Windows event log, and execute database operations. You can grant permissions to the ASPNET account in the same way that you would grant them to any other Windows user account. However, the process isn't always obvious—so you might want to consult a good handbook about Windows system administration before you take these steps.

If you're using a computer for development testing only, you can use a shortcut to give the ASP.NET service greater privileges. Instead of using the ASPNET account, you can configure ASP.NET code so that it runs under the *local system* account. The local system account is a built-in Windows account with administrator-level permissions. Code that runs under this account has the ability to do almost anything on the current computer. Using the local system account is a poor idea on a production system, but it isn't a bad approach for testing a new web application on a development computer.

NOTE The ASP.NET account is a global setting that affects all web applications on the computer, provided you're using IIS 5. If you're using Windows Server 2003, you must use configure the IIS 6 application pool settings instead. Editing the machine.config will have no effect.

To change the ASP.NET settings to use the local system account, you need to perform the following steps.

1. Open the machine.config file in the C:\[WinDir]\Microsoft.NET\[Version]\Config directory using Notepad. (If you've installed the .NET Framework 1.1 on a Windows XP computer, this directory will be C:\Windows\Microsoft.NET\v1.1.4322\Config.

2. Search for the text userName="Machine". You'll find this setting in the processModel tag, which looks something like this:

```
<processModel enable="true" ...
 userName="Machine" password="AutoGenerate" ... />
```

3. The userName="Machine" instruction tells ASP.NET to run using the special ASPNET account. Modify this attribute to be userName="System". This tells ASP.NET to use the local system account.

```
<processModel enable="true" ...
 userName="System" password="AutoGenerate" ... />
```

4. Now you must restart the ASP.NET service. To do this, you can either reboot the computer, or you can use Task Manager to manually terminate the ASP.NET service. In the latter case, look for the process named aspnet_wp.exe. Select it and click End Process.

The effect of the ASP.NET account is explored in Chapter 25, which tackles security in more depth.

NOTE You might wonder how virtual directory permissions and the ASP.NET account settings interact. Essentially, the virtual directory permissions determine what files a user can request. If the user successfully requests an ASP.NET file, the ASP.NET engine will then execute the corresponding web page code. The ASP.NET account settings determine what this code is allowed to do.

The Last Word

In this chapter, you learned how to make sure your computer is ready to host ASP.NET websites. Before you continue to the next part, make sure you've verified that you can request the sample ASP.NET page (as described in the section "Verifying that ASP.NET Is Correctly Installed"). This ensures that both ASP.NET and IIS are installed and configured properly. Once that's in place, you're ready to begin designing full-fledged ASP.NET applications and web pages. You can start with Chapter 3, which presents a comprehensive overview of the new Visual Basic .NET language.

CHAPTER 3

Learning the Visual Basic .NET Language

Before you can create an ASP.NET application, you need to choose a .NET language to program it. If you're an ASP or Visual Basic developer, the natural choice is VB .NET. If you're a longtime Java programmer or old-hand C++ coder, C# will probably suit you best. VBScript isn't an option—it just doesn't have the range, flexibility, and elegance a modern language demands.

This chapter presents an overview of the Visual Basic .NET language. You'll learn about the data types you can use, the operations you can perform, and the code you'll need to define functions, loops, and conditional logic. This chapter assumes that you've programmed before and that you're already familiar with most of these concepts—you just need to see how they're implemented in VB .NET.

If you've programmed with an earlier version of Visual Basic, you might find that the most beneficial way to use this chapter is to browse through it without reading every section. This approach will give you a general overview of the VB .NET language. You can then return to this chapter later as a reference when needed. But remember, though you can program an ASP.NET application without mastering all the language details, this deep knowledge is often what separates the casual programmer from the legendary programming guru.

NOTE The examples in this chapter show individual lines and code snippets. You won't actually be able to use these code snippets in an application until you've learned about objects and .NET types. But don't despair—the next chapter builds on this information, fills in the gaps, and presents an ASP.NET example for you try out.

The .NET Languages

The .NET Framework 1.1 ships with four languages: VB .NET, C#, JScript .NET, and J#. These languages are, to a large degree, functionally equivalent. Microsoft has worked hard to eliminate language conflicts in the .NET Framework. These battles slow down adoption, distract from the core framework features, and make it difficult for the developer community to solve problems together and share solutions. According to Microsoft, choosing to program in VB .NET instead of C# is just a lifestyle choice and won't affect the performance, interoperability, feature set, or development time of your applications. Surprisingly, this ambitious claim is essentially true.

.NET also allows other third-party developers to release languages that are just as feature rich as VB .NET or C#. These languages (which already include Eiffel, Perl, Python, and even COBOL) "snap in" to the .NET Framework effortlessly. The secret is the special machine.config configuration file that is installed with the .NET Framework. In one of its sections, the machine.config file lists the language compilers that are currently installed.

```
<!-- Other configuration settings omitted. -->
<compilers>
    <compiler language="c#;cs;csharp" extension=".cs"
     type="Microsoft.CSharp.CSharpCodeProvider, System, Version=1.0.5000.0"/>

    <compiler language="vb;vbs;visualbasic;vbscript" extension=".vb"
     type="Microsoft.VisualBasic.VBCodeProvider, System, Version=1.0.5000.0"/>

    <compiler language="js;jscript;javascript" extension=".js"
     type="Microsoft.JScript.JScriptCodeProvider, Microsoft.JScript,
     Version=7.0.5000.0"/>

    <compiler language="VJ#;VJS;VJSharp" extension=".jsl"
     type="Microsoft.VJSharp.VJSharpCodeProvider, VJSharpCodeProvider,
     Version=7.0.5000.0"/>
</compilers>
```

TIP To view the machine.config file, look for the directory [WinDir]\Microsoft.NET\Framework\[Version]\Config. For example, after installing .NET 1.1 on a Windows XP computer, the machine.config file is placed in the directory C:\Windows\Microsoft.NET\Framework\v1.1.4322\Config.

To install another .NET language, all you need to do is copy the compiler to your computer and add a line to the machine.config file. (Typically, a setup program will perform these steps for you automatically.) The new compiler will then transform your code creations into a sequence of IL (Intermediate Language) instructions.

IL is the only "language" that the CLR recognizes. When you create the code for an ASP.NET web form, it's changed into IL using the VB .NET compiler (vbc.exe), the C# compiler (csc.exe), the JScript compiler (jsc.exe), or the J# compiler (vjc.exe). You can perform the compilation manually or let ASP.NET handle it automatically when a web page is requested. We'll discuss the difference between these two techniques in Chapter 5.

The Evolution of VB .NET

Traditional ASP development was restricted to the VBScript programming language, which was first developed as a basic scripting language for writing macros and other simple code that would be used by another application. VBScript was never intended for sophisticated, interactive web applications, hence expert programmers had to strain the language to its limit to create first-rate ASP pages. To get around many limitations in VBScript, advanced pages needed to rely on separate components written in other languages, which generally had to be installed and configured separately on the web server. In the end, even though VBScript was intended to be easier to use than ordinary Visual Basic, writing advanced ASP pages actually became much more complicated because of the additional effort needed to circumvent VBScript's limitations.

Just replacing VBScript with Visual Basic would have been a significant advantage. Some of the features Visual Basic 6 offers that VBScript lacks include the following:

- **Access to the platform services.** VBScript, on the other hand, is automatically isolated by the scripting host and has many security-related restrictions.
- **Typed programming.** VBScript doesn't allow you strict control over data types, and works with special "variant" variables instead, which are supposed to be easier to use. Unfortunately, they also introduce data type conversion problems and difficult-to-detect errors.
- **Event-driven programming.** Unlike Visual Basic, VBScript is notoriously disorganized and has little flexibility to group or organize code so that code can be easily debugged and reused.
- **Support for objects.** Visual Basic doesn't have perfect object-oriented features, but they are still light years over what VBScript can accomplish.

However, ASP.NET has completely skipped over this stage in evolution and moved directly to the advanced capabilities of Visual Basic .NET. This latest version of Visual Basic is a complete redesign that answers years of unmet complaints and extends the VB language into new territory. Some of the new features include the following:

- **Structured error handling.** The end of the aggravating "On Error Goto" construct has finally arrived. VB .NET introduces .NET's new standard: clean, concise, structured exception handling. You'll see it in Chapter 11.
- **Language refinements.** Every aspect of the VB language has been tweaked and refined. You can now overload functions, declare and assign variables on the same line, and use shortened assignment syntax.
- **Strong typing.** Even Visual Basic 6 performed some automatic variable conversions that could cause unusual bugs. VB .NET allows you to rein in your program and prevent possible errors with strict type checking.
- **True object-oriented programming.** Inheritance, interfaces, polymorphism, constructors, shared members and abstract classes...the list goes on, and Visual Basic .NET integrates them all into the language.

These are only some of the changes, but they're enough to show you that VB .NET is separated from VBScript by two major evolutionary leaps. All of these features are available in other .NET languages such as C#, but Visual Basic and VBScript developers will have to adjust the most.

Variables and Data Types

As with all programming languages, you keep track of data in VB .NET using *variables*. Variables can store numbers, text, dates, and times, and can even point to full-fledged objects.

When you declare a variable, you give it a name, and you specify the type of data it will store. To declare a local variable, you use the Dim statement, as shown here:

```
' Create an integer variable named ErrorCode.
Dim ErrorCode As Integer

' Create a string variable named MyName.
Dim MyName As String
```

NOTE This example shows one other ingredient in VB .NET programming: *comments*. Comments are descriptive text that is ignored by the compiler. VB .NET comments always start with an apostrophe (') and continue for the entire line.

Every .NET language uses the same variable data types. Different languages may provide slightly different names (for example, a VB .NET Integer is the same as a C# int), but the CLR makes no distinction. This allows for deep language integration. Because languages share the same data types, you can easily use objects written in one .NET language in an application written in another .NET language. No data type conversions are required.

In order to create this common data type system, Microsoft needed to iron out many of the inconsistencies that existed between VBScript, Visual Basic 6, C++, and other languages. Their solution was to create a set of basic data types, which are provided in the .NET class library. These core data types are shown in Table 3-1.

Table 3-1. Common Data Types

Class Library Name	VB .NET Name	C# Name	Contains
Byte	Byte	byte	An integer from 0 to 255.
Int16	Short	short	An integer from –32768 to 32767.
Int32	Integer	int	An integer from –2,147,483,648 to 2,147,483,647.
Int64	Long	long	An integer from about –9.2e18 to 9.2e18.

Table 3-1. Common Data Types (Continued)

Class Library Name	VB .NET Name	C# Name	Contains
Single	Single	float	A single-precision floating point number from approximately –3.4e38 to 3.4e38.
Double	Double	double	A double-precision floating point number from approximately –1.8e308 to 1.8e308.
Decimal	Decimal	decimal	A 128-bit fixed-point fractional number that supports up to 28 significant digits.
Char	Char	char	A single 16-bit Unicode character.
String	String	string	A variable-length series of Unicode characters.
Boolean	Boolean	bool	A True or False value.
DateTime	Date	N/A*	Represents any date and time from 12:00:00 AM, January 1 of the year 1 in the Gregorian calendar to 11:59:59 PM, December 31, year 9999. Time values can resolve values to 100 nanosecond increments. Internally, this data type is stored as a 64-bit integer.
TimeSpan	N/A*	N/A*	Represents a period of time, as in 10 seconds or 3 days. The smallest possible interval is 1 "tick" (100 nanoseconds).
Object	Object	object	The ultimate base class of all .NET types. Can contain any data type or object.

* If the language does not provide an alias for a given type, you can just use the .NET class name.

You can also define a variable by using the type name from the .NET class library. This approach produces identical variables. It's also a requirement when the data type doesn't have an alias built into the language. For example, you can rewrite the earlier example that used VB .NET data type names with this code snippet that uses the class library names:

```
Dim ErrorCode As System.Int32
Dim MyName As System.String
```

This code snippet uses fully qualified type names that indicate that the Int32 type is found in the System namespace (along with all of the most fundamental types). In Chapter 4, we'll discuss types and namespaces in more detail.

Data Type Changes from Visual Basic 6

Luckily for VB developers, the list of data types in .NET is quite similar to the data types from earlier versions. Some changes, however, were unavoidable:

- Visual Basic defined an Integer as a 16-bit number with a maximum value of 32,767. VB .NET, on the other hand, defines an Integer as a 32-bit number. Long now refers to a 64-bit integer, while Short refers to a 16-bit integer.
- The Currency data type has been replaced by Decimal, which supports more decimal places (and thus greater accuracy).
- Fixed-length strings are no longer supported.
- Variants are no longer supported and have been replaced with the generic Object type, which can hold any object or simple data type.
- The Date data type has increased range and precision and works slightly differently. If you're migrating legacy code that manipulates dates from a previous version of Visual Basic, you may need to rewrite it.

Assignment and Initializers

Once you've created your variable you can freely assign values to them, as long as these values have the correct data type. Here's the code that shows this two step process:

```
' Define variables.
Dim ErrorCode As Integer
Dim MyName As String

' Assign values.
ErrorCode = 10
MyName = "Matthew"
```

You can also assign a value to a variable in the same line that you create it. This feature is familiar to most C++ programmers, but it's a new addition to VB .NET. Here's an example that compresses four lines of code into two:

```
Dim ErrorCode As Integer = 10
Dim MyName As String = "Matthew"
```

Visual Basic .NET is kind enough to let you use simple data types without initializing them. Numbers are automatically initialized to 0 and strings are initialized to an empty string (""). That means the following code will succeed in VB .NET:

```
Dim Number As Integer     ' Number now contains 0.
Number = Number + 1       ' Number now contains 1.
```

What's in a Name? Not the Data Type.

You'll notice that the preceding examples don't use variable prefixes. Most Visual Basic and C++ programmers are in the habit of adding a few characters to the start of a variable name to indicate its data type. In .NET, this practice is discouraged, because data types can be used in a much more flexible range of ways without any problem, and most variables hold references to full objects anyway. In this book, variable prefixes aren't used, except for web controls, in which it helps to distinguish lists, text boxes, buttons, and other common user interface elements. In your own programs, you should follow a consistent (typically companywide) standard that may or may not adopt a system of variable prefixes.

Arrays

Arrays allow you to store a series of values that have the same data type. Each individual value in the array is accessed using one or more index numbers. It's often convenient to picture arrays as lists of data (if the array has one dimension), or grids of data (if the array has two dimensions). Typically, arrays are laid out contiguously in memory.

Visual Basic programmers will find that arrays are one of the most profoundly changed language elements. In seeking to harmonize .NET languages, Microsoft decided that all arrays must start at a fixed lower bound of 0. There are no exceptions. When you create an array in VB .NET, you simply specify the upper bound.

```
' Create an array with four strings (from index 0 to index 3).
Dim StringArray(3) As String

' Create a 2 x 4 grid array (with a total of eight integers).
Dim IntArray(1, 3) As Integer
```

By default, if your array includes simple data types they are all initialized to default values (0, False, or "", depending on whether you are using some type of number, a Boolean variable, or a string). You can also fill an array with data at the same time that you create it. In this case, you don't need to explicitly specify the number of elements, because .NET can determine it automatically.

```
' Create an array with four strings, one for each number from 1 to 4.
Dim StringArray() As String = {"1", "2", "3", "4"}
```

The same technique works for multidimensional arrays, except that two sets of curly brackets are required:

```
' Create a 4 x 2 array (a grid with four rows and two columns).
Dim IntArray() As Integer = {{1, 2}, {3, 4}, {5, 6}, {7, 8}}
```

Figure 3-1 shows what this array looks like in memory.

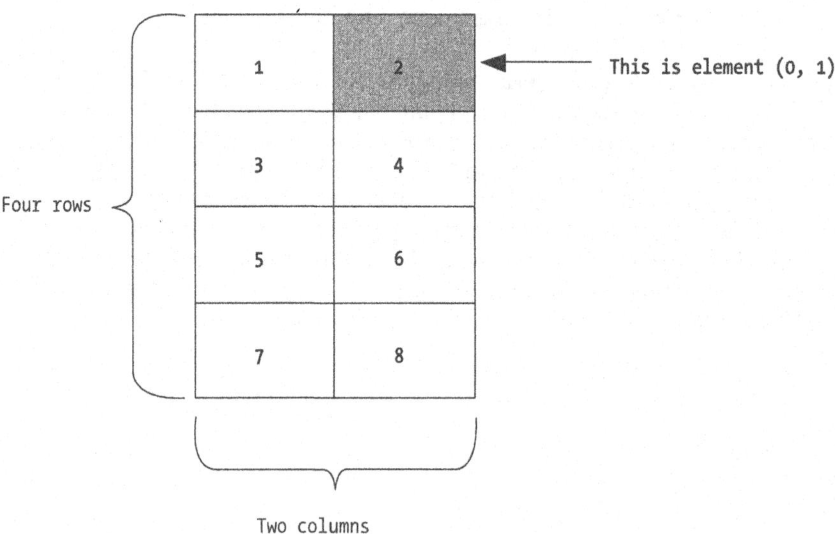

Figure 3-1. A sample array of integers

To access an element in an array, you specify the corresponding index number in parentheses. Array indices are always zero-based. That means that MyArray(0) accesses the first cell in a one-dimensional array, MyArray(1) accesses the second cell, and so on.

```
' Access the value in row 0 (first row), column 1 (second column).
Dim Element As Integer
Element = intArray(0, 1)     ' Element is now set to 2.
```

One nice feature that VB .NET offers is array redimensioning. In VB .NET, all arrays start with an initial size, and any array can be resized. To resize an array, you use the ReDim keyword.

```
Dim MyArray(10, 10) As Integer
ReDim MyArray(20, 20)
```

In this example, all the contents in the array will be erased when it's resized. To preserve the contents, you can use the optional Preserve keyword when redimensioning the array. However, if you're using a multidimensional array you'll only be able to change the last dimension, or a runtime error will occur.

```
Dim MyArray(10, 10) As Integer
ReDim Preserve MyArray(10, 20)   ' Allowed, and the contents will remain.
ReDim Preserve MyArray(20, 20)   ' Not allowed. A runtime error will occur.
```

TIP In many cases, it's easier to dodge counting issues and use a full-fledged collection rather than an array. Collections are generally better suited to modern object-oriented programming and are used extensively in ASP.NET. The .NET class library provides many types of collection classes, including simple collections, sorted lists, key-indexed lists (dictionaries), and queues. You'll see examples of collections throughout this book.

Enumerations

An enumeration is a group of related constants, each of which is given a descriptive name. Every enumerated value corresponds to a preset integer. In your code, however, you can refer to an enumerated value by name, which makes your code clearer and helps to prevent errors. For example, it's much more straightforward to set the border of a label to the enumerated value BoderStyle.Dashed rather than the obscure numeric constant 3. In this case, Dashed is a value in the BorderStyle enumeration, and it represents the number 3.

Here's an example of an enumeration that defines different types of users:

```
' Define an enumeration called UserType with three possible values.
Enum UserType
    Admin
    Guest
    Invalid
End Enum
```

Now you can use the UserType enumeration as a special data type that is restricted to one of three possible values. You assign or compare the enumerated value using the dot notation shown in the following example.

```
' Create a new value and set it equal to the UserType.Admin constant.
Dim NewUserType As UserType
NewUserType = UserType.Admin
```

Internally, enumerations are maintained as numbers. In the preceding example, 0 is automatically assigned to Admin, 1 to Guest, and 2 to Invalid. You can set a number directly into an enumeration variable, although this can lead to an undetected error if you use a number that doesn't correspond to one of the defined values.

In some scenarios, you might want to control what numbers are used for various values in an enumeration. This technique is typically used when the number has some specific meaning or corresponds to some other piece of information. For example, the following code defines an enumeration that represents the error code returned by a legacy component.

```
Enum ErrorCode
    NoResponse = 166
    TooBusy = 167
    Pass = 0
End Enum
```

Now you can use the ErrorCode enumeration, which was defined earlier, with a function that returns an integer representing an error condition, as shown here:

```
Dim Err As ErrorCode
Err = DoSomething()
If Err = ErrorCode.Pass
    ' Operation succeeded.
End If
```

TIP Enumerations are widely used in .NET. You won't need to create your own enumerations to use in ASP.NET applications, unless you're designing your own components. However, the concept of enumerated values is extremely important, because the .NET class library uses it extensively. For example, you set colors, border styles, alignment, and various other web control styles using enumerations provided in the .NET class library.

Variable Operations

You can use all the standard type of variable operations in VB .NET. When working with numbers, you can use various math symbols, as listed in Table 3-2. Visual Basic .NET follows the conventional order of operations, performing exponentiation first, followed by multiplication and division, and then addition and subtraction. You can also control order by grouping subexpressions with parentheses.

```
Dim Number As Integer

Number = 4 + 2 * 3
' Number will be 10.

Number = (4 + 2) * 3
' Number will be 18.
```

Table 3-2. Arithmetic Operations

Operator	Description
+	Addition. `1 + 1 = 2.`
-	Subtraction (and to indicate negative numbers). `5 - 2 = 3.`
*	Multiplication. `2 * 5 = 10.`
/	Division. `5 / 2 = 2.5.`
^	Exponentiation. `3 ^ 2 = 9.`
\	Integer division (any remainder is discarded). `7 \ 3 = 2.`
Mod	Gets the remainder left after integer division. `7 Mod 3 = 1.`

When dealing with strings, you can use the concatenation operator (&), which joins together two strings.

```
' Join two strings together. Could also use the + operator.
MyName = FirstName & " " & LastName
```

The addition operator (+) can also be used to join strings, but it's generally clearer to use the concatenation operator. The concatenation operator automatically attempts to convert both variables in the expression to the string data type, if they are not already strings.

In addition, Visual Basic .NET now provides special shorthand assignment operators. A few examples are shown here:

```
' Add 10 to MyValue (the same as MyValue = MyValue + 10).
MyValue += 10

' Multiple MyValue by 3 (the same as MyValue = MyValue * 3).
MyValue *= 3

' Divide MyValue by 12 (the same as MyValue = MyValue / 12).
MyValue /= 12
```

Line Termination

Sometimes, code statements are too long to efficiently fit on a single line. In Visual Basic, you can break a code statement over multiple lines by adding a space followed by the line-continuation character (an underscore) to the end of the line. Here's an example:

```
' A long line of code.
MyValue = MyValue1 + MyValue2 + MyValue3

' A code statement split over several lines in VB.
MyValue = MyValue1 + MyValue2 + _
        MyValue3
```

Advanced Math

In the past, every language has had its own set of keywords for common math operations such as rounding and trigonometry. In .NET languages, many of these keywords remain. However, you can also use a centralized Math class that's part of the .NET Framework. This has the pleasant side effect of ensuring that the code you use to perform mathematical operations can easily be translated into equivalent statements in any .NET language with minimal fuss.

To use the math operations, you invoke the methods of the System.Math class. These methods are *shared*, which means that they are always available and ready to use. (The next chapter explores the difference between shared and instance members in more detail.)

The following code snippet shows some sample calculations that you can perform with the Math class.

```
Dim MyValue As Integer
MyValue = Math.Sqrt(81)             ' MyValue = 9
MyValue = Math.Round(42.889, 2)     ' MyValue = 42.89
MyValue = Math.Abs(-10)             ' MyValue = 10
MyValue = Math.Log(24.212)          ' MyValue = 3.18.. (and so on)
MyValue = Math.PI                   ' MyValue = 3.14159265358979323846
```

The features of the Math class are too numerous to list here in their entirety. The preceding examples show some common numeric operations. For more information about the trigonometric and logarithmic functions that are available, refer to the MSDN reference for the Math class.

Type Conversions

Converting information from one data type to another is a fairly common programming task. For example, you might retrieve text input for a user that contains the number you want to use for a calculation. Or, you might need take a calculated value and transform it into text you can display in a web page.

The Visual Basic .NET rules for type conversion are slightly less strict than some other languages, like C#. For example, VB .NET will automatically allow the conversions shown here:

```
Dim BigValue As Integer = 100
Dim SmallValue As Short
Dim MyText As String = "100"

' Convert your 32-bit BigValue number into a 16-bit number.
SmallValue = BigValue

' Convert your MyText into a number.
BigValue = MyText
```

The problem with code like this, is that it isn't guaranteed to work. Conversions are of two types: narrowing and widening. *Widening conversions* always succeed. For example, you can always convert a number into a string, or a 16-bit integer into a 32-bit integer. On the other hand, *narrowing conversions* may or may not succeed, depending on the data. If you're converting a 32-bit integer to a 16-bit integer (as in the previous code snippet), you'll encounter an error if the 32-bit number is larger than the maximum value that can be stored in a 16-bit data type. Similarly, some strings can't be converted to numbers. A failed narrowing conversion will lead to an unexpected runtime error.

It's possible to tighten up Visual Basic's type conversion habits by adding an Option Strict instruction to the beginning of your code files.

```
Option Strict On
```

In this case, VB .NET will not allow automatic or *implicit* data type conversions if they could cause an error or lose data. Instead, you'll need to explicitly indicate that you want to perform a conversion.

To perform an *explicit* data type conversion in VB .NET, you use the CType() function. This function takes two arguments. The first specifies the variable you want to convert, and the second specifies the data type you're converting it to. Here's how you would rewrite the earlier example with explicit conversions:

```
Dim BigValue As Integer = 100
Dim SmallValue As Short
Dim MyText As String = "100"

' Explicitly convert your 32-bit number into a 16-bit number.
SmallValue = CType(BigValue, Short)

' Explicitly convert your string into a number.
BigValue = CType(MyText, Integer)
```

Just like implicit conversions, explicit conversions can still fail and produce a runtime error. The difference is that when you add the CType() function, you clearly indicate that you're aware that a conversion is taking place. At the same time that you use CType(), you should add code that either validates your data before you attempt to convert it, or catches any errors using the error-handling techniques described in Chapter 11.

You can also use the classic Visual Basic keywords such as Val(), CStr(), CInt(), CBool(), and so on to perform data type conversions with the standard data types. However, the CType() function is a nice generic solution that works for all scenarios. The examples in this book almost always use explicit conversion with the CType() function. A few exceptions apply. For example, Visual Basic's built-in Val() function is more convenient than CType() in some scenarios because it just returns a zero if it fails to convert a string to a number.

```
Dim TextString As String = "Hello"

Dim Number As Integer
Number = Val(TextString)
' Number is now 0, because TextString contains no numeric information.
```

You'll also find that you can use object methods to perform some conversions a little more elegantly. The next section demonstrates this approach.

Object-Based Manipulation

.NET is object-oriented to the core. In fact, even ordinary variables are really full-fledged objects in disguise. That means that common data types have the built-in smarts to handle basic operations (like counting the number of letters in a string). Even better, it means that you can manipulate strings, dates, and numbers in exactly the same way in C# and in VB .NET. This wouldn't be true if developers used special keywords that were built into the C# or VB .NET language.

As an example, every type in the .NET class library includes a ToString() method. The default implementation of this method returns the class name. In simple variables, a more useful result is returned: the string representation of the given variable. The following code snippet demonstrates the use of the ToString() method with an integer.

```
Dim MyString As String
Dim MyInteger As Integer = 100

' Convert a number to a string. MyString will have the contents "100".
MyString = MyInteger.ToString()
```

To understand this example, you need to remember that all integers are based on the Int32 class in the .NET class library. The ToString() method is built in to the Int32 class, so it's available when you use an integer in any language. You should also notice that the line of code that uses the ToString() method is virtually identical in both languages.

The next few sections explore the object-oriented underpinnings of the .NET data types in more detail.

NOTE Object-based code isn't just easier to translate from one language to another, it's also more elegant. From an object-oriented perspective, it makes more sense when the functionality you use to manipulate a data type originates from the data type itself.

The String Class

One of the best examples of how class members can replace built-in functions is found with strings. You might be familiar with the standard Visual Basic string functions such as Len(), Left(), Right(), and Instr(). These functions have been a part of Visual Basic and VBScript for years, and they're still available in VB .NET. However, a better solution is to use the methods of the String class, which provides greater consistency between .NET languages.

The following code snippet shows several ways to manipulate a string using its object nature.

```
Dim MyString As String = "This is a test string       "
MyString = MyString.Trim()                    ' = "This is a test string"
MyString = MyString.Substring(0, 4)           ' = "This"
MyString = MyString.ToUpper()                 ' = "THIS"
MyString = MyString.Replace("IS", "AT")       ' = "THAT"

Dim Length As Integer = MyString.Length      ' = 4
```

The first few statements use built-in methods, like Trim(), Substring(), ToUpper(), and Replace(). These methods generate new strings, and each of these statements replaces the current MyString with the new string object. The final statement uses a built-in Length property, which returns an integer that represents the number of letters in the string.

TIP A method is just a function or procedure that's hard-wired into an object. A property is similar to a variable—it's a piece of data that's associated with an object. You'll learn more about methods and properties in the next chapter.

Note that the Substring() method requires a starting offset and a character length. Strings use zero-based counting. That means that the first letter is in position 0, the second letter is in position 1, and so on. This marks a sharp change from the traditional

Visual Basic functions, which used one-based counting. This change is found throughout the .NET Framework for the sake of consistency.

You can even use these methods in succession in a single (rather ugly) line:

```
MyString = MyString.Trim.SubString(0, 4).ToUpper().Replace("IS", "AT")
```

Or, to make life more interesting, you can use the string methods on string literals just as easily as string variables:

```
MyString = "hello".ToUpper()     ' Sets MyString to "HELLO"
```

Table 3-3 lists some useful members of the System.String class.

Table 3-3. Useful String Members

Member	Description
Length	Returns the number of characters in the string (as an integer).
ToUpper() and ToLower()	Changes the string to contain all uppercase or all lowercase characters.
Trim(), TrimEnd(), and TrimStart()	Removes spaces or some other characters from either (or both) ends of a string.
PadLeft() and PadRight()	Adds the specified character to either side of a string, the number of times you indicate. For example, PadLeft(3, " ") adds three spaces to the left side.
Insert()	Puts another string inside a string at a specified (zero-based) index position. For example, Insert(1, "pre") adds the string "pre" after the first character of the current string.
Remove()	Removes a specified number of strings from a specified position. For example, Remove(0, 1) removes the first character.
Replace()	Replaces a specified substring with another string. For example, Replace("a", "b") changes all "a" characters in a string into "b" characters.
Substring()	Extracts a portion of a string of the specified length at the specified location. For example, Substring(0, 2) retrieves the first two characters.
StartsWith() and EndsWith()	Determines whether a string ends or starts with a specified substring. For example, StartsWith("pre") will return either True or False, depending on whether the string begins with the letters "pre" in lowercase.

Table 3-3. Useful String Members (Continued)

Member	Description
IndexOf() and LastIndexOf()	Finds the zero-based position of a substring in a string. This returns only the first match, and can start at the end or beginning. You can also use overloaded versions of these methods that accept a parameter that specifies the position to start the search.
Split()	Divides a string into an array of substrings delimited by a specific substring. For example, with Split(".") you could chop a paragraph into an array of sentence strings.
Join()	Joins an array of strings together. You can also specify a separator that will be inserted between each element.

The DateTime and TimeSpan Classes

The DateTime and TimeSpan data types also have built-in methods and properties. These class members allow you to perform the following three useful tasks:

- Extract a part of a DateTime (for example, just the year), or convert a TimeSpan to a specific representation (such as the total number of days or total number of minutes).
- Easily perform date calculations.
- Determine the current date and time and other information (such as the day of the week or whether or not the date occurs in a leap year).

For example, the following block of code creates a DateTime object, sets it to the current date and time, and adds a number of days. It then creates a string that indicates the year that the new date falls in ("for example, "2003").

```
Dim MyDate As DateTime = DateTime.Now
MyDate = MyDate.AddDays(365)
Dim DateString As String = MyDate.Year.ToString()
```

The next example shows how you can use a TimeSpan object to find the total number of minutes between two DateTime objects.

```
Dim MyDate1 As DateTime = DateTime.Now
Dim MyDate2 As DateTime = DateTime.Now.AddHours(3000)

Dim Difference As TimeSpan
Difference = MyDate2.Subtract(MyDate1)

Dim NumberOfMinutes As Double
NumberOfMinutes = Difference.TotalMinutes
```

These examples give you an idea of the flexibility .NET provides for manipulating date and time data. Tables 3-4 and 3-5 list some of the more useful built-in features of the DateTime and TimeSpan objects.

Table 3-4. Useful DateTime Members

Member	Description
Now	Gets the current date and time.
Today	Gets the current date, and leaves time set to 00:00:00.
Year, Date, Day, Hour, Minute, Second, and Millisecond	Returns one part of the DateTime object as an integer. For example, Month will return 12 for any day in December.
DayOfWeek	Returns an enumerated value that indicates the day of the week for this DateTime, using the DayOfWeek enumeration. For example, if the date falls on Sunday, this will return DayOfWeek.Sunday.
Add() and Subtract()	Adds or subtracts a TimeSpan from the DateTime.
AddYears(), AddMonths(), AddDays(), AddHours(), AddMinutes(), AddSeconds(), AddMilliseconds()	Adds an integer that represents a number of years, months, and so on, and returns a new DateTime. You can use a negative integer to perform a date subtraction.
DaysInMonth()	Returns the number of days in the month represented by the current DateTime.
IsLeapYear()	Returns True or False depending on whether the current DateTime is in a leap year.
ToString()	Changes the current DateTime to its string representation. You can also use an overloaded version of this method that allows you to specify a parameter with a format string.

Table 3-5. Useful TimeSpan Members

Member	Description
Days, Hours, Minutes, Seconds, Milliseconds	Returns one component of the current TimeSpan. For example, the Hours property can return an integer from 0 to 23.
TotalDays, TotalHours, TotalMinutes, TotalSeconds, TotalMilliseconds	Returns the total value of the current TimeSpan, indicated as a number of days, hours, minutes, and so on. For example, the TotalDays property might return a number like 234.342.
Add() and Subtract()	Combines TimeSpan objects together.
FromDays(), FromHours(), FromMinutes(), FromSeconds(), FromMilliseconds()	Allows you to quickly specify a new TimeSpan. For example, you can use TimeSpan.FromHours(24) to define a TimeSpan object exactly 24 hours long.
ToString()	Changes the current TimeSpan to its string representation. You can also use an overloaded version of this method that allows you to specify a parameter with a format string.

The Array Class

Arrays also behave like objects in the new world of .NET. For example, if you want to find out the size of an array, you won't use the old-fashioned UBound() function that's built into the Visual Basic language. Instead, you can use the Array.GetUpperBound() method in any language. The following code snippet shows this technique in action.

```
Dim MyArray() As Integer = {1, 2, 3, 4, 5}
Dim Bound As Integer

' Zero represents the first dimension of an array.
Bound = MyArray.GetUpperBound(0)    ' Bound = 4
```

Arrays also provide a few other useful methods, which allow you to sort them, reverse them, and search them for a specified element. Table 3-6 lists some useful members of the System.Array class.

Table 3-6. Useful Array Members

Member	Description
Length	Returns an integer that represents the total number of elements in all dimensions of an array. For example, a 3 × 3 array has a length of 9.
GetLowerBound() and GetUpperBound()	Determines the dimensions of an array. As with just about everything in .NET, you start counting at zero (which represents the first dimension).
Clear()	Empties an array's contents.
IndexOf() and LastIndexOf()	Searches a one-dimensional array for a specified value and returns the index number. You cannot use this with multidimensional arrays.
Sort()	Sorts a one-dimensional array made up of comparable data such as strings or numbers.
Reverse()	Reverses a one-dimensional array so that its elements are backward, from last to first.

Conditional Structures

In many ways, conditional logic—deciding which action to take based on user input, external conditions, or other information—is the heart of programming.

All conditional logic starts with a *condition*: a simple expression that can be evaluated to True or False. Your code can then make a decision to execute different logic depending on the outcome of the condition. To build a condition, you can use any combination of literal values or variables, along with *logical operators*. Table 3-7 lists the basic logical operators.

Table 3-7. Logical Operators

Operator	Description
=	Equal to
<>	Not equal to
<	Less than
>	Greater than
<=	Less than or equal to
>=	Greater than or equal to
And	And (evaluates to True only if both expressions are True)
Or	Or (evaluates to True if either expression is True)

You can use the comparison operators (<, >, <=, >=) with numeric types and strings. A string is deemed to be "less than" another string if it occurs earlier in an alphabetic sort. Thus "apple" is less than "attach."

The If ... End If Block

The If ... End If block is the powerhouse of conditional logic, able to evaluate any combination of conditions and deal with multiple and different pieces of data. Here's an example with an If ... End If block that features two conditions:

```
If MyNumber > 10 Then
    ' Do something.
ElseIf MyString = "hello" Then
    ' Do something.
Else
    ' Do something.
End If
```

Keep in mind that the If ... End If block matches one condition at most. For example, if MyNumber is greater than 10, the first condition will be met. That means the code in the first conditional block will run, and no other conditions will be evaluated. Whether or not MyString contains the text "hello" becomes irrelevant, because that condition will not be evaluated.

The Select Case Block

VB .NET also provides a Select Case structure that you can use to evaluate a single variable or expression for multiple possible values. In the following code, each case examines the MyNumber variable, and tests if it's equal to a specific integer.

```
Select Case MyNumber
    Case 1
        ' Do something if MyNumber = 1.
    Case 2
        ' Do something if MyNumber = 2.
    Case Else
        ' Do something if MyNumber is anything else.
End Select
```

If desired, you can handle multiple cases with one segment of code by including a list of comma-separated values in the Case statement.

```
Select Case MyNumber
    Case 1, 2
        ' Do something if MyNumber = 1 Or MyNumber = 2.
    Case Else
        ' Do something if MyNumber is anything else.
End Select
```

Unlike the If ... End If block, Select Case is limited to evaluating a single piece of information at a time. However, it provides a leaner, clearer syntax than the If ... End If block for situations in which you need to test a single variable.

Loop Structures

Loop structures allow you to repeat a segment of code multiple times. There are three basic types of loops in Visual Basic .NET. You choose the type of loop based on the type of task you need to perform. Your choices are as follows:

- You can loop a set number of times with a For ... Next loop.
- You can loop through all the items in a collection of data using a For Each loop.
- You can loop until a certain condition is met, using a Do ... Loop.

For ... Next and For Each loops are ideal for chewing through sets of data that have a known, fixed size. Do ... Loop is a more flexible construct that allows you to continue processing until a complex condition is met. Do ... Loop is often used with repetitive tasks or calculations that don't have a set number of iterations.

The For ... Next Block

The For ... Next block is a basic ingredient in many programs. It allows you to repeat a block of code a set number of times, using a built-in counter. To create a For ... Next loop, you need to specify a starting value, an ending value, and the amount to increment with each pass. Here's one example:

```
Dim i As Integer
For i = 1 To 10 Step 1
    ' This code executes 10 times.
    Debug.Write(i)
Next
```

In this example, the counter you're using is a variable named i. The loop begins at 1 and ends at 10. The "Step 1" clause specifies that i will be increased by 1 each time the code passes through the loop. You can omit this part of the code, because 1 is the default increment. Once i reaches 10 the final pass is made through the loop.

If you run this code using a tool like Visual Studio .NET, it will write the following numbers in the Debug window:

```
1 2 3 4 5 6 7 8 9 10
```

It often makes sense to set the counter variable based on the number of items you're processing. For example, you can use a For ... Next loop to step through the elements in an array by checking the size of the array before you begin. Here's the code you would use:

```
Dim StringArray() As String = {"one", "two", "three"}

Dim i As Integer
For i = 0 To StringArray.GetUpperBound(0)
    Debug.Write(StringArray(i) & " ")
Next
```

This code produces the following output:

```
one two three
```

Scope Changes from Visual Basic 6

In traditional Visual Basic, there were only two types of scope for a variable: form level and procedure level. VB .NET tightens these rules a notch by introducing block scope. Block scope means that any variables created inside a block structure (such as a conditional If… End If or a For… Next or a Do… Loop) are only accessible inside that block of code.

```
For i = 0 To 10
    Dim TempVariable As Integer
    ' (Do some calculation with TempVariable.)
Next
' You cannot access TempVariable here.
```

This change won't affect many programs. It's really designed to catch a few more accidental errors. If you need to access a variable inside and outside of some type of block structure, just define the variable before the block starts.

The For Each Block

VB .NET also provides a For Each block that allows you to loop through the items in a set of data. With a For Each block, you don't need to create an explicit counter variable. Instead, you create a variable that represents the type of data you're looking for. Your code will then loop until you've had a chance to process each piece of data in the set.

For Each is particularly useful for traversing the data in collections and arrays. For example, the next code segment loops through the items in an array using For Each. This code is identical to the previous example, but a little simpler.

```
Dim StringArray() As String = {"one", "two", "three"}

Dim Element As String
For Each Element In StringArray
    ' This code loops three times, with the Element variable set to
    ' "one", then "two", and then "three".
    Debug.Write(Element & " ")
Next
```

In this case, the For Each loop is looking for string in the array. Thus, if defines a string variable named Element. If you used code like this, you wouldn't retrieve any information at all:

```
Dim StringArray() As String = {"one", "two", "three"}

Dim Element As Integer
For Each Element In StringArray
    ' This code never executes, because there are
    ' no integers in this array.
Next
```

For Each iteration has one key limitation: It's read-only. For example, if you wanted to loop through an array and change the values in that array at the same time, For Each code wouldn't work. Instead, you would need to fall back on a For ... Next block with a counter.

The Do ... Loop Block

Finally, Visual Basic supports a Do ... Loop structure that tests a specific condition after each pass through the loop. To build your condition, you use the While or Until keyword. These two keywords are opposites. While means "as long as this is true," and Until means "as long as this is not true."

Here's an example that loops ten times. After each pass, the code evaluates whether the counter (i) has exceeded a set value.

```
Dim i As Integer = 1
Do
    i += 1
    ' This code executes 10 times.
Loop While i < 10
```

You can also place the condition at the beginning of the loop. In this case, the condition is tested before the loop is started. The following code is equivalent to the previous example, unless the condition you're testing is False to begin with. In that case, none of the code in the loop will execute.

```
Dim i As Integer = 1
Do While i < 10
    i += 1
    ' This code executes 10 times.
Loop
```

On the other hand, if you place the condition at the end of the loop, the code will always be executed at least once.

TIP Sometimes you need to exit a loop in a hurry. To do so, you'll need to use the corresponding Exit statement. For example, you can jump out of a For ... Next or For Each loop using the Exit For statement, and you can escape from a Do ... Loop with Exit Do.

Functions and Subroutines

Functions and subroutines are the most basic building block you can use to organize your code. Ideally, each function or subroutine will perform a distinct, logical task. By breaking your code down into procedures, you not only simplify your life, but you also make it easier to organize your code into classes and step into the world of object-oriented programming.

Visual Basic distinguishes between two types of procedures: ordinary subroutines and functions. The only difference between the two is that functions return a value. To set the return value of a function, you can assign a value to the function name, just as in previous versions of Visual Basic. VB .NET also introduces the useful Return keyword, which allows you to exit a function and return a result in one quick, clear step.

Subroutines are declared with the Sub keyword, and functions are declared with the Function keyword. Here is an example of each one:

```
Private Sub MySub()
    ' Code goes here.
End Sub

Private Function MyFunc() As Integer
    ' As an example, return the number 10.
    Return 10
End Function
```

You'll notice that both of these procedures are preceded with the accessibility keyword Private. This indicates that these procedures won't be accessible to code in a different class or module. The next chapter considers classes and accessibility in more detail.

Calling your procedures is straightforward—you simply enter the name of procedure, followed by parentheses. If you call a function, you have the option of using the data it returns, or just ignoring it.

```
' This call is allowed.
MySub()

' This call is allowed.
MyFunc()

' This call is allowed.
Dim MyNumber As Integer
MyNumber = MyFunc()
```

```
' This call isn't allowed.
' MySub does not return any information.
MyNumber = MySub()
```

Parameters

Procedures can also accept information through parameters. Parameters are declared in a similar way to variables. By convention, parameter names always begin with a lowercase first letter in any language.

Here's how you might create a function that accepts two parameters and returns their sum.

```
Private Function AddNumbers(number1 As Integer, number2 As Integer) As Integer
    Return (number1 + number2)
End Sub
```

When calling a procedure, you specify any required parameters in parentheses, or use an empty set of parentheses if no parameters are required.

```
' Call a subroutine with no parameters.
MySub()

' Call a subroutine with two Integer parameters.
MySub2(10, 20)

' Call a function with two Integer parameters and an Integer return value.
Dim ReturnValue As Integer = AddNumbers(10, 10)
```

Procedure Overloading

VB .NET supports overloading, which allows you to create more than one function or subroutine with the same name, but with a different set of parameters. When you call the procedure, the CLR automatically chooses the correct version by examining the parameters you supply.

This is old hat to C programmers, but a valuable new introduction to the Visual Basic world. It allows you to collect different versions of several functions together. For example, you might allow a database search that returns an author name. Rather than create three functions with different names depending on the criteria, such as GetNameFromID(), GetNameFromSSN(), GetNameFromBookTitle(), you could create three versions of the GetCustomerName() function. Each function would have the same name, but a different *signature*, meaning it would require different parameters.

To overload a procedure, you use the Overloads keyword. Here's an example that provides two overloaded versions for the GetProductPrice() method.

```
Private Overloads Function GetProductPrice(ID As Integer) As Decimal
    ' Code here.
End Function

Private Overloads Function GetProductPrice(name As String) As Decimal
    ' Code here.
End Function

' And so on...
```

You can look up product prices based on the unique product ID, or the full product name, depending on whether you supply an integer or string argument:

```
Dim Price As Decimal

' Get price by product ID (the first version).
Price = GetProductPrice(1001)

' Get price by product name (the second version).
Price = GetProductPrice("DVD Player")
```

You cannot overload a function with versions that have the same *signature*—that is, the same number of parameters and parameter data types—because the CLR will not be able to distinguish them from each other. When you call an overloaded function, the version that matches the parameter list you supply is used. If no version matches, an error occurs.

NOTE .NET uses overloaded methods in most of its classes. This approach allows you to use a flexible range of different parameters, while centralizing functionality under common names. Even the methods we've looked at so far (like the String methods for padding or replacing text) have multiple versions that provide similar features with various different options.

Delegates

Delegates are a new feature of the .NET languages. They allow you to create a variable that "points" to a procedure. You can use this variable at any time to invoke the procedure. Delegates help you write flexible code that can be reused in many different situations.

The first step when using a delegate is to define its signature. A delegate variable can only point to a function or procedure that matches its specific signature (list of parameters). For example, if you have a subroutine that accepts a single string parameter, and another subroutine that accepts two string parameters, you'll need to use a separate delegate type for each subroutine. This enforces a level of type safety that isn't found with traditional function pointers in languages like C++.

Here's the code you use to define a delegate and its signature:

```
' Define a delegate that can represent any function that accepts a single
' string parameter and returns a string.
Private Delegate Function StringFunction(in As String) As String
```

Once you've defined a type of delegate, you can create and assign a delegate variable. For example, assume your program has the following function:

```
Private Function TranslateEnglishToFrench(english As String) As String
    ' Code goes here.
End Function
```

This function requires one string parameter and returns a string. Thus, it matches the signature used in the definition of the StringFunction delegate. That means you can create a StringFunction delegate variable, and use it to store a reference to the TranslateEnglishToFrench() function. To actually store the reference to the TranslateEnglishToFrench() function, you use the AddressOf statement.

The following code demonstrates this technique:

```
' Create a delegate variable.
Dim FunctionReference As StringFunction

' Store a reference to a matching procedure.
FunctionReference = AddressOf TranslateEnglishToFrench
```

Once you have a delegate variable that references a function, you can invoke the function through the delegate. To do this, you just use the delegate name as though it were the function name:

```
Dim FrenchString As String

' Run the method that functionReference points to.
' In this case, it will be TranslateEnglishToFrench().
FrenchString = FunctionReference("Hello")
```

In the previous code example, the procedure that the FunctionReference delegate points to will be invoked with the parameter "Hello" and the return value will be stored in the FrenchString variable.

Delegates Are the Basis of Events

Wouldn't it be nice to have a delegate that could refer to more than one function at once, and invoke them simultaneously? That would allow the client application to have multiple "listeners," and notify the listeners all at once when something happens.

In fact, delegates do have this functionality, but you're more likely to see it in use with .NET events. Events, which are described in the next chapter, are based on delegates, but work at a slightly higher level. In a typical ASP.NET program, you'll use events extensively, but you'll probably never work directly with delegates.

The Last Word

It's impossible to do justice to an entire language in a single chapter. However, if you've programmed before, you'll find that this chapter provides all the information you need to get started with the .NET languages. As you work through the full ASP.NET examples in the following chapters, you can refer to this chapter to clear up any language issues. In the next chapter, you'll learn about more important language concepts, and the object-oriented nature of .NET.

CHAPTER 4

Types, Objects, and Namespaces

OBJECT-ORIENTED PROGRAMMING has been a popular buzzword over the last several years. In fact, one of the few places that object-oriented programming *wasn't* emphasized was in ordinary ASP pages. With .NET, the story changes considerably. Not only does .NET allow you to use objects, it demands it. Almost every ingredient you'll need to use to create a web application is, on some level, really a kind of object.

So how much do you need to know about object-oriented programming to write .NET pages? It depends on whether you want to follow existing examples and cut and paste code samples, or have a deeper understanding of the way .NET works and gain more control. This book assumes that if you're willing to pick up a thousand-page book, then you're the type of programmer who excels by understanding how and why things work the way they do. It also assumes that you're interested in some of the advanced ASP.NET programming tasks that *will* require class-based design, like designing custom controls (see Chapter 23) and creating your own components (see Chapter 22).

This chapter explains objects from the point of view of the .NET Framework. I won't rehash the typical object-oriented theory, because there are already countless excellent programming books on the subject. Instead, I'll show you the types of objects .NET allows, how they're constructed, and how they fit into the larger framework of namespaces and assemblies.

The Basics About Classes

As a developer, you've probably already created classes, or at least heard about them. *Classes* are the code definitions for objects. The nice thing about a class is that you can use it to create as many objects as you need. For example, you might have a class that represents an XML file, which can be used to read some data. If you want to access multiple XML files at once, you can create several instances of your class, as shown in Figure 4-1. These instances are called *objects.*

Classes consist of three key ingredients:

- **Properties.** Properties allow you to access an object's data. Some properties may be read-only, so they cannot be modified, while others can be changed. For example, the previous chapter demonstrated how you can use the read-only Length property of a String object to find out how many letters are in a string.

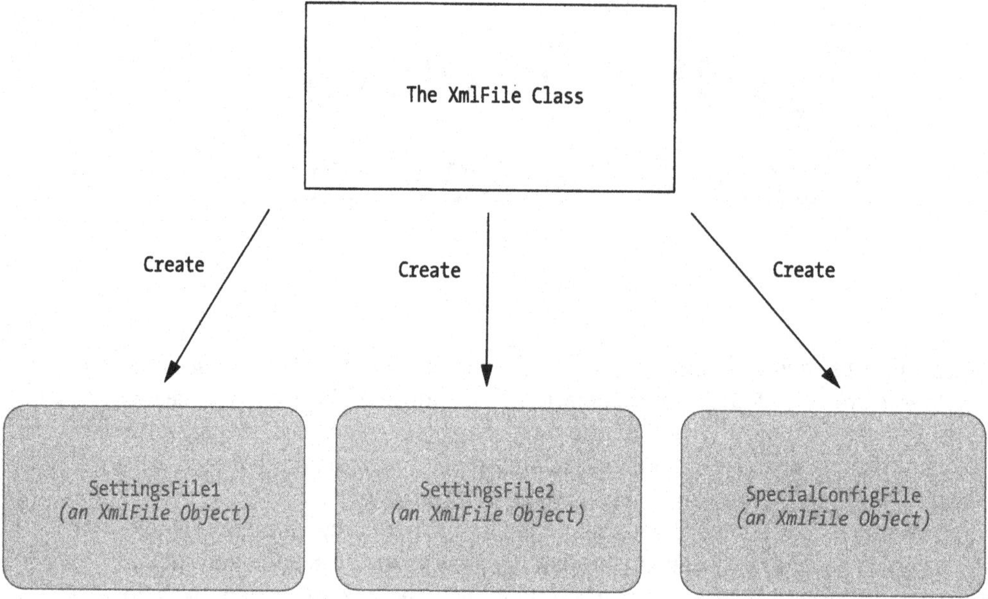

Figure 4-1. Classes are used to create objects

- **Methods.** Methods allow you to perform an action with an object. Unlike properties, methods are used for actions that perform a distinct task or may change the object's state significantly. For example, to open a connection to a database you might call an Open() method in a Connection object.
- **Events.** Events provide notification that something has happened. If you've ever programmed an ordinary desktop application in Visual Basic, you know how controls can fire events to trigger your code. For example, if a user clicks on a button, the Button object fires a Click event, which your code can react to. ASP.NET controls also provide events.

In addition, classes contain their own code and internal set of private data. Classes behave like *black boxes,* which means that when you use an object, you shouldn't waste any time wondering about how it works, or what low-level information it's using. Instead, you only need to worry about the public interface of a class, which is the set of properties, methods, and events that are available for you to work with. Together, these elements are called class *members.*

In ASP.NET, you'll create your own custom classes to represent individual web pages. In addition, you'll create custom classes if you design any special components (as shown in Chapter 22). For the most part, however, you'll be using prebuilt classes from the .NET class library, rather than programming your own.

Shared Members

One of the tricks about .NET classes is that there are really two ways to use them. Some class members can be used without creating an object first. These are called *shared* members, and they're accessed by class name. For example, you can use the shared property DateTime.Now to retrieve a DateTime object that represents the current date and time. You don't need to create a DateTime object first.

On the other hand, the majority of the DateTime members require a valid instance. For example, you can't use the AddDays() method or the Hour property without a valid object. These *instance* members have no meaning without a live object and some valid data to draw on.

The following code snippet uses shared and instance members:

```
' Get the current date using a shared method.
' Note that you need to use the class name: DateTime.
Dim MyDate As DateTime = DateTime.Now

' Use an instance method to add a day.
' Note that you need to use the object name: MyDate.
MyDate = MyDate.AddDays(1)

' The following code makes no sense.
' It tries to use the instance method AddDays with the class name DateTime!
MyDate = DateTime.AddDays(1)
```

Both properties and methods can be designated as shared. Shared methods are a major part of the .NET Framework, and you will make frequent use of them in this book. Remember, some classes may consist entirely of shared members (like the Math class shown in the previous chapter), and some may use only instance members. Other classes, like DateTime, provide a combination of the two.

In the next example, which introduces a basic class, we'll use only instance members. This is the most common design, and a good starting point.

A Simple Class

To create a class, you must define it using a special block structure:

```
Public Class Product
    ' Class code goes here.
End Class
```

You can define as many classes as you need in the same file (which is a departure from Visual Basic 6, which required a separate file for each class). However, a class cannot span more than one file.

Classes exist in many forms. They may represent an actual thing in the real world (as they do in most programming textbooks), they may represent some programming abstraction (such as a rectangle or color structure), or they may just be a convenient way to group together related functionality (like the Math class). Deciding what a class should represent and breaking down your code into a group of interrelated classes is part of the art of programming.

Building a Basic Class

In the next example, you'll see how to construct a .NET class piece by piece. This class will represent a product from the catalog of an e-commerce company. The Product class will store product data, and it will include the built-in functionality needed to generate a block of HTML that displays the product on a web page. When this class is complete, you'll be able to put it to work with a sample ASP.NET test page.

Once you've defined a class, the first step is to add some basic data. The next example defines three member variables that store information about the product: namely, its name, price, and a URL that points to an image file.

```
Public Class Product
    Private Name As String
    Private Price As Decimal
    Private ImageUrl As String
End Class
```

Notice that when you create variables in a class, you don't use the Dim keyword. The Dim keyword is used to create a *local variable* inside a procedure. A local variable only exists until the current procedure ends. On the other hand, a *member variable* (or *field*) is declared as part of a class. It's available to all the procedures in the class, and it lives as long as the containing object lives.

When you create a member variable, you need to explicitly set its *accessibility*. The accessibility determines whether other parts of your code will be able to read and alter this variable. For example, if one ObjectA contains a private variable, ObjectB will not be able to read or modify it. Only ObjectA will have that ability. On the other hand, if ObjectA has a public variable, any other object in your application is free to read and alter the information it contains. Local variables don't support any accessibility keywords, because they can never be made available to any code beyond the current procedure.

Generally, in a simple ASP.NET application most of your variables will be private because the majority of your code will be self-contained in a single web page class. As you start creating separate components to reuse functionality, however, accessibility becomes much more important. Table 4-1 explains the different access levels you can use.

Table 4-1. Accessibility Keywords

VB .NET Keyword	Accessibility
Public	Can be accessed by any other class
Private	Can only be accessed by code procedures inside the current class
Friend	Can be accessed by code procedures in any of the classes in the current assembly
Protected	Can be accessed by code procedures in the current class, or any class that inherits from this class
Protected Friend	Can be accessed by code procedures in the current application, or any class that inherits from this class

The accessibility keywords don't just apply to variables. They also apply to methods, properties, and events, all of which will be explored in this chapter.

Creating a Live Object

From the client's point of view, the only difference between creating a simple data type (like a string or integer) and creating an object is the fact that the New keyword must be used with objects. The New keyword *instantiates* the object, which means it creates a copy of the class in memory. If you define an object but don't instantiate it, you'll receive the infamous "null reference" error when you try to use the object. That's because the object doesn't actually exist yet.

The following code snippet creates an object based on the Product class and then releases it.

```
Dim SaleProduct As New Product()

' Optionally you could do this in two steps:
' Dim SaleProduct As Product
' SaleProduct = New Product()

' Now release the class from memory.
SaleProduct = Nothing
```

In many cases, you can omit the last line, which releases the product. That's because objects are automatically released when the appropriate variable goes out of scope. Objects are also released when your application ends. In an ASP.NET web page, your application is only given a few seconds to live. Once the web page is rendered to HTML, the application ends, and all objects are automatically released.

TIP Just because an object is released doesn't mean the memory it uses is immediately reclaimed. The CLR uses a long running service (called *garbage collection*) that periodically scans for released objects, and reclaims the memory they hold.

In some cases you will want to define an object variable without using the New keyword to create it. For example, you might want to assign an instance that already exists to your object variable. Or you might receive a live object as a return value from a function. The following code shows one such example.

```
' Define but don't create the product.
Dim SaleProduct As Product

' Call a function that accepts a numeric product ID parameter,
' and returns a product object.
SaleProduct = FetchProduct(23)
```

In these cases, when you aren't actually creating the class, you shouldn't use the New keyword.

Class Creation Changes from Visual Basic 6

In Visual Basic 6, it was a bad idea to define an object with the New keyword in the definition. This would not actually create the class, but cause it to be automatically created the first time you refer to it in a code statement. The problem was that you could release the object, try to use the variable again, and end up with a new blank copy of the object automatically re-created. This bizarre behavior has been stamped out in VB .NET. You'll also notice that the Set keyword is no longer needed. VB .NET can distinguish between variables and objects automatically, and doesn't need your help.

Adding Properties

The simple Product class is essentially useless because there's no way your code can manipulate it. All its information is private and unreachable. Other classes won't be able to set or read this information.

To overcome this limitation, you could make the member variables public. Unfortunately, that approach could lead to problems because it would give other objects free access to change everything, even allowing them to apply invalid or inconsistent data. Instead, you need to add a "control panel" through which your code can manipulate Product objects in a safe way. You do this by adding *property procedures*.

Property procedures usually have two parts. The property *get* procedure allows your code to retrieve data from the object. The property *set* procedure allows your code to set the object's data. In some cases, you might omit one of these parts, such as when you want to create a property that can be examined but not modified.

Property procedures are similar to any other type of procedure in that you can write as much code as you need. For example, your property set procedure could raise an error to alert the client code of invalid data and prevent the change from being applied. Or, your property set procedure could change multiple private variables at once, thereby making sure that the object's internal state remains consistent. In the Product class example, this sophistication isn't required. Instead, the property procedures just provide straightforward access to the private variables.

To prevent confusion between the private variable names and the property names, the private variables have been renamed to start with an underscore in the VB .NET code. This is a common convention, but it doesn't represent the only possible approach.

```
Public Class Product
    Private _Name As String
    Private _Price As Decimal
    Private _ImageUrl As String

    Public Property Name() As String
        Get
            Return _Name
        End Get
        Set(Value As String)
            _Name = Value
        End Set
    End Property

    Public Property Price() As Decimal
        Get
            Return _Price
        End Get
        Set(Value As Decimal)
            _Price = Value
        End Set
    End Property

    Public Property ImageUrl() As String
        Get
            Return _ImageUrl
        End Get
        Set(Value As String)
            _ImageUrl = Value
        End Set
    End Property

End Class
```

The client can now create and configure the class by using its properties and the familiar dot syntax. For example, if the object is named SaleProduct, you can set the product name using the SaleProduct.Name property. Here's an example:

```
Dim SaleProduct As New Product()
SaleProduct.Name = "Kitchen Garbage"
SaleProduct.Price = 49.99
SaleProduct.ImageUrl = "http://mysite/garbage.png"
```

Adding a Basic Method

The current Product class consists entirely of data. This type of class is often useful in an application. For example, you might use it to send information about a product from one function to another. However, it's more common to add functionality to your classes along with the data. This functionality takes the form of *methods*.

Methods are simply public functions and subroutines that are built into your class. When a method is called on an object, your code responds to do something useful, like returning some calculated data. In our example, we'll add a GetHtml() method to the Product class. This method will return a string representing a formatted block of HTML based on the current data in the Product object. You could then take this block of HTML and placed it on a web page to represent the product.

```
Public Class Product
    ' (Variables and property procedures omitted for clarity.)

    Public Function GetHtml() As String
        Dim HtmlString As String
        HtmlString = "<h1>" & _Name & "</h1><br>"
        HtmlString &= "<h3>Costs: " & _Price.ToString() & "</h3><br>"
        HtmlString &= "<img src=" & _ImageUrl & ">"
        Return HtmlString
    End Function

End Class
```

All the GetHtml() method does is read the private data, and format it in some attractive way. This really targets our class as a user interface class rather than a pure data class or "business object."

Adding a Constructor

Currently, the Product class has a problem. Ideally, classes should ensure that they are always in a valid state. However, unless you explicitly set all the appropriate properties, the Product object won't correspond to a valid product. This could cause an error if you try to use a method that relies on some of the data that hasn't been supplied. In the past, this was a major limitation of classes in Visual Basic programming. Today, .NET brings Visual Basic up to the level of other modern languages by introducing *constructors*.

A constructor is a method that automatically runs when the class is first created. In VB .NET, the constructor always has the name New.

The next code example shows a new version of the Product class. It adds a constructor that requires the product price and name as arguments.

```
Public Class Product
    ' (Additional class code omitted for clarity.)

    Public Sub New(name As String, price As Decimal)
        ' These parameters have the same name as the property procedures,
        ' but that doesn't cause a problem. The local variables have priority.
        _Name = name
        _Price = price
    End Sub

End Class
```

Here's an example of the code you need to create an object based on the new Product class, using its constructor:

```
Dim SaleProduct As New Product("Kitchen Garbage", 49.99)
```

The preceding code is much leaner than the code that was required to create and initialize the previous version of the Product class. With the help of the constructor, you can create the Product object and configure it with the basic data it needs in a single line.

If you don't create a constructor, .NET supplies a default constructor that does nothing. If you create at least one constructor, .NET will not supply a default constructor. Thus, in the preceding example, the Product class has exactly one constructor, which is the one that is explicitly defined in code. In order to create a Product class, you *must* use this constructor. This restriction prevents a client from creating an object without specifying the bare minimum amount of data that's required.

```
' This will not be allowed, because there is
' no zero-argument constructor.
Dim SaleProduct As New Product()
```

Most of the classes you use will have constructors that require parameters. As with ordinary methods, constructors can be overloaded with multiple versions, each providing a different set of parameters. When creating an object, you can choose the constructor that suits you best based on the information that you have available. The .NET Framework classes use overloaded constructors extensively.

NOTE When creating multiple constructors in VB .NET, you don't use the Overloads keyword that was introduced in Chapter 3. There's no technical reason for this discrepancy; it's just a harmless quirk.

Adding a Basic Event

Classes can also use events to notify your code. To define an event in VB .NET, you use the Event keyword, followed by the name of the event, and a list of parameters that the event will use. Once you've defined the event, you can fire it any time using the RaiseEvent statement.

As an illustration, the Product class example has been enhanced with a NameChanged event that occurs whenever the Name is modified through the property procedure. This event won't fire if code inside the class changes the underlying private name variable without going through the property procedure.

```
Public Class Product
    ' (Additional class code omitted for clarity.)

    ' Define the event.
    Public Event NameChanged()

    Public Property Name() As String
        Get
            Return _Name
        End Get
        Set(Value As String)
            _Name = Value

            ' Fire the event to all listeners.
            RaiseEvent NameChanged()
        End Set
    End Property

End Class
```

It's quite possible that you'll create dozens of ASP.NET applications without once defining a custom event. However, you'll be hard-pressed to write a single ASP.NET web page without *handling* an event. To handle an event, you first create a subroutine called an *event handler*. The event handler contains the code that should be executed when the event occurs. Then, you connect the event handler to the event.

To handle the Product class you need to begin by creating an event handler in another class. The event handler needs to have the exact same syntax as the event it's handling. In the Product example, the event has no parameters, so the event handler would look like the simple subroutine as shown here:

```
Public Sub ChangeDetected()
    ' This code executes in response to the NameChanged event.
End Sub
```

There are two ways to connect an event handler. The first option is to connect an event handler at runtime using the AddHandler statement. Here's an example:

```
Dim SaleProduct As New Product()

' This connects the SaleProduct.NameChanged event to an event handling
' procedure called ChangeDetected.
AddHandler SaleProduct.NameChanged, AddressOf ChangeDetected

' Now the event will occur in response to this code:
SaleProduct.Name = "Kitchen Garbage"
```

You'll notice that this code is quite similar to the delegate example in the previous chapter. In fact, events use delegates behind the scenes to keep track of the event handlers they need to notify.

Instead of connecting events programmatically, you can connect them declaratively with the WithEvents keyword and the Handles clause. You'll see this technique in the web form examples in the next few chapters. However, it's worth noting that if you're using Visual Studio .NET, you won't need to manually hook up event handlers for web controls at all. Instead, Visual Studio .NET will add the necessary code to connect all the event handlers you create.

NOTE In traditional Visual Basic programming, events were connected to event handlers based on the procedure name. In .NET, this clumsy system is abandoned. Your event handler can have any name you want, and it can even be used to handle more than one event, provided they pass the same type of information in their parameters.

ASP.NET uses a new event-driven programming model, and you'll soon become very used to writing code that reacts to events. Unless you're creating your own components, however, you won't need to fire your own custom events. For an example where custom events make sense, refer to Chapter 23, which discusses how you can build your own controls.

Testing the Product Class

To learn a little more about how the Product class works, it helps to create a simple web page. This web page will create a Product object, get its HTML representation, and then display it in the web page. To try out this example, you'll need several files that are provided with the online samples in the Chapter04 directory. These include the following:

- **Product.vb.** This file contains the code for the Product class.
- **Product.dll.** This file contains the compiled code for the Product class.
- **Garbage.jpg.** This is the image that the Product class will use.
- **ProductTest.aspx.** This file contains the web page code that uses the Product class.

The first step is to choose a virtual directory where you can set up your test. You can create a new virtual directory, as described in Chapter 2, or you can use the default directory (c:\Inetpub\wwwroot). Once you've made your choice, follow these steps:

1. First, copy Garbage.jpg and ProductTest.aspx to the directory you've chosen.
2. Next, create a subdirectory named bin.
3. Copy the Product.dll file into the \bin subdirectory. This ensures that the Product class will be available to all the web pages in this virtual directory—a topic explored in more detail in the next chapter.

Now you can request the ProductTest.aspx page. If you've used the root website directory c:\Inetpub\wwwroot, you would request http://localhost/ProductTest.aspx.

The ProductTest.aspx page creates a new Product object, configures it, and uses the the GetHtml() method. The HTML is written to the web page using the Response.Write() method. Here's the code:

```
<%@ Page Language="VB" %>
<script runat="server">
    Sub Page_Load(sender As Object, e As EventArgs)
        Dim SaleProduct As New Product("Kitchen Garbage", 49.99)
        SaleProduct.ImageUrl = "garbage.jpg"
        Response.Write(SaleProduct.GetHtml())
    End Sub
</script>

<html>
<head>
</head>
<body>
    <form runat="server">
    </form>
</body>
</html>
```

The <script> block holds a subroutine named Page_Load. This subroutine is triggered when the page is first created. Once this code finished, the HTML is sent to the client. The web page that you'll see is shown in Figure 4-2.

The interesting thing about the GetHtml() method is that it's similar to how an ASP.NET web control works, but on a much cruder level. To use an ASP.NET control, you create an object (explicitly or implicitly), and configure some properties. Then ASP.NET automatically creates a web page by examining all these objects and requesting their associated HTML (by calling a hidden GetHtml() method, or something conceptually similar).[1] It then sends the completed page to the user. The end result is that you work with objects, instead of dealing directly with raw HTML code.

When using a web control, you only see the public interface made up of properties, methods, and events. However, understanding how class code actually works will help you master advanced development.

Now that you've seen the basics of classes, and a demonstration of how you can use a class, it's time to introduce a little more theory about .NET objects, and revisit the basic data types introduces in the last chapter.

---

1. In actual fact, the ASP.NET engine calls a method named Render() in every web control.

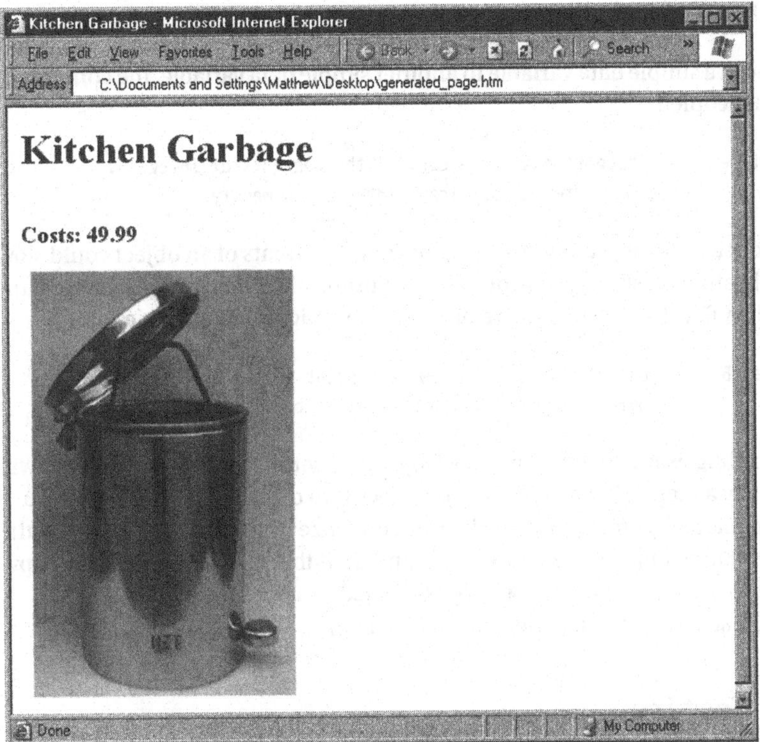

Figure 4-2. Output generated by a Product object

Value Types and Reference Types

In Chapter 3, you learned how simple data types such as strings and integers are actually objects created from the class library. This allows some impressive tricks, like built-in string handling and date calculation. However, simple data types differ from more complex objects in one important way. They work like *value types,* while classes behave like *reference types.*

What this means is that a variable for a simple data type contains the actual information you put in it (such as the number 7). On the other hand, object variables actually store a reference that points to a location in memory where the full object is stored. In most cases, .NET masks you from this underlying reality, and you won't notice any difference in the way you work with reference objects and the way you manipulate simple value type variables. However, there are three cases when you will notice that object variables act a little differently than ordinary data types: in assignment operations, in comparison operations, and when passing parameters.

Assignment Operations

When you assign a simple data variable to another simple data variable, the contents of the variable are copied.

```
IntegerA = IntegerB   ' IntegerA now has a copy of the contents of IntegerB.
                      ' There are two duplicate integers in memory.
```

Objects work a little differently. Copying the entire contents of an object could slow down an application, particularly if you were performing multiple assignments. With objects, the default is to just copy the reference in an assignment operation.

```
ObjectA = ObjectB    ' ObjectA and ObjectB now both point to the same thing.
                     ' There is one object, and two ways to access it.
```

In the preceding example, if you modify ObjectB by setting a property, ObjectA will be automatically affected. In fact, ObjectA is ObjectB. To override this behavior, you would need to manually create a new object and initialize its information to match the existing object. Some objects provide a Clone() method that allows you to easily copy the object. One example is the DataSet, which is used to store information from a database. You'll see this trick in action later in the book.

Equality Testing

A similar distinction between objects and simple data types appears when you compare two variables. When you compare simple variables, you're comparing the contents:

```
If IntegerA = IntegerB Then
    ' This is True as long as the integers have the same content.
End If
```

When you compare object variables you're actually testing whether they're the same instance. In other words, you're testing if the references are pointing to the same object in memory, not if their contents match. VB .NET emphasizes this difference by forcing you to use the Is keyword to compare objects. Using the equals (=) sign will generate a compile-time error.

```
If ObjectA Is ObjectB Then
    ' This is True if both ObjectA and ObjectB point to the same thing.
    ' This is False if they are separate, yet identical objects.
End If
```

Passing Parameters by Reference and by Value

You can create two types of procedure parameters. The standard type (known as ByVal in Visual Basic) ensures that any changes don't propagate back to the calling code and modify the original variable. In other words, when you use a ByVal parameter, a copy of the parameter is submitted to the procedure. The second type of parameter is ByRef. If a procedure changes the value of a ByRef parameter, the original variable will also be modified.

The following code shows a procedure that uses a reference parameter. When the procedure modifies this parameter (multiplying it by two), the calling code is also affected.

```
Private Sub ProcessNumber(ByRef number As Integer)
    number *= 2
End Sub
```

Here's a code snippet that shows the effect of calling the ProcessNumber procedure:

```
Dim Num As Integer = 10
ProcessNumber(Num)          ' Once this call completes, Num will be 20.
```

This behavior is straightforward when you're using value types, like integers. However, if you use reference types, like a Product object or an array, you won't see this behavior. The reason is because the entire object isn't passed in the parameter. Instead, it's just the *reference* that's transmitted. This is a whole lot more efficient for large objects (it saves having to copy a large block of memory), but it doesn't always lead to the behavior you expect.

One notable quirk occurs if you use ByVal. In this case, you aren't creating a copy of the object, but a copy of the reference. This reference still points to the same in-memory object. That means that any changes a subroutine makes to an object that has been passed in as a parameter will affect the calling code.

Reviewing .NET Types

So far the discussion has focused on simple data types and classes. The .NET class library is actually composed of *types*, which is a catch-all term that includes several object-like relatives:

- **Classes.** This is the most common type in .NET Framework. Strings and arrays are two examples of .NET classes, although you can easily create your own.
- **Structures.** Structures, like classes, can include properties, methods, and events. Unlike classes, they are value types, which alters the way they behave with assignment and comparison operations. Structures also lack some of the more advanced class features (like inheritance), and are generally simpler. Integers, dates, and chars are all structures.
- **Enumerations.** An enumeration defines a set of integer constants with descriptive names. Enumerations were introduced in the previous chapter.
- **Delegates.** A delegate is a function pointer that allows you to invoke a procedure indirectly. Delegates are the foundation for .NET event handling, and were introduced in the previous chapter.
- **Interfaces.** They define contracts that a class must adhere to. Interfaces are an advanced technique of object-oriented programming, and they're useful when standardizing how objects interact. You'll learn about interfaces with custom control programming in Chapter 23.

Would the Real Reference Types Please Stand Up?

Occasionally, a class can override its behavior to act more like a value type. For example, the String type is a full-featured class, not a simple value type. (This is required to make strings efficient, because they can contain a variable amount of data.) However, the String type overrides its equality and assignment operations so that these operations work like those of a simple value type. This makes the String work in the way that programmers intuitively expect. Arrays, on the other hand, are reference types through and through. If you assign one array variable to another, you copy the reference, not the array (although the Array class also provides a Clone() method that returns a duplicate array to allow true copying).

Table 4-2 sets the record straight, and explains exactly which data types are value types, and which data types are really reference types.

Table 4-2. Common Reference and Value Types

Data Type	Nature	Behavior
Integer, Decimal, Single, Double, and all other basic numeric types	Value Type	Equality and assignment operations work with the variable contents, not a reference.
DateTime, TimeSpan	Value Type	Equality and assignment operations work with the variable contents, not a reference.
Char, Byte, and Boolean	Value Type	Equality and assignment operations work with the variable contents, not a reference.
String	Reference Type	Equality and assignment operations appear to work with the variable contents, not a reference.
Array	Reference Type	Equality and assignment operations work with the reference, not the contents.
Object	Reference Type	Equality and assignment operations work with the reference, not the contents.

Advanced Class Programming

Part of the art of object-oriented programming is determining class relations. For example, you could create a Product object that contains a ProductFamily object, or a Car object that contains four Wheel objects. To create this sort of class relationship, all you need to do is define the appropriate variable or properties in the class. This type of relationship is called *containment*.

For example, the following code shows a ProductCatalog class, which holds an array of Products.

```
Public Class ProductCatalog
    Private _Products() As Product

    ' (Other class code goes here.)
End Class
```

In ASP.NET programming, you'll find special classes called collections that have no purpose other than to group together various objects. Some collections also allow you to sort and retrieve objects using a key name. You'll learn more about collections in Chapter 10.

In addition, classes can have a different type of relationship known as *inheritance*.

Inheritance

Inheritance is a form of code reuse. It allows one class to acquire and extend the functionality of another class. For example, you could create a class called TaxableProduct that inherits from Product. The TaxableProduct class would gain all the same methods, properties, and events of the Product class. You could then add additional members that relate to taxation.

```
Public Class TaxableProduct
    Inherits Product

    Private _TaxRate As Decimal = 1.15

    Public ReadOnly Property TotalPrice() As Decimal
        Get
            ' The code can access the Price property because it's
            ' a public part of the base class Product.
            ' The code cannot access the private _Price variable, however.
            Return (Price * _TaxRate)
        End Get
    End Property

End Class
```

This technique appears much more useful than it really is. In an ordinary application, most classes use containment and other relationships instead of inheritance, which can complicate life needlessly without delivering many benefits. Dan Appleman, a renowned VB guru, once described inheritance as "the coolest feature you'll almost never use."

In all honesty, there is one place that you'll see inheritance at work in ASP.NET. Inheritance allows you to create a custom class that inherits the features of a class in the .NET class library. For example, when you create a custom web form, you actually inherit from a basic Page class to gain the standard set of features. Similarly, when you create a custom web service, you inherit from the WebService class. You'll see this type of inheritance throughout the book.

There are many more subtleties of class-based programming with inheritance. For example, you can override parts of a base class, prevent classes from being inherited, or create a class that must be used for inheritance and can't be directly created. These topics aren't covered in this book, and they don't affect most ASP.NET programmers.

Shared Members

The beginning of this chapter introduced the idea of shared properties and methods, which can be used without a live object. Shared members are often used to provide useful functionality related to an object. The .NET class library uses this technique heavily. For example, the System.Math class is entirely composed of shared methods for performing mathematical operations. You never need to specifically create a Math object.

Shared members have a wide variety of possible uses. Sometimes they provide basic conversions and utility functions that support a class. To create a shared property or method, you just need to use the shared keyword, right after the accessibility keyword.

The following example shows a TaxableProduct class that contains a shared TaxRate property and private variable. That means that there is one copy of the tax rate information, and it applies to all TaxableProduct objects.

```
Public Class TaxableProduct
    Inherits Product

    ' (Other class code omitted for clarity.)

    Private Shared _TaxRate As Decimal = 1.15

    ' Now you can call TaxableProduct.TaxRate, even without an object.
    Public Shared Property TaxRate() As Decimal
        Get
            Return _TaxRate
        End Get
        Set(Value As Decimal)
            _TaxRate = Value
        End Set
    End Property

End Class
```

You can now retrieve the tax rate information directly from the class, without needing to create an object first.

```
' Change the TaxRate. This will affect all TotalPrice calculations for any
' TaxableProduct object.
TaxableProduct.TaxRate = 1.24
```

Shared data isn't tied to the lifetime of an object. In fact, it's available throughout the life of the entire application. That means shared members are the closest thing .NET programmers have to global data.

A shared member can't access an instance member. In order to access a nonshared member, it needs an actual instance of your object—in which case it must also be an instance member.

Converting Objects

Objects can be converted with the same syntax that's used for simple data types. However, an object can only be converted into three types of things: itself, an interface that it supports, or a base class that it inherits from. You can't convert an object into a string or an integer. Instead, you will need to call a conversion method, if it's available, such as ToString() or Parse().

For example, you could convert a TaxableProduct into a Product. You wouldn't actually lose any information, but you would no longer be able to access the TotalPrice property—unless you converted the reference back to a TaxableProduct. This underscores an important point: when you convert an object, you don't actually change that object. The exact same object remains floating as a blob of binary data somewhere in memory. What you change is the way that you access that object.

For example, if you have a Product variable that points to a TaxableProduct object, your object really *is* a TaxableProduct. However, you can only use the properties and methods that are defined in the Product class. This is one of the subtleties of manipulating objects, and it's demonstrated in the next example.

The following example creates a TaxableProduct object, converts it to a Product reference, and then checks if the object can be safely transformed back into a TaxableProduct (it can). You'll notice that the actual conversion uses the CType() function introduced in the previous chapter.

```
' Declare two empty variables (don't use the New keyword).
Dim TheProduct As Product
Dim TheTaxableProduct As TaxableProduct

' This works, because TaxableProduct derives from Product.
TheProduct = New TaxableProduct()

' This will be True.
If TypeOf TheProduct Is TaxableProduct Then
    ' Convert the object and assign to the other variable.
    TheTaxableProduct = CType(TheProduct, TaxableProduct)
End If
```

```
Dim TotalPrice As Decimal

' This works.
TotalPrice = TheTaxableProduct.TotalPrice

' This won't work, even though TheTaxableProduct and TheProduct are the same
' object. The Product class doesn't provide a TotalPrice property.
TotalPrice = TheProduct.TotalPrice
```

At this point, it might seem that being able to convert objects is a fairly specialized technique that will only be required in cases for which you're using inheritance. This isn't always true. Object conversions are also required when you use certain types of generic classes.

One example is a collections class, which you'll use in Chapter 10. Most collection classes are built in such a way that they can store any type of object. In order to have this ability, they need to treat all objects in the same way—as instances of the root System.Object class. (Remember, all classes in .NET inherit from System.Object at some point, even if this relationship isn't explicitly defined in the class code.) The end result is that when you retrieve an object from a collection, you need to convert it from a System.Object to its real type. If you don't take this step, you won't be able to use its methods and properties.

Understanding Namespaces and Assemblies

Whether you realize it at first or not, every piece of code in .NET exists inside a .NET type (typically a class). In turn, every type exists inside a namespace. Figure 4-3 shows this arrangement for your own code and the DateTime class. Keep in mind that this is an extreme simplification—the System namespace alone is stocked with several hundred classes. This diagram is only designed to show you the layers of organization.

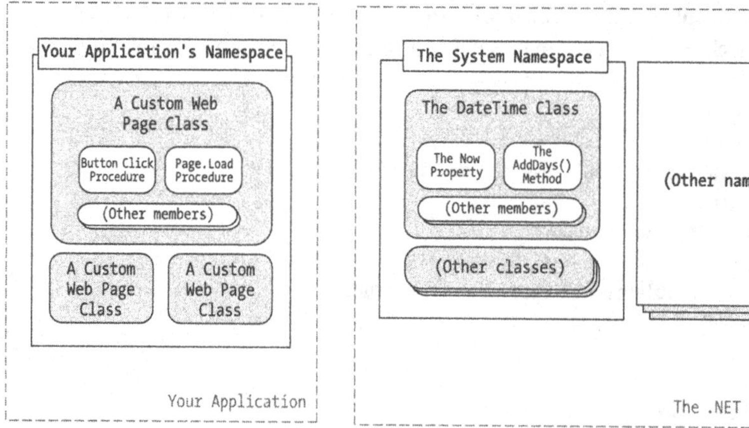

Figure 4-3. A look at two namespaces

Namespaces are used to organize all the different types in the class library. Without namespaces, these types would all be grouped into a single long and messy list. This type of organization is practical for a small set of information, but it would be useless for the thousands of types included with .NET.

Many of the chapters in this book introduce you new .NET classes and namespaces. For example, in the chapters on web controls, you'll learn how to use the objects in the System.Web.UI namespace. In the chapters about web services, you'll study the types in the System.Web.Services namespace. For databases, you'll turn to the System.Data namespace. In fact, you've already learned a little about one namespace: the basic System namespace that contains all the simple data types explained in the previous chapter.

To continue your exploration after you've finished the book, you'll need to turn to the MSDN reference, which painstakingly documents the properties, methods, and events of every class in every namespace (see Figure 4-4). If you have Visual Studio .NET installed, you can view the MSDN Help by selecting Start ➤ Programs ➤ Microsoft Visual Studio .NET ➤ Microsoft Visual Studio .NET Documentation. You can find class reference information, grouped by namespace, under the Visual Studio .NET ➤ .NET Framework ➤ Reference ➤ Class Library node.

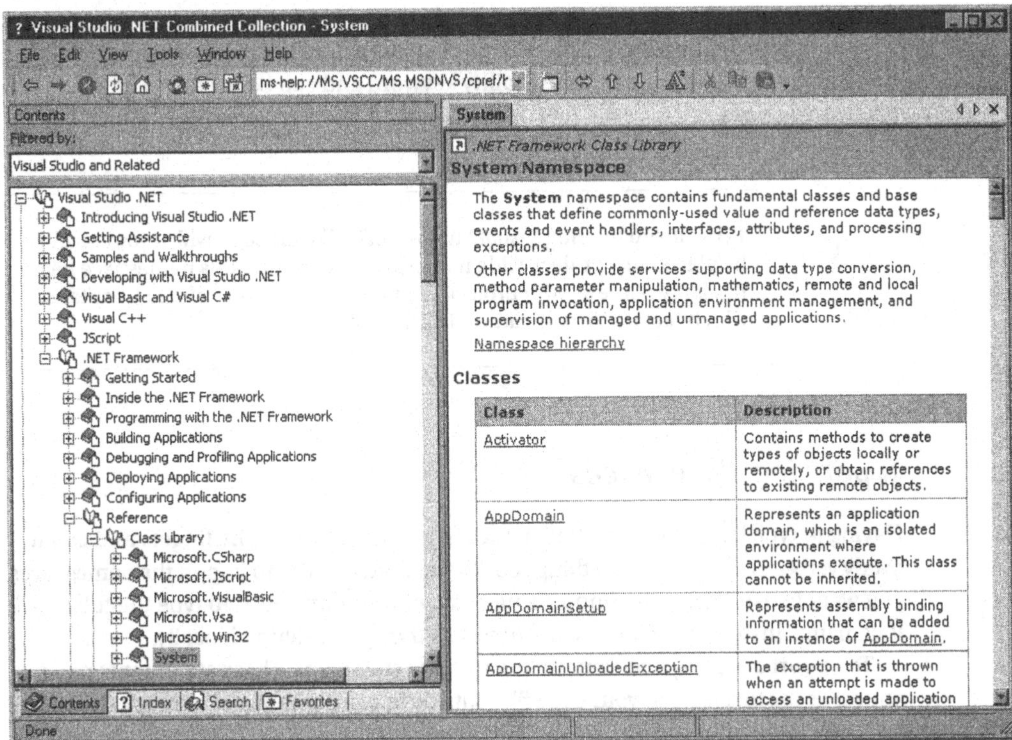

Figure 4-4. The MSDN Class Library reference

Using Namespaces

Often when you write ASP.NET code, you'll just use the default namespace. If, however, you want to organize your code into multiple namespaces, you can define the namespace using a simple block structure, as shown here:

```
Namespace MyCompany
    Namespace MyApp

        Public Class Product
            ' Code goes here.
        End Class

    End Namespace
End Namespace
```

In the preceding example, the Product class is in the namespace MyCompany.MyApp. Code inside this namespace can access the Product class by name. Code outside it needs to use the fully qualified name, as in MyCompany.MyApp.Product. This ensures that you can use the components from various third-party developers without worrying about a name collision. If those developers follow the recommended naming standards, their classes will always be in a namespace that uses the name of their company and software product. The fully qualified name of a class will then almost certainly be unique.

Namespaces don't take an accessibility keyword and can be nested as many layers deep as you need.

TIP If you're using Visual Studio .NET, all your code will automatically be placed in a project-wide namespace. By default, this namespace has the same name as your project. For more information, refer to Chapter 8, which tackles Visual Studio .NET in detail.

Importing Namespaces

Having to type long, fully qualified names is certain to tire out the fingers and create overly verbose code. To tighten things up, it's standard practice to import the namespaces you want to use. When you import a namespace, you don't need to type the fully qualified name. Instead, you can use the object as though it's defined locally.

To import a namespace, you use the Imports statement. These statements must appear as the first lines in your code file, outside of any namespaces or block structures.

```
Imports MyCompany.MyApp
```

Consider the situation without importing a namespace:

```
Dim SalesProduct As New MyCompany.MyApp.Product()
```

It's much more manageable when you import the MyCompany.MyApp namespace. Once you do, you can use this syntax instead:

```
Dim SalesProduct As New Product()
```

Importing namespaces is really just a convenience. It has no effect on the performance of your application. In fact, whether you use namespace imports or not, the compiled IL code will look exactly the same. That's because the language compiler will translate your relative class references into fully qualified class names when it generates an EXE or DLL file.

Assemblies

You might wonder what gives you the ability to use the class library namespaces in a .NET program. Are they hard-wired directly into the language? The truth is that all .NET classes are contained in *assemblies*. Assemblies are the physical files that contain compiled code. Typically, assembly files have the extension .exe if they are stand-alone applications, or .dll if they're reusable components.

TIP The .dll extension is also used for code that needs to be executed (or "hosted") by another type of program. If you compile your ASP.NET web pages, you'll create one or more DLL files, because your code doesn't represent a stand-alone application. Instead, it's executed by the ASP.NET engine when a web request is received.

There isn't a strict relationship between assemblies and namespaces. An assembly can contain multiple namespaces. Conversely, more than one assembly file can contain classes in the same namespace. Technically, namespaces are a *logical* way to group classes. Assemblies, however, are a *physical* package for distributing code.

The .NET classes are actually contained in a number of different assemblies. For example, the basic types in the System namespace come from the mscorlib.dll assembly. Many ASP.NET types are found in the System.Web.dll assembly. In addition, you might want to use other, third-party assemblies. Often, assemblies and namespaces have the same names. For example, you'll find the namespace System.Web in the assembly file System.Web.dll. However, this is a convenience, not a requirement.

When compiling an application, you need to tell the language compiler what assemblies the application uses. If you're compiling your code by hand, you'll need to specify this on the command line, as described in Chapter 5. If you're using Visual Studio .NET, you can link to other assemblies by adding references, as described in Chapter 8. Visual Studio .NET will start you out with a basic set of assembly references, which is all you need to create most .NET web pages.

The Last Word

At its simplest, object-oriented programming is the idea that your code should be organized into separate classes. If followed carefully, this approach leads to code that's easier to alter, enhance, debug, and reuse. Now that you know the basics of object-oriented programming, you're ready to see how it's implemented in ASP.NET with web pages and server controls.

Part Two

Developing ASP.NET Applications

CHAPTER 5

ASP.NET Applications

THE LAST FEW CHAPTERS have presented an up-close, intensive look at .NET and the Visual Basic .NET language. They also described how to set up your computer with the web-hosting software and virtual directories you need to make ASP.NET applications. Equipped with this knowledge, you're now ready to dive into real ASP.NET programming with your first .aspx page.

In this chapter, you'll learn some of the core topics that every ASP.NET developer must master. You'll learn what makes up an ASP.NET site, and what types of files it can include. Even more important, you'll see how an ASP.NET application works behind the scenes, how to configure it, and how to use the *code-behind* model of development to separate your application code from the user interface of a web page. These concepts are the foundation of every ASP.NET programming project.

The Anatomy of an ASP.NET Application

It's sometimes difficult to define exactly what a web application is. Unlike a traditional desktop program (which is usually contained in a single EXE file), ASP.NET applications are divided into multiple web pages. This division means that a user can enter an ASP.NET application at several different points, or follow a link out of the application to another part of the website or another web server. So does it make sense to consider a website as an application?

In ASP.NET, the answer is yes. Every ASP.NET application shares a common set of resources and configuration settings. Web pages from other ASP.NET applications don't share these resources, even if they're on the same web server. Technically speaking, every ASP.NET application is executed inside a separate *application domain*. Application domains are isolated areas in memory, and they ensure that even if one web application causes a fatal error, it won't affect any other application that is currently running on the same computer. Similarly, application domains restrict a web page in one application from accessing the in-memory information of another application. Each web application is maintained separately, and has its own set of caching, application, and session data.

The standard definition of an ASP.NET application describes it as a combination of files, pages, handlers, modules, and executable code that can be invoked from a virtual directory (and, optionally, its subdirectories) on a web server. In other words, the virtual directory is the basic grouping structure that delimits an application. Figure 5-1 shows a web server that hosts four separate web applications.

In Chapter 2, you saw how to create virtual directories. The next step is to examine what a virtual directory can contain.

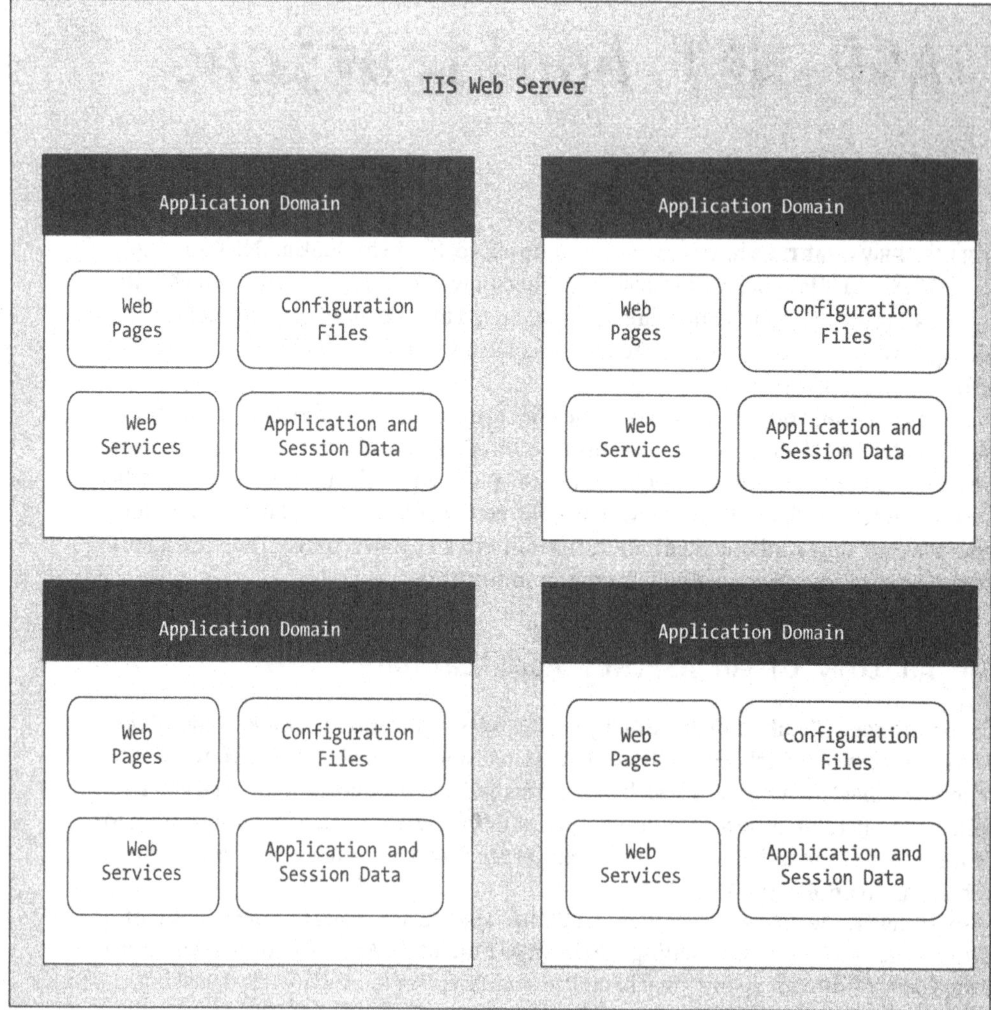

Figure 5-1. ASP.NET applications

ASP.NET File Types

ASP.NET applications can include several different types of files. Table 5-1 introduces all these file types.

Table 5-1. ASP.NET File Types

File Name	Description
Ends with .aspx	These are ASP.NET web pages (the .NET equivalent of the .asp file in an ASP application). They contain the user interface and optionally the underlying application code. Users request or navigate directly to one of these pages to start your web application.
Ends with .ascx	These are ASP.NET user controls. User controls are similar to web pages, except that they can't be accessed directly. Instead, they must be hosted inside an ASP.NET web page. User controls allow you to develop an important piece of the user interface and reuse it in as many web forms as you want without repetitive code.
Ends with .asmx	These are ASP.NET web services, which are described in the Part Four of this book. Web services work differently than web pages, but they still share the same application resources, configuration settings, and memory.
web.config	This is the XML-based configuration file for your ASP.NET application. It includes settings for customizing security, state management, memory management, and much more. This file is explained throughout the book, and dissected in Chapter 29.
global.asax	This is the global application file (the .NET equivalent of the global.asa file in an ASP application). You can use this file to define global variables and react to global events, such as when a web application first starts.
Ends with .disco or .vsdisco	These are special *discovery* files that are used to advertise the web services a web application provides. You'll learn more about discover files in the fourth part of this book.
Ends with .vb	These are code-behind files that contain Visual Basic code. They allow you to separate the application from the user interface of a web page. The code-behind model is introduced in this chapter, and used extensively in this book.
Ends with .resx	These files typically exist if you're using Visual Studio .NET. They're used to store localization information (like text in multiple languages), and information that you post to the web page at design time.
Ends with .sln, .suo, and .vbproj, and .csproj	These files are used by Visual Studio .NET to group together projects (a collection of files in a web application) and solutions (a collection of projects that you're developing or testing at once). These files are only used during development and should not be deployed to a web server. However, even if you *do* copy these files to a web server, the default ASP.NET security settings will prevent a user from viewing them.

In addition, your web application can contain other resources that aren't special ASP.NET files. For example, your virtual directory can hold image files, HTML files, or CSS (cascading style sheets) files. These resources might be used in one of your ASP.NET web pages, or they might be used independently. There's no reason that a website can't combine static HTML pages with dynamic ASP.NET pages.

Most of the files in Table 5-1 types are optional. You can create a legitimate ASP.NET application with a single web page (.aspx file) or web service (.asmx file).

What About ASP Files?

ASP.NET doesn't use any of the same files as ASP (such as .asp pages and the global.asa file). If you have a virtual directory that contains both .aspx and .asp files, you really have two applications: an ASP.NET web application, and a legacy ASP application.

In fact, the process that manages and renders .asp files, and the ASP.NET service that compiles and serves .aspx files, are two separate programs that don't share any information. This design has a couple of important implications:

- You can't share state information between ASP and ASP.NET applications. The Session and Application collections, for example, are completely separate.
- You specify ASP and ASP.NET configuration settings in different ways. If you specify an ASP setting, it won't apply to ASP.NET, and vice versa.

Generally, you should keep ASP and ASP.NET files in separate virtual directories to avoid confusion. However, if you're migrating a large website, you can safely use both types of files as long as they don't try to share resources.

The bin Directory

Every web application directory can use a special subdirectory called \bin. This directory holds the .NET assemblies (compiled code files) used by your application. There are two reasons you might place an assembly in the \bin directory:

- If you're precompiling your web pages and web services, they will be stored in a DLL assembly file in the \bin directory. This topic, which is a common source of confusion for new ASP.NET developers, is explained in detail a little later in this chapter.
- If you're using separate components in a web application, you can install them in the \bin directory to make them available to your web pages and web services. This technique was demonstrated in Chapter 4 with the Product class..

For example, you can develop a database component in any .NET language, compile it to a DLL assembly file, and place it in the \bin directory of a web application. ASP.NET will automatically detect the assembly, and any page in the web application will be able to use it. This seamless deployment model is far easier than working with traditional COM components, which must be registered before they can be used (and often re-registered when they change).

Application Updates

One of the most useful features of ASP.NET has nothing to do with new controls or enhanced functionality. Instead, it's the so-called "zero-touch" deployment and application updating that means you can modify your ASP.NET application easily and painlessly without needing to restart the server.

Page Updates

If you modify a code file or a web form, ASP.NET automatically recompiles an updated version with the next client request. This means that new client requests always use the most recent version of the page. ASP.NET even compiles the page automatically to native machine code and caches it to improve performance.

Component Updates

You can replace any assembly in the \bin directory with a new version, even if it's currently in use. The file will never be locked. You can also add or delete assembly files without any problem. ASP.NET continuously monitors the \bin directory for changes. When a change is detected, it creates a new application domain and uses it to handle any new requests. Existing requests are completed using the old application domain, which contains a cached copy of all the old versions of the components. When all the existing requests are completed, the old application domain is removed from memory.

This automatic rollover feature, sometimes called *shadow copy*, allows you to painlessly update a website without taking it offline, even if it uses separate components.

Configuration Changes

In the somewhat painful early days of ASP programming, configuring a web application was no easy task. You needed to either create a script that modified the IIS (Internet Information Services) metabase or use IIS Manager. Once a change was made, you would often need to stop and start the IIS web service (again by using IIS Manager or the iisreset utility). Sometimes you would even need to reboot the server before the modification would take effect!

Fortunately, these administrative headaches are no longer required for ASP.NET, which manages its own configuration independently from IIS. The configuration of an ASP.NET web application is defined using the web.config file, which is described at the end of this chapter. The web.config file stores information in a plain text XML format, so you can easily edit it with a tool like Notepad. If you change a web.config setting,

ASP.NET uses the same automatic rollover as it does when you update a component. Existing requests complete with the original settings, and new requests are served by a new application domain that uses the new web.config settings. Once again, modifying live sites is surprisingly easy (and relieving) in ASP.NET.

NOTE There are still a few settings that need to be made at the IIS level and can't be controlled through the web.config file. One example is security—because IIS processes the request before ASP.NET, both IIS and ASP.NET security settings come into play. These minor exceptions are noted in this book, wherever they apply.

A Simple Application from Start to Finish

Now that you're familiar with all the essential ingredients of an ASP.NET application, it's a good time to walk through the process of creating a simple web application from start to finish. In this case, we won't be using ASP.NET's new code-behind feature. We'll also steer away from Visual Studio .NET, and rely entirely on Notepad.

1. First of all, create the virtual directory for your application. For this example, create the directory C:\ASP.NET\TestWeb using Windows Explorer.
2. The next step is to turn this folder into a virtual directory and a web application. This process is described in detail in Chapter 2. Essentially, you must start the IIS Manager (select Start ➤ Programs ➤ Administrative Tools ➤ Internet Information Services), right-click the Default Website item and select New Virtual Directory. Internet Information Services is shown in Figure 5-2.

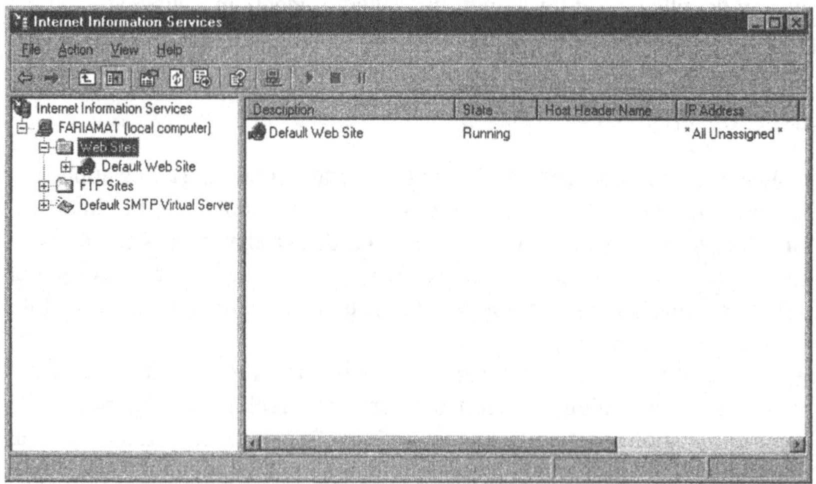

Figure 5-2. Internet Information Services

3. Follow the Virtual Directory Creation wizard, choosing MyFirstWebApp for the virtual folder name (see Figure 5-3), and using the default settings.

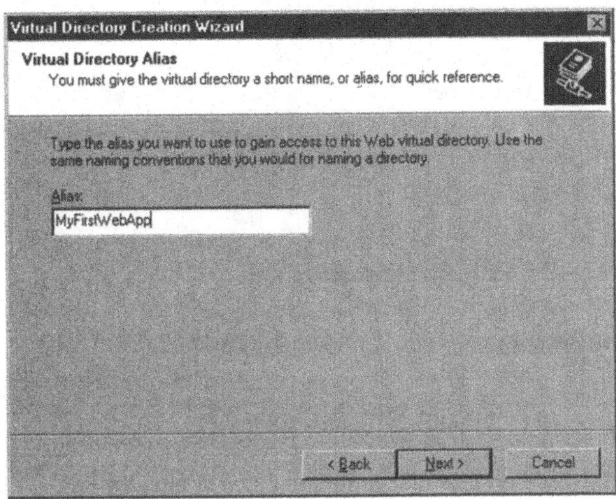

Figure 5-3. The Virtual Directory Creation wizard

4. Now, return to the C:\ASP.NET\TestWeb directory, and create a new text file called HelloWorld.aspx. Using Notepad, you can create the simple web page shown here. (This page will be explained in just a moment.)

```
<html>
<script language="VB" runat="server">
    Private Sub Page_Load()
        lblTest.Text = "Hello, the Page.Load event occurred."
    End Sub
</script>

<body>
<form id="Form" runat="server">
    <asp:Label id="lblTest" runat="server" />
</form>

</body>
</html>
```

5. Save this file, open your browser, and request the web page. Remember, when you request the web page you need to specify the virtual directory name, which isn't necessarily the same as the real directory name. You also need to know your computer name. For example, I set C:\ASP.NET\TestWeb to be a virtual directory called MyFirstWebApp, and my computer is called fariamat. That means I need to request http://fariamat/MyFirstWebApp/HelloWorld.aspx. The output for the HelloWorld.aspx page is shown in Figure 5-4.

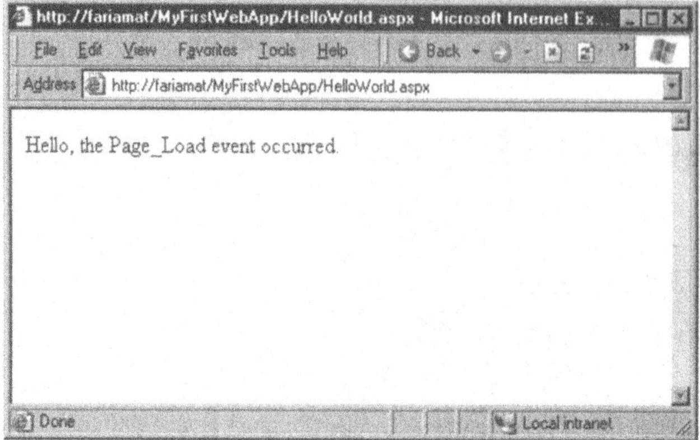

Figure 5-4. The output of HelloWorld.aspx

TIP You can always determine your computer name by opening up Windows Explorer and looking at the network section. Alternatively, you can try the special TCP/IP "loopback" address 127.0.0.1, or the special computer name localhost, both of which are configured to always access the local server. The web address would then become http://127.0.0.1/MyFirstWebApp/HelloWorld.aspx or http://localhost/MyFirstWebApp/HelloWorld.aspx.

Line by Line with HelloWorld.aspx

The HelloWorld.aspx web page has two parts: a script block that contains VB .NET code, and a form tag that holds all the ASP.NET server controls used on the page. The script block is the code portion of the page. The rest of the page defines the user interface.

The easiest way to analyze the HelloWorld.aspx is to start with the controls. ASP.NET controls are always nested inside a <form> tag. In this case, there is only control—a special Label represented by the <asp:Label> tag. The Label control outputs plain text in a browser.

```
<form id="Form" runat="server">
    <asp:Label id="lblTest" runat="server" />
</form>
```

When creating an ASP.NET control, you need to use the runat="server" attribute. This specifies that your control executes on the server and allows your code to interact with the control directly. On the other hand, anything you create that doesn't have the runat="server" attribute is treated as a static unchangeable piece of user interface, just like an ordinary HTML tag. A unique name is also assigned to the control (in this case, lblTest) so it can be uniquely identified in your code.

In the script block, there is a special .NET-defined event handler called Page_Load. This event handler is triggered when the page is first loaded.

```
Private Sub Page_Load()
    lblTest.Text = "Hello, the Page.Load event occurred."
End Sub
```

This event handler manipulates the lblTest object. Specifically, the code sets the Text property of the Label control to a string with a greeting message.

If you're a seasoned ASP developer, this code snippet probably seems extremely unusual, because it uses ASP.NET's new web control model. You'll probably be more familiar with this type of interaction if you're a traditional Visual Basic developer. In the web control model, you don't generate dynamic content by writing out HTML tags. Instead, you simply modify the properties of a web control. The web control then generates its own HTML output when the page is rendered. In this example, the HelloWorld.aspx page actually looks like this (in a slightly simplified format) when it's received in the browser:

```
<html>
<body>

<form id="Form" method="post">
    <span id="lblTest">Hello, the Page_Load event occurred.<br></span>
</form>

</body>
</html>
```

Note that the label control tag has disappeared. It's been replaced with the HTML required to show the label text. You'll also notice that the code has been stripped out as well, which prevents the end user from viewing it.

This is just a taste of the new web control model. In Chapter 6 you'll study how it works—and its many advantages—in much more detail.

Behind the Scenes with HelloWorld.aspx

So what really happens when ASP.NET receives a request for the HelloWorld.aspx file? The process actually unfolds over several steps.

1. First of all, IIS determines that the .aspx file extension belongs to ASP.NET and passes it along to the ASP.NET worker process. If the file extension belonged to another service (as it would for .asp files), ASP.NET would never get involved.

2. If this is the first time a page in this application has been requested, ASP.NET automatically creates the application domain and a special application object (technically, an instance derived from the .NET class System.Web.HttpApplication). If there are any global.asax variables that need to be created or application event handlers that need to be executed, ASP.NET performs those tasks now.

NOTE ASP.NET applications are only created once and are shared by all clients. Once the application is running, it will never shut down unless you reboot the computer or terminate the ASP.NET process manually.

3. ASP.NET considers the specific .aspx file. If it has never been executed, ASP.NET compiles and caches the page. If this task has already been performed (for example, someone else has already requested this page) and the file hasn't been changed, ASP.NET will use the precompiled version.

4. The compiled HelloWorld.aspx acts like a miniature program. It starts running and executes all its code (in this case the Page_Load event handler). At this stage, everything is working together as a set of in-memory .NET objects.

5. When the code is finished, ASP.NET asks every control in the web page to render itself. For example, the label control takes its text property and transforms it into the standard HTML that is required.

TIP In fact, ASP.NET performs a little sleight of hand, and may customize the output with additional client-side JavaScript or DHTML if it detects that the client browser supports it. In the case of HelloWorld.aspx, the output of the label control is too simple to require this type of automatic tweaking.

6. The final page is sent to the user and the application ends.

The description is lengthy, but it's important to start off with a good understanding of the fundamentals. Figure 5-5 illustrates the stages in a web page request.

The most important detail is the fact that your code works with objects. The final step is to transform these objects into the appropriate HTML output. A similar conversion from objects to output happens with a Windows program in Visual Basic 6 or VB .NET, but it's so automatic that programmers rarely give it much thought. Also, in those environments the code is always being run locally. In an ASP.NET application, the code runs in a protected environment on the server. The client only sees the results once the web page processing has ended and the program has been released from memory.

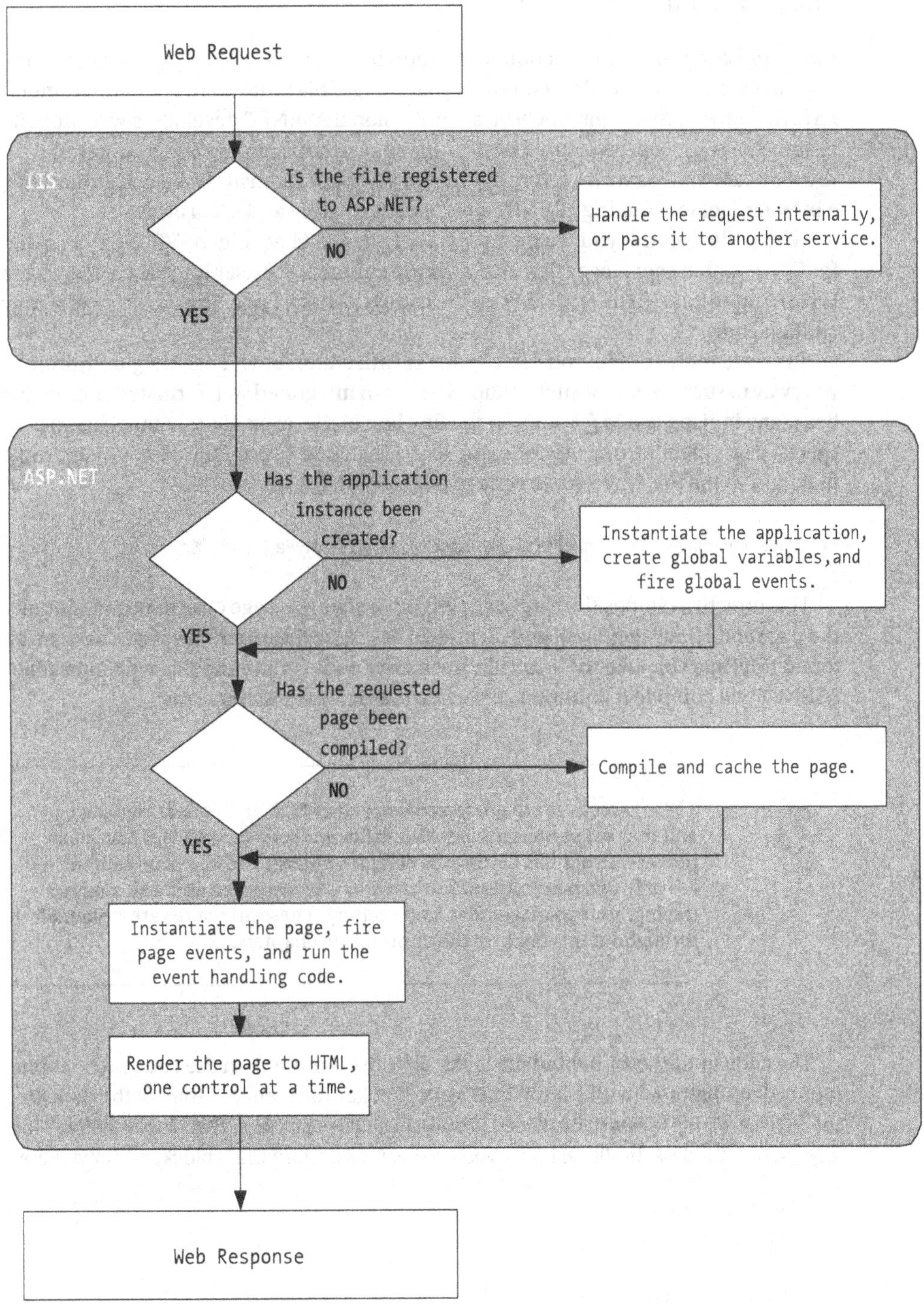

Figure 5-5. The stages in an ASP.NET request

Code-Behind

Before finishing your introduction to web application with ASP.NET, you need to consider the technique of code-behind programming. This innovation is so important to ASP.NET development that I believe all professional ASP.NET developers will adopt it eventually. Microsoft-sponsored best-of-breed platform samples (for example, the IBuySpy case studies we'll explore in Chapter 26) use it extensively. Visual Studio .NET, a premier tool for creating ASP.NET sites, uses it natively and exclusively.

With code-behind, you create a separate code file (a .vb file for VB .NET or .cs file for C#) to match every .aspx file. The .aspx file contains the user interface which is the HTML code and ASP.NET tags that create controls on the page. The .vb or .cs files only contain code.

To create the .aspx file, you can use any HTML editor, or you can drag-and-drop your way to success with Visual Studio .NET's own integrated web form designer, which has many indispensable features. In the first line of the .aspx file, you must insert a special Page directive that identifies the matching code-behind file. Here's an example that links to the VB .NET source code in the file MyPage.vb:

```
<%@ Page Language="VB" Inherits="MyPageClass" Src="MyPage.vb" %>
```

This directive defines the language (VB), identifies the page class that contains all the page code (MyPageClass), and identifies the source file where the page class can be found (MyPage.vb). Like the .aspx file, the source code is contained in a plain text file. ASP.NET will compile it automatically when the web page is requested.

TIP Directives are processed before any ASP.NET code is executed, and they set various options that influence how the ASP.NET compiler processes your file. Setting the default language and the code-behind file are only two possibilities. You can also add attributes that will configure tracing, state management, and caching. These attributes are explained throughout this book, in the appropriate chapters.

The code in the code-behind file looks slightly different than the code in the inline model demonstrated with HelloWorld.aspx. The key difference is that all the code in the MyPage.vb file needs to be placed inside a custom page class. This class is defined like any other .NET class. In Visual Basic, you use the Class... End Class block, as shown here:

```
Private Class MyPageClass
  Inherits System.Web.UI.Page

    ' (Code goes here.)

End Class.
```

The only trick is that your custom page class must inherit from a generic Page class in the .NET Framework. If you remember the object-oriented primer in Chapter 4, you'll recognize that the Page class is in the namespace System.Web.UI, which contains all sorts of types used for ASP.NET user interfaces.

You can now add code inside the page class. For example, you could rewrite HelloWorld.aspx with code-behind as the two files shown here:

HelloWorld2.aspx

```
<%@ Page Language="VB" Inherits="HelloWorldClass"

    Src="HelloWorld2.vb" %>
<html>
<body>
<form id="Form" runat="server">
    <asp:Label id="lblTest" runat="server" />
</form>

</body>
</html>
```

HelloWorld2.vb

```
Private Class HelloWorldClass
  Inherits System.Web.UI.Page
    Protected lblTest As System.Web.UI.WebControls.Label

    Public Sub Page_Load()
        lblTest.Text = "Hello, the Page_Load event occurred."
    End Sub

End Class
```

In the HelloWorld2.vb code-behind file, you need to add an additional line to define the Label control. All ASP.NET controls must be defined using the Protected keyword.

```
Protected lblTest As System.Web.UI.WebControls.Label
```

You should make sure that the control name matches the id attribute in the <asp:Label> tag exactly. This allows ASP.NET to connect the controls in your .aspx template file to the controls that you manipulate in your code. It also allows code editors like Visual Studio .NET to check for syntax errors, such as an attempt to use an undeclared variable or a property that the label control doesn't support. You'll learn more about how Visual Studio .NET automates some of the chores associated with ASP.NET development in Chapter 8.

In the case of HelloWorld.aspx, the code is so simple that you don't receive much of a benefit from code-behind development. However, the advantage increases dramatically as you begin to add more complex ASP.NET controls and code routines.

Web Form Inheritance Explained

One potentially confusing aspect in the preceding example is the fact that the word "Inherits" is used twice: once in the .aspx template file, and once in the code file. You might be wondering who is inheriting from what, and why?

There are actually three stages involved, as shown in Figure 5-6.

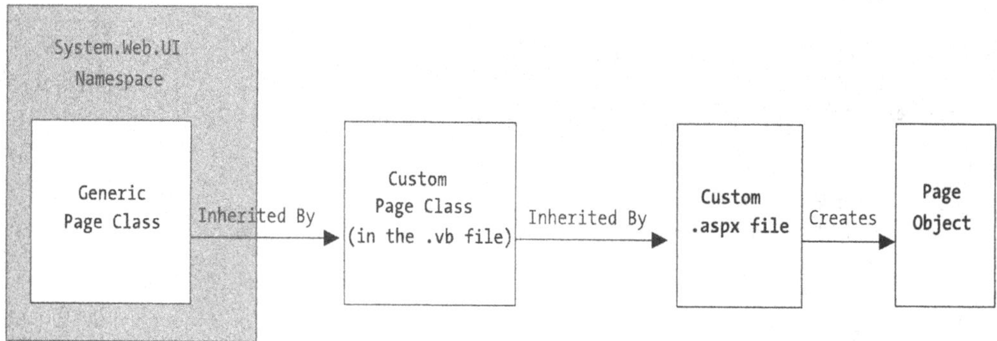

Figure 5-6. Web form inheritance

1. First, there is the Page class from the .NET class library. This class defines the basic functionality that allows a web page to host other controls, render itself to HTML, and provide access to the traditional ASP objects such as Request, Response, and Session.

2. Second, there is your code-behind class (for example, HelloWorldPage). This class inherits from the Page class to acquire the basic set of ASP.NET web page functionality. (And believe me, you wouldn't want to code that yourself.)

3. Finally, the .aspx page (for example, HelloWorld2.aspx) inherits the code from the custom form class you created. This allows it to combine the user interface with the code that supports it.

Incidentally, this is also the reason that you need to declare all control variables with the Protected keyword instead of the Private keyword. Protected variables, unlike private variables, are accessible to derived classes. In other words, using protected variables in your code-behind class ensures that the variables are accessible in the derived page class. If you tried to make the variables private instead or protected, they wouldn't be accessible in the derived page class, and ASP.NET wouldn't be able to connect your control variables to your control tags. Try it out—you'll see it leads to an unhandled error when ASP.NET tries to compile your code.

The Page Class Isn't Just a Code-Behind Feature

Even if you aren't using code-behind development, the System.Web.UI.Page class is still being used. Every time an .aspx file is requested, ASP.NET derives a special custom class from the generic Page class to represent the page. That means you can use all the properties and features of the Page class in your code, even if you write your code routines in a script block inside the .aspx file.

The only difference is the syntax. In code-behind development, you explicitly inherit from the Page class. This technique provides you with increased clarity and an extra layer of flexibility. For example, you could create your own template class that inherits from Page and defines some additional features. Then you could inherit from this class in your code-behind files to create several different web pages in your site. This technique might not be used by most programmers, but it's a key to .NET's extensible, object-oriented design vision. It also becomes much more important when you start to design custom controls like those described in Chapter 23.

Compiled Code-Behind Files

There is another way to use code-behind files: as precompiled assemblies. This technique is important because Visual Studio .NET uses it automatically. It's also a point of confusion that confounds many new ASP.NET programmers.

TIP An assembly is just a logical container for compiled code. It usually takes the form of a DLL or EXE file.

Essentially, you can precompile your code-behind file into a .NET assembly. When compiling a code-behind file, you create a DLL assembly. You can then create an .aspx file that uses the compiled code-behind assembly. The end result is the same, but the actual syntax is a little different.

First of all, you create a code-behind file as normal. Then you compile it using the command-line compiler. For Visual Basic, you use the vbc.exe utility included with the .NET Framework. All the .NET language compilers are found in a directory like C:\[WinDir]\Microsoft.NET\Framework\[Version]. For example, after installing .NET 1.1 on a Windows XP computer, the language compilers are placed in the directory C:\Windows\Microsoft.NET\Framework\v1.1.4322.

To compile a code-behind file, you can open a command prompt window and type something like the following:

```
vbc /t:library /r:System.dll /r:System.Web.dll HelloWorld.vb
```

The /t:library parameter indicates that you want to create a DLL assembly instead of an EXE assembly. The compiled assembly will have the name HelloWorld.dll, because the source file is named HelloWord.vb. Additionally, you use the /r parameter to specify any dependent assemblies that you use. In the case of HelloWorld, you'll use the standard system and web classes, which are contained in two namespaces: System.dll and System.Web.dll.

Figure 5-7 shows a successful command-line compilation. A DLL file has been created, but no feedback is provided.

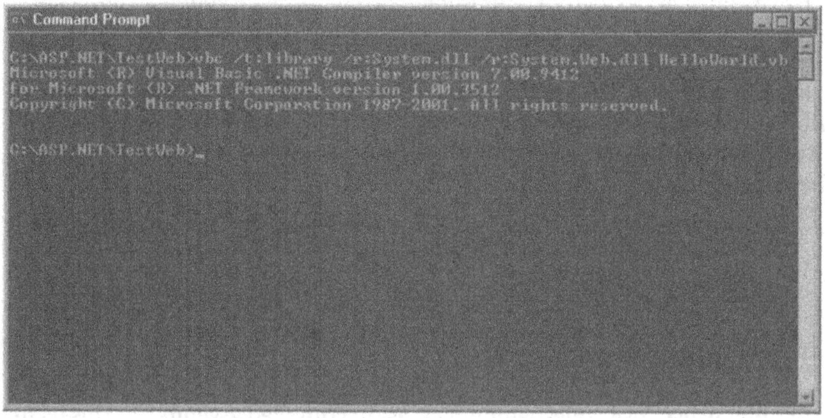

Figure 5-7. Command-line compilation

Figure 5-8 shows the problem caused by leaving out a required assembly—an unrecognized class is found and the code isn't compiled. Interestingly, this problem is reduced with the .NET 1.1 compiler, which can resolve many references on its own.

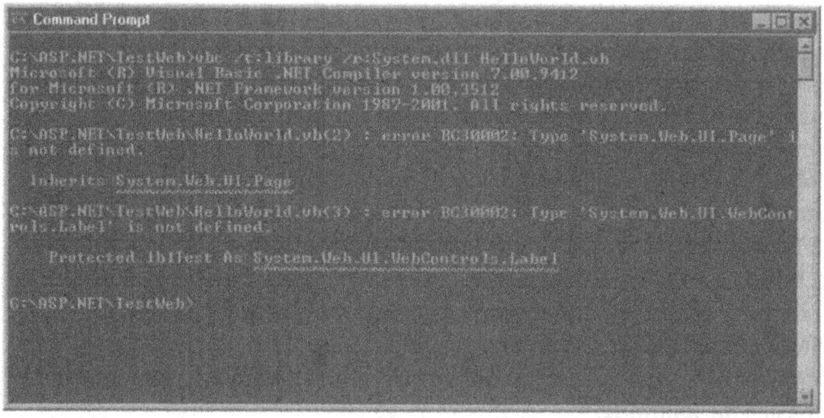

Figure 5-8. A failed compilation attempt

Once the file is compiled, you must copy it to the ASP.NET application's \bin directory. Now you can reference it in your .aspx file by class name.

```
<%@ Page Language="VB" Inherits="HelloWorldClass" %>
```

You no longer need to specify a source file, because ASP.NET automatically registers and recognizes every class name in every assembly in your web application's \bin directory. If you specify a class that ASP.NET can't find, you'll receive an error page like the one shown in Figure 5-9.

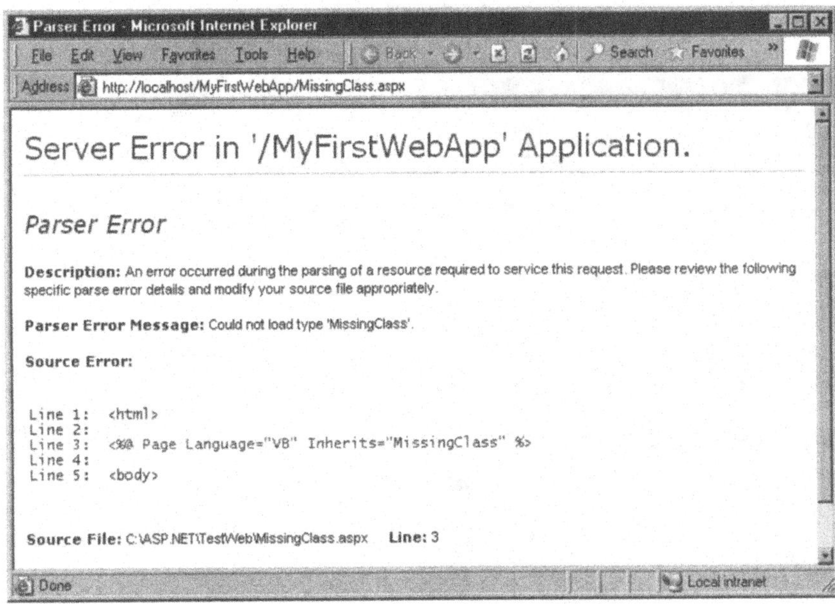

Figure 5-9. A web page with a missing code-behind class

That's all there is to it. The samples for this chapter include a set of three files—CompiledHelloWorld.aspx, CompiledHelloWorld.vb, and CompiledHelloWorld.dll—that allow you to test the compiled code-behind option. Note that in the sample files, slightly different class names are used for each example, because you can't define the same class in two different places as a part of the same web application.

Remember, you don't need to perform the extra step of precompilation. ASP.NET will compile your source files for you automatically the first time they're requested by a client, and either way, your web application will function the same. However, there are a few reasons you might want to. First of all, precompiling ensures that ASP.NET won't need to compile the page the first time it's requested, which speeds up the first web request. More importantly, precompiling can help if you don't want to leave source code files on the server. If you use precompilation, you can deploy your application in a compiled form, ensuring that it can never be tampered with or easily inspected. Even better, if you understand the basics of compiling a code-behind file, you know most of what you need to understand to create a .NET component.

The Path Variable

The preceding examples assume that the Microsoft.NET Framework directory C:\[WinDir]\Microsoft.NET\Framework\[Version] is added to the global Path variable. That way, you can run the vbc.exe and csc.exe utilities in any directory without having to type the whole directory name each time. By default, this convenience isn't enabled, and if you often compile files manually, you should make this change so you can save a few keystrokes.

Start by selecting Settings ➤ Control Panel ➤ System from the Start menu. Then select the Advanced tab and click Environment Variables. The Path variable is located in the System Variables list, as shown in Figure 5-10.

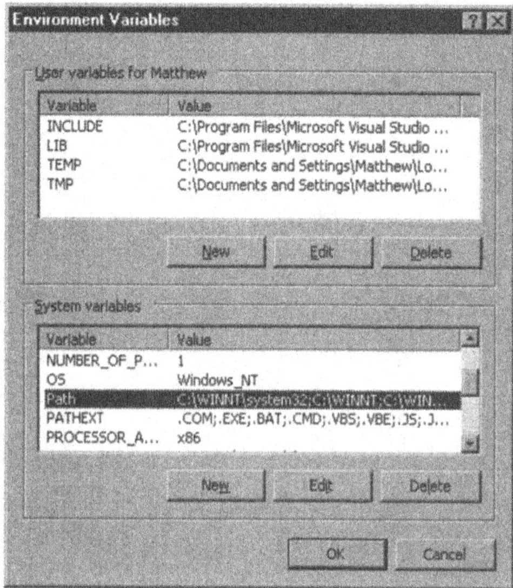

Figure 5-10. The Path environment variable

Modify this variable by adding a semicolon followed by your .NET Framework directory at the end of the path string. Then click OK to accept and apply your changes. You can now run the programs from this directory at the command line without needing to type the directory name.

TIP If you're using Visual Studio .NET, you don't need to go this trouble. Instead, you can use a special shortcut. Simply select Start ➤ Programs ➤ Microsoft Visual Studio .NET ➤ Visual Studio .NET Tools ➤ Visual Studio .NET Command Prompt. This opens a command prompt window and sets the Path variable to include the .NET Framework directory, all in one step. The modified Path only takes effect inside the new command window.

Compiling Multiple Files into One Assembly

When compiling a code-behind file, you don't need to create a separate DLL for each page. Instead, you can compile all your web page classes into one assembly, provided each web page class has a different name (or is located in a different namespace).

The next example (split over two lines) combines three .vb files into one assembly, named MyWebApp.dll.

```
vbc /out:MyWebApp.dll /t:library /r:System.dll /r:System.Web.dll
   HelloWorld.vb GoodbyeCruelWorld.vb MainPage.vb
```

The Page directive doesn't require any changes. The .aspx web pages still inherit from the appropriate class, just as before.

You can also use a wildcard to automatically compile a selection of files.

```
vbc /out:MyWebApp.dll /t:library /r:System.dll /r:System.Web.dll *.vb
```

Code-Behind and Visual Studio .NET

Visual Studio .NET use multifile compilation to compile all the web page classes in your project into one DLL file. This process takes place automatically when you run the web application in the development environment. The vbc.exe or csc.exe compiler is used behind the scenes.

In addition, Visual Studio .NET adds a special Codebehind attribute in the Page directive of each .aspx file.

```
<%@ Page Language="VB" Inherits="HelloWorldPage"
    Codebehind="HelloWorld.vb" %>
```

ASP.NET doesn't pay any attention to the Codebehind attribute. It will not attempt to retrieve or compile this file. Instead, the Codebehind attribute is used by Visual Studio .NET so it can track the name and location of code-behind files, and provide them to you for editing in the design environment. Unlike the Src attribute, the Codebehind attribute doesn't establish a link between the two files. In the previous example, if you change the HelloWorld.vb file outside of Visual Studio .NET, it will not automatically be recompiled and used when you request the corresponding web page.

Importing Namespaces

There is one additional nicety that our code-behind file has left out. To make it easier to work with a namespace, you can use the Imports statement, which was introduced in Chapter 4. For example, if you import the System.Web.UI.WebControls namespace, you can shorten the fully qualified class name System.Web.UI.WebControls.Label to just Label, saving some keystrokes.

The following is a revised code-behind example for the HelloWorld page (the changed lines are highlighted in bold). Note that the Page and Label class can be used without fully qualified names, because the relevant namespaces have been imported.

```
Imports System.Web.UI
Imports System.Web.UI.WebControls

Public Class MyPageClass
  Inherits Page
    Protected lblTest As Label

    Private Sub Page_Load()
        lblTest.Text = "Hello, the Page_Load event occurred."
    End Sub

End Class
```

You can also import namespaces into an .aspx file using a directive. This is a technique you might use if you *don't* use code-behind development. It allows the code in the script block to use short class names instead of long, fully qualified names.

```
<%@ Import Namespace="System.Web.UI" %>
<%@ Import Namespace="System.Web.UI.WebControls" %>
```

Generally, every code file imports a common set of basic namespaces for standard types, web controls, and web utility classes. To make life a little easier, you might want to get into the habit of copying this block of code into the beginning of every code-behind file:

```
Imports System
Imports System.Web
Imports System.Web.UI
Imports System.Web.UI.WebControls
Imports System.Web.UI.HtmlControls
```

Visual Studio .NET will add these basic imports to your code-behind files automatically.

Assessing Code-Behind

Code-behind represents a major change in philosophy, and it brings ASP.NET in line with modern programming practices. The advantages of code-behind don't appear until you begin to develop complex, multilayered applications. Some of the reasons you might want to use code-behind include the following:

- **Better organization.** ASP pages are infamous for their tangle of script commands and HTML formatting tags. This confusion often results in a spaghetti-like mess that is difficult to debug, impossible to reuse, and even harder for other programmers to work with. With code-behind, your code is encapsulated in a neat class. It's easier to read, and it's easier to isolate and reuse pieces of useful functionality. The only way you could do this with ASP was to create separate COM components.

- **Separation of the user interface.** One of the most well-known problems with traditional ASP development is that it mingles formatting and content (the information displayed to the user) with programming logic. This means that programmers are often the only ones able to perform the graphic design for an ASP website. If professional web designers get involved, you need to give them the source code files, raising the possibility that sensitive information will leak out or some code will be inadvertently broken. With code-behind, the .aspx file can be manipulated, polished, and perfected by any other user as long as the control names remain the same. It can even be modified in a third-party designer like Microsoft FrontPage or Macromedia Dreamweaver.

- **The ability to use advanced code editors.** Embracing code-behind programming allows you to benefit from indispensable tools—namely Visual Studio .NET, which can automatically verify the syntax of your code-behind files, provide IntelliSense statement completion, and allow you to design the corresponding .aspx web form. Even if you're an unredeemed Notepad user, I heartily encourage you to try out Visual Studio .NET. It's light years ahead of early ASP editors like Visual Interdev, which were generally more trouble than they were worth.

This book uses code-behind for all its examples. That said, you don't need to use code-behind programming to use ASP.NET or follow the examples in this book. You can just take the code out of its page class and paste it into a script block in a normal .aspx file.

This Book Focuses on Code, Not HTML

The focus in this book is on programming ASP.NET pages, which means that most examples only show you the code, not the control tags from the .aspx page layout. When a new control is introduced, I'll show you the ASP.NET tag and how to use it. In some cases, you'll dive right into the .aspx file to create control templates and other user interface code. However, for the most part I assume you'll learn more from a code example that focuses on objects and code statements rather than one that repeats the standard control tags.

To see the .aspx template files for examples in this book, you should refer to the online samples. You can also find a comprehensive control tag reference at the end of this book, in Chapters 27 and 28. However, in an ideal world you should think, like .NET does, in terms of objects, and use Visual Studio .NET to draw your controls and configure their properties.

Three Ways to Code Web Forms

To summarize, there are three different ways that you can program web forms, as outlined in Table 5-2.

Table 5-2. Web Form Development Models

Development Model	You Create	You Deploy (to the Web Server)
Traditional inline code	.aspx files that contain code and user interface layout	.aspx files
Code-behind	.aspx files with user interface and .vb files with code	.aspx and .vb files
Compiled code-behind	.aspx files with user interface and .vb files with code	.aspx files and the compiled DLL files (which go in the \bin directory)

The Global.asax Application File

The global.asax file allows you to write global application code. The global.asax file looks similar to a normal .aspx file, except for the fact that it can't contain any HTML or ASP.NET tags. Instead, it contains event-handling code that reacts to application or session events that can be triggered by a request for any web page or web service.

For example, the following global.asax file reacts to the Application.EndRequest event, which happens just before the page is sent to the user.

```
<script runat="server">
    Private Sub Application_OnEndRequest()
        Response.Write("<hr>This page was served at " & _
          DateTime.Now.ToString())
    End Sub
</script>
```

This event handler uses the Write() method of the built-in Response object to write a footer at the bottom of the page with the date and time that the page was created.

Each ASP.NET application can have one global.asax file. Once you place it in the appropriate virtual directory, ASP.NET recognizes it and uses it automatically. For example, if you place it in the TestWeb directory, the HelloWorld.aspx file will be affected, as shown in Figure 5-11.

Adding an automatic footer is generally not a useful function for a professional website. A more typical use might be writing an entry to a database log. That way, usage information would be tracked automatically. However, the global.asax file is a minor ingredient, and many web applications won't use it at all.

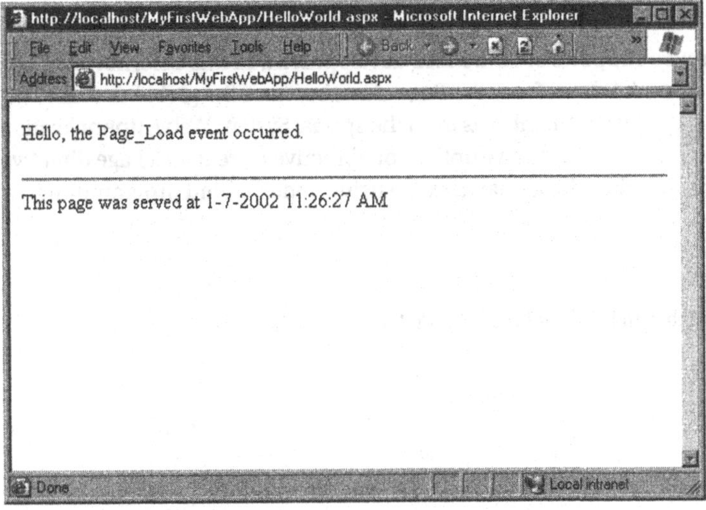

Figure 5-11. HelloWorld.aspx with an automatic footer

What Is DateTime.Now?

Your ASP.NET code can use the full range of features from the .NET class library. The preceding example used the special System.DateTime class, which allows you to store and manipulate date information. The DateTime class provides a special shared property, Now, which can be called at any time to retrieve a DateTime object that represents the current date and time. (You might remember from Chapter 4 that shared properties can always be accessed, even without creating an instance of the class.)

The DateTime object is then converted to its string representation, using the ToString() method that every .NET object supports. The string representation is created based on the web server's current regional settings. In traditional ASP development, you would need to use a built-in language function instead of an object method to accomplish the same task.

Global.asax Code-Behind

The global.asax file also supports code-behind development. In this case, however, the code-behind class doesn't inherit from the Page class, because the global.asax file doesn't represent a page. Instead, it inherits from the special System.Web.HttpApplication class. Similarly, the global.asax uses an Application directive instead of a Page directive.

The next example rewrites the global.asax file using code-behind programming.

global.asax

```
<%@ Application Codebehind="Global.vb" Inherits="GlobalApp" %>
```

global.vb

```
Imports System
Imports System.Web

Public Class GlobalApp
  Inherits System.Web.HttpApplication

    Private Sub Application_OnEndRequest()
        Response.Write("This page was served at " & _
          DateTime.Now.ToString())
    End Sub

End Class
```

As described in the "Behind the Scenes with HelloWorld.aspx" section earlier in this chapter, ASP.NET always creates a custom HttpApplication class to represent your application when it's first started. This is true whether you use code-behind development or not—the difference with code-behind development is that you need to understand and specify that detail explicitly.

Application Events

Application.EndRequest is only one of more than a dozen events you can respond to in your code. To create a different event handler, you simply need to create a subroutine with the defined name. Table 5-3 lists some of the most common application events that you'll use.

Table 5-3. Basic Application Events

Method Name	Description
Application_OnStart	Occurs when the application starts, which is the first time it receives a request from any user. It doesn't occur on subsequent requests. This event is commonly used to create or cache some initial information that will be reused later.
Application_OnEnd	Occurs when the application is shutting down, generally because the web server is being restarted. You can create cleanup code here.
Application_OnBeginRequest	Occurs with each request the application receives, just before the page code is executed.
Application_OnEndRequest	Occurs with each request the application receives, just after the page code is executed.
Session_OnStart	Occurs whenever a new user request is received and a session is started. Sessions are described in Chapter 10.
Session_OnEnd	Occurs when a session times out or is programmatically ended.
Application_OnError	Occurs when an unhandled error occurs. You can find more information about error handling in Chapter 11.

Understanding the ASP.NET Classes

Once you understand that all web pages are instances of the Page class and all global.asax files are instances of the HttpApplication class, many mysteries are cleared up.

For example, consider this line from the global.asax (or global.vb) file:

```
Response.Write("This page was served at " & DateTime.Now.ToString())
```

You might wonder what gives you the ability to use the Response object. In previous versions of ASP, Response was just a special object built into ASP programming. ASP.NET, however, uses a more consistent object-oriented approach. In ASP.NET, the Response object is available because it's a part of the HttpApplication class.

When you inherit from HttpApplication (either explicitly in a code-behind file or automatically), your class acquires all the features of the HttpApplication class. These include properties such as Request, Response, Session, Application, and Server. In turn, each of these properties holds an instance of a special ASP.NET object. For example, HttpApplication.Response holds a reference to the HttpResponse object, which provides a method called Write().

Similarly, when you create an .aspx page, you're creating a class that inherits from ASP.NET's Page class. This class also provides properties such as Request, Response, Session, and Application, along with a number of additional user-interface related members.

TIP ASP.NET provides the traditional built-in objects through properties in basic classes such as Page and Application. For backward compatibility, these objects still support almost all the ASP syntax, and they add some new properties. However, the major change between ASP and ASP.NET is that these built-in objects are used much less often. For example, dynamic pages are usually created by setting control properties rather than using the Response.Write() command. These controls are introduced in Chapter 6.

The MSDN Reference

Understanding the underlying object model is probably the best way to become an ASP.NET guru and distinguish yourself from other, less experienced ASP.NET programmers. It allows you to use the MSDN to find out the full set of capabilities available to you. For example, now that you understand all global.asax files are custom HttpApplication instances, you can refer to the documentation for the HttpApplication class (see Figure 5-12). You can use any of the HttpApplication properties inside your global.asax or global.vb file. Similarly, you can write event handlers for any of its events. If you also understand that the Response property is an instance of the HttpResponse class, you can find out more information about the ways you can use the Response object.

TIP If you have Visual Studio .NET installed, you can view the MSDN help by selecting Start ➤ Programs ➤ Microsoft Visual Studio .NET ➤ Microsoft Visual Studio .NET Documentation. You can find class reference information, grouped by namespace, under the Visual Studio .NET ➤ .NET Framework ➤ Reference ➤ Class Library node.

The basic set of ASP.NET objects is described in the next chapter. However, knowing the classes that these objects are based on allows you to get a better understanding of ASP.NET development.

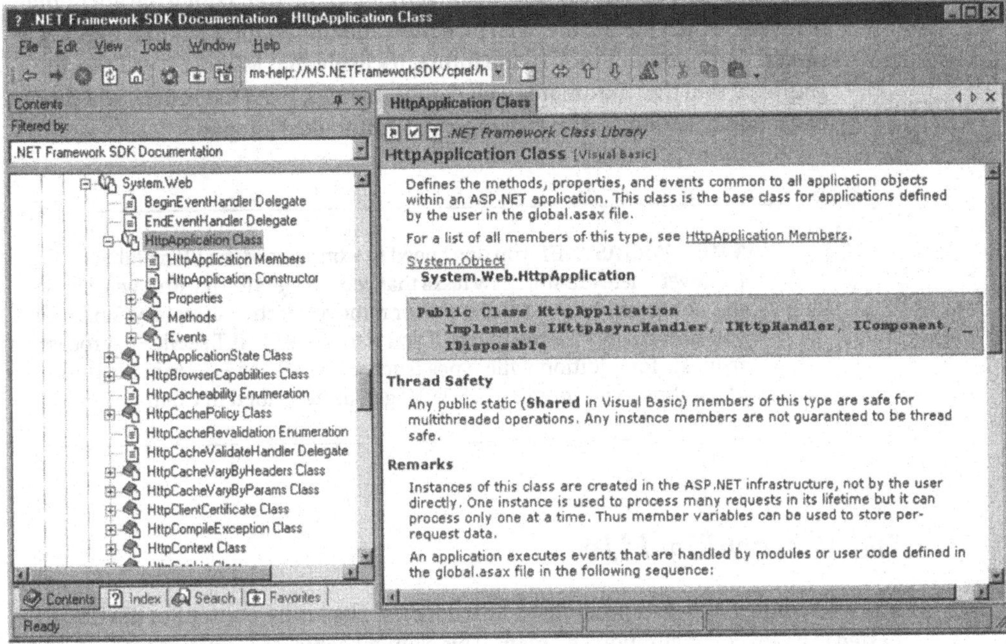

Figure 5-12. The MSDN help for HttpApplication

ASP.NET Configuration

The last topic we'll consider in this chapter is the web.config configuration file. In the MyFirstWebApp application, there is currently no web.config file. That means that the default settings are used from the server's machine.config file.

Every web server has a single machine.config file that defines the default options. This file is found in the directory C:\[WinDir]\Microsoft.NET\Framework\[Version]\Config, where [Version] is the version number of the .NET Framework. Generally, you won't edit this file manually. It contains a complex mess of computer-specific settings. Instead, you can create a web.config file for your application that contains additional or overridden settings.

The web.config files has several advantages over traditional ASP configuration:

- **It's never locked.** As described in the beginning of this chapter, you can update web.config settings at any point, and ASP.NET will smoothly transition to a new application domain.

- **It's easily accessed and replicated.** Provided you have the appropriate network rights, you can change a web.config file from a remote computer. You can also copy the web.config file and use it to apply identical settings to another application or another web server that runs the same application in a web farm scenario.

- **It's easy to edit and understand.** The settings in the web.config file are human-readable, which means they can be edited and understood without needing a special configuration tool. In the future, it's likely that Microsoft will provide a graphical tool that automates web.config changes. Even without it, you can easily add or modify settings using a text editor like Notepad.

NOTE With ASP.NET, you don't need to worry about the IIS metabase. However, there are still a few tasks that you can't perform with a web.config file. For example, you can't create or remove a virtual directory. Similarly, you can't change file mappings. If you want the ASP.NET service to process requests for additional file types (such as HTML, or a custom file type you define), you must use IIS Manager, as described in Chapter 2.

The Web.config File

The web.config file uses a predefined XML format. The entire content of the file is nested in a root <configuration> element. This element contains a <system.web> element, which is used for ASP.NET settings. Inside the <system.web> element are separate elements for each aspect of configuration.

Here's the basic skeletal structure of the web.config file:

```
<?xml version="1.0" encoding="utf-8" ?>
<configuration>
    <system.web>

        <!-- Configuration sections go here. -->

    </system.web>
</configuration>
```

You can include as few or as many configuration sections as you want. For example, if you need to specify special error settings, you could add just the <customError> group. If you create an ASP.NET web application project in Visual Studio .NET, a web.config file is created for you with a basic structure that includes all the important sections. Visual Studio .NET adds comments to each section that describe the purpose and syntax of various options. XML comments are bracketed with the <!-- and --> character sequences, as shown here:

```
<!-- This is the format for an XML comment. -->
```

The following example shows a web.config file with its most important sections, but no settings. Note that the web.config file is case-sensitive, like all XML documents, and starts every setting with a lowercase letter. That means you cannot write <CustomErrors> instead of <customErrors>.

```
<?xml version="1.0" encoding="utf-8" ?>
<configuration>
    <system.web>

        <httpRuntime />
        <pages />
        <compilation />
        <customErrors />
        <authentication />
        <authorization />
        <identity />
        <trace />
        <sessionState />
        <httpHandlers />
        <httpModules />
        <globalization />
        <compilation />

    </system.web>
</configuration>
```

If you want to learn about all the settings that are available in the web.config file, you have two options:

- Individual configuration sections are described in this book when the appropriate topic is discussed. For example, in Chapter 10, the settings in the <sessionState> group are described.
- In Chapter 29, you can find a detailed list of configuration settings.

To learn more about XML, the format used for the web.config file, you can refer to Chapter 18.

Nested Configuration

ASP.NET uses a multilayered configuration system that allows you to use different settings for different parts of your application. To use this technique, you need to create additional subdirectories inside your virtual directory. These subdirectories can contain their own web.config files with additional settings.

Subdirectories inherit web.config settings from the parent directory. For example, consider the web request http://localhost/MyFirstWebApp/Special/SpecialHelloWorld.aspx, which accesses a file in Special, which is a subdirectory of the application virtual directory MyFirstWebApp. The corresponding physical directory is C:\TestWeb\Special.

The web request for SpecialHelloWorld.aspx can acquire settings from three different files, as shown in Figure 5-13.

Any machine.config or TestWeb\web.config settings that aren't explicitly overridden in the TestWeb\Special\web.config file will still apply to the SpecialHelloWorld.aspx page. In this way, subdirectories can specify just a small set of settings that differ from

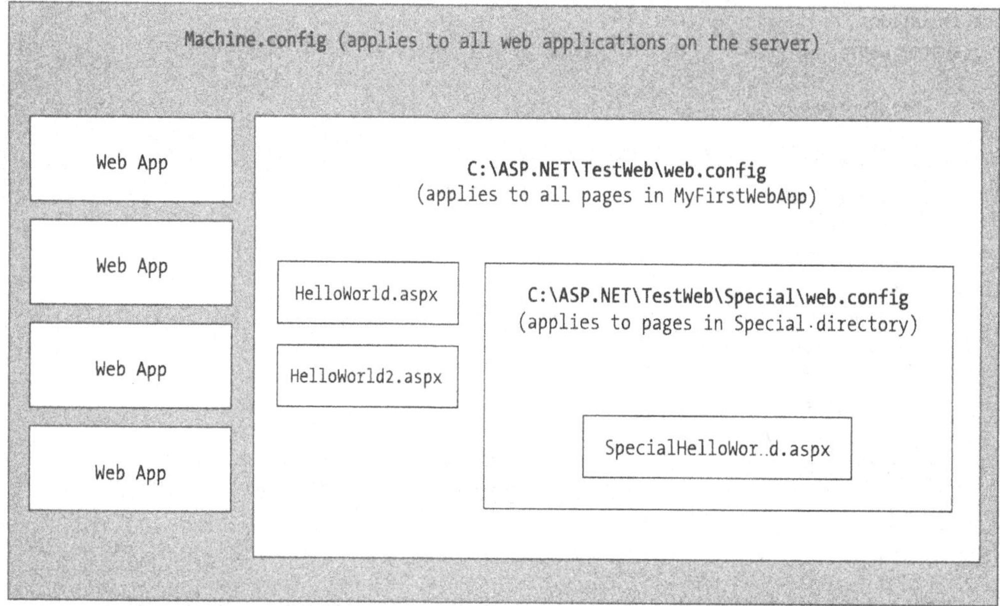

Figure 5-13. Configuration inheritance

the rest of the web application. One reason you might want to use multiple directories in an application is to apply different security settings. Files that need to be secured would then be placed in a special directory with a web.config file that defines more stringent security settings.

Storing Custom Settings in the Web.config File

Before rounding up our discussion of configuration, it's worth examining how you can add some of your own settings to the web.config file, and use them with the simple HelloWorld.aspx page.

You add custom settings to a web.config file in a special element called <appSettings>. Note that the <appSettings> element is nested in the root <configuration> element, not the <system.web> element, which contains the other groups of predefined settings. Here's the basic structure:

```
<?xml version="1.0" encoding="utf-8" ?>
<configuration>

   <appSettings>
      <!-- Special application settings go here. -->
   </appSettings>
```

```
    <system.web>
        <!-- Configuration sections go here. -->
    </system.web>

</configuration>
```

The custom settings that you add are written as simple string variables. There are several reasons that you might want to use a special web.config setting:

- **To centralize an important setting that needs to be used in many different pages.** For example, you could create a variable that contains a database connection string. Any page that needs to connect to the database could then retrieve this value and use it. (As you'll learn later in this book, it's a good idea to always use the exact same database connection string in all your pages, because this ensures that SQL Server can reuse connections for different clients. The technical term for this performance-enhancing feature is connection pooling.)
- **To make it easy to quickly switch between different modes of operation.** For example, you might create a special debugging variable. Your web pages could check for this variable, and if it's set to a specified value, output additional information to help you test the application.
- **To set some initial values.** Depending on the operation, the user might be able to modify these values, but the web.config file could supply the defaults.

Custom settings are entered using an <add> element that identifies a unique variable name (key) and the variable contents (value). The following example adds two special variables, one that contains a database connection string, and one that defines a suitable SQL statement for retrieving sales records.

```
<?xml version="1.0" encoding="utf-8" ?>
<configuration>

    <appSettings>
      <add key="ConnectionString"
       value="Data Source=localhost;Initial Catalog=Pubs;User ID=sa"/>

      <add key="SelectSales" value="SELECT * FROM Sales"/>
    </appSettings>

  <system.web>
        <!-- Configuration sections go here. -->
  </system.web>

</configuration>
```

You can create a simple test page to query this information and display the results, as shown in the following example (which is provided with the sample code as ShowSettings.aspx and ShowSettings.vb). You retrieve custom settings from the web.config by key name, using the System.Configuration.ConfigurationSettings class. This class provides a shared property called AppSettings.

```
Imports System.Web.UI
Imports System.Web.UI.WebControls
Imports System.Configuration

Public Class ShowSettings
  Inherits Page
    Protected lblTest As Label

    Private Sub Page_Load()
        lblTest.Text = "This app will connect with"
        lblTest.Text &= "the connection string:<br><b>"
        lblTest.Text &= _
          ConfigurationSettings.AppSettings("ConnectionString")
        lblTest.Text &= "</b><br><br>"
        lblTest.Text &= "And will execute the SQL Statement:<br>"
        lblTest.Text &= "<b>"
        lblTest.Text &= ConfigurationSettings.AppSettings("SelectSales")
        lblTest.Text &= "</b>"
    End Sub

End Class
```

Dissecting the Code ...

This example introduces a few new details:

- The System.Configuration namespace is imported to make it easier to access the ConfigurationSettings class.
- The &= operator is used to quickly add information to the label. This is equivalent to writing lblTest.Text = lblText.Text & "[extra content]".
- A few HTML tags are added to the label, including bold tags (<b>) to emphasize certain words, and a line break (<br>) to split the output over multiple lines.

Later, in the third part of this book, you'll learn how to use connection strings and SQL statements with a database. For now, our simple application just displays the custom web.config settings, as shown in Figure 5-14.

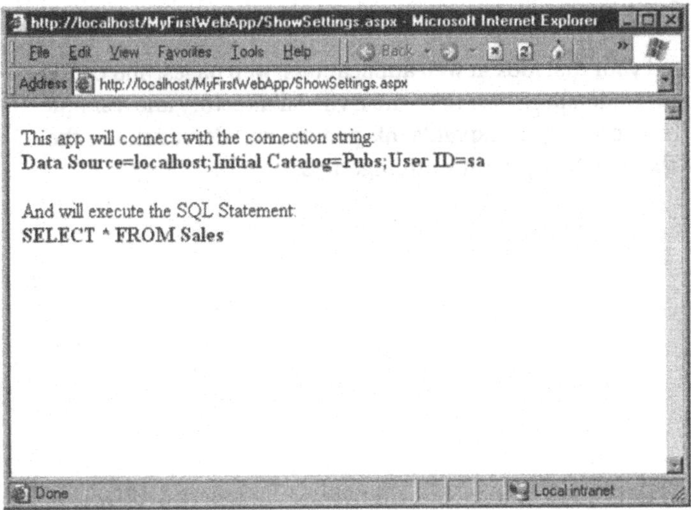

Figure 5-14. Displaying custom application settings

It's commonly asked whether or not this approach constitutes a security risk. Unlike code files, the web.config file can't be deployed in a compiled form. For that reason, it might seem like a potential security risk to store information such as a database access password in plain text. However, ASP.NET is configured, by default, to deny any requests for .config files. That means a remote user will not be able to access the file through IIS. Instead, they'll receive the error message shown in Figure 5-15.

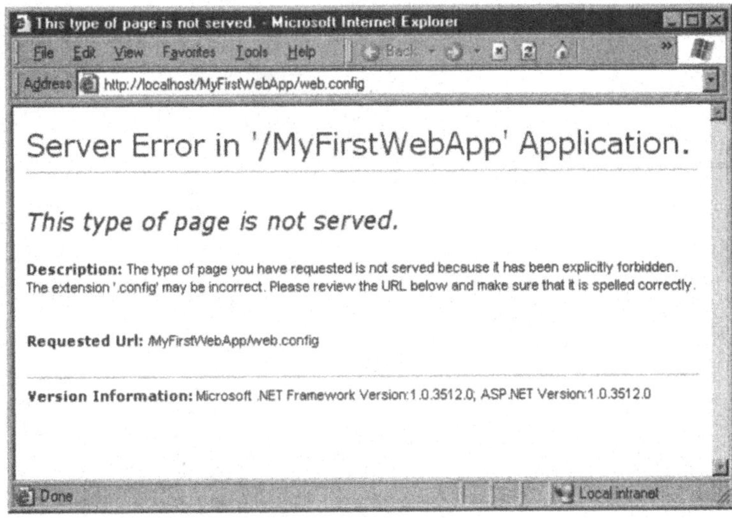

Figure 5-15. Requests for web.config are denied

The Last Word

This chapter presented your first look at web applications, web pages, and configuration. You should now understand how to create a virtual directory and a simple ASP.NET web page. The next chapter expands this picture, and demonstrates the server-side controls that ASP.NET puts at your fingertips.

CHAPTER 6

Web Form Fundamentals

ASP.NET INTRODUCES a remarkable new model for creating web pages. In traditional ASP development, programmers had to master the quirks and details of HTML markup before being able to design dynamic web pages. Pages had to be carefully tailored to a specific task, and additional content could only be generated by outputting raw HTML tags. Worst of all, ASP.NET programs usually required extensive code changes whenever a website's user interface was updated with a new look.

In ASP.NET, you can use a higher-level model of server-side web controls. These controls are created and configured as objects, and automatically provide their own HTML output. Even better, ASP.NET allows web controls to behave like their Windows counterparts by maintaining state and even raising events that you can react to in code.

This chapter explains the basics of the server controls. You'll learn how to handle events, interact with control objects, and understand the object hierarchy of HTML server controls. These topics are entirely different from traditional ASP programming, and they represent an innovative new way to program the Web.

A Simple Page Applet

The first example you'll see demonstrates how server-based controls work using a single-page applet. This type of program, which combines user input and the program output on the same page, is used to provide popular tools on many sites. Some examples include calculators for mortgages, taxes, health or weight indices, retirement savings plans, single-phrase translators, and stock tracking utilities.

The following page allows the user to convert a number of U.S. dollars to the equivalent amount of Euros (see Figure 6-1).

The HTML for this page is shown here. To make it as clear as possible, the style attribute of the <div> tag used for the border has been omitted. There are two <input> tags: one for the text box and one for the submit button. These elements are enclosed in a <form> tag, so they can submit information back to the server when the button is clicked. The rest of the page consists of static text.

```
<html><body>
  <form method="post">
    <div>

      Convert:  
      <input type="text">  US dollars to Euros.<br><br>
      <input type="submit" value="OK">

    </div>
  </form>
</body></html>
```

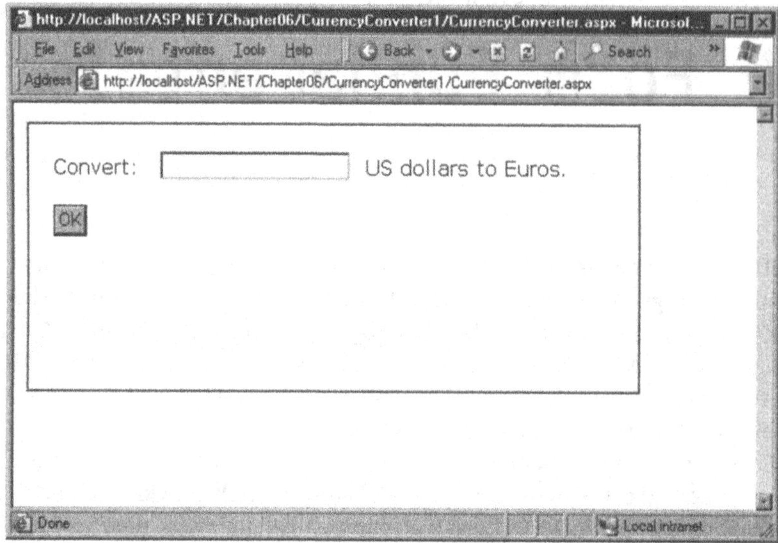

Figure 6-1. A simple currency converter

As it stands, this page looks nice but provides no functionality. It consists entirely of the user interface (HTML tags), and contains no code.

The Least You Need to Know About HTML

If you're new to HTML, the previous web page might look a little perplexing. To help understand it, you need to know a few basic rules of HTML:

- Anything enclosed in angled brackets (< >) is a tag, which is interpreted by the browser. For example, in the currency converter page the "Convert" text is displayed directly, but the <div> tag indicates something else: the graphical box that surrounds the text. Similarly, the <input> tags represent a text box and a button, respectively.
- HTML documents always start with an <html> tag and end with an </html> tag.
- Inside the HTML document, you can place code, additional information like the web page title, and the actual web page content. The web page content is always placed between <body> and </body> tags.
- White space is ignored in HTML. That means that spaces, line breaks, and so on are collapsed. If you need to explicitly insert additional spaces, you use the character entity   (stands for nonbreaking space). To insert line breaks, you can use the break tag: <br>.

Remember, you don't need to understand HTML to program ASP.NET web pages. You just need to know what server controls you want to use. However, you'll be able to get started more quickly if you have basic HTML knowledge. For a quick primer, you can refer to one of the excellent HTML tutorials on the Internet, such as `http://www.w3schools.com/html` or `http://archive.ncsa.uiuc.edu/General/Internet/WWW/HTMLPrimer.html`.

The ASP Solution—and Its Problems

In a traditional ASP program, you would add the currency conversion functionality to this page by examining the posted form values and manually writing the result to the end of the page with the Response.Write() command. This approach works well for a simple page, but it encounters the following difficulties as the program becomes more sophisticated:

- **"Spaghetti" code.** The order of the Response.Write() statements determines the output. If you want to tailor different parts of the output based on a condition, you'll need to reevaluate that condition at several different places in your code.
- **Lack of flexibility.** Once you've perfected your output in an ASP application, it's very difficult to change it. If you decide to modify the page several months later, you have to read through the code, follow the logic, and try to sort out numerous details.
- **Combining content and formatting.** Depending on the complexity of your user interface, your Response.Write() may need to add new HTML tags and style attributes. This encourages programs to tangle formatting and content details together, making it difficult to change just one or the other at a later date.
- **Complexity.** Your code becomes increasingly intricate and disorganized as you add different types of functionality. For example, it could be extremely difficult to track the effects of different conditions and different Response.Write() blocks if you created a combined tax-mortgage-interest calculator. The only way to handle this realistically in ASP programming is to write separate web pages.

Quite simply, an ASP application that needs to create a sizable portion of interface using Response.Write() commands encounters the same dilemmas that a Windows program would find if it needed to manually draw its text boxes and command buttons on an application window in response to every user action.

The ASP.NET Solution: Server Controls

In ASP.NET, you can still use Response.Write() to create a dynamic web page. But ASP.NET provides a better approach. It allows you to turn static HTML tags into objects—called *server controls*—that you can program on the server.

ASP.NET provides two sets of server controls:

- **HTML server controls.** These are server-based equivalents for standard HTML elements. These controls are ideal if you're a seasoned web programmer who prefers to work with familiar HTML tags (at least at first). They are also useful when migrating existing ASP pages to ASP.NET, because they require the fewest changes. You'll learn about HTML server controls in this chapter.
- **Web controls.** These are similar to the HTML server controls, but provide a richer object model with a variety of properties for style and formatting details. They also provide more events and more closely resemble the controls used for Windows development. Web controls also feature some user interface elements that have no HTML equivalent, such as the DataGrid and the validation controls. You'll learn about web controls in the next chapter.

HTML Server Controls

HTML server controls provide an object interface for standard HTML elements. They provide three key features:

- **They generate their own interface.** You set properties in code, and the underlying HTML tag is updated automatically when the page is rendered and sent to the client.
- **They retain their state.** You can write your program the same way you would write a traditional Windows program. There's no need to re-create a web page from scratch each time you send it to user.
- **They fire events.** Your code can respond to these events, just like ordinary controls in a Windows application. In ASP code, everything is grouped into one block that executes from start to finish. With event-based programming, you can easily respond to individual user actions and create more structured code. If a given event doesn't occur, the event handler code won't be executed.

To convert the currency converter to an ASP.NET page that uses server controls, all you need to do is add the special attribute runat="server" to each tag that you want to transform into a server control. You should also add an id attribute to each control that you need to interact with in code. The id attribute assigns the unique name that you'll use to refer to the control in code.

In the currency converter application, the input text box and submit button can be changed into server controls. In addition, the <form> element must also be processed as a server control to allow ASP.NET to access the controls it contains, as shown here:

```
<html><body>
  <form method="post" runat="server">
    <div>

      Convert:  
      <input type="text" id="US" runat="server">
        US dollars to Euros.
      <br><br>
      <input type="submit" value="OK" id="Convert" runat="server">

    </div>
  </form>
</body></html>
```

The web page still won't do anything, because you haven't written any code. However, now that you've converted the static HTML elements to HTML server controls, you're ready to work with them.

NOTE ASP.NET controls are always placed inside the <form> tag of the page. The <form> tag is a part of the standard for HTML forms, and it allows the browser to send information back to the web server.

View State

If you look at the HTML that is sent to you when you request the page, you'll see it's slightly different than the information in the .aspx file. First of all, the runat="server" attributes are stripped out (because they have no meaning to the client browser, which can't interpret them). More importantly, an additional hidden field has been added to the form.

```
<html><body>
  <form method="post" runat="server">
  <input type="hidden" name="__VIEWSTATE"
   value="dDw3NDg2NTI5MDg7Oz4=" />
    <div>

      Convert:  
      <input type="text" id="US" runat="server">  US dollars to Euros.
      <br><br>
      <input type="submit" value="OK" id="Convert" runat="server">

    </div>
  </form>
</body></html>
```

This hidden field stores information about the state of every control in the page, in a compressed format. It allows you to manipulate control properties in code and have the changes automatically persisted. This is a key part of the web forms programming model. Thanks to view state, you can often forget about the stateless nature of the Internet and treat your page like a continuously running application.

Even though the currency converter program doesn't yet include any code, you'll already notice one change. If you enter information in the text box and click the submit button to post the page, the refreshed page will still contain the value you entered in the text box. (In the original example that uses ordinary HTML elements, the value will be cleared every time the page is posted back.) This change occurs because ASP.NET controls automatically retain state.

The HTML Control Classes

Before you can continue any further with the currency calculator, you need to know about the control objects you've created. All the HTML server controls are defined in the System.Web.UI.HtmlControls namespace. There is a separate class for each kind of control. Table 6-1 describes the basic HTML server controls, and shows you the related HTML element.

Table 6-1. The HTML Server Control Classes

Class Name	HTML Tag Represented	Description
HtmlAnchor	<a>t	A hyperlink that the user can click to jump to another page.
HtmlButton	<button>	A button that the user clicks to perform an action. It's not supported by all browsers, so HtmlInputButton is usually used instead.
HtmlForm	<form>	The form wraps all the controls on a web page. Controls that appear inside a form will send their data to the server when the page is submitted.
HtmlImage	<img>	A link that points to an image, which will be inserted into the web page at the current location.
HtmlInputButton	<input type="button">, <input type="submit">, and <input type="reset">	A button that the user clicks to perform an action (often it's used to submit all the input values on the page to the server).

Table 6-1. The HTML Server Control Classes (Continued)

Class Name	HTML Tag Represented	Description
HtmlInputCheckBox	<input type="checkbox">	A checkbox that the user can check or clear. Doesn't include any text of its own.
HtmlInputFile	<input type="file">	A Browse button and text box that can be used to upload a file to your web server, as described in Chapter 17.
HtmlInputHidden	<input type="hidden">	Contains text-based information that will be sent to the server when the page is posted back, but won't be visible to the user.
HtmlInputImage	<input type="image">	Similar to the <img> tag, but it inserts a "clickable" image that submits the page.
HtmlInputRadioButton	<input type="radio">	A radio button that can be selected in a group. Doesn't include any text of its own.
HtmlInputText	<input type="text"> and <input type="password">	A single-line text box where the user can enter information. Can also be displayed as a password field (which displays asterisks instead of characters to hide the user input).
HtmlSelect	<select>	A drop-down or regular list box, where the user can select an item.
HtmlTable, HtmlTableRow, and HtmlTableCell	<table>, <tr>, <th> and <td>	A table that displays multiple rows and columns of static text.
HtmlTextArea	<textarea>	A large text box where the user can type multiple lines of text.
HtmlGenericControl	Any other HTML element	Can represent a variety of HTML elements that don't have dedicated control classes.

So far, the currency converter defines three controls, which are instances of the HtmlForm, HtmlInputText, and HtmlInputButton classes, respectively. It's important that you know the class names, because you need to define each control class in the code-behind file if you want to interact with it. (Visual Studio .NET simplifies this task: Whenever you add a control using its web designer, the appropriate tag is added to the .aspx file and the appropriate variables are defined in the code-behind class.)

TIP This chapter introduces many new server controls. As you work your way through the examples, I'll explain many of the corresponding properties and events and the class hierarchy. However, for single-stop shopping, you're encouraged to refer to Chapter 27, which provides a complete HTML server control reference. Each control is featured separately, with a picture, example tag, and a list of properties, events, and methods. In the meantime, Table 6-2 gives a quick overview of some of the most important control properties.

Table 6-2. Important HTML Control Properties

Control	Most Important Properties
HtmlAnchor	Href, Target, Title
HtmlImage and HtmlInputImage	Src, Alt, Width, and Height
HtmlInputCheckBox and HtmlInputRadioButton	Checked
HtmlInputText	Value
HtmlSelect	Items (collection)
HtmlTextArea	Value
HtmlGenericControl	InnerText

In order to actually add some functionality to the currency converter, you need to add some ASP.NET code. Web forms are event-driven, which means that every piece of code acts in response to a specific event. In the simple currency converter page example, the most useful event occurs when the user clicks the submit button (named Convert). The HtmlInputButton allows you to react to this action by handling the ServerClick event.

Before you continue, it makes sense to add another control that can be used to display the result of the calculation. In this case, you can use a <div> tag named Result. The <div> tag is one way to insert a block of formatted text into a web page. Here's the line of HTML that you'll need:

```
<div style="FONT-WEIGHT: bold" id="Result" runat="server">
```

The example now has the following four server controls:

- A form (HtmlForm object). This is the only control you do not need to use in your code-behind class.
- An input text box named US (HtmlInputText object).
- A submit button named Convert (HtmlInputButton object).
- A div tag named Result (HtmlGenericControl object).

The following code shows the revised web page (CurrencyConverter.aspx) and the code-behind class (CurrencyConverter.vb), which calculates the currency conversion and displays the result. For the purpose of this example, the page and code-behind file have been created by hand using Notepad. However, they follow the conventions used in Visual Studio .NET.

CurrencyConverter.aspx

```
<%@ Page Language="VB" Inherits="CurrencyConverter"
    Src="CurrencyConverter.vb" AutoEventWireup="False" %>
<html><body>
  <form method="post" runat="server">
    <div>
      Convert:  
      <input type="text" id="US" runat="server">  US dollars to Euros.
      <br><br>
      <input type="submit" value="OK" id="Convert" runat="server">
      <div style="FONT-WEIGHT: bold" id="Result" runat="server"></div>
    </div>
  </form>
</body></html>
```

CurrencyConverter.vb

```
Imports Microsoft.VisualBasic
Imports System
Imports System.Web
Imports System.Web.UI
Imports System.Web.UI.WebControls
Imports System.Web.UI.HtmlControls

Public Class CurrencyConverter
  Inherits Page

    Protected Result As HtmlGenericControl
    Protected WithEvents Convert As HtmlInputButton
    Protected US As HtmlInputText
```

```
    Private Sub Convert_ServerClick(sender As Object, e As EventArgs) _
     Handles Convert.ServerClick

        Dim USAmount As Decimal = Val(US.Value)
        Dim EuroAmount As Decimal = USAmount * 1.12
        Result.InnerText = USAmount.ToString() & " US dollars = "
        Result.InnerText &= EuroAmount.ToString() & " Euros."

    End Sub

End Class
```

The code-behind class is a typical example of an ASP.NET page. You'll notice the following conventions:

- **It uses the Imports statement.** This provides access to all the important namespaces. This is a typical first step in any code-behind file. You'll notice that the namespace Microsoft.VisualBasic is included. This allows you to use the traditional Visual Basic Val method to convert the text box entry into a number. Otherwise, you would need to use the static Parse() method of one of the number types to accomplish the same thing.

  ```
  ' This line is equivalent to the traditional Val function.
  Dim Amount As Decimal = Decimal.Parse(US.Value)
  ```

- **It defines a custom Page class and control variables.** This is also the standard format of all code-behind files. You'll notice that the variable names match the id attribute set in each control tag. The WithEvents keyword is used for the HtmlInputButton control so the page can receive its ServerClick event. You could define all controls using the WithEvents keyword, but in this case it isn't needed.

- **It defines a single event handler.** This event handler retrieves the value from the text box, multiplies it by a preset conversion ratio (which would typically be stored in another file or a database), and sets the text of the <div> tag.

The complete program works seamlessly. When the button is clicked, the page is resubmitted, the event handling code is triggered, and the page is resent (see Figure 6-2). Note that the ToString() method, which converts the numbers into strings before they are displayed, isn't strictly necessary. In most cases, Visual Basic .NET will perform this conversion automatically. However, it's always a good practice to handle conversions explicitly to prevent unexpected problems.

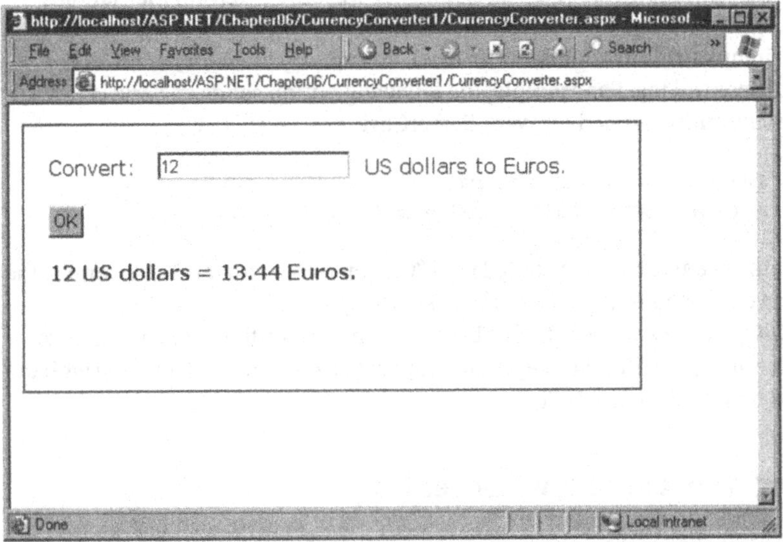

Figure 6-2. The ASP.NET currency converter

Event Handling Changes

The currency converter adds a few refinements that weren't found in the previous chapter's HelloWorld.aspx page. The most important differences are found in the event handler definition. (Note that the underscore is used to split this code over two lines. In your programs, you can include this on a single line without the underscore.)

```
Private Sub Convert_ServerClick(sender As Object, e As EventArgs) _
    Handles Convert.ServerClick
```

First of all, the event handler now accepts two parameters (sender and e). This is the recommended .NET standard for all events. It allows your code to identify the control that sent the event (through the sender parameter) and retrieve any other information that may be associated with the event (through the e parameter). You'll see examples of these advanced techniques later in the next chapter.

Secondly, the event handler explicitly connects itself to the appropriate event using the Handles clause. This allows the event handler subroutine to take any name and ensures that an error will be raised if the event or control isn't found. The example also adds the AutoEventWireup="False" attribute to the Page directive of the .aspx file to indicate that event handlers are being connected manually.

```
<%@ Page Language="VB" Inherits="CurrencyConverter"
    Src="CurrencyConverter.vb" AutoEventWireup="False" %>
```

When AutoEventWireup is set to False, ASP.NET will always rely on the Handles keyword to connect events to event handlers. Alternatively, you can leave out the AutoEventWireup attribute (it defaults to True), and specify the name of the event handler in the control tag. For example, the following button sends its ServerClick event to the subroutine named Convert_ServerClick.

```
<input type="submit" value="OK" id="Convert"
 OnServerClick="Convert_ServerClick" runat="server">
```

Note that the event name is preceded with "On" in the control tag. For example, the ServerClick event becomes the OnServerClick attribute.

Both techniques are equivalent. This book uses the first option, which connects event handlers using the Handles keyword. This brings our examples into line with the code created by Visual Studio .NET.

Improving the Currency Converter

Now that you've looked at the basic server controls, it might seem that their benefits are fairly minor compared with the cost of learning a whole new system of web programming. In this next section, you'll start to extend the currency calculator applet. You'll see how additional functionality can be snapped in to our existing program in an elegant, modular way. As the program grows, ASP.NET handles its complexity easily, steering you away from the tangled and intricate code that would be required in traditional ASP applications.

Adding Multiple Currencies

The first task is to allow the user to choose a destination currency. In this case, you need to use a drop-down list box. In HTML, a drop-down list is represented by a <select> element that contains one or more <option> elements. Each <option> element corresponds to a separate item in the list.

To reduce the amount of HTML in the currency converter, you can define a drop-down list without any list items by adding an empty <select> tag. As long as you ensure that this <select> tag is a server control (by giving it a name and adding the runat="server" attribute), you'll be able to interact with it in code and add the required items when the page loads.

Here's the revised HTML for the CurrencyConverter.aspx page:

```
<%@ Page Language="VB" Inherits="CurrencyConverter"
    Src="CurrencyConverter.vb" AutoEventWireup="False" %>

<html><body>
  <form method="post" runat="server">

    <!-- div tag used for formatting. -->
      Convert:  
      <input type="text" id="US" runat="server">
        US dollars to Euros.
      <select style="WIDTH: 155px" id="Currency" runat="server"></select>
```

```
      <br><br>
      <input type="submit" value="OK" id="Convert" runat="server">
      <br><br>
      <div style="FONT-WEIGHT: bold" id="Result" runat="server"></div>
    </div>

  </form>
</body></html>
```

Next, you must add the corresponding control variable to the CurrencyConverter class:

```
Protected Currency As HtmlSelect
```

The currency list can now be filled using code at runtime. In this case, the ideal event is the Page.Load event, because this is the first event that occurs when the page is executed. Here's the code you need to add to the CurrencyConverter page class:

```
Private Sub Page_Load(sender As Object, e As EventArgs) _
  Handles MyBase.Load

    If Me.IsPostBack = False
        Currency.Items.Add("Euro")
        Currency.Items.Add("Japanese Yen")
        Currency.Items.Add("Canadian Dollars")
    End If

End Sub
```

Dissecting the Code...

This example illustrates several important points:

- You can specify MyBase to define an event handler for a Page event. The MyBase keyword always refers to the class that your page inherited from (in this case, the Page class).
- You can use the Items property to get items in a list control. This allows you to append, insert, and remove <option> elements. Remember, when generating dynamic content with a server control you set the properties, and the control creates the appropriate HTML tags.
- Before adding any items to this list, you need to make sure that this is the first time the page is being served. Otherwise, the page will continuously add more items to the list or inadvertently overwrite the user's selection every time the user interacts with the page. To perform this test, you check the Me.IsPostBack property. The Me keyword points to the current instance of the page class. In other words, IsPostback is a property of the CurrencyConverter class, which CurrencyConverter inherited from the generic Page class. If IsPostBack is False, the page is being created for the first time, and it's safe to initialize it.

Storing Information in the List

Of course, if you're a veteran HTML coder, you know that a select list also provides a value attribute that you can use to store additional information. As the currency converter uses a short list of hard-coded values, this would be an ideal place to store the conversion rate.

To set the value tag, you need to create a ListItem object and add that to the HtmlInputSelect control. The ListItem class provides a constructor that lets you to specify the text and value at the same time that you create it, thereby allowing condensed code like this:

```
Private Sub Page_Load(sender As Object, e As EventArgs) _
  Handles MyBase.Load

    If Me.IsPostBack = False
        ' The HtmlInputSelect control accepts text or ListItem objects.
        Currency.Items.Add(New ListItem("Euro", "1.12"))
        Currency.Items.Add(New ListItem("Japanese Yen", "122.33"))
        Currency.Items.Add(New ListItem("Canadian Dollar", "1.48"))
    End If

End Sub
```

To complete the example, the calculation code must be rewritten to take the selected currency into account, as follows:

```
Private Sub Convert_ServerClick(sender As Object, e As EventArgs) _
  Handles convert.ServerClick

    Dim Amount As Decimal = Val(US.Value)

    ' Retrieve the select ListItem object by its index number.
    ' Each ListItem object provides a Text and Value property.
    Dim Item As ListItem
    Item = Currency.Items(Currency.SelectedIndex)

    Dim NewAmount As Decimal = Amount * Val(Item.Value)
    Result.InnerText = Amount.ToString() & " US dollars = "
    Result.InnerText &= NewAmount.ToString() & " " & Item.Text

End Sub
```

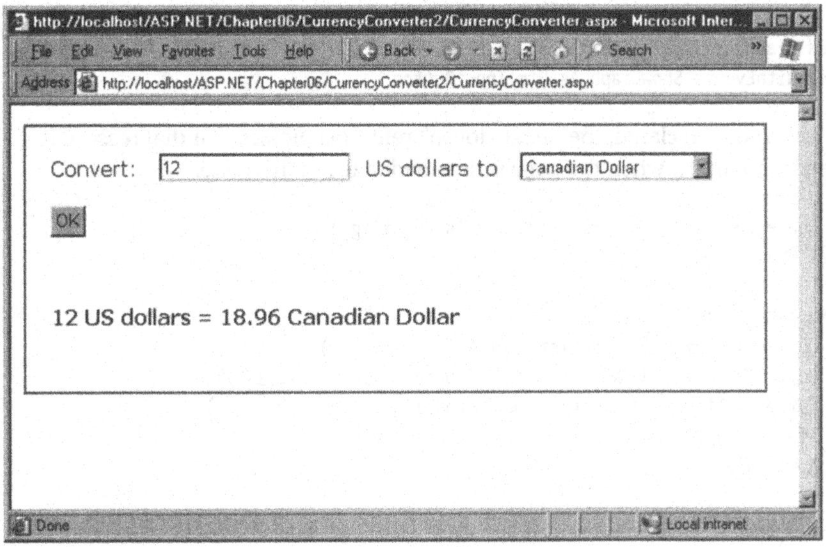

Figure 6-3. The multicurrency converter

Adding Linked Images

Adding a different set of functionality to the currency converter is just as easy as adding a new button. For example, it might be useful for the utility to display a currency conversion rate graph. To provide this feature, the program would need an additional button and image control.

Here's the revised HTML:

```
<%@ Page Language="VB" Inherits="CurrencyConverter"
         Src="CurrencyConverter.vb" AutoEventWireup="False" %>

<html><body>
  <form method="post" runat="server">

    <!-- div tag used for formatting. -->
      Convert:  
      <input type="text" id="US" runat="server">
        US dollars to Euros.
      <select style="WIDTH: 155px" id="Currency"
       runat="server"></select><br><br>
      <input type="submit" value="OK" id="Convert" runat="server">
      <input type="submit" value="Show Graph" id="ShowGraph"
       runat="server">
      <br><br>
      <img id="Graph" runat="server"><br><br>
      <div style="FONT-WEIGHT: bold" id="Result" runat="server"></div>
    </div>

  </form>
</body></html>
```

The new controls are also defined in the code-behind file.

```
Protected Graph As HtmlImage
Protected WithEvents ShowGraph As HtmlInputButton
```

As it's currently declared, the image doesn't refer to a picture. For that reason, it makes sense to hide it when the page is first loaded using this code.

```
Private Sub Page_Load(sender As Object, e As EventArgs) _
  Handles MyBase.Load

    If Me.IsPostBack = False
        Currency.Items.Add(New ListItem("Euro", "1.12"))
        Currency.Items.Add(New ListItem("Japanese Yen", "122.33"))
        Currency.Items.Add(New ListItem("Canadian Dollar", "1.58"))
    End If
    Graph.Visible = False

End Sub
```

Interestingly, when a sever control is hidden, ASP.NET leaves it out of the final HTML page.

Now you can handle the click event of the new button to display the appropriate picture. In the currency converter, there are three possible picture files: pic0.png, pic1.png, and pic2.png, depending on the selected currency.

```
Private Sub ShowGraph_ServerClick(sender As Object, e As EventArgs) _
  Handles ShowGraph.ServerClick

    Graph.Src = "Pic" & Currency.SelectedIndex & ".png"
    Graph.Alt = "Currency Graph"
    Graph.Visible = True

End Sub
```

Already, the currency calculator is beginning to look more interesting, as shown in Figure 6-4.

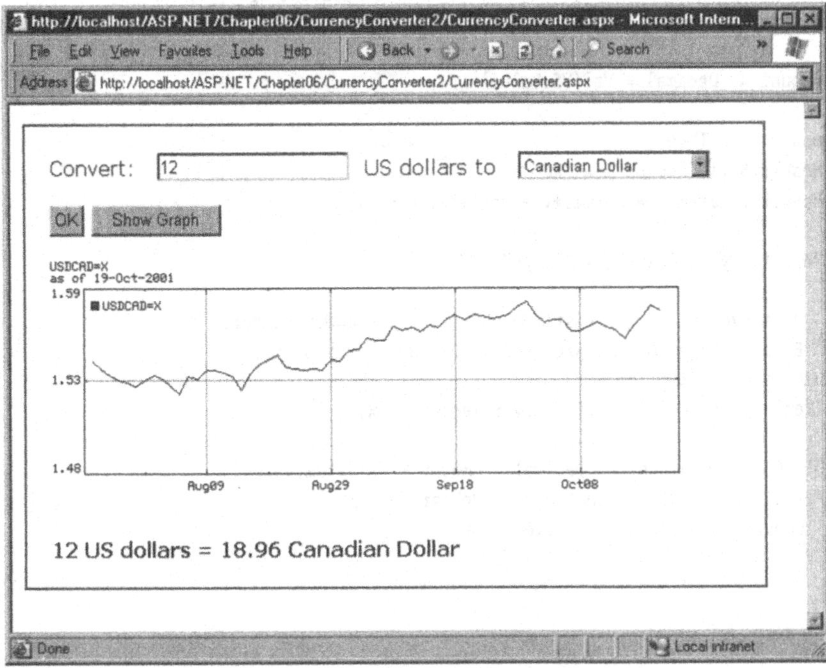

Figure 6-4. The currency converter with an image control

Setting Styles

In addition to a limited set of properties, each HTML control also provides access to the CSS (cascading style sheet) style attributes through its Style collection. To use this collection, you need to specify the name of the CSS style attribute and the value that you want to assign to it. Here's the basic syntax:

```
ControlName.Style("AttributeName") = "AttributeValue"
```

For example, you could use this technique to emphasize an invalid entry in the currency converter with the color red. In this case, you'll also need to reset the color to its original value for valid input, as the control uses view state to remember all its settings, including its style properties.

```
Private Sub Convert_ServerClick(sender As Object, e As EventArgs) _
  Handles convert.ServerClick

    Dim Amount As Decimal = Val(US.Value)

    If Amount <= 0 Then
        Result.Style("color") = "Red"
        Result.InnerText = "Specify a positive number"
    Else
        Result.Style("color") = "Black"

        ' Retrieve the select ListItem object by its index number.
        ' Each ListItem object provides a Text and Value property.
        Dim Item As ListItem
        Item = Currency.Items(Currency.SelectedIndex)

        Dim ConvertedAmount As Decimal = Amount * Val(Item.Value)
        Result.InnerText = Amount & " US dollars = " & _
          ConvertedAmount & " " & Item.Text
    End If

End Sub
```

TIP The Style collection is used to set the style attribute in the HTML tag with a list of formatting options such as font family, size, and color. But if you aren't familiar with CSS styles, there's no need to learn them now. Instead, you should use the web control equivalents, which provide higher-level properties that allow you to configure their appearance and automatically create the appropriate style attributes. You'll learn about web controls in the next chapter.

This concludes the simple currency converter applet, which now boasts automatic calculation, linked images, and dynamic formatting. In the following sections, we'll look at the building blocks of ASP.NET interfaces more closely.

A Deeper Look at HTML Control Classes

Related classes in the .NET Framework use inheritance to share functionality. For example, every HTML control inherits from the base class HtmlControl. The HtmlControl class provides essential features every HTML server control uses. The inheritance diagram is shown in Figure 6-5.

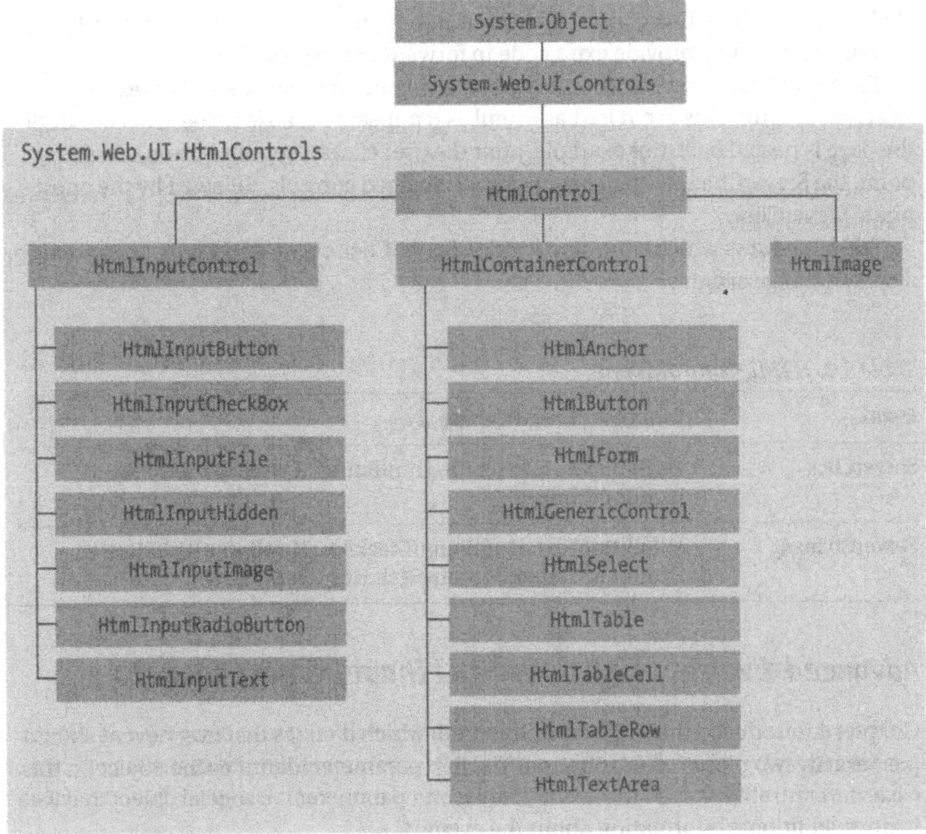

Figure 6-5. HTML control inheritance

The next few sections dissect the ASP.NET classes that are used for HTML server controls. You can use this material to help understand the common elements that are shared by all HTML controls. For the specific details about each individual HTML control, you can refer to the reference in Chapter 27.

HTML server controls generally provide properties that closely match their tag attributes. For example, the HtmlImage class provides Align, Alt, Border, Src, Height, and Width properties. For this reason, users who are familiar with HTML syntax will find that HTML server controls are the most natural fit. Users who aren't as used to HTML will probably find that web controls (described in the next chapter) have a more intuitive set of properties.

HTML Control Events

HTML server controls also provide one of two possible events: ServerClick or ServerChange. The ServerClick is simply a click that is processed on the server side. It's provided by most button controls, and it allows your code to take immediate action.

This action might override the expected behavior. For example, if you intercept the click event of a hyperlink control (the <a> element), the user won't be redirected to a new page unless you provide extra code to forward the request.

The ServerChange event responds when a change has been made to a text or selection control. This event isn't as useful as it appears because it doesn't occur until the page is posted back (for example, after the user clicks a submit button). At this point, the ServerChange event occurs for all changed controls, followed by the appropriate ServerClick.

Table 6-3 shows which controls provide a ServerClick event, and which ones provide a ServerChange event.

Table 6-3. HTML Control Events

Event	Controls that Provide It
ServerClick	HtmlAnchor, HtmlForm, HtmlButton, HtmlInputButton, HtmlInputImage
ServerChange	HtmlInputText, HtmlInputCheckBox, HtmlInputRadioButton, HtmlInputHidden, HtmlSelect, HtmlTextArea

Advanced Events with the HtmlInputImage Control

Chapter 4 introduced the .NET event standard, which dictates that every event should pass exactly two pieces of information. The first parameter identifies the object (in this case, the control) that fired the event. The second parameter is a special object that can include additional information about the event.

In the examples you've looked at so far, the second parameter (e) has always been used to pass an empty System.EventArgs object. This object doesn't contain any additional information—it's just a glorified placeholder. Here's one such example:

```
Private Sub Convert_ServerClick(sender As Object, e As EventArgs) _
  Handles convert.ServerClick
```

In fact, there is only one HTML server control that sends additional information: the HtmlInputImage control. It sends a special ImageClickEventArgs object (from the System.Web.UI namespace) that provides X and Y properties representing the location where the image was clicked. You'll notice that the definition for the HtmlInputImage.ServerClick event handler is a little different from the event handlers used with other controls:

```
Private Sub ImgButton_ServerClick(sender As Object, _
  e As ImageClickEventArgs) Handles ImgButton.ServerClick
```

Using this additional information, you can replace multiple button controls and image maps with a single, intelligent HtmlInputImage control. The sample ImageTest.aspx page shown in Figure 6-6 puts this feature to work with a simple graphical button. Depending on whether the user clicks the button border or the button surface, a different message is displayed.

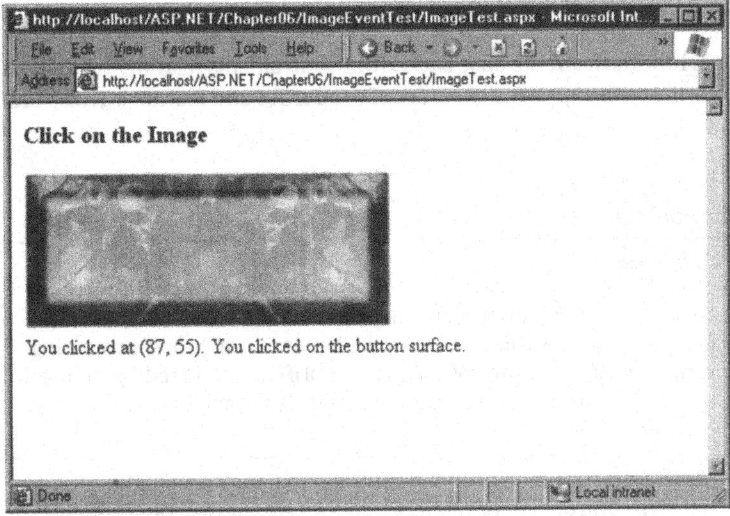

Figure 6-6. Using an HtmlInputImage control

The page code examines the click coordinates provided by the ImageClickEventArgs object, and displays them in another control. Here's the page code you need:

```
Public Class ImageTest
  Inherits Page

    Protected Result As HtmlGenericControl
    Protected WithEvents ImgButton As HtmlInputImage

    Private Sub ImgButton_ServerClick(sender As Object, _
      e As ImageClickEventArgs) Handles ImgButton.ServerClick

        Result.InnerText = "You clicked at (" & e.X.ToString() & _
                           ", " & e.Y.ToString() & "). "

        If e.Y < 100 And e.Y > 20 And e.X > 20 and e.X < 275 Then
            Result.InnerText &= "You clicked on the button surface."
        Else
            Result.InnerText &= "You clicked the button border."
        End If
    End Sub

End Class
```

The HtmlControl Base Class

Every HTML control inherits from the base class HtmlControl. This relationship means that every HTML control will support a basic set of properties and features. These are shown in Table 6-4.

Table 6-4. HtmlControl Properties

Property	Description
Attributes	Provides a collection of all the tag attributes and their values. Rather than setting an attribute directly, it's better to use the corresponding property. However, this collection is useful if you need to add or configure a custom attribute or an attribute that doesn't have a corresponding property.
Controls	Provides a collection of all the controls contained inside the current control. (For example, a <div> server control could contain an <input> server control.) Each object is provided as a generic System.Web.UI.Control object, so you may need to cast the reference with the CType() function to access control-specific properties.
Disabled	Set this to True to disable the control, thereby ensuring that the user cannot interact with it and its events will not be fired.
EnableViewState	Set this to False to disable the automatic state management for this control. In this case, the control will be reset to the properties and formatting specified in the control tag every time the page is posted back. If this is set to True (the default), the control uses a hidden input field to store information about its properties, thereby ensuring that any changes you make in code are remembered.
Page	Provides a reference to the web page that contains this control as a System.Web.UI.Page object.
Parent	Provides a reference to the control that contains this control. If the control is placed directly on the page (rather than inside another control), it will return a reference to the page object.
Style	Provides a collection of CSS style properties that can be used to format the control.
TagName	Indicates the name of the underlying HTML element (for example, "img" or "div").
Visible	When set to False, the control will be hidden and will not be rendered to the final HTML page that is sent to the client.

The HtmlControl class also provides built-in support for data binding, which you'll examine in Chapter 15.

Properties Can Be Set in Code or in the Tag

To set the initial value of a property, you can configure the control in the Page.Load event handler, or you can adjust the control tag in the .aspx file by adding special attributes. Note that the Page.Load event occurs after the page is initialized with the default values and the tag settings. That means that your code can override the properties set in the tag (but not vice versa).

The following HtmlImage control is an example that sets properties through attributes in the control tag. The control is automatically disabled and will not have its view state information stored.

```
<img EnableViewState="False" Disabled="True" id="Graph" runat="server">
```

The only disadvantage with using control tag attributes is that errors will not necessarily be detected before they occur. An invalid property assignment in the code-behind, on the other hand, will almost always generate a compile-time error informing you about the problem.

The HtmlContainerControl Class

Any HTML control that requires a closing tag also inherits from the HtmlContainer control. For example, elements such as <a>, <form>, and <div> always use a closing tag, because they can contain other HTML elements. On the other hand, <img> and <input> are only used as stand-alone tags. Thus, the HtmlAnchor, HtmlForm, and HtmlGenericControl classes inherit from HtmlContainerControl, while HtmlImage and HtmlInput do not.

The HtmlContainer control adds two properties, as described in Table 6-5.

Table 6-5. HtmlContainerControl Properties

Property	Description
InnerHtml	The HTML content between the opening and closing tags of the control. Special characters that are set through this property will not be converted to the equivalent HTML entities. This means you can use this property to apply formatting with nested tags like <b>, <i>, and <h1>.
InnerText	The text content between the opening and closing tags of the control. Special characters will be automatically converted to HTML entities and displayed like text (for example, the less than character (<) will be converted to < and will be displayed as < in the web page). That means that you can't use HTML tags to apply additional formatting with this property. The simple currency converter page used the InnerText property to enter results into a <div> tag.

The HtmlInputControl Class

This control defines some properties (shown in Table 6-6) that are common to all the HTML controls that are based on the <input> tag, including the <input type="text">, <input type="submit">, and <input type="file"> elements.

Table 6-6. HtmlInputControl Properties

Property	Description
Type	Provides the type of input control. For example, a control based on <input type="file"> would return "file" for the type property.
Value	Returns the contents of the control as a string. In the simple currency converter, this property allowed the code to retrieve the information entered in the text input control.

The Page Class

One control that hasn't been discussed in detail is the Page class. As explained in the previous chapter, every web page is a custom class that inherits from System.Web.UI.Page. By inheriting from this class, your web page class acquires a number of properties that your code can use. These include properties for enabling caching, validation, and tracing, which are discussed throughout this book.

Some of the more fundamental properties are described in Table 6-7, including the traditional built-in objects that ASP developers often used, such as Response, Request, and Session.

Table 6-7. Basic Page Properties

Property	Description
Application and Session	These collections are used to hold state information on the server. This topic is discussed in Chapter 10.
Cache	This collection allows you to store objects for reuse in other pages or for other clients. Caching is described in Chapter 24.
Controls	Provides a collection of all the controls contained on the web page. You can also use the methods of this collection to add new controls dynamically.
EnableViewState	When set to False, this overrides the EnableViewState property of the contained controls, thereby ensuring that no controls will maintain state information.

Table 6-7. Basic Page Properties (Continued)

Property	Description
IsPostBack	This Boolean property indicates whether this is the first time the page is being run (False), or whether the page is being resubmitted in response to a control event, typically with stored view state information (True). This property is often used in the Page.Load event handler, thereby ensuring that basic setup is only performed once for controls that maintain view state.
Request	Refers to an HttpRequest object that contains information about the current web request, including client certificates, cookies, and values submitted through HTML form elements. It supports the same features as the built-in ASP Request object.
Response	Refers to an HttpResponse object that allows you to set the web response or redirect the user to another web page. It supports the same features as the built-in ASP Response object, although it's used much less in .NET development.
Server	Refers to an HttpServerUtility object that allows you to perform some miscellaneous tasks, such as URL and HTML encoding. It supports the same features as the built-in ASP Server object.
User	If the user has been authenticated, this property will be initialized with user information. This property is described in more detail in Chapter 25.

The Controls Collection

The Page.Controls collection includes all the controls on the current web form. You can loop through this collection and access each control. For example, the following code writes out the name of every control on the current page to a server control called Result.

```
Result.InnerText = "List of controls: "
Dim ctrl As Control
For Each ctrl In Me.Controls
    Result.InnerText &= " " & ctrl.ID
Next
```

You can also use the Controls collection to add a dynamic control. The following code creates a new button with the caption Dynamic Button and adds it to the bottom of the page.

```
Dim ctrl As New HtmlButton()
ctrl.InnerText = "Dynamic Button"
ctrl.ID = "DynamicButton"
Me.Controls.Add(ctrl)
```

The best place to generate new controls is in the Page.Load event handler. This ensures that the control will be created each time the page is served. In addition, if you're adding an input control that uses view state, the view state information will be restored to the control after the Page.Load event fires. That means a dynamically generated text box will retain its text over multiple postbacks, just like a text box that is defined in the .aspx file. Dynamically created controls are difficult to position, however. By default, they appear at the bottom of the page. The only way to change this behavior is to create a container control that acts as a placeholder, like a server-side <div> tag. You can then add the dynamic control to the Controls collection of the container control.

The HttpRequest Class

The HttpRequest class encapsulates all the information related to a client request for a web page (see Table 6-8). Most of this information corresponds to low-level details such as posted-back form values, server variables, the response encoding, and so on. If you're using ASP.NET to its fullest, you'll almost never dive down to that level. Other properties are generally useful for retrieving information, particularly about the capabilities of the client browser. You'll learn about some of the security-related properties in Chapter 25.

Table 6-8. HttpRequest Properties

Property	Description
ApplicationPath and PhysicalPath	ApplicationPath gets the ASP.NET application's virtual directory (URL), while PhysicalPath gets the "real" directory.
Browser	Provides a link to an HttpBrowserCapabilities object that contains properties describing various browser features, such as support for ActiveX controls, cookies, VBScript, and frames. This replaces the BrowserCapabilities component that was sometimes used in ASP development.
ClientCertificate	An HttpClientCertificate object that gets the security certificate for the current request, if there is one.
Cookies	Gets the collection cookies sent with this request. Cookies are discussed in more detail in Chapter 10.

Table 6-8. HttpRequest Properties (Continued)

Property	Description
Headers and ServerVariables	Provides a name/value collection of HTTP headers and server variables. You can get the low-level information you need if you know the corresponding header or variable name.
IsAuthenticated and IsSecureConnection	Returns True if the user has been successfully authenticated and if the user is connected over SSL (also known as secure sockets).
QueryString	Provides the parameters that were passed along with the query string. Chapter 10 discusses how you can use the query string to transfer information between pages.
Url and UrlReferrer	Provides a Uri object that represents the current address for the page, and the page where the user is coming from (the previous page that linked to this page).
UserAgent	A string representing the browser type. Internet Explorer provides the value "MSIE" for this property.
UserHostAddress and UserHostName	Gets the IP address and the DNS name of the remote client. You could also access this information through the ServerVariables collection.
UserLanguages	Provides a sorted string array that lists the client's language preferences. This can be useful if you need to create multilingual pages.

The HttpResponse Class

The HttpResponse class allows you to send information directly to the client. In traditional ASP development, the Response object was used heavily to create dynamic pages. Now, with the introduction of the new server-based control model, these relatively crude methods are no longer needed.

The HttpResponse does still provide some important functionality: namely caching support, cookie features, and the Redirect method, which allows you to transfer the user to another page. A list of HttpResponse members is provided in Table 6-9.

```
' You can redirect to a file in the current directory.
Response.Redirect("newpage.aspx")

' You can redirect to another website.
Response.Redirect("http://www.prosetech.com")
```

Table 6-9. HttpResponse Members

Member	Description
BufferOutput	When set to True (the default), the page isn't sent to the client until it's completely rendered and ready to send, as opposed to being sent piecemeal.
Cache	References an HttpCachePolicy object that allows you to configure how this page will be cached. Caching is discussed in Chapter 24.
Cookies	The collection of cookies sent with the response. You can use this property to add additional cookies, as described in Chapter 10.
Write(), BinaryWrite(), and WriteFile()	These methods allow you to write text or binary content directly to the response stream. You can even write the contents of a file. These methods are de-emphasized in ASP.NET, and shouldn't be used in conjunction with server controls.
Redirect()	This method transfers the user to another page in your application or a different website.

The ServerUtility Class

The ServerUtility class provides some miscellaneous helper methods, as listed in Table 6-10. The most commonly used are UrlEncode()/UrlDecode() and HtmlEncode()/HtmlDecode(). These functions change a string into a representation that can safely be used as part of a URL or displayed in a web page.

Table 6-10. ServerUtility Methods

Method	Description
CreateObject()	Creates an instance of the COM object that is identified by its programmatic ID (progID). This is included for backward compatibility, because it will generally be easier to interact with COM objects using the .NET Framework services.
HtmlEncode() and HtmlDecode()	Changes an ordinary string into a string with legal HTML characters and back again.
UrlEncode() and UrlDecode()	Changes an ordinary string into a string with legal URL characters and back again.
MapPath()	Returns the physical file path that corresponds to a specified virtual file path on the web server.

Table 6-10. ServerUtility Methods (Continued)

Method	Description
Transfer()	Transfers execution to another web page in the current application. This is similar to the Response.Redirect() method, but slightly faster. It cannot be used to transfer the user to a site on another web server, or to a non-ASP.NET page (like an HTML page or a ASP page).

For example, imagine you want to display this text on a web page:

```
Enter a word <here>
```

If you try to write this information to a page or place it inside a control, you would end up with this instead:

```
Enter a word
```

The problem is that the browser has tried to interpret the text "<here>" as an HTML tag. A similar problem occurs if you actually use valid HTML tags. For example, consider this text:

```
To bold text use the <b> tag.
```

Not only will the text "<b>" not appear, but the browser will interpret it as an instruction to make the text that follows bold. To circumvent this automatic behavior, you need to convert potential problematic values to their special HTML equivalents. For example < becomes < in your final HTML page, which the browser displays as the < character.

You can perform this transformation on your own, or you can circumvent the problem by using the InnerText property. When you set the contents of a control using InnerText, any illegal characters are automatically converted into their HTML equivalents. However, this won't help if you want to set a tag that contains a mix of embedded HTML tags and encoded characters. It also won't be of any use for controls that don't provide an InnerText property, such as the Label web control you'll examine in the next chapter. In these cases, you can use the HtmlEncode() method to replace the special characters. Here's an example:

```
' Will output as "Enter a word &lt;here&gt;" in the HTML file, but the
' browser will display it as "Enter a word <here>".
ctrl.InnerHtml = Server.HtmlEncode("Enter a word <here>")
```

Or consider this example, which mingles real HTML tags with text that needs to be encoded.

```
ctrl.InnerHtml = "To <b>bold</b> text use the "
ctrl.InnerHtml &= Server.HtmlEncode("<b>") & " tag."
```

Figure 6-7 shows the results of successfully and incorrectly encoding special HTML characters. You can try out this sample as the HtmlEncodeTest.aspx page included with the examples for this chapter.

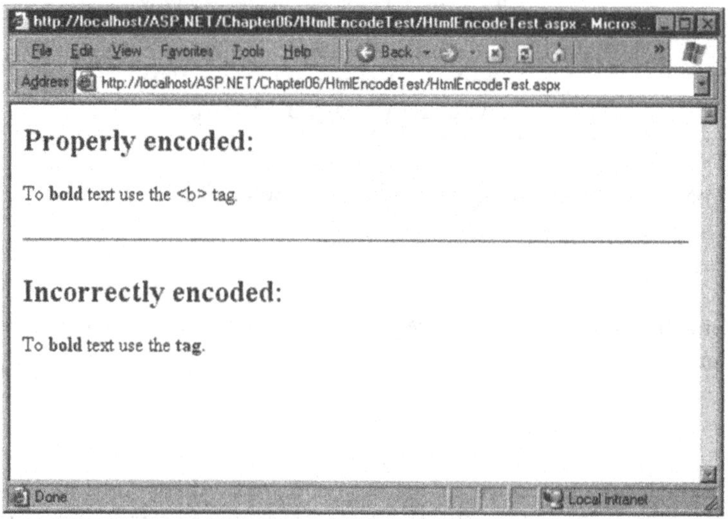

Figure 6-7. Encoding special HTML characters

The HtmlEncode() method is particularly useful if you're retrieving values from a database, and you aren't sure if the text is valid HTML. You can use the HtmlDecode() method to revert the text to its normal form if you need to perform additional operations or comparisons with it in your code. Table 6-11 lists some special characters that need to be encoded.

Table 6-11. Common HTML Special Characters

Result	Description	Encoded Entity
	Nonbreaking space	
<	Less-than symbol	<
>	Greater-than symbol	>
&	Ampersand	&
"	Quotation mark	"

Similarly, the UrlEncode() method changes text into a form that can be used in a URL. Generally, this allows information to work as a query string variable, even if it contains spaces and other characters that aren't allowed in a URL. You'll see this technique demonstrated in Chapter 10.

The Last Word

HTML controls are a compromise between web controls and traditional ASP.NET programming. They use the familiar HTML elements, but provide a limited object-oriented interface. Essentially, HTML controls are designed to be straightforward, predictable, and automatically compatible with existing programs. With HTML controls, the final HTML page that is sent to the client closely resembles the original .aspx page.

In the next chapter, you'll learn about web controls, which provide a more sophisticated object interface that abstracts away the underlying HTML. If you're starting a new project or need to add some of ASP.NET's most powerful controls, web controls are the best option.

CHAPTER 7

Web Controls

THE LAST CHAPTER introduced one of ASP.NET's most surprising changes: the shift to event-driven and control-based programming. This change allows you to create programs for the web using the same object-oriented, modern code you would use to write a Windows application.

However, HTML server controls really only show a glimpse of what is possible with ASP.NET's new server control model. To see some of the real advantages, you need to dive into the richer and more extensible web controls. In this chapter, you'll explore the basic web controls and their class hierarchy. You'll also delve deeper into ASP.NET's event handling, learn the details of the web page life cycle, and put your knowledge to work by creating a web page for designing greeting cards.

Stepping Up to Web Controls

Now that you've seen the new model of server controls, you might wonder why we need additional web controls. But in fact, HTML controls are much more limited than server controls need to be. For example, every HTML control corresponds directly to an HTML tag, meaning that you're bound by the limitations and abilities of the HTML language. Web controls, on the other hand, have no such restriction. They emphasize the future of web design.

Some of the reasons you should switch to web controls include the following:

- **They provide a rich user interface.** A web control is programmed as an object, but doesn't necessarily correspond to a single tag in the final HTML page. For example, you might create a single Calendar or DataGrid control, which will be rendered as dozens of HTML elements in the final page. When using ASP.NET programs, you don't need to know anything about HTML. The control creates the required HTML tags for you.

- **They provide a consistent object model.** The HTML language is full of quirks and idiosyncrasies. For example, a simple text box can appear as one of three elements, including <textarea>, <input type="text">, and <input type="password">. With web controls, these three elements are consolidated as a single TextBox control. Depending on the properties you set, the underlying HTML element that ASP.NET renders may differ. Similarly, the names of properties don't follow the HTML attribute names. Controls that display text, whether it's a caption or a text box that can be edited by the user, expose a Text property.

- **They tailor their output automatically.** ASP.NET server controls can detect the type of browser and automatically adjust the HTML code they write to take advantage of features such as support for DHTML. You don't need to know about the client because ASP.NET handles that layer and automatically uses the best possible set of features.

- **They provide high-level features.** You'll see that web controls allow you to access additional events, properties, and methods that don't correspond directly to typical HTML controls. ASP.NET implements these features by using a combination of tricks.

Throughout this book, you'll see examples that use the full set of web controls. In order to master ASP.NET development, you need to become comfortable with these user-interface ingredients and understand all their abilities. HTML server controls, on the other hand, are less important for web development, unless you need to have fine-grained control over the HTML code that will be generated and sent to the client. They are de-emphasized in .NET.

NOTE This chapter is the first one to include examples that are created in Visual Studio .NET. Visual Studio .NET makes it much easier to lay out complex user interfaces, such as the greeting-card maker applet demonstrated at the end of this chapter. If you want to modify or recompile the code in these examples, you'll find it easiest if you use Visual Studio .NET. The next chapter presents a guided tour of the Visual Studio .NET design environment.

Basic Web Control Classes

If you've ever created a Windows application before, you're probably familiar with the basic set of standard controls, including labels, buttons, and text boxes. ASP.NET provides web controls for all these standbys. (And if you've created .NET Windows applications, you'll notice that the class names and properties have many striking similarities, which are designed to make it easy to transfer the experience you acquire in one type of application to another.)

Table 7-1 lists the basic control classes and the HTML elements they generate. Note that some controls, such as Button and TextBox, can be rendered as different HTML elements. ASP.NET uses the element that matches the properties you've set. Also, some controls have no single HTML equivalent. For example, the CheckBoxList and RadioButtonList controls output as a <table> that contains multiple HTML checkboxes or radio buttons. ASP.NET wraps them into a single object on the server side for convenient programming, thus illustrating one of the primary strengths of web controls.

Table 7-1. Basic Web Controls

Control Class	Underlying HTML Element
Label	<span>
Button	<input type="submit"> or <input type="button">
TextBox	<input type="text">, <input type="password">, or <textarea>
CheckBox	<input type="checkbox">
RadioButton	<input type="radio">
Hyperlink	<a>
LinkButton	<a> with a contained <img> tag
ImageButton	<input type="image">
Image	<img>
ListBox	<select size="X"> where X is the number of rows that are visible at once
DropDownList	<select>
CheckBoxList	A list or <table> with multiple <input type="checkbox"> tags
RadioButtonList	A list or <table> with multiple <input type="radio"> tags
Panel	<div>
Table, TableRow, and TableCell	<table>, <tr>, and <td> or <th>

This table omits some of the more specialized rich controls, which you'll see in Chapter 9, and the advanced data controls, which you'll see in Chapter 16.

The Web Control Tags

ASP.NET tags have a special format. They always begin with the prefix asp: followed by the class name. If there is no closing tag, the tag must end with />. Each attribute in the tag corresponds to a control property, except for the runat="server" attribute, which signals that the control should be processed on the server.

The following, for example, is an ASP.NET TextBox:

```
<asp:TextBox id="txt" runat="server" />
```

When a client requests this .aspx page, the following HTML is returned. The name is a special attribute that ASP.NET uses to track the control.

```
<input type="text" name="ctrl0" />
```

Alternatively, you could place some text in the TextBox, set its size, make it read-only, and change the background color. All these actions have defined properties. For example, the TextBox.TextMode property allows you to specify SingleLine (the default), MultiLine (for a textarea type of control), or Password (for an input control that displays all asterisks when the user types in a value). The Color can be adjusted using the BackColor and ForeColor properties. And the size of the TextBox can be tweaked using the Rows property. Here's an example of a customized TextBox:

```
<asp:TextBox id="txt" BackColor="Yellow" Text="Hello World"
 ReadOnly="True" TextMode="MultiLine" Rows="5" runat="server" />
```

The resulting HTML uses the textarea element and sets all the required style attributes. It's shown in the browser in Figure 7-1.

```
<textarea name="txt" rows="5" readonly="readonly" id="txt"
 style="background-color:Yellow;">Hello World</textarea>
```

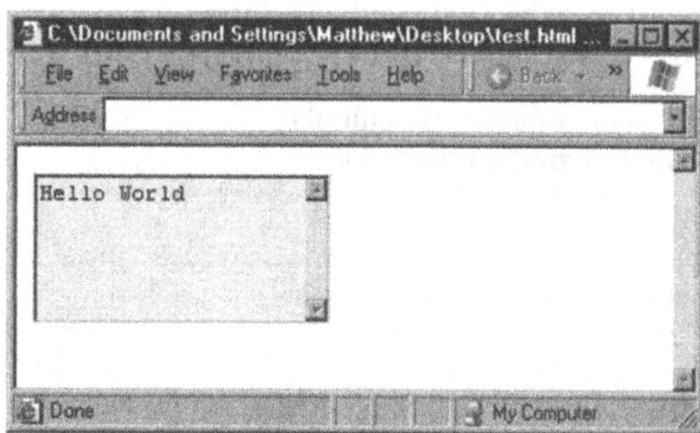

Figure 7-1. A customized text box

Clearly, it's easy to create a web control tag. It doesn't require any understanding of HTML. However, you *will* need to understand the control class and the properties that are available to you.

Web Control Classes

Web control classes are defined in the System.Web.UI.WebControls namespace. They follow a slightly more tangled object hierarchy than HTML server controls, as shown in Figure 7-2.

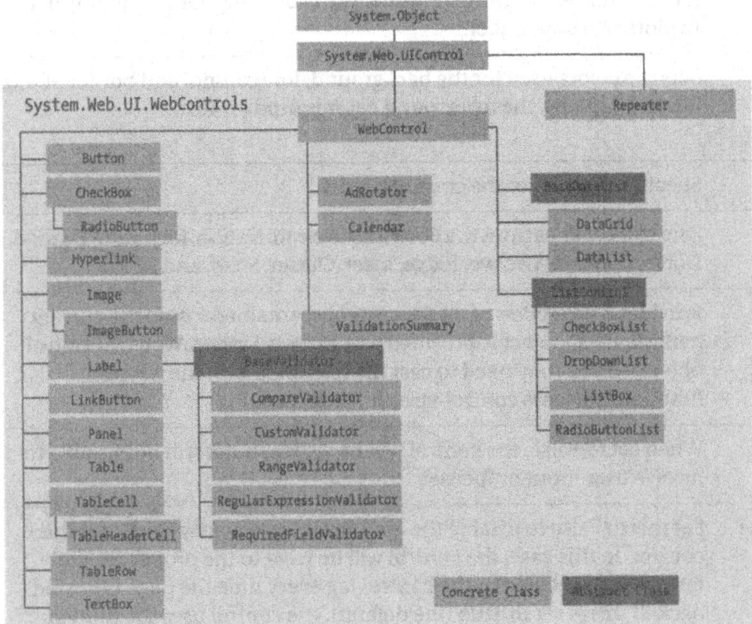

Figure 7-2. The web control hierarchy

This inheritance diagram includes some controls that you won't study in this chapter, including the data controls such as the Repeater, DataList, and DataGrid, and the validation controls. These controls are explored in later chapters.

The WebControl Base Class

All web controls begin by inheriting from the WebControl base class. This class defines the essential functionality for tasks such as data binding and includes some basic properties that you can use with any control, as described in Table 7-2.

Table 7-2. WebControl Properties

Property	Description
AccessKey	Specifies the keyboard shortcut as one letter. For example, if you set this to "Y" the Alt-Y keyboard combination will automatically change focus to this web control. This feature is only supported on Internet Explorer 4.0 and higher.
BackColor, BorderColor, and ForeColor	Sets the colors used for the background, foreground, and border of the control. Usually, the foreground color is used for text.
BorderWidth	Specifies the size of the control border.
BorderStyle	One of the values from the BorderStyle enumeration, including Dashed, Dotted, Double, Groove, Ridge, Inset, Outset, Solid, and None.
Controls	Provides a collection of all the controls contained inside the current control. Each object is provided as a generic System.Web.UI.Control object, so you may need to cast the reference with the CType() function to access control-specific properties.
Enabled	When set to False, the control will be visible, but it will not be able to receive user input or focus.
EnableViewState	Set this to False to disable the automatic state management for this control. In this case, the control will be reset to the properties and formatting specified in the control tag every time the page is posted back. If this is set to True (the default), the control uses the hidden input field to store information about its properties, ensuring that any changes you make in code are remembered.
Font	Specifies the font used to render any text in the control as a special System.Drawing.Font object.
Height and Width	Specifies the width and height of the control. For some controls, these properties will be ignored when used with older browsers.
Page	Provides a reference to the web page that contains this control as a System.Web.UI.Page object.
Parent	Provides a reference to the control that contains this control. If the control is placed directly on the page (rather than inside another control), it will return a reference to the page object.
TabIndex	A number that allows you to control the tab order. The control with a TabIndex of 0 has the focus when the page first loads. Pressing Tab moves the user to the control with the next lowest TabIndex, provided it is enabled. This property is only supported in Internet Explorer 4.0 and higher.
Tool	Displays a text message when the user hovers the mouse above the control. Many older browsers don't support this property.
Visible	When set to False, the control will be hidden and will not be rendered to the final HTML page that is sent to the client.

The next few sections describe some of the common concepts you'll use with almost any web control, including how to set properties that use units and enumerations, and how to use colors and fonts.

Units

All the properties that use measurements, including BorderWidth, Height, and Width, require the Unit structure, which combines a numeric value with a type of measurement (pixels, percentage, and so on). That means that when you set these properties in a control tag, you must make sure to append px (pixel) or % (for percentage) to the number to indicate the type of unit.

Here's an example with a Panel control that is 300 pixels wide, and has a height equal to 50 percent of the current browser window:

```
<asp:Panel Height="300px" Width="50%" id="pnl" runat="server" />
```

If you're assigning a unit-based property through code, you need to use one of shared method of the Unit type. Use Pixel() to supply a value in pixels, and Percentage() to supply a percentage value.

```
' Convert the number 300 to a Unit object
' representing pixels, and assign it.
pnl.Height = Unit.Pixel(300)

' Convert the number 50 to a Unit object
' representing percent, and assign it.
pnl.Width = Unit.Percentage(50)
```

You could also manually create a Unit object and initialize it using one of the supplied constructors and the UnitType enumeration. This requires a few more steps, but allows you to easily assign the same unit to several controls.

```
' Create a Unit object.
Dim MyUnit as New Unit(300, UnitType.Pixel)

' Assign the Unit object to several controls or properties.
pnl.Height = MyUnit
pnl.Width = MyUnit
```

Enumerated Values

Enumerations are used heavily in the .NET class library to group together a set of related constants. For example, when you set a control's BorderStyle property, you can choose one of several predefined values from the BorderStyle enumeration. In code, you set an enumeration using the dot syntax:

```
ctrl.BorderStyle = BorderStyle.Dashed
```

In the .aspx file, you set an enumeration by specifying one of the allowed values as a string. You don't include the name of the enumeration type, which is assumed automatically.

```
<asp:TextBox BorderStyle="Dashed" Text="Border Test" id="txt"
 runat="server" />
```

Figure 7-3 shows the TextBox with the altered border.

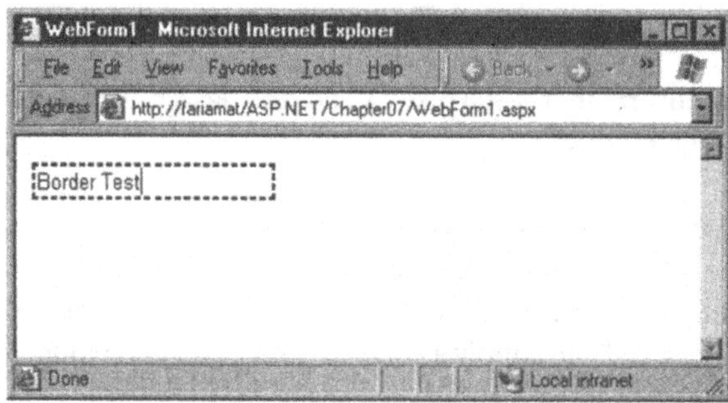

Figure 7-3. Modifying the border style

Colors

The Color property refers to a Color object from the System.Drawing namespace. Color objects can be created in several different ways:

- **Using an ARGB (alpha, red, green, blue) color value.** You specify each value as integer.
- **Using a predefined .NET color name.** You choose the correspondingly named read-only property from the Color class. These properties include all the HTML colors.
- **Using an HTML color name.** You specify this value as a string using the ColorTranslator class.

To use these any of techniques, you must import the System.Drawing namespace, as follows:

```
Import System.Drawing
```

The following code shows several ways to specify a color in code.

```
' Create a color from an ARGB value
Dim Alpha As Integer = 255, Red As Integer = 0
Dim Green As Integer = 255, Blue As Integer = 0
ctrl.ForeColor = Color.FromARGB(Alpha, Red, Green, Blue)

' Create a color using a .NET name
ctrl.ForeColor = Color.Crimson

' Create a color from an HTML code
ctrl.ForeColor = ColorTranslator.FromHtml("Blue")
```

When defining a color in the .aspx file, you can use any one of the known color names.

```
<asp:TextBox ForeColor="Red" Text="Test" id="txt" runat="server" />
```

The color names that you can use are listed in Chapter 28. Alternatively, you can use a hexadecimal color number (in the format #<red><green><blue>) as shown here:

```
<asp:TextBox ForeColor="#ff50ff" Text="Test"
    id="txt" runat="server" />
```

Fonts

The Font property actually references a full FontInfo object, which is defined in the System.Drawing namespace. Every FontInfo object has several properties that define its name, size, and style. This properties are shown in Table 7-3.

Table 7-3. FontInfo Properties

Property	Description
Name	A string indicating the font name (such as "Verdana").
Size	The size of the font as a FontUnit object. This can represent an absolute or relative size.
Bold, Italic, Strikeout, Underline, and Overline	Boolean properties that either apply the given style attribute or ignore it.

In code, you can assign to the various font properties using the familiar dot syntax.

```
ctrl.Font.Name = "Verdana"
ctrl.Font.Bold = True
```

You can also set the size using the FontUnit type.

```
' Specifies a relative size.
ctrl.Font.Size = FontUnit.Small

' Specifies an absolute size of 14 pixels.
ctrl.Font.Size = FontUnit.Point(14)
```

In the .aspx file, you need to use a special "object walker" syntax to specify object properties such as font. The object walker syntax uses a hyphen (-) to separate properties. For example, you could set a control with a specific font (Tahoma) and font size (40 point) like this:

```
<asp:TextBox Font-Name="Tahoma" Font-Size="40" Text="Size Test" id="txt"
 runat="server" />
```

Or with a relative size:

```
<asp:TextBox Font-Name="Tahoma" Font-Size="Large" Text="Size Test"
 id="txt" runat="server" />
```

The altered TextBox in this example is shown in Figure 7-4.

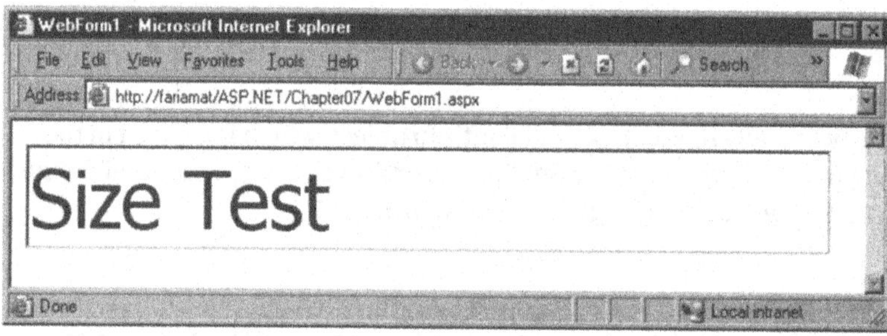

Figure 7-4. Modifying a control's font

List Controls

The list controls include the ListBox, DropDownList, CheckBoxList, and RadioButtonList. They all work in essentially the same way, but are rendered differently in the browser. The ListBox, for example, is a rectangular list that displays several entries, while the DropDownList shows only the selected item. The CheckBoxList and RadioButtonList are similar to the ListBox, but every item is rendered as a check box or option button, respectively.

Like the HtmlSelect control described in the previous chapter, all the list controls provide a SelectedIndex property that indicates the selected row as a zero-based index. For example, if the first item in the list is selected, ctrl.SelectedIndex will be 0. List controls also provide an additional SelectedItem property, which allows your code to retrieve the ListItem object that represents the selected item. The ListItem object provides three important properties: Text (the displayed content), Value (the hidden value from the HTML markup), and Selected (True or False depending on whether the item is selected).

In the last chapter, you used code like this to retrieve the selected ListItem object from an HtmlSelect control called Currency, as follows:

```
Dim Item As ListItem
Item = Currency.Items(Currency.SelectedIndex)
```

With a web control, this can be simplified with a clearer syntax.

```
Dim Item As ListItem
Item = Currency.SelectedItem
```

Multiple-Select List Controls

Some list controls can allow multiple selections. This isn't allowed for the DropDownList or RadioButtonList, but it is supported for a ListBox, provided you have set the SelectionMode property to the enumerated value ListSelectionMode.Multiple. The user can then select multiple items by holding down the Ctrl key while clicking the items in the list. With the CheckBoxList, multiple selections are always possible.

If you have a list control that supports multiple selection, you can find all the selected items by iterating through the Items collection of the list control, and checking the ListItem.Selected property of each item. Figure 7-5 shows a simple web page example. It provides a list of computer languages and indicates which selections the user made when the OK button is clicked.

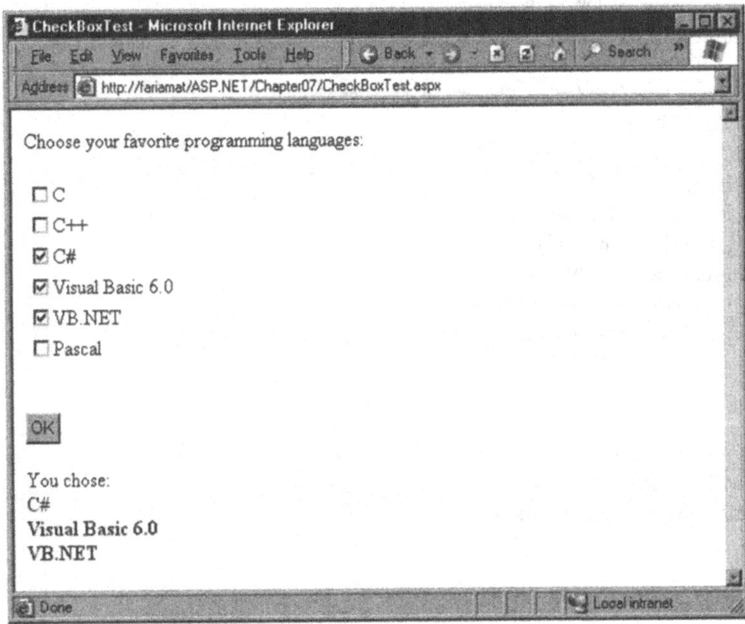

Figure 7-5. A simple CheckListBox test

The .aspx file for this page defines CheckListBox, Button, and Label controls, as shown here:

```
<%@ Page Language="VB" Inherits="CheckListTest" Src="CheckListTest.vb"
    AutoEventWireup="False" %>

<html><body>
  <form method="post" runat="server">

  Choose your favorite programming languages:<br><br>
  <asp:CheckBoxList id="chklst" runat="server" /><br><br>
  <asp:Button id="cmdOK" Text="OK" runat="server" /><br><br>
  <asp:Label id="lblResult" runat="server" />

  </form>
</body></html>
```

The code adds items to the CheckListBox at startup, and iterates through the collection when the button is clicked.

```
Imports System
Imports System.Web
Imports System.Web.UI
Imports system.Web.UI.WebControls
Imports System.Web.UI.HtmlControls

Public Class CheckListTest
  Inherits Page

    Protected chklst as CheckBoxList
    Protected WithEvents cmdOK As Button
    Protected lblResult as Label

    Private Sub Page_Load(sender As Object, e As EventArgs) _
      Handles MyBase.Load
        If Me.IsPostBack = False
            chklst.Items.Add("C")
            chklst.Items.Add("C++")
            chklst.Items.Add("C#")
            chklst.Items.Add("Visual Basic 6.0")
            chklst.Items.Add("VB.NET")
            chklst.Items.Add("Pascal")
        End If
    End Sub

    Private Sub cmdOK_Click(sender As Object, e As EventArgs) _
      Handles cmdOK.Click
        lblResult.Text = "You chose:<b>"
```

```
        Dim lstItem As ListItem
        For Each lstItem In chklst.Items
            If lstItem.Selected = True Then
                ' Add text to label.
                lblResult.Text &= "<br>" & lstItem.Text
            End If
        Next

        lblResult.Text &= "</b>"
    End Sub

End Class
```

Control Prefixes

When working with web controls, it's often useful to use a three-letter lowercase prefix to identify the type of control. The preceding example (and those in the rest of this book) follow this convention to make user interface code as clear as possible. Some recommended control prefixes are as follows:

- Button: cmd
- CheckBox: chk
- Image: img
- Label: lbl
- List control: lst
- Panel: pnl
- RadioButton: opt
- TextBox: txt

If you're a veteran VB programmer, you'll also notice that this book doesn't use prefixes to identify data types. This is in keeping with the new philosophy of .NET, which recognizes that data types can often change freely and without consequence, and where variables often point to full-featured objects instead of simple data variables.

Table Controls

Essentially, the Table control is built out of a hierarchy of objects. Each Table object contains one or more TableRow objects. In turn, each TableRow object contains one or more TableCell objects. Each TableCell object contains other ASP.NET controls of HTML content that displays information. If you're familiar with the HTML table tags, this relationship (shown in Figure 7-6) will seem fairly logical.

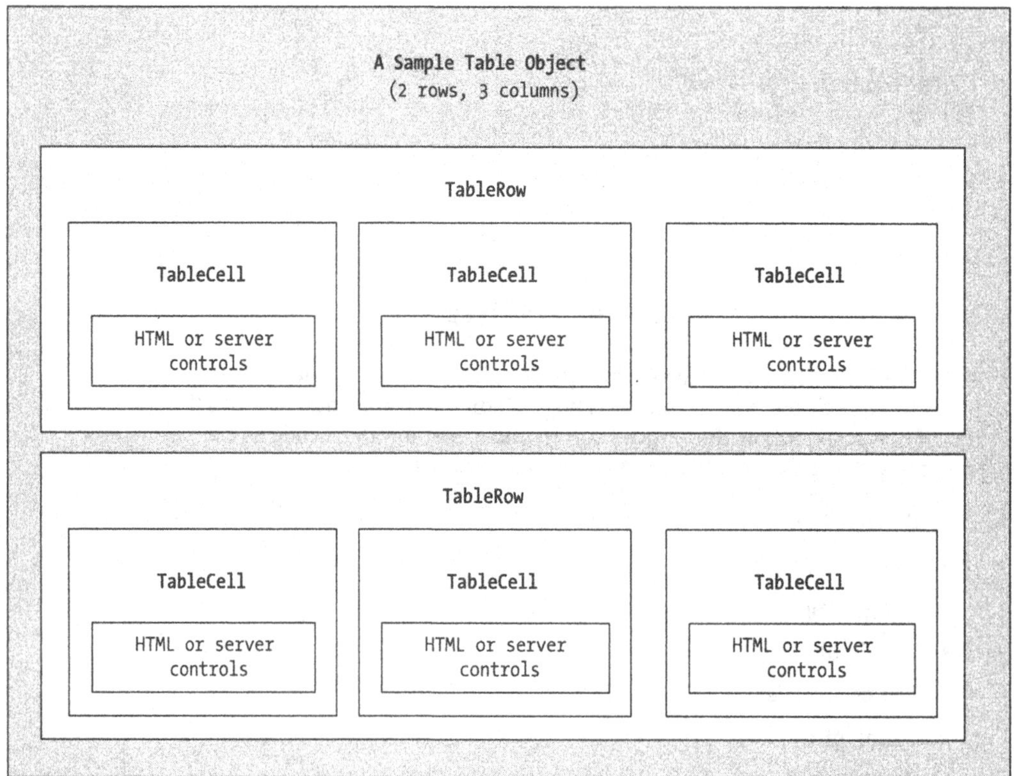

Figure 7-6. Table control containment

To create a table dynamically, you follow the same philosophy as you would for any other web control. First, you create and configure the necessary ASP.NET objects. Then ASP.NET converts these objects to their final HTML representation before the page is sent to the client.

Consider the example shown in Figure 7-7. It allows the user to specify a number of rows and columns as well as whether cells should have borders. When the user clicks the generate button, the table is filled dynamically with sample data according to the selected options, as shown in Figure 7-8.

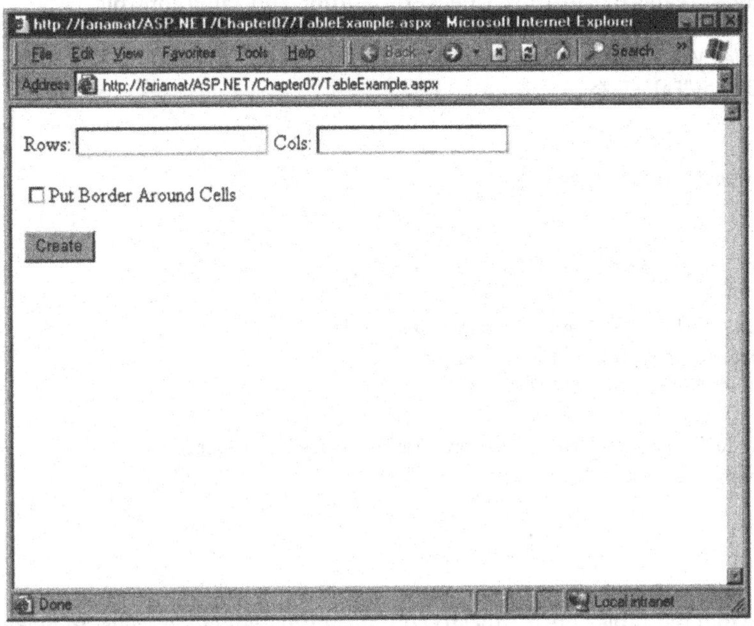

Figure 7-7. The table test options

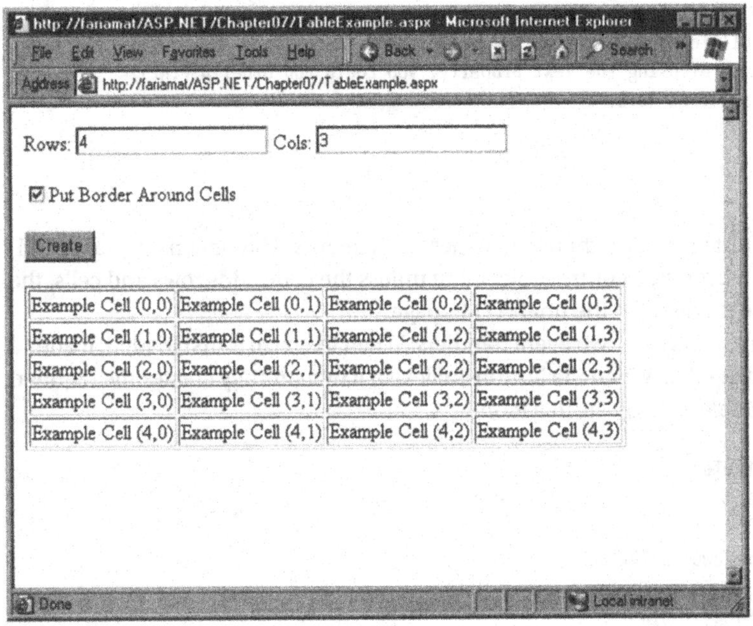

Figure 7-8. A dynamically generated table

The .aspx code creates the TextBox, CheckBox, Button, and Table controls.

```
<%@ Page Language="VB" Inherits="TableTest" Src="TableTest.vb"
    AutoEventWireup="False" %>

<html><body>
  <form method="post" runat="server">

    Rows:
    <asp:TextBox id="txtRows" runat="server" /> 
    Cols:
    <asp:TextBox id="txtCols" runat="server" /><br><br>
    <asp:CheckBox id="chkBorder" runat="server"
        Text="Put Border Around Cells" />
    <br><br>
    <asp:Button id="cmdCreate" runat="server" Text="Create" /><br><br>
    <asp:Table id="tbl" runat="server" />

  </form>
</body></html>
```

You'll notice that the Table control doesn't contain any actual rows or cells. To make a valid table, you would need to nest several layers of tags. The following example creates a table with a single cell that contains the text "A Test Row."

```
<asp:Table id="tbl" runat="server">
  <asp:TableRow id="row" runat="server">
    <asp:TableCell Text="A Test Row" id="cell" runat="server">
      <!-- Instead of using the Text property, you could add other ASP.NET
           control tags here. -->
    </asp:TableCell>
  </asp:TableRow>
</asp:Table>
```

In the table test web page, there are no nested elements. That means the table will be created as a server-side control object, but unless the code adds rows and cells, the table will not be rendered in the final HTML page.

The TablePage class uses two event handlers. When the page is first loaded, it adds a border around the table. When the button is clicked, it dynamically creates the required TableRow and TableCell objects in a loop.

```
Public Class TableTest
  Inherits Page

    Protected txtRows As TextBox
    Protected txtCols As TextBox
    Protected tbl As Table
    Protected chkBorder As CheckBox
    Protected WithEvents cmdCreate As Button
```

```
    Private Sub Page_Load(sender As Object, e As EventArgs) _
      Handles MyBase.Load
        ' Configure the table's appearance.
        ' This could also be performed in the .aspx file,
        ' or in the cmdCreate_Click event handler.
        tbl.BorderStyle = BorderStyle.Inset
        tbl.BorderWidth = Unit.Pixel(1)
    End Sub

    Private Sub cmdCreate_Click(sender As Object, e As EventArgs) _
      Handles cmdCreate.Click

        ' Remove all the current rows and cells.
        ' This is not necessary if EnableViewState is set to False.
        tbl.Controls.Clear()

        Dim i, j As Integer
        For i = 0 To Val(txtRows.Text)

            ' Create a new TableRow object.
            Dim rowNew As New TableRow()

            ' Put the TableRow in the Table.
            tbl.Controls.Add(rowNew)

            For j = 0 To Val(txtCols.Text)

                ' Create a new TableCell object.
                Dim cellNew As New TableCell()
                cellNew.Text = "Example Cell (" & i.ToString() & ","
                cellNew.Text &= j.ToString & ")"

                If chkBorder.Checked = True Then
                    cellNew.BorderStyle = BorderStyle.Inset
                    cellNew.BorderWidth = Unit.Pixel(1)
                End If
                ' Put the TableCell in the TableRow.
                rowNew.Controls.Add(cellNew)

            Next
        Next

    End Sub

End Class
```

This code uses the Controls collection to add child controls. Every container control provides this property. You could also add use the TableCell.Controls collection to add special web controls to each TableCell. For example, you could place an Image control and a Label control in each cell. In this case, you can't set the TableCell.Text property. The following code snippet uses this technique, and the results are shown in Figure 7-9.

```
' Create a new TableCell object.
Dim cellNew As New TableCell()

' Create a new Label object.
Dim lblNew As New Label()
lblNew.Text = "Example Cell (" & i.ToString() & "," & j.ToString() & ")<br>"

Dim imgNew As New System.Web.UI.WebControls.Image()
imgNew.ImageUrl = "cellpic.png"

' Put the label and picture in the cell.
cellNew.Controls.Add(lblNew)
cellNew.Controls.Add(imgNew)

' Put the TableCell in the TableRow.
rowNew.Controls.Add(cellNew)
```

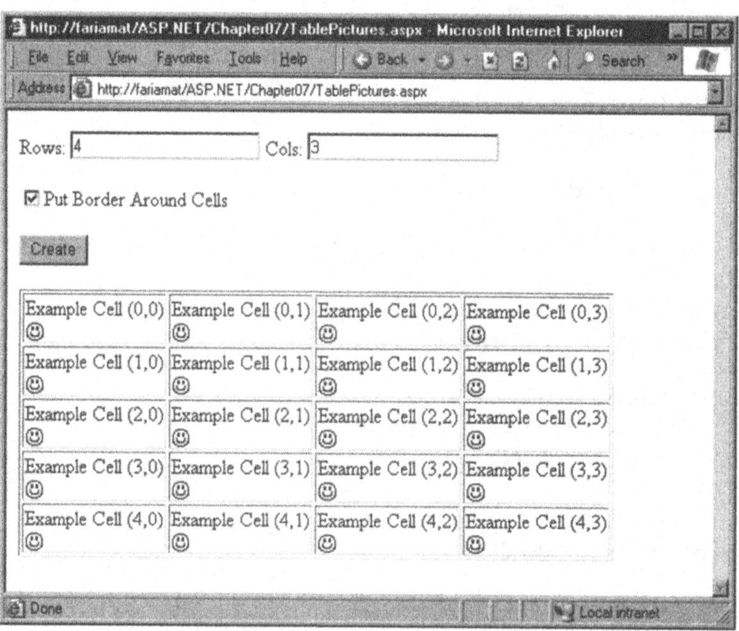

Figure 7-9. A table with contained controls

The real flexibility of the table test page is the fact the each TableRow and TableCell is a full-featured object. If you want, you can give each cell a different border style, border color, and text color. The full list of TableRow and TableCell properties is described in Chapter 28.

AutoPostBack and Web Control Events

The previous chapter explained that one of the main limitations of HTML server controls is their limited set of useful events—there are exactly two. HTML controls that trigger a postback, such as buttons, raise a ServerClick event. Input controls provide a ServerChange event that doesn't actually fire until the page is posted back.

Server controls are really an ingenious illusion. You'll recall that the code in an ASP.NET page is processed on the server. It's then sent to the user as ordinary HTML. Figure 7-10 illustrates the order of events in page processing.

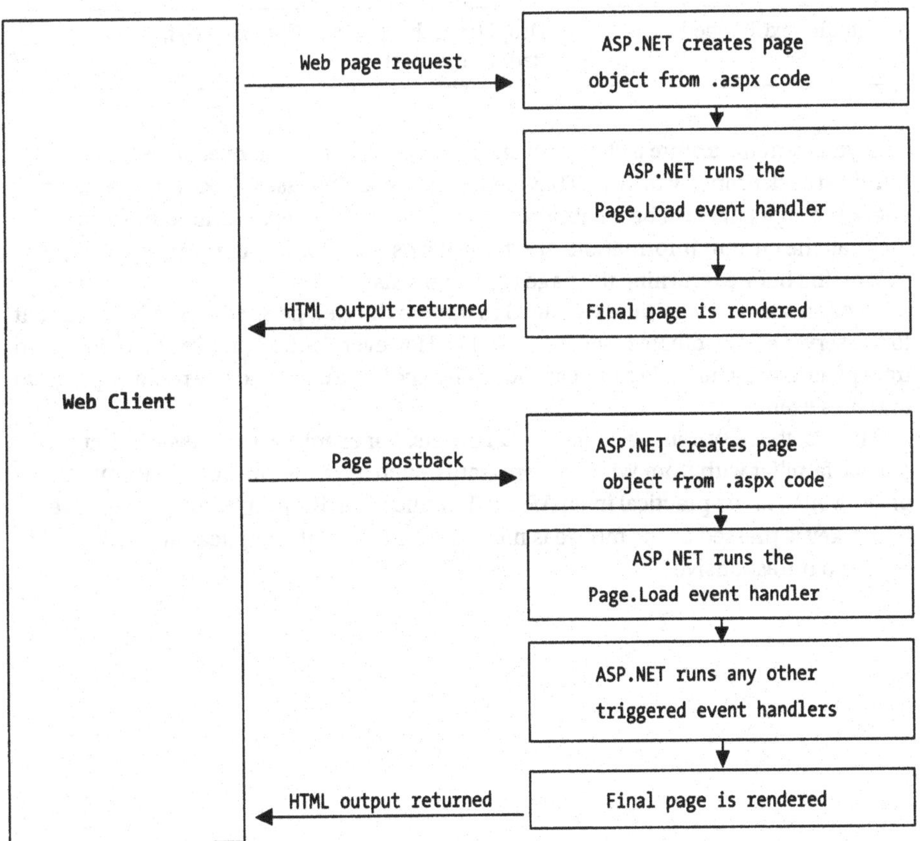

Figure 7-10. The page processing sequence

This is the same in ASP.NET as it was in traditional ASP programming. The question is, how can you write server code that will react to an event that occurs on the client? The answer is a new innovation called the *automatic postback.*

The automatic postback submits a page back to the server when it detects a specific user action. This gives your code the chance to run again and create a new, updated page. Controls that support automatic postbacks include almost all input web controls. Table 7-4 provides a basic list of web controls and their events.

Table 7-4. Web Control Events

Event	Web Controls That Provide It
Click	Button, ImageButton
TextChange	TextBox (only fires after the user changes the focus to another control)
CheckChanged	CheckBox, RadioButton
SelectedIndexChanged	DropDownList, ListBox, CheckBoxList, RadioButtonList

If you want to capture a change event for a web control, you need to set its AutoPostBack property to True. That means that when the user clicks a radio button or check box, the page will be resubmitted to the server. The server examines the page, loads all the current information, and then allows your code to perform some extra processing before returning the page back to the user.

In other words, every time you need to update the web page, it's actually being sent to the server and re-created (see Figure 7-11). However, ASP.NET makes this process so transparent that your code can treat your web page like a continuously running program that fires events.

This postback system isn't ideal for all events. For example, some events that you may be familiar with from Windows programs, such as mouse movement events or key press events, aren't practical in an ASP.NET application. Resubmitting the page every time a key is pressed or the mouse is moved would make the application unbearably slow and unresponsive.

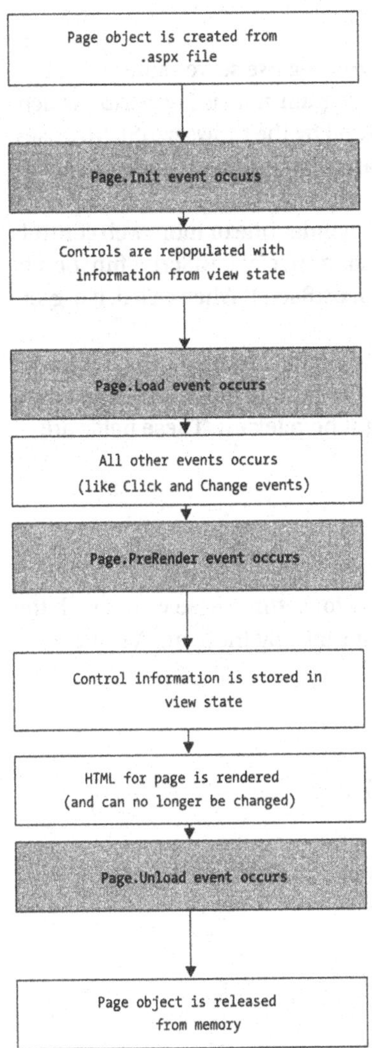

Figure 7-11. The postback processing sequence

How Postback Events Work

Chapter 1 explained that not all types of web programming use server-side code like ASP.NET. One common example of client-side web programming is JavaScript, which uses simple code that's limited in scope and is executed by the browser. ASP.NET uses the client-side abilities of JavaScript to bridge the gap between client-side and server-side code.

Here's how it works. If you create a web page that includes one or more web controls that are configured to use AutoPostBack, ASP.NET adds a special JavaScript function to the rendered HTML page. This function is named __doPostBack(). When called, it triggers a postback, sending data back to the web server.

ASP.NET also adds two additional hidden input fields that are used to pass information back to the server. This information consists of the ID of the control that raised the event, and any additional information that might be relevant. These fields are initially empty, as shown here:

```
<input type="hidden" name="__EVENTTARGET" value="" />
<input type="hidden" name="__EVENTARGUMENT" value="" />
```

The __doPostBack() function has the responsibility for setting these values with the appropriate information about the event, and then submitting the form. A sample __doPostBack() function is shown here:

```
<script language="javascript">
<!--
    function __doPostBack(eventTarget, eventArgument) {
        var theform = document.Form1;
        theform.__EVENTTARGET.value = eventTarget;
        theform.__EVENTARGUMENT.value = eventArgument;
        theform.submit();
    }
// -->
</script>
```

Remember, ASP.NET generates the __doPostBack() function automatically. This code grows lengthier as you add more AutoPostBack controls to your page, because the event data must be set for each control.

Finally, any control that has its AutoPostBack property set to True is connected to the __doPostBack() function using the onclick or onchange attributes. These attributes indicate what action the browser should take in response to the client-side JavaScript events onclick and onchange.

The following example shows the tag for a list control named lstBackColor, which posts back automatically. Whenever the user changes the selection in the list, the client side onchange event fires. The browser then calls the __doPostBack() function, which sends the page back to the server.

```
<select id="lstBackColor" onchange="__doPostBack('lstBackColor','')"
 language="javascript">
```

In other words, ASP.NET automatically changes a client-side JavaScript event into a server-side ASP.NET event, using the __doPostBack() function as an intermediary. Figure 7-12 shows this process.

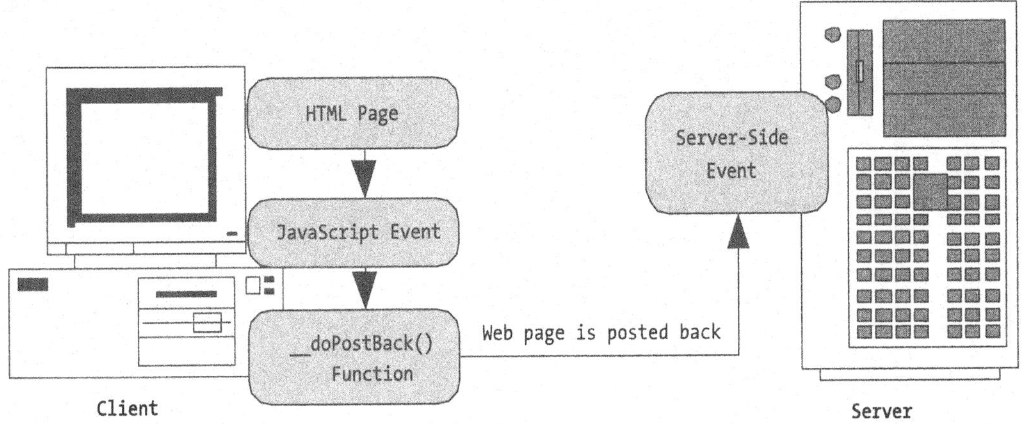

Figure 7-12. An automatic postback

If you're a seasoned ASP developer, you may have manually created a solution like this for traditional ASP web pages. ASP.NET handles these details for you automatically, simplifying life a great deal.

The Page Life Cycle

To understand how web control events work, you need to have a solid understanding of the page life cycle. Consider what happens when a user changes a control that has the AutoPostBack property set to True.

1. On the client side, the JavaScript __doPostBack event is invoked, and the page is resubmitted to the server.
2. ASP.NET re-creates the Page object using the .aspx file.
3. ASP.NET retrieves state information from the hidden view state field, and updates the controls accordingly.
4. The Page.Load event is fired.
5. The appropriate change event is fired for the control.
6. The Page.Unload event fires and the page is rendered (transformed from a set of objects to an HTML page).
7. The new page is sent to the client.

To watch these events in action, it helps to create a simple event tracker application (see Figure 7-13). All this application does is write a new entry to a list control every time one of the events it's monitoring occurs. This allows you to see the order in which events are triggered.

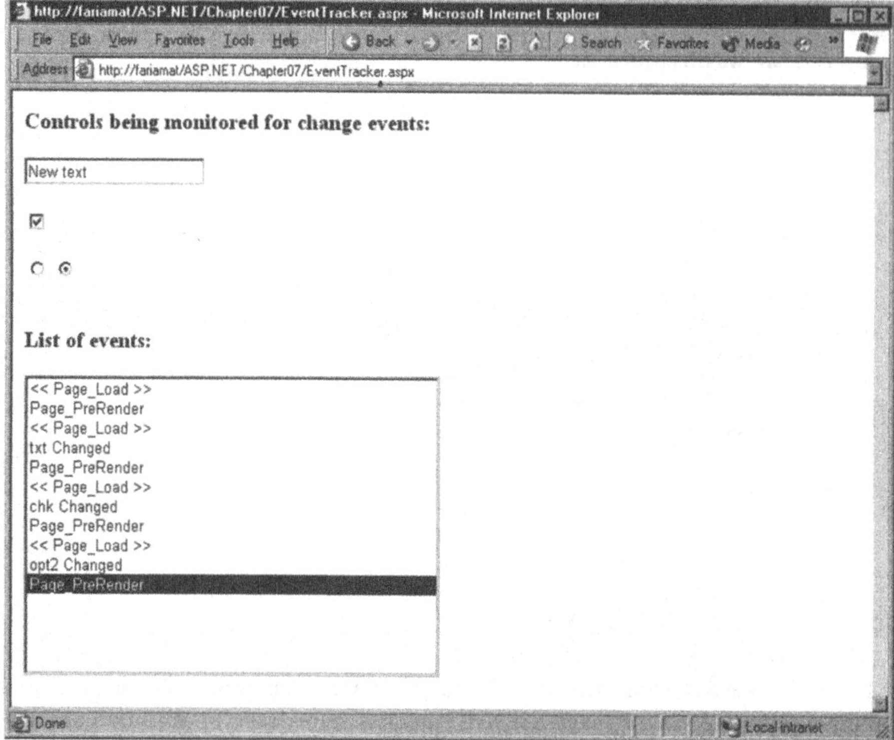

Figure 7-13. The event tracker

EventTracker.aspx

```
<%@ Page Language="VB" Src="EventTracker.vb" Inherits="EventTracker"
    AutoEventWireup="False"%>

<html><body>
  <form method="post" runat="server">
    <h3>Controls being monitored for change events:</h3>
    <asp:TextBox id=txt runat="server" AutoPostBack="True" /><br><br>
    <asp:CheckBox id=chk runat="server" AutoPostBack="True" /><br><br>
    <asp:RadioButton id=opt1 runat="server" GroupName="Sample"
         AutoPostBack="True" />
    <asp:RadioButton id=opt2 runat="server" GroupName="Sample"
         AutoPostBack="True" /><br><br><br>
    <h3>List of events:</h3>
    <asp:ListBox id=lstEvents runat="server" Width="355px"
         Height="505px" /><br>
  </form>
</body></html>
```

EventTracker.vb

```
Public Class EventTracker
  Inherits System.Web.UI.Page

    Protected WithEvents lstEvents As ListBox
    Protected WithEvents chk As CheckBox
    Protected WithEvents txt As TextBox
    Protected WithEvents opt1 As RadioButton
    Protected WithEvents opt2 As RadioButton

    Private Sub Page_Load(sender As Object, e As EventArgs) _
      Handles MyBase.Load
        Log("<< Page_Load >>")
    End Sub

    Private Sub Page_PreRender(sender As Object, e As EventArgs) _
      Handles MyBase.PreRender
        ' When the Page.UnLoad event occurs it is too late
        ' to change the list.
        Log("Page_PreRender")
    End Sub

    Private Sub CtrlChanged(sender As Object, e As System.EventArgs) _
      Handles chk.CheckedChanged, opt1.CheckedChanged, _
      opt2.CheckedChanged, txt.TextChanged
        ' Find the control ID of the sender.
        ' This requires converting the Object type into a Control class.
        Dim ctrlName As String = CType(sender, Control).ID
        Log(ctrlName & " Changed")
    End Sub

    Private Sub Log(entry As String)
        lstEvents.Items.Add(entry)

        ' Select the last item to scroll the list so the most recent
        ' entries are visible.
        lstEvents.SelectedIndex = lstEvents.Items.Count - 1
    End Sub

End Class
```

Dissecting the Code ...

The following points are worth noting about this code:

- The code writes to the ListBox using a private Log() subroutine. The Log() subroutine adds the text and automatically scrolls to the bottom of the list each time a new entry is added, thereby ensuring that the most recent entries remain visible.
- All the change events are handled by the same subroutine, CtrlChanged(). The event handling code uses the source parameter to find out what control sent the event, and it incorporates that information in the log string.
- All the controls that use automatic postback have to be defined using the WithEvents keyword, or the Handles clause will not work.

A Simple Web Page Applet

Now that you've had a whirlwind tour of the basic web control model, it's time to put it to work with the second single-page utility. In this case, it's a simple example for a dynamic e-card generator (see Figure 7-14). You could extend this sample (for example, allowing users to store e-cards to the database, or using the techniques in Chapter 17 to mail notification to card recipients), but even on its own this example is a good demonstration of basic control manipulation with ASP.NET.

The web page is divided into two regions. On the left is an ordinary <div> tag containing a set of web controls for specifying card options. On the right is a Panel control (named pnlCard), which contains two other controls (lblGreeting and imgDefault) that are used to display user-configurable text and a picture. This text and picture represents the greeting card.

TIP The <div> tag is useful when you want to group text and controls together, and apply a set of formatting properties (such as a color or font) to all of them. The <div> tag is used in many of the examples in this book, but it can safely be left out—the only change will be the appearance of the formatted page.

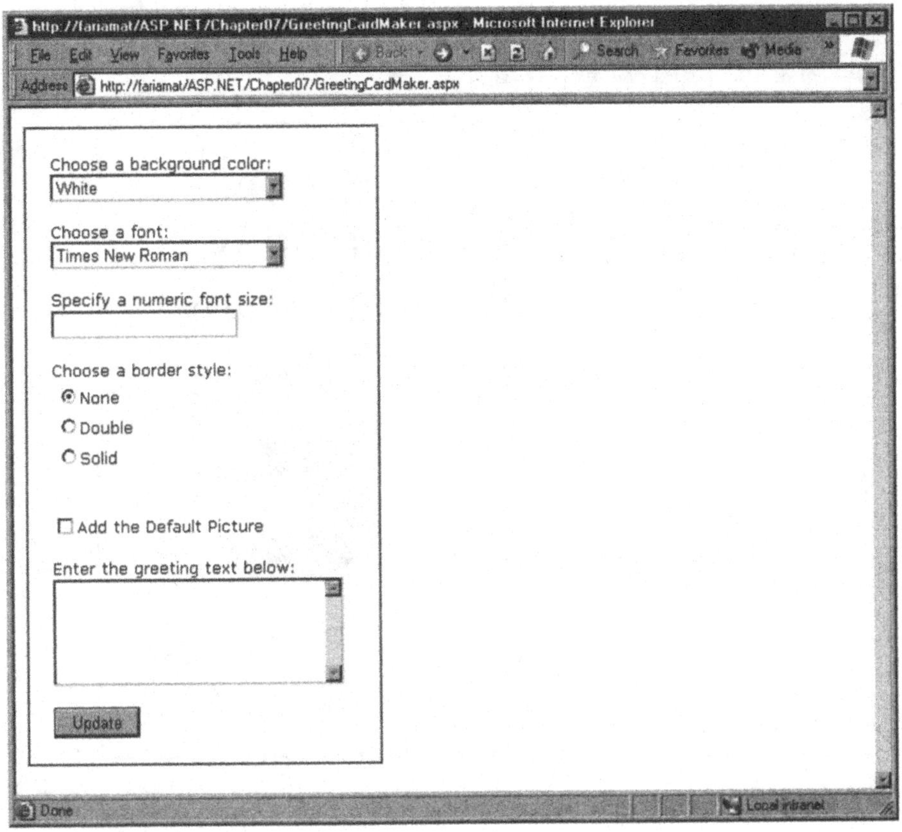

Figure 7-14. The e-card generator

Whenever the user clicks the OK button, the page is posted back and the "card" is updated (see Figure 7-15).

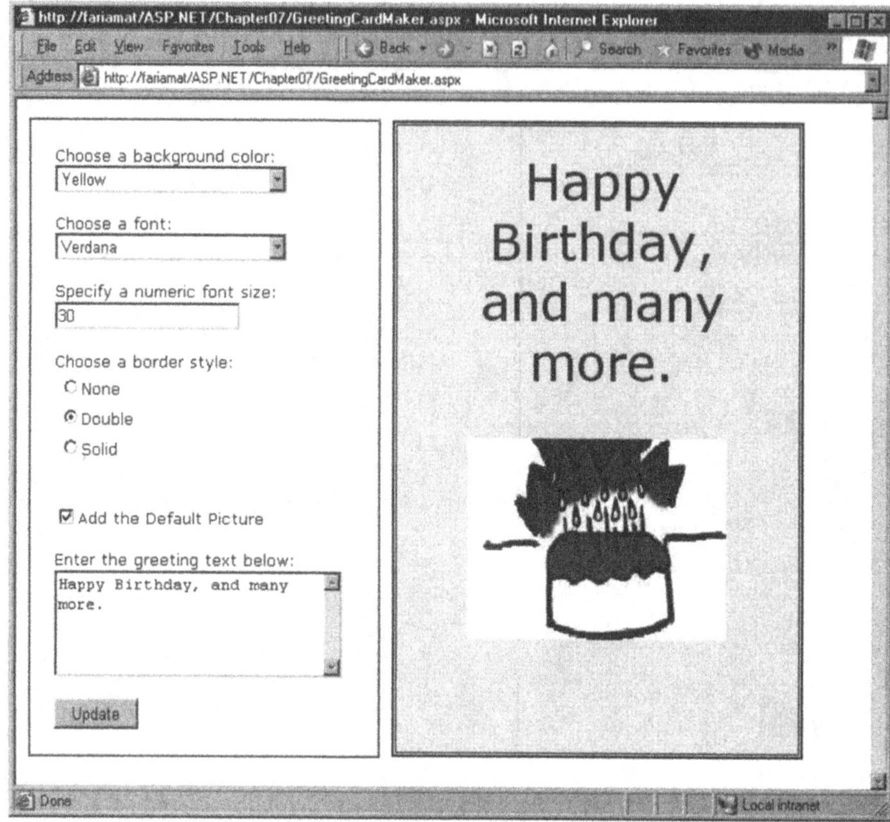

Figure 7-15. A user-configured greeting card

The .aspx layout code is very straightforward. Of course, the sheer length of it makes it difficult to work with efficiently. This is an ideal point to start considering Visual Studio .NET, which will handle the .aspx details for you automatically and won't require you to painstakingly format and organize the user interface markup tags.

```
<%@ Page Language="VB" Src="GreetingCardMaker.vb"
    Inherits="GreetingCardMaker" AutoEventWireup="False"%>

<html><body>
  <form method="post" runat="server">
  <!-- div formatting tag left out for clarity. -->

  <!-- Here are the controls: -->
  Choose a background color:<br>
  <asp:DropDownList id="lstBackColor" runat="server" Width="194px"
       Height="22px"/><br><br>
  Choose a font:<br>
  <asp:DropDownList id="lstFontName" runat="server" Width="194px"
       Height="22px" /><br><br>
```

```
  Specify a numeric font size:<br>
  <asp:TextBox id="txtFontSize" runat="server" /><br><br>
  Choose a border style:<br>
  <asp:RadioButtonList id="lstBorder" runat="server" Width="177px"
       Height="59px" /><br><br>
  <asp:CheckBox id="chkPicture" runat="server"
       Text="Add the Default Picture"></asp:CheckBox><br><br>
  Enter the greeting text below:<br>
  <asp:TextBox id="txtGreeting" runat="server" Width="240px" Height="85px"
       TextMode="MultiLine" /><br><br>
  <asp:Button id="cmdUpdate" runat="server" Width="71px" Height="24px"
       Text="Update" />
  </div>

  <!-- Here is the card: -->
  <asp:Panel id="pnlCard" style="Z-INDEX: 101; LEFT: 313px; POSITION: absolute;
       TOP: 16px" runat="server" Width="339px" Height="481px"
       HorizontalAlign="Center"><br> 
  <asp:Label id="lblGreeting" runat="server" Width="256px"
       Height="150px" /><br><br><br>
  <asp:Image id="imgDefault" runat="server" Width="212px"
       Height="160px" />
  </asp:Panel>

  </form>
</body></html>
```

The code follows the familiar pattern with an emphasis on two events: the Page.Load event, where initial values are set, and the Button.Click event, where the card is generated. The Imports statements are left out of the following listing, because the basic set of required namespaces should be familiar to you by now.

```
Public Class GreetingCardMaker
  Inherits Page
    Protected lstBackColor As DropDownList
    Protected lstFontName As DropDownList
    Protected txtFontSize As TextBox
    Protected chkPicture As CheckBox
    Protected txtGreeting As TextBox
    Protected pnlCard As Panel
    Protected lblGreeting As Label
    Protected lstBorder As RadioButtonList
    Protected imgDefault As Image
    Protected WithEvents cmdUpdate As Button

    Private Sub Page_Load(sender As Object, e As EventArgs) _
      Handles MyBase.Load
        If Me.IsPostBack = False Then
```

```
            ' Set color options.
            lstBackColor.Items.Add("White")
            lstBackColor.Items.Add("Red")
            lstBackColor.Items.Add("Green")
            lstBackColor.Items.Add("Blue")
            lstBackColor.Items.Add("Yellow")

            ' Set font options.
            lstFontName.Items.Add("Times New Roman")
            lstFontName.Items.Add("Arial")
            lstFontName.Items.Add("Verdana")
            lstFontName.Items.Add("Tahoma")

            ' Set border style options by adding a series of
            ' ListItem objects.
            ' Each item indicates the name of the option, and contains the
            '  corresponding integer in the Value property.
            lstBorder.Items.Add(New _
              ListItem(BorderStyle.None.ToString(), BorderStyle.None))
            lstBorder.Items.Add(New _
              ListItem(BorderStyle.Double.ToString(), BorderStyle.Double))
            lstBorder.Items.Add(New _
              ListItem(BorderStyle.Solid.ToString, BorderStyle.Solid))

            ' Select the first border option.
            lstBorder.SelectedIndex = 0

            ' Set the picture.
            imgDefault.ImageUrl = "defaultpic.png"
        End If
    End Sub

    Private Sub cmdUpdate_Click(sender As Object, e As EventArgs) _
      Handles cmdUpdate.Click

        ' Update the color.
        pnlCard.BackColor = Color.FromName(lstBackColor.SelectedItem.Text)

        ' Update the font.
        lblGreeting.Font.Name = lstFontName.SelectedItem.Text

        If Val(txtFontSize.Text) > 0 Then
            lblGreeting.Font.Size = FontUnit.Point(Val(txtFontSize.Text))
        End If

        ' Update the border style.
        pnlCard.BorderStyle = Val(lstBorder.SelectedItem.Value)
```

```
        ' Update the picture.
        If chkPicture.Checked = True Then
            imgDefault.Visible = True
        Else
            imgDefault.Visible = False
        End If

        ' Set the text.
        lblGreeting.Text = txtGreeting.Text

    End Sub

End Class
```

As you can see, this example limits the user to a few preset font and color choices. The code for the BorderStyle option is particularly interesting. The lstBorder control has a list that displays the text name of one of the BorderStyle enumerated values. You'll remember from the introductory chapters that every enumerated value is really an integer with a name assigned to it. The lstBorder also secretly stores the corresponding number so that the code can retrieve the number and set the enumeration easily when the user makes a selection and the cmdUpdate_Click event handler fires.

Improving the Greeting Card Applet

ASP.NET pages have access to the full .NET class library. With a little exploration, you'll find classes that might help the greeting-card maker, such as tools that let you retrieve all the known color names and all the fonts installed on the web server.

For example, you can fill the lstFontName control with a list of fonts using the special System.Drawing.Text.InstalledFontCollection class (see Figure 7-16). Here's the code you'll need:

```
' Get the list of available fonts and add them to the font list.
Dim Family As FontFamily
Dim Fonts As New System.Drawing.Text.InstalledFontCollection()
For Each Family In Fonts.Families
    lstFontName.Items.Add(Family.Name)
Next
```

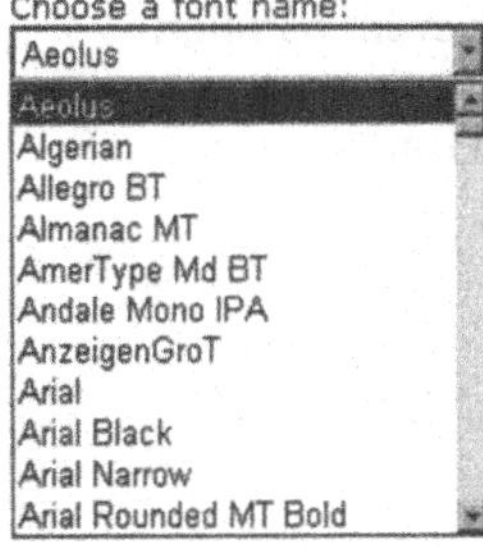

Figure 7-16. The font list

You can also get a list of color names from the System.Drawing.KnownColor enumeration. In order to do this, you use one of basic enumeration features: the shared Enum.GetNames() method, which inspects an enumeration and provides an array of strings, with one string for each value in the enumeration. A minor problem with this approach is that it includes system environment colors (for example "Active Border") in the list. It may not be obvious to the user what colors these values represent. Still, this approach works well for this simple application.

```
' Get the list of colors.
Dim ColorArray As String() = System.Enum.GetNames( _
                             GetType(System.Drawing.KnownColor))
lstBackColor.DataSource = ColorArray
lstBackColor.DataBind()
```

This web page can then use data binding to automatically fill the list control with information from the ColorArray. You'll explore data binding in much more detail in Chapter 15.

A similar technique can be used to fill in BorderStyle options:

```
' Set border style options.
Dim BorderStyleArray As String()
BorderStyleArray = System.Enum.GetNames(GetType(BorderStyle))
lstBorder.DataSource = BorderStyleArray
lstBorder.DataBind()
```

This code raises a new challenge: How do you convert the value that the user selects into the appropriate constant for the enumeration? When the user chooses a border style from the list, the SelectedItem property will have a text string like "Groove." But in order to apply this border style to the control, you need a way to determine the enumerated constant that matches this text.

There are a few different ways to handle this problem. (Earlier, you saw an example in which the enumeration integer was stored as a value in the list control.) In this case, the most direct approach involves using an advanced feature called a TypeConverter. A TypeConverter is a special class that is able to convert from a specialized type (in this case, the BorderStyle enumeration) to a simpler type (such as a string) and vice versa.

To access this class, you need to import the System.ComponentModel namespace.

```
Imports System.ComponentModel
```

You can then add the following code to the cmdUpdate_Click event handler:

```
' Find the appropriate TypeConverter for the BorderStyle enumeration.
Dim cnvrt As TypeConverter
cnvrt = TypeDescriptor.GetConverter(GetType(BorderStyle))

' Update the border style using the value from the converter.
pnlCard.BorderStyle = cnvrt.ConvertFromString(_
  lstBorder.SelectedItem.Text)
```

Don't worry if this example introduces a few features that look entirely alien! These features are more advanced (and they aren't tied specifically to ASP.NET). However, they show you some of the flavor that the full .NET class library can provide for a mature application.

Generating the Cards Automatically

The last step is to use ASP.NET's automatic postback events to make the card update dynamically every time an option is changed. The OK button could now be used to submit the final, perfected greeting card, which might then be e-mailed to a recipient or stored in a database.

To configure the controls so they automatically trigger a page postback, simply add the AutoPostBack="True" attribute to each user input control. An example is shown here:

```
Choose a background color:<br>
<asp:DropDownList id="lstBackColor" AutoPostBack="True" runat="server"
     Width="194px" Height="22px"/><br><br>
```

Next, you need to make sure the control variables are defined in your class with the WithEvents keyword. This enables your code to access their events.

```
Protected WithEvents lstBackColor As DropDownList
```

Lastly, you need to create an event handler for each control's change event. To save a few steps, you can use the same event handler for all of the input controls. All the event handler needs to do is call the update routine that regenerates the greeting card.

```
Private Sub ControlChanged(sender As Object, e As System.EventArgs) _
  Handles lstBackColor.SelectedIndexChanged, _
  chkPicture.CheckedChanged, txtFontSize.TextChanged, _
  lstBackColor.SelectedIndexChanged, _
  lstBorder.SelectedIndexChanged, _
  lstFontName.SelectedIndexChanged, _
  lstForeColor.SelectedIndexChanged

    ' Call the button event handler to refresh the greeting card.
    cmdUpdate_Click(Nothing, Nothing)

End Sub
```

With these features, it's easy to perfect the more extensive card-generating program shown in Figure 7-17. The full code for this application is provided with the online samples.

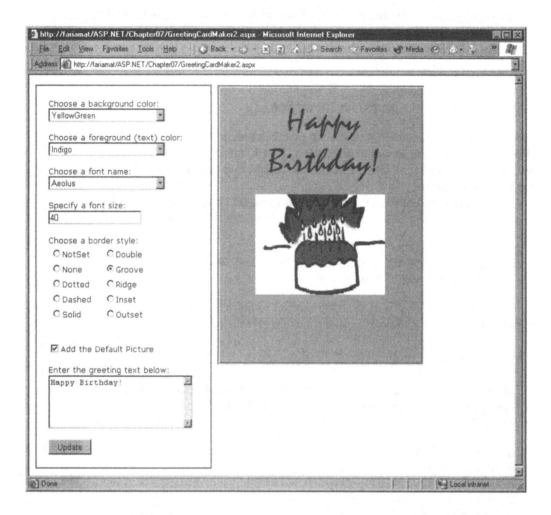

Figure 7-17. A more extensive card generator

TIP Automatic postback isn't always best. Sometimes an automatic postback can annoy a user, especially when the user is working over a slow connection, or when the server needs to perform a time-consuming option. For that reason, it's sometimes best to use an explicit submit button and not enable AutoPostBack for most input controls.

A Word About Conventions

From this point on, the examples will adopt a few conventions designed to make code examples more clear, concise, and readable.

- The .aspx layout file is rarely shown with an example, unless it requires special coding (such as the creation of a template or data-binding syntax, two topics you'll explore in Part Three of this book). The .aspx files are really nothing more than an ordering of standard control tags.
- The Imports directives in the code-behind file are left out, unless they reference an unusual namespace that hasn't been identified. Generally, you'll reuse the same standard block of Imports statements for each code-behind file.
- The control variables in the page class are sometimes omitted and replaced with a comment. The control variable declarations are also standard boilerplate code.

These changes won't affect you at all if you're using an IDE such as Visual Studio .NET, which generates the .aspx file, control variables, and most Imports statements automatically.

The Last Word

This chapter introduced you to web controls and their object interface. As you continue through this book, you'll learn more about the web controls. The following highlights are still to come:

- In Chapter 9, you'll learn about advanced controls such as the AdRotator, the Calendar, and the validation controls. You'll also learn about third-party controls such as the advanced Internet Explorer web controls.
- In Chapter 16, you'll learn about the DataGrid, DataList, and Repeater—high-level web controls that let you manipulate a complex table of data from any data source.
- In Chapter 23, you'll learn how you can use .NET inheritance to create your own customized web controls.

For a good reference that shows each web control and lists its important properties, refer to Chapter 28.

CHAPTER 8

Using Visual Studio .NET

In the past, ASP developers have overwhelmingly favored simple text editors like Notepad for programming web pages. Other choices were available, but each one suffered from its own quirks and limitations. Tools like Visual Interdev and web classes for Visual Basic were useful for rapid development, but often made deployment more difficult or obscured important features. The standard was a gloves-off approach of raw HTML with blocks of code inserted wherever necessary.

Visual Studio .NET provides the first design tool that can change that. First of all, it's extensible, and can even work in tandem with other straight HTML editors like FrontPage or Dreamweaver. It also inherits the best features from editors like Visual Interdev and Visual Basic 6.

This chapter provides a lightning tour that shows how to create a web application in the Visual Studio .NET environment. You'll also learn how IntelliSense can dramatically reduce the number of errors you'll make, and how to use the renowned single-step debugger that lets you look under the hood and "watch" your program in action.

The Promise of Visual Studio .NET

All .NET applications are built out of plain-text source files. C# code is stored in .cs files and VB code is stored in .vb files, regardless of whether this code is targeted for the Windows platform, the Web, or a simple command prompt utility. Despite this fact, you'll rarely find VB or C# developers creating Windows applications by hand in a text editor. The process is not only tiring, but also opens the door to a host of possible errors that could be easily caught at design time. The same is true for ASP.NET programmers. Although you can write your web page classes and arrange your web page controls by writing it all by hand, you'll spend hours developing and testing it.

Visual Studio .NET is an indispensable tool for developers on any platform. It provides a few impressive benefits, including the following:

- **Integrated error checking.** Visual Studio .NET can detect a wide range of problems, such as data-type conversion errors, missing namespaces or classes, and undefined variables. Errors are detected as you type, underlined, and added to an error list for quick reference.

- **The Web Form designer.** To create a web page in Visual Studio .NET, you simply drag ASP.NET controls to the appropriate location, resize them, and configure their properties. Visual Studio .NET does the heavy lifting: automatically creating the underlying .aspx template file for you with the appropriate tags and attributes, and adding the control variables to your code-behind file.

- **Productivity enhancements.** Visual Studio .NET makes coding quick and efficient, with a collapsible code display, automatic statement completion, and color-coded syntax. You can even create sophisticated macro programs that automate repetitive tasks.

- **Fine-grained debugging.** Visual Studio .NET's integrated debugger allows you to watch code execution, pause your program at any point, and inspect the contents of any variable. These debugging tools can save endless headaches when writing complex code routines.

- **Easy deployment.** When you start an ASP.NET project in Visual Studio .NET, all the files you need are generated automatically, including a sample web.config configuration file. When you compile the application, all your page classes are compiled into one DLL for easy deployment.

- **Complete extensibility.** You can add your own custom add-ins, controls, and dynamic help plug-ins to Visual Studio .NET, and customize almost every aspect of its appearance and behavior.

Visual Studio .NET is available in two different versions. The first release, often called Visual Studio .NET 2002 or just Visual Studio .NET, targets the .NET 1.0 Framework. Visual Studio .NET 2003 is designed to use the .NET 1.1 Framework. Both versions of Visual Studio .NET work almost identically, and you can use either one with the instructions in this chapter.

Starting a Visual Studio .NET Project

You start Visual Studio .NET from the Start menu by selecting Programs ➤ Microsoft Visual Studio .NET ➤ Microsoft Visual Studio .NET. The IDE will load up with a special start page (see Figure 8-1).

At the top of the start page are the following three tabs:

- **Projects.** This tab provides a list of recent projects that you can open with a single mouse click (these projects are also available through the File ➤ Recent Projects submenu). Each project is identified with a last modified date. At the bottom of the page are two buttons that allow you to open a project (by browsing) or create a new one. The Projects tab is selected by default.

- **Online Resources.** This tab provides a set of resources for retrieving .NET information from the Internet and performing other web-related tasks.

- **My Profile.** This tab provides configuration options that let you set the default language and help options, as well as the window layout and action on startup. Many more configuration options are provided in the Options dialog box (select Tools ➤ Options from the menu). You can also configure toolbars, menus, and create keyboard shortcuts from the Customize window (select Tools ➤ Customize from the menu).

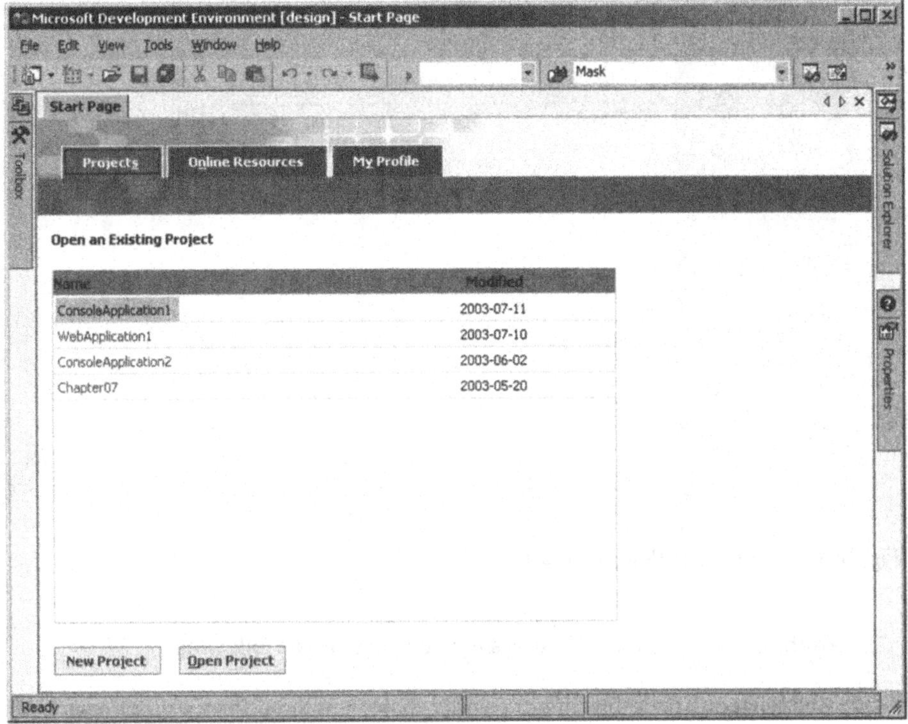

Figure 8-1. The Visual Studio .NET start page

The Online Resources tab is shown in Figure 8-2. It provides a number of options, which are listed on the left of the window.

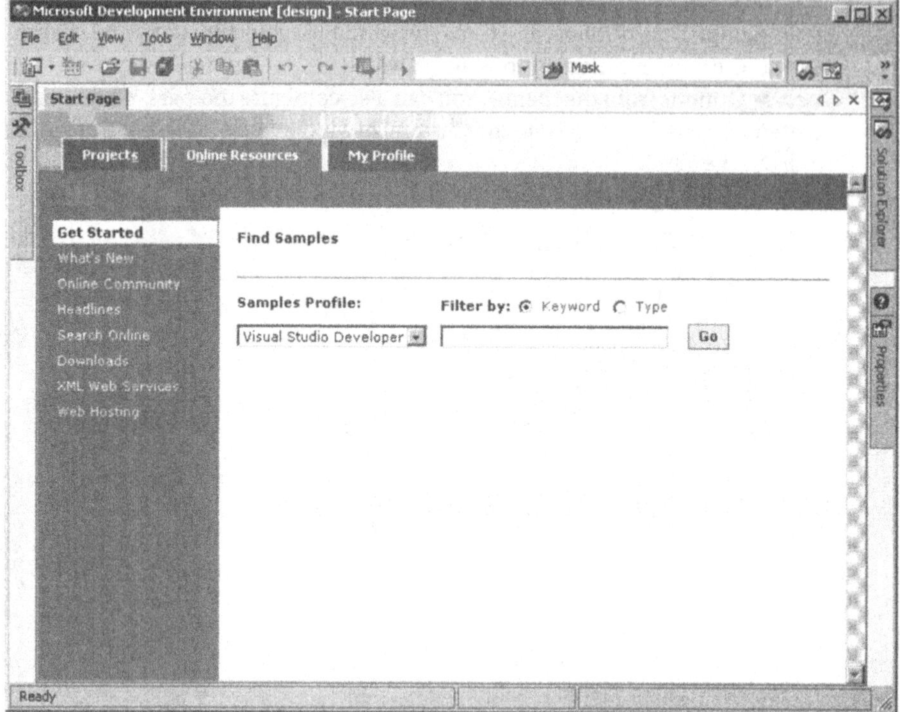

Figure 8-2. The Online Resources tab

The options in the Online Resources window include the following:

- **Get Started.** This is the default page. It allows you to perform a quick search for Microsoft samples that deal with a specific technology or topic. The examples can be seamlessly downloaded and installed from inside Visual Studio .NET.
- **What's New.** This option takes you to an MSDN home page with Visual Studio .NET information. It provides access to late-breaking .NET news, downloadable service packs, and other information.
- **Online Community.** This option allows you to download sample .NET code from Microsoft-affiliated sites and browse a number of .NET newsgroups that are hosted by Microsoft on the Internet. When you click on a newsgroup, your default newsreader (such as Microsoft Outlook) will open to allow you to read and browse postings. Newsgroups are an excellent place to ask programming questions and communicate with other ASP.NET programmers.

TIP The Internet is full of great places to get tips and advice from other ASP.NET developers. For some helpful web-based forums, surf to `http://www.asp.net/Forums`.

- **Headlines.** This option includes a wealth of information from Microsoft's MSDN developer site. You can use this section to read recent articles from the knowledge base (answers to technical problems or fixes and workarounds for known bugs), technical articles, and news releases. When you click on a link, the related web page will open inside Visual Studio .NET. If you want more comfortable browsing using your default Internet browser, just right-click on the link and choose External Window.
- **Search Online.** This option allows you to search the MSDN online library (see Figure 8-3). This search option is available through the MSDN site (`http://msdn.microsoft.com/`), but Visual Studio .NET makes it easy to search for information without needing to leave the comfort of your development environment.

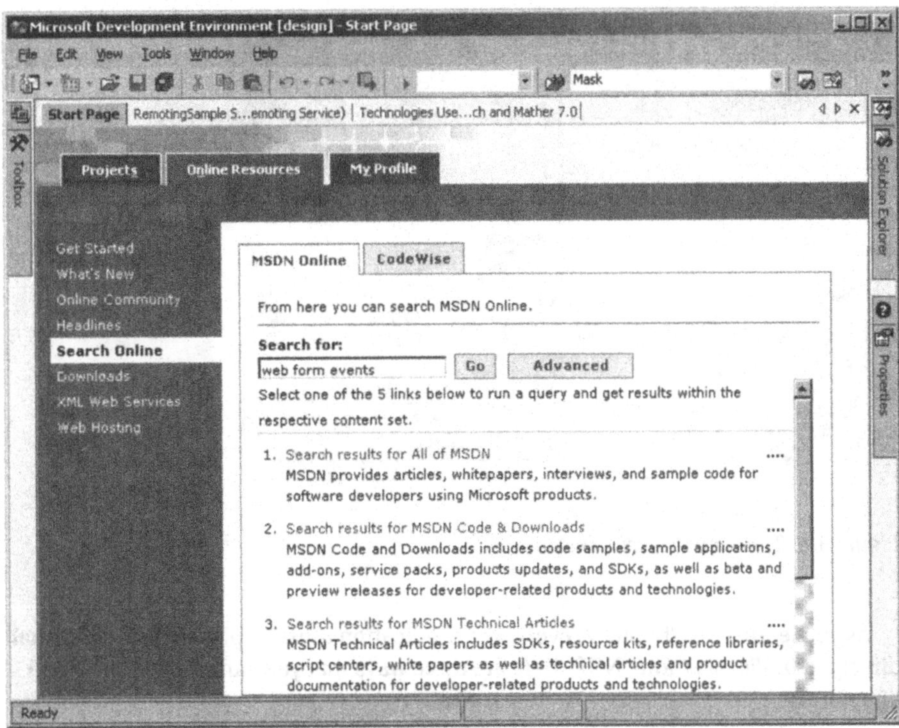

Figure 8-3. Searching the MSDN online library

- **Downloads.** This option provides access to source code, service packs, and other updates. You'll also find add-ons beyond just program updates. For example, you might find case studies or optional programming add-ons.
- **XML Web Services.** This option allows you to search for published web services, and advertise your own web services. Web services are covered in detail in Part Four of this book.
- **Web Hosting.** This option allows you to find companies that host ASP.NET sites for a subscription fee, such as iNNERHOST, Brinkster, and EraServer. In many cases, if you have a hosting plan with one of these providers, you can directly upload your ASP.NET pages from inside Visual Studio .NET.

Creating a New Application

To start your first Visual Studio .NET application, click the New Project button on the start page or select File ➤ New ➤ Project.

The New Project window (shown in Figure 8-2) allows you to choose the type of project and the location where it will be created. You should choose the Visual Basic Projects node, and the ASP.NET Web Application template.

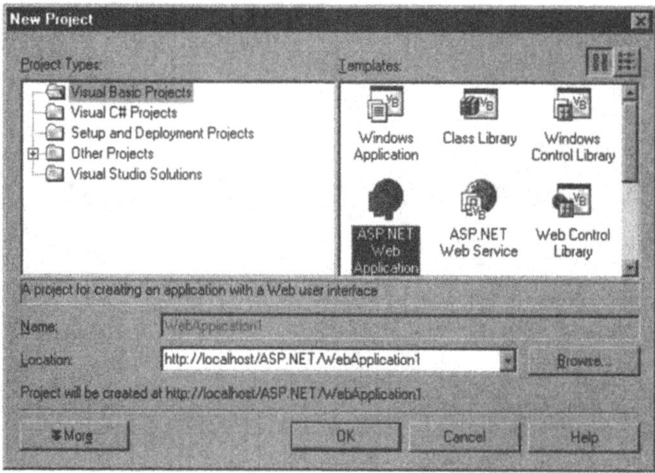

Figure 8-4. The New Project window

As you learned in Chapter 2, every web application must be placed inside a virtual directory. In Visual Studio .NET, there are three ways that you can work with virtual directories:

- Create a new virtual directory in c:\Inetpub\wwwroot using Visual Studio .NET.
- Create the virtual directory manually using IIS, and then create a Visual Studio .NET project in that virtual directory.
- Create a new virtual directory inside an existing virtual directory using Visual Studio .NET.

The approach you use is a matter of personal preference. However, the second choice is the most flexible, because you won't be forced into storing all your web projects in the c:\Inetpub\wwwroot directory. To use this approach, simply supply the path to the existing virtual directory when you create the project. For example, if you create a virtual directory http://localhost/MySite and map it to c:\MySite, you can create a web project in this directory by specifying the location http://localhost/MySite.

If you want to create a new virtual directory using only Visual Studio .NET, you must place this virtual directory inside the website root or another virtual directory that already exists. For example, if you specify http://localhost/WebApplication1, then Visual Studio .NET will create the directory c:\Inetpub\wwwroot\WebApplication1, and configure it to be a virtual directory. Or, if you've created the virtual directory http://localhost/MySite and mapped it to c:\MySite, you can use Visual Studio .NET to create the new virtual directory http://localhost/MySite/NewSite. The new virtual directory will be placed inside the first one, so in this case it will map to c:\MySite\NewSite. However, despite the fact that one virtual directory will be nested inside the other, the two virtual directories will not share any characteristics, and they won't be a part of the same web application.

NOTE When Visual Studio .NET creates a new virtual directory, it automatically configures it to be a web application (much like the IIS virtual directory wizard does). This means that all the web pages in this directory will have their own configuration settings and memory space, which is a requirement for debugging them in Visual Studio .NET.

Project Files

When you create a web application, Visual Studio .NET will add a collection of files. You can see all the files that your project contains in the Solution Explorer window (see Figure 8-5).

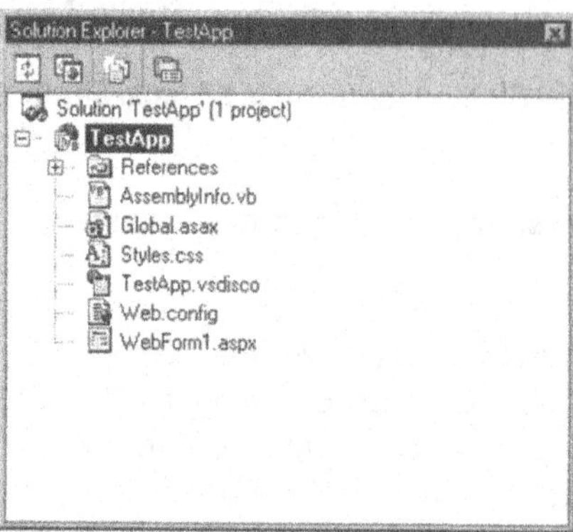

Figure 8-5. The Solution Explorer window

Some of the files that make up a project include the .aspx files for your web pages, a global.asax global application file, a web.config configuration file, a .vsdisco file used with web services, and a Styles.css file you can use to create CSS (cascading style sheet) styles for applying consistent formatting to different HTML elements.

Visual Studio .NET also creates a single .vbproj project file that references all these files. In addition, you can group more than one project together for testing purposes with an .sln solution file. This technique is useful if you want to test a component with a website, or a web service project with a Windows application. It's demonstrated in Chapter 21.

The relationship between Visual Studio .NET project and solution files is shown in Figure 8-6.

The Solution Explorer also includes a file called AssemblyInfo.vb, which defines some additional information that will be added to the compiled DLL file with your web application. This includes information such as the web application version number, your company name, and so on. This information doesn't affect the performance or behavior of your web application, but it can make it easier to track multiple versions.

A typical AssemblyInfo.vb file is shown here:

```
<Assembly: AssemblyTitle("MyWebApp")>
<Assembly: AssemblyDescription("ProseTech Inc. E-Commerce Site.")>
<Assembly: AssemblyCompany("ProseTech")>
<Assembly: AssemblyCopyright("Copyright 2001")>
<Assembly: AssemblyTrademark("ProseTech™")>
```

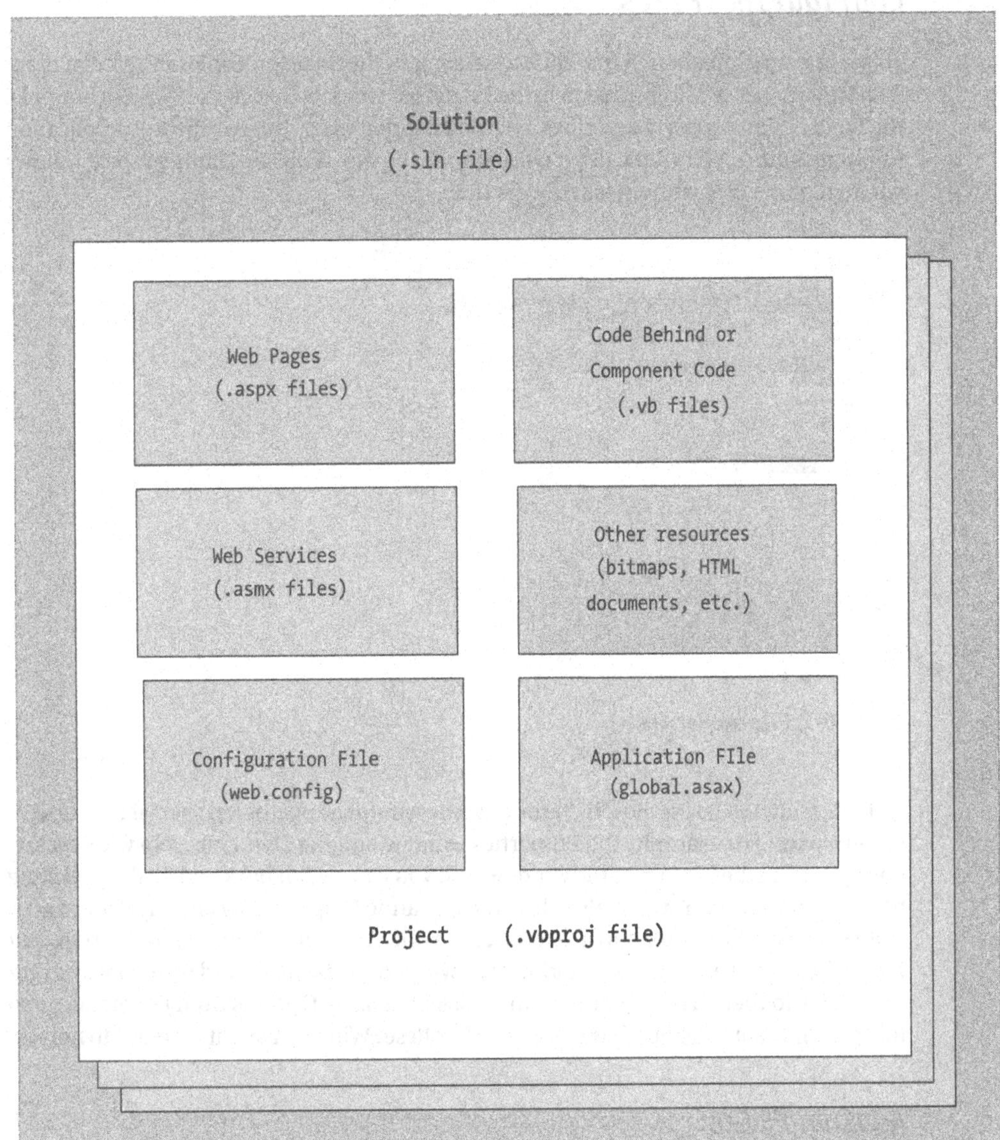

Figure 8-6. Project files

Configuring Files

To get information about a file, click to select it in the Solution Explorer. You can then read various pieces of information in the Properties window (see Figure 8-7). For example, the Build Action property describes what will happen when you run the web application in Visual Studio .NET (typically, it will compile the file). The File Name property allows you to rename files without leaving the IDE.

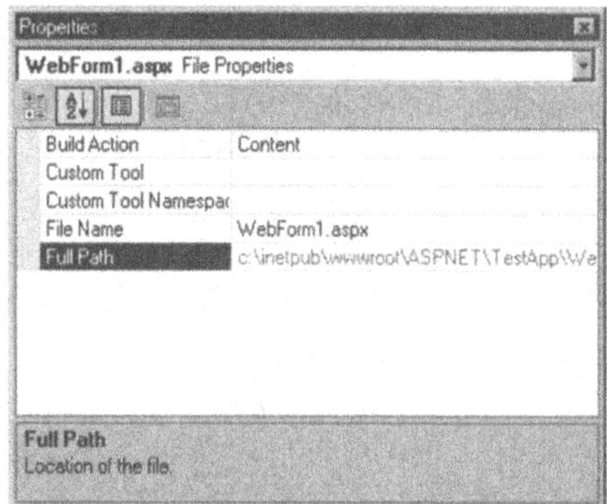

Figure 8-7. File properties

By default, Visual Studio .NET groups some windows together in special tabs to save screen space. For example, the Properties window and the Dynamic Help window are both placed at the bottom of the window, and you can switch back and forth by clicking the appropriate tab. You can also close the Dynamic Help window entirely if you find it is slowing your computer down, or drag it and dock it to a different screen location. Just remember, if you end up with windows strewn all over the place and no easy way to get them back to their original configuration, select Tools ➤ Options from the menu, go to the Environment ➤ General settings, and click Reset Window Layout to return to normal.

Adding Files

When you first create a web application, you'll begin with one web page called WebForm1.aspx. You can add additional web pages by right-clicking on your project in the Solution Explorer and selecting Add ➤ Add New Item.

You can add various different types of files to your project, including web forms, web services, stand-alone components, resources you want to track like bitmaps and text files, and even ordinary HTML files. Visual Studio .NET event provides some basic designers that allow you to edit these types of files directly in the IDE. Figure 8-8 shows the file types that you can add to a web application.

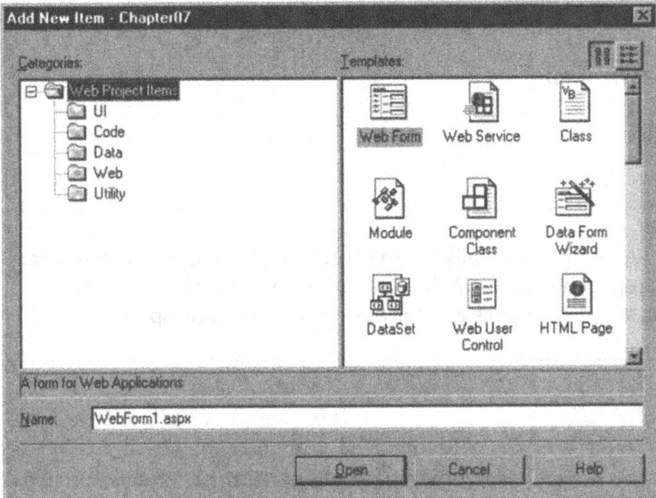

Figure 8-8. Supported file types

You can also add files that already exist by selecting Add ➤ Add Existing Item. You can use this technique to add pages from the sample code provided with this book into your own web applications, allowing you to test the examples without needing to create the corresponding virtual directories. However, you must remember that a web page in Visual Studio .NET actually consists of three files: the .aspx template, the .vb code-behind, and the .resx resource file, with any localizable data. To add an existing web page, you must add all these three files at once by following these steps:

1. Right-click the project in the Solution Explorer and choose Add ➤ Add Existing Item.
2. In the "Files of type" field, choose All Files (*.*).
3. Select the three related files, by clicking on each one while holding down the Ctrl key. For example, if you want to add WebPage1.aspx, make sure you also select WebPage1.vb and WebPage1.resx.
4. Click Open to insert the web page into your project.

Adding an Assembly Reference

The Solution Explorer also shows all the references configured for your project. These are the .NET assemblies that your code-behind files link to automatically. By default, every Visual Studio .NET web project includes the following referenced assemblies:

- System.dll
- System.Data.dll

- System.Drawing.dll
- System.Web.dll
- System.Web.Services.dll
- System.Xml.dll

TIP Remember, assemblies can contain more than one namespace: for example, the System.Web.dll assembly includes classes in the System.Web namespace and the System.Web.UI namespace.

When creating files outside of Visual Studio .NET, you don't need to manually specify these references because they're resolved dynamically at runtime. However, if you want to precompile a code-behind file, you need to list all the referenced namespaces as parameters on the vbc.exe command line. Because Visual Studio .NET precompiles all code-behind files, it needs to explicitly reference them. In addition, because Visual Studio .NET can resolve all the references and inspect all the classes that you're using, it can provide IntelliSense and verify your code to ensure that you're using the classes correctly.

If you want to use additional features or a third-party component, you may need to import more assemblies. For example, if you want to use advanced classes for transactions, you need to add a reference to the System.EnterpriseServices.dll. To add a reference, follow these steps:

1. Right-click the References item in the Solution Explorer and choose Add Reference.
2. In the Add Reference window, select the component you want to use. If the component isn't located in the centralized component registry on your computer (known as the Global Assembly Cache, or GAC), you'll need to click the Browse button and select the DLL file from the appropriate directory.
3. Click OK to add the reference to your web project.

Adding a reference isn't the same as using the Imports statement. The Imports statement allows you to use the classes in a namespace without typing the long, fully qualified class names. However, if you're missing a reference, it doesn't matter what imports you use—the classes won't be available. For example, if you import the System.Web.UI namespace, you can write Page instead of System.Web.UI.Page in your code. But if you haven't added a reference to the System.Web.dll assembly that contains these classes, you won't be able to import the System.Web.UI namespace at all.

Designing Web Pages

Now that you understand the basic organization of Visual Studio .NET, you can begin designing a simple web page. To start, double-click the web page you want to design (start with WebPage1.aspx if you haven't added any additional pages). A blank designer page will appear.

Before you begin, you may want to switch to grid layout, which gives you complete freedom to place controls wherever you want on the page. Select DOCUMENT in the Properties window (or just click the blank web form once), and find the pageLayout property. You have the following two options:

- **FlowLayout.** In a FlowLayout page, elements are positioned line by line, like in a word processor document. To add a control, you need to drag and drop it to an appropriate place. You also need to add spaces and hard returns to position elements the way you want them.
- **GridLayout.** In a GridLayout page, elements can be positioned with absolute coordinates. You can draw controls directly onto the web form surface. The disadvantage is that the controls won't adjust their position if the page content changes. For example, if you add a significant amount of text to a label control, forcing it to become much larger, it might overwrite another nearby control.

To add controls, choose the control type from the toolbox on the right. By default, the toolbox is enabled to automatically hide itself when your mouse moves away from it, somewhat like the AutoHide feature for the Windows taskbar. This behavior is often exasperating, so you may want to click the pushpin in the top-right corner of the toolbox to make it stop in its fully expanded position.

You Can Combine Layout Modes

Although you must choose GridLayout or FlowLayout for the page, you can place controls inside special Grid Layout or Flow Layout panels. This allows you to align some controls relative to one another, but place them at a specific location on the page. (It also allows you to do the converse: align controls absolutely in a Grid Layout box, but have this box change position to accommodate the content on the rest of a FlowLayout page.)

You'll find the Grid Layout Panel and Flow Layout Panel in the HTML tab on the toolbox. These controls look like boxes. You can configure the border and background of a panel by right-clicking it and choosing Build Style. These controls are actually just <div> tags that use a special attribute to tell Visual Studio .NET how to treat them:

```
<div ms_positioning="FlowLayout">[HTML and controls go here.]</div>
```

In the online examples, you'll find many cases in which these panels are used.

Using the toolbox, you can add two types of controls. Click the Web Forms tab to see the web controls that are available. Click the HTML tab to see all the HTML elements you can use. Once you've chosen the type of control, you can place it on your web form and resize it to the right dimensions, as shown in Figure 8-9.

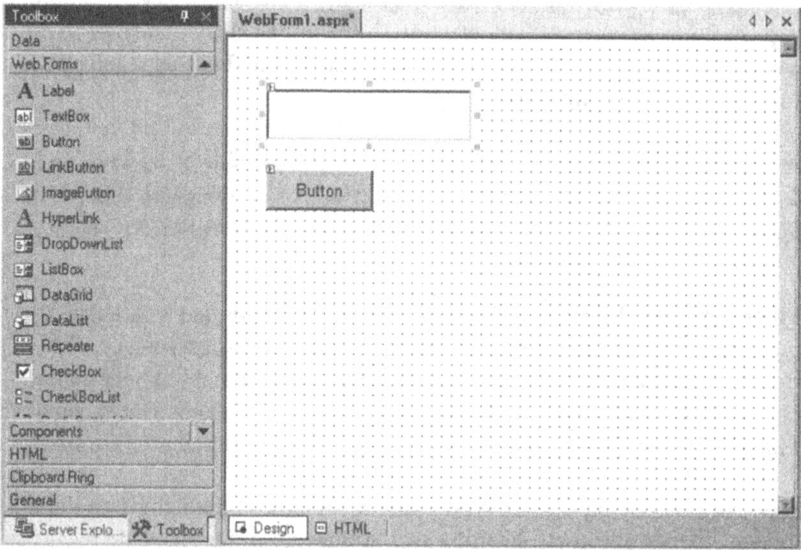

Figure 8-9. The Web Form designer

Every time you add a web control, Visual Studio automatically adds the corresponding tag to your .aspx file. You can even look at the .aspx code, or add server control tags and HTML elements manually by typing them in. To switch your view, click the HTML button at the bottom of the web designer. You can click Design to revert back to the graphical web form designer.

Figure 8-10 shows what you might see in the HTML view after you add a TextBox control to a web page.

Using the HTML view, you can manually add attributes or rearrange controls. In fact, Visual Studio .NET even provides limited IntelliSense features that automatically complete opening tags and alert you if you use an invalid tag. Generally, however, you won't need to use the HTML view in Visual Studio .NET. Instead, you can use the design view and configure controls through the Properties window.

To configure a control, click once to select it, or choose it by name in the drop-down list at the top of the Properties window. Then, modify the appropriate properties in the window, such as Text, ID, and ForeColor. These settings are automatically translated to the corresponding ASP.NET control tag attributes and define the initial appearance of your control. Visual Studio .NET even provides special "choosers" that allow you to select extended properties. For example, you can select a color from a drop-down list that shows you the color (Figure 8-11), and you can configure the font from a standard font selection dialog box.

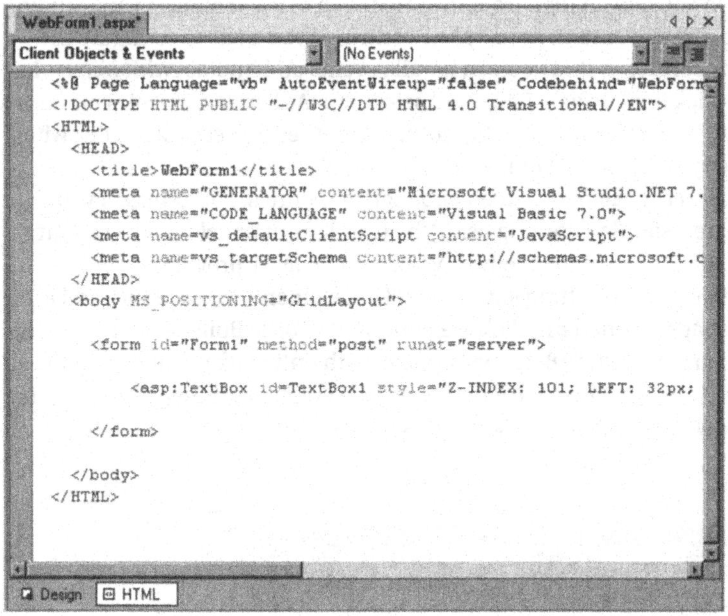

Figure 8-10. The HTML view for a page

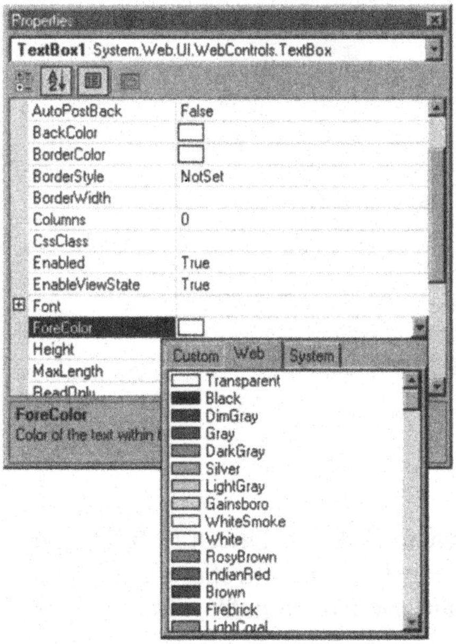

Figure 8-11. Setting the color property

By default, when you add an item from the HTML tab of the toolbox, Visual Studio .NET adds a static HTML element, not a server control. If you want to configure the element as a server control so that you can handle events and interact with it in code, you need to right-click it in the web page, and select Run As Server Control. This adds the required runat="server" attribute to the control tag. Alternatively, you could switch to design view and type this in on your own.

Of course, not all HTML elements need to be server controls. For example, you might want to create a simple <div> tag using the Grid Layout panel or Flow Layout panel items in the HTML tab of the toolbox. Visual Studio .NET provides an indispensable style builder for formatting any static HTML element. To test it out, add a panel to your web page. Then, right-click the panel and choose Build Style. The Style Builder window (shown in Figure 8-12) will appear, with options for configuring the colors, font, layout, and border for the element. As you configure these properties, the web page HTML will be updated to reflect your settings.

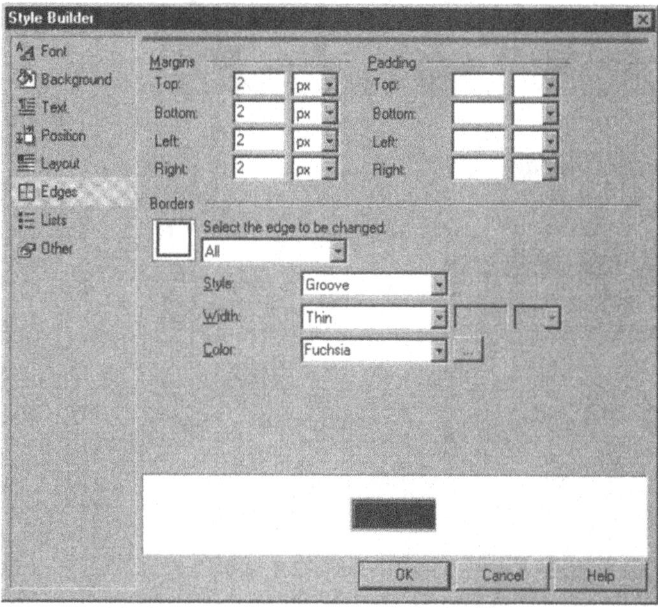

Figure 8-12. Building HTML styles

Finally, the Properties window also allows you to configure the DOCUMENT object, which represents the web page itself. These settings have different effects. For example, if you set enableSessionState to False, the Page directive in the .aspx file will automatically include the attribute EnableSessionState=False.

```
<%@ Page Language="vb" AutoEventWireup="false"
    Codebehind="WebForm1.aspx.vb" Inherits="TestProject.WebForm1"%>
```

The Page directive also provides a couple of other interesting attributes:

- **AutoEventWireup.** This attribute indicates that Visual Studio .NET will use the Handles keyword to connect all event handlers explicitly. This is the same pattern you used in the examples in the previous chapters.
- **Codebehind.** This attribute indicates the file where the code-behind source is stored. Examining this attribute, you'll see that Visual Studio .NET's standard is to create a code-behind file with the same name as the .aspx file, but with the extension .aspx.vb. The examples in Chapter 5 and Chapter 6 used a slightly different convention, and gave code-behind files the same name with the extension .vb (as in WebForm1.vb instead of WebForm1.aspx.vb). Remember, the Codebehind attribute is only used by Visual Studio .NET to track source-code files. It's not used by ASP.NET. When you deploy a web application with Visual Studio .NET, all the code will be compiled into a single DLL assembly, and the location of the original source code will no longer be important.
- **Inherits.** This attribute indicates the class that contains the code for this web page. In Visual Studio .NET, the class always has the same name as the page, and is in a namespace defined by your project. In other words, when you create a project called Test and a web page TestPage.aspx, the code-behind class will be Test.TestPage. The default namespace can be configured using the project options, as you'll see later in this chapter.

Writing Code

Some of Visual Studio .NET's most welcome enhancements appear when you start to write the code that supports your user interface. To start coding, you need to switch to the code-behind view. To switch back and forth, you can use two buttons that are placed just above the Solution Explorer window (see Figure 8-13). The ToolTips identify these buttons as View Code and View Designer, respectively. The "code" in question is the VB code, not the HTML markup in the .aspx file.

Figure 8-13. Switching from design view to code view

When you switch to code view, you'll see the Page class for your web page. Visual Studio .NET creates the Page class automatically and adds a special block of code into a collapsible region titled Web Form Designer Generated Code. This code, which simply initializes the page so it will work with Visual Studio .NET in the design environment, can safely be ignored.

```
#Region " Web Form Designer Generated Code "

    'This call is required by the Web Form Designer.
    <System.Diagnostics.DebuggerStepThrough()>_
    Private Sub InitializeComponent()
    End Sub

    Private Sub Page_Init(ByVal sender As System.Object, _
      ByVal e As System.EventArgs) Handles MyBase.Init
        'CODEGEN: This method call is required by the Web Form Designer.
        'Do not modify it using the code editor.
        InitializeComponent()
    End Sub

#End Region
```

In addition, each time you add a control to the web page, Visual Studio .NET declares the control in the Page-behind class, thereby saving many extra keystrokes. These variable declarations are also hidden in the Web Form Designer Generated Code region. For example, if you add a text box named txtInput to a web page, you'll find the following line of code in the Page class:

```
Protected WithEvents txtInput As System.Web.UI.TextBox
```

You may notice that the code-behind files don't appear in the Solution Explorer. In fact, the code-behind files *are* a part of your project, but they're hidden by default to present a simpler programming model to new users. This gives the illusion that the .aspx file and the .vb file are combined in a single entity.

To see the code-behind files, select Project ➤ Show All Files from the menu. Now the Solution Explorer will show an .aspx.vb code-behind file under each .aspx page. Figure 8-14 shows an example with two code-behind pages (one for a web form and one for a global.asax application file). You'll also be able to see the contents of the \bin directory, which holds the compiled web page code.

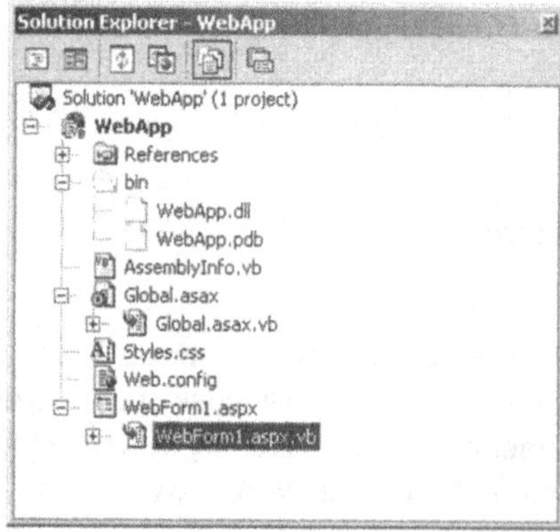

Figure 8-14. The hidden code-behind files in a project

Adding Event Handlers

Most of the code in an ASP.NET web page is placed inside event handlers that react to web control events. Using Visual Studio .NET, there are three ways to add an event handler to your code:

- **Type it in manually.** In this case, you add the subroutine directly to the page class. You must specify the appropriate parameters and the Handles clause, just like when creating a code-behind file by hand.
- **Double-click a control in design view.** In this case, Visual Studio .NET will create an event handler for that control's default event. For example, if you double-click on the page, it will create a Page.Load event handler. If you double-click on a button or input control, it will create an event handler for the Click or Change event.
- **Choose the event from the drop-down list.** At the top of the code view, there are two drop-down lists. To add an event handler, choose the control in the list on the left, and the event you want to react to in the list on the right (see Figure 8-15). To add an event for the page, choose MyBase for the control name.

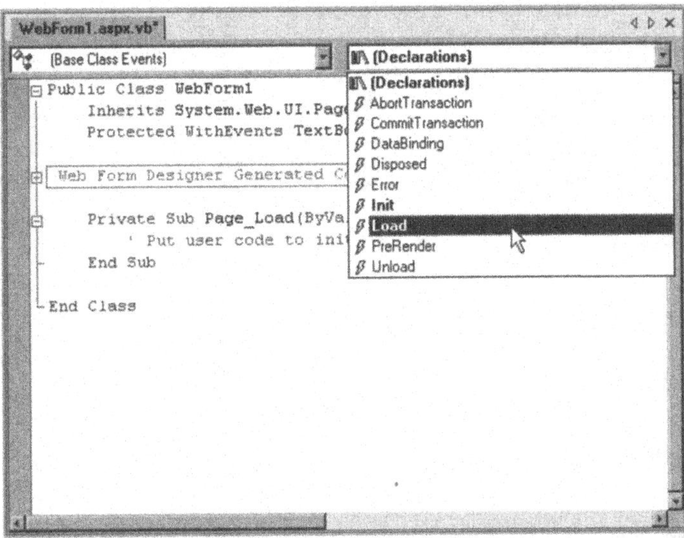

Figure 8-15. Creating an event handler

When Visual Studio .NET creates an event handler for you, it automatically adds the required Handles clause. It also adds ByVal before each parameter name to indicate that parameters are passed by value (as explained in Chapter 4). This keyword is purely optional—in fact, in most of the examples in this book it's left out to save space.

IntelliSense and Outlining

Visual Studio .NET provides a number of automatic timesavers through its IntelliSense technology. They are similar to features such as automatic spell checking and formatting in Microsoft Office applications, but they're much less intrusive. Most of these features are introduced in this chapter, but you'll need several hours of programming before you'll become familiar with all of VS .NET's time savers. There isn't enough space to describe advanced tricks, such as the intelligent search and replace features, and Visual Studio .NET's programmable macros. These features could occupy an entire book of their own!

Outlining

Outlining allows Visual Studio .NET to "collapse" a subroutine, block structure, or region to a single line. It allows you to see the code that interests you, while hiding unimportant code. To collapse a portion of code, click the minus box next to the first line. Click the box again (which will now have a plus symbol) to expand it (see Figure 8-16).

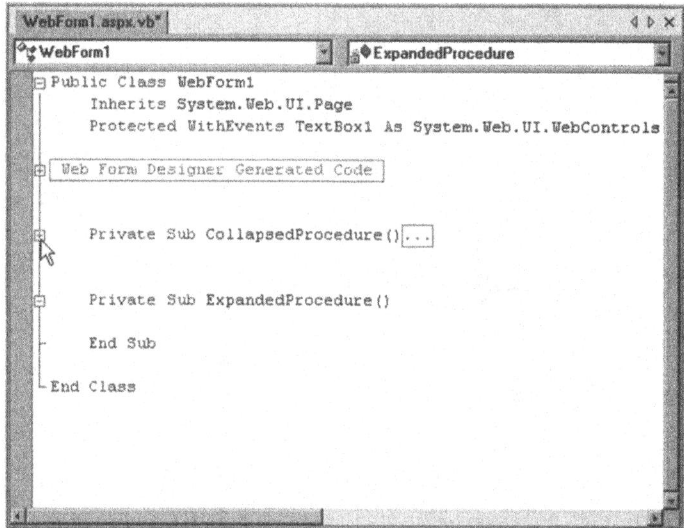

Figure 8-16. Collapsing code

You can hide any section of code that you want. Simply select the code, right-click the selection, and choose Outlining ➤ Hide Selection.

Member List

Visual Studio .NET makes it easy for you to interact with controls and classes. When you type a class or object name, it pops up a list of available properties and methods (see Figure 8-17). It uses a similar trick to provide a list of data types when you define a variable, or to provide a list of valid values when you assign to an enumeration.

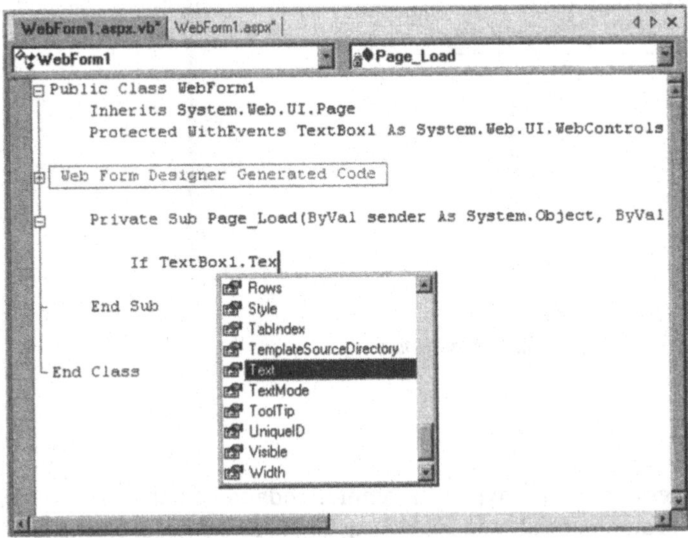

Figure 8-17. IntelliSense at work

Visual Studio .NET also provides a list of parameters and their data types when you call a method or invoke a constructor. This information is presented in a ToolTip above the code and is shown as you type. Because the .NET class library makes heavy use of function overloading, these methods may have multiple different versions. When they do, Visual Studio .NET indicates the number of versions and allows you to see the method definitions for each one by clicking the small up and down arrows in the ToolTip. Each time you click the arrow, the ToolTip displays a different version of the overloaded method (see Figure 8-18).

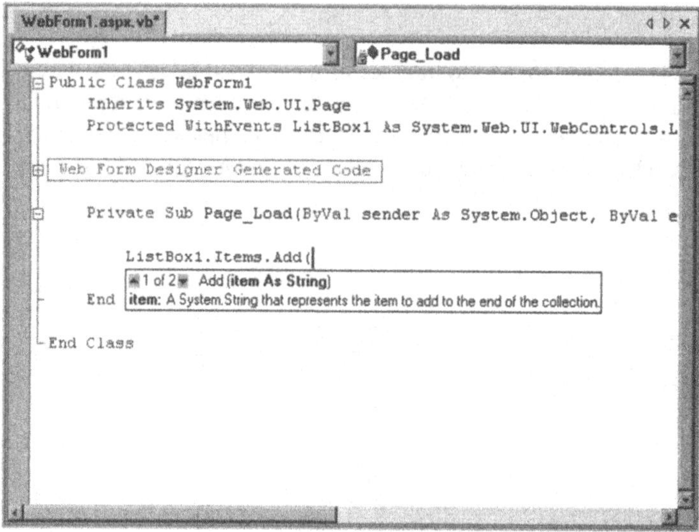

Figure 8-18. IntelliSense with overloaded methods

Block Completion

You'll also save a few keystrokes when typing in common code constructs. For example, Visual Studio .NET will automatically add the closing End If, End Case, or Next line when you type an If, Select Case, or For statement.

Error Underlining

One of the code editor's most useful features is error underlining. Visual Studio .NET is able to detect a variety of error conditions, such as undefined variables, properties or methods, invalid data type conversions, and missing code elements. Rather than stopping you to alert you that a problem exists (an annoying feature in previous versions of Visual Basic), the VS .NET editor quietly underlines the offending code. You can hover your mouse over an underlined error to see a brief ToolTip description of the problem (Figure 8-19).

If you try to compile your program with errors in it, Visual Basic .NET stops you and displays the Task List window with a list of all the errors it detected (see Figure 8-20). You can then jump quickly to a problem by double-clicking it in the list.

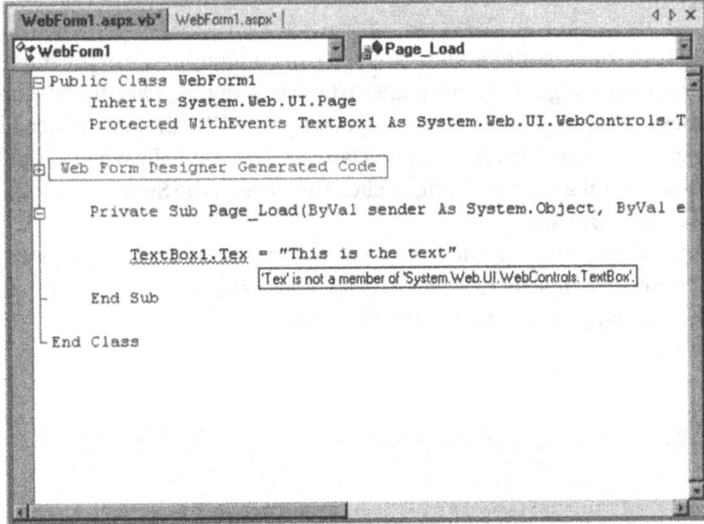

Figure 8-19. Highlighting errors at design time

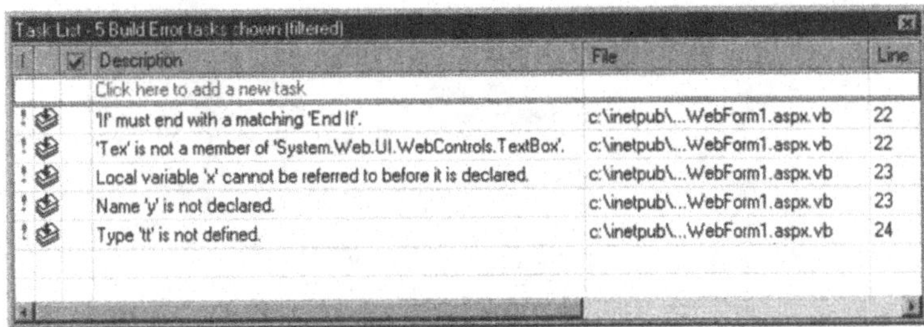

Figure 8-20. Build errors in the Task List

Auto Format and Color

Visual Studio .NET also provides some cosmetic conveniences. It automatically colors your code, making comments green, keywords blue, and normal code black. The result is much more readable code. You can even configure the colors Visual Studio .NET uses by selecting Tools ➤ Options and then choosing the Environment ➤ Fonts and Colors section.

In additional, Visual Studio .NET is configured by default to automatically format your code. This means you can type your code lines freely without worrying about tabs and positioning. As soon as you move on to the next line, Visual Studio .NET applies the "correct" indenting.

Project Settings

There are several types of project-wide settings that you can configure. One of the most important is setting your *start page.* The start page isn't necessarily the page that users will start with when they use the application—that depends on the URL they use. Instead, the start page is the page that Visual Studio .NET will launch automatically when you're testing your application. To set a start page, right-click the page in the Solution Explorer and select Set As Start Page.

To access the full set of project properties, right-click your project in the Solution Explorer and select Properties (or select Project ➤ Properties from the menu). The project properties window shown in Figure 8-21 will appear.

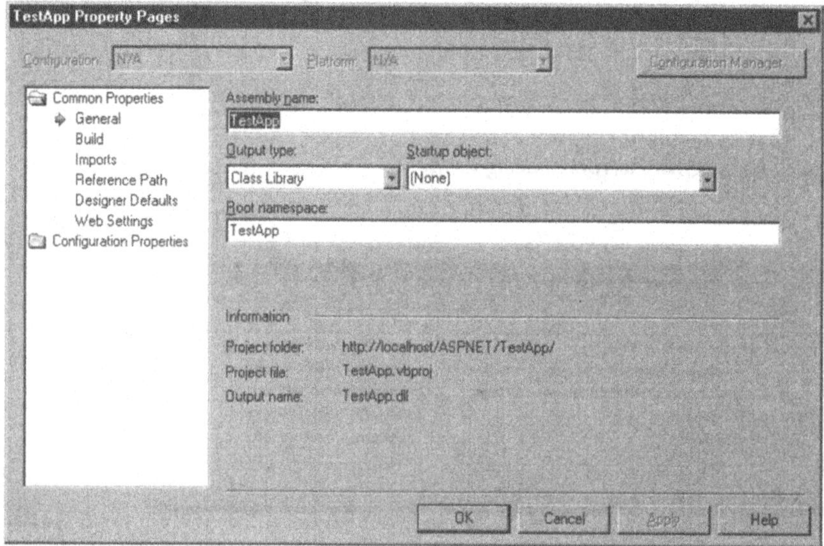

Figure 8-21. Project properties

There are two groups of project settings: Common Properties, which always apply, and Configuration Properties, which are tied to a specific configuration mode (for example, release mode or debug mode). The Common Properties are explained in Table 8-1.

Table 8-1. Common Project Properties

Group	Description
General	You can configure the Assembly name setting to change the name of the DLL file that VS .NET generates. You can change the Root namespace to change the name of the namespace that contains all your web classes (the page directive in the .aspx files will be updated automatically). Note that the Output type will always be class library. A web application is not a stand-alone executable, but a DLL that the ASP.NET engine loads in response to a user request.
Build	You can set the project-wide values for Option Explicit, Option Strict, and Option Compare. Option Explicit should always be enabled to prevent variable naming mistakes. Option Strict forces you to use explicit data type conversion (for example, you must the CType() function to convert a string into a number), which can help eliminate accidental errors.
Imports	You can use this section to import namespaces and make them locally available to all the code in your project. When you take this approach, you don't need to use the Imports statement at the beginning of each file.
Designer Defaults	You can set the default Page layout style (grid or layout) that will be used in all new web pages. You can also specify that client event handling and postback code should be created using VBScript. Generally, you won't use this option because it limits your application to Internet Explorer browsers.

Visual Studio .NET Debugging

Once you've created an application, you can compile and run it by choosing Debug ➤ Start from the menu, or by clicking the Start button on the toolbar. When you compile your project in debug mode, Visual Studio .NET adds to your code special debugging symbols, which allow it to work with the built-in debugging services. When you're ready to deploy your web application, you change the build configuration in the toolbar from Debug to Release, which instructs Visual Studio .NET to compile your program without debug symbols, improving overall performance. Figure 8-22 shows the portion of the Visual Studio .NET toolbar that you use to configure the build mode.

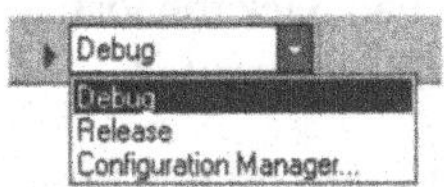

Figure 8-22. Configuring the build mode

When you compile your application, Visual Studio .NET creates a single DLL file with the name of your project and compiles all the page classes into this file. (This process was described with the explanation of code-behind development in Chapter 5.) Visual Studio .NET then starts one of the pages in your application by launching Internet Explorer and browsing to your application's start page.

Single-Step Debugging

Single-step debugging allows you to test your assumptions about how your code works, and see what's really happening under the hood of your application. It's incredibly easy to use. Just follow these steps:

1. Find a location in your code where you want to pause execution, and start single-stepping (you can use any executable line of code, but not a variable declaration, comment, or blank line). Click in the margin next to the line code and a red breakpoint will appear (see Figure 8-23).

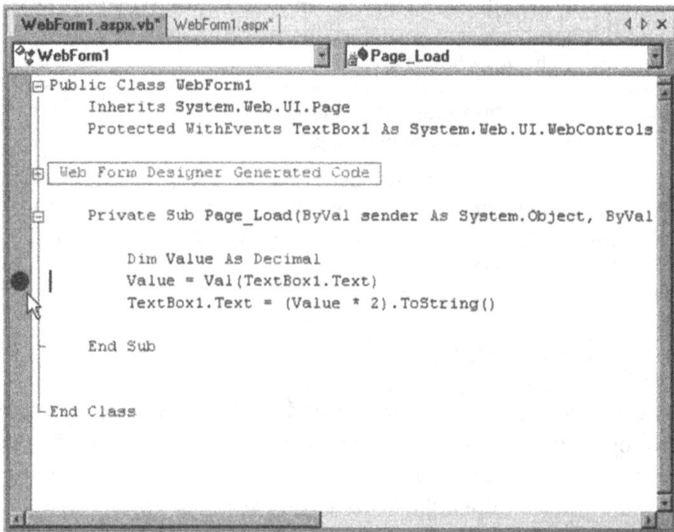

Figure 8-23. Setting a breakpoint

2. Now start your program as you would ordinarily. When the program reaches your breakpoint, execution will pause, and you'll be switched back the Visual Studio .NET code window. The breakpoint statement won't be executed.

3. At this point, you have several options. You can execute the current line by pressing F8. The following line in your code will be highlighted with a yellow arrow, indicating that this is the next line that will be executed. You can continue like this through your program, running one line at a time by pressing F8, and following the code's path of execution.

4. Whenever the code is in break mode, you can hover over variables to see their current contents (see Figure 8-24). This allows you to verify that variables contain the values you expect.

5. You can also use any of the commands listed in Table 8-2 while in break mode. These commands are available from the context menu by right-clicking the code window, or by using the associated hotkey.

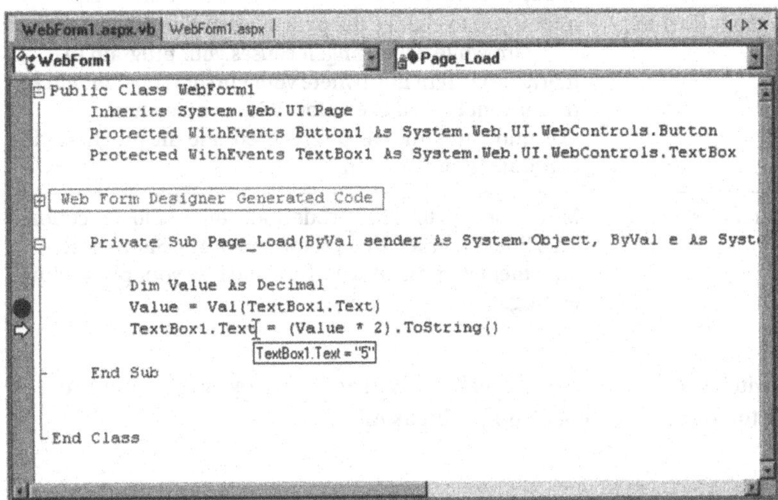

Figure 8-24. Viewing variable contents in break mode

Table 8-2. Commands Available in Break Mode

Command (Hot Key)	Description
Step Into (F8)	Executes the currently highlighted line and then pauses. If the currently highlighted line calls a procedure, execution will pause at the first executable line inside the method or function (which is why this feature is called stepping "into").
Step Over (Shift-F8)	The same as Step Into, except it runs procedures as though they are a single line. If you press Step Over while a procedure call is highlighted, the entire procedure will be executed. Execution will pause at the next executable statement in the current procedure.
Step Out (Ctrl-Shift-F8)	Executes all the code in the current procedure, and then pauses at the statement that immediately follows the one that called this method or function. In other words, this allows you to step "out" of the current procedure in one large jump.

Table 8-2. Commands Available in Break Mode (Continued)

Command (Hot Key)	Description
Continue (F5)	Resumes the program and continues to run it normally, without pausing until another breakpoint is reached.
Run To Cursor (Ctrl-F8)	Allows you to run all the code up to a specific line (where your cursor is currently positioned). You can use this technique to skip a time-consuming loop.
Set Next Statement (Ctrl-F9)	Allows you to change the path of execution of your program while debugging. It causes your program to mark the current line (where your cursor is positioned) as the current line for execution. When you resume execution, this line will be executed, and the program will continue from that point.
Show Next Statement	Moves focus to the line of code that is marked for execution. This line is marked by a yellow arrow. The Show Next Statement command is useful if you lose your place while editing.

You can switch your program into break mode at any point by clicking the pause button in the toolbar or selecting Debug ➤ Break All.

Advanced Breakpoints

Choose Debug ➤ Windows ➤ Breakpoints to see a window that lists all the breakpoints in your current project. The Breakpoints window provides a hit count, showing you the number of times a breakpoint has been encountered (see Figure 8-25). You can jump to the corresponding location in code by double-clicking a breakpoint. You can also use the Breakpoints window to disable a breakpoint without removing it. That allows you to keep a breakpoint to use in testing later, without leaving it active. Breakpoints are automatically saved with the Visual Studio .NET project files, although they aren't used when you compile the application in release mode.

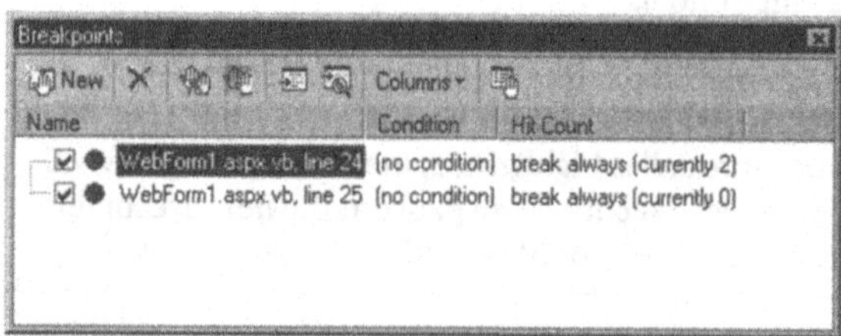

Figure 8-25. The Breakpoints window

Visual Studio .NET allows you to customize breakpoints so they only occur if certain conditions are true. To customize a breakpoint, right-click it and select Breakpoint Properties. In the window that appears you can take one of the following actions:

- Click the Condition button to set an expression. You can choose to break when this expression is True or when it has changed since the last time the breakpoint was hit.
- Click the Hit Count button to create a breakpoint that only pauses after a breakpoint has been hit a certain number of times (for example, at least 20), or a specific multiple of times (for example, every fifth time).

Variable Watches

In some cases, you might want to track the status of a variable without switching into break mode repeatedly. In this case, it's more useful to use the Autos, Locals, and Watch windows, which allow you track variables across an entire application. These windows are described in Table 8-3.

Table 8-3. Variable Watch Windows

Window	Description
Locals	Automatically displays all the variables that are in scope in the current procedure. This offers a quick summary of important variables.
Autos	Automatically displays variables that VS .NET determines are important for the current code statement. For example, this might include variables that are accessed or changed in the previous line.
Watch	Displays variables you have added. Watches are saved with your project, so you can continue tracking a variable at a later time. To add a watch, right-click a variable in your code and select Add Watch, or double-click the last row in the Watch window and type in the variable name.

Each row in the Locals, Autos, and Watch windows provides information about the type or class of the variable and its current value. If the variable holds an object instance, you can expand the variable and see its private members and properties. For example, in the Locals window you'll see the variable Me, which is a reference to the current page class. If you click the plus (+) box next to the word Me, a full list will appear that describes many page properties (and some system values), as shown in Figure 8-26.

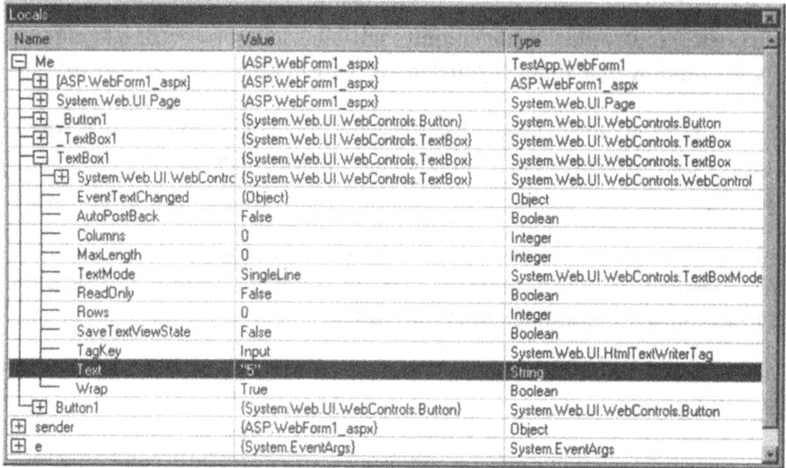

Figure 8-26. Viewing the page class in the Locals window

If you are missing one of the Watch windows, you can show it manually by selecting it from the Debug ➤ Windows submenu.

TIP The Watch, Locals, and Autos windows allow you to change simple variables while your program is in break mode. Just double-click the current value in the Value column and type in a new value. This allows you to simulate scenarios that are difficult or time consuming to re-create manually, or test specific error conditions.

Debugging Problems

In order to debug a web application with Visual Studio .NET, you must meet a few specific requirements. If these requirements aren't met, you'll receive an "unable to start debugging" error message when you attempt to start the application. This error signals that Visual Studio .NET was able to compile the web application, but can't execute it in debug mode.

Unfortunately, this error can be caused by a dizzying range of different problems. The following are some possible causes:

- IIS (Internet Information Services), the Windows component that hosts web applications, isn't installed or is installed incorrectly.
- The user running Visual Studio .NET isn't a member of the Debugger Users group for the web server.

- The user running Visual Studio .NET doesn't have permission to debug the ASP.NET process. For example, if the ASP.NET process is running under the local system account, the user must have Administrator privileges to debug it.
- The Web application doesn't have a web.config file, or the web.config file doesn't enable debugging.
- Integrated Windows authentication isn't enabled for the virtual directory.

The first step that you should take when diagnosing this error is to verify that IIS and ASP.NET are installed correctly. Try to run your application by selecting Debug ➤ Start Without Debugging from the Visual Studio .NET menu. If your web application still doesn't execute properly, or a blank or garbled page appears, you may need to repair the .NET Framework. This process is described in Chapter 2. If your web application *does* run properly, continue with the following steps to enable debugging.

The next step is to verify that the virtual directory exists and is correctly configured in IIS. Problems can occur if you've changed the virtual directory settings or removed it. To investigate in more detail, start the IIS Manager utility by selecting Settings ➤ Control Panel ➤ Administrative Tools ➤ Internet Information Services from the Start menu. Find the virtual directory you're using, right-click it, and choose Properties.

First, verify that the virtual directory is configured as web application. If you see the Remove button in the Application Settings section, the directory is configured correctly. If you see the Create button instead, the directory isn't configured correctly. Click Create to designate the virtual directory as a web application, and then try to run your web application in Visual Studio .NET

Another problem can occur if Visual Studio .NET isn't allowed to authenticate itself to the application. To check if this is the problem, right-click the virtual directory and choose Properties. Then, select the Directory Security tab, and in the Anonymous access and authentication control section, click the Edit button. In the Authentication Methods dialog box, under Authenticated access, select Integrated Windows authentication, and click OK to apply your changes. (You can learn more about these settings in Chapter 25.)

Finally, if the problem persists, you should check that you have a correctly configured web.config file. The web.config file should follow the structure shown here:

```
<configuration>
    <system.web>
        <compilation defaultLanguage="VB" debug="true" >

    <!-- Other settings omitted. -->

    </system.web>
</configuration>
```

By default, Visual Studio .NET adds the compilation tag to the automatically generated web.config file with the debug setting set to true.

For more information, refer to the Microsoft white paper at `http://msdn.microsoft.com/library/en-us/vsdebug/html/vxtbshttpservererrors.asp`, which describes these steps and some other troubleshooting steps for remote servers.

Web Matrix

As impressive as it is, Visual Studio .NET isn't for everyone. If you're looking for a web development application that provides many of the conveniences of Visual Studio .NET without the cost, you may be interested in Microsoft's Web Matrix project. Web Matrix is a freely downloadable editor for ASP.NET sites that includes drag-and-drop web page design and a stand-alone web server that you can use for testing web pages without IIS. (Best of all, this web server is supported on some operating systems that don't support IIS, such as Windows XP Home Edition.) Web Matrix doesn't include all of Visual Studio .NET's timesaving features, though—you'll find that there isn't support for statement completion or InteliSense, which makes the .NET learning curve a little steeper. To download Web Matrix, or read the free tour and frequently asked questions, go to `http://www.asp.net/webmatrix`.

Unfortunately, the files you'll create with Web Matrix differ from those generated by Visual Studio .NET. In Visual Studio .NET, you use the code-behind model, which places the web page source code into separate files. Visual Studio .NET also precompiles all the source code into a single DLL. With Web Matrix, you use the inline code approach, which combines code and HTML in a single file. The Web Matrix display simplifies life a little—it allows you to display just the code portion or just the HTML portion of the file using its configurable viewer—but the model is still different. There's no way to open a web page that uses code-behind in Web Matrix. In Visual Studio .NET, you can open a web page with inline code, but you'll use the ability to debug the code, or edit it with Visual Studio .NET IntelliSense. It's likely that both Web Matrix and Visual Studio .NET will be combined into a single, more flexible product in a future release. Until that time, you will need to do a little extra work to bridge the format gap.

The examples in this book are compatible with Visual Studio .NET or with any other type of code-behind development. The online code includes the standard .aspx and .vb files that you can use independently, and the optional .vbproj and .sln project and solution files for use with Visual Studio .NET. If you use Web Matrix, you'll need to resign yourself to the tedious process of cutting and pasting the sample code. If you're using Notepad on its own, you won't need to change the code, but you'll need to precompile it using the vbc.exe compiler described in Chapter 5.

The Last Word

This chapter extolled the many benefits of Visual Studio .NET. However, if you prefer to work with a simpler, leaner utility (such as Notepad), you can still create equally advanced ASP.NET applications. You might even discover a third-party IDE that you prefer to use, like Web Matrix. One of the best features of ASP.NET programming is that it isn't hard-wired to a particular design environment—you're free to use anything from a plain text editor to a professional development tool like Visual Studio .NET.

CHAPTER 9

Validation and Rich Controls

THIS CHAPTER LOOKS AT some of the real promise of ASP.NET and the web control model. First, you'll consider two controls that have no equivalent in the ordinary HTML world: the Calendar and AdRotator. The controls demonstrate how the web control model can invent entirely new types of web page user interface without needing to break browser compatibility.

Next, you'll learn about ASP.NET's validation controls. These controls take a previously time-consuming and complicated task—verifying user input and reporting errors—and automate it with an elegant, easy-to-use collection of validators. You'll learn how to add these controls to an existing page and use regular expression, custom validation functions, and manual validation. And as usual, you'll peer under the hood to take a look at how ASP.NET implements these new features.

Finally, you'll consider the next generation of controls, which promises to bring a new world of rich user interface to the Web. These new controls, prepared by other developers, represent one of the most exciting new directions for ASP.NET.

The Calendar Control

The Calendar control is one of the most impressive web controls. It's commonly called a rich control because it can be programmed as a single object (and defined in a single simple tag), but rendered in dozens of lines of HTML output.

```
<asp:Calendar id="Dates" runat="server" />
```

The Calendar control presents a single month view, as shown in Figure 9-1. The user can navigate from month to month using the navigational arrows, at which point the page is posted back and ASP.NET automatically provides a new page with the correct month values. You don't need to write any additional event-handling code to manage this process. When the user clicks on a date, it becomes highlighted in a gray box. You can retrieve the selected day in your code as a DateTime object from the Calendar.SelectedDate property.

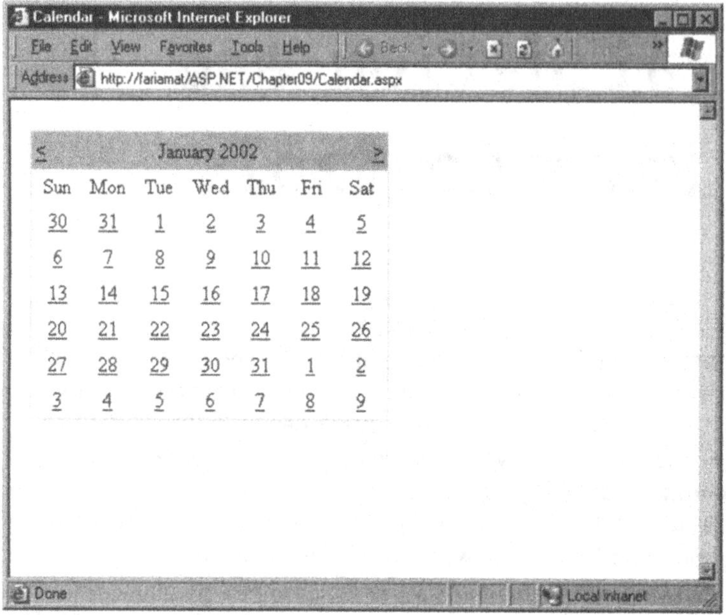

Figure 9-1. The default Calendar

This basic set of features may provide everything you need in your application. Alternatively, you can configure different selection modes to allow users to select entire weeks or months, or render the control as a static calendar that doesn't allow selection. The only fact you must remember is that if you allow month selection, the user can also select a single week or a day. Similarly, if you allow week selection, the user can also select a single day.

The type of selection is set through the Calendar.SelectionMode property. You may also need to set the Calendar.FirstDayOfWeek property to configure how a week is selected. (For example, set FirstDayOfWeek to the enumerated value Monday, and weeks will be selected from Monday to Sunday.)

When you allow multiple date selection, you need to examine the SelectedDates property, which provides a collection of all the selected dates. You can loop through this collection using the For Each syntax. The following code demonstrates this technique:

```
lblDates.Text = "You selected these dates:<br>"

Dim dt As DateTime
For Each dt In MyCalendar.SelectedDates
    lblDates.Text &= dt.ToLongDateString() & "<br>"
Next
```

Figure 9-2 shows the resulting page after this code has been executed.

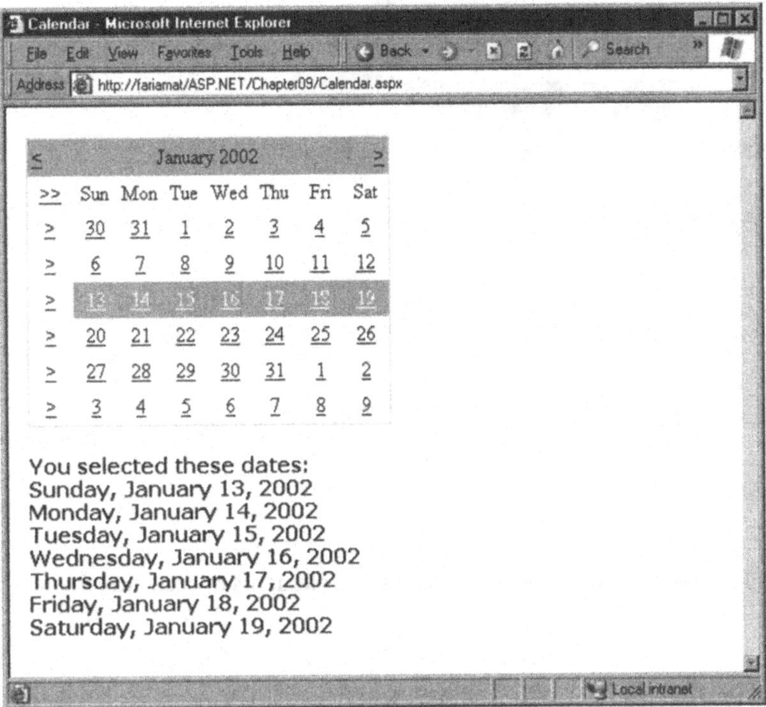

Figure 9-2. Selecting multiple dates

Formatting the Calendar

The Calendar control provides a whole host of formatting-related properties. Various parts of the Calendar, like the header, selector, and various day types can be set using one of the style properties (for example, WeekendDayStyle). Each of these style properties references a full-featured TableItemStyle object that provides properties for coloring, border style, font, and alignment. Taken together, they allow you to modify almost any part of the Calendar's appearance. For more information about the Calendar styles, you can refer to the web control reference in Chapter 28.

If you're using a design tool like Visual Studio .NET, you can even set an entire related color scheme using the built-in designer. Simply right-click the control on your design page and select Auto Format. You'll be presented with a list of predefined formats that set the style properties, as shown in Figure 9-3.

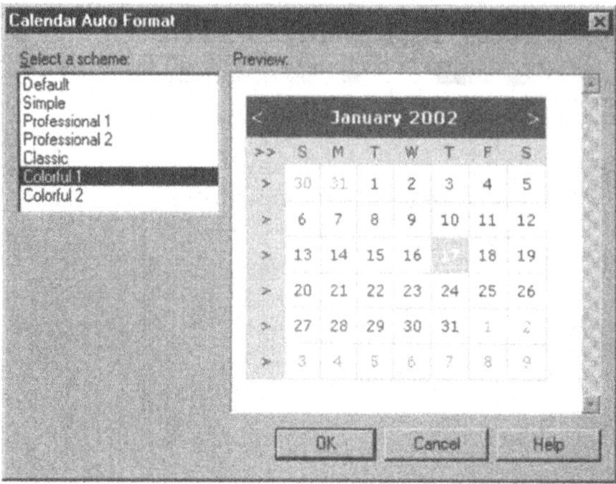

Figure 9-3. Calendar styles

You can also use additional properties to hide some elements or configure the text they display.

Restricting Dates

In most situations where you need to use a calendar for selection, you don't want to allow the user to select any date in the calendar. For example, the user might be booking an appointment or choosing a delivery date, two services that are generally only provided on set days. The Calendar makes it surprisingly easy to implement this logic. In fact, if you've worked with the date and time controls on the Windows platform, you'll quickly recognize that the ASP.NET versions are far superior.

The basic approach to restricting dates is to write an event handler for the Calendar.DayRender event. This event occurs when the Calendar is about to create a month to display to the user. This event gives you the chance to examine the date that is being added to the current month (through the e.Day property), and decide whether it should be selectable or restricted.

The following code makes it impossible to select any weekend days or days in years greater than 2010.

```
Private Sub DayRender(source As Object, e As DayRenderEventArgs) _
  Handles Calendar.DayRender

    ' Restrict dates after the year 2100, and those on the weekend.
    If e.Day.IsWeekend Or e.Day.Date.Year > 2010 Then
        e.Day.IsSelectable = False
    End If

End Sub
```

The e.Day object is an instance of the CalendarDay class, which provides various useful properties. These are described in Table 9-1.

Table 9-1. CalendarDay Properties

Property	Description
Date	The DateTime object that represents this date.
IsWeekend	True if this date falls on a Saturday or Sunday.
IsToday	True if this value matches the Calendar.TodaysDate property, which is set to the current day by default.
IsOtherMonth	True if this date doesn't belong to the current month, but is displayed to fill in the first or last row. For example, this might be the last day of the previous month or the next day of the following month.
IsSelectable	Allows you to configure whether the user can select this day.

The DayRender event is extremely powerful. Besides allowing you to tailor what dates are selectable, it also allows you to configure the cell where the date is located through the e.Cell property (the Calendar is really a sophisticated HTML table). For example, you could highlight an important date or even add extra information. Here's an example that highlights a single day—the fifth of May:

```
Private Sub DayRender(source As Object, e As DayRenderEventArgs) _
  Handles Calendar.DayRender

    ' Check for May 5 in any year, and format it.
    If e.Day.Date.Day = 5 And e.Day.Date.Month = 5 Then
        e.Cell.BackColor = System.Drawing.Color.Yellow

        ' Add some static text to the cell.
        Dim lbl As New Label
        lbl.Text = "<br>My Birthday!"
        e.Cell.Controls.Add(lbl)
    End If

End Sub
```

Figure 9-4 shows the resulting calendar display.

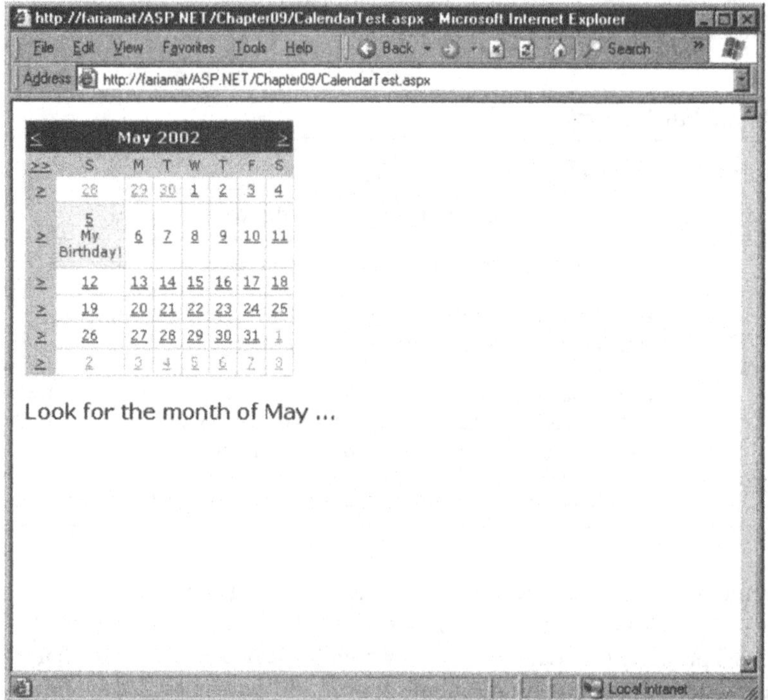

Figure 9-4. Highlighting a day

The Calendar control provides two other useful events: SelectionChanged and VisibleMonthChanged. These occur immediately after a change, but before the page is returned to the user. You can react to this event and update other portions of the web page to correspond to the current calendar month. For example, you might want to set a corresponding list of times in a list control. The following code demonstrates this approach, using a different set of time values if a Monday is selected in the Calendar.

```
Private Sub SelectionChanged(source As Object, e As EventArgs) _
  Handles Calendar.SelectionChanged

    lstTimes.Items.Clear()

    Select Case MyCalendar.SelectedDate.DayOfWeek
        Case DayOfWeek.Monday
            ' Apply special Monday schedule.
            lstTimes.Items.Add("10:00")
            lstTimes.Items.Add("10:30")
            lstTimes.Items.Add("11:00")
```

```
        Case Else
            lstTimes.Items.Add("10:00")
            lstTimes.Items.Add("10:30")
            lstTimes.Items.Add("11:00")
            lstTimes.Items.Add("11:30")
            lstTimes.Items.Add("12:00")
            lstTimes.Items.Add("12:30")
    End Select
End Sub
```

To try out these features of the Calendar control, run the Appointment.aspx page from the online samples. It provides a formatted calendar that restricts some dates, formats others specially, and updates a corresponding list control when the selection changes.

The AdRotator

The AdRotator has been available as an ASP component for some time. The new ASP.NET AdRotator adds some new features, such as the ability to filter the full list of banners to the best matches for a given page. The AdRotator also uses a new XML file format.

The basic purpose of the AdRotator is to provide a banner-type graphic on a page (often used as an advertisement link to another site) that is chosen randomly from a group of possible banners. In other words, every time the page is requested, a different banner could be chosen and displayed, which is the "rotation" indicated by the name AdRotator.

In ASP.NET, it wouldn't be too difficult to implement an AdRotator type of design on your own. You could react to the Page.Load event, generate a random number, and then use that number to choose from a list of predetermined image files. You could even store the list in the web.config file so that it can be easily modified separately as part of the application's configuration. Of course, if you wanted to enable several pages with a random banner you would either have to repeat the code or create your own custom control. The AdRotator provides these features for free.

The Advertisement File

The AdRotator stores its list of image files in a special XML file. This file uses the format shown here.

```
<Advertisements>

  <Ad>
    <ImageUrl>prosetech.jpg</ImageUrl>
    <NavigateUrl>http://www.prosetech.com</NavigateUrl>
    <AlternateText>ProseTech Site</AlternateText>
    <Impressions>1</Impressions>
    <Keyword>Computer</Keyword>
  </Ad>

</Advertisements>
```

This example shows a single possible advertisement. To add more advertisements, you would create multiple <Ad> elements, and place them all inside the root <Advertisements> element.

```
<Advertisements>

  <Ad>
    <!-- First ad here. -->
  </Ad>

  <Ad>
    <!-- Second ad here. -->
  </Ad>
</Advertisements>
```

Each <Ad> element has a number of other important properties that configure the link, the image, and the frequency, as described in Table 9-2.

Table 9-2. Advertisement File Elements

Element	Description
ImageUrl	The image that will be displayed. This can be a relative link (a file in the current directory) or a fully qualified Internet URL.
NavigateUrl	The link that will be followed if the user clicks on the banner.
AlternateText	The text that will be displayed instead of the picture if it cannot be displayed. This text will also be used as a tooltip in some newer browsers.
Impressions	A number that sets how often an advertisement will appear. This number is relative to the numbers specified for other ads. For example, a banner with the value 10 will be shown twice as often as the banner with the value 5.
Keyword	A keyword that identifies a group of advertisements. This can be used for filtering. For example, you could create ten advertisements, and give half of them the keyword "Retail" and the other half the keyword "Computer." The web page can then choose to filter the possible advertisements to include only one of these groups.

The AdRotator Class

The actual AdRotator class only provides a limited set of properties. You specify the appropriate advertisement file in the AdvertisementFile property, and the type of window that the link should follow (the Target window). The target can name a specific frame, or it can use one of the special values defined in Table 9-3.

Table 9-3. Special Frame Targets

Target	Description
_blank	The link opens a new unframed window.
_parent	The link opens in the parent of the current frame.
_self	The link opens in the current frame.
_top	The link opens in the topmost frame of the current window (so the site appears in the full, unframed window).

Optionally, you can set the KeywordFilter property so that the banner will be chosen from a specific keyword group. A fully configured AdRotator tag is shown here.

```
<asp:AdRotator id="Ads" runat="server" AvertisementFile="MainAds.xml"

   Target="_blank" KeywordFilter="Computer" />
```

TIP In Visual Studio .NET, you can't link to an advertisement file unless you have added it to the current project.

Additionally, you can react to the AdRotator.AdCreated event. This occurs when the page is being created, and an image is randomly chosen from the file. This event provides you with information about the image that you can use to customize the rest of your page. For example, you might display some related content or a link, as shown in Figure 9-5.

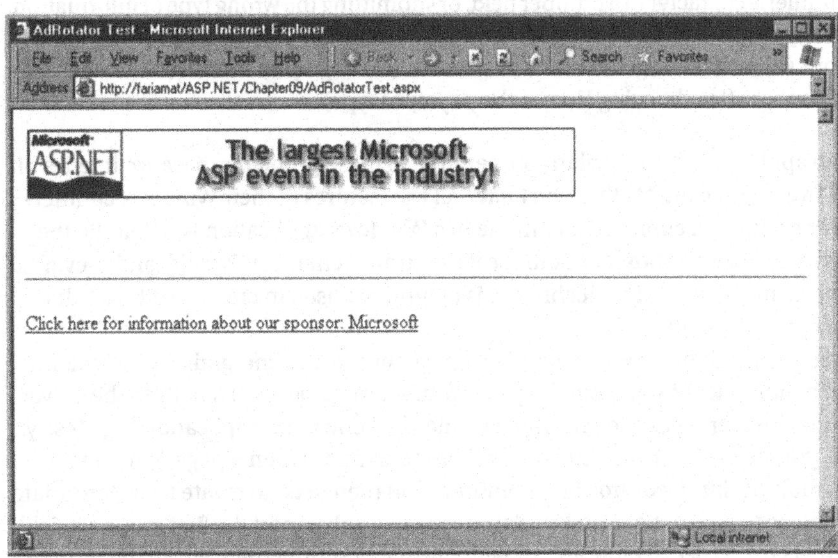

Figure 9-5. An AdRotator with synchronized content

The event-handling code for this example simply configures the hyperlink control based on the randomly selected advertisement:

```
Private Sub Ads_AdCreated(sender As Object, _
  e As AdCreatedEventArgs) Handles Ads.AdCreated
    ' Synchronize the Hyperlink control.
    lnkBanner.NavigateUrl = e.NavigateUrl

    ' Syncrhonize the text of the link.
    lnkBanner.Text = "Click here for information about our sponsor: "
    lnkBanner.Text &= e.AlternateText
End Sub
```

As you can see, rich controls like the Calendar and AdRotator don't just add a sophisticated HTML output, they also include an event framework that allows you to take charge of the control's behavior and integrate it into your application.

Validation

As a seasoned developer, you probably realize that you can't assume users won't make mistakes. What's particularly daunting is the range of possible mistakes that users can make, such as the following:

- Users might ignore an important field and leave it blank.
- Users might try to type a short string of "nonsense" to circumvent a required field check, thereby creating endless headaches on your end, such as e-mail addresses that aren't valid that cause problems for your automatic mailing programs.
- Users might make an honest mistake, including a typing error, entering a non-numeric character in a number field, or submitting the wrong type of information. They might even enter several pieces of information that are individually correct, but when taken together are inconsistent (for example, entering a MasterCard number after choosing Visa as the payment type).

A web application is particularly susceptible to these problems, because it relies on basic HTML input controls that don't have all the features of their Windows counterparts. For example, a common technique in a Windows application is to handle the KeyPress event of a text box, check to see if the current character is valid, and prevent it from appearing if it isn't. This technique is commonly used to create text boxes that only accept numeric input.

In web applications, however, you don't have that sort of fine-grained control. In order to handle a KeyPress event the page would have to be posted back to the server every time the user types a letter, which would slow down the application hopelessly. Instead, you need to perform all your validation at once when a page (which may contain multiple input controls) is submitted. You then need to create the appropriate user interface to report the mistakes. Some websites only report the first incorrect field, while others use a special table, list, or window that describes them all. By the time you have perfected your validation routines, a considerable amount of fine-tuned effort has gone into writing validation code.

ASP.NET aims to save you this trouble and provide you with a reusable framework of validation controls that manages validation details by checking fields and reporting on errors automatically. These controls can even make use of client-side DHTML and JavaScript to provide a more dynamic and responsive interface, while still providing ordinary validation for older down-level browsers.

The Validation Controls

ASP.NET provides five different validator controls, which are described in Table 9-4. Four are targeted at specific types of validation, while the fifth allows you to apply custom validation routines.

Table 9-4. Validator Controls

Control Class	Description
RequiredFieldValidator	Validation succeeds as long as the input control doesn't contain an empty string.
RangeValidator	Validation succeeds if the input control contains a value within a specific numeric, alphabetic, or date range.
CompareValidator	Validation succeeds if the input control contains a value that matches the value in another, specified input control.
RegularExpressionValidator	Validation succeeds if the value in an input control matches a specified regular expression.
CustomValidator	Validation is performed by a user-defined function.

Each validation control can be bound to a single input control. In addition, you can apply more than one validation control to the same input control to provide multiple types of validation.

If you use the RangeValidator, CompareValidator, or RegularExpressionValidator, validation will automatically succeed if the input control is empty, because there is no value to validate. If this isn't the behavior you want, you should add an additional RequiredFieldValidator to the control. That ensures that two types of validation will be performed, effectively restricting blank values.

Like all other web controls, you add a validator as a tag in the form <asp:ControlClassName />. There is one additional validation control, called ValidationSummary, which doesn't perform any actual control checking. Instead, it can be used to provide a list of all the validation errors for the entire page.

The Validation Process

You can use the validator controls to verify a page automatically when the user submits it, or manually in your code. The first approach is the most common.

When using automatic validation, the user receives a normal page, and begins to fill in the input controls. When finished, the user clicks a button to submit the page. Every button has a CausesValidation property, which can be set to True or False. What happens when the user clicks the button depends on the value of the CausesValidation property.

- If CausesValidation is False, ASP.NET will ignore the validation controls, the page will be posted back, and your event-handling code will run normally.
- If CausesValidation is True (the default), ASP.NET will automatically validate the page when the user clicks the button. It does this by performing the validation for each control on the page. If any control fails to validate, ASP.NET will return the page with some error information, depending on your settings. Your click event handling code may or may not be executed—meaning that you'll have to specifically check in the event handler whether the page is valid or not.

Based on this description, you'll realize that validation happens automatically when certain buttons are clicked. It doesn't happen when the page is posted back due to a change event (like choosing a new value in an AutoPostBack list) or if the user clicks a button that has CausesValidation set to False. However, you can still validate one or more controls manually, and then make a decision in your code based on the results. We'll look at this process in more detail a little later.

Client-Side Validation

In browsers that support it (currently only Internet Explorer 5 and above), ASP.NET will automatically add code for client-side validation. In this case, when the user clicks on a CausesValidation button, the same error messages will appear without the page needing to be submitted and returned from the server. This increases the responsiveness of the application.

However, if the page validates successfully on the client side, ASP.NET will still revalidate it when it's received at the server. This is because it's easy for an experienced user to circumvent client-side validation. For example, a malicious user might delete the block of JavaScript validation code and continue working with the page. By performing the validation at both ends, your application can be as responsive as possible, but remain secure.

The Validator Classes

The validation control classes are found in the System.Web.UI.WebControls namespace and inherit from the BaseValidator class. This class defines the basic functionality for a validation control. Its properties are described in Table 9-5.

Table 9-5. Properties of the BaseValidator Class

Property	**Description**
ControlToValidate	Identifies the control that this validator will check. Each validator can verify the value in one input control.
ErrorMessage, ForeColor, and Display	If validation fails, the validator control can display a text message (set by the ErrorMessage property). The Display property allows you to configure whether this error message will be added dynamically as needed (Dynamic), or whether an appropriate space will be reserved for the message (Static). Static is useful when the validator is in a table, and you don't want the width of the cell to collapse when no message is displayed.
IsValid	After validation is performed, this returns True or False depending on whether it succeeded or failed. Generally, you'll check the state of the entire page by looking at its IsValid property instead, to find out if all the validation controls succeeded.
Enabled	When set to False, automatic validation will not be performed for this control when the page is submitted.
EnableClientSideScript	If set to True, ASP.NET will add special JavaScript and DHTML code to allow client-side validation on browsers that support it.

When using a validation control, the only properties you need to use are ControlToValidate and ErrorMessage. In addition, you may need to use the properties that are used for your specific validator. These properties are outlined in Table 9-6.

Table 9-6. Validator-Specific Properties

Validator Control	**Added Members**
RequiredFieldValidator	None required
RangeValidator	MaximumValue, MinimumValue, Type
CompareValidator	ControlToCompare, Operator, Type, ValueToCompare
RegularExpressionValidator	ValidationExpression
CustomValidator	ClientValidationFunction, ServerValidate event

A detailed explanation for each validation control is provided in Chapter 28. Also, the customer validation form example later in this chapter demonstrates each type of validation.

A Simple Validation Example

To get an understanding of how validation works, you can create a simple example. This test uses a single Button web control, two TextBox controls, and a RangeValidation control that validates the first text box. If validation fails, an error message will be shown in the RangeValidation control, so this control should be placed immediately next to the TextBox it's validating. Figure 9-6 shows the appearance of the page after a failed validation attempt.

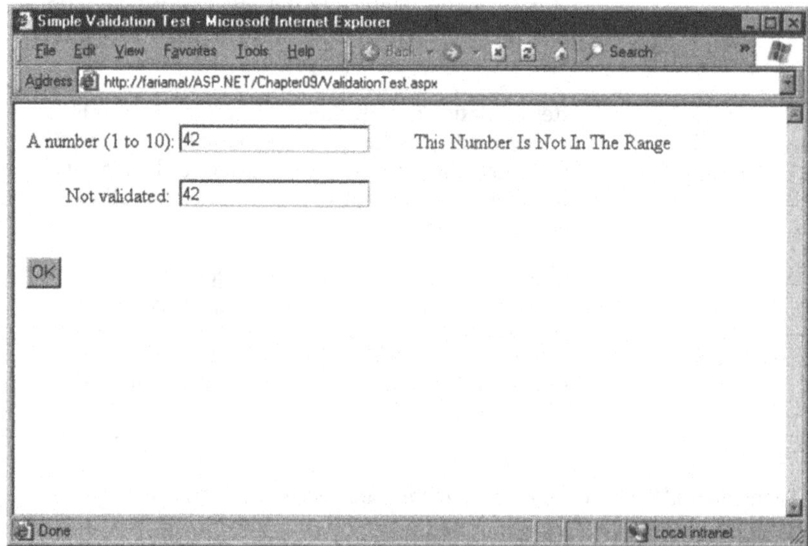

Figure 9-6. Failed validation

In addition, a Label control is placed at the bottom of the form. This label will report when the page has been successfully posted back and the button click event handling code is executed. Its EnableViewState property is disabled to ensure that it will be cleared every time the page is posted back.

The layout code defines a RangeValidator control, sets the error message, identifies the control that will be validated, and requires an integer from 1 to 10. These properties are set in the .aspx file, but they could also be configured in the event handler for the Page.Load event. The Button automatically has its CauseValidation property set to True, as this is the default.

```
<html><body>
  <form method="post" runat="server">

    A number (1 to 10):
    <asp:TextBox id=txtValidated runat="server" />
    <asp:RangeValidator id="RangeValidator" runat="server"
         ErrorMessage="This Number Is Not In The Range"
         ControlToValidate="txtValidated"
         MaximumValue="10" MinimumValue="1"
         Type="Integer" />
    <br><br>
    Not validated:
    <asp:TextBox id=txtNotValidated runat="server" /><br><br>
    <asp:Button id=cmdOK runat="server" Text="OK" /><br><br>
    <asp:Label id=lblMessage runat="server"
         EnableViewState="False" />

  </form>
</body></html>
```

Finally, here is the code that responds to the button click:

```
Private Sub cmdOK_Click(sender As Object, e As EventArgs) _
  Handles cmdOK.Click
    lblMessage.Text = "cmdOK_Click event handler executed."
End Sub
```

If you're testing this web page in Internet Explorer 5 or later, you'll notice an interesting trick. When you first open the page, the error message is hidden. But if you type an invalid number (remember, validation will succeed for an empty value), and press the Tab key to move to the second text box, an error message will appear automatically next to the offending control. This is because ASP.NET adds a special JavaScript function that detects when the focus changes. This code uses the special WebUIValidation.js script library file that is installed on your server with the .NET Framework (in the c:\Inetpub\wwwroot\aspnet_client\system_web\[Version] directory), and is somewhat complicated. However, ASP.NET handles all the details for you automatically. If you try to click the OK button with an invalid value in txtValidated, your actions will be ignored, and the page won't be posted back.

These features are relatively high-level, because they combine DHTML and JavaScript. Clearly, not all browsers will support this client-side validation. To see what will happen on a down-level browser, set the RangeValidator.EnableClientScript property to False and rerun the page. Now error messages won't appear dynamically as you change focus. However, when you click the OK button, the page will be returned from the server with the appropriate error message displayed next to the invalid control.

The potential problem in this scenario is the fact that the click event handling code will still execute, even though the page is invalid. To correct this problem, and ensure that your page behaves the same on modern and older browsers, you must specifically abort the event code if validation hasn't been performed successfully.

```
Private Sub cmdOK_Click(sender As Object, e As EventArgs) _
  Handles cmdOK.Click
    ' Abort the event if the control isn't valid.
    If RangeValidator.IsValid = False Then Exit Sub
    lblMessage.Text = "cmdOK_Click event handler executed."
End Sub
```

This code solves our current problem, but it isn't much help if the page contains multiple validation controls. Fortunately, every web form provides its own IsValid property. This property will be False if *any* validation control has failed. It will be True if all the validation controls completed successfully, or if validation was not performed (for example, if the validation controls are disabled or if the button has CausesValidation set to False).

```
Private Sub cmdOK_Click(sender As Object, e As EventArgs) _
  Handles cmdOK.Click
    ' Abort the event if the page isn't valid.
    If Me.IsValid = False Then Exit Sub
    lblMessage.Text = "cmdOK_Click event handler executed."
End Sub
```

Remember, client-side validation is just a nice frosting on top of your application. Server-side validation will always be performed, ensuring that crafty users can't "spoof" pages.

Other Display Options

In some cases, you might have already created a carefully designed form that combines multiple input fields. Perhaps you want to add validation to this page, but you can't reformat the layout to accommodate all the error messages for all the validation controls. In this case, you can save some work by using the ValidationSummary control.

To try this out, set the Display property of the RangeValidator control to None. This ensures that the error message will never be displayed. However, validation will still be performed, and the user will still be prevented from successfully clicking the OK button if some invalid information exists on the page.

Next, add the ValidationSummary in a suitable location (such as the bottom of the page).

```
<asp:ValidationSummary id="Errors" runat="server" />
```

When you run the page, you won't see any dynamic messages as you enter invalid information and tab to a new field. However, when you click the OK button, the ValidationSummary will appear with a list of all error messages, as shown in Figure 9-7. In this case, it retrieves one error message (from the RangeValidator control). However, if you had a dozen validators, it would retrieve all of their error messages and create a list.

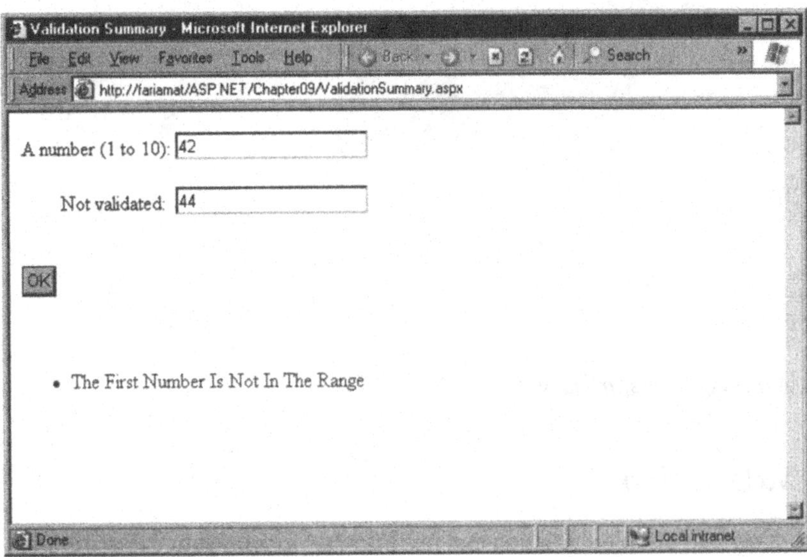

Figure 9-7. The validation summary

The ValidationSummary control also provides some useful properties you can use to fine-tune the error display. You can set the HeaderText property to display a special title at the top of the list (such as "Your page contains the following errors:"). You can also change the ForeColor and choose a DisplayMode. The possible modes are BulletList (the default), List, and Paragraph.

Finally, you choose to have the validation summary displayed in a pop-up dialog box instead of on the page (see Figure 9-8). This approach has the advantage of leaving the user interface of the page untouched, but it also forces the user to dismiss the error messages by closing the window before being able to modify the input controls. If users will need to refer to these messages while they fix the page, the inline display is better.

To show the summary in a dialog box, set the ValidationSummary.ShowMessageBox property to True.

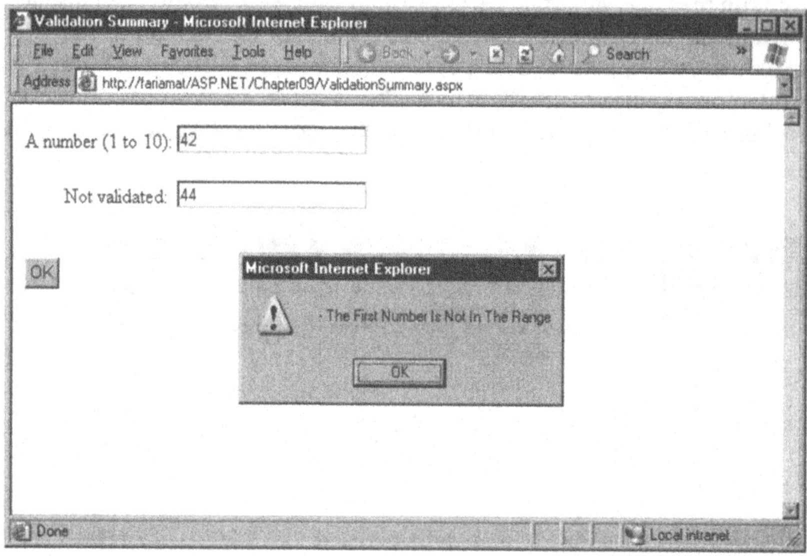

Figure 9-8. A message box summary

Manual Validation

Your final option is to disable validation and perform the work on your own, with the help of the validation controls. This allows you to take other information into consideration, or create a specialized error message that involves other controls (such as images or buttons).

The following are three ways that you can create manual validation:

- Use your own code to verify values. In this case, you won't use any of the ASP.NET validation controls.
- Disable the EnableClientScript property for each validation control. This allows an invalid page to be submitted, after which you can decide what to do with it depending on the problems.
- Add a button with CausesValidation set to False. When this button is clicked, manually validate the page by calling the Page.Validate method. Then examine the IsValid property and decide what to do.

The next example uses the second approach. Once the page is submitted, it examines all the validation controls on the page, by looping through the Page.Validators collection. Every time it finds a control that hasn't validated successfully, it retrieves the invalid value from the input control and adds it to a string. At the end of this routine, it displays a message that describes which values were incorrect, as shown in Figure 9-9.

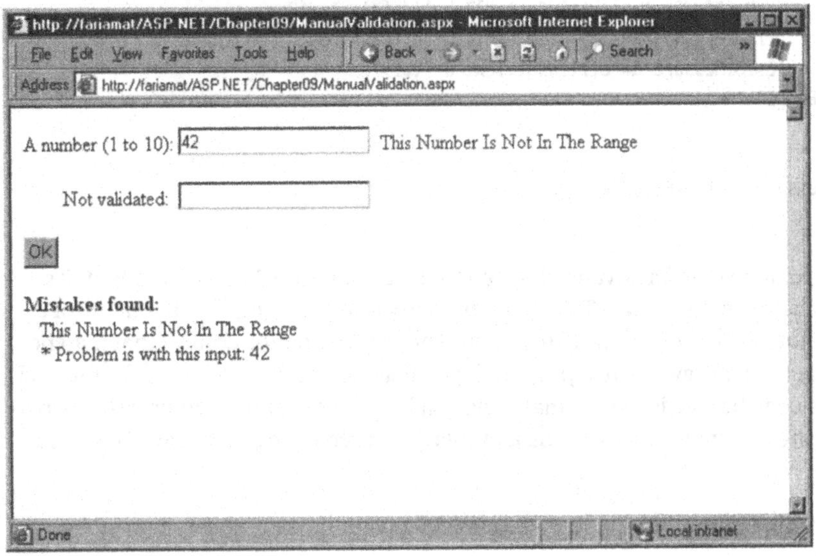

Figure 9-9. Manual validation

This technique adds a feature that wouldn't be available with automatic validation, which uses the static ErrorMessage property. In that case, it isn't possible to include the actual incorrect values in the message.

Here's the event handler that checks for invalid values:

```
Private Sub cmdOK_Click(sender As Object, e As EventArgs) _
  Handles cmdOK.Click

    Dim ErrorMessage As String = "<b>Mistakes found:</b><br>"

    ' Create a variable to represent the input control.
    Dim ctrlInput As TextBox

    ' Search through the validation controls.
    Dim ctrl As BaseValidator
```

```
    For Each ctrl In Me.Validators
        If ctrl.IsValid = False Then
            ErrorMessage &= ctrl.ErrorMessage & "<br>"

            ' Find the corresponding input control, and change the
            ' generic Control variable into a TextBox variable.
            ' This allows access to the Text property.
            ctrlInput = CType( _
              Me.FindControl(ctrl.ControlToValidate), TextBox)
            ErrorMessage &= " * Problem is with this input: "
            ErrorMessage &= ctrlInput.Text & "<br>"
        End If
    Next

    lblMessage.Text = ErrorMessage
End Sub
```

This example uses an advanced technique: the Page.FindControl() method. It's required because the ControlToValidate property is just a string with the name of a control, not a reference to the actual control object. To find the control that matches this name (and retrieve its Text property), you need to use the FindControl() method. Once the code has retrieved the matching text box, it can perform other tasks such as clearing the current value, tweaking a property, or even changing the text box color.

Understanding Regular Expressions

Regular expressions are an advanced tool for matching patterns. They have appeared in countless other languages and gained popularity as an extremely powerful way to work with strings. In fact, Visual Studio .NET even allows programmers to perform a search and replace operation through their code using a regular expression (which may represent a new height of computer geekdom).

Regular expressions can almost be considered an entire language of their own. To master all the ways that you can use regular expressions—including pattern matching, back references, and named groups—could occupy an entire small book. Fortunately, you can understand the basics of regular expressions without nearly that much work.

Literals and Metacharacters

All regular expressions are made up of two kinds of characters: literals and metacharacters. Literals are not unlike the string literals you type in code. They represent a specific defined character. For example, if you search for the string literal "l" you'll find the character "l" and nothing else.

Metacharacters provide the true secret to unlocking the full power of regular expressions. You're probably already familiar with two metacharacters from the DOS world (? and *). Consider the command-line expression shown here:

```
Del *.*
```

The expression *.* contains one literal (the period) and two metacharacters (the asterisks). This translates as "delete every file that starts with any number of characters, contains a dot, and ends with an extension of any number of characters." Because all files in DOS implicitly have extensions, this has the well-documented effect of deleting everything in the current directory.

Another DOS metacharacter is the question mark, which means "any single character." For example, the following statement deletes any file named "hello" that has an extension of exactly one character.

```
Del hello.?
```

The regular expression language provides many flexible metacharacters—far more than the DOS command line. For example, \s represents any whitespace character (such as a space or Tab). \d represents any digit. Thus, the following expression would match any string that starts with the numbers 333, followed by a single whitespace character and any three numbers. Valid matches include 333 333, 333 945, but not 334 333 or 3334 945.

```
333\s\d\d\d
```

Part of the reason that regular expressions are confusing to new users is because they use special metacharacters that are more than one character long. In the previous example, \s represents a single character, as does \d, even though they both occupy two characters in the expression.

You can use the plus sign to represent a repeated character. For example 5+7 means "any number of 5 characters, followed by a single 7." The number 57 would match, as would 555557. You can also use the brackets to group together a subexpression. For example, (52)+7 would find match any string that starts with a sequence of 52. Matches includes 527, 52527, 52552527, and so on.

You can also delimit a range of characters using square brackets. [a-f] would match any single character from "a" to "f" (lowercase only). The following expression would match any word that starts with a letter from "a" to "f", contains one or more "word" characters (letters), and ends with "ing"—possible matches include acting and developing.

```
[a-f]\w+ing
```

The following is a more useful regular expression that can match any e-mail address by verifying that it contains the @ symbol. The dot is a metacharacter used to indicate any character except newline. Some invalid e-mail addresses would still be allowed, however, including those that contain spaces, and the regular expression doesn't verify that a dot (.) is present. We'll introduce a better example a little later.

```
.+@.+
```

Finding a Regular Expression

Clearly, to pick the perfect regular expression may require some testing. In fact, there are numerous reference materials (on the Internet and in paper form) that include useful regular expressions for validating common values such as postal codes. To experiment on your own, you can use the simple RegularExpressionTest page included with the online samples, which is shown in Figure 9-10. It allows you to set a regular expression that will be used to validate a control. Then you can try typing in some sample values, and see if the regular expression validator succeeds or fails.

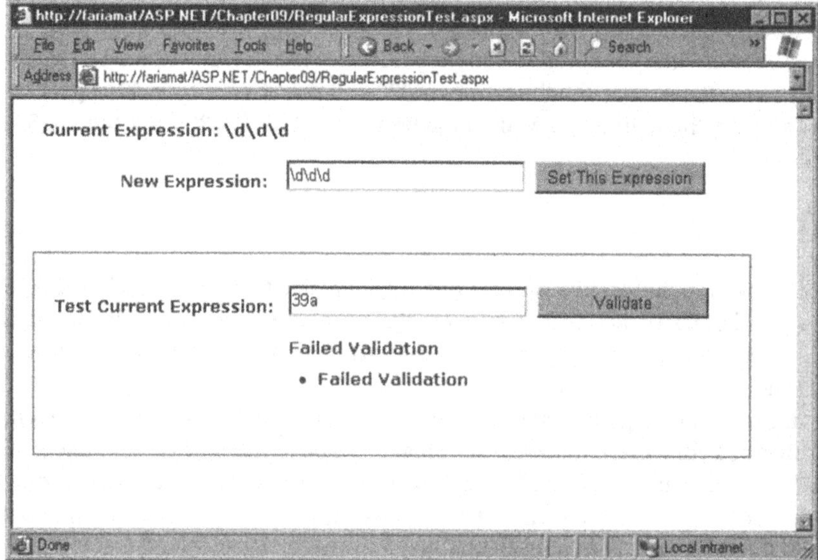

Figure 9-10. A regular expression test page

The code is quite simple. The Set This Expression button assigns a new regular expression to the RegularExpressionValidator control (using whatever text you have typed). The Validation button simply triggers a postback, which causes ASP.NET to perform validation automatically. If an error message appears, validation has failed. Otherwise, it's successful.

```
Public Class RegularExpressionTest
  Inherits Page

    Protected txtExpression As TextBox
    Protected txtValidate As TextBox
    Protected lblExpression As Label
    Protected WithEvents cmdSetExpression As Button
    Protected WithEvents cmdValidate As Button
    Protected TestValidator As RegularExpressionValidator
    Protected ValidationSummary1 As ValidationSummary
```

```
    Private Sub cmdSetExpression_Click(sender As Object, _
      e As EventArgs) Handles cmdSetExpression.Click
        TestValidator.ValidationExpression = txtExpression.Text
        lblExpression.Text = "Current Expression: "
        lblExpression.Text &= txtExpression.Text
    End Sub

End Class
```

Table 9-7 shows some of the fundamental regular expression building blocks. If you need to match a literal character with the same name as a special character, you generally precede it with a \ character. For example *hello* matches the text *hello* in a string, because the special asterisk (*) character is preceded by a slash (\).

Table 9-7. Regular Expression Characters

Character	Description
*	Zero or more occurrences of the previous character or subexpression. For example, 7*8 matches 7778 or just 8.
+	One or more occurrences of the previous character or subexpression. For example, 7+8 matches 7778 but not 8.
( )	Groups a subexpression that will be treated as a single element. For example, (78)+ matches 78 and 787878.
|	Either of two matches. For example, 8|6 matches 8 or 6.
[ ]	Matches one character in a range of valid characters. For example, [A-C] matches A, B, or C.
[^]	Matches a character that isn't in the given range. For example, [^A-B] matches any character except A and B.
.	Any character except newline. For example, .here matches where and there.
\s	Any whitespace character (such as a Tab or space).
\S	Any nonwhitespace character (such as a Tab or space).
\d	Any digit character.
\D	Any character that is not a digit.
\w	Any "word" character (letter, number, or underscore).

A few of common (and useful) regular expressions are shown in Table 9-8.

Table 9-8. Commonly Used Regular Expressions

Content	Regular Expression	Description
Email address*	\S+@\S+\.\S+	Check for an ampersand (@), dot (.), and only allow nonwhitespace characters.
Password	\w+	Any sequence of word characters (letter, space, or underscore).
Specific length password	\w{4,10}	A password that must be at least four characters long, but no longer than ten characters.
Advanced password	[a-zA-Z]\w{3,9}	As with the specific length password, this regular expression will allow four to ten total characters. The twist is that the first character must fall in the range of a–z or A–Z (that is to say it must start with a letter).
Another advanced password	[a-zA-Z]\w*\d+\w*	This password starts with a letter character, followed by zero or more word characters, a digit, and then zero or more word characters. In short, it forces a password to contain a number somewhere inside it. You could use a similar pattern to require two numbers or any other special character.
Limited-length field	\S{4,10}	Like the password example, this allows four to ten characters, but it allows special characters (asterisks, ampersands, and so on).
Social Security number	\d{3}-\d{2}-\d{4}	A sequence of three, two, then four digits, with each group separated by a dash. A similar pattern could be used when requiring a phone number.

* There are many different ways to validate e-mail addresses, with regular expressions of varying complexity. See `http://www.4guysfromrolla.com/webtech/validateemail.shtml` for a discussion of the subject and numerous examples.

Some logic is much more difficult to model in a regular expression. An example is the Luhn algorithm, which verifies credit card numbers by first doubling every second digit, adding these doubled digits together, and then dividing the sum by ten. The number is valid (although not necessarily connected to a real account) if the final result is zero. To use the Luhn algorithm, you need a CustomValidator control that runs this logic on the supplied value.

A Validated Customer Form

To end our discussion, we'll consider a full-fledged web form that combines a variety of different pieces of information that might be needed to add a user record (for example, an e-commerce site shopper or a content site subscriber). This form is shown in Figure 9-11.

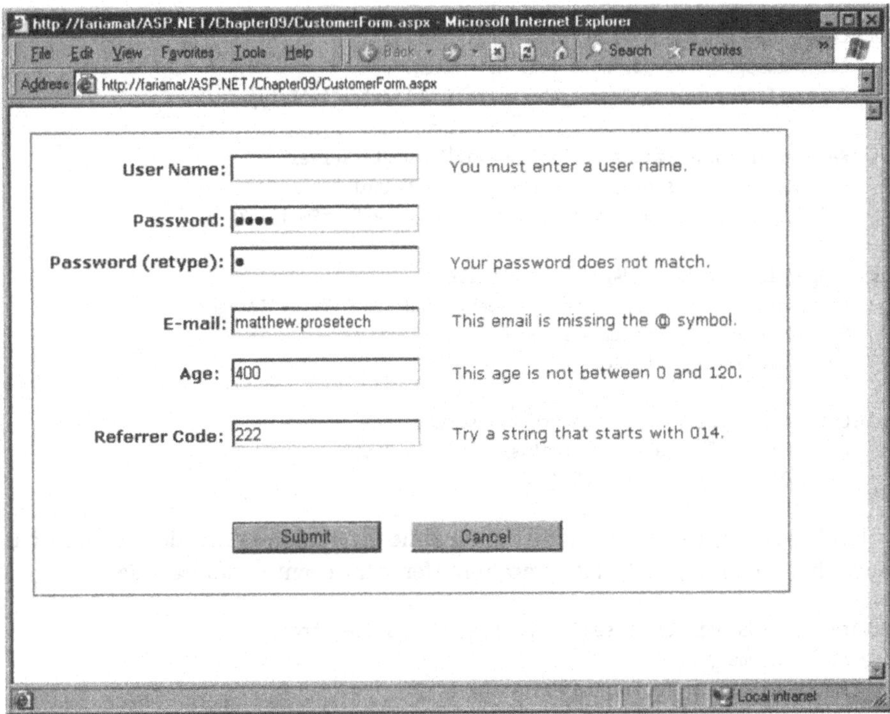

http://fariamat/ASP.NET/Chapter09/CustomerForm.aspx - Microsoft Internet Explorer

File Edit View Favorites Tools Help

Address http://fariamat/ASP.NET/Chapter09/CustomerForm.aspx

User Name: [ ] You must enter a user name.

Password: [••••]

Password (retype): [•] Your password does not match.

E-mail: [matthew.prosetech] This email is missing the @ symbol.

Age: [400] This age is not between 0 and 120.

Referrer Code: [222] Try a string that starts with 014.

[Submit] [Cancel]

Local intranet

Figure 9-11. A sample customer form

There are several types of validation being performed on the customer form:

- A RequiredFieldValidator is used for the user name and the password.
- A CompareValidator ensures that the two versions of the masked password match.

- A RegularExpressionValidator checks that the e-mail address contains an @ symbol.
- A RangeValidator ensures the age is a number from 0 to 120.
- A CustomValidator performs a special validation on the server of a "referrer code." This code verifies that the first three characters make up a number that is divisible by 7.

The tags for the validator controls are as follows:

```
<asp:RequiredFieldValidator id="vldUserName" runat="server"
     ErrorMessage="You must enter a user name."
     ControlToValidate="txtUserName" />

<asp:RequiredFieldValidator id="vldPassword" runat="server"
     ErrorMessage="You must enter a password."
     ControlToValidate="txtPassword" />

<asp:CompareValidator id="vldRetype" runat="server"
     ErrorMessage="Your password does not match."
     ControlToCompare="txtPassword" ControlToValidate="txtRetype" />

<asp:RegularExpressionValidator id="vldEmail" runat="server"
     ErrorMessage="This email is missing the @ symbol."
     ValidationExpression=".+@.+" ControlToValidate="txtEmail" />

<asp:RangeValidator id="vldAge" runat="server"
     ErrorMessage="This age is not between 0 and 120." Type="Integer"
     MaximumValue="120" MinimumValue="0"
     ControlToValidate="txtAge" />

<asp:CustomValidator id="vldCode" runat="server"
     ErrorMessage="Try a string that starts with 014."
     ControlToValidate="txtCode" />
```

The form provides two validation buttons, one that requires validation and one that allows the user to cancel the task gracefully. Here's the event-handling code:

```
Private Sub cmdSubmit_Click(sender As Object, e As EventArgs) _
  Handles cmdSubmit.Click
    If Page.IsValid = False Then Exit Sub
    lblMessage.Text = "This is a valid form."
End Sub

Private Sub cmdCancel_Click(sender As Object, e As EventArgs) _
  Handles cmdCancel.Click
    lblMessage.Text = "No attempt was made to validate this form."
End Sub
```

The only form-level code that is required for validation is the custom validation code. The validation takes place in the event handler for the CustomValidator.ServerValidate event. This method receives the value it needs to validate (e.Value) and sets the result of the validation to True or False (e.IsValid).

```
Private Sub vldCode_ServerValidate(source As Object, _
  e As ServerValidateEventArgs) Handles vldCode.ServerValidate
    ' Check if the first three digits are divisible by seven.
    If Val(Left(e.Value, 3)) Mod 7 = 0 Then
        e.IsValid = True
    Else
        e.IsValid = False
    End If
End Sub
```

TIP In some cases, you might be able to replace custom validation with a particularly ingenious use of a regular expression. However, custom validation can be used to ensure that validation code is only executed at the server. That prevents users from seeing your regular expression template (in the rendered JavaScript code) and using it to determine how they can outwit your validation routine. For example, a user may not have a valid credit card number, but if they know the algorithm you use to test credit card numbers, they can create a false one more easily.

You'll notice that this validation isn't performed until the page is posted back. That means that if you enable the client script code (the default), dynamic messages will appear informing the user when the other values are incorrect, but they will not indicate any problem with the referral code until the page is posted back.

This isn't really a problem, but if it troubles you, use the CustomValidator's ClientValidationFunction property. First, add a client-side JavaScript or VBScript validation function to the .aspx portion of the web page (ideally, it will be JavaScript, for compatibility with browsers other than Internet Explorer). You can't use ASP.NET code, only code that will be recognized by the client browser.

Your JavaScript function will accept two parameters (in true .NET style), which identify the source of the event and the additional validation parameters. In fact, the client-side event is modeled on the .NET ServerValidate event. Just as you did in the ServerValidate event handler, in the client validation function you retrieve the value to validate from the Value property of the event argument object. You then see the IsValid property to indicate whether validation succeeds or fails.

Here's the client-side equivalent for the code in the ServerValidate event handler. You'll notice that the JavaScript code resembles C# superficially.

```
<script language="JavaScript">
<!--
function MyCustomValidation(objSource, objArgs)
{
    // Get value.
    var number = objArgs.Value;

    // Check value and return result.
    number = number.substr(0, 3);
    if (number % 7 == 0)
    {
        objArgs.IsValid = true;
        return;
    }
    else
    {
        objArgs.IsValid = false;
        return;
    }
}
// -->
</script>
```

Once you've added the function, set the ClientValidationFunction property of the CustomValidator control to the name of the function. You can add this information manually, or by using the Properties window in Visual Studio .NET.

```
<asp:CustomValidator id="vldCode" runat="server"
     ErrorMessage="Try a string that starts with 014."
     ControlToValidate="txtCode"
     ClientValidationFunction="MyCustomValidation" />
```

ASP.NET will now call this function on your behalf when it's required.

TIP Even when you use client-side validation, you should still include the ServerValidate event handler, both to provide server-side validation for clients that don't support the required JavaScript and DHTML features, and to prevent clients from circumventing your validation by modifying the HTML page they receive.

You Can Validate List Controls

The examples in this chapter have concentrated exclusively on validating text entry, which is the most common requirement in a web application. While you can't validate RadioButton or CheckBox controls, you can validate most single-select list controls.

When validating a list control, the value that is being validated is the Value property of the selected ListItem object. Remember, the Value property is the special hidden information attribute that can be added to every list item. If you don't use it, you can't validate the control (validating the text of the selection isn't a supported option).

Other Rich Controls

One of the best features of ASP.NET's new control model is that other developers can create their own rich controls, which can then be incorporated into any ASP.NET application. You'll get a taste of this in Chapter 23, when you learn to create your own controls. Even without this knowledge, however, you can already start to use some of these advanced third-party controls. These controls provide features unlike any HTML element—including advanced grids, charting tools, and tree views.

ASP.NET custom controls act like web controls in every sense. Your web page interacts with the appropriate control object, and the final output is rendered automatically every time the page is sent to the client as HTML. That means the controls only need to be installed on your server, and any client can benefit from them. To access a custom control, you generally need to copy the assembly DLL to your application's bin directory or add a reference to it using Visual Studio .NET. You can then import the namespace and even add the control to the Visual Studio .NET toolbox (a process demonstrated in the next section with the Internet Explorer controls). You may even find that some controls support data binding and templates, and provide specialized designers that let you customize them from the development environment.

The Internet contains many hubs for control sharing. One such location is Microsoft's own `http://www.asp.net`, which provides a control gallery where developers can submit their own ASP.NET web controls (see Figure 9-12). Some of these controls are free (at least in a limited version), while others require a purchase.

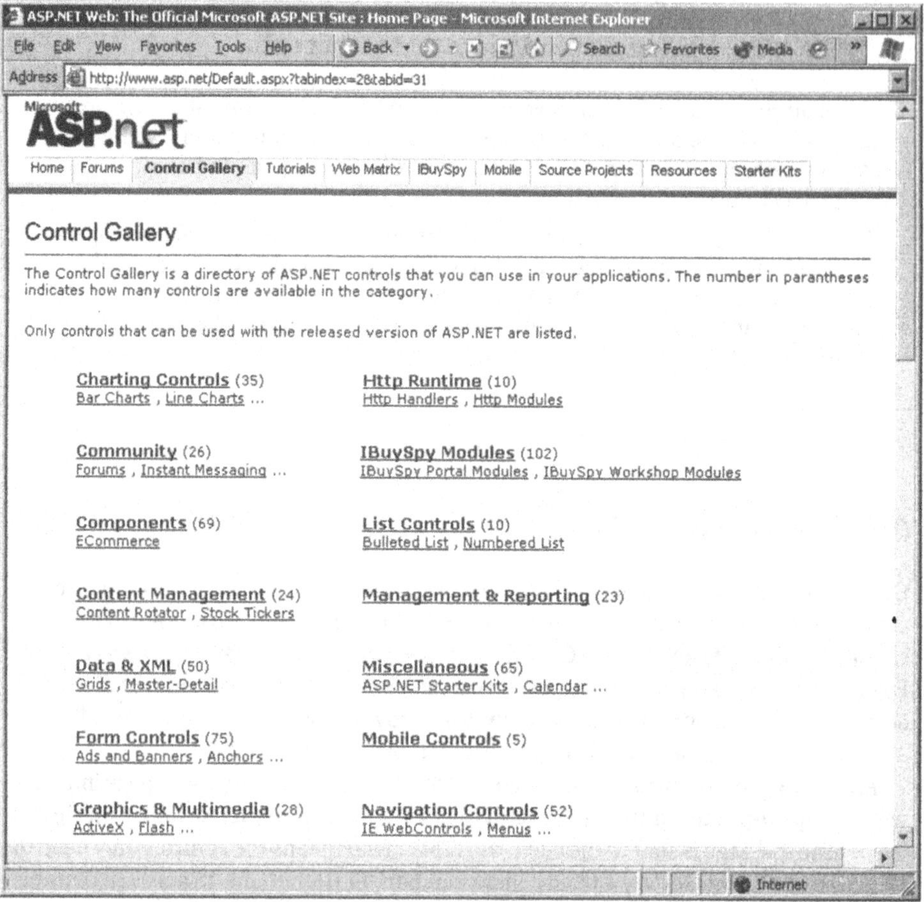

Figure 9-12. The `http://www.asp.net` *control gallery*

For example, one omission in the set of ASP.NET web controls is a menu control. On the `http://www.asp.net/ControlGallery` page you'll find no less than 19 menu controls (at the time of this writing), including the freely downloadable RadMenu from Telerik and SlideMenu from obout.

The Microsoft Internet Explorer Controls

Microsoft's Internet Explorer team has developed its own toolkit of controls for the ASP.NET platform. The Internet Explorer controls correspond to a few standards seen in the Windows world, including the following:

- A toolbar with a collection of graphical buttons.
- A TreeView that displays a hierarchy of items (as used in Windows Explorer to show directories).

- MultiPage and TabStrip controls, which are often used together to provide a set of tabbed "pages." The user can display a different set of controls (contained in one page in a MultiPage) by clicking a different button on the TabStrip.

The Internet Explorer controls can send HTML output for any current browser, but they shine when used with Internet Explorer 5.5 or later, where they use special DHTML code automatically to create a more responsive and dynamic user interface. You can download the Internet Explorer controls from `http://msdn.microsoft.com/downloads/samples/internet/ASP_DOT_NET_ServerControls/WebControls`. You can see the Internet Explorer Web control documentation at `http://msdn.microsoft.com/workshop/WebControls/webcontrols_entry.asp`.

The Internet Explorer web controls include the C# source code for all controls. To use the controls, you must first run the build.bat batch file in the install directory (typically c:\Program Files\IE Web Controls). This compiles an assembly named Microsoft.Web.UI.WebControls.dll in the build subdirectory of the install directory. The easiest way to use this assembly is to add the Internet Explorer controls to the Visual Studio .NET toolbox. To do so, right-click the toolbox and select Add/Remove Items (or Customize Toolbox in Visual Studio .NET 2002). Select the .NET Framework Components tab, click Browse, and select the Microsoft.Web.UI.WebControls.dll assembly from the appropriate directory. The controls will be selected automatically, as shown in Figure 9-13. Click OK to add them to the toolbox.

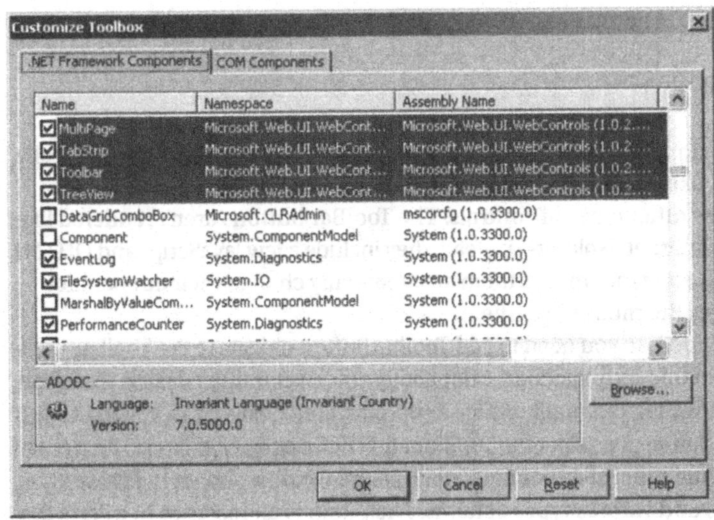

Figure 9-13. Adding the Internet Explorer controls to the toolbox

Now, you can use the web controls in any project you create with Visual Studio .NET. When you drop them onto a web page, the required assembly will be referenced automatically and copied to the \bin directory of your web application. The following directive will be added to the web page, indicating that controls that start with the prefix iewc are in the Microsoft.Web.UI.WebControls namespace, which is found in the Microsoft.Web.UI.WebControls.dll assembly.

```
<%@ Register TagPrefix="iewc" Namespace="Microsoft.Web.UI.WebControls"
    Assembly="Microsoft.Web.UI.WebControls" %>
```

To simplify your code, you should also import this namespace in your code-behind file:

```
Imports Microsoft.Web.UI.WebControls
```

For more information about how ASP.NET works with custom controls and assemblies, you can refer to the discussion in Chapter 23. The next few sections demonstrate the individual Internet Explorer controls. All of the test pages you'll see are included with the online code.

NOTE The Internet Explorer controls are not officially supported by Microsoft. This means there is no guarantee that these controls will work with every release of the .NET Framework (although they do work with both 1.0 and 1.1), or that these controls won't be discontinued (possibly with some of the functionality being integrated into a future version of ASP.NET).

The Toolbar

The Toolbar is a column or row of controls that appear on a rectangular bar. Typically, these controls look like buttons, although they can include text boxes, labels, drop-down lists, and a few other types of controls. The ToolBar buttons aren't rendered like ordinary buttons in Internet Explorer—instead, they include a few JavaScript and DHTML niceties, like a hover style that makes them automatically change their appearance when the user moves the mouse over them.

To configure the Toolbar, you need to add ToolbarButton objects to the Toolbar.Items property. You can do this through code, but usually you'll set it up at design time. You can modify the control tag manually, or use a sophisticated designer in Visual Studio .NET. To use the designer, just select the Toolbar and click on the ellipsis (...) next to the Items property in the Properties window. You'll see the window shown in Figure 9-14, which allows you to add various types of items. Each item is an instance of a class that derives from ToolbarItem. With a ToolbarButton you can set the button text (through the Text property) and add a picture (through the ImageUrl property).

You can modify all the customary web control properties for the Toolbar, including the font, color, and size. In addition, you can set the Toolbar.Orientation property to Vertical or Horizontal. Figure 9-15 shows an example of a vertical toolbar with four buttons. Whenever a button is clicked, a nearby label is updated with the corresponding text.

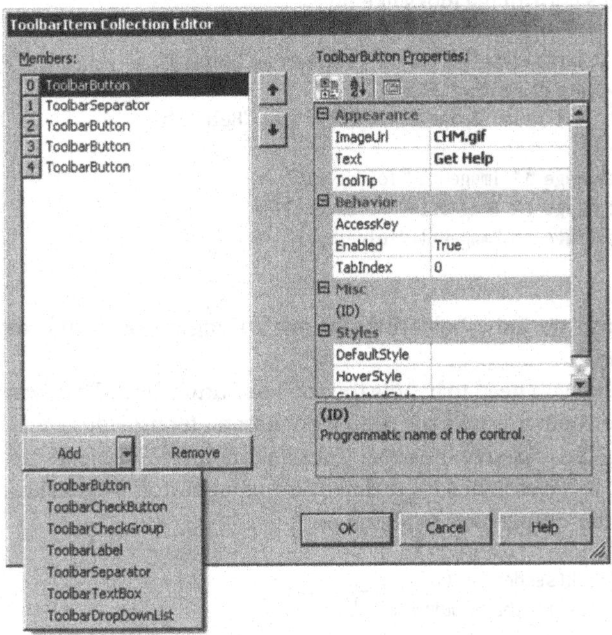

Figure 9-14. Adding Toolbar items through the designer

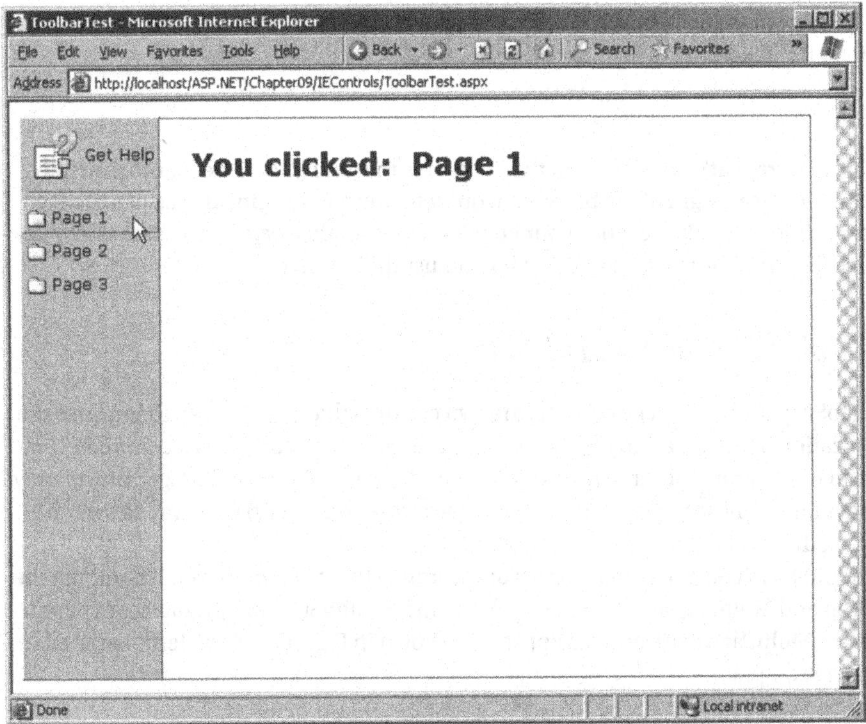

Figure 9-15. A web page with a Toolbar

In the .aspx, the <Toolbar> control tag looks like this:

```
<iewc:Toolbar id="Toolbar1" Orientation="Vertical" Font-Names="Verdana"
 Font-Size="X-Small" Height="440px" Width="114px">
    <iewc:ToolbarButton Text="Get Help" ImageUrl="CHM.gif" ID="Help" />
    <iewc:ToolbarSeparator />
    <iewc:ToolbarButton Text="Page 1" ImageUrl="folder.gif" />
    <iewc:ToolbarButton Text="Page 2" ImageUrl="folder.gif" />
    <iewc:ToolbarButton Text="Page 3" ImageUrl="folder.gif" />
</iewc:Toolbar>
```

Each button is added using a nested <ToolbarButton> tag. The tag attributes indicate the appropriate text and image.

To react to the button clicks, you need to handle the Toolbar.ButtonClick. This event fires when *any* button in the Toolbar is clicked. The sender parameter provides a reference to the ToolbarButton that triggered the event. You can examine this object's Text property (or its ID property, if you assigned it), to determine what button was clicked.

Here's the code used for the simple page in Figure 9-15:

```
Private Sub Toolbar1_ButtonClick(sender As Object, _
  e As System.EventArgs) Handles Toolbar1.ButtonClick

    Dim ClickedButton As ToolbarButton = CType(sender, ToolbarButton)
    If ClickedButton.ID = "Help" Then
        lblInfo.Text = "You clicked the Help button."
    Else
        lblInfo.Text = "You clicked: " & ClickedButton.Text
    End If

End Sub
```

One feature that's missing from the Toolbar is the ability to make it automatically take the width or height of the browser in order to present the appearance of a "docked" control. Unfortunately, because your code executes on the server, there's no way you can retrieve this information and use it to adjust the Toolbar.

The TabStrip and MultiPage

The TabStrip and MultiPage controls are two controls that you can use to improve the organization of information on a web page. The MultiPage control is a container that you can use to group other controls into separate "pages." The MultiPage control only displays one of these pages at a time, so it gives you a quick and easy way to switch between different content on a web page.

The TabStrip control displays a row or column of buttons. Often, you'll combine the TabStrip and MultiPage controls on a page, using the TabStrip to navigate from page to page in a MultiPage control. This approach (shown in Figure 9-16) is demonstrated in the next example.

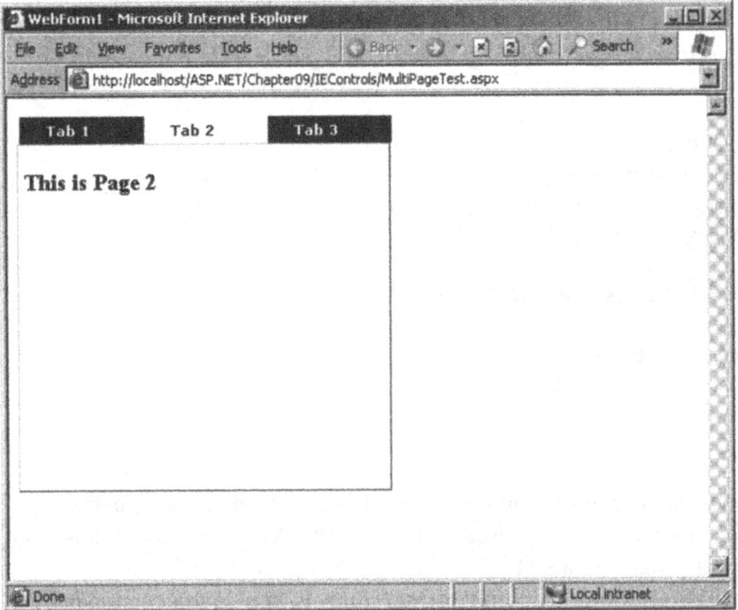

Figure 9-16. A linked TabStrip and MultiPage

The first step is to add the TabStrip control to the web page. Each page in the TabStrip is represented by a separate Tab object in the TabStrip.Items collection. You can add tabs to this collection through code, or you can set it up at design time. In Visual Studio .NET, simply click the ellipsis (...) next to the Items property to open a designer that allows you to add, remove, rearrange, and configure tabs. The important property of each Tab object is Text, which contains the display caption.

TIP Many of the Internet Explorer controls include options for defining styles to customize their appearance. For example, you can alter the style attributes in the TabDefaultStyle, TabSelectedStyle, and TabHoverStyle to change how the TabStrip is rendered in HTML. For more information, refer to the Internet Explorer control reference.

Once you've configured the TabStrip control, you can add and configure the MultiPage control. Unfortunately, the MultiPage control doesn't allow you to drag-and-drop controls onto its pages at design time using Visual Studio .NET. Instead, you need to modify the MultiPage tags in the .aspx file. In Visual Studio .NET, you would do this by switching to HTML view in the web page designer. Keep in mind that if you wanted to handle the events of a control you add in HTML view, you'll also need to declare the control in the code-behind class, because Visual Studio .NET will not do this automatically.

Each page in a MultiPage is defined with a <PageView> tag, and each <PageView> can contain any other HTML content or ASP.NET controls. The following example defines three pages (one for each TabStrip button), and places different content on each page:

```
<iewc:MultiPage id="MultiPage1" >
    <iewc:PageView id="page1">
        <br><h3> This is Page 1</h3>
     </iewc:PageView>
    <iewc:PageView id="page2">
        <br><h3> This is Page 2</h3>
    </iewc:PageView>
    <iewc:PageView id="page3">
        <br><h3> This is Page 3</h3>
    </iewc:PageView>
</iewc:MultiPage>
```

The currently visible page is determined by the SelectedIndex property of the MultiPage control. The number 0 represents the first page. You can set the visible page in the control tag, or programmatically.

The final step in this example is to link the two controls. You do this manually by handling the TabStrip1.SelectedIndexChanged event, but the TabStrip provides an easier option. All you need to do is set the TabStrip.TargetID property to the ID of the corresponding MultiPage control. Once you've established this link, navigation will take place automatically. Every time the user clicks a new TabStrip button, the page will post back, and the MultiPage.SelectedIndex property will be modified accordingly.

The TreeView

The TreeView is a hierarchical tree of nodes. It mimics the behavior of the well-known Windows TreeView, which is found everywhere from Windows Explorer to IIS Manager. The TreeView even maintains its state, remembering what levels are expanded and which ones are collapsed when the page is posted back to the server.

Each node in the TreeView is represented by a TreeNode object, and can include text and an image. In order to use images, you need to define a named TreeView style that indicates the picture you want to use. The following control declaration defines two types: one named Folder that shows a directory folder icon, and one named Page that shows a blank web page icon.

```
<iewc:TreeView id="TreeView1" runat="server" >
    <iewc:TreeNodeType Type="Folder" ImageUrl="folder.gif" />
    <iewc:TreeNodeType Type="Page" ImageUrl="page.gif" />
</iewc:TreeView>
```

Now you can add nodes to the TreeView and optionally use one of these styles. As with the TabStrip and MultiPage controls, you can add nodes to the TreeView at design time using the Visual Studio .NET designer or by typing the tag into the .aspx file by hand. However, it's often more useful to fill the TreeView programmatically in the Page.Load event handler. You might even want to read information from a database (as described in Chapter 14) and use that to populate the TreeView.

To add a node, you use the Add() method of the node collection. For example, the following code shows how to add a single root-level node to the TreeView. In this example, the node is titled "My Site" and uses the image from the Folder style.

```
Dim Node As New TreeNode()
Node.Text = "My Site"
Node.Type = "Folder"
TreeView1.Nodes.Add(Node)
```

The TreeView can contain as many levels of nodes as you need. To add a subnode, you need to use the Add() method of the parent's node collection. For example, the following code snippet adds the same "My Site" node, places two other nodes under this node, and then expands the TreeView so that all nodes will be visible when the page is first displayed:

```
Dim SiteNode As New TreeNode()
SiteNode.Text = "My Site"
SiteNode.Type = "Folder"
TreeView1.Nodes.Add(SiteNode)

Dim PageNode As New TreeNode()
PageNode.Text = "Home Page"
PageNode.Type = "Page"
SiteNode.Nodes.Add(PageNode)

PageNode = New TreeNode()
PageNode.Text = "Search Page"
PageNode.Type = "Page"
SiteNode.Nodes.Add(PageNode)

' Make sure the tree is expanded.
SiteNode.Expanded = True
```

Because adding a new node takes four lines of code, it's easiest to create a private helper method that can handle the job. The following code uses this approach to add a larger catalog of pages to the TreeView:

```
Private Sub Page_Load(sender As Object, e As EventArgs) _

  Handles MyBase.Load
    If Not Me.IsPostBack
        Dim RootNode As TreeNode
        RootNode = AddNode("default.aspx", "My Site", "Folder", _
          TreeView1.Nodes)
```

```
        AddNode("home.aspx", "Home Page", "Page", RootNode.Nodes)
        AddNode("search.aspx", "Search Page", "Page", RootNode.Nodes)
        AddNode("contact.aspx", "Contact Page", "Page", RootNode.Nodes)
        AddNode("info.aspx", "Contact Page", "Page", RootNode.Nodes)
        RootNode.Expanded = True

        RootNode = AddNode("links.aspx", "Links", "Folder", _
          TreeView1.Nodes)
        AddNode("http://www.nytimes.com", "New York Times", "Page",  _
          RootNode.Nodes)
        AddNode("http://www.theonion.com", "The Onion", "Page", _
          RootNode.Nodes)
        AddNode("http://www.zdnet.com", "ZDNet", "Page", RootNode.Nodes)
        AddNode("http://www.google.com", "Google", "Page", _
          RootNode.Nodes)
        RootNode.Expanded = True
    End If
End Sub

Private Function AddNode(id As String, text As String, _
  type As String, nodeCollection As TreeNodeCollection) As TreeNode
    Dim Node As New TreeNode()
    Node.Text = text
    Node.Type = type
    Node.ID = id
    nodeCollection.Add(Node)
    Return Node
End Function
```

The result is shown in Figure 9-17.

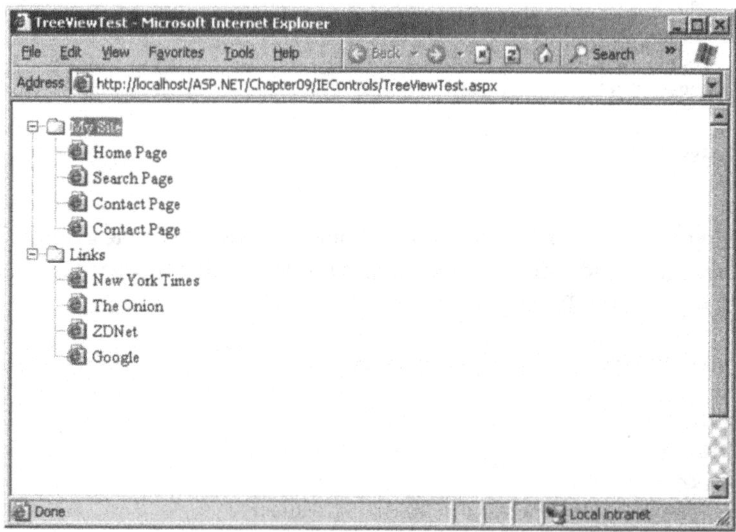

Figure 9-17. A sample TreeView

You can read the currently selected node from the TreeView at any time using the SelectedNodeIndex property. To get the TreeNode object based on the index number, use the helper method TreeView.GetNodeFromIndex(). The TreeView control also provides several events, including Collapse, Expand, and SelectedIndexChanged.

You'll notice in the previous example that each node was given a unique ID that corresponds to a relative web page or absolute URL. You can use this information as the basis for a simple page navigation system. Essentially, it works like this:

- You set the TreeView to post back every time a node is selected by setting its AutoPostBack property to True.
- You handle the TreeView.SelectedIndexChanged event. You can determine the new node in this event handler using the e.NewNode index and the TreeView.GetNodeFromIndex()method.
- Once you have the TreeNode that was selected, you can retrieve the ID property, which corresponds to the new selected page.
- Use the Response.Redirect() to navigate to the new page.

Here's the event-handling code you need to implement this approach:

```
Private Sub TreeView1_SelectedIndexChange(sender As Object, _
  e As TreeViewSelectEventArgs) Handles TreeView1.SelectedIndexChange

    Dim SelectedNode As TreeNode = TreeView1.GetNodeFromIndex(e.NewNode)
    Response.Redirect(SelectedNode.ID)

End Sub
```

Practical Site Navigation

There's still a fair bit you could do to make the previous example into a more realistic navigation control. First of all, instead of hard-coding the page names, you would probably want to retrieve them from a database, as explained in Chapter 14. This allows you to update the website structure without needing to recompile your web page code.

In addition, you'll probably want to keep the TreeView visible, at least while the user is browsing through the links on the current site. To accomplish this, you'll need to use *frames*. Frames allow you to display more than one HTML document in the same browser window. In the case of a site with a navigational menu, you could split the page vertically into two frames. The frame on the left would contain the TreeView, while the frame on the right would show the selected content. For more information about frames, refer to the tutorial `http://www.w3schools.com/html/html_frames.asp` or the FAQ at `http://www.htmlhelp.com/faq/html/frames.html`. Frames are completely independent of ASP.NET. They are simply a part of the HTML standard.

The online samples include a page that uses frames with the TreeView. But be warned: Because frames only exist on the client side, it's a little more work to manipulate them in your ASP.NET code. In the TreeView example, you'll need to send a few lines of JavaScript code to the browser to force the other frame to navigate to a new page. For a simpler alternative, consider using a control that renders HTML links directly, like one of the custom menus on `http://www.asp.net`. Or, you can create a menu with a user control, as demonstrated in the IBuySpy e-commerce store in Chapter 26.

The Last Word

One of the most impressive features of ASP.NET is its customizability and extensibility. This chapter showed you how web controls can go far beyond the limitations of ordinary HTML elements, but it only scratched the surface of third-party controls. For more information about the Internet Explorer web controls and other third-party creations, take your search online to the .NET community with sites like `http://www.asp.net`.

CHAPTER 10

State Management

THE MOST SIGNIFICANT DIFFERENCE between programming for the Internet and programming for the desktop is state management. In a traditional Windows application, state is managed automatically and transparently. Memory is plentiful, and always available. In a web application, it's a different story. Thousands of users might simultaneously run the same application on the same computer (the web server), each one communicating over the stateless HTTP protocol of the Internet. These conditions make it impossible to program a web application like a traditional Windows program.

Understanding these state limitations is the key to creating efficient, robust web applications. In this chapter you'll learn why state is no trivial issue in the world of Internet programming, and you'll see how you can use ASP.NET's state management features to store and manage information carefully and consistently. You'll explore different state options, including view state, session state, and custom cookies, and consider how to transfer information from page to page using the query string.

The Problem of State

In a traditional Windows program, users interact with a continuously running application. A portion of memory on the desktop computer is allocated to store the current set of working information.

In a web application, the story is quite a bit different. A professional ASP.NET site might look like a continuously running application, but it's really just a clever illusion. Web applications use a highly efficient disconnected access pattern. In a typical web request, the client connects to the web server and requests a page. When the page is delivered, the connection is severed and the web server abandons any information it has about the client. By the time the user receives a page, the "application" has already stopped running.

Because clients only need to be connected for a few seconds, a web server can handle thousands of requests without a performance hit. However, if you need to retain information between user actions (and you almost always do), you need to take additional steps.

Is ASP.NET State Management Like ASP?

If you're a seasoned ASP programmer, most of the content in this chapter will sound familiar. State management in ASP.NET is refined, not revolutionized. You'll see some changes, such as a new object model (from the .NET class library) and view state, which is an entirely new option for storing data. You'll also learn advanced session state configuration options that weren't available in any previous version of ASP. These options allow you to persist state to a database or another process, thus making it shareable between servers in a web farm and durable between server restarts. On the whole, however, many of the same state considerations that are found in ASP applications apply to ASP.NET.

View State

In the previous chapters, you learned how ASP.NET controls use view state to remember their state. View state information is maintained in a hidden field and automatically sent back to the server with every postback. However, view state isn't limited to server controls. Your web page code can add additional bits of information directly to the view state collection of the containing page, and retrieve it later after the page is posted back. The type of information you can store includes simple data types and your own custom objects.

The view state collection is provided through the ViewState property of the page. This property is an instance of the StateBag collection class. To add and remove items in this class, you use a dictionary-based syntax, where every item has a unique string name.

For example, consider this code:

```
' The Me keyword refers to the current Page object.
Me.ViewState("Counter") = 1
```

This places the value 1 (or rather, an integer that contains the value 1) into the view state collection, and gives it the descriptive name Counter. If there is currently no item with the name Counter, a new item will be added automatically. If there is already an item indexed under the name Counter, it will be removed from the collection.

When retrieving a value, you use the key name and perform the necessary conversion. If you haven't enabled Option Strict, you may be able to perform some conversions automatically. However, it's always a better idea to handle the conversion explicitly to make your code clearer, and less prone to error. Conversions can be performed to any type using the CType() statement, as explained in Chapters 3 and 4.

Here's the code that retrieves the counter from view state:

```
Dim Counter As Integer
Counter = CType(Me.ViewState("Counter"), Integer)
```

NOTE ASP.NET provides many collections that use the exact same dictionary syntax. This includes the collections you'll use for session and application state, as well as those used for caching and cookies. You'll see several of these collections in this chapter.

A View State Example

The following example is a simple counter program that records how many times a button was clicked. Without any kind of state management, the counter will be locked perpetually at 1. With a careful use of view state, the counter works as expected.

```
Public Class SimpleCounter
  Inherits Page

    Protected lblCount As Label
    Protected WithEvents cmdIncrement As Button

    Private Sub cmdIncrement_Click(sender As Object, _
      e As EventArgs) Handles cmdIncrement.Click
        Dim Counter As Integer
        If Me.ViewState("Counter") = Nothing Then
            Counter = 1
        Else
            Counter = CType(Me.ViewState("Counter"), Integer) + 1
        End If

        Me.ViewState("Counter") = Counter
        lblCount.Text = "Counter: " & Counter.ToString()
    End Sub

End Class
```

The code checks first for a null reference before assigning to the Counter variable. This is not strictly necessary, because Visual Basic .NET will automatically convert an empty value to the number 0 in an addition statement. However, this technique *is* required for more complex objects, which may need to be specially created or have various properties set before being placed into state for the first time.

The output for this page is shown in Figure 10-1.

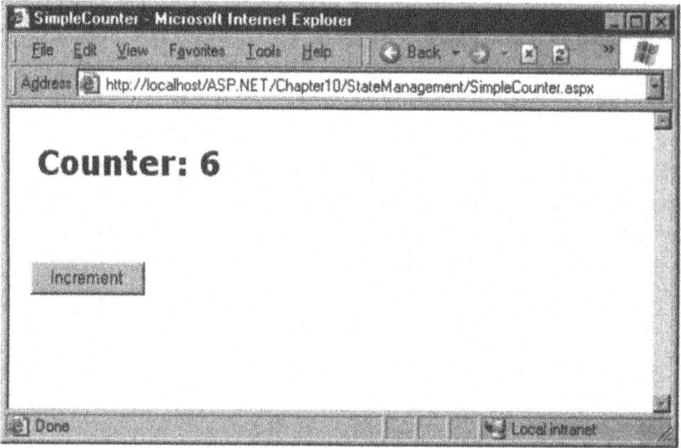

Figure 10-1. A simple view state counter

There are other ways to solve the state management problem with the simple counter example. For example, you could enable view state for the label control, and use the label control to store the counter. Every time the Increment button is clicked, you could then retrieve the current value from the label text and convert it to an integer. However, this technique isn't always appropriate. For example, you might create a program that tracks button clicks, but doesn't display them on the screen. In this case, you could still store this information in a web control, but you would have to make it hidden. That, of course, is exactly what view state does: it stores information automatically in a special hidden field in the page. Because ASP.NET handles these lower-level details for you, your code becomes more clear and concise.

View State Is Also Used When Creating Custom Controls

Every control provides a ViewState property. However, in web page code you can only access the view state for the current object. This means that when you're authoring an ASP.NET web page, you can only access the view state for your custom Page object. On the other hand, if you're creating a custom control, you can use the control's ViewState property to store any extra state information you need to maintain the control's appearance and data. The hidden view state field that you see in HTML contains the view state information for every object on the page, and it includes the information you add explicitly, and the information various controls add automatically. You'll find more information about custom controls in Chapter 23.

Making View State Secure

You probably remember from Chapter 6 that view state information is stored in a single jumbled string that looks like this:

```
<input type="hidden" name="__VIEWSTATE" value="dDw3NDg2NTI5MDg7Oz4="/>
```

As you add more information to view state, this value can become much longer. Because this value isn't formatted as clear text, many ASP.NET programmers assume that their view state data is encrypted. It isn't. Instead, the view state information is simply patched together in memory and converted to a Base64 string. A clever hacker could reverse-engineer this string and examine your view state data in a matter of seconds.

If you want to make view state more secure, you have two choices. First, you can make sure that the view state information is tamper-proof by instructing ASP.NET to use a *hash code*. You do this by adding the EnableViewStateMAC attribute to the Page directive in your .aspx file, as shown here:

```
<%@Page EnableViewStateMAC="True" %>
```

A hash code is a cryptographically strong checksum. When you set the EnableViewStateMAC, ASP.NET calculates the checksum and adds it to the view state data. When the page is posted back, ASP.NET recalculates the checksum and ensures that it matches. If a malicious user changes the view state data, ASP.NET will be able to detect the change, and it will reject the postback.

Even when you use hash codes, the view state data will still be readable. To prevent users from getting any view state information, you can enable view state *encryption*. In this case, you need to find the <machineKey> tag in the machine.config file. (Remember, the machine.config file is found in a directory like C:\[WinDir]\Microsoft.NET\[Version]\Config.) Set the validation attribute to 3DES, which stands for Triple DES encryption:

```
<configuration>
   <system.web>
      <!-- Other settings omitted. -->

      <machineKey validation="3DES" >

   </system.web>
</configuration>
```

Make sure you also set the EnableViewStateMAC attribute for the page, as described earlier. Now the view state information for the page will be completely encrypted.

When hashing or encrypting data, ASP.NET uses a special machine-specific key. Because no one else has this key, no user will be able to generate a fake hash code or decrypt encrypted view state information.

TIP Don't encrypt view state data if you don't need to. The encryption will impose a performance penalty, because the web server needs to perform the encryption and decryption with each postback. Also, the size of the view state field will increase because encrypted data is larger than raw unencrypted data, which means it will take slightly longer to transmit the page.

Retaining Member Variables

You have probably noticed that any information you set in a member variable for an ASP.NET page is automatically abandoned when the page processing is finished and the page is sent to the client. (The Counter variable in the previous code listing is an example.) Interestingly, you can work around this limitation using view state.

The basic principle is to save all member variables to view state when the Page.PreRender event occurs, and retrieve them when the Page.Load event occurs. Remember, Page.Load happens every time the page is created. In the case of a postback, the Page.Load event occurs first, followed by any other control events.

The following example uses this technique with a single user variable (named Contents). The page provides a text box and two buttons. The user can choose to save a string of text, and then restore it at a later time (see Figure 10-2). The Button.Click event handlers store and retrieve this text using the Contents member variable. These event handlers don't need to save or restore this information using view state, because the PreRender and Load event handlers perform these tasks when page processing starts and finishes.

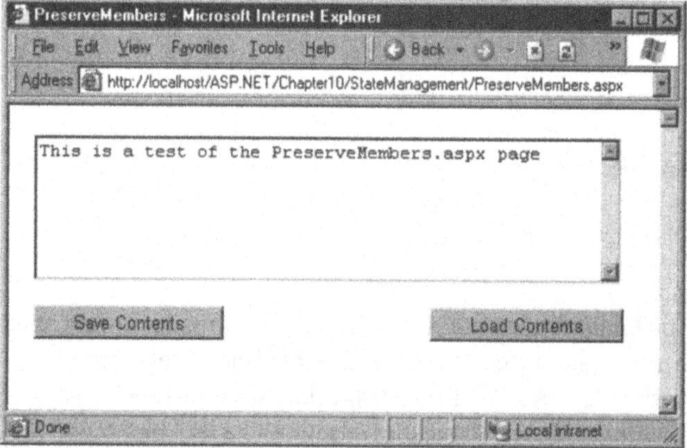

Figure 10-2. A page with state

```
Public Class PreserveMembers
  Inherits Page

    Protected txtContents As TextBox
    Protected WithEvents cmdSave As Button
    Protected WithEvents cmdLoad As Button

    ' A member variable that will be cleared with every postback.
    Private Contents As String

    Private Sub Page_Load(sender As Object, e As EventArgs) _
      Handles MyBase.Load
        If Me.IsPostBack = True Then
            ' Restore variables.
            Contents = CType(Me.ViewState("Text"), String)
        End If
    End Sub

    Private Sub Page_PreRender(sender As Object, _
      e As System.EventArgs) Handles MyBase.PreRender
        ' Persist variables.
        Me.ViewState("Text") = Contents
    End Sub

    Private Sub cmdSave_Click(sender As Object, e As EventArgs) _
      Handles cmdSave.Click
        ' Transfer contents of text box to member variable.
        Contents = txtValue.Text
        txtValue.Text = ""
    End Sub

    Private Sub cmdLoad_Click(sender As Object, e As EventArgs) _
      Handles cmdLoad.Click
        ' Restore contents of member variable to text box.
        txtValue.Text = Contents
    End Sub

End Class
```

The logic in the Load and PreRender event handlers allows the rest of your code to work more or less as it would in a desktop scenario. However, you must be careful not to store needless amounts of information when using this technique. If you store unnecessary information in view state, it will enlarge the size of the final page output, and can thus slow down page transmission times. Another disadvantage with this approach is that it hides the low-level reality that every piece of data must be explicitly saved and restored. When you hide this reality, it's more likely that you'll forget to respect it and design for it.

If you decide to use this approach to save member variables in view state, use it *exclusively*. In other words, refrain from saving some view state variables at the PreRender stage and others in control event handlers, because this is sure to confuse yourself and any other programmer who looks at your code.

TIP The previous example reacted to the Page.PreRender event, which occurs just after page processing is complete and just before the page is rendered into HTML. This is an ideal place to store any leftover information that is required. You cannot store view state information in an event handler for the Page.Unload event. Though your code will not cause an error, the information will not be stored in view state, because the final HTML page output is already rendered.

Storing Custom Objects

You can store your own objects in view state just as easily as you store numeric and string types. However, in order to store an item in view state, ASP.NET must be able to convert it into a stream of bytes so that it can be added to the hidden input field in the page. This process is called *serialization*. If your objects aren't serializable (and by default they're not), you'll receive an error message when you attempt to place them in view state.

To make your objects serializable, you need to add a special <Serializable> attribute before your class declaration. For example, here's an exceedingly simple Customer class:

```
<Serializable> _
Public Class Customer
    Public FirstName As String
    Public LastName As String

    Public Sub New(firstName As String, lastName As String)
        Me.FirstName = firstName
        Me.LastName = lastName
    End Sub
End Class
```

Because the Customer class is marked as serializable, it can be stored in view state:

```
' Store a customer in view state.
Dim Cust As New Customer("Marsala", "Simons")
Me.ViewState("CurrentCustomer") = Cust
```

Remember, when using custom objects, you'll need to cast your data when you retrieve it from view state.

```
' Retrieve a customer from view state.
Dim Cust As Customer
Cust = CType(Me.ViewState("CurrentCustomer", Customer)
```

Once you understand this principle, you'll also be able to determine what .NET objects can be placed in view state. You simply need to find the class information in the MSDN Help. If you have Visual Studio .NET installed, select Start ➤ Programs ➤ Microsoft Visual Studio .NET ➤ Microsoft Visual Studio .NET Documentation. You can find class reference information, grouped by namespace, under the Visual Studio .NET ➤ .NET Framework ➤ Reference ➤ Class Library node. Find the class you're interested in and examine the documentation. If the class declaration is preceded with the <Serializable> attribute, the object can be placed in view state. If the <Serializable> attribute isn't present, the object isn't serializable, and you won't be able to store it in view state. However, you will still be able to use other types of state management, like session state, which is described later in this chapter.

Transferring Information

One of the most significant limitations with view state is that it's tightly bound to a specific page. If the user navigates to another page, this information is lost. There are several solutions to this problem, and the best approach depends on your requirements. One common approach is to pass information using the query string. This approach is commonly found in search engines. For example, if you perform a search on the popular "Ask Jeeves" website for organic gardening, you'll be redirected to a new URL that incorporates your search parameters. Figure 10-3 shows the URL you'll see.

Figure 10-3. A URL with query string information

The query string is the portion of the URL after the question mark. In this case, it defines a single variable named ask, which contains the string "organic+gardening".

The advantage of the query string is that it's very lightweight and doesn't exert any kind of burden on the server. There are some limitations, however:

- Information is limited to simple strings, which must contain URL-legal characters.
- Information is clearly visible to the user and by anyone else who cares to eavesdrop on the Internet.
- The enterprising user might decide to modify the query string and supply new values, which your program won't expect and can't protect against.
- Many browsers impose a limit on the length of a URL (usually from 1 to 2 KB). For that reason, you can't place a large amount of information in the query string and still be assured of compatibility with most browsers.

Adding information to the query string is still a useful technique. It's particularly well suited in database applications where you present the user with a list of items that correspond to records in a database, like products. The user can then select an item and be forwarded to another page with detailed information about the selected item. One easy way to implement this design is to have the first page send the item ID to the second page. The second page then looks that item up in the database, and displays the detailed information. You'll notice this technique in e-commerce sites like Amazon.com.

To store information in the query string, you need to place it there yourself. Unfortunately, there is no collection-based way to do. Typically, this means using a special HyperLink control, or a special Response.Redirect() statement like the one shown here.

```
' Go to newpage.aspx. Submit a single query string argument
' named recordID and set to 10.
Response.Redirect("newpage.aspx?recordID=10")
```

Multiple parameters can be sent as long as they're separated with an ampersand (&).

```
' Go to newpage.aspx. Submit two query string arguments:
' recordID (10) and mode (full).
Response.Redirect("newpage.aspx?recordID=10&mode=full")
```

The receiving page has an easier time working with the query string. It can receive the values from the QueryString dictionary collection exposed by the built-in Request object.

```
Dim ID As String
ID = Request.QueryString("recordID")
```

Note that information is always retrieved as a string, which can then be converted to another simple data type. Values in the QueryString collection are indexed by the variable name.

A Query String Example

The next program presents a table of entries. When the user chooses an item by clicking on the appropriate hyperlink, the user is forwarded to a new page. This page displays the received ID number. This provides a quick and simple query string test. In a sophisticated application, you would want to combine some of the data control features that are described later in this book in the ADO.NET chapters.

The first page provides a list of items, a check box, and a submission button (see Figure 10-4).

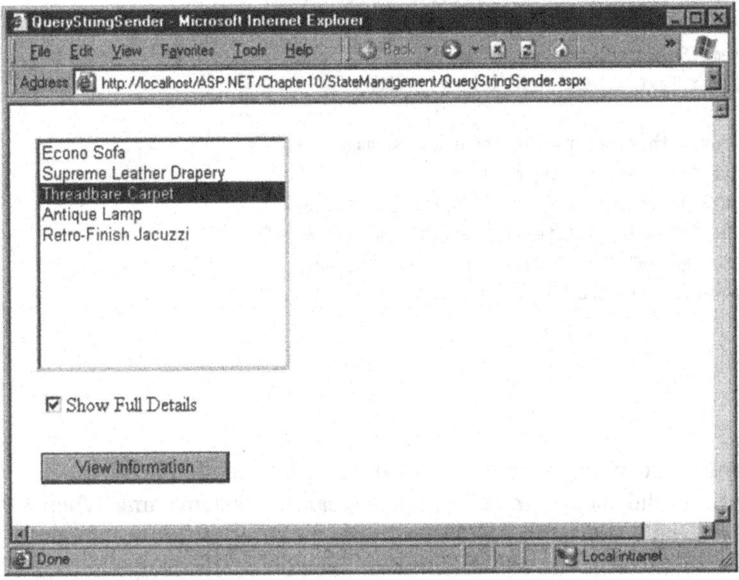

Figure 10-4. A query string sender

Here's the code for the first page:

```
Public Class QueryStringSender
  Inherits Page

    Protected lstItems As ListBox
    Protected chkDetails As CheckBox
    Protected WithEvents cmdGo As Button

    Private Sub Page_Load(sender As Object, e As EventArgs) _
      Handles MyBase.Load
        ' Add sample values.
        lstItems.Items.Add("Econo Sofa")
        lstItems.Items.Add("Supreme Leather Drapery")
        lstItems.Items.Add("Threadbare Carpet")
        lstItems.Items.Add("Antique Lamp")
        lstItems.Items.Add("Retro-Finish Jacuzzi")
    End Sub
```

```
    Private Sub cmdGo_Click(sender As Object, e As EventArgs) _
      Handles cmdGo.Click
        If lstItems.SelectedIndex = -1 Then
            lblError.Text = "You must select an item."
        Else
            ' Forward the user to the information page,
            ' with the query string data.
            Dim Url As String = "QueryStringRecipient.aspx?"
            Url &= "Item=" & lstItems.SelectedItem.Text & "&"
            Url &= "Mode=" & chkDetails.Checked.ToString()
            Response.Redirect(Url)
        End If
    End Sub

End Class
```

One interesting aspect of this example is that it places information in the query string that really isn't valid, namely the space that appears in the item name. When you run the application, you'll notice that ASP.NET encodes the string for you automatically, converting spaces to the valid %20 equivalent escape sequence. The recipient page reads the original values from the QueryString collection without any trouble. The recipient page is shown in Figure 10-5.

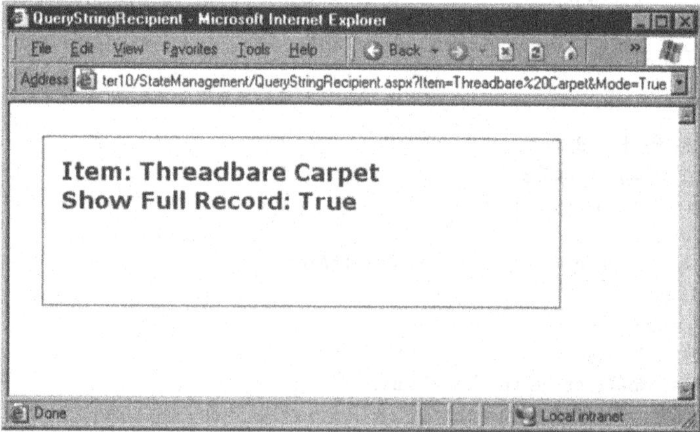

Figure 10-5. A query string recipient

```
Public Class QueryStringRecipient
  Inherits Page

    Protected lblInfo As Label

    Private Sub Page_Load(sender As Object, e As EventArgs) _
      Handles MyBase.Load
        lblInfo.Text = "Item: " & Request.QueryString("Item")
        lblInfo.Text &= "<br>Show Full Record: "
        lblInfo.Text &= Request.QueryString("Mode")
    End Sub

End Class
```

Custom Cookies

Custom cookies provide another way that you can store information for later use. Cookies are small files that are created on the client's hard drive (or, if they're temporary, in the web browser's memory). One advantage of cookies is that they work transparently without the user being aware that information needs to be stored. They also can be easily used by any page in your application, and even retained in between visits, which allows for truly long-term storage. They suffer from some of the same drawbacks that affect query strings. Namely, they're limited to simple string information, and they're easily accessible and readable if the user finds and opens the corresponding file. These factors make them a poor choice for complex or private information or large amounts of data.

Some users disable cookies on their browsers, which will cause problems for web applications that require them. For the most part, cookies are widely adopted because so many sites use them. However, they can limit your potential audience, and they aren't suited for the embedded browsers used with mobile devices. Also, a user might manually delete a cookie file that is stored on their hard drive.

A good rule of thumb is to use cookies to retain preference-related information, such as a customer's last order item or e-mail address. You can then use this information to provide a richer experience. However, you shouldn't require the use of cookies or assume that they'll always be present.

Before you can use cookies, you should import the System.Net namespace so you can easily work with the appropriate types.

```
Imports System.Net
```

Cookies are fairly easy to use. Both the Request and Response objects (which are provided through Page properties) provide a Cookies collection. The important trick to remember is that you retrieve cookies from the Request object, and you set cookies using the Response object.

To set a cookie, just create a new System.Net.HttpCookie object. You can then fill it with string information (using the familiar dictionary pattern) and attach it to the current web response.

```
' Create the cookie object.
Dim Cookie As New HttpCookie("Preferences")

' Set a value in it.
Cookie("LanguagePref") = "English"

' Add it to the current web response.
Response.Cookies.Add(Cookie)
```

A cookie added in this way will persist until the user closes the browser and will be sent with every request. To create a longer-lived cookie, you can set an expiration date.

```
' This cookie lives for 1 year.
Cookie.Expires = DateTime.Now.AddYears(1)
```

Cookies are retrieved by cookie name using the Request.Cookies collection.

```
Dim Cookie As HttpCookie = Request.Cookies("Preferences")
Dim Language As String

' Check to see if a cookie was found with this name.
' This is a good precaution to take,
' because the user could disable cookies,
' in which case the cookie will not exist.
If Not Cookie Is Nothing Then
    Language = Cookie("LanguagePref")
End If
```

The only way to remove a cookie is by replacing it with a cookie that has an expiration date that has already passed. The code here demonstrates this technique:

```
Dim Cookie As New HttpCookie("LanguagePref")
Cookie.Expires = DateTime.Now.AddDays(-1)
Response.Cookies.Add(Cookie)
```

A Cookie Example

The next example shows a typical use of cookies to store a customer name. If the name is found, a welcome message is displayed, as shown in Figure 10-6.

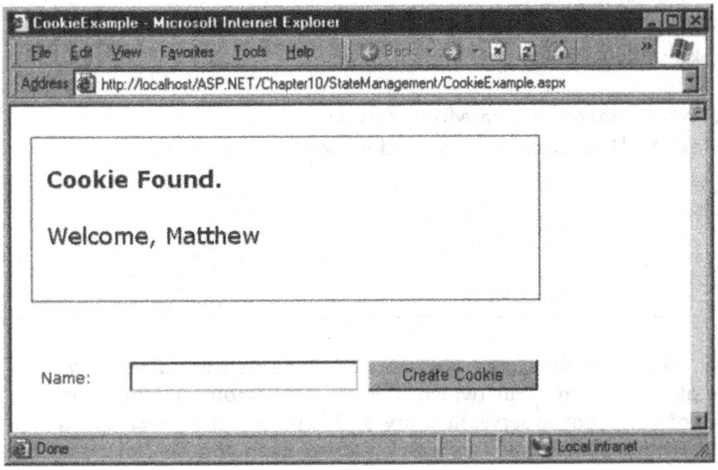

Figure 10-6. Displaying information from a custom cookie

Here's the code for this page:

```
Imports System.Net

Public Class CookieExample
  Inherits Page

    Protected lblWelcome As Label
    Protected txtName As TextBox
    Protected WithEvents cmdStore As Button

    Private Sub Page_Load(sender As Object, e As EventArgs) _
      Handles MyBase.Load
        Dim Cookie As HttpCookie = Request.Cookies("Preferences")
        If Cookie Is Nothing Then
            lblWelcome.Text = "<b>Unknown Customer</b>"
        Else
            lblWelcome.Text = "<b>Cookie Found.</b><br><br>"
            lblWelcome.Text &= "Welcome, " & Cookie("Name")
        End If
    End Sub

    Private Sub cmdStore_Click(sender As Object, e As EventArgs) _
      Handles cmdStore.Click
        Dim Cookie As HttpCookie = Request.Cookies("Preferences")
        If Cookie Is Nothing Then
            Cookie = New HttpCookie("Preferences")
        End If
```

```
        Cookie("Name") = txtName.Text
        Cookie.Expires = DateTime.Now.AddYears(1)
        Response.Cookies.Add(Cookie)

        lblWelcome.Text = "<b>Cookie Created.</b><br><br>"
        lblWelcome.Text &= "New Customer: " & Cookie("Name")
    End Sub

End Class
```

NOTE You'll find that some other ASP.NET features use cookies. Two examples are session state (which allows you to temporarily store user-specific information in server memory) and forms security (which allows you to restrict portions of a website, and force users to access it through a login page). Forms security is discussed in Chapter 25, while session state is described in the next section of this chapter.

Session State

There comes a point in the life of most applications when they begin to have more sophisticated storage requirements. An application might need to store and access complex information such as DataSets or custom data objects, which can't be easily persisted to a cookie or sent through a query string. Or the application might have stringent security requirements that prevent it from storing information on the client in view state or a custom cookie. In these situations, you can use ASP.NET's built-in session state facility.

Session state management is one of ASP.NET's premiere features. It allows you to store any type of data in memory on the server. The information is protected, because it is never transmitted to the client, and it's uniquely bound to a specific session. Every client that accesses the application has a different session and a distinct collection of information. Session state is ideal for storing information like the items in the current user's shopping basket when the user browses from one page to another.

Session Tracking

ASP.NET tracks each session using a unique 120-bit identifier. ASP.NET uses a special algorithm to generate this value, thereby guaranteeing that it's unique and random, so a malicious user can't reverse engineer or "guess" what session ID a given client will be using. This special ID is the only piece of information that is transmitted between the web server and the client. When the client presents the session ID, ASP.NET looks up the corresponding session, retrieves the serialized data from the state server, converts it to live objects, and places these objects into a special collection so they can be accessed in code. This process takes place automatically.

In order for this system to work, the client must present the appropriate session ID with each request. There are two ways this can be accomplished:

- **Using cookies.** In this case, the session ID is transmitted in a special cookie (named "ASP.NET_SessionId"), which ASP.NET creates automatically when the session collection is used. This is the default, and it's also the same approach that was used in earlier versions of ASP.

- **Using modified URLs.** In this case, the session ID is transmitted in a specially modified (or "munged") URL. This is a new feature in ASP.NET that allows you to create applications that use session state with clients that don't support cookies.

Session state doesn't come for free. Though it solves many of the problems associated with other forms of state management, it forces the server to store additional information in memory. This extra memory requirement, even if it is small, can quickly grow to performance-destroying levels as hundreds or thousands of clients access the site.

In other words, any use of session state must be carefully thought out. A careless use of session state is one of the most common reasons that a web application can't scale to serve a large number of clients. Sometimes, a better approach is to use caching, as described in Chapter 24.

Using Session State

You can interact with session state using the System.Web.SessionState.HttpSessionState class, which is provided in an ASP.NET web page as the built-in Session object. The syntax for adding items to the collection and retrieving them is basically the same as for adding items to a page's view state.

For example, you might store a DataSet in session memory like this:

```
Session("dsInfo") = dsInfo
```

You can then retrieve it with an appropriate conversion operation:

```
dsInfo = CType(Session("dsInfo"), DataSet)
```

Session state is global to your entire application for the current user. Session state can be lost in several ways:

- If the user closes and restarts the browser.

- If the user accesses the same page through a different browser window, although the session will still exist if a web page is accessed through the original browser window. Browsers differ on how they handle this situation.

- If the session times out due to inactivity. More information about session timeout can be found in the configuration section.

- If the programmer ends the session in code.

In the first two cases, the session actually remains in memory, because the web server has no idea that the client has closed the browser or changed windows. The session will linger in memory, remaining inaccessible, until it eventually expires.

Table 10-1 describes the methods and properties of the HttpSessionState class.

Table 10-1. HttpSessionState Members

Member	Description
Count	The number of items in the current session collection.
IsCookieless	Identifies whether this session is tracked with a cookie, or using modified URLs.
IsNewSession	Identifies whether this session was just created for the current request. If there is currently no information in session state, ASP.NET won't bother to track the session or create a session cookie. Instead, the session will be re-created with every request.
Mode	Provides an enumerated value that explains how ASP.NET stores session state information. This storage mode is determined based on the web.config configuration settings discussed later in this chapter.
SessionID	Provides a string with the unique session identifier for the current client.
StaticObjects	Provides a collection of read-only session items that were declared by <object runat=server> tags in the global.asax. Generally, this technique isn't used, and is a holdover from ASP programming that is included for backward compatibility.
Timeout	The current number of minutes that must elapse before the current session will be abandoned, provided that no more requests are received from the client. This value can be changed programmatically, giving you the change to make the session collection longer term when required for more important operations.
Abandon()	Cancels the current session immediately and releases all the memory it occupied. This is a useful technique in a logoff page to ensure that server memory is reclaimed as quickly as possible.
Clear()	Removes all the session items, but doesn't change the current session identifier.

A Session State Example

The next example uses session state to store several Furniture data objects. The data object combines a few related variables and uses a special constructor so that it can be created and initialized in one easy line. Rather than use full property procedures, the class takes a shortcut and uses public member variables.

```
Public Class Furniture

    Public Name As String
    Public Description As String
    Public Cost As Decimal

    Public Sub New(Name As String, Description As String, _
      Cost As Decimal)
        Me.Name = Name
        Me.Description = Description
        Me.Cost = Cost
    End Sub

End Class
```

Three Furniture objects are created the first time the page is loaded, and they're stored in session state. The user can then choose from a list of furniture piece names. When a selection is made, the corresponding object will be retrieved, and its information will be displayed, as shown in Figure 10-7.

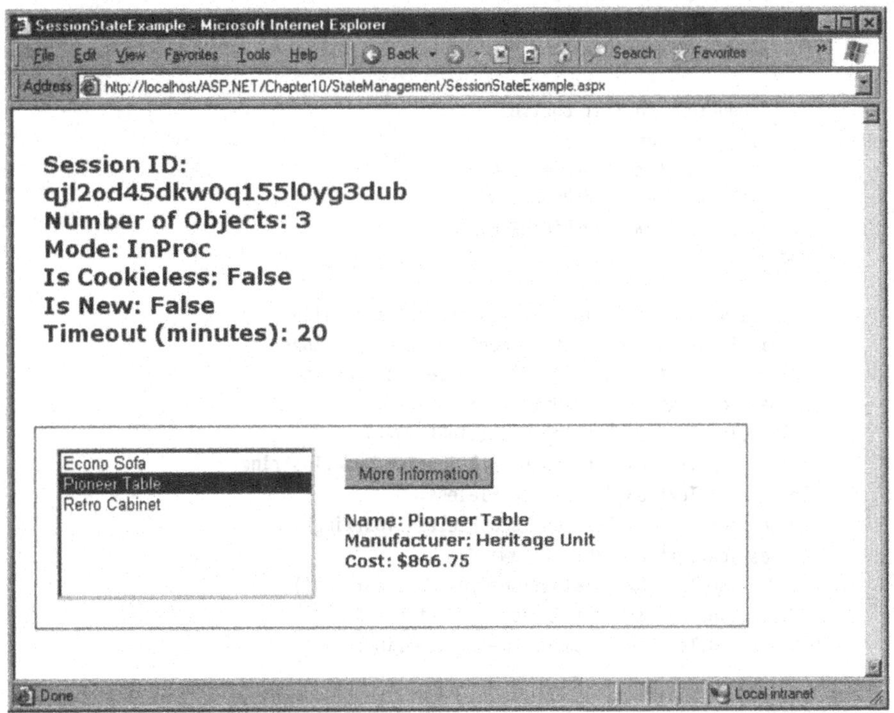

Figure 10-7. A session state example with data objects

```
Public Class SessionStateExample
  Inherits Page

    Protected cmdMoreInfo As Button
    Protected lblRecord As Label
    Protected lblSession As Label
    Protected lstItems As ListBox

    Private Sub Page_Load(sender As Object, e As EventArgs) _
      Handles MyBase.Load

        If Me.IsPostBack = False Then
            ' Create Furniture objects.
            Dim Piece1 As New Furniture("Econo Sofa", _
                                        "Acme Inc.", 74.99)
            Dim Piece2 As New Furniture("Pioneer Table", _
                                        "Heritage Unit", 866.75)
            Dim Piece3 As New Furniture("Retro Cabinet", _
                                        "Sixties Ltd.", 300.11)

            ' Add objects to session state.
            Session("Furniture1") = Piece1
            Session("Furniture2") = Piece2
            Session("Furniture3") = Piece3

            ' Add rows to list control.
            lstItems.Items.Clear()
            lstItems.Items.Add(Piece1.Name)
            lstItems.Items.Add(Piece2.Name)
            lstItems.Items.Add(Piece3.Name)
        End If

        ' Display some basic information about the session.
        ' This is useful for testing configuration settings.
        lblSession.Text = "Session ID: " & Session.SessionID
        lblSession.Text &= "<br>Number of Objects: "
        lblSession.Text &= Session.Count.ToString()
        lblSession.Text &= "<br>Mode: " & Session.Mode.ToString()
        lblSession.Text &= "<br>Is Cookieless: "
        lblSession.Text &= Session.IsCookieless.ToString()
        lblSession.Text &= "<br>Is New: "
        lblSession.Text &= Session.IsNewSession.ToString()
        lblSession.Text &= "<br>Timeout (minutes): "
        lblSession.Text &= Session.Timeout.ToString()

    End Sub

    Private Sub cmdMoreInfo_Click(sender As Object, _
      e As EventArgs) Handles cmdMoreInfo.Click

        If lstItems.SelectedIndex = -1 Then
            lblRecord.Text = "No item selected."
```

```
        Else
            ' Construct the right key name based on the index.
            Dim Key As String
            Key = "Furniture" & _
                  (lstItems.SelectedIndex + 1).ToString()

            ' Retrieve the Furniture object from session state.
            Dim Piece As Furniture = CType(Session(Key), Furniture)

            ' Display the information for this object.
            lblRecord.Text = "Name: " & Piece.Name
            lblRecord.Text &= "<br>Manufacturer: "
            lblRecord.Text &= Piece.Description
            lblRecord.Text &= "<br>Cost: $" & Piece.Cost.ToString()
        End If

    End Sub

End Class
```

It's also a good practice to add a few session-friendly features in your application. For example, you could add a logout button to the page that automatically cancels a session using the Session.Abandon() method. This way, the user will be encouraged to terminate the session rather than just close the browser window, and the server memory will be reclaimed faster.

Making Session State Scalable

When web developers need to store a large amount of state information, they face a confounding problem. They can use session state and ensure excellent performance for a small set of users, but risk poor scalability for large numbers. Alternatively, they can use a database to store temporary session information. This allows you to store a large amount of session information for long periods of time (potentially weeks or months instead of mere minutes). However, it also slows performance because the database must be queried for almost every page request.

There is a compromise, and it involves caching. The basic approach is to create a temporary database record with session information, and store its unique ID in session state. This ensures that the in-memory session information is always minimal, but your web page code can easily find the corresponding session record. To reduce the number of database queries, you'll also add the session information to the cache (indexed under the session identifier). On subsequent requests, your code can check for the session information in the cache first. If the information is no longer in the cache, your code can retrieve it from the database as a last resort. This process becomes even more transparent if you create a custom component that provides the session information and performs the required cache lookup for you.

For more information, read about custom components in Chapter 22 and caching in Chapter 24.

Session State Configuration

Session state is configured through the web.config file for your current application (which is found in the same virtual directory as the .aspx web page files). The configuration file allows you to set advanced options such as the timeout and the session state mode. If you're creating your web application in Visual Studio .NET, your project will include an automatically generated web.config file.

A typical web.config file is shown here. The settings that don't relate to session state have been omitted.

```
<?xml version="1.0" encoding="utf-8" ?>
<configuration>
    <system.web>
        <!-- Other settings omitted. -->

        <sessionState
            mode="InProc"
            stateConnectionString="tcpip=127.0.0.1:42424"
            sqlConnectionString="data source=127.0.0.1;user id=sa"
            cookieless="false"
            timeout="20"
        />
    </system.web>
</configuration>
```

In total, there are five settings related to session state. They're described in the following sections.

Cookieless

You can set the cookieless setting to true or false (the default).

```
<sessionState
    cookieless="false"
/>
```

When set to true, the session ID will automatically be inserted into the URL. When ASP.NET receives a request, it will remove the ID, retrieve the session collection, and forward the request to the appropriate directory. A munged URL is shown in Figure 10-8.

Figure 10-8. A munged URL with the session ID

ASP.NET is even intelligent enough to automatically convert relative links in the web page by adding the session ID into the URL automatically in the final HTML page that is sent to the client.

For example, consider the following project (included with the online samples in the CookielessSessions directory). It contains two pages and uses cookieless mode. The first page is shown in Figure 10-9. It contains a HyperLink control and a button. The HyperLink's NavigateUrl property is set to Cookieless2.aspx. When ASP.NET renders this page, it transforms the hyperlink control to an HTML anchor tag (as it always does). However, it also updates the anchor, changing the fixed URL to include the current session ID. This way, session state will still be preserved when the user clicks this link.

```
<a id="HyperLink1"
   href="/localhost/ASP.NET/(ddugkx55qmzqm355bzshxz55)/
   Cookieless2.aspx">HyperLink
</a>
```

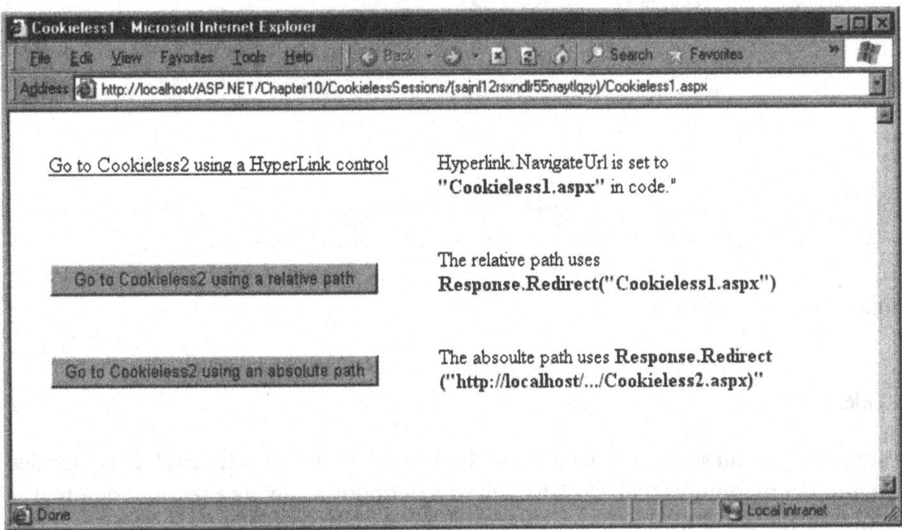

Figure 10-9. Three tests of cookieless sessions

Even manual redirects in the code are successfully intercepted by and modified to preserve session information. For example, the button uses the Response.Redirect() method to forward the user to the Cookieless2.aspx page. The following relative redirect statement preserves the munged URL, with no extra steps required:

```
Private Sub cmdLink_Click(sender As Object, e As EventArgs _
  Handles cmdLink.Click
    Response.Redirect("Cookieless2.aspx")
End Sub
```

The only real limitation of cookieless state is that you cannot use absolute links, because ASP.NET will not insert the session ID into them. For example, if you use the third command button, the current session will be abandoned. The result is shown in Figure 10-10, and the code is shown here:

```
Private Sub cmdLinkAbsolute_Click(sender As Object, e As EventArgs) _
  Handles cmdLinkAbsolute.Click
    Dim Url As String
    Url = "http://localhost/ASP.NET/Chapter10/CookielessSessions/"
    Url &= "Cookieless2.aspx"
    Response.Redirect(Url)
End Sub
```

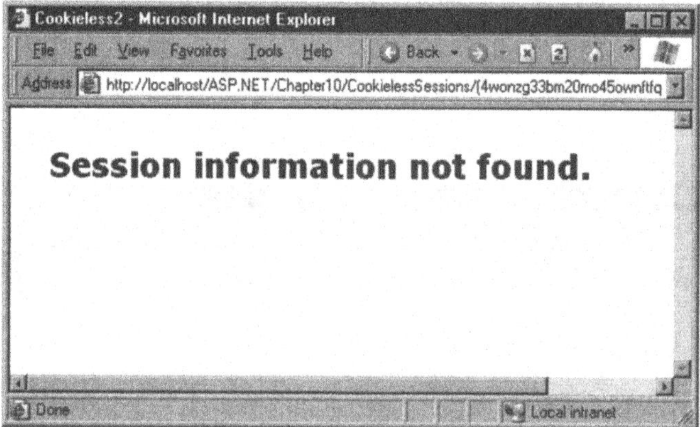

Figure 10-10. A lost session

Timeout

Another important session state setting in the web.config file is the timeout. This specifies the number of minutes that ASP.NET will wait, without receiving a request, before it abandons the session.

```
<sessionState
    timeout="20"
/>
```

This setting represents one of the most important compromises of session state. A difference of minutes can have a dramatic effect on the load of your server and the performance of your application. Ideally, you will choose a timeframe that is short enough to allow the server to reclaim valuable memory after a client stops using the application, but long enough to allow a client to pause and continue a session without losing it.

You can also programmatically change the session timeout in code. For example, if you know a session contains an unusually large amount of information, you may need to limit the amount of time the session can be stored. You would then warn the user and change the timeout property. Here's a sample line of code that changes the timeout to ten minutes:

```
Session.Timeout = 10
```

Mode

The other session state settings allow you to configure special session state services.

```
<sessionState
    mode="InProc"
    stateConnectionString="tcpip=127.0.0.1:42424"
    sqlConnectionString="data source=127.0.0.1;user id=sa;password="
/>
```

The different mode options are described in the next few sections.

InProc

For the default mode (InProc), the other two settings have no effect. They are just included as place holders to show you the appropriate format. InProc is similar to how session state was stored in previous versions of ASP. It instructs information to be stored in the same process as the ASP.NET worker threads, which provides the best performance, but the least durability. If you restart your server, the state information will be lost.

Generally, InProc is the best option for most websites. The one most notable exception is in a web farm scenario. In order to allow session state to be shared between servers, you must use the out-of-process or SQL Server–based session state service.

Off

This setting disables session state management for every page in the application. This can provide a slight performance improvement for websites that are not using session state.

StateServer

With this setting, ASP.NET will use a separate Windows Service for state management. This service runs on the same web server, but it's outside the main ASP.NET process, which gives it a basic level of protection if the ASP.NET process needs to be restarted. The cost is the increased time delay imposed when state information is transferred between two processes. If you frequently access and change state information, this can make for a fairly unwelcome slowdown.

When using the StateServer setting, you need to specify a value for the stateConnectionString setting. This string identifies the TCP/IP address of the computer that is running the StateServer service and its port number (which is defined by ASP.NET and doesn't usually need to be changed). This allows you to host the StateServer on another computer. If you don't change this setting, the local server will be used (set as address 127.0.0.1).

Of course, before your application can use the service, you need to start it. The easiest way to do this is to use the Microsoft Management Console. Select Start ➤ Programs ➤ Administrative Tools ➤ Computer Management (you can also access the Administrative Tools group through Control Panel). Then select the Services and Applications ➤ Services node. Find the service called ASP.NET State in the list, as shown in Figure 10-11.

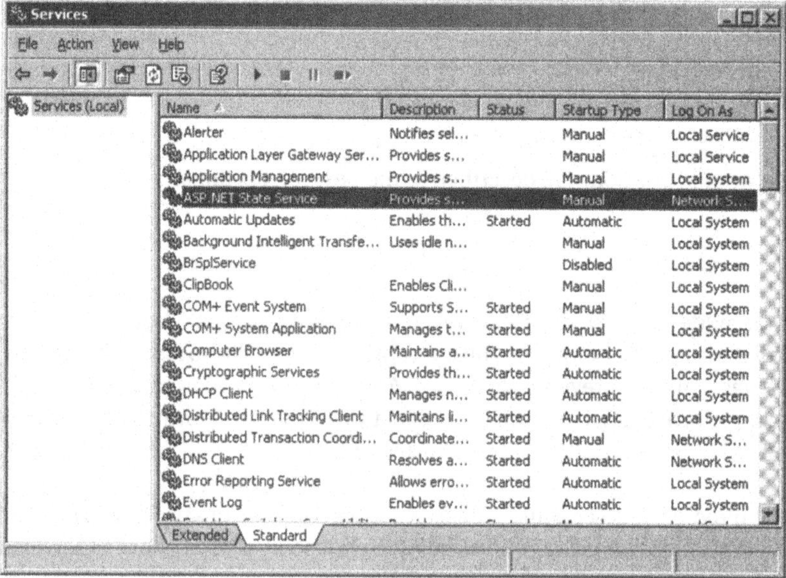

Figure 10-11. The ASP.NET state service

Once you find the service in the list, you can manually start and stop it by right-clicking it. Generally, you'll want to configure Windows to automatically start the service. Right-click it, select Properties, and modify the Startup type setting to Automatic, as show in Figure 10-12.

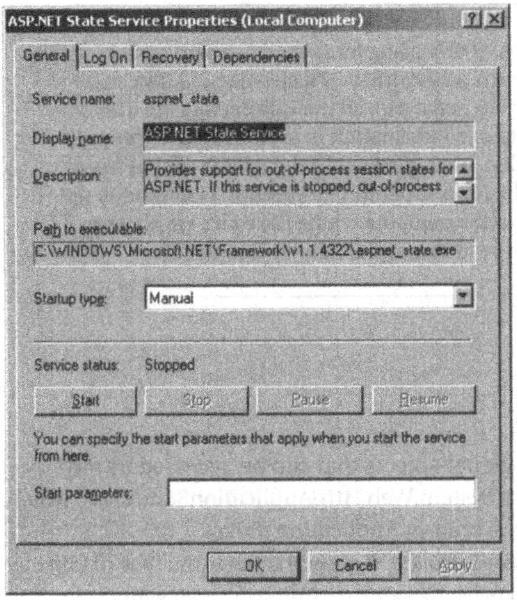

Figure 10-12. Service properties

SqlServer

This setting instructs ASP.NET to use an SQL Server database to store session information, as identified by the sqlConnectionString attribute. This is the most resilient state store, but also the slowest by far. To use this method of state management, you'll need to have a server with SQL Server installed.

When setting the sqlConnectionString, you follow the same sort of pattern you use with ADO.NET data access. Generally, you'll need to specify a data source (the server address) and a user ID and password, unless you're using SQL integrated security.

In addition, you need to install the special stored procedures and temporary session databases. These stored procedures take care of storing and retrieving the session information. ASP.NET includes a Transact-SQL script for this purpose called InstallSqlState.sql. It's found in the C:\[WinDir]\Microsoft.NET\Framework\[Version] directory. You can run this script using an SQL Server utility like OSQL.exe or Query Analyzer. It only needs to be performed once.

NOTE If you're hosting ASP.NET using more than one web server (which is affectionately known as a *web farm*), you'll also need to take some extra configuration steps to make sure all the web servers are in sync. Otherwise, one might encode information in session state differently than another, which will cause a problem if the user is routed from one server to another during a session. The solution is to modify the <machineKey> section of the machine.config file so it's consistent across all servers. For more information, refer to Chapter 29.

Application State

Application state allows you to store global objects that can be accessed by any client. Application state is based on the System.Web.HttpApplicationState class, which is provided in all web pages through the built-in Application object.

Application state is very similar to session state. It supports the same type of objects, retains information on the server, and uses the same dictionary-based syntax. A common example with application state is a global counter that tracks how many times an operation has been performed by all of the web application's clients.

For example, you could create a global.asax event handler that tracks how many sessions have been created or how many requests have been received into the application. Or you can use similar logic in the Page.Load event handler to track how many times a given page has been requested by various clients. Here's an example of the latter:

```
Private Sub Page_Load(sender As Object, e As EventArgs) _
  Handles MyBase.Load

    Dim Count As Integer = CType(Application("HitCounter", Integer)
    Count += 1
    Application("HitCounter") = Count
    lblCounter.Text = Count.ToString()

End Sub
```

Once again, application state items are stored as objects, so it's always a good idea to convert them manually. Items in application state never time out. They last until the application or server is restarted.

Application state isn't often used, because it's generally inefficient. In the previous example, the counter would probably not keep an accurate count, particularly in times of heavy traffic. For example, if two clients requested the page at the same time, you could have a sequence of events like this:

1. User A retrieves the current count (432).

2. User B retrieves the current count (432).

3. User A sets the current count to 433.

4. User B sets the current count to 433.

In other words, one request isn't counted because two clients access the counter at the same time. To prevent this problem, you need to use the Lock() and Unlock() methods, which explicitly allow only one client to access the Application state collection at a time.

```
Private Sub Page_Load(sender As Object, e As EventArgs) _
  Handles MyBase.Load

    ' Acquire exclusive access.
    Application.Lock()

    Dim Count As Integer = CType(Application("HitCounter", Integer)
    Count += 1
    Application("HitCounter") = Count

    ' Release exclusive access.
    Application.Unlock()

    lblCounter.Text = Count.ToString()

End Sub
```

Unfortunately, all other clients requesting the page will now be stalled until the Application collection is released. This can drastically reduce performance. Generally, frequently modified values are poor candidates for application state. In fact, application state is rarely used in the .NET world because its two most common uses have been replaced by easier, more efficient methods:

- In the past, application state was used to store application-wide constants, such as a database connection string. As you saw in Chapter 5, this type of constant can now be stored in the web.config file, which is generally more flexible because you can change it easily without needing to hunt through web page code or recompile your application.

- Application state can also be used to store frequently used information that is time-consuming to create, such as a full product catalog that requires a database lookup. However, using application state to store this kind of information raises all sorts of problems about how to check if the data is valid and how to replace it when needed. It can also hamper performance if the product catalog is too large. Chapter 24 introduces a similar but much more sensible approach—storing frequently used information in the ASP.NET cache. Many uses of application state can be replaced more efficiently with caching.

An Overview of State Management Choices

Each state management choice has a different lifetime, scope, performance overhead, and level of support. Table 10-2 and Table 10-3 show an at-a-glance comparison of your state-management options.

Table 10-2. State Management Options Compared (part 1)

	View State	Query String	Custom Cookies
Allowed Data Types	All serializable .NET data types.	A limited amount of string data.	String data.
Storage Location	A hidden field in the current web page.	The browser's URL string.	The client's computer (in memory or a small text file, depending on its lifetime settings).
Lifetime	Retained permanently, for postbacks to a single page.	Lost when the user enters a new URL or closes the browser. However, can be stored in a bookmark.	Set by the programmer. Can be used in multiple pages and can persist between visits.
Scope	Limited to the current page.	Limited to the target page.	The whole ASP.NET application.
Security	By default it's insecure, although you can use page directives to enforce encryption and hashing.	Clearly visible and easy for the user to modify.	Insecure, and can be modified by the user.
Performance Implications	Storing a large amount of information will slow transmission, but will not affect server performance.	None, because the amount of data is trivial.	None, because the amount of data is trivial.
Typical Use	Page-specific settings.	Sending a Product ID from a catalog page to a details page.	Personalization preferences for a website.

Table 10-3. State Management Options Compared (part 2)

	Session State	Application State
Allowed Data Types	All .NET data types.	All .NET data types.
Storage Location	Server memory.	Server memory.
Lifetime	Times out after a predefined period (usually 20 minutes, but can be altered globally or programmatically).	The lifetime of the application (typically, until the server is rebooted).
Scope	The whole ASP.NET application.	The whole ASP.NET application. Unlike other methods, application data is global to all users.
Security	Very secure, because data is never transmitted to the client.	Very secure, because data is never transmitted to the client.
Performance Implications	Storing a large amount of information can slow down the server severely, especially if there are a large number of users at once, because each user will have a separate copy of session data.	Storing a large amount of information can slow down the server, because this data will never timeout and be removed.
Typical Use	Store items in a shopping basket.	Storing any type of global data.

The Last Word

State management is the art of retaining information between requests. Usually, this information is user-specific (like a list of items in a shopping cart, a user name, or an access level), but sometimes it's global to the whole application (like usage statistics that track site activity). Because ASP.NET uses a disconnected architecture, you need to explicitly store and retrieve state information with each individual request. The approach you choose to store this data can have a dramatic effect on the performance, scalability, and security of your application. Remember to consult the tables in the last section of this chapter to help evaluate different types of state management, and determine what is best for your needs.

CHAPTER 11

Tracing, Logging, and Error Handling

NO SOFTWARE CAN RUN free from error, and ASP.NET applications are no exception. Sooner or later your code will be interrupted by a programming mistake, invalid data, unexpected circumstances, or even hardware failure. Novice programmers spend sleepless nights worrying about errors. Professional developers recognize that bugs are an inherent part of software applications and code defensively, testing assumptions, logging problems, and writing error-handling code to deal with the unexpected.

In this chapter, you'll learn the error handling and debugging practices that can defend your ASP.NET applications against common errors, track user problems, and help you solve mysterious issues. You'll learn how to use VB .NET's new structured exception handling, how to use logs to keep a record of unrecoverable errors, and how to configure custom web pages for common HTTP errors. You'll also learn how to use page tracing to see diagnostic information about ASP.NET pages.

Common Errors

Errors can occur in a variety of situations. Some of the most common causes of errors include attempts to divide by zero (usually caused by invalid input or missing information) and attempts to connect to a limited resource such as a file or a database (which can fail if the file doesn't exist, the database connection times out, or the code has insufficient security credentials).

Another infamous type of error is the *null reference exception*, which usually occurs when a program attempts to use an uninitialized object. As a .NET programmer, you'll quickly learn to recognize and resolve this common, but annoying mistake. The following code example shows the problem in action:

```
Dim conOne As OleDbConnection
' The next line will fail and generate a null reference exception.
' You cannot modify a property (or use a method) of an object that
' doesn't exist!
conOne.ConnectionString = ConnectionString

Dim conTwo As New OleDbConnection()
' This works, because the object has been initialized
' with the New keyword.
conTwo.ConnectionString = ConnectionString
```

When an error occurs in your code, .NET checks to see if there are any active error handlers in the current scope. If the error occurs inside a function, .NET searches for local error handlers, and then checks for any active error handlers in the calling code. If no error handlers are found, the current procedure is aborted, and an error page is displayed in the browser. Depending on whether the request came from the local computer or a remote client, the error page may show a detailed description (as shown in Figure 11-1) or a generic message. You'll explore this topic a little later in the "Error Pages" section of this Chapter.

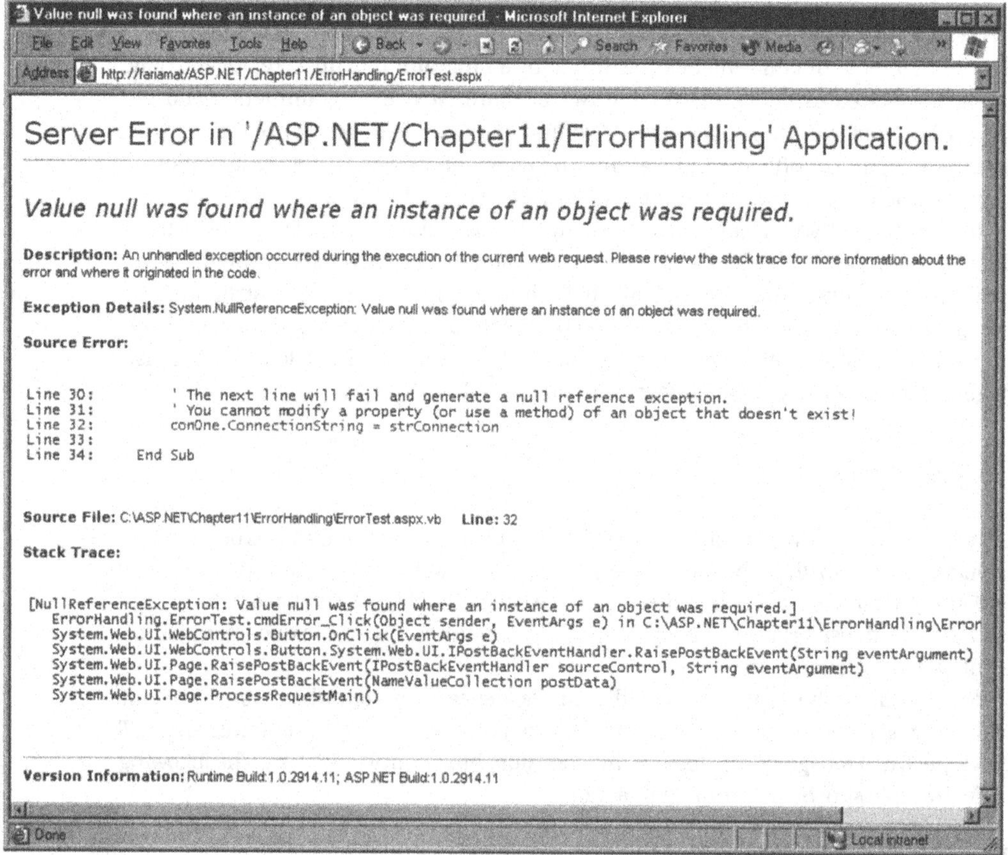

Figure 11-1. A sample error page

Even if an error is the result of invalid input or the failure of a third-party component, an error page can shatter the professional appearance of any application. The application users end up with a feeling that the application is unstable, insecure, or of poor quality—and they're at least partially correct.

If an ASP.NET application is carefully designed and constructed, an error page will almost never appear. Errors may still occur due to unforeseen circumstances, but they will be caught in the code and identified. If the error is a critical one that the application cannot solve on its own, it will report a more useful (and user-friendly) page of information that might include a link to a support e-mail or phone number where the customer can receive additional assistance. You'll look at those techniques in this chapter.

On Error Go Home

Traditional ASP pages and other Visual Basic or VBScript applications use an error-handling system based on the On Error Goto statement. In order to support backward compatibility, the On Error Goto command is still available in the modern ASP.NET environment. However, there's no good reason to use this old-fashioned approach, except if you need to migrate legacy code. Instead, structured exception handling, a technique that's existed in most other programming languages for years, finally makes its debut in VB .NET.

Structured exception handling offers a long list of improvements over the traditional On Error Goto statement:

- **Exceptions handlers use a modern block structure.** This makes it easy to activate and deactivate different error handlers for different sections of code, and handle their errors individually.
- **Exceptions are caught based on their type.** This allows you to streamline error-handling code without needing to sift through obscure error codes.
- **Exceptions are object-based.** Each exception provides a significant amount of diagnostic information wrapped into a neat object, instead of a simple message and error code. These exception objects also support an InnerException property that allows you to wrap a generic error over the more specific error that caused it. Best of all, exception objects can be easily transferred between different procedures in your code, unlike the traditional Err object (which was automatically reset when the point of execution moved to another procedure or another error occurred). You can even create and throw your own exception objects.
- **Exception handlers are multilayered.** You can easily layer exception handlers on top of other exception handlers, some of which may only check for a specialized set of errors.
- **Exceptions are a generic part of the .NET framework.** That means they're completely cross-language compatible. Thus, a .NET component written in C# can throw an exception that you can catch in a web page written in VB.

The .NET Exception Object

Every exception object derives from the base class System.Exception. The Exception class includes the essential functionality for identifying any type of error. Table 11-1 lists its most important members.

Table 11-1. Exception Properties

Member	Description
HelpLink	A link to a help document, which can be a relative or fully qualified URL or URN (file:///C:/ACME/MyApp/help.html#Err42). The .NET Framework doesn't use this property, but you can set it in your custom exceptions if you want to use it in your web page code.
InnerException	A nested exception. For example, a method might catch a simple file IO error, and create a higher-level "operation failed" error. The details about the original error could be retained in the InnerException property of the higher-level error.
Message	Contains a text description with a significant amount of information describing the problem.
Source	The name of the assembly where the error occurred.
StackTrace	A string that contains a list of all the current method calls on the stack, in order of most to least recent. This is useful for determining where the problem occurred.
TargetSite	A reflection object (an instance of the System.Reflection.MethodBase class) that provides some information about the method where the error occurred. This information includes generic method details like the procedure name and the data types for its parameter and return value. It doesn't contain any information about the actual parameter values that were used when the problem occurred.
GetBaseException()	This method is useful for nested exceptions that may have more than one layer. It retrieves the original (deepest nested) exception by moving to the base of the InnerException chain.

Exception Flavors

When you catch an exception in an ASP.NET, it won't be an instance of the generic System.Exception class. Instead, it will be an object that represents a specific type of error. This object will be based on one of the many classes that inherit from System.Exception. These include diverse classes like DivideByZeroException, ArithmeticException, System.IO.IOException, System.Security.SecurityException, and many more. Some of these classes provide additional details about the error in additional properties.

Visual Studio .NET provides a useful tool to browse through the exceptions in the .NET class library. Simply select Debug ➤ Exceptions from the menu (you'll need to have a project open in order for this work). The Exceptions window will appear with exceptions organized in a hierarchical tree control, grouped by namespace (see Figure 11-2).

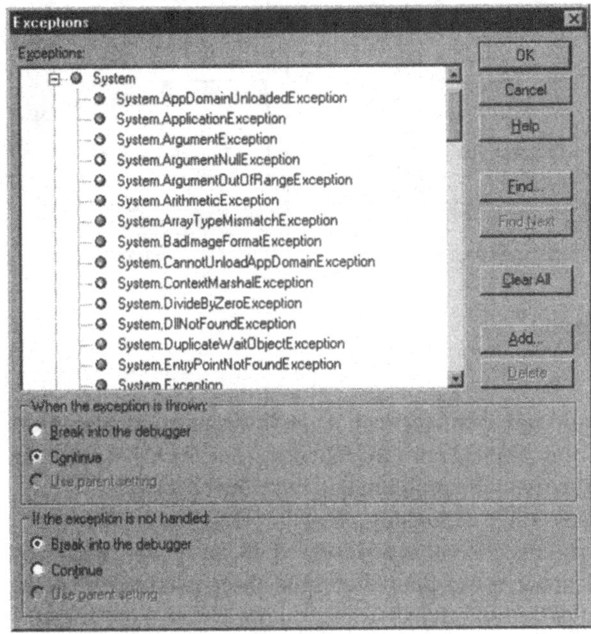

Figure 11-2. Visual Studio .NET's exception viewer

The Exceptions window allows you to specify what exceptions should be handled by your code when debugging, and what exceptions will cause Visual Studio .NET to enter break mode immediately. That means you don't need to disable your error-handling code to troubleshoot a problem.

For example, you could choose to allow your program to handle a common FileNotFoundException (which could be caused by an invalid user selection), but instruct Visual Studio .NET to pause execution if an unexpected DivideByZero exception occurs.

The Exception Chain

Figure 11-3 shows how the InnerException property works. In this case, a FileNotFoundException led to a NullReferenceException, which led to a custom UpdateFailedException. The code returns an UpdateFailedException that references the NullReferenceException, which references the original FileNotFoundException.

The InnerException property is an extremely useful tool for component-based programming. Generally, it's not much help if a component reports a low-level problem

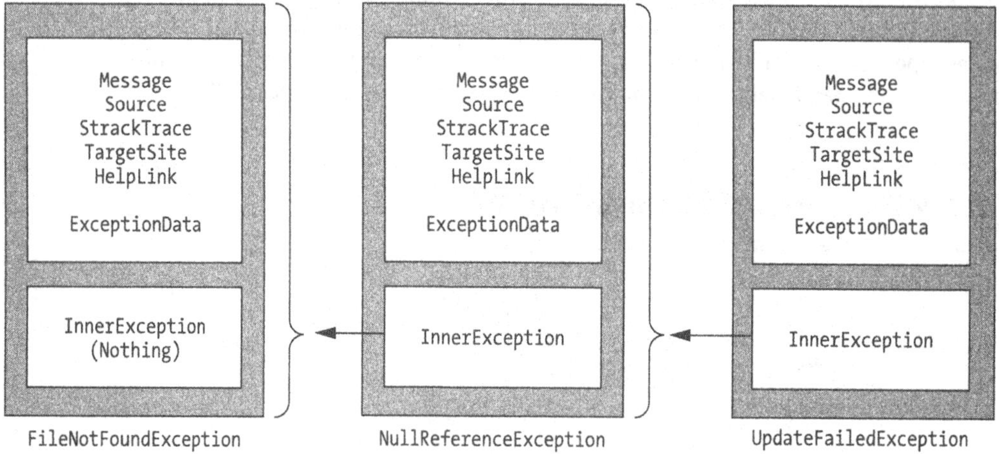

Figure 11-3. Exceptions can be chained together

like a null reference or a divide-by-zero error. Instead, it needs to communicate a more detailed message about which operation failed, and what input may have been invalid. The calling code can then often correct the problem and retry the operation.

On the other hand, sometimes you're debugging a bug that lurks deep inside the component itself. In this case, you need to know precisely what caused the error—you don't want to replace it with a higher-level exception that could obscure the root problem. Using an exception chain handles both these scenarios: You receive as many linked exception objects as needed, which can specify information from the least to the most specific error condition.

Handling Exceptions

The first line of defense in an application is to check for potential error conditions before performing an operation. For example, a program can explicitly check if the divisor is 0 before performing a calculation or if a file exists before attempting to open it.

```
If System.IO.File.Exists("myfile.txt") = True Then
    ' Safe to open the myfile.txt file.
End If

If Divisor <> 0 Then
    ' Safe to divide some number by Divisor.
End If
```

Even if you perform this basic level of "quality assurance," your application is still vulnerable. For example, there is no way to protect against all the possible file access problems that occur, including hardware failures or network problems that could arise spontaneously in the middle of an operation. Similarly, there's no way to validate a user ID and password for a database before attempting to open a connection—and even if there were, that technique would be subject to its own set of potential errors. In some cases, it may not be practical to perform the full range of defensive checks, because they may impose a noticeable performance drag on your application. For all these reasons, you need a way to detect and deal with errors when they occur.

.NET languages provide this technique with structured exception handling. To use structured exception handling, you wrap potentially problematic code in the special block structure shown here:

```
Try
    ' Risky code goes here (such as opening a file or
    ' connecting to a database).
Catch
    ' An error has been detected. You can deal with it here.
Finally
    ' Time to clean up, regardless of whether there was an error or not.
End Try
```

The Try statement enables error handling. Any exceptions that occur in the following lines can be "caught" automatically. The code in the Catch block will be executed when an error is detected. And either way, whether a bug occurs or not, the optional Finally section of the code will be executed last. This allows you to perform some basic cleanup, like closing a database connection. The Finally code is important because it will execute even if an error has occurred that will prevent the program from continuing. In other words, if an unrecoverable exception halts your application, you'll still have the chance to release resources.

The act of catching an error neutralizes it. If all you want to do is render a specific error harmless, you don't even need to add any code in the Catch block of your error handler. Usually, however, this portion of the code will be used to report the error to the user or log it for future reference. In a separate component (such as a business object), this code might actually create a new exception object with additional information and throw it to the calling code, which will be in the best position to remedy it or alert the user.

Catching Specific Exceptions

Structured exception handling is particularly flexible because it allows you to catch specific types of exceptions. To do so, you add multiple Catch statements, each one identifying the type of exception (and providing a new variable to catch it in), as follows:

```
Try
    ' Risky database code goes here.
Catch err As System.Data.OleDbException
    ' Catches common problems like connection errors.
Catch err As System.NullReferenceException
    ' Catches problems resulting from an uninitialized object.
End Try
```

An exception will be caught as long as it's of the same class, or if it's derived from the indicated class. In other words, the statement "Catch err As Exception" will catch any exception, because every exception object is derived from the System.Exception base class.

Exception blocks work like an If/End If or Select Case block structure. That means that as soon as a matching exception handler is found, the appropriate catch code is invoked. Therefore, you should organize your Catch statements from most specific to least specific:

```
Try
    ' Risky database code goes here.
Catch err As System.Data.OleDbException
    ' Catches common problems like connection errors.
Catch err As System.NullReferenceException
    ' Catches problems resulting from an unitialized object.
Catch err As System.Exception
    ' Catches any other errors.
End Try
```

Ending with a Catch statement for the generic Exception class is often a good idea to make sure no errors slip through. However, in component-based programming you should make sure you only intercept an exception you can deal with or recover from. Otherwise, it's better to let the calling code catch the original error.

Nested Exception Handlers

When an exception is thrown, .NET tries to find a matching Catch statement in the current procedure. If the code isn't in a local structured exception block, or if none of the Catch statements match the exception, VB .NET will move up the call stack, searching for active exception handlers.

Consider the example shown here, where the Page.Load event handler calls a private DivideNumbers() function.

```
Private Sub Page_Load(sender As Object, e As EventArgs) _
  Handles MyBase.Load
    Try
        DivideNumbers(5, 0)
    Catch err As DivideByZeroException
        ' Report error here.
    End Try
End Sub

Private Function DivideNumbers(number As Decimal, divisor As Decimal) _
  As Decimal
    Return (number/divisor)
End Function
```

In this example, the DivideNumbers() function lacks any sort of exception handler. However, the DivideNumbers() function call is made inside an exception handler, which means that the problem will be caught further upstream in the calling code. This is a good approach because the DivideNumbers() routine could be used in a variety of different circumstances (or if it's part of a component, in a variety of different types of applications). It really has no access to any kind of user interface and can't directly report an error. Only the calling code is in a position to determine if the problem is a serious or minor one, and only the calling code can prompt the user for more information or report error details in the web page.

Exception handlers can also be overlapped in such a way that different exception handlers filter out different types of problems. Here's one such example:

```
Private Sub Page_Load(sender As Object, e As EventArgs) _
  Handles MyBase.Load
    Try
        Dim Average As Integer = GetAverageCost(DateTime.Now)
    Catch err As DivideByZeroException
        ' Report error here.
    End Try
End Sub

Private Function GetAverageCost(saleDate As Date) As Integer
    Try
        ' Use Database access code here to retrieve all the sale records
        ' for this date, and calculate the average.
    Catch err As OleDbException
        ' Handle a database related problem.
    Finally
        ' Close the database connection.
    End Try
End Function
```

Dissecting the Code ...

- If an OleDbException occurs during the database operation, it will be caught in the GetAverageCost() function.
- If a DivideByZeroException occurs (for example, the function attempts to calculate an average based on a DataSet that contains no rows), the exception will be caught in the calling Page.Load event handler.
- If another problem occurs (such as a null reference exception), there is no active exception handler that can catch it. In this case, .NET will search through the entire call stack without finding a matching Catch statement in an active exception handler, and will generate a runtime error, end the program, and return a page with exception information.

Exception Handling in Action

You can use a simple program to test exceptions and see what sort of information is retrieved. This sample program allows a user to enter two values and attempts to divide them. It then reports all the related exception information in the page (see Figure 11-4).

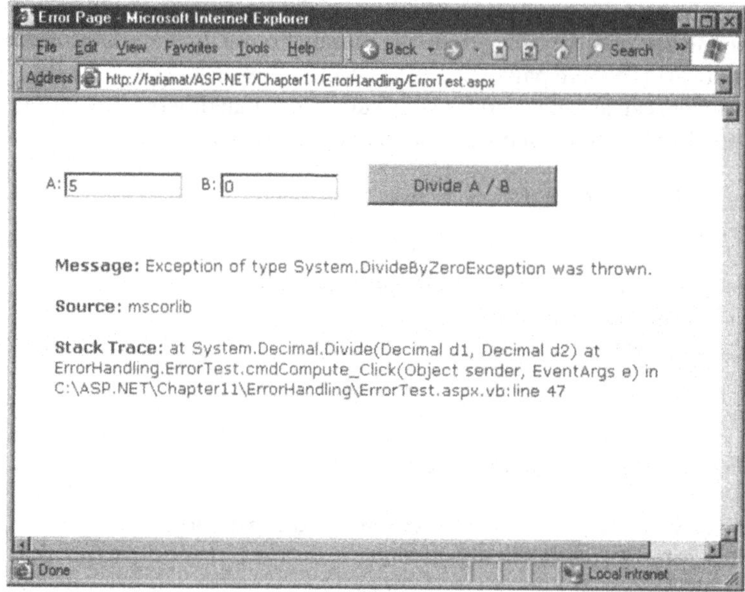

Figure 11-4. Catching and displaying exception information

Obviously, this problem could be easily avoided with extra code-safety checks, or elegantly resolved using the validation controls. However, this code provides a good example of how you can deal with the properties of an exception object. It also gives you a good idea about what sort of information will be returned.

Here's the page class code for this example:

```
Public Class ErrorTest
  Inherits Page
    Protected lblResult As Label
    Protected WithEvents cmdCompute As Button
    Protected txtB As TextBox
    Protected txtA As TextBox

    Private Sub cmdCompute_Click(sender As Object, e As EventArgs) _
      Handles cmdCompute.Click

        Try
            Dim A, B, Result As Decimal
            A = Val(txtA.Text)
            B = Val(txtB.Text)
            Result = A / B
            lblResult.Text = Result.ToString()
            lblResult.ForeColor = Color.Black
```

```
        Catch err As Exception
            lblResult.Text = "<b>Message:</b> " & err.Message
            lblResult.Text &= "<br><br>"
            lblResult.Text &= "<b>Source:</b> " & err.Source
            lblResult.Text &= "<br><br>"
            lblResult.Text &= "<b>Stack Trace:</b> " & err.StackTrace
            lblResult.ForeColor = Color.Red
        End Try

    End Sub

End Class
```

Note that as soon as the error occurs, execution is transferred to an exception handler. The code in the Catch block isn't completed. It's for that reason that the contents of the label are set in the Catch block. These lines will only be executed if the division code runs error-free.

You'll see many more examples of exception handling throughout this book. The data access chapters in the third part of this book show the best practices for exception handling when accessing a database.

Mastering Exceptions

There are a number of useful points to keep in mind when working with VB .NET's new structured exception handling:

- **Break down your code into multiple Try/Catch blocks.** If you put all of your code into one exception handler, you'll have trouble determining where the problem occurred. Also, unlike with the On Error Goto system, there is no way to "resume" the code in a Try block. That means that if an error occurs early on and you have a great deal of code in a single exception handler, many lines will be skipped. The rule of thumb is to use one exception handler for one related task (like opening a file and retrieving information).

- **Use ASP.NET's error pages during development.** During development, you may not want to implement portions of your application's error-handling code because it may mask easily correctable mistakes in your application.

- **Don't use for exception handlers for every statement.** Simple code statements (assigning a constant value to a variable, interacting with a control, and so on) may cause errors during development testing, but will not cause any future problems once perfected. Error handling should be used when you're accessing an outside resource or dealing with supplied data that you have no control over (and thus may be invalid).

Throwing Your Own Exceptions

You can also define and create your own exception objects to represent special error conditions. All you need to do is create an instance of the appropriate exception class, and then use the Throw statement.

The next example introduces a modified DivideNumbers() function. It explicitly checks if the specified divisor is 0, and then manually creates and throws an instance of the DivideByZeroException class to indicate the problem, rather than attempt the operation. Depending on the code, this pattern can save time by eliminating some unnecessary steps, or prevent a task from being initiated if it can't be successfully completed.

```
Private Sub Page_Load(sender As Object, e As EventArgs) _
  Handles MyBase.Load
    Try
        DivideNumbers(5, 0)
    Catch err As DivideByZeroException
        ' Report error here.
    End Try
End Sub

Private Function DivideNumbers(number As Decimal, divisor As Decimal) _
  As Decimal
    If divisor = 0
        Dim err As New DivideByZeroException()
        Throw err
    Else
        Return (number/divisor)
    End If
End Function
```

Alternatively, you can create a .NET exception object, but you must specify a custom error message by using a different constructor:

```
Private Function DivideNumbers(number As Decimal, divisor As Decimal) _
  As Decimal
    If divisor = 0
        Dim err As New DivideByZeroException( _
         "You supplied 0 for the divisor parameter. You must be stopped.")
        Throw err
    Else
        Return (number/divisor)
    End If
End Function
```

In this case, the DivideByZeroException will still be caught by any ordinary exception handlers. The only difference is that the error object has a modified Message property that contains the custom string. The resulting exception is shown in Figure 11-5.

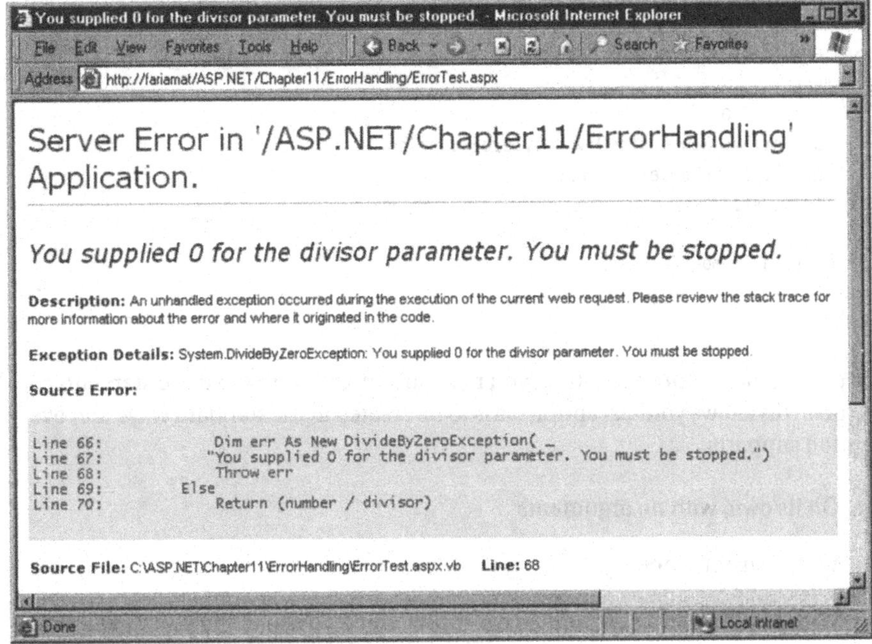

Figure 11-5. Standard exception, custom message

Throwing an error is most useful in component-based programming. In component-based programming, your ASP.NET page is creating objects and calling methods from a class defined in a separately compiled assembly. In this case, the class in the component needs to be able to notify the calling code (the web application) of any errors. The component should handle recoverable errors quietly, and not pass them up to the calling code. On the other hand, if an unrecoverable error occurs, it should always be indicated with an exception, and never through another mechanism (like a return code). For more information about component-based programming, refer to Chapter 22.

If you can find an exception in the class library that accurately reflects the problem that has occurred, you should throw it. If you need to return additional or specialized information, you can create your own custom exception class.

Custom exception classes should always inherit from System.ApplicationException. In addition, you can add properties to record additional information. For example, here is a special class that records information about the failed attempt to divide by zero:

```
Public Class CustomDivideByZeroException
  Inherits ApplicationException

    ' Add a variable to specify the "other" number.
    ' This might help diagnose the problem.
    Public DividingNumber As Integer

End Class
```

You can throw this custom error like this:

```
Private Function DivideNumbers(number As Integer, divisor As Integer) _
  As Integer
    If divisor = 0
        Dim err As New CustomDivideByZeroException()
        err.DividingNumber = number
        Throw err
    Else
        Return (number/divisor)
    End If
End Function
```

To perfect the custom exception, you need to supply it with the three standard constructors. This allows your exception class to be created in the standard ways that every exception supports:

- On its own, with no arguments
- With a custom message
- With a custom message and an exception object to use as the inner exception

All these constructors need to do is forward the parameters to the base class (the constructors in the inherited ApplicationException class) using the MyBase keyword, as shown here:

```
Public Class CustomDivideByZeroException
  Inherits ApplicationException

    ' Add a variable to specify the "other" number.
    Public DividingNumber As Integer

    Public Sub New()
        MyBase.New()
    End Sub

    Public Sub New(message As String)
        MyBase.New(message)
    End Sub

    Public Sub New(message as String, inner As Exception)
        MyBase.New(message, inner)
    End Sub

End Class
```

The third constructor is particularly useful for component programming. Using it you could intercept a low-level exception (like DivideByZero) and replace it with a higher-level exception without losing the original exception. The next example shows you could use this constructor with a component class called ArithmeticUtility:

```
Public Class ArithmeticUtilityException
  Inherits ApplicationException

    Public Sub New()
        MyBase.New()
    End Sub

    Public Sub New(message As String)
        MyBase.New(message)
    End Sub

    Public Sub New(message as String, inner As Exception)
        MyBase.New(message, inner)
    End Sub

End Class

Public Class ArithmeticUtility

    Private Function Divide(number As Decimal, divisor As Decimal) _
      As Decimal
        Try
            Return (number/divisor)
        Catch err As Exception
            ' Create an instance of the specialized exception class,
            ' and place the original error in the InnerException property.
            Dim errNew As New ArithmeticUtilityException(err)

            ' Now "rethrow" the new exception.
            Throw errNew
        End Try
    End Function

End Class
```

Remember, custom exception classes are really just a special, standardized way for one class to communicate an error to a different portion of code. If you aren't using components or your own utility classes, you probably don't need to create custom exception classes.

Logging Exceptions

In many cases, it's best not only to detect and catch errors, but to log them as well. For example, some problems may only occur when your web server is dealing with a particularly large load. Other problems might recur intermittently, with no obvious causes. To diagnose these errors and build a larger picture of site problems, you need to log errors automatically so they can be reviewed at a later date.

The .NET Framework provides a wide range of logging tools. When certain errors occur, you can send an e-mail, add a database record, or create and write to a file. Many of these techniques are described in other parts of this book. However, you should keep your logging code as simple as possible. For example, you'll probably run into trouble if you try to log a database error to another table in the database.

One of the best logging tools is provided in the Windows event logs, described in Table 11-2. To view these logs, select Settings ➤ Control Panel ➤ Administrative Tools ➤ Event Viewers from the Start menu. By default, you'll see three logs, as shown in Figure 11-6). You can right-click a log to clear the events in the log, save log entries, and import an external log file.

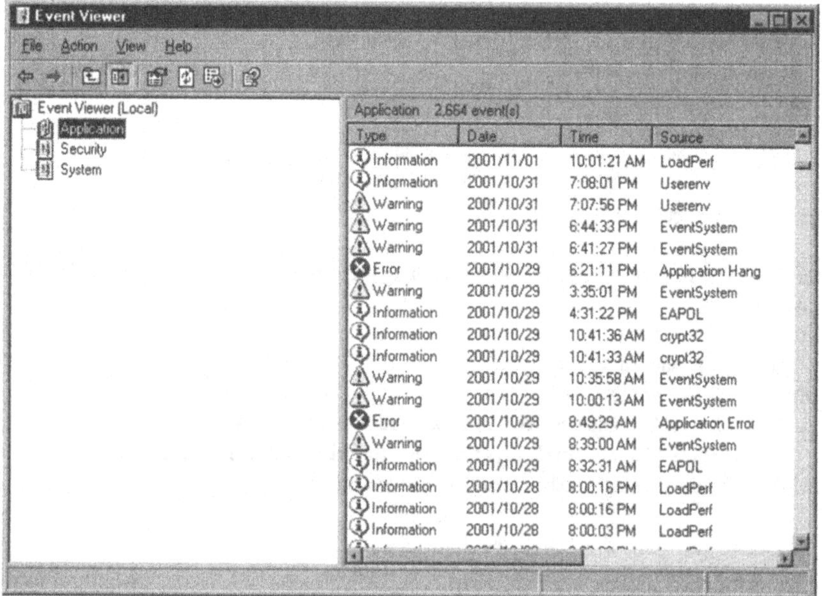

Figure 11-6. The event viewer

Table 11-2. Windows Event Logs

Log Name	**Description**
Application log	Used to track errors or notifications from any application. Generally, you'll use this log, or create your own.
Security log	Used to track security-related problems, but generally used exclusively by the operating system.
System log	Used to track operating system events.

Each event record identifies the source (generally, the application or service that created the record), the type of notification (error, information, warning), and the time it was left. You can also double-click a record to view additional information such as a text description (see Figure 11-7).

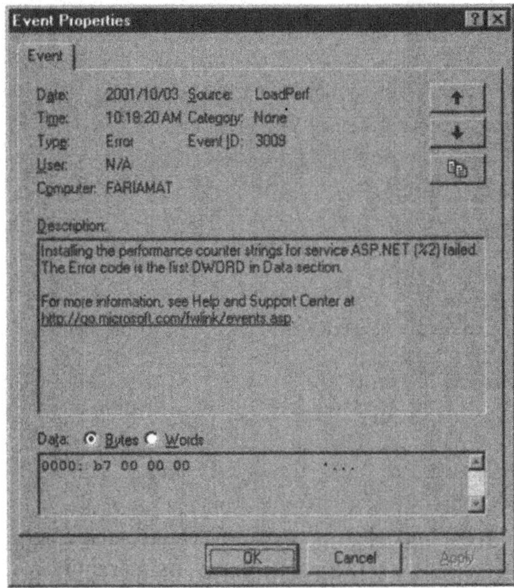

Figure 11-7. Event information

One of the potential problems with event logs is that they're automatically overwritten when the maximum size is reached (typically half a megabyte) as long as they're of at least a certain age (typically seven days). This means that application logs can't be used to log critical information that you need to retain for a long period of time. Instead, they should be used to track information that is only valuable for a short amount of time. For example, you can use event logs to review errors and diagnose strange behavior immediately after it happens, not a month later.

You do have some ability to configure the amount of time a log will be retained and the maximum size it will be allowed to occupy. To configure these settings, right-click the application log and select Properties. You'll see the Application Properties window shown in Figure 11-8.

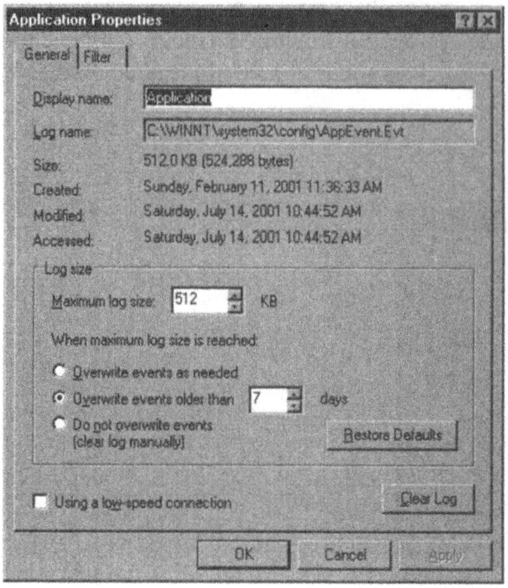

Figure 11-8. Log properties

Generally, you should not disable automatic log deletion, because it could cause a large amount of wasted space and slowed performance if information isn't being regularly removed. Instead, if you want to retain more log information, set a larger disk space limit.

Using the EventLog Class

You can interact with event logs in an ASP.NET page by using the classes in the System.Diagnostics namespace. First, import the namespace at the beginning of your code-behind file:

```
Imports System.Diagnostics
```

The following example rewrites the simple ErrorTest page to use event logging:

```
Public Class ErrorTestLog
  Inherits Page
    Protected lblResult As Label
    Protected WithEvents cmdCompute As Button
    Protected txtB As TextBox
    Protected txtA As TextBox
```

```
    Private Sub cmdCompute_Click(sender As Object, e As EventArgs) _
      Handles cmdCompute.Click
        Try
            Dim A, B, Result As Decimal
            A = Val(txtA.Text)
            B = Val(txtB.Text)
            Result = A / B
            lblResult.Text = Result.ToString()
            lblResult.ForeColor = Color.Black
        Catch err As Exception
            lblResult.Text = "<b>Message:</b> " & err.Message & "<br><br>"
            lblResult.Text &= "<b>Source:</b> " & err.Source & "<br><br>"
            lblResult.Text &= "<b>Stack Trace:</b> " & err.StackTrace
            lblResult.ForeColor = Color.Red

            ' Write the information to the event log.
            Dim Log As New EventLog()
            Log.Source = "DivisionPage"
            Log.WriteEntry(err.Message, EventLogEntryType.Error)
        End Try
    End Sub

End Class
```

The event log record will now appear in the Event Viewer utility, as shown in Figure 11-9. Note that logging is intended for the system administrator or developer. It doesn't replace the code you use to notify the user and explain that a problem has occurred.

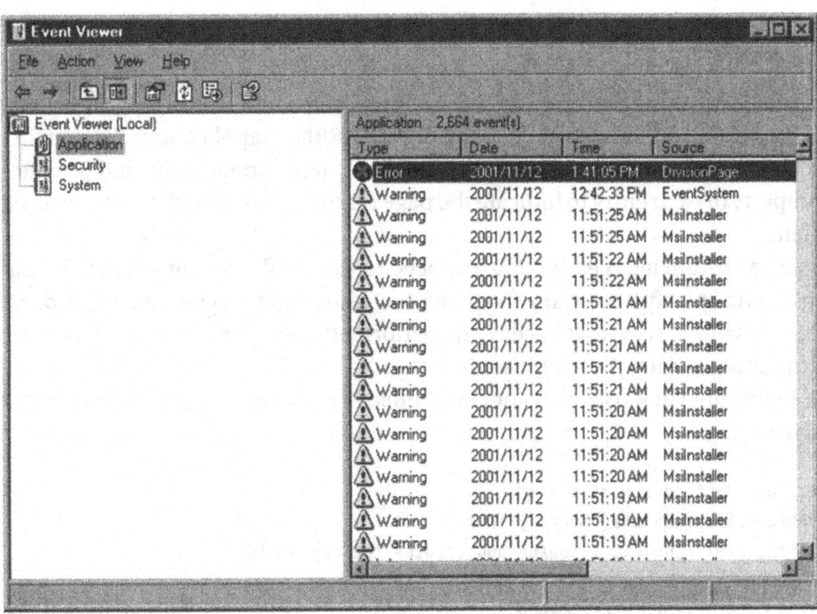

Figure 11-9. A custom event

Event Log Security

There is one potential problem that could prevent this code example from working on your computer. By default, the ASP.NET service runs using a special account named ASPNET, which won't have the permissions to create event log entries. In order to remedy this problem, you can instruct ASP.NET to use a different account (as explained in Chapter 4), or you can grant the required permissions to the ASPNET account. To do the latter, you need to modify the registry as described in these steps:

1. Run regedit.exe, either from a command-line prompt or by choosing Run from the Start menu.
2. Browse to the HKEY_Local_Machine\SYSTEM\CurrentControlSet\Services\EventLog section of the registry.
3. Select the EventLog folder if you want to give ASP.NET permission to all areas of the event log. Or, select a specific folder that corresponds to the event log that ASP.NET needs to access.
4. Choose Security ➤ Permissions.
5. Add the account ASPNET to the list. To do this, click the Add button, type in ASPNET, and then click OK.
6. Give the ASPNET account Full Control for this section of the registry, by selecting the Allow check box next to Full Control.

Custom Logs

You can also log errors to a custom log. For example, you could create a log with your company name, and add records in it for all of your ASP.NET applications. You might even want to create an individual log for a particularly large application, and use the Source property of each entry to indicate the page (or web service method) that caused the problem.

Accessing a custom log is easy—you just need to use a different constructor for the EventLog class to specify the custom log name. You also need to register an *event source* for the log. This initial step only needs to be performed once. Typically, you'll use the name of the application as the event source.

Here's an example that uses a custom log named MyNewLog and registers the event source MyNewLog.

```
' Register the event source if needed.
If Not EventLog.SourceExists("MyApp") Then
    ' This registers the event source and creates the custom log,
    ' if needed.
    EventLog.CreateEventSource("MyApp", "MyNewLog")
End If
```

```
' Open the log. If the log doesn't exist,
' it will be created automatically.
Dim Log As New EventLog("MyNewLog")
log.WriteEntry(err.Message, EventLogEntryType.Error)
```

If you specify the name of a log that doesn't exist when you use the CreateEventSource() method, the system will create a new, custom event log for you the first time you write an entry.

The new log is shown in Figure 11-10.

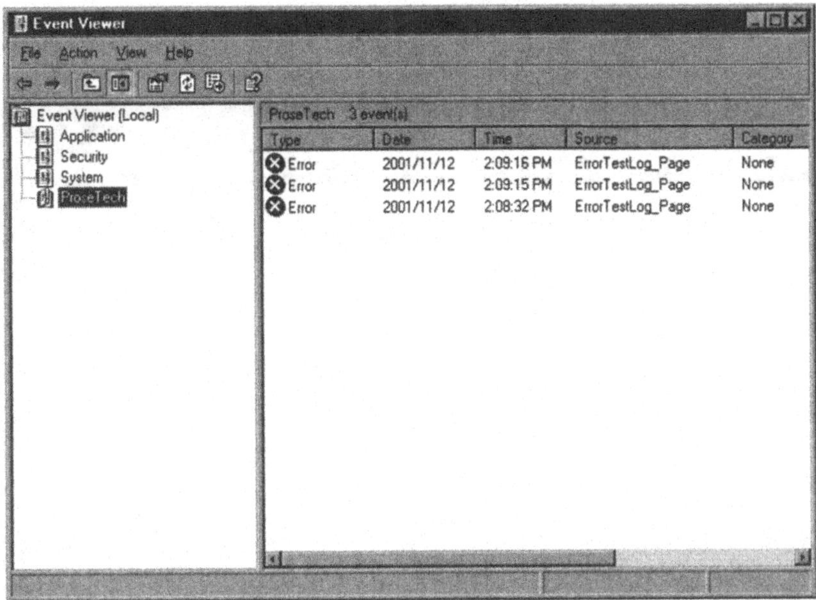

Figure 11-10. A custom log

TIP Event logging uses disk space and takes processor time away from web applications. Don't store unimportant information, large quantities of data, or information that would be better off in another type of storage (such as a relational database). Generally, an event log should be used to log unexpected conditions or errors, not customer actions or performance tracking information.

Retrieving Log Information

One of the disadvantages of the event logs is that they're tied to the web server. This can make it difficult to review log entries if you don't have a way to access the server. There are several possible solutions to this problem. One interesting technique involves using a special administration page. This ASP.NET page can use the EventLog class to retrieve and display all the information from the event log.

The following example retrieves all the entries that were left by the ErrorLogTest, and displays them in a simple web page (shown in Figure 11-11). A more sophisticated approach would use similar code, but one of the data controls discussed in Chapter 16 instead.

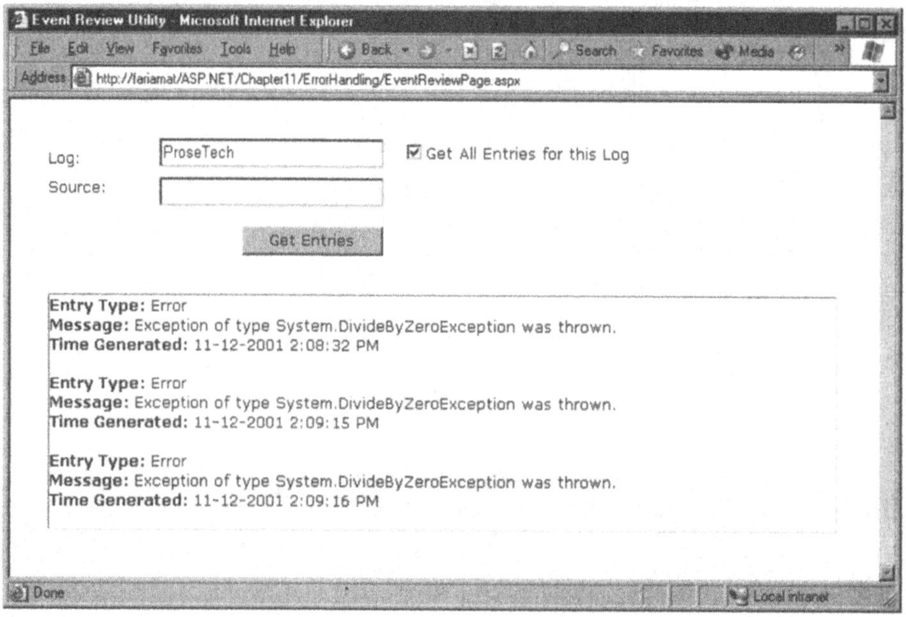

Figure 11-11. A log viewer page

Here's the web page code you'll need:

```
Public Class EventReviewPage
  Inherits Page

    Protected lblResult As Label
    Protected txtSource As TextBox
    Protected WithEvents cmdGet As Button
    Protected WithEvents chkAll As CheckBox
    Protected txtLog As TextBox
```

```
    Private Sub cmdGet_Click(sender As Object, e As EventArgs) _
      Handles cmdGet.Click

        lblResult.Text = ""

        ' Check if the log exists.
        If Not EventLog.Exists(txtLog.Text) Then
            lblResult.Text = "The event log " & txtLog.Text
            lblResult.Text &= " doesn't exist."
        Else
            Dim log As New EventLog(txtLog.Text)
            Dim entry As EventLogEntry
            For Each entry In log.Entries
                ' Write the event entries to the page.
                If chkAll.Checked = True Or _
                  entry.Source = txtSource.Text Then
                    lblResult.Text &= "<b>Entry Type:</b> "
                    lblResult.Text &= entry.EntryType.ToString()
                    lblResult.Text &= "<br><b>Message:</b> "
                    lblResult.Text &= entry.Message
                    lblResult.Text &= "<br><b>Time Generated:</b> "
                    lblResult.Text &= entry.TimeGenerated
                    lblResult.Text &= "<br><br>"
                End If
            Next
        End If

    End Sub

    Private Sub chkAll_CheckedChanged(sender As Object, _
      e As EventArgs) Handles chkAll.CheckedChanged
        ' The chkAll control has AutoPostback = True.
        If chkAll.Checked = True Then
            txtSource.Text = ""
            txtSource.Enabled = False
        Else
            txtSource.Enabled = True
        End If
    End Sub

End Class
```

TIP You can get around some of the limitations involved with the event log by using your own custom logging system. All the ingredients you need are built into the common class library. You could store error information in a database (as described in Chapter 14), or just send it to an e-mail account (as described in Chapter 17).

Error Pages

As you create and test an ASP.NET application, you'll become familiar with the rich information pages that are shown to describe unhandled errors. These pages are extremely useful for diagnosing problems during development, because they contain a wealth of information. Some of this information includes the source code where the problem occurred (with the offending line highlighted), the type of error, and a detailed error message describing the problem. A sample rich error page is shown in Figure 11-12.

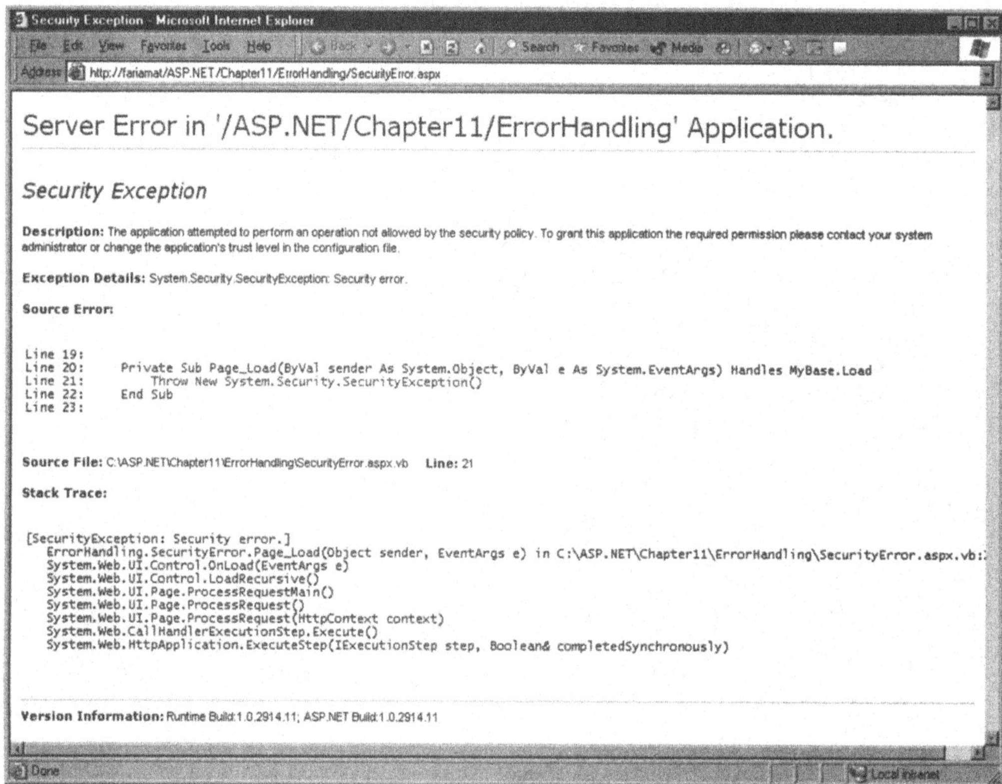

Figure 11-12. A rich ASP.NET error page

This error page is only shown for local requests that access the ASP.NET application through the http://localhost domain. (This domain always refers to the current computer, regardless of its actual server name or Internet address.) ASP.NET doesn't create a rich error page for requests from other computers, which receive the rather unhelpful generic page shown in Figure 11-13.

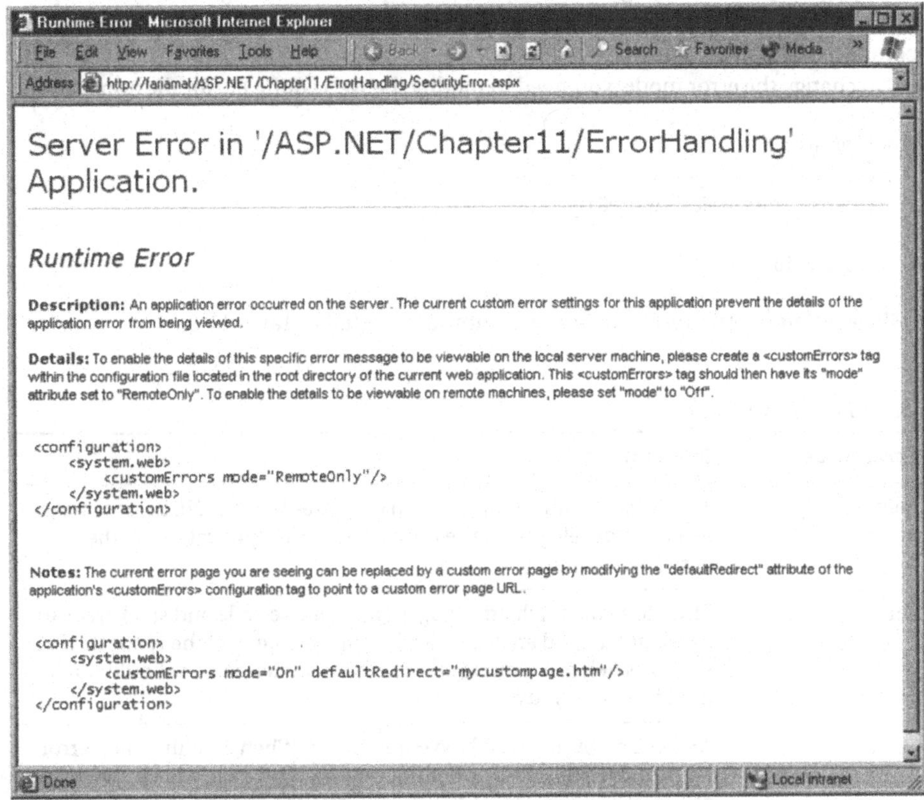

Figure 11-13. A generic client error page

This generic page lacks any specific details about the type of error or the offending code. Sharing this information with end users would be a security risk (potentially exposing sensitive details about the source code) and it would be completely unhelpful, because clients are never in a position to modify the source code themselves. Instead, the page includes a generic message explaining that an error has occurred and describing how to enable remote error pages.

Error Modes

Remote error pages remove this restriction, and allow ASP.NET to display detailed information for problems regardless of the source of the request. Remote error pages are intended as a testing tool. For example, in the initial rollout of an application beta, you might use field testers. These field testers would need to report specific information about application errors to aid in the debugging process. Similarly, you could use remote error pages if you're working with a team of developers and testing an ASP.NET application from a live web server. In this case, you might follow the time-honored code, compile, and upload pattern.

To change the error mode, you need to modify the web.config file for the application:

```
<configuration>
  <system.web>
    <customErrors mode="RemoteOnly" />
  </system.web>
</configuration>
```

The different options for the mode attribute are listed in Table 11-3.

Table 11-3. Error Modes

Error Mode	Description
RemoteOnly	This is the default setting, which only uses rich ASP.NET error pages when the developer is accessing an ASP.NET application on the current machine.
Off	This configures rich error pages (with source code and stack traces) for all unhandled errors, regardless of the source of the request. This setting is helpful in many development scenarios, but should not be used in a deployed application.
On	ASP.NET error pages will never be shown. When an unhandled error is encountered, a corresponding custom error page will be shown if one exists. Otherwise, ASP.NET will show the generic message explaining that application settings prevent the error details from being displayed, and describing how to change the configuration.

A Custom Error Page

In a deployed application, you should use the On or RemoteOnly error mode. Any errors in your application should be dealt with through error-handling code, which can then present a helpful and user-oriented message (rather than the developer-oriented code details in ASP.NET's rich error messages).

However, it isn't possible to catch every possible error in an ASP.NET application. For example, a hardware failure could occur spontaneously in the middle of an ordinary code statement that could not normally cause an error. More commonly, the user might encounter an HTTP error by requesting a page that doesn't exist. ASP.NET allows you to handle these problems with custom error pages.

There are two ways to implement custom error pages. You can create a single generic error page, and configure ASP.NET to use by modifying the web.config file as shown here:

```
<configuration>
  <system.web>
    <customErrors defaultRedirect="DefaultError.aspx" />
  </system.web>
</configuration>
```

ASP.NET will now exhibit the following behavior:

- If ASP.NET encounters an HTTP error while serving the request, it will forward the user to the DefaultError.aspx web page.
- If ASP.NET encounters an unhandled application error, and it isn't configured to display rich error pages, it will forward the user to the DefaultError.aspx. Remote users will never see the generic ASP.NET error page.
- If ASP.NET encounters an unhandled application error and it is configured to display rich developer-targeted error pages, it will display the rich error page instead.

NOTE What happens if an error occurs in the error page itself? If an error occurs in custom error page (in this case, DefaultError.aspx), ASP.NET will not be able to handle it. It will not try to re-forward the user to the same page. Instead, it will display the normal client error page with the generic message.

Specific Custom Error Pages

You can also create error pages targeted at specific types of HTTP errors (such as the infamous 404 Not Found error, or Access Denied). This technique is commonly used with websites to provide friendly equivalents for common problems. Figure 11-14 shows how Excite handles this issue.

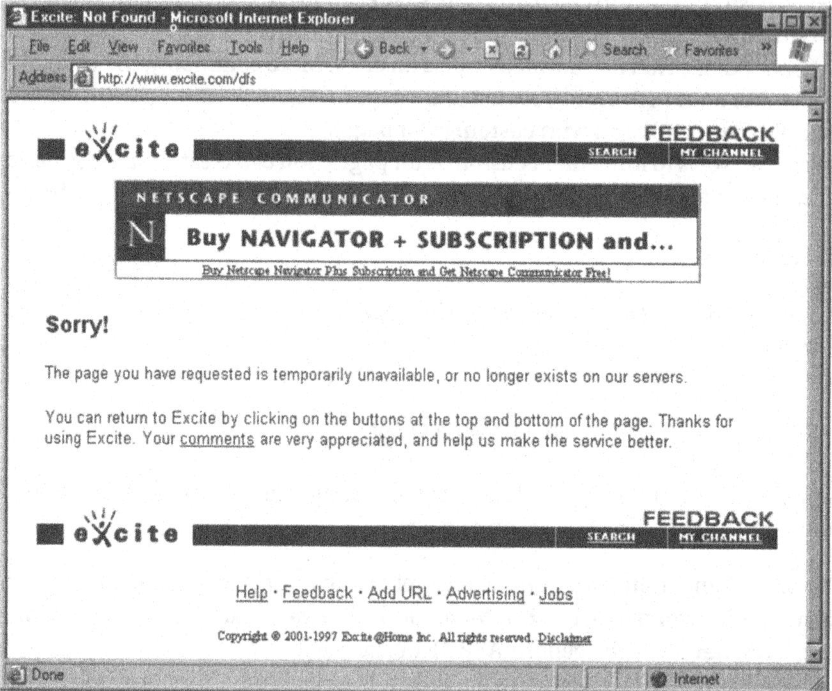

Figure 11-14. A sample custom error page

To define a error-specific custom page, you add an <error> element to the <customErrors> element. The <error> element identifies the HTTP error code, and the redirect page.

```
<configuration>
  <system.web>
    <customErrors defaultRedirect="DefaultError.aspx">
      <error statusCode="404" redirect="404.aspx" />
    <customErrors>
  </system.web>
</configuration>
```

In this example, the user will be redirected to the 404.aspx page when requesting an ASP.NET page that doesn't exist. This custom error page may not work exactly the way that you expect, because it only comes into effect if ASP.NET is handling the request.

For example, if you request the nonexistent page whateverpage.aspx, you'll be redirected to 404.aspx, because the .aspx file extension is registered to the ASP.NET service. However, if you request the nonexistent page whateverpage.html, ASP.NET will not process the request, and the default redirect setting specified in IIS will be used. Typically, this means that the user will see the page C:\[WinDir]\Help\IISHelp\common\404b.htm. You could change the set of registered ASP.NET file types to include .html and .htm files, but this will slow down performance. Optionally, you could change your ASP.NET application to use the custom IIS error page:

```
<configuration>
  <system.web>
    <customErrors defaultRedirect="/defaulterror.aspx">
      <error statusCode="404" redirect="/Errors/404b.htm" />
    <customErrors>
  </system.web>
</configuration>
```

When an error occurs that isn't specifically addressed by a custom <error> element, the default error page will be used.

Page Tracing

ASP.NET's detailed error pages are extremely helpful when you're testing and perfecting an application. However, sometimes you need more information to verify that your application is performing properly or to track down logic errors, which may produce invalid data but no obvious exceptions. In traditional ASP development, programmers often resorted to using Response.Write() to display debug information directly on the web page. Unfortunately, this technique is fraught with problems:

- **Code entanglement.** It's difficult to separate the ordinary code from the debugging code. Before the application can be deployed, you need to painstakingly search through the code and remove or comment out all the Response.Write() statements.
- **No single point of control.** If problems occur later down the road, there's no easy way to "re-enable" the write statements. Response.Write() statements are tightly integrated into the code.
- **User interface problems.** Response.Write() outputs information directly into the page. Depending on the current stage of page processing, the information can appear in just about any location, potentially scrambling your layout.

These problems can be overcome with additional effort and some homegrown solutions. However, ASP.NET provides a far more convenient and flexible method built into the framework services. It's called tracing.

Enabling Tracing

In order to use tracing, you need to explicitly enable it. There are several ways to switch tracing on. One of the easiest ways is by adding an attribute to the Page directive in the .aspx portion of your page:

```
<%@ Page Trace="True" %>
```

You can also enable tracing with using the built-in Trace object (which is an instance of the System.Web.TraceContext class). Here's an example of how you might turn tracing on in the Page.Load event hander:

```
Private Sub Page_Load(sender As Object, e As EventArgs) _
  Handles MyBase.Load
    Trace.IsEnabled = True
End Sub
```

This technique is particularly useful because it allows you to enable or disable tracing for a page programmatically. For example, you could examine the query string collection, and only enable tracing if a special Tracing variable is received. This could allow developers to run tracing diagnostics on deployed pages, without revealing that information for normal requests from end users.

```
Private Sub Page_Load(sender As Object, e As EventArgs) _
  Handles MyBase.Load
    If Request.QueryString("Tracing") = "On"
        Trace.IsEnabled = True
    End If
End Sub
```

Lastly, you can enable application-level tracing with the web.config file. This topic is discussed later in this chapter.

Note that by default, once you enable tracing it will only apply to local requests. That prevents actual end users from seeing the tracing information. If you need to trace a web page from an offsite location, you should use a technique like the one shown previously (for query string activation). You'll also need to change some web.config settings to enable remote tracing. Information about modifying these settings is found at the end of this chapter, in the "Application-Level Tracing" section.

What About Visual Studio .NET?

Visual Studio .NET provides a full complement of debugging tools that allow you to set breakpoints, step through code, and view the contents of variables while your program executes. Though you can use Visual Studio .NET in conjunction with page tracing, you probably won't need to. Instead, page tracing will become more useful for debugging problems after you have deployed the application to a web server. Visual Studio .NET error handling is discussed in Chapter 8.

Tracing Information

ASP.NET tracing automatically provides a lengthy set of standard, formatted information. For example, Figure 11-15 shows a rudimentary ASP.NET page with a single label control and button.

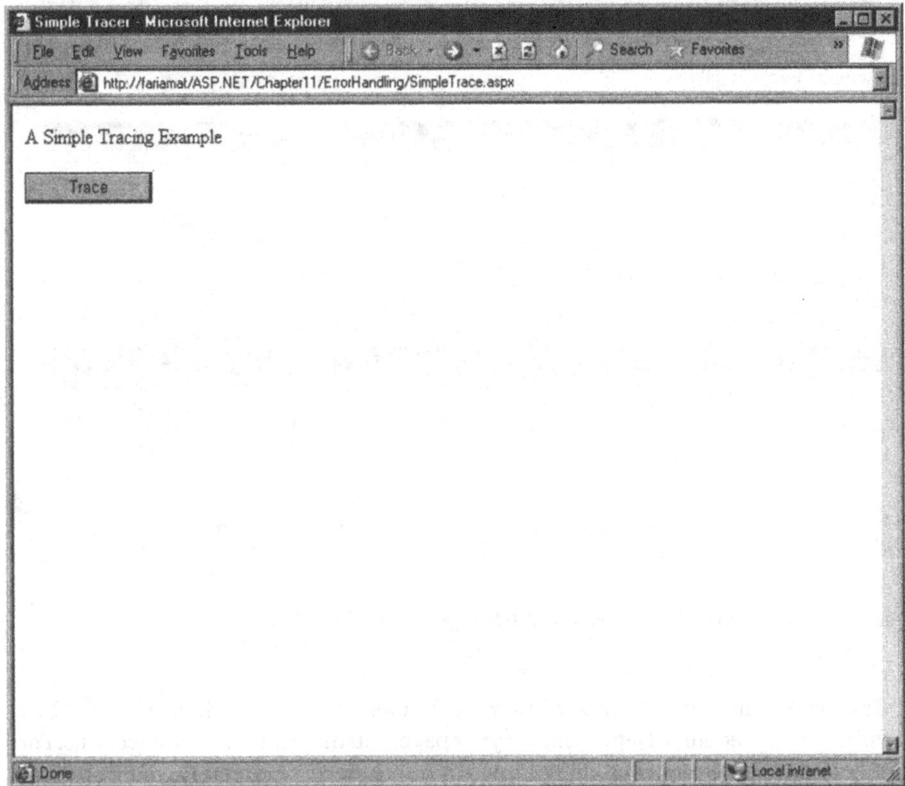

Figure 11-15. A simple ASP.NET page

On its own, this page does very little, displaying a single line of text. When you click the button to enable tracing, however, you end up with a lot of extra diagnostic information, as shown in Figure 11-16.

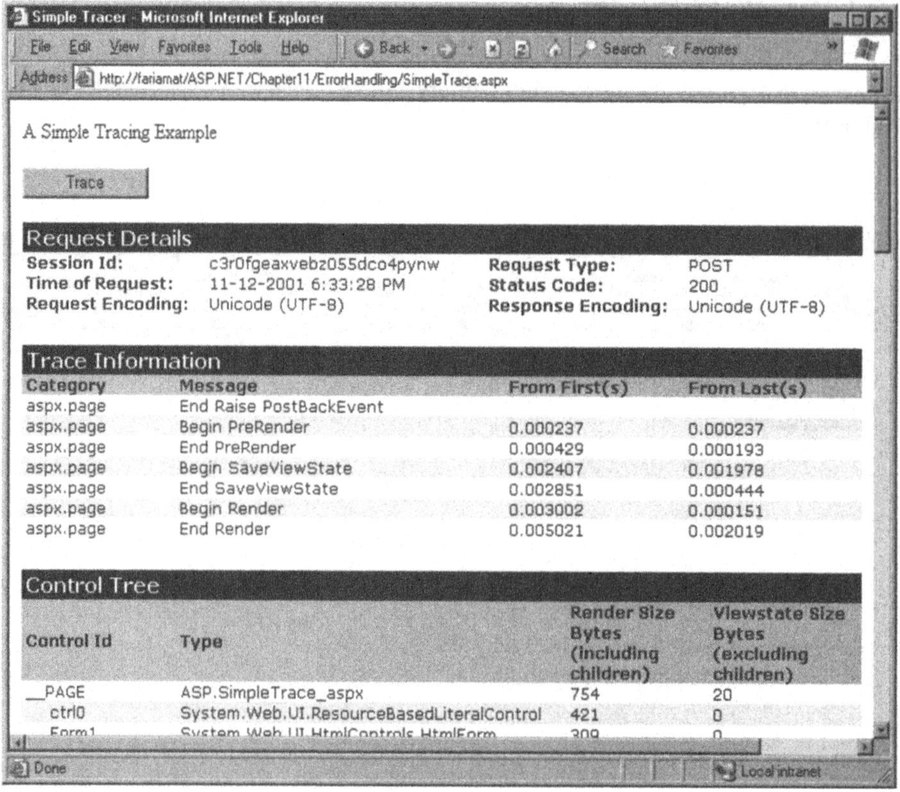

Figure 11-16. Tracing the simple ASP.NET page

Tracing information is provided in several different categories, which are described in the following sections. Depending on your page, you may not see all the sections. For example, if the page request didn't supply any query string parameters, you won't see the QueryString collection. Similarly, if there's no data currently being held in application or session state, you won't see those sections either.

TIP If you're designing your web pages with Visual Studio .NET, you'll have better success if you use flow layout mode for the page instead of grid layout mode. In grid layout mode, the tracing information will probably overwrite your page content. Another option is to use application-level tracing, as described at the end of this chapter.

Request Details

This section includes some basic information such as the current Session ID, the time the web request was made, and the type of web request and encoding (see Figure 11-17).

Request Details			
Session Id:	vqa22245szjcs545kripra45	**Request Type:**	POST
Time of Request:	11-12-2001 6:49:35 PM	**Status Code:**	200
Request Encoding:	Unicode (UTF-8)	**Response Encoding:**	Unicode (UTF-8)

Figure 11-17. Request Details

Trace Information

This section shows the different stages of processing the page went through before being sent to the client. Each section has additional information about how long it took to complete, as a measure from the start of the first stage (From First) and as a measure from the start of the previous stage (From Last). If you add your own trace messages (a technique described shortly), they will also appear in this section (see Figure 11-18).

Category	Message	From First(s)	From Last(s)
aspx.page	Begin ProcessPostData Second Try		
aspx.page	End ProcessPostData Second Try	0.000164	0.000164
aspx.page	Begin Raise ChangedEvents	0.000320	0.000156
aspx.page	End Raise ChangedEvents	0.000455	0.000134
aspx.page	Begin Raise PostBackEvent	0.000586	0.000131
aspx.page	End Raise PostBackEvent	0.003737	0.003152
aspx.page	Begin PreRender	0.004063	0.000326
aspx.page	End PreRender	0.004235	0.000173
aspx.page	Begin SaveViewState	0.007149	0.002914
aspx.page	End SaveViewState	0.007771	0.000621
aspx.page	Begin Render	0.007975	0.000204
aspx.page	End Render	0.011350	0.003375

Figure 11-18. Trace Information

Control Tree

The control tree shows you all the controls on the page, indented to show their hierarchy (which controls are contained inside other controls). In this simple page example, the only explicitly created controls are the label (lblMessage) and the web page. However, ASP.NET adds additional literal controls automatically to represent spacing and any other static elements that aren't server controls (such as text or ordinary HTML tags). One useful feature of this section of the Viewstate column, which tells you how many bytes of space are required to persist the current information in the control. This can help you gauge whether enabling control state is detracting from performance, particularly when working with data-bound controls like the DataGrid or DataList (see Figure 11-19).

Control Tree			
Control Id	Type	Render Size Bytes (including children)	Viewstate Size Bytes (excluding children)
__PAGE	ASP.TraceExample_aspx	1691	24
ctrl0	System.Web.UI.ResourceBasedLiteralControl	427	0
Form1	System.Web.UI.HtmlControls.HtmlForm	1236	0
ctrl1	System.Web.UI.LiteralControl	137	0
cmdWrite	System.Web.UI.WebControls.Button	201	0
ctrl2	System.Web.UI.LiteralControl	2	0
Label1	System.Web.UI.WebControls.Label	113	0
ctrl3	System.Web.UI.LiteralControl	2	0
cmdWriteCategory	System.Web.UI.WebControls.Button	232	0
ctrl4	System.Web.UI.LiteralControl	2	0
cmdError	System.Web.UI.WebControls.Button	203	0
ctrl5	System.Web.UI.LiteralControl	2	0
cmdSession	System.Web.UI.WebControls.Button	171	0
ctrl6	System.Web.UI.LiteralControl	14	0
ctrl7	System.Web.UI.LiteralControl	28	0

Figure 11-19. Control Tree

Session State and Application State

These sections display every item that is in the current session or application state. Each item is listed with its name, type, and value. If you're storing simple pieces of string information, the value is straightforward. If you're storing an object, .NET calls the objects ToString() method to get an appropriate string representation. For complex objects, the result may just be the class name (see Figure 11-20).

Session State		
Session Key	Type	Value
Test	System.String	This is just a string
MyDataSet	System.Data.DataSet	System.Data.DataSet

Figure 11-20. Session State

Cookies Collection

This section displays all the cookies that are sent with the response, and the content and size of each cookie in bytes. Even if you haven't explicitly created a cookie, you'll see the ASP.NET_SessionId cookie, which contains the current session ID. If you're using forms-based authentication, you'll also see the security cookie (see Figure 11-21).

Cookies Collection		
Name	Value	Size
ASP.NET_SessionId	vqa22245szjcs545kripra45	42

Figure 11-21. Cookies Collection

Headers Collection

This section lists all the HTTP headers. Generally, you don't need to use this information, although it can be useful for troubleshooting unusual network problems (see Figure 11-22).

Headers Collection	
Name	Value
Cache-Control	no-cache
Connection	Keep-Alive
Content-Length	68
Content-Type	application/x-www-form-urlencoded
Accept	image/gif, image/x-xbitmap, image/jpeg, image/pjpeg, application/vnd.ms-excel, application/msword, application/pdf, */*
Accept-Encoding	gzip, deflate
Accept-Language	en-us
Host	fariamat
Referer	http://fariamat/ASP.NET/Chapter11/ErrorHandling/TraceExample.aspx
User-Agent	Mozilla/4.0 (compatible; MSIE 6.0; Windows NT 5.1; .NET CLR 1.0.2914)

Figure 11-22. Headers Collection

Forms Collection

This section lists the posted-back form information (see Figure 11-23).

Form Collection	
Name	Value
__VIEWSTATE	dDwtMjA5NDAxOTA1OTs7Pg==
cmdSession	Add Session Item

Figure 11-23. Forms Collection

QueryString Collection

This section lists the variables and values submitted in the query string. Generally, you'll be able to see this information directly in the Address box in the browser, so you won't need to refer to the information here (see Figure 11-24).

Querystring Collection	
Name	Value
search	cat
style	full

Figure 11-24. QueryString Collection

Server Variables

This section lists all the server variables and their contents. You don't generally need to examine this information. Note also that if you want to examine a server variable programmatically, you can do so by name with the built-in Request.ServerVariables collection, or by using one of the more useful higher-level properties from the Request object.

Writing Trace Information

The default trace log provides a set of important information that can allow you to monitor some important aspects of your application, such as the current state contents and the time taken to execute portions of code. In addition, you'll often want to generate your own tracing messages. For example, you might want to output the value of a variable at various points in execution, so you can compare it with an expected value. Similarly, you might want to output messages when the code reaches certain points in execution, so you can verify that various procedures are being used (and are used in the order you expect).

To write a custom trace message, you use the Write() or the Warn() method of the built-in Trace object. These methods are equivalent. The only difference is that Warn() displays the message in red lettering, which makes it easier to distinguish from other messages in the list. Here's a code snippet that writes a trace message when the user clicks a button:

```
Private Sub cmdWrite_Click(sender As Object, e As EventArgs) _
  Handles cmdWrite.Click

    Trace.IsEnabled = True
    Trace.Write("About to place an item in session state.")
    Session("Test") = "Contents"
    Trace.Write("Placed item in session state.")

End Sub
```

These messages appear in the trace information section of the page, along with the default messages that ASP.NET generates automatically (see Figure 11-25).

You can also use an overloaded method of Write() or Warn() that allows you to specify the category. A common use of this field is to indicate the current procedure, as shown in Figure 11-26.

```
Private Sub cmdWriteCategory_Click(sender As Object, _
  e As System.EventArgs) Handles cmdWriteCategory.Click

    Trace.IsEnabled = True
    Trace.Write("Page_Load", "About to place an item in session state.")
    Session("Test") = "Contents"
    Trace.Write("Page_Load", "Placed item in session state.")

End Sub
```

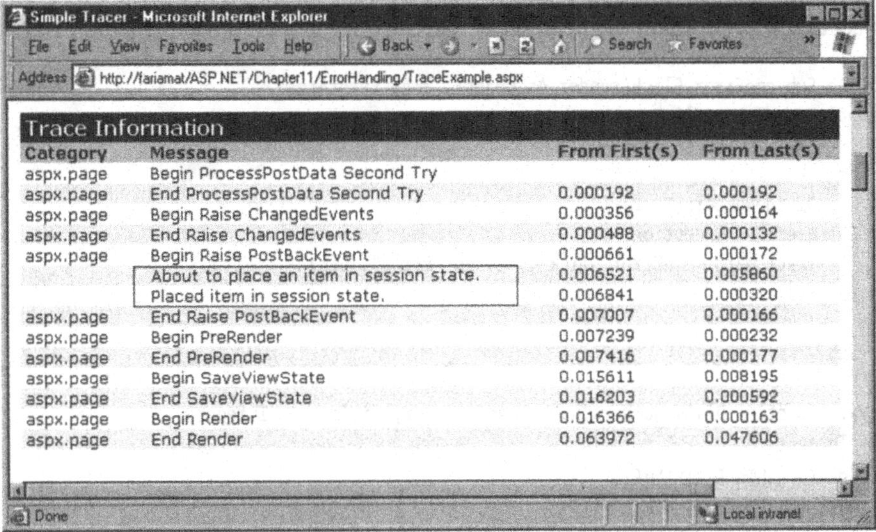

Simple Tracer - Microsoft Internet Explorer

http://fariamat/ASP.NET/Chapter11/ErrorHandling/TraceExample.aspx

Trace Information

Category	Message	From First(s)	From Last(s)
aspx.page	Begin ProcessPostData Second Try		
aspx.page	End ProcessPostData Second Try	0.000192	0.000192
aspx.page	Begin Raise ChangedEvents	0.000356	0.000164
aspx.page	End Raise ChangedEvents	0.000488	0.000132
aspx.page	Begin Raise PostBackEvent	0.000661	0.000172
	About to place an item in session state.	0.006521	0.005860
	Placed item in session state.	0.006841	0.000320
aspx.page	End Raise PostBackEvent	0.007007	0.000166
aspx.page	Begin PreRender	0.007239	0.000232
aspx.page	End PreRender	0.007416	0.000177
aspx.page	Begin SaveViewState	0.015611	0.008195
aspx.page	End SaveViewState	0.016203	0.000592
aspx.page	Begin Render	0.016366	0.000163
aspx.page	End Render	0.063972	0.047606

Figure 11-25. Custom trace messages

Simple Tracer - Microsoft Internet Explorer

http://fariamat/ASP.NET/Chapter11/ErrorHandling/TraceExample.aspx

Trace Information

Category	Message	From First(s)	From Last(s)
aspx.page	Begin ProcessPostData Second Try		
aspx.page	End ProcessPostData Second Try	0.000195	0.000195
aspx.page	Begin Raise ChangedEvents	0.000410	0.000215
aspx.page	End Raise ChangedEvents	0.000551	0.000141
aspx.page	Begin Raise PostBackEvent	0.000680	0.000129
Page_Load	About to place an item in session state.	0.005326	0.004646
Page_Load	Placed item in session state.	0.005640	0.000313
aspx.page	End Raise PostBackEvent	0.005808	0.000169
aspx.page	Begin PreRender	0.005947	0.000139
aspx.page	End PreRender	0.006108	0.000161
aspx.page	Begin SaveViewState	0.008451	0.002343
aspx.page	End SaveViewState	0.008959	0.000508
aspx.page	Begin Render	0.009122	0.000162
aspx.page	End Render	0.016037	0.006915

Figure 11-26. A categorized trace message

Alternatively, you can supply category and message information with an exception object that will automatically be described in the trace log, as shown in Figure 11-27.

```
Private Sub cmdError_Click(sender As Object, e As EventArgs) _
  Handles cmdError.Click

    Try
        DivideNumbers(5, 0)
    Catch err As Exception
        Trace.Warn("cmdError_Click", "Caught Error", err)
    End Try

End Sub

Private Function DivideNumbers(number As Integer, divisor As Integer) _
  As Integer
    Return (number/divisor)
End Sub
```

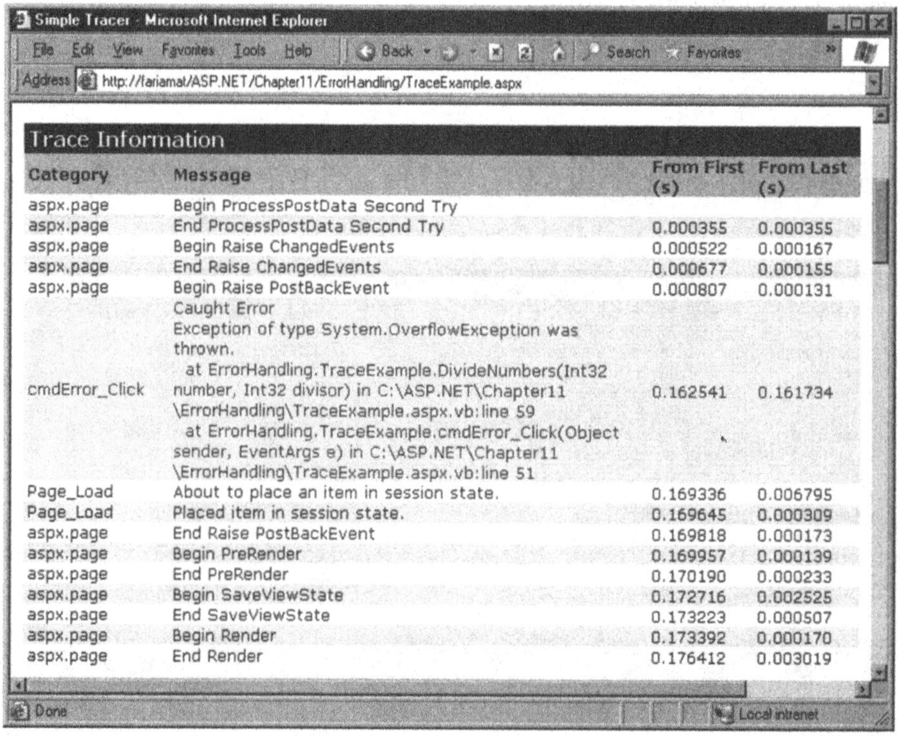
Simple Tracer - Microsoft Internet Explorer
File Edit View Favorites Tools Help
Back Search Favorites
Address http://fariamat/ASP.NET/Chapter11/ErrorHandling/TraceExample.aspx
Trace Information
Category
Message
From First (s)
From Last (s)
aspx.page Begin ProcessPostData Second Try
aspx.page End ProcessPostData Second Try 0.000355 0.000355
aspx.page Begin Raise ChangedEvents 0.000522 0.000167
aspx.page End Raise ChangedEvents 0.000677 0.000155
aspx.page Begin Raise PostBackEvent 0.000807 0.000131
cmdError_Click Caught Error
Exception of type System.OverflowException was thrown.
at ErrorHandling.TraceExample.DivideNumbers(Int32 number, Int32 divisor) in C:\ASP.NET\Chapter11\ErrorHandling\TraceExample.aspx.vb:line 59
at ErrorHandling.TraceExample.cmdError_Click(Object sender, EventArgs e) in C:\ASP.NET\Chapter11\ErrorHandling\TraceExample.aspx.vb:line 51
0.162541 0.161734
Page_Load About to place an item in session state. 0.169336 0.006795
Page_Load Placed item in session state. 0.169645 0.000309
aspx.page End Raise PostBackEvent 0.169818 0.000173
aspx.page Begin PreRender 0.169957 0.000139
aspx.page End PreRender 0.170190 0.000233
aspx.page Begin SaveViewState 0.172716 0.002525
aspx.page End SaveViewState 0.173223 0.000507
aspx.page Begin Render 0.173392 0.000170
aspx.page End Render 0.176412 0.003019
Done
Local intranet

Figure 11-27. An exception trace message

By default, trace messages are listed in the order they were outputted by your code. Alternatively, you can specify that messages should be sorted by category, using the TraceMode attribute in the Page directive:

```
<%@ Page Trace="True" TraceMode="SortByCategory" %>
```

or the TraceMode property of the Trace object in your code:

```
Trace.TraceMode = TraceMode.SortByCategory
```

Application-Level Tracing

Application-level tracing allows you to enable tracing for an entire application. To do this, you need to modify settings in the web.config file, as shown here:

```
<configuration>
  <system.web>
    <trace enabled="true" requestLimit="10" pageOutput="false"
     traceMode="SortByTime" localOnly="true" />
  </system.web>
</configuration>
```

The full list of tracing options is described in Table 11-4.

Table 11-4. Tracing Options

Attribute	Values	Description
Enabled	True, False	Turns application-level tracing on or off.
requestLimit	Any integer (e.g., 10)	This is the number of HTTP requests for which tracing information will be stored. Unlike page-level tracing, this allows you collect a batch of information from multiple requests. When the maximum is reached, the information for the oldest request is abandoned every time a new request is received.
pageOutput	True, False	Determines whether tracing information will be displayed on the page (as it is with page-level tracing). If you choose False, you'll still be able to view the collected information by requesting trace.axd from the virtual directory where your application is running.
traceMode	SortByTime, SortByCategory	Determines the sort order of trace messages.
localOnly	True, False	Determines whether tracing information will be shown only to local clients (clients using the same computer) or can be shown to remote clients as well. By default, this is True and remote clients cannot see tracing information.

To view tracing information, you request the trace.axd file in the web application's root directory. This file doesn't actually exist; instead, ASP.NET automatically intercepts the request and interprets it as a request for the tracing information. It will then provide a list of the most recent collected requests (see Figure 11-28), provided you're making the request from the local machine or have enabled remote tracing.

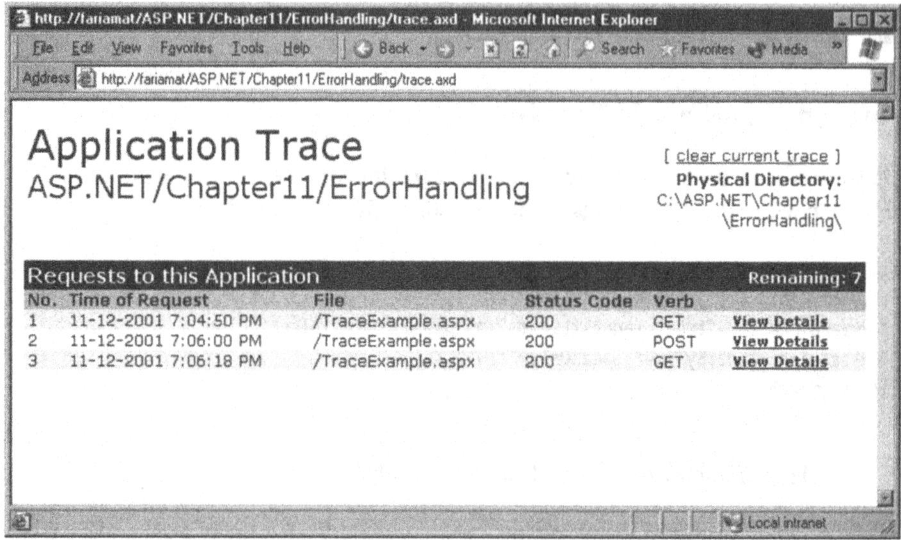

Figure 11-28. Traced application request

You can see the detailed information for any request by clicking the View Details link (see Figure 11-29). This provides a useful way to store tracing information for a short period of time, and allows you to review it without needing to see the actual pages. It also works best if you're using Visual Studio .NET's grid layout, which uses absolute positioning that can conflict with the tracing display and lead to overwritten or obscured text.

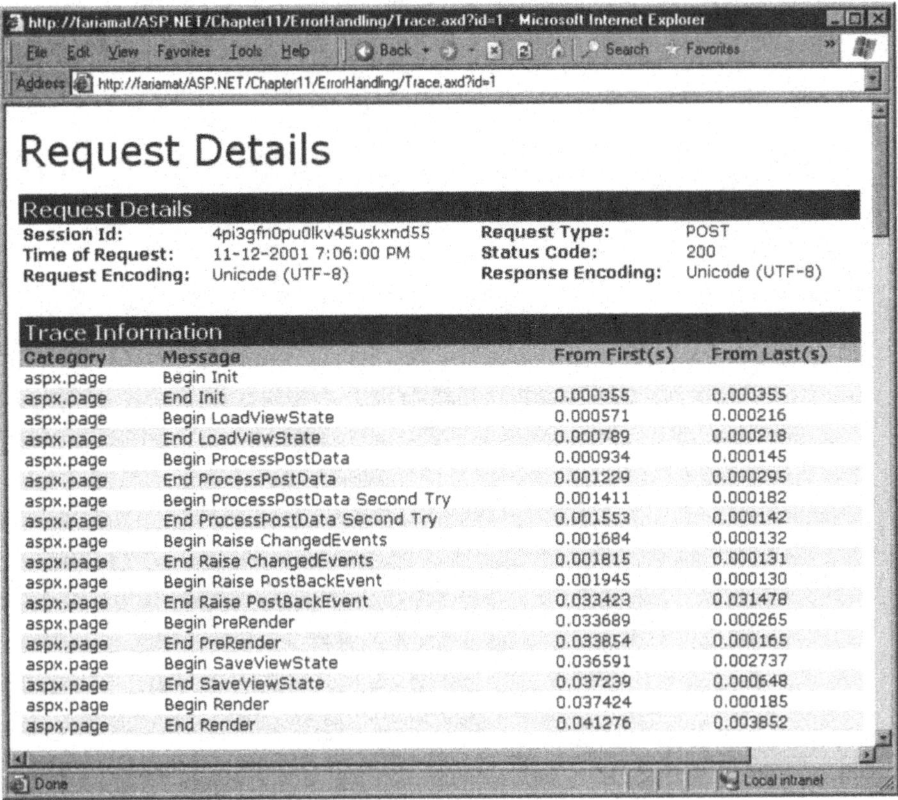

Figure 11-29. Request trace information

The Last Word

The difference between an ordinary website and a professional web application is often in how it deals with errors. In this chapter, you've learned the different lines of defense you can use in .NET, including structured error handling, logging, custom error pages, and tracing. This rounds out the basics of ASP.NET programming. In the next chapter, you'll learn how to take a complete web application and deploy it to a remote web server.

CHAPTER 12

Deploying ASP.NET

THE .NET FRAMEWORK makes it almost painless to deploy any type of application, including ASP.NET websites. Often, you won't need to do much more than copy your web application directory to the web server, and then configure it as a virtual directory. The headaches of the past—registering components and troubleshooting version conflicts—are gone.

This simplicity makes it practical to deploy websites by manually copying files, rather than relying on a dedicated setup tool. The first part of this chapter focuses on this approach. Next, you'll see how the tools in Visual Studio .NET can simplify website deployment, and how you can package your web application for easy distribution with a full-fledged setup program. Finally, the chapter ends by introducing some of the considerations you'll face if you want to migrate a legacy ASP website to ASP.NET—and how difficult that might be.

Making Your Website Visible

ASP.NET applications can be used in a variety of different environments, including LANs (local area networks) and over the Internet. To understand the difference, it helps to review a little about how web servers work with networks and the Internet.

A network is defined simply as a group of devices connected by communication links. A traditional LAN connects devices over a limited area, like a company site or an individual's house. Multiple LANs are connected into a WAN (wide area network) using a variety of technologies. In fact, the Internet is nothing more than a high-speed backbone that joins together millions of LANs.

The cornerstone of the Internet is *IP*, the Internet Protocol. On an IP network, each computer is given a unique 32-bit number called an IP address. An IP address is typically written as four numbers from 0–255 separated by periods (as in 192.145.0.1). To access another computer over a network, you need to use its IP address.

Of course, IP addresses aren't easy to remember and don't make for great marketing campaigns. To make life easier, web servers on the Internet usually register unique *domain names* like www.amazon.com. This domain name is mapped to the IP address by a special catalog, which is maintained by a network of servers on the Internet. This network, called the DNS (Domain Name Service), is a core part of the infrastructure of the Internet. When you type **www.microsoft.com** in a web browser, the browser contacts the nearest DNS server, looks up the IP address that's mapped to http://www.microsoft.com, and contacts it.

So what effect does all this have on the accessibility of your website? In order to be easily reached over the Internet, the web server you use needs to be registered in the DNS registry. In order to be registered in the DNS registry, you must have a fixed IP address. Commercial Internet service providers won't give you a fixed IP address unless you're willing to pay a sizable fee. In fact, most will place you behind a firewall or some type of network address translation, which will hide your computer's IP address. The same is true in most company networks, which are shielded from the outside world.

However, ASP.NET applications don't *need* to be accessible over the Internet. Many are useful within an internal network. In this case, you don't need to worry about the DNS registry. Other computers can access your website using either the IP address of your machine or, more likely, the network computer name.

For example, imagine you deploy an application to a virtual directory name MyWebApp. On the web server, you can access it like this:

```
http://localhost/MyWebApp
```

Assuming the computer is named MyWebServer, here's how you can access the virtual web directory on another computer on the same LAN:

```
http://MyWebServer/MyWebApp
```

Now, assume that MyWebServer is registered in the DNS as www.MyWebServer.com and exposed to the Internet. You could then use the following URL:

```
http://www.MyWebServer.com/MyWebApp
```

Finally, you can always use the computer's IP address, provided the computer is on the same network or visible on the Internet. Assuming the IP address is 123.5.123.4 here's the URL you would use:

```
http://123.5.123.4/MyWebApp
```

Internal networks often use dynamic IP addresses, and DNS registration changes. For these reasons, using the computer name or domain name to access a website is usually the best approach for accessing a website.

Deploying a Simple Site

To run your web application, a web server needs exactly two things:

- Your application and configuration files
- A virtual directory

Consider the simple websites created in Chapter 6. They consist of web pages (.aspx), code-behind files (.vb), and a few miscellaneous details, like image files. To deploy these applications, you simply need to copy all the files to a new directory on the web server. How you transfer these files depends on the Internet hosting service you're using. Usually, you'll need to use an FTP program to upload the files to a designated area. However, if both your computer and the web server are on the same internal network, you might just use Windows Explorer or the command prompt to copy files.

Once the files are in place, an administrator can follow the steps described in Chapter 2 to expose the new directory as a virtual directory. In the case of a commercial provider, this step will probably be completed as soon as you subscribe and won't need any work on your part.

If your web application uses a web.config file, you should make sure debug mode isn't enabled in the deployed version. To do so, find the debug attribute in the compilation tag, if it is present, and set it to false, as follows:

```
<configuration>
  <system.web>

    <compilation defaultLanguage="vb" debug="false" />

    <!-- Other settings omitted. -->
  </system.web>
<configuration>
```

When debugging is enabled, the compiled ASP.NET web pages will be larger and execute more slowly. For that reason, debugging should only be used while testing your web application.

Deploying a Visual Studio .NET Project

ASP.NET web applications can be deployed in much the same way regardless of the tool you use to create them. However, if you're using Visual Studio .NET to create web applications, there are a number of files that you *won't* need to transfer to the web server. Here's a list of files that you can safely ignore:

- **All .vb files.** Visual Studio .NET compiles all your code to a DLL assembly. There's no need for you to deploy the source, because it won't be used.
- **All .resx files.** By default, each web page will have a .resx file to store binary and localizable data. This data is also compiled into the web application assembly, so it doesn't need to be deployed separately.
- **The .vbproj, .webinfo, and .sln files.** These are used by Visual Studio .NET to track the files in the project, and various debugging and build settings. They have no effect on the application at runtime.
- **The .pdb files in the \bin directory.** These files allow you to attach a debugger to your web application.

You should also ignore the Styles.css, .vsdisco, and global.asax files that Visual Studio .NET generates automatically, unless your web application uses them.

The only files that you *do* need to deploy are the .aspx web pages, the web.config file, the DLL files in the \bin directory, and any other resources you use (like image files, HTML files, and so on). For example, if you wanted to deploy the GreetingCardMaker project from Chapter 7, you would deploy the following five files:

```
\GreetingCardMaker.aspx
\GreetingCardMaker2.aspx
\web.config
\defaultpic.png
\bin\GreetingCardMaker.dll
```

It's perfectly reasonable to deploy the GreetingCardMaker project to a directory on the web server that has a different name. However, you can't rename the \bin directory or move the files it contains to another directory.

NOTE Before you deploy an application that was created in Visual Studio .NET, make sure that you compile the code in release mode. Otherwise, your web application performance will suffer. To compile a web application in release mode, select Release from the Solution Configurations drop-down list on the toolbar. Then, start the application (or just right-click the project in the Solution Explorer and choose Rebuild).

Transplanting Visual Studio .NET Projects

In some cases, you might want to copy the complete Visual Studio .NET project from one computer to another, perhaps to allow debugging, testing, or editing at another site. In this case, you'll need to copy all the files in the project directory, and make sure that the virtual directory and local path on the target web server matches the virtual directory and local path of the source computer. This information is hard-coded in the .vbproj and .webinfo files. If you change the local path or virtual directory you'll need to create a new project, or manually edit the paths in these files using Notepad.

If you try to run a transplanted application and receive an ASP.NET error page warning you that a setting in the configuration file is invalid, the virtual directory may not be configured correctly. This problem typically occurs if the virtual directory exists, but isn't configured as a web application. If this is the case, certain configuration settings aren't allowed. To resolve this problem, make sure that the virtual directory is a web application using IIS Manager, as described in Chapter 2.

Web Applications and Components

It's just as straightforward to deploy web applications that use other components. That's because all the components your website uses are copied in the \bin subdirectory. There are no additional steps required to register assemblies or copy them to a specific system directory.

NOTE Private assemblies are quite a boon for web-hosting companies, who need to host dozens, hundreds, or thousands of web applications on the same computer. Their web servers can't install risky components into a system directory just because one website requires it—especially when the version that one site requires might conflict with the version needed by another site on the same computer!

For example, consider the IEControls web project included with the sample code in Chapter 9. It used the Microsoft Internet Explorer controls. All the code for these controls is found in the Microsoft.Web.UI.WebControls.dll file in the \bin directory. When you deploy this application, you need to copy this assembly with your web application code. That means your application will continue working seamlessly on the remote web server. There's no need to run a setup program or install the Microsoft Internet Explorer controls into a system directory.

Of course, this principle doesn't hold true if you're using *shared assemblies*, which are stored in a special system location called the GAC (global assembly cache). Usually, you won't store components in this location, because it complicates development and offers few benefits. The core .NET assemblies are located in the GAC because they're large and likely to be used in almost every .NET application. It doesn't make sense to force you to deploy the .NET assemblies with every website you create. However, this does mean that it's up to the administrator of the web server to install the version of the .NET Framework that you require. This detail just isn't in your website's control.

Other Configuration Steps

The simple model of deployment that you've seen so far is often called *zero-touch deployment*, because you don't need to manually configure web server resources. (It's also sometimes called *XCopy deployment*, because transferring websites is as easy as copying directories.) However, some applications are more difficult to set up on a web server. Here are some common factors that will require additional configuration steps:

- **Databases.** If your web application uses a database, you'll need to transfer the database to the web server. You can do this by generating an SQL script that will automatically create the database and load it with data. Alternately, you could back up the database and then restore it on the web server. In either case, an administrator needs to use a database management tool.

- **Alternate machine.config settings.** You can control the settings for your web application in the web.config file that you deploy. However, problems can occur if your web application relies on settings in the machine.config that aren't present on the web server.

- **Windows account permissions.** Usually, a web server will run web page code under a restricted account like the local ASPNET account. This account might not be allowed to perform the tasks you rely on, like writing to files or the Windows event log. In this case, an administrator needs to specifically grant the permissions you need to the ASPNET account.
- **IIS security settings.** If your website uses SSL encryption or Windows authentication (as described in Chapter 25), the virtual directory settings will need to be tweaked. This also requires the help of an administrator.

To solve these problems in the most effective way, it helps to work with an experienced Windows administrator. That's especially true if the web server is using IIS 6 (the version of IIS provided with Windows 2003). IIS 6 provides a number of configuration options, and allows every web application on a server to run under a different Windows account. This ensures that your website can be granted the exact permission set it requires, without affecting any other web application.

Deploying with Visual Studio .NET

Visual Studio .NET aims to simplify web application deployment in the same way that it simplifies the task of designing rich web pages. There are two key innovations that you'll explore in this chapter:

- **The Copy Project feature.** This allows you to transfer your files directly to a web server on the same network, or over the Internet using Front Page Server extensions. The appropriate files are copied, and the virtual directory is created automatically.
- **Web setup projects.** Using Visual Studio .NET, you can create an installer that will copy your files, create the required virtual directory, and perform any other setup tasks you need.

Copy Project

The Copy Project feature is a quick and easy way to transfer your web application files without using a separate program or leaving the design environment. You simply need to open your web project, rebuild it in release mode, and then select Project ➤ Copy Project from the menu. The Copy Project window (shown in Figure 12-1) will appear.

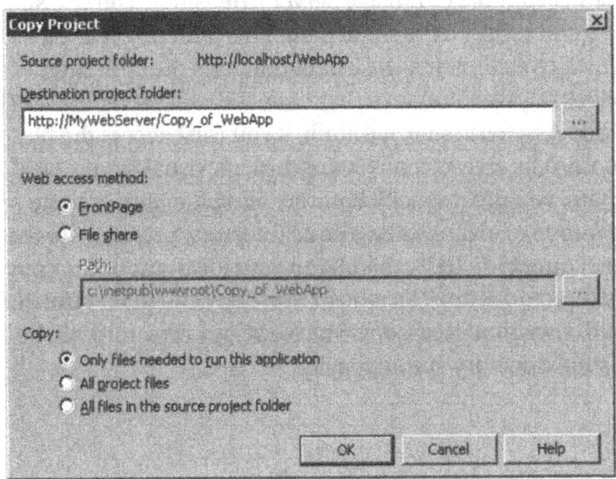

Figure 12-1. The Copy Project window

The first step is to specify the URL where you want to copy your web application. The URL reflects two pieces of information: the computer name or domain name for the web server, and the virtual directory name for your project. In Figure 12-1, the project is about to be transferred to the computer named MyWebServer, and the files will be placed in the virtual directory Copy_Of_WebApp. The web access method is set to FrontPage, which means that the file transfer will work entirely over HTTP, and the destination web server must have FrontPage Server Extensions installed. At the bottom of the window, the copy option indicates that only required files will be transferred. This means the source code will not be copied.

TIP Even if you choose to copy only the required files, the .pdb debugging files will still be transferred. If you don't need to debug your web application on the web server, remove these files before you copy the project.

When you click OK, Visual Studio .NET will connect and transfer the files. You will probably be prompted to enter your user ID and password for the web server. When performing the file transfer, Visual Studio .NET transfers all the required files, regardless of whether or not the same version already exists on the web server. This is different than the behavior seen when uploading websites in Microsoft FrontPage, and it will make it more time-consuming to perform minor updates to large sites.

If the remote web server doesn't support FrontPage Server Extensions, you can still transfer your files, provided you can supply a file share path. This path might use a mapped drive (like f:\WebSites\MyWebSite) or a UNC path that uses the computer name (like \\WebServer\WebSites\MyWebSite). In either case, the web server must be accessible over the local network. As a basic rule of thumb, if you can't access the file share in Windows Explorer, you won't be able to connect to it through Visual Studio .NET.

When copying with a file share, you must specify both the file share path and the web URL. You can use this technique to create a new virtual directory, provided it's the root website or in another virtual directory. To try this out on your local computer, copy a web application to the virtual directory http://localhost/NewCopy and make sure the specified file share is c:\Inetpub\wwwroot\NewCopy. The NewCopy directory will be created and configured as a virtual directory automatically.

Web Setup Projects

Copying files by hand or with the Copy Project feature will meet the needs of most web application programmers. However, in some cases you might need to deploy an application that has a complex set of requirements. Perhaps you need to add databases, registry settings, and Start menu shortcuts to the target computer. Or perhaps you want to deploy the same web application to multiple computers. In these cases, it's easiest to create a dedicated installer. In Visual Studio .NET, you can create this installer using the web setup project type.

The web setup project is a special type of Visual Studio .NET project. Unlike other project types, it isn't language-specific. In fact, you won't have the ability to write any code. Instead, you'll configure setup options through setup designers and property windows. When you compile the final setup project, Visual Studio .NET will generate an .msi installation file. You can then run this file on a web server to install your web application.

The easiest way to start creating a web setup project is to add it to the solution that contains the web application you want to deploy.

First, open an existing project. Then, right-click the solution item in the Solution Explorer window, and choose Add ➤ New Project. Choose Web Setup Project from the Setup and Deployment Projects group, as shown in Figure 12-2. Then, enter the name, and click OK to add the project.

TIP Your solution now contains two projects. Before continuing, right-click the web application and choose Set As StartUp Project. This way the setup application will only be built when you chose. Compiling a setup file can take some time, and it's only required when you want to deploy the finished application, not during testing.

The setup project is unlike any other type of .NET application. Instead of writing code, you configure options in a variety of different designers. Finding the designer you need and setting the appropriate options are the keys to creating your setup project.

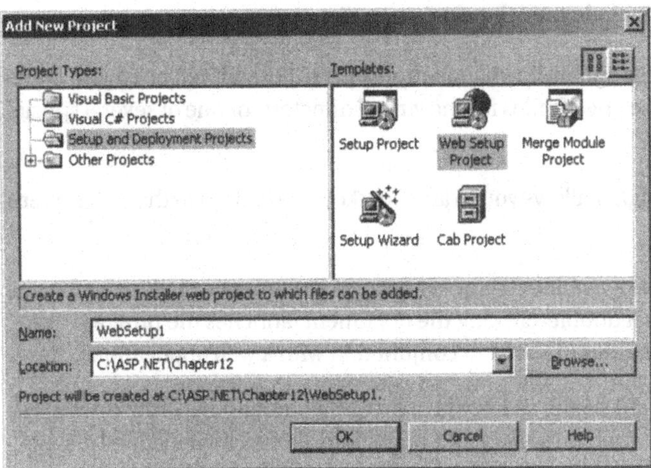

Figure 12-2. Creating a web setup project

The Setup Designers

The web setup project provides six different designers. To navigate to a designer, right-click your setup project in the Solution Explorer, select View, and choose the appropriate designer, as shown in Figure 12-3.

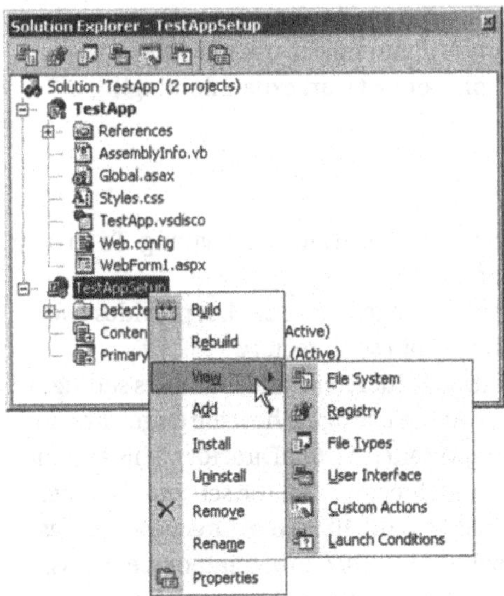

Figure 12-3. The setup designers

The setup designers include the following:

- **File System.** This designer allows you to specify the files that will be copied to the web server. You can specify files for the virtual directory, or one of several special system directories.
- **Registry.** This designer allows you to add new keys and values to the web server's registry.
- **File Types.** This designer allows you to register a document extension with your application (so that double-clicking the document launches the program automatically). This setting isn't used in conjunction with a web application.
- **User Interface.** This designer allows you to tweak the wording and order of windows used in the setup wizard. However, your options are limited to predefined dialog boxes. There is no way to create your own custom windows with .NET code.
- **Custom Actions.** This designer allows you to link to another program, which will launch at the end of the setup to perform an extra configuration. One common reason to use a custom action is to launch a database setup script.
- **Launch Conditions.** This designer allows you to specify special conditions that must be met in order for a setup to run.

You can also set some basic options like Author, ProductName, and Version by selecting the project in the Solution Explorer and using the Properties window. Most of these are descriptive settings used in the setup wizard or other Windows dialog boxes, like the Add/Remove Programs dialog box.

To create a simple setup project, you only need to use the file system designer, which is described in the next section. For information about how to use the other designers, refer to the Visual Studio .NET documentation—or just start experimenting!

Transferring Files

Initially, your setup project is a blank template that doesn't install anything. To change this, you need to use the file system designer.

The default file system designer window is shown in Figure 12-4. It provides two directories: the Web Application Folder, and the \bin subdirectory.

Before continuing, select the Web Application Folder item, and look at its settings in the Properties window. Using these settings, you can configure how the target directory will be created on the web server. The most important is VirtualDirectory. This specifies the default name that will be given to the virtual directory that the setup will create. Many of the other directory settings map directly to the IIS virtual directory settings. For example, AllowDirectoryBrowsing, AllowReadAccess, AllowScriptSourceAccess, AllowWriteAccess, and ExecutePermissions all correspond to the virtual directory permissions described in Chapter 2. Similarly, DefaultDocument identifies the default file that should be served if you request the virtual directory without specifying a page.

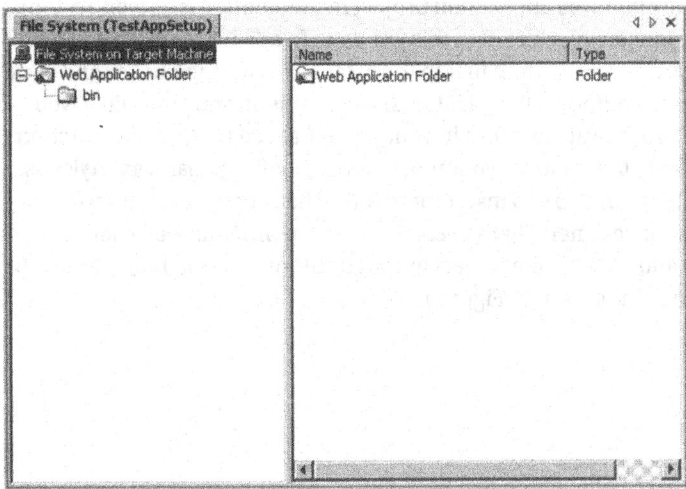

Figure 12-4. The file system designer

When you start your web setup project, both folders will be empty. However, you can add your website files from the web application project that's in the same solution. To do so, right-click the Web Application Folder item and choose Add ➤ Project Output. You'll see the window shown in Figure 12-5.

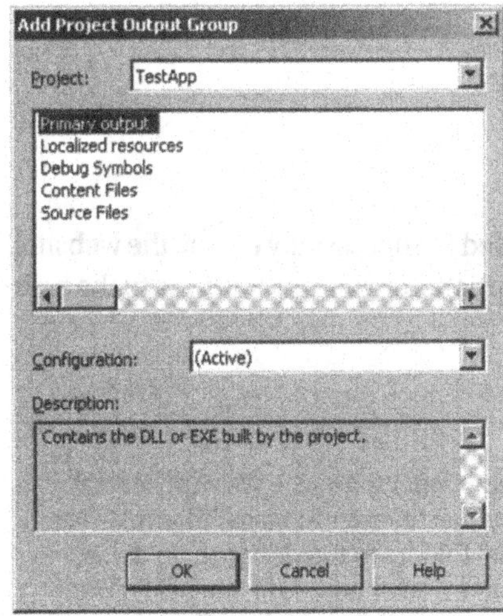

Figure 12-5. Adding project output to a setup

In this example, the other web application project in the solution is named TestApp. You'll see that it's automatically selected in this window. To add files from this project, select both primary output and content files in the list (hold down the Ctrl key and click both items). The primary output is the DLL file that contains all your compiled web application. The content files are any files in your project that have their Build Action set to Content. By default, this includes your project's web.config, global.asax, Styles.css, and .aspx and .asmx files. Click OK to insert these files. The actual file names won't appear in the file system designer. That's because the setup program won't actually read the content files and compile the project output until you chose to build the setup. Instead, you'll see the items shown in Figure 12-6.

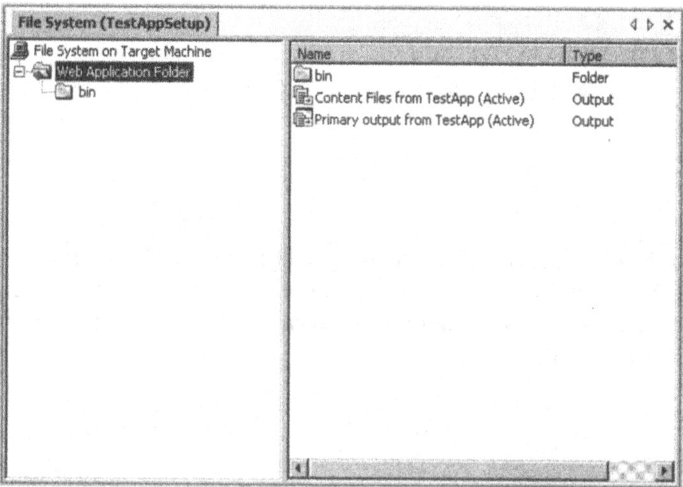

Figure 12-6. The website files in the designer

At this point, your project has all the files needed to successfully deploy the website. You can still add more files and configure other options, or you can continue to the next section to build the setup.

TIP By default, the file system designer only shows the Web Application Folder and the \bin directory it contains. In order to install files to other locations, you need to add additional folders to the designer. To do so, simply right-click in the directory pane and choose Add Special Folder. There are options that map to the computer's Fonts folder, Favorites folder, Startup folder, and many more. Folders that have already been added to the list are grayed out so that you can't choose them again. Once you've added the folder to the designer, you can choose to add shortcuts or files to the folder.

Building and Running the Setup

To create the setup file, set Visual Studio .NET to release mode (using the toolbar). Right-click the setup project in the Solution Explorer and choose Build. The web application will be compiled first, and then it will be added to the setup project. Finally, an .msi file will be generated in the \Release subdirectory of your setup project directory. The whole process can take several minutes.

For example, in the online samples for this chapter you'll find a TestApp project and a TestAppSetup project, both of which are a part of the same solution. When you build the TestAppSetup in release mode, the setup files will appear in the TestAppSetup\Release directory.

In this example, the generated setup files will include the following:

- **TestAppSetup.msi.** This is the complete Microsoft Installer package for your website, with the compressed data. You can run this setup directly.
- **InstMsiA.exe and InstMsiW.exe.** These files are used to install the Windows installer service. This should already be installed on computers with the .NET Framework, but these files are included if required.
- **Setup.exe and Setup.ini.** Run this setup file if you aren't sure if the computer supports the Microsoft Installer service. The setup program will install the required MSI service if needed, and will then head straight to the TestAppSetup.msi file to install your website.

When you run the setup application, you'll see the default wizard that walks you through a few simple steps, and gives you a chance to modify the target virtual directory (as shown in Figure 12-7). The virtual directory will be created in the default web root, and the website files will be copied.

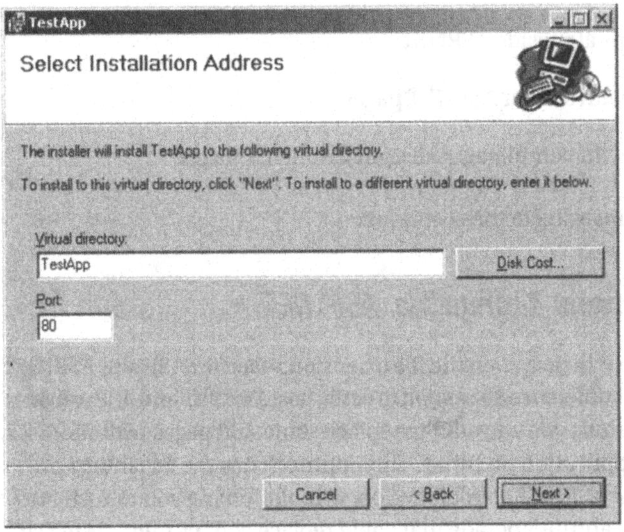

Figure 12-7. The setup wizard

Remember, if you want to customize the wizard, just work use the user interface designer in the web setup project. As a standard setup application, you can rerun your installer to repair or uninstall the website.

NOTE Web setup projects will not install the .NET Framework. If the web server doesn't already have the .NET Framework installed, you can install it using the Windows Update feature, or by downloading the redistributable from `http://www.asp.net`.

Migrating from ASP

Before continuing to the third part of this book, where you'll dive into ADO.NET, it makes sense to consider what will happen to the legacy ASP sites that exist today. If you're an ASP developer, you've probably created numerous websites already. You may be interested in turning these ASP sites into full-featured ASP.NET applications so you can gain some of the benefits discussed in this book. Unfortunately, migration is often a tricky issue, and ASP.NET doesn't represent a minor upgrade. If you have a complex application that relies on COM components, client-side scripting, and Response.Write() commands to create a sophisticated interface, you may have a substantial migration task on your hand. This section gives you a preview of the difficulties and changes that lie ahead. I won't try to hide the painful truth—properly migrating an application to .NET isn't a quick task.

Fortunately, migration isn't always necessary. The .NET Framework is designed with interoperability in mind, because Microsoft recognizes that it just isn't possible to abandon the last several years of development effort. With ASP.NET, you have the following three options:

- Run ASP applications alongside ASP.NET
- Replace ASP pages with similar ASP.NET pages
- Replace ASP pages with completely redesigned ASP.NET pages

The following sections investigate these options.

Run ASP Applications Alongside ASP.NET

ASP.NET doesn't replace ASP. In fact, even the file extensions used for ASP and ASP.NET web pages are different. This difference allows you to easily host ASP.NET and ASP websites on the same server. Given time, you can start to replace some ASP pages with ASP.NET pages and upgrade your application bit by bit. This approach has the advantage of allowing you to learn about ASP.NET as you develop, without forcing you to rush into extra work or commit to an abrupt upgrade that could replace your current, tested site with new bug-ridden software.

The main drawback to mingling ASP and ASP.NET pages in the same application is the fact that you cannot share state information. For example, if you add an object to application state in an ASP page, you cannot retrieve it in an ASP.NET page, because the ASP.NET page uses an entirely different memory space and set of data on the server. Similarly, session information won't be shared. Even worse, if you set information into the Session collection in an ASP page and redirect the user to a series of ASP.NET pages, the current ASP session could actually time out because IIS will not detect any new requests to the ASP application. Mingling ASP with ASP.NET is generally easiest when you have a content-driven site that doesn't use much state management.

Replace ASP Pages with Similar ASP.NET Pages

This approach tries to minimize development time by creating ASP.NET pages that resemble ASP pages. Often, this approach is to rename .asp files to give them the .aspx extension. In many cases, this solution will work, because ASP.NET supports most of the syntax that was used in ASP. However, this solution loses many of the advantages that ASP.NET offers, such as the web control model.

In this case, it's worth asking whether it makes any sense to transfer an application to a different platform without cleaning up the mess traditional ASP code imposed. If you need a specific advanced feature that's offered in ASP.NET—for example, if you need to enable web farm session state support—and you aren't interested in much else, this solution may make good sense. But in any other case, you'll be wasting time tweaking your code and ironing out new inconsistencies when you really should be redesigning your application.

Replace ASP Pages with Redesigned ASP.NET Pages

This, of course, is the ideal solution. In this case, you'll benefit from all of ASP.NET's new features, and create an application that is easier to debug, modify, and enhance. This approach also has a very significant drawback: It is by far the most time-consuming. If your ASP application works fine the way it is, there may not be much of a business case for replacing it with a new and improved version.

The actual difficulty required to move an application to ASP.NET depends on its sophistication, and how many custom workarounds or unusual solutions you're already using in ASP. Pages that make heavy use of Response.Write() to create dynamic interfaces will need to be completely redesigned with the new event-driven server control model (see Chapters 6 and 7). Custom authentication routines may be replaced with ASP.NET's new forms-based security (see Chapter 25). COM components should be removed and replaced with similar .NET assemblies (see Chapter 22). Database code must be rewritten from scratch using the new disconnected model and ADO.NET (see Chapters 13 and 14). If you've created a sophisticated e-commerce website with a well-thought-out design that uses separate components, it may be easier to start a new application from scratch than to attempt a migration—but it won't be quick.

The Last Word

This chapter considered the new deployment model of the .NET Framework and took a whirlwind tour through Visual Studio .NET web setup projects. This rounds out the second part of this book, and you now have all the fundamentals you need to create a basic ASP.NET website. In the next part, you'll dive into practical database programming with ADO.NET.

Part Three

Working with Data

CHAPTER 13

Introducing ADO.NET

SO FAR, YOU'VE DISCOVERED that ASP.NET isn't just a new way to create modern web applications—it's also part of an ambitious multilayered strategy called .NET. ASP.NET is only one component in Microsoft's .NET platform, which includes new languages, a new philosophy for cross-language integration, a new way of looking at components and deployment, and a shared class library with components that allow you to do everything from handling errors to analyzing XML documents. In this chapter, you'll discover that the .NET Framework has yet another surprise in store: ADO.NET, Microsoft's latest data access model.

ADO.NET allows you to interact with relational databases and other data sources. Quite simply, ADO.NET is the technology that ASP.NET applications use to communicate with a database, whether they need to add a new customer record, log a purchase, or display a product catalog. If you've worked with ADO before, you'll discover that ADO.NET is much more than a slightly enhanced .NET version of the ADO data access technology. As with ASP and Visual Basic, the .NET moniker signals some revolutionary changes. ADO.NET is now optimized for distributed applications (like web applications), integrated with XML, and outfitted with an entirely new object model.

In this chapter, you'll look at some of the defining features of ADO.NET with a high-level overview. You won't actually get into any real coding—that's all to come in the next few chapters—but you will prepare yourself by learning the basic organization and philosophy of ADO.NET. Along the way, I'll answer some common questions about how ADO and ADO.NET differ, why web developers need a new data access technology, and what ingredients make up a data-driven web application.

Introducing ADO.NET and Data Management

Almost every piece of software ever written works with data. In fact, a typical Internet application is often just a thin user interface shell on top of a sophisticated database program that reads and writes information from a database on the web server. At its simplest, a database program might allow a user to perform simple searches and display results in a formatted table. A more sophisticated ASP.NET application might use a database behind the scenes to retrieve information, which is then processed and displayed in the appropriate format and location in the browser. The user might not even be aware (or care) that the displayed information originates from a database. Using a database is an excellent way to start dividing the user interface logic from the content, which allows you to create a site that can work with dynamic, easily updated data.

In most ASP.NET applications you'll need to use a database for some tasks. Here are some basic examples of data-driven ASP.NET applications:

- E-commerce sites involve managing sales, customer, and inventory information. This information might be displayed directly on the screen (as with a product catalog) or used unobtrusively to record transactions or customer information.
- Online knowledge bases and customized search engines involve less structured databases that store vast quantities of information, or links to various documents and resources.
- Information-based sites such as web portals can't be easily scalable or manageable unless all the information they use is stored in a consistent, strictly defined format. Typically, a site like this is matched with another ASP.NET program that allows an authorized user to add or update the displayed information by modifying the corresponding database records through a browser interface. In Chapter 26 you'll look at a portal application that is completely configurable and draws all its information from a database.

You probably won't have any trouble thinking about where you need to use database technology in an ASP.NET application. What Internet application couldn't benefit from a guest book that records user comments, or a simple e-mail address submission form that uses a back-end database to store a list of potential customers or contacts?

A Quick Overview of Databases

The most common way to manage data is by using a database. Database technology is particularly useful for business software, which typically requires hierarchical sets of related information. For example, a typical database for a sales ordering program consists of a list of customers, a list of products, and a list of sales that draws on information from the other two tables. This type of information is best described using a relational model, which is the philosophy that underlies all modern database products, including SQL Server, Oracle, and even Microsoft Access.

In a relational model, information is broken down into its smallest and most concise units. For example, a sales record doesn't store all the information about the products that were sold. Instead it just stores a product ID that refers to a full record in a product table, as shown in Figure 13-1.

While it's technically possible to organize data into tables and store it on the hard drive as an XML file, this wouldn't be very flexible. Instead, a web application needs full relational database management system (RDBMS), such as SQL Server. The RDBMS handles the data infrastructure, ensuring optimum performance and reliability. These products take the responsibility of providing data to multiple users simultaneously, and making sure that certain rules are followed (for example, disallowing conflicting changes or invalid data types).

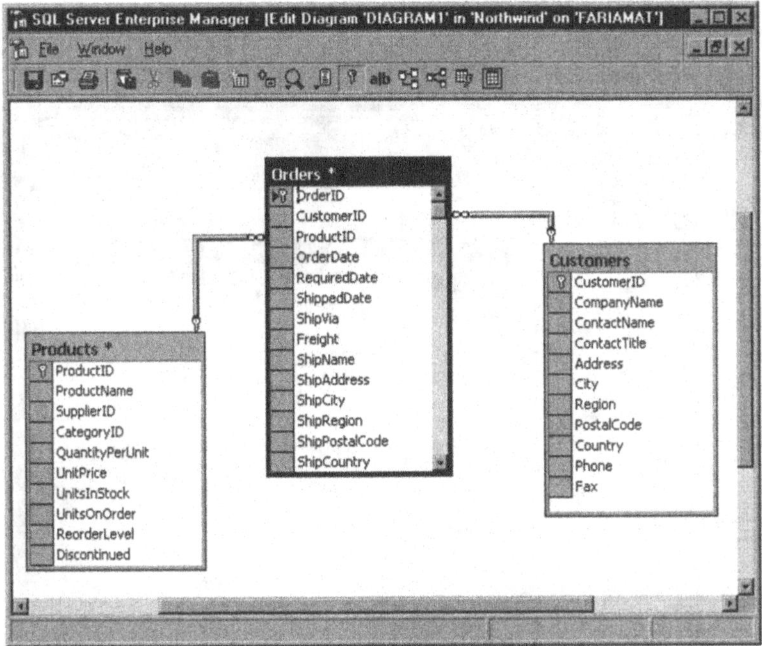

Figure 13-1. Simple table relationships

Relational database products also provide tools that you can usually use to create and modify the structure of the database. Figure 13-2 shows the Enterprise Manager in SQL Server, which allows you to perform a host of administrative tasks, including designing and creating tables. As an ASP.NET developer, you may have the responsibility of creating the database required for a web application. Alternatively, it may already exist, or it may be the responsibility of a dedicated database administrator.

This is where ADO.NET comes into the picture. ADO.NET is a technology designed to let an ASP.NET program (or any other .NET program, for that matter) access data. Typically, you'll use ADO.NET to access a relational database, but you could also use it to work with raw XML information, or other data sources that aren't necessarily databases. More and more, ADO.NET is becoming a standard way to access and exchange any type of information.

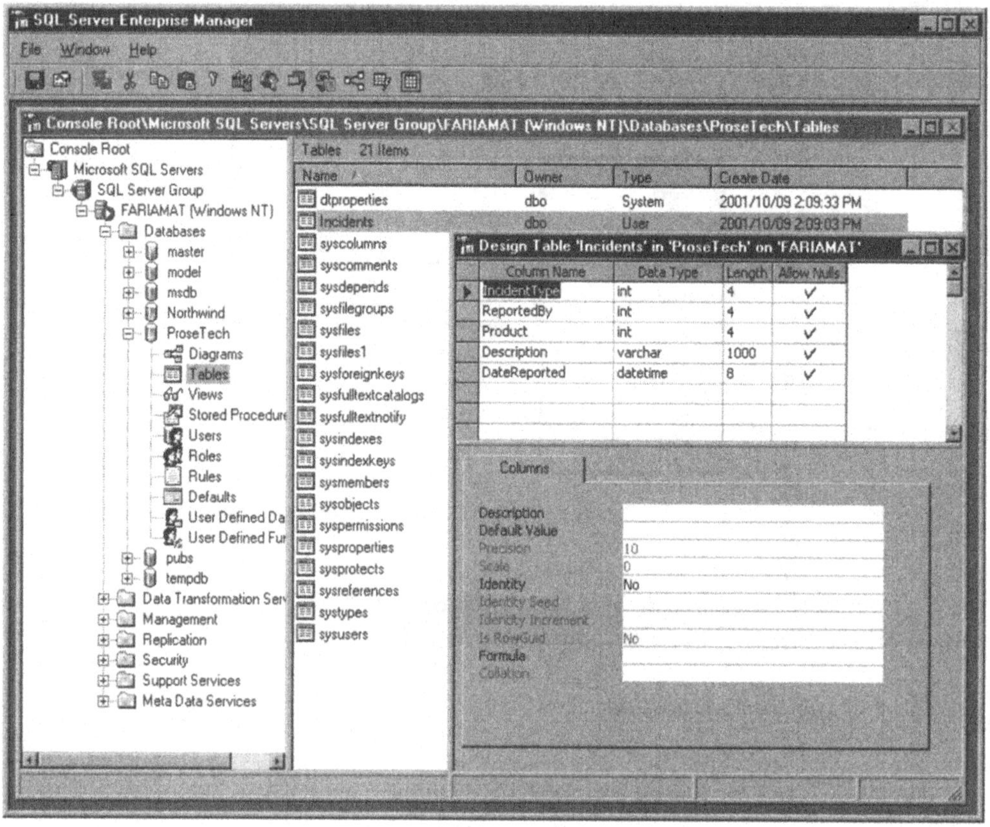

Figure 13-2. Enterprise Manager lets you create databases

Database Access in the Internet World

Accessing a database in an Internet application is a completely different scenario than accessing a database in a typical desktop or client server program. Most developers hone their database skills in the desktop world, and run into serious problems when they try to apply what they have learned with stand-alone applications in the world of the Web. Quite simply, web applications raise a whole new set of considerations and potential problems. These problems have plagued ASP developers for years and are finally dealt with directly by ADO.NET's new design.

NOTE Some of the discussion in this chapter compares ADO.NET to ADO, Microsoft's previous data access technology. If you haven't programmed with ADO before, feel free to disregard these comparisons. You'll get a full tutorial on ADO.NET programming from the ground up in the next chapter.

Problems of Scale

A web application has the potential to be used by hundreds of simultaneous users. This means that it can't be casual about using server memory or limited resources like database connections. If you design an ASP application that acquires a database connection and holds it for even a few minutes, other users may notice a definite slowdown or even be locked out of the database completely. And if database concurrency issues aren't carefully thought out, problems such as locked records and conflicting updates can make it difficult to provide consistent data to all users.

All of these problems are possible with traditional client/server database development. The difference is that they are far less likely to have any negative effect because the typical load (the number of simultaneous users) is dramatically lower. Database practices that might slightly hamper the performance of a client/server application can multiply rapidly and cause significant problems in a web application.

Problems of State

You probably know that HTTP is a stateless protocol. This means that connections between a browser and the web server aren't maintained. When a user browses to a page in an ASP.NET application, a connection is made, code is processed, an HTML page is returned, and the connection is immediately severed. While users may have the illusion that they are interacting with a continuously running application, they are really just receiving a string of static pages. (ASP.NET makes this illusion so convincing that it's worth asking if it can really be considered an illusion at all.)

With data-driven web applications, the stateless nature of HTTP can be quite a thorny problem. The typical approach is to connect to a database, read information, display it, and then close the database connection. This approach runs into difficulties if you want the user to be able to modify the retrieved information. In this scenario, the application requires a certain amount of intelligence in order to be able to identify the original record, build an SQL statement to select it, and update it with the new values. This approach might work for an application that only allows simple changes or additions, but if you need to allow a user to perform extensive modifications, the process is far from easy.

Problems of Communication and Compatibility

Sending data over an internal network is easy. Sending information over the Internet is also easy, as long as you stick to standard text and the HTTP protocol. ADO worked fine while you were using it on a Windows web server. However, if you needed to send data to another computer or a component written in another language, the Microsoft-centric nature of ADO started to show through. Not only would these other computers and components need to understand the complex rules of COM, they would also need to punch holes through Internet firewalls, which reject ADO's proprietary data format. And don't even ask how you can work with ADO data on a non-Microsoft platform like Linux or Mac OS—you can't!

Characteristics of ADO.NET

ADO.NET is interesting because in many ways it *inverts* Microsoft's previous database access philosophy. Features that were optional add-ons in ADO, like disconnected data access, are now part of the core feature set in ADO.NET. Other features that were commonly used in ADO, like server-side cursors, are completely removed. In the following sections, you'll get your first taste of the dramatic changes in ADO.NET.

Disconnected Access

Disconnected access is the most important characteristic of ADO.NET, the greatest change from ADO, and perhaps the single best example of the new .NET philosophy for accessing data.

In a typical ADO application, you connect to the database, create a Recordset, display the information, and then abandon the Recordset and close the connection. While the connection is open, you have a "live" (or cursor-based) connection with the database. This live connection allows you to make immediate updates and you can even see the changes made by other users in real time. Unfortunately, database servers can only provide a limited number of connections before they reject connection requests. The longer you keep a connection open, the greater the chance becomes that another user will be prevented from accessing the database. In a poorly written program, the database connection is kept open while other tasks are being performed. But even in a well-written program using ADO, the connection must be kept open until all the data is processed and the Recordset is no longer needed.

ADO.NET has an entirely different philosophy. In ADO.NET you still create a connection to a database, but you can't use a cursor. Instead, you fill a DataSet object with a *copy* of the information drawn from the database. If you change the information in the DataSet, the information in the corresponding table in the database isn't changed. That means you can easily process and manipulate the data without worry, because you aren't using a valuable database connection. If needed, you can reconnect to the original data source, and apply all your DataSet changes in a single batch operation.

Disconnected Access Raises New Issues

Disconnected access is a key requirement for Internet applications, and it's also an approach that often requires additional consideration and precautions. Disconnected access makes it easy for users to create inconsistent updates, a problem that won't be resolved (or even identified) until the update is committed back to the original data source. Disconnected access can also require special considerations because changes aren't applied in the order they were entered. This design can cause problems when you modify related records.

Fortunately, ADO.NET provides a rich set of features to deal with all these possibilities, and provide performance that is almost always superior to ADO. However, you do need to be aware that the new disconnected model may introduce new considerations and require extra care. You'll examine these issues in the following ADO.NET chapters.

XML Integration

ADO.NET has deep support for XML. This fact isn't automatically obvious when you're working with the ADO.NET DataSet, because you'll usually use the built-in methods and properties of the DataSet to perform all the data manipulation you need. But if you delve a little deeper, you'll discover that you can access the information in the DataSet as an XML document. You can even write this modify values, remove rows, and add new records by modifying the XML, without losing any information.

Figure 13-3 shows a sample customer table in SQL Server's Enterprise Manager. Figure 13-4 shows the XML document ADO.NET creates for the customer table. The XML is displayed courtesy of a simple utility included with the online samples for this chapter. I haven't included the code yet, because you won't explore the specifics of how to connect to a database until the next chapter. The important concept to understand now is that your ASP.NET application doesn't need to perform any additional steps to convert the data into XML.

SQL Server Enterprise Manager - [Data in Table 'Customers' in 'Northwind' on 'FARIAMAT']

File Window Help

CustomerID	CompanyName	ContactName	ContactTitle	Address
ALFKI	Alfreds Futterkiste	Maria Anders	Sales Representative	Obere Str. 57
ANATR	Ana Trujillo Emparedados y helados	Ana Trujillo	Owner	Avda. de la Constitu
ANTON	Antonio Moreno Taquería	Antonio Moreno	Owner	Mataderos 2312
AROUT	Around the Horn	Thomas Hardy	Sales Representative	120 Hanover Sq.
BERGS	Berglunds snabbköp	Christina Berglund	Order Administrator	Berguvsvägen 8
BLAUS	Blauer See Delikatessen	Hanna Moos	Sales Representative	Forsterstr. 57
BLONP	Blondesddsl père et fils	Frédérique Citeaux	Marketing Manager	24, place Kléber
BOLID	Bólido Comidas preparadas	Martín Sommer	Owner	C/ Araquil, 67
BONAP	Bon app'	Laurence Lebihan	Owner	12, rue des Boucher
BOTTM	Bottom-Dollar Markets	Elizabeth Lincoln	Accounting Manager	23 Tsawassen Blvd.
BSBEV	B's Beverages	Victoria Ashworth	Sales Representative	Fauntleroy Circus
CACTU	Cactus Comidas para llevar	Patricio Simpson	Sales Agent	Cerrito 333
CENTC	Centro comercial Moctezuma	Francisco Chang	Marketing Manager	Sierras de Granada
CHOPS	Chop-suey Chinese	Yang Wang	Owner	Hauptstr. 29
COMMI	Comércio Mineiro	Pedro Afonso	Sales Associate	Av. dos Lusíadas, 2
CONSH	Consolidated Holdings	Elizabeth Brown	Sales Representative	Berkeley Gardens 1
DRACD	Drachenblut Delikatessen	Sven Ottlieb	Order Administrator	Walserweg 21
DUMON	Du monde entier	Janine Labrune	Owner	67, rue des Cinquan
EASTC	Eastern Connection	Ann Devon	Sales Agent	35 King George
ERNSH	Ernst Handel	Roland Mendel	Sales Manager	Kirchgasse 6
FAMIA	Familia Arquibaldo	Aria Cruz	Marketing Assistant	Rua Orós, 92
FISSA	FISSA Fabrica Inter. Salchichas S.A.	Diego Roel	Accounting Manager	C/ Moralzarzal, 86
FOLIG	Folies gourmandes	Martine Rancé	Assistant Sales Agent	184, chaussée de T
FOLKO	Folk och fä HB	Maria Larsson	Owner	Åkergatan 24
FRANK	Frankenversand	Peter Franken	Marketing Manager	Berliner Platz 43

Figure 13-3. Partial listing of a database table

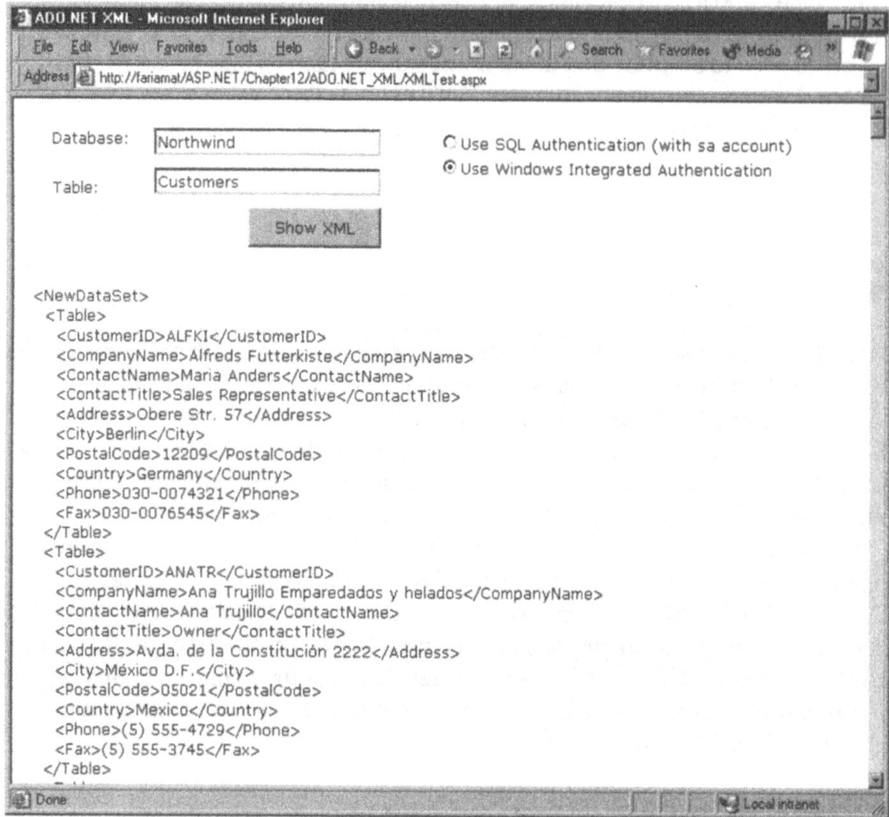

Figure 13-4. Partial XML listing for the table

In other words, ADO.NET is built on XML technology from the ground up.

When Does XML Programming Make Sense?

In the excitement over ADO.NET's new XML features, web developers often forget to ask why—or if—they should use XML. The short answer is that if you don't already know why you need XML, you probably don't need it at all.

ADO.NET's deep XML integration isn't required for a typical self-contain web application. In fact, if you modify relational data through an XML model, you can run into several types of problems that you won't face using the DataSet object directly, like data type conversion problems and errors with duplicated data or violated relationships. Where ADO.NET XML really shines is if you need to exchange the information in the DataSet with another application, particularly one that isn't written in .NET, or even running on a non-Microsoft operating system. These other applications won't be able to recognize a proprietary data format, but they will be able to process an XML document. Because you can convert the information in a DataSet into XML, you'll be able to exchange data with these other applications.

This book focuses on using the ADO.NET objects to interact with a database. This approach is more useful, straightforward, and robust than processing XML documents. However, you'll learn more about XML in later chapters. Chapter 18 describes XML processing in detail, including its ADO.NET integration, and the fourth part of this book demonstrates how you can use XML to send data to and from a cross-platform web service.

The Enhanced DataSet

ADO.NET has a self-sufficiency that previous data access technologies never had. Because the ADO.NET DataSet is designed to be useful without a database connection, it needs to retain much more information than the classic ADO Recordset. Thus, DataSets can store multiple distinct tables, information about the relations between them, and extended information about columns and constraints.

In ADO, the only way to put data from more than one table into a Recordset is by using a Join query. Join queries are great for retrieving data, but they cause problems if you need to update the data source with changes. For example, consider a Join query that combines sales and customer information to create a sales report. If you modify the customer name, it isn't obvious whether you're trying to change the customer record (correcting a misspelled customer name), or trying to modify the data for the sales report (trying to indicate that a given sales order actually applies to a different customer).

ADO.NET gives you the flexibility to avoid these problems. You can add information for several related tables to a DataSet, link them together, and have the functional equivalent of a miniature, disconnected relational database. When changes need to be flushed back to the data source, each table is updated separately. You'll see these techniques in action in the next chapter.

.NET Code

Like all the .NET class library components, ADO.NET is built with .NET, or *managed code*, which runs under the control of the CLR (common language runtime). The traditional ADO components, on the other hand, use unmanaged COM-based code. Though you can still use COM components in ASP.NET, every time you call a method or set a property you have to jump over the boundary between managed and unmanaged code. This switch causes a performance lag that reduces efficiency. ADO.NET avoids this problem, ensuring better performance.

The ADO.NET Object Model

This section introduces the ADO.NET classes and explains how they interact. These objects are the foundation of ADO.NET programming, and you'll return to them consistently over the next three chapters to create, read, update, and process data.

ADO.NET relies on the functionality in a small set of core objects. These objects can be divided into two groups: those that are used to contain and manage data (like DataSet, DataTable, DataRow, and DataRelation) and those that are used to connect to a specific data source (like Connection, Command, and DataReader).

The data container objects are completely generic. No matter what data source you use, once you extract the data it's stored using the same DataSet class. Think of the DataSet as playing the same role as a collection or array—it's a package for data. The difference is that the DataSet is customized for relational data, which means it understands concepts like rows, columns, and table relationships natively.

The second group of objects exists in several different flavors. Each set of data interaction objects is called an ADO.NET *data provider*. Data providers are customized so that each one uses the best performing way of interacting with its data source. For example, the SQL Server data provider is designed to work with SQL Server 7 or later. Internally, it uses SQL Server's TDS (tabular data stream) protocol for communicating, guaranteeing the best possible performance. If you're using Oracle, you'll need to use the Oracle provider objects instead.

It's important to understand that you can use any data provider in almost exactly the same way, with almost exactly the same code. The provider objects derive from the same base classes, implement the same interfaces, and expose the same set of methods and properties. In some cases, a data provider object will provide custom functionality that's only available with certain data sources, like SQL Server's ability to perform XML queries. However, the basic members used for retrieving and modifying data are identical.

In .NET 1.0, Microsoft included the following two providers:

- **SQL Server provider.** Provides optimized access to a SQL Server database (version 7.0 or later).

- **OLE DB provider.** Provides access to any data source that has an OLE DB driver.

In .NET 1.1, Microsoft added two more providers:

- **Oracle provider.** Provides optimized access to an Oracle database (version 8i or later).

- **ODBC provider.** Providers access to any data source that has an ODBC driver.

These two additional providers are also available as a separate download from the MSDN site, which is useful if you want to use them but you're still programming with .NET 1.0. In addition, third-party developers and database vendors have released their own ADO.NET providers, which follow the same conventions and can be used in the same way as those that are included with the .NET Framework.

When choosing a provider, you should first try to find one that's customized for your data source. If you can't find a suitable provider, you can use the OLE DB provider, as long as you have an OLE DB driver for your data source. The OLE DB technology has been around for many years as a part of ADO, so most data sources provide an OLE DB driver (including SQL Server, Oracle, Access, MySQL, and many more). In the rare situation that you can't find a full provider or an OLE DB driver, you can fall back on the ODBC provider, which works in conjunction with an ODBC driver.

TIP Microsoft includes the OLE DB provider with ADO.NET so that you can use your existing OLE DB drivers. However, if you can find a provider that's customized specifically for your data source, you should use it instead. For example, you can connect to SQL Server database using either the SQL Server provider or the OLE DB provider, but the first will perform best.

To help understand the different layers that come into play with ADO.NET, refer to Figure 13-5.

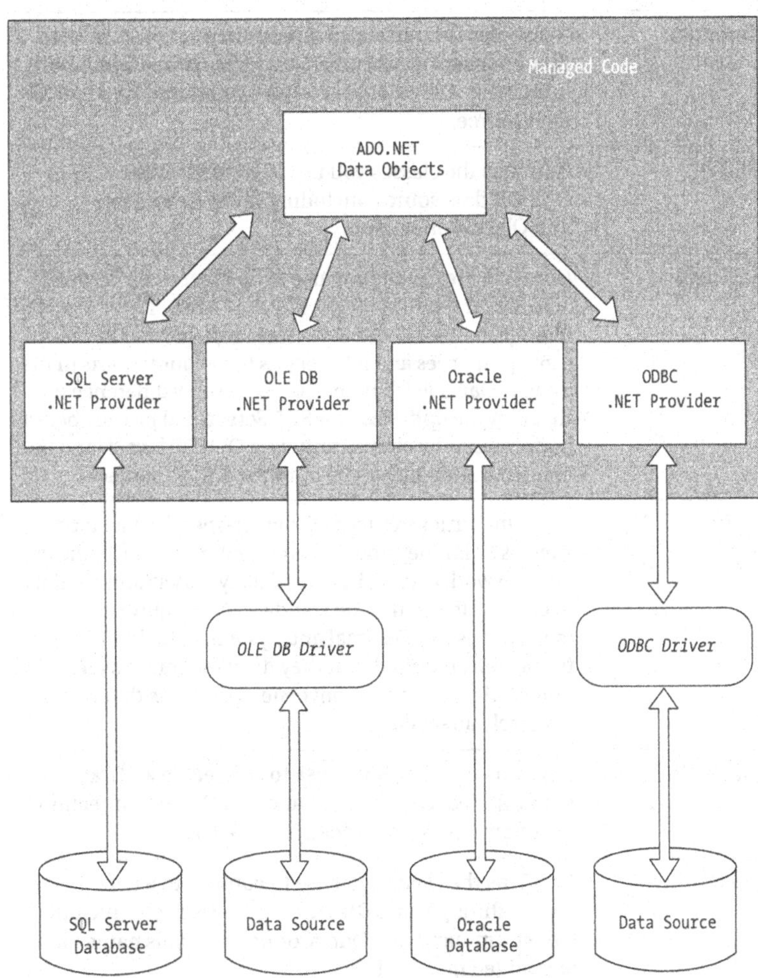

Figure 13-5. The layers between your code and the data source

Data Namespaces

The ADO.NET components live in seven different namespaces in the .NET class library. Together, these namespaces hold all the functionality of ADO.NET. Table 13-1 describes each data namespace.

Table 13-1. ADO.NET Namespaces

Namespace	Purpose
System.Data	Contains fundamental classes with the core ADO.NET functionality. This includes DataSet and DataRelation, which allow you to manipulate structured relational data. These classes are totally independent of any specific type of database or the way you use to connect to it.
System.Data.Common	These classes aren't used directly in your code. Instead, they are used by other data provider classes that inherit from them and provide versions customized for a specific data source.
System.Data.OleDb	Contains the classes you use to connect to an OLE DB data source, including OleDbCommand and OleDbConnection.
System.Data.SqlClient	Contains the classes you use to connect to a Microsoft SQL Server database (version 7.0 or later). These classes, like SqlCommand and SqlConnection, provide all the same properties and methods as their counterparts in the System.Data.OleDb namespace. The only difference is that they are optimized for SQL Server, and provide better performance by eliminating extra OLE DB layers (and by connecting directly to the optimized TDS interface).
System.Data.SqlTypes	Contains structures for SQL Server-specific data types such as SqlMoney and SqlDateTime. You can use these types to work with SQL Server data types without needing to convert them into the standard .NET equivalents (such as System.Decimal and System.DateTime). These types aren't required, but they do allow you to avoid any potential rounding or conversion problems that could adversely affect data.
System.Data.OracleClient	Contains the classes you use to connect to an Oracle database, like OracleCommand and OracleConnection. This namespace was added in .NET 1.1.
System.Data.Odbc	Contains the classes you use to connect to a data source through an ODBC driver. These classes include OdbcCommand and OdbcConnection. This namespace was added in .NET 1.1.

The Data Objects

The data objects allow you to store a local disconnected copy of data. They don't store a connection to a data source—in fact, you can create all the data objects by hand without even using a database. No matter what type of data source you use, objects like DataSet and DataRelation are generic.

The object model is shown in Figure 13-6.

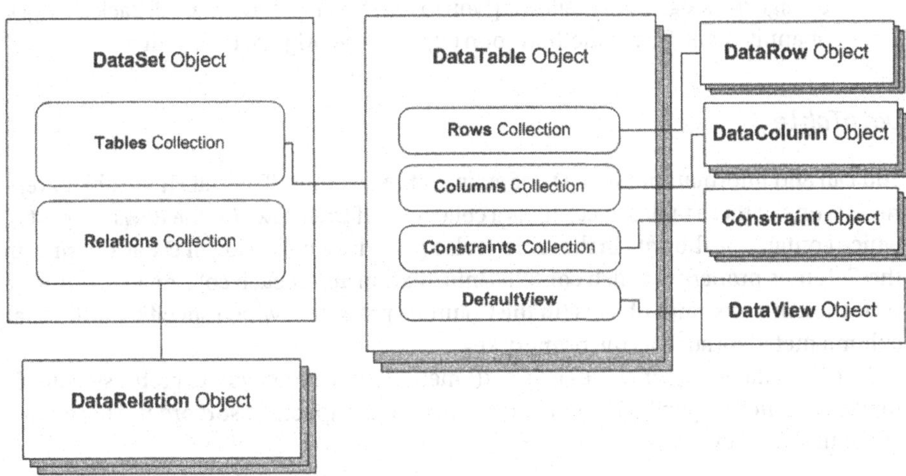

Figure 13-6. The data modeling objects

In the following chapters, you'll become very familiar with all these objects. In the remaining sections of this chapter, I'll briefly introduce them all and give a high-level overview of how they work together.

DataSet

The DataSet class is at the core of the ADO.NET disconnected data model. The DataSet class stores disconnected information drawn from a database and allows you to manipulate it as a single neatly packaged object. The DataSet class has no direct connection to a data source. In fact, you can create a DataSet by hand without needing to involve a database at all.

DataSet contains two main types of objects: DataTables (provided in the Tables property) and DataRelations (provided in the Relations property). The DataSet also incorporates some basic change-tracking, which allows you to apply the changes you make back to a data source at a later time.

The DataSet supports the following key methods:

- WriteXml() and ReadXml() allow the DataSet to be serialized to an XML file and read back from a file.
- Merge() adds the contents of one DataSet into another.
- Clear() removes all the information in the DataSet. You can also just destroy the object (by setting it to Nothing or letting it go out of scope) without using this method.
- AcceptChanges(), GetChanges(), and RejectChanges() work with the DataSet's change tracking, thereby allowing you to retrieve changed rows, roll back changes, or apply them. These methods don't update the original data source.

DataTable

You can add information into a DataSet one table at a time. The DataTable object represents one of these tables. It contains a collection of DataRows (in the Rows property), which contains all the data in the table. It also provides a collection of DataColumns (in the Columns property), which contains information about each column in the table, a collection of Constraint objects (in the Columns property), which specifies additional column metadata such as the primary key.

The DataTable class includes a Select() method that allows you to grab a subset of rows that match a specified filter expression, and in a specified sort order. These rows are returned as an array.

DataRow

Each DataRow represents a single row of information in the table. You can access individual values using the field name or a field index. You can also add new rows and use the following methods:

- BeginEdit(), EndEdit(), and CancelEdit() allow you to use edit mode to make a series of changes to a row, and apply or cancel them all at once.
- Delete() marks a row as deleted, and hides it from the default view used for the table, which means it won't appear when you bind the data to a control. However, the row will still be present in the DataTable until you update the data source and refresh the DataSet. (In fact, the row needs to be present so that your program can find and remove the row from the original data source when you update it.) You'll delve into this in the next chapter.
- GetChildRows() uses the table relations you've defined to get rows from a linked table. For example, when using a Customers table you can use GetChildRows() to retrieve all the corresponding order records from the Orders table.

DataColumn

Unlike the DataRow objects, the DataColumn objects don't contain any actual data. Instead, they store information about the column, such as the column's data type, its default value, and various restrictions (its length, whether null values are allowed, and so on).

DataRelation

Each DataRelation object specifies a single parent/child relationship between two different tables in a DataSet. For example, a DataRelation could indicate the CustomerID column in the Orders table corresponds to the CustomerID column in the Customers table. In this case, the Customers table is the parent, and Orders table is the child, because each customer (the parent) can have multiple orders (children). As with any relational database, using a relation implies certain restrictions. For example, you can't create a child row that refers to a nonexistent parent, and you can't delete a parent that has corresponding child rows.

While it's easy to add a table from a data source into a DataSet, there is currently no corresponding way to get information about relationship from a data source, and apply it automatically to the DataSet. If you want to create a DataRelation in a DataSet to mirror the logic in your database, you need to do it manually.

DataView

The DataView object provides a window onto a DataTable. Each DataTable has at least one DataView (provided through the DefaultView property), which is used for data binding. By default, the DataView simply shows all the information in the DataTable, with no changes. However, you can use the DataView to apply special filtering or sorting options. These frills aren't available in a DataTable, because they affect the presentation of data. The DataTable object is only concerned with data content.

DataViews also allow you to format a single DataTable in more than one way by creating separate DataView objects. However, DataViews don't have any capabilities to hide specific columns or change the order of columns. To hide or rearrange columns, you have to work with the actual ASP.NET control.

The Data Provider Objects

On their own, the data objects can't accomplish much. You might want to add tables, rows, and data by hand, but in most cases the information you need is located in a data source such as a relational database. To access this information, extract it, and insert it into the appropriate data objects, you need the objects described in this section. Remember, each one of these objects has a database-specific implementation. That means you use a different, essentially equivalent object depending on whether you're interacting with SQL Server, Oracle, or the OLE DB provider.

The goal of the data source objects is to create a connection and move information into a DataSet or into a DataReader. The overall interaction of these objects is shown in Figure 13-7. This diagram shows the simplest way of accessing a database—going straight to the source with Command objects and retrieving read-only rows through a DataReader.

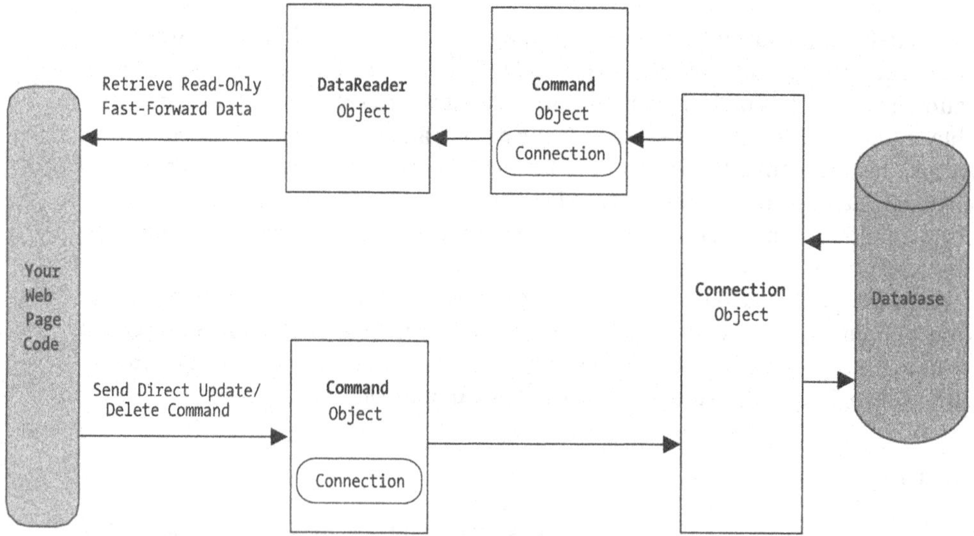

Figure 13-7. Direct data access with ADO.NET

Figure 13-8 shows your other option: placing data into a disconnected DataSet to work with it over an extended period of time. You'll consider both of these approaches in the next chapter.

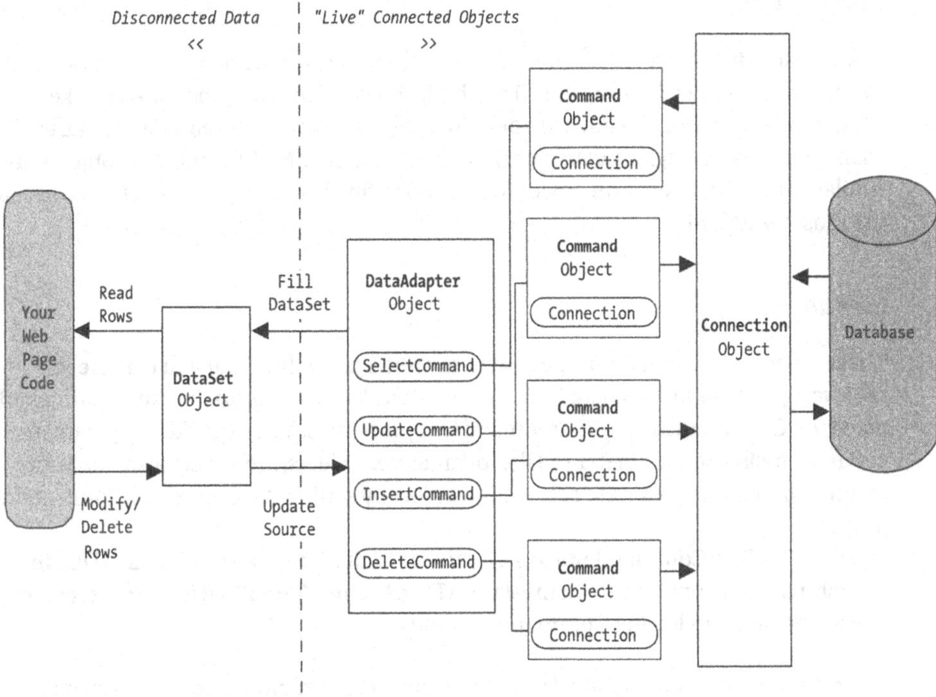

Figure 13-8. Using a DataSet with ADO.NET.

Each provider uses a different string prefix to name its objects. For example, the SQL Server provider uses the string "Sql" and so its Connection object is named SqlConnection. Table 13-2 shows the names of the different provider objects that are provided with .NET 1.1.

Table 13-2. The ADO.NET Data Provider Objects

	SQL Server .NET Provider	OLE DB .NET Provider	Oracle .NET Provider	ODBC .NET Provider
Connection	SqlConnection	OleDbConnection	OracleConnection	OdbcConnection
Command	SqlCommand	OleDbCommand	OracleCommand	OdbcCommand
DataReader	SqlDataReader	OleDbDataReader	OracleDataReader	OdbcDataReader
DataAdapter	SqlDataAdapter	OleDbDataAdapter	OracleDataAdapter	OdbcDataAdapter

The next few sections outline the four basic types of data provider objects.

Connection

The first step in any database operation is to create a Connection object and establish the connection by calling its Open() method. You can then use other objects, like Commands, to perform database operations. Connections also allow you to start a transaction, using BeginTransaction() method. The ADO.NET Connection objects are similar to ADO's Connection object. When you're finished using a connection, you call the Close() method.

Command

These objects represent a SQL statement or stored procedure that you can use to retrieve, update, or modify data from a data source. You set information into a command using the CommandType and CommandText properties. You can add any parameters you need (using SqlParameter or OleDbParameter objects). You must also link your command to the appropriate connection object by setting the Command.Connection property.

The ADO.NET Command objects are similar to the Command object in ADO. To actually use your command, you must use a DataAdapter (described in the next section), or use one of the following Command methods:

- ExecuteNonQuery() allows you to execute a command without retrieving any information. This is ideal for an Insert, Update, or Delete operation using a SQL statement or stored procedure.
- ExecuteReader() is ideal for Select queries. It creates a DataReader object that allows you to retrieve rows from the data source.
- ExecuteScalar() returns the first value in a query. This is useful if you're executing a function that returns only one value (for example, a function that counts the number of rows in a table or calculates a maximum, minimum, or average value).

DataReader

The DataReader objects allow you to process a set of records from start to finish, one row at a time. They are the fastest way to read data if you simply need to display it in a web page, and you don't need to be able to manipulate or update the data later on. These classes are the equivalent of ADO's fast-forward-only cursor. They maintain a live connection with a data source, but they don't allow any changes. To get a single row of information from a DataReader object, you use the Read() method.

DataAdapter

These objects act as a bridge between a Command and a DataSet. For example, you can create a SQL statement that selects a set of rows, create a Command that represents it, and use the DataAdapter object to automatically retrieve all the matching values and insert them into a supplied DataSet. Similarly, you can use the DataAdapter for the reverse procedure: to update a data source based on a modified DataSet.

Every DataAdapter can hold a reference to four different commands, one for each type of operation. You set these commands through the DeleteCommand, InsertCommand, SelectCommand, and UpdateCommand properties. You don't need to create Command objects for all these properties if you don't want to perform the corresponding task. For example, you only need to set the SelectCommand if you're just interested in retrieving rows.

Once you've set the appropriate commands, you can use one of the following methods:

- Fill() executes the SelectCommand and places the results into the DataSet you supply.
- FillSchema() uses the SelectCommand to retrieve information about a table, such as column constraints, and add it to a DataSet. No data rows are transferred.
- Update() scans through the supplied DataSet, and applies all the changes it finds to the data source. In the process, it uses the InsertCommand, UpdateCommand, or DeleteCommand as required. For example, if it finds new rows that didn't exist before, it uses the InsertCommand.

Comparing ADO and ADO.NET

Earlier versions of ADO were designed for desktop use and added Internet functionality as an afterthought. ADO.NET is a revolutionary change that reverses this picture. This means that .NET programmers can use ADO.NET in exactly the same way—whether they're designing for the desktop, client/server, or web environment. These changes don't come without some growing pains for the ADO programmer, however. Not only has the object model been entirely redesigned, but common tasks like updating data have changed considerably.

The scenarios that follow illustrate the difference between ADO and ADO.NET in some common situations. If you've never programmed with ADO before, you'll be starting from scratch—so feel free to skip the historical comparison and move directly to the next chapter. But if you've worked with ADO, the next few sections will help you understand how your skills will map to ADO.NET programming.

Scenario 1: Looping Through a Table

Consider the case in which you need to display a list of database information by moving through a table of data from start to finish. In ADO, you would create a fast-forward read-only connection with the Connection object, fill a Recordset, and loop through it using the MoveNext() method. As soon as the operation was complete, you would close the connection.

In this case, ADO.NET is quite similar. You still use the Connection and Command objects, but instead of going through a Recordset (or DataSet, the ADO.NET replacement), you can use a DataReader. A DataReader is a special object designed to move quickly through a stream of data. It's always configured as a read-only, forward-only reader, which ensures optimum performance.

Scenario 2: Looping Through Parent-Child Tables

Sometimes you'll want to display a set of hierarchical information in a way that clearly shows the parent-child relationship. For example, you might need to show a nested table listing sales orders information inside a list of customers.

In ADO, this type of table is easy to create, but requires a significant amount of manual work. One approach is to fill multiple Recordsets (in this case a Customers Recordset and a Sales Recordset). For every record in the Customers table, you would need to search through the Sales table to find any links. Another approach would be to use a Join query to create a single compound Recordset, and sort it by customer. In this case, as you loop through the table you would need to continuously check the current customer. Whenever a new customer appears, you would start a new customer group. These approaches, which are both fairly simple on the surface, often lead to a lot of extra coding and repeated database queries.

In ADO.NET, this type of manual work is greatly simplified through a collection-based approach. You would just retrieve the Customers and Sales tables, add them both separately to a DataSet, and define the relation. You could then loop through all the sales for each customer using a standard For/Each statement like this:

```
For Each CustomerRow In CustomerTable.Rows
    ' (Display the customer group.)

    For Each SalesRow In CustomerRow.GetChildRows(SalesRelationship)
        ' (Display each sale for that customer.)
    Next
Next
```

You'll explore this technique in more detail in the next chapter.

Scenario 3: Retrieving, Processing, and Updating Data

In ADO, retrieving, processing, and updating data is more or less automatic, because a connection to the database is always present. Typically, you read information using a Connection (and possibly a Command) object, place it in a Recordset, and make changes, which take effect automatically.

In ADO.NET, the DataSet is *never* directly connected to the database. This change is designed to prevent the bad habits (such as leaving connections open) that often limit the scalability of database applications. To get information from the database into the DataSet, and to move changes from the DataSet back to the database, you need to use a special adapter object. This adapter bridges the gap between the DataSet and the data source, and allows information to shuttle back and forth.

Scenario 4: Disconnected Use

In ADO, you create a disconnected Recordset by creating a Connection and filling the Recordset as you would normally, and then you remove the Connection. To commit changes, you reconnect and use the Update() or UpdateBatch() method of the Recordset.

As discussed earlier, you could have problems updating the original information if your Recordset was composed out of multiple joined tables.

In ADO.NET, no special steps need to be taken. DataSets are automatically disconnected, and information isn't transmitted directly, but through the appropriate data adapter object.

Can I Still Use ADO?

ADO provides some features that ADO.NET cannot. For example, ADO allows you to create a Recordset that automatically refreshes itself when another user changes data on the server, thereby guaranteeing that it's always up-to-date. ADO also allows you to lock records that you might be about to change, making it easy to guarantee exclusive access without worrying about stored procedures or transactions. However, while these concepts may still play a role in some client/server and desktop programs, they are fundamentally incompatible with Internet applications. No ASP.NET application can effectively maintain a connection for a user over the Internet—and even if you could, it would never make sense for a single user to have exclusive access to information that needs to be shared with a broad community of users. For all these reasons, ADO.NET is the only practical database access model for ASP.NET applications.

The Last Word

This chapter has covered a lot of ground in exploring the ADO.NET architecture. The two key enhancements that ADO.NET introduces are first-class support for a disconnected programming model and rich XML integration. The first change is designed to improve performance, while the second broadens the reach of your data, allowing it to be easily shared with other applications.

In the next chapter, you'll put ADO.NET to use with some practical examples.

CHAPTER 14

ADO.NET Data Access

THE PREVIOUS CHAPTER introduced ADO.NET and the family of objects that provides its functionality. This family includes objects for modeling data (representing tables, rows, columns, and relations) and objects designed for communicating with a data source. In this chapter, you'll learn how to put these objects to work by creating pages that use ADO.NET to retrieve information from a database and apply changes. You'll also learn how to retrieve and manage disconnected data, and deal with the potential problems that it presents.

About the ADO.NET Examples

One of the goals of ADO.NET is to provide data access universally and with a consistent object model. This means that you should be able to access data the same way regardless of what type of database you're using (or even if you're using a data source that isn't actually a database). In this chapter, most examples will use the "lowest common denominator" of data access—the OLE DB data classes. These types, found in the System.Data.OleDb namespace, allow you to communicate with just about any database that has a matching OLE DB provider, including SQL Server. However, when you develop a production-level application, you'll probably want to use a pure .NET provider that's customized for your database, because it will offer the best performance.

Regardless which provider you use, your code will look almost the same. Often, the only differences will be the namespace that's used, and the name of the ADO.NET data access objects.

Each provider designates its own prefix for naming objects. Thus, the SQL Server provider includes SqlConnection and SqlCommand objects, while the Oracle provider includes OracleConnection and OracleCommand objects. Internally, these objects work quite differently, because they need to connect to different databases using different low-level protocols. Externally, however, these objects look quite similar, and provide an identical set of basic methods. This means that your application is shielded from the complexity of different standards, and can use the SQL Server provider in the same way the Oracle provider uses it. In fact, a block of code for interacting with an SQL Server database can often be translated into a block of Oracle-specific code just by renaming the objects.

In the examples in this chapter, I'll make note of any differences between the OLE DB and SQL Server providers. Remember, though the underlying technical details differ, and the objects are almost identical. The only real differences are as follows:

- The names of the Connection, Command, DataReader, and DataAdapter classes are different in order to help you distinguish them.
- The connection string (the information you use to connect to the database) differs depending on what data source you're using, where it's located, and what type of security you're using.
- The OLE DB objects support a wider variety of data types, while the SQL Server objects only support valid SQL Server data types.

TIP When programming with ADO.NET, it always helps to know your database. If you have information on hand about the data types it uses, the stored procedures it provides, and the user account you need to use, you'll be able to work more quickly and with less chance of error.

Obtaining the Sample Database

This chapter uses examples drawn from the *pubs* database, a sample database included with Microsoft SQL Server and designed to help you test database access code. If you aren't using SQL Server, you won't have this database available. Instead, you can use MSDE, the free data engine included with Visual Studio .NET. MSDE is a scaled-down version of SQL Server that's free to distribute. Its only limitations are that it's restricted to five simultaneous users and that it doesn't provide any graphical tools for creating and managing databases. To install the pubs database in MSDE or SQL Server, you can use the SQL script included with the samples for this chapter. Alternatively, you can use a different relational database engine and tweak the examples in this section accordingly. For more information about installing, configuring, and using MSDE, refer to the .NET documentation.

SQL Basics

When you interact with a data source through ADO.NET, you use the SQL language to retrieve, modify, and update information. In some cases, ADO.NET will hide some of the details for you, or even generate required SQL statements automatically. However, to design an efficient database application with a minimal amount of frustration, you need to understand the basic concepts of SQL.

SQL (Structured Query Language) is a standard data access language used to interact with relational databases. Different databases differ in their support of SQL or add additional features, but the core commands used to select, add, and modify data are common. In a database product like SQL Server, it's possible to use SQL to create fairly sophisticated SQL scripts for stored procedures and triggers (although they have little of the power of a full object-oriented programming language). When working with ADO.NET, however, you'll probably only use the following standard types of SQL statements:

- A Select statement retrieves records.
- An Update statement modifies existing records.
- An Insert statement adds a new record.
- A Delete statement deletes existing records.

If you already have a good understanding of SQL, you can skip the next few sections. Otherwise, read on for a quick tour of SQL fundamentals.

Experimenting with SQL

If you've never used SQL before, you may want to play around with it and create some sample queries before you start using it in an ASP.NET site. Most database products provide some sort of tool for testing queries. If you're using SQL Server, you can try the SQL Query Analyzer, shown in Figure 14-1. (Just select Programs ➤ Microsoft SQL Server ➤ Query Analyzer from the Start menu.) This program lets you type in SQL statements, run them, and see the retrieved results, thereby allowing you to test your SQL assumptions and try out new queries.

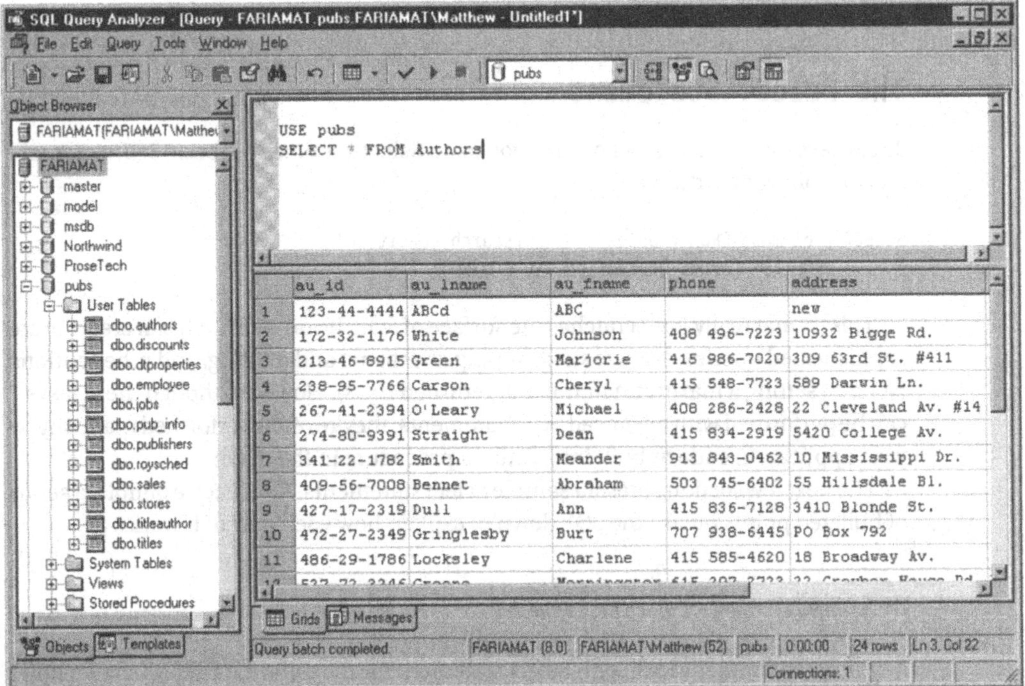

Figure 14-1. The Query Analyzer

You can try out all the examples in this section without generating an ASP.NET program. Just use the SQL Query Analyzer or a similar query tool. In Query Analyzer, you can type in the SQL statement you want to run, and then click the start button (which appears on the toolbar as a green play button). If you're executing a query, a table of records with the returned information will appear at the bottom of the screen. Otherwise, you'll see a single-line response indicating how many rows in the database were affected by your query. If you enter a syntax error, the Query Analyzer will prompt you with an explanation.

Before you can use any of the SQL examples in this chapter, make sure you select the pubs database. You can do this by choosing Query ➤ Change Database from the menu, or just by typing **USE pubs** into the query window before you add any other SQL statements.

TIP To learn more about SQL, use one of the online SQL tutorials available on the Internet, such as the one at `http://www.w3schools.com/sql`. If you're working with SQL Server you can use Microsoft's thorough Books Online reference to become a database guru. One topic you might want to investigate is Join queries, which allow you to connect related tables into one set of results.

The Select Statement

To retrieve one or more rows of data, you use a Select statement. A basic SQL statement has the following structure:

```
SELECT [columns] FROM [tables] WHERE [search_condition]
      ORDER BY [order_expression ASC | DESC]
```

This format really just scratches the surface of SQL. If you want, you can create more sophisticated queries that use subgrouping, averaging and totaling, and other options (such as setting a maximum number of returned rows). However, though these tasks can be performed with advanced SQL statements, they're often performed manually by your application code or built into a stored procedure in the database.

The next few sections present sample Select statements. After each example, a series of bulleted points breaks the SQL down to explain how each part of it works.

A Sample Select Statement

A typical (and rather inefficient) Select statement for the pubs database is shown here. It works with the Authors table, which contains a list of authors:

```
SELECT * FROM Authors
```

- The asterisk (*) retrieves all the columns in the table. This isn't the best approach for a large table if you don't need all the information. It increases the amount of data that has to be transferred and can slow down your server.
- The From clause identifies that the Authors table is being used for this statement.
- There is no Where clause. This means that all the records will be retrieved from the database, regardless of whether there are ten or ten million. This is a poor design practice, because it often leads to applications that appear to work fine when they're first deployed, but gradually slow down as the database grows. In general, you should always include a Where clause to limit the possible number of rows. Often, queries are limited by a date field (for example, including all orders that were placed in the last three months).
- There is no Order By clause. This is a perfectly acceptable approach, especially if order doesn't matter or you plan to sort the data on your own using the tools provided in ADO.NET.

Improving the Select Statement

Here's another example that retrieves a list of author names:

```
SELECT au_lname, au_fname FROM Authors WHERE State='MI' ORDER BY au_lname ASC
```

- Only two columns are retrieved (au_lname and au_fname). They correspond to the first and last names of the author.
- A Where clause restricts results to those authors who live in the specified state. Note that the Where clause requires apostrophes around the value you want to match (unless it is a numeric value).
- An Order By clause sorts the information alphabetically by the author's last name.

An Alternative Select Statement

Here's one last example:

```
SELECT TOP 100 au_lname, au_fname FROM Authors ORDER BY au_lname, au_fname ASC
```

- This example uses the Top clause instead of a Where statement. The database rows will be sorted, and the first one hundred matching results will be retrieved. The Top clause is useful for user-defined search operations where you want to ensure that the database isn't tied up in a long operation retrieving unneeded rows.
- This example uses a more sophisticated Order By expression, which sorts authors with identical last names in a subgroup by their first name.

The Where Clause

In many respects, the Where clause is the most important part of the Select statement. You can combine multiple conditions with the And keyword, and you can specify greater than and less than comparisons by using the greater than (>) and less than (<) operators.

The following is an example with a different table and a more sophisticated Where statement:

```
SELECT * FROM Sales WHERE ord_date < '2000/01/01' AND ord_date > '1987/01/01'
```

- This example uses the international date format to compare date values. Although SQL Server supports many different date formats, yyyy/mm/dd is recommended to prevent ambiguity.
- If you were using Access, you would need to use the US date format mm/dd/yyyy, and replace the apostrophes around the date with the number (#) symbol.

Aggregate Queries

The SQL language also defines special *aggregate functions*. Aggregate functions return work with a set of values, but only return a single value. For example, you can use an aggregate function to count the number of records in a table, or calculate the average price of a product. The most commonly used aggregate functions are listed in Table 14-1.

Table 14-1. SQL Aggregate Functions

Command	Description
Avg(fieldname)	Calculates the average of all values in a given numeric field.
Sum(fieldname)	Calculates the sum of all values in a given numeric field.
Min(fieldname) and Max(fieldname)	Finds the minimum or maximum value in a number field.
Count(*)	Returns the number of rows in the result set.
Count(DISTINCT fieldname)	Returns the number of unique (and non-null) rows in the result set.

For example, here's a query that returns a single value: the number of records in the Authors table:

```
SELECT COUNT(*) FROM Authors
```

And here's how you could calculate the total quantity of all sales by adding together the qty field in each record:

```
SELECT SUM(qty) FROM Sales
```

The SQL Update Statement

The SQL Update statement selects all the records that match a specified search expression and then modifies them all according to an update expression. At its simplest, the Update statement has the following format:

```
UPDATE [table] SET [update_expression] WHERE [search_condition]
```

Typically, you'll use an Update statement to modify a single record. The following example adjusts the phone column in a single author record. It uses the unique author ID to find the correct row.

```
UPDATE Authors SET phone='408 496-2222' WHERE au_id='172-32-1176'
```

In the Query Analyzer, this statement will return the number of rows affected, but it will not display the change. To do that, you need to request the row by performing another SQL statement (see Figure 14-2).

```
SELECT Authors WHERE au_id='172-32-1176'
```

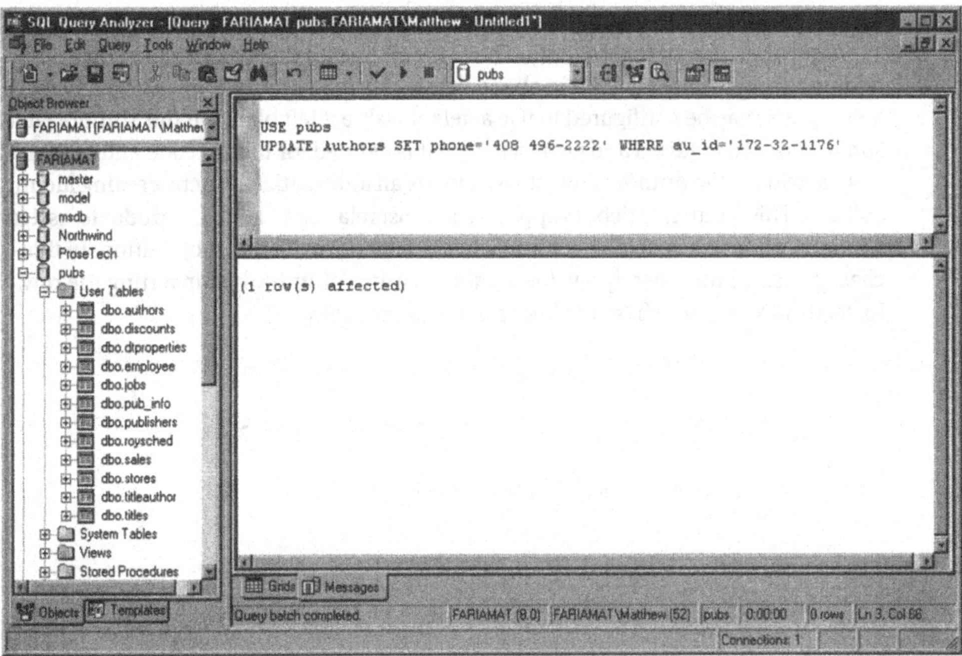

Figure 14-2. An Update statement in the Query Analyzer

As with a Select statement, you can use an Update statement to make several changes at once or to search for a record based on several different criteria:

```
UPDATE Authors SET au_lname='Whiteson', au_fname='John'
    WHERE au_lname='White' AND au_fname='Johnson'
```

You can even use the Update statement to update an entire range of matching records. The following example modifies the phone number for every author who lives in California:

```
UPDATE Authors SET phone='408 496-2222' WHERE state='CA'
```

The SQL Insert Statement

The SQL Insert statement adds a new record to a table with the information you specify. It takes the following form:

```
INSERT INTO [table] ([column_list]) VALUES ([value_list])
```

You can provide the information in any order you want, as long as you make sure that the list of column names and the list of values correspond exactly.

```
INSERT INTO Authors (au_id, au_lname, au_fname, zip, contract)
      VALUES ('998-72-3566', 'John', 'Khan', 84152, 0)
```

This example leaves out some information, such as the city and address, in order to provide a simple example. The previous example shows the bare minimum required to create a new record in the Authors table. The new record is featured in Figure 14-3.

Remember, database tables often have requirements that can prevent you from adding a record unless you fill in all the fields with valid information. Alternatively, some fields may be configured to use a default value if left blank. In the Authors table, some fields are required and a special format is defined for the zip code and author ID.

One feature the Authors table doesn't use is an automatically incrementing identity column. This feature, which is supported in most relational database products, assigns a unique value to a specified column when you perform an insert operation. In this case, you shouldn't specify a value for the identity column when inserting the row. Instead, allow the database to choose one automatically.

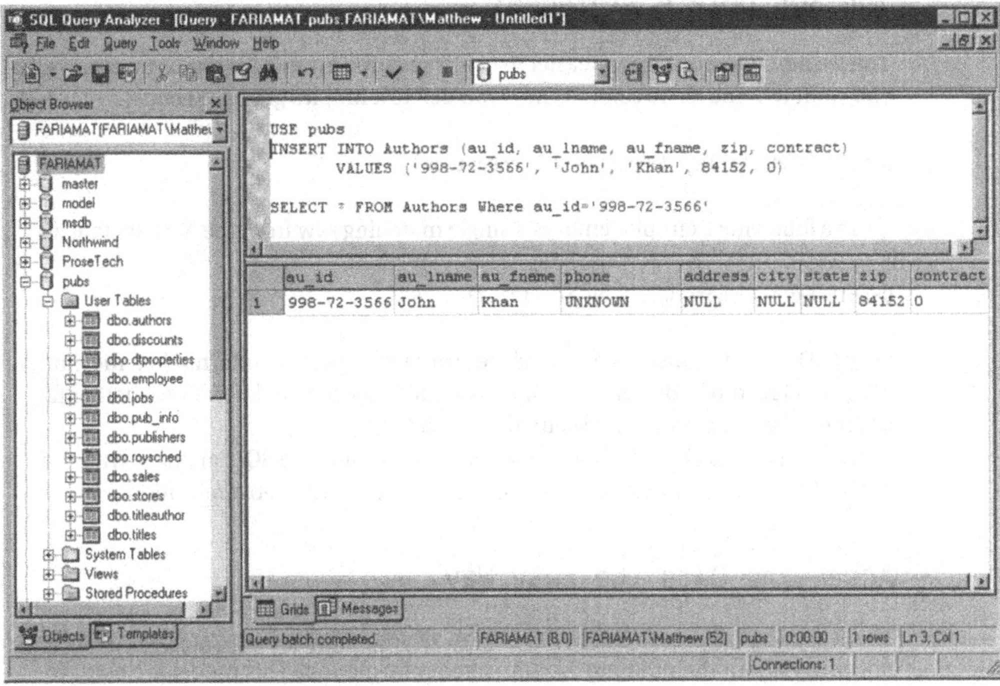

Figure 14-3. Inserting a new record

Auto-Increment Fields Are Indispensable

If you're designing a database, make sure that you add an auto-incrementing identity field to every table. It's the fastest, easiest, and least error-prone way to assign a unique "identification number" to every record. Without an automatically generated identity field, you'll need to go to considerable effort to create and maintain your own unique field. Often, programmers fall into the trap of using a data field for a unique identifier, such as a Social Security number or name. This almost always leads to trouble at some inconvenient time far in the future, when you need to add a person who doesn't have an SSN or social security number (for example, a foreign national) or account for an SSN or name change (which will cause problems for other related tables, such as a purchase order table that identifies the purchaser by the name or SSN field). A much better approach is to use a unique identifier, and have the database engine assign an arbitrary unique number to every row automatically.

If you create a table without a unique identification column, you'll have trouble when you need to select that specific row for deletion or updates. Selecting records based on a text field can also lead to problems if the field contains special embedded characters (like apostrophes). You'll also find it extremely awkward to create table relationships.

The SQL Delete Statement

The Delete statement is even easier to use. It specifies criteria for one or more rows that you want to remove. Be careful: Once you delete a row, it's gone for good!

```
DELETE FROM [table] WHERE [search_condition]
```

The following example removes a single matching row from the Authors table:

```
DELETE FROM Authors WHERE au_id='172-32-1176'
```

SQL Delete and Update commands return a single piece of information: the number of affected records. You can examine this value and use it to determine whether the operation was successful or executed as expected.

The rest of this chapter shows how you can combine the SQL language with the ADO.NET objects to retrieve and manipulate data in your web applications.

Accessing Data the Easy Way

The "easy way" to access data is to perform all your database operations directly and not worry about maintaining disconnected information. This model is closest to traditional ADO programming, and it allows you to sidestep potential concurrency problems, which occur when multiple users try to update information at once. It's also well suited to ASP.NET web pages, which don't need to store disconnected information for long periods of time. Remember, an ASP.NET web page is loaded when the page is requested, and shut down as soon as the response is returned to the user. That means a page typically has a lifetime of only a few seconds.

With simple data access, a disconnected copy of the data isn't retained. That means that data selection and data modifications are performed separately. Your program must keep track of the changes that need to be committed to the data source. For example, if a user deletes a record, you need to explicitly specify that record using an SQL Delete statement.

Simple data access is ideal if you only need to read information or if you only need to perform simple update operations, such as adding a record to a log or allowing a user to modify values in a single record (for example, the customer information for an e-commerce site). Simple data access may not be as useful if you want to modify several different records or tables at the same time.

To retrieve information with simple data access, follow these steps:

1. Create Connection, Command, and DataReader objects.

2. Use the DataReader to retrieve information from the database and display it in a control on a web form.

3. Close your connection.

4. Send the page to the user. At this point, the information your user sees and the information in the database no longer have any connection, and all the ADO.NET objects have been destroyed.

To add or update information, follow these steps:

1. Create new Connection and Command objects.
2. Execute the Command (with the appropriate SQL statement).

Both of these approaches are demonstrated in this chapter.

Importing the Namespaces

Before continuing any further, make sure you import the ADO.NET namespaces, as shown here.

```
Imports System.Data
Imports System.Data.OleDb
```

If you wanted to use the SQL server provider instead of the OLE DB provider, you would use these two lines instead:

```
Imports System.Data
Imports System.Data.SqlClient
```

Creating a Connection

Before you can retrieve or update data, you need to make a connection to the data source. Generally, connections are limited to some fixed number, and if you exceed that number (either because you run out of licenses or because your database server can't accommodate the user load), attempts to create new connections will fail. For that reason, you should try to hold a connection open for as short a time as possible. You should also write your database code inside a Try/Catch error-handling structure, so that you can respond if an error does occur, and make sure you close the connection even if you can't perform all your work.

When creating a Connection object, you need to specify a value for its ConnectionString property. This ConnectionString defines all the information the computer needs to find the data source, log in, and choose an initial database. Out of all the details in the examples in this chapter, the ConnectionString is the one value you might have to tweak before it works for the database you want to use. Luckily, it's quite straightforward. Here's an example that uses a connection string to connect to the SQL Server OLE DB provider:

```
Dim MyConnection As New OleDbConnection()
MyConnection.ConnectionString = "Provider=SQLOLEDB.1;Data Source=localhost;" & _
 "Initial Catalog=Pubs;User ID=sa"
```

The connection string for the SqlConnection object is quite similar, and just leaves out the Provider setting:

```
Dim MyConnection As New SqlConnection()
MyConnection.ConnectionString = "Data Source=localhost;" & _
 "Initial Catalog=Pubs;User ID=sa"
```

The Connection String

The connection string is actually a series of distinct pieces of information, separated by semicolons (;). In the preceding example, the connection string identifies the following pieces of information:

- **Provider.** This is the name of the OLE DB provider, which allows communication between ADO.NET and your database. SQLOLEDB is the OLE DB provider for SQL). Other providers include MSDAORA (the OLE DB provider for an Oracle database) and Microsoft.Jet.OLEDB.4.0 (the OLE DB provider for Access).
- **Data Source.** This indicates the name of the server where the data source is located. In this case, the server is on the same computer that hosts the ASP.NET site, so localhost is sufficient.
- **Initial Catalog.** This is the name of the database that this connection will be accessing. It's only the "initial" database because you can change it later, by using the Connection.ChangeDatabase() method.
- **User ID.** This is a user ID used to connect access the database. The user ID "sa" corresponds to the system administrator account provided with databases such as SQL Server.
- **Password.** By default, the sa account doesn't have a password. Typically, in a production-level site, this account would be modified or replaced. To specify a password for a user, just add the Password settings to the connection string (as in "Password=letmein"). Note that as with all connection string settings, you don't need quotation marks, but you do need to separate the setting with a semicolon.
- **ConnectionTimeout.** This determines how long your code will wait, in seconds, before generating an error if it cannot establish a database connection. Our example connection string doesn't set the ConnectionTimeout, so the default of 15 seconds is used. Use 0 to specify no limit, which is a bad idea. This means that, theoretically, the code could be held up indefinitely while it attempts to contact the server.

There are some other, lesser-used options you can set for a connection string, such as parameters that specify how long you'll wait while trying to make a connection before timing out. For more information, refer to the .NET Help files. Look under the appropriate connection object (such as SqlConnection or OleDbConnection).

Windows Authentication

The previous examples use SQL Server authentication, where you explicitly place the user ID and password information in the connection string. However, SQL Server authentication is disabled by default in SQL Server 2000, because a more secure alternative exists: *integrated Windows authentication.*

Here's the lowdown on both types of authentication:

- With SQL Server authentication, SQL Server maintains its own user account information in the database. It uses this information to determine if you are allowed to access specific parts of a database.With Windows authentication, SQL Server automatically uses the Windows account information for the currently logged-in user. In the database, it stores information about what database privileges each user should have.

TIP You can set what type of authentication your SQL Server uses through Enterprise Manager. Just right-click on your server in the tree, which will be named (local), and select Properties. Choose the Security tab to change the type of authentication. You can choose either "Windows only" or "SQL Server and Windows," which allows both Windows authentication and SQL Server authentication. This option is also known as mixed-mode authentication.

To connect to SQL Server using Windows authentication, you need to use the Integrated Security setting in the connection string. The following connection string uses integrated authentication. Note that it doesn't define a username and password, because the Windows operating system will automatically pass the identity of the current user to SQL Server.

```
MyConnection.ConnectionString = "Provider=SQLOLEDB.1;Data Source=localhost;" & _
  "Initial Catalog=Pubs;Integrated Security=SSPI"
```

For Windows authentication to work, the currently logged-on Windows user must have the required authorization to access the SQL database. In the case of an ASP.NET application, the "current user" is the account that's defined in machine.config file. By default, this is the ASPNET account, which probably won't have the permissions required to access your database.

You can solve this problem in two ways. You can grant the required database permissions to the ASPNET account using Enterprise Manager. (One useful shortcut is to use Enterprise Manager's Create Login wizard. This process is described in the SQL Server documentation.) The other option is to configure the ASP.NET service to use an account with greater privileges. Chapter 2 describes how you can give the ASP.NET service full system privileges for testing purposes.

TIP Windows authentication is the most secure approach to interacting with a database. It ensures that you don't need to enter sensitive user ID and password information directly in a configuration file, where other users might see it.

Connection String Tips

Typically, all the database code in your application will use the same connection string. For that reason, it usually makes the most sense to store a connection string in a class member variable or, even better, a configuration file.

```
Dim ConnectionString As String = "Provider=SQLOLEDB ..."
```

You can also create a Connection object and supply the connection string in one step by using a different constructor:

```
Dim MyConnection As New OleDbConnection(ConnectionString)
' MyConnection.ConnectionString is now set to ConnectionString.
```

Making the Connection

Before you can use a connection, you have to explicitly open it, as shown here:

```
MyConnection.Open()
```

To verify that you have successfully connected to the database, you can try displaying some basic connection information. The following example writes some basic information to a label control named lblInfo (see Figure 14-4).

Here's the code using a Try/Catch error-handling block:

```
' Define the ADO.NET Connection object.
Dim MyConnection As New OleDbConnection(ConnectionString)

Try
    ' Try to open the connection.
    MyConnection.Open()
    lblInfo.Text = "<b>Server Version:</b> " & MyConnection.ServerVersion
    lblInfo.Text &= "<br><b>Connection Is:</b> " & MyConnection.State.ToString()
Catch err As Exception
    ' Handle an error by displaying the information.
    lblInfo.Text = "Error reading the database. "
    lblInfo.Text &= err.Message
```

```
Finally
    ' Either way, make sure the connection is properly closed.
    ' (Even if the connection wasn't opened successfully,
    '  calling Close() won't cause an error.)
    MyConnection.Close()
    lblInfo.Text &= "<br><b>Now Connection Is:</b> "
    lblInfo.Text &=  MyConnection.State.ToString()
End Try
```

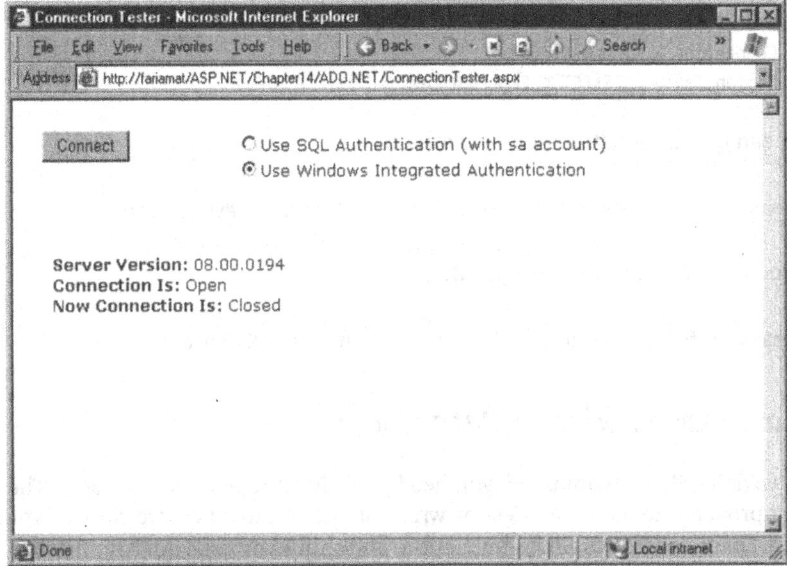

Figure 14-4. Testing your connection

Once you use the Open() method, you have a live connection to your database. One of the most fundamental principles of data access code is that you should reduce the amount of time you hold a connection open as much as possible. Imagine that as soon as you open the connection, you have a live, ticking time bomb. You need to get in, retrieve your data, and throw the connection away as quickly as possible in order to ensure your site runs efficiently.

Closing a connection is just as easy, as shown here:

```
MyConnection.Close()
```

Defining a Select Command

The Connection object provides a few basic properties that supply information about the connection, but that's about all. To actually retrieve data, you need a few more ingredients:

- An SQL statement that selects the information you want
- A Command object that executes the SQL statement
- A DataReader or DataSet object to catch the retrieved records

Command objects represent SQL statements. To use a Command, you define it, specify the SQL statement you want to use, specify an available connection, and execute the command.

You can use one of our earlier SQL statements as shown here:

```
Dim MyCommand As New OleDbCommand()
MyCommand.Connection = MyConnection
MyCommand.CommandText = "SELECT * FROM Authors"
```

Or you can use the constructor as a shortcut:

```
Dim MyCommand As New OleDbCommand("SELECT * FROM Authors", MyConnection)
```

The process is identical for the SqlCommand:

```
Dim MyCommand As New SqlCommand("SELECT * FROM Authors", MyConnection)
```

Using a Command with a DataReader

Once you've defined your command, you need to decide how you want to use it. The simplest approach is to use a DataReader, which allows you to quickly retrieve all your results. The DataReader uses a live connection, and should be used quickly and then closed. The DataReader is also extremely simple. It supports fast forward-only read-only access to your results, which is generally all you need when retrieving information. Because of the DataReader's optimized nature, it provides better performance than the DataSet. It should always be your first choice for simple data access.

Before you can use a DataReader, make sure you've opened the connection:

```
MyConnection.Open()
```

To create a DataReader, you use the ExecuteReader() method of the command object, as shown here:

```
' You don't need the New keyword, as the Command will create the DataReader.
Dim MyReader As OleDbDataReader
MyReader = MyCommand.ExecuteReader()
```

The process is identical for the SqlDataReader:

```
Dim MyReader As SqlDataReader
MyReader = MyCommand.ExecuteReader()
```

These two lines of code define a DataReader object, and then create it by executing your command. Once you have the reader, you retrieve a single row at a time using the Read method:

```
MyReader.Read()   ' The first row in the result set is now available.
```

You can then access the values in the current row using the corresponding field names. The following example adds an item to a list box with the first name and last name for the current row:

```
lstNames.Items.Add(MyReader("au_lname") & ", " & MyReader("au_fname"))
```

To move to the next row, use the Read() method again. If this method returns True, a row of information has been successfully retrieved. If it returns False, you've attempted to read past the end of your result set. There is no way to move backward to a previous row.

As soon as you've finished reading all the results you need, close the DataReader and Connection:

```
MyDataReader.Close()
MyConnection.Close()
```

Putting It All Together

The next example demonstrates how you can use all the ADO.NET ingredients together to create a simple application that retrieves information from the Authors table. You can select an author record by last name using a drop-down list box, as shown in Figure 14-5.

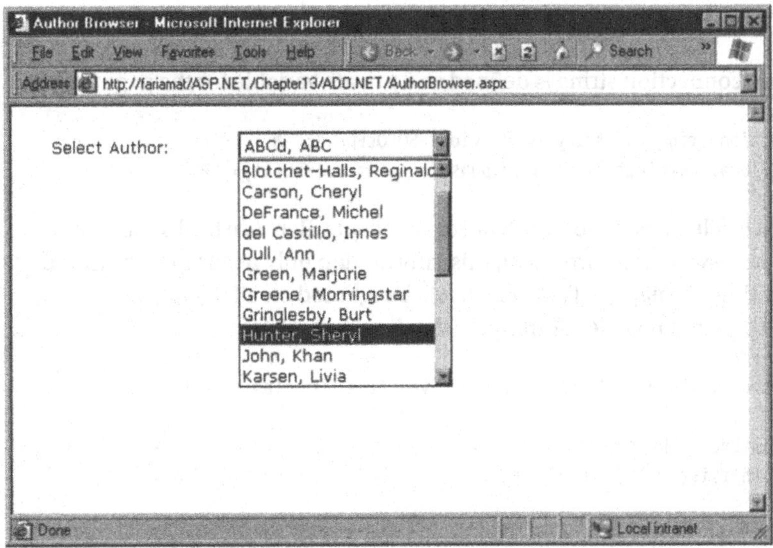

Figure 14-5. Selecting an author

The full record is then retrieved and displayed in a simple label control, as shown in Figure 14-6.

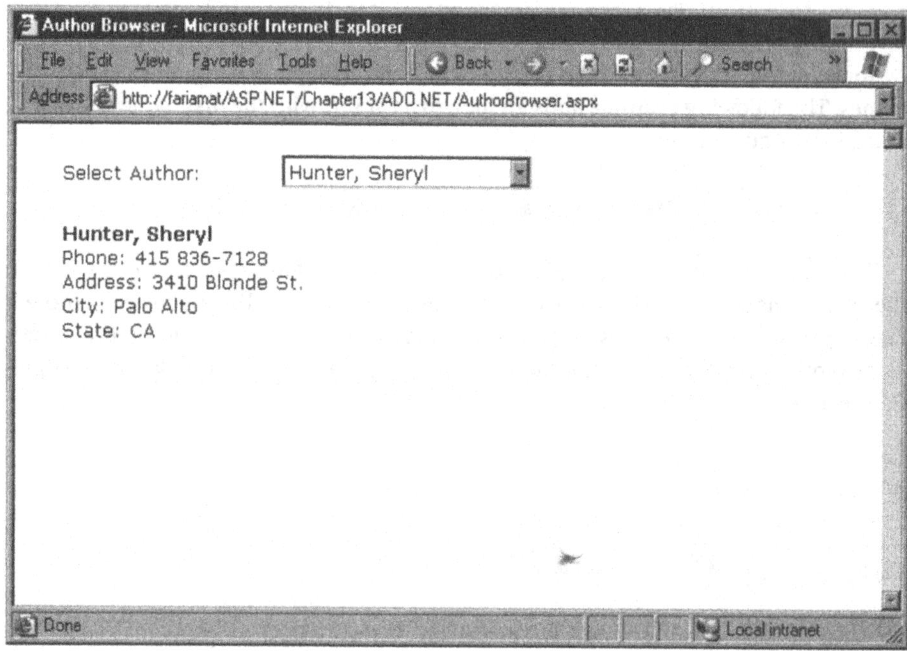

Figure 14-6. Author information

Filling the List Box

To start off, the connection string is defined as a private variable for the page class:

```
Private ConnectionString As String = "Provider=SQLOLEDB.1;" & _
 "Data Source=localhost;Initial Catalog=pubs;Integrated Security=SSPI"
```

The list box is filled when the Page.Load event occurs. Because the list box control is set to persist its view state information, this information only needs to be retrieved once, the first time the page is displayed. It will be ignored on all postbacks.

Here's the code that fills the list from the database:

```
Private Sub Page_Load(sender As Object, e As EventArgs) Handles MyBase.Load

    If Me.IsPostBack = False Then
        FillAuthorList()
    End If

End Sub
```

```
Private Sub FillAuthorList()

    lstAuthor.Items.Clear()

    ' Define the Select statement.
    ' Three pieces of information are needed: the unique id,
    ' and the first and last name.
    Dim SelectSQL As String
    SelectSQL = "SELECT au_lname, au_fname, au_id FROM Authors"

    ' Define the ADO.NET objects.
    Dim con As New OleDbConnection(ConnectionString)
    Dim cmd As New OleDbCommand(SelectSQL, con)
    Dim reader As OleDbDataReader

    ' Try to open database and read information.
    Try
        con.Open()
        reader = cmd.ExecuteReader()

        ' For each item, add the author name to the displayed
        ' list box text, and store the unique ID in the Value property.
        Do While reader.Read()
            Dim NewItem As New ListItem()
            NewItem.Text = reader("au_lname") & ", " & reader("au_fname")
            NewItem.Value = reader("au_id")
            lstAuthor.Items.Add(NewItem)
        Loop

        reader.Close()

    Catch err As Exception
        lblResults.Text = "Error reading list of names. "
        lblResults.Text &= err.Message
    Finally
        con.Close()
    End Try

End Sub
```

This example looks more sophisticated than the previous bite-sized snippets in this chapter, but it really doesn't introduce anything new. The standard Connection, Command, and DataAdapter objects are used. The Connection is opened inside an error-handling block, so that your page can handle any unexpected errors and provide information. A Finally block makes sure that the connection is properly closed, even if an error occurs.

The actual code for reading the data uses a loop. With each pass, the Read() method is called to get another row of information. When the reader has read all the available information, this method will return False, the While condition will evaluate to False, and the loop will end gracefully.

The unique ID (the value in the au_id field) is stored in the Value property of the list box for reference later. This is a crucial ingredient that is needed to allow the corresponding record to be queried again. If you tried to build a query using the author's name, you would need to worry about authors with the same name, and invalid characters (such as the apostrophe in O'Leary) that would invalidate your SQL statement.

Retrieving the Record

The record is retrieved as soon as the user changes the selection in the list box. To make this possible, the AutoPostBack property of the list box is set to True so that its change events are detected automatically.

```
Private Sub lstAuthor_SelectedIndexChanged(sender As Object, _
  e As EventArgs) Handles lstAuthor.SelectedIndexChanged

    ' Create a Select statement that searches for a record
    ' matching the specific author id from the Value property.
    Dim SelectSQL As String
    SelectSQL = "SELECT * FROM Authors "
    SelectSQL &= "WHERE au_id='" & lstAuthor.SelectedItem.Value & "'"

    ' Define the ADO.NET objects.
    Dim con As New OleDbConnection(ConnectionString)
    Dim cmd As New OleDbCommand(SelectSQL, con)
    Dim reader As OleDbDataReader

    ' Try to open database and read information.
    Try
        con.Open()
        reader = cmd.ExecuteReader()
        reader.Read()
        lblResults.Text = "<b>" & reader("au_lname")
        lblResults.Text &= ", " & reader("au_fname") & "</b><br>"
        lblResults.Text &= "Phone: " & reader("phone") & "<br>"
        lblResults.Text &= "Address: " & reader("address") & "<br>"
        lblResults.Text &= "City: " & reader("city") & "<br>"
        lblResults.Text &= "State: " & reader("state") & "<br>"
        reader.Close()
    Catch err As Exception
        lblResults.Text = "Error getting author. "
        lblResults.Text &= err.Message
    Finally
        con.Close()
    End Try

End Sub
```

The process is similar to the procedure used to retrieve the last names. There are only a couple of differences:

- The code dynamically creates an SQL statement based on the selected item in the drop-down list box. It uses the Value property of the selected item, which stores the unique identifier. This is a common (and very useful) technique.
- Only one record is read. The code assumes that only one author has the matching au_id, which is reasonable as this field is unique.

NOTE This example shows how ADO.NET works to retrieve a simple result set. Of course, ADO.NET also provides handy controls that go beyond this generic level, and let you provide full-featured grids with sorting and editing. These controls are described in Chapter 16. For now, you should concentrate on understanding the fundamentals about ADO.NET and how it works with data.

Updating Data

Now that you understand how to retrieve data, it isn't much more complicated to perform simple delete and update operations. Once again, you use the Command object, but this time you don't need a DataReader because no results will be retrieved. You also don't need an SQL Select command. Instead, you can use one of three new SQL commands: Update, Insert, or Delete.

To execute an Update, Insert, or Delete statement, you need to create a Command object. You can then execute the command with the ExecuteNonQuery() method. This method returns the number of rows that were affected, which allows you to check your assumptions. For example, if you attempt to update or delete a record and are informed that no records were affected, you probably have an error in your Where clause that is preventing any records from being selected. (If, on the other hand, your SQL command has a syntax error or attempts to retrieve information from a nonexistent table, an exception will occur.)

Enhancing the Author Page

To demonstrate how to Update, Insert, and Delete simple information, the previous example has been enhanced. Instead of being displayed in a label, the information from each field is added to a separate text box. Two additional buttons allow you to update the record (Update), or delete it (Delete). You can also insert a new record by clicking Create New, entering the information in the text boxes, and then clicking Insert New. The updated web page is shown in Figure 14-7.

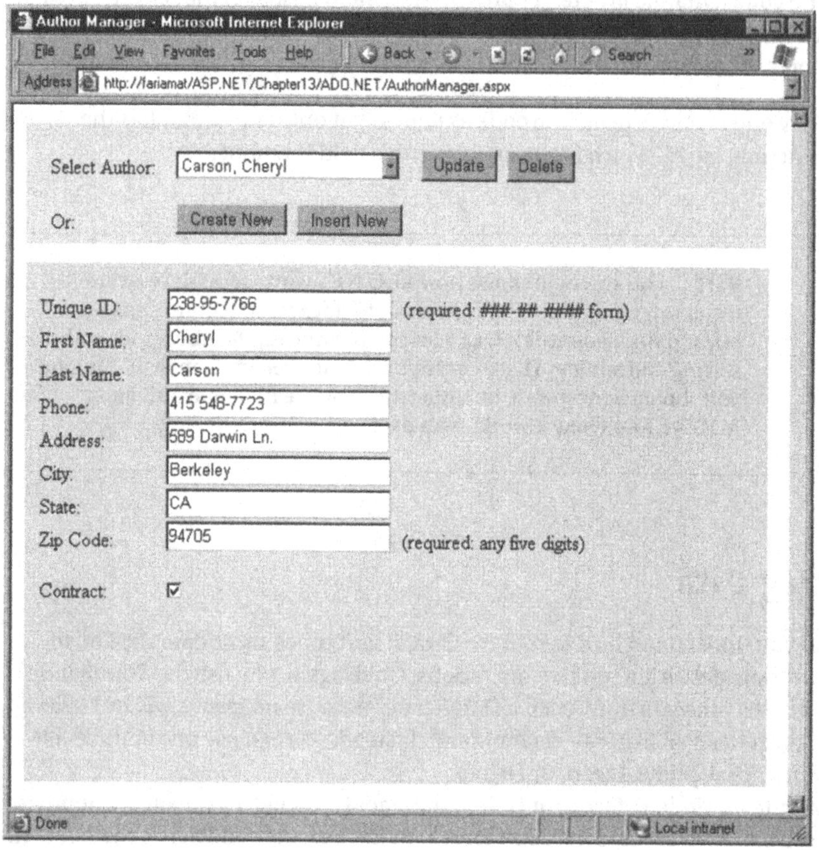

Figure 14-7. A more advanced author manager

The record selection code is identical from an ADO.NET perspective, but it now uses the individual text box controls.

```
Private Sub lstAuthor_SelectedIndexChanged(sender As Object, _
  e As EventArgs) Handles lstAuthor.SelectedIndexChanged

    ' Define ADO.NET objects.
    Dim SelectSQL As String
    SelectSQL = "SELECT * FROM Authors "
    SelectSQL &= "WHERE au_id='" & lstAuthor.SelectedItem.Value & "'"
    Dim con As New OleDbConnection(ConnectionString)
    Dim cmd As New OleDbCommand(SelectSQL, con)
    Dim reader As OleDbDataReader

    ' Try to open database and read information.
    Try
        con.Open()
        reader = cmd.ExecuteReader()
        reader.Read()
```

```
        ' Fill the controls.
        txtID.Text = reader("au_id")
        txtFirstName.Text = reader("au_fname")
        txtLastName.Text = reader("au_lname")
        txtPhone.Text = reader("phone")
        txtAddress.Text = reader("address")
        txtCity.Text = reader("city")
        txtState.Text = reader("state")
        txtZip.Text = reader("zip")
        chkContract.Checked = CType(reader("contract"), Boolean)
        reader.Close()
        lblStatus.Text = ""
    Catch err As Exception
        lblStatus.Text = "Error getting author. "
        lblStatus.Text &= err.Message
    Finally
        con.Close()
    End Try

End Sub
```

To see the full code, refer to the online samples for this chapter. If you play with the example at length, you'll notice that it lacks a few niceties that would be needed in a professional website. For example, when creating a new record, the name of the last selected user is still visible, and the Update and Delete buttons are still active, which can lead to confusion or errors. A more sophisticated user interface could prevent these problems by disabling inapplicable controls (perhaps by grouping them in a Panel control) or using separate pages. In this case, however, the page is useful as a quick way to test some basic data access code.

Updating a Record

When the user clicks the Update button, the information in the text boxes is applied to the database as follows:

```
Private Sub cmdUpdate_Click(sender As Object, _
  e As EventArgs) Handles cmdUpdate.Click

    ' Define ADO.NET objects.
    Dim UpdateSQL As String
    UpdateSQL = "UPDATE Authors SET "
    UpdateSQL &= "au_id='" & txtID.Text & "', "
    UpdateSQL &= "au_fname='" & txtFirstName.Text & "', "
    UpdateSQL &= "au_lname='" & txtLastName.Text & "', "
    UpdateSQL &= "phone='" & txtPhone.Text & "', "
    UpdateSQL &= "address='" & txtAddress.Text & "', "
    UpdateSQL &= "city='" & txtCity.Text & "', "
    UpdateSQL &= "state='" & txtState.Text & "', "
    UpdateSQL &= "zip='" & txtZip.Text & "', "
    UpdateSQL &= "contract='" & Int(chkContract.Checked) & "' "
    UpdateSQL &= "WHERE au_id='" & lstAuthor.SelectedItem.Value & "'"
```

```
    Dim con As New OleDbConnection(ConnectionString)
    Dim cmd As New OleDbCommand(UpdateSQL, con)

    ' Try to open database and execute the update.
    Try
        con.Open()
        Dim Updated As Integer
        Updated = cmd.ExecuteNonQuery
        lblStatus.Text = Updated.ToString() & " records updated."
    Catch err As Exception
        lblStatus.Text = "Error updating author. "
        lblStatus.Text &= err.Message
    Finally
        con.Close()
    End Try

End Sub
```

The update code is similar to the record selection code. The main differences are as follows:

- No DataReader is used, because no results are returned.
- A dynamically generated Update command is used for the Command object. It selects the corresponding author records, and changes all the fields to correspond to the values entered in the text boxes.
- The ExecuteNonQuery() method returns the number of affected records. This information is displayed in a label to confirm to the user that the operation was successful.

Deleting a Record

When the user clicks the Delete button, the author information is removed from the database. The number of affected records is examined, and if the Delete operation was successful, the FillAuthorList() function is called to refresh the page.

```
Private Sub cmdDelete_Click(sender As Object, _
  e As EventArgs) Handles cmdDelete.Click

    ' Define ADO.NET objects.
    Dim DeleteSQL As String
    DeleteSQL = "DELETE FROM Authors "
    DeleteSQL &= "WHERE au_id='" & lstAuthor.SelectedItem.Value & "'"

    Dim con As New OleDbConnection(ConnectionString)
    Dim cmd As New OleDbCommand(DeleteSQL, con)

    ' Try to open the database and delete the record.
    Dim Deleted As Integer
    Try
        con.Open()
        Deleted = cmd.ExecuteNonQuery()
```

```
    Catch err As Exception
        lblStatus.Text = "Error deleting author. "
        lblStatus.Text &= err.Message
    Finally
        con.Close()
    End Try

    ' If the delete succeeded, refresh the author list.
    If Deleted > 0 Then
        FillAuthorList()
    End If

End Sub
```

Interestingly, delete operations rarely succeed with the records in the pubs database, because they have corresponding child records linked in another table of the pubs database. Specifically, each author can have one or more related book titles. Unless the author's records are removed from the TitleAuthor table first, the author cannot be deleted. Because of the careful error handling used in the previous example, this problem is faithfully reported in your application (see Figure 14-8) and doesn't cause any real problems.

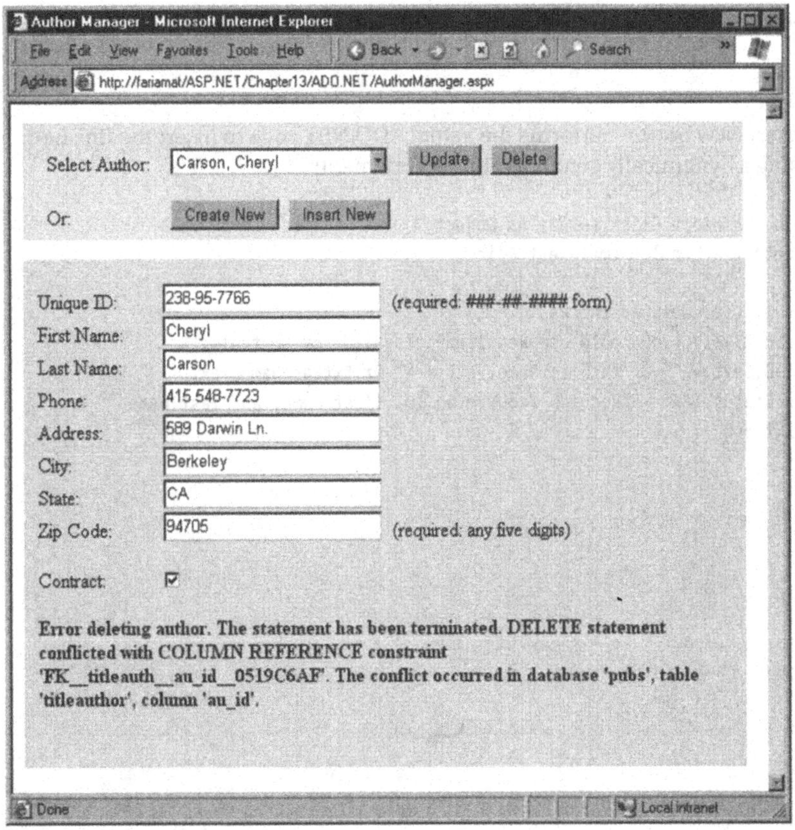

Figure 14-8. A failed delete attempt

To get around this limitation, you can use the Create New and Insert New buttons to add a new record, and then delete this record. Because this new record won't be linked to any other records, its deletion will be allowed.

Adding a Record

To start adding a new record, click Create New to blank the fields. Technically speaking, this step isn't required, but it simplifies the user's life.

```
Private Sub cmdNew_Click(sender As Object, _
  e As EventArgs) Handles cmdNew.Click

    txtID.Text = ""
    txtFirstName.Text = ""
    txtLastName.Text = ""
    txtPhone.Text = ""
    txtAddress.Text = ""
    txtCity.Text = ""
    txtState.Text = ""
    txtZip.Text = ""
    chkContract.Checked = False

    lblStatus.Text = "Click Insert New to add the completed record."

End Sub
```

The Insert New button performs the actual ADO.NET code to insert the finished record using a dynamically generated Insert statement:

```
Private Sub cmdInsert_Click(sender As Object, _
  e As EventArgs) Handles cmdInsert.Click

    ' Perform user-defined checks.
    ' Alternatively, you could use RequiredFieldValidator controls.
    If txtID.Text = "" Or txtFirstName.Text = "" Or txtLastName.Text = "" Then
        lblStatus.Text = "Records require an ID, first name, and last name."
        Exit Sub
    End If
```

```
    ' Define ADO.NET objects.
    Dim strInsert As String
    strInsert = "INSERT INTO Authors ("
    strInsert &= "au_id, au_fname, au_lname, "
    strInsert &= "phone, address, city, state, zip, contract) "
    strInsert &= "VALUES ('"
    strInsert &= txtID.Text & "', '"
    strInsert &= txtFirstName.Text & "', '"
    strInsert &= txtLastName.Text & "', '"
    strInsert &= txtPhone.Text & "', '"
    strInsert &= txtAddress.Text & "', '"
    strInsert &= txtCity.Text & "', '"
    strInsert &= txtState.Text & "', '"
    strInsert &= txtZip.Text & "', '"
    strInsert &= Int(chkContract.Checked) & "')"

    Dim con As New OleDbConnection(ConnectionString)
    Dim cmd As New OleDbCommand(strInsert, con)

    ' Try to open the database and execute the update.
    Dim Added As Integer
    Try
        con.Open()
        Added = cmd.ExecuteNonQuery
        lblStatus.Text = Added.ToString() & " records inserted."
    Catch err As Exception
        lblStatus.Text = "Error inserting record. "
        lblStatus.Text &= err.Message
    Finally
        con.Close()
    End Try

    ' If the insert succeeded, refresh the author list.
    If Added > 0 Then
        FillAuthorList()
    End If

End Sub
```

If the insert fails, the problem will be reported to the user in a rather unfriendly way (see Figure 14-9). This is typically the result of not specifying valid values. In a more polished application, you would use validators (as shown in Chapter 9) and provide more useful error messages. If the insert operation is successful, the page is updated with the new author list.

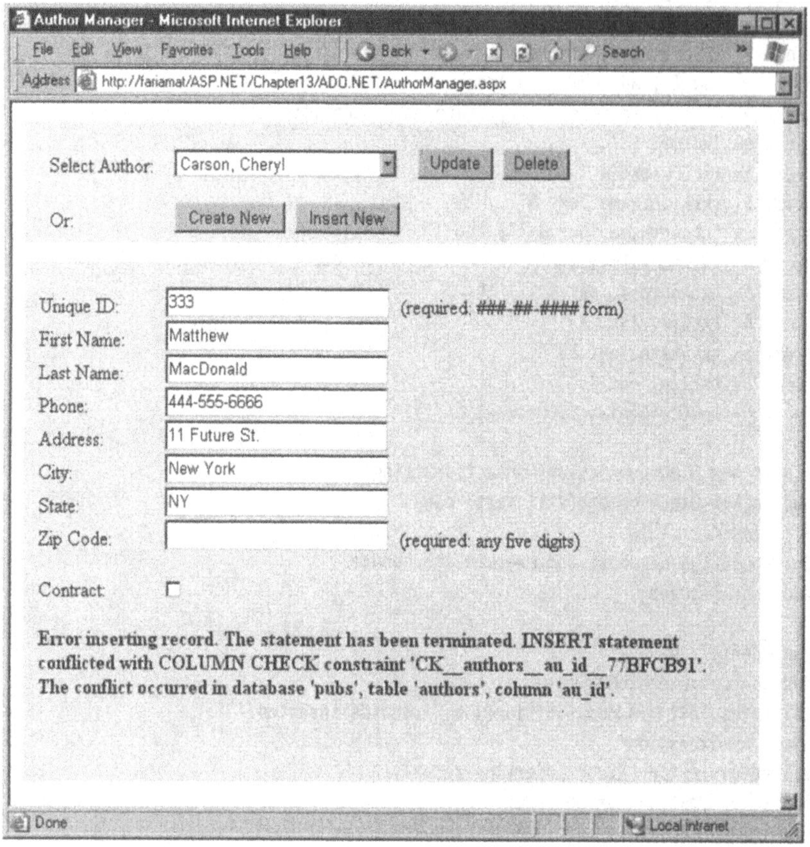

Figure 14-9. A failed insertion

Using Disconnected Data

With disconnected data, you need to code a little differently. Because you make your changes through the DataSet rather than with direct commands, you can often write less SQL code. However, you'll need to watch for the problems that can occur if more than one user attempts to make conflicting changes at the same time, or if you need to commit changes to multiple tables. In this simple one-page scenario, disconnected data access won't present much of a problem. If, however, you use disconnected data access to make a number of changes and commit them all at once, you're more likely to run into trouble.

With disconnected data access, a copy of the data is retained in memory while your code is running. Changes are tracked automatically using the built-in features of the DataSet object. You fill the DataSet in much the same way that you connect a DataReader. However, although the DataReader held a live connection, information in the DataSet is always disconnected.

Selecting Disconnected Data

The following example shows how you could rewrite the FillAuthorList() subroutine to use a DataSet instead of a DataReader. The changes are highlighted in bold.

```
Private Sub FillAuthorList()

    lstAuthor.Items.Clear()

    ' Define ADO.NET objects.
    Dim SelectSQL As String
    SelectSQL = "SELECT au_lname, au_fname, au_id FROM Authors"
    Dim con As New OleDbConnection(ConnectionString)
    Dim cmd As New OleDbCommand(SelectSQL, con)
    Dim adapter As New OleDbDataAdapter(cmd)
    Dim Pubs As New DataSet()

    ' Try to open database and read information.
    Try
        con.Open()
        ' All the information in transferred with one command.
        adapter.Fill(Pubs, "Authors")
    Catch err As Exception
        lblStatus.Text = "Error reading list of names. "
        lblStatus.Text &= err.Message
    Finally
        con.Close()
    End Try

    Dim row As DataRow
    For Each row In Pubs.Tables("Authors").Rows
        Dim NewItem As New ListItem()
        NewItem.Text = row("au_lname") & ", " & _
          row("au_fname")
        NewItem.Value = row("au_id")
        lstAuthor.Items.Add(NewItem)
    Next

End Sub
```

Every DataAdapter can hold four different commands: SelectCommand, InsertCommand, UpdateCommand, and DeleteCommand. This allows you to use a single DataAdapter object for multiple tasks. The Command object supplied in the constructor is automatically assigned to the DataAdapter.SelectCommand property.

The DataAdapter.Fill() method takes a DataSet and inserts one table of information. In this case, the table is named Authors, but any name could be used. That name is used later to access the appropriate table in the DataSet.

To access the individual DataRows, you can loop through the Rows collection of the appropriate table. Each piece of information is accessed using the field name, as it was with the DataReader.

Selecting Multiple Tables

Some of the most impressive features of the DataSet appear when you retrieve multiple different tables. A DataSet can contain as many tables as you need, and you can even link these tables together to better emulate the underlying relational data source. Unfortunately, there's no way to connect tables together automatically based on relationships in the underlying data source. However, you can add relations with a few extra lines of code, as shown in the next example.

In the pubs database, authors are linked to titles using three tables. This arrangement (called a many-to-many relationship, shown in Figure 14-10) allows several authors to be related to one title, and several titles to be related to one author. Without the intermediate TitleAuthor table, the database would be restricted to a one-to-many relationship, which would only allow a single author for each title.

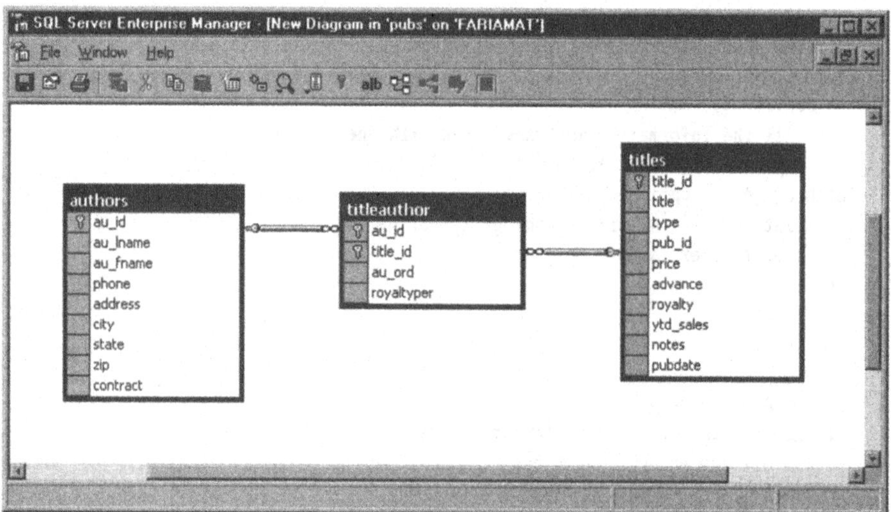

Figure 14-10. A many-to-many relationship

In an application, you would rarely need to access these tables individually. Instead, you would need to combine information from them in some way (for example, to find out what author wrote a given book). On its own, the Titles table only indicates the author ID. It doesn't provide additional information such as the author's name and address. To link this information together, you can use a special SQL Select statement called a Join query. Alternatively, you can use the features built into ADO.NET, as demonstrated in this section.

The next example provides a simple page that lists authors and the titles they have written. The interesting thing about this page is that it's generated using ADO.NET table linking.

To start, the standard ADO.NET data access objects are created, including a DataSet. All these steps are performed in a custom CreateList() subroutine, which is called from the Page.Load event handler so that the output is created when the page is first generated.

```
' Define ADO.NET objects.
Dim SelectSQL As String
SelectSQL = "SELECT au_lname, au_fname, au_id FROM Authors"
Dim con As New OleDbConnection(ConnectionString)
Dim cmd As New OleDbCommand(SelectSQL, con)
Dim adapter As New OleDbDataAdapter(cmd)
Dim dsPubs As New DataSet()
```

Next, the information for all three tables is pulled from the database and placed in the DataSet. This task could be accomplished with three separate Command objects, but to make the code a little leaner, this example uses only one, and modifies the CommandText property as needed.

```
Try
    con.Open()
    adapter.Fill(dsPubs, "Authors")

    ' This command is still linked to the data adapter.
    cmd.CommandText = "SELECT au_id, title_id FROM TitleAuthor"
    adapter.Fill(dsPubs, "TitleAuthor")

    ' This command is still linked to the data adapter.
    cmd.CommandText = "SELECT title_id, title FROM Titles"
    adapter.Fill(dsPubs, "Titles")

Catch err As Exception
    lblList.Text = "Error reading list of names. "
    lblList.Text &= err.Message
Finally
    con.Close()
End Try
```

Now that all the information is in the database, two DataRelation objects can be created to make it easier to navigate through the linked information. In this case, these DataRelation objects match the foreign key restrictions that are defined in the database.

To create a DataRelation, you need to specify the linked fields from two different tables, and you need to give your DataRelation a unique name. The order of the linked fields is important. The first field is the parent, and the second field is the child. (The idea here is that one parent can have many children, but each child can only have one parent. In other words, the *parent-to-child* relationship is another way of saying a *one-to-many* relationship.) In our example, each book title can have more than one entry in the TitleAuthor table. Each author can also have more than one entry in the TitleAuthor table.

```
Dim Titles_TitleAuthor As New DataRelation("Titles_TitleAuthor", _
  dsPubs.Tables("Titles").Columns("title_id"), _
  dsPubs.Tables("TitleAuthor").Columns("title_id"))
Dim Authors_TitleAuthor As New DataRelation("Authors_TitleAuthor", _
  dsPubs.Tables("Authors").Columns("au_id"), _
  dsPubs.Tables("TitleAuthor").Columns("au_id"))
```

Once these DataRelation objects have been created, they must be added to the DataSet:

```
dsPubs.Relations.Add(Titles_TitleAuthor)
dsPubs.Relations.Add(Authors_TitleAuthor)
```

The remaining code loops through the DataSet. However, unlike the previous example, which moved through one table, this example uses the DataRelation objects to branch to the other linked tables. It works like this:

1. Select first record from the Author table.
2. Using the Authors_TitleAuthor relationship, find the child records that correspond to this author. This step uses the GetChildRows method of the DataRow.
3. For each matching record in TitleAuthor, look up the corresponding Title record to get the full text title. This step uses the GetParentRows method of the DataRow.
4. Move to the next Author record, and repeat the process.

The code is lean and economical:

```
Dim rowAuthor, rowTitleAuthor, rowTitle As DataRow

For Each rowAuthor In dsPubs.Tables("Authors").Rows

    lblList.Text &= "<br><b>" & rowAuthor("au_fname")
    lblList.Text &= " " & rowAuthor("au_lname") & "</b><br>"

    For Each rowTitleAuthor In rowAuthor.GetChildRows(Authors_TitleAuthor)
        For Each rowTitle In rowTitleAuthor.GetParentRows(Titles_TitleAuthor)
            lblList.Text &= "  "   ' Non-breaking spaces.
            lblList.Text &= rowTitle("title") & "<br>"
        Next
    Next
Next
```

The final result is shown in Figure 14-11.

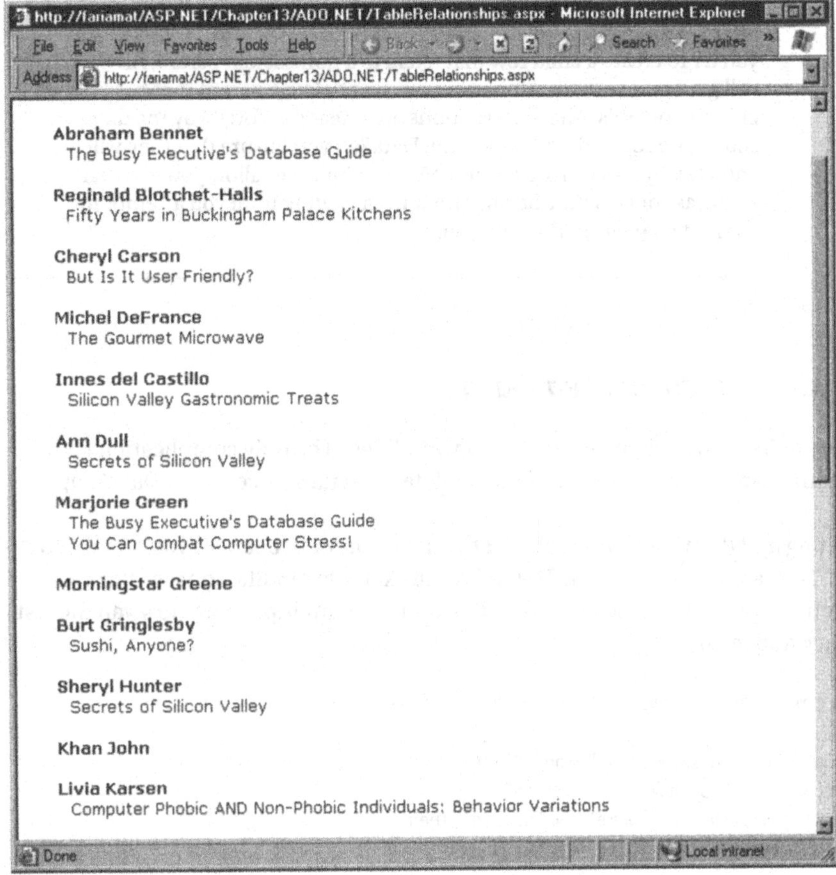

Figure 14-11. Hierarchical information from two tables

If there were a simple one-to-many relationship between authors and titles, you could leave out the inner For Each statement, and use simpler code, as follows:

```
For Each rowAuthor In dsPubs.Tables("Authors").Rows
    ' Display Author
    For Each rowTitle In rowAuthor.GetChildRows(Authors_Titles)
        ' Display Title
    Next
Next
```

However, having seen the more complicated example, you're ready to create and manage multiple DataRelation objects on your own.

NOTE Using a DataRelation implies certain restrictions. For example, if you try to create a child row that refers to a nonexistent parent, ADO.NET will generate an error. Similarly, you can't delete a parent that has linked children records. These restrictions are already enforced by the data source, but by adding them to the DataSet, you ensure that they will be enforced by ADO.NET as well. This technique can allow you to catch errors as soon as they occur, rather than waiting until you attempt to commit changes to the data source.

Modifying Disconnected Data

The information in the DataSet can be easily modified. The only complication is that these changes aren't committed until you update the data source with a DataAdapter object.

Updating and deleting rows are two of the most common changes you'll make to a DataSet. They are also the easiest. The following example modifies one author's last name. You can place this logic into a function and call it multiple times to swap the last name back and forth.

```
For Each rowAuthor In dsPubs.Tables("Authors").Rows

    If rowAuthor("au_lname") = "Bennet" Then
        rowAuthor("au_lname") = "Samson"
    Else If rowAuthor("au_lname") = "Samson" Then
        rowAuthor("au_lname") = "Bennet"
    End If

Next
```

Deleting a record is just as easy:

```
For Each rowAuthor In dsPubs.Tables("Authors").Rows

    If rowAuthor("au_fname") = "Cheryl" Then
        rowAuthor.Delete
    End If

Next
```

Alternatively, if you know the exact position of a record, you can modify or delete it using the index number rather than enumerating through the collection:

```
dsPubs.Tables("Authors").Rows(3).Delete
```

The DataSet is always disconnected. Any changes you make will appear in your program, but won't affect the original data source unless you take additional steps. In fact, when you use the Delete method, the row isn't actually removed, only marked for deletion. (If the row were removed entirely, ADO.NET would be unable to find it and delete it from the original data source when you reconnect later.)

If you use the Delete() method, you need to be aware of this fact and take steps to avoid trying to use deleted rows, as follows:

```
For Each row In dsPubs.Tables("Authors").Rows
    If row.RowState <> DataRowState.Deleted Then
        ' It's OK to display the row value, modify it, or use it.
    Else
        ' This record is scheduled for deletion.
        ' You should just ignore it.
    End If
Next
```

If you try to read a field of information from a deleted item, an error will occur. As I warned earlier—life with disconnected data isn't always easy.

NOTE You can use the DataSet.Rows.Remove() method to delete a record completely. However, if you use this method the record won't be deleted from the data source when you reconnect and update it with your changes. Instead, it will just be eliminated from your DataSet.

Adding Information to a DataSet

You can also add a new row using the Add() method of the Rows collection. Before you can add a row, however, you need to use the NewRow() method first to get a blank copy. The following example uses this technique with the original web page for viewing and adding authors:

```
Dim rowNew As DataRow
rowNew = dsPubs.Tables("Authors").NewRow
rowNew("au_id") = txtID.Text
rowNew("au_fname") = txtFirstName.Text
rowNew("au_lname") = txtLastName.Text
rowNew("phone") = txtPhone.Text
rowNew("address") = txtAddress.Text
rowNew("city") = txtCity.Text
rowNew("state") = txtState.Text
rowNew("zip") = txtZip.Text
rowNew("contract") = Int(chkContract.Checked)
dsPubs.Tables("Authors").Rows.Add(rowNew)
```

The full code needed to update the data source with these changes is included a little later in this chapter.

Updating Disconnected Data

Earlier, you saw how the DataAdapter object allows you to retrieve information. Unlike the DataReader, DataAdapter objects can transfer data in both directions.

Updating the data source is a more complicated operation than reading from it. Depending on the changes that have been made, the DataAdapter may need to perform Insert, Update, or Delete operations. Luckily, you don't need to create these Command objects by hand. Instead, you can use ADO.NET's special utility class: the CommandBuilder object. Each provider includes its own CommandBuilder. SqlCommandBuilder in the class used with the SQL Server provider, and OleDbCommandBuilder is used with the OLE DB provider.

The CommandBuilder

The CommandBuilder examines the DataAdapter object you used to create the DataSet, and it adds the additional Command objects for the InsertCommand, DeleteCommand, and UpdateCommand properties. The process works like this:

```
' Create the CommandBuilder.
Dim cb As New OleDbCommandBuilder(adapter)

' Retrieve an updated DataAdapter.
adapter = cb.DataAdapter
```

NOTE Using a CommandBuilder is a convenient approach, but it's not always ideal. That's because you have no real control over the commands that the CommandBuilder generates. If you want to tweak these commands to optimize performance (for example, using a stored procedure), or to enforce different types of concurrency, you'll need to create your Command objects by hand. For more information about getting into the nitty-gritty details of ADO.NET, consult one of the books referenced at the end of this chapter.

Updating a DataTable

With the correctly configured DataAdapter, you can update the data source using the Update() method. Here's the code to commit the changes for the Authors table:

```
con.Open()
Dim RowsAffected As Integer
RowsAffected = adapter.Update(dsPubs, "Authors")
con.Close()
```

If you need to update more than one table, you'll need to create a separate DataAdapter for each table. You must then use the CommandBuilder to configure the DataAdapter so that it has the commands required to update the given table. You can then open the connection, use the Update() method of each DataAdapter, and close the connection.

The DataSet stores information about the current state of all the rows and their original state. This allows ADO.NET to find the changed rows. It adds every new row (rows with the state DataRowState.Added) with the DataAdapter.InsertCommand. It removes every deleted row (DataRowState.Deleted) using the DataAdapter.Delete-Command. It also updates every changed row (DataRowState.Modified) with the DataAdapter.UpdateCommand. There is no guaranteed order in which these operations will take place. Once the update is successfully completed, all rows will be reset to DataRowState.Unchanged.

TIP If you use the DataAdapter.Update() method without opening the connection, the connection will be opened automatically, and closed once the update is complete. However, it's usually best to explicitly control when the connection is opened and closed. That allows you more flexibility. For example, you could open the connection once, and perform two operations, rather than opening the connection separately for each table you want to update.

Controlling Updates

If you used linked tables, the standard way of updating the data source can cause some problems, particularly if you've deleted or added records. These problems occur because changes usually aren't committed in the same order that they were made. (To provide this type of tracking, the DataSet object would need to store much more information and waste valuable memory on the server.)

You can control the order in which tables are updated, but that's not always enough to prevent a conflict. For example, if you update the Authors table first, ADO.NET might try to delete an Author record before it deletes the TitleAuthor record that is still using it. If you update the TitleAuthor table first, ADO.NET might try to create a TitleAuthor that references a nonexistent Title. At some point, ADO.NET may be enhanced with the intelligence needed to avoid these problems, provided you use DataRelations. Currently, you need to resort to other techniques for more fine-grained control.

Using features built into the DataSet, you can pull out the rows that need to be added, modified, or deleted into separate DataSets, and choose an update order that will not place the database into an inconsistent state at any point. Generally, you can safely update a database by performing all the record inserts, followed by all the modifications, and then all the deletions. Start with the child tables, and then update the parent table.

By using the DataSet.GetChanges() method, you can implement this exact pattern:

```
' Create three DataSets, and fill them from dsPubs.
Dim dsNew As DataSet = dsPubs.GetChanges(DataRowState.Added)
Dim dsModify As DataSet = dsPubs.GetChanges(DataRowState.Modified)
Dim dsDelete As DataSet = dsPubs.GetChanges(DataRowState.Deleted)

' Update these DataSets separately. Remember, each DataSet has three tables!
' Also note that the "add" operation for the Authors and Titles tables
' must be carried out before the add operation for the TitleAuthor table.
AuthorsAdapter.Update(dsNew, "Authors")
TitlesAdapter.Update(dsNew, "Titles")
TA_Adapter.Update(dsNew, "TitleAuthor")
AuthorsAdapter.Update(dsModify, "Authors")
TitlesAdapter.Update(dsModify, "Titles")
TA_Adapter.Update(dsModify, "TitleAuthor")
AuthorsAdapter.Update(dsDelete, "Authors")
TitlesAdapter.Update(dsDelete, "Titles")
TitlesAdapter.Update(dsDelete, "TitleAuthor")
```

This adds a layer of complexity, and a significant amount of extra code. However, in cases where you make many different types of modifications to several different tables at once, this is the only solution. To avoid these problems, you could commit changes earlier (rather than committing an entire batch of changes at once), or use Command objects directly instead of relying on the disconnected data features of the DataSet. Batched updates are almost always more trouble than they're worth in a web application. (On the other hand, they are indispensable in some desktop applications that need to work with data even when a network connection isn't present.)

An Update Example

The next example rewrites the code for adding a new author in the update page with equivalent DataSet code. You can find this example in the online samples as AuthorManager2.aspx. (AuthorManager.aspx is the original, command-based version.)

```
Private Sub cmdInsert_Click(sender As Object, e As EventArgs) _
  Handles cmdInsert.Click

    ' Define ADO.NET objects.
    Dim SelectSQL As String
    SelectSQL = "SELECT * FROM Authors"
    Dim con As New OleDbConnection(ConnectionString)
    Dim cmd As New OleDbCommand(SelectSQL, con)
    Dim adapter As New OleDbDataAdapter(cmd)
    Dim dsPubs As New DataSet()
```

```
    ' Get the schema information.
    Try
        con.Open()
        adapter.FillSchema(dsPubs, SchemaType.Mapped, "Authors")
    Catch err As Exception
        lblStatus.Text = "Error reading schema. "
        lblStatus.Text &= err.Message
    Finally
        con.Close()
    End Try

    Dim rowNew As DataRow
    rowNew = dsPubs.Tables("Authors").NewRow
    rowNew("au_id") = txtID.Text
    rowNew("au_fname") = txtFirstName.Text
    rowNew("au_lname") = txtLastName.Text
    rowNew("phone") = txtPhone.Text
    rowNew("address") = txtAddress.Text
    rowNew("city") = txtCity.Text
    rowNew("state") = txtState.Text
    rowNew("zip") = txtZip.Text
    rowNew("contract") = Int(chkContract.Checked)
    dsPubs.Tables("Authors").Rows.Add(rowNew)

    ' Insert the new record.
    Dim Added As Integer
    Try
        ' Create the CommandBuilder.
        Dim cb As New OleDbCommandBuilder(adapter)
        ' Retrieve an updated DataAdapter.
        adapter = cb.DataAdapter

        ' Update the database using the DataSet.
        con.Open()
        Added = adapter.Update(dsPubs, "Authors")
    Catch err As Exception
        lblStatus.Text = "Error inserting record. "
        lblStatus.Text &= err.Message
    Finally
        con.Close()
    End Try

    ' If the insert succeeded, refresh the author list.
    If Added > 0 Then
        FillAuthorList()
    End If

End Sub
```

In this case, the example is quite inefficient. In order to add a new record, a DataSet needs to be created, with the required tables and a valid row. To retrieve information about what this row should look like, the DataAdapter.FillSchema() method is used. The FillSchema() method creates a table with no rows, but with other information about the table, such as the name of each field and the requirements for each column (the data type, the maximum length, any restriction against null values, and so on). If you wanted, you could use the FillSchema() method followed by the Fill() method.

After this step, the information is entered into a new row in the DataSet, the DataAdapter is updated with the CommandBuilder, and the changes are committed to the database. The whole operation took two database connections and required the use of a DataSet that was then abruptly abandoned. In this scenario, disconnected data is probably an extravagant solution to a problem that would be better solved with ordinary Command objects.

TIP Many database tables use identity columns that increment automatically. For example, an alternate design of the Authors table might use au_id as an auto-incrementing column. In this case, the database would automatically assign a unique ID to each inserted author record. When adding new authors, you wouldn't specify any value for the au_id field; instead, this number would be generated when the changes are committed to the database.

Concurrency Problems

As you discovered earlier, ADO.NET maintains information in the DataSet about the current and the original value of every piece of information in the DataSet. When updating a row, ADO.NET searches for a row that matches every "original" field exactly, and then updates it with the new values. If another user changes even a single field in that record while your program is working with the disconnected data, an exception is thrown. The update operation is then halted, potentially preventing other valid rows from being updated.

There is an easier way to handle these potential problems: using the DataAdapter.RowUpdated event. This event occurs after every individual insert, update, or delete operation, but before an exception is thrown. It gives you the chance to examine the results, note any errors, and prevent an error from occurring.

The first step is to create an appropriate event handler for the DataAdapter.RowUpdated event, as follows:

```
Private Sub OnRowUpdated(sender As Object, e As OleDbRowUpdatedEventArgs)

    ' Check if any records were affected.
    ' If no records were affected, the statement didn't execute as expected.
    If e.RecordsAffected() < 1 Then
        ' Find out the type of failed error.
        Select Case e.StatementType
            Case StatementType.Delete
                lstErrors.Items.Add("Not deleted: " & e.Row("au_id"))
            Case StatementType.Insert
                lstErrors.Items.Add("Not inserted: " & e.Row("au_id"))
            Case StatementType.Update
                lstErrors.Items.Add("Not updated: " & e.Row("au_id"))
        End Select

        ' Using the OledDbRowUpdatedEventArgs class, you can tell ADO.NET
        ' to ignore the problem and keep updating the other rows.
        e.Status = UpdateStatus.SkipCurrentRow
    End If

End Sub
```

The OleDbRowUpdatedEventArgs object provides this event handler with information about the row that ADO.NET just attempted to modify (e.Row), the type of modification (e.StatementType), and the result (e.RecordsAffected). In this example, errors are detected, and information about the unsuccessfully updated rows is added to a list control. Now that the problem has been noted, the e.Status property can be used to instruct ADO.NET to continue updating other changed rows in the DataSet.

Remember, this event occurs while the DataAdapter is in mid-update and using a live database connection. For that reason, you should not try to perform anything too complicated or time-consuming in this event handler. Instead, quickly log or display the errors and continue.

Now that the event handler has been created, you need to attach it to the DataSet before your perform the update. To do this, you use the AddHandler statement as follows:

```
' Connect the event handler.
AddHandler adapter.RowUpdated, AddressOf OnRowUpdated

' Perform the update.
Dim RowsAffected As Integer
RowsAffected = adapter.Update(dsPubs, "Authors")
```

A Concurrency Example

It can be hard to test the code you write to deal with concurrency problems, because it's only executed in specific circumstances. These circumstances may be common for a fully deployed large-scale application, but they're more difficult to re-create when a single developer is doing the testing.

The ConcurrencyHandler.aspx file in the online samples shows simulates a concurrency problem by making invalid changes to a database using two separate DataSets. When the code attempts to commit these changes, the OnRowUpdated code springs into action and reports the problem (see Figure 14-12).

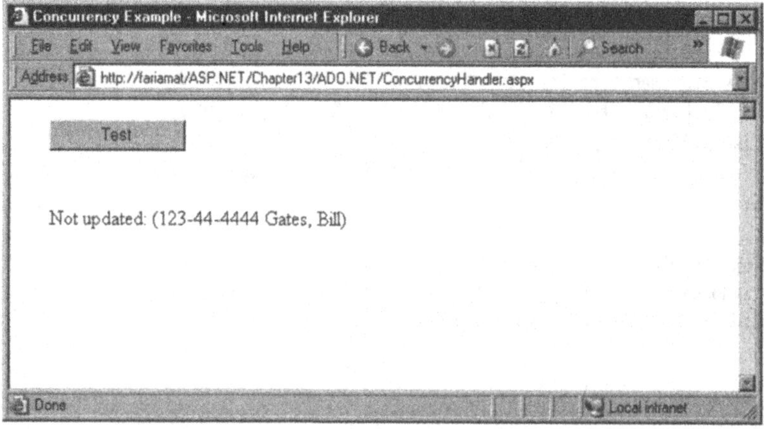

Figure 14-12. Reporting concurrency problems

The full page code is shown here:

```
Public Class ConcurrencyHandler
  Inherits Page
    Protected WithEvents cmdTest As Button
    Protected lblResult As System.Web.UI.WebControls.Label

    ' Connection string used for all connections.
    Private ConnectionString As String = "Provider=SQLOLEDB.1;" & _
     "Data Source=localhost;Initial Catalog=pubs;Integrated Security=SSPI"

    Private Sub OnRowUpdated(sender As Object, e As OleDbRowUpdatedEventArgs)
        ' Check if any records were affected.
        If e.RecordsAffected() < 1 Then
            ' Find out the type of failed error.
            Select Case e.StatementType
                Case StatementType.Delete
                    lblResult.Text &= "<br>Not deleted: "
                Case StatementType.Insert
                    lblResult.Text &= "<br>Not inserted: "
                Case StatementType.Update
                    lblResult.Text &= "<br>Not updated: "
            End Select
```

```
        lblResult.Text &= "(" & e.Row("au_id") & " " & e.Row("au_lname")
        lblResult.Text &= ", " & e.Row("au_fname") & ")"

        ' Continue processing.
        e.Status = UpdateStatus.SkipCurrentRow
    End If

End Sub

Private Sub cmdTest_Click(sender As Object, e As EventArgs) _
  Handles cmdTest.Click

    lblResult.Text = ""

    ' Define ADO.NET objects.
    Dim SelectSQL As String
    SelectSQL = "SELECT * FROM Authors"
    Dim con As New OleDbConnection(ConnectionString)
    Dim cmd As New OleDbCommand(SelectSQL, con)
    Dim adapter As New OleDbDataAdapter(cmd)

    ' Create the CommandBuilder.
    Dim cb As New OleDbCommandBuilder(adapter)
    ' Retrieve an updated DataAdapter.
    adapter = cb.DataAdapter

    ' Connect the event handler.
    AddHandler adapter.RowUpdated, AddressOf OnRowUpdated

    ' Create two DataSets... perfect for conflicting data.
    Dim dsPubs1 As New DataSet(), dsPubs2 As New DataSet()

    Try
        con.Open()

        ' Fill both DataSets with the same table.
        adapter.Fill(dsPubs1, "Authors")
        adapter.Fill(dsPubs2, "Authors")

        ' "Flip" the contract field in the first row of dsPubs1.
        If dsPubs1.Tables(0).Rows(0).Item("contract") = True Then
            dsPubs1.Tables(0).Rows(0).Item("contract") = False
        Else
            dsPubs1.Tables(0).Rows(0).Item("contract") = True
        End If

        ' Update the database
        adapter.Update(dsPubs1, "Authors")
```

```
            ' Make a change in the second DataSet.
            dsPubs2.Tables(0).Rows(0).Item("au_fname") = "Bill"
            dsPubs2.Tables(0).Rows(0).Item("au_lname") = "Gates"

            ' Try to update this row. Even though these changes don't conflict,
            ' the update will fail because the row has been changed.
            adapter.Update(dsPubs2, "Authors")

        Catch err As Exception
            lblResult.Text &= "Error reading schema. "
            lblResult.Text &= err.Message
        Finally
            con.Close()
        End Try

    End Sub

End Class
```

Direct Commands or the DataSet—Which Works Best?

As you've seen in this chapter, ADO.NET gives you two different ways to solve the same problems. Direct commands are the leanest, most straightforward approach, and they side-step some of the headaches you'll face with disconnected data. On the other hand, DataSets really shine when you need to work with more than one related table, and they also work well with the data binding techniques you'll use in Chapter 16. Which one you use depends on the situation, but in many cases both approaches will work equally well.

The key fact you should realize is that the simpler approach—using direct commands—often makes perfect sense. Over-eager .NET converts sometimes try to use the DataSet everywhere, needlessly complicating life. But if you're happy with forward-only read-only data, and you don't need to convert your data to XML or send it to another component, there's no embarrassment in using ADO.NET's DataReader.

The Last Word

The chapter gave you a comprehensive introduction to ADO.NET and its new disconnected data model. Although you've seen all the core concepts, there's still more you can learn. For a comprehensive book that focuses exclusively on ADO.NET, you may be interested in *Microsoft ADO.NET (Core Reference)* from Microsoft Press or *ADO.NET: From Novice to Pro* from Apress. Both books investigate some of the techniques you can use to optimize ADO.NET data access code.

In the next two chapters, you'll learn about ASP.NET's new data binding features, and see how you can use them with a little ADO.NET code to write practical data-driven pages.

CHAPTER 15

Data Binding

IN THE LAST CHAPTER, you learned how to use ADO.NET to retrieve information from a database, how to work with it an ASP.NET application, and how to apply your changes back to the original data source. These techniques are flexible and powerful, but they aren't always convenient.

For example, you can use the DataSet or the DataReader to retrieve rows of information, format them individually, and add them to an HTML table on a web page. Conceptually, this isn't too difficult. However, it still requires a lot of repetitive code to move through the data, format columns, and display it in the correct order. Repetitive code may be easy, but it's also error-prone, difficult to enhance, and unpleasant to look at. Fortunately, ASP.NET adds a feature that allows you to skip this process and pop data directly into HTML elements and fully formatted controls. It's called *data binding*.

Introducing Data Binding

The basic principle of data binding is this: You tell a control where to find your data and how you want it displayed, and the control handles the rest of the details. Data binding in ASP.NET is superficially similar to data binding in the world of desktop or client/server applications, but in truth it's fundamentally different. In those environments, data binding involves the creation of a direct connection between a data source and a control in an application window. If the user changes a value in the onscreen control, the data in the linked database is modified automatically. Similarly, if the database changes while the user is working with it (for example, another user commits a change), the display can be refreshed automatically.

This type of data binding isn't practical in the ASP.NET world, because you can't effectively maintain a database connection over the Internet. This "direct" data binding also severely limits scalability and reduces flexibility. In fact, data binding has acquired a bad reputation for exactly these reasons.

ASP.NET data binding, on the other hand, has little in common with direct data binding. ASP.NET data binding works in one direction only. Information moves *from* a data object *into* a control. Then the data objects are thrown away and the page is sent to the client. If the user modifies the data in a data bound control, your program can update the corresponding record in the database, but nothing happens automatically.

ASP.NET data binding is much more flexible than traditional data binding. Many of the most powerful data binding controls, such as the Repeater, DataList, and DataGrid, allow you to configure formatting options and even add repeating controls and buttons for each record. This is all set up through special templates, which are a new addition to ASP.NET. Templates are examined in detail in the next chapter.

Types of ASP.NET Data Binding

There are actually two types of ASP.NET data binding: single-value and repeated-value binding. Single-value data binding is by far the simpler of the two, while repeated-value binding provides the foundation for the most advanced ASP.NET data controls.

Single-Value or "Simple" Data Binding

Single-value data binding is used to add information anywhere on an ASP.NET page. You can even place information into a control property or as plain text inside an HTML tag. Single-value data binding doesn't necessarily have anything to do with ADO.NET. In fact, because ADO.NET usually works with entire lists or tables of information, single-value data binding is rarely of much use. Instead, single-value data binding allows you to take a variable, property, or expression and insert it dynamically into a page.

Repeated-Value or List Binding

Repeated-value data binding is more useful for handling complex tasks, such as displaying an entire table or all the values from a single field in a table. Unlike single-value data binding, this type of data binding requires a special control that supports it. Typically, this will be a list control like CheckBoxList or ListBox, but it can also be a much more sophisticated control like the DataGrid. You'll know that a control supports repeated-value data binding if it provides a DataSource property. As with single-value binding, repeated-value binding doesn't necessarily need to use data from a database, and it doesn't have to use the ADO.NET objects. For example, you can use repeated-value binding to bind data from a collection or an array.

How Data Binding Works

Data binding works a little differently depending on whether you're using single-value or repeated-value binding. In single-value binding, a data binding expression is inserted right into the HTML markup in the .aspx file (not the code-behind file). In repeated-value binding, data binding is configured by setting the appropriate control properties (typically in the Page.Load event handler). You'll see specific examples of both these techniques later in this chapter.

Once you specify data binding, you need to activate it. You accomplish this task by calling the DataBind() method. The DataBind() method is a basic piece of functionality supplied in the Control class. It automatically binds a control and any child controls that it contains. With repeated-value binding, you can use the DataBind() method of the specific list control you're using. Alternatively, you can bind the whole page at once, by calling the DataBind() method of the current Page object. Once you call this method, all the data binding expressions in the page are evaluated and replaced with the specified value.

Typically, you call the DataBind() method in the Page.Load event handler. If you forget to use it, ASP.NET will ignore your data binding expressions, and the client will receive a page that contains empty values.

This is a general description of the whole process. To really understand what's happening, you need to work with some specific examples.

Single-Value Data Binding

Single-value data binding is really just a different approach to dynamic text. To use it, you add special data binding expressions into your .aspx files. These expressions have the following format:

```
<%# expression_goes_here %>
```

This may look like a script block, but it isn't. If you try to write any code inside this tag, you will receive an error. The only thing you can add is valid data binding expressions. For example, if you have a public variable on your page named Country, you could write the following:

```
<%# Country %>
```

When you call the DataBind() method for the page, this text will be replaced with the value for Country (for example, Spain). Similarly, you could use a property or a built-in ASP.NET object as follows:

```
<%# Request.Browser.Browser %>
```

This would substitute a string with the current browser name (for example, IE). In fact, you can even call a public function defined on your page or execute a simple expression, provided it returns a result that can be converted to text and displayed on the page. Thus, the following data binding expressions are all valid:

```
<%# GetUserName(ID) %>
<%# 1 + (2 * 20) %>
<%# "John " & "Smith" %>
```

Remember, these data binding expressions are placed in the HTML tags of your .aspx file. That means that if you're relying on Visual Studio .NET to manage your HTML code automatically, you may have to venture into slightly unfamiliar territory. To examine how you can add a data binding expression, and see why you might want to, it helps to review a simple example.

A Simple Data Binding Example

This section considers a simple example of single-value data binding. The example has been stripped to the bare minimum amount of detail needed to illustrate the concept.

You start with a special variable defined in your Page class, which is called TransactionsCount:

```
Public Class DataBindingPage
  Inherits Page
    Public TransactionCount As Integer

    ' (Additional code omitted.)
End Class
```

Note that this variable must be designated as Public, not Private. Otherwise, ASP.NET will not be able to access it when it's evaluating the data binding expression.

Now, assume that this value is set in the Page.Load event handler using some database lookup code. For testing purposes, our example skips this step and hard-codes a value:

```
Private Sub Page_Load(sender As Object, e As EventArgs) Handles MyBase.Load

    ' (You could use database code here to look up a value for TransactionCount.)
    TransactionCount = 10
    ' Now convert all the data binding expressions on the page.
    Me.DataBind()

End Sub
```

Two things actually happen in this event handler: The TransactionCount variable is set to 10, and all the data binding expressions on the page are bound. Currently, there aren't any data binding expressions, so this method has no effect. Notice that this example uses the Me keyword to refer to the current page. You could just write DataBind() without the Me keyword, because the default object is the current Page object. However, using the Me keyword makes it a bit clearer what object is being used.

To actually make this data binding accomplish something, you need to add a data binding expression. Usually, it's easiest to add this value directly to the presentation code in the .aspx file. If you're using Notepad to create your ASP.NET pages, you won't have any trouble with this approach. If, on the other hand, you're using Visual Studio .NET to create your controls, you can add a label control, and then configure the data binding expression in the HTML view by clicking the HTML button at the bottom of the web page window (see Figure 15-1).

You could also type this data binding expression in the Properties window, but Visual Studio .NET doesn't always refresh this information correctly. In this case, it's better to work on a slightly lower level.

To add your expression, find the tag for the label control. Modify the Text property as shown in the following code. Note that some of the label attributes (such as its size and position) have been left out to help make it clearer. You should not, however, delete this information in your code!

```
<asp:Label id=lblDynamic runat="server" Font-Size="X-Large" Font-Names="Verdana">
There were <%# TransactionCount %> transactions today.
I see that you are using <%# Request.Browser.Browser %>.
</asp:Label>
```

```
<%@ Page Language="vb" AutoEventWireup="false" Codebehind="SimpleDataBindi
<!DOCTYPE HTML PUBLIC "-//W3C//DTD HTML 4.0 Transitional//EN">
<HTML>
    <HEAD>
        <title>Simple Data Binding</title>
        <meta content="Microsoft Visual Studio.NET 7.0" name="GENERATOR">
        <meta content="Visual Basic 7.0" name="CODE_LANGUAGE">
        <meta content="JavaScript" name="vs_defaultClientScript">
        <meta content="http://schemas.microsoft.com/intellisense/ie5" name
    </HEAD>
    <body MS_POSITIONING="GridLayout">
        <form id="Form1" method="post" runat="server">

            <asp:Label id="lblDynamic" runat="server" Font-Size="X-Large"
            </asp:Label>

        </form>
    </body>
</HTML>
```

Figure 15-1. HTML view

This example uses two separate data binding expressions, which are inserted along with the normal static text. The first data binding expression references the TransactionCount variable, and the second uses the built-in Request object to find out some information about the user's browser. When you run this page, the output looks like Figure 15-2.

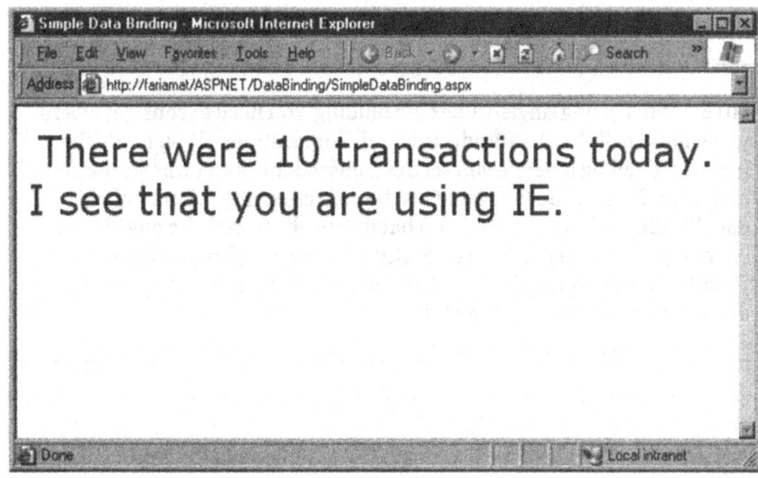

Figure 15-2. The result of data binding

The data binding expressions have been automatically replaced with the appropriate values. If the page is posted back, you could use additional code to modify TransactionCount, and as long as you call the DataBind() method, that information will be popped into the page in the data binding expression you've defined.

If, however, you forget to call the DataBind() method, the data binding expressions will be ignored, and the user will see a somewhat confusing window that looks like Figure 15-3.

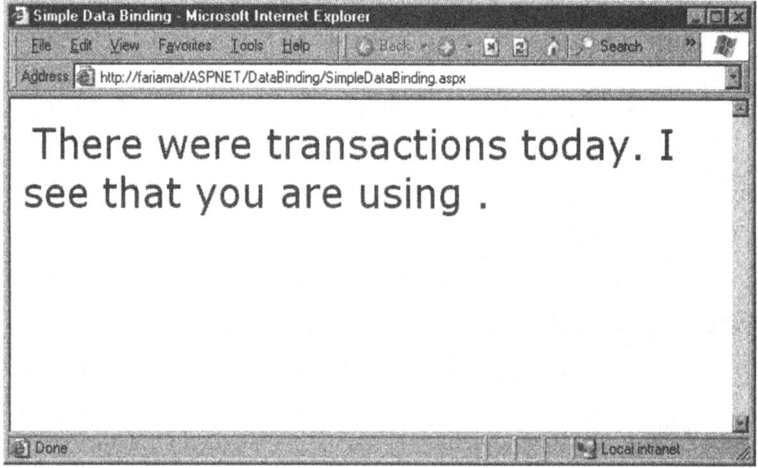

Figure 15-3. The nondata-bound page

You also need to be a little careful with your data-bound control in the design environment. If you modify its properties in the Properties window of Visual Studio .NET, the editor can end up thoughtlessly obliterating your data binding expressions.

NOTE When using single-value data binding, you need to consider when you should call the DataBind() method. For example, if you made the mistake of calling it before you set the TransactionCount variable, the corresponding expression would just be converted into 0. Remember, data binding is a one-way street. That means there won't be any visible effect if you change the TransactionCount variable after you've used the DataBind() method. Unless you call the DataBind() method again, the displayed value won't be updated.

Simple Data Binding with Properties

In the example so far, data binding expressions are used to set static text information inside a label tag. However, you can also use single-value data binding to set other types of information on your page, including control properties. To do this, you simply have to know where to put the data binding expression.

For example, consider the following page, which defines a variable named URL and uses it to point to a picture in the application directory:

```
Public Class DataBindingPage
  Inherits Page

    Public URL As String

    Private Sub Page_Load(sender As Object, e As EventArgs) Handles MyBase.Load
        URL = Server.MapPath("picture.jpg")
        Me.DataBind()
    End Sub

End Class
```

This URL can now be used to create a label, as in the previous example:

```
<asp:Label id=lblDynamic runat="server"><%# URL %></asp:Label>
```

You can also use it for a caption for a check box:

```
<asp:CheckBox id="chkDynamic" Text="<%# URL %>" runat="server" />
```

Or for a target for a hyperlink control:

```
<asp:Hyperlink id="lnkDynamic" Text="Click here!" NavigateUrl="<%# URL %>"
 runat="server" />
```

Or even for a picture:

```
<asp:Image id="imgDynamic" Src="<%# URL %>" runat="server" />
```

The only trick is that you need to edit these control tags manually. A final combined page that uses all these elements would look something like Figure 15-4.

To examine this example in more detail, try out the sample code for this chapter.

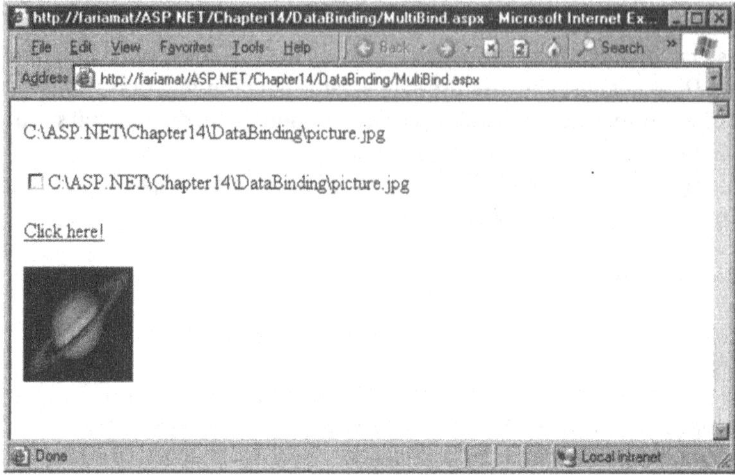

Figure 15-4. Multiple ways to bind the same data

Problems with Single-Value Data Binding

Before you start using single-value data binding techniques in every aspect of your ASP.NET programs, you should consider some of the serious drawbacks that this approach can present. These include the following:

- **Putting code into a page's user interface.** One of ASP.NET's great advantages is that it finally allows developers to separate the user interface code (the HTML and control tags in the .aspx file) from the actual code used for data access and all other tasks (in the code-behind file). However, over-enthusiastic use of single-value data binding can encourage you to disregard that distinction and start coding function calls and even operations into your page. If not carefully managed, this can lead to complete disorder.

- **Code fragmentation.** When data binding expressions are used, it may not be obvious to other developers where the functionality resides for different operations. This is particularly a problem if you blend both approaches (modifying the same control using a data binding expression, and then directly in code). Even worse, the data binding code may have certain dependencies that aren't immediately obvious. If the page code changes, or a variable or function is removed or renamed, the corresponding data binding expression could stop providing valid information without any explanation or even an obvious error.

- **No design-time error checking.** When you type a data binding expression, you need to remember the corresponding variable, property, or method name and enter it exactly. If you don't, you won't realize your mistake until you try to run the page, at which point you'll receive an error (see Figure 15-5). This is a significant drawback for those who are used to Visual Studio .NET's automatic error checking. You also can't take advantage of Visual Studio .NET's IntelliSense features to automatically complete code statements.

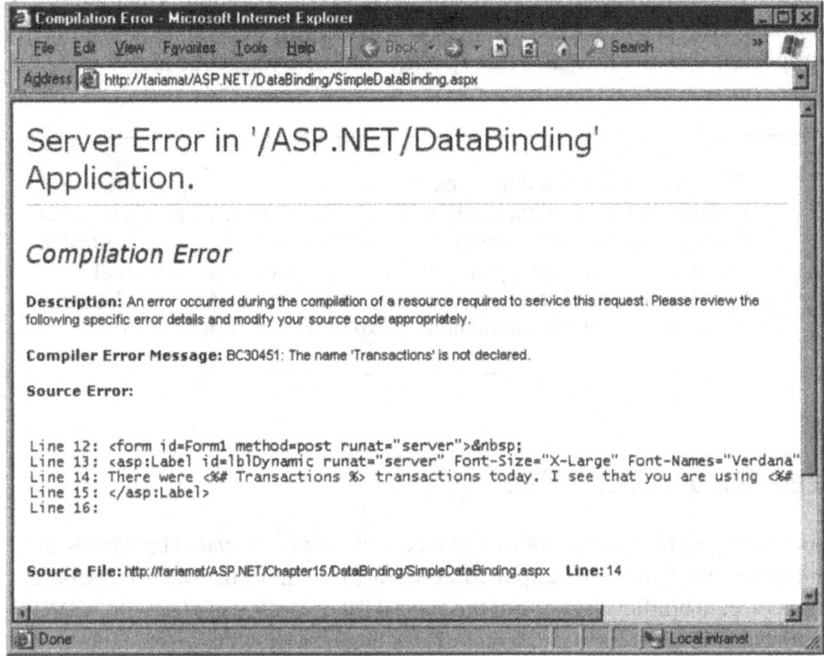

Figure 15-5. A common error

Of course, some developers love the flexibility of single-value data binding, and use it to great effect, making the rest of their code more economical and streamlined. It's up to you to be aware of (and avoid) the potential drawbacks. Often, single-value data binding suits developers who prefer to write code directly in .aspx files without Visual Studio .NET. These developers manually write all the control tags they need, and can thus use single-value data binding to create a shorter, more concise file without adding extra code. Visual Studio .NET developers rely on simple data binding much less often.

Using Code Instead of Simple Data Binding

If you decide not to use single-value data binding, you can accomplish the same thing using code. For example, you could use this event handler to display the same output as the first label example:

```
Private Sub Page_Load(sender As Object, e As EventArgs) Handles MyBase.Load

    TransactionCount = 10
    lblDynamic.Text = "There were " & TransactionCount.ToString()
    lblDynamic.Text &= "transactions today. "
    lblDynamic.Text &= "I see that you are using " & Request.Browser.Browser

End Sub
```

This code dynamically fills in the label without using data binding. The trade-off is more code. Instead of importing ASP.NET code into the .aspx file, you end up doing the reverse: importing the user interface (the specific text) into your code file!

TIP As much as possible, stick to one approach for using dynamic text. If you decide to use data binding, try to reduce the number of times you modify a control's text in code. If you do both, you may end up confusing others, or just canceling your own changes! For example, if you call the DataBind() method on a control that uses a data expression after changing its values in code, your data binding expression will not be used.

Repeated-Value Data Binding

While using simple data binding is an optional choice, repeated-value binding is so useful that almost every ASP.NET application will want to make use of it somewhere. Repeated-value data binding uses one of the special list controls included with ASP.NET. You link one of these controls to a data list source (such as a field in a data table), and the control automatically creates a full list using all the corresponding values. This saves you from having to write code that loops through the array or data table and manually adds elements to a control. Repeated-value binding can also simplify your life by supporting advanced formatting and template options that automatically configure how the data should look when it's placed in the control.

To create a data expression for list binding, you need to use a list control that explicitly supports data binding. Luckily, ASP.NET provides a whole collection, many of which you've probably already used in other applications or examples:

- **ListBox, DropDownList, CheckBoxList, and RadioButtonList.** These web controls provide a list for a single-column of information.
- **HtmlSelect.** This server-side HTML control represents the HTML <select> element, and works essentially the same as the ListBox web control. Generally, you'll only use this control for backward compatibility or when upgrading an existing ASP page.
- **DataList, DataGrid, and Repeater.** These rich web controls allow you to provide repeating lists or grids that can display more than one column (or field) of information at a time. For example, if you were binding to a hashtable (a special type of collection), you could display both the key and value of each item. If you were binding to a full-fledged table in a DataSet, you could display multiple fields in any combination. These controls offer the most powerful and flexible options for data binding.

With repeated-value data binding, you can write a data binding expression in your .aspx file, or you can apply the data binding by setting control properties. In the case of the simpler list controls, you'll usually just set properties. Of course, you can set properties in many ways, using code in a code-behind file, or by modifying the control tag in the .aspx file, possibly with the help of Visual Studio .NET's Properties window. The approach you take doesn't matter. The important detail is that you don't use any <%# expression %> data binding expressions.

For more sophisticated and flexible controls, such as the Repeater and DataList, you need to set some properties and enter data binding expressions in the .aspx file, generally using a special template format. Understanding the use of templates is the key to mastering data binding, and you'll explore templates in detail in the next chapter.

To continue any further with data binding, it helps to divide the subject into a few basic categories. You'll start by looking at data binding with the list controls.

Data Binding with Simple List Controls

In some ways, data binding to a list control is the simplest kind of data binding. You only need to follow three steps:

1. Create and fill some kind of data object. There are numerous options, including an Array, ArrayList, Collection, Hashtable, DataTable, and DataSet. Essentially, you can use any type of collection that supports the IEnumerable interface, although there are specific advantages and disadvantages that you'll discover in each class.

2. Link the object to the appropriate control. To do this, you only need to set a couple of properties, including DataSource. If you're binding to a full DataSet, you'll also need to set the DataMember property to identify the appropriate table that you want to use.

3. Activate the binding. As with single-value binding, you activate data binding by using the DataBind() method, either for the specific control or for all contained controls at once by using the DataBind() method for the current page.

This process is the same whether you're using the ListBox, DropDownList, CheckBoxList, RadioButtonList, or even HtmlSelect control. All these controls provide the exact same properties and work the same way. The only difference is in the way they appear on the final web page.

A Simple List Binding Example

To try out this type of data binding, add a ListBox control to a new web page. Use the Page.Load event handler to create a collection to use as a data source as follows:

```
Dim colFruit As New Collection()
colFruit.Add("Kiwi")
colFruit.Add("Pear")
colFruit.Add("Mango")
colFruit.Add("Blueberry")
colFruit.Add("Apricot")
colFruit.Add("Banana")
colFruit.Add("Peach")
colFruit.Add("Plum")
```

Now, you can link this collection to the list box control.

```
lstItems.DataSource = colFruit
```

Because a collection is a straightforward, unstructured type of object, this is all the information you need to set. If you were using a DataTable (which has more than one field) or a DataSet (which has more than one DataTable), you would have to specify additional information.

To activate the binding, use the DataBind() method:

```
Me.DataBind()    ' Could also use lstItems.DataBind() to bind just the list box.
```

The resulting web page is shown in Figure 15-6.

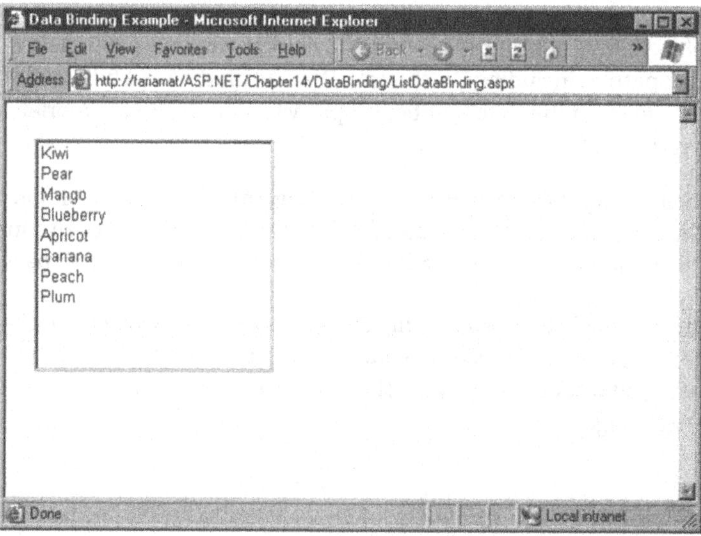

Figure 15-6. A data-bound list

This technique can save quite a few lines of code. In this example, there isn't a lot of savings because the collection is created just before it's displayed. In a more realistic application, however, you might be using a function that returns a ready-made collection to you.

```
Dim colFruit As Collection    ' No New keyword is needed this time.
colFruit = GetFruitsInSeason("Summer")
```

In this case, it's extremely simple to add the extra two lines needed to bind and display the collection in the window.

```
lstItems.DataSource = colFruit
Me.DataBind()
```

Or even change it to this:

```
lstItems.DataSource = GetFruitsInSeason("Summer")
Me.DataBind()
```

On the other hand, consider the extra trouble you would have to go through if you didn't use data binding. This type of savings adds up rapidly, especially when you start to combine data binding with multiple controls, advanced objects like DataSets, or advanced controls that apply formatting through templates.

Multiple Binding

You can bind the same data list object to multiple different controls. Consider the following example, which compares all the different types of list controls at your disposal by loading them with the same information:

```
Private Sub Page_Load(sender As Object, e As EventArgs) Handles MyBase.Load

    ' Create and fill the collection.
    Dim colFruit As New Collection()
    colFruit.Add("Kiwi")
    colFruit.Add("Pear")
    colFruit.Add("Mango")
    colFruit.Add("Blueberry")
    colFruit.Add("Apricot")
    colFruit.Add("Banana")
    colFruit.Add("Peach")
    colFruit.Add("Plum")

    ' Define the binding for the list controls.
    MyListBox.DataSource = colFruit
    MyDropDownListBox.DataSource = colFruit
    MyHTMLSelect.DataSource = colFruit
    MyCheckBoxList.DataSource = colFruit
    MyRadioButtonList.DataSource = colFruit

    ' Activate the binding.
    Me.DataBind()

End Sub
```

The rendered page is shown in Figure 15-7.

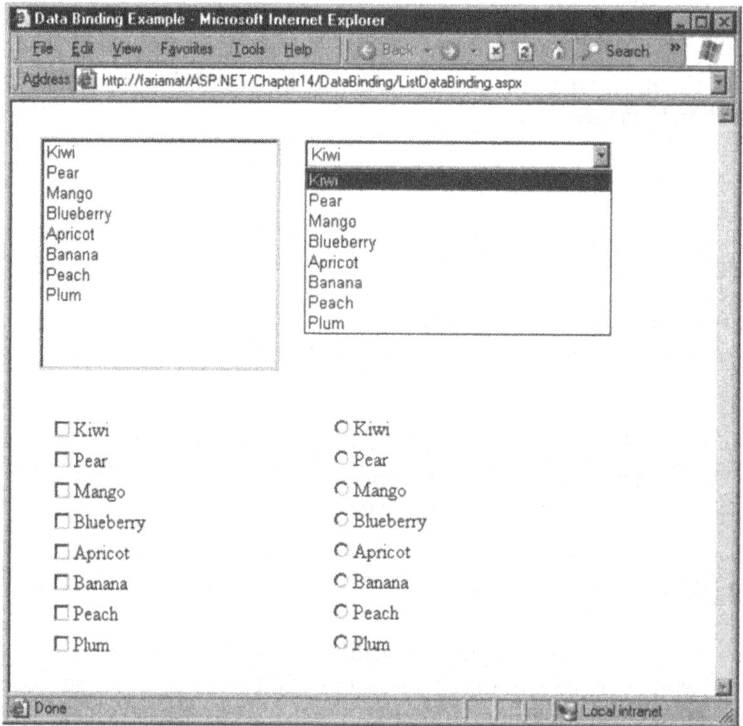

Figure 15-7. Multiple bound lists

This is another area where ASP.NET data binding may differ from what you have experienced in a desktop application. In traditional data binding, all the different controls are sometimes treated like "views" on the same data source, and you can only work with one record from the data source at a time. In this type of data binding, when you select Pear in one list control, the other list controls would automatically refresh so that they too have Pear selected (or the corresponding information from the same row). This isn't how ASP.NET uses data binding.

Data Binding and View State

Remember, the original collection is destroyed as soon as the page is completely processed into HTML and sent to the user. However, the information will remain in the controls if you've set their EnableViewstate properties to True. That means that you don't need to re-create and rebind the control every time the Page.Load event occurs, and you should check the IsPostBack property first.

Of course, in many cases, especially when working with databases, you'll want to rebind on every pass. For example, if you presented information corresponding to values in a database table, you might want to let the user make changes or specify a record to be deleted. As soon as the page is posted back, you would execute an SQL command and rebind the control to show the new data (thereby confirming to the user that the data source was updated with the change). In this case, you'll rebind the data with every postback.

The next chapter will examine this situation a little more closely. The important concept to realize now is that you need to be consciously evaluating state options. If you don't need view state for a data-bound list control, you should disable it, because it can slow down response times if a large amount of data is displayed on the screen. This is particularly true for the multiple binding example, because each control will have its own view state and its own separate copy of the identical data.

Data Binding with a Hashtable

Basic collections certainly aren't the only kind of data source you can use with list data binding. Other popular choices include various types of arrays and specialized collections. The concepts are virtually identical, so this chapter won't spend much time looking at different possibilities. Instead, you'll look at one more example with a hashtable before continuing straight to DataSets and DataReaders, which allow information to be displayed from a database.

A *hashtable* is a special kind of collection in which every item has a corresponding key. It's also called a dictionary, because every item (or "definition," to use the dictionary analogy) is indexed with a specific key (or dictionary "word"). This is similar to the way that built-in ASP.NET collections like Session, Application, and Cache work.

You might already know that the standard collection used in the previous example allows you to specify a key for every inserted item. However, it doesn't require one. This is the main difference between a generic collection and the hashtable. Hashtables always need keys, which make them more efficient for retrieval and sorting. Generic collections, on the other hand, are like large canvas bags that accommodate anything. Generally, you need to go through every item in a generic collection to find what you need, which makes them ideal for cases where you always need to display or work with all the items at the same time.

You create a hashtable in much the same way that you create a collection. The only difference is that you need to supply a unique key for every item. The next example uses the lazy practice of assigning a sequential number for each key:

```
Private Sub Page_Load(sender As Object, e As EventArgs) Handles MyBase.Load

    If Page.IsPostBack = False Then
        Dim colFruit As New Hashtable()
        colFruit.Add(1, "Kiwi")
        colFruit.Add(2, "Pear")
        colFruit.Add(3, "Mango")
        colFruit.Add(4, "Blueberry")
        colFruit.Add(5, "Apricot")
        colFruit.Add(6, "Banana")
```

```
        colFruit.Add(7, "Peach")
        colFruit.Add(8, "Plum")

        ' Define the binding for the list controls.
        MyListBox.DataSource = colFruit

        ' Activate the binding.
        Me.DataBind()
    End If

End Sub
```

However, when you try to run this code, you'll receive the unhelpful page shown in Figure 15-8.

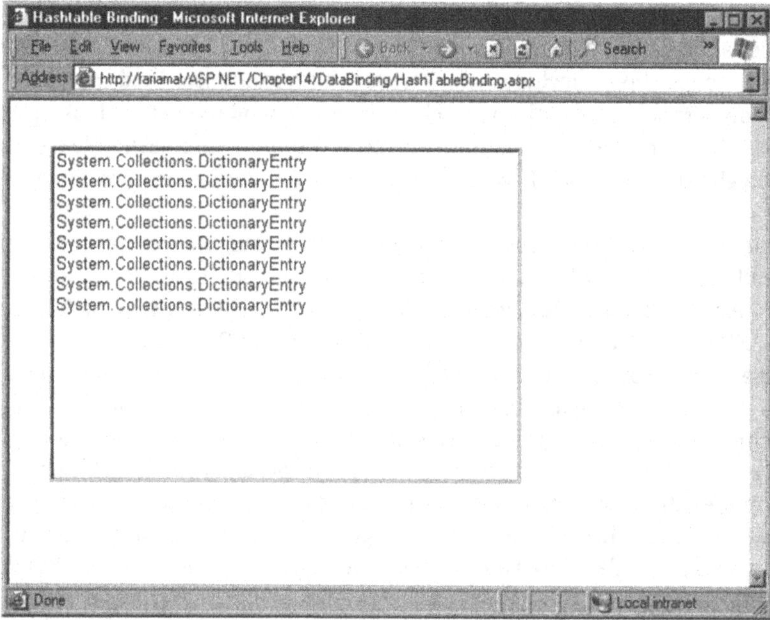

Figure 15-8. Unhelpful data binding

What happened? ASP.NET doesn't know how to handle hashtables without additional information. Instead, it defaults to using the ToString() method to get the class name for each item in the collection, which is probably not what you had in mind.

To solve this problem, you have to specify the property that you're interested in. Add the following line before the Me.DataBind() statement:

```
MyListBox.DataTextField = "Value"      ' To use the Value property of each item.
```

The page will now appear as expected, with all the fruit names. Notice that you need to enclose the property name in quotation marks. ASP.NET uses reflection to inspect your object and find the property that has the name Value at runtime.

You might want to experiment with what other types of collections you can bind to a list control. One interesting option is to use a built-in ASP.NET control such as the Session object. An item in the list will be created for every currently defined Session variable, making this trick a nice little debugging tool to quickly check current session information.

Using the DataValueField Property

Along with the DataTextField property, all list controls that support data binding also provide a DataValueField, which adds the corresponding information to the value attribute in the control element. This allows you to store extra (undisplayed) information that you can access later. For example, you could use these two lines to define your data binding:

```
MyListBox.DataTextField = "Value"
MyListBox.DataValueField = "Key"
```

The control will appear exactly the same, with a list of all the fruit names in the hashtable. However, if you look at the rendered HTML that's sent to the client browser, you'll see that value attributes have been set with the corresponding numeric key for each item:

```
<select name="MyListBox" id="MyListBox" >
    <option value="8">Plum</option>
    <option value="7">Peach</option>
    <option value="6">Banana</option>
    <option value="5">Apricot</option>
    <option value="4">Blueberry</option>
    <option value="3">Mango</option>
    <option value="2">Pear</option>
    <option value="1">Kiwi</option>
</select>
```

You can retrieve this value later on using the SelectedItem class to get additional information. For example, you could enable AutoPostBack for the list control, and add the following code:

```
Private Sub MyListBox_SelectedIndexChanged(sender As Object, _
 e As EventArgs) Handles MyListBox.SelectedIndexChanged

    lblMessage.Text = "You picked: " & MyListBox.SelectedItem.Text
    lblMessage.Text &= " which has the key: " & MyListBox.SelectedItem.Value

End Sub
```

The result is demonstrated in Figure 15-9. This technique is particularly useful with a database. You could embed a unique ID into the value property and be able to quickly look up a corresponding record depending on the user's selection by examining the value of the SelectedItem object.

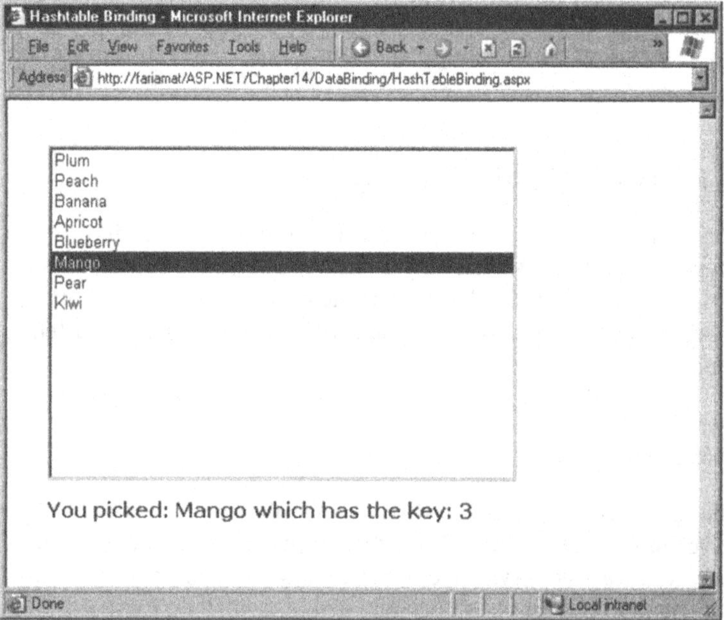

Figure 15-9. Binding to the text and value properties

Note that in order for this to work, you must not be regenerating the list with every postback. If you are, the selected item information will be lost, and an error will occur. The preceding example uses the Page.IsPostBack property to determine whether to build the list.

Data Binding with Databases

So far the examples in this chapter have dealt with data binding that doesn't involve databases or any part of ADO.NET. While this is an easy way to familiarize yourself with the concepts, and a useful approach in its own right, the greatest advantage from data binding is achieved when you use it in conjunction with a database.

Remember, in order to work with databases you should import the related namespaces. Here's the two namespaces you would import to use the OLE DB provider:

```
Imports System.Data
Imports System.Data.OleDb
```

The data binding process still takes place in the same three steps with a database. First you create your data source, which will be a DataReader or DataSet object. A

DataReader generally offers the best performance, but it limits your data binding to a single control, so a DataSet is a more common choice. In the following example, the DataSet is filled by hand, but it could just as easily be filled using a DataAdapter object.

```
' Define a DataSet with a single DataTable.
Dim dsInternal As New DataSet()
dsInternal.Tables.Add("Users")

' Define two columns for this table.
dsInternal.Tables("Users").Columns.Add("Name")
dsInternal.Tables("Users").Columns.Add("Country")

' Add some actual information into the table.
Dim rowNew As DataRow
rowNew = dsInternal.Tables("Users").NewRow()
rowNew("Name") = "John"
rowNew("Country") = "Uganda"
dsInternal.Tables("Users").Rows.Add(rowNew)

rowNew = dsInternal.Tables("Users").NewRow()
rowNew("Name") = "Samantha"
rowNew("Country") = "Belgium"
dsInternal.Tables("Users").Rows.Add(rowNew)

rowNew = dsInternal.Tables("Users").NewRow()
rowNew("Name") = "Rico"
rowNew("Country") = "Japan"
dsInternal.Tables("Users").Rows.Add(rowNew)
```

Next, a table from the DataSet is bound to the appropriate control. In this case, you need to specify the appropriate field using the DataTextField property:

```
' Define the binding.
lstUser.DataSource = dsInternal.Tables("Users")
lstUser.DataTextField = "Name"
```

Alternatively, you could use the entire DataSet for the data source, instead of just the appropriate table. In this case, you have to select a table by setting the control's DataMember property. This is an equivalent approach, but the code looks slightly different:

```
' Define the binding.
lstUser.DataSource = dsInternal
lstUser.DataMember = "Users"
lstUser.DataTextField = "Name"
```

As always, the last step is to activate the binding:

```
Me.DataBind()    ' Could also use lstItems.DataBind() to bind just the list box.
```

The final result is a list with the information from the specified database field, as shown in Figure 15-10. The list box will have an entry for every single record in the table, even if it appears more than once, from the first row to the last.

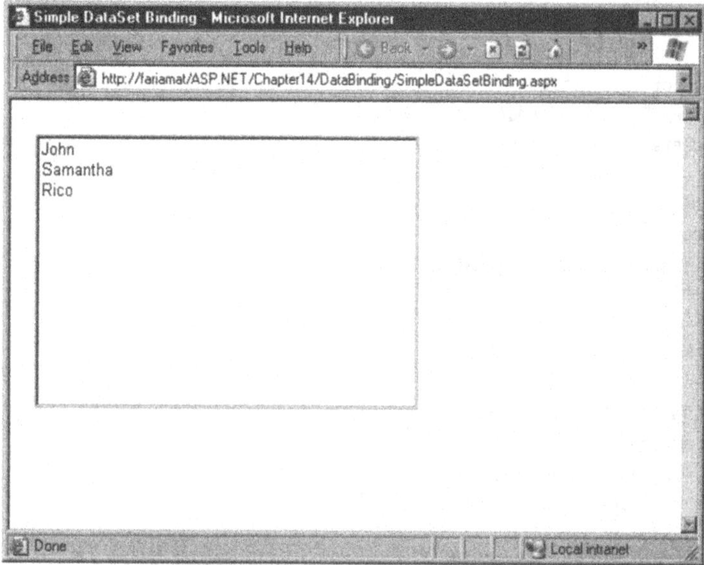

Figure 15-10. DataSet binding

TIP The simple list controls require you to bind their Text or Value property to a single data field in the data source object. However, much more flexibility is provided by the more advanced data binding controls examined in the next chapter. They allow fields to be combined in any way using templates.

Creating a Record Editor

The next example is more practical. It's a good example of how data binding might be used in a full ASP.NET application. This example allows the user to select a record and update one piece of information by using data-bound list controls. This example uses the Products table from the Northwind database included with SQL Server. A private variable in the Page class is used to define a connection string that every part of the code can access as follows:

```
Private ConnectionString As String = "Provider=SQLOLEDB.1;" & _
 "DataSource=localhost;Initial Catalog=Northwind;Integrated Security=SSPI"
```

The first step is to create a drop-down list that allows the user to choose a product for editing. The Page.Load event handler takes care of this task, retrieving the data, binding it to the drop-down list control, and then activating the binding:

```
Private Sub Page_Load(sender As Object, e As EventArgs) Handles MyBase.Load

    If Me.IsPostBack = False Then
        ' Define the ADO.NET objects for selecting Products.
        Dim selectSQL As String = "SELECT ProductName, ProductID FROM Products"
        Dim con As New OleDbConnection(ConnectionString)
        Dim com As New OleDbCommand(selectSQL, con)

        ' Open the connection.
        con.Open()

        ' Define the binding.
        lstProduct.DataSource = com.ExecuteReader()
        lstProduct.DataTextField = "ProductName"
        lstProduct.DataValueField = "ProductID"

        ' Activate the binding.
        lstProduct.DataBind()

        con.Close()

        ' Make sure nothing is currently selected.
        lstProduct.SelectedIndex = -1

    End If

End Sub
```

The actual database code is very similar to what was used in the previous chapter. The example uses a Select statement, but carefully limits the returned information to just the ProductName field, which is the only piece of information it will use. The resulting window shows a list of all the products defined in the database, as shown in Figure 15-11.

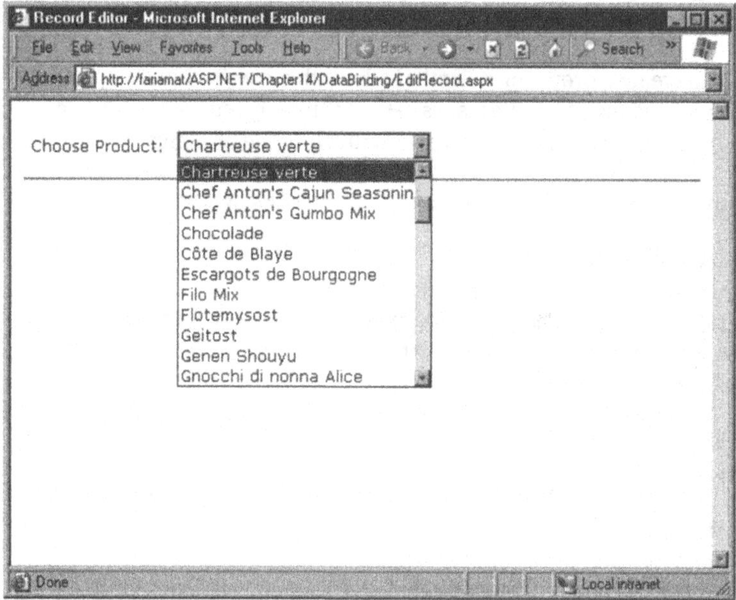

Figure 15-11. Product choices

The drop-down list enables AutoPostBack, so as soon as the user makes a selection, a lstProduct.SelectedItemChanged event fires. At this point, your code performs the following tasks:

- It reads the corresponding record from the Products table and displays additional information about it in a label control. In this case, a special Join query is used to link information from the Products and Categories table. The code also determines what the category is for the current product. This is the piece of information it will allow the user to change.
- It reads the full list of CategoryNames from the Categories table and binds this information to a different list control.
- It highlights the row in the category list box that corresponds to the current product. For example, if the current product is a Seafood category, the Seafood entry in the list box will be selected.

This logic appears fairly involved, but it's really just an application of what you've learned over the last two chapters. The full listing is shown here. All this code is placed inside the event handler for the lstProdcut.SelectedIndexChanged.

```
' Create a command for selecting the matching product record.
Dim ProductCommand As String
ProductCommand = "SELECT ProductName, QuantityPerUnit, " & _
 "CategoryName FROM Products INNER JOIN Categories ON " & _
 "Categories.CategoryID=Products.CategoryID " & _
 "WHERE ProductID='" & lstProduct.SelectedItem.Value & " '"

' Create the Connection and Command objects.
Dim con As New OleDbConnection(ConnectionString)
Dim comProducts As New OleDbCommand(ProductCommand, con)

' Retrieve the information for the selected product.
con.Open()
Dim reader As OleDbDataReader = comProducts.ExecuteReader()
reader.Read()

' Update the display.
lblRecordInfo.Text = "<b>Product:</b> " & reader("ProductName") & "<br>"
lblRecordInfo.Text &= "<b>Quantity:</b> " & reader("QuantityPerUnit") & "<br>"
lblRecordInfo.Text &= "<b>Category:</b> " & reader("CategoryName")

' Store the corresponding CategoryName for future reference.
Dim MatchCategory As String = reader("CategoryName")

' Close the reader.
reader.Close()

' Create a new Command for selecting categories.
Dim CategoryCommand As String = "SELECT CategoryName, CategoryID FROM Categories"
Dim comCategories As New OleDbCommand(CategoryCommand, con)

' Retrieve the category information, and bind it.
lstCategory.DataSource = comCategories.ExecuteReader()
lstCategory.DataTextField = "CategoryName"
lstCategory.DataValueField = "CategoryID"
lstCategory.DataBind()
con.Close()

' Highlight the matching category in the list.
lstCategory.Items.FindByText(MatchCategory).Selected = True

lstCategory.Visible = True
cmdUpdate.Visible = True
```

This code could be improved in several ways. In probably makes most sense to remove these data access routines from this event handler, and put them into more generic functions. For example, you could use a function that accepts a ProductName and returns a single DataRow with the associated product information. Another improvement would be to use a stored procedure to retrieve this information, rather than a full-fledged DataReader.

The end result is a window that updates itself dynamically whenever a new product is selected, as shown in Figure 15-12.

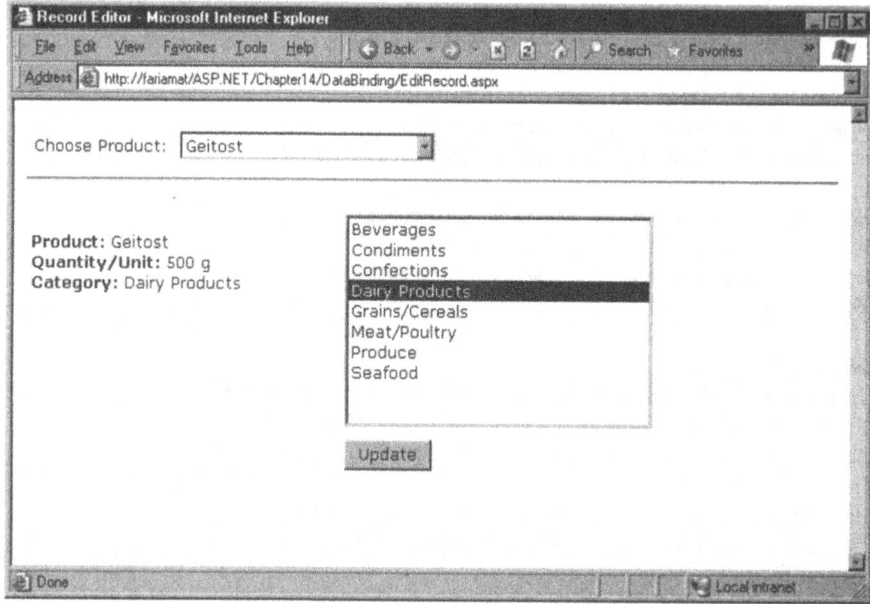

Figure 15-12. Product information

This example still has one more trick in store. If the user selects a different category and clicks Update, the change is made in the database. Of course, this means creating new Connection and Command objects, as follows:

```
Private Sub cmdUpdate_Click(sender As Object, _
 e As EventArgs) Handles cmdUpdate.Click

    ' Define the Command.
    Dim UpdateCommand As String = "UPDATE Products " & _
     "SET CategoryID=" & stCategory.SelectedItem.Value & _
     "WHERE ProductID=" & lstProduct.SelectedItem.Value

    Dim con As New OleDbConnection(ConnectionString)
    Dim com As New OleDbCommand(UpdateCommand, con)

    ' Perform the update.
    con.Open()
    com.ExecuteNonQuery()
    con.Close()

End Sub
```

This example could easily be extended so that it allows you to edit all the properties in a product record. But before you try that, you might want to experiment with template-based data binding, which is introduced in the next chapter. Using templates, you can create sophisticated lists and grids that provide automatic features for selecting, editing, and deleting records.

The Last Word

This chapter presented a thorough overview of data binding in ASP.NET. Using the techniques in this chapter, you can create simple data-bound pages. However, if you want to create a page that incorporates record editing, sorting, and other more advanced tricks, these data binding features offer little help. Instead, you'll need to turn to specialized controls, like the DataList and DataGrid, which build upon these data binding features. You'll explore these controls in the next chapter.

CHAPTER 16

The DataList, DataGrid, and Repeater

WHEN IT COMES TO data binding, not all ASP.NET controls are created equal. In the last chapter, you saw how data binding could help you automatically insert single values and lists into all kinds of common controls and even ordinary HTML. In this chapter, you'll concentrate on three more advanced controls—the DataList, DataGrid, and Repeater—which allow you to bind entire tables of data. These controls are sometimes known as *template controls* because they allow you to use significant formatting and customization features by creating templates. Some of these controls even have additional built-in functionality for selecting, editing, and sorting the displayed information.

Introducing Templates

Templates are special blocks of HTML that allow you to define the content and formatting for part of a control. Controls that support templates allow a great deal of flexibility. Rather than just setting an individual value (such as a Text property) and related formatting properties (such as a Color property), you define an entire block of HTML that can include controls, styles, and information in any arrangement. The drawback is that you need to enter this information manually in its tag form. If you're used to the conveniences of Visual Studio .NET, diving back into markup may seem like a rather unfriendly approach. However, in many ways templates are just an extension of the data binding syntax you saw in the examples in the previous chapter, and that means the tags are easy to understand.

Unlike single-value data binding, the repeated-value data binding used in the Repeater, DataList, and DataGrid controls almost always uses information drawn from a database and provided in a DataSet object. This chapter returns to the pubs database. All the data binding examples use the Authors table, which contains a list of author information. Because the focus of this chapter is on designing and using templates and other features of the ASP.NET data controls, you don't need examples that involve complex or unusual data access code. In fact, you could duplicate these examples by creating and filling a DataSet object manually, and not using a database at all.

Using Templates with the DataList

To see a simple example of how data binding works with a template control, add a DataList control to your web page. If you're working with Visual Studio .NET, you won't see a default graphical representation. Instead, a special box will appear informing you that this control requires templates (Figure 16-1).

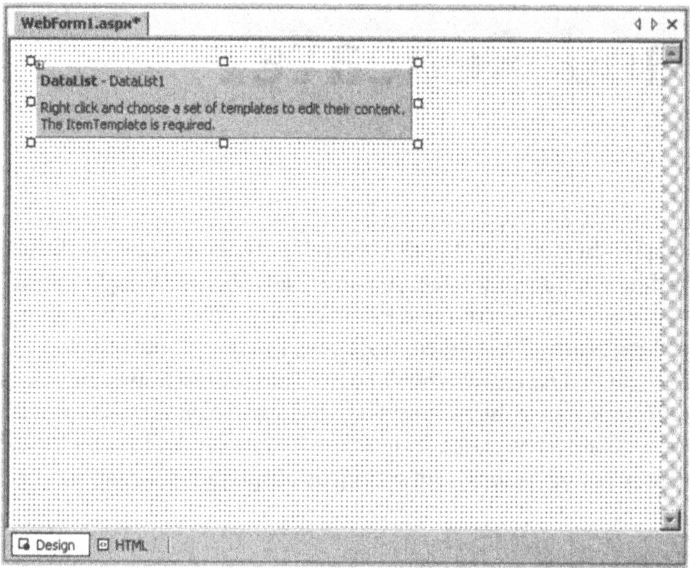

Figure 16-1. A template control at design time

Creating a Template

As in the previous chapter, you need to work with the markup in your .aspx file to implement data binding. All the templates for controls like the DataList are defined in the .aspx file. To view it in Visual Studio .NET, click the HTML button at the bottom of the form designer.

Find the line that represents your DataList control. It's made up of an opening and closing tag. If you're using grid layout for your page, the opening tag will have additional information about the size and position of the DataList.

```
<asp:DataList id=listAuthor runat="server"></asp:DataList>
```

To make your DataList functional, you need to add at least one template: the item template. All templates are coded in between the opening and ending tags of the DataList control. If you're working with Visual Studio .NET, you'll receive an IntelliSense list that provides you with the names of all the templates as soon as you type the less-than (<) character (see Figure 16-2).

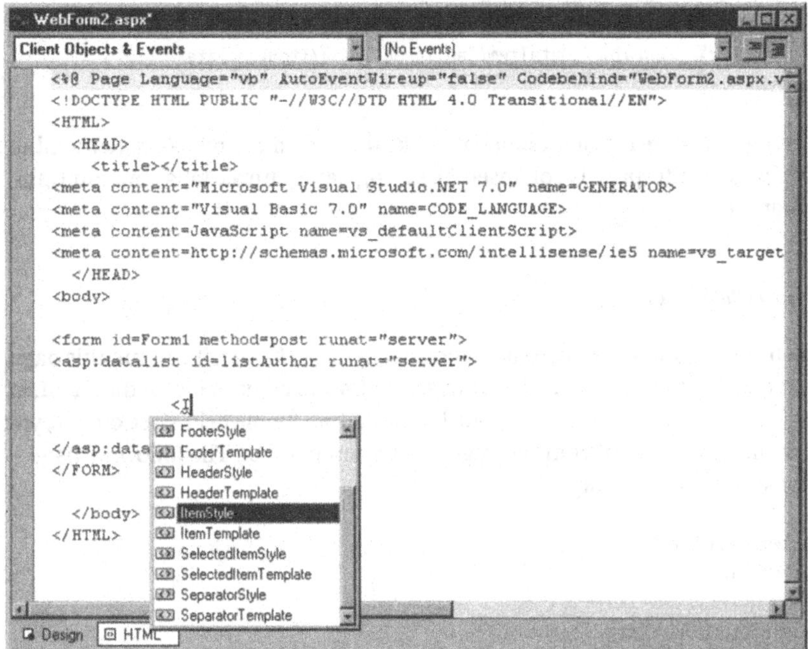

Figure 16-2. An IntelliSense template list

The item template is added like this:

```
<asp:DataList id=listAuthor runat="server">
    <ItemTemplate></ItemTemplate>
</asp:DataList>
```

Inside the item template, you can add a data binding expression using the special <%# %> data binding expression syntax. As with the examples in the last chapter, you can use any combination of expressions and variables inside an expression. You also use the special Container.DataItem() method to refer to the object that is bound to the DataSource property.

For example, the DataList that follows binds a table and displays the author's last name (drawn from the au_lname field):

```
<asp:DataList id=listAuthor runat="server">
    <ItemTemplate><%# Container.DataItem("au_lname") %></ItemTemplate>
</asp:DataList>
```

In order for this syntax to work, a DataSet with the au_lname field must be bound to the DataSource property of the listAuthor DataList at runtime.

The following example shows a more sophisticated example of data binding that combines two fields to display an author's full name in a standard format.

```
<asp:DataList id=listAuthor runat="server">
    <ItemTemplate><%# Container.DataItem("au_lname") %>,
                  <%# Container.DataItem("au_fname") %></ItemTemplate>
</asp:DataList>
```

The spacing used here is just intended to make the code more readable. Remember, in an HTML page, whitespace is collapsed, meaning hard returns, tabs, and multiple spaces are ignored.

Using a Template

On its own, this template still doesn't accomplish anything. In fact, if you run this page, no information will be displayed in the browser window. To actually create the DataList, you need to bind a data source that has an au_lname and au_fname field. For example, you could create and bind a DataSet in the Page.Load event handler. The following page class demonstrates this technique.

```
Imports System.Data.OleDb
Imports System.Data

Public Class BasicAuthorList
  Inherits Page

    Protected listAuthor As DataList

    Private ConnectionString As String = "Provider=SQLOLEDB.1;" & _
    "Data Source=localhost;Initial Catalog=pubs;Integrated Security=SSPI"

    Private Sub Page_Load(sender As Object, e As EventArgs) _
      Handles MyBase.Load
        ' Create and fill a DataSet.
        Dim SQL As String
        SQL = "SELECT * FROM Authors"
        Dim con As New OleDbConnection(ConnectionString)
        Dim cmd As New OleDbCommand(SQL, con)
        Dim adapter As New OleDbDataAdapter(cmd)
        Dim Pubs As New DataSet()
        con.Open()
        adapter.Fill(Pubs, "Authors")
        con.Close()

        ' Bind the DataSet, and activate the data bindings for the page.
        listAuthor.DataSource = Pubs.Tables("Authors")
        Me.DataBind()
    End Sub

End Class
```

This is standard ADO.NET code. The end result is a list of names in a simple, unformatted HTML table, as shown in Figure 16-3.

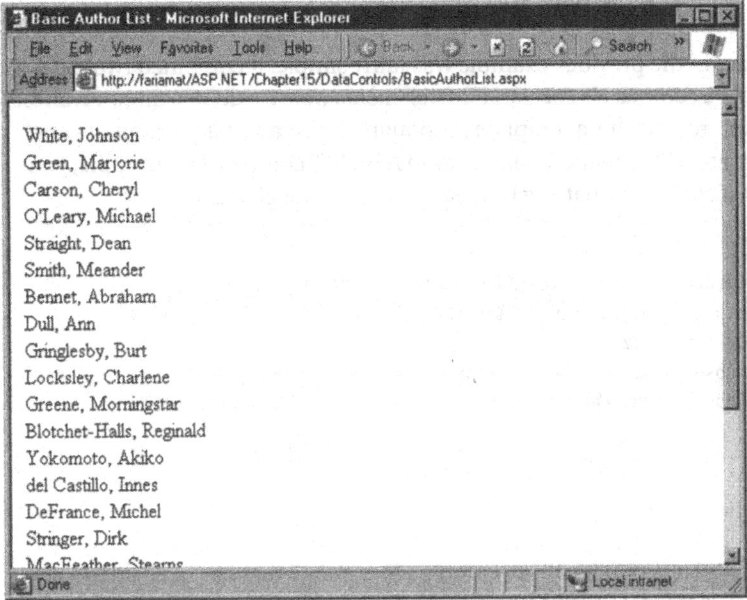

Figure 16-3. The author list

Unfortunately, at design time you won't see all this information, because the data binding is set up dynamically through code. Instead, in Visual Studio .NET you'll only see any hard-coded, static elements in the template (in this case, the comma), as shown in Figure 16-4.

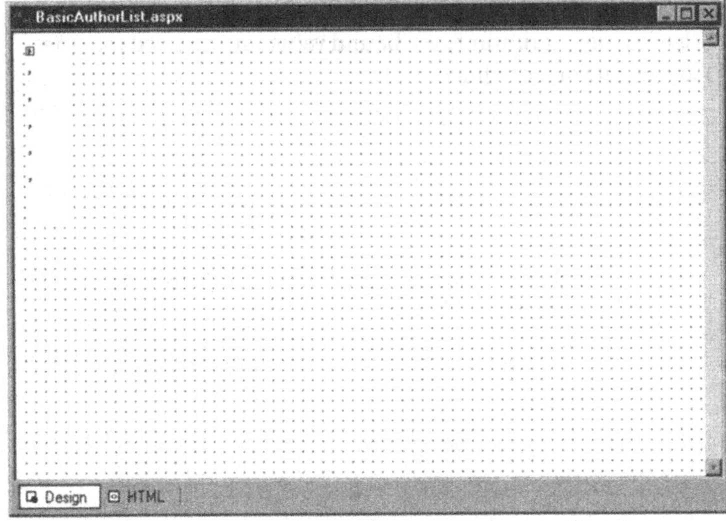

Figure 16-4. The author list at design time

Templates with HTML

The item template in the previous example was fairly simple. It combined two data fields, separated by a comma. No special HTML elements were used. For a more advanced template, you can treat the item template as though it's just another portion of your .aspx file, and insert HTML markup tags or even ASP.NET controls. For example, you could make use of special formatting by creating a template like this:

```
<ItemTemplate>
    <font face="Verdana" size="2"><b><%# Container.DataItem("au_fname") %>
    <%# Container.DataItem("au_lname") %></b></font><br>
    <font face="Verdana" size="1">
        Address: <%# Container.DataItem("address") %><br>
        City: <%# Container.DataItem("city") %></font><br><br>
</ItemTemplate>
```

Dissecting the Code . . .

This template looks considerably more complicated, but all that has been added are some stock HTML elements, including the following:

- The <font> tag to change the font style and size for the displayed text
- The <b> tag to bold the heading (the author's name)
- Nonbreaking spaces ( ) and hard breaks (<br>) to align the text

The result is a more attractive list that incorporates formatting along with information from your data source, as shown in Figure 16-5.

At design time, you'll see a list that defaults to five items and only shows the static information (the headings), as shown in Figure 16-6. This gives you an idea why this code is referred to as a template. At runtime, the bound values are inserted into the appropriate slots in the layout you've defined.

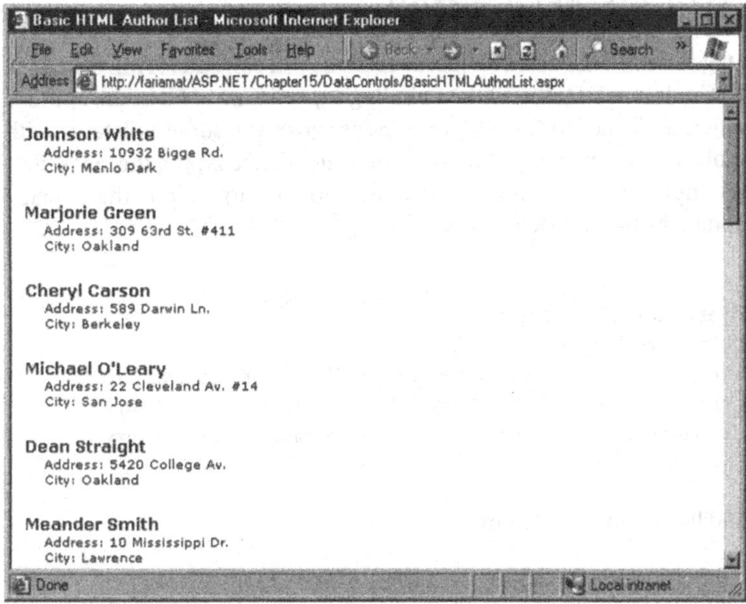

Figure 16-5. A more attractive author list

Figure 16-6. The author list at design time

Templates with ASP.NET Controls

You can add the tags for ASP.NET controls just as easily as you can add HTML elements. You can then add Container.DataItem() data binding expressions to fill in the appropriate control values. In Visual Studio .NET, IntelliSense gives you some assistance with a drop-down list of elements you might want to use when you're typing the .aspx file.

The following template uses text boxes to hold the values returned from the DataSet. It also adds an update button to each record.

```
<ItemTemplate>
    <b><%# Container.DataItem("au_fname") %>
    <%# Container.DataItem("au_lname") %></b><br>
    <asp:TextBox Text='<%# Container.DataItem("address") %>' runat=server /><br>
    <asp:TextBox Text='<%# Container.DataItem("city") %>' runat=server /><br>
    <asp:Button id=cmdUpdate Text='Update' runat=server></asp:Button><br><br>
</ItemTemplate>
```

The data bound list is shown in Figure 16-7.

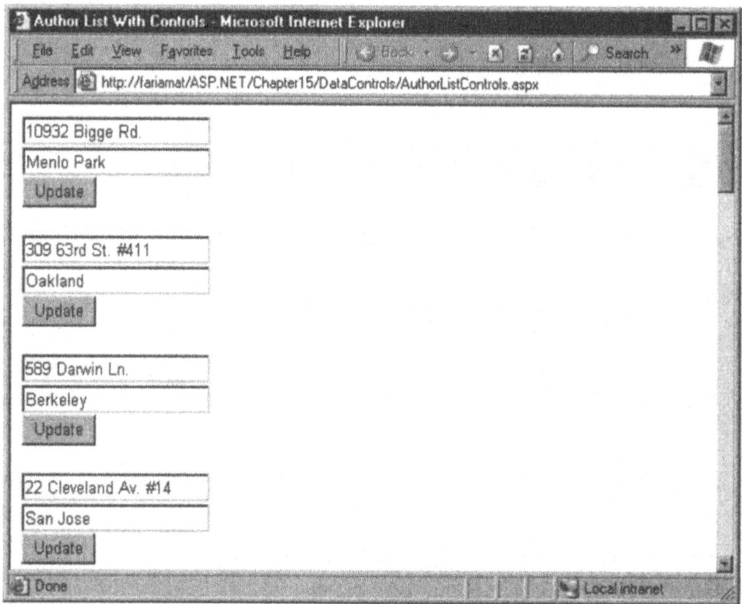

Figure 16-7. The author list with ASP.NET controls

As it stands, there's one problem: The button isn't connected to any event handler. In fact, even if you manually connect it by defining it in the Page class with the WithEvents keyword, you won't be able to distinguish one button from another. That means that when the event occurs you won't be able to tell which item the button belongs to, and you won't know what record should be updated.

The easiest way to resolve this problem is to use an event from the DataList control, not the contained button. The DataList.ItemCommand event serves this purpose. It fires whenever any button in the DataList is clicked. It also provides the item where the event occurred (through the e.Item property). Later in this chapter, you'll look at more specific examples that show how you can use this event to update or delete records in a DataList.

Formatting with DataBinder.Eval()

So far, the examples in this chapter have used the Container.DataItem() syntax for data binding. There's one other option, which includes the System.Web.UI.DataBinder class. The following example retrieves an author's last name using this syntax:

```
DataBinder.Eval(Container.DataItem, "au_lname")
```

From a performance standpoint, the DataBinder.Eval() data binding expression is slightly slower because it uses runtime-type inspection (also known as reflection). However, it's useful in some situations in which you need to apply additional formatting, because it accepts a format string as an optional third parameter. In the authors table from the pubs database, this notation isn't very useful because almost all the information is stored in strings. If you need to work with numbers or date values, however, this formatting can become extremely useful.

Format strings are generally made up of a placeholder and format indicator, which are wrapped inside curly brackets. It looks something like this:

```
"{0:C}"
```

In this case, the 0 represents the value that will be formatted, and the letter indicates a predetermined format style. In this case, C means currency format, which formats a number as a dollar figure (so 3400.34 becomes $3,400.34). To use this format string when data binding, you could use code like this:

```
DataBinder.Eval(Container.DataItem, "Price", "{0:C}")
```

Some of the other formatting options for numeric values are shown in Table 16-1.

Table 16-1. Numeric Format Strings

Type	Format String	Example
Currency	{0:C}	$1,234.50
Brackets indicate negative values: ($1,234.50). Currency sign is locale-specific: (£1,234.50).		
Scientific (Exponential)	{0:E}	1.234.50E+004
Percentage	{0:P}	45.6%
Fixed Decimal	{0:F?}	Depends on the number of decimal places you set. {0:F3} would be 123.400. {0:F0} would be 123.

Other examples can be found in the MSDN Help database. For date or time values, there is also an extensive list. Some examples are shown in Table 16-2.

Table 16-2. Time and Date Format Strings

Type	*Format String*	*Example*
Short Date **(for example: 10/30/2002)**	{0:d}	M/d/yyyy
Long Date **(for example: Monday, January 30, 2002)**	{0:D}	dddd, MMMM dd, yyyy
Long Date and Short Time **(for example: Monday, January 30, 2002 10:00 AM)**	{0:f}	dddd, MMMM dd, yyyy HH:mm aa
Long Date and Long Time **(for example: Monday, January 30, 2002 10:00:23 AM)**	{0:F}	dddd, MMMM dd, yyyy HH:mm:ss aa
ISO Sortable Standard **(for example: 2002-01-30 10:00:23)**	{0:s}	yyyy-MM-dd HH:mm:ss
Month and Day **(for example: January 30)**	{0:M}	MMMM dd
General **(for example: 10/30/2002 10:00:23 AM)**	{0:G}	M/d/yyyy HH:mm:ss aa (depends on locale-specific settings)

Data Binding with Multiple Templates

The examples so far have worked exclusively with the item template. Part of the power of template controls is that they define several different styles that allow you to configure different types of rows. For example, you can also create a template for the header row (HeaderTemplate) and the divider in between rows (SeparatorTemplate). You can also set items to alternate row by row (by adding an AlternateItemTemplate).

The following example shows a number of different templates in a DataList control.

```
<asp:datalist id=listAuthor runat="server">
    <HeaderTemplate>
        <h2>Author List</h2><br><hr>
    </HeaderTemplate>
    <ItemTemplate>
        <b><%# Container.DataItem("au_fname") %>
        <%# Container.DataItem("au_lname") %></b><br>
        Address: <%# Container.DataItem("address") %><br>
        City: <%# Container.DataItem("city") %>
    </ItemTemplate>
    <AlternatingItemTemplate>
            <b><%# Container.DataItem("au_fname") %>
        <%# Container.DataItem("au_lname") %></b><br>
            Address: <%# Container.DataItem("address") %><br>
            City: <%# Container.DataItem("city") %>
    </AlternatingItemTemplate>
    <SeparatorTemplate>
        <br><hr><br>
    </SeparatorTemplate>
    <FooterTemplate>
        <br>This list provided on <%# System.DateTime.Now %>
    </FooterTemplate>
</asp:datalist>
```

Note that these templates can be listed in the .aspx file in any order. The resulting DataList looks quite a bit different, and is shown in Figure 16-8.

Special templates are also the key to unlocking the selecting and editing features you'll consider shortly.

Figure 16-8. The author list with multiple templates

Formatting with Template Styles

Every template has a corresponding style. For example, you can configure the appearance of a header template inside a <HeaderStyle> tag. You can manually code these tags in the .aspx file, or you can set them using the Property window in Visual Studio .NET, which will add the corresponding information to your code automatically (see Figure 16-9).

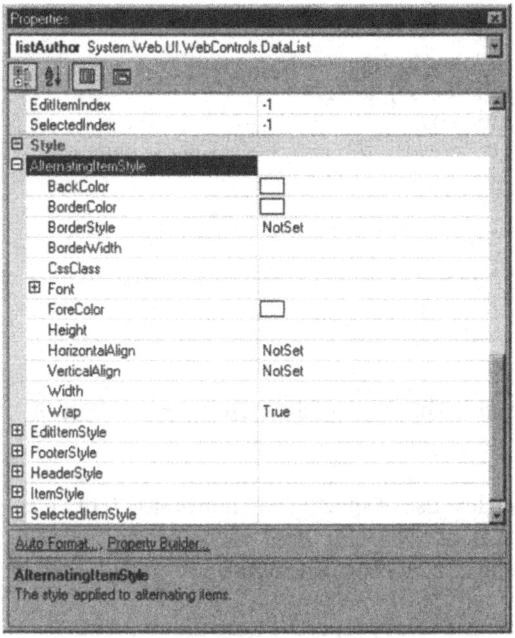

Figure 16-9. Configuring styles in Visual Studio

Each style has a significant amount of associated information that allows you to set background and foreground colors, borders, fonts, and alignment as attributes of the style tag. Here's an example of a control that makes full use of the different styles:

```
<asp:datalist id=listAuthor runat="server" BorderColor="#DEBA84"
 BorderStyle="None" CellSpacing="2" BackColor="#DEBA84" CellPadding="3"
 GridLines="Both" BorderWidth="1px">
    <HeaderStyle Font-Bold="True" ForeColor="White" BackColor="#A55129">
    </HeaderStyle>
    <ItemStyle Font-Size="Smaller" Font-Names="Verdana" ForeColor="#8C4510"
    BackColor="#FFF7E7"></ItemStyle>
    <AlternatingItemStyle BackColor="#FFE0C0"></AlternatingItemStyle>
    <FooterStyle ForeColor="#8C4510" BackColor="#F7DFB5"></FooterStyle>

    <HeaderTemplate>
        <h2>Author List</h2>
    </HeaderTemplate>
    <FooterTemplate>
        <br>This list provided on <%# System.DateTime.Now %>
    </FooterTemplate>
```

```
    <ItemTemplate>
        <b><%# Container.DataItem("au_fname") %>
        <%# Container.DataItem("au_lname") %></b><br>
        Address: <%# Container.DataItem("address") %><br>
        City: <%# Container.DataItem("city") %>
    </ItemTemplate>
    <SeparatorTemplate>
        <hr>
    </SeparatorTemplate>
</asp:datalist>
```

Dissecting the Code ...

The template is shown in Figure 16-10 with a basic list of data. There are a couple of interest points about this template:

- The actual templates make much less use of spacing and line breaks (
 elements) because some basic information is set for the DataList setting border style and cell padding for the table that will contain all the rows.
- Initially, all the styles inherit the basic color properties from the containing control (in this case, the DataList). In addition, the AlternatingItemStyle tag inherits all the formatting you apply to the ItemStyle element.

The templates, combined with the corresponding style tags, allow you to have a very fine-grained control over every aspect of your data control's appearance. This control is quite different than the features data binding has historically offered. In fact, data binding has acquired a bad reputation because it's typically very inflexible, often allowing no way to modify or combine values, and forcing you to use every field retrieved from a database with no control over order or layout. With ASP.NET templates, the situation is reversed. Every field is explicitly placed using a Container.DataItem() expression, and additional formatting can be applied at every level using the DataBinder.Eval() method and the powerful set of built-in styles.

Auto Format

One other interesting feature is Visual Studio .NET's "auto format" ability for data controls. (You may have already used a similar feature when formatting tables in Microsoft Word.) To automatically format a DataList, click the Auto Format link at the bottom of the Properties window. A window will appear that allows you to choose a grouped set of themed styles, as shown in Figure 16-11.

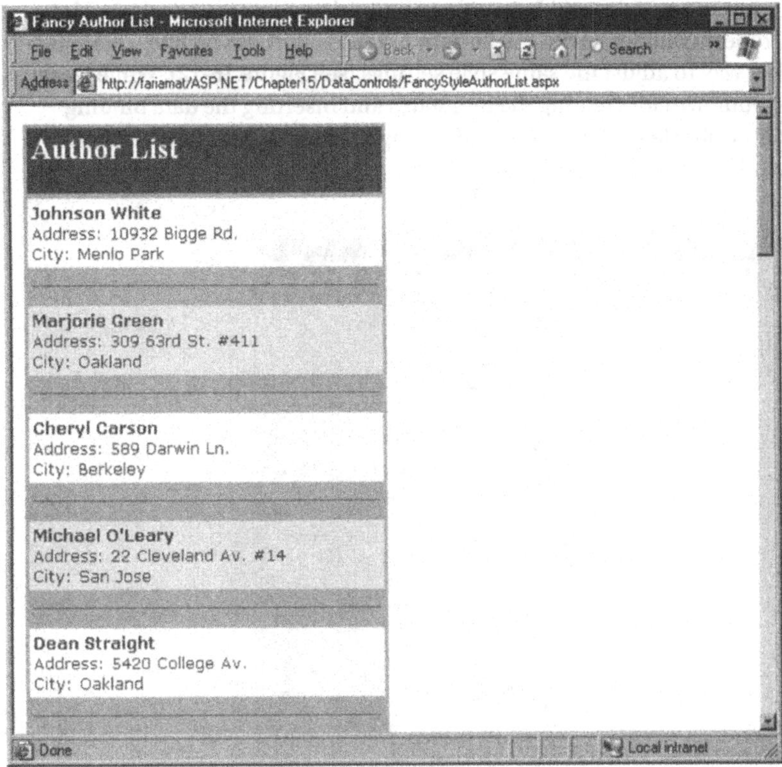

Figure 16-10. Fancy style author list

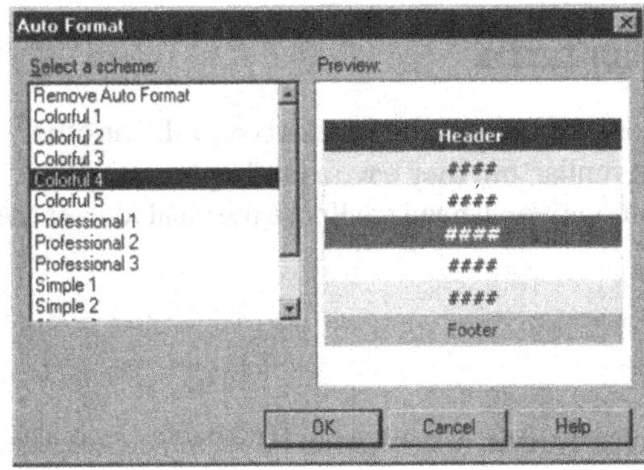

Figure 16-11. Applying a control theme

When you choose a style set from this window, all the code is added to configure the DataList control and the corresponding styles. You can then fine-tune it with the Properties window or manually in the .aspx code view.

Similarly, you can set styles and formatting options in an integrated window by clicking the Property Builder link at the bottom of the Properties window. This gives you yet another way to adjust the same style settings (see Figure 16-12). While you're essentially on your own for creating the templates and inserting the data binding syntax, there is no shortage of tools for configuring the look of your data control.

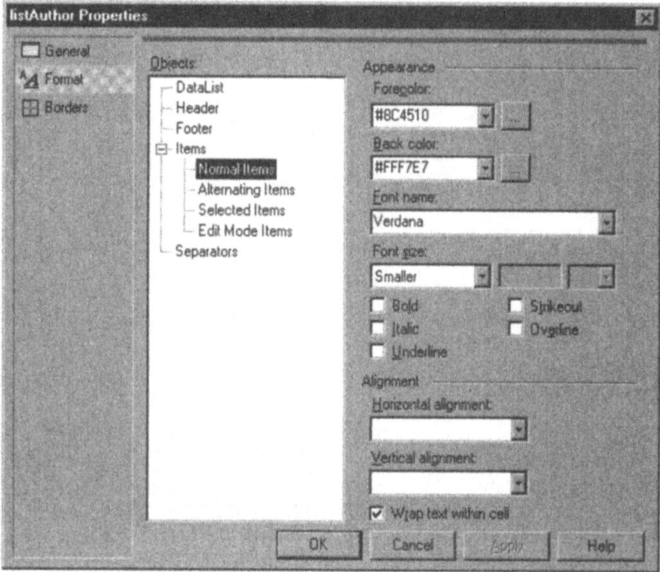

Figure 16-12. The Property Builder

Comparing the Template Controls

Up to this point, the examples have concentrated on the DataList control. The other data controls provided in ASP.NET are similar, but they have a few important differences. As you design your web applications, you'll need to choose the ideal tool for the task at hand.

The DataList

The DataList is a versatile control that displays a list of items in an HTML table. Generally, each item is contained in a single column on a single row. That makes the DataList ideal for customized displays in which multiple fields are grouped and formatted in one block of HTML. If you look at the HTML code that is generated for the DataList when it's sent to the client, you'll see that a DataList encloses every item in a separate table row. (Alternatively, you can use the DataGrid control for a multicolumned grid display.)

The DataList supports automatic selection and editing. Compared to the DataGrid, it lacks automatic paging (the ability to break a table into multiple pages that are displayed separately) and sorting.

Data List Layout

The DataList provides some additional layout features that let you change how the cells in the table are ordered. For example, you can set the RepeatDirection property to Horizontal to make a row of cells from left to right. Every item will occupy a separate column on the same row. In Figure 16-13, you can see the result when the RepeatDirection is changed for the previous example with a list of authors.

You can also create a DataList that lays out items in a grid with a maximum number of columns with the RepeatColumns property. By default, RepeatColumns is set to 0 and no specific maximum number of columns is used. In Horizontal alignment, the table will have one column for each item, and in Vertical alignment, the table will have only one column, with all the items in separate rows.

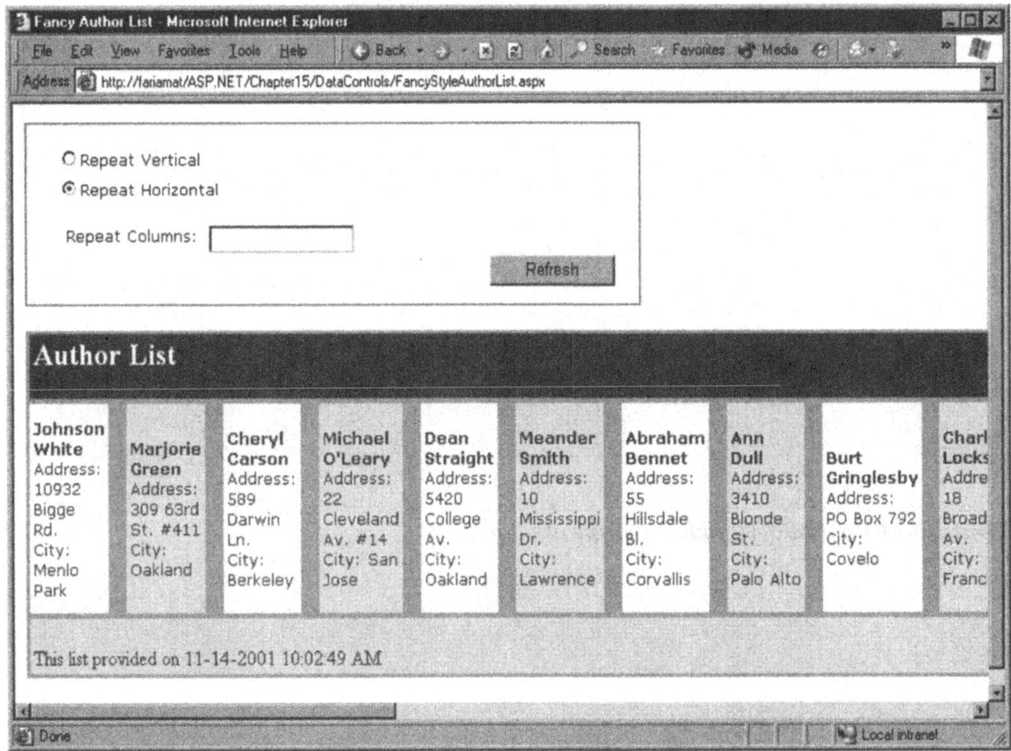

Figure 16-13. A horizontal author list

Once you set the RepeatColumns property, ASP.NET will create a table with that many columns (provided enough items exist) and will fill it from left to right (if RepeatDirection is Horizontal) or top to bottom (if RepeatDirection is Vertical). Figure 16-14 shows the results of setting RepeatColumns to 5 and RepeatDirection to Vertical.

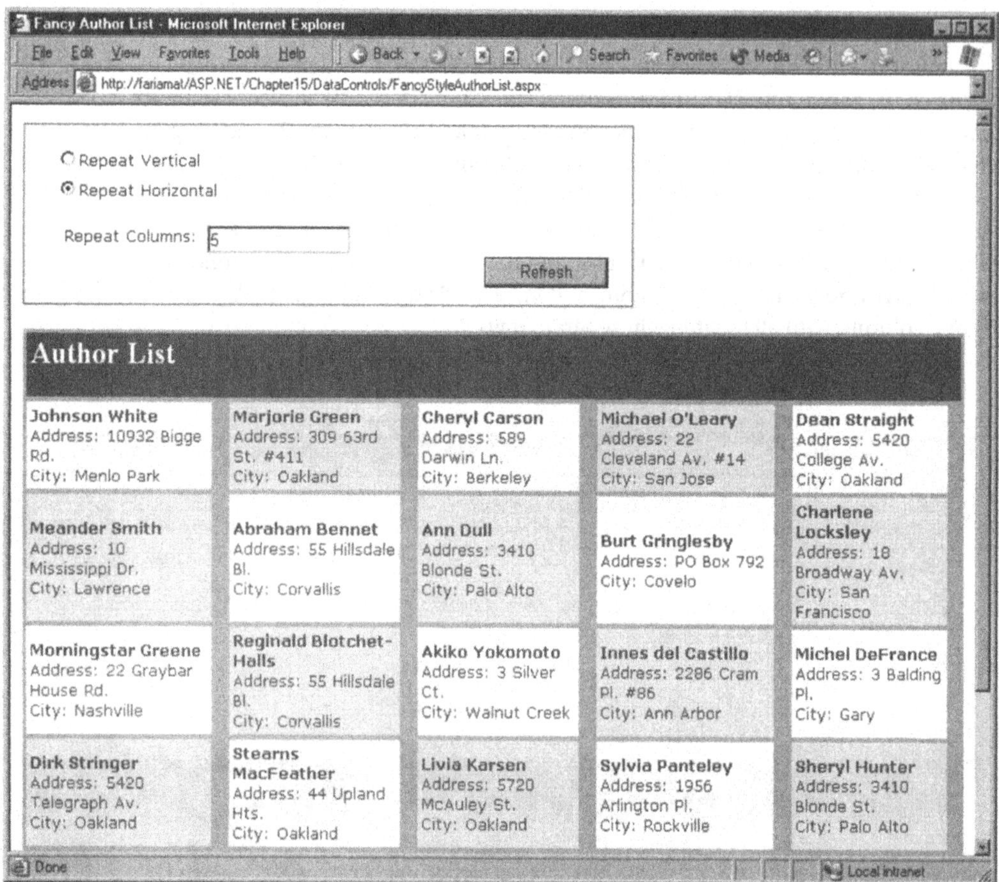

Figure 16-14. Controlling layout with RepeatColumns

To play around with these different layout options, try the sample code for this chapter, which includes an example that lets the user choose the RepeatDirection and number of RepeatColumns for a table (the file FancyStyleAuthorList.aspx). The important point for DataLists is that each item is fully contained in a single cell.

The DataGrid

The DataGrid is designed for displaying a multicolumn table, in which every item in a list has a single row with multiple columns. Typically, each column corresponds to information in an individual database field, although templates allow you to precisely configure the content.

The DataGrid is probably the most powerful data control, because it comes equipped with the most ready-made functionality. These include features for automatic paging, sorting, selecting, and editing.

Automatically Generating Columns

Interestingly, the DataGrid is the only data control described in this chapter that can work without templates. As long as you have the AutoGenerateColumns property set to True (the default), columns will be created for every field in a DataSet as soon as you bind it.

Here's an example of how you bind the DataGrid with auto-generated columns:

```
' (Data access code omitted.)

gridAuthor.AutoGenerateColumns = True
gridAuthor.DataSource = Pubs.Tables("Authors")

' Columns are generated automatically when the DataGrid is bound.
' No templates are required.
Me.DataBind()
```

The output is automatic, and appears in the exact same way that it's stored in the DataSet (Figure 16-15).

This approach loses many of the advantages of data binding, however, because you cannot precisely define the order, appearance, and formatting of the columns. In other words, you should be aware of this functionality, but you'll probably want to avoid it, and explicitly set AutoGenerateColumns to False and define specific column tags.

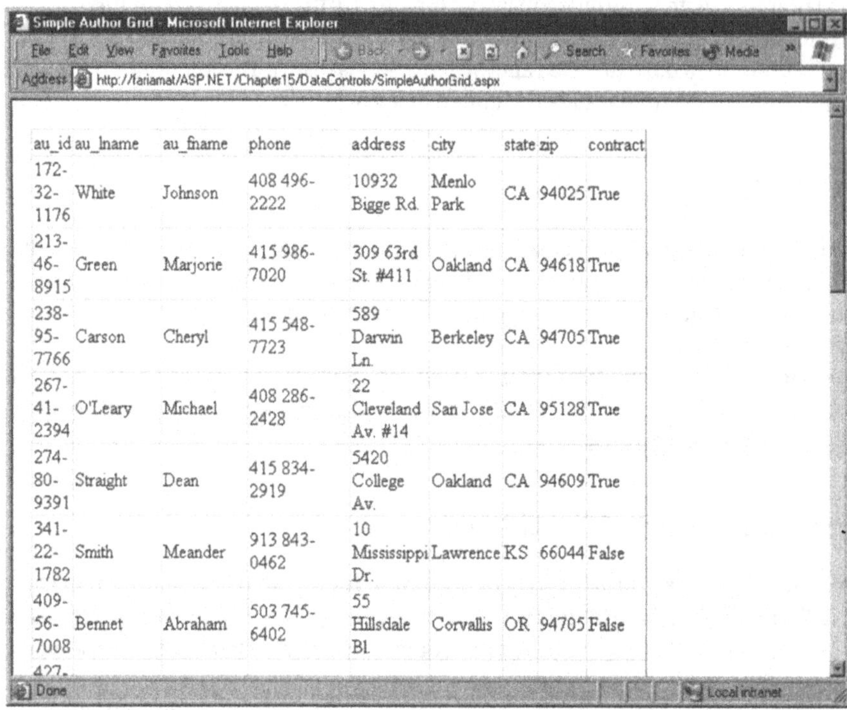

au_id	au_lname	au_fname	phone	address	city	state	zip	contract
172-32-1176	White	Johnson	408 496-2222	10932 Bigge Rd.	Menlo Park	CA	94025	True
213-46-8915	Green	Marjorie	415 986-7020	309 63rd St. #411	Oakland	CA	94618	True
238-95-7766	Carson	Cheryl	415 548-7723	589 Darwin Ln.	Berkeley	CA	94705	True
267-41-2394	O'Leary	Michael	408 286-2428	22 Cleveland Av. #14	San Jose	CA	95128	True
274-80-9391	Straight	Dean	415 834-2919	5420 College Av.	Oakland	CA	94609	True
341-22-1782	Smith	Meander	913 843-0462	10 Mississippi Dr.	Lawrence	KS	66044	False
409-56-7008	Bennet	Abraham	503 745-6402	55 Hillsdale Bl.	Corvallis	OR	94705	False
427-								

Figure 16-15. An auto-generated DataGrid

Defining Columns

With DataGrids, the content and formatting of each column is defined in a special nested <Columns> tag. Inside this tag, you add one column control tag for each column you want in your DataGrid. Columns are displayed from right to left in the grid, based on the order the column tags are listed in the .aspx file.

When you create a column, you have several possible choices. Each of these column types corresponds to a control class in the System.Web.UI.WebControls namespace.

- **BoundColumn.** This column displays text from a field in the DataSource.
- **ButtonColumn.** This column displays a command button for each item in the list.
- **EditCommandColumn.** This column displays editing buttons for each item in the list.
- **HyperlinkColumn.** This column displays its contents (a field from the data source or static text) as a hyperlink.
- **TemplateColumn.** This column allows you to specify multiple fields, custom controls, and anything you would normally put in an item template for a DataList control.

To create a DataGrid with these column types, set the AutoGenerateColumns property of your DataGrid to False. You can then add the columns using the Property Builder available in Visual Studio .NET or by writing the appropriate tags in the .aspx file. The latter approach is the best way to understand what is actually taking place, and it's similar to creating templates for a DataList.

The layout code for a sample grid is shown here:

```
<asp:DataGrid id=gridAuthor runat="server" AutoGenerateColumns="False">
  <Columns>
    <asp:TemplateColumn HeaderText="Author Name">
      <ItemTemplate><%# Container.DataItem("au_fname") %>
      <%# Container.DataItem("au_lname") %></ItemTemplate>
    </asp:TemplateColumn>

    <asp:BoundColumn DataField="city" HeaderText="City" />
    <asp:BoundColumn DataField="address" HeaderText="Address" />
  </Columns>
</asp:DataGrid>
```

Once the DataGrid is bound to the author information in the DataSet, a grid is generated, as shown in Figure 16-16.

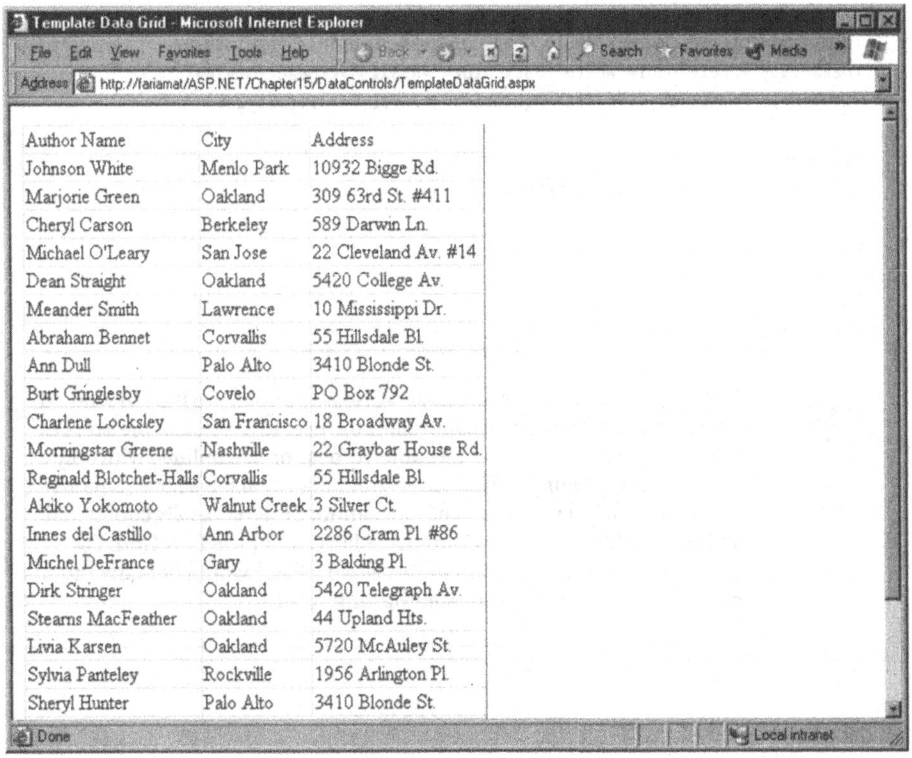
Template Data Grid - Microsoft Internet Explorer
File Edit View Favorites Tools Help
Search Favorites Media
Address http://fariamat/ASP.NET/Chapter15/DataControls/TemplateDataGrid.aspx
Author Name City Address
Johnson White Menlo Park 10932 Bigge Rd.
Marjorie Green Oakland 309 63rd St. #411
Cheryl Carson Berkeley 589 Darwin Ln.
Michael O'Leary San Jose 22 Cleveland Av. #14
Dean Straight Oakland 5420 College Av.
Meander Smith Lawrence 10 Mississippi Dr.
Abraham Bennet Corvallis 55 Hillsdale Bl.
Ann Dull Palo Alto 3410 Blonde St.
Burt Gringlesby Covelo PO Box 792
Charlene Locksley San Francisco 18 Broadway Av.
Morningstar Greene Nashville 22 Graybar House Rd.
Reginald Blotchet-Halls Corvallis 55 Hillsdale Bl.
Akiko Yokomoto Walnut Creek 3 Silver Ct.
Innes del Castillo Ann Arbor 2286 Cram Pl. #86
Michel DeFrance Gary 3 Balding Pl.
Dirk Stringer Oakland 5420 Telegraph Av.
Stearns MacFeather Oakland 44 Upland Hts.
Livia Karsen Oakland 5720 McAuley St.
Sylvia Panteley Rockville 1956 Arlington Pl.
Sheryl Hunter Palo Alto 3410 Blonde St.
Done
Local intranet

Figure 16-16. A DataGrid using templates

This example presents a few interesting details:

- Columns are the first level of nested items in the DataGrid tag, not templates.
- Predefined column are added by using the appropriate ASP.NET column control with the properties configured through tag attributes.
- For greater control, you can insert a TemplateColumn, which can contain a series of templates specifying the header, footer, and item appearance. The preceding example uses the item template to create a column that displays an author's first and last name together. Note that this is the only case where data binding expressions are required. The bound columns take care of data binding automatically when you specify the DataField attribute.

Styles

Styles can be configured in the same way they were for the DataList, through the Property Builder window or by using the Auto Format window to apply a themed set of matching styles. The example below adds three styles.

```
<asp:DataGrid id=gridAuthor runat="server" AutoGenerateColumns="False"
 BorderColor="#DEBA84" BorderStyle="None" CellSpacing="2"
 BackColor="#DEBA84" CellPadding="3" BorderWidth="1px">

   <FooterStyle ForeColor="#8C4510" BackColor="#F7DFB5"></FooterStyle>
   <HeaderStyle ForeColor="White" BackColor="#A55129"></HeaderStyle>
   <ItemStyle ForeColor="#8C4510" BackColor="#FFF7E7"></ItemStyle>

   <Columns>
      <!-- Column information omitted. -->
   </Columns>

</asp:DataGrid>
```

TIP One useful feature of the DataGrid is the ability to hide individual columns. For example, you could allow the user to set certain preferences that configure the display to be either verbose or streamlined with only a few important columns. This differs from the DataList, which contains all its information in a single cell and cannot be dynamically configured. To hide a column, use the Columns collection for the DataGrid. For example, gridAuthors.Columns(2).Visible = False would hide the third columns (columns are numbered starting at zero).

The Repeater

The Repeater is the simplest of the template controls, and it doesn't provide any extra support for selection, editing, or sorting. For that reason, the Repeater is mostly left out of the discussion in this chapter.

One interesting feature about the Repeater is that it doesn't apply any of its own formatting. In other words, the item template you define for a Repeater is simply repeated the required number of times on a page with no additional HTML tags. The DataList and DataGrid, on the other hand, supply a basic HTML table to delimit items. Consider the Repeater shown here:

```
<asp:Repeater id=repeatAuthor runat="server">
    <ItemTemplate><%# Container.DataItem("au_fname") %></ItemTemplate>
</asp:Repeater>
```

This Repeater creates the list of first names shown in Figure 16-17, which run together into a single long string of text.

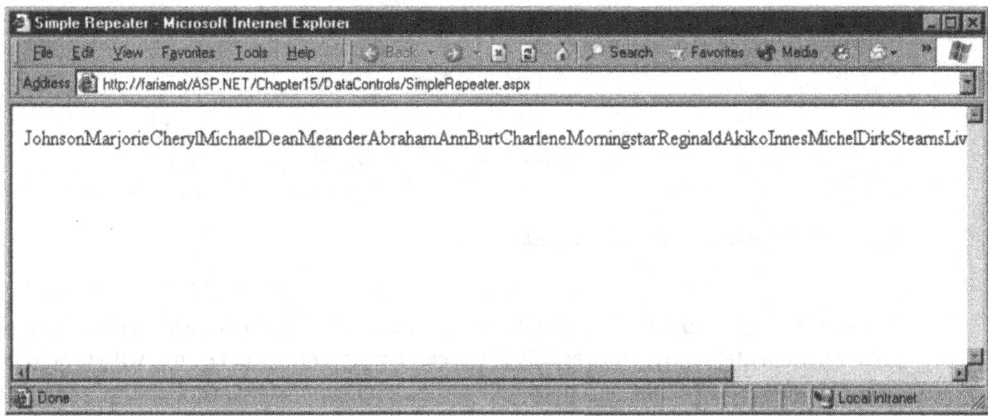

Figure 16-17. A no-frills repeater

To create a table in a Repeater, you must include the begin table tag (<table>) in the HeaderTemplate, a single table row tag (<tr>) in the ItemTemplate, and the end table tag (</table>) in the FooterTemplate.

```
<asp:Repeater id=repeatAuthor runat="server">
    <HeaderTemplate><table></HeaderTemplate>
    <ItemTemplate><tr><%# Container.DataItem("au_fname") %>
    </tr></ItemTemplate>
    <FooterTemplate></table></FooterTemplate>
</asp:Repeater>
```

This construct is underlined in red in the Visual Studio .NET editor because the <table> tag overlaps the template tags. However, it's perfectly valid for a Repeater, and it creates the desired output (Figure 16-18).

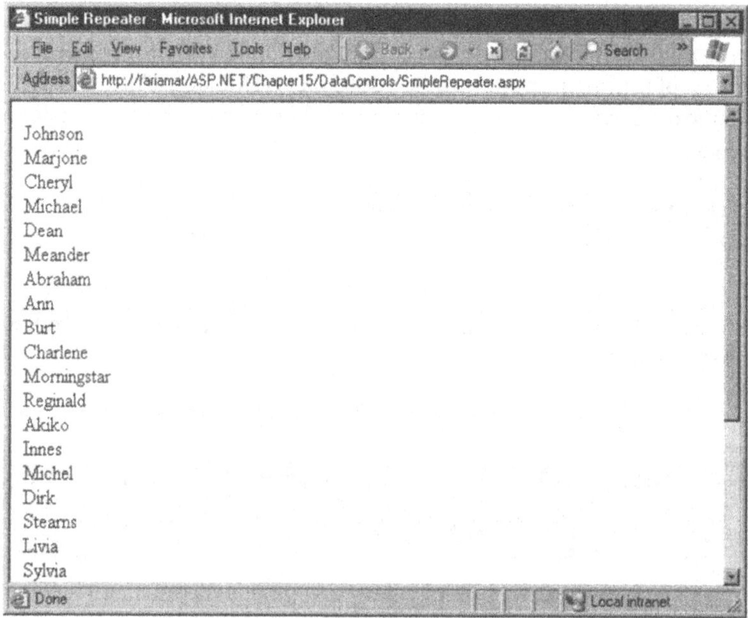

Figure 16-18. A repeater with an added table

Incidentally, this ability to overlap tags and the complete lack of any preset formatting gives the Repeater control its flexibility. You can create a repeater control with tags that span templates, which just isn't possible for the DataList or DataGrid. Usually, however, you'll prefer one of these more fully featured controls.

Styles and Templates

The DataList, DataGrid, and Repeater are described in detail in the MSDN Help. Tables 16-3 and 16-4 present an overview that compares what styles and templates each control offers. You should also examine the additional properties of the DataGrid and DataList controls. For example, both allow you to configure a default background color and cell padding, and hide or display the header and footer.

Table 16-3. Data Control Styles

DataList	DataGrid	Repeater
AlternatingItemStyle	AlternatingItemStyle	No predefined styles
EditItemStyle	EditItemStyle	
FooterStyle	FooterStyle	
HeaderStyle	HeaderStyle	
ItemStyle	ItemStyle	
SelectedItemStyle	SelectedItemStyle	
SeparatorStyle	PagerStyle	

Table 16-4. Data Control Templates

DataList	DataGrid (only supported by the TemplateColumn)	Repeater
AlternatingItemTemplate	HeaderTemplate	ItemTemplate
EditItemTemplate	ItemTemplate	AlternatingItemTemplate
HeaderTemplate	EditItemTemplate	SeparatorTemplate
ItemTemplate	FooterTemplate	FooterTemplate
SelectedItemTemplate		
SeparatorTemplate		
FooterTemplate		

Preparing Your List for Selection and Editing

Before you can use more advanced features with your template control, you need to straighten out a couple of details. First of all, you should move the code for querying the database and binding the grid to a separate procedure. You'll need to call this procedure frequently, so that you can update the grid when the user makes a change or applies a new sorting order. You also need to make sure that the grid isn't indiscriminately re-bound. For example, if you bind the grid in the Page.Load event handler at the beginning of every postback, you'll end up losing information about what button the user clicked or what item the user selected.

Ideally, your code should follow a pattern like that shown here, which splits the data binding and data retrieval into separate procedures:

```
Private Sub Page_Load(sender As Object, e As EventArgs) Handles MyBase.Load
    If Me.IsPostBack = False Then
        Dim ds As DataSet = GetDataSet()
        BindGrid(ds)
    End If
End Sub

Private Function GetDataSet() As DataSet
    Dim SQL As String
    SQL = "SELECT * FROM Authors"
    Dim con As New OleDbConnection(ConnectionString)
    Dim cmd As New OleDbCommand(SQL, con)
    Dim adapter As New OleDbDataAdapter(cmd)
    Dim dsPubs As New DataSet()
    adapter.Fill(dsPubs, "Authors")
    con.Close()
    Return dsPubs
End Sub

Private Sub BindGrid(ds As DataSet)
    gridAuthor.DataSource = ds.Tables("Authors")
    Me.DataBind()
End Sub
```

Selecting Items

"Selecting" an item generally refers to the ability to click a row and have it change color (or become highlighted) to indicate that the user is currently working with this record. At the same time, you might want to display additional information about the record in another control. With the DataGrid and DataList, selection happens almost automatically.

Before you can use item selection, you must define a different style for selected items. The SelectedItemStyle determines how the selected row or cell will appear. If you don't set this style, it will default to the same value as ItemStyle, which means the user won't be able to determine which row is currently selected. If you're using a DataList, you'll also need to define a SelectedItemTemplate.

To find out what item is currently selected (or to change the selection) you can use the SelectedItem property. It will be set to -1 if no item is currently selected. Also, you can react to the SelectedIndexChanged event to handle any additional related tasks. For example, you might want to update another control with additional information about the selected record.

Selection with the DataGrid

To start, define formatting for the selected item, as shown here. Remember, you can also set this style using the Properties window at design time.

```
<SelectedItemStyle Font-Bold="True" ForeColor="White" BackColor="#738A9C">
</SelectedItemStyle>
```

Next, you need to create a button the user can click to select the row. For a DataGrid, this means adding a bound button column with the CommandName property set to Select. You also need to specify the text that will appear in the button. Depending on the ButtonType you set, this button can appear as a hyperlink or a graphical push button.

```
<asp:ButtonColumn Text="Select" ButtonType="PushButton"
    CommandName="Select">
</asp:ButtonColumn>
```

When you compile and run the page, the button will automatically select the column and change the appearance when clicked (see Figure 16-19).

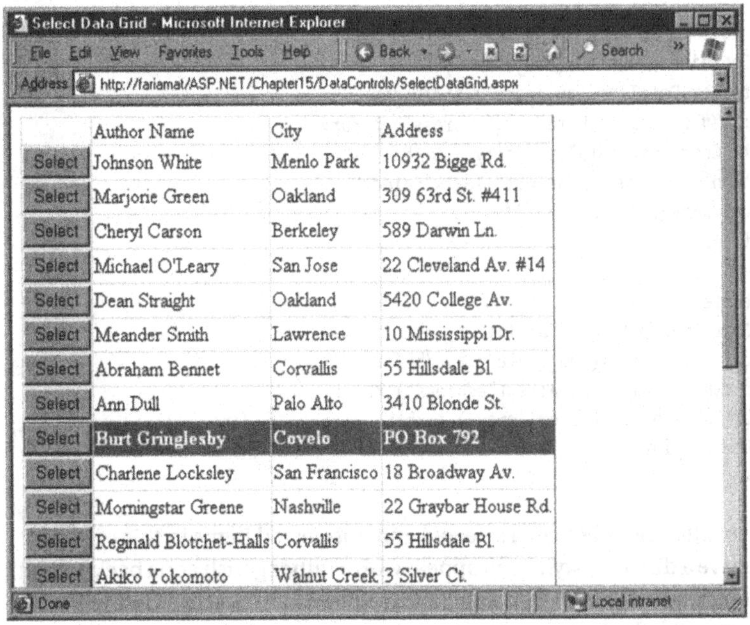

	Author Name	City	Address
Select	Johnson White	Menlo Park	10932 Bigge Rd.
Select	Marjorie Green	Oakland	309 63rd St. #411
Select	Cheryl Carson	Berkeley	589 Darwin Ln.
Select	Michael O'Leary	San Jose	22 Cleveland Av. #14
Select	Dean Straight	Oakland	5420 College Av.
Select	Meander Smith	Lawrence	10 Mississippi Dr.
Select	Abraham Bennet	Corvallis	55 Hillsdale Bl.
Select	Ann Dull	Palo Alto	3410 Blonde St.
Select	Burt Gringlesby	Covelo	PO Box 792
Select	Charlene Locksley	San Francisco	18 Broadway Av.
Select	Morningstar Greene	Nashville	22 Graybar House Rd.
Select	Reginald Blotchet-Halls	Corvallis	55 Hillsdale Bl.
Select	Akiko Yokomoto	Walnut Creek	3 Silver Ct.

Figure 16-19. DataGrid selection

Selection with the DataList

To start, define the SelectedItemStyle and SelectedItemTemplate. You'll also need to add a Select button of some sort to the ItemTemplate. A complete example is shown here:

```
<asp:DataList id=listAuthor runat="server" BorderColor="#DEBA84"
 BorderStyle="None" CellSpacing="2" BackColor="#DEBA84" CellPadding="3"
 GridLines="Both" BorderWidth="1px">

    <HeaderStyle Font-Bold="True" ForeColor="White" BackColor="#A55129">
    </HeaderStyle>
    <ItemStyle Font-Names="Verdana" ForeColor="#8C4510" BackColor="#FFF7E7">
    </ItemStyle>
    <AlternatingItemStyle BackColor="#FFE0C0"></AlternatingItemStyle>
    <SelectedItemStyle Font-Italic="True" BorderColor="Aqua"
                       BackColor="#FFC0FF">
    </SelectedItemStyle>

    <HeaderTemplate>
       <h2>Author List</h2>
    </HeaderTemplate>

    <ItemTemplate>
       <b><%# Container.DataItem("au_fname") %>
       <%# Container.DataItem("au_lname") %></b><br>
       Address: <%# Container.DataItem("address") %><br>
       City: <%# Container.DataItem("city") %><br>
       <asp:Button CommandName="Select" Text="Select"
            Runat=server ID="Button1"/>
    </ItemTemplate>

    <SelectedItemTemplate>
       <b><%# Container.DataItem("au_fname") %>
       <%# Container.DataItem("au_lname") %></b><br>
       Address: <%# Container.DataItem("address") %><br>
       City: <%# Container.DataItem("city") %><br>
    </SelectedItemTemplate>
</asp:DataList>
```

There are two differences between selected and unselected items in this example. Selected items have a different style (and appear with a rather garish aqua background) and selected items use a different template (appearing without a select button).

Unlike the DataGrid, the DataList doesn't natively recognize a special type of select button column. This means that you need to handle the DataList.ItemCommand event and make sure the corresponding row is selected. The ItemCommand event is fired whenever any button is clicked in a DataList. You need to examine either the source parameter or the e.CommandName property to determine what button was clicked.

```
Private Sub listAuthor_ItemCommand(source As Object, _
  e As DataListCommandEventArgs) Handles listAuthor.ItemCommand

    ' Was the select button clicked?
    If e.CommandName = "Select" Then
        ' Select the appropriate row.
        listAuthor.SelectedIndex = e.Item.ItemIndex
```

```
        ' Rebind the grid to update its appearance.
        Dim ds As DataSet = GetDataSet()
        BindGrid(ds)
    End If

End Sub
```

To select a row, all you need to do is set the SelectedIndex property of the DataList. The ItemCommand event makes it easy, by supplying the row that was clicked in the e.Item property. A DataList with a selected item is shown in Figure 16-20.

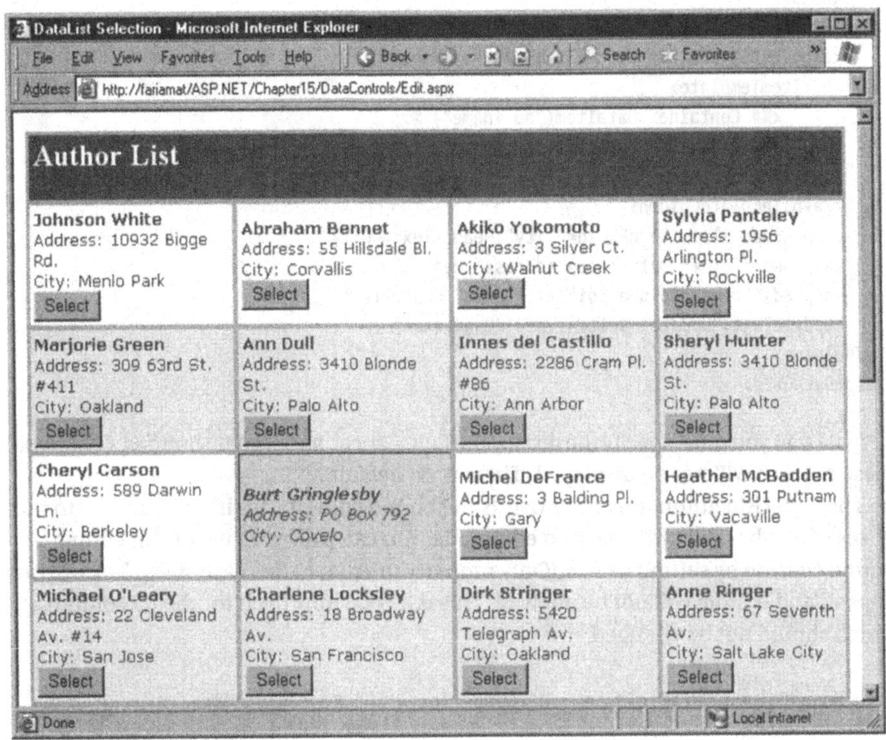

Figure 16-20. DataList selection

Editing Items

Editing an item in ASP.NET is similar to selecting it. The only difference is that you use the EditItemIndex property instead of SelectedIndex. You also need to add additional database code to change the information in the data source.

Editing with the DataGrid

The DataGrid uses a special type of column that automatically displays the edit buttons, called EditCommandColumn. Initially, this column displays an edit button for every row. Once this button is clicked, the corresponding row switched into edit mode, and the EditCommandColumn displays two buttons: Cancel and Update. Cancel returns the row to normal, while Update applies the changes and updates the database (with the help of your code).

The following is a sample DataGrid with an edit column:

```
<asp:DataGrid id=gridAuthor runat="server" AutoGenerateColumns="False" >
  <Columns>
    <asp:BoundColumn DataField="au_id" HeaderText="ID" />
    <asp:TemplateColumn HeaderText="Author Name">
      <ItemTemplate>
        <%# Container.DataItem("au_fname") %>
        <%# Container.DataItem("au_lname") %>
      </ItemTemplate>
    </asp:TemplateColumn>
    <asp:BoundColumn DataField="city" HeaderText="City" />
    <asp:BoundColumn DataField="address" HeaderText="Address" />
    <asp:EditCommandColumn EditText="Edit" CancelText="Cancel"
     UpdateText="Update" ButtonType="PushButton" />
  </Columns>
</asp:DataGrid>
```

Note that you must specify the text for the Edit, Cancel, and Update buttons. Otherwise, these buttons will not be displayed. There is no default text.

The DataGrid automatically converts the bound columns in the current row to text boxes when the user switches into edit mode. You can prevent a user from editing a bound column by setting its ReadOnly property to True. In this case, a text box will not appear, and editing will not be allowed. This is a good approach for the ID column, which should not be changed.

```
<asp:BoundColumn DataField="au_id" HeaderText="ID" ReadOnly="True" />
```

In this example, no edit controls will be provided for the first column (the author name), because it's defined as a special template column. In order for a template column to support edit mode, it must define an EditItemTemplate as well as an ItemTemplate.

```
<asp:TemplateColumn HeaderText="Author Name">
    <ItemTemplate>
        <%# Container.DataItem("au_fname") %>
        <%# Container.DataItem("au_lname") %>
    </ItemTemplate>
    <EditItemTemplate>
        <asp:TextBox Text='<%# Container.DataItem("au_fname") %>'
                     id="txtfname" runat=server /><br>
        <asp:TextBox Text='<%# Container.DataItem("au_lname") %>'
                     id="txtlname" runat=server /><br>
    </EditItemTemplate>
</asp:TemplateColumn>
```

You might also want to use TemplateColumns with special edit templates to allow the user to use controls other than text boxes to edit the data. For example, you could create a drop-down list box and fill it in the Page.Load event.

The EditCommand Event

To actually add some functionality to the edit buttons, you need to react to a few basic DataGrid events. To start, you must use the EditCommand event to put the appropriate row in your list into edit mode, as shown here:

```
Private Sub gridAuthor_EditCommand(source As Object, _
  e As DataGridCommandEventArgs) Handles gridAuthor.EditCommand

    gridAuthor.EditItemIndex = e.Item.ItemIndex
    Dim ds As DataSet = GetDataSet()
    BindGrid(ds)

End Sub
```

When you place a DataGrid into edit mode, it automatically provides a text box that allows the user to edit every field, as shown in Figure 16-21.

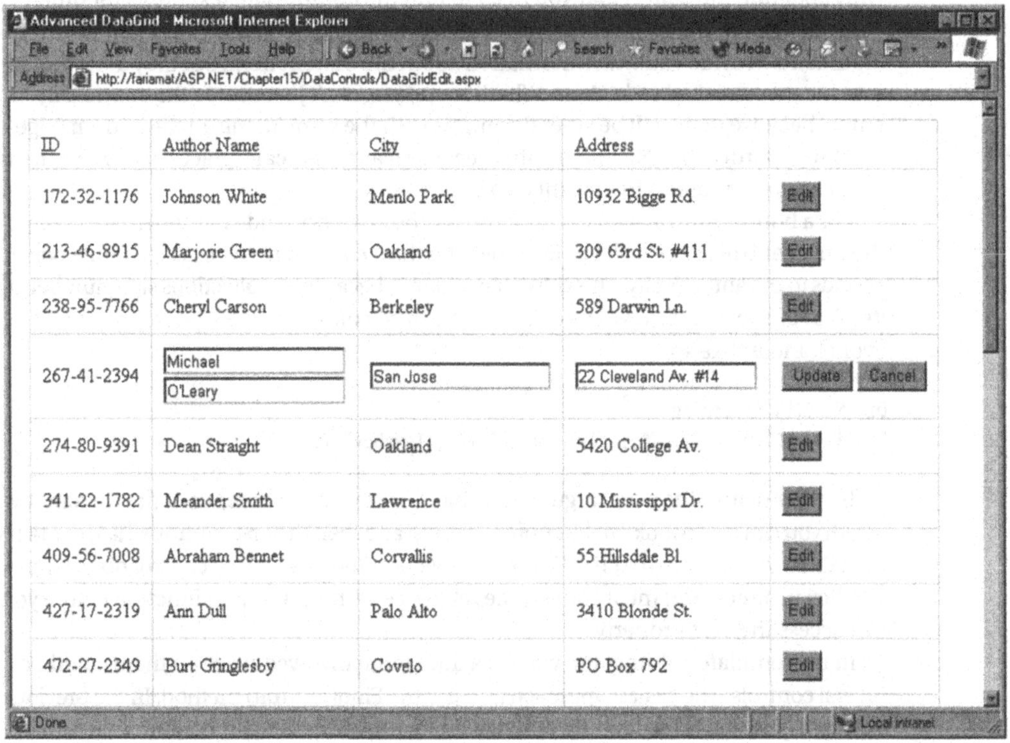

Figure 16-21. DataGrid editing

The CancelCommand Event

The next possible event is CancelCommand, which occurs when the user clicks Cancel to end editing. In this event handler, you need to switch off editing for the DataGrid and rebind the row.

```
Private Sub gridAuthor_CancelCommand(source As Object, _
  e As DataGridCommandEventArgs) Handles gridAuthor.CancelCommand

    gridAuthor.EditItemIndex = -1
    Dim ds As DataSet = GetDataSet()
    BindGrid(ds)

End Sub
```

The UpdateCommand Event

The UpdateCommand event is probably the most important event. It has two tasks: to apply the change to the database, and to switch the row out of edit mode, as the CancelCommand event handler does. You don't need to actually modify the DataGrid itself, because the new values will appear automatically when the data is retrieved from the data source and re-bound.

Updates are applied with an SQL statement and a Command object. The only trick with updating the data is that you need to find the appropriate text boxes (or other controls) where the new values have been entered. The UpdateCommand event arguments provide you with information about the current item, but they don't directly provide the actual edited values. What's more, you can't just access the controls by name, because there will be several controls with the same name on the current page—one for each row. (ASP.NET allows this because it automatically places each row into its own naming container to prevent a conflict.)

For a bound control, you can find the text box using an index number, because it's the only control in the cell. For example, the third column in the example table corresponds to the author's city. This cell is at position 2, because all collections start numbering items at 0. You can retrieve the cell from the third column in the UpdateCommand event handler like so:

```
Dim NewCity As String
NewCity = CType(e.Item.Cells(2).Controls(0), TextBox).Text
```

In other words, the event arguments object e provides a reference to the current row, which you can use to look up the appropriate cell and then the first control, which contains the edited value. Note that the Controls collection returns a basic control object, not a TextBox instance. You must convert the reference with the CType() function before you can access the Text property.

In the template column, the work is a little more involved because there could be several controls. The easiest approach is to use the FindControl() method. In the previous example, you could retrieve the author's first name from the first column as follows:

```
Dim NewFirstName As String
NewFirstName = CType(e.Item.FindControl("txtfname"), TextBox).Text
```

Now that you know the fundamentals for accessing cells and controls, you can combine these techniques with some standard ADO.NET code to create a fully functional update routine like the one shown here:

```
Private Sub gridAuthor_UpdateCommand(source As Object, _
 e As DataGridCommandEventArgs) Handles gridAuthor.UpdateCommand

    ' Create variables to hold new values.
    Dim NewFirstName, NewLastName As String
    Dim NewCity, NewAddress As String

    ' Retrieve the new values.
    NewFirstName = CType(e.Item.FindControl("txtfname"), TextBox).Text
    NewLastName = CType(e.Item.FindControl("txtlname"), TextBox).Text
    NewCity = CType(e.Item.Cells(2).Controls(0), TextBox).Text
    NewAddress = CType(e.Item.Cells(3).Controls(0), TextBox).Text

    ' Retrieve the author ID to look up the record.
    Dim ID As String
    ID = e.Item.Cells(0).Text

    ' Define the SQL Update statement.
    Dim Update As String
    Update = "UPDATE Authors SET "
    Update &= "au_fname='" & NewFirstName & "', "
    Update &= "au_lname='" & NewLastName & "', "
    Update &= "city='" & NewCity & "', "
    Update &= "address='" & NewAddress & "' "
    Update &= "WHERE au_id='" & ID & "'"

    ' Create the ADO.NET objects.
    Dim con As New OleDbConnection(ConnectionString)
    Dim cmd As New OleDbCommand(Update, con)

    ' Try to open database and execute the update.
    Try
        con.Open()
        Dim NumberUpdated As Integer
        NumberUpdated = cmd.ExecuteNonQuery()
        lblStatus.Text = NumberUpdated.ToString()
        lblStatus.Text &= " records updated."
    Catch err As Exception
        lblStatus.Text = "Error updating author. "
        lblStatus.Text &= err.Message
    Finally
        If Not (con Is Nothing) Then
            con.Close()
        End If
    End Try
```

```
        ' Cancel edit mode.
        gridAuthor.EditItemIndex = -1

        ' Rebind the grid.
        Dim ds As DataSet = GetDataSet()
        BindGrid(ds)

    End Sub
```

Editing with the DataList

DataList editing is very similar to DataGrid editing. You simply need to keep these points in mind:

- The DataList uses templates. Editing for a DataList item works the same as it does for a TemplateColumn in a DataGrid. This means that you need to explicitly create an EditItemTemplate and use Container.DataItem() statements to place information into text boxes or other controls.
- The DataList goes in and out of edit mode by setting the EditItemIndex, exactly like the DataGrid.
- The DataList raises EditCommand, UpdateCommand, and CancelCommand events, just like the DataGrid. The code you use in your event handlers is essentially the same.
- The DataList doesn't have predefined editing controls. That means you need to add your own buttons for editing. Usually, you accomplish this by adding the required edit button to the SeletecedItemTemplate or ItemTemplate, and the cancel and update buttons to the EditItemTemplate.
- The DataList does provide some built-in smarts. If you set the command name of your button to Edit, Update, or Cancel, the corresponding EditCommand, UpdateCommand, or CancelCommand event will be fired automatically, along with the more generic ItemCommand. This is different than record selection, where you needed to use the generic ItemCommand event and check the command name to find out what type of button was clicked.

The Templates

When you examine the DataList editing code, you'll recognize that it's very similar to the DataGrid and DataList selection examples. First you define the appropriate templates. The following example (see Figure 16-22) creates an edit button and allows editing for two fields (in the txtCity and txtAddress text boxes).

```
<asp:DataList id=listAuthor runat="server" Width="189px" Height="556px"
 BorderStyle="Ridge" BorderWidth="3px" CellPadding="5">
    <ItemTemplate>
        <b><%# Container.DataItem("au_fname") %>
        <%# Container.DataItem("au_lname") %></b>
        (<%# Container.DataItem("au_id") %>)<br>
        Address: <%# Container.DataItem("address") %><br>
        City: <%# Container.DataItem("city") %><br>
        <asp:Button CommandName="Edit" Text="Edit" Runat=server />
    </ItemTemplate>

    <EditItemTemplate>
        <b><%# Container.DataItem("au_fname") %>
        <%# Container.DataItem("au_lname") %></b>
        (<asp:Label Text='<%# Container.DataItem("au_id") %>'
                id=lblID runat=server />)<br>
        Address:
        <asp:TextBox Text='<%# Container.DataItem("address") %>'
                 id="txtAddress" runat=server /><br>
        City:
        <asp:TextBox Text='<%# Container.DataItem("city") %>'
                 id="txtCity" runat=server /><br>
        <asp:Button CommandName="Update" Text="Update" Runat=server />
        <asp:Button CommandName="Cancel" Text="Cancel" Runat=server />
    </EditItemTemplate>

    <SeparatorTemplate><hr></SeparatorTemplate>

</asp:DataList>
```

One interesting trick in this code is that the edit template stores the author ID in a label control so that it can be retrieved easily with the FindControl() method and used to look up the corresponding database record for the update. There are other possible approaches to retrieving the author ID of the record in edit mode. For example, you can set the DataList.DataKeyField property to the name of the key field (like "au_id"). You can then find the key for a given row using the DataList.DataKeys collection. This approach allows you to store a key that you don't want to display in the control. It's also quite a convenience—as long as you've set the DataKeyField property before filling the control, the DataKeys collection will be populated automatically from the data source.

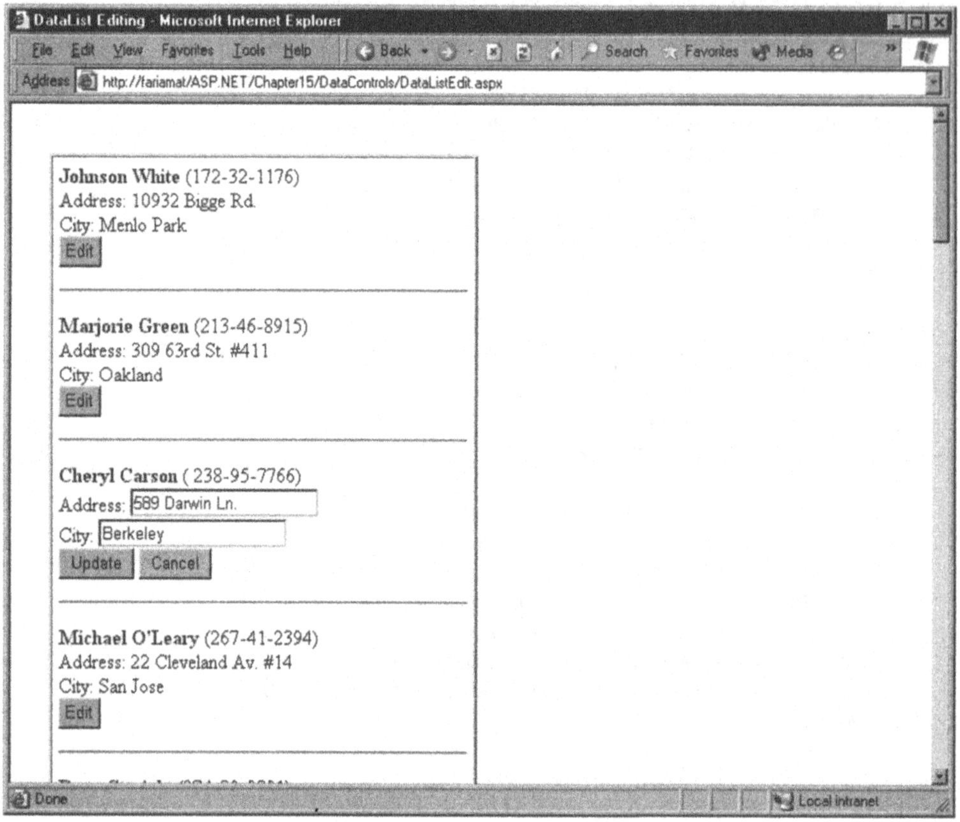

Figure 16-22. DataList editing

The Event Handler Code

Then basic event handler code is almost identical to the DataGrid example. The EditCommand event turns on edit mode:

```
Private Sub listAuthor_EditCommand(source As Object, _
 e As DataListCommandEventArgs) Handles listAuthor.EditCommand

    listAuthor.EditItemIndex = e.Item.ItemIndex
    Dim ds As DataSet = GetDataSet()
    BindGrid(ds)

End Sub
```

The CancelCommand turns off edit mode:

```
Private Sub listAuthor_CancelCommand(source As Object, _
 e As DataListCommandEventArgs) Handles listAuthor.CancelCommand

    listAuthor.EditItemIndex = -1
    Dim ds As DataSet = GetDataSet()
    BindGrid(ds)

End Sub
```

The UpdateCommand turns off edit mode after updating the database. In this case, you must use the FindControl() method to look up the values you need:

```
Private Sub listAuthor_UpdateCommand(source As Object, _
  e As DataListCommandEventArgs) Handles listAuthor.UpdateCommand

    ' Create variables to hold new values.
    Dim NewCity, NewAddress As String

    ' Retrieve the new values.
    NewCity = CType(e.Item.FindControl("txtCity"), TextBox).Text
    NewAddress = CType(e.Item.FindControl("txtAddress"), TextBox).Text

    ' Retrieve the author ID to look up the record.
    Dim ID As String
    ID = CType(e.Item.FindControl("lblID"), Label).Text

    ' Define the SQL Update statement.
    Dim Update As String
    Update = "UPDATE Authors SET "
    Update &= "city='" & NewCity & "', "
    Update &= "address='" & NewAddress & "' "
    Update &= "WHERE au_id='" & ID & "'"

    ' Create the ADO.NET objects.
    Dim con As New OleDbConnection(ConnectionString)
    Dim cmd As New OleDbCommand(Update, con)

    ' Try to open database and execute the update.
    Try
        con.Open()
        Dim NumberUpdated As Integer
        NumberUpdated = cmd.ExecuteNonQuery
        lblStatus.Text = NumberUpdated.ToString() & " records updated."
    Catch err As Exception
        lblStatus.Text = "Error updating author. "
        lblStatus.Text &= err.Message
    Finally
        If Not (con Is Nothing) Then
            con.Close()
        End If
    End Try
```

```
    ' Cancel edit mode.
    listAuthor.EditItemIndex = -1

    ' Rebind the grid.
    Dim ds As DataSet = GetDataSet()
    BindGrid(ds)

End Sub
```

Paging with the DataGrid

Often, a database search will return too many rows to be realistically displayed in a single page. If the client is using a slow connection, sending an extremely large DataGrid can take a frustrating amount of time to arrive. Once the data is retrieved, the user may find out that it doesn't contain the right content anyway, or that the search was too broad and there is no easy way to wade through all the results to find the important information.

The DataGrid handles this scenario with an automatic paging feature. When you use automatic paging, the full results are retrieved from the data source and placed into a DataSet. Once you bind that DataSet to the DataGrid, however, the data is subdivided into smaller groupings (typically of 10 or 20 rows) and only a single batch is sent to the user. The other groups are abandoned when the page finishes processing. To allow the user to skip from one page to another, the DataGrid automatically displays a group of pager controls at the bottom of the DataGrid. These pager controls look like a less-than (<) and greater-than (>) sign (see Figure 16-23).

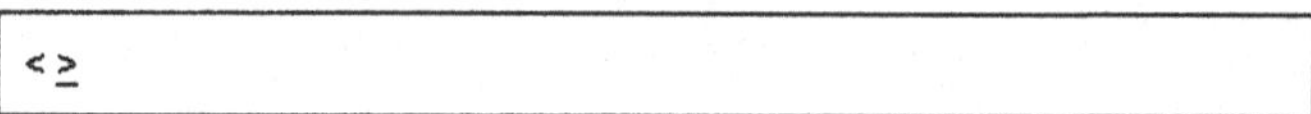

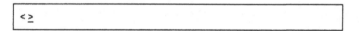

Figure 16-23. The hyperlinks for page navigation

Implementing automatic paging is quite easy. You just need to follow these steps:

- Set the AllowPaging property of the DataGrid to True, and specify a number of rows for the PageSize property. This ensures that the paging controls will be displayed at the bottom of the DataGrid.
- Configure the PagerStyle as desired. These settings determine the color and appearance of the pager row, and they also determine the type of pager controls. For example, you can set DataGrid.PagerStyle.Mode to NextPrev to show next and previous buttons for stepping through the pages (< and >) or to NumericPages to show a group of number buttons that allow the user to jump immediately to the specified page (1 2 3 4 5 ...).

- Handle the PageIndexChanged event, and use it to set the CurrentPageIndex and rebind the DataGrid. The value you should use for the CurrentPageIndex is provided in the event arguments.

Here's the code you need to use to respond to when the user navigates from one page to another in a paged DataGrid:

```
Private Sub gridAuthor_PageIndexChanged(source As Object, _
 e As DataGridPageChangedEventArgs) Handles gridAuthor.PageIndexChanged

    ' Set the new page.
    gridAuthor.CurrentPageIndex = e.NewPageIndex
    ' Rebind the grid.
    Dim ds As DataSet = GetDataSet()
    BindGrid(ds)

End Sub
```

Figure 16-24 shows the DataGrid with paging support.

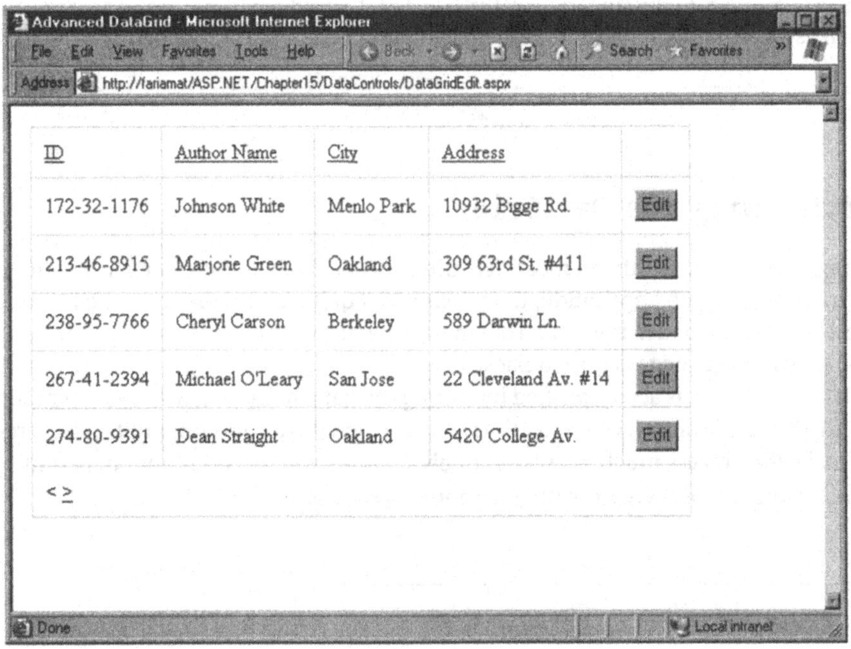

ID	Author Name	City	Address	
172-32-1176	Johnson White	Menlo Park	10932 Bigge Rd.	Edit
213-46-8915	Marjorie Green	Oakland	309 63rd St. #411	Edit
238-95-7766	Cheryl Carson	Berkeley	589 Darwin Ln.	Edit
267-41-2394	Michael O'Leary	San Jose	22 Cleveland Av. #14	Edit
274-80-9391	Dean Straight	Oakland	5420 College Av.	Edit
< >				

Figure 16-24. DataGrid paging

Paging and Performance

Keep in mind that when you use paging, every time a new page is requested the full DataSet is queried from the database. That means there is no performance increase on the database side. In fact, because the information is split into multiple pages, and you need to repeat the query every time the user moves to a new page, the database load actually *increases*. However, the client will see an improvement. Because any given page only contains a subset of the total data, the page size is smaller and will be transmitted faster, reducing the client's wait. The end result is a more responsive and manageable page.

There are ways that you can use paging without increasing the amount of work the database needs to perform. One option is to store the entire DataSet in server memory using the Session collection. That way, every time the user moves to a different page, you simply need to retrieve the data from memory and rebind it, avoiding the database altogether. However, you'll need to be extremely careful that you don't overburden the server. If multiple clients use your web application at the same time there could be dozens or hundreds of DataSet objects left in memory, waiting to timeout, and draining your web server performance. A much more scalable option is to store the DataSet in global cache memory, using the techniques described in Chapter 24. And as always, once you've decided to try a new technique, make sure you profile it in a real-world environment so that you can assess whether it helps or hinders your application performance.

Sorting with the DataGrid

Sorting is a standard feature in most rich grid controls, such as those seen in Windows applications. In a web application, the process isn't quite as easy, because the DataSet object isn't maintained in memory. That means that the data needs to be requeried and re-bound when the page is posted back.

DataGrid sorting is accomplished by sorting the data in the DataSet before binding it to the DataGrid control. However, the DataGrid includes a couple of built-in features that make the process much simpler. Namely, it allows you to use column hyperlinks (shown in Figure 16-25) to implement automatic sorting.

ID	Author Name	City	Address

Figure 16-25. The hyperlinks for column sorting

To use DataGrid sorting, you must specify the SortExpression property for every column that should allow sorting. The SortExpression is ultimately applied to the source table in the DataSet. It should name the column that you want to use for sorting (followed by a space and the letters DESC if you want to sort in descending or reverse order). If you want to sort by more than one row, you can separate field names with a comma. Remember, this is the database field name, not necessarily the name you use in the DataGrid header. A complete example is shown here:

```
<asp:datagrid id=gridAuthor runat="server" AutoGenerateColumns="False"
 AllowPaging="True" AllowSorting="True">
  <Columns>
    <asp:TemplateColumn HeaderText="Author Name"
                        SortExpression="au_fname, au_lname">
        <ItemTemplate>
            <%# Container.DataItem("au_fname") %>
            <%# Container.DataItem("au_lname") %>
        </ItemTemplate>
    </asp:TemplateColumn>

    <asp:BoundColumn DataField="city" HeaderText="City"
                     SortExpression="city"></asp:BoundColumn>
    <asp:BoundColumn DataField="address" HeaderText="Address"
                     SortExpression="address"></asp:BoundColumn>
  </Columns>
</asp:datagrid>
```

Next, set the AllowSorting property of the DataGrid to True. This ensures that the column headings appear as hyperlinks.

Finally, you must handle the SortCommand event. This event provides you with the name of the column that was clicked. You can use this information to build a sort expression and apply it before rebinding the data.

```
Private Sub gridAuthor_SortCommand(source As Object, _
 e As DataGridSortCommandEventArgs) Handles gridAuthor.SortCommand

    Dim ds As DataSet = GetDataSet()
    ' Apply the sort expression to the default view for the table.
    ds.Tables("Authors").DefaultView.Sort = e.SortExpression
    BindGrid(ds)

End Sub
```

You Can Also Implement Sorting for a DataList

You now know enough about sorting to implement it for a DataList control. In fact, the process is very similar, but requires a few extra steps. First of all, you would need to add your own sort buttons, either in the control or, more likely, as separate controls above or below the DataList. When one of these sort buttons is clicked, you would then programmatically set a sort expression for your DataSet and rebind the data. The only difference between a DataGrid and a DataList control is that the DataGrid provides a convenient set of sort buttons (the column headers) and allows you to specify the corresponding sort expression directly in the column tag.

Sorting and Filtering with the DataView

Although you may not realize it, when you bind to a DataTable, you actually make use of another object called the DataView. The DataView sits between ASP.NET web page binding and your DataTable. Usually it does very little aside from providing the information from the associated DataTable. However, you can customize the DataView so that it applies its own sort order or filter settings. That way you can customize the data that will be shown in the web page, without needing to actually modify your data.

You can create a new DataView object by hand, and bind directly to that DataView. However, every DataTable object has an associated default DataView, which is provided through the DataTable.DefaultView property. You can modify the settings of this DataView to change how the bound data will look.

Typically, there are two tasks that you'll perform with a DataView:

- **Sorting.** This allows you to modify the order in which rows will appear.
- **Filtering.** This allows you to hide some of the rows in the DataTable.

Both of these tasks can be performed by the database server, provided you craft the right SQL using the Order By and Where clauses. However, DataView filtering becomes very useful if you need to work the full, unfiltered data for one task, but you only want to display a subset of that data. It's also useful if you need to show data in several different ways.

Sorting

To apply a sort to bound data, you simply set the DataView.Sort property with a string with the corresponding sort information. DataView sorting uses the same syntax as the Order By clause in an SQL query. You add ASC after a column name for an ascending sort (with smallest values first), or DESC for a descending sort. The default is ASC.

For example, you might retrieve a list of authors sorted by ID using this SQL Select statement:

```
SELECT * FROM Authors ORDER BY au_ID ASC
```

The equivalent DataView sort expression is as follows:

```
ds.Tables("Authors").DefaultView.Sort = "au_ID ASC"
```

The DataView sorts according to the data type of the column. For example, string columns are sorted alphanumerically without regard to case (assuming the DataTable.CaseSensitive property is False). Numeric columns are ordered using a numeric sort. Columns that contain binary data cannot be sorted.

Filtering

To filter a DataView, you set a filter expression in the DataView.RowFilter property. The only rows that will be displayed are those that match the filter criteria. Filtering by column works similarly to the SQL Where clause.

For example, you might use the following SQL statement to select author records that don't have a contract, as follows:

```
SELECT * FROM Authors WHERE contract='false'
```

This translates into the ADO.NET code shown here:

```
ds.Tables("Authors").DefaultView.RowFilter = "contract='false'"
```

Here's a complete example that queries the database, applies a custom sort and filter expression, and then binds the grid:

```
' Create and fill a DataSet.
Dim SQL As String
SQL = "SELECT au_lname, au_fname, phone, address, state, contract FROM Authors"
Dim con As New OleDbConnection(ConnectionString)
Dim cmd As New OleDbCommand(SQL, con)
Dim adapter As New OleDbDataAdapter(cmd)
Dim Pubs As New DataSet()
adapter.Fill(Pubs, "Authors")
con.Close()

' Apply custom sorting and filtering.
Pubs.Tables("Authors").DefaultView.Sort = "au_lname ASC"
Pubs.Tables("Authors").DefaultView.RowFilter = "state='CA' AND contract='true'"

' Bind the DataSet, and activate the data bindings for the page.
gridAuthor.AutoGenerateColumns = True
gridAuthor.DataSource = Pubs.Tables("Authors")
Me.DataBind()
```

The filtered table will include 13 rows sorted by the author's last name. It's shown in Figure 16-26.

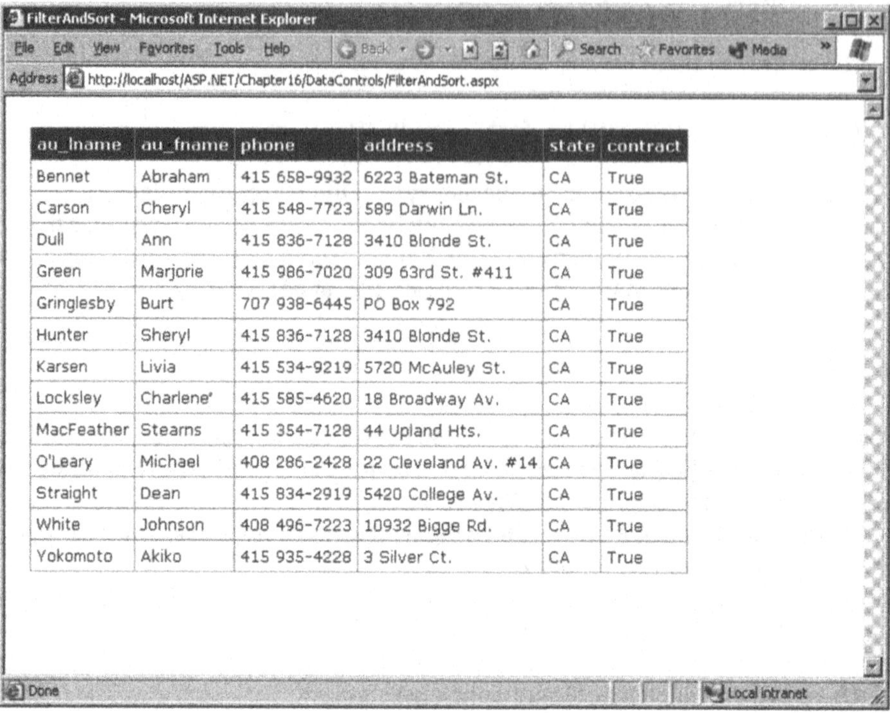

au_lname	au_fname	phone	address	state	contract
Bennet	Abraham	415 658-9932	6223 Bateman St.	CA	True
Carson	Cheryl	415 548-7723	589 Darwin Ln.	CA	True
Dull	Ann	415 836-7128	3410 Blonde St.	CA	True
Green	Marjorie	415 986-7020	309 63rd St. #411	CA	True
Gringlesby	Burt	707 938-6445	PO Box 792	CA	True
Hunter	Sheryl	415 836-7128	3410 Blonde St.	CA	True
Karsen	Livia	415 534-9219	5720 McAuley St.	CA	True
Locksley	Charlene'	415 585-4620	18 Broadway Av.	CA	True
MacFeather	Stearns	415 354-7128	44 Upland Hts.	CA	True
O'Leary	Michael	408 286-2428	22 Cleveland Av. #14	CA	True
Straight	Dean	415 834-2919	5420 College Av.	CA	True
White	Johnson	408 496-7223	10932 Bigge Rd.	CA	True
Yokomoto	Akiko	415 935-4228	3 Silver Ct.	CA	True

Figure 16-26. A sorted and filtered table

TIP You should never get into the habit of querying more data than you need and relying on the DataView filtering abilities. This forces the database server to do unnecessary work and transmit an unnecessarily large amount of information.

The Last Word

In this chapter you explored the details of the DataGrid, DataList, and Repeater. These controls contain a wealth of customizable features, and are far more flexible than previous data binding models. The ASP.NET data controls are also an excellent example of how the ASP.NET web control model allows you to focus on objects, not HTML.

CHAPTER 17

Files, Streams, and E-mail

THERE'S A GOOD REASON why you examined ADO.NET before considering simpler data-access techniques such as writing and reading to ordinary files. Traditional file access is generally much less useful in a web application than it is in a desktop program. Databases, on the other hand, are designed from the ground up to support a large load of simultaneous users with speed, safety, and efficiency. Most web applications will rely on a database for some features, but many won't have any use for straight file access.

Of course, enterprising ASP.NET developers can find a use for almost any technology. There's no doubt in my mind that if file access was left out of this book, many developers would be frustrated when they designed web applications with legitimate (and innovative) uses for ordinary files. In fact, file access is so easy and straightforward in .NET that it may be the perfect ticket for simple, small-scale solutions that don't need a full external database.

This chapter explains how you can use the input/output classes in .NET to read and change file system information, create simple text and binary files, and allow users to upload their own files. The chapter winds up with another important ASP.NET feature: e-mailing. You'll learn how you can send an e-mail message from your web server just by creating and configuring the right .NET object.

Files and Web Applications

Why is it that most web applications don't make direct use of files? There are actually several limitations:

- **File naming.** Every file you create needs to have a unique name (or it will overwrite another file). Unfortunately, there is no easy way to ensure that a file's name is unique. While relational databases provide auto-incrementing fields that automatically fill with a unique number when you create the record, files have no such niceties. Usually, you need to let the user specify the file name or fall back on some random number system. For example, you might create a file name based on a random number combined with the current date and time, or a file name that uses a GUID (globally unique identifier). With both of these approaches file names would be statistically unique, which means that duplicates would be extremely unlikely.

- **Multiuser limitations.** As you've seen in the ADO.NET chapters, relational databases provide features to manage locking, inconsistent updates, and transactions. Comparatively, the web server's file system is woefully backward. Opening a file generally locks other users out of it, and there is no possibility for more than one user to update a file at once without catastrophe.
- **Scalability problems.** File operations suffer from some overhead. In a simple scenario, file access may be faster than connecting to a database and performing a query. But when multiple users are working with files at the same time, these advantages disappear, and your web server may slow down dramatically.
- **Security risks.** If you allow the user to specify a file or path name, there's a chance the user could devise a way to trick your application into accessing or overwriting a protected system file. Even without this ability, a malicious or careless user might use an ASP.NET page that creates or uploads files to fill up your web server hard drive and cause it to stop working.

Generally, file access is best for smaller internal applications (such as those hosted on an intranet). In these situations, you can assume a smaller number of simultaneous users, as well as a set of trusted users who are less likely to try to battle your web server. Alternatively, you can force internal users to be explicitly authenticated using their network accounts before being allowed access to your site. Authentication is discussed in more detail in Chapter 25.

File System Information

Many of the considerations mentioned previously apply to web applications that create their own files. However, the simplest level of file access just involves retrieving information about existing files and directories, and performing typical file system operations such as copying files and creating directories.

ASP.NET provides four basic classes for retrieving this sort of information. They are all located in the System.IO namespace (and, incidentally, can be used in desktop applications in the exact same way that they are used in web applications).

- The Directory and File classes provide shared methods that allow you to retrieve information about any files and directories that are visible from your server. They are best suited for quick "one off" operations.
- The DirectoryInfo and FileInfo classes use similar instance methods and properties to retrieve the same sort of information. They are ideal for situations when you need to perform a series of operations or retrieve several pieces of information from the same file or directory.

In Chapter 4, you saw how a class can provide two different types of members. Shared members are always available—you just use the name of the class. To access an instance member, you need to create an object first, and then access the property or method through the object's variable name.

With the file-access classes, shared methods are more convenient to use because they don't require you to create the class. On the other hand, if you need to retrieve several pieces of information, it's easier to use an instance class. That way you don't need to keep specifying the name of the directory or file each time you call a method. It's also faster. That's because the FileInfo and DirectoryInfo classes perform their security checks once—when you create the object instance. The Directory and File classes perform a security check every time you invoke a method.

The Directory and File Classes

The Directory and File classes provide a number of useful methods. Tables 17-1 and 17-2 tell the whole story. Note that every method takes the same parameter: a fully qualified path name identifying the directory or file you want the operation to act on. A few methods, like Delete(), have optional parameters.

Table 17-1. Directory Class Members

Method	Description
CreateDirectory()	Creates a new directory. If you specify a directory inside another nonexistent directory, ASP.NET will thoughtfully create *all* the required directories.
Delete()	Deletes the corresponding empty directory. To delete a directory along with its contents (subdirectories and files), add the optional second parameter of True.
Exists()	Returns True or False to indicate if the specified directory exists.
GetCreationTime(), GetLastAccessTime(), and GetLastWriteTime()	Returns a DateTime object that represents the time the directory was created, accessed, or written to. Each "Get" method has a corresponding "Set" method, which isn't shown in this table.
GetDirectories(), GetFiles(), and GetLogicalDrives()	Returns an array of strings, one for each subdirectory, file, or drive in the specified directory (depending on which method you're using). This method can accept a second parameter that specifies a search expression (like "ASP*.*"). Drive letters are in the format "c:\".
GetParent()	Parses the supplied directory string and tells you what the parent directory is. You could do this on your own by searching for the \ character, but this function makes life a little easier.

Table 17-1. Directory Class Members (Continued)

Method	Description
GetCurrentDirectory() and SetCurrentDirectory()	Allows you to set and retrieve the current directory, which is useful if you need to use relative paths instead of full paths. Generally, these functions shouldn't be relied on and aren't necessary.
Move()	Accepts two parameters: the source path and the destination path. The directory and all its contents can be moved to any path, as long as it's located on the same drive.

Table 17-2. File Class Members

Method	Description
Copy()	Accepts two parameters: the fully qualified source file name and the fully qualified destination file name. To allow overwriting, add the optional third parameter set to True.
Delete()	Deletes the specified file, but doesn't throw an exception if the file can't be found.
Exists()	Indicates True or False whether a specified file exists.
GetAttributes() and SetAttributes()	Retrieves or sets an enumerated value that can include any combination of the values from the FileMode enumeration.
GetCreationTime(), GetLastAccessTime(), and GetLastWriteTime()	Returns a DateTime object that represents the time the file was created, accessed, or last written to. Each "Get" method has a corresponding "Set" method, which isn't shown in this table.
Move()	Accepts two parameters: the fully qualified source file name and the fully qualified destination file name. You can move a file across drives, and even rename it while you move it (or rename it without moving it).

The File class also includes some methods that allow you to create and open files as streams. You'll explore these features a little later in the chapter. The only feature that the File class lacks (and the FileInfo class provides) is the ability to retrieve the size of a specified file.

The File and Directory methods are completely intuitive. For example, consider the code for a simple page that displays some information about the files in a specific directory. You might use this code to create a simple admin page that allows you to review the contents of an FTP directory. Clients could use this page to review their documents and remove suspicious files (see Figure 17-1).

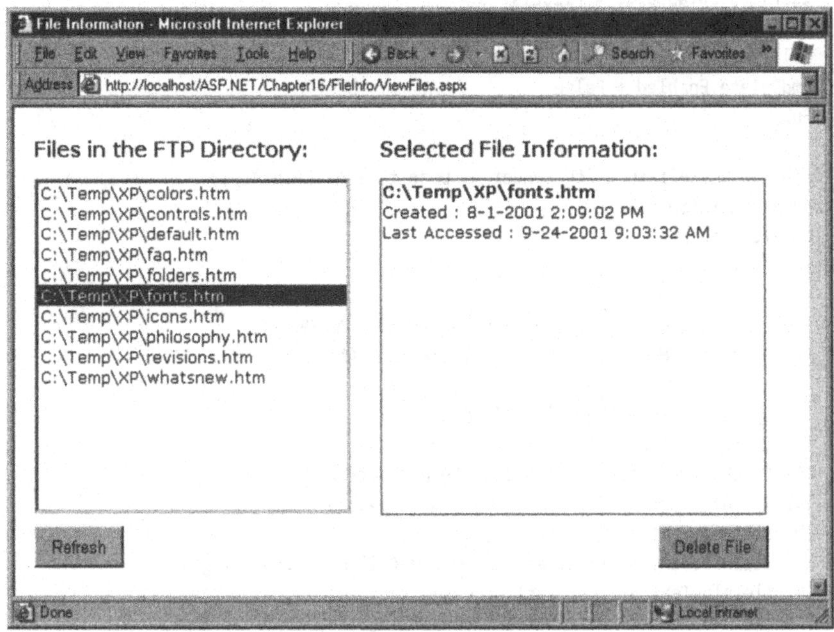

Figure 17-1. An admin page with file information

The code for this page is as follows:

```
' Import the namespace that includes the I/O classes.
Imports System.IO

Public Class ViewFiles
  Inherits Page

    Protected WithEvents lstFiles As ListBox
    Protected WithEvents cmdRefresh As Button
    Protected lblFileInfo As Label
    Protected WithEvents cmdDelete As Button

    Public FTPDirectory As String = "c:\FTPSite\Current"

    Private Sub Page_Load(sender As Object, e As EventArgs) _
      Handles MyBase.Load
        If Me.IsPostBack = False Then
            CreateFileList()
        End If
    End Sub
```

```
Private Sub CreateFileList()
    ' Retrieve the list of files, and display it in the page.
    ' This code also disables the delete button, ensuring the
    ' user must view the file information before deleting it.
    Dim FileList() As String = Directory.GetFiles(FTPDirectory)
    lstFiles.DataSource = FileList
    lstFiles.DataBind()
    lblFileInfo.Text = ""
    cmdDelete.Enabled = False
End Sub

Private Sub cmdRefresh_Click(sender As Object, e As EventArgs) _
  Handles cmdRefresh.Click
    CreateFileList()
End Sub

Private Sub lstFiles_SelectedIndexChanged(sender As Object, _
  e As EventArgs) Handles lstFiles.SelectedIndexChanged

    ' Display the selected file information.
    ' This control has AutoPostback = True.
    Dim FileName As String = lstFiles.SelectedItem.Text
    lblFileInfo.Text = "<b>" & FileName & "</b><br>"
    lblFileInfo.Text &= "Created : "
    lblFileInfo.Text &= File.GetCreationTime(FileName).ToString()
    lblFileInfo.Text &= "<br>Last Accessed : "
    lblFileInfo.Text &= File.GetLastAccessTime(FileName).ToString()
    lblFileInfo.Text &= "<br>"

    ' Show attribute information. GetAttributes can return a combination
    ' of enumerated values, so you need to evaluate it with the
    ' And keyword.
    Dim Attr As FileAttributes = File.GetAttributes(FileName)
    If (Attr And FileAttributes.Hidden) = FileAttributes.Hidden Then
        lblFileInfo.Text &= "This is a hidden file." & "<br>"
    End If
    If (Attr And FileAttributes.ReadOnly) = FileAttributes.ReadOnly Then
        lblFileInfo.Text &= "This is a read-only file." & "<br>"
    End If

    ' Allow the file to be deleted.
    If (Attr And FileAttributes.ReadOnly) <> _
     FileAttributes.ReadOnly Then
        cmdDelete.Enabled = True
    End If

End Sub
```

```
    Private Sub cmdDelete_Click(sender As Object, e As EventArgs) _
      Handles cmdDelete.Click
        File.Delete(lstFiles.SelectedItem.Text)
        CreateFileList()
    End Sub

End Class
```

Dissecting the Code . . .

- The CreateFileList() procedure is easy to code, because it uses the data-binding feature of the ListBox. The array returned from the GetFiles() methods can be attached to the list with no extra code.
- When the user chooses an item in the list, the control posts the page back immediately, and allows your code to refresh the file information.
- When evaluating the FileAttributes enumeration, you need to use the And keyword to perform *bitwise arithmetic*. The reason is that the value returned from GetAttributes() can actually contain a combination of more than one attribute.
- The code that displays file information could benefit from a switch to the FileInfo class. As it is, every method needs to specify the file, which requires a separate security check.

NOTE In order for this code to work, the account that is used to run the ASP.NET worker process must have rights to the directory you're using. Otherwise, a SecurityException will be thrown when your web page attempts to access the file system. You can modify the permissions for a directory, and control who is allowed to access it by right-clicking the directory, selecting Properties, and choosing the Security tab. Alternatively, you might find it easier to modify the account that ASP.NET uses so you don't need to change these permissions at all. For more information, refer to Chapter 2, which explains how to configure the account used for ASP.NET applications.

The DirectoryInfo and FileInfo Classes

The DirectoryInfo and FileInfo classes mirror the functionality in the Directory and File classes. In addition, they make it easy to walk through directory and file relationships. For example, you can easily retrieve the FileInfo objects of files in a directory represented by a DirectoryInfo object.

Note that while the Directory and File classes only exposed methods, DirectoryInfo and FileInfo provide a combination of properties and methods. For example, while the File class had separate GetAttributes and SetAttributes methods, the FileInfo class exposes a read-write Attributes property.

Another nice thing about the DirectoryInfo and FileInfo classes is that they share a common set of properties and methods. Table 17-3 describes the members they have in common.

Table 17-3. DirectoryInfo and File Members

Member	**Description**
Attributes	Allows you to retrieve or set attributes using a combination of values from the FileAttributes enumeration.
CreationTime, LastAccessTime, and LastWriteTime	Allows you to set or retrieve the creation time, last-access time, and last-write time, using a DateTime object.
Exists	Returns True or False depending on whether the file or directory exists. In other words, you can create FileInfo and DirectoryInfo objects that don't actually correspond to current physical directories, although you obviously won't be able to use properties like CreationTime and methods like MoveTo().
FullName, Name and Extension	Returns a string that represents the fully qualified name, the directory or file name (with extension), or the extension on its own, depending on which property you use.
Delete()	Removes the file or directory, if it exists. When deleting a directory, it must be empty or you must specify an optional parameter set to True.
Refresh()	Updates the object so it's synchronized with any file system changes that have happened in the meantime (for example, if an attribute was changed manually using Windows Explorer).
Create()	Creates the specified directory or file.
MoveTo()	Copies the directory and its contents or the file. For a DirectoryInfo object, you need to specify the new path; for a FileInfo object you specify a path and file name.

In addition, the FileInfo and DirectoryInfo classes have a couple of unique members, as indicated in Tables 17-4 and 17-5.

Table 17-4. Unique DirectoryInfo Members

Member	Description
Parent, and Root	Returns a DirectoryInfo object that represents the parent or root directory.
CreateSubdirectory()	Creates a directory with the specified name in the directory represented by the DirectoryInfo object. It also returns a new DirectoryInfo object that represents the subdirectory.
GetDirectories()	Returns an array of DirectoryInfo objects that represent all the subdirectories contained in this directory.
GetFiles()	Returns an array of FileInfo objects that represent all the files contained in this directory.

Table 17-5. Unique FileInfo Members

Member	Description
Directory	Returns a DirectoryInfo object that represents the parent directory.
DirectoryName	Returns a string that identifies the name of the parent directory.
Length	Returns a Long with the file size in bytes.
CopyTo()	Copies a file to the new path and file name specified as a parameter. It also returns a new FileInfo object that represents the new (copied) file. You can supply an optional additional parameter of True to allow overwriting.

When you create a DirectoryInfo or FileInfo object, you specify the full path in the constructor.

```
Dim MyDirectory As New DirectoryInfo("c:\Temp")
Dim MyFile As New FileInfo("c:\Temp\readme.txt")
```

This path may or may not correspond to a real physical file or directory. If it doesn't, you can always use the Create() method to create the corresponding file or directory.

```
' Define the new directory and file.
Dim MyDirectory As New DirectoryInfo("c:\Temp\Test")
Dim MyFile As New FileInfo("c:\Temp\Test\readme.txt")

' Now create them. Order here is important.
' You can't create a file in a directory that doesn't exist yet.
MyDirectory.Create()
MyFile.Create()
```

A Sample File Browser

You can use methods such as DirectoryInfo.GetFiles() and DirectoryInfo.GetDirectories() to create a simple file browser. Be warned that while this code is a good example of how to use the DirectoryInfo and FileInfo classes, it isn't a good example of security. Generally, you wouldn't want a user to find out so much information about the files on your web server.

The sample file browser program allows the user to see information about any file in any directory in the current drive, as shown in Figure 17-2.

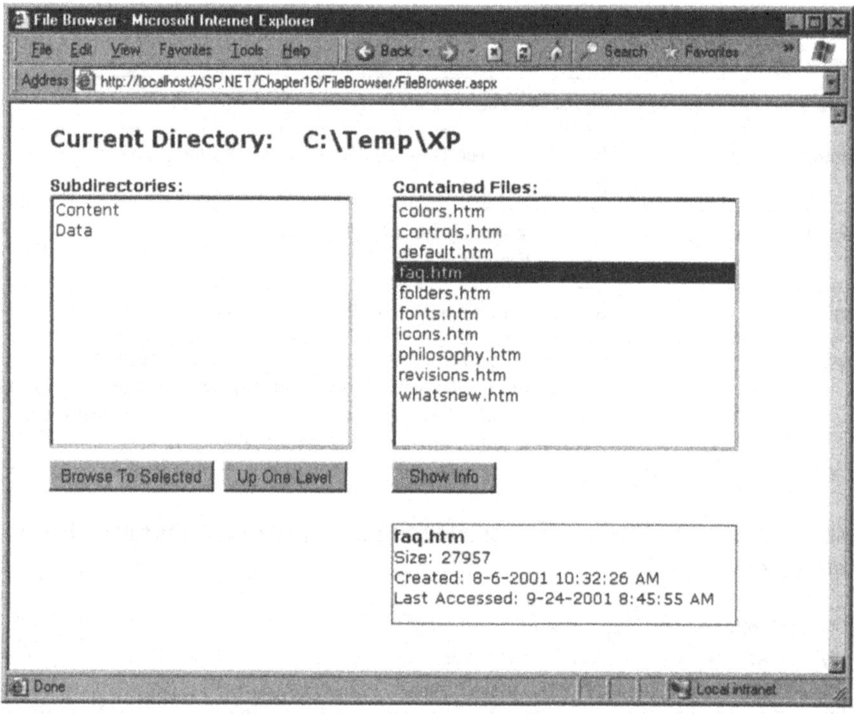

Figure 17-2. A web server file browser

```
Imports System.IO

Public Class FileBrowser
  Inherits Page

    Protected WithEvents cmdBrowse As Button
    Protected lblFileInfo As Label
    Protected lstDirs As ListBox
    Protected lstFiles As ListBox
    Protected lblCurrentDir As Label
    Protected WithEvents cmdParent As Button
    Protected WithEvents cmdShowInfo As Button

    Private Sub Page_Load(sender As Object, e As EventArgs) _
      Handles MyBase.Load
        If Me.IsPostBack = False Then
            Dim StartingDir As String = "c:\Temp"
            lblCurrentDir.Text = StartingDir
            ShowFilesIn(StartingDir)
            ShowDirectoriesIn(StartingDir)
        End If
    End Sub

    Private Sub ShowFilesIn(Dir As String)
        Dim DirInfo As New DirectoryInfo(Dir)
        Dim FileItem As FileInfo

        lstFiles.Items.Clear()
        For Each FileItem In DirInfo.GetFiles()
            lstFiles.Items.Add(FileItem.Name)
        Next
    End Sub

    Private Sub ShowDirectoriesIn(Dir As String)
        Dim DirInfo As New DirectoryInfo(Dir)
        Dim DirItem As DirectoryInfo

        lstDirs.Items.Clear()
        For Each DirItem In DirInfo.GetDirectories()
            lstDirs.Items.Add(DirItem.Name)
        Next
    End Sub
```

```
    Private Sub cmdBrowse_Click(sender As Object, e As EventArgs) _
      Handles cmdBrowse.Click
        ' Browse to the currently selected subdirectory.
        If lstDirs.SelectedIndex <> -1 Then
            Dim NewDir As String = lblCurrentDir.Text.TrimEnd("\")
            NewDir &= "\" & lstDirs.SelectedItem.Text
            lblCurrentDir.Text = NewDir
            ShowFilesIn(NewDir)
            ShowDirectoriesIn(NewDir)
        End If
    End Sub

    Private Sub cmdParent_Click(sender As Object, e As EventArgs) _
      Handles cmdParent.Click
        ' Browse up to the current directory's parent.
        ' The Directory.GetParent method helps us out.
        Dim NewDir As String
        If Directory.GetParent(lblCurrentDir.Text) Is Nothing Then
            ' This is the root directory; there are no more levels.
            Exit Sub
        Else
            NewDir = Directory.GetParent(lblCurrentDir.Text).FullName
        End If

        lblCurrentDir.Text = NewDir
        ShowFilesIn(NewDir)
        ShowDirectoriesIn(NewDir)
    End Sub

    Private Sub cmdShowInfo_Click(sender As Object, e As EventArgs) _
      Handles cmdShowInfo.Click
        ' Show information for the currently selected file.
        If lstFiles.SelectedIndex <> -1 Then
            Dim FileName As String = lblCurrentDir.Text.TrimEnd("\")
            FileName &= "\" & lstFiles.SelectedItem.Text
            Dim SelFile As New FileInfo(FileName)
            lblFileInfo.Text = "<b>" & SelFile.Name & "</b><br>"
            lblFileInfo.Text &= "Size: " & SelFile.Length & "<br>"
            lblFileInfo.Text &= "Created: "
            lblFileInfo.Text &= SelFile.CreationTime.ToString()
            lblFileInfo.Text &= "<br>Last Accessed: "
            lblFileInfo.Text &= SelFile.LastAccessTime.ToString()
        End If
    End Sub

End Class
```

Dissecting the Code ...

- The list controls in this example don't post back immediately. Instead, the web page relies on Browse To Selected and Show Info buttons.

- By default, directory names don't end with a trailing backslash (\) character. (For example, c:\Temp is used instead of c:\Temp\.) However, when referring to the root drive, a slash is required. This is because only c:\ refers to the root drive; c: refers to the current directory, whatever it may be. This can cause problems when handling file names because you don't want to add an extra trailing slash to a path (as in the invalid path c:\\myfile.txt). To solve this problem, the preceding code uses the String.TrimEnd() method, which removes the slash if it's present. Another approach would be to use the dedicated Path class in the System.IO namespace, which provides methods to manipulate strings that contain directory and file paths.

- The ShowFilesIn() and ShowDirectoriesIn() subroutines loop through the file and directory collections to build the lists. Another approach is to use data binding instead, as shown in the following code sample. Just remember that when you bind a collection of objects, you need to specify which property will be used for the list. In this case, it's the DirectoryInfo.Name or FileInfo.Name property.

```
' Another way to fill lstFiles.
lstFiles.DataSource = DirInfo.GetFiles()
lstFiles.DataMember = "Name"
lstFiles.DataBind()
```

Reading and Writing with Streams

The .NET Framework makes it easy to create simple "flat" files in text or binary format. Unlike a database, these files don't have any internal structure (that's why they're called "flat"). Instead, these files are really just a list of whatever information you want—the programmer's equivalent to a large canvas bag.

Text Files

You can write to a file and read from a file using a StreamWriter and a StreamReader—special classes that abstract away the process of file interaction. There really isn't much to it. You can create the StreamWriter and StreamReader classes on your own, or you can use one of the helpful shared methods included in the File class, like CreateText() or OpenText().

Here's an example that gets a StreamWriter for writing data to the file c:\myfile.txt.

```
' Define a StreamWriter (which is designed for writing text files).
Dim w As StreamWriter

' Create the file, and get a StreamWriter for it.
w = File.CreateText("c:\myfile.txt")
```

Once you have the StreamWriter, you can use the WriteLine() method to add information into the file. The WriteLine method is overloaded so that it can write many simple data types, including strings, integers, and other numbers. These values are essentially all converted into strings when they're written to a file, and must be converted back into the appropriate types manually when you read the file.

```
w.WriteLine("This file generated by ASP.NET")  ' Write a string.
w.WriteLine(42)                                 ' Write a number.
```

When you finish with the file, you must make sure to close it. Otherwise, the changes may not be properly written to disk, and the file could be locked open. Before closing it, it's a good idea to call the Flush() method to make sure all data is written to disk, as the StreamWriter will perform some in-memory caching to optimize performance.

```
' Tidy up.
w.Flush()
w.Close()
```

Finally, it's always a good idea to take a look at what you wrote in Notepad, while debugging an application that writes to files. Figure 17-3 shows the contents that are created in c:\myfile.txt with the simple code you've considered.

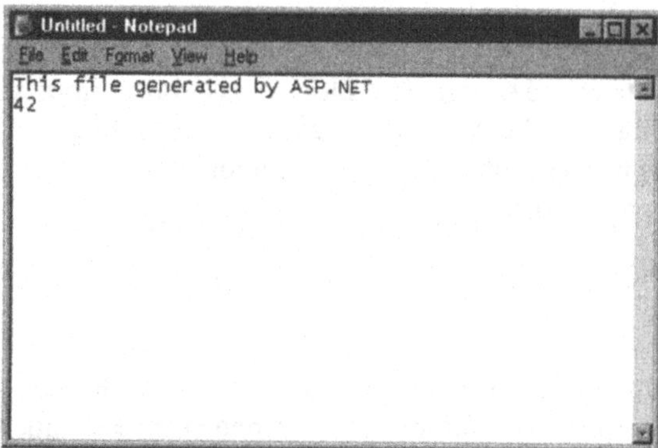

Figure 17-3. A sample text file

To read the information, you use the corresponding StreamReader class. It provides a ReadLine() method that gets the next available value, and returns it as a string. ReadLine() starts at the first line, and advances the position to the end of the file, one line at a time.

```
Dim r As StreamReader = File.OpenText("c:\myfile.txt")
Dim InputString As String
InputString = r.ReadLine()    ' = "This file generated by ASP.NET"
InputString = r.ReadLine()    ' = "42"
```

ReadLine() returns Nothing when there is no more data in the file. This means that you can read all the data in a file using code like this:

```
' Read and display the lines from the file until the end
' of the file is reached.
Dim Line As String
Do
    Line = sr.ReadLine()
    ' (Process the line here.)
Loop Until line Is Nothing
```

TIP In Chapter 10, you saw how you could create a cookie for the current user, which could be persisted to disk as a simple text file. This is probably a more common technique for a web application, but it's quite a bit different than the file access code you've looked at in this chapter. Cookies are created on the client side rather than on the server. This means that your ASP.NET code may be able to use them on subsequent requests, but they aren't useful for tracking other information that you need to retain.

Binary Files

You can also write to a binary file. Binary data uses space more efficiently, but also creates files that aren't as easy to read on your own. If you open a file in Notepad, you'll see a lot of extended ASCII characters (politely known as gibberish).

To open a file for binary writing, you need to create a new BinaryWriter class. The class constructor accepts a stream, which you can retrieve using the File.OpenWrite() method. Here's the code to open the file c:\binaryfile.bin for binary writing:

```
Dim w As New BinaryWriter(File.OpenWrite("c:\binaryfile.bin"))
```

.NET concentrates on stream objects, rather than the source or destination for the data. This means that you can write binary data to any type of stream, whether it represents a file or some other type of storage location, using the same code. In addition, writing to a binary file is almost the same as writing to a text file.

```
Dim str As String = "ASP.NET Binary File Test"
Dim int As Integer = 42
w.Write(str)
w.Write(int)

w.Flush()
w.Close()
```

Unfortunately, binary files require that you know the data type you want to retrieve. To retrieve a string, you use the ReadString() method. To retrieve an integer, you must use ReadInt32(). That's why the preceding code example writes variables instead of literal values. If the value 42 were hard-coded as the parameter for the Write() method, it wouldn't be clear if the value would be written as a 17-bit integer, 32-bit integer, decimal, or something else. Unfortunately, you may need to micromanage binary files in this way to prevent errors.

```
Dim r As New BinaryReader(File.OpenRead("c:\binaryfile.bin"))
Dim str As String
Dim int As Integer
str = r.ReadString()
int = r.ReatInt32()
```

NOTE There's no easy way to jump to a location in a text or binary file without reading through all the information in order. While you can use methods like Seek() on the underlying stream, you need to specify an offset in bytes, which involves some fairly involved calculations to determine variable sizes. If you need to store a large amount of information and move through it quickly, you need a dedicated database, not a binary file.

A Simple Guest Book

The next example demonstrates the file-access techniques described in the previous sections to create a simple guest book. The page actually has two parts. If there are no current guest entries, the client will only see the controls for adding a new entry, as shown in Figure 17-4.

When the user clicks Submit, a file will be created for the new guest book entry. As long as there is at least one guest book entry, a DataList control will appear at the top of the page, as shown in Figure 17-5.

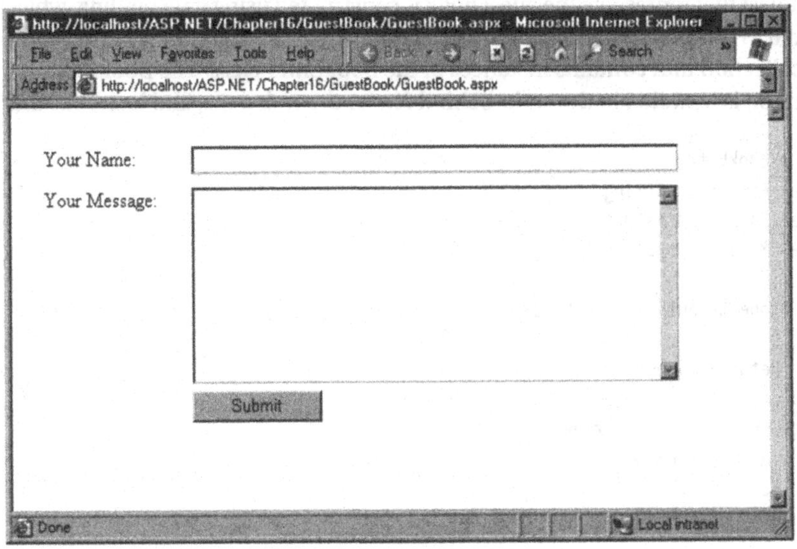

Figure 17-4. The initial guest book page

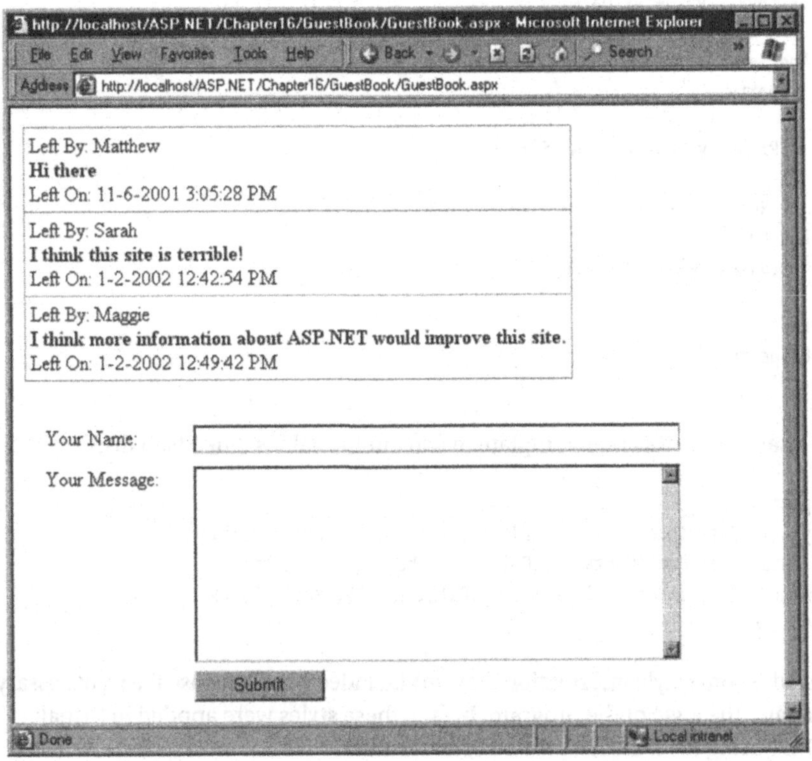

Figure 17-5. The full guest book page

The DataList that represents the guest book is constructed using data binding, which you explored in Chapters 15 and 16. Technically speaking, the DataList is bound to an ArrayList collection that contains instances of the BookEntry class. The BookEntry class definition is included in the code-behind file for the web page, and looks like this:

```
Public Class BookEntry
    Private _Author As String
    Private _Submitted As Date
    Private _Message As String

    Public Property Author() As String
        Get
            Return _Author
        End Get
        Set(ByVal Value As String)
            _Author = Value
        End Set
    End Property

    Public Property Submitted() As Date
        Get
            Return _Submitted
        End Get
        Set(ByVal Value As Date)
            _Submitted = Value
        End Set
    End Property

    Public Property Message() As String
        Get
            Return _Message
        End Get
        Set(ByVal Value As String)
            _Message = Value
        End Set
    End Property
End Class
```

The DataList uses this item template to fish out the values it needs to display:

```
<ItemTemplate>
  Left By: <%# Databinder.Eval(Container.DataItem, "Author") %><br>
  <b><%# Databinder.Eval(Container.DataItem, "Message") %></b><br>
  Left On: <%# Databinder.Eval(Container.DataItem, "Submitted") %>
</ItemTemplate>
```

It also adds some style information that isn't included here, because it isn't necessary to understand the logic of the program. In fact, these styles were applied in Visual Studio .NET using the DataList's Auto Format feature.

As for the entries, the guest book page uses a special directory (GuestBook) to store a collection of files. Each file represents a separate entry in the guest book. A better approach would usually be to create a GuestBook table in a database, and make each entry a separate record.

The code for the web page is shown here.

```
Imports System.IO

Public Class GuestBook
  Inherits Page

    Protected GuestBookList As DataList
    Protected WithEvents cmdSubmit As Button
    Protected txtMessage As TextBox
    Protected txtName As TextBox

    Private GuestBookName As String
    GuestBookName = Server.MapPath("GuestBook")

    Private Sub Page_Load(sender As Object, e As EventArgs) _
      Handles MyBase.Load
        If Me.IsPostBack = False Then
            GuestBookList.DataSource = GetAllEntries()
            GuestBookList.DataBind()
        End If
    End Sub

    Private Sub cmdSubmit_Click(sender As Object, e As EventArgs) _
      Handles cmdSubmit.Click
        ' Create a new BookEntry object.
        Dim NewEntry As New BookEntry()
        NewEntry.Author = txtName.Text
        NewEntry.Submitted = DateTime.Now
        NewEntry.Message = txtMessage.Text

        ' Let the SaveEntry procedure create the corresponding file.
        SaveEntry(NewEntry)

        ' Refresh the display.
        GuestBookList.DataSource = GetAllEntries()
        GuestBookList.DataBind()

        txtName.Text = ""
        txtMessage.Text = ""
    End Sub

    Private Function GetAllEntries() As ArrayList
        ' Return an ArrayList that contains BookEntry objects
        ' for each file in the GuestBook directory.
        ' This function relies on the GetEntryFromFile function.
        Dim Entries As New ArrayList()
        Dim GuestBookDir As New DirectoryInfo(GuestBookName)
```

```
        Dim FileItem As FileInfo
        For Each FileItem In GuestBookDir.GetFiles()
            Entries.Add(GetEntryFromFile(FileItem))
        Next

        Return Entries
    End Function

    Private Function GetEntryFromFile(ByVal EntryFile As FileInfo) _
      As BookEntry
        ' Turn the file information into a Book Entry object.
        Dim NewEntry As New BookEntry()
        Dim r As StreamReader = EntryFile.OpenText()
        NewEntry.Author = r.ReadLine()
        NewEntry.Submitted = DateTime.Parse(r.ReadLine())
        NewEntry.Message = r.ReadLine()
        r.Close()

        Return NewEntry
    End Function

    Private Sub SaveEntry(ByVal Entry As BookEntry)
        ' Create a new file for this entry, with a file name that should
        ' be unique.
        Dim Rand As New Random()
        Dim FileName As String = GuestBookName & "\"
        FileName &= DateTime.Now.Ticks.ToString() & Rand.Next(100)
        Dim NewFile As New FileInfo(FileName)
        Dim w As StreamWriter = NewFile.CreateText()

        ' Write the information to the file.
        w.WriteLine(Entry.Author)
        w.WriteLine(Entry.Submitted.ToString())
        w.WriteLine(Entry.Message)
        w.Flush()
        w.Close()
    End Sub
End Class
```

Dissecting the Code ...

- The code uses text files so you can easily review the information on your own with Notepad. Binary files could be used just as easily and would save a small amount of space.
- The file name for each entry is generated using a combination of the current date and time (in ticks) and a random number. Practically speaking, this makes it impossible for a file to be generated with a duplicate file name.

- This program doesn't use any error handling, which is an obvious limitation. Whenever you try to access a file, you should use a Try/Catch block, because all kinds of unexpected events can occur and cause problems.
- Careful design makes sure that this program isolates file writing and reading code in separate functions, such as SaveEntry(), GetAllEntries(), and GetEntryFromFile(). For even better organization, you could move these routines into a separate class or even a separate component. For more information, read Chapter 22.

Allowing File Uploads

Although you've seen detailed examples about how to work with files and directories on the web server, you haven't yet considered the question of how to allow file uploads. The problem with file uploading is that you need some way to retrieve information from the client—and as you already know, all ASP.NET code executes on the server.

Fortunately, ASP.NET includes a special HTML server control that can help you with this task. It's called HtmlInputFile, and it represents the <input type="file"> HTML tag. While it doesn't give you much choice as far as user interface is concerned (it's limited to a text box that contains a file name and a Browse button), it does accomplish what you need.

To create a working file upload page, you need three ingredients:

- You must set the encoding type of the form to "multipart/form-data." You can do this by setting a property of the HtmlForm control class, or you can just find the tag in your .aspx file and modify as shown in the following code sample. (If you're using Visual Studio .NET, you need to switch to HTML view to see this tag.) If you don't make this change, your uploading code will not work.

```
<form id="Form1" enctype="multipart/form-data" runat="server">
  <!-- Server controls go here, including the HtmlInput control. -->
</form>
```

- You need to add the HtmlInputFile control, either by hand as an <input type="file" runat="server"> tag, or using Visual Studio .NET. In Visual Studio .NET, you need to choose the File Field control from the HTML tab in the toolbox. After you drop the File Field onto your web, right-click it and select Run As Server Control to change it into a full-fledged ASP.NET server control.
- You need to add a button that triggers the upload and saves the file to the server's hard drive. (The Browse button functionality is hard-wired into the browser.) In the event handler for this button, you can use the HtmlInputFile.PostedFile.SaveAs() method to save the file to the server's hard drive.

```
FileInput.PostedFile.SaveAs("c:\newfile")
```

Figure 17-6 shows a complete web page that demonstrates how to upload a user-specified file:

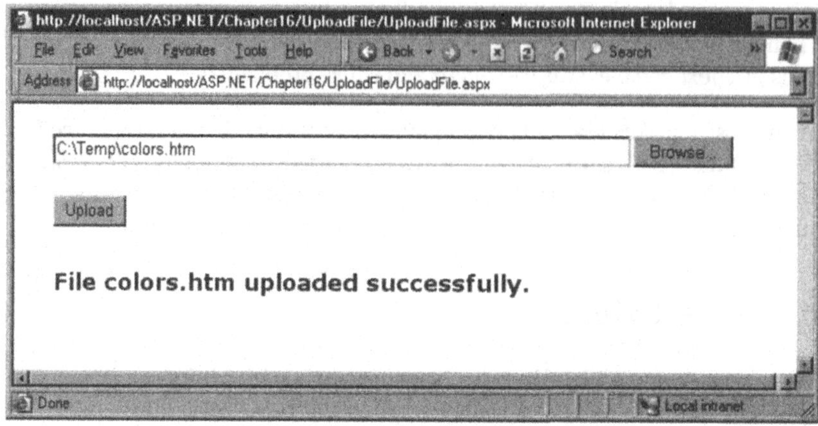

Figure 17-6. A simple file uploader

```
Imports System.IO

Public Class UploadFile
  Inherits Page
    Protected WithEvents cmdUpload As Button
    Protected lblInfo As Label
    Protected FileInput As HtmlInputFile

    Private Sub Page_Load(sender As Object, e As EventArgs) _
      Handles MyBase.Load
        ' Only accept image types.
        FileInput.Accept = "image/*"
    End Sub

    Private Sub cmdUpload_Click(sender As Object, e As EventArgs) _
      Handles cmdUpload.Click

        ' Check that a file is actually being submitted.
        If FileInput.PostedFile = "" Then
            lblInfo.Text = "No file specified."
        Else
            Try
                ' The saved file will retain its original filename,
                ' but be stored in the current server application directory.
                Dim ServerFileName As String
                ServerFileName = Path.GetFileName _
                  (FileInput.PostedFile.FileName)
                FileInput.PostedFile.SaveAs("c:\Uploads\" & ServerFileName)
                lblInfo.Text = "File " & ServerFileName
                lblInfo.Text &= " uploaded successfully."
```

```
        Catch err As Exception
            lblInfo.Text = err.Message
        End Try
    End If

End Sub

End Class
```

Dissecting the Code ...

- The saved file keeps its original (client-side) name. The code uses the Path.GetFileName() shared method, to transform the fully qualified name provided by FileInput.PostedFile.FileName and retrieve just the file, without the path.
- The FileInput.PostedFile object only contains a few properties. One interesting property is ContentLength, which returns the size of the file in bytes. You could examine this setting and use it to prevent a user from uploading excessively large files.

The Maximum Size of a File Upload

By default, ASP.NET will reject a request that's larger than four megabytes. However, you can alter this maximum by modifying the maxRequestLength setting in the web.config. This sets the largest allowed file in kilobytes. The following sample setting configures the server to accept files up to eight megabytes in size.

```
<?xml version="1.0" encoding="utf-8" ?>
<configuration>
  <system.web>
    <!-- Other settings omitted for clarity. -->
    <httpRuntime maxRequestLength="8192"
    />
  </system.web>
</configuration>
```

Be careful, though. When you allow an eight megabyte upload, your code won't run until that full request has been received. That means that a malicious server could cripple your server by sending large request messages to your application. Even if your application ultimately rejects these messages, the ASP.NET worker process threads will still be tied up waiting for the requests to complete. This type of attack is called a denial of service attack, and the larger your allowed request size is, the more susceptible your website becomes.

Sending Mail

I've saved the easiest for last. Sending mail in an ASP.NET application involves little more than creating a single object. Behind the scenes, the ASP.NET mailing features use the built-in SMTP service included with IIS (Internet Information Services). The technology is similar to the CDO component often used in traditional ASP development.

The first step when working with mail messages is to import the appropriate namespace, as follows:

```
Import System.Web.Mail
```

Next, you create a new MailMessage object, and set properties to identify the recipient, the priority, the subject, and the message itself. When entering the message, you can use standard HTML tags, provided you've set the BodyFormat property to MailFormat.Html.

```
Dim MyMessage As New MailMessage()
MyMessage.To = "someone@mycompany.com"
MyMessage.From = "ASP.NET Test Application <me@mycompany.com>"
MyMessage.Subject = "This is a test"
MyMessage.Priority = MailPriority.High
MyMessage.Body = "<b>Hello world (of email).</b>"
```

To send the mail, you use the shared Send() method of the SmtpMail class. You can also specify the SMTP server you want to use, which is required if you're behind a firewall that blocks direct SMTP traffic.

```
SmtpMail.SmtpServer = "localhost"
SmtpMail.Send(MyMessage)
```

Imagine the warm feeling you'll get when your application sends you its first e-mail, as shown in Figure 17-7.

You can also add an attachment to an e-mail message by creating a MailAttachment object. This class has two important properties: Encoding (which is set to MailEncoding.UUEncode by default), and Filename, which identifies a file on the server. You can set the Filename property in the MailAttachment constructor.

```
Dim MyAttachment As New MailAttachment("c:\Temp\SampleFile.rtf")
```

You then link the MailAttachment to a MailMessage using the Attachments collection.

```
MyMessage.Attachments.Add(MyAttachment)
```

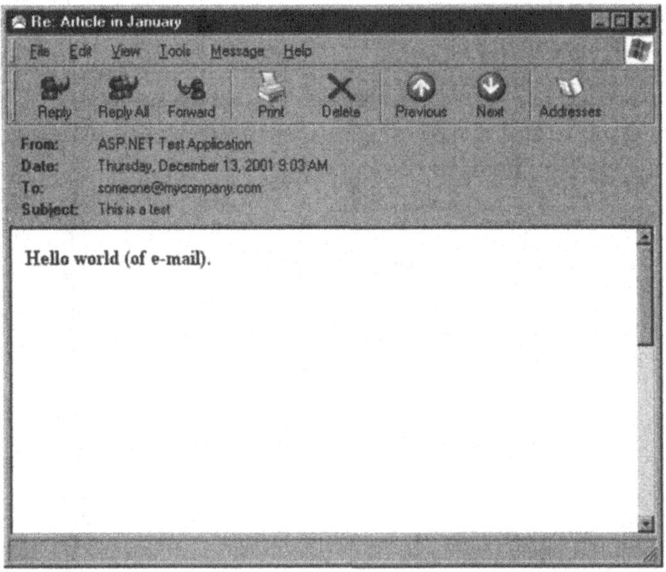

Figure 17-7. An e-mail delivered from your web application

The only catch is that in order to use this mail ability, you'll need to have a local SMTP server or relay server on your network. To configure your SMTP settings, fire up IIS Manager again, and select Default SMTP Server under your computer name (or the name of the computer that is the SMTP server). Right-click, and select properties. The important configuration details are under the Delivery tab, although server configuration is beyond the scope of this book. Instead, consult a good guide for IIS administration.

NOTE The SMTP service sends mail—it doesn't receive it. Unfortunately, .NET doesn't include any classes for retrieving e-mail from a mail account, although there are third-party components that fill this gap.

An Issue Reporting Form

A common place where ASP.NET's mail features can be put to use is the common issue/comment reporting form. Sometimes these pages are connected directly to a database. In other cases, the page might send an e-mail to a technical support address, as shown in Figure 17-8.

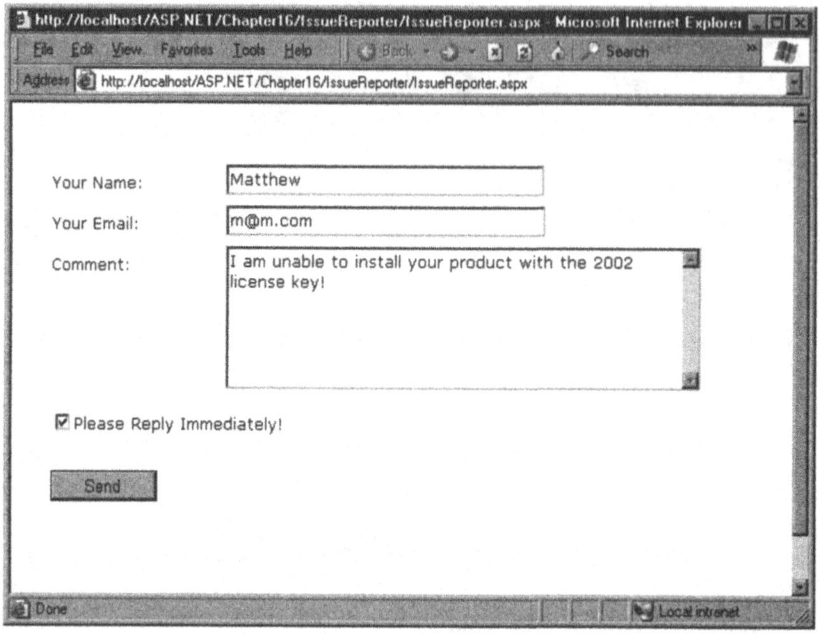

Figure 17-8. Reporting an issue

```
Imports System.Web.Mail
Public Class IssueReporter
  Inherits Page

    Protected chkPriority As CheckBox
    Protected txtName As TextBox
    Protected txtSender As TextBox
    Protected txtComment As TextBox
    Protected WithEvents cmdSend As Button
    Protected lblResult As Label

    Private Sub cmdSend_Click(sender As Object, e As EventArgs) _
      Handles cmdSend.Click
        ' Create the message.
        Dim Msg As New MailMessage()
        Msg.Subject = "Issue Report"
        Msg.Body = "Submitted By: " & txtName.Text & Chr(10)
        Msg.Body &= txtComment.Text
        Msg.From = txtSender.Text
        If chkPriority.Checked Then Msg.Priority = MailPriority.High

        ' Send the message.
        SmtpMail.SmtpServer = "localhost"
        SmtpMail.Send(Msg)
    End Sub

End Class
```

TIP When specifying the "From" address of a message, make sure you include a valid e-mail address. If you want to include the sender's name, use the format "Sender Name <senderaddress@somewhere.com>". IIS may refuse to send messages that don't include reply addresses, which leads to disappearing e-mail.

E-mail Can Be Used for Automatic Logging

In the previous example, you saw how a customer can fill out a form that triggers the sending of an e-mail. Many sites take this idea a step further, and automatically report on problems with the web application by sending an e-mail to an administrator's account. This is an extremely interesting technique, but requires a few considerations:

- Don't attach an automatic e-mail feature to a noncritical error or a known issue that occurs occasionally. In these cases, it's better to log some sort of aggregate information to a database table that can be examined later, rather than clogging up an important e-mail account.
- Will someone actually read the mail? If the messages aren't being checked, they do little good.
- In some cases, an error could occur with the e-mail service, thereby preventing this technique from working. In these situations, an even simpler error-logging method is better. Consider the Windows event log, as described in Chapter 11.

The Last Word

Although databases and websites make a perfect fit, there's nothing that prevents you from using the classes in the .NET Framework to access other types of data, including files. In fact, the code you use to interact with the file system is exactly the same as what you would use in a desktop application, or any .NET program. Thanks to the .NET Framework, common programming problems can finally be solved in the same way, regardless of the type of application you're creating.

CHAPTER 18

Using XML

XML IS WOVEN right into the fabric of .NET, and it powers key parts of ASP.NET technology. In this chapter, you'll learn why XML plays a part in every ASP.NET web application—whether you realize it or not.

You'll also learn how you can create and read XML documents on your own, by using the classes of the .NET library. Along the way, I'll sort through some of the near-hysteric XML hype and consider what practical role XML can play in a web application. You may find that ASP.NET's low-level XML support is all you need, and decide that you don't want to manually create and manipulate XML data. On the other hand, you might want to use the XML classes to communicate with other applications and components, or just as a convenient replacement for simple text files. This chapter assesses all these issues realistically—which is a major departure from most of today's ASP.NET articles, seminars, and books. We'll begin with a whirlwind introduction to XML that explains how it works, and why it exists.

XML's Hidden Role in .NET

The most useful place for XML isn't in your web applications, but in the infrastructure that supports them. Microsoft has taken this philosophy to heart with ASP.NET. Instead of providing separate components that allow you to add in a basic XML parser or similar functionality, ASP.NET uses XML quietly behind the scenes to accomplish a wide range of different tasks. If you don't know much about XML yet, the first thing you should realize is that you're already using it.

Configuration Files

ASP.NET stores settings in a human-readable XML format using configuration files like machine.config and web.config, which were first introduced in Chapter 5. Arguably, a plain text file could be just as efficient. However, that would force the designers of the ASP.NET platform to create their own proprietary format, which developers would then need to learn. XML provides an all-purpose syntax for storing any data in a customized, yet consistent and standardized way using tags. Anyone who understands XML will immediately understand how the ASP.NET configuration files are organized.

ADO.NET Data Access

The ADO.NET DataSet can represent any data as an XML document, without requiring an error-prone conversion step. This has a number of interesting consequences. One change (which you won't see in this book) occurs with distributed systems, which use multiple components on different computers that communicate over a network. With ADO, these components would exchange data in a proprietary binary format, which would have difficulty crossing firewall boundaries. With ADO.NET, these components exchange pure text-based XML. This XML data exchange could even be extended to components on another operating system or in a non-Microsoft development language. All they need to do is be able to read XML.

As an ASP.NET developer, you're more likely to see some interesting but less useful XML features with ADO.NET. For example, you can store the results of a database query in an XML file, and retrieve it later in the same page or in another application. You can also use other XML standards, like XSLT (XML transformations) and XPath (XML searching) with the data in a DataSet.

Web Services

Web services, which are described in the fourth part of this book, are one of the best examples of integrated XML in ASP.NET. In order to create or use a web service in a .NET program, you don't actually have to understand anything about XML, because the .NET Framework handles all the details for you. However, because web services are built on these accepted standards, other programmers can develop clients for your web services in completely different programming languages, operating systems, and computer platforms, with little extra work. In fact, they can even use a competitor's toolkit to create a web service that you can call from a .NET application! Cross-platform programming is clearly one of XML's key selling points.

Anywhere Miscellaneous Data Is Stored

Just when you think you've identified everywhere that XML markup is used, you'll find it appearing somewhere new. You'll find XML when you write an advertisement file defining the content for the AdRotator control, or if you use .NET serialization to write an object to a file. The fact that these formats use XML probably won't change the way they work, but it does open up other possibilities for integrating the data with other applications and tools. It's also one more example that the developers of the .NET Framework have embraced XML in unprecedented ways, abandoning Microsoft's traditional philosophy of closed standards and proprietary technologies.

XML Explained

The basic premise of XML is fairly simple, although the possible implementations of it (and the numerous extensions to it) can get quite complex. XML is designed as an all-purpose format for organizing data. In almost every case, when you decide to use XML, you're deciding to store data in a standardized way, rather than creating your own new (and to other developers, unfamiliar) format. The actual location of this data—in memory, in a file, in a network stream—is irrelevant.

The best way to understand the role XML plays is to consider the evolution of a simple file format *without* XML. For example, consider a simple program that stores product items as a list in a file. When you first create this program, you decide that it will store three pieces of product information (ID, name, and price), and that you'll use a simple text file format for easy debugging and testing. The file format you use looks like this:

```
1
Chair
49.33
2
Car
43399.55
3Fresh Fruit Basket
49.99
```

This is the sort of format that you might create by using .NET classes like the StreamWriter. It's easy to work with—you just write all the information, in order, from top to bottom. Of course, it's a fairly fragile format. If you decide to store an extra piece of information in the file (such as a flag that indicates if an item is available), your old code won't work. Instead you might need to resort to adding a header that indicates the version of the file.

```
SuperProProductList
Version 2.0
1
Chair
49.33
True
2
Car
43399.55
True
3
Fresh Fruit Basket
49.99
False
```

Now, you could check the file version when you open it and use different file reading code appropriately. Unfortunately, as you add more and more possible versions, the file reading code will become incredibly tangled, and you may accidentally break compatibility with one of the earlier file formats without realizing it. A better approach would be to create a file format that indicates where every product record starts and stops. Your code would then just set some appropriate defaults if it finds missing information in an older file format.

Here's a relatively crude solution that improves the SuperProProductList by adding a special sequence of characters (##Start##) to show where each new record begins.

```
SuperProProductList
Version 3.0
```

```
##Start##
1
Chair
49.33
True
3
##Start##
2
Car
43399.55
True
3
##Start##
3
Fresh Fruit Basket
49.99
False
4
```

All in all, this isn't a bad effort. Unfortunately, you may as well use the binary file format at this point—the text file is becoming hard to read, and it's even harder to guess what piece of information each value represents. On the code side, you'll also need some basic error-checking abilities of your own. For example, you should make your code able to skip over accidentally entered blank lines, detect a missing ##Start## tag, and so on, just to provide a basic level of protection.

The central problem with this homegrown solution is that you're reinventing the wheel. While you're trying to write basic file-access code and create a reasonably flexible file format for a simple task, other programmers around the world are creating their own private, ad hoc solutions. Even if your program works fine and you can understand it, other programmers will definitely not find it easy.

Improving the List with XML

This is where XML comes into the picture. XML is an all-purpose way to identify any type of data using tags. These tags use the same sort of format found in an HTML file, but while HTML tags indicate formatting, XML tags indicate content. (Because an XML file is just about data, there is no standardized way to display it in a browser.)

The SuperProProductList could use the following, clearer XML syntax:

```
<?xml version="1.0"?>
<SuperProProductList>
    <Product>
        <ID>1</ID>
        <Name>Chair</Name>
        <Price>49.33</Price>
        <Available>True</Available>
        <Status>3</Status>
    </Product>
    <Product>
        <ID>2</ID>
```

```
        <Name>Car</Name>
        <Price>43399.55</Price>
        <Available>True</Available>
        <Status>3</Status>
    </Product>
    <Product>
        <ID>3</ID>
        <Name>Fresh Fruit Basket</Name>
        <Price>49.99</Price>
        <Available>False</Available>
        <Status>4</Status>
    </Product>
</SuperProProductList>
```

This format is clearly readable. Every product item is enclosed in a <Product> tag, and every piece of information has its own tag with an appropriate name. Tags are nested several layers deep to show relationships. Essentially, XML provides the basic tag syntax, and you (the programmer) define the tags that you want to use. That's why XML is often described as a *meta-language*—it's a language you use to create your own language. In the SuperProProductList example, this custom XML language defines tags like <Product>, <ID>, <Name>, and so on.

Best of all, when you read this XML document in most programming languages (including those in the .NET Framework), you can use XML parsers to make your life easier. In other words, you don't need to worry about detecting where a tag starts and stops, collapsing whitespace, and identifying attributes (although you do need to worry about capitalization, because XML is case-sensitive). Instead, you can just read the file into some helpful XML data objects that make navigating through the entire document much easier.

XML Files vs. Databases

XML can do an incredible number of things—perhaps including some that it was never designed for. This book is not intended to teach you XML programming, but good ASP.NET application design. For most ASP.NET programmers, XML is an ideal replacement for custom file-access routines, and works best in situations where you need to store a small amount of data for relatively simple tasks.

XML files aren't a good substitution for a database, because they have the same limitations as any other type of file access. In a web application, only a single user can access a file at a time without causing an error, regardless of whether the file contains an XML document or binary content. Database products provide a far richer set of features for managing multiuser concurrency and providing optimized performance. Of course, there's nothing to stop you from storing XML data in a database, which many database products actively encourage. In fact, the newest versions of leading database products like SQL Server and Oracle even included extended XML features that support some of the standards you'll see in this chapter.

XML Basics

Part of XML's popularity is the result of its simplicity. When creating your own XML document, there are only a few rules you need to remember. The following two considerations apply to both XML and HTML markup:

- Whitespace is automatically collapsed, so you can freely use tabs and hard returns to properly align your information. To add a real space, you need to use the   entity equivalent, as in HTML.
- You can only use valid characters. Special characters, such as the angle brackets (< >) and the ampersand (&), can't be entered as content. Instead, you'll have to use the entity equivalents (such as < and > for angle brackets, and & for the ampersand). These equivalents are the same as in HTML coding, and will be automatically converted back to the original characters when you read them into your program with the appropriate .NET classes.

In addition, XML imposes rules that aren't found in ordinary HTML:

- XML tags are case-sensitive, so <ID> and <id> are completely different tags.
- Every start tag must have an end tag, or you must use the special "empty tag" format, which includes a forward slash at the end. For example, you can use <Name>Content</Name> or <Name />, but you cannot use <Name> on its own. This is similar to the syntax for ASP.NET controls.
- All tags must be nested in a root tag. In SuperProProductList example, the root tag is <SuperProProductList>. As soon as the root tag is closed, the document is finished, and you cannot add any more content. In other words, if you omit the <SuperProProductList> tag and start with a <Product> tag, you'll only be able to enter information for one product, because as soon as you add the closing </Product> the document is complete.
- Every tag must be fully enclosed. In other words, when you open a subtag, you need to close it before you can close the parent. <Product><ID></ID></Product> is valid, but <Product><ID></Product></ID> isn't. As a general rule, indent when you open a new tag, because this will allow you to see the document's structure and notice if you accidentally close the wrong tag first.

If you meet these requirements, your XML document can be parsed and displayed as a basic tree. This means that your document is well formed, but it doesn't mean that is valid. For example, you may still have your elements in the wrong order (for example, <ID><Product></Product></ID>), or you may have the wrong type of data in a given field (for example, <ID>Chair</ID><Name>2</Name>). There are ways to impose these additional rules on your XML documents, as you'll see shortly.

XML tags are also known as *elements*. These elements are the primary units for organizing information, but they aren't the only option. You can also use *attributes*.

Attributes

Attributes are used to add extra information to an element. Instead of putting information into a subtag, you can use an attribute. In the XML community, deciding whether to use subtags or attributes—and what information should go into an attribute—is a matter of great debate, with no clear consensus.

Here's the SuperProProductList example with an ID and Name attribute instead of an ID and Name subtag:

```
<?xml version="1.0"?>
<SuperProProductList>
    <Product ID="1" Name="Chair">
        <Price>49.33</Price>
        <Available>True</Available>
        <Status>3</Status>
    </Product>
    <Product ID="2" Name="Car">
        <Price>43399.55</Price>
        <Available>True</Available>
        <Status>3</Status>
    </Product>
    <Product ID="3" Name="Fresh Fruit Basket">
        <Price>49.99</Price>
        <Available>False</Available>
        <Status>4</Status>
    </Product>
</SuperProProductList>
```

Of course, you've already seen this sort of syntax with HTML tags and ASP.NET server controls.

```
<asp:DropDownList id="lstBackColor" AutoPostBack="True"
                  runat="server" Width="194px"
                  Height="22px"/>
```

Attributes are also common in the configuration file.

```
<sessionState mode="Inproc"
              cookieless="false"
              timeout="20" />
```

Note that the use of attributes in XML is more stringent than in HTML. In XML, attributes must always have values, and these values must use quotation marks. For example, <Product Name="Chair" /> is acceptable, but <Product Name=Chair /> or <Product Name /> isn't. (ASP.NET control tags don't always follow these rules.)

Comments

You can also add comments to an XML document. Comments go anywhere and are ignored for data processing purposes. Comments are bracketed by the <!-- and --> character sequences.

```
<?xml version="1.0"?>
<SuperProProductList>
<!-- This is a test file. -->
    <Product ID="1" Name="Chair">
        <Price>49.33<!-- Why so expensive? --></Price>
        <Available>True</Available>
        <Status>3</Status>
    </Product>
    <!-- Other products omitted for clarity. -->
</SuperProProductList>
```

The XML Classes

.NET provides a rich set of classes for XML manipulation in several namespaces. One of the most confusing aspects of using XML with .NET is deciding which combination of classes you should use. Many of them provide similar functionality in a slightly different way, optimized for specific scenarios or for compatibility with specific standards.

The majority of the examples you'll explore use the types in this namespace, which allow you to read and write XML files, manipulate XML data in special objects, and even validate XML documents. You'll look at the following options for dealing with XML data:

- Reading and writing XML directly, just like you read and write text files, using XmlTextWriter and XmlTextReader
- Dealing with XML as a collection of in-memory objects, such as XmlDocument and XmlNode
- Dealing with XML as an interface to relational data, using the XmlDataDocument class

The XML TextWriter

One of the simplest ways to create or read any XML document is to use the basic XmlTextWriter and XmlTextReader classes. These classes work like their StreamWriter and StreamReader relatives, except for the fact that they write and read XML documents instead of ordinary text files. This means that you follow the same process that you saw in Chapter 17 for creating a file. First, you create or open the file. Then you write to it or read from it, moving from top to bottom. Finally, you close it, and get to work using the retrieved data in whatever way you'd like.

Before beginning this example, you'll need to import the namespaces for file handling and XML.

```
Imports System.IO
Imports System.Xml
```

Here's an example that creates a simple version of the SuperProProductList document.

```
Dim fs As New FileStream("c:\SuperProProductList.xml", _
                         FileMode.Create)
Dim w As New XmlTextWriter(fs, Nothing)

w.WriteStartDocument()
w.WriteStartElement("SuperProProductList")
w.WriteComment("This file generated by the XmlTextWriter class.")

' Write the first product.
w.WriteStartElement("Product")
w.WriteAttributeString("ID", "", "1")
w.WriteAttributeString("Name", "", "Chair")

w.WriteStartElement("Price")
w.WriteString("49.33")
w.WriteEndElement()

w.WriteEndElement()

' Write the second product.
w.WriteStartElement("Product")
w.WriteAttributeString("ID", "", "2")
w.WriteAttributeString("Name", "", "Car")

w.WriteStartElement("Price")
w.WriteString("43399.55")
w.WriteEndElement()

w.WriteEndElement()

' Write the third product.
w.WriteStartElement("Product")
w.WriteAttributeString("ID", "", "3")
w.WriteAttributeString("Name", "", "Fresh Fruit Basket")

w.WriteStartElement("Price")
w.WriteString("49.99")
w.WriteEndElement()

w.WriteEndElement()

' Close the root element.
w.WriteEndElement()
w.WriteEndDocument()
w.Close()
```

This code is similar to the code used for writing a basic text file. It does have a few advantages, however. You can close elements quickly and accurately, the angle brackets (< >) are included for you automatically, and some errors (such as closing the root element too soon) are caught automatically, thereby ensuring a well-formed XML document as the final result.

To check that your code worked, open the file in Internet Explorer, which automatically provides a collapsible view for XML documents (see Figure 18-1).

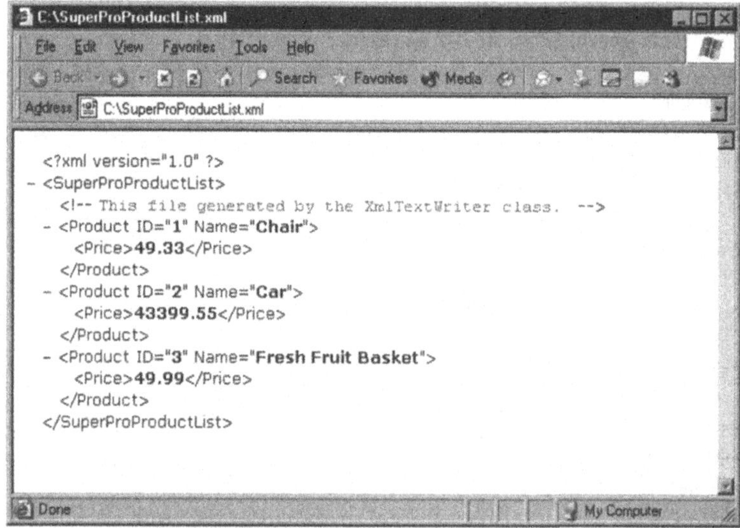

Figure 18-1. SuperProProductList.xml

Formatting Your XML

By default, the XmlTextWriter will create an XML file that has all its tags lumped together in a single line without any helpful carriage returns or indentation. Although additional formatting isn't required (and doesn't change how the data will be processed), it can make a significant difference if you want to read your XML files in Notepad or another text editor. Fortunately, the XmlTextWriter supports formatting, you just need to enable it, as follows:

```
' Set it to indent output.
w.Formatting = Formatting.Indented

' Set the number of indent spaces.
w.Indentation = 5
```

The XML Text Reader

Reading the XML document in your code is just as easy with the corresponding XmlTextReader class. The XmlTextReader moves through your document from top to bottom, one node at a time. You call the Read() method to move to the next node. This method returns True if there are more nodes to read, or False once it has read the final node. The current node is provided through the properties the XmlTextReader class, like NodeType and Name.

A node is a designation that includes comments, whitespace, opening tags, closing tags, content, and even the XML declaration at the top of your file. To get a quick understanding of nodes, you can use the XmlTextReader to run through your entire document from start to finish, and display every node it encounters. The code for this task is shown here:

```
Dim fs As New FileStream("c:\SuperProProductList.xml", FileMode.Open)
Dim r As New XmlTextReader(fs)

' Parse the file and read each node.
Do While r.Read()
    lblStatus.Text &= "<b>Type:</b> " & r.NodeType.ToString & "<br>"

    If r.Name <> "" Then
        lblStatus.Text &= "<b>Name:</b> " & r.Name & "<br>"
    End If

    If r.Value <> "" Then
        lblStatus.Text &= "<b>Value:</b> " & r.Value & "<br>"
    End If

    If r.AttributeCount > 0 Then
        lblStatus.Text &= "<b>Attributes:</b> "
        Dim i As Integer
        For i = 0 To r.AttributeCount() - 1
            lblStatus.Text &= "  " & r.GetAttribute(i) & " "
        Next
        lblStatus.Text &= "<br>"
    End If

    lblStatus.Text &= "<br>"
Loop
r.Close()
```

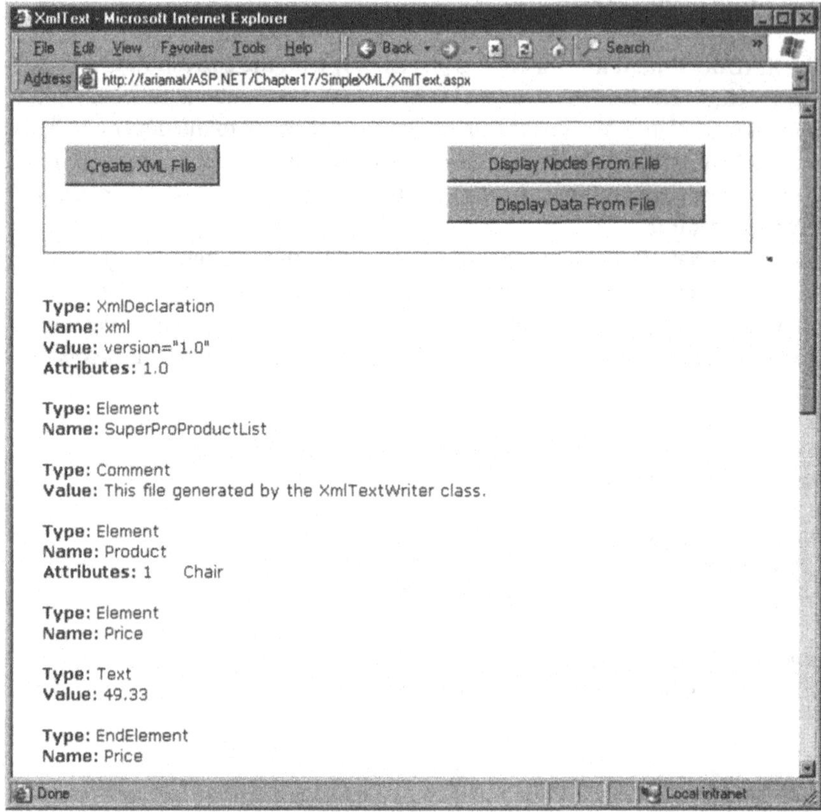

Figure 18-2. Reading XML structure

To test this out, try the XmlText.aspx page included with the online samples (as shown in Figure 18-2). The following is a list of all the nodes that are found, shortened to include only one product:

```
Type: XmlDeclaration
Name: xml
Value: version="1.0"
Attributes: 1.0

Type: Element
Name: SuperProProductList

Type: Comment
Value: This file generated by the XmlTextWriter class.

Type: Element
Name: Product
Attributes: 1, Chair

Type: Element
Name: Price
```

```
Type: Text
Value: 49.33

Type: EndElement
Name: Price

Type: EndElement
Name: Product

Type: EndElement
Name: SuperProProductList
```

In a typical application, you would need to go "fishing" for the elements that interest you. For example, you might read information from an XML file such as SuperProProductList.xml and use it to create Product objects, based on the Product class shown here:

```
Public Class Product
    Private _ID As Integer
    Private _Name As String
    Private _Price As Decimal

    Public Property ID() As Integer
        Get
            Return _ID
        End Get
        Set(ByVal Value As Integer)
            _ID = Value
        End Set
    End Property

    Public Property Name() As String
        Get
            Return _Name
        End Get
        Set(ByVal Value As String)
            _Name = Value
        End Set
    End Property

    Public Property Price() As Decimal
        Get
            Return _Price
        End Get
        Set(ByVal Value As Decimal)
            _Price = Value
        End Set
    End Property

End Class
```

There's nothing particularly special about this class—all it does is allow you to store three related pieces of information (a price, name, and ID). Note that this class uses property procedures and so is eligible for data binding.

A typical application might read data out of an XML file and place it directly into the corresponding objects. The next example (also a part of the XmlText.aspx page) shows how you can easily create a group of Product objects based on the SuperProProductList.xml file.

```
' Open a stream to the file.
Dim fs As New FileStream("c:\SuperProProductList.xml", FileMode.Open)
Dim r As New XmlTextReader(fs)

Dim Products As New ArrayList()

' Loop through the products.
Do While r.Read()

    If r.NodeType = XmlNodeType.Element And r.Name = "Product" Then
        Dim NewProduct As New Product()
        NewProduct.ID = Val(r.GetAttribute(0))
        NewProduct.Name = r.GetAttribute(1)

        ' Get the rest of the subtags for this product.
        Do Until r.NodeType = XmlNodeType.EndElement
            r.Read()

            ' Look for Price subtags.
            If r.Name = "Price" Then
                Do Until (r.NodeType = XmlNodeType.EndElement)
                    r.Read()
                    If r.NodeType = XmlNodeType.Text Then
                        NewProduct.Price = Val(r.Value)
                    End If
                Loop
            End If

            ' You could check for other Product nodes
            ' (like Available, Status, etc.) here.
        Loop

        ' Add the product to the list.
        Products.Add(NewProduct)
    End If
Loop

r.Close()

' Display the retrieved document.
dgResults.DataSource = Products
dgResults.DataBind()
```

Dissecting the Code ...

- This code uses a nested looping structure. The outside loop iterates over all the products, and the inner loop searches through all the product tags (in this case, there is only a possible Price tag). This keeps the code well organized. The EndElement node alerts you when a node is complete and the loop can end. Once all the information is read for a product, the corresponding object is added into the ArrayList collection.
- All the information is retrieved from the XML file as a string. Thus, the Val function is used to extract numbers, although there are other possibilities.
- Data binding is used to display the contents of the collection. A DataGrid set to generate columns automatically creates the table shown in Figure 18-3.

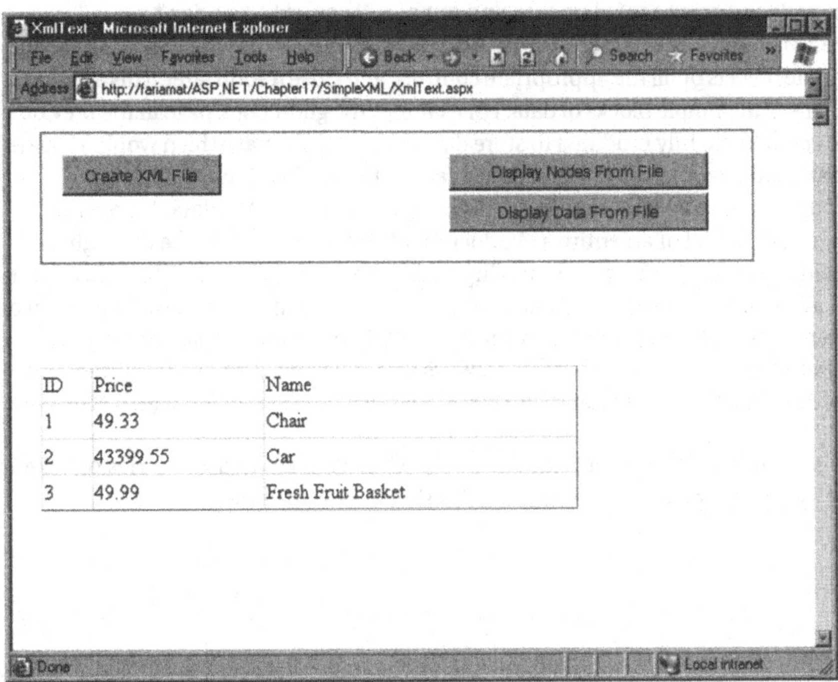

Figure 18-3. Reading XML content

NOTE The XmlTextReader provides many more properties and methods. These additional members don't add new functionality; they allow for increased flexibility. For example, you can read a portion of an XML document into a string using methods such as ReadString(), ReadInnerXml(), and ReadOuterXml(). These members are all documented in the MSDN class library reference. Generally, the most straightforward approach is just to work your way through the nodes as shown in the SuperProProductList example.

Working with XML Documents

The XmlTextReader and XmlTextWriter use XML as a *backing store*. These classes are streamlined for getting XML data into and out of a file quickly. You don't actually work with the XML data in your program. Instead, you open the file, use the data to create the appropriate objects or fill the appropriate controls, and close it soon after. This approach is ideal for storing simple blocks of data. For example, the guest book page in the previous chapter could be slightly modified to store data in an XML format, which would provide greater standardization, but wouldn't change how the application works.

The XmlDocument class provides a different approach to XML data. It provides an in-memory model of an entire XML document. You can then browse through the document, reading, inserting, or removing nodes at any location. The XML document can be saved to or retrieved from a file, but the XmlDocument class doesn't maintain a direct connection to the file. In this respect, the XmlDocument is analogous to the DataSet in ADO.NET programming: It's always disconnected. The XmlTextWriter and XmlTextReader, on the other hand, are always connected to a stream, which is usually a file.

When you use the XmlDocument class, your XML file is created as a series of linked .NET objects in memory. The object model is shown in Figure 18-4.

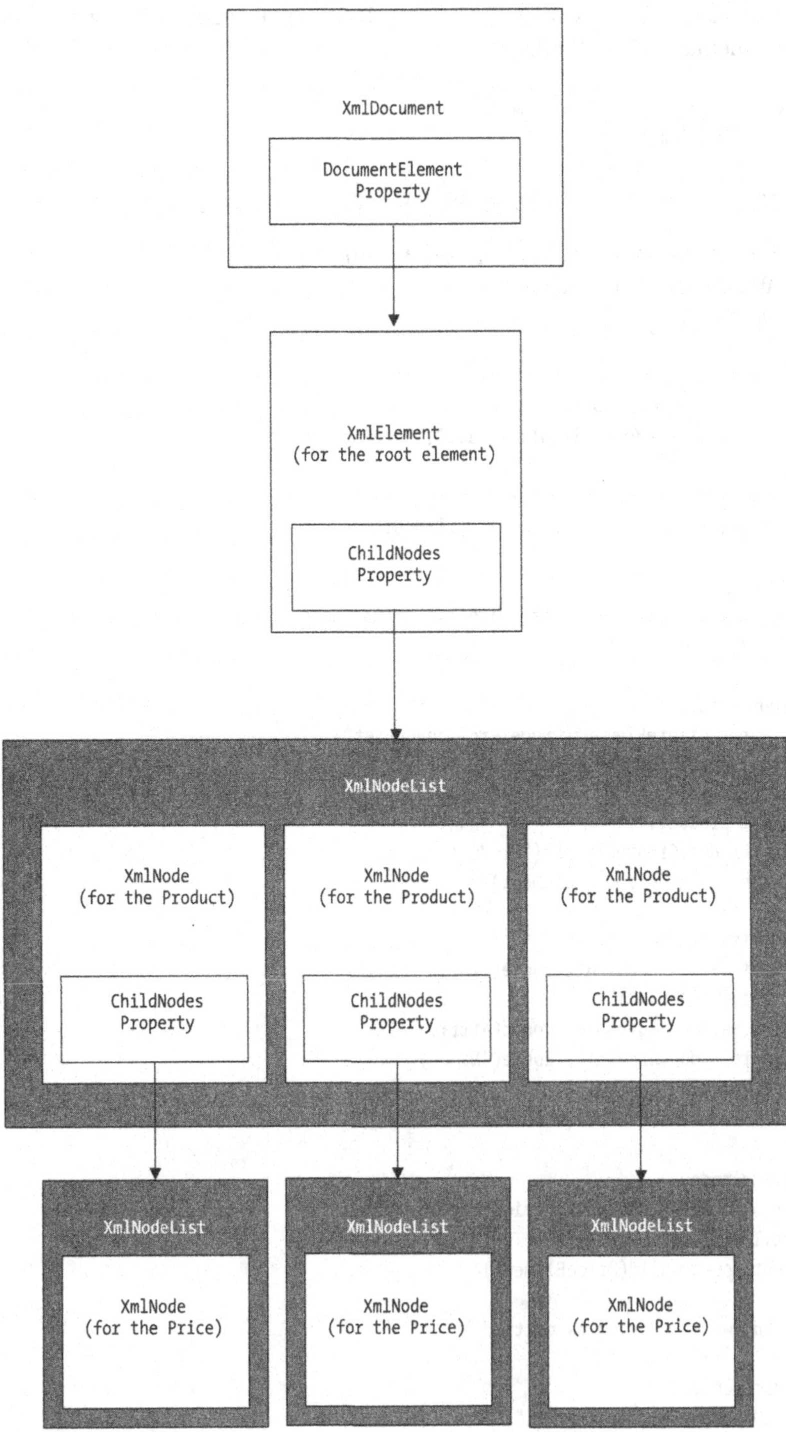

Figure 18-4. An XML document in memory

Next is an example that creates the SuperProProductList in memory, using an XmlDocument class. When it's finished, the XML document is transferred to a file using the XmlDocument.Save() method.

```
' Start with a blank in-memory document.
Dim doc As New XmlDocument()

' Create some variables that will be useful for
' manipulating XML data.
Dim RootElement, ProductElement, PriceElement As XmlElement
Dim ProductAttribute As XmlAttribute
Dim Comment As XmlComment

' Create the declaration.
Dim Declaration As XmlDeclaration
Declaration = doc.CreateXmlDeclaration("1.0", Nothing, "yes")

' Insert the declaration as the first node.
doc.InsertBefore(Declaration, doc.DocumentElement)

' Add a comment.
Comment = doc.CreateComment("Created with the XmlDocument class.")
doc.InsertAfter(Comment, Declaration)

' Add the root node.
RootElement = doc.CreateElement("SuperProProductList")
doc.InsertAfter(RootElement, Comment)

' Add the first product.
ProductElement = doc.CreateElement("Product")
RootElement.AppendChild(ProductElement)

' Set and add the product attributes.
ProductAttribute = doc.CreateAttribute("ID")
ProductAttribute.Value = "1"
ProductElement.SetAttributeNode(ProductAttribute)
ProductAttribute = doc.CreateAttribute("Name")
ProductAttribute.Value = "Chair"
ProductElement.SetAttributeNode(ProductAttribute)

' Add the price node.
PriceElement = doc.CreateElement("Price")
PriceElement.InnerText = "49.33"
ProductElement.AppendChild(PriceElement)

' (Code to add two more products omitted.)

' Save the document.
doc.Save("c:\SuperProProductList.xml")
```

One of the best features of the XmlDocument class is that it doesn't rely on any underlying file. When you use the Save() method, the file is created, a stream is opened, the information is written, and the file is closed, all in one line of code. That means that this is probably the only line that you need to put inside a Try/Catch error-handling block.

While you're manipulating data with the XML objects, your text file isn't being changed. Once again, this is conceptually similar to the ADO.NET DataSet.

Dissecting the Code ...

- Every separate part of the XML document is created as an object. Elements (tags) are created as XmlElement objects, comments are created as XmlComment objects, and attributes are represented as XmlAttribute objects.

- To create a new element, comment, or attribute for your XML document, you need to use one of the XmlDocument class methods, such as CreateComment(), CreateAttribute(), or CreateElement(). This ensures that the XML is generated correctly for your document, but it doesn't actually place any information into the XmlDocument.

- Once you have created the appropriate object and entered any additional inner information, you need to add it to your document. You can do so using XmlDocument methods such as InsertBefore() or InsertAfter(). To add a child element (such as the Product element inside the SuperProProductList element), you need to find the appropriate parent object and use its AppendChild() method. In other words, you need to keep track of some object references; you can't write a child element directly to the document in the same way that you could with the XmlTextWriter.

- You can insert nodes anywhere. While the XmlTextWriter and XmlTextReader forced you to read every node, from start to finish, the XmlDocument is a much more flexible collection of objects.

The file written by this code is shown in Figure 18-5 (as displayed by Internet Explorer).

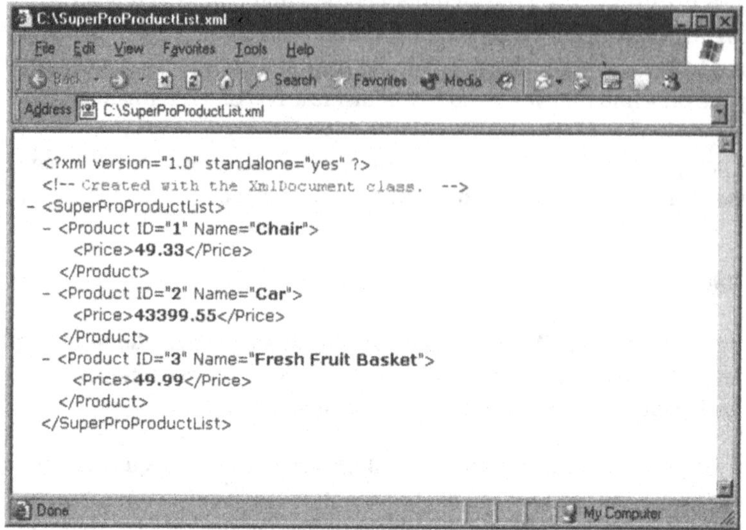

Figure 18-5. The XML file

Reading an XML Document

To read information from your XML file, all you need to do is create an XmlDocument object and use its Load() method. Depending on your needs, you may want to keep the data in its XML form, or you can extract by looping through the collection of linked XmlNode objects. This process is similar to the XmlTextReader example, but the code is noticeably cleaner.

```
' Create the document.
Dim doc As New XmlDataDocument()
doc.Load("c:\SuperProProductList.xml")

' Loop through all the nodes, and create the ArrayList..
Dim Element As XmlElement
Dim Products As New ArrayList()

For Each Element In doc.DocumentElement.ChildNodes
    Dim NewProduct As New Product()
    NewProduct.ID = Element.GetAttribute("ID")
    NewProduct.Name = Element.GetAttribute("Name")
```

```
    ' If there were more than one child node, you would probably use
    ' another For Each loop here, and move through the
    ' Element.ChildNodes collection.
    NewProduct.Price = Element.ChildNodes(0).InnerText

    Products.Add(NewProduct)
Next

' Display the results.
dgResults.DataSource = Products
dgResults.DataBind()
```

TIP Whether you use the XmlDocument or the XmlTextReader class depends on a number of factors. Generally, XmlDocument is used when you want to deal directly with XML, rather than just use XML as a way to persist some information. In general, the XmlTextReader is best for large XML files, because it won't attempt to load the entire document into memory at once.

The Difference Between XmlNode and XmlElement

You may have noticed that the XmlDocument is created with specific objects like XmlComment and XmlElement, but read back as a collection of XmlNode objects. The reason is that XmlComment and XmlElement are customized classes that inherit their basic functionality from XmlNode.

The ChildNodes collection allows you to retrieve all the content contained inside any portion of an XML document. Because this content could include comments, elements, and any other types of node, the ChildNodes collection uses the lowest common denominator. Thus, it provides child nodes as a collection of standard XmlNode objects. Each XmlNode has basic properties similar to what you saw with the XmlTextReader, including NodeType, Name, Value, and Attributes. You'll find that you can do all of your XML processing with XmlNode objects.

You have a variety of other options for manipulating your XmlDocument and extracting or changing pieces of data. Table 18-1 provides an overview.

Table 18-1. XmlNode Manipulation

Technique	Description
Finding a node's relative	Every XmlNode leads to other XmlNode objects. You can use properties such as FirstChild, LastChild, PreviousSibling, NextSibling, and ParentNode to return a reference to a related node.
An example is ParentNode = MyNode.ParentNode.	
Cloning a portion of an XmlDocument	You can use the CloneNode() method with any XmlNode to create a duplicate copy. You need to specify True or False to indicate whether you want to clone all children (True) or just the single node (False).
An example is NewNode = MyNode.Clone(True).	
Removing or adding nodes	Find the parent node, and then use one of its node-adding methods. You can use AppendChild() to add the child to the end of the child list, and PrependChild() to add the node to the start of the child list. You can also remove nodes with RemoveChild(), ReplaceChild(), and RemoveAll(), which deletes all the children and all the attributes for the current node.
An example is MyNode.RemoveChild(NodeToDelete).	
Adding inner content	Find the node, and add a NodeType.Text child node. One possible shortcut is just to set the InnerText property of your node, but that will erase any existing child nodes.
Manipulating attributes	Every node provides an XmlAttributeCollection of all its attributes through the XmlNode.Attributes property. To add an attribute, you must create an XmlAttribute object, and use methods such as Append(), Prepend(), InsertBefore(), or InsertAfter(). To remove an attribute, you can use Remove() and RemoveAll().
An example is MyNode.Attributes.Remove(AttributeToDelete).	
Working with content as string data	You can retrieve or set the content inside a node using properties such as InnerText, InnerXml, and OuterXml. Be warned that the inner content of a node includes all child nodes. Thus, setting this property carelessly could wipe out other information, like subtags.

The XmlDocument class provides a rich set of events that fire before and after nodes are inserted, removed, and changed. The likelihood of using these events in an ordinary ASP.NET application is fairly slim, but it represents an interesting example of the features .NET puts at your fingertips.

Searching an XML Document

One of the pleasures of the XmlDocument is its support of searching, which allows you to find nodes when you know they are there—somewhere—but you aren't sure how many matches there are or where the elements are.

To search an XmlDocument, all you need to do is use the GetElementById() or GetElementsByTagName() method. The following code example puts the GetElementsByTagName method() to work, and creates the output shown in Figure 18-6.

```
Dim doc As New XmlDataDocument()
doc.Load("c:\SuperProProductList.xml")
Dim Results As XmlNodeList
Dim Result As XmlNode

' Find the matches.
 Results = doc.GetElementsByTagName("Price")

' Display the results.
lblStatus.Text = "<b>Found " & Results.Count.ToString() & " Matches "
lblStatus.Text &= " for the Price tag: </b><br><br>"
For Each Result In Results
    lblStatus.Text &= Result.FirstChild.Value & "<br>"
Next
```

This technique works well if you want to find an element based on its name. If you want to use more sophisticated searching, match only part of a name, or examine only part of a document, you'll have to fall back on the traditional standard: looping through all the nodes in the XmlDocument.

TIP The search method provided by the XmlDocument class is relatively primitive. For a more advanced tool, you might want to learn the XPath language, which is a W3C recommendation (defined at `http://www.w3.org/TR/xpath/`) designed for performing queries on XML data. .NET provides XPath support through the classes in the System.Xml.XPath namespace, which include an XPath parser and evaluation engine. Of course, these aren't much use unless you learn the syntax of the XPath language itself.

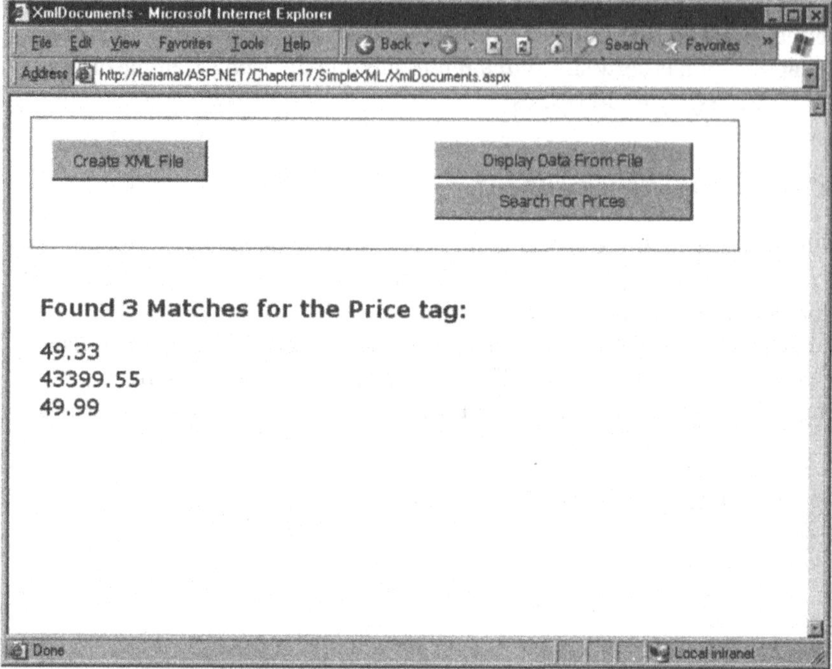

Figure 18-6. Searching an XML document

XML Validation

XML has a rich set of supporting standards, many of which are far beyond the scope of this book. One of the most useful in this family of standards is XSD (XML Schema Definition). XSD defines the rules that a specific XML document should conform to. When you're creating an XML file on your own, you don't need to create a corresponding XSD file—instead, you might just rely on the ability of your code to behave properly. While this is sufficient for tightly controlled environments, if you want to open up your application to other programmers, or allow it to interoperate with other applications, you should create an XSD document. Think of it this way: XML allows you to create your own custom language for storing data, and XSD allows you to define the syntax of the language you create.

XML Namespaces

Before you can create an XSD document, you'll need to understand about one other XML standard, called XML namespaces. XML namespaces are used to uniquely identify different XML-based languages. For example, you could tell the difference between your SuperProProductList standard and another organization's product catalog because it would use different namespaces. Namespaces are particularly important for applications, which need an easy way to determine what type of XML file they're processing. By examining the namespace, your code can determine if it will be able to process a given XML file.

NOTE XML namespaces aren't directly related to .NET namespaces. XML namespaces identify different XML languages. .NET namespaces are a code construct used to organize types.

To specify that an element belongs to a specific namespace, you simply need to add the xmlns attribute to the start tag, and indicate the namespace. For example, here's how you could put all of the elements in an XML document into the namespace SuperProProductList.

```
<?xml version="1.0"?>
<SuperProProductList xmlns="SuperProProductList">
    <Product>
        <ID>1</ID>
        <Name>Chair</Name>
        <Price>49.33</Price>
        <Available>True</Available>
        <Status>3</Status>
    </Product>

    <!-- Other products omitted. -->
</SuperProProductList>
```

This code example defines a default namespace. All elements, including the Product, ID, and Name elements, are automatically placed in this namespace.

Many XML namespaces use URIs (Universal Resource Identifiers). Typically, these URIs look like a web page URL. For example, http://www.mycompany.com/mystandard is a typical name for a namespace. Though the namespace looks like it points to a valid location on the Web, this isn't required (and shouldn't be assumed). The reason that URIs are used for XML namespaces is because they're more likely to be unique. Typically, if you create a new XML markup, you'll use a URI that points to a domain or website you control. That way, you can be sure that no one else is likely to use that URI.

Another approach is to use namespace prefixes. A namespace prefixes a short character sequence that you can insert in front of a tag name to indicate its namespace. You define the prefix in the xmlns attribute by inserting a colon (:) followed by the characters you want to use for the prefix. Here's how the SuperProProductList would look using this commonly used technique:

```
<?xml version="1.0"?>
<super:SuperProProductList xmlns:super="SuperProProductList">
    <super:Product>
        <super:ID>1</super:ID>
        <super:Name>Chair</super:Name>
        <super:Price>49.33</super:Price>
        <super:Available>True</super:Available>
        <super:Status>3</super:Status>
    </super:Product>

    <!-- Other products omitted. -->
</super:SuperProProductList>
```

Namespace prefixes are simply used to map an element to a namespace. The actual prefix you use isn't important as long as it remains consistent. It also doesn't matter whether you use namespace prefixes or a default namespace, provided the namespaces match.

TIP Namespace names must match exactly. If you change the capitalization in part of a namespace, add a trailing / character, or modify any other detail, it will be interpreted as a different namespace by the XML parser.

XSD Documents

An XSD document, or *schema*, defines what elements a document should contain and the way that these elements are organized (the structure). It can also identify the appropriate data types for all the content. XSD documents are written using an XML syntax with special tag names. All the XSD tags are placed in the http://www.w3.org/2001/XMLSchema namespace. Often, this namespace uses the prefix xsd: or xs: as in the following example.

The full XSD specification is out of the scope of this chapter, but you can learn a lot from a simple example. The following is the slightly abbreviated SuperProProductList.xsd file. All it does is define the elements and attributes used in the SuperProProductList.xml document and their data types. It indicates that the file is a list of Product elements, which are a complex type made up of a string (Name), a decimal value (Price), and an integer (ID). This example uses the second version of the SuperProProductList.xsd document, in order to demonstrate the use of attributes in a schema file.

```
<?xml version="1.0"?>
<xs:schema id="SuperProProductList"
    targetNamespace="SuperProProductList"
    xmlns:xs=" http://www.w3.org/2001/XMLSchema" >
  <xs:element name="SuperProProductList">
    <xs:complexType>
      <xs:choice maxOccurs="unbounded">
        <xs:element name="Product">
          <xs:complexType>
            <xs:sequence>
              <xs:element name="Price" type="xs:decimal"
                  minOccurs="0" />
            </xs:sequence>
            <xs:attribute name="ID" form="unqualified"
                type="xs:string" />
            <xs:attribute name="Name" form="unqualified"
                type="xs:int" />
          </xs:complexType>
        </xs:element>
      </xs:choice>
    </xs:complexType>
  </xs:element>
</xs:schema>
```

In the XSD file, you need to specify the namespace for the documents you want to validate. You do this by adding the targetNamespace attribute to the first element in the XSD document:

```
<xs:schema id="SuperProProductList"
    targetNamespace="SuperProProductList"
    xmlns:xs=" http://www.w3.org/2001/XMLSchema" >
```

Validating an XML File

To validate an XML document against a schema, you use the XmlValidatingReader class. This class is based on the XmlTextReader, but includes the ability to verify that the document follows the rules specified in an XSD schema file. The XmlValidatingReader throws an exception (or raises an event) to indicate errors as you move through the XML file.

The first step when performing validation is to import the System.Xml.Schema namespace, which contains types like XmlSchema and XmlSchemaCollection.

```
Imports System.Xml.Schema
```

The following example shows how you can create an XmlValidatingReader that uses the SuperProProductList.xsd file, and use it to verify that the XML in SuperProProductList.xml is valid.

```
' Open the XML file.
Dim fs As New FileStream(Request.ApplicationPath & _
  "\SuperProProductList.xml", FileMode.Open)
Dim r As New XmlTextReader(fs)

' Create the validating reader.
Dim vr As New XmlValidatingReader(r)
vr.ValidationType = ValidationType.Schema

' Add the XSD file to the validator.
Dim Schemas As New XmlSchemaCollection()
Schemas.Add("SuperProProductList", _
  Request.ApplicationPath & "\SuperProProductList.xsd")
vr.Schemas.Add(Schemas)

' Read through the document.
Do While vr.Read()
    ' Process document here.
    ' If an error is found, an exception will be thrown.
Loop

vr.Close()
```

Using the current file, this code will succeed, and you'll be able to access the current node through the XmlValidatingReader object in the same way that you could with the XmlTextReader. However, consider what happens if you make the minor modification shown here.

```
<Product ID="A" Name="Chair">
```

Now when you try to validate the document, an XmlSchemException (from the System.Xml.Schema namespace) will be thrown, alerting you to the invalid data type, as shown in Figure 18-7.

Instead of catching errors, you can react to the ValidationEventHandler event. If you react to this event, you'll be provided with information about the error, but no exception will be thrown. Typically, you would use the AddHandler statement to connect your event handling procedure to the XmlValidatingReader.ValidationEventHandler event just before you started to read the XML file.

```
AddHandler vr.ValidationEventHandler, AddressOf MyValidateHandler
```

The event handler receives a ValidationEventArgs class, which contains the exception, a message, and a number representing the severity:

```
Public Sub MyValidateHandler(sender As Object, e As ValidationEventArgs)
    lblStatus.Text &= "Error: " & e.Message & "<br>"
End Sub
```

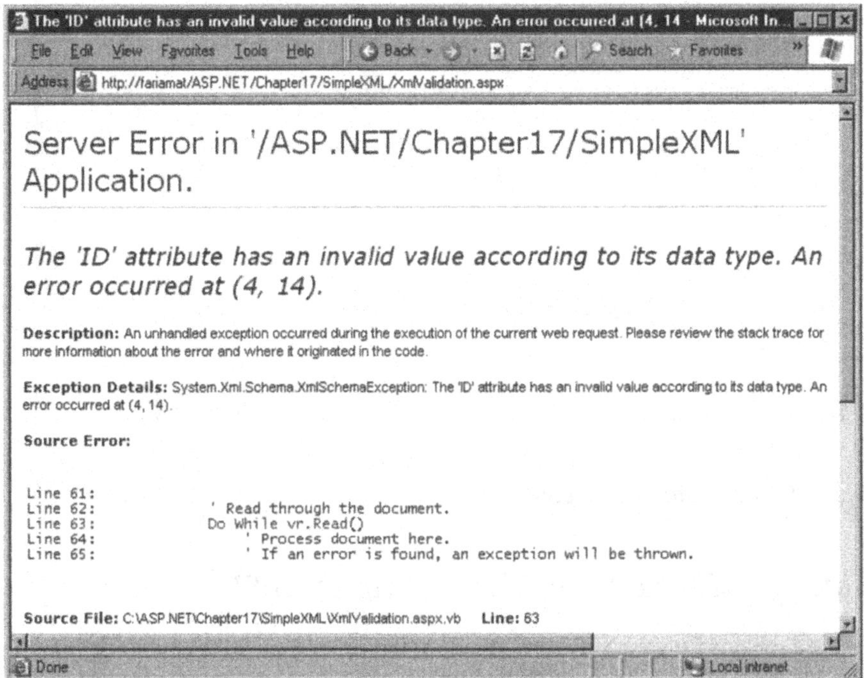

Figure 18-7. An XmlSchemException

To try out validation, you can use the XmlValidation.aspx page in the online samples. It allows you to validate a valid SuperProProductList, as well as two other versions, one with incorrect data and one with an incorrect tag (see Figure 18-8).

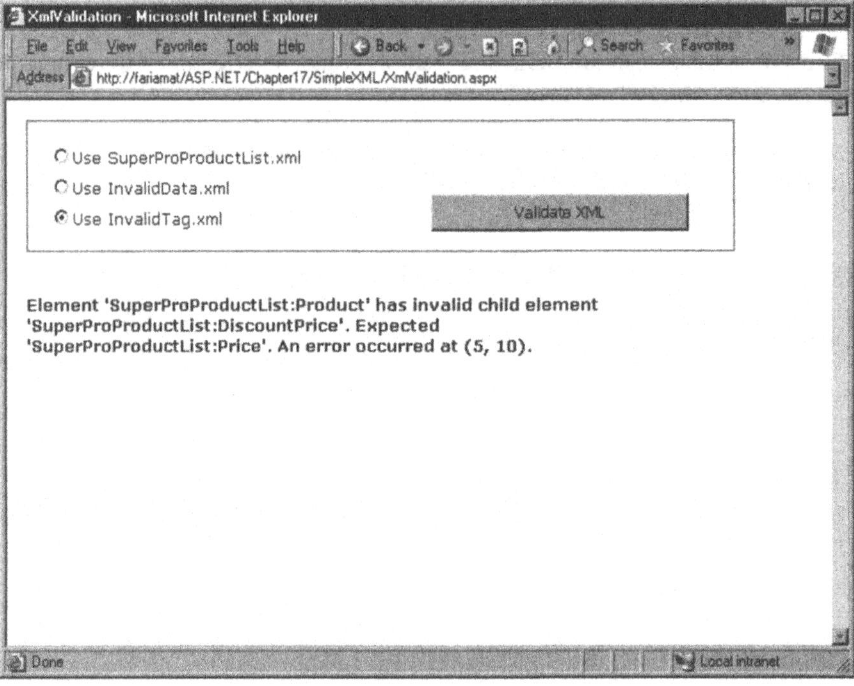

Figure 18-8. The validation test page

Creating XSD Files in Visual Studio .NET

To create a schema for your XML files, you don't have to master all the subtleties of XSD syntax. Visual Studio .NET provides an impressive graphical designer that lets you point and click your way to success.

Start by adding the appropriate XML file to your project. You can then edit your XML data in one of two ways: in direct text view, which provides a color-coded display of the XML tags, or through a graphical editor that makes your XML content look like one or more database tables (see Figure 18-9). You can add new rows or change existing data with ease.

To create the schema, just right-click anywhere on either of the XML views, and choose Create Schema from the context menu. An XSD file with the same name as your XML file will be generated automatically and added to your project.

There are also two views for editing your XSD file: text view and another graphical designer. By default, Visual Studio .NET will assume that all the data in an XML file is made up of strings. You can use the graphical tool to choose better options for each field (see Figure 18-10), and the XSD document will be updated automatically.

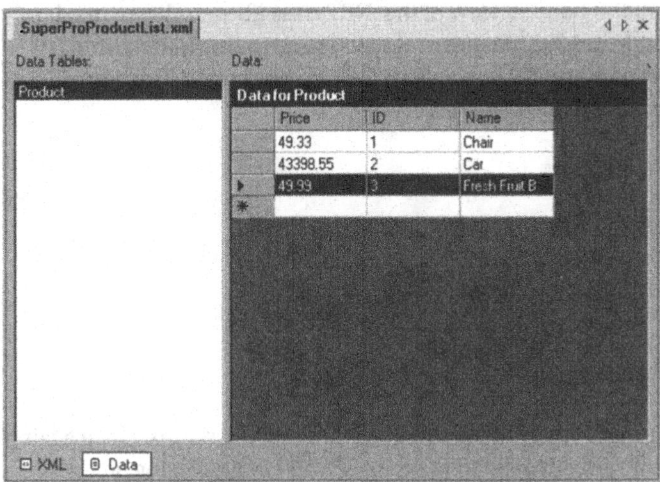

Figure 18-9. The graphical XML designer

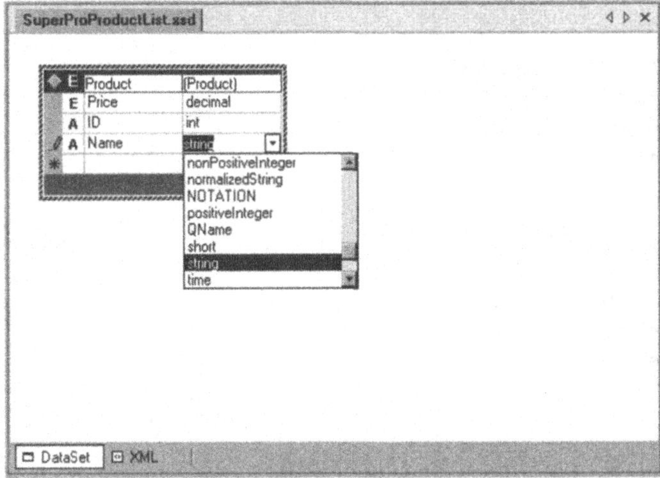

Figure 18-10. The graphical XSD designer

XML Display and Transforms

Another standard associated with XML is XSL, which uses a stylesheet to transform an XML document. XSL can be used to extract a portion of an XML document, or convert an XML document into another type of XML document. An even more popular use of XSL transformations is to convert an XML document into an HTML document that can be displayed in a browser.

XSL is easy to use from the point of view of the .NET class library. All you need to understand is how to create an XmlTransform object (found in the System.Xml.Xsl namespace). You use its Load() method to specify a stylesheet and its Transform() method to output the result to a file or stream.

```
Dim Transformer As New XmlTransform

' Load the XSL stylesheet.
Transformer.Load("SuperProProductList.xslt")

' Create a transformed XML file.
' SuperProProductList.xml is the starting point.
Transformer.Transform("SuperProProductList.xml", "New.xml")
```

However, that doesn't spare you from needing to learn the XSL syntax. Once again, the intricacies of XSL aren't directly related to core ASP.NET programming, and so they're outside the scope of this book. To get started with XSL, however, it helps to review a simple stylesheet example:

```
<?xml version="1.0" encoding="UTF-8" ?>
<xsl:stylesheet xmlns:xsl="http://www.w3.org/1999/XSL/Transform"
    version="1.0" >

  <xsl:template match="SuperProProductList">
    <html><body><table border="1">
    <xsl:apply-templates select="Product"/>
    </table></body></html>
  </xsl:template>

  <xsl:template match="Product">
    <tr>
    <td><xsl:value-of select="@ID"/></td>
    <td><xsl:value-of select="@Name"/></td>
    <td><xsl:value-of select="Price"/></td>
    </tr>
  </xsl:template>

</xsl:stylesheet>
```

Every XSL file has a root xsl:stylesheet element. The stylesheet can contain one or more templates (the sample file SuperProProductList.xslt has two). In this example, the first template searches for the root SuperProProductList element. When it finds it, it outputs the tags necessary to start an HTML table, and then uses the xsl:apply-templates command to branch off and perform processing for any contained Product elements.

```
<xsl:template match="SuperProProductList">
  <html><body><table border="1">
  <xsl:apply-templates select="Product"/>
```

When that process is complete, the HTML tags for the end of the table will be written.

```
</table></body></html>
```

When processing each Product element, information about the ID, Name, and Price is extracted and written to the output using the xsl:value-of command. The @ sign indicates that the value is being extracted from an attribute, not a subtag. Every piece of information is written inside a table row. For more advanced formatting, you could use additional HTML tags to format some text in bold or italics, for example.

```
<xsl:template match="Product">
  <tr>
  <td><xsl:value-of select="@ID"/></td>
  <td><xsl:value-of select="@Name"/></td>
  <td><xsl:value-of select="Price"/></td>
  </tr>
</xsl:template>
```

The final result of this process is the HTML file shown here.

```
<html>
  <body>
    <table border="1">
      <tr>
        <td>1</td>
        <td>Chair</td>
        <td>49.33</td>
      </tr>
      <tr>
        <td>2</td>
        <td>Car</td>
        <td>43398.55</td>
      </tr>
      <tr>
        <td>3</td>
        <td>Fresh Fruit Basket</td>
        <td>49.99</td>
      </tr>
    </table>
  </body>
</html>
```

In the next section, you'll take a look at how this output appears in an Internet browser.

Generally speaking, if you aren't sure that you need XSL, you probably don't. The .NET Framework provides a rich set of tools for searching and manipulating XML files using objects and code, which is the best approach for small-scale XML use.

The Xml Web Control

If you use an XLST transform like the one demonstrated in the previous example, you might wonder what your code should do with the generated HTML. You could try to write it directly to the browser or save it to the hard drive, but these approaches are awkward, especially if you want to display the generated HTML inside a normal ASP.NET web page that contains other controls. The XmlTransform object just converts XML files—it doesn't provide any way to insert the output into your web page.

ASP.NET includes an Xml web control that fills this gap, and can display XML content. You can specify the XML content for this control in several ways: by assigning an XmlDocument object to the Document property, by assigning a string containing the XML content to the DocumentContent property, or by specifying a string that refers to an XML file using the DocumentSource property.

```
' Display the information from an XML file in the Xml control.
MyXml.DocumentSource = Request.ApplicationPath & _
  "\SuperProProductList.xml"
```

If you assign the SuperProProductList.xml file to the Xml control, you're likely to be disappointed. The result is just a string of the inner text (the price for each product), bunched together without a space (see Figure 18-11).

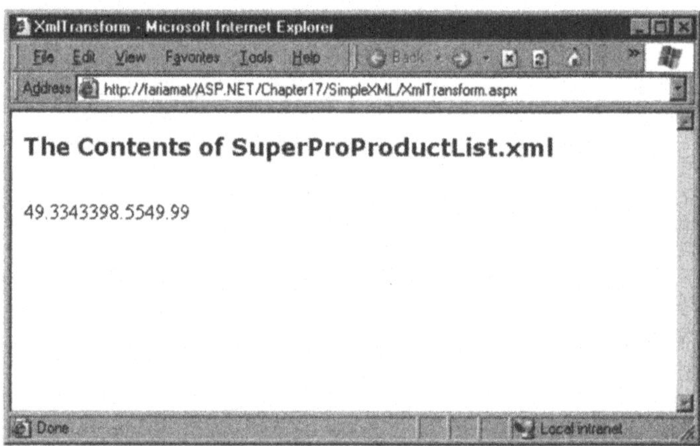

Figure 18-11. Unformatted XML content

However, you can also apply an XSL transformation, either by assigning an XslTransform object to the Transform property or by using a string that refers to the XSLT file with the TransformSource property.

```
' Specify a XSLT file.
MyXml.TranformSource = Request.ApplicationPath & _
  "\SuperProProductList.xslt"
```

Now the output is automatically formatted according to your stylesheet (see Figure 18-12).

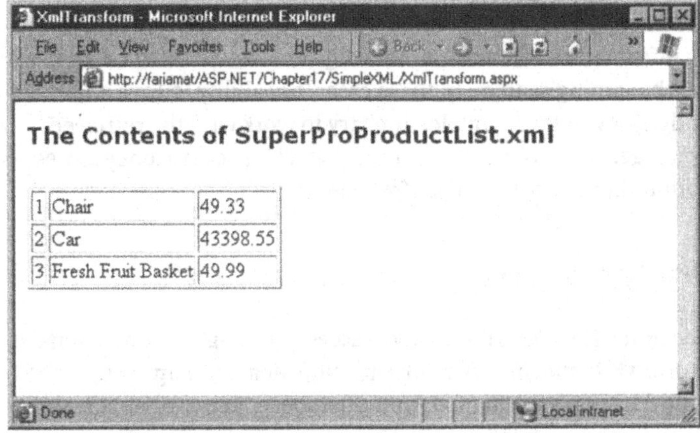

Figure 18-12. Transformed XML content

XML in ADO.NET

The integration between ADO.NET and XML is straightforward and effortless, but it isn't likely to have a wide range of usefulness. Probably the most interesting feature is the ability to serialize a DataSet to an XML file (with or without a corresponding XSD schema file). The following code example demonstrates this technique:

```
' Save a DataSet.
MyDataSet.WriteXml(Request.ApplicationPath & "\datasetfile.xml")

' Save a DataSet schema that defines the structure of the DataSet tables.
MyDataSet.WriteSchema(Request.ApplicationPath & "\datasetfile.xsd")

' Retrieve the DataSet with its schema. Using the schema
' means no data types are corrupted and no structural information is lost.
Dim MyDataSet2 As New DataSet()
MyDataSet2.ReadXmlSchema(Request.ApplicationPath & "\datasetfile.xsd")
MyDataSet2.ReadXml(Request.ApplicationPath & "\datasetfile.xml")
```

This technique could be useful for permanently storing the results of a slow-running query. A web page that needs this information could first check for the presence of the file before trying to connect to the database. This type of system is similar to many homegrown solutions used in traditional ASP programming. It's useful, but it raises additional issues. For example, every web page that needs the data must check the file's age to determine whether it's still valid. Presumably, the XML file will need to be refreshed at periodic intervals, but if more than one executing web page finds that the file needs to be refreshed and tries to create it at the same time, a file-access problem will occur.

All these problems can be resolved with a little painful coding, although caching provides a more streamlined and elegant solution. It also offers much better performance, because the data is stored in memory. Caching is described in Chapter 24.

Of course, there could be some cases in which you need to exchange the results of a query with an application on another platform, or when you need to store the results permanently (caching information will be automatically removed if it isn't being used or the server memory is becoming scarce). In these cases, the ability to save a DataSet can come in quite handy. But whatever you do, don't try to work with the retrieved DataSet and commit changes back to the data source. Handling concurrency issues is difficult enough without trying to use stale data from a file!

Accessing a DataSet as XML

Another option provided by the DataSet is the ability to access it through an XML interface. This allows you to perform XML-specific tasks (like hunting for a tag or applying an XSL transformation) with the data you've extracted from a database. To do so, you create an XmlDataDocument that wraps the DataSet. When you create the XmlDataDocument, you supply the DataSet you want as a parameter:

```
Dim DataDocument As New XmlDataDocument(MyDataSet)
```

Now you can look at the DataSet in two different ways. Because XmlDataDocument inherits from XmlDocument class, it provides all the same properties and methods for examining nodes and modifying content. You can use this XML-based approach to deal with your data, or you can manipulate the DataSet through the XmlDataDocument.DataSet property. In either case, the two views are kept automatically synchronized—when you change the DataSet, the XML is updated immediately, and vice versa.

For example, consider the pubs database, which includes a table of authors. Using the XmlDataDocument, you could examine a list of authors as an XML document, and even apply an XSL transformation with the help of the Xml web control. Here's the complete code you'd need:

```
Dim ConnectionString As String = "Provider=SQLOLEDB.1;" & _
  "Data Source=localhost;Initial Catalog=pubs;Integrated Security=SSPI"
Dim SQL As String = "SELECT * FROM authors WHERE city='Oakland'"

' Create the ADO.NET objects.
Dim con As New OleDbConnection(ConnectionString)
Dim cmd As New OleDbCommand(SQL, con)
Dim adapter As New OleDbDataAdapter(cmd)
Dim ds As New DataSet("AuthorsDataSet")

' Retrieve the data.
con.Open()
adapter.Fill(ds, "AuthorsTable")
con.Close()
```

```
' Create the XmlDataDocument that wraps this DataSet.
Dim DataDoc As New XmlDataDocument(ds)

' Display the XML data (with the help of an XSLT) in the XML web control.
XmlControl.Document = DataDoc
XmlControl.TransformSource = "authors.xslt"
```

The processed data is shown in Figure 8-13.

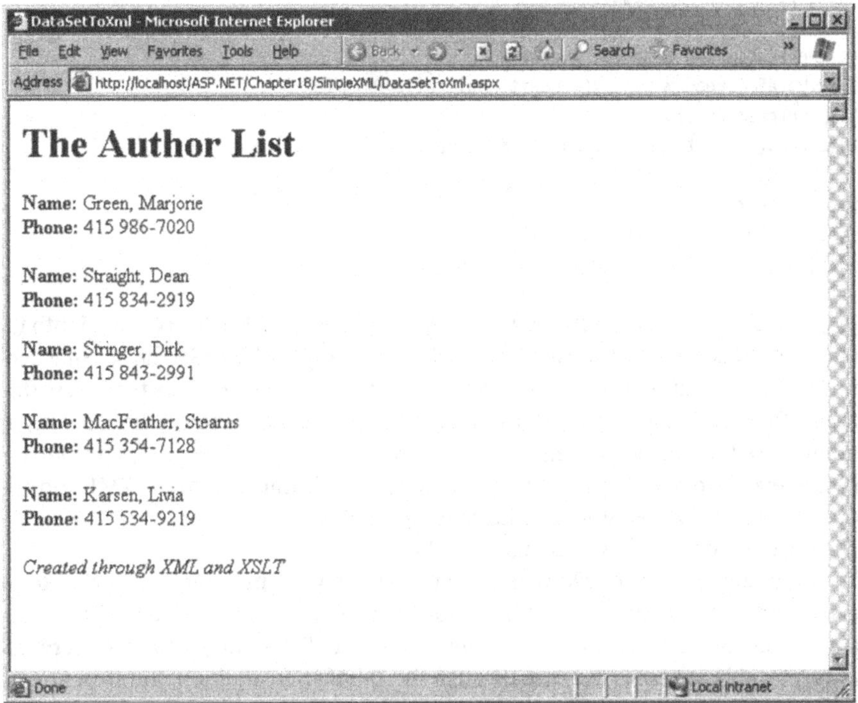

Figure 18-13. Displaying the results of a query through XML and XSLT

Remember, when you interact with your data as XML, all the customary database-oriented concepts like relationships and unique constraints go out the window. The only reason you should interact with your DataSet as XML is if you need to perform an XML-specific task, not to replace the approaches used in Chapter 14 to update data. In most cases, you'll find it easier to use advanced controls like the DataList and DataGrid, rather than creating a dedicated XSL transform to transform data into the HTML you want to display.

Accessing XML Through the DataSet

Often, a more useful way to use the XmlDataDocument is to access an ordinary XML file as though it were one or more tables. This means you don't need to work with the XML syntax you've explored, and you don't need to go to the work of extracting all the information and creating the appropriate objects and collections. Instead, you can use the familiar ADO.NET objects to manipulate the underlying XML document.

Consider these few remarkable lines of code:

```
Dim DataDoc As New XmlDataDocument()

' Set the schema and retrieve the data.
DataDoc.DataSet.ReadXmlSchema(Request.ApplicationPath & _
  "\SuperProProductList.xsd")
DataDoc.Load(Request.ApplicationPath & "\SuperProProductList.xml")

' Display the retrieved data.
dgResults.DataSource = DataDoc.DataSet
dgResults.DataBind()
```

In this example, a new XmlDataDocument is created, an XML file is loaded into it, and the information is automatically provided through a special DataSet that is "attached" to the XmlDataDocument. This allows you to use the ADO.NET objects to work with data (like the DataTable and DataRow objects), as well as the standard XmlDocument members (like the GetTagsByElementName() method and the ChildNodes property). You could even use both approaches at the same time, because both the XML and the ADO.NET interface access the same underlying data.

The retrieved data is shown in Figure 18-14.

The only catch is that your XML file must have a schema in order for ASP.NET to be able to determine the proper structure of your data. Before you retrieve the XML file, you must use the XmlDataDocument.DataSet.ReadXmlSchema() method. Otherwise, you won't be able to access the data through the DataSet. In addition, the structure of your XML document must conform to the table-based and row-based structure used by ADO.NET. You'll find that some XML files can be loaded into an XmlDataDocument more successfully than others

Clearly, if you need to store hierarchical data in an XML file and are willing to create an XSD schema, the XmlDataDocument is a great convenience. It also allows you to bridge the gap between ADO.NET and XML—some clients can look at the data as XML, while others can access it through the database objects without losing any information or requiring an error-prone conversion process.

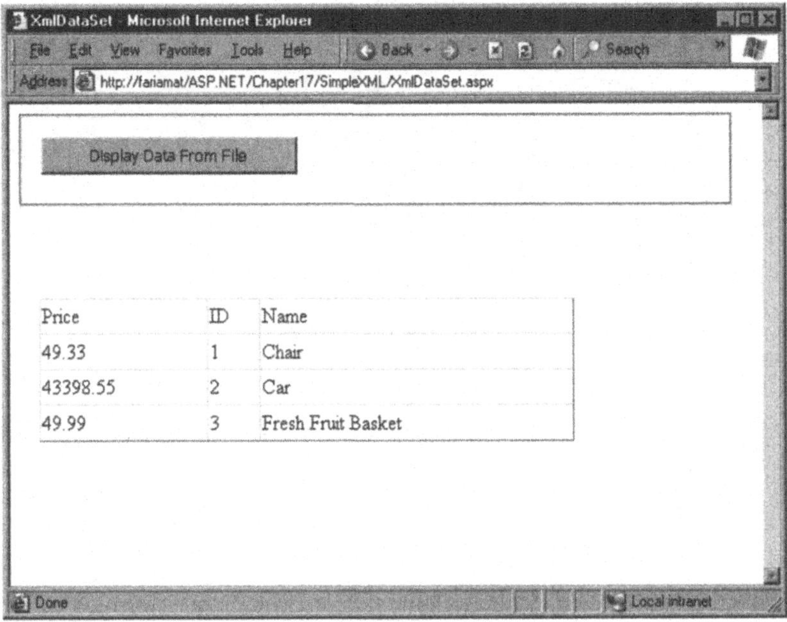

Figure 18-14. Accessing XML data through ADO.NET

The Last Word

Now that your lightning tour of XML and ASP.NET is drawing to a close, you should have a basic understanding of what XML is, how it looks, and why you might use it in a web page. XML represents a new tool for breaking down the barriers between different businesses and platforms—it's nothing less than a universal model for storing and communicating all types of information.

XML on its own is a remarkable innovation. However, to get the most out of XML you need to embrace other standards that allow you to validate XML, transform XML, and search XML for specific information. The .NET Framework provides classes for all of these tasks in the System.Xml namespaces. To continue your exploration, start with a comprehensive review of different XML standards (like the one provided at `http://www.w3schools.com/xml`) and then dive into the class library.

Part Four

Web Services

CHAPTER 19

Web Services Architecture

MICROSOFT HAS PROMOTED ASP.NET's new web services more than almost any other part of the .NET Framework. But despite their efforts, confusion is still widespread about what a web service is and, more importantly, what it's meant to accomplish. This chapter introduces web services and explains their role in Microsoft's vision of the programmable web. Along the way, you'll learn about the open standards plumbing that allows web services to work and removes some of the confusion surrounding technical terms like WSDL (Web Service Description Language), SOAP, and UDDI (universal description, discovery, and integration).

Internet Programming Then and Now

In order to understand the place of web services, you have to understand the shortcomings with the current architecture of Internet applications. In many respects, Internet applications are at the same point in their development that client/server desktop applications were seven years ago—the "monolithic" era. Today's Internet is dominated by full-featured websites that are written entirely from scratch, and aren't able to share functionality between each other.

The Era of Monolithic Applications

Most of the applications you use over the Internet today can be considered "monolithic," because they combine a variety of different services behind a single proprietary user interface. For example, you may already use your bank's website to do everything from checking exchange rates and reviewing stock quotes to paying bills and transferring funds. This is a successful model of development, but it has the following unavoidable shortcomings:

- Monolithic applications take a great deal of time and resources to create. They are often tied to a specific platform or to specific technologies, and they can't be easily extended and enhanced.

- Getting more than one application to work together is a full project of its own. Usually, an integration project involves a lot of custom work that's highly specific to a given scenario. And what's worse, every time you need to interact with another business, you need to start the integration process all over again. Currently, most websites limit themselves to extremely simple methods of integration. For example, you might be provided with a link that opens up another website in an existing frame on the current web page.

- Most importantly, units of application logic can't easily be reused between one application and another. With ASP.NET, source code can be shared using .NET classes, but this isn't possible for applications created by different companies or written using different programming languages. And if you want to perform more sophisticated or subtle integration, such as between a website and a Windows application, or between applications hosted on different platforms, there are no easy solutions available.
- Sometimes, you might want to get extremely simple information from a web application, such as an individual stock quote. In order to get this information, you usually need to access and navigate through the entire web application, locate the correct page, and then perform the required task. There's no way to access information or perform a task without working through the graphical user interface, which can be cumbersome over a slow connection or unworkable on a portable device like a cell phone.

Components and the COM Revolution

This state of affairs may sound familiar if you know the history of the Windows platform. A similar situation existed in the world of desktop applications many years ago. Developers found that they were spending the majority of their programming time solving problems they had already solved before. Programmers needed to structure in-house applications very carefully with DLLs or source code components in order to have any chance or reusing their work. Third-party applications usually could only be integrated through specific "pipelines." For example, one program might need to export to a set file format, which would then be manually imported into a different application. Companies focused on features and performance, but had no easy way to share data or work together.

The story improved dramatically when Microsoft introduced their COM technology (parts of which also goes by the more market-friendly name ActiveX). With COM, developers found that they could develop components in their language of choice, and reuse them in a variety of different programming environments, without needing to share source code. Similarly, there was less of a need to export and import information using proprietary file formats. Instead, COM components allowed developers to package functionality into succinct and reusable chunks with well-defined interfaces.

COM helped end the era of monolithic applications. Even though you still use database and office productivity applications like Microsoft Word, which seem to be monolithic, integrated applications, much of the functionality in these applications is delegated to separate components behind the scenes. As with all object-oriented programming, this makes code easier to debug, alter, and extend.

Web Services and the Programmable Web

Web services enable the same evolution that COM did, with a twist. Web services are individual units of programming logic that exist on a web server. They can be easily integrated into all sorts of applications, including everything from other ASP.NET applications to simple command-line applications. The twist is that, unlike COM, which is a platform-specific standard, web services are built on a foundation of open standards. These standards allow web services to be created with .NET but consumed on other platforms—or vice versa. In fact, the idea of web services didn't originate at Microsoft. Other major computer forces like IBM helped to develop the core standards that Microsoft uses natively in ASP.NET.

The root standard for all the individual web service standards is XML. Because XML is text-based, web service invocations can pass over normal HTTP channels. Other distributed object technologies, like DCOM, are much more complex and, as a result, they are exceedingly difficult to configure correctly, especially if you need to use them over the Internet. So not only are web services governed by cross-platform standards, but they're also easier to use.

The starting point for understanding a web service is seeing it as an individual function that's called over the Internet. Of course, this "function" has all the powerful capabilities that ASP.NET programmers are used to, such as the automatic security (see Chapter 25) and session-state facilities (see Chapter 10) discussed in other parts of this book.

When Web Services Make Sense

With the overbearing web services hype, developers sometimes forget to ask tough questions about when web services should and should *not* be used. Although web services are an impressive piece of technology, they aren't the best choice for all applications.

Microsoft recommends that web services be used when your application needs to cross *platform boundaries* or *trust boundaries*. You cross a platform boundary when your system incorporates a non-.NET application. In other words, web services are a perfect choice if you need to provide data to a Java client running on a Unix computer. Because web services are based on open standards, the Java developer simply needs to use a web service toolkit that's designed for the Java platform. The Java programmer can then call your .NET web services seamlessly, without worrying about any conversion issues.

You cross a trust boundary when your system incorporates applications from more than one company or organization. In other words, web services work well if you need to provide some information from a database (like a product catalog or customer list) to an application written by other developers. If you use web services, you won't need to supply the third-party developers with any special information—instead, they can get all the information using an automated tool that reads the WSDL document. You also won't need to give them access to privileged resources. For example, instead of connecting directly to your database or to a proprietary component, they can interact with the web service, which will retrieve the data for them. In fact, you can even use the same IIS (Internet Information Services) security settings that you use with web pages (see Chapter 25) to protect your web services!

If you aren't crossing platform or trust boundaries, web services might not be a great choice. For example, web services are generally a poor way to share functionality between two web applications on your web server, or between different types of applications in your company. Instead, it's a much better idea to develop and share a dedicated .NET component. This technique ensures optimum performance, because there is no need to translate data into XML or send messages over the network. It's described in more detail in Chapter 22, which tackles component-based development.

The Open Standards Plumbing

Before using web services, it helps to understand a little about the architecture that makes it all possible. Strictly speaking, this knowledge isn't required to work with web services. In fact, you can skip to the next chapter and start creating your first web service right now. However, understanding a little bit about the way web services work can help you determine how to use them best.

Remember, web services are designed from the ground up with open standard compatibility in mind. To ensure the greatest possible compatibility and extensibility, the web service architecture has been made as generic as possible. That means that very few assumptions are made about the format and encoding used to send information to and from a web service. Instead, all of these details are explicitly defined, in a very flexible way, using standards like SOAP and WSDL. And as you'll see, in order for a client to be able to connect to a web service, a lot of mundane work has to go on behind the scenes processing and interpreting this SOAP and WSDL information. This mundane work does exert a bit of a performance overhead, but it won't hamper most well-designed web services.

Table 19-1 summarizes the standards this chapter examines.

Table 19-1. Web Service Standards

Standard	Description
WSDL	The Web Service Description Language tells a client what methods are present in a web service, what parameters and return values each method uses, and how to communicate with them.
SOAP	The preferred way to encode information (such as data values) before sending it to a web service.
HTTP	The protocol over which all web service communication takes place. For example, SOAP message are sent over HTTP channels.
DISCO	The discovery standard that contains links to web services or can be used to provide a dynamic list of web services in a specified path.
UDDI	The business registry that lists information about companies, the web services they provide, and the corresponding URLs for DISCO file or WSDL contracts. Unfortunately, it's still too new to be widely accepted and useful.

Web Service Description Language

WSDL is an XML-based standard that specifies how a client can interact with a web service, including details such as how parameters and return values should be encoded in a message, and what protocol should be used for transmission over the Internet. Currently, three standards are supported for the actual transmission of web service information: HTTP GET, HTTP POST, and SOAP (over HTTP).

The full WSDL standard can be found at `http://www.w3.org/TR/wsdl`. The standard is fairly complex, but its underlying logic is hidden from the developer in ASP.NET programming, just as ASP.NET web controls abstract away the messy details of HTML tags and attributes. As you'll see in the next chapter, ASP.NET creates WSDL documents for your web services automatically. ASP.NET can also create a proxy class based on a WSDL document. This proxy class allows a client to call a web service without worrying about networking or formatting issues. Many non-.NET platforms provide similar tools to make these chores relatively painless. For example, Visual Basic 6 or C++ developers can use Microsoft's SOAP Toolkit (which is freely downloadable from `http://msdn.microsoft.com/downloads/list/websrv.asp`).

In the next few sections, you'll examine a sample WSDL document for a very simple web service, made up of a single method called GetStockQuote(). This method accepts a string specifying a stock ticker and returns a numeric value that represents a current price quote. The web service itself is called MyWebService, and you'll peer into its actual ASP.NET code in the next chapter.

NOTE The WSDL document contains information for communication between a web service and client. It doesn't contain any information that has anything to do with the code or implementation of your web service methods—that is unnecessary and would compromise security.

The <definitions> Element

The WSDL document is quite long, so the next few sections will consider it section by section, in order. Don't worry about understanding it in detail—the .NET Framework will handle that—but do use it to get an idea about how web services communicate.

The header and root namespace looks like this:

```
<?xml version="1.0" encoding="utf-8" ?>
<definitions xmlns:s="http://www.w3.org/2001/XMLSchema"
  xmlns:http="http://schemas.xmlsoap.org/wsdl/http/"
  xmlns:mime="http://schemas.xmlsoap.org/wsdl/mime/"
  xmlns:tm="http://microsoft.com/wsdl/mime/textMatching/"
  xmlns:soap="http://schemas.xmlsoap.org/wsdl/soap/"
  xmlns:soapenc="http://schemas.xmlsoap.org/soap/encoding/"
  xmlns:s0="http://tempuri.org/" targetNamespace="http://tempuri.org/"
  xmlns="http://schemas.xmlsoap.org/wsdl/">

  <!-- This is where all the rest of the WSDL document goes.
  I've snipped it into the individual pieces shown in the
  rest of the chapter. -->

</definitions>
```

Looking at the WSDL document, you'll notice that an XML tag structure is used. All the information is contained in a root <definitions> element.

The <types> Element

The first element contained inside the <description> element is a <types> element that defines information about the data types of the return value and parameters your web service method uses. If your web service returns an instance of a custom class, ASP.NET will add an extra entry to define your class (although only data members will be preserved, not methods, which can't be converted into an XML representation).

The <types> element for the sample MyWebService is shown here. By looking at it, you can tell that the function, GetStockQuote(), uses a string parameter, called Ticker, and a decimal return value. The corresponding lines are highlighted in bold.

```
<types>
  <s:schema attributeFormDefault="qualified" elementFormDefault="qualified"
  targetNamespace="http://tempuri.org/">
    <s:element name="GetStockQuote">
      <s:complexType>
        <s:sequence>
          <s:element minOccurs="1" maxOccurs="1" name="Ticker"
             nillable="true" type="s:string"/>
        </s:sequence>
      </s:complexType>
    </s:element>
    <s:element name="GetStockQuoteResponse">
      <s:complexType>
        <s:sequence>
          <s:element minOccurs="1" maxOccurs="1"
             name="GetStockQuoteResult" type="s:decimal"/>
        </s:sequence>
      </s:complexType>
    </s:element>
    <s:element name="decimal" type="s:decimal"/>
  </s:schema>
</types>
```

Incidentally, the information in the <types> section is defined using the XML schema standard (XSD). Chapter 18 introduced this standard with a look at XML validation. The same technique is used in web services to validate the messages that are exchanged between a web service and a client, although the process is completely seamless.

The <message> Elements

Messages represent the information exchanged between a web service method and a client. When you request a stock quote from the simple web service, ASP.NET sends a message, and the web service sends a different message back. The definition for these messages is found in the <message> section of the WSDL document. Here's an example:

```
<message name="GetStockQuoteSoapIn">
  <part name="parameters" element="s0:GetStockQuote"/>
</message>
<message name="GetStockQuoteSoapOut">
  <part name="parameters" element="s0:GetStockQuoteResponse"/>
</message>
```

In this example, you'll notice that ASP.NET creates both a GetStockQuoteSoapIn and a GetStockQuoteSoapOut message. The naming is optional, but it underscores the fact that a separate message is required for input (sending parameters and invoking a web service method) and output (retrieving a return value from a web service method).

The data used in these messages is defined in terms of the information in the <types> section. For example, the GetStockQuoteSoapIn request message sends the GetStockQuote element, which is defined in the <types> section as a string named Ticker.

Similar message definitions are used for the other two types of communication, HTTP POST and HTTP GET. These are simpler communication methods that are primarily used for testing. Instead of using a full-fledged SOAP message, they just send simple XML.

```
<message name="GetStockQuoteHttpGetIn">
  <part name="Ticker" type="s:string"/>
</message>
<message name="GetStockQuoteHttpGetOut">
  <part name="Body" element="s0:decimal"/>
</message>
<message name="GetStockQuoteHttpPostIn">
  <part name="Ticker" type="s:string"/>
</message>
<message name="GetStockQuoteHttpPostOut">
  <part name="Body" element="s0:decimal"/>
</message>
```

Remember, MyWebService only contains one method. The three versions of it that you see in WSDL are provided and supported by ASP.NET automatically to allow the client the chance to choose a preferred method of communication.

The <portType> Elements

The information in the <portType> section of the WSDL document provides an overview of all the methods available in the web service. Each method is defined as an <operation>, and each operation includes the request and response message.

For example, you'll see that for the SOAP port type (MyWebServiceSoap), the GetStockQuote() method requires an input message called GetStockQuoteIn and a matching output message called GetStockQuoteOut.

```
<portType name="MyWebServiceSoap">
  <operation name="GetStockQuote">
    <input message="s0:GetStockQuoteSoapIn"/>
    <output message="s0:GetStockQuoteSoapOut"/>
  </operation>
</portType>
<portType name="MyWebServiceHttpGet">
  <operation name="GetStockQuote">
    <input message="s0:GetStockQuoteHttpGetIn"/>
    <output message="s0:GetStockQuoteHttpGetOut"/>
  </operation>
</portType>
<portType name="MyWebServiceHttpPost">
  <operation name="GetStockQuote">
    <input message="s0:GetStockQuoteHttpPostIn"/>
    <output message="s0:GetStockQuoteHttpPostOut"/>
  </operation>
</portType>
```

The <binding> Elements

The <binding> elements link the abstract data format to the concrete protocol used for transmission over an Internet connection. So far, the WSDL document has specified the data type used for various pieces of information, the required messages used for an operation, and the structure of each message. With the <binding> element, the WSDL document specifies the low-level communication protocol that you can use to talk to a web service.

For example, the MyWebService WSDL document specifies that the SOAP-specific GetStockQuote operation communicates using SOAP messages. The HTTP POST and HTTP GET operations receive information as an XML document (type mimeXML), and send it encoded as either a query string argument (type http:urlEncded) or in the body of a posted form (type application/x-www-form-urlencoded).

```
<binding name="MyWebServiceSoap" type="s0:MyWebServiceSoap">
  <soap:binding transport="http://schemas.xmlsoap.org/soap/http"
   style="document"/>
  <operation name="GetStockQuote">
    <soap:operation soapAction="http://tempuri.org/GetStockQuote"
     style="document"/>
    <input>
      <soap:body use="literal"/>
    </input>
    <output>
      <soap:body use="literal"/>
    </output>
  </operation>
</binding>
```

```
<binding name="MyWebServiceHttpGet" type="s0:MyWebServiceHttpGet">
  <http:binding verb="GET"/>
  <operation name="GetStockQuote">
    <http:operation location="/GetStockQuote"/>
    <input>
      <http:urlEncoded/>
    </input>
    <output>
      <mime:mimeXml part="Body"/>
    </output>
  </operation>
</binding>
<binding name="MyWebServiceHttpPost" type="s0:MyWebServiceHttpPost">
  <http:binding verb="POST"/>
  <operation name="GetStockQuote">
    <http:operation location="/GetStockQuote"/>
    <input>
      <mime:content type="application/x-www-form-urlencoded"/>
    </input>
    <output>
      <mime:mimeXml part="Body"/>
    </output>
  </operation>
</binding>
```

The <service> Element

The <service> element defines the "entry points" into your web service. This is how a client accesses the web service.

An ASP.NET web service defines three different <port> elements in the <service> element, one for each protocol. Inside each <port> element is another element that identifies the Internet address (URL) needed to access the web service. Most web services (and all ASP.NET web services) use the same URL address for all types of communication.

```
<service name="MyWebService">
  <port name="MyWebServiceSoap" binding="s0:MyWebServiceSoap">
    <soap:address
        location="http://localhost/MyWebService/MyWebService.asmx"/>
  </port>
  <port name="MyWebServiceHttpGet" binding="s0:MyWebServiceHttpGet">
    <http:address
        location="http://localhost/MyWebService/MyWebService.asmx"/>
  </port>
  <port name="MyWebServiceHttpPost" binding="s0:MyWebServiceHttpPost">
    <http:address
        location="http://localhost/MyWebService/MyWebService.asmx"/>
  </port>
</service>
```

TIP Here's a neat trick: Any existing ASP.NET service will display its corresponding WSDL document if you add L?WSDL to the query string. For example, you could look at the WSDL document for the preceding web service example by navigating to `http://localhost/MyWebService/MyWebService.asmx?WSDL`. One of the greatest benefits of web services is their auto-discovery and self-description features.

SOAP

As the WSDL document shows, there are three different protocols a client can use to communicate with a web service:

- HTTP GET, which communicates with a web service by encoding information in the query string, and retrieves information as a basic XML document.
- HTTP POST, which places parameters in the request body (as form values), and retrieves information as a basic XML document.
- SOAP, which uses XML for both request and response messages. Like HTTP GET and HTTP POST, SOAP works over HTTP, but it uses a more detailed XML-based language for bundling up information. SOAP messages are widely supported by many platforms.

A Sample SOAP Message

Essentially, when you use the SOAP protocol, you're simply using the SOAP standard to encode the information in your messages. SOAP messages follow an XML-based standard, and look something like this:

```
<?xml version="1.0" encoding="UTF-8" standalone="no"?>
<soap:Envelope xmlns="http://schemas.xmlsoap.org/soap/envelope/">
  <soap:Body>
    <GetStockQuote xmlns ="http://tempuri.org/message/">
      <Ticker>MSFT</Ticker>
    </GetStockQuote>
  </soap:Body>
</soap:Envelope>
```

Looking at the preceding SOAP message, you can see that the root element is a <soap:envelope>, which contains the <soap:body> of the request. Inside the body is information indicating that the GetStockQuote() method is being called, with a Ticker parameter of MSFT. While this is a fairly straightforward method call, SOAP messages can easily contain entire structures representing custom objects or DataSets.

In response to this request, a SOAP output message will be returned. Here's an example of what you might expect:

```
<?xml version="1.0" encoding="utf-8"?>
<soap:Envelope xmlns="http://schemas.xmlsoap.org/soap/envelope/">
  <soap:Body>
    <GetStockQuoteResponse xmlns="http://www.prosetech.com/Stocks">
      <GetStockQuoteResult>29.23</GetStockQuoteResult>
    </GetStockQuoteResponse>
  </soap:Body>
</soap:Envelope>
```

NOTE You may have already noticed why the SOAP message format is superior to HTTP GET and HTTP POST. When using SOAP, both request and response messages are formatted using XML. When using HTTP GET and HTTP POST, the response messages use XML, but the request messages use simple name/value pairs to supply the parameter information. This means that HTTP GET and HTTP POST won't allow you to use complex objects as parameters, and won't be natively supported on most non-.NET platforms. HTTP GET and HTTP POST are primarily included for testing purposes.

Remember, your applications won't directly handle SOAP messages. Instead, .NET will translate the information in a SOAP message into the corresponding .NET data types before it reaches your code. This allows you to interact with web services in the same way that you interact with any other object.

For information about the SOAP standard, you can read the full specification at `http://www.w3.org/TR/SOAP`. (Once again, these technical details explain a lot about how SOAP works, but are rarely implemented in day-to-day programming.)

Communicating with a Web Service

The WSDL and SOAP standards enable the communication between web service and client, but they don't show how it happens. The following three components play a role:

- A custom web service class that provides some piece of functionality.
- A client application that wants to use this functionality.
- A proxy class that acts as the interface between the two. The proxy class contains a representation of all the web service methods, and takes care of the details involved with communicating with the web service by the chosen protocol.

The actual process works like this (see Figure 19-1):

1. The client creates an instance of a proxy class.
2. The client invokes the method on the proxy class, exactly as though it were using a normal, local class.

3. Behind the scenes, the proxy class sends the information to the web service in the appropriate format (usually SOAP) and receives the corresponding response, which is deserialized into the corresponding data or object.

4. The proxy class returns the result to the calling code.

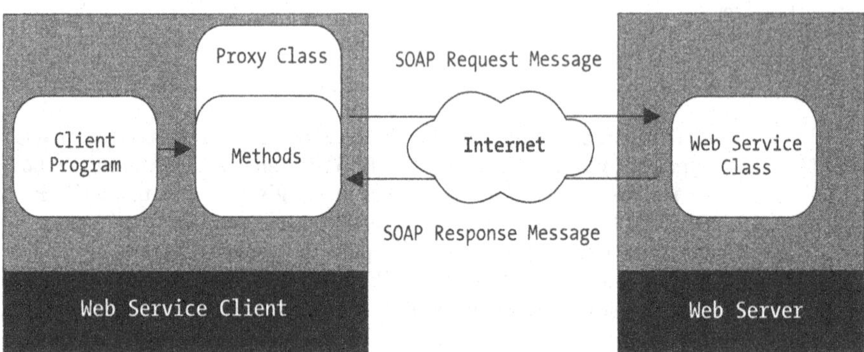

Figure 19-1. Web service communication

Perhaps the most significant detail lies in the fact that the client doesn't need to be aware that a remote function call to a web service is being made. The process is completely transparent and works as though you were calling a function in your own local code!

Of course, the following additional limitations and considerations apply:

- Not all data types are supported for method parameters and return values. For example, you can't pass many .NET class library objects (the DataSet is one important exception).

- The network call takes a short but measurable amount of time. If you need to use several web service methods in a row, this delay can start to add up.

- Unless the web service takes specific steps to remember its state information, this data will be lost. Basically, this means that you should treat a web service like a stateless utility class, composed of as many independent methods as you need. You shouldn't think of a web service as an ordinary object with properties and member variables.

- There are a variety of new errors that can occur and interrupt your web method (for example, network problems). You may need to take this into account when building a robust application.

You'll examine all of these issues in detail throughout the next two chapters.

Web Service Discovery and UDDI

Imagine you've created a web service that uses WSDL to describe how it works and transmits information in SOAP packets. Inevitably, you'll start to ask how clients can find your web services. At first thought, it seems to be a trivial question. Clearly, a web service is available at a specific URL address. Once the client has this address, the WSDL document can be retrieved by adding ?WSDL to the URL, and all the necessary information is available. So why is a discovery standard required at all?

The straightforward process described earlier works great if you only need to share a web service with specific clients or inside a single organization. However, as web services become more and more numerous and eventually evolve into a common language for performing business transactions over the Web, this manual process seems less and less practical. For one thing, if a company provides a dozen web services, how does it communicate each of these 12 URLs to prospective clients? Emailing them to individual developers is sure to take up time and create inefficiency. Trying to recite them over the telephone is worse. Providing an HTML page that consolidates all the appropriate links is a start, but it will still force client application developers to manually enter information into their programs. If this information changes later on, it will result in painstaking minor changes that could cause countless headaches. Sometimes, trivial details aren't so trivial.

The DISCO Standard

The DISCO standard picks up where the "HTML page with links" concept ends. When following the DISCO standard you provide a .disco file that specifies where a web service is located. Tools such as Visual Studio .NET can read the discover file and automatically provide you with the list of corresponding web services.

Here is a sample .disco file:

```
<disco:discovery  xmlns:disco="http://schemas.xmlsoap.org/disco"
  xmlns:wsdl="http://schemas.xmlsoap.org/disco/wsdl">
    <wsdl:contractRef
          ref="http://localhoust/MyWebService/MyWebService.asmx?WSDL"/>
</disco:discovery>
```

The benefit of a .disco file is that it is clearly used for web services (while .html and .aspx files can contain any kind of content). The other advantage is that you can insert <disco> elements for as many web services as you want, including ones that reside on other web servers. In other words, a .disco file provides a straightforward way to create a repository of web service links that can be used automatically by .NET.

Dynamic Discovery

ASP.NET can also use dynamic discovery. An example is shown here:

```
<?xml version="1.0" encoding="utf-8" ?>
<dynamicDiscovery xmlns="urn:schemas-dynamicdiscovery:disco.2000-03-17">
<exclude path="_vti_cnf" />
<exclude path="_vti_pvt" />
<exclude path="_vti_log" />
<exclude path="_vti_script" />
<exclude path="_vti_txt" />
<exclude path="Web References" />
</dynamicDiscovery>
```

A <dynamicDiscovery> element doesn't specifically reference individual web services. Instead, it instructs ASP.NET to search all the subdirectories under the current directory for web services. By creating a dynamic discovery file, you can be certain that your discovery will always provide an up-to-date list of all the web services you have.

The <exclude> elements tell the discovery process not to look in those folders. This can be used to save time (for example, by restricting directories that just contain images). It can also restrict a web service from appearing publicly in a discovery process, although it will still be accessible unless you have specifically written authentication or security code.

TIP Do you need discovery files? ASP.NET web services don't require any kind of discovery file. You may not need to make a web service easily available. But in many scenarios this standard makes the business aspect of using web services a lot easier. Visual Studio .NET automatically creates a discovery document for your computer that references all the web services you create. When Visual Studio .NET creates a discovery file, it uses the extension .vsdisco.

Universal Description, Discovery, and Integration

UDDI is one of the youngest and most rapidly developing standards in the web service family. UDDI is a Microsoft-led initiative designed to make it easier for you to locate web services on any server.

With discovery files, the client still needs to know the specific URL location of the discovery file. Discovery files may make life easier by consolidating multiple web services into one document, but they don't provide any obvious way to examine the web services offered by a company without navigating to their website and looking for a .disco hyperlink. The goal of UDDI, on the other hand, is to provide a repository where businesses can advertise all the web services they have. For example, a company might list the services it has for business document exchange, which describe how purchase orders can be submitted and tracking information can be retrieved. In order to submit this information, a business must be registered with the service. In some ways, UDDI is the equivalent of a Yahoo! for web services.

There are three main sections to the UDDI:

- White pages, which provide business contact information
- Yellow pages, which organize XML web services into categories
- Green pages, which provide detailed technical information about individual services (this information may be provided by referencing discovery documents or WSDL contracts)

Interestingly enough, the UDDI registry defines a complete programming interface that specifies how SOAP messages can be used to retrieve information about a business or register the web services for a business. In other words, the UDDI registry is itself a web service! This standard is still too new to really be of use, but you can find detailed specifications at `http://uddi.microsoft.com`.

Where Are Web Services Today?

Currently, first-generation web services are being used to bridge the gaps between modern applications and older technologies. For example, an organization might use a web service to provide access to a legacy database. Internal applications can then contact the web service instead of needing to interact directly with the database, which could be much more difficult. Similar techniques are being used to allow different applications to interact. For example, web services can act as a kind of "glue" that allows a payroll system to interact with another type of financial application in the same company.

The second generation of web services are those that allow partnering companies to work together. For example, an e-commerce company might need to submit orders or track parcels through the web service provided by a shipping company. Second-generation web services require two companies to work closely together to devise a strategy for exposing the functionality they each need. Second-generation web services are in their infancy, but are gaining ground quickly.

The third generation of web services will allow developers to create much more modular applications by aggregating many different services into one application. For example, you might add a virtual hard drive to your web applications using a third-party web service. You would pay a subscription fee to the web service provider, but the end user wouldn't be aware of what application functionality is provided by you and what functionality relies on third-party web services. This third generation of web services will require new standards and enhancements that will allow web services to better deal with issues like reliability, discovery, and performance. These standards are constantly evolving, and it's anyone's guess how long it will be before third-generation web services begin to flourish, but it's probably just a matter of time.

The Last Word

This chapter introduced web services, explained the role they play in distributed applications, and dissected the standards and technologies they rely on to provide their magic. In the next chapter you'll see just how easy .NET makes it to create your own web services.

CHAPTER 20

Creating Web Services

WEB SERVICES HAVE the potential to simplify web development dramatically. They might even lead to a new generation of applications that seamlessly integrate multiple remote services into a single web page or desktop interface. However, the greatest programming concept in the world is doomed to fail if it isn't supported by powerful, flexible tools that make its use not only possible, but convenient. Fortunately, ASP.NET doesn't disappoint. It provides classes that allow you to create a web service quickly and easily.

In the previous chapter you looked at the philosophy that lead to the creation of web services, and the XML infrastructure that makes it all possible. This chapter delves into the practical side of web services, leading you through the process of designing and coding web services. You'll also consider how a web service can use transactions, caching, and security.

Web Service Basics

As you've already seen in this book, ASP.NET is based on object-oriented principles. The traditional (and primitive) script-based programming used in ASP has been replaced with classes that wrap code into neat reusable objects. Web services follow that pattern—in fact, every web service is really an ordinary class. A client can create an instance of your web service and use its methods just as though it were any other locally defined class. The underlying HTTP transmission and data type conversion that must happen are handled behind the scenes.

How does this magic work? It's made possible by the .NET Framework and the types in the System.Web.Services namespace.

A typical web service consists of a few basic ingredients:

- **An .asmx text file that contains the web service code.** Alternatively, if you're using Visual Studio .NET, the web service code will be in a separate code-behind file. You'll see both of these techniques in this chapter.

- **The web service class code.** Typically, this class will inherit from System.Web.Services.WebService, but it doesn't need to.

- **One or more web service methods.** These are ordinary methods in the web service class that are with a special WebMethod attribute. This attribute indicates that the corresponding method should be exposed over the Internet.

ASP.NET will manage the lower-level details for you. For example, you never need to create a WSDL (Web Service Description Language) document or a SOAP message. ASP.NET automatically generates the WSDL document for your web methods when it's requested, and converts ordinary .NET method calls to SOAP messages behind the scenes.

The only layer you need to worry about is the business-specific code that actually performs the task (like inserting data into a database, creating a file, performing a calculation, and so on). This code is written like any other Visual Basic .NET method.

The StockQuote Web Service

The previous chapter examined the WSDL document generated for a simple web service that contained only one method. The following example shows the corresponding web service code in an .asmx text file:

```
<%@ WebService Language="VB" Class="StockQuote" %>

Imports System.Web.Services

Public Class StockQuote
    Inherits WebService

    <WebMethod> Public Function GetStockQuote(Ticker As String) _
      As Decimal
        ' (Insert some database code here to look up
        ' and return the quote.)
    End Function

End Class
```

The StockQuote class looks more or less the same as any .NET class. The two differences—inheriting from WebService and using the WebMethod attribute—are highlighted in the example.

An .asmx file is similar to the standard .aspx file used for graphical ASP.NET pages. As with .aspx files, .asmx files start with a directive that specifies the language, and are compiled the first time they are requested in order to increase performance. They can be created with Notepad or any other text editor. The letter "m" indicates "method"—because all web services are built out of one or more web methods that provide the actual functionality.

Understanding the StockQuote Service

The code for the StockQuote web service is quite straightforward. The first line specifies that the file is used for a web service and is written in Visual Basic .NET code. The next line imports the web service namespace so that all the classes you need are at your fingertips. As with other core pieces of ASP.NET technology, web service functionality is provided through prebuilt types in the .NET class library.

The remainder of the code is the actual web service, which is built out of a single class that derives from WebService. In the previous example, the web service class contains a method called GetStockQuote(). This is a normal Visual Basic .NET function, with a special <WebMethod> attribute before its definition.

.NET attributes are used to describe code. The WebMethod attribute doesn't change how your function works, but it does tell ASP.NET that this is one of the procedures it must make available over the Internet. Functions or subroutines that don't have this attribute won't be accessible (or even visible) to remote clients, regardless of whether they are defined with the Private or Public keyword.

You Don't Need to Inherit from WebService

The .NET Framework contains the functionality for communicating over the Internet and generating WSDL documents for your code. This functionality is automatically provided to any method marked with the WebMethod attribute, even if you don't inherit from the WebService class. So why bother?

Inheriting from WebService is a convenience that makes sure you can access the built-in ASP.NET objects (such as Application Session, and User) just as easily as you can in a web form. These objects are provided as properties of the WebService class, which your web service acquires through inheritance. If you don't need to use any of these objects (or if you're willing to go through the shared HttpContext.Current property to access them), you don't need to inherit.

Here's how you would access Session state in a web service if you derive from the base WebService class:

```
' Store a number in session state.
Session("Counter") = 10
```

Here's the equivalent code you would need to use if your web service class doesn't derive from WebService:

```
' Store a number in session state.
HttpContext.Current.Session("Counter") = 10
```

The best way to understand a web service is to think of it as a *business object*. Business objects support your programs, but don't take part in creating any user interface. For example, business objects might have helper functions that retrieve information from a database, perform calculations, or process custom data and return the results. Your code creates business objects whenever it needs to retrieve or store specific information, such as report information from a database. Sometimes business objects are called *service providers*, because they perform a task (a service), but they rarely retain any information in memory.

Probably the most amazing part of this example is that the StockQuote web service is now complete. All you need to do is copy the .asmx file to your web server in a virtual directory that other clients can access over the Internet, as you would with an .aspx page. Other clients can then start creating instances of your class and can call the GetStockQuote() method as though it were a locally defined procedure. All they need to do is use .NET to create a proxy class. The process of creating a client is demonstrated in Chapter 21.

Web Services with Code-Behind

As you've seen with web pages, Visual Studio .NET uses code-behind files so you can separate design and code. In the case of .asmx files, this feature isn't really necessary. Web service files consist entirely of code and don't contain any user interface elements. However, to maintain consistency, Visual Studio .NET uses the same system that it uses with web pages, which means that every web service you create will have both an .asmx and a .vb file. You won't notice this while you're using the Visual Studio .NET IDE, because the .asmx file is hidden from you. However, when you deploy your web service to the server, you'll have to be sure to copy both the .asmx file and the compiled code-behind DLL.

The code-behind version of the StockQuote web service would look like this:

StockQuote.asmx

```
<%@ WebService Language="vb"
    Codebehind="StockQuote.asmx.vb"
    Class="StockApp.StockQuote" %>
```

StockQuote.asmx.vb

```
Imports System.Web.Services

Public Class StockQuote
    Inherits WebService

    #Region " web services Designer Generated Code "
        ' The infrastructure code in this region is added
        ' automatically. It contains information for any
        ' components you add from the toolbox.
        ' Generally, this region won't have any important code for
        ' web services.
    #End Region

    <WebMethod()> Public Function GetStockQuote(Ticker As String) _
      As Decimal
        ' (Lookup code goes here.)
    End Function

End Class
```

Note that the client always connects to web service using a URL that points to the .asmx file, much as a client requests a web page using a URL that points to an .aspx file.

Documenting Your Web Service

Web services are self-describing, which means that ASP.NET automatically provides all the information the client needs about what methods are available and what parameters they require. This is all accomplished through the WSDL document. However, while the WSDL document describes the mechanics of the web service, it doesn't describe its purpose, or the meaning of the information supplied to and returned from each method. Most web services will provide this information in separate developer documents. However, you can (and should) include a bare minimum of information with your web service by using attributes.

TIP Attributes are a special language construct built into the .NET Framework. Essentially, attributes describe your code to the .NET runtime by adding extra metadata. The attributes you use for web service description are recognized by the .NET Framework, and provided to clients in automatically generated description documents and through the Internet Explorer test page. Attributes are used in many other situations, and even if you haven't encountered them before, you're sure to encounter them again in .NET programming.

Descriptions

You can add descriptions to each function through the WebMethod attribute, and to the entire web service as a whole using a WebService attribute. For example, the StockQuote service could be described like this:

```
<WebService(Description:="Retrieve information about a stock.")> _
Public Class StockQuote
    Inherits WebService

    <WebMethod(Description:="Gets a quote for a NASDAQ stock.")> _
    Public Function GetStockQuote(Ticker As String) As Decimal
        (Lookup code goes here.)
    End Function

End Class
```

In this example, the line continuation character (_) is used to put the attributes on a separate line. You might also notice that the Description is added as a named argument using the := operator.

These custom descriptions will appear in two important places. First of all, they will be added to the WSDL document that ASP.NET generates automatically. The descriptive information is added as <documentation> tags:

```
<service name="StockQuote">
  <documentation>Methods to get information about a NASDAQ
stock.</documentation>

  <!-- Port elements are defined here. -->
</service>
```

The descriptive information will also appear in the automatically generated browser test page, which is more likely to be viewed by the client. The test page is described later in this chapter.

Specifying an XML Namespace

You should specify a unique namespace for your web service that can't be confused with the namespaces used for other web services on the Internet. Note that this is an XML namespace, not a .NET namespace. It doesn't affect how your code works, or how the client uses your web service. Instead, this namespace is used to uniquely identify your web service in the WSDL document. XML namespaces look like URLs, but they don't need to correspond to a valid Internet location. For more information, refer to the XML overview in Chapter 18.

Ideally, the namespace you use will refer to a URL address that you control. Often, this will incorporate your company's Internet domain name as part of the namespace. For example, if your company uses the website http://www.mycompany.com, you might give the stock quote web service a namespace like http://www.mycompany.com/StockQuote. If you don't specify a namespace, the default (http://tempuri.org/) will be used. This is fine for development, but you'll see a warning message in the test page advising you to use something more distinctive.

The namespace is specified through the WebService attribute, as shown here. As with any VB code statement, you need to use the line continuation character (an underscore) to split it over more than one line.

```
<WebService(Description:="Methods to ...", _
Namespace:="http://www.prosetech.com/Stocks")>
```

TIP Before you continue, you should specify a custom namespace using the Namespace property of the WebService attribute. Without it, you'll receive a warning message and the Internet Explorer test page will contain a lengthy (and somewhat annoying) description about how to change namespaces.

Testing Your Web Service

Even without creating a client for your web service, you can use the built-in features of the .NET Framework to view information about your web service and perform a rudimentary test.

The most useful testing feature is the ASP.NET test page: an automatically generated HTML page that lets you execute the methods in a web service and review its WSDL document. There are no special steps required to see this page—ASP.NET generates it automatically when you request an .asmx web service file without specifying any additional information.

Before continuing any further, you should modify the GetStockQuote() method in the same web service so that it returns a hard-coded number. This will allow you to test that it's working with the test page. For example, you could use the statement Return Ticker.Length. That way, the return value will be the number of characters you supplied in the Ticker parameter.

```
<WebMethod(Description:="Gets a quote for a NASDAQ stock.")> _
Public Function GetStockQuote(Ticker As String) As Decimal
   Return Ticker.Length
End Function
```

The Web Service Test Page

To view the IE test page, you can do one of two things:

- If you're creating your .asmx file using a text editor, place the file in an appropriate virtual directory, and then request it with your browser (using a URL like http://localhost/MyVirtualDirectory/StockQuote.asmx).
- If you're creating your web service in Visual Studio .NET, just click the Run button.

This window (shown in Figure 20-1) lists all the available web service methods (in this case only one, GetStockQuote(), is available). It also lists whatever description information you may have added through the WebMethod and WebService attributes.

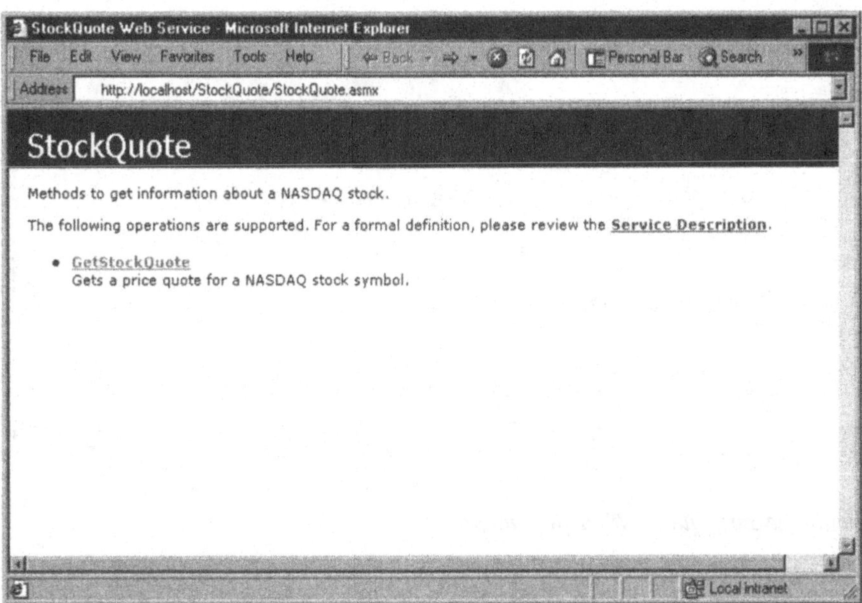

Figure 20-1. The web service test page

Remember, you don't need to write any special code to make this page appear. It's generated for you automatically by ASP.NET, and is intended purely as a testing convenience. Clients using your web service won't browse to this page to interact with your web service, but they might use it to find out some basic information about how to use it.

Service Description

You can also click the Service Descriptions link to display the WSDL description of your web service (see Figure 20-2), which you examined in detail in Chapter 19.

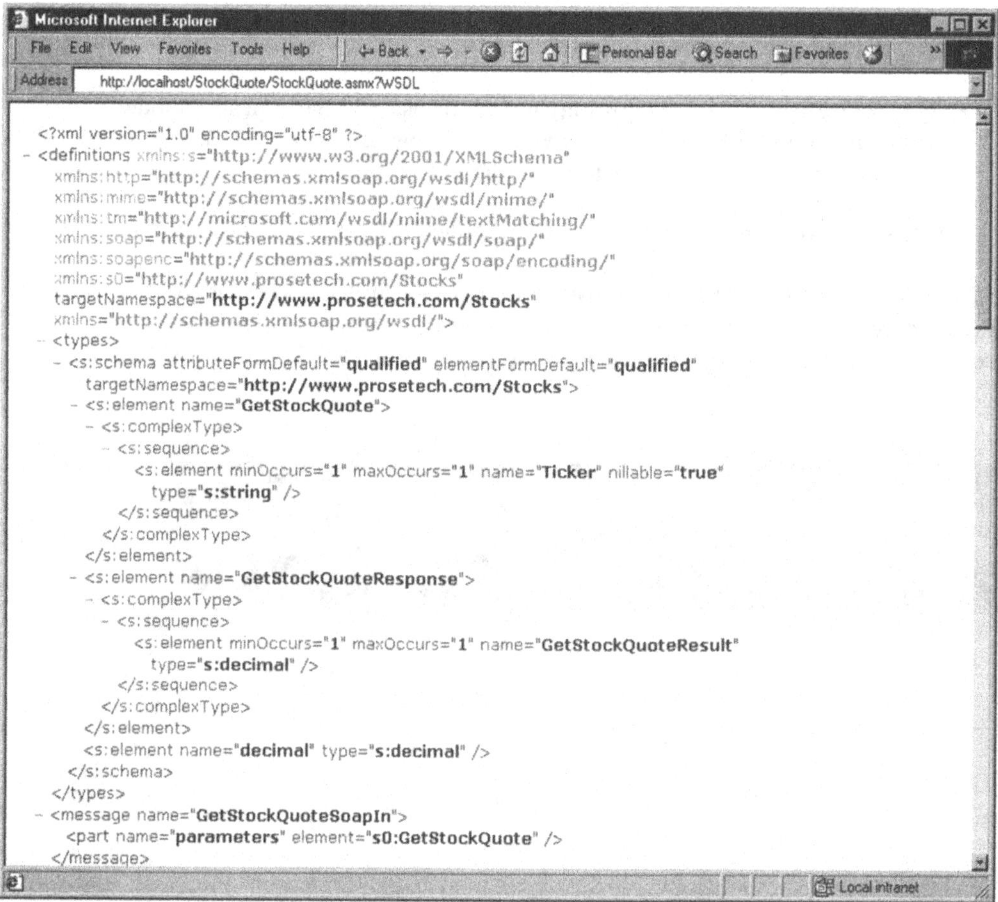

Figure 20-2. Viewing the StockQuote WSDL document

When you click on this link, the browser makes a request to the .asmx file with a WSDL parameter in the query string.

```
http://localhost/StockQuote/StockQuote.asmx?WSDL
```

If you know the location of an ASP.NET web service file, you can always retrieve its WSDL document by adding ?WSDL to the URL. This provides a standard way for a client to find all the information it needs to make a successful connection. Whenever ASP.NET receives a URL in this format, it generates and returns the WSDL document for the web service.

Method Description

You can find out information about the methods in your web service by clicking the corresponding link. For example, in the StockQuote web service you can click the GetStockQuote() link (see Figure 20-3).

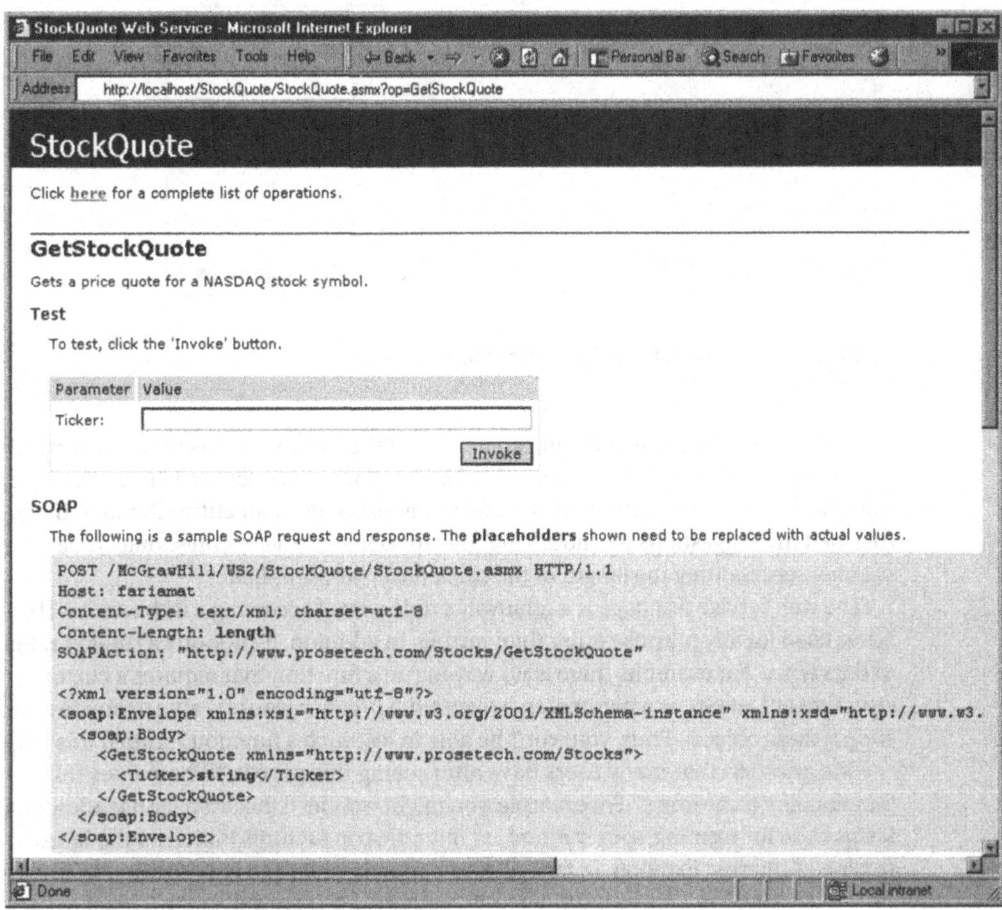

Figure 20-3. The GetStockQuote() method description

This window provides two sections. The first part is made up of a text box and Invoke button that allow you to run the function without needing to create a client. The second part is a list of the different protocols you can use to connect with the web service (HTTP POST, HTTP GET, and SOAP), and a technical description of the message format for each one.

Testing a Method

To test your method, enter a ticker and click the Invoke button. The result will be returned to you as an HTML page (see Figure 20-4).

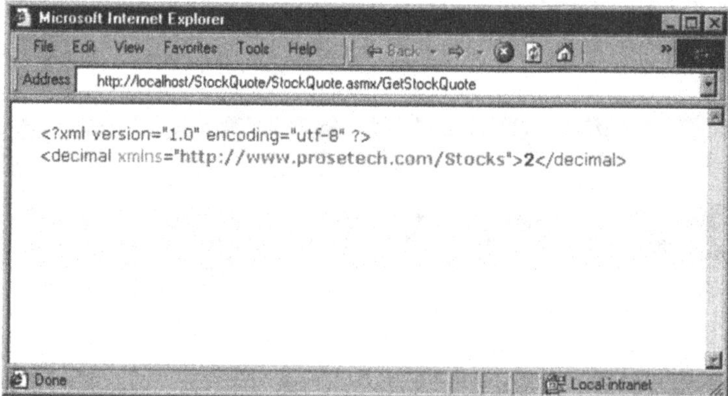

Figure 20-4. The result from GetStockQuote()

This may not be the result you expected, but the information is there—wrapped inside the tags of an XML document. This format allows a web service to return complex information, such as a class with several members or even an entire DataSet. If you followed the suggestions for modifying the StockQuote service, you should see a number representing the length of the stock ticker you supplied.

The web service test page is a relatively crude way of accessing a web service. It's never used for any purpose other than testing. In addition, it supports a smaller range of data types. For example, there is no way to run a function that requires a custom structure or DataSet as a parameter, because the browser won't be able to create and supply these objects. Thus, you won't be able to test such a function through this page.

One question that many users have after seeing this page is "Where does this functionality come from?" For example, you might wonder if the test page has additional script code for running your method, or if it relies on features built into the latest version of Internet Explorer. In fact, all that happens when you click the Invoke button is a normal HTTP operation. In version 1.1 of the .NET Framework, this operation is an HTTP POST that submits the parameters you supply. If you look at the URL for the result page, you'll see the following:

```
http://localhost/StockQuote/StockQuote.asmx/GetStockQuote
```

In version 1.0 of the .NET Framework, the test page performs an HTTP GET request when you click the Invoke button. In this case, the parameters you supply are sent using the query string. The URL will look slightly different because you'll be able to clearly see the parameter values that are being submitted, as shown here:

```
http://localhost/StockQuote/StockQuote.asmx/GetStockQuote?Ticker=MSFT
```

In fact, you can receive the same XML document with the same information by manually typing this URL into any browser's address bar. (In .NET 1.1, the same feat is technically possible, but it's disabled by default to ensure a greater level of security, as explained in the previous chapter.)

In both cases, the request URL follows this format:

```
http://localhost/[VirtualDirectory]/[AsmxFile]/[Method]?[Parameters]
```

If you're using HTTP GET the parameters are supplied as a list of query string variables after the question mark. Otherwise, this portion of the URL is omitted. However, both HTTP GET and HTTP POST retrieve the results as an XML document. This XML document will look exactly the same, no matter which operation the test page uses.

The clients that use your web service won't use HTTP GET or HTTP POST requests. Instead, they will send full SOAP messages over HTTP. In all cases, the actual physical connection (also known as the *transport protocol*) is the same. The only difference is in the data that you send (otherwise known as the *message protocol*). With HTTP GET, you send the name of the method you want to invoke and any required parameters in the query string. With HTTP POST you send the same information in the body of a request. With SOAP over HTTP, you post the data in an XML package called a SOAP message.

SOAP allows for more flexibility. Because it was designed with web services in mind, it lets you send custom objects or DataSets as parameters. But the fact that you can access your web method through a simple HTTP request demonstrates the simplicity of web services. Surely, if you can run your code this easily in a basic browser, true cross-platform integration can't be that much harder.

Web Service Data Types

Although the client can interact with a web service method as though it were a local function or subroutine, there are some differences. The most significant of these are the restrictions on the data types that you can use. Table 20-1 provides a list of data types that are supported for web service parameters and return values.

TIP These limitations are designed to ensure cross-platform compatibility. There's no reason that .NET couldn't create a way to convert objects to XML and back, and use that to allow you to send complex objects to a web service. However, this "extension" would limit the ability of non-.NET clients to use the web services.

Table 20-1. Web Service Data Types

Data Type	Description
The Basics	Standard types such as integers and floating-point numbers, Boolean variables, dates and times, and strings are fully supported.
Enumerations	Enumerations types (defined in Visual Basic .NET with the Enum keyword) are fully supported.
DataSets	ADO.NET DataSets allow you to use information from a relational database in your methods. DataTables and DataRows, however, aren't supported.
XmlNode	Objects based on System.Xml.XmlNode are representations of a portion of an XML document. Under the hood, all web service data is passed as XML. This class allows you to directly support a portion of XML information whose structure may change.
Custom Objects	You can pass any object you create based on a custom class or structure. The only limitation is that only data members can be transmitted. If you use a class with defined methods, the copy of the object that is transmitted will only have its properties and variables. You won't be able to successfully use most other .NET classes (except instances of the DataSet and XmlNode classes).
Arrays	You can use arrays of any supported type, including DataSets, XmlNodes, and custom objects.

The full set of objects is supported for return values, and for parameters when you're communicating through SOAP. If you're communicating through HTTP GET or HTTP POST, you'll only be able to use basic types, enumerations, and arrays of basic types or enumerations. This is because complex classes and other types cannot be represented in the query string (for HTTP GET) or form body (for an HTTP POST operation).

The StockQuote Service with a Data Object

If you've ever used a stock quote service over the Internet, you've probably noticed that the example so far is somewhat simplified. The GetStockQuote() function returns one piece of information—a price quote—whereas popular financial sites usually produce a full quote with a 52-week high and 52-week low, and other information about the volume of shares traded on a particular day. You could add more methods to the web service to supply this information, but that would require multiple similar function calls, which would slow down performance, because more time would be spent sending messages back and forth over the Internet. The client code would also become more tedious.

A better solution is to use a data object that encapsulates all the information you need. You can define the class for this object in the same file, and then use it as a parameter or return value for any of your functions. The data object is a completely ordinary Visual Basic .NET class, and shouldn't derive from System.Web.Services.WebService. It can contain public member variables that use any of the data types supported for web services. It can't contain methods—if it does, they will simply be ignored, and won't be available to the client. Similarly, you shouldn't use full property procedures, as they will just be converted into ordinary public variables on the client side.

The client will receive the data object and be able to work with it exactly as though it were defined locally. In fact, it will be—the automatically generated proxy class will contain a copy of the class definition, as you'll see in Chapter 21.

Here's how the StockQuote service would look with the addition of a convenient data object:

```
Imports System.Web.Services

<WebService(Description:="Methods to get stock information.", _
Namespace:="http://www.prosetech.com/Stocks")> _
Public Class StockQuote_BusinessObject
  Inherits System.Web.Services.WebService

    <WebMethod(Description:="Gets a price quote for a stock.")> _
    Public Function GetStockQuote(Ticker As String) As StockInfo
        Dim Quote As New StockInfo()
        Quote.Symbol = Ticker
        Quote = FillQuoteFromDB(Quote)
        Return Quote
    End Function

    Private Function FillQuoteFromDB(Lookup As StockInfo) _
      As StockInfo
        ' You can add the appropriate database code here.
        ' For test purposes this function hard-codes
        ' some sample information.
        Lookup.CompanyName = "Trapezoid"
        Lookup.Price = 400
        Lookup.High_52Week = 410
        Lookup.Low_52Week = 20
        Return Lookup
    End Function

End Class
```

```
Public Class StockInfo
    Public Price As Decimal
    Public Symbol As String
    Public High_52Week As Decimal
    Public Low_52Week As Decimal
    Public CompanyName As String
End Class
```

Dissecting the Code ...

Here's what happens in the GetStockQuote() function:

1. A new StockInfo object is created.
2. The corresponding Symbol is specified for the StockInfo object.
3. The StockInfo object is passed to another function that fills it with information. This function is called FillQuoteFromDB().

The FillQuoteFromDB() function isn't visible to remote clients because it lacks the WebMethod attribute. It isn't even visible to other classes or code modules, because it's defined with the Private keyword. Typically, this function will perform some type of database lookup. It might return information that is confidential and should not be made available to all clients. By putting this logic into a separate function, you can separate the code that determines what information the client should receive, and still have the ability to retrieve the full record if your web service code needs to examine or modify other information. Generally, most of the work that goes into creating a web service—once you understand the basics—will be spent trying to decide the best way to divide its functionality into separate procedures.

You might wonder how the client will understand the StockInfo object. In fact, the object is really just returned as a blob of XML or SOAP data. If you invoke this method through the test page, you'll see the result shown in Figure 20-5.

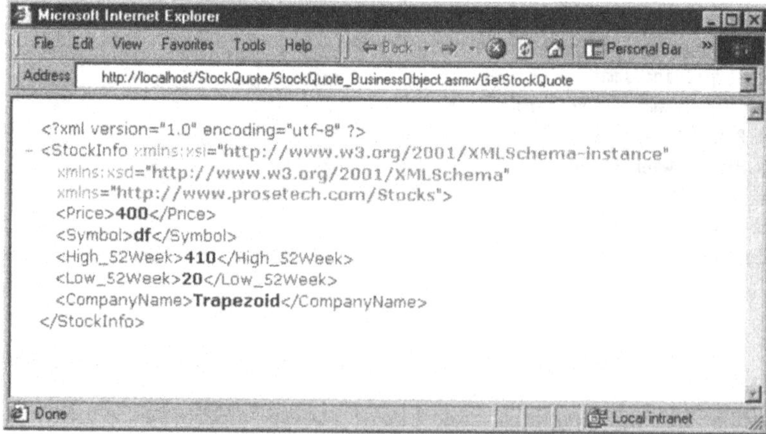

Figure 20-5. The result from GetStockQuote() as a data object

But ASP.NET is extremely clever about custom objects. When you use a class like StockInfo in your web service, it adds the definition directly into the WSDL document:

```
<types>
  <-- Other types omitted. -->
  <s:complexType name="StockInfo">
    <s:sequence>
      <s:element minOccurs="1" maxOccurs="1" name="Price"
        type="s:decimal" />
      <s:element minOccurs="1" maxOccurs="1" name="Symbol"
        nillable="true" type="s:string" />
      <s:element minOccurs="1" maxOccurs="1" name="High_52Week"
        type="s:decimal" />
      <s:element minOccurs="1" maxOccurs="1" name="Low_52Week"
        type="s:decimal" />
      <s:element minOccurs="1" maxOccurs="1" name="CompanyName"
        nillable="true" type="s:string" />
    </s:sequence>
  </s:complexType>
</types>
```

When you generate a client for this web service, a proxy class will be created automatically. It will define the StockInfo class and convert the XML data back into a StockInfo object. The end result is that all the information will return to your application in the form you expect, just as if you had used a local function. You'll see an example in the next chapter.

Returning Historical Data from StockQuote

It may interest you to model a class for a web service that returns historical information that can be used to create a price graph. You could implement this in a few different ways. For example, you might use a function that requires the starting and ending dates, and returns an array that contains a number of chronological price quotes. Your client code would then determine how much information was returned by checking the upper bound of the array. The web method definition would look something like this:

```
<WebMethod()> Public Function GetHistory _
  (Ticker As String, Start As DateTime, End As DateTime) _
  As Decimal()
```

Alternatively, you might use a function that accepts a parameter specifying the number of required entries and the time span.

```
<WebMethod()> Public Function GetHistory (Ticker As String, _
  Period As TimeSpan, NumberOfEntries As Integer) _
  As Decimal()
```

In either case, it's up to you to find the best way to organize a web service. The process is a long and incremental one that often involves performance tuning and usability concerns. Of course, it also gives you a chance to put everything you've learned into practice, and get right into the fine details of ASP.NET programming.

The ASP.NET Intrinsic Objects

When you inherit from System.Web.Services.WebService, you gain access to several of the standard built-in ASP.NET objects that you can use in an ordinary Web Forms page. These include the following:

- **Application.** Used to store data globally, so that it's available to all clients (as described in Chapter 10).
- **Server.** Used for utility functions, such as encoding strings so they can be safely displayed on a web page (as described in Chapter 6).
- **Session.** Used for client-specific state information (as described in Chapter 10).
- **User.** Used to retrieve information about the current client, if the client has been authenticated (as described in Chapter 25).
- **Context.** Provides access to Request and Response and, more usefully, the Cache object (described in Chapter 24).

On the whole, these built-in objects won't often be used in web service programming, with the possible exception of the Cache object. Generally, a web service should look and work like a business object, and not rely on retrieving or setting additional information through a built-in ASP.NET object. However, if you need to use per-user security or state management, these objects will be very useful. For example, you could create a web service that requires the client to log on, and subsequently stores important information in the Session collection. Or you could create a web service that creates a custom object on the server (such as a DataSet), stores it in the Session collection, and returns whatever information you need through various separate functions that can be invoked as required.

State Management

Web services are usually designed as *stateless* classes. That means that a web service provides a collection of utility functions that don't need to be called in any particular order, and don't retain any information between requests.

There are a number of reasons that this design is used. First of all, retaining any kind of state uses memory on the web server, which reduces performance as the number of clients grows. Another problem is the fact that contacting a web service takes time. If you can retrieve all the information you need at once, and process it on the client, it's generally faster than making several separate calls to a web service that maintains state.

There are several different kinds of state management available in ASP.NET, including using the Application and Session collections, or using custom cookies. All of these techniques are also applicable to web services. However, with web services session management is disabled by default. Otherwise, the server needs to check for session information each time a request is received, which imposes a slight overhead.

You can enable session state management for a specific method by using the EnableSession property of the WebMethod attribute.

```
<WebMethod(EnableSession:=True)>
```

Before you implement state management, make sure you review whether there is another way to accomplish your goal. Many ASP.NET gurus believe that maintaining state is at best a performance drag, and at worse a contradiction to the philosophy of lightweight stateless web services. For example, instead of using a dedicated function to submit client preferences, you could add extra parameters to all your functions to accommodate the required information. Similarly, instead of allowing a user to manipulate a large DataSet stored in the Session collection on the server, you could return the entire object to the client and then clear it from memory.

TIP When evaluating state management, you have to consider many application-specific details. But in general, it's always a good idea to reduce the amount of information stored in memory on the web server, especially if you want to create a web service that can scale to serve hundreds of simultaneous users.

What happens when you have a web service that enables session state management for some methods but disables it for others? Essentially, disabling session management just tells ASP.NET to ignore any in-memory session information, and withhold the Session collection from the current procedure. It doesn't cause existing information to be cleared out of the collection (that will only happen when the session times out). The only performance benefit you're receiving is from not having to look up session information when it isn't required.

The StockQuote Service with State Management

The following example introduces state management into the StockQuote web service.

```
Public Class StockQuote_SessionState
  Inherits WebService

    <WebMethod(EnableSession:=True)> _
    Public Function GetStockQuote(Ticker As String) As Decimal
        ' Increment counters. This function locks the application
        ' collection to prevent synchronization errors.
        Application.Lock()
        Application(Ticker) = CType(Application(Ticker), Integer) + 1
        Application.UnLock()
        Session(Ticker) = CType(Session(Ticker), Integer) + 1

        ' Return a value representing the length of the ticker.
        Return Ticker.Length
    End Function

    <WebMethod(EnableSession:=True)> _
    Public Function GetStockUsage(Ticker As String) As CounterInfo
        Dim Result As New CounterInfo()
        Result.GlobalRequests = CType(Application(Ticker), Integer)
        Result.SessionRequests = CType(Session(Ticker), Integer)
        Return Result
    End Function

End Class

Public Class CounterInfo
    Public GlobalRequests As Integer
    Public SessionRequests As Integer
End Class
```

This example allows the StockQuote service to record how much it has been used. Every time the GetStockQuote() method is called, two counters are incremented. One is a global counter that tracks the total number of requests for that stock quote from all clients. The other one is a session-specific counter that represents how many times the current client has requested a quote for the specified stock. The Ticker string is used to name the stored item. That means that if a client requests quotes for 50 different stocks, 50 different counter variables will be created. Clearly, this system wouldn't be practical for large-scale use. One practice that this example does follow correctly is that of locking the Application collection before updating it. This can cause a significant performance slowdown, but it guarantees that the value will be accurate even if multiple clients are accessing the web service simultaneously.

To view the counter information, you can call the GetStockUsage() function with the ticker for the stock you're interested in. A custom object, CounterInfo, is returned to you with both pieces of information.

It's unlikely that you'd design an application to store this much usage information in memory, but it gives you a good indication of how you can use session and application state management in a web service just as easily as you can an ASP.NET page. Note that session state automatically expires after a preset amount of time, and both the session and Application collections will be emptied when the application is stopped. For more information about ASP.NET state management, refer to Chapter 10.

NOTE As you've seen, a web service needs to specifically enable session state with the WebMethod attribute. This allows session state to work for one method. However, in most cases you want session state to persist between method calls. For example, you might want to set session state data in one web method and retrieve it in another. To allow this, the client must support ASP.NET's session state cookie. The steps you need to enable this support are described in Chapter 21.

Other Web Service Options

The final section of this chapter explores how you can extend your web services with support for transactions, caching, and ASP.NET security. None of these features are customized for web service use. Instead, they are built into the ASP.NET platform, the .NET Framework, and the Windows operating system. This section shows you how to access them.

Transactions

Transactions are an important feature in many business applications. They ensure that a series of operations either succeeds or fails as a unit. Transactions also prevent the possibility of inconsistent or corrupted data that can occur if an operation fails midway through after committing only some of its changes. The most common example of a transaction is a bank account transfer. When you move $100 from one account to another, two actions take place: a withdrawal in the first account, and a deposit in the second. If these two tasks are a part of a single transaction they will either both succeed or both fail. It will be impossible for one account to be debited if the other isn't credited.

Web services can participate in COM+ transactions, but in a somewhat limited way. Because of the stateless nature of the HTTP protocol, web service methods can only act as the root object in a transaction. That means that a web service method can start a transaction and use it to perform a series of related tasks, but multiple web services cannot be grouped into one transaction. As a result, you may have to put in some extra thought when you're creating a transactional web service. For example, it won't make sense to create a financial web service with a separate DebitAccount() and CreditAccount() methods, because they won't be able to be grouped into a transaction. Instead, you can make sure both tasks executed as a single unit using a transactional TransferFunds() method.

To use a transaction in a web service, you first have to add a reference to the System.EnterpriseServices assembly. In order to do this in Visual Studio .NET, right-click References in the Solution Explorer, select Add Reference, and choose System.EnterpriseServices (see Figure 20-6).

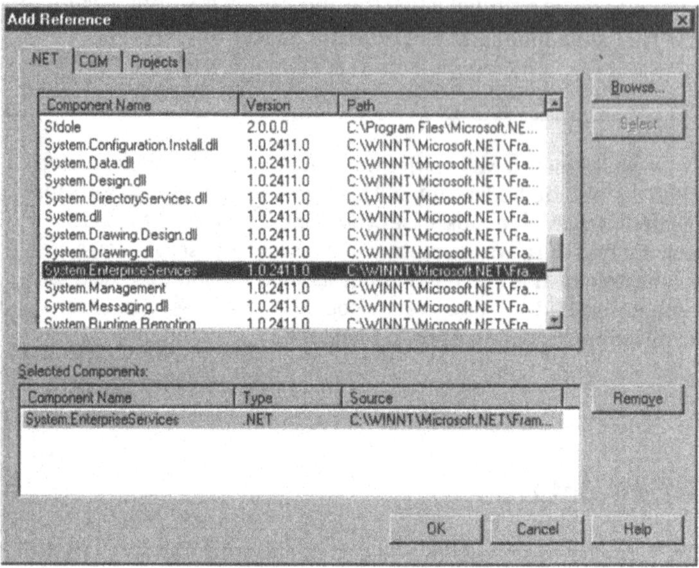

Figure 20-6. Adding a reference to System.EnterpriseServices

You can now import the corresponding namespace so the types you need (TransactionOption and ContextUtil) are at your fingertips.

```
Imports System.EnterpriseServices
```

To start a transaction in a web service method, set the TransactionOption property of the WebMethod attribute. TransactionOption is an enumeration that provides several values that allow you to specify whether a code component uses or requires transactions. Because web services must be the root of a transaction, most of these options don't apply. To create a web service method that starts a transaction automatically, use the following attribute:

```
<WebMethod(TransactionOption:=TransactionOption.RequiresNew)>
```

The transaction is automatically committed when the web method completes. The transaction is rolled back if any unhandled exception occurs, or if you explicitly instruct the transaction to fail using the following code:

```
ContextUtil.SetAbort()
```

Most databases support COM+ transactions. The moment you use these databases in a transactional web method, they will automatically be enlisted in the current transaction. If the transaction is rolled back, the operations you perform with these databases (like adding, modifying, or removing records) will be automatically reversed. However, some operations (like writing a file to disk) aren't inherently transactional. That means that these operations will not be rolled back if the transaction fails.

Now consider the following web method, which takes two actions: it deletes records in a database and then tries to read from a file. However, if the file operation fails and the exception isn't handled, the entire transaction will be rolled back, and the deleted records will be restored.

```
Din ConnectionString As String = "Provider=SQLOLEDB.1;Data Source=localhost;" & _
  "Initial Catalog=Pubs;Integrated Security=SSPI"

<WebMethod(TransactionOption:=TransactionOption.RequiresNew)> _
Public Sub UpdateDatabase()
    ' Create ADO.NET objects.
    Dim con As New SqlConnection(ConnectionString)
    Dim cmd As New SqlCommand("DELETE * FROM authors", Con)

    ' Apply the update. This will be registered as part of the transaction.
    con.Open()
    cmd.ExecuteNonQuery()
    con.Close()

    ' Try to access a file. This generates an exception which isn't handled.
    ' The web method will be aborted and the changes will be rolled back.
    Dim fs As New System.IO.FileStream("does_not_exist.bin", IO.FileMode.Open)

    ' (If no errors have occured, the database changes
    ' are committed here when the method ends).
End Sub
```

Another way to handle this code is to catch the error, perform any cleanup that's required, and then explicitly roll back the transaction if necessary:

```
<WebMethod(TransactionOption:=TransactionOption.RequiresNew)> _
Public Sub UpdateDatabase()
    ' Create ADO.NET objects.
    Dim con As New SqlConnection(ConnectionString)
    Dim cmd As New SqlCommand("DELETE * FROM authors", Con)

    ' Apply the update.
    Try
        con.Open()
        cmd.ExecuteNonQuery()
        con.Close()

        Dim fs As New System.IO.FileStream("does_not_exist.bin", _
          IO.FileMode.Open)
    Catch
        If con.State <> ConnectionState.Closed Then con.Close()
        ContextUtil.SetAbort()
    End Try
End Sub
```

Does a web service need to use COM+ transactions? It all depends on the situation. If multiple updates are required in separate data stores, you may need to use transactions to ensure your data's integrity. If, on the other hand, you're only modifying values in a single database (such as SQL 2000) you can probably make use of the data provider's built-in transaction features instead.

Caching

The simplest kind of web service caching is output caching. Output caching works with web services in the same way that it does with web pages: identical requests (in this case, requests for the same method and with the same parameters) will receive identical responses from the cache, until the cached information expires. This can greatly increase performance in heavily trafficked sites, even if you only store a response for a few seconds.

Output caching should only be used for straightforward information retrieval or data processing functions. It should not be used in a method that needs to perform other work, such as changing session items, logging usage, or modifying a database. This is because subsequent calls to a cached method will receive the cached result, and the web method code will not be executed.

To enable caching for a function, you use the CacheDuration property of the WebMethod attribute.

```
<WebMethod(CacheDuration:=30)> _
Public Function GetProducts() As DataSet
    ' (Code omitted.)
End Sub
```

This example caches the product catalog for 30 seconds. Any user who calls the GetProducts() method in this time span will receive the same DataSet, directly from ASP.NET's output cache.

Generally, you should determine the amount of time depending on how long the underlying data will remain valid. For example, if a stock quote were being retrieved, you would use a much smaller number of seconds than you might for a weather forecast. If you were storing a piece of information that seldom changes, like the results of a yearly census poll, your considerations would be entirely different. In this case, the information is almost permanent, but the amount of returned information will be larger than the capacity of ASP.NET's output cache. Your goal in this situation would be to limit the cache duration enough to ensure that only the most popular requests are stored.

Of course, caching decisions should also be based on how long it will take to re-create the information and how many clients will be using the web service. You may need to perform substantial real-world testing and tuning to achieve perfection.

ASP.NET also supports data caching, which allows you to store full-fledged objects in the cache. As with all ASP.NET code, you can use data caching through the Cache object (which is available through the Context.Cache property in your web service code). This object can temporarily store information that is expensive to create so that it can be reused by other clients calling the same method, or even other web services or ASP.NET web pages. For more information on data caching and output caching, refer to Chapter 24.

Security

You have two options for web service security. You can create and use your own login and authentication features, or you can use the standard security features that are built into IIS and ASP.NET. These standard security features are described in detail in Chapter 25. The only difference between ASP.NET security in a web service and a web page is that a web service doesn't present any user interface, it cannot request user credentials on its own. It has to rely on the calling code, or rely on having the user logged on under an authorized account.

If you decide to design your own web service authentication system, you'll probably begin by adding a dedicated Login() method. This method will create a license key, stores it in a database, and the return it to the user. Every other method in your web service will then require the license key as an additional parameter. Before performing any code, each web method will validate the license key by examining the database.

The following example shows how the StockQuote service uses this system. Once again, only the conceptual design is shown. To actually finish this into a full-featured application, you'd need to add some rudimentary database code, as described in Chapter 14.

```
Public Class StockQuote_Security
  Inherits System.Web.Services.WebService

    <WebMethod> _
    Public Function Login(ID As String, Password As String) _
     As LicenseKey
        If VerifyUser(ID, Password) = True Then
            ' Generate a license key made up of
            ' some random sequence of characters.
            Dim Key As New LicenseKey()
            Key.Key = Guid.NewGuid().ToString()

            ' (The key would then be added to some temporary
            ' license database.)

            Return Key
        Else
            ' Cause an error that will be returned to the client.
            ' The function uses a special SecurityException
            ' from the .NET class library.
            Throw New System.Security.SecurityException()
        End If
    End Function
```

```
<WebMethod> _
Public Function GetStockQuote(Ticker As String, _
 Key As LicenseKey) As Integer
    If VerifyKey(Key) = False Then
        Throw New System.Security.SecurityException()
    Else
        ' Normal GetStockQuote code goes here.
        Return Ticker.Length
    End If
End Function

Private Function VerifyUser(ID As String, Password As String) As Boolean
    ' (Add database lookup code here to verify the user.
    '  In this example, you validate the user no matter what.)
    Return True
End Function

Private Function VerifyKey(Key As LicenseKey) As Boolean
    ' (Look up key in key database. If it's not there
    '  or it's expired, return False. In this example,
    '  you validate the user no matter what.)
    Return True
End Function
End Class

Public Class LicenseKey
    Public Key As String
End Class
```

Dissecting the Code...

- Before using any method in this class, the client must call the Login() method and store the received license key. Every other web method will require that license key.

- The LicenseKey class uses a GUID, or global unique identifier. This is a randomly generated 128-bit number that is guaranteed to be statistically unique. (In other words, the chance of generating two unique GUIDs in a web service or guessing another user's GUID are astronomically small.)

- The same private function—VerifyKey()—is used regardless of what web method is invoked. This ensures that the license verification code is only written in one place, and is used consistently.

- Currently, this design requires a trip to the database to verify that a license key exists for each web method invocation. Data caching could be added to this design to solve this problem. In this case, every key would be stored in two places—in the database, which would be used as a last resort and duplicated in the in-memory cache. The VerifyKey() function would only perform the database lookup if the cached item was not found. For more information about caching, refer to Chapter 24.

Security with SOAP Headers

The potential problem with this example is that it requires a license key (or a user ID and password, depending on your design) to be submitted with each method call as a parameter. This can be a bit tedious. To streamline this process, you can use a custom SOAP header.

SOAP headers are special pieces of information that are sent with every SOAP message. They can contain any type of data that you could use as a method parameter or return value for web service method. The advantage of SOAP headers is just the convenience. The client specifies a SOAP header once, and the header is automatically sent to every method that needs it, making the coding clearer and more concise.

To create a custom SOAP header, you first need to define a class that inherits from System.Web.Services.Protocols.SoapHeader. You can then add all the additional pieces of information you want it to contain as member variables. In the following example, three pieces of information are added: a user ID, password, and key:

```
Public Class SecurityHeader
  Inherits System.Web.Services.Protocols.SoapHeader

    Public UserID As String
    Public Password As String
    Public Key As String
End Class
```

Next, your web service needs a public member variable to receive the SOAP header.

```
Public Class StockQuote_SoapSecurity
  Inherits System.Web.Services.WebService

    Public KeyHeader As SecurityHeader

    ' (Other web service code goes here.)
End Class
```

The client can create an instance of the SecurityHeader, set the UserID and Password, and attach the SecurityHeader to the web service by assigning it to the KeyHeader variable of the proxy class. This process is demonstrated in Chapter 21, in the section "Using Custom SOAP Headers."

The web service requires one last ingredient. Each web service method that wants to access the SecurityHeader must explicitly indicate this requirement with a SoapHeader attribute. The attribute indicates the web service member variable where the header should be placed.

```
Public Class StockQuote_SoapSecurity
  Inherits System.Web.Services.WebService

    Public KeyHeader As SecurityHeader

    <WebMethod>, _
    <SoapHeader("KeyHeader", Direction:=SoapHeaderDirection.InOut)> _
    Public Function GetStockQuote(Ticker As String) As Integer
        ' (Code omitted.)
    End Function

End Class
```

In this example, the header is sent bi-directionally. It goes to the web method and back to the client. This allows for a useful trick: The user can set the user ID and password, and the web service can remove these pieces of information from the header (for security) and replace them with a key once the verification has been performed. The advantage of this method is that the client doesn't need to explicitly call the Login() method. It's all handled transparently.

The complete web service would look like this:

```
Public Class StockQuote_Security
  Inherits System.Web.Services.WebService

    Public KeyHeader As SecurityHeader

    <WebMethod>, _
    <SoapHeader("KeyHeader", Direction:=SoapHeaderDirection.InOut)> _
    Public Function GetStockQuote(Ticker As String) As Integer
        If VerifyKey(KeyHeader) = False Then
            Throw New System.Security.SecurityException()
        Else
            ' Normal GetStockQuote code goes here.
            Return Ticker.Length
        End If
    End Function

    Private Function VerifyKey(Key As SecurityHeader) As Boolean
        If Key.Key = "" Then
            ' (Look up the user in the database and assign the key.
            '  Add the key to temporary database and return True.)
        Else
            ' (Look up key in key database. If it's not there
            '  or it's expired, return False).
        End If
```

```
        ' This test function always returns true.
        Key.UserID = ""
        Key.Password = ""
        Key.Key = Guid.NewGuid().ToString()
        Return True
    End Function

End Class
```

CAUTION SOAP messages are sent over the network as ordinary text. This means that if you create an authentication system like this, malicious users could watch network traffic and intercept passwords as they are sent from the client to the web service. To solve this problem, you can use SSL (Secure Sockets Layer) with your web service to encrypt all the messages that are exchanged. Refer to Chapter 25 for more information.

The Last Word

In ASP.NET, designing a web service is almost as easy as creating an ordinary business class. But to use web services *well*, you need to understand the role they play in enterprise applications. Web services aren't the best way to share functionality between different web pages or web applications on a web server, because of the overhead needed to send SOAP messages over the network. However, they are an excellent way to connect different software packages, or glue together the internal systems of separate companies.

In the next chapter, you'll learn how to call web services in any type of .NET application.

CHAPTER 21

Using Web Services

THE PAST COUPLE OF CHAPTERS examined how to design and code web services. By now you realize that web services are really standard business objects that provide a powerful built-in communication framework that allows you to interact with them over the Internet. However, you still don't know how this interaction takes place. In this chapter, you'll examine how to create a simple ASP.NET client for your StockQuote web service. Then, for a little more fun, you'll see how to access a real, mature web service on the Internet: Microsoft's TerraService, which exposes a vast library of millions of satellite pictures from a database that is 1.5 TB in size.

Consuming a Web Service

Microsoft has repeatedly declared that their ambition with programming tools such as Visual Studio .NET, the CLR (common language runtime), and the .NET class library is to provide the common infrastructure for application developers, who will then only need to create the upper layer of business-specific logic. Web services hold true to that promise, with ASP.NET automating communication between web services and clients. Before this chapter is finished, you'll see how you can call a web service method as easily as a method in a local class.

Web services communicate with other .NET applications through a special proxy class. You can create this proxy class automatically through Visual Studio .NET or by using a command-line tool. When you wish to call a web method, you call the corresponding method of the proxy object, which then fetches the results for you using SOAP calls. Strictly speaking, you don't need to use a proxy class—you could create and receive the SOAP messages on your own. However, this process is quite difficult and involves a degree of low-level understanding and complexity that would make web services much less useful.

Configuring a Web Service Client in Visual Studio .NET

When developing and testing a web service in Visual Studio .NET, it's often easiest to add both the web service and the client application to the same solution. This allows you to test and change both pieces at the same time. You can even use the integrated debugger to set breakpoints and step through the code in both the client and the server, as though they were really a single application!

To work with both projects at once in Visual Studio .NET, follow these steps:

1. Open the web service project (in this case, the StockQuote service).

2. Select File ➤ Add Project ➤ New Project.

3. Choose ASP.NET Web Application, give it a title (for example, StockQuoteClient), and click OK.

4. You should set the new project as the startup project (otherwise, you'll just see the web service test page when you click the start button). To make this adjustment, right-click the new project in the Solution Explorer, and choose Set As StartUp Project.

5. If you create the projects in this order, the build order will be automatically set correctly, and the web service will be compiled before the ASP.NET application is compiled and launched. To verify the build order, right-click one of the projects in the Solution Explorer, and click Project Build Order. The StockQuote service should be first in the list.

6. Your Solution Explorer should now look like Figure 21-1.

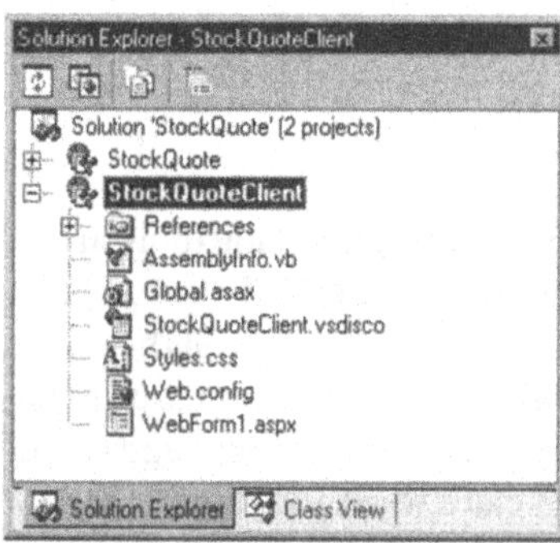

Figure 21-1. Two projects in Solution Explorer

Creating a Web Reference in Visual Studio .NET

Even after you add two projects to the same solution, they still have no way to communicate with each other. To set up this layer of interaction, you need to create a special proxy class. In Visual Studio .NET, you create this proxy class by adding a web reference. Web references are similar to ordinary references, but instead of pointing to assemblies with ordinary .NET types, they point to a URL with a WSDL (Web Service Description Language) contract for a web service.

To create a web reference, follow these steps:

1. Right-click the client project in the Solution Explorer, and select Add Web Reference.

2. The Add Web Reference window opens, as shown in Figure 21-2. This window provides options for searching web registries or entering a URL directly. In Visual Studio .NET 2003, there's also a link that allows you to browse all the web services on the local computer.

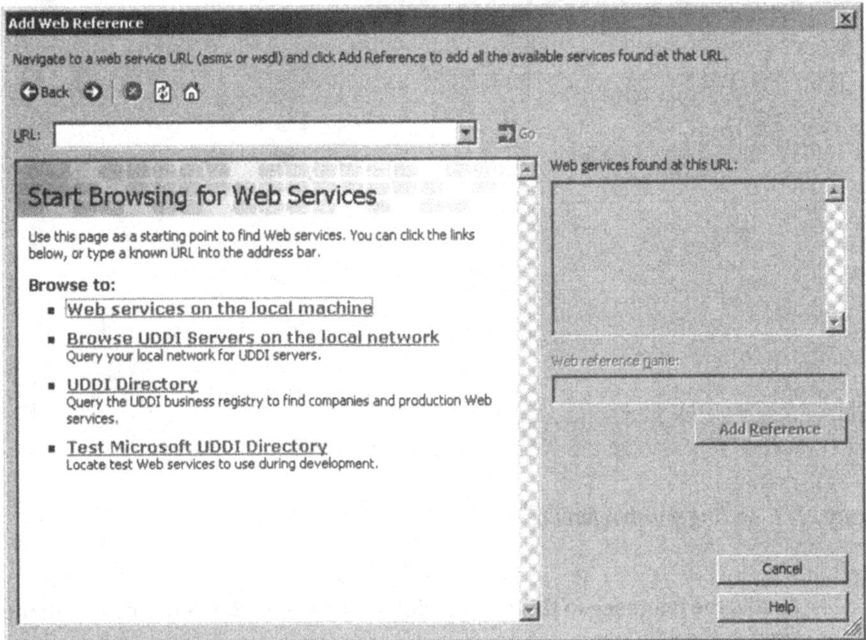

Figure 21-2. The Add Web Reference window

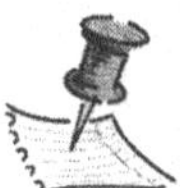

NOTE The figures in this chapter show the web reference windows in Visual Studio .NET 2003. The functionality is the same in Visual Studio .NET 2002, but the appearance and layout is slightly different.

3. You can browse directly to your web service by entering a URL that points to the .asmx file. The test page will appear in the window (as shown in Figure 21-3), and the Add Reference button will be enabled.

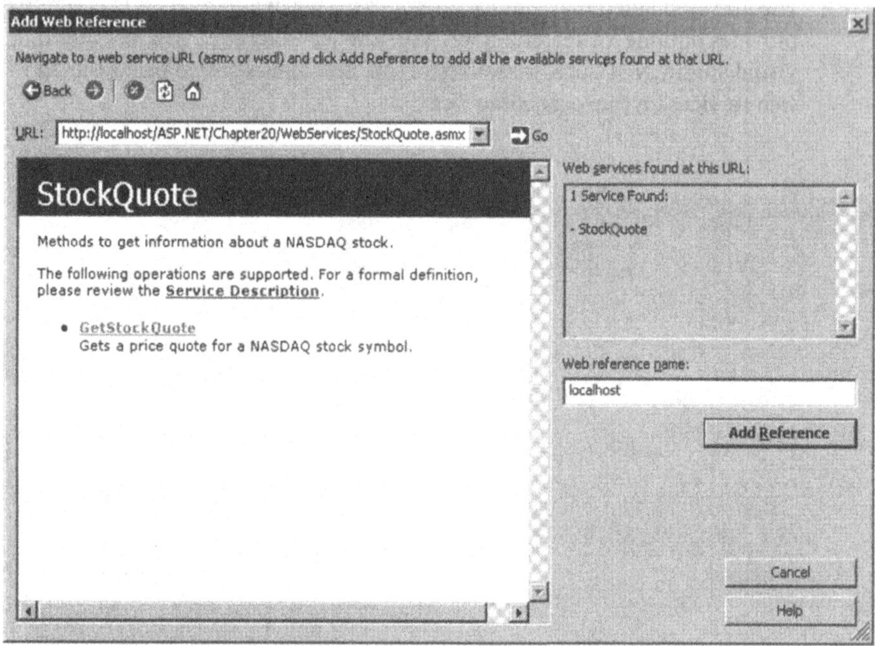

Figure 21-3. Adding a web reference

4. To add the reference to this web service, click the Add Reference button to the right of the window.
5. Now your computer (the web server for this service) will appear in the Web References group for your project in the Solution Explorer window. A copy of the corresponding discovery document and WSDL contract will also be added to the client project, and you can browse them as well (Figure 21-4).

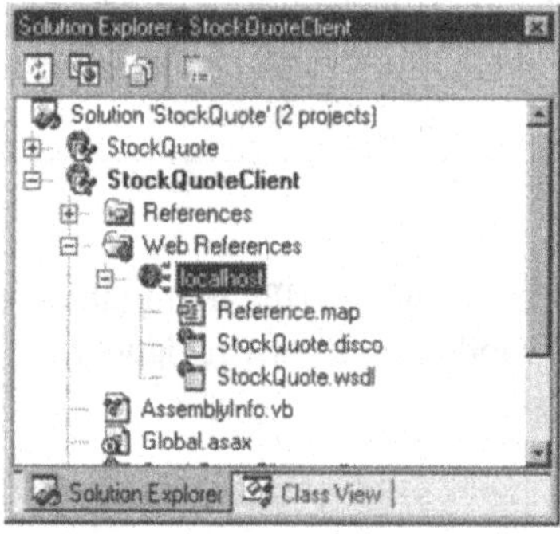

Figure 21-4. The WSDL contract

NOTE The web reference you create uses the WSDL contract and information that exists at the time you add the reference. If the web service is changed, you'll need to update your proxy class by right-clicking the server name (localhost, in this case) and choosing Update Web Reference.

The Proxy Class

On the surface, Visual Studio .NET makes it seem like all you need is a simple link to your web service. In reality, whenever you add a web reference Visual Studio .NET creates a proxy class for you automatically. To really understand how web service clients work, you need to take a look at this class.

First, select Project ➤ Show All Files from the Visual Studio .NET menu. This reveals additional files that are usually hidden, such as resource files and code-behind files for web pages (for example, WebForm1.aspx.vb), which usually appear as if they are all contained in one file (WebForm1.aspx). In a web service client, you'll find a file named Reference.vb under the corresponding web reference (see Figure 21-5).

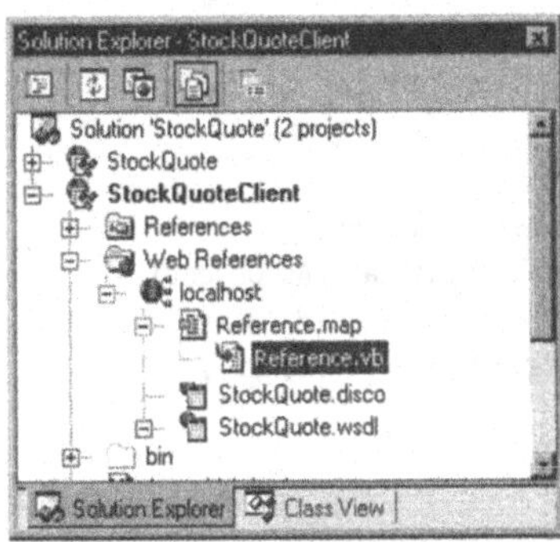

Figure 21-5. The proxy class

This file contains the proxy class code that's used to interact with the web service. You can double-click the file in the Solution Explorer to view its source code. It's shown below, in a slightly simplified form. I've left out the attributes that tell Visual Studio .NET how to treat this code when debugging, and replaced some of the attributes that configure the SOAP transmission with comments.

```
'------------------------------------------------------------------------------
'     This code was generated by a tool.
'     Runtime Version: 1.1.4322.573
'------------------------------------------------------------------------------
Imports System
Imports System.Diagnostics
Imports System.Web.Services
Imports System.Web.Services.Protocols
Imports System.Xml.Serialization

Namespace localhost

    ' (A WebServiceBindingAttribute is declared here.)
    Public Class StockQuote
        Inherits System.Web.Services.Protocols.SoapHttpClientProtocol

        Public Sub New()
            MyBase.New
            Me.Url = "http://localhost/WebServices/StockQuote.asmx"
        End Sub

        ' (A SoapDocumentMethodAttribute is declared here.)
        Public Function GetStockQuote(ByVal Ticker As String) As StockInfo
            Dim results() As Object = Me.Invoke ( _
             "GetStockQuote", New Object() {Ticker})
            Return CType(results(0),StockInfo)
        End Function

        Public Function BeginGetStockQuote(ByVal Ticker As String, _
         ByVal callback As System.AsyncCallback, ByVal asyncState As Object) _
         As System.IAsyncResult
            Return Me.BeginInvoke("GetStockQuote", New Object() {Ticker}, _
             callback, asyncState)
        End Function

        Public Function EndGetStockQuote(ByVal asyncResult As _
          System.IAsyncResult) As StockInfo
            Dim results() As Object = Me.EndInvoke(asyncResult)
            Return CType(results(0),StockInfo)
        End Function

    End Class

    Public Class StockInfo
        Public Price As Decimal
        Public Symbol As String
        Public High_52Week As Decimal
        Public Low_52Week As Decimal
        Public CompanyName As String
    End Class

End Namespace
```

Dissecting the Code...

Several interesting details appear in this example:

- The entire class is contained inside a namespace that is named after the server. For example, to use the StockQuote proxy code (and the StockQuote web service), you have to access the .NET namespace called localhost.
- At the end of this file, a copy of the StockInfo class definition is provided. This class is used to return some information from the StockQuote service. Now that Visual Studio .NET has placed its definition in the proxy class, you can create your own StockInfo objects, without needing to add any new code. Unlike the StockQuote proxy class, the StockInfo class doesn't participate in any SOAP messages or Internet communication; it's just a simple data class.
- The StockQuote class contains the same methods as the StockQuote web service. This class acts as a "stand-in" for the remote StockQuote web service. When you call a StockQuote method, you're really calling a method of this local class. This class then performs the SOAP communication as required to contact the "real" remote web service. The proxy class acquires its ability to communicate in SOAP through the .NET class library. It inherits from the SoapHttpClientProtocol class, and binds its local methods to web service methods with prebuilt .NET attributes. In other words, the low-level SOAP details are hidden not only from you, but also from the proxy class, which relies on ready-made .NET components from the System.Web.Services.Protocols namespace.
- If you peer into the GetStockQuote() method, you'll notice that it doesn't actually retrieve a StockInfo object from the remote web service. Instead, it receives a generic Object type (which corresponds to a blob of XML data). It then handles the conversion into a StockInfo object before it returns the information to your code. In other words, the proxy layer not only handles the SOAP communication layer, but also handles the conversion from XML to .NET objects and data types, as needed. If .NET types were used directly with web services, it would be extremely difficult to use them from other non-Microsoft platforms.
- The proxy class has three methods for every method in the remote web service. The first method, which is named after the corresponding web service method (such as GetStockQuote), is used like an ordinary Visual Basic function. The other two methods are used to retrieve the same information from the same method asynchronously. In other words, you submit a request with the BeginGetStockQuote method, and pick up your results later with the EndGetStockQuote method. This is a useful technique in desktop applications where you don't want to become bogged down waiting for a slow Internet connection. However, the examples in this chapter focus on ASP.NET clients, which don't really benefit from asynchronous consumption because the page isn't returned to the client until all the code has finished processing.

- The proxy class uses a constructor that sets the URL property to point to the web service .asmx file. You can query this property in your code to find out what web service the proxy is using, or you could change it to connect to an identical web service at another location.

Dynamic Web Service URLs

By default, when you add a web reference in Visual Studio .NET, the web service URL is hard-coded in the constructor of the proxy class. However, Visual Studio .NET allows you to change this behavior, and configure the proxy class to use a dynamic URL endpoint. This way, the URL will be stored in a separate configuration file. As a result, if the web service is moved to a different web server, you won't need to rebuild the application. Instead, you can simply update the configuration file so that it uses the new URL.

To set a web service to use a dynamic URL, you should change the URL Behavior option in the Properties window, as shown in Figure 21-6.

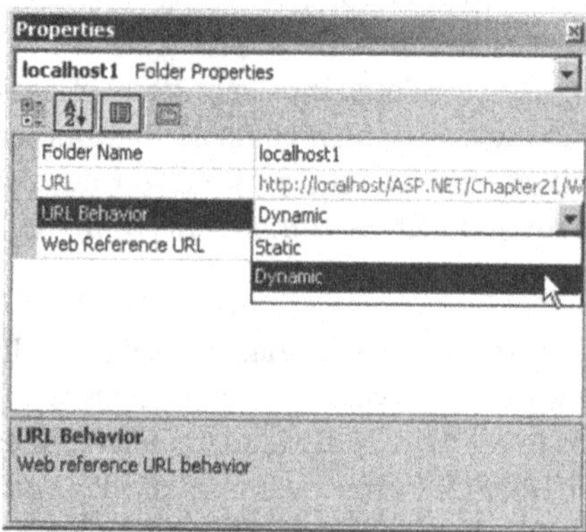

Figure 21-6. Configuring a dynamic web service URL

When you make this change, the web service URL will be added to the <appSettings> section of the client's configuration file. If the client is a web application, this information will be added to the web.config file. If you're creating a different type of client application, like a Windows application, the configuration file will have a name in the format [AppName].exe.config. For example, if your application is named SimpleClient.exe, the configuration file will be SimpleClient.exe.config. You must follow this naming convention.

TIP Visual Studio .NET uses a little sleight-of-hand with named configuration files. In the design environment, the configuration file will have the name App.config. However, when you build the application, this file will be copied to the build directory and given the appropriate name (to match the executable file). The only exception is web clients. All web applications use a configuration file named web.config, no matter what file names you use. That's what you'll see in the design environment as well.

An example of the automatically generated configuration file setting is shown here:

```
<?xml version="1.0" encoding="utf-8"?>
<configuration>

  <appSettings>
    <add key="AppName.ServerName.ServiceName"
     value=" http://localhost/WebServices/MyService.asmx "/>
  </appSettings>

</configuration>
```

The code in the proxy class is modified so that it attempts to read whatever information is in the configuration file. If it doesn't find the required value, it defaults to the URL that was used during development. Here's how the constructor looks:

```
Public Sub New()
    MyBase.New()
    Dim urlSetting As String = _
      ConfigurationSettings.AppSettings("AppName.ServerName.ServiceName")

    If Not urlSetting Is Nothing Then
        Me.Url = urlSetting
    Else
        Me.Url = "http://localhost/WebServices/MyService.asmx"
    End If
End Sub
```

This allows you to modify the web service URL after compiling and deploying the application, simply by editing the configuration file.

Creating a Proxy with WSDL.exe

Even if you aren't using Visual Studio to design your client application, you still interact with a web service through a proxy class. However, this proxy class needs to be generated with another tool. In this case, you must use the WSDL.exe utility that is included with the .NET Framework. (You can find this file in the .NET Framework directory, such as C:\Program Files\Microsoft.NET\FrameworkSDK\Bin. Visual Studio .NET users have the WSDL.exe utility in the C:\Program Files\Microsoft Visual Studio .NET\FrameworkSDK\Bin directory.) This file is a command-line utility, so it's easiest to use by opening a command prompt window. (Click the Start button, and choose Programs ➤ Accessories ➤ Command Prompt.)

The syntax for WSDL.exe is as follows:

```
Wsdl /language:language  /protocol:protocol /namespace:myNameSpace /out:filename
    /username:username /password:password /domain:domain <url or path>
```

Each field is described in Table 21-1.

Table 21-1. WSDL.exe Command-Line Parameters

Parameter	Meaning
Language	This is the language the class is written in. It really doesn't matter—you shouldn't modify the proxy class anyway, because your changes will be lost every time you need to regenerate it. However, if you want to examine it and understand the proxy class, you should probably specify VB. If you don't make a choice, the default is C#.
Protocol	Usually, you'll omit this option and use the default (SOAP). However, you could also specify HttpGet and HttpPost, for slightly more limiting protocols.
Namespace	This is the .NET namespace that your proxy class will use. If you omit this parameter, no namespace is used, and the classes in this file are available globally. For better organization, you should probably choose a logical namespace.
Out	This allows you to specify the name for the generated file. By default this is the name of the service, followed by an extension indicating the language (such as StockQuote.vb). You can always rename this file after it's generated.
Username, Password, and Domain	You should specify these values if the web server requires authentication to access the discovery and WSDL documents.
URL or Path	This is the last portion of the Wsdl command line, and it specifies the location of the WSDL file for the web service.

A typical WSDL.exe command might look something like this:

```
wsdl /language:VB /namespace:localhost http://localhost/pub/StockQuote.asmx?WSDL
```

In this case, a StockQuote.vb file would be created, and it would look almost identical to the example shown in the previous section. Before you can use this class in an ASP.NET application, you'll need to compile the file. Assuming that it's a VB .NET file, you must use the vbc.exe compiler included with the .NET Framework (C# developers use csc.exe instead). To turn your StockQuote class into a DLL, use the following statement in the command prompt window:

```
vbc /t:library /out:StockQuote.dll StockQuote.vb
```

Now you can copy the DLL file to the bin directory of your ASP.NET client application. Web pages in that application can access the classes in this DLL as long as they use the correct namespace. ASP.NET searches the bin directory to find available classes automatically.

NOTE You can use a web service without WSDL.exe or Visual Studio .NET. In fact, you don't even need a proxy class. All you need is a program that can send and receive SOAP messages. After all, web services are designed to be cross-platform. However, unless you have significant experience with another tool (such as the Microsoft SOAP Toolkit), the details are generally frustrating and unpleasant. .NET provides the prebuilt infrastructure you need to guarantee easy, error-free operation.

Using the Proxy Class

Using the proxy class is easy. In most respects, it isn't any different than using a local class. The following sample page uses the StockQuote service and displays the information it retrieves in a label control. You could place this snippet of code into a Page.Load event handler.

```
' Create a StockInfo object for your results.
Dim WSInfo As localhost.StockInfo

' Create the actual web service proxy class.
Dim WS As New localhost.StockQuote

' Call the web service method.
WSInfo = WS.GetStockQuote("MSFT")

lblResult.Text = WSInfo.CompanyName & " is at: " & WSInfo.Price
```

The whole process is quite straightforward. First, the code creates a StockInfo object to hold the results. Then the code creates an instance of the proxy class, which allows access to all the web service functionality. Finally, the code calls the web service method using the proxy class and catches the returned data in the StockInfo object.

As you experiment with your project, remember that it doesn't have a direct connection to your web service. Whenever you change the web service, you'll have to rebuild the web service (right-click the web service project and select Build), and then update the web reference (right-click the client project's localhost reference and select Update Web Reference). Until you perform these two steps, your client will not be able to access any new methods, or methods that have modified signatures (different parameter lists).

Waiting and Timeouts

You might have noticed that the proxy class (StockQuote) really contains many more members than just the three methods shown in the source code. In fact, it acquires a substantial amount of extra functionality because it inherits from the SoapHttpClientProtocol class. In many scenarios, you won't need to use any of these additional features. In some cases, however, they will become very useful. One example is with the Timeout property.

The Timeout property allows you to specify the maximum amount of time you're willing to wait, in milliseconds. The default (–1) indicates that you'll wait as long as it takes, which could make your web application unacceptably slow if you attempt to perform a number of operations with an unresponsive web service.

When using the Timeout property, you need to include error handling. If the Timeout period expires without a response, an exception will be thrown, giving you the chance to notify the user about the problem.

In the following example, the simple StockQuote client is rewritten to use a timeout.

```
Dim WSInfo As localhost.StockInfo
Dim WS As New localhost.StockQuote()

' This timeout will apply to all WS method calls, until it's changed.
WS.Timeout = 3000  ' 3000 milliseconds is 3 seconds.

Try
    ' Call the web service method.
    WSInfo = GetStockQuote("MSFT")
    lblResult.Text = WSInfo.CompanyName & " is at: " & WSInfo.Price
Catch e As Exception
    lblResult.Text = "web service timed out after 3 seconds."
End Try
```

By default, the timeout is 100000 milliseconds (10 seconds).

Connecting Through a Proxy

The proxy class also has some built-in intelligence that allows you to reroute its HTTP communication with special Internet settings. By default, the proxy class uses the

Internet settings on the current computer. In some networks, this may not be the best approach. You can override these settings by using the Proxy property of the web service proxy class.

TIP In this case, "proxy" is being used in two different ways: as a proxy that manages communication between a client and a web service, and as a proxy server in your organization that manages communication between a computer and the Internet.

For example, if you need to connect through a computer called ProxyServer using port 80, you could use the following code before you called any web service methods:

```
Dim ConnectionProxy As New WebProxy("ProxyServer", 80)

Dim WS As New localhost.StockQuote()
WS.Proxy = ConnectionProxy
```

There are many other options for the WebProxy class that allow you to configure connections in a more complicated scenario.

State Management

If you try to use a stateful web service, you're likely to be frustrated. Every time you re-create the proxy class, a new session ID is automatically assigned, which means you won't be able to access the session information from the previous request. To counter this problem, you need to take extra steps to preserve the cookie that has the session ID.

In a web client, you'll need to store the session ID between requests, and then reapply it to the proxy object just before you make a call to the web service. Just about any type of storage can be used: a database, a local cookie, view state, or even the session collection for the current web page. In other words, you could store information for your web service session in your current (local) page session.

If the previous discussion seems a little confusing, it's because you need to remind yourself that there are really two active sessions in this example. The web service client has one session, which is maintained as long as the user reading your site doesn't close his browser. The web service itself also has its own session. (In fact, the web service could even be hosted on a different web server). The web service session can't be maintained automatically because you don't communicate with it directly. Instead, the proxy class bears the burden of holding the web service session information. Figure 21-7 illustrates the difference.

The next example sheds some light on this situation. This example uses a variant of the original web service, called StockQuote_SessionState, which you saw in the previous chapter. It provides two methods: the standard GetStockQuote() method and a GetStockUsage() method that returns a CounterInfo object with information about how many times the web method was used.

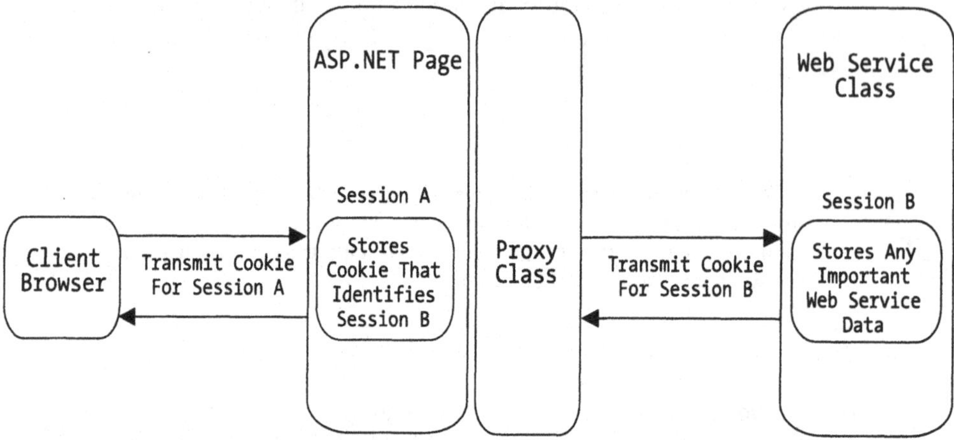

Figure 21-7. Session cookies with a web client

Your client is a simple web page with two buttons and a label control. Every time the Call Service button is clicked, the GetStockQuote() method is invoked with a default parameter. When the Get Usage Info button is clicked, the GetStockUsage() method is called, which returns the current usage statistics. Information is added to the label, creating a log that records every consecutive action.

```
Public Class FailedSessionServiceTest
  Inherits Page
    Protected WithEvents cmdCallService As Button
    Protected lblResult As Label
    Protected WithEvents cmdGetCounter As Button

    Private WS As New localhost.StockQuote_SessionState()

    Private Sub cmdGetCounter_Click(sender As Object, e As EventArgs) _
      Handles cmdGetCounter.Click
        Dim WSInfo As localhost.CounterInfo
        WSInfo = WS.GetStockUsage("MSFT")

        ' Add usage information to the label.
        lblResult.Text &= "<b>Global: " & WSInfo.GlobalRequests.ToString()
        lblResult.Text &= "<br>Session: "
        lblResult.Text &= WSInfo.SessionRequests.ToString() & "<br></b>"
    End Sub

    Private Sub cmdCallService_Click(sender As Object, e As EventArgs) _
      Handles cmdCallService.Click
        Dim Result As Decimal = WS.GetStockQuote("MSFT")
```

```
        ' Add confirmation message to the label.
        lblResult.Text &= "GetStockQuote With MSFT Returned "
        lblResult.Text &= Result.ToString() & "<br>"
    End Sub

End Class
```

Unfortunately, every time this button is clicked, the proxy class is re-created, and a new session is used. The output on the page tells an interesting story: after clicking cmdCallService four times and cmdGetCounter once, the web service reports the right number of global application requests, but the wrong number of session requests, as shown in Figure 21-8.

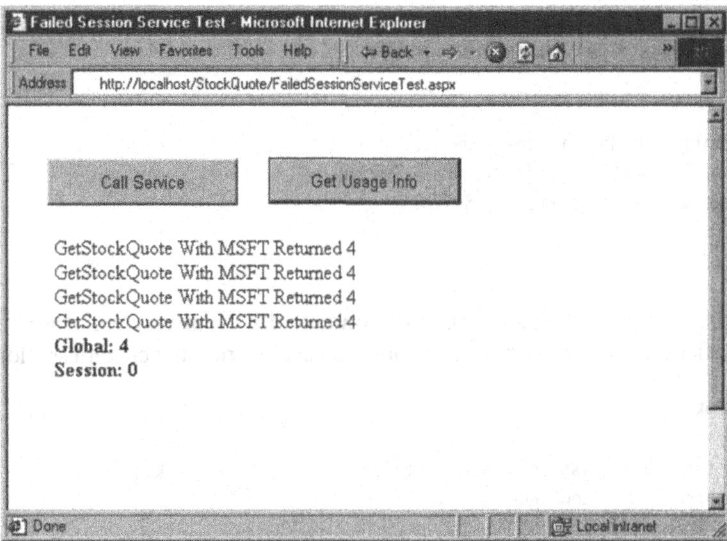

Figure 21-8. A failed attempt to use session state

To fix this problem, you need to set the CookieContainer property of the proxy class. First, be sure to import the System.Net class, which has the cookie classes this example needs:

```
Imports System.Net
```

The event handlers are modified to add calls to two private functions: GetCookie() and SetCookie(). These methods are called immediately before and after the web method call.

```
Private Sub cmdGetCounter_Click(sender As Object, e As EventArgs) _
  Handles cmdGetCounter.Click
    Dim WSInfo As localhost.CounterInfo
    GetCookie()
    WSInfo = WS.GetStockUsage("MSFT")
    SetCookie()

    ' Add usage information to the label.
    lblResult.Text &= "<b>Global: " & WSInfo.GlobalRequests.ToString()
    lblResult.Text &= "<br>Session: "
    lblResult.Text &= WSInfo.SessionRequests.ToString() & "<br></b>"
End Sub

Private Sub cmdCallService_Click(sender As Object, e As EventArgs) _
  Handles cmdCallService.Click
    GetCookie()
    Dim Result As Decimal = WS.GetStockQuote("MSFT")
    SetCookie()

    ' Add confirmation message to the label.
    lblResult.Text &= "GetStockQuote With MSFT Returned "
    lblResult.Text &= Result.ToString() & "<br>"

End Sub
```

The GetCookie() method initializes the CookieContainer for the proxy class, enabling it to send and receive cookies. It also tries to retrieve the cookie from the current session.

```
Private Sub GetCookie()

    ' Initialize the proxy class CookieContainer so it can receive cookies.
    WS.CookieContainer = New CookieContainer()

    ' Create a cookie object, and try to retrieve it from session state.
    Dim SessionCookie As Cookie
    SessionCookie = CType(Session("WebServiceCookie"), Cookie)

    ' If a cookie was found, place it in the proxy class.
    ' The only reason it won't be found is if this is the first time the
    ' button has been clicked.
    If IsNothing(SessionCookie) = False Then
        WS.CookieContainer.Add(SessionCookie)
    End If

End Sub
```

The SetCookie() method explicitly stores the web service session cookie in session state.

```
Private Sub SetCookie()

    ' Retrieve and store the current cookie for next time.
    ' The session is always stored in a special cookie
    ' called ASP.NET_SessionId.

    Dim WSUri As New Uri("http://localhost")

    Dim Cookies As CookieCollection = WS.CookieContainer.GetCookies(WSUri)
    Session("WebServiceCookie") = Cookies("ASP.NET_SessionId")

End Sub
```

The code could have been simplified somewhat if it stored the whole cookie collection instead of just the session cookie, but this approach is more controlled.

Now the page works correctly, as shown in Figure 21-9.

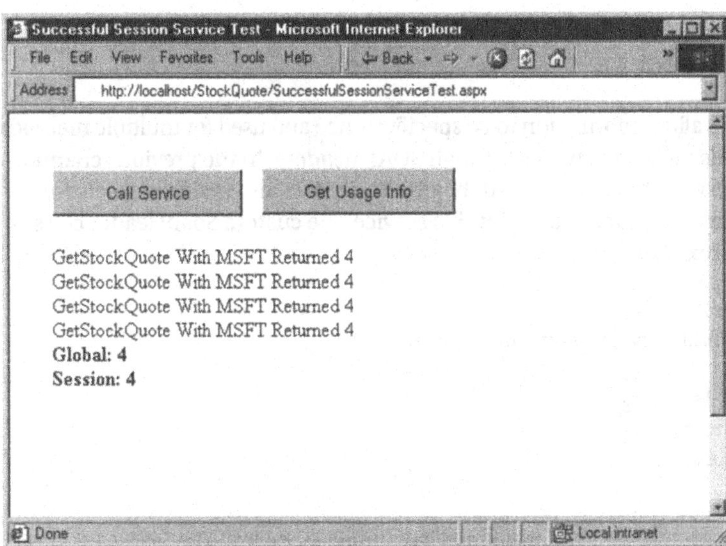

Figure 21-9. A successful use of session state

Does Session State Management Make Sense with a Web Service?

Because web services are destroyed after every method call, they don't provide a natural mechanism for storing state information. You can use the Session collection to compensate for this limitation, but this approach raises the following complications:

- Session state will disappear when the session times out. The client will have no way of knowing when the session times out, which means the web service may behave unpredictably.
- Session state is tied to a specific user, not to a specific class or object. This can cause problems if the same client wants to use the same web service in two different ways, or creates two instances of the proxy class at once.
- Session state is only maintained if the client preserves the session cookie. The state management you use in a web service won't work if the client fails to take these steps.

Using SOAP Headers

Some web services allow information to be specified once and used for multiple methods automatically. This technique works through SOAP headers. In the previous chapter, you saw a web service that used a SOAP header to receive and maintain security credentials. When you create a client for this service, the custom SoapHeader class is copied into the proxy file:

```
Public Class SecurityHeader
  Inherits System.Web.Services.Protocols.SoapHeader

    Public UserID As String
    Public Password As String
    Public Key As String
End Class
```

To use the web service, you create an instance of this header, supply the appropriate information, and then attach it to the appropriate variable in the proxy class.

```
' Create an instance of the header.
Dim Header As New SecurityHeader()
Header.UserID = "Matthew"
Header.Password = "OpenSesame"

' Create the proxy class.
Dim WS As New localhost.StockQuote_SoapSecurity()

' Assign the header.
WS.SecurityHeaderValue = Header
```

When you assign the custom header to the proxy class, no information is transmitted. However, from this point onward, whenever you call a web method that needs the SecurityHeader, it will be transmitted automatically. In other words, you set the header once and don't need to worry about supplying any additional security information, as long as you use the same instance of the proxy class. The online examples include a simple example of a web service client that uses a SOAP header for authentication.

An Example with TerraService

Now that you know how to use a web service, you aren't just limited to using the web services that you create. In fact, the Internet is brimming with sample services that you can use to test your applications or try out new techniques. In the future, you'll even be able to buy prebuilt functionality that you can integrate into your ASP.NET applications by calling a web service. Typically, you'll pay for these services using some kind of subscription model. Because they're implemented through .NET web services and WSDL contracts, you won't need to install anything extra on your web server.

The next section considers how to use one of the more interesting web services: Microsoft's TerraService. TerraService is based on the hugely popular TerraServer site where web surfers can view topographic maps and satellite photographs of most of the globe. The site was developed by Microsoft's research division to test SQL Server and increase Microsoft's boasting ability. Under the hood, a 1.5 TB SQL Server 2000 database stores all the pictures that are used, as a collection of millions of different tiles. You can find out more about TerraServer at `http://terraservice.net`.

To promote .NET, Microsoft has equipped TerraServer with a web service interface that allows you to access the TerraServer information. Using this interface (called TerraService) isn't difficult, but creating a polished application with it would be. Before you can really understand how to stitch together different satellite tiles to create a large picture, you need to have some basic understanding of geography and projection systems. There's plenty of additional information about it at the TerraServer site. However, because this book is about .NET and not geography, your use of the TerraService will be fairly straightforward. Once you understand the basics, you can continue experimenting with additional web methods and create a more extensive application based on TerraService.

Adding the Reference

The first step is to create a new ASP.NET application and add a web reference. In Visual Studio .NET, you start by returning to the Add Web Reference window. The TerraService web service is located at `http://terraservice.net/TerraService.asmx`. Type it in to the Address text box, and press Enter. The TerraService test page will appear (see Figure 21-10).

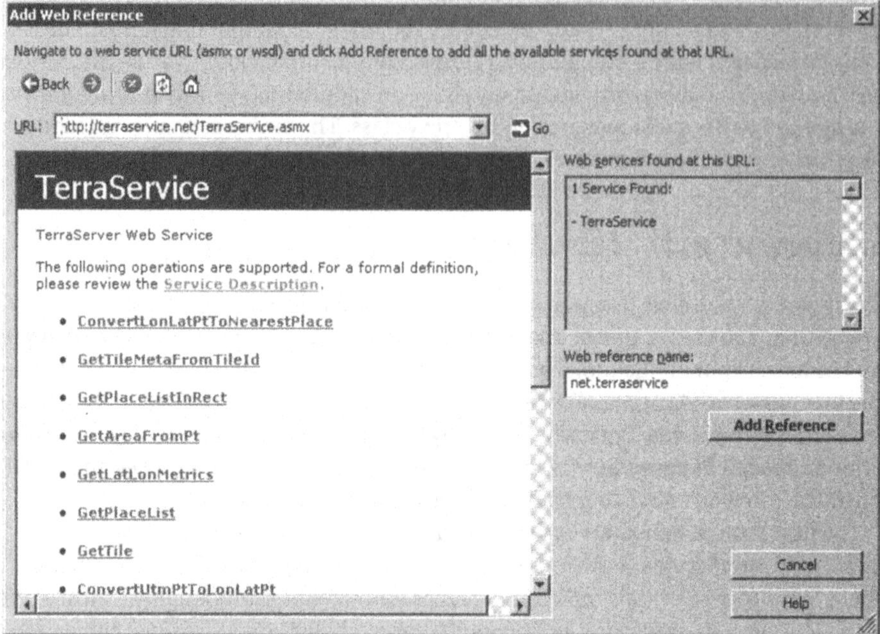

Figure 21-10. Adding a TerraService web reference

You can see from the displayed test page that there are approximately 15 functions. At the time of this writing, no additional information is provided on the test page (indicating that Microsoft doesn't always follow its own recommendations). To read about these methods, you'll have to browse the site on your own.

Click Add Reference to create the Web Reference. The WSDL document, discovery file, and proxy class will be created under the namespace net.terraservice, as shown in Figure 21-11.

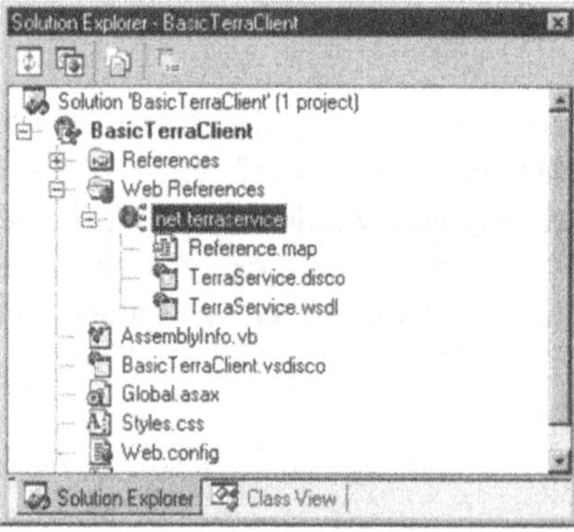

Figure 21-11. The TerraService files in Visual Studio .NET

Trying It Out

Before continuing too much further, it makes sense to try out a simple method to see if the web service works as expected. A good choice to start is the simple GetPlaceFacts() method, which retrieves some simple information about a geographic location that you supply. In this case, the TerraService documentation (and Visual Studio .NET IntelliSense) informs you that this method requires the use of two special classes: a Place class (which specifies what you're searching for), and a PlaceFacts class (which provides you with the information about your place). These classes are available in the net.terraservice namespace.

The following example retrieves information about a place named "Seattle" when a button is clicked, and displays it in a label control. The process is split into two separate subroutines for better organization, although this isn't strictly required.

```
Private Sub cmdShow_Click(sender As Object, e As EventArgs) _
  Handles cmdShow.Click

    ' Create the Place object for Seattle.
    Dim SearchPlace As New net.terraservice.Place()
    SearchPlace.City = "Seattle"

    ' Create the PlaceFacts objects to retrieve your information.
    Dim Facts As net.terraservice.PlaceFacts

    ' Call the web service method.
    Facts = ts.GetPlaceFacts(SearchPlace)

    ' Display the results with the help of a subroutine.
    ShowPlaceFacts(Facts)

End Sub

Private Sub ShowPlaceFacts(Facts As net.terraservice.PlaceFacts)
    lblResult.Text &= "<b>Place: " & Facts.Place.City & "</b><br><br>"
    lblResult.Text &= Facts.Place.State & ", " & Facts.Place.Country
    lblResult.Text &= "<br> Lat: " & Facts.Center.Lat.ToString()
    lblResult.Text &= "<br> Long: " & Facts.Center.Lon.ToString()
    lblResult.Text &= "<br><br>"
End Sub
```

The result is a successful retrieval of information about the city of Seattle, including its longitude, latitude, and country, as shown in Figure 21-12.

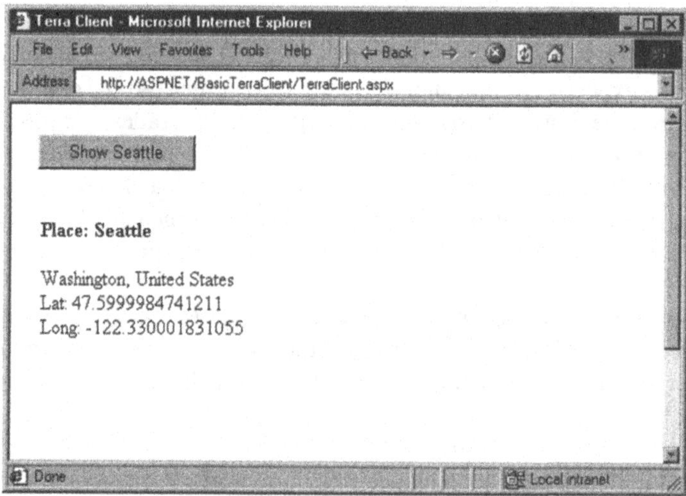

Figure 21-12. Retrieving information from the TerraService

Searching for More Information

The TerraService documentation recommends against using the GetPlaceFacts() method, because it's only able to retrieve information about the first place with the matching name. Typically, there are many locations that share the same name. Even in the case of Seattle, there are several landmark locations stored in the TerraServer database along with the city itself. All of these places start with the word "Seattle."

The GetPlaceList() method provides a more useful approach, because it returns an array with all the matches. When using GetPlaceList() you have to specify a maximum number of allowed matches, to prevent your application from becoming tied up with an extremely long query. You also have a third parameter, which you can set to True to retrieve only results that have corresponding picture tiles in the database, or False to return any matching result. Typically, you would use True if you were creating an application that displays the satellite images for searched locations. You'll also notice that the GetPlaceList() function accepts a place name directly and doesn't use a Place object.

To demonstrate this method, add a second button to the test page and use the following code:

```
Private Sub cmdShowAll_Click(sender As Object, e As EventArgs) _
  Handles cmdShowAll.Click

    ' Create the TerraService objects.
    Dim FactsArray() As net.terraservice.PlaceFacts
    Dim Facts As net.terraservice.PlaceFacts

    ' Retrieve the matching list (for the city "Kingston").
    FactsArray = ts.GetPlaceList("Kingston", 100, False)
```

```
    ' Loop through all the results, and display them.
    For Each Facts In FactsArray
        ShowPlaceFacts(Facts)
    Next

End Sub
```

The result is a list of about 50 matches for places with the name "Kingston," as shown in Figure 21-13.

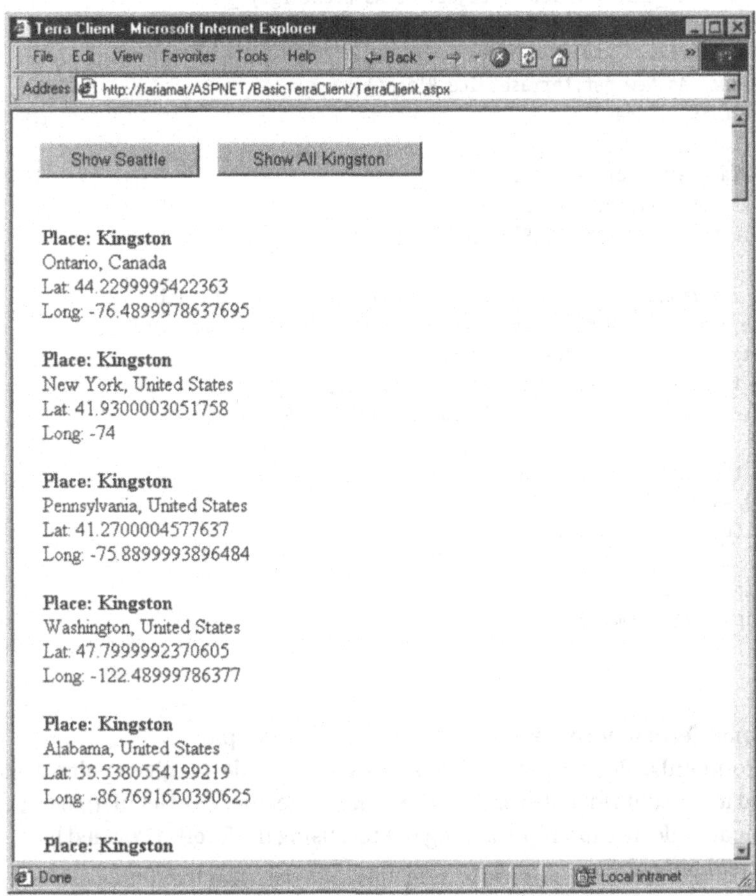

Figure 21-13. Retrieving place matches

Displaying a Tile

By this point, you've realized that using the TerraService isn't really different than using any other DLL or code library. The only difference is that you're accessing it over the Internet. In this case, it's no small feat: the TerraServer database contains so much information that it would never be practical to create a network-based or local application. Also, this information, if not carefully managed, would be extremely difficult to download over the Internet. Providing it through a web service interface solves all these problems.

The next example shows your last trick for a web service. It retrieves the closest matching tile for the city of Seattle and displays it. To display the tile, the example takes the low-level approach of using Response.WriteBinary(). In a more advanced application, a significant amount of in-memory graphical manipulation might be required to get the result you want. The retrieved tile is shown in Figure 21-14.

```
Private Sub cmdShowPic_Click(sender As Object, e As EventArgs) _
  Handles cmdShowPic.Click
    ' Define the search.
    Dim SearchPlace As New net.terraservice.Place()
    SearchPlace.City = "Seattle"

    ' Get the PlaceFacts for Seattle.
    Dim Facts As net.terraservice.PlaceFacts
    Facts = ts.GetPlaceFacts(SearchPlace)

    ' Retrieve information about the tile at the center of Seattle, using
    ' the Scale and Theme enumerations from the terraservice namespace.
    Dim TileData As net.terraservice.TileMeta
    TileData = ts.GetTileMetaFromLonLatPt(Facts.Center, _
     net.Terraservice.Theme.Photo, net.terraservice.Scale.Scale16m)

    ' Retrieve the image.
    Dim Image() As Byte
    Image = ts.GetTile(TileData.Id)

    ' Display the image.
    Response.BinaryWrite(Image)

End Sub
```

Two additional TerraService methods are used in this example. GetTileMetaFromLonLatPt() retrieves information about the tile at a given point. This function is used to find out what tile contains the center of Seattle. The GetTile() method retrieves the binary information representing the tile, using the TileID provided by GetTileMetaFromLonLatPt().

You'll probably also want to combine several tiles together, which requires the use of other TerraService methods. The full set of supported methods is documented at `http://terraservice.net`. Once again, using these methods requires an understanding of graphics and geography, but they don't require any unusual use of web services. The core concept—remote method calls through SOAP communication—remains the same.

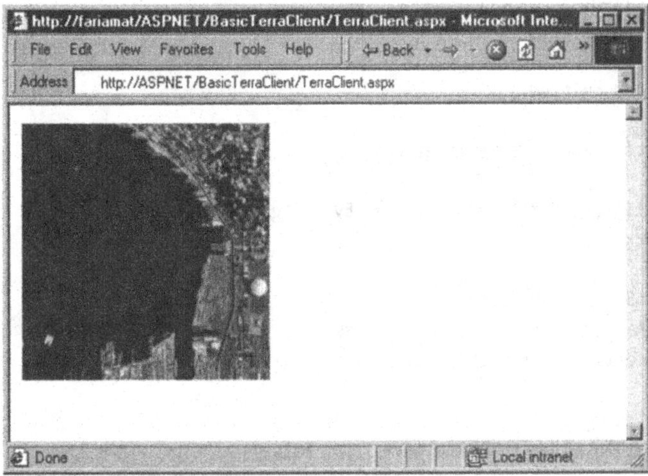

Figure 21-14. A tile from TerraService

Windows Clients

Because this is book is focused squarely on ASP.NET, you haven't had the chance to see one of the main advantages of web services. Quite simply, they allow desktop applications to use pieces of functionality from the Internet. This allows you to provide a rich, responsive desktop interface that periodically retrieves any real-time information it needs from the Internet. The process is almost entirely transparent. As high-speed access becomes more common, you may not even be aware which portions of functionality depend on the Internet and which ones don't.

You can use web service functionality in a Windows application in exactly the same way that you would use it in an ASP.NET application. First, you would create the proxy class using Visual Studio .NET or the WSDL.exe utility. Then you would add code to create an instance of your web service and call a web method. The only different is the upper layer: the user interface the application uses.

If you haven't explored desktop programming with .NET yet, you'll be happy to know that you can reuse much of what you've learned in ASP.NET development. Many web controls (such as labels, buttons, text boxes, and lists) closely parallel their .NET desktop equivalents, and the code you write to interact with them can often be transferred from one environment to the other with very few changes. In fact, the main difference between desktop programming and web programming in .NET is the extra steps you need to take in web applications to preserve information between postbacks and when transferring the user from one page to another.

The following example shows the form code for a simple Windows TerraService client that uses the GetPlaceList() web method. It's been modified to search for a place that the user enters in a text box, and display the results in a list box control. The basic designer code, which creates the controls and sets their initial properties, has been omitted. (This plays the same role as the control tags in the .aspx web page file.)

```
Public Class WindowsTerraClient
  Inherits System.Windows.Forms.Form

    ' (Windows designer code omitted.)

    Private ts As New net.terraservice.TerraService()

    Private Sub cmdShow_Click(sender As Object, e As EventArgs) _
      Handles cmdShow.Click

        ' Create the TerraService objects.
        Dim FactsArray() As net.terraservice.PlaceFacts
        Dim Facts As net.terraservice.PlaceFacts

        ' Retrieve the matching list.
        FactsArray = ts.GetPlaceList(txtPlace.text, 100, False)

        ' Loop through all the results, and display them.
        For Each Facts In FactsArray
            ShowPlaceFacts(Facts)
        Next

    End Sub

    Private Sub ShowPlaceFacts(Facts As net.terraservice.PlaceFacts)

        Dim NewItem As String
        NewItem = "Place: " & Facts.Place.City & ", "
        NewItem &= Facts.Place.State & ", " & Facts.Place.Country
        lstPlaces.Items.Add(NewItem)

    End Sub

End Class
```

The interface for this application is shown in Figure 21-15.

Of course, Windows development contains many other possibilities, which are covered in many other excellent books. The interesting part from your vantage point is the way that a Windows client can interact with a web service just like an ASP.NET application does. This raises a world of new possibilities for integrated Windows and web applications.

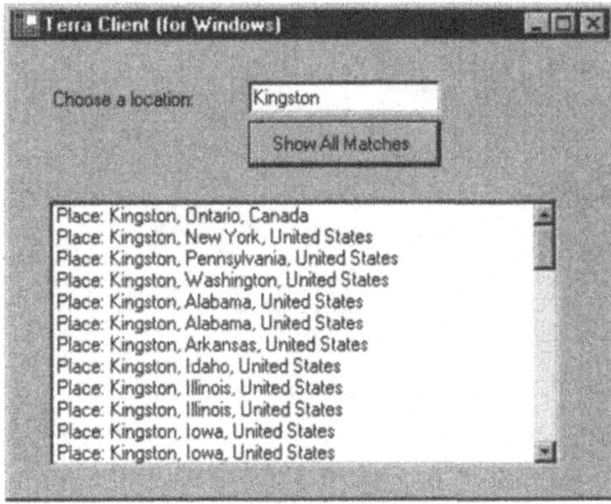

Figure 21-15. A Windows client for TerraService

The Last Word

This chapter demonstrated how you can use your own web methods, and other web services on the Internet. If you would like to hone your skills with other examples, consider some of the following web services:

- GotDotNet (`http://www.gotdotnet.com/playground/services`) is a Microsoft-sponsored site with some basic web services such as a thumbnail generator, e-mail sender, and quote of the day. Best of all, you can also see the .NET implementation code for these services.
- XMethods (`http://www.xmethods.com`) is a more general web service catalog. It includes many non-Microsoft web services that you can use in .NET applications, like the BabelFish translator.
- Microsoft's MapPoint is an interesting example that enables you to access high-quality maps and geographical information. MapPoint isn't free, but you can use a free trial of the web service. See `http://msdn.microsoft.com/library/en-us/dnmapnet/html/mapintronet.asp` for more information.

Part Five
Advanced ASP.NET

CHAPTER 22

Component-Based Programming

COMPONENT-BASED PROGRAMMING is a simple, elegant idea. When used properly, it allows your code to be more organized, consistent, and reusable. It's also incredibly easy to implement in a .NET application, because you never need to use the Windows registry or perform any special configuration.

To create a .NET component, you separate a portion of your program's functionality and compile it to a separate assembly (DLL file). Your web pages (or any other .NET application) can then use this component in the same way that they use any other .NET class. Best of all, your component provides exactly the features your code requires, and hides all the other messy details.

When combined with careful organization, component-based programming is the basis of good ASP.NET application design. In this chapter, you'll examine how you can create components (and why you should), and consider examples that show you how to encapsulate database functionality with a well-written business object. You'll also take a detour into the world of COM, and show how you can access legacy components by adding .NET wrappers around them.

Why Use Components?

To master ASP.NET development, you need to become a skilled user of the .NET class library. So far, you've learned how to use .NET components designed for sending mail, reading files, and interacting with databases. Though these class library ingredients are powerful, they aren't customizable, which is both an advantage and a weakness.

For example, it's convenient to be able to access any database in almost exactly the same way, irrespective of what type of information it contains. However, it's much less helpful to have to weave database details (such as SQL queries and connection strings) directly into your web page code. Though you can improve on this situation by storing some database constants in a web.config application file, you'll still end up with a significant amount of data access code scattered throughout your web pages. If the structure of the database changes even slightly, you could be left with dozens of pages to update and retest. To solve these problems, you need to create an extra layer between your web page code and the database. This "extra layer" takes the form of a custom component.

This database scenario is only one of the reasons you might want to create your own components. Component-based programming is really just a logical extension of good code-organizing principles, and it offers a long list of advantages:

- **Increased security.** For example, you could configure your component to only allow access to certain tables, fields, or rows in a database. This is often easier than setting up complex permissions in the database itself. Because the application has to go through the component, it needs to play by its rules.
- **Better organization.** Components move the clutter out of your web page code. It also becomes easier for other programmers to understand your application's logic when it's broken down into separate components.
- **Easier troubleshooting.** It's impossible to oversell the advantage of components when testing and debugging an application. Component-based programs are broken down into smaller, tighter blocks of code, making it easier to isolate exactly where a problem is occurring.
- **More manageable.** Component-based programs are much easier to enhance and modify because common tasks are coded once (in the component), and used in as many places as required. Without components, commonly used code has to be copied and pasted throughout an application, making it extremely difficult to change and synchronize.
- **Code reuse.** Components can be shared with any ASP.NET application that needs the component's functionality. Even better, a component can be used by any .NET application, meaning you could create a common "backbone" of logic that's used by a web application and an ordinary Windows application.
- **Simplicity.** Components can provide multiple related tasks for a single client request (writing several records to a database, opening and reading a file in one step, or even starting and managing a database transaction). Similarly, components hide details—an application programmer can use a database component without worrying about the database name, location of the server, or the user account needed to connect. Even better, you can perform a search using certain criteria, and the component itself can decide whether to use a dynamically generated SQL statement or stored procedure.
- **Performance.** If you need to perform a long, time-consuming operation, you can create an asynchronous component to handle the work for you. That allows you to perform other tasks with the web page code, and return to pick up the result at a later time.

Components in ASP

In ASP programming, components were also required to overcome the limitations of VBScript. Unlike ASP pages, components could be written in Visual Basic 6, which provided a richer syntax, a speedier compiled language, and the ability to perform tasks that just weren't allowed in ordinary script code. ASP.NET, as you've learned, doesn't suffer from any of these limitations, and hence components aren't required to compensate for ASP deficiencies. However, components still make good sense and are required to design a large-scale, well-organized ASP.NET application.

Component Jargon

Component-based programming is sometimes shrouded in a fog of specialized jargon. Understanding these terms helps sort out exactly what a component is supposed to do, and it also allows you to understand MSDN articles about application design. If you're already familiar with the fundamentals of components, feel free to skip ahead.

Three-Tier Design

The idea of three-tier design is that the functionality of most complete applications can be divided into three main levels (see Figure 22-1). The first level is the user interface (or presentation tier), which displays controls, and receives and validates user input. All the event handlers in your web page are in this first level. The second level is the business layer, where the application-specific logic takes place. For an e-commerce site, application-specific logic includes rules such as how shipping charges are applied to an order, when certain promotions are valid, and what customer actions should be logged. It doesn't involve generic .NET details such as how to open a file or connect to a database. The third layer is the data layer, where the application's information is stored in files or a database. The third layer contains logic about how to retrieve and update data, such as SQL queries or stored procedures.

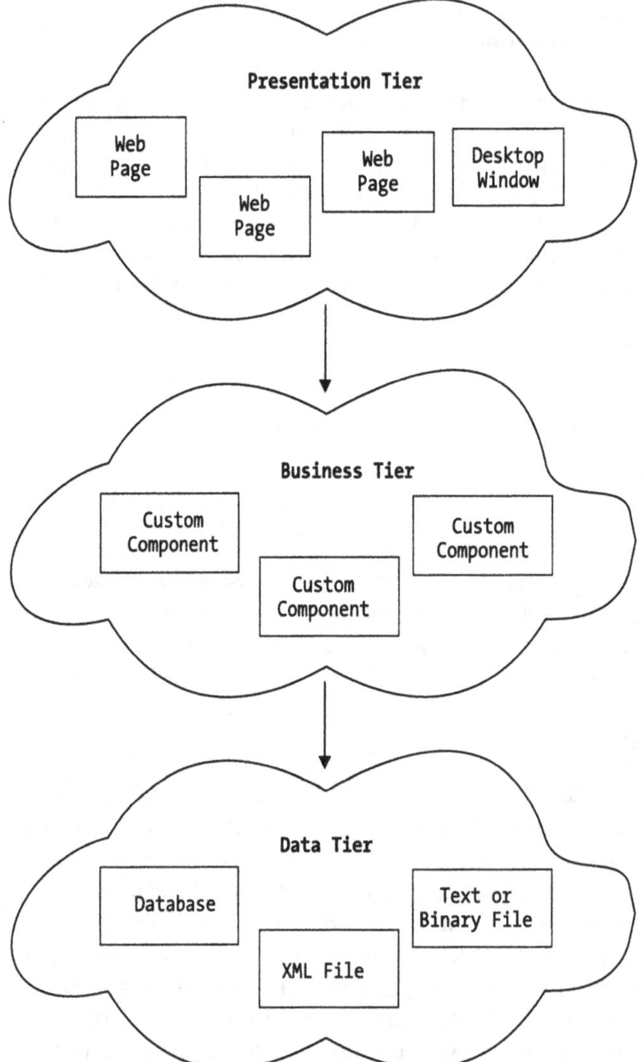

Figure 22-1. Three-tier design

The important detail about three-tier design is that information only travels from one level to an adjacent level. In other words, your user interface code shouldn't try to directly access the database and retrieve information. Instead, it should go through the second layer and then arrive at the database.

This basic organization principle can't always be adhered to, but it's a good model to follow. When you create a component, it's almost always used in the second layer to bridge the gap between the data and the user interface. In other words, if you want to fill a list of product categories in a list box, your user interface code would call a component, which would get the list from the database, and then return it to your code. Your web page code is isolated from the database—and if the database structure changes you need to change one concise component, instead of every page on your site.

Encapsulation

If three-tier design is the overall goal of component-based programming, encapsulation is the best rule of thumb. Encapsulation is the principle that you should create your application out of "black boxes" that hide information. For example, if you have a component that logs a purchase on an e-commerce site, that component handles all the details and allows only the essentially variables to be specified.

For example, this component might accept a user ID and an order item ID, and then handle all the other details. The calling code would not need to worry about how the component works or where the data is coming from—it just needs to understand how to use the component. (This principle is described in a lot of picturesque ways. For example, you know how to drive a car because you understand its component interface—the steering wheel and pedals—not because you understand the low-level details about internal combustion and the engine.)

Data Objects

Data objects are used in a variety of ways. In this book, the term refers to a custom object that you make that represents a certain grouping of data. For example, you could create a Person class that has properties like Height, Age, and EyeColor. Your code can then create data objects based on this class. You might want to use a data object to pass information from one portion of code to another. (Note that data objects are sometimes used to describe objects that handle data management. This isn't the way you'll see it used in this book.)

Business Objects

The term *business object* often means different things to different people. Generally, business objects are the components in the second layer of your application that provide the extra layer between your code and the data source. They are called business objects because they enforce *business rules.* For example, if you try to submit a purchase order without any items, the appropriate business object would throw an exception and refuse to continue. In this case, no .NET error has occurred—instead, you've detected the presence of a condition that should not be allowed according to your application's logic.

In your examples, business objects are also going to contain data access code. In an extremely complicated, large, and changeable system, you might want to further subdivide components, and actually have your user interface code talking to a business object, which in turn talks to a data object that interacts with the data source. However, for most programmers this extra step is overkill, especially with the increased level of consistency that is provided by ADO.NET.

Creating a Simple Component

Technically, a component is just a collection of one or more classes that are compiled together as a unit. For example, Microsoft's System.Web.dll is a single (but very large) component that provides the objects found in many of the System.Web namespaces. So far, the code examples in this book have only used a few types of class—mainly custom web page classes that inherit from System.Web.UI.Page and contain mostly event-handling procedures. Component classes, on the other hand, won't interact directly with a web page and rarely inherit from anything. They are more similar to the custom Web Service classes described in the fourth part of this book, which collect related features together in a series of utility methods.

Web Services vs. Components

Web services provide some of the same opportunities for code reuse as custom components. However, web services are primarily designed as an easy way to share functionality across different computers and platforms. A component, on the other hand, isn't nearly as easy to share with the wide world of the Internet, but is far more efficient for sharing internally (for example, between different applications in the same company or different websites on the same server). For that reason, web services and components don't directly compete—in fact, a web service could even make use of a component (or vice versa). In some cases you might find yourself programming a site with a mixture of the two, putting the code that needs to be reused in-house into components, and the functionality that needs to be made publicly available into web services.

The Component Class

You have two options when writing a component.

- You can code it by hand in a .vb text file, and then compile it with the vbc.exe command-line compiler described in earlier chapters.
- You can use Visual Studio .NET, and start a new Class Library project. When choosing the project directory, you need to specify a real (physical) directory, not the virtual directory name. Figure 22-2 shows Visual Studio .NET's New Project window with a Class Library project.

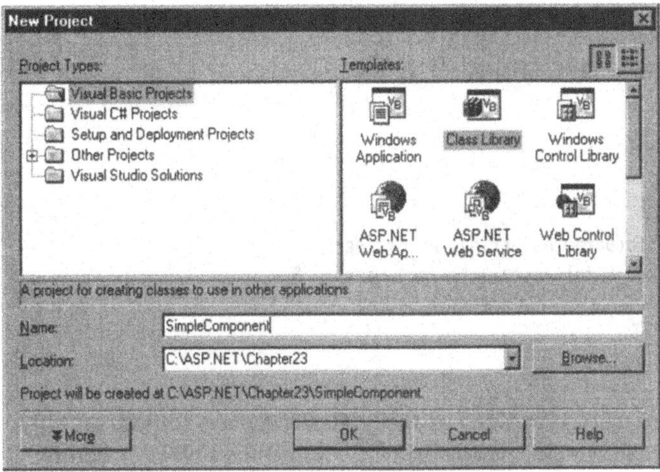

Figure 22-2. Creating a component in Visual Studio .NET

These options are equivalent. In your .vb file, you define the component as a class.

```
Public Class SimpleTest
    ' (Code goes here, inside one or more methods.)
End Class
```

Remember, a component can contain more than one class. You can create other classes in the same file, or in separate files, which will be compiled together into one assembly.

```
Public Class SimpleTest
End Class

Public Class SimpleTest2
End Class
```

To add functionality to your class, you add public methods (functions or subroutines). The web page code calls these methods to retrieve information or perform a task. The following example shows one of the simplest possible components, which does nothing more than return a string to the calling code.

```
Public Class SimpleTest
    Public Function GetInfo(param As String) As String
        Return "You invoked SimpleTest.GetInfo() with '" & _
               param & "'"
    End Function
End Class

Public Class SimpleTest2
    Public Function GetInfo(param As String) As String
        Return "You invoked SimpleTest2.GetInfo() with '" & _
               param & "'"
    End Function
End Class
```

Usually, these classes will be organized in a special namespace. You can group classes into a namespace at the file level by using the Namespace block structure. In the following example, the classes will be accessed in other applications as SimpleComponent.SimpleTest and SimpleComponent.SimpleTest2. If needed, you can create multiple levels of nested namespaces.

```
Namespace SimpleComponent

    Public Class SimpleTest
        ' (Class code omitted.)
    End Class

    Public Class SimpleTest2
        ' (Class code omitted.)
    End Class

End Namespace
```

In Visual Studio .NET, your component is automatically placed in a root namespace that has the project name. This code doesn't appear in the .vb file (although you can add additional namespaces there). To change the name of your root namespace, right-click the project in the Solution Explorer and select Properties. Look under the Common Properties ➤ General group for the root namespace setting (see Figure 22-3). You can also use this window to configure the name that will be given to the compiled assembly file.

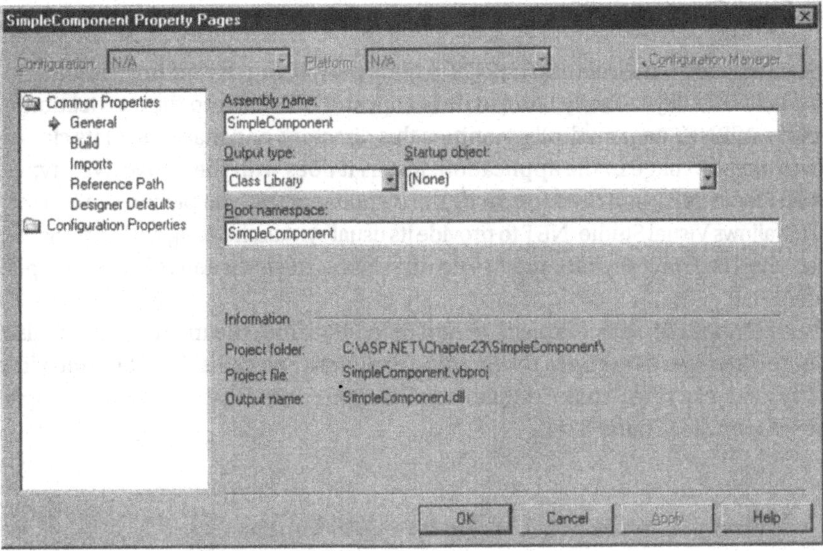

Figure 22-3. Setting the root namespace

Compiling the Component Class

In Visual Studio .NET, you can compile this class just by right-clicking the project in the Solution Explorer and choosing Build. You can't actually run the project, because it isn't an application, and it doesn't provide any user interface.

If you're writing the class by hand in a text file, you can compile it in more or less the same way as you compile a .aspx code-behind file or .asmx web service.

```
vbc /t:library /r:System.dll /r:System.Web.dll SimpleComponent.vb
```

The /t:library parameter indicates that you want to create a DLL assembly instead of an EXE assembly. The compiled assembly will have the name SimpleComponent.dll. The /r parameter specifies any dependent assemblies you use. The compilation process is the same as that described with web pages in Chapter 5.

NOTE Unlike web pages and web services, you must compile a component before you can use it. Components aren't hosted by the ASP.NET service and IIS (Internet Information Services), and thus cannot be compiled automatically when they are needed.

Using the Component

Using the component in an actual ASP.NET page is easy. If you're working without Visual Studio .NET, all you really need to do is copy the DLL file into the application's bin directory. ASP.NET automatically monitors this directory, and makes all of its classes available to any web page in the application, just as it does with the native .NET types.

In Visual Studio .NET, you need to specify the component that you plan to use as a reference. This allows Visual Studio .NET to provide its usual syntax checking and IntelliSense. Otherwise, it will interpret your attempts to use the class as mistakes and refuse to compile your code.

To link a component, select Project ➤ Add Reference from the menu (you can also right-click the References group in the Solution Explorer). Select the .NET tab, and click Browse. Find and select the SimpleComponent.dll file you created in the previous example, and choose Open (see Figure 22-4).

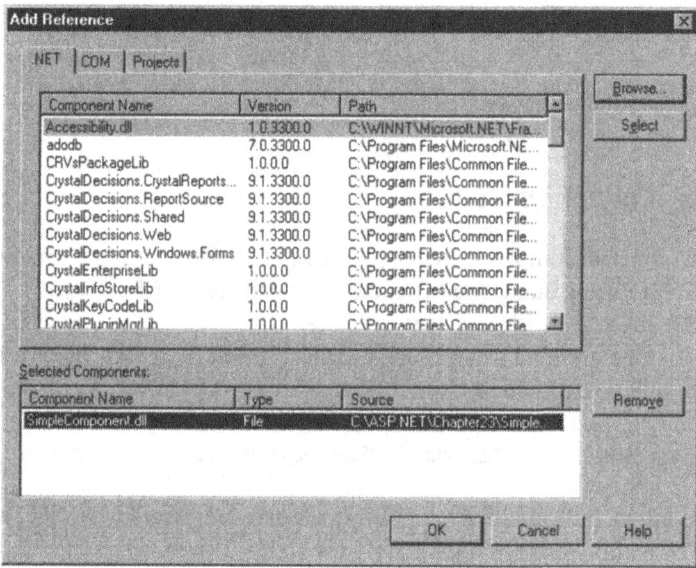

Figure 22-4. Adding a custom component reference

Once you add the reference, the DLL file will be automatically copied to the bin directory of your current project. You can verify this by checking the Full Path property of the SimpleComponent reference, or just browsing to the directory in Windows Explorer. The nice thing is that this file will automatically be overwritten with the most recent compiled version of the assembly every time you run the project.

TIP You can also create a Visual Studio .NET solution that combines a class library project with an ASP.NET application project. This technique, which you examined with web services in the Chapter 21, allows you to debug a component while it's in use alongside the application. In this case, you don't add a reference to the DLL file. Instead, you add a special project reference to the class library project in the same solution, using the Projects tab of the Add Reference window. With project references, Visual Studio .NET automatically compiles the component for you when run the application that uses it.

You can now use the component by creating instances of the SimpleTest or SimpleTest2 class.

```
Public Class TestPage
  Inherits Page

    Protected lblResult As Label

    Private Sub Page_Load(sender As Object, e As EventArgs) _
      Handles MyBase.Load
        Dim TestComponent As New SimpleComponent.SimpleTest()
        Dim TestComponent2 As New SimpleComponent.SimpleTest2()
        lblResult.Text = TestComponent.GetInfo("Hello") & "<br><br>"
        lblResult.Text &= TestComponent2.GetInfo("Bye")
    End Sub

End Class
```

The output for this page, shown in Figure 22-5, combines the return value from both GetInfo() methods.

To make this code slightly simpler, you could have chosen to use shared methods, so that you don't need to create an object before using the method. A shared GetInfo() method would look like this:

```
Public Class SimpleTest
    Public Shared Function GetInfo(param As String) As String
        Return "You invoked SimpleTest.GetInfo() with '" & _
               param & "'"
    End Function
End Class
```

The web page would access the shared GetInfo() method through the class name, and would not need to create an object.

```
Private Sub Page_Load(sender As Object, e As EventArgs) _
  Handles MyBase.Load
    lblResult.Text = SimpleComponent.SimpleTest.GetInfo("Hello")
End Sub
```

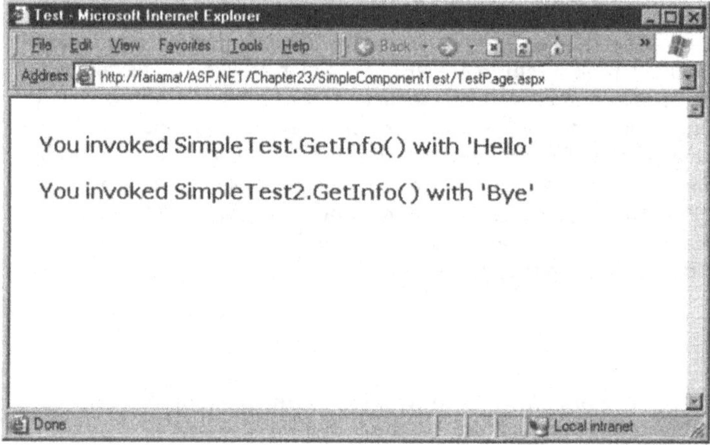

Figure 22-5. The SimpleTest component output

Properties and State

The SimpleTest classes provide functionality through public methods. If you're familiar with class-based programming (as described in Chapter 4), you'll remember that classes can also store information in private member variables, and provide property procedures that allow the calling code to modify this information. For example, a Person class might have a FirstName property.

When you create classes that use property procedures, you're using stateful design. In stateful design, the class has the responsibility of maintaining certain pieces of information. In stateless design, like the one found in the SimpleTest component, no information is retained between method calls. Compare that to the stateful SimpleTest class shown here:

```
Public Class SimpleTest

    Private _Data As String
    Public Property Data() As String
        Get
            Return _Data
        End Get
        Set(Value As String)
            _Data = Value
        End Set
    End Property

    Public Function GetInfo() As String
        Return "You invoked SimpleTest.GetInfo()," & _
               "and _Data is '" & _Data & "'"
    End Function

End Class
```

In the programming world, there have been a number of great debates arguing whether stateful or stateless programming is best. Stateful programming is the most natural, object-oriented approach, but it also has a few disadvantages. In order to accomplish a common task, you might need to set several properties before calling a method. Each of these individual steps adds a little bit of unneeded overhead. A stateless design, on the other hand, often performs all its work in a single method call. However, because no information is retained in state, you may need to specify several parameters, which can make for tedious programming. A good example of stateful versus stateless objects is shown by the FileInfo and File classes, which are described in Chapter 17.

There is no short answer about whether stateful or stateless design is best, and it often depends on the task at hand. High-performance components, components that use transactions, or components that need to be invoked remotely (like web services), usually use stateless design, which is the simplest and most reliable approach. Because no information is retained in memory, there's fewer server resources being used, and there's no danger of losing valuable data if a software or hardware failure occurs. The next example illustrates the difference with two ways to design an Account class.

A Stateful Account Class

Consider a stateful account class that represents a single customers account. Information is read from the database when it's first created in the constructor method, and can be updated using the Update() method.

```
Public Class CustomerAccount

    Private _AccountNumber As Integer
    Private _Balance As Decimal

    Public Property Balance() As Decimal
        Get
            Return _Balance
        End Get
        Set(Value As Decimal)
            _Balance = Value
        End Set
    End Property

    Public Sub New(AccountNumber As Integer)
        ' (Code to read account record from database goes here.)
    End Sub

    Public Sub Update()
        ' (Code to update database record goes here.)
    End Sub

End Class
```

If you have two CustomerAccount objects that expose a Balance property, you need to perform two separate steps to transfer money from one account to another. Conceptually, the process works like this:

```
' Create an account object for each account,
' using the account number.
Dim AccountOne As New Bank.CustomerAccount(122415)
Dim AccountTwo As New Bank.CustomerAccount(123447)
Dim Amount As Decimal = 1000

' Withdraw money from one account.
AccountOne.Balance -= Amount

' Deposit money in the other account.
AccountTwo.Balance += Amount

' Update the underlying database records using an Update method.
AccountOne.Update()
AccountTwo.Update()
```

The problem here is that if this task is interrupted halfway through by an error, you'll end up with at least one unhappy customer.

A Stateless AccountUtility Class

A stateless object, on the other hand, might only expose a shared method called FundTransfer(), which performs all its work in one method.

```
Public Class AccountUtility

    Public Shared Sub FundTransfer(AccountOne As Integer, _
      AccountTwo As Integer, Amount As Decimal)
        ' (The code here retrieves the two database records,
        '  changes them, and updates them.)
    End Sub

End Class
```

The calling code can't use the same elegant CustomerAccount objects, but it can be assured that account transfers are protected from error. Because all the database operations are performed at once, they can use a database stored procedure for greater performance, and a transaction to ensure that the withdrawal and deposit either succeed or fail as a whole.

```
' Store the account and transfer details.
Dim Amount As Decimal = 1000
Dim AccountIDOne As Integer = 122415
Dim AccountIDTwo As Integer = 123447

Bank.AccountUtility.FundTransfer(AccountIDOne, AccountIDTwo, _
  Amount)
```

In a mission-critical system, transactions are often a requirement. For that reason, classes that retain very little state information are often the best design approach, even though they aren't quite as satisfying from an object-oriented perspective.

Database Components

Clearly, components are extremely useful. But if you're starting a large programming project, you may not be sure what features are the best candidates for being made into separate components. Learning how to break an application into components and classes is one of the great arts of programming, and it takes a good deal of practice and fine-tuning.

One of the most common types of components is a database component. Database components are an ideal application of component-based programming for several reasons:

- **Databases require extraneous details.** These details include connection strings, field names, and so on, all of which can distract from the application logic, and can easily be encapsulated by a well-written component.
- **Databases change frequently.** Even if the underlying table structure remains constant and additional information is never required (which is far from certain), queries may be replaced by stored procedures, and stored procedures may be redesigned.
- **Databases have special connection requirements.** You may even need to change the database access code for reasons unrelated to the application. For example, after profiling and testing a database, you might discover that you can replace a single query with two queries or a more efficient stored procedure. In either case, the returned data remains constant, but the data access code is dramatically different.
- **Databases are used repetitively in a finite set of ways.** In other words, a common database routine should be written once and is certain to be used many times over.

A Simple Database Component

To examine the best way to create a database component, you'll consider a simple application that provides a classifieds page listing items that various individuals have for sale. The database uses two tables: an Items table that lists the description and price of a specific sale item, and a Categories table that lists the different groups you can use to categorize an item. The relationship is shown in Figure 22-6.

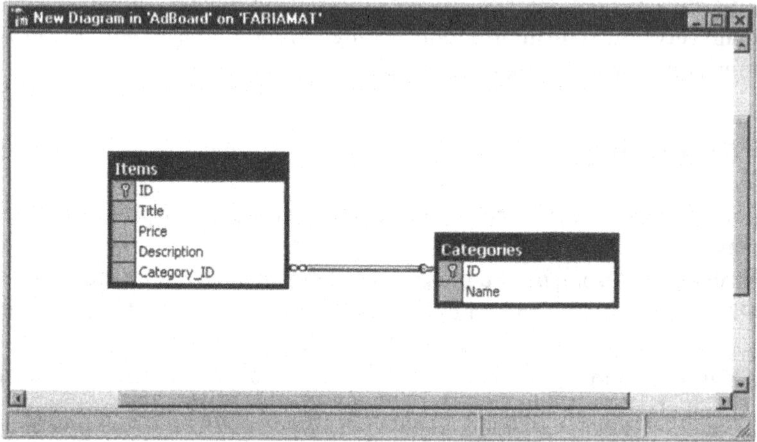

Figure 22-6. The AdBoard database relationships

In this example, you're connecting with an SQL server database using the OLE DB part of the class library. You can create this database yourself, or you can refer to the online samples, which include an SQL script that will generate it automatically. To start, the Categories table is preloaded with a standard set of allowed categories.

The database component is simple. It's an instance class that retains some basic information (such as the connection string to use), but it doesn't allow the client to change this information, and therefore doesn't need any property procedures. Instead, it performs most of its work in methods such as GetCategories() and GetItems(). These methods return DataSets with the appropriate database records. This type of design creates a fairly thin layer over the database—it handles some details, but the client is still responsible for working with familiar ADO.NET classes such as the DataSet.

```
Imports System.Data
Imports System.Data.OleDb
Imports System.Configuration

Public Class DBUtil
    Private ConnectionString As String

    Public Sub New()
        ConnectionString = ConfigurationSettings.AppSettings( _
                           "ConnectionString")
    End Sub

    Public Function GetCategories() As DataSet
        Dim Query As String = "SELECT * FROM Categories"
        Dim ds As DataSet = FillDataSet(Query, "Categories")
        Return ds
    End Function
```

```
    Public Overloads Function GetItems() As DataSet
        Dim Query As String = "SELECT * FROM Categories"
        Dim ds As DataSet = FillDataSet(Query, "Items")
        Return ds
    End Function

    Public Overloads Function GetItems(categoryID As Integer) _
      As DataSet
        Dim Query As String = "SELECT * FROM Items "
        Query &= "WHERE Category_ID='" & categoryID & "'"
        Dim ds As DataSet = FillDataSet(Query, "Items")
        Return ds
    End Function

    Public Sub AddCategory(name As String)
        Dim Insert As String = "INSERT INTO Categories "
        Insert &= "(Name) VALUES ('" & name & "')"

        Dim con As New OleDbConnection(ConnectionString)
        Dim cmd As New OleDbCommand(Insert, con)

        con.Open()
        cmd.ExecuteNonQuery()
        con.Close()
    End Sub

    Public Sub AddItem(title As String, description As String, _
                       price As Decimal, categoryID As Integer)
        Dim Insert As String = "INSERT INTO Items "
        Insert &= "(Title, Description, Price, Category_ID)"
        Insert &= "VALUES ('" & title & "', '" & description & "', "
        Insert &= price & ", '" & categoryID & "')"

        Dim con As New OleDbConnection(ConnectionString)
        Dim cmd As New OleDbCommand(Insert, con)
        con.Open()
        cmd.ExecuteNonQuery()
        con.Close()
    End Sub

    Private Function FillDataSet(query As String, _
                                 tableName As String) As DataSet
        Dim con As New OleDbConnection(ConnectionString)
        Dim cmd As New OleDbCommand(query, con)
        Dim adapter As New OleDbDataAdapter(cmd)

        Dim ds As New DataSet()
        adapter.Fill(ds, tableName)
        con.Close()

        Return ds
    End Function

End Class
```

Dissecting the Code ...

- This code automatically retrieves the connection string from the web.config file when the class is created, as described in Chapter 5. This trick enhances encapsulation, but if the client web application doesn't have the appropriate setting, the component will not work.
- This class uses an overloaded GetItems() method. This means the client can call GetItems() with no parameters to return the full list, or with a parameter indicating the appropriate category. (Chapter 3 provides an introduction to overloaded functions.)
- Each method that accesses the database opens and closes the connection. This is a far better approach than trying to hold a connection open over the lifetime of the class, which is sure to result in performance degradation in multiuser scenarios.
- The code uses its own private FillDataSet() function to make the code more concise. This isn't made available to clients. Instead, the FillDataSet() function is then used by the GetItems() and GetCategories() methods.

NOTE In a real-world application, you probably wouldn't create an SQL command by stitching together multiple strings. If you did, you could run into problems when the user-supplied values contained special characters like apostrophes (') or the semi-colon (;). These problems could lead to an error, or even a security violation if the user is able to craft invalid input that would lead your code to execute a different SQL statement than you intend. The solution to these problems is to use parameterized commands like stored procedures. The IBuySpy case studies (described in Chapter 26) demonstrate this technique.

Consuming the Database Component

To use this component in a web application, you first have to make sure that the appropriate connection string is configured in the web.config file, as shown here.

```
<?xml version="1.0" encoding="utf-8" ?>
<configuration>

  <appSettings>
    <add key="ConnectionString"
         value="Provider=SQLOLEDB.1;Data Source=localhost;Initial
                Catalog=AdBoard;Integrated Security=SSPI" />
  </appSettings>

  <system.web>
    <!-- Configuration sections go here. -->
  </system.web>

</configuration>
```

Next, compile and copy the component DLL file, or add a reference to it if you're using Visual Studio .NET. The only remaining task is to add the user interface.

To test out this component, you can create a simple test page. In your example, shown in Figure 22-7, this page allows users to browse the current listing by category and add new items. When the user first visits the page, it prompts the user to select a category.

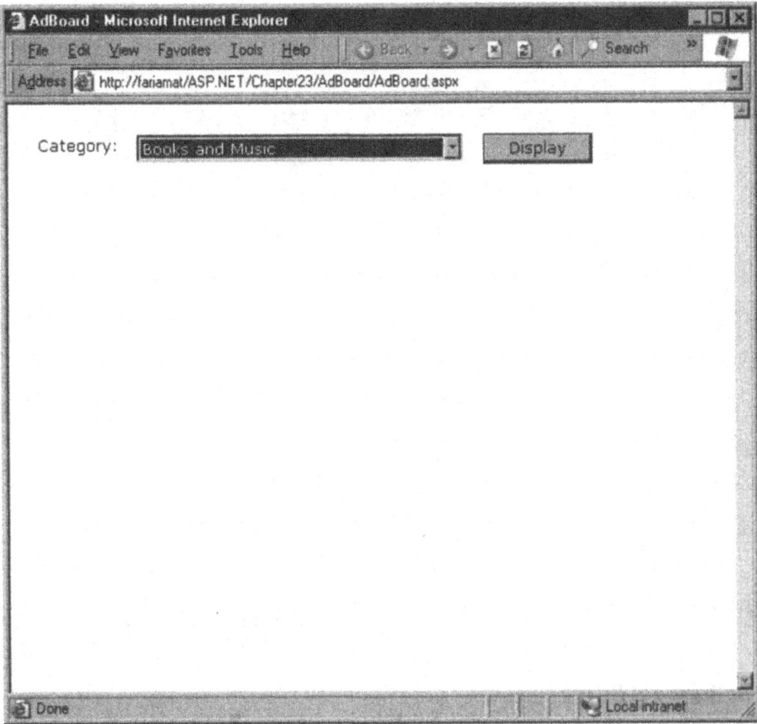

Figure 22-7. The AdBoard categories

Once a category is chosen, the matching items are displayed, and a panel of controls appears, which allows the user to add a new entry to the ad board under the current category, as shown in Figure 22-8.

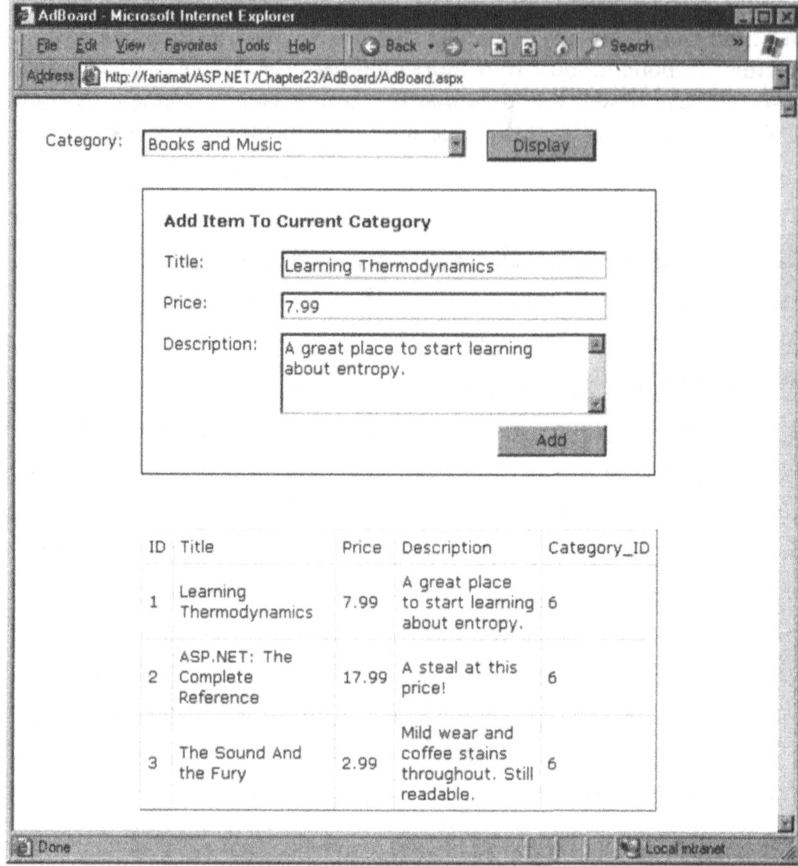

Figure 22-8. The AdBoard listing

The page code creates the component when needed, and displays the appropriate database information by binding the DataSet to the drop-down list or DataGrid control.

```
Public Class AdBoard
  Inherits Page

    Protected lstCategories As DropDownList
    Protected WithEvents cmdDisplay As Button
    Protected pnlNew As Panel
    Protected txtDescription As TextBox
    Protected txtPrice As TextBox
    Protected txtTitle As TextBox
    Protected gridItems As DataGrid
    Protected WithEvents cmdAdd As Button
```

```
    Private Sub Page_Load(sender As Object, e As EventArgs) _
      Handles MyBase.Load
        If Me.IsPostBack = False Then
            Dim DB As New SimpleDB.DBUtil()

            lstCategories.DataSource = DB.GetCategories()
            lstCategories.DataTextField = "Name"
            lstCategories.DataValueField = "ID"
            lstCategories.DataBind()
            pnlNew.Visible = False
        End If
    End Sub

    Private Sub cmdDisplay_Click(sender As Object, e As EventArgs) _
      Handles cmdDisplay.Click
        Dim DB As New SimpleDB.DBUtil()

        gridItems.DataSource = DB.GetItems( _
          lstCategories.SelectedItem.Value)
        gridItems.DataBind()
        pnlNew.Visible = True
    End Sub

    Private Sub cmdAdd_Click(sender As Object, e As EventArgs) _
      Handles cmdAdd.Click
        Dim DB As New SimpleDB.DBUtil()

        DB.AddItem(txtTitle.Text, txtDescription.Text, _
                   txtPrice.Text, lstCategories.SelectedItem.Value)

        gridItems.DataSource = DB.GetItems(_
          Val(lstCategories.SelectedItem.Value))
        gridItems.DataBind()
    End Sub

End Class
```

Dissecting the Code . . .

- Not all the functionality of the component is used in this page. For example, the page doesn't use the AddCategory() method or the version of GetItems() that doesn't require a category number. This is completely normal. Other pages may use different features from the component.

- The page is free of data access code. It does, however, need to understand how to use a DataSet, and it would need to know specific field names in order to create a more attractive DataGrid with custom templates for layout (instead of automatically generated columns).

- The page could be improved with error-handling code or validation controls. As it is, no validation is performed to ensure that the price is numeric, or to even ensure that the required values are supplied.

Enhancing the Component with Error Handling

One way the component could be enhanced is with better support for error reporting. As it is, any database errors that occur will be immediately returned to the calling code. In some cases (for example, if there is a legitimate database problem), this is a reasonable approach, because the component can't handle the problem.

However, there is one common problem that the component fails to handle properly. This problem occurs if the connection string isn't found in the web.config file. Though the component tries to read the connection string as soon as it's created, the calling code won't realize there is a problem until it tries to use a database method.

A better approach is to notify the client as soon as the problem is detected, as shown in the following code example.

```
Public Class DBUtil
    Private ConnectionString As String

    Public Sub New()
        ConnectionString = ConfigurationSettings.AppSettings(_
                           "ConnectionString")
        If ConnectionString = "" Then
            Throw New ApplicationException(_
              "Missing ConnectionString variable in web.config.")
        End If
    End Sub

      (Other class code omitted.)

End Class
```

This code throws an ApplicationException with a custom error message that indicates the problem. To provide even better reporting, you could create your own exception class that inherits from ApplicationException, as described in Chapter 11.

TIP If you're debugging your code in Visual Studio .NET, you'll find that you can single step from your web page code right into the code for the component, even if it isn't a part of the same solution. The appropriate source code file will be loaded into your editor automatically, as long as it's available.

Enhancing the Component with Aggregate Information

The component doesn't have to limit the type of information it provides to DataSets. Other information can also be useful. For example, you might provide a read-only property called ItemFields that returns an array of strings representing the names for fields in the Items table. Or you might add another method that retrieves aggregate information about the entire table, such as the average cost of an item or the total number of currently listed items, as shown here:

```
Public Class DBUtil
    ' (Other class code omitted.)

    Public Function GetAveragePrice() As Decimal
        Dim Query As String = "SELECT AVG(Price) FROM Items"

        Dim con As New OleDbConnection(ConnectionString)
        Dim cmd As New OleDbCommand(Query, con)

        con.Open()
        Dim Average As Decimal = cmd.ExecuteScalar()
        con.Close()

        Return Average
    End Function

    Public Function GetTotalItems() As Integer
        Dim Query As String = "SELECT Count(*) FROM Items"

        Dim con As New OleDbConnection(ConnectionString)
        Dim cmd As New OleDbCommand(Query, con)

        con.Open()
        Dim Count As Integer = cmd.ExecuteScalar()
        con.Close()

        Return Count
    End Function

End Class
```

These commands use some customized SQL that may be new to you (namely, the Count and AVG functions). However, these methods are just as easy to use from the client's perspective as GetItems() and GetCategories().

```
Dim DB As New SimpleDB.DBUtil()
Dim AveragePrice As Decimal = DB.GetAveragePrice()
Dim TotalItems As Integer = DB.GetTotalItems()
```

It may have occurred to you that you could return information such as the total number of items through a read-only property procedure (like TotalItems) instead of a method (in this case, GetTotalItems). Though this would work, property procedures are better left to information that is maintained with the class (in a private variable) or is easy to reconstruct. In this case, it takes a database operation to count the number of rows, and this database operation could cause an unusual problem or slow down performance if used frequently. To help reinforce that fact, a method is used instead of a property.

Enhancing the Component with a Data Object

Sometimes a DataSet isn't the best way to return information to the client. One possible reason could be that the field names are unusual, unintuitive, or subject to change. Another reason might be that the client isn't using data binding, and doesn't want to worry about using the ADO.NET objects to extract the appropriate information.

In these cases, you can create a more advanced component that returns information using a custom data class. This approach takes encapsulating one step further, and isolates the calling code from most of the underlying database details. For example, you could create the following classes to represent the important details for items and categories.

```
Public Class Item
    Public ID As Integer
    Public Title As String
    Public Price As Decimal
    Public Description As String
    Public Category As String
End Class

Public Class Category
    Public ID As Integer
    Public Name As String
End Class
```

For the most part, the member variable names match the actual field names, although they don't need to do so. You can add these classes directly to the .vb file that contains the DBUtil component class.

The DBUtil class requires a slight bit of rewriting to use the new classes. To simplify matters, this version only uses the category-specific version of the GetItems() method. You'll notice, however, that this method has been enhanced to perform a Join query, and return the matching category name (instead of just the ID) for each item row.

```
Public Class DBUtil
    ' (Other class code omitted.)

    Public Function GetCategories() As Collection
        Dim Query As String = "SELECT * FROM Categories"
        Dim ds As DataSet = FillDataSet(Query, "Categories")
        Dim dr As DataRow
        Dim Categories As New Collection()

        For Each dr In ds.Tables("Categories").Rows
            Dim Entry As New Category()
            Entry.ID = dr("ID")
            Entry.Name = dr("Name")
            Categories.Add(Entry)
        Next

        Return Categories
    End Function

    Public Function GetItems(categoryID As Integer) As Collection
        Dim Query As String = "SELECT * FROM Items "
        Query &= "INNER JOIN Categories ON "
        Query &= "Category_ID=Categories.ID "
        Query &= "WHERE Category_ID='" & categoryID & "'"
        Dim ds As DataSet = FillDataSet(Query, "Items")
        Dim dr As DataRow
        Dim Items As New Collection()

        For Each dr In ds.Tables("Items").Rows
            Dim Entry As New Item()
            Entry.ID = dr("ID")
            Entry.Title = dr("Title")
            Entry.Price = dr("Price")
            Entry.Description = dr("Description")
            Entry.Category = dr("Name")
            Items.Add(Entry)
        Next

        Return Items
    End Function

End Class
```

Now the GetCategories() and GetItems() methods return a collection of Category or Item objects. Whether this information is drawn from a file, database, or created manually is completely transparent to the calling code.

Unfortunately, this change has broken the original code. The problem is that you can't use data binding with the member variables of an object. Instead, your class needs to provide property procedures. For example, you can rewrite the classes for a quick test, using the following code.

```
Public Class Item
    Public ID As Integer
    Public Price As Decimal
    Public Description As String

    Private _Title As String
    Public Property Title() As String
        Get
            Return _Title
        End Get
        Set(Value As String)
            _Title = Value
        End Set
    End Property

    Private _Category As String
    Public Property Category() As String
        Get
            Return _Category
        End Get
        Set(Value As String)
            _Category = Value
        End Set
    End Property
End Class

Public Class Category

    Private _ID As Integer
    Public Property ID() As Integer
        Get
            Return _ID
        End Get
        Set(Value As Integer)
            _ID = Value
        End Set
    End Property
```

```
    Private _Name As String
    Public Property Name() As String
        Get
            Return _Name
        End Get
        Set(Value As String)
            _Name = Value
        End Set
    End Property

End Class
```

Now data binding will be supported for the ID and Name properties of any Category objects, and the Title and Category properties of all Item objects. The original AdBoard code won't require any changes (unless you've changed the component's namespace or class names), but it will work with one slight difference. Because the DataGrid can only bind to two pieces of information, it will only display two columns, as shown in Figure 22-9.

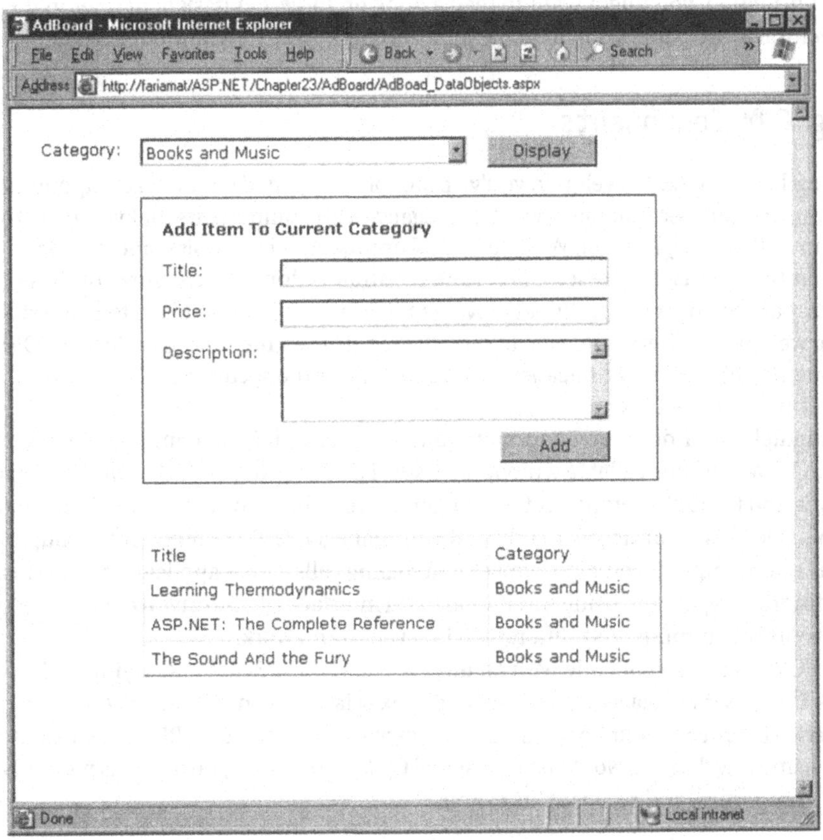

Figure 22-9. The AdBoard with the new component

Of course, the calling code doesn't need to use data binding. Instead, it can work with the Item and Category objects directly, just as you can work with .NET structures such as DateTime and Font. Here's an example of how you could fill the list box manually.

```
Dim DB As New DataObjectDB.DBUtil()
Dim Item As New DataObjectDB.Category()
Dim Categories As Collection = DB.GetCategories()

For Each Item In Categories
    lstCategories.Items.Add(New ListItem(Item.Name, Item.ID))
Next
```

The Category and Item objects are really just special structures that group together related data. You could rewrite the AddItem() method in the DBUtil component so that it required an Item object parameter. The Item object could provide some basic error checking when you create and set its properties, which would notify you of invalid information before you attempt to add it to the database.

This approach can streamline a multilayered application, but it can also add unneeded complexity, and risks mingling database details deep into your classes and code. For more information, you might want to read a book on three-tier design, or refer to the architectural white papers provided by Microsoft in the MSDN Knowledge Base.

Using COM Components

If you're a longtime ASP developer, you've probably developed your own components at one time or another. You may even have legacy COM components that you need to use in an ASP.NET application. While the ideal approach is to redesign and recode these components as .NET assemblies, time constraints don't always allow for these changes, particularly if you're already involved in a large migration effort to convert existing web pages. There is no way to directly mingle the unmanaged code in a COM component with .NET code, because this would violate the security and verification services built into the CLR.

Fortunately, .NET does provide a method to interact with COM components. It's called an RCW (runtime callable wrapper)—a special .NET proxy class that sits between your code and the COM component (see Figure 22-10). The RCW handles the transition from managed Visual Basic .NET code to the unmanaged COM component. Though this may seem simple, it actually involves marshaling calls across application domains, converting data types, and using traditional COM interfaces. It also involves converting COM events to the completely different .NET event framework.

The RCW presents your code with an interface that mimics the underlying COM object—it's the same idea as the web service proxy class, which "pretends" to be the web service in order to simplify your coding. Once you've created an RCW, you can use it in the same way that you would use the actual COM component, invoking its methods, using its properties, and receiving its events.

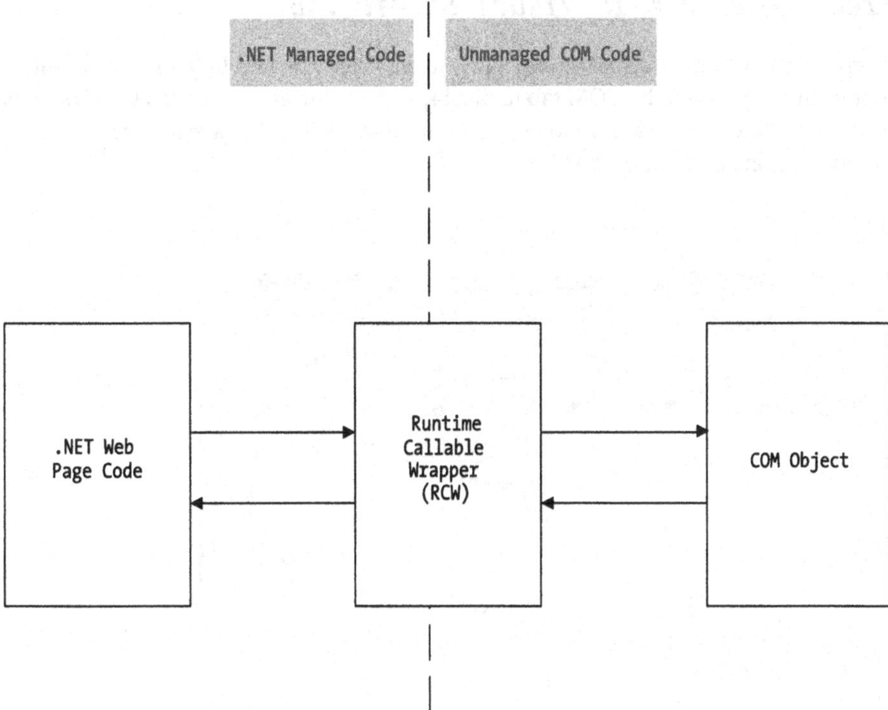

Figure 22-10. Accessing a COM object through an RCW

You have three options for using a RCW:

- You can obtain one from the author of the original COM component. In this case, the RCW is called a *primary interop assembly.* For example, Microsoft provides primary interop assemblies for many of their COM components, like the classic ADO library and the Microsoft Office components.
- Generate a RCW using Visual Studio .NET or the tblimp.exe (Type Library Importer) command-line utility. These are the two approaches shown in this chapter.
- Create your own using the types in the System.Runtime.InteropServices namespaces. This is an advanced task that is extremely tedious and complicated.

Microsoft has invested a great deal of effort in perfecting the COM interoperability in .NET. When you generate an RCW, the process is quick and painless. In most cases, the RCW will expose all the functionality of the COM component seamlessly.

Creating an RCW in Visual Studio .NET

To create an RCW with Visual Studio .NET, select Project ➤ Add Reference from the menu, and then select the COM tab to display a list of currently installed COM objects. Find the COM object you want to use and double-click it, or browse to it using the Browse button (see Figure 22-11).

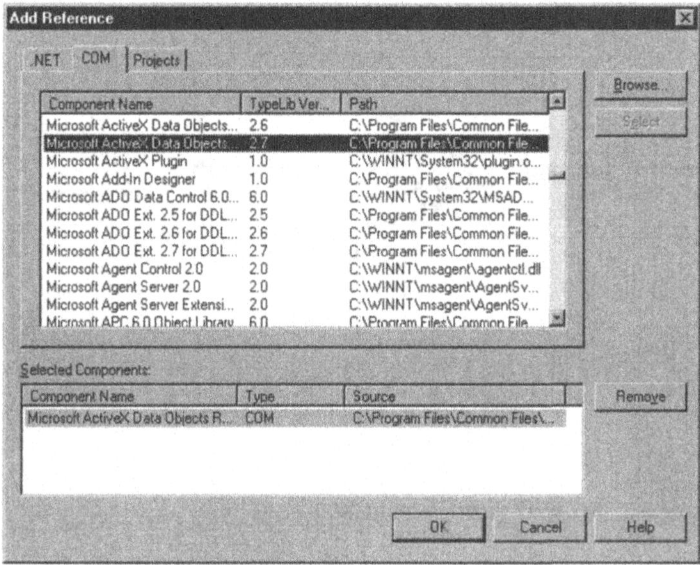

Figure 22-11. Adding a COM reference

When you click OK, .NET will first check for a primary interop assembly, which is an RCW that has been created by the same company organization that created the original COM component. If it cannot find a primary interop assembly, it will prompt you with a warning and generate the RCW DLL file automatically. This file will be placed in the bin directory of your application (as are all components), and will automatically be given the name of the COM component's type library.

For example, in Figure 22-11, a reference is being added to the COM-based ADO data access library (the precursor to ADO.NET). The RCW has the name ADODDB.dll and is made available through the namespace ADODB. This primary interop assembly is provided with the .NET Framework, but you can create your own RCW assemblies for other COM components just as easily through the Add Reference window.

You can find the component's namespace by examining the current references for your project in the Solution Explorer (see Figure 22-12).

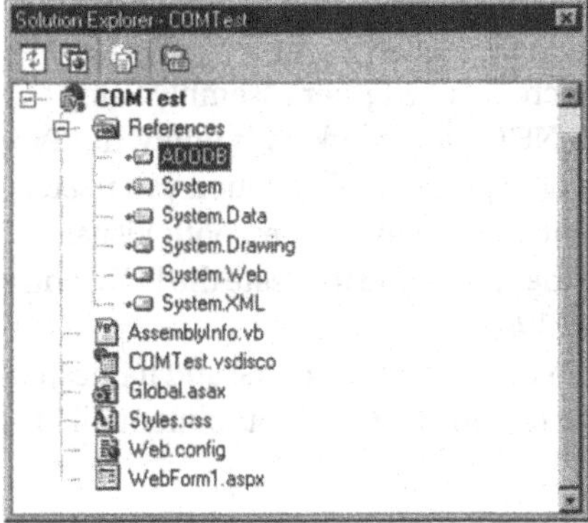

Figure 22-12. The Runtime Callable Wrapper

You can now create classes from the COM component, and use them as though they are native .NET classes (which, of course, they now are). This means that you use the .NET syntax to create an object or receive an event using the classes in the RCW. Figure 22-13 demonstrates with the Recordset object from the ADO component.

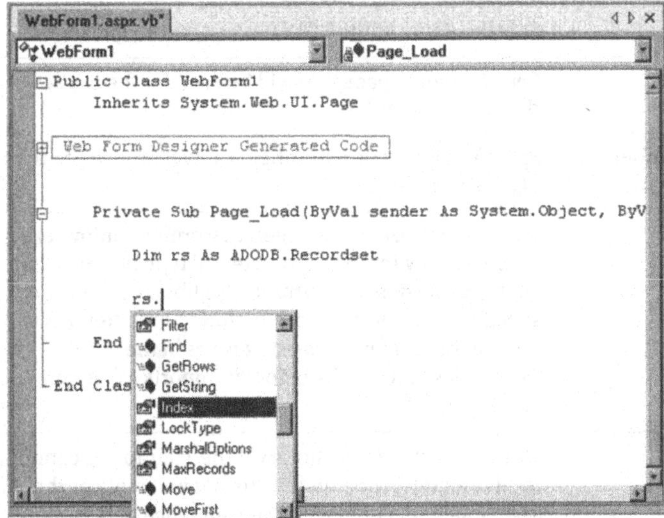

Figure 22-13. Using an RCW class

Creating an RCW with the Type Library Importer

If you aren't using Visual Studio .NET, you can create a wrapper assembly using a command-line utility that is included with the .NET Framework. This utility, the Type Library Importer, is quite straightforward. The only piece of information you need is the file name that contains the COM component. Behind the scenes, both Visual Studio .NET and the Type Library Importer use the same code to create the RCW, and as a result both approaches produce equivalent RCWs.

The following statement creates an RCW with the default file name and namespace (as it would be in Visual Studio .NET), assuming that the MyCOMComponent.dll file is in the current directory.

```
tlbimp MyCOMComponent.dll
```

Assuming that the MyCOMComponent has a type library named MyClasses, the generated RCW file will have the name MyClasses.dll and will expose its classes through a namespace named MyClasses. You can also configure these options with command-line parameters, as described in Table 22-1.

Table 22-1. Type Library Import Parameters

Parameter	Description
/out:Filename	Sets the name of the RCW file that will be generated.
/namespace:Namespace	Sets the namespace that will be used for the classes in the RCW assembly.
/asmversion:VersionNumber	Specifies the version number that will be given to the RCW assembly.
/reference:Filename	If you don't specify the /reference option, tlbimp.exe automatically imports any external type libraries that are referenced by the current type library. If you specify the /reference option, tlbimp.exe attempts to resolve these references using types in the .NET assemblies you specify before it imports other type libraries.
/strictref	Doesn't import a type library if the Tblimp.exe cannot resolve all references in the current assembly or the assemblies specified with the /reference option.

There are also additional options for creating signed assemblies, which is useful if you're a component vendor who needs to distribute a .NET assembly to other clients. These features are described in the MSDN reference. Additionally, you can use .NET classes to manually write your own wrapper class. This process is incredibly painstaking, however, and in the words of Microsoft's own documentation, "seldom performed."

The Last Word

The components used in this chapter are business objects. They perform a service like querying a database. Generally, business components return data, but don't get involved in how this data is formatted or displayed to the user. The next chapter shows how you can use the same component-oriented approach to reuse user interface in multiple web pages with custom controls.

CHAPTER 23

Custom Controls

COMPONENT-BASED DEVELOPMENT encourages you to divide the logic in your application into discrete, independent blocks. Once you've made the jump to custom classes and objects, you can start creating modular web applications (and even desktop applications) that are built out of reusable units of code. But while these objects help work out thorny data access procedures or custom business logic, they don't offer much when it comes to simplifying your user interface code. If you want to create web applications that reuse a customized portion of user interface, you're still stuck rewriting control tags and reconfiguring page initialization code in several different places.

It doesn't have to be this way. ASP.NET includes tools for modularizing and reusing portions of user interface code that are just as powerful as those that allow you to design custom business objects. There are two main tools at your fingertips, both of which you'll explore in this chapter:

- User controls allow you to reuse a portion of a page, by placing it in a special .ascx file. ASP.NET also allows you to make smart user controls that provide methods and properties, and configure their contained controls automatically.

- Custom-derived controls allow you to build a new control by inheriting from an ASP.NET control class. With custom controls there is no limit to what you can do, whether it's adding a new property or tweaking the rendered HTML output.

User Controls

User controls look pretty much the same as ASP.NET web forms. Like web forms, they are composed of an HTML-like portion with control tags (the .ascx file) and can optionally use a .vb code-behind file with event-handling logic. They can also include the same range of HTML content and ASP.NET controls, and they experience the same events as the Page object (such as Load and PreRender). The only differences between user controls and web pages are as follows:

- User controls begin with a <%@ Control %> directive instead of a <%@ Page %> directive.

- User controls use the file extension .ascx instead of .aspx, and their code-behind files inherit from the System.Web.UI.UserControl class. In fact, the UserControl class and the Page class both inherit from the same base classes, which is why they share so many of the same methods and events, as shown in the inheritance diagram in Figure 23-1.

- User controls can't be requested directly by a client. Instead, user controls are embedded inside other web pages.

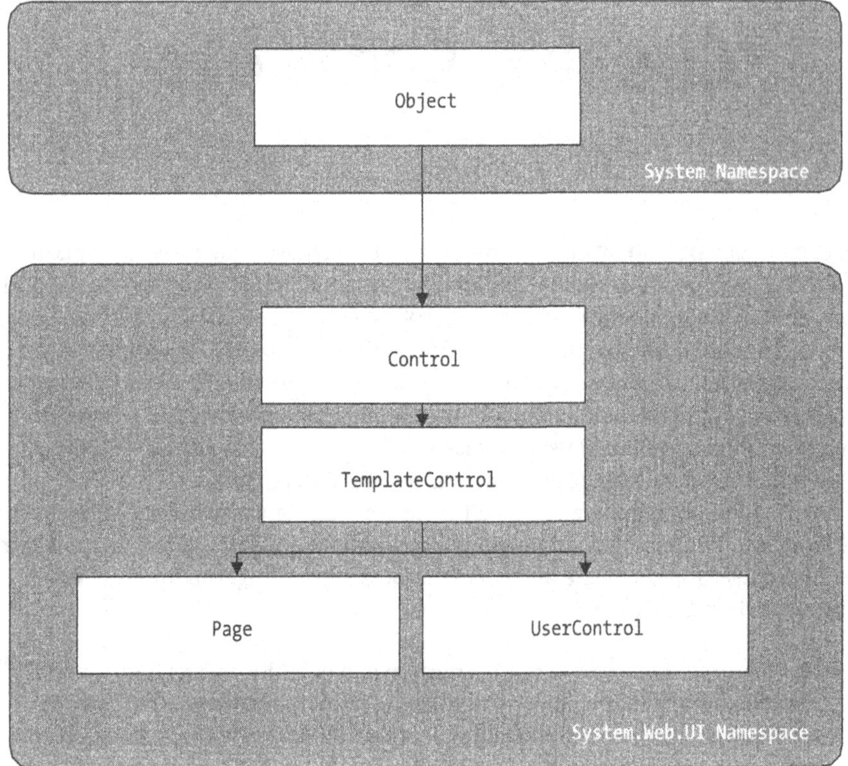

Figure 23-1. The Page and UserControl inheritance chain

Creating a Simple User Control

You can create a user control in Visual Studio .NET in much the same way that you add a web page. Just right-click the project in the Solution Explorer, and select Add ➤ Add User Control. If you aren't using Visual Studio .NET, you simply begin by creating an .ascx text file.

The following user control contains a single label control.

```
<%@ Control Language="VB" AutoEventWireup="false"
    Inherits="Footer" %>

<asp:Label id="lblFooter" runat="server" />
```

Note that the Control directive uses the same attributes that are used in the Page directive for a web page, including Language, AutoEventWireup, and Inherits. Optionally, you could add a Src attribute if you aren't precompiling your code-behind class. Visual Studio .NET will add a Codebehind attribute to track the file while editing. To refresh your memory about page attributes, refer to Chapter 5.

The code-behind class for this sample user control is similarly straightforward. It uses the UserControl.Load event to add some text to the label.

```
Public MustInherit Class Footer
  Inherits UserControl

    Protected lblFooter As Label

    Private Sub Load(sender As Object, e As EventArgs) _
      Handles MyBase.Load
        lblFooter.Text = "This page was served at "
        lblFooter.Text &= DateTime.Now.ToString()
    End Sub

End Class
```

Note that the class has the addition of the MustInherit keyword in its class definition. This indicates that the user control cannot be accessed directly; instead, a control derived from this class must be placed on a web page.

To test this user control, you need to insert it into a web page. Two steps are required. First, you need to add a <%@ Register %> directive that identifies the control you want to use and associates it with a unique control prefix.

```
<%@ Register TagPrefix="cr" TagName="Footer" Src="Footer.ascx" %>
```

The Register directive specifies a tag prefix and name. Tag prefixes group sets of related controls (for example, all ASP.NET web controls use the tag prefix "asp"). Tag prefixes are usually lowercase—technically, they are case-insensitive—and should be unique for your company or organization. The Src directive identifies the location of the user control template file, not the code-behind file.

You can then add the user control whenever you want (and as many times as you want), by inserting its control tag. Consider this page example:

```
<%@ Page Language="VB" AutoEventWireup="false"
    Inherits="FooterHost"%>
<%@ Register TagPrefix="cr" TagName="Footer" Src="Footer.ascx" %>

<HTML>
<body>

<form id=Form1 method=post runat="server">
    <h2>A Page With a Footer</h2><hr>
    Static Page Text<br><br>
    <cr:Footer id=Footer1 runat="server" />
</form>

</body>
</HTML>
```

This example (shown in Figure 23-2) demonstrates a simple way that you could create a header or footer and reuse it in all the pages in your web site, just by adding a user control. In the case of your simple footer, you won't save much code. However, this approach will become much more useful for a complex control with extensive formatting or several contained controls.

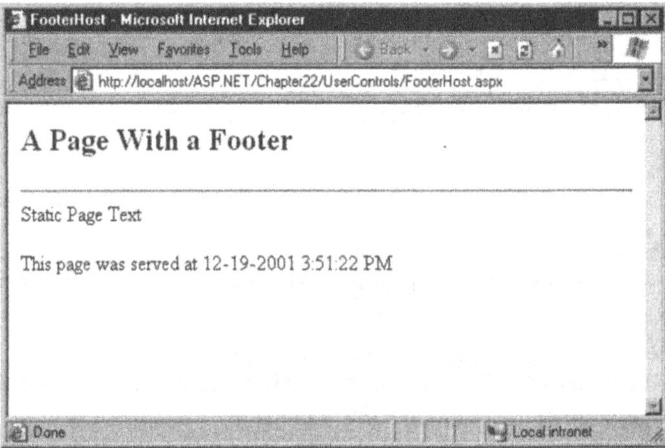

Figure 23-2. A page with a user control footer

Of course, this is only scratching the surface of what you can do with a user control. In the following sections, you'll learn how to enhance a control with properties, methods, and events—transforming it from a simple "include file" into a full-fledged object.

NOTE The Page class provides a special LoadControl() method that allows you to create a user control dynamically at runtime from an .ascx file. The user control is returned to you as a control object, which you can then add to the Controls collection of a container control on the web page (like PlaceHolder or Panel) to display it on the page. This technique isn't recommended as a substitute for declaratively using a user control, but it does have some interesting applications if you need to generate user interface dynamically. Chapter 26 shows how the LoadControl() method is used with the IBuySpy portal application.

Visual Studio .NET User Control Support

In Visual Studio .NET, you have a few shortcuts available when working with user controls. Once you've created your user control, simply build your project, and then drag the .ascx file from the Solution Explorer and drop it onto the drawing area of a web form. Visual Studio .NET will automatically add the Register directive for you, as well as an instance of the user control tag.

In the design environment, the user control will be displayed as a familiar gray box, as shown in Figure 23-3. This is the same nondescript package used for data-bound controls that don't have any templates configured.

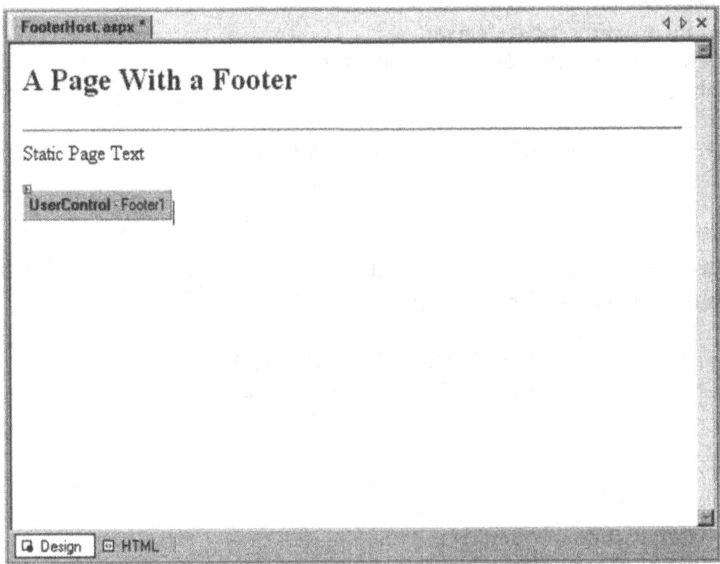

Figure 23-3. A user control at design time

Independent User Controls

Conceptually, there are really two types of user controls: independent and integrated. Independent user controls don't interact with the rest of the code on your form. The Footer user control is one such example. Another example might be a list of buttons that offer links to other pages. A menu user control like this could handle the events for all the buttons, and then run the appropriate Response.Redirect() code to move to another web page. Or it could just be an ordinary HyperLink control that doesn't have any associated server-side code. Every page in the website could then include the same menu user control—enabling painless website navigation with no need to worry about frames. In fact, this is exactly the approach you'll see in practice in Chapter 26 with the IBuySpy e-commerce application.

The following sample defines a simple menu control that just requests a given page with a different query string argument. Note that the style attribute of the <div> tag (which defines fonts and formatting) is omitted for clarity. I've also left out the Inherits attribute in the Control tag, because the user control doesn't require any code-behind logic.

```
<%@ Control Language="VB" AutoEventWireup="false" %>

<div>
  Products:
  <asp:HyperLink id="lnkBooks" runat="server"
    NavigateUrl="MenuHost.aspx?product=Books">Books
  </asp:HyperLink><br>
  <asp:HyperLink id=lnkToys runat="server"
    NavigateUrl="MenuHost.aspx?product=Toys">Toys
  </asp:HyperLink><br>
  <asp:HyperLink id=lnkSports runat="server"
    NavigateUrl="MenuHost.aspx?product=Sports">Sports
  </asp:HyperLink><br>
  <asp:HyperLink id=lnkFurniture runat="server"
    NavigateUrl="MenuHost.aspx?product=Furniture">Furniture
  </asp:HyperLink>
</div>
```

The MenuHost.aspx file includes two controls, the Menu control and a label that displays the product query string parameter.

```
<%@ Page Language="VB" AutoEventWireup="false" Inherits="MenuHost"%>
<%@ Register TagPrefix="cr" TagName="Menu" Src="Menu.ascx" %>

<HTML>
<body>

<form id=Form1 method=post runat="server">
    <cr:Menu id="Menu1" runat="server" />
    <asp:Label id="lblSelection" / >
</form>

</body>
</HTML>
```

When the MenuHost.aspx page loads, it adds the appropriate information to the lblSelection control.

```
Private Sub Page_Load(sender As Object, e As EventArgs) _
  Handles MyBase.Load
    If Request.Params("product") <> "" Then
        lblSelection.Text = "You chose: "
        lblSelection.Text &= Request.Params("product")
    End If
End Sub
```

The end result is shown in Figure 23-4. Whenever you click a button, the page is posted back, and the text is updated.

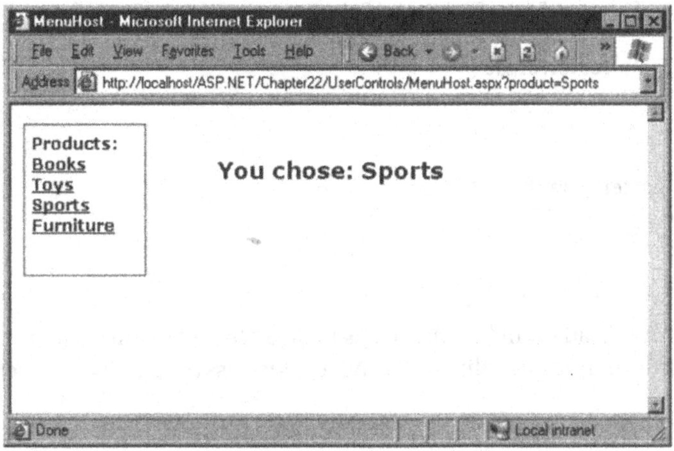

Figure 23-4. The Menu user control

Integrated User Controls

Integrated user controls interact with the web page that hosts them, in one way or another. When designing these controls, the class-based design tips you learned in Chapter 4 really become useful.

A typical example is a user control that allows some level of configuration through properties. For example, you could create a footer that supports two different display formats: long date and short time. To add a further level of refinement, the Footer user control allows the web page to specify the appropriate display format using an enumeration.

The first step is to create an enumeration in the custom Footer class. Remember, an enumeration is simply a type of constant that is internally stored as an integer, but is set in code by using one of the allowed names that you specify. Variables that use the FooterFormat enumeration can take the value FooterFormat.LongData or FooterFormat.ShortTime.

```
Public Enum FooterFormat
    LongDate
    ShortTime
End Enum
```

The next step is to add a property to the Footer class that allows the web page to retrieve or set the current format applied to the footer. The actual format is stored in a private variable called _Format, which is set to the long data format by default when the class is first created. (The same effect could be accomplished, in a slightly sloppier way, by using a public member variable named Format instead of a full property procedure.) If you're hazy on how property procedures work, feel free to review the explanation in Chapter 4.

```
Private _Format As FooterFormat = FooterFormat.LongDate

Public Property Format() As FooterFormat
    Get
        Return _Format
    End Get
    Set(ByVal Value As FooterFormat)
        _Format = Value
    End Set
End Property
```

Finally, the UserControl.Load event handler needs to take account of the current footer state and format the output accordingly. The full Footer class code is shown here:

```
Public MustInherit Class Footer
  Inherits UserControl

    Protected lblFooter As Label

    Public Enum FooterFormat
        LongDate
        ShortTime
    End Enum

    Private _Format As FooterFormat = FooterFormat.LongDate
    Public Property Format() As FooterFormat
        Get
            Return _Format
        End Get
        Set(ByVal Value As FooterFormat)
            _Format = Value
        End Set
    End Property

    Private Sub Page_Load(sender As Object, e As EventArgs) _
      Handles MyBase.Load
        lblFooter.Text = "This page was served at "

        If _Format = FooterFormat.LongDate Then
            lblFooter.Text &= DateTime.Now.ToLongDateString()
        ElseIf _Format = FooterFormat.ShortTime Then
            lblFooter.Text &= DateTime.Now.ToShortTimeString()
        End If
    End Sub

End Class
```

To test out this footer, you need to create a page that includes the user control and defines a variable in the custom Page class that represents the user control. (Note that Visual Studio .NET doesn't add this variable automatically when you create the control, as it does for ordinary web controls.) You can then modify the Format property through the user control variable. An example is shown in Figure 23-5, which automatically sets the Format property for the user control to match a radio button selection whenever the page is posted back.

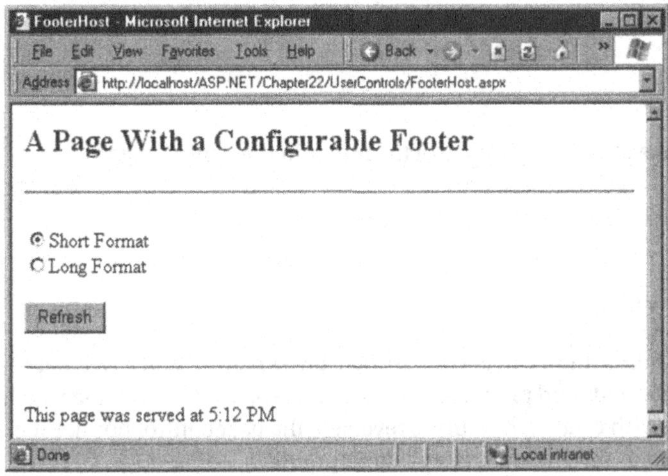

Figure 23-5. The modified footer

Note that the user control property is modified in the Page.Load event handler, not the cmdRefresh.Click event handler. The reason is that the Load event occurs before the user control has been rendered each time the page is created. The Click event occurs after the user control has been rendered, and though the property change will be visible in your code, it won't affect the user control's HTML output, which has already been added to the page.

```
Public Class FooterHost
  Inherits Page

    Protected optShort As RadioButton
    Protected optLong As RadioButton
    Protected cmdRefresh As Button
    Protected Footer1 As Footer
```

```
    Private Sub Page_Load(sender As Object, e As EventArgs) _
      Handles MyBase.Load

        If optLong.Checked = True Then
            Footer1.Format = Footer.FooterFormat.LongDate
        ElseIf optShort.Checked = True Then
            Footer1.Format = Footer.FooterFormat.ShortTime
        Else
            ' The default value in the Footer class will apply.
        End If

    End Sub

End Class
```

You could also set the initial appearance of the footer in the control tag.

```
<cr:Footer Format="ShortTime" id="Footer1" runat="server" />
```

User Control Events

Another way that communication can occur between a user control and a web page is through events. With methods and properties, the user control reacts to a change made by the web page code. With events, the story is reversed: the user control notifies the web page about an action, and the web page code responds.

Creating a web control that uses events is fairly easy. Consider the next example, which uses a special login box that verifies a user's credentials. This type of control could be used in a variety of sources to restrict access to a variety of different pages. For that reason, you can't hard-code any logic in the user control that redirects the user to a specific page. Instead, the LoginBox user control needs to raise an event to alert the web page code if the login process was successful. At that point, the web page can display the appropriate resource.

The first step in creating the LoginBox user control is to define the events using the Event keyword. (You can refer to Chapter 4 for a quick overview of how to use events in .NET.)

The LoginBox control defines two events, one that indicates a failed login attempt and one that indicates success.

```
Event LoginFailed()
Event LoginAuthenticated()
```

The LoginBox code can now fire either of these events by using the RaiseEvent command.

```
RaiseEvent LoginFailed()
```

These events are raised after the Login button is clicked, and the user's information is examined. The full user control code is shown here:

```
Public MustInherit Class LoginBox
  Inherits UserControl

    Protected txtUser As TextBox
    Protected txtPassword As TextBox
    Protected WithEvents cmdLogin As Button

    Event LoginFailed()
    Event LoginAuthenticated()

    Private Sub cmdLogin_Click(sender As Object, e As EventArgs) _
      Handles cmdLogin.Click

        ' Typically, this code would use the FormsAuthentication
        ' class described in Chapter 24, or some custom
        ' database-lookup code to authenticate the user.
        ' This example simply checks for a "secret" code.
        If txtPassword.Text = "opensesame" Then
            RaiseEvent LoginAuthenticated()
        Else
            RaiseEvent LoginFailed()
        End If

    End Sub

End Class
```

The page hosting this code can then add an event handler for either one of these events, in the same way that event handlers are created for any control—by declaring the control variable with the WithEvents keyword, and adding a Handles statement to a procedure with the appropriate signature.

Figure 23-6 shows a simple example of a page that uses the LoginBox control. If the login fails three times, the user is forwarded to another page. If the login succeeds, the LoginBox control is disabled and a message is displayed.

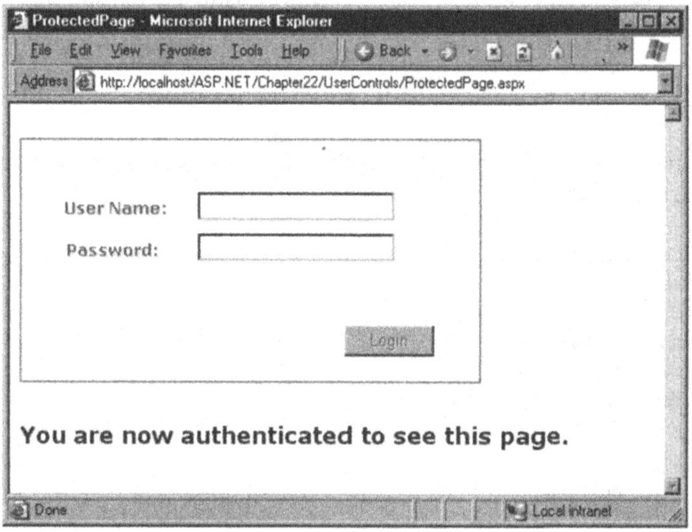

Figure 23-6. Using the LoginBox user control

The code for this example is refreshingly straightforward.

```
Public Class ProtectedPage
  Inherits Page

    Protected lblSecretMessage As Label
    Protected pnlControls As Panel
    Protected WithEvents Login As UserControls.LoginBox

    Private Sub Failed() Handles Login.LoginFailed
        ' Retrieve the number of failed attempts from view state.
        Dim Attempts As Integer
        Attempts = CType(ViewState("Attempts"), Integer)

        Attempts += 1
        If Attempts >= 3 Then Response.Redirect("default.aspx")

        ' Store the new number of failed attempts in view state.
        ViewState("Attempts") = Attempts
    End Sub

    Private Sub Succeeded() Handles Login.LoginAuthenticated
        pnlControls.Enabled = False
        lblSecretMessage.Text = "You are now authenticated" & _
                                "to see this page."
    End Sub

End Class
```

Note that the user control is declared using the full namespace name (UserControls.LoginBox). This is always a good idea, and it's required if the namespace used for the user control is different than that used for the web page.

Using Events with Parameters

In the LoginBox example, there is no information passed along with the event. In many cases, however, you want to convey additional information that relates to the event. For example, you could create a LoginRequest event that passes information about the user ID and password that were entered. This would allow your code to decide whether the user has sufficient security permissions for the requested page, while retaining a common look for login boxes throughout your web application.

The .NET standard for events specifies that every event should use two parameters. The first one provides a reference to the control that sent the event, while the second one incorporates any additional information. This additional information is wrapped into a custom EventArgs object, which inherits from the System.EventArgs class. (If your event doesn't require any additional information, you can just use the generic System.EventArgs object, which doesn't contain any additional data. Many events in ASP.NET, such as Page.Load or Button.Click, follow this pattern.)

The EventArgs class that follows allows the LoginBox user control to pass the name of the authenticated user to the event handler.

```
Public Class LoginAuthenticatedEventArgs
  Inherits EventArgs

    Public UserName As String

End Class
```

To use this class, you need to modify the LoginAuthenticated event definition to the .NET standard shown here. At the same time, you should also modify the LoginFailed event definition, which can use the default (empty) System.EventArgs class.

```
Event LoginAuthenticated(sender As Object, _
  e As LoginAuthenticatedEventArgs)
Event LoginFailed(sender As Object, e As EventArgs)
```

Next, your code for raising the event needs to submit the required two pieces of information as event parameters.

```
Private Sub cmdLogin_Click(sender As Object, e As EventArgs) _
  Handles cmdLogin.Click

    If txtPassword.Text = "opensesame" Then
        Dim EventInfo As New LoginAuthenticatedEventArgs()
        EventInfo.UserName = txtUser.Text
        RaiseEvent LoginAuthenticated(Me, EventInfo)
    Else
        ' You can define the EventArgs object on the same line
        ' that you use it to make more economical code.
        RaiseEvent LoginFailed(Me, New EventArgs())
    End If

End Sub
```

Lastly, your receiving code needs to update its event handler to use the new signature.

```
Private Sub Succeeded(sender As Object, _
  e As LoginAuthenticatedEventArgs) Handles Login.LoginAuthenticated

    pnlControls.Enabled = False
    lblSecretMessage.Text = "You are now authenticated"
    lblSecretMessage.Text &= "to see this page, " & e.UserName

End Sub

Private Sub Failed(sender As Object, e As EventArgs) _
  Handles Login.LoginFailed

        ' Retrieve the number of failed attempts from view state.
        Dim Attempts As Integer
        Attempts = CType(ViewState("Attempts"), Integer)

        Attempts += 1
        If Attempts >= 3 Then Response.Redirect("default.aspx")

        ' Store the new number of failed attempts in view state.
        ViewState("Attempts") = Attempts

End Sub
```

Now the user will see a page like the one shown in Figure 23-7 after a successful login.

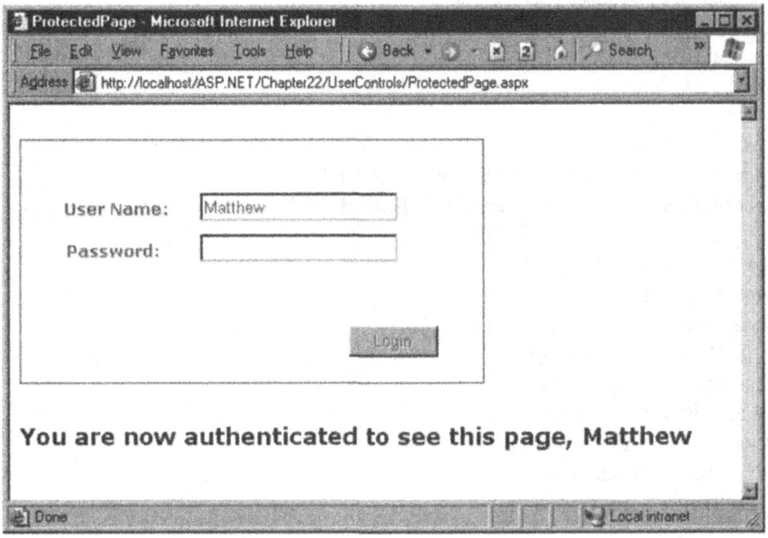

Figure 23-7. Retrieving the user name through an event

User Control Limitations

User controls provide a great deal of flexibility when you want to combine several web controls (and additional HTML content) in a single unit, and possibly add some higher-level business logic. However, they are less useful when you want to modify or extend individual web controls.

For example, imagine you want to create a text-box-like control for name entry. This text box might provide GetFirstName and GetLastName methods, which examine the entered text and parse it into a first and last name using one of two recognized formats: space-separated ("FirstName LastName") or comma-separated ("LastName, FirstName"). This way the user can enter a name in either format, and your code doesn't have to go through the work of parsing the text. Instead, the user control handles it automatically.

The full code for this user control would look something like this:

```
Public MustInherit Class NameTextBox
  Inherits System.Web.UI.UserControl

    Protected txtName As TextBox

    Private _FirstName As String
    Private _LastName As String

    Public Function GetFirstName() As String
        UpdateNames()
        Return _FirstName
    End Function
```

```
    Public Function GetLastName() As String
        UpdateNames()
        Return _LastName
    End Function

    Private Sub UpdateNames()
        Dim CommaPos As Integer = txtName.Text.IndexOf(",")
        Dim SpacePos As Integer = txtName.Text.IndexOf(" ")

        Dim NameArray() As String
        If CommaPos <> -1 Then
            NameArray = txtName.Text.Split(",")
            _FirstName = NameArray(1)
            _LastName = NameArray(0)
        ElseIf SpacePos <> -1 Then
            NameArray = txtName.Text.Split(" ")
            _FirstName = NameArray(0)
            _LastName = NameArray(1)
        Else
            ' The text has no comma or space.
            ' It cannot be converted to a name.
            Throw New InvalidOperationException()
        End If
    End Sub

End Class
```

The online samples include a simple page that allows you to test this control (shown in Figure 23-8). It retrieves the first and last name that are entered in the text box when the user clicks a button.

```
Private Sub cmdGetNames_Click(sender As Object, e As EventArgs) _
  Handles cmdGetNames.Click
    lblNames.Text = "<b>First name:</b> "
    lblNames.Text &= NameTextBox1.GetFirstName()
    lblNames.Text &= "<br><b>Last name:</b> "
    lblNames.Text &= NameTextBox1.GetLastName()
End Sub
```

Using a full user control is overkill in this case, and it also makes it difficult for the web page programmer to further configure the text box. For example, if a programmer wants to set the text box font or change its size, you either need to add the corresponding properties to the user control class or provide access to the text box through a public member variable. (Technically, the web page programmer could access the text box by using the Controls collection of the user control, but this is a less structured approach that can run into problems if other controls are added to the user control or the ID of the text box changes.) There's also no way to set these values in the user control tag.

The next section describes a better, more fine-grained approach for extending or fine-tuning individual controls.

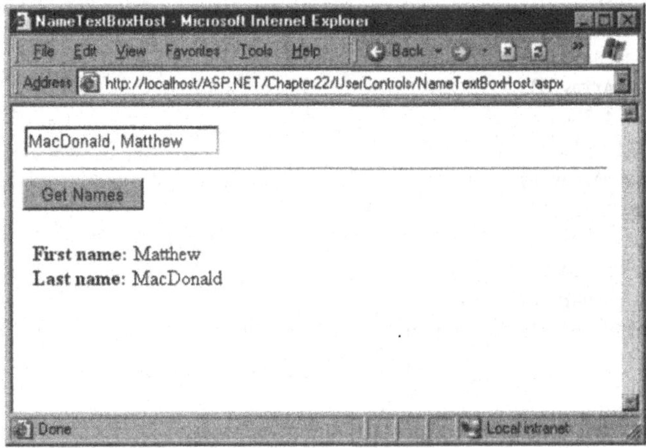

Figure 23-8. A custom user control based on the text box

Derived Custom Controls

Thanks to the class-based .NET Framework, there is an easier solution for creating specialized controls using inheritance. All you need to do is find the control you want to extend in the .NET class library, and derive a new class from it that adds the additional functionality you need.

Here's an example of the name text box implemented through a custom control.

```
Public Class NameTextBox
  Inherits System.Web.UI.WebControls.TextBox

    Private _FirstName As String
    Private _LastName As String

    Public Function GetFirstName() As String
        UpdateNames()
        Return _FirstName
    End Function

    Public Function GetLastName() As String
        UpdateNames()
        Return _LastName
    End Function

    Private Sub UpdateNames()
        Dim CommaPos As Integer = Text.IndexOf(",")
        Dim SpacePos As Integer = Text.IndexOf(" ")

        Dim NameArray() As String
```

```
        If CommaPos <> -1 Then
            NameArray = Text.Split(",")
            _FirstName = NameArray(1)
            _LastName = NameArray(0)
        ElseIf SpacePos <> -1 Then
            NameArray = Text.Split(" ")
            _FirstName = NameArray(0)
            _LastName = NameArray(1)
        Else
            ' The text has no comma or space.
            ' It cannot be converted to a name.
            Throw New InvalidOperationException()
        End If
    End Sub

End Class
```

In this example, the custom NameTextBox class inherits from the TextBox class (which is found in the System.Web.UI.WebControls namespace). Because the NameTextBox class extends the TextBox class, all the original TextBox members (such as Font and ForeColor) are still available to the web page programmer, and can be set in code or through the control tag. The only differences in the code between the user control version and the custom control version is that the custom version adds an Inherits statement and works natively with the Text property of the NameTextBox class (not a TextBox member variable).

Consuming a Custom Control

To test the control, you should compile it into an assembly using the vbc.exe compiler, and place it in the bin directory for the application. This is the exact same process you used in Chapter 22 for custom components. You can then register the custom control using a Register directive with a slightly different set of attributes than the one you used for user controls.

```
<%@ Register TagPrefix="CR" Namespace="CustomControls" Assembly="CustomCtrls" %>
```

This register directive identifies the compiled assembly file and the namespace that holds the custom control. When you register a custom control assembly in this fashion, you gain access to all the control classes in it. You can insert a control by using the tag prefix, followed by a colon (:) and the class name.

```
<CR:NameTextBox id="NameTextBox1" runat="server" />
```

You can set properties of the NameTextBox in code or through the tag. These can include any additional properties you've defined or the properties from the base class:

```
<CR:NameTextBox id="NameTextBox1" BackColor="LightYellow"
    Font="Verdana" Text="Enter Name Here" runat="server" />
```

The technique of deriving custom control classes is known as subclassing, and it allows you to easily add the functionality you need without losing the basic set of features inherent in a control. Subclassed controls can add new properties, events, and methods, or override the existing ones. For example, you could add a ReverseText() or EncryptText() method to the NameTextBox class that loops through the text contents and modifies them. The process of defining and using custom control events, methods, and properties is the same as with user controls.

One common reason for subclassing a control is to add default values. For example, you might create a custom Calendar control that automatically modifies some properties in its constructor. When the control is first created, these default properties will automatically be applied.

```
Public Class FormattedCalendar
  Inherits Calendar

    Public Sub New()
        ' Configure the appearance of the calendar table.
        Me.CellPadding = 8
        Me.CellSpacing = 8
        Me.BackColor = Color.LightYellow
        Me.BorderStyle = BorderStyle.Groove
        Me.BorderWidth = Unit.Pixel(2)
        Me.ShowGridLines = True

        ' Configure the font.
        Me.Font.Name = "Verdana"
        Me.Font.Size = FontUnit.XXSmall

        ' Set some special calendar settings.
        Me.FirstDayOfWeek = FirstDayOfWeek.Monday
        Me.PrevMonthText = "<--"
        Me.NextMonthText = "-->"

        ' Select the current date by default.
        Me.SelectedDate = Date.Today
    End Sub

End Class
```

You could even add additional event-handling logic to this class that will use the Calendar's DayRender event to configure custom date display. This way, the Calendar class itself handles all the required formatting and configuration; your page code doesn't need to work at all! Note that the Handles clause specifies the MyBase keyword, indicating an event of the current (inherited) class.

```
Private Sub FormattedCalendar_DayRender(sender As Object, _
  e As DayRenderEventArgs) Handles MyBase.DayRender

    If e.Day.IsOtherMonth Then
        e.Day.IsSelectable = False
        e.Cell.Text = ""
    Else
        e.Cell.Font.Bold = True
    End If

End Sub
```

The preferred way to handle this is actually to override the OnDayRender() method, which is automatically called just before the event is fired. When you override a method like this, make sure you call the base method using the MyBase keyword. This ensures that any basic tasks (like firing the event) are performed.

The effect of the following code is equivalent to the event-based approach:

```
Protected Overrides Sub OnDayRender(cell As TableCell, _
  day As CalendarDay)

    ' Call the base Calendar.OnDayRender method.
    MyBase.OnDayRender(cell, day)

    If day.IsOtherMonth Then
        day.IsSelectable = False
        cell.Text = ""
    Else
        cell.Font.Bold = True
    End If

End Sub
```

Figure 23-9 contrasts two Calendar controls: the normal one, and the custom FormattedCalendar control class.

TIP Even though you set these defaults in the custom class code, that doesn't prevent you from modifying them in your web page code. The constructor code runs when the Calendar control is created, after which the control tag settings are applied. Finally, the event-handling code in your web page also has the chance to modify the FormattedCalendar properties.

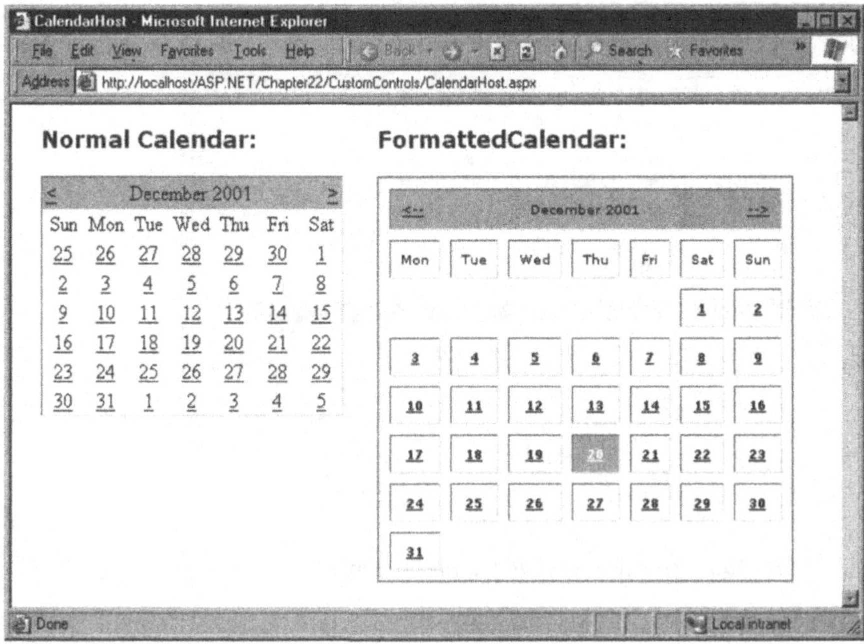

Figure 23-9. A subclassed Calendar control

Visual Studio .NET Custom Control Support

In Visual Studio .NET, it's often easiest to develop custom controls in a separate class library project, compile the code into a DLL, and add a reference to the assembly in the new project. This allows you to easily place the custom controls and the web page classes in separate namespaces, and update them separately.

The process of adding a reference to a custom control assembly is very similar to the process you used to add a reference to a normal compiled component. Start by right-clicking the toolbox, and choose Add/Remove Items (or Customize Toolbox in Visual Studio .NET 2002). Click the .NET Framework Components tab (shown in Figure 23-10), and then click the Browse button. Then choose the custom control assembly from the file browser. The controls will be added to the list of available .NET controls.

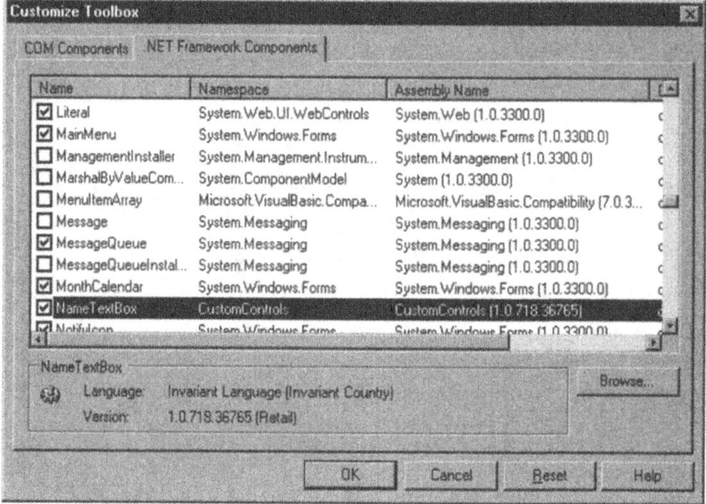

Figure 23-10. Adding a reference to the NameTextBox

All checkmarked controls will appear in the toolbox (see Figure 23-11). You can then draw them on your web forms just as you would with an ordinary control. Note that controls aren't added on a per-project basis. Instead, they will remain in the Toolbox until you delete them. To remove a control, right-click it and select Delete. This removes the icon only, not the referenced assembly.

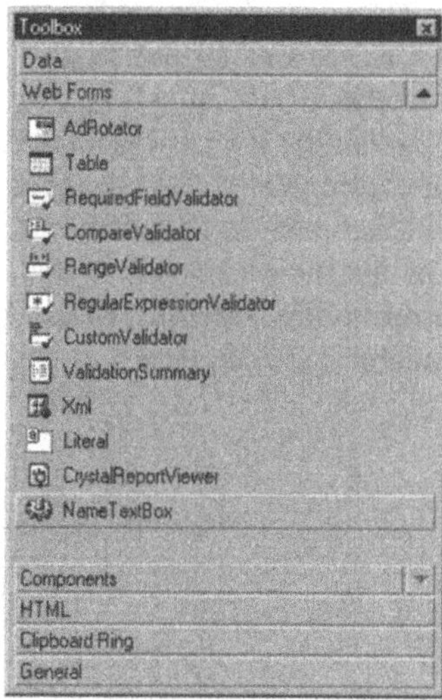

Figure 23-11. The toolbox with a custom control

Any properties you add for the custom control automatically appear in the Properties window under the Misc heading. You can further customize the design-time behavior of your control by using various attributes from the System.ComponentModel namespace.

```
Imports System.ComponentModel
```

For example, the property defined here (part of the ConfigurableRepeater control you will consider later in this chapter) will always appear in a "Layout" category in the Properties window. It indicates this to Visual Studio .NET through a System.ComponentModel.Category attribute. Note that attributes are always enclosed in angled brackets and must appear on the same line as the code element they refer to (in this case, the property procedure declaration) or be separated from it using the underscore-line continuation character. (You may remember that .NET attributes were also used when programming web services. In that case, the attributes were named WebMethod and WebService.)

```
<Category("Layout")> _
Public Property RepeatTimes() As Integer
    Get
        Return _RepeatTimes
    End Get
    Set(ByVal Value As Integer)
        _RepeatTimes = Value
    End Set
End Property
```

You can specify more than one attribute at a time, as long as you separate them using commas. The example here includes a Category and a Description attribute. The result is shown in the Properties window in Figure 23-12.

```
<Description("The number of times Text will be repeated"), Category("Layout")> _
```

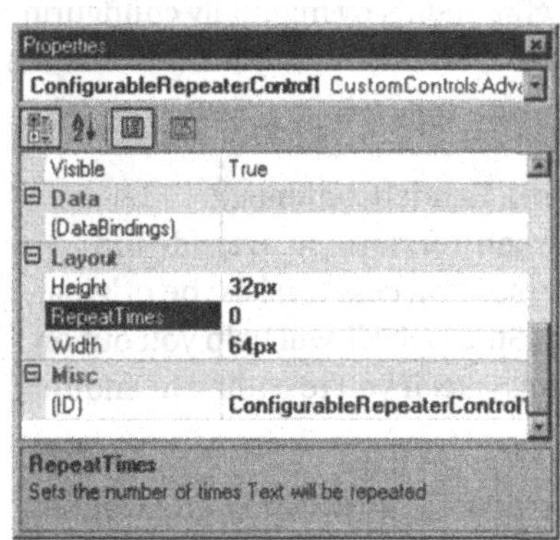

Figure 23-12. Configuring custom control design-time support

A list of useful attributes for configuring a controls design time support is shown in Table 23-1.

Table 23-1. Attributes for Design-Time Support

Attribute	Description
<Browsable(True|False)>	If False, this property will not appear in the Properties window (although the programmer can still modify it in code or by manually adding the control tag attribute, as long as you include a Set property procedure).
<Bindable(True|False)>	If True, Visual Studio .NET will display this property in the DataBindings dialog box and allow it to be bound to a field in a data source.
<Category("")>	A string that indicates the category under which the property will appear in the Properties window.
<Description("")>	A string that indicates the description the property will have when selected in the Properties window.
<DefaultValue()>	Sets the default value that will be displayed for the property in the Properties window.
<ParenthesizePropertyName(True|False)>	If True, Visual Studio .NET will display parentheses around this property in the Properties window (as it does with the ID property).

Other Custom Control Tricks

You can also subclass a control and add low-level refinements by manually configuring the HTML that will be generated from the control. To do this, you only need to follow a few basic guidelines:

- Override one of the render methods (Render(), RenderContents(), RenderBeginTag(), and so on) from the base control class. To override the method successfully, you need to specify the same access level as the original method (such as Public or Protected). Visual Studio .NET will help you out on this account by warning you if you make a mistake. If you're coding in another editor, just check the MSDN reference first.
- Use the MyBase keyword to call the base method. In other words, you want to make sure you're adding functionality to the method, not replacing it with your code. The original method may perform some required cleanup task that you aren't aware of, or it may raise an event that the web page could be listening for.
- Add the code to write out any additional HTML. Usually, this code will use the HtmlWriter class, which supplies a helpful Write() method for direct HTML output.

The following is an example of a text box control that overrides the Render() method to add a title. The content for this title is taken from the custom Title property.

```
Public Class TitledTextBox
  Inherits TextBox

    Private _Title As String
    Public Property Title() As String
        Get
            Return _Title
        End Get
        Set(ByVal Value As String)
            _Title = Value
        End Set
    End Property

    Protected Overrides Sub Render(writer As HtmlTextWriter)
        ' Add new HTML.
        writer.Write("<h1>" & _Title & "</h1><br>")

        ' Call the base method (so that the text box is rendered).
        MyBase.Render(writer)
    End Sub

End Class
```

Figure 23-13 shows what the TitledTextBox control looks like in the design environment.

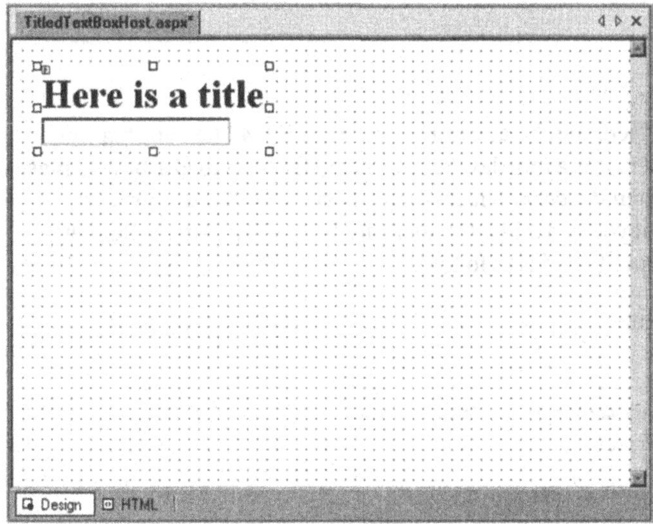

Figure 23-13. A subclassed text box with a title

Remember, ASP.NET creates a page by moving through the list of controls and instructing each one to render itself (by calling the Render() method). It collects the total HTML output and sends it as a complete page (nested in root <HTML><body> tags).

Problems with Grid Layout and the TitledTextBox

As written, the TitledTextBox will work properly in basic HTML pages, but it won't work if you add style attributes to give the TitledTextBox an absolute position on the page. You'll see this behavior if you use grid layout mode with Visual Studio .NET—the text box will be positioned correctly, but the title will be left behind.

The problem in this situation is that all the attributes the user adds to the TitledTextBox are written to the page in the base class Render() method, which means they will only be added to the text box, not the title. To solve this problem, you have the following options:

- You can use a grid layout page, but put the custom control inside a Flow Layout Panel. This way, the title and label will stay together.
- You can redesign the control as a composite control, instead of a custom TextBox control. In this case, you need to inherit from WebControl, and add both a text box and the title in the RenderContents() method. Composite controls are described later in this chapter.
- You can completely replace the rendering logic in the custom TextBox, which is the most complex approach. In this case, you won't call MyBase.Render(). You'll also need to wrap both the title and text box in another HTML element, like a <div> tag. To make sure the control remains in the correct position, you would add the style attribute to the <div>.

You can use a similar technique to add attributes to the HTML text box tag. For example, you might want to link a little JavaScript code to the OnBlur attribute to make a message box appear when the control loses focus. There is no TextBox property that exposes this attribute, but you can add it manually in the AddAttributesToRender() method. The code you would need is as follows:

```
Public Class LostFocusTextBox
  Inherits TextBox

    Protected Overrides Sub AddAttributesToRender( _
      writer As HtmlTextWriter)

        MyBase.AddAttributesToRender(writer)
        writer.AddAttribute("OnBlur", _
          "javascript:alert('You Lost Focus')")

    End Sub

End Class
```

The resulting HTML for the LostFocusTextBox looks something like this:

```
<input type="text" id="LostFocusTextBox2"
       OnBlur="javascript:alert('You Lost Focus')" />
```

Figure 23-14 shows what happens when the text box loses focus. You could extend the usefulness of this control by making the alert message configurable, as shown here:

```
Public Class LostFocusTextBox
  Inherits TextBox

    Private _Alert As String
    Public Property AlertCode() As String
        Get
            Return _Alert
        End Get
        Set(Value As String)
            _Alert = Value
        End Set
    End Property

    Protected Overrides Sub AddAttributesToRender( _
      writer As HtmlTextWriter)

        MyBase.AddAttributesToRender(writer)
        writer.AddAttribute("OnBlur", _
          "javascript:alert('" & _Alert & "')")

    End Sub

End Class
```

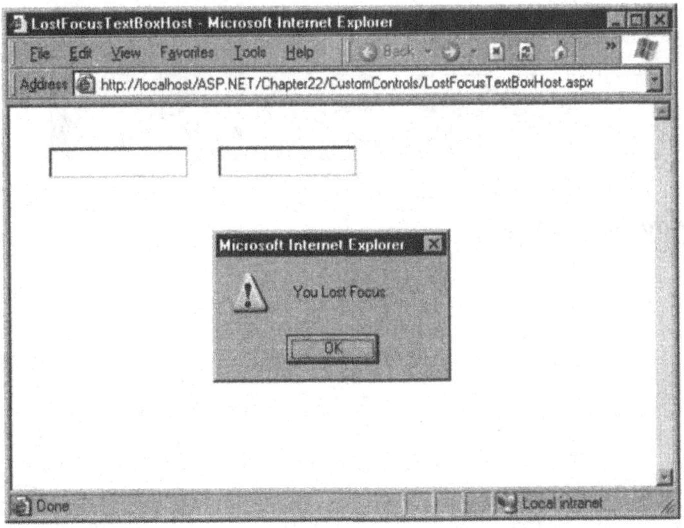

Figure 23-14. The LostFocusTextBox control

Creating a Web Control from Scratch

Once you start experimenting with altering the TextBox control's HTML, it might occur to you to design a control entirely from scratch. This is an easy task in ASP.NET—all you need to do is inherit from the System.Web.UI.WebControls.WebControl class, which is the base of all ASP.NET web controls. Figure 23-15 shows the inheritance hierarchy for web controls.

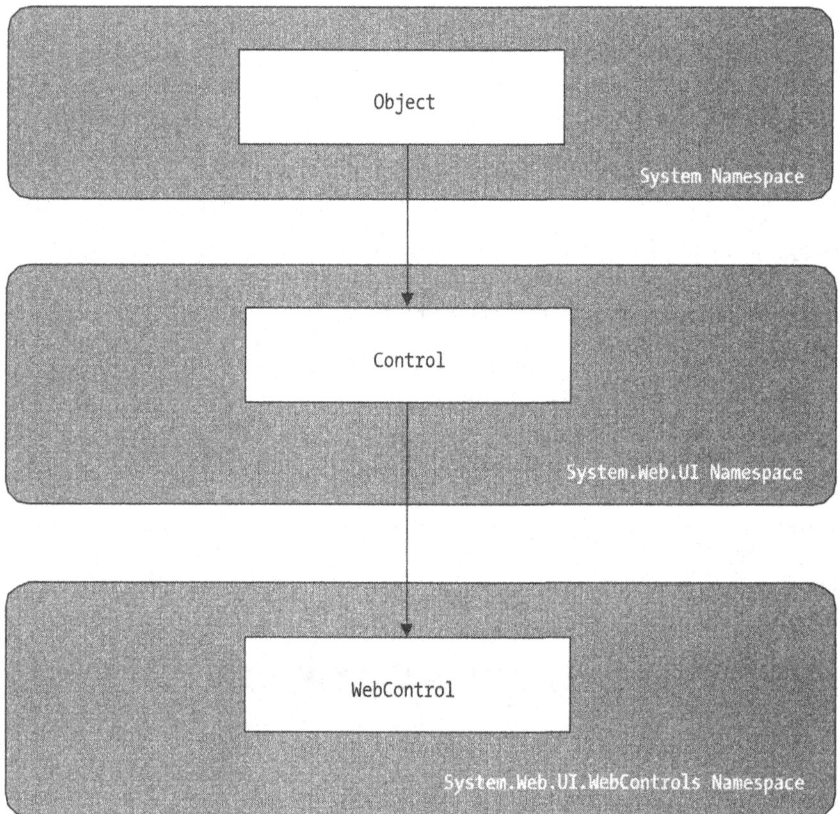

Figure 23-15. Web control inheritance

NOTE Technically, you could inherit from the base System.Web.UI.Control class instead, but it provides fewer features. The main difference with the WebControl class is that it provides a basic set of formatting properties such as Font, BackColor, and ForeColor. These properties are automatically implemented by adding the appropriate HTML attributes to your HTML tag, and are also persisted in view state for you automatically. If you inherit from the more basic Control class, you need to provide your own style-based properties, add them as attributes using the HtmlTextWriter, and store the settings in view state so they will be remembered across postbacks.

To create your own control from scratch, you need to do little more than add the appropriate properties, and implement your own custom RenderContents() or Render() method, which writes the HTML output using the HtmlTextWriter class. The RenderContents() method takes place after the Render() method, which means that the formatting attributes have already been applied.

The code is quite similar to the earlier TextBox examples. It creates a repeater type of control that lists a given line of text multiple times. The number of repeats is set by the RepeatTimes property.

```
Public Class ConfigurableRepeaterControl
  Inherits WebControl

    Private _RepeatTimes As Integer = 3
    Private _Text As String = "Text"
    Public Property RepeatTimes() As Integer
        Get
            Return _RepeatTimes
        End Get
        Set(ByVal Value As Integer)
            _RepeatTimes = Value
        End Set
    End Property

    Public Property Text() As String
        Get
            Return _Text
        End Get
        Set(ByVal Value As String)
            _Text = Value
        End Set
    End Property
```

```
    Protected Overrides Sub RenderContents(writer As HtmlTextWriter)
        MyBase.RenderContents(writer)
        Dim i As Integer
        For i = 1 To _RepeatTimes
            writer.Write(_Text & "<br>")
        Next
    End Sub

End Class
```

Because you've used a WebControl-derived class instead of an ordinary Control-derived class, and because the code writes the output inside the RenderContents() method, the web page programmer can set various style attributes. A sample formatted ConfigurableRepeaterControl is shown in Figure 23-16. If you want to include a title or another portion that you don't want rendered with formatting, add it to the Render method.

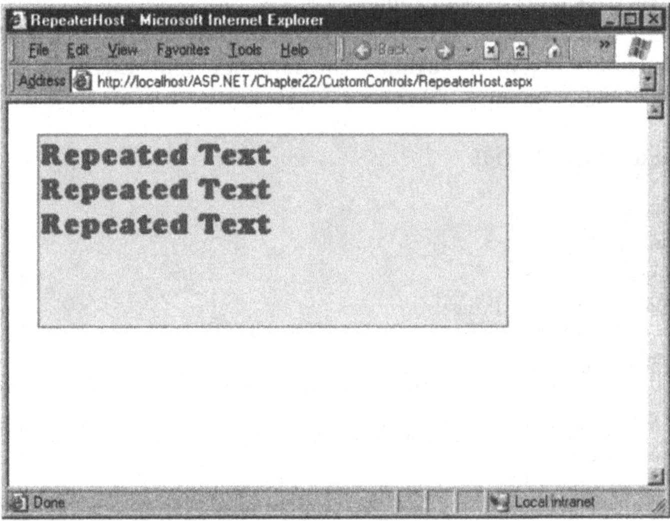

Figure 23-16. WebControl formatting for repeating control

Creating Adaptive Controls

One interesting approach you can take with custom controls is to vary their output based on the browser. ASP.NET uses this technique for some of its more complex controls (such as the validators), ensuring that they are always rendered in the form best suited to the client's browser.

Depending on the sophistication of your control, a lot of thought may need to go into making it support multiple browsers. (Cross-browser support is one of the main criteria that distinguishes the best-of-breed custom ASP.NET controls.) However, the actual implementation details are trivial—all you need to do is retrieve the browser type and respond accordingly in the Render() or RenderContents() method.

A sample control is shown next that simply evaluates the capabilities of its container. It generates the output shown in Figure 23-17.

```
Protected Overrides Sub RenderContents(writer As HtmlTextWriter)
    MyBase.RenderContents(writer)

    If Me.Page.Request.Browser.JavaScript = True Then
        writer.Write("<i>You support JavaScript.</i><br>")
    End If

    If Me.Page.Request.Browser.Browser = "IE" Then
        writer.Write("<i>Output configured for IE.</i><br>")
    ElseIf Me.Page.Request.Browser.Browser = "Netscape" Then
        writer.Write("<i>Output configured for Netscape.</i><br>")
    End If

    Dim i As Integer
    For i = 1 To _RepeatTimes
        writer.Write(_Text & "<br>")
    Next

End Sub
```

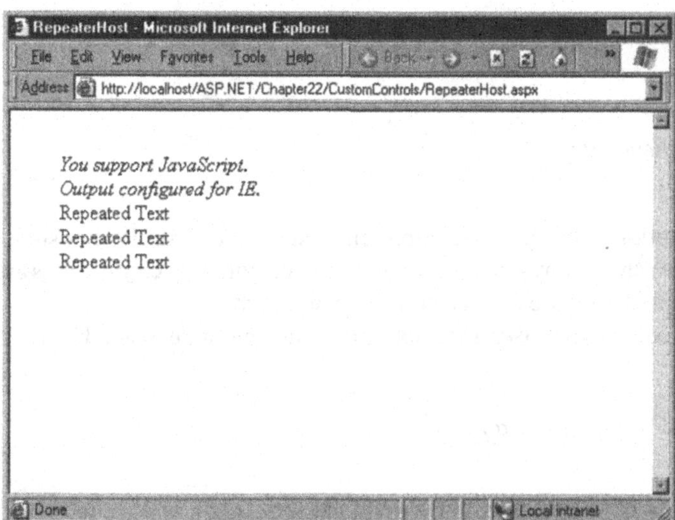

Figure 23-17. An adaptive repeater

Maintaining Control State

Currently, the repeater control provides an EnableViewState property, but it doesn't actually abide by it. You can test this out by creating a simple page with two buttons (see Figure 23-18). One button changes the RepeatTimes to 5, while the other button simply triggers a postback. You'll find that every time you click the Postback button, RepeatTimes is reset to the default of 3. If you change the Text property in your code, you'll also find that it reverts to the value specified in the control tag.

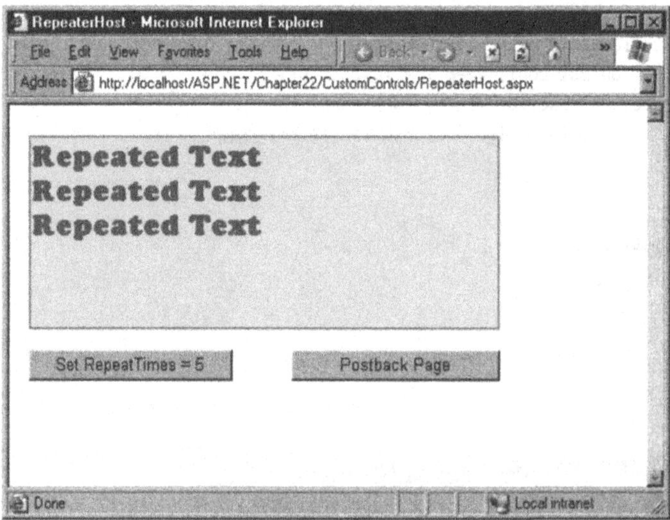

Figure 23-18. Testing view state

There's an easy solution to this problem: Store the value in the control's view state. As with web pages, the value in any member variables in a custom web control class are automatically abandoned after the page is returned to the client.

Here's a rewritten control that uses a variable stored in view state instead of a member variable.

```
Public Class ConfigurableRepeaterControl
  Inherits WebControl

    Public Sub New()
        ViewState("RepeatTimes") = 3
        ViewState("Text") = "Text"
    End Sub
```

```
    Public Property RepeatTimes() As Integer
        Get
            Return CType(ViewState("RepeatTimes"), Integer)
        End Get
        Set(ByVal Value As Integer)
            ViewState("RepeatTimes") = Value
        End Set
    End Property

    Public Property Text() As String
        Get
            Return CType(ViewState("Text"), String)
        End Get
        Set(ByVal Value As String)
            ViewState("Text") = Value
        End Set
    End Property

    Protected Overrides Sub RenderContents(writer As HtmlTextWriter)
        MyBase.RenderContents(writer)
        Dim i As Integer
        For i = 1 To RepeatTimes
            writer.Write(Text & "<br>")
        Next
    End Sub

End Class
```

The code is essentially the same, although it now uses a constructor to initialize the RepeatTimes and Text values. Extra care must also be taken to make sure that the view state object is converted to the correct data type. Performing this conversion manually ensures that you won't end up with difficult-to-find bugs or quirks. Note that though the code looks the same as the code used to store a variable in a Page object's view state, the collections are different. This means that the web page programmer won't be able to access the control's view state directly.

You'll find that if you set the EnableViewState property to False, changes will not be remembered, but no error will occur. When view state is disabled, ASP.NET still allows you to write items to view state, but they won't persist across postbacks.

Creating a Composite Control

So far, you've seen how user controls are generally used for aggregate groups of controls with some added higher-level business logic, while custom controls allow you to create the final HTML output from scratch. You'll also find that user controls are generally quicker to create, easier to work with in a single project, and simpler to program. Custom controls, on the other hand, provide extensive low-level control features you haven't even considered in this chapter, such as templates and data binding.

One technique you haven't considered is composite controls—custom controls that are built out of other controls. Composite controls are a little bit closer to user controls, because they render their user interface at least partly out of other controls. For example, you might find that you need to generate a complex user interface using an HTML table. Rather than write the entire block of HTML manually in the Render() method (and try to configure it based on various higher-level properties), you could dynamically create and insert a Table web control. This pattern is quite common with ASP.NET server controls—for example, it's logical to expect that advanced controls such as the Calendar and DataGrid rely on simpler table-based controls like Table to generate their user interface.

Generating composite controls is quite easy. All you need to do is create the control objects you want to use and add them to the Controls collection of your custom control. (Optionally, you could use one or more container controls, such as the PlaceHolder or Panel, and add the controls to the Controls collection of a container control.) By convention, this task is carried out by overriding the CreateChildControls() method.

The following example creates a grid of buttons, based on the Rows and Cols properties. A simple test page for this control is pictured in Figure 23-19.

```
Public Class ButtonGrid
  Inherits WebControl

    Public Sub New()
        ViewState("Rows") = 2
        ViewState("Cols") = 2
    End Sub

    Public Property Cols() As Integer
        Get
            Return CType(ViewState("Cols"), Integer)
        End Get
        Set(ByVal Value As Integer)
            ViewState("Cols") = Value
        End Set
    End Property

    Public Property Rows() As Integer
        Get
            Return CType(ViewState("Rows"), Integer)
        End Get
        Set(ByVal Value As Integer)
            ViewState("Rows") = Value
        End Set
    End Property
```

```
    Protected Overrides Sub CreateChildControls()
        Dim i, j, k As Integer

        For i = 1 To CType(ViewState("Rows"), Integer)

            For j = 1 To CType(ViewState("Cols"), Integer)
                k += 1

                ' Create and configure a button.
                Dim ctrlB As New Button()
                ctrlB.Width = Unit.Pixel(60)
                ctrlB.Text = k.ToString()

                ' Add the button.
                Me.Controls.Add(ctrlB)
            Next

            ' Add a line break.
            Dim ctrlL As New LiteralControl("<br>")
            Me.Controls.Add(ctrlL)
        Next
    End Sub

End Class
```

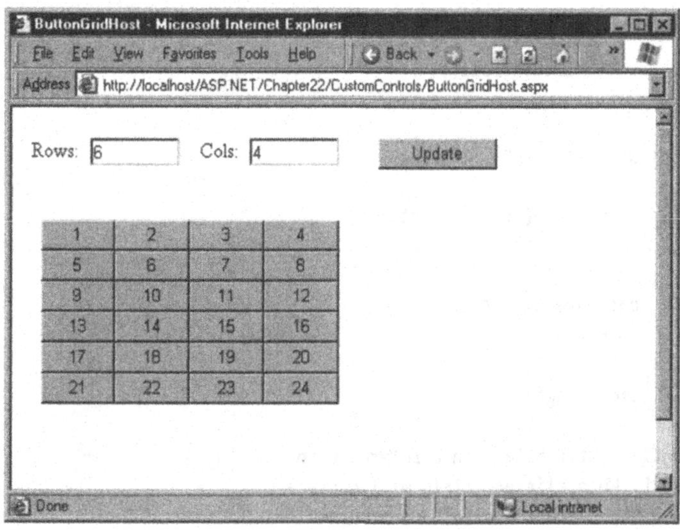

Figure 23-19. A composite control using buttons

Custom Control Events and Postbacks

Raising an event from a control is just as easy as it was with a user control. All you need to do is define the event (and any special EventArgs class) and then fire it with the RaiseEvent statement.

However, to raise an event, your code needs to be executing—and for your code to be triggered, the web page needs to be posted back to the server. If you need to create a control that reacts to user actions instantaneously, and then refreshes itself or fires an event to the web page, you need a way to trigger and receive a postback.

In an ASP.NET web page, web controls fire postbacks by calling a special JavaScript function called __doPostBack(). This function was described in Chapter 7. The __doPostBack() function accepts two parameters: the name of the control that triggered the postback, and a string representing additional postback data. You can retrieve a reference to the __doPostBack() function using the special Page.GetPostBackEventReference() method in your rendering code. (Every control provides the Page property, which provides a reference to the web page where the control is situated.)

The GetPostBackEventReference() method allows you to perform an interesting trick—namely, creating a control or HTML link that invokes the __doPostBack function. The easiest way to perform this magic is usually to add a JavaScript onClick attribute to an HTML element. Anchors, images, and buttons all support the onClick attribute.

Consider the ButtonGrid control. Currently, the buttons are created, but there is no way to receive their events. This can be changed by setting each button's onClick attribute to refer to the __doPostBack() function. The added lines are highlighted in bold, as follows:

```
Protected Overrides Sub CreateChildControls()
    Dim i, j, k As Integer

    For i = 1 To CType(ViewState("Rows"), Integer)

        For j = 1 To CType(ViewState("Cols"), Integer)
            k += 1

            ' Create and configure a button.
            Dim ctrlB As New Button()
            ctrlB.Width = Unit.Pixel(60)
            ctrlB.Text = k.ToString()

            ' Set the onClick attribute with a reference to
            ' __doPostBack. When clicked, ctrlB will cause a
            ' postback to the current control and return
            ' the assigned text of ctrlB.
            ctrlB.Attributes("onClick") = _
              Page.GetPostBackEventReference(Me, ctrlB.Text)
```

```
            ' Add the button.
            Me.Controls.Add(ctrlB)
        Next

        ' Add a line break.
        Dim ctrlL As New LiteralControl("<br>")
        Me.Controls.Add(ctrlL)
    Next
End Sub
```

To handle the postback, your custom control also needs to implement the IPostBackEventHandler interface, as shown here:

```
Public Class ButtonGrid
  Inherits WebControl
  Implements IPostBackEventHandler

    ' (Control code goes here.)

End Class
```

You then need to create a method that implements the IPostBackEventHandler.RaisePostBackEvent() method. This method will be triggered when your control fires the postback, and it will receive any additional information that is submitted through the GetPostBackEventReference() method. In the ButtonGrid control, this extra information will be the text of the button that was clicked.

```
Public Overridable Overloads Sub RaisePostBackEvent(eventArgument _
  As String) Implements IPostBackEventHandler.RaisePostBackEvent

    ' (Respond to postback here.)

End Sub
```

Once you receive the postback, you can modify the control, or even raise another event to the web page. To enhance the ButtonGrid example to use this method, you'll define an additional event in the control:

```
Event GridClick(ByVal ButtonName As String)
```

This event handler raises an event to the web page, with information about the selected button. You'll notice that the event definition doesn't follow the .NET standard for simplicity's sake.

The RaisePostBackEvent() method can then trigger the GridClick event. Here's the complete, revised code for the ButtonGrid:

```
Public Class ButtonGrid
  Inherits WebControl
  Implements IPostBackEventHandler

    Event GridClick(ByVal ButtonName As String)

    Public Sub New()
        Viewstate("Rows") = 2
        Viewstate("Cols") = 2
    End Sub

    Public Overridable Overloads Sub RaisePostBackEvent(eventArgument _
      As String) Implements IPostBackEventHandler.RaisePostBackEvent
        RaiseEvent GridClick(eventArgument)
    End Sub

    Public Property Cols() As Integer
        Get
            Return CType(Viewstate("Cols"), Integer)
        End Get
        Set(ByVal Value As Integer)
            Viewstate("Cols") = Value
        End Set
    End Property

    Public Property Rows() As Integer
        Get
            Return CType(Viewstate("Rows"), Integer)
        End Get
        Set(ByVal Value As Integer)
            Viewstate("Rows") = Value
        End Set
    End Property

    Protected Overrides Sub CreateChildControls()
        Dim i, j, k As Integer

        For i = 1 To CType(Viewstate("Rows"), Integer)

            For j = 1 To CType(Viewstate("Cols"), Integer)
                k += 1
                Dim ctrlB As New Button()
                ctrlB.Width = Unit.Pixel(60)
                ctrlB.Text = k.ToString()
                ctrlB.Attributes("OnClick") = _
                  Page.GetPostBackEventReference(Me, ctrlB.Text)

                ' Add a button.
                Me.Controls.Add(ctrlB)
            Next
```

```
            ' Add a line break.
            Dim ctrlL As New LiteralControl("<br>")
            Me.Controls.Add(ctrlL)
        Next
    End Sub

End Class
```

Figure 23-20 shows a web page that allows you to test the ButtonGrid. It handles the GridClick event, and displays a message indicating which button was clicked. It also allows the user to specify the number of rows and columns that should be added to the grid.

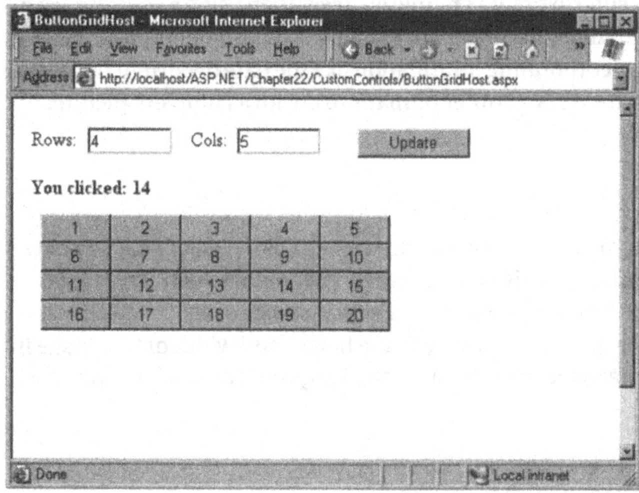

Figure 23-20. Handling custom control events

Here's the web page code:

```
Public Class ButtonGridHost
  Inherits System.Web.UI.Page

    Protected txtRows As System.Web.UI.WebControls.TextBox
    Protected txtCols As System.Web.UI.WebControls.TextBox
    Protected WithEvents cmdUpdate As System.Web.UI.WebControls.Button
    Protected lblInfo As System.Web.UI.WebControls.Label
    Protected WithEvents ButtonGrid1 As CustomControls.ButtonGrid

    Private Sub cmdUpdate_Click(sender As Object, e As EventArgs) _
      Handles cmdUpdate.Click
        ButtonGrid1.Rows = txtRows.Text
        ButtonGrid1.Cols = txtCols.Text
    End Sub
```

```
    Private Sub ButtonGrid1_GridClick(ButtonName As String) _
      Handles ButtonGrid1.GridClick
        lblInfo.Text = "You clicked: " & ButtonName
    End Sub
End Class
```

Dynamic Graphics

One of the features of the .NET Framework is GDI+, a set of classes designed for creating bitmaps. You can use GDI+ in a Windows or an ASP.NET application to draw dynamic graphics. In a Windows application, the graphics you draw would be copied to a window for display. In ASP.NET, the graphics can be rendered right into the HTML stream, and sent directly to the client browser.

In general, using GDI+ code to draw a graphic is slower than using a static image file. However, it gives you much more freedom. For example, you can tailor the graphic to suit a particular purpose, incorporating information like the date or current user name. You can also mingle text, shapes, and other bitmaps to create a complete picture.

Basic Drawing

There are four basic steps you need to follow when using GDI+. First of all, you have to create an in-memory bitmap. This is the drawing space where you'll create your masterpiece. To create the bitmap, you declare a new instance of the System.Drawing.Bitmap class. You must specify the height and width of the image in pixels. Be careful—don't make the bitmap larger than required, or you'll needlessly waste memory.

```
' Create an in-memory bitmap where you will draw the image.
' The Bitmap is 300 pixels wide and 50 pixels high.
Dim Image As New Bitmap(300, 50)
```

The next step is to create a GDI+ graphics context for the image, which is represented by the System.Drawing.Graphics object. This object provides the methods that allow you to render content to the in-memory bitmap. To create a Graphics object from an existing Bitmap object, you just use the shared Graphics.FromImage() method as shown here:

```
Dim g As Graphics = Graphics.FromImage(Image)
```

Now comes the interesting part. Using the methods of the Graphics class, you can draw text, shapes, and image on the bitmap. Table 23-2 lists some of the most fundamental Graphics class methods. The methods that begin with the word "Draw" draw outlines, while the methods that begin with the word "Fill" draw solid regions. The only exception is the DrawString() method which draws filled in text using a font you specify, and the methods for copying bitmap images, like DrawIcon() and DrawImage().

Table 23-2. Graphics Class Methods for Drawing

Method	Description
DrawArc()	Draws an arc representing a portion of an ellipse specified by a pair of coordinates, a width, and a height.
DrawBezier() and DrawBeziers()	The infamous and attractive Bezier curve, which is defined by four control points.
DrawClosedCurve()	Draws a curve, and then closes it off by connecting the end points.
DrawCurve()	Draws a curve (technically, a cardinal spline).
DrawEllipse()	Draws an ellipse defined by a bounding rectangle specified by a pair of coordinates, a height, and a width.
DrawIcon() and DrawIconUnstreched()	Draws the icon represented by an Icon object, and (optionally) stretches it to fit a given rectangle.
DrawImage() and DrawImageUnscaled()	Draws the image represented by an Image-derived object, and (optionally) stretches it to fit a given rectangle.
DrawLine() and DrawLines()	Draws a line connecting the two points specified by coordinate pairs.
DrawPie()	Draws a "piece of pie" shape defined by an ellipse specified by a coordinate pair, a width, a height, and two radial lines.
DrawPolygon()	Draws a multisided polygon defined by an array of points.
DrawRectangle() and DrawRectangles()	Draws an ordinary rectangle specified by a starting coordinate pair and width and height.
DrawString()	Draws a string of text in a given font.
FillClosedCurve()	Draws a curve, closes it off by connecting the end points, and fills it.
FillEllipse()	Fills the interior of an ellipse.
FillPie()	Fills the interior of a "piece of pie" shape.
FillPolygon()	Fills the interior of a polygon.
FillRectangle() and FillRectangles()	Fills the interior of a rectangle.
FillRegion()	Fills the interior of a Region object.

When calling the Graphics class methods, you'll need to specify several parameters to indicate the pixel coordinates for what you want to draw. For example, when drawing a rectangle, you'll need to specify the location of the top-left corner, and the width and height of the rectangle. Here's an example of how you might draw a solid rectangle in yellow:

```
' Draw a rectangle starting at location (0, 0)
' that is 300 pixels wide and 50 pixels high.
g.FillRectangle(Brushes.Yellow, 0, 0, 300, 50)
```

When measuring pixels, the point (0, 0) is the top-left corner of your image in (x, y) coordinates. The x coordinate increases as you go further to the right, and the y coordinate increases as you go further down. In the current example, the image is 300 pixels wide and 50 pixels high, which means the point (300, 50) is the bottom-right corner.

You'll also notice that you need to specify either a Brush or a Pen object when you create any graphic. Methods that draw shape outlines require a Pen, while methods that draw filled-in regions require a Brush. You can create your own custom Pen and Brush objects, but .NET provides an easier solution with the Brushes and Pens classes. These classes expose shared properties that provide various Brushes and Pens for different colors. For example, Brushes.Yellow returns a Brush object that fills regions in using a solid yellow color.

Once the image is complete, you can send it to the browser using the Image.Save() method. Conceptually, you "save" the image to the browser's response stream. It then gets sent to the client, and displayed in the browser.

```
' Render the image to the HTML output stream.
Image.Save(Response.OutputStream, _
  System.Drawing.Imaging.ImageFormat.Gif)
```

TIP You can save an image to any valid stream, including a FileStream. This technique allows you to save dynamically generated images to disk, so you can use them later in other web pages.

Finally, you should explicitly release your image and graphics context when you're finished, because both hold on to some unmanaged resources that might not be released right away if you don't.

```
g.Dispose()
Image.Dispose()
```

GDI+ is a specialized approach, and its more advanced features are beyond the scope of this book. However, you can learn a lot by considering a couple of simple examples.

Drawing Custom Text

Using the techniques you've learned, it's easy to create a simple web page that uses GDI+. The next example uses GDI+ to render some text in a bordered rectangle with a happy face graphic next to it.

Here's the code you'll need:

```
Private Sub Page_Load(sender As Object, _
  e As EventArgs) Handles MyBase.Load

    ' Create an in-memory bitmap where you will draw the image.
    ' The Bitmap is 300 pixels wide and 50 pixels high.
    Dim Image As New Bitmap(300, 50)

    ' Get the graphics context for the bitmap.
    Dim g As Graphics = Graphics.FromImage(Image)

    ' Draw a solid yellow rectangle with a red border.
    g.FillRectangle(Brushes.LightYellow, 0, 0, 300, 50)
    g.DrawRectangle(Pens.Red, 0, 0, 299, 49)

    ' Draw some text using a fancy font.
    Dim Font As New Font("Alba Super", 20, FontStyle.Regular)
    g.DrawString("This is a test.", Font, Brushes.Blue, 10, 0)

    ' Copy a smaller gif into the image from a file.
    Dim Icon As System.Drawing.Image
    Icon = Image.FromFile(Server.MapPath("smiley.gif"))
    g.DrawImageUnscaled(Icon, 240, 0)

    ' Render the entire bitmap to the HTML output stream.
    Image.Save(Response.OutputStream, _
      System.Drawing.Imaging.ImageFormat.Gif)

    ' Clean up.
    g.Dispose()
    Image.Dispose()

End Sub
```

Figure 23-21 shows the resulting web page.

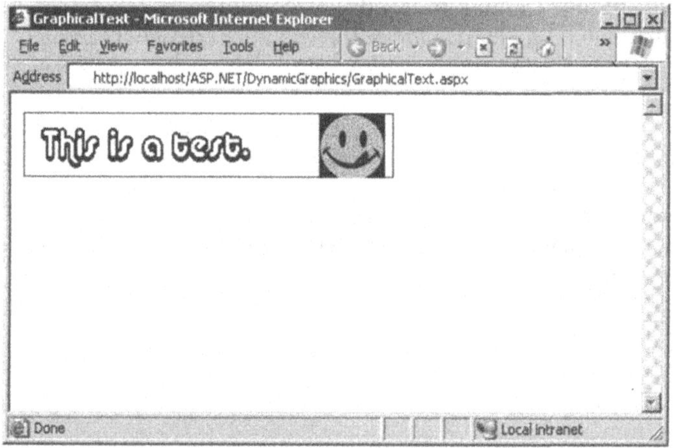

Figure 23-21. Drawing a custom image

TIP Because this image is generated on the server, you can use any font that the server has installed when creating the graphic. The client won't need to have the same font, because the client will receive the text as a rendered image.

Placing Custom Images Inside Web Pages

There is one problem with the Image.Save() approach demonstrated so far. When you save an image to the response stream, you overwrite whatever information ASP.NET would otherwise use. If you have a web page that includes other static content and controls, this content won't appear at all in the final web page. Instead, the dynamically rendered graphics will replace it.

Fortunately, there is a simple solution: You can link to a dynamically generated image using the HTML <img> tag, or the Image web control. But instead of linking your image to a static image file, link it to the .aspx file that generates the picture.

For example, you could create a file named GraphicalText.aspx that writes a dynamically generated image to the response stream. In another page, you could show the dynamic image by adding an Image web control, and setting the ImageUrl property to GraphicalText.aspx. In fact, you'll even see the image appear in Visual Studio .NET's design-time environment before you run the web page!

When you use this technique to embed dynamic graphics in web pages, you also need to think about how the web page can send information to the dynamic graphic. For example, what if you don't want to show a fixed piece of text, but you want to generate a dynamic label that incorporates the name of the current user? (In fact, if you do want to show a static piece of text, it's probably better to create the graphic ahead of time and store it in a file, rather than generating it using GDI+ code each time the user requests the page.) One solution is to pass the information using the query string. The page that renders the graphic can then check for the query string information it needs.

Here's how you would rewrite the dynamic graphic generator with this in mind:

```
' Get the user name.
Dim Name As String = Request.QueryString("Name")

If Name = "" Then
    ' No name was supplied.
    ' Don't display anything.

Else
    ' Create an in-memory bitmap where you will draw the image.
    Dim Image As New Bitmap(300, 50)

    ' Get the graphics context for the bitmap.
    Dim g As Graphics = Graphics.FromImage(Image)

    g.FillRectangle(Brushes.LightYellow, 0, 0, 300, 50)
    g.DrawRectangle(Pens.Red, 0, 0, 299, 49)

    ' Draw some text based on the query string.
    Dim Font As New Font("Alba Super", 20, FontStyle.Regular)
    g.DrawString(Name, Font, Brushes.Blue, 10, 0)

    ' Render the entire bitmap to the HTML output stream.
    Image.Save(Response.OutputStream, _
      System.Drawing.Imaging.ImageFormat.Gif)

    g.Dispose()
    Image.Dispose()

End If
```

Figure 23-22 shows a page that uses this dynamic graphic page, along with two Label controls. The page passes the query string argument "Joe Brown" to the page. The full Image.ImageUrl thus becomes GraphicalText.aspx?Name=Joe%20Brown.

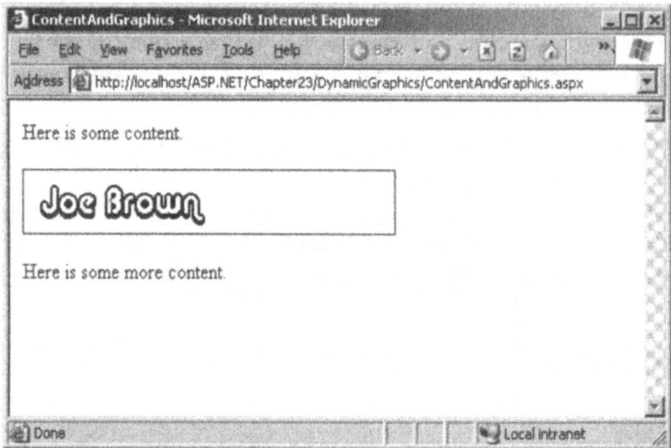

Figure 23-21. Mingling custom images and controls on the same page

The Last Word

ASP.NET custom control creation could be a book in itself. To master it, you'll want to experiment with the online samples for this chapter. Once you've perfected your controls, pay special attention to the attributes described in Table 23-1. These are the key to making your control behave properly and work conveniently in design environments like Visual Studio .NET.

CHAPTER 24

Caching and Performance Tuning

ASP.NET APPLICATIONS are a bit of a contradiction. On the one hand, because they're hosted over the Internet, they have unique requirements—namely, they need to be able to serve hundreds of clients as easily and quickly as they deal with a single user. On the other hand, ASP.NET includes some remarkable tricks that let you design and code a web application in the same way you program a desktop application. These tricks are useful, but they can lead developers into trouble. The problem is that ASP.NET makes it easy to forget you're creating a web application—so easy that you might introduce programming practices that will slow or cripple your application when it's used by a large number of users in the real world.

Fortunately, there is a middle ground. You can use the incredible timesaving features like view state, web controls, and session state that you've spent the last twenty-odd chapters learning about, and still create a robust web application. But to finish the job properly, you'll need to invest a little extra time to profile and optimize your website's performance.

This chapter discusses the strategies you can use to ensure performance. They fall into three main categories:

- **Design for scalability.** There are a few key guidelines that, if kept in mind, can steer you toward efficient, scalable designs.
- **Profile your application.** One problem with web applications is that it's sometimes hard to test them under the appropriate conditions and really get an idea of what their problems may be. However, Microsoft provides several useful tools that allow you to benchmark your application and put it through a rigorous checkup.
- **Implement caching.** A little bit of caching may seem like a novelty in a single-user test, but it can make a dramatic improvement in real-world scenarios. You can easily incorporate output and fragment caching into most pages, and use data caching to replace less memory-friendly approaches like state management.

Designing for Scalability

The chapters throughout this book have combined practical how-to information with tips and insight about the best designs you can use (and the possible problems you'll face). Now that you're a more accomplished ASP.NET programmer, it's a good idea to review a number of considerations—and a few minor ways that you can tune up all aspects of your application.

ASP.NET Code Compilation

ASP.NET provides dramatically better performance than ASP, although it's hard to quote a hard statistic because the performance increases differ widely depending on the ways you structure your pages and the type of operations you perform. The greatest performance increase results from ASP.NET's automatic code compilation. With traditional ASP pages, the script code in a web page was processed for every client request. With ASP.NET, each page class is compiled to native code the first time it's requested, and then cached for future requests.

This system has one noticeable side effect. The very first time that a user accesses a particular web page (or the first time a user accesses it after it has been modified), there will be a longer delay while the page is compiled. In some cases, this time for the first request may actually be slightly slower than the equivalent ASP page request. However, this phenomenon will be much more common during development than in an actual deployed web site. With a live web site, a page will be compiled for the first request and then reused for the rest of the application's lifetime. With ASP.NET's ability to automatically recycle memory and recover from most problems without requiring a restart, and with the increased stability of the Windows 2000, Windows XP, and Windows 2003 Server platforms, an ASP.NET application could be running around the clock for weeks with little user intervention and very few page recompiles.

The Ideal Web Server

Microsoft recommends a two-processor web server for the best price to performance ratio. A single-CPU computer is only marginally cheaper and will provide reduced performance, particularly for applications that use ADO.NET extensively, or in cases where an administrator is using a logging or administrative tool on the web server computer itself (which is almost never a good idea). More sophisticated servers, such as those with four CPUs, are significantly more expensive. A better way to achieve a similar performance increase for a heavily trafficked website is by using multiple servers to host it (this is known as a web farm or web garden).

These techniques aren't required for typical websites, unless you're building the next Amazon.com. If you plan to host an ASP.NET application with a web farm or web garden, you'll probably also need some outside technical help. At least one book is in print that is completely dedicated to describing the hardware and software configuration for these large-scale setups.

Server Controls

Most of the examples in this book use server controls extensively. Server controls are the basic ingredient in an ASP.NET page, and they don't carry a significant performance overhead—in fact, they usually provide better performance than dynamically writing a page with tricks such as the Response.Write() method.

However, ASP.NET server controls can be unnecessary in some situations. For example, if you have static text that never needs to be accessed or modified in your code, you don't need to use a Label web control. Instead, you can enter the text as static HTML in your .aspx layout file. In Visual Studio .NET, you can use the HTML label control, which is actually created as an ordinary <div> tag. Unless you specifically check the Run As Server Control option, it will be created as a static element rather than a full server control.

Another potential refinement involves view state. If you don't need view state for a control, you should disable it by setting the control's EnableView state to False. Two cases in which you don't need view state are if the control is set at design time and never changes, or if the control is refreshed with every postback and doesn't need to keep track of its previous set of information. In the latter case, there is one catch: If you need to retrieve the user's selection when the page is posted back, you'll still need to enable view state for the control. For example, this is why you use view state with data-bound web pages, even though the controls are refilled from the data source after every postback.

Generally, view state becomes most significant when dealing with large controls that can contain significant amounts of data. The problem is that this data exerts a greater toll on your application because it's added to the web page twice: directly in the HTML for the control, and again in the hidden label control used for view state. It's also sent both to the client and then back to the server with each postback. To get a handle on whether view state could be an issue, use page tracing (as described in Chapter 11) to see how many bytes the current page's view state is consuming.

TIP Both of these issues (static text and view state) are fairly minor refinements. They can speed up download times, particularly if your application is being used by clients with slow Internet connections. However, they will almost never cause a serious problem in your application the way poor database or session state code can. Don't spend too much time tweaking your controls, but do keep these issues in mind while programming so that you can optimize your pages where the opportunity presents itself.

ADO.NET Database Access

The rules for accessing a database are relatively straightforward, but they can't be overemphasized. Open a connection to the database only at the point where you need it, and close it properly as soon as possible. Database connections are a limited resource, and represent a potential bottleneck if you don't design your web pages carefully.

In addition to making sure you treat your database with this basic degree of respect, there are a number of additional steps you can take to improve performance:

- **Improve your database with stored procedures.** Relational database management systems like SQL Server are remarkably complex products. They provide a number of configuration options that have nothing to do with ASP.NET, but can make a substantial difference in performance. For example, a database that uses intelligently designed stored procedures instead of dynamically generated queries will often perform much better, because stored procedures can be compiled and optimized in advance. This is particularly true if a stored procedure needs to perform several related operations at once.

- **Improve your database with profiling and indexes.** Defining indexes that match the types of searches you need to perform can result in much quicker row-lookup capabilities. To perfect your database, you'll need to examine it with a profiling tool (such as Profiler for SQL Server). These tools record database activity into a special log that can be reviewed, analyzed, and replayed. The profiling utility can usually identify problem areas (such as slow executing queries) and even recommend a new set of indexes that will provide better performance. However, to properly profile the database you'll need to simulate a typical load by running your application.

- **Get only the information you need.** One of the simplest ways to improve any database code is to reduce the amount of information it retrieves, which will reduce the network load, the amount of time the connection needs to be open, and the size of the final page. For example, all searches should be limited to present a small set of rows at a time (perhaps by filtering by date) and should only include the fields that are truly important. Note, however, that while this is an excellent rule of thumb, it isn't always the right solution. For example, if you're providing a page that allows a user to edit a database record, it's often easier to retrieve all the information for all the rows at once, rather than requery the database every time the user selects a record to get additional information.

- **Use connection pooling.** In a typical web application, your RDBMS receives requests on behalf of countless different clients, from several different web pages. Generally, these connections are open and active for only a short amount of time, and creating them is the most time-consuming step. However, if every web page uses the exact same connection string, database products such as SQL Server will be able to use their built-in connection pooling to reuse a connection for more than one consecutive client, speeding up the process dramatically. This happens transparently and automatically, provided you always use the exact same connection string (even a minor difference like the order of settings will prevent a connection from being reused). To ensure that the connection string is the same, centralize it in the web.config file, as described in Chapter 5.

- **Use data binding.** The fastest way to get information out of a database and into a page is to use a DataReader or DataSet and bind it directly to a data control. This approach may involve a little more work with custom templates, but it's better than moving through the rows manually and writing to the page yourself.

- **Use caching.** If a certain set of data is frequently requested and changes slowly, it's an ideal candidate for caching. With caching, the information will be read from the database and loaded into temporary memory the first time a client requests it, and made directly available to future requests without any database access required. Output and data caching are discussed later in this chapter.

Session State

Session state was the single greatest restriction on performance in traditional ASP development. Although ASP.NET introduces some features that make session state more scalable, it still needs to be used carefully.

Generally, you won't run into problems if you're just storing a customer's ID in session state. You can create a simple shopping basket by storing a list of currently selected products. However, if you plan to store large amounts of information such as a DataSet, you need to tread carefully and consider the multiplying effect of a successful application. If each session reserves about 1 MB of information, 100 simultaneous sessions (not necessarily all corresponding to users who are still at your site) can easily chew up more than 100 MB of memory. To solve this sort of problem, you have two design choices:

- Store everything in a database record, and store the ID for that database in session state. When the client returns, look up the information. Nothing is retained in memory, and the information is durable—it won't expire until you remove the record. Of course, this option can reclaim server memory, but slows down the application with database access, which is the other vulnerable part of your application.

- A better solution is often to store information in a database record, and then cache some of the information in memory. Then the information can still be retrieved quickly when needed, but the memory can be reclaimed by ASP.NET if the server's performance is suffering. More information about data caching can be found later in this chapter.

Also keep in mind that with session state, the best state facility is almost always the default in-process session state store. The other options (such as storing session state in an SQL database) impose additional performance overhead, and are only necessary when hosting your website in a web farm with multiple web servers.

Profiling

To judge the success of an attempted performance improvement, you need to be able to measure the performance of your application. In cases where performance is lagging, you also need enough information to diagnose the possible bottleneck, so you can make a meaningful change.

The Process Model

The simplest option you have to see how ASP.NET is functioning is to retrieve its vital statistics through the ProcessModelInfo class. This class (in the System.Web namespace) provides two useful shared methods. The first, GetProcessInfo(), retrieves a ProcessInfo object that contains information about the current ASP.NET worker process running on the server. The second method, GetProcessHistory(), returns an array with up to 100 ProcessInfo objects that contain information about recent worker processes. For example, if ASP.NET has been restarted three times since the server was powered on, you'll be able to retrieve up to three ProcessInfo objects. (ASP.NET restarts aren't necessarily due to errors or instability. You might be using advanced configuration settings to automatically restart the ASP.NET worker process after a certain period of idle time or when a certain amount of memory is used, as described in Chapter 29.) The ProcessInfo object provides several useful pieces of information, as shown in Table 24-1.

NOTE If you're hosting your application on IIS 6 (the version of Internet Information Services that is included with Windows 2003 Server), the IIS 6 process model will be used instead of the IIS process model, and you won't be able to use the ProcessModelInfo class to retrieve any diagnostic information.

Table 24-1. ProcessInfo Properties

Property	Description
Age	A TimeSpan object that indicates the length of time that the process was in use (or the length of time since inception for a currently running process).
PeakMemoryUsed	The maximum amount of memory, in megabytes, that this process has used at any one time.
ProcessID	The ASP.NET-assigned ID number.
RequestCount	The number of requests that have been served by this process.
ShutdownReason	If the process has shut down, this indicates a value from the ProcessShutdownReason enumeration. This can be an automatic process recycling (such as MemoryLimitExceeded, RequestsLimit, or Timeout), or it could be a serious failure (such as PingFailed or Unexpected).
StartTime	A DateTime object indicating when the process started.
Status	A value from the ProcessStatus enumeration that indicates the current state of the process (such as Alive, ShutDown, ShuttingDown, or Terminated).

To keep an eye on the ASP.NET worker process from another computer, you can create a simple test page that displays the current process information. The following ProcessModelReport.aspx page displays all the statistics for the current process when the user clicks a button. The results are shown in Figure 24-1.

```
Dim Current As ProcessInfo = ProcessModelInfo.GetCurrentProcessInfo
lblInfo.Text = "<b>Process: </b>" & Current.ProcessID.ToString()
lblInfo.Text &= "<br><b>Start: </b>" & Current.StartTime.ToString()
lblInfo.Text &= "<br><b>Age: </b>" & Current.Age.ToString()
lblInfo.Text &= "<br><b>Peak Memory: </b>" & Current.PeakMemoryUsed.ToString()
lblInfo.Text &= "<br><b>Status: </b>" & Current.Status.ToString()
```

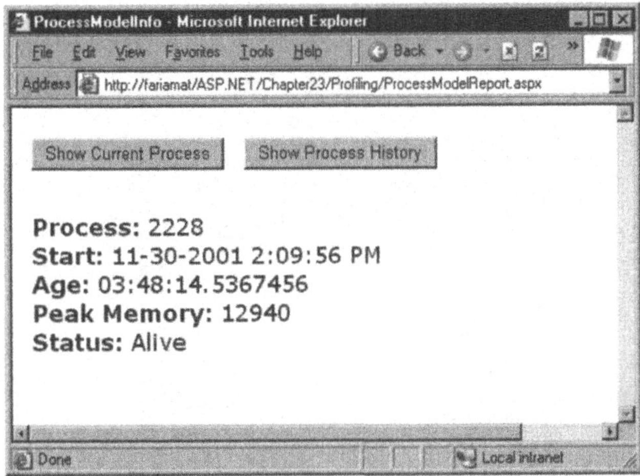

Figure 24-1. The current process

The same page also provides summary information about the recent worker processes. Thanks to ASP.NET's data binding, the most important information in the ProcessInfo array can be sent straight into the DataGrid control in two easy lines, as shown in Figure 24-2.

```
dgProcess.DataSource = ProcessModelInfo.GetHistory(100)
dgProcess.DataBind()
```

The process model information is a basic starting point when checking up on the health of your application. However, it won't give you any idea about the strengths and shortcomings of your code. For that, you need to perform stress testing.

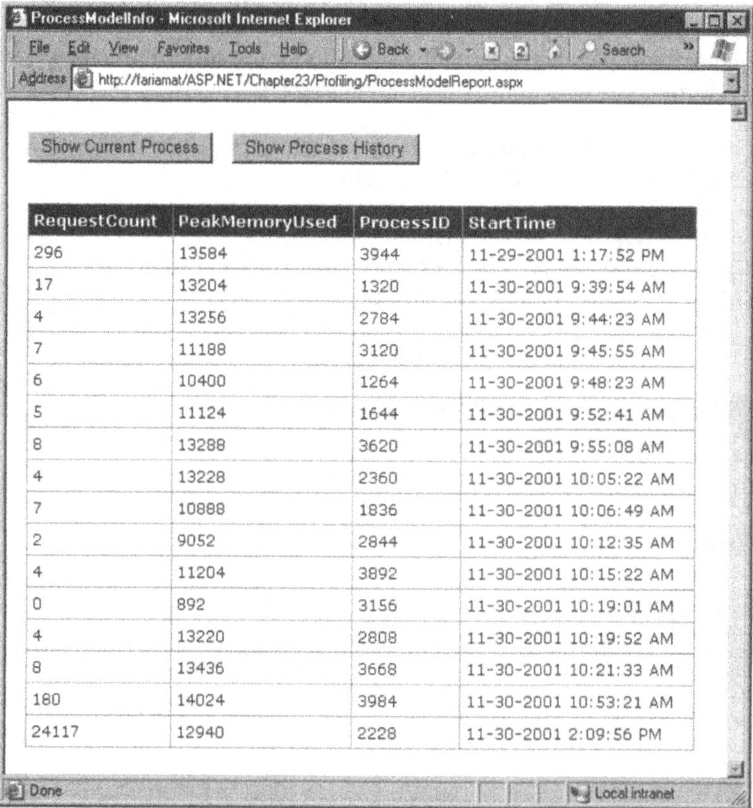

RequestCount	PeakMemoryUsed	ProcessID	StartTime
296	13584	3944	11-29-2001 1:17:52 PM
17	13204	1320	11-30-2001 9:39:54 AM
4	13256	2784	11-30-2001 9:44:23 AM
7	11188	3120	11-30-2001 9:45:55 AM
6	10400	1264	11-30-2001 9:48:23 AM
5	11124	1644	11-30-2001 9:52:41 AM
8	13288	3620	11-30-2001 9:55:08 AM
4	13228	2360	11-30-2001 10:05:22 AM
7	10888	1836	11-30-2001 10:06:49 AM
2	9052	2844	11-30-2001 10:12:35 AM
4	11204	3892	11-30-2001 10:15:22 AM
0	892	3156	11-30-2001 10:19:01 AM
4	13220	2808	11-30-2001 10:19:52 AM
8	13436	3668	11-30-2001 10:21:33 AM
180	14024	3984	11-30-2001 10:53:21 AM
24117	12940	2228	11-30-2001 2:09:56 PM

Figure 24-2. The process history

Stress Testing

There is no shortage of testing tools and .NET Framework features that you can use to profile your ASP.NET applications. Being able to bridge the gap from test results to application insight is often not as easy. You may be able to record important information such as TTFB and TTLB (the time taken to serve the first byte and the time taken to deliver the last byte, and complete the delivery). But without a way to gauge the meaning of these settings, it isn't clear whether your application is being held back by a slow hard drive, a poor choice of ASP.NET settings, an overtasked database, or bad application design. In fact, performance testing is an entire science of its own.

Most basic tests use a dedicated web server, a set of dedicated client machines that are interacting with your web server over a fast isolated network, and a load-generating tool that runs on each client. The load-generating tool automatically requests a steady stream of pages, simulating a heavy load. You might use a utility like Application Center Test (included with some versions of Visual Studio .NET) or the ASP favorite, WAST (Web Service Applications Stress Tool), which is available for a free download from `http://www.microsoft.com/technet/itsolutions/intranet/downloads/webstres.asp`. (The nice thing about Application Center Test is that you can create tests directly in Visual Studio .NET simply by adding the appropriate project type to your solution, as shown in Figure 24-3.) Note that if you try to test the server using a load-testing tool running from the same computer, you'll retrieve data that is much less accurate and much less useful.

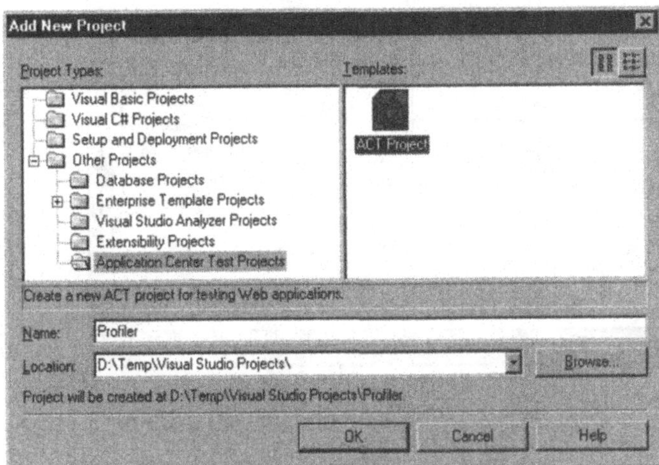

Figure 24-3. Creating an Application Center Test project

Both Application Center Test and Web Service Applications Stress Tool simulate real-world conditions by continuously requesting pages through several different connections simultaneously. You can configure how many requests are made at once and what files are requested. You can even use a wizard that records typical browser activity while you use the site, and then replays it later. Figure 24-4 shows an Application Center Test in progress.

Most load-generating tools record some kind of report as they work. Both Application Center Test and Web Service Application Stress Tool create text summaries. Additionally, you can record results using Windows performance counters, which you'll examine in the next section.

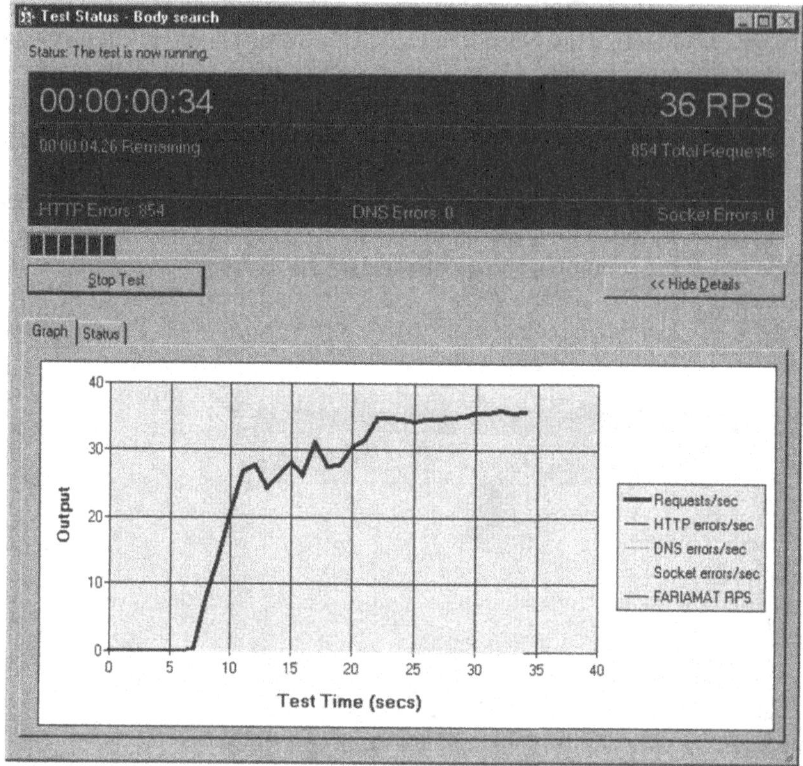

Figure 24-4. Running an Application Center Test project

Performance Counters

Windows performance counters are the basic unit of measurement for gauging the performance of your application. You can add or configure counters from a testing utility like Web Service Application Stress Tool, or you can monitor performance directly from the system Performance window. To do so, choose Settings ➤ Control Panel ➤ Administrative Tools ➤ Performance from the Start menu. Figure 24-5 shows the Performance window.

By default, you'll only see performance counters for measuring basic information such as the computer's CPU and disk drive use. However, ASP.NET installs much more useful counters for tracking web application performance. To add these counters, right-click the counter list and choose Properties. You can configure numerous options (such as changing the appearance of the graph and logging information to a report), but the most important tab is Data, which allows you to add and remove counters from the current list. To start, remove the default counters, and click Add to choose more useful ones, as shown in Figure 24-6.

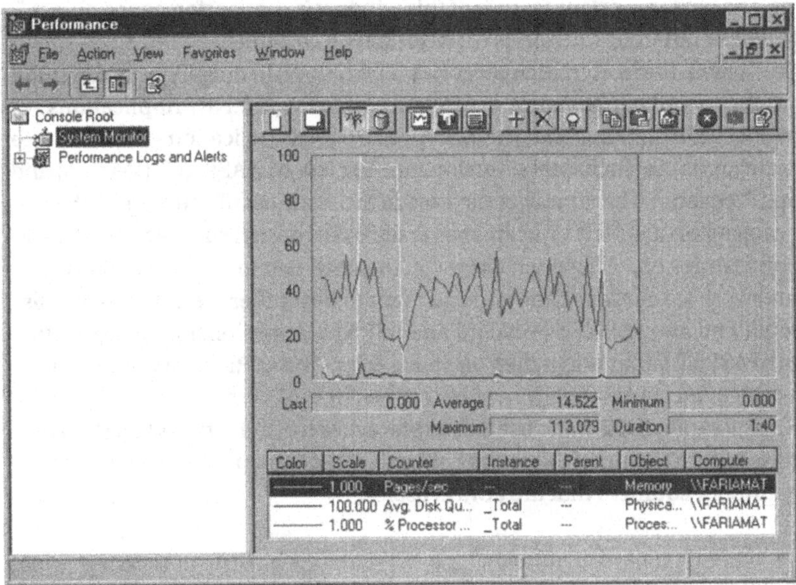

Figure 24-5. Monitoring performance counters

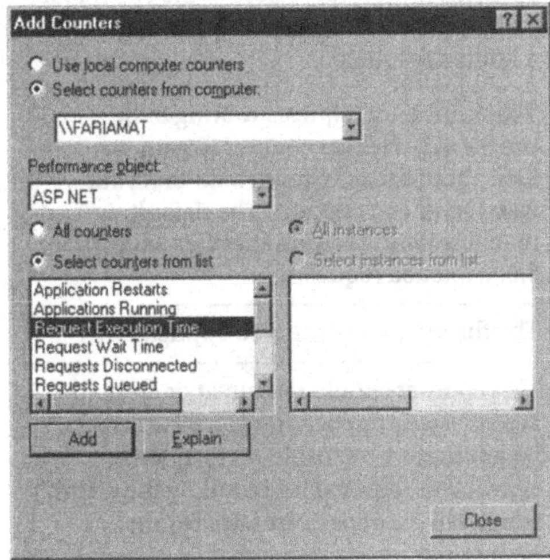

Figure 24-6. Adding ASP.NET performance counters

You'll notice several important features about the Add Counters window. First of all, you can specify a computer name—in other words, you can monitor the performance of a remote computer. Monitoring the web server's performance on a client computer is ideal, because it ensures that the act of monitoring doesn't have as much of an effect on the server. The next important feature of this window is the "performance object." There are dozens of different categories of performance counters.

For ASP.NET, you'll find four main categories. The ASP.NET category provides information about the overall performance of ASP.NET, while the ASP.NET Applications category provides information about a single specified web application. There are also two similar categories that include the version number (such as ASP.NET [Version] and ASP.NET Apps [Version]). These categories provide the same list of counters as the corresponding categories that don't indicate the version. This design supports the side-by-side execution features of .NET, which allow you to install two (or more) versions of the.NET Framework at the same time and use them to host different websites. In this case, you would find one ASP.NET [Version] and ASP.NET Apps [Version] category for each version of ASP.NET that is installed on your server. The ASP.NET and ASP.NET Application categories automatically map to the most recent version.

Table 24-2 lists some of the most useful counter types by category and name. The asterisked rows indicate counters that can help you diagnose a problem, while the other rows represent counters that are always useful.

Table 24-2. Useful Performance Counters

Category	**Counter**	**Description**
Processor	% CPU Utilization	The percentage of the CPU's processing time that is being used. If your CPU use remains consistently low regardless of the client load, your application may be trapped waiting for a limited resource.
ASP.NET	Requests Queued	The number of requests waiting to be processed. Use this counter to gain an idea about the maximum load that your web server can support. The default machine.config setting specifies a limit of 5,000 queued requests.
ASP.NET Applications	Requests/Sec	The throughput of the web application.
ASP.NET Applications	* Errors Total	This counter should remain at or close to zero. If a web application generates errors, it can exert a noticeable performance slowdown (required for handling the error), which will skew performance results.
ASP.NET	* Application Restarts, Worker Process Restarts	The ASP.NET process may restart based on a fatal crash, or automatically in response to recycling options set in the machine.config file (see the <processModel> settings in Chapter 29 for more information). These counters can give you an idea about how often the ASP.NET process is being reset, and can indicate unnoticed problems.

Table 24-2. Useful Performance Counters (Continued)

Category	Counter	Description
System	* Context Switches/sec	Indicates the rate that thread contexts are switched. A high number may indicate that various threads are competing for a limited resource.
ASP.NET Applications	Pipeline Instance Count	The number of request pipelines that exist for an application. This gives an idea of the maximum number of concurrent requests that are being served. If this number is low under a load, it often signifies that the CPU is being used well.
.NET	* CLR Exceptions, # of Exceps Thrown	The number of exceptions thrown in a .NET application. This can indicate that unexpected errors are occurring (as with the ErrorsTotal counter), but it can also indicate the normal operation of error-handling code in response to a missing file or invalid user action.

.NET provides some interesting features that let you interact with the system performance counters programmatically. For example, you can add new performance counters, or retrieve the current value of a performance counter in your code, and display relevant information in a web page or desktop application. To use these features, you simply need to explore the types in the System.Diagnostics namespace. Table 24-3 gives an overview of the .NET classes you can use to interact with performance counters. For more information, refer to the MSDN class library reference.

Table 24-3. Performance-Counter Classes

Class	Description
PerformanceCounter	Represents an individual counter, which includes information like the counter name and the type of data it records. You can create your own counter to represent application-specific performance measures (such as number of purchases per second).
PerformanceCounterCategory	Represents a counter category, which will contain one or more counters.
CounterCreationData	Represents the data required to create a new counter. It can be used for more control or as a shortcut when creating PerformanceCounter objects.
CounterSample	Represents a single piece of information recorded by the counter. It provides a RawValue (the recorded number), a TimeStamp (when the value was recorded), and additional information about the type of counter and how frequently the counter is read. A typical performance counter might create samples several times per second.

Caching

ASP.NET has taken some dramatic steps forward with caching. Many developers who first learn about caching see it as a bit of a frill, but nothing could be further from the truth. Used intelligently, caching could provide a twofold, threefold, or even tenfold performance improvement by retaining important data for just a short period of time.

In ASP.NET, there are really two types of caching. Your applications can and should use both types, as they complement each other.

- **Output caching** is the simplest type of caching. It stores a copy of the final rendered HTML page that is sent to the client. The next client that submits a request for this page doesn't actually run the page. Instead, the final HTML output is sent automatically. The time that would have been required to run the page and its code is completely reclaimed.
- **Data caching** is carried out manually in your code. To use data caching, you store important pieces of information that are time-consuming to reconstruct (such as a DataSet retrieved from a database) in the cache. Other pages can check for the existence of this information, and use it, thereby bypassing the steps ordinarily required to retrieve it. Data caching is conceptually the same as using Application state (described in Chapter 10), but it's much more server-friendly because items will be removed from the cache automatically when it grows too large and performance could be affected. Items can also be set to expire automatically.
- **Fragment caching** is really a specialized type of output caching. It stores and reuses the compiled HTML output of a portion of a user control on a page. Thus, when the page is requested some code may be executed, but the code for the appropriate user control isn't.

Output Caching

To see output caching in action, you can create a simple page that displays the current time of day. This page is shown in Figure 27-7.

The code for this task is elementary:

```
Public Class OutputCaching
  Inherits Page
    Protected lblDate As Label

    Private Sub Page_Load(sender As Object, e As EventArgs) _
      Handles MyBase.Load

        lblDate.Text = "The time is now:<br>"
        lblDate.Text &= DateTime.Now.ToString()

    End Sub

End Class
```

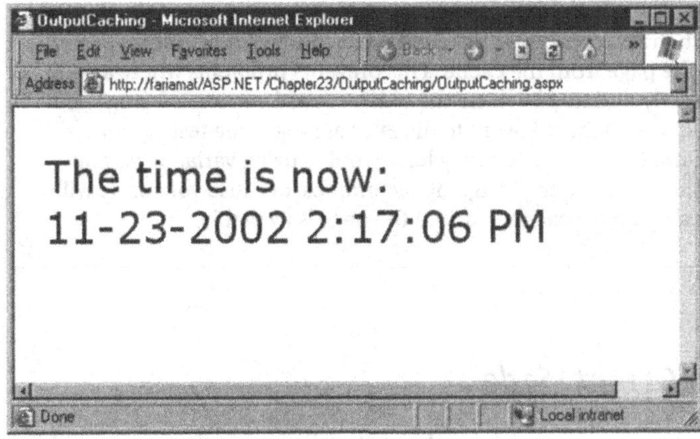

Figure 24-7. Displaying the page's creation date

There are two ways to cache an ASP.NET page. The most common approach is to insert the OutputCache directive at the top of your .aspx file, as shown here:

```
<%@ OutputCache Duration="20" VaryByParam="None" %>
```

The Duration attribute instructs ASP.NET to cache the page for 20 seconds. The VaryByParam attribute is also required—but you'll learn about its effect a little later.

When you run the test page, you'll discover some interesting behavior. The first time you access the page, the current date will be displayed. If you refresh the page a short time later, however, the page will not be updated. Instead, ASP.NET will automatically send the cached HTML output to you, until it expires in 20 seconds. When the cached page expires, ASP.NET will run the page code again, generate a new cached copy, and use that for the next 20 seconds.

Twenty seconds may seem like a trivial amount of time, but in a high-volume site, it can make a dramatic difference. For example, you might cache a page that provides a list of products from a catalog. By caching the page for 20 seconds, you limit database access for this page to three operations per minute. Without caching, the page will try to connect to the database once for each client, and could easily make dozens of requests in the course of a minute.

Of course, just because you request that a page should be stored for 20 seconds doesn't mean that it actually will be. The page could be evicted out of the cache early if the system finds that memory is becoming scarce. This allows you to use caching freely, without worrying too much about hampering your application by using up vital memory.

TIP When you recompile a cached page, ASP.NET will automatically remove the page from the cache. This prevents problems where a page isn't properly updated because the older, cached version is being used. However, you might still want to disable caching while testing your application. Otherwise, you may have trouble using variable watches, breakpoints, and other debugging techniques, because your code will not be executed if a cached copy of the page is available.

Caching on the Client Side

Another option is to cache the page exclusively on the client side. In this case, the browser stores a copy, and will automatically use this page if the client browses back to the page or retypes the page's URL. However, if the user clicks the Refresh button, the cached copy will be abandoned and the page will be re-requested from the server, which will run the appropriate page code once again. You can cache a page on the client side using the Location attribute, which specifies a value from the System.Web.UI.OutputCacheLocation enumeration. Possible values include Server (the default), Client, None, and All.

```
<%@ OutputCache Duration="20" VaryByParam="None" Location="Client" %>
```

Client-side caching is less common than server-side caching. Because the page is still re-created for every separate user, it won't cut down on code execution or database access nearly as dramatically as server-side caching (which shares a single cached copy among all users). However, client-side caching can be a useful technique if your cached page uses some sort of personalized data. For example, there is no point in caching a page on the server that displays a "hello" message with the user's name. Even though each user is in a separate session, the page will only be created once and reused for all clients, ensuring that most will receive the wrong greeting. Instead, you can either use fragment caching to cache the generic portion of the page, or client-side caching to store a user-specific version on each client's computer.

Caching and the Query String

One of the main considerations in caching is deciding when a page can be reused and when information must be accurate up to the latest second. Developers, with their love of instant gratification (and lack of patience), generally tend to overemphasize the importance of real-time information. You can usually use caching to efficiently reuse slightly stale data without a problem, and with a considerable performance improvement.

Of course, sometimes information needs to be dynamic. One example is if the page uses information from the current user's session to tailor the user interface. In this case, full page caching just isn't appropriate (although fragment caching may help). Another example is if the page is receiving information from another page through the query string. In this case, the page is too dynamic to cache—or is it?

Our current example sets the VaryByParam attribute to None, which effectively tells ASP.NET that you only need to store one copy of the cached page, which is suitable for all scenarios. If the request for this page adds query string arguments to the URL, it makes no difference—ASP.NET will always reuse the same output until it expires. You can test this by adding a query string parameter manually in the browser window (such as ?a=b), as shown in Figure 24-8.

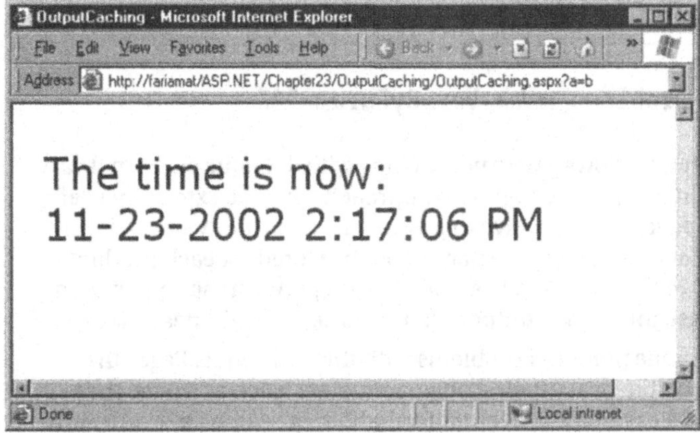

Figure 24-8. Adding a query string parameter

Caching Multiple Page Versions

Based on this experiment, you might assume that output caching isn't suitable for pages that use query string arguments. But ASP.NET actually provides another option. You can set the VaryByParam attribute to "*" to indicate that the page uses the query string, and to instruct ASP.NET to cache separate copies of the page for different query string arguments.

```
<%@ OutputCache Duration="20" VaryByParam="*" %>
```

Now, when you request the page with additional query string information, ASP.NET will examine the query string. If the string matches a previous request, and a cached copy of that page exists, it will be reused. Otherwise, a new copy of the page will created and cached separately.

To get a better idea how this process works, consider the following series of requests:

1. You request a page without any query string parameter, and receive page copy A.
2. You request the page with the parameter ProductID=1. You receive page copy B.
3. Another user requests the page with the parameter ProductID=2. That user receives copy C.

4. Another user requests the page with ProductID=1. If the cached output B has not expired, it's sent to the user.

5. The user then requests the page with no query string parameters. If copy A has not expired, it's sent from the cache.

You can try this out on your own, although you might want to lengthen the amount of time that the cached page is retained to make it easier to test.

Problems with VaryByParam="*"

Setting VaryByParam="*" allows you to use caching with dynamic pages that vary their output based on the query string. This approach could be extremely useful for a product detail page, which receives a product ID in its query string. With vary-by-parameter caching, a separate page could be stored for each product, thereby saving a trip to the database. However, to gain performance benefits you might have to increase the cached output lifetime to several minutes or longer.

Of course, there are some potential problems with this technique. Pages that accept a wide range of different query string parameters (such as a page that receives numbers for a calculation, client information, or search keywords) just aren't suited to output caching. The possible number of variations is enormous, and the potential reuse is very low. Though these pages will be evicted from the cache when the memory is needed, they could inadvertently force other more important information out of the cache first, or slow down other operations.

Caching with Specific Parameters

Setting VaryByParam to the wildcard asterisk (*) is unnecessarily vague. It's usually better to specifically identify an important query string variable by name. Here's an example:

```
<%@ OutputCache Duration="20" VaryByParam="ProductID" %>
```

In this case, ASP.NET will examine the query string looking for the ProductID parameter. Requests with different ProductID parameters will be cached separately, but all other parameters will be ignored. This is particularly useful if the page may be passed additional query string information that it doesn't use. ASP.NET has no way to distinguish the "important" query string parameters without your help.

You can specify several parameters, as long as you separate them with semicolons.

```
<%@ OutputCache Duration="20" VaryByParam="ProductID;CurrencyType" %>
```

In this case, query string will cache separate versions provided the query string differs by ProductID or CurrencyType.

A Multiple Caching Example

The following example uses two web pages to demonstrate how multiple versions of a web page can be cached separately. The first page, QueryStringSender.aspx, isn't cached. It provides three buttons, and is shown in Figure 24-9.

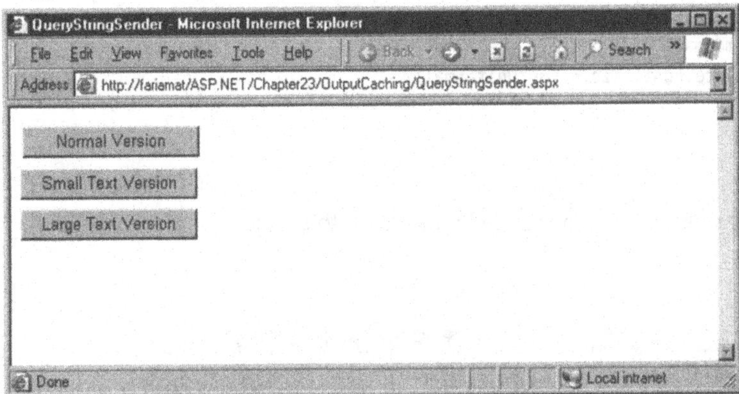

Figure 24-9. Three page options

A single event handler handles the Click event for all three buttons. The event handler navigates to the QueryStringRecipient.aspx page, and adds a Version parameter to the query string to indicate which button was clicked—cmdNormal, cmdLarge, or cmdSmall.

```
Private Sub cmdVersion_Click(sender As Object, e As EventArgs) _
  Handles cmdLarge.Click, cmdNormal.Click, cmdSmall.Click

        Response.Redirect(QueryStringRecipient.aspx & "?Version=" & _
          CType(sender, Control).ID)

End Sub
```

The QueryStringRecipient.aspx destination page displays the familiar date message. The page uses an OutputCache directive that looks for a single query string parameter (named Version).

```
<%@ OutputCache Duration="60" VaryByParam="Version" %>
```

In other words, there are three separately maintained HTML outputs for this page, one where Version equals cmdSmall, one where Version equals cmdLarge, and one where Version equals cmdNormal.

Although it isn't necessary for this example, the Page.Load event handler tailors the page by changing the font size of the label accordingly. This makes it easy to distinguish the three different versions of the page, and verify that the caching is working as expected.

```
Private Sub Page_Load(sender As Object, e As EventArgs) _
  Handles MyBase.Load

    lblDate.Text = "The time is now:<br>" & DateTime.Now.ToString()
    Select Case Request.QueryString("Version")
        Case "cmdLarge"
            lblDate.Font.Size = FontUnit.XLarge
        Case "cmdNormal"
            lblDate.Font.Size = FontUnit.Large
        Case "cmdSmall"
            lblDate.Font.Size = FontUnit.Small
    End Select

End Sub
```

Figure 24-10 shows one of the cached outputs for this page.

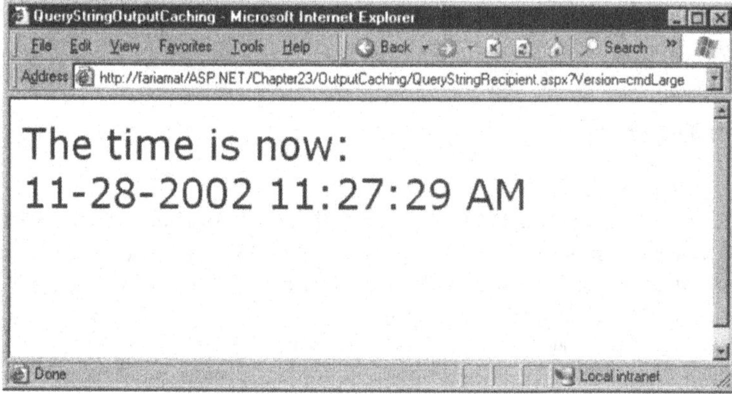

Figure 24-10. One page with three cached outputs

Caching and Events

The same problems you witnessed with cached pages and query string values can occur with a cached page that runs events. With VaryByParam="None" ASP.NET will cache one version of the page for all POST requests, and reuse that when any postback is triggered. This means that if you click a button multiple times, it will really only be executed once. Even worse, if you have a page with multiple buttons, their Click events may be ignored altogether. A static page will be re-sent no matter what button the user clicks, effectively disabling the page.

To compensate for these problems, you can specify the specific postback values that will require separately cached versions of the page using the VaryByParam attribute. For example, set VaryByParam="txtName" to vary the result based on the txtName contents that are posted back with the page. However, this is generally not a recommended approach. Because you can't directly see the values that are being posted back (as you can with query string information), it's very easy to create a problem for yourself.

One such problem occurs with view state, which is contained in a special hidden control. This hidden input control is sent back to the page with each postback. This means that if you include a VaryByParam="*" attribute with a page that maintains view state, you could quickly end up with dozens of versions of the cached page. Every time ASP.NET receives the page, it will examine the information that's posted back. It will then determine that the page request isn't the same as any other previous request because the hidden field has changed, and it will add yet another copy of the page to the cache. If, on the other hand, you try to solve this problem by using VaraByParams="None", the caching won't be conditional, and some values may not be correctly restored.

The bottom line is this: For effective, straightforward caching, don't try to implement output caching with an event-driven page. Instead, use fragment caching to cache a portion of the page, or use data caching to cache specific information. Both of these techniques are described later in this chapter.

Custom Caching Control

Varying by query string parameters isn't the only option when storing multiple cached versions of a page. ASP.NET also allows you to create your own special procedure that decides whether to cache a new page version or reuse an existing one. This code examines whatever information is appropriate, and then returns a string. ASP.NET uses this string to implement caching. If your code generates the same string for different requests, ASP.NET will reuse the cached page. If your code generates a new string value, ASP.NET will generate a new cached version, and store it separately.

One way you could use custom caching is to cache different versions of a page based on the browser type. That way, Netscape browsers will always receive Netscape-optimized pages, and Internet Explorer users will receive IE-optimized HTML. To set up this sort of logic, you start by adding the OutputCache directive to the pages that will be cached. Use the VaryByCustom attribute to specify a name that represents the type of custom caching you're creating. The following example uses the name "Browser" because pages will be cached based on the client browser.

```
<%@ OutputCache Duration="10" VaryByParam="None" VaryByCustom="Browser" %>
```

Next, you need to create the procedure that will generate the custom caching string. This procedure must be coded in the global.asax application file (or its code-behind file), and must use the following syntax:

```
Public Overrides Function GetVaryByCustomString( _
  context As HttpContext, arg As String) As String

    ' Check for the requested type of caching.
    If arg = "Browser"
        ' Determine the current browser.
        Dim BrowserName As String
        BrowserName = Context.Request.Browser.Browser

       ' Indicate that this string should be used to vary caching.
       Return BrowserName
    End If

End Function
```

The GetVaryByCustomString() function passes the VaryByCustom name in the arg parameter. This allows you to create an application that implements several different types of custom caching in the same function. Each different type would use a different VaryByCustom name (such as "Browser," "BrowserVersion," or "DayOfWeek"). Your GetVaryByCustomString() function would examine the VaryByCustom name, and then return the appropriate caching string. If the caching strings for different requests match, ASP.NET will reuse the cached copy of the page. Or to look at it another way, ASP.NET will create and store a separate cached version of the page for each caching string it encounters.

The OutputCache directive has a third attribute that you can use to define caching. This attribute, VaryByHeader, allows you to store separate versions of a page based on the value of an HTTP header received with the request. You can specify a single header or a list of headers separated by semicolons. This technique could be used with multilingual sites to cache different versions of a page based on the client browser language.

```
<%@ OutputCache Duration="20" VaryByParam="None"
    VaryByHeader="Accept-Language" %>
```

Caching with the HttpCachePolicy Class

Using the OutputCache directive is generally the preferred way to cache a page, because it separates the caching instruction from the rest of your code. The OutputCache directive also makes it easy to configure several advanced properties in one line.

However, there is one other choice: You can write code that uses the built-in special Response.Cache property, which provides an instance of the System.Web.HttpCachePolicy class. This object provides properties that allow you to turn on caching for the current page.

In the following example, the date page has been rewritten so that it automatically enables caching when the page is first loaded. This code enables caching with the SetCacheability() method, which specifies that the page will be cached on the server, and that any other client can use the cached copy of the page. The SetExpires() method defines the expiration date for the page, which is set to be the current time plus 60 seconds.

```
Private Sub Page_Load(sender As Object, e As EventArgs) _
  Handles MyBase.Load

    ' Cache this page on the server.
    Response.Cache.SetCacheability(HttpCacheability.Public)

    ' Use the cached copy of this page for the next 60 seconds.
    Response.Cache.SetExpires(DateTime.Now.AddSeconds(60))

    ' This additional line ensures that the browser can't
    ' invalidate the page when the user clicks the Refresh button
    ' (which some rogue browsers attempt to do).
    Response.Cache.SetValidUntilExpires(True)

    lblDate.Text = "The time is now:<br>" & DateTime.Now.ToString()

End Sub
```

TIP Always test your caching strategies after implementing them. For some completely mysterious reason, caching with the HttpCachePolicy class works slightly different than with the OutputCache directive. Namely, event procedures bypass the cached page unless you set the HttpCachePolicy.VaryByParam property. This means that you can enable caching for an event-driven page, and this caching will only be used for ordinary GET requests, not postbacks. Strange, but true.

Fragment Caching

In some cases, you may find that you can't cache an entire page, but you would still like to cache a portion that is expensive to create and doesn't vary. One way to implement this sort of scenario is to use data caching to store just the underlying information used for the page. You'll examine this technique in the next section. Another option is to use fragment caching.

To implement fragment caching, you need to create a user control for the portion of the page you want to cache. You can then add the OutputCache directive to the user control. The result is that the page will not be cached, but the user control will.

Fragment caching is conceptually the same as page caching. There is only one catch—if your page retrieves a cached version of a user control, it cannot interact with it in code. For example, if your user control provides properties, your web page code cannot modify or access these properties. When the cached version of the user control is used, a block of HTML is simply inserted into the page. The corresponding user control object is not available.

Output Caching in a Web Service

You can also use output caching for individual methods in a web service. To do so, you need to add the CacheDuration value to the WebMethod before the appropriate method declaration. The following example caches a web method's result for 30 seconds:

```
<WebMethod(CacheDuration:=30)> _
Private Function MyMethod(myParameter As Integer) As String
    ' (Code goes here.)
End Function
```

When using output caching with a web service, you don't need to enable any type of cache varying. Responses are only reused for requests that supply an identical set of parameters. For example, if three clients invoke MyMethod(), each with a different value of myParameter, three separate strings will be stored in the cache. If another client calls MyMethod() with a matching myParameter value before the 30 second time limit elapses, that client will receive the cached data, and the web method code will not be executed.

Data Caching

Data caching is the most flexible type of caching, but it also forces you to take specific additional steps in your code to implement it. The basic principle of data caching is that you add items that are expensive to create to a special built-in collection object (called Cache). This object works much like the Application object you saw in Chapter 10. It's globally available to all requests from all clients in the application. There are only two differences:

- **The Cache object is thread-safe.** This means that you don't need to explicitly lock or unlock the Cache collection before adding or removing an item. However, the objects in the Cache collection will still need to be thread-safe themselves. For example, if you create a custom business object, more than one client could try to use that object at once, which could lead to invalid data. There are various ways to code around this limitation—one easy approach that you'll see in this chapter is just to make a duplicate copy of the object if you need to work with it in a web page.

- **Items in the Cache collection are removed automatically.** ASP.NET will remove an item if it expires, if one of the objects or files it depends on is changed, or if the server becomes low on memory. This means you can freely use the cache without worrying about wasting valuable server memory, because ASP.NET will remove items as needed. But because items in the cache can be removed, you always need to check if a cache object exists before you attempt to use it. Otherwise, you could generate a null-reference exception.

There are several ways to insert an object into the cache. You can simply assign it to a new key name (as you would with the Session or Application collections), but this approach is generally discouraged because it does not allow you to have any control over the amount of time the object will be retained in the cache. A better approach is to use the Insert() method.

The Insert() method has four overloaded versions. The most useful and commonly used one requires four parameters and is shown here.

```
Cache.Insert(key, item, dependencies, absoluteExpiration, slidingExpiration)
```

The parameters are described in Table 24-4.

Table 24-4. Cache.Insert() Parameters

Parameter	Description
key	A string that assigns a name to this cached item in the collection and allows you to look it up later.
item	The actual object that you want to cache.
dependencies	A CacheDependency object that allows you to create a dependency for this item in the cache. If you don't want to create a dependent item, just specify Nothing for this parameter.
absoluteExpiration	A DateTime object representing the time at which the item will be removed from the cache.
slidingExpiration	A TimeSpan object represents how long ASP.NET will wait between requests before removing a cached item. For example, if this value is 20 minutes, ASP.NET will evict the item if it isn't used by any code for a 20-minute period.

Typically, you won't use all of these parameters at once. Cache dependencies, for example, are a special tool you'll consider a little later in this chapter. Also, you cannot set both a sliding expiration and an absolute expiration policy at the same time. If you want to use an absolute expiration, set the slidingExpiration parameter to TimeSpan.Zero.

```
Cache.Insert("MyItem", obj, Nothing, _
          DateTime.Now.AddMinutes(60), TimeSpan.Zero)
```

Absolute expirations are best when you know the information in a given item can only be considered valid for a specific amount of time (such as a stock chart or weather report). Sliding expiration, on the other hand, is more useful when you know that a cached item will always remain valid (such as historical data or a product catalog), but should still be allowed to expire if it isn't being used. To set a sliding expiration policy, set the absoluteExpiration parameter to DateTime.Max, as shown here.

```
Cache.Insert("MyItem", obj, Nothing, _
          DateTime.MaxValue, TimeSpan.FromMinutes(10))
```

A Simple Cache Test

The following page presents a simple caching test. An item is cached for 30 seconds and reused for requests in that time. The page code always runs (because the page itself isn't cached), checks the cache, and retrieves or constructs the item as needed. It also reports whether the item was found in the cache.

```
Public Class SimpleCacheTest
  Inherits Page

    Protected lblInfo As Label

    Private Sub Page_Load(sender As Object, e As EventArgs) _
      Handles MyBase.Load

        If Me.IsPostBack = True Then
            lblInfo.Text &= "Page posted back.<br>"
        Else
            lblInfo.Text &= "Page created.<br>"
        End If

        If Cache("TestItem") Is Nothing Then
            lblInfo.Text &= "Creating TestItem...<br>"
            Dim TestItem As Date = DateTime.Now()

            lblInfo.Text &= "Storing TestItem in cache"
            lblInfo.Text &= "for 30 seconds.<br>"
            Cache.Insert("TestItem", TestItem, Nothing, _
                         DateTime.Now.AddSeconds(30), TimeSpan.Zero)
        Else
            lblInfo.Text &= "Retrieving TestItem...<br>"
            Dim testitem As Date = CType(Cache("TestItem"), Date)
            lblInfo.Text &= "TestItem is '" & TestItem.ToString()
            lblInfo.Text &= "'<br>"
        End If

        lblInfo.Text &= "<br>"

    End Sub

End Class
```

Figure 24-11 shows the result after the page has been loaded and posted back several times in the 30-second period.

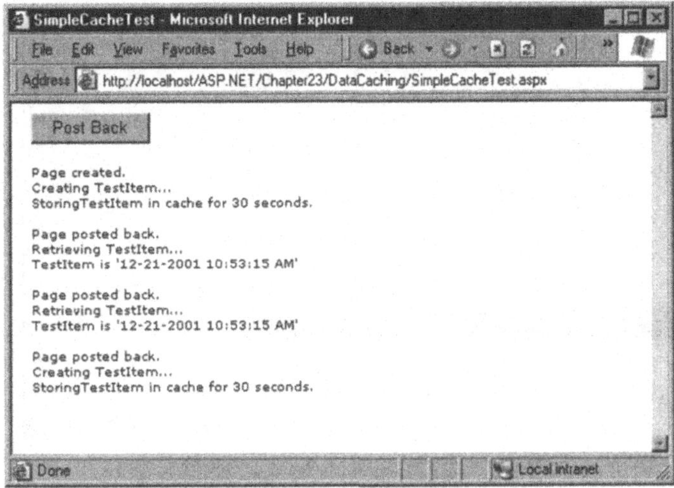

Figure 24-11. A simple cache test

Caching to Provide Multiple Views

A more interesting demonstration of caching is shown in the next example, which retrieves information from a database and stores it in a DataSet. This information is then displayed in a web page. However, the output for the web page can't be efficiently cached because the user is given the chance to customize the display by hiding any combination of columns. Note that even with just ten columns, you can construct more than one thousand different possible views by hiding and showing various columns. These are far too many columns for successful output caching!

Figure 24-12 shows the page.

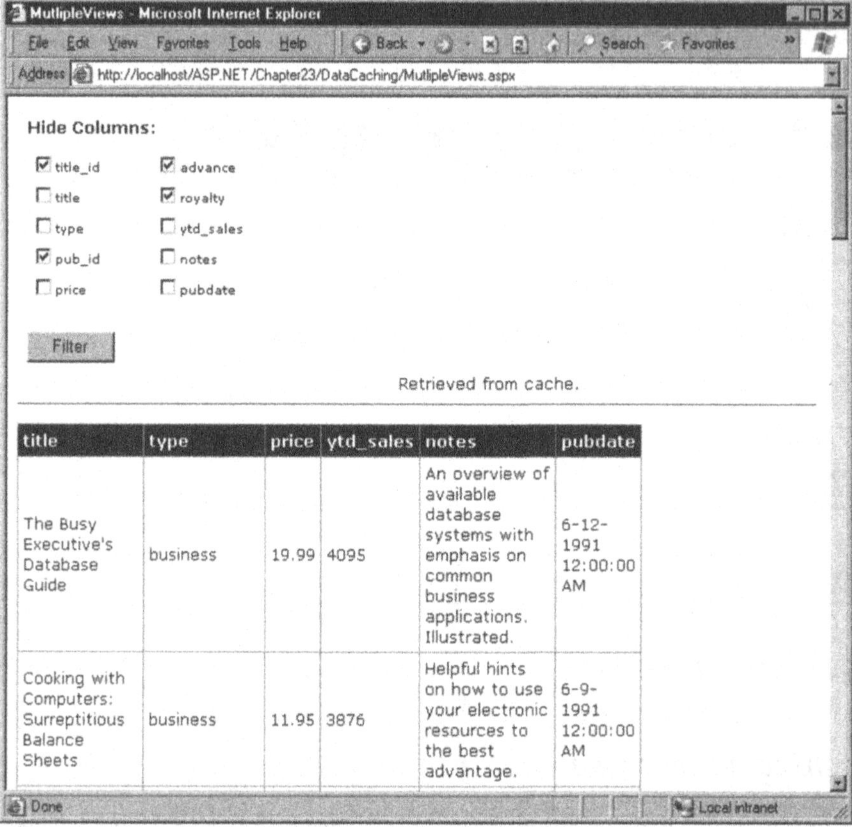

Figure 24-12. Filtering information from a cached DataSet

The DataSet is constructed in the dedicated RetrieveData() function shown here:

```
Private Function RetrieveData() As DataSet
    Dim ConnectionString As String
    ConnectionString = "Provider=SQLOLEDB.1; " & _
      "Data Source=localhost;Initial Catalog=Pubs;Integrated Security=SSPI"

    Dim SQLSelect As String
    SQLSelect = "SELECT * FROM Titles"

    ' Define ADO.NET objects.
    Dim con As New OleDbConnection(ConnectionString)
    Dim cmd As New OleDbCommand(SQLSelect, con)
    Dim adapter As New OleDbDataAdapter(cmd)
    Dim dsPubs As New DataSet()
```

```
    con.Open()
    adapter.Fill(dsPubs, "Titles")
    con.Close()

    Return dsPubs

End Function
```

When the page is first loaded, the check box list of columns is filled:

```
chkColumns.DataSource = dsPubs.Tables(0).Columns
chkColumns.DataMember = "Item"
chkColumns.DataBind()
```

The DataSet is inserted into the cache with a sliding expiration of two minutes when the page is loaded:

```
Cache.Insert("Titles", dsPubs, Nothing, DateTime.MaxValue, _
  TimeSpan.FromMinutes(2))
```

Every time the Filter button is clicked, the page attempts to retrieve the DataSet from the cache. If it cannot retrieve the DataSet, it calls the RetrieveData function and then adds the DataSet to the cache. It then reports on the page whether the DataSet was retrieved from the cache or generated manually.

To provide the configurable grid, the code actually loops through the DataTable, removing all the columns that the user has selected to hide before binding the data. Many other alternatives are possible (another approach is just to hide columns), but this strategy demonstrates an important fact about the cache. When you retrieve an item, you actually retrieve a reference to the cached object. If you modify that object, you're actually modifying the cached item as well. For the page to be able to delete columns without affecting the cached copy of the DataSet, the code needs to create a duplicate copy before performing the operations, using the DataSet.Copy() method.

The full code for the Filter button is shown here:

```
Private Sub cmdFilter_Click(sender As Object, e As EventArgs) _
  Handles cmdFilter.Click

    Dim dsPubs As DataSet
    If Cache("Titles") Is Nothing Then
        dsPubs = RetrieveData()
        Cache.Insert("Titles", dsPubs, Nothing, DateTime.MaxValue, _
                    TimeSpan.FromMinutes(2))
        lblCacheStatus.Text = "Created and added to cache."
    Else
        dsPubs = CType(Cache("Titles"), DataSet)
        dsPubs = dsPubs.Copy()
        lblCacheStatus.Text = "Retrieved from cache."
    End If
```

```
    Dim Item As ListItem
    For Each Item In chkColumns.Items
        If Item.Selected = True Then
            dsPubs.Tables(0).Columns.Remove(Item.Text)
        End If
    Next

    gridPubs.DataSource = dsPubs.Tables(0)
    gridPubs.DataBind()

End Sub
```

Caching with Dependencies

You can also specify that a cache item will expire automatically when another cache item expires or when a file is modified. This logic is referred to as a cache dependency, because your cached item is dependent on another resource, and is only valid while that resource remains unchanged.

To create a cache dependency, you need to create a CacheDependency object, and then use it when adding the dependent cached item. For example, the following code creates a cached item that will automatically be evicted from the cache when an XML file is changed.

```
' Create a dependency for the ProductList.xml file.
Dim ProdDependency As New CacheDependency( _
  Server.MapPath("ProductList.xml"))

' Add a cache item that will be dependent on this file.
Cache.Insert("ProductInfo", ProdInfo, ProdDependency)
```

CacheDependency monitoring begins as soon as the object is created. If the XML file changes before you have added the dependent item to the cache, the item will expire immediately once it's added.

The CacheDependency object provides several different constructors. You've already seen how it can make a dependency based on a file by using the file name constructor. You can also specify a directory that needs to be monitored for changes, or you can use a constructor that accepts an array of strings that represent multiple files and directories.

Yet another constructor accepts an array of file names and an array of cache keys. The following example uses this constructor to create an item that is dependent on another item in the cache.

```
Cache("Key 1") = "Cache Item 1"

' Make Cache("Key 2") dependent on Cache("Key 1").
Dim DependencyKey(0) As String
DependencyKey(0) = "Key 1"
Dim Dependency As New CacheDependency(Nothing, dependencyKey)

Cache.Insert("Key 2", "Cache Item 2", dependency)
```

Now, when Cache("Key 1") changes or is removed from the cache, Cache("Key 2") will automatically be dropped.

Figure 24-13 shows a simple test page that is included with the online samples for this chapter. It sets up a dependency, modifies the file, and allows you to verify that the cache item has been dropped from the cache.

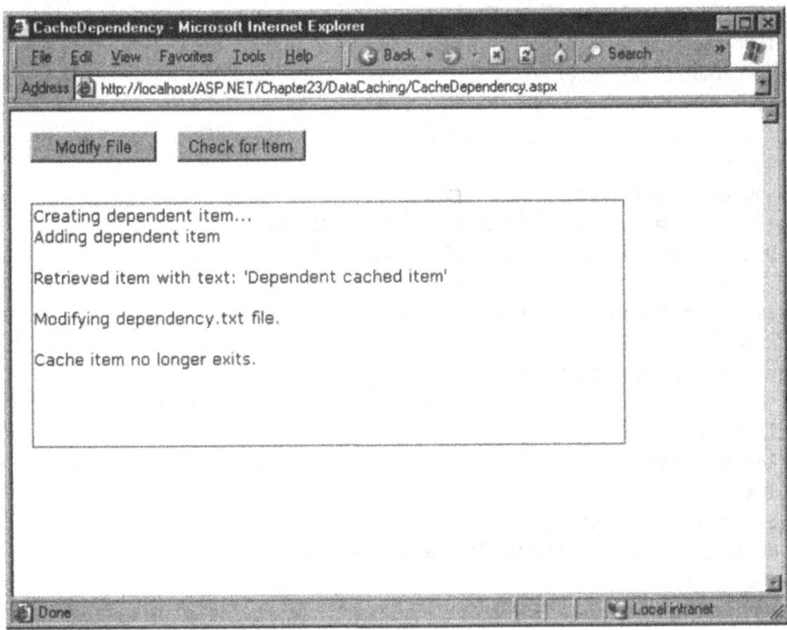

Figure 24-13. Testing cache dependencies

Data Caching in a Web Service

A web service can use data caching just as easily as a web page. In fact, you can store data in a web method and retrieve it in a web page, or vice versa. The only difference is that to access the Cache object in a web service, you need to use the Http-Context.Current.Cache property. It isn't provided as a default property.

The following web service presents a simple example of caching at work. It provides two web methods: GetAuthorData() and GetAuthorNames(). Both of these web methods call the same private GetAuthorDataSet() method, which returns a DataSet with the full customer table. GetAuthorData() returns this DataSet directly, while the GetAuthorNames() retrieves this DataSet, extracts just the author names, and returns it as an array of strings.

```
<WebService()> _
Public Class DataCachingTest
  Inherits System.Web.Services.WebService

    Private ConnectionString As String = "Provider=SQLOLEDB.1;" & _
      "Data Source=localhost;Initial Catalog=Pubs;Integrated Security=SSPI"

    <WebMethod()> _
    Public Function GetAuthorData() As DataSet
        ' Return the full author DataSet (from the cache if possible).
        Return GetAuthorDataSet()
    End Function

    <WebMethod()> _
    Public Function GetAuthorNames() As String()
        ' Get the customer DataSet (from the cache if possible).
        Dim Dt As DataTable = GetAuthorDataSet().Tables(0)

        ' Create an array that will hold the name of each customer.
        Dim Names() As String
        ReDim Names(Dt.Rows.Count - 1)

        ' Fill the array.
        Dim Row As DataRow
        Dim i As Integer
        For Each Row In Dt.Rows
            Names(i) = Row("au_fname") & " " & Row("au_lname")
            i += 1
        Next
        Return Names
    End Function

    Private Function GetAuthorDataSet() As DataSet
        Dim Cache As System.Web.Caching.Cache
        Cache = HttpContext.Current.Cache

        ' Check for cached item.
        Dim ds As DataSet
        ds = CType(Cache("DataSet"), DataSet)ds = Cache("DataSet")
        If ds Is Nothing Then
            ' Recreate the item.
            ds = New DataSet("DataSet")
            Dim con As New OleDbConnection(ConnectionString)
            Dim cmd As New OleDbCommand("SELECT * FROM Authors", con)
            Dim adapter As New OleDbDataAdapter(cmd)
            Try
                con.Open()
                adapter.Fill(ds, "Authors")
            Finally
                con.Close()
            End Try
```

```
            ' Store the item in the cache (for 60 seconds).
            Cache.Insert("DataSet", ds, Nothing, _
              DateTime.Now.AddSeconds(60), TimeSpan.Zero)
        End If
        Return ds
    End Function

End Class
```

The GetCustomerDataSet() method includes all the caching logic. If the DataSet is in the cache, it returns it immediately. Otherwise, it queries the database, creates the DataSet, and inserts it in the cache. The end result is that both web methods can use the same cached data.

The Last Word

The most performance-critical area in most web applications is the data layer. But many ASP.NET developers don't realize that you can dramatically reduce the burden on your database and increase the scalability of all your web applications with just a little caching code. The IBuySpy examples presented in the next chapter use caching broadly and consistently, guaranteeing good performance.

However, with any performance-optimization strategy, the only way to gauge the value of a change is to perform stress testing and profiling. Without this step, you might spend a great deal of time perfecting code that will achieve only a minor improvement in performance or scalability, at the expense of more effective changes.

CHAPTER 25

Implementing Security

BY DEFAULT, your ASP.NET applications are available to any user who can access the Internet. While this is ideal for many web applications (and it suits the original spirit of the Internet), it isn't always appropriate. For example, an e-commerce site needs to provide a secure shopping experience in order to win customers. A subscription-based site needs to limit content or site access in order to extract a fee. Even a wide-open public site may provide some resources or features (such as an administrative report or configuration page) that shouldn't be available to all users.

ASP.NET provides a multilayered security model that makes it easy to protect your web applications. While this security is powerful and profoundly flexible, it can appear somewhat confusing, due in large part to the number of different layers where security can be applied. Most of the work in applying security to your application doesn't come from writing code, but from determining the appropriate places to implement your strategy.

In this chapter, you'll sort out the different security subsystems, and consider how you can use Windows, IIS, and ASP.NET services to protect your application. You'll also look at some custom examples that use ASP.NET's new forms-based security, which provides a quick and easy model for adding a user login page.

Determining Security Requirements

Over the past few years, security has become one of the hottest buzzwords in application design. Media reports constantly emerge about nefarious hackers lifting mailing lists or credit card numbers from e-commerce sites. In most cases, these break-ins are not due to computer wizardry, but to simple carelessness or the lack of a security policy.

The first step in securing your applications is deciding where you need security, and what it needs to protect. For example, you may need to block access in order to protect private information or maybe just to enforce a subscription policy. Perhaps you don't need any sort of security at all, but you want a login system to provide personalization for frequent visitors. These requirements will determine the approach you use.

Security doesn't need to be complex, but it does need to be wide-ranging. For example, even if you force users to log in to a part of your site, you still need to make sure that the information is stored in the database under a secure account with a password that couldn't easily be guessed by a user on your local network. You also need to guarantee that your application can't be tricked into sending private information (a possibility if the user modifies a page or a query string to post back different information than you expect).

Restricted File Types

ASP.NET automatically provides a basic level of security by blocking requests for certain file types (such as configuration and source code files). These file types are identified in the web server's machine.config file in the framework configuration directory (typically C:\[WindowsDir]\Microsoft.NET\Framework\[version]\Config), and are assigned to the special HttpForbiddenHandler.

```
<add verb="*" path="*.asax" type="System.Web.HttpForbiddenHandler" />
<add verb="*" path="*.ascx" type="System.Web.HttpForbiddenHandler" />
<add verb="*" path="*.config" type="System.Web.HttpForbiddenHandler" />
<add verb="*" path="*.cs" type="System.Web.HttpForbiddenHandler" />
<add verb="*" path="*.csproj" type="System.Web.HttpForbiddenHandler" />
<add verb="*" path="*.vb" type="System.Web.HttpForbiddenHandler" />
<add verb="*" path="*.vbproj" type="System.Web.HttpForbiddenHandler" />
<add verb="*" path="*.webinfo" type="System.Web.HttpForbiddenHandler" />
<add verb="*" path="*.asp" type="System.Web.HttpForbiddenHandler" />
<add verb="*" path="*.licx" type="System.Web.HttpForbiddenHandler" />
<add verb="*" path="*.resx" type="System.Web.HttpForbiddenHandler" />
<add verb="*" path="*.resources" type="System.Web.HttpForbiddenHandler" />
```

Security Concepts

There are three concepts that form the basis of any discussion about security:

- **Authentication.** This is the process of determining a user's identity and forcing users to prove they are who they claim to be. Usually, this involves entering credentials (typically a user name and password) into some sort of login page or window. These credentials are then authenticated against the Windows user accounts on the computer, a list of users in a file, or a back-end database.

- **Authorization.** Once a user is authenticated, authorization is the process of determining if that user has sufficient permissions to perform a given action (such as viewing a page or retrieving information from a database). Windows imposes some authorization checks (for example, when you open a file), but your code will probably want to impose its own checks (for example, when a user performs a task in your web application like submitting an order, assigning a project, or giving a promotion).

- **Impersonation.** In ASP.NET, all code runs under a fixed account defined in the machine.config file. Impersonation allows a portion of your code to run under a different identity, with a different set of Windows permissions.

The ASP.NET Security Model

As you've seen in previous chapters, web requests are fielded first by IIS, which then passes the request on to ASP.NET if the file type is registered with the ASP.NET service. Figure 25-1 shows how these levels interact.

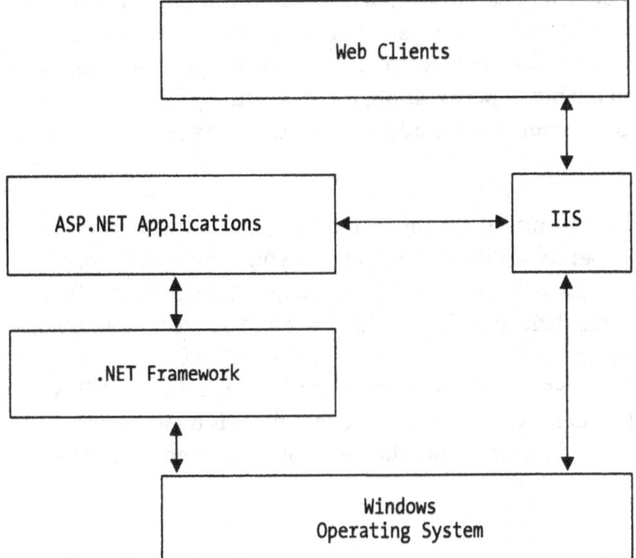

Figure 25-1. IIS and ASP.NET interaction

Security can be applied at several different places in this chain. First, consider the process for an ordinary (non-ASP.NET) web page request:

1. IIS attempts to authenticate the user. Generally, IIS allows requests from all anonymous users and automatically logs them in under the IUSR_[ServerName] account. IIS security settings are configured on a per-directory basis.

2. If IIS authenticates the user successfully, it attempts to send the user the appropriate HTML file. The operating system performs its own security checks to verify that the authenticated user (typically IUSR_[ServerName]) is allowed access to the specified file and directory.

The first and last steps are similar for an ASP.NET request, but there are several additional intermediary layers:

1. IIS attempts to authenticate the user. Generally, IIS allows requests from all anonymous users and automatically logs them in under the IUSR_[ServerName] account.

2. If IIS authenticates the user successfully, it passes the request to ASP.NET with additional information about the authenticated user. ASP.NET can then use its own security services, depending on the settings in the web.config file and the page that was requested.

3. If ASP.NET authenticates the user, it allows requests to the .aspx page or .asmx web service. Your code can perform additional custom security checks (for example, manually asking for another password before allowing a specific operation).

4. When the ASP.NET code requests resources (for example, tries to open a file or connect to a database) the operating system performs its own security checks. All ASP.NET code runs under a fixed account that's defined in the machine.config file. However, if you enable impersonation, these system operations will be performed under the account of the authenticated user (or a different account you specify).

One very important and easily missed concept is the fact that the ASP.NET code doesn't run under the IUSR_[ServerName] account, even if you're using anonymous user access. The reason is that the IUSR_[ServerName] account doesn't have sufficient privileges for ASP.NET code, which needs to be able to create and delete temporary files in order to manage the compilation process. Instead, the ASP.NET account is set through the machine.config file, as described in Chapter 2. When designing ASP.NET pages, you must keep this fact in mind, and make sure that there is no way your program could be used to make dangerous modifications or delete important files.

Security Strategies

There are a number of different ways that the IIS and ASP.NET security settings can interact, and these combinations often give new ASP.NET developers endless headaches. In reality, there are two central strategies that can be used to add ASP.NET security or personalization to a site.

- Allow anonymous users, but use ASP.NET's forms authentication model to secure parts of your site. This allows you to create a subscription site or e-commerce store, allows you to manage the login process easily, and lets you write your own login code for authenticating users against a database or simple user account list.
- Forbid anonymous users, and use IIS authentication to force every user to log in using Basic, Digest, or Integrated Windows authentication. This system requires that every user has a Windows user account on the server (although users could share accounts). This scenario is poorly suited for a public web application, but often ideal with an intranet or company-specific site designed to provide resources for a limited set of users. This approach can also be used to secure web services.

You'll concentrate on these two approaches in this chapter.

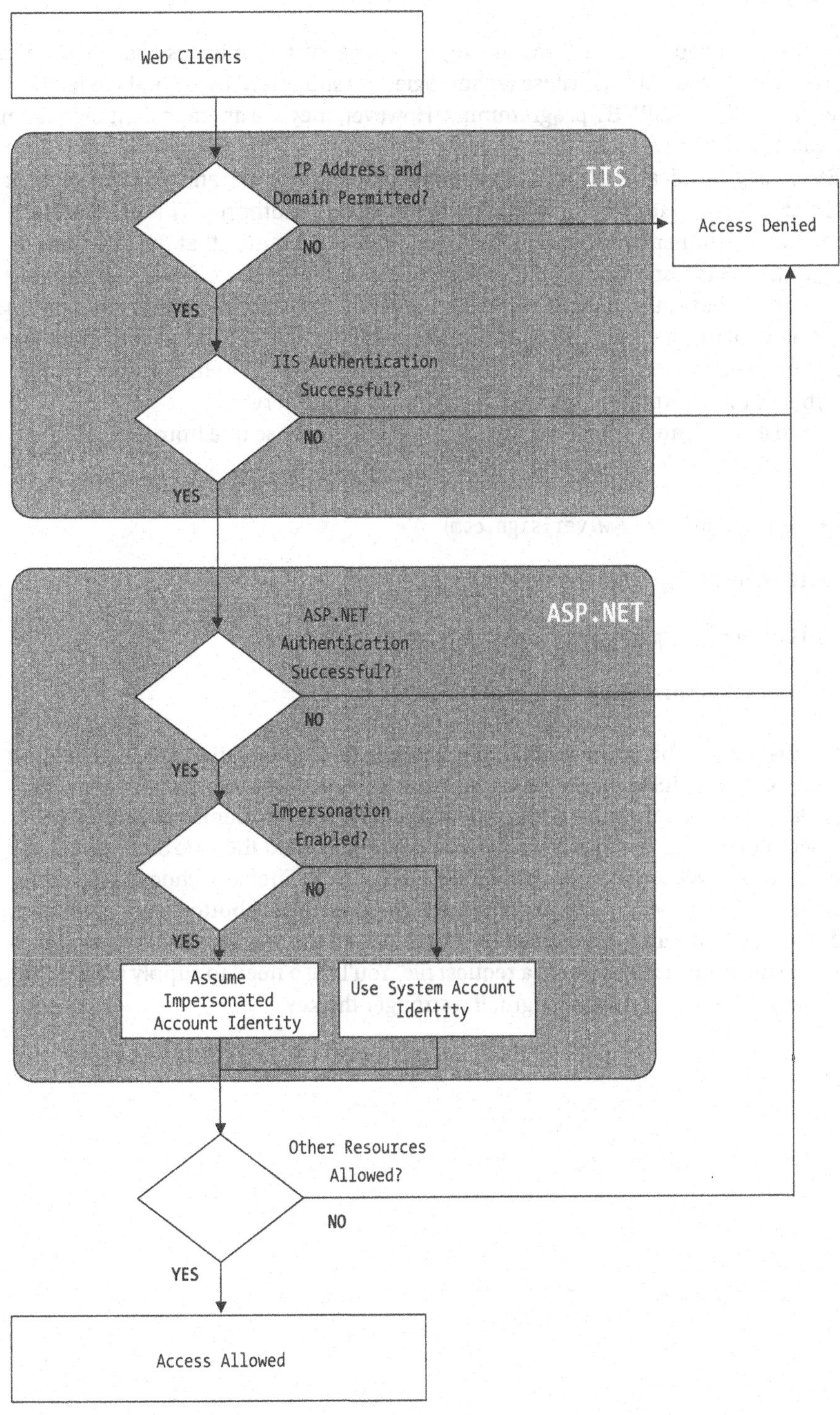

Figure 25-2. Authenticating a request

Certificates

One topic this chapter doesn't treat in detail is user server certificates and SSL (Secure Sockets Layer) connections. These technologies are supported by IIS and are really independent from ASP.NET programming. However, they are an important ingredient in creating a secure website.

Essentially, certificates allow you to demonstrate that your site and your organization information are registered and verified with a certificate authority. This generally encourages customer confidence, although it doesn't guarantee that the company or organization acts responsibly or fairly. A certificate is a little like a driver's license—it doesn't prove that you can drive, but it demonstrates that a third-party (in this case, a department of the government) is willing to attest to your identity and your qualifications. Your web server requires a certificate in order to use SSL, which automatically encrypts all the information sent between the client and server.

To add a certificate to your site, you first need to purchase one from a certificate authority. Some well-known certificate authorities include the following:

- Verisign (`http://www.verisign.com`)
- GeoTrust (`http://www.geotrust.com`)
- GloalSign (`http://www.globalsign.com`)
- Thawte (`http://www.tawte.com`)

The first step in this process of getting a certificate is to e-mail a certificate request for your web server. IIS Manager allows you to create a certificate request automatically. First, start IIS Manager (select Settings ➤ Control Panel ➤ Administrative Tools ➤ Internet Information Services from the Start menu). Expand the Web Sites group, and right-click your web site item (usually titled Default Web Site) and choose Properties. Under the Directory Security tab, you'll find a Server Certificate button (see Figure 25-3). Click this button to start a Web Server Certificate Wizard that requests some basic organization information and generates a request file. You'll also need to supply a bit length for the key—the higher the bit length, the stronger the key.

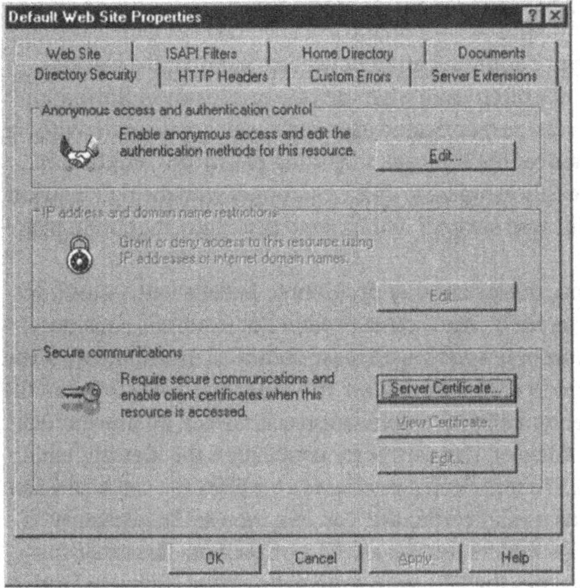

Figure 25-3. Directory security settings

The generated file can be saved as a text file, but it must ultimately be e-mailed to a certificate authority (along with the required fee). A sample (slightly abbreviated) request file is shown here.

```
Webmaster: administrator@certificatecompany.com
Phone: (555) 555-5555
Server: Microsoft Key Manager for IIS Version 4.0

Common-name: www.yourcompany.com
Organization: YourOrganization

-----BEGIN NEW CERTIFICATE REQUEST-----
MIIB1DCCAToCAQAwgZMxCzAJBgNVBAYTAlVTMREwDwYDVQQIEwhOZXcgWW9yazEQ
MA4GA1UEBxMHQnVmZmFsbzEeMBwGA1UEChMVVW5pdmVyc2l0eSBhdCBCdWZmYWxv
MRwwGgYDVQQLExNSZXNlYXJjaCBGb3VuZGF0aW9uMSEwHwYDVQQDExh3d3cucmVz
ZWFyY2guYnVmZmFsby5lZHUwgZ8wDQYJKoZIhvcNAQEBBQADgYOAMIGJAoGBALJO
hbsCagHN4KMbl7uzOGwvcjJeWH8JqIUFVFi352tnoA15PZfCxW18KNtFeBtrbOpf
-----END NEW CERTIFICATE REQUEST-----
```

The certificate authority will return a certificate that you can install according to their instructions.

Secure Sockets Layer

SSL technology is used to encrypt communication between a client and a website. Although it slows performance, it's often used when private or sensitive information needs to be transmitted between an authenticated user and a web application. Without SSL, any information that's sent over the Internet, including passwords, credit card numbers, and employee lists, is easily viewable to an eavesdropper with the right network equipment. This is also true with web services, which send their information in plain-text SOAP messages.

Even with the best encryption, there's another problem to wrestle with—just how can a client be sure that a web server is who it claims to be? For example, consider a clever attacker that uses some sort of IP spoofing to masquerade as Amazon.com. Even if you use SSL to transfer your credit card information, the malicious web server on the other end will still be able to decrypt all your information seamlessly. To prevent this type of deception, SSL uses certificates. The certificate establishes the identity, while SSL protects the communication. If a malicious user abuses a certificate, it can be revoked.

To use SSL, you need to install a valid certificate. You can then set IIS directory settings specifying that individual folders require an SSL connection. To access this page over SSL, the client simply types the URL with a preceding https instead of http at the beginning of the request.

In your ASP.NET code, you can check if a user is connecting over a secure connection using code like this:

```
Private Sub Page_Load(sender As Object, e As EventArgs) _
  Handles MyBase.Load

    If Request.IsSecureConnection = True Then
        lblStatus.Text = "This page is running under SSL."
    Else
        lblStatus.Text = "This page isn't secure."
        lblStatus.Text &= "<br>Please request it with the "
        lblStatus.Text &= "prefix https:// instead of http://"
    End If

End Sub
```

Figure 25-4 shows the page that you'll see in the browser when connecting over a normal connection.

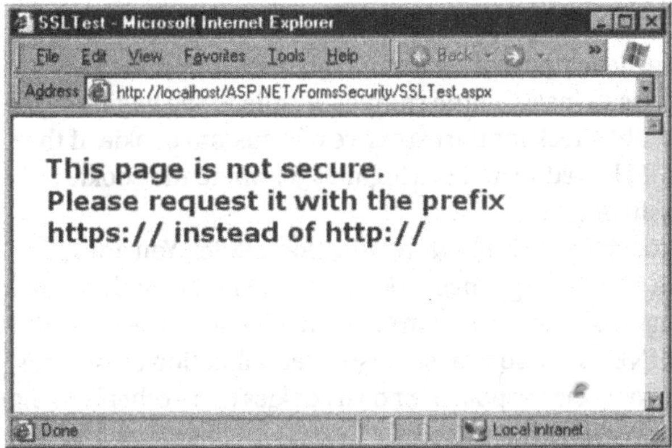

Figure 25-4. Testing for an SSL connection

How Does SSL Work?

With SSL, the client and web server start a secure session before they communicate any information. This secure session uses a randomly generated encryption key. Here's how the process works:

1. The client requests an SSL connection.
2. The server signs its digital certificate and sends it to the client.
3. The client verifies that the certificate was issued by a CA it trusts, matches the web server it wants to communicate with, and has not expired or been revoked. If the certificate is valid, the client continues to the next step.
4. The client tells the server what encryption key sizes it supports.
5. The server chooses the strongest key length that is supported by both the client and server. It then informs the client what size this is.
6. The client generates a session key (a random string of bytes). It encrypts this session key using the server's public key (which was provided through the server's digital certificate). It then sends this encrypted package it to the server.
7. The server decrypts the session key using its private key. Both the client and server now have the same random session key, which they can use to encrypt communication for the duration of the session.

Forms Authentication

In traditional ASP programming, developers often had to create their own security systems. A common approach was to insert a little snippet of code to the beginning of every secure page. This code would check for the existence of a custom cookie. If the cookie didn't exist, the user would be redirected to a login page, where the cookie would be created after a successful login.

ASP.NET uses the same approach in its forms authentication model. You are still responsible for writing the code for your login page. However, you no longer have to create or check for the cookie manually, and you don't need to add any code to secure pages. You also benefit from ASP.NET's support for sophisticated validation algorithms, which make it all but impossible for users to spoof their own cookies or try other hacking tricks to fool your application into giving them access.

Figure 25-5 shows a simplified security diagram of the forms authentication model in ASP.NET.

To implement forms-based security, you need to follow three steps:

1. Set the authentication mode in the web.config file.
2. Restrict anonymous users from a specific page or directory in your application.
3. Create the login page.

Web.config Settings

The type of security used by ASP.NET is defined in the web.config file, through three tags: <authentication>, <authorization>, and <identity>. For a quick reference of these sections and their settings, you can refer to Chapter 29.

The <authentication> tag defines the ASP.NET authentication mode that will be used to validate the user. In the following listing, the application is configured to use ASP.NET's forms authentication model. In addition, a <forms> subtag defines some additional settings required for this mode. Namely, it sets the name of the security cookie, the length of time it will be considered valid, and the page that will be used for user login.

```
<configuration>
    <system.web>
        <!-- Other settings omitted. -->
        <authentication mode="Forms">
            <forms name="MyAppCookie"
                   loginUrl="Login.aspx"
                   protection="All"
                   timeout="30" path="/" />
        </authentication>
    </system.web>
</configuration>
```

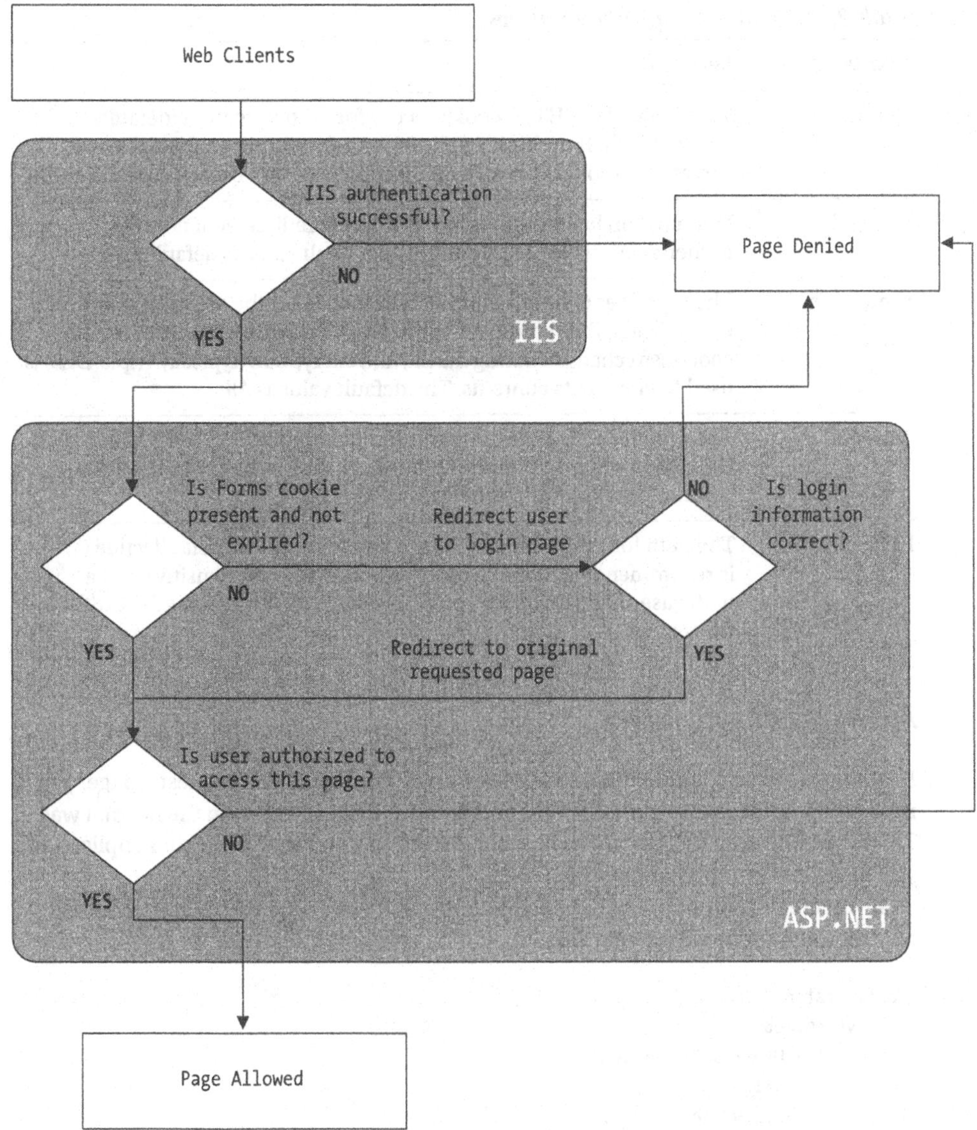

Figure 25-5. ASP.NET forms authentication

The settings are described briefly in Table 25-1. They all supply default values and do not need to be set explicitly.

Table 25-1. Form Authentication Settings

Attribute	Description
Name	The name of the HTTP cookie to use for authentication (defaults to .ASPXAUTH). If multiple applications are running on the same web server, you should give each application's security cookie a unique name.
loginUrl	Your custom login page, where the user is redirected if no valid authentication cookie is found. The default value is default.aspx.
protection	The type of encryption and validation used for the security cookie (can be All, None, Encryption, or Validation). Validation ensures that the cookie isn't changed during transit, and encryption (typically Triple-DES) is used to encode its contents. The default value is All.
Timeout	The number of minutes before the cookie expires. ASP.NET will refresh the cookie when it receives a request, as long as half of the cookie's lifetime has expired. The default value is 30.
Path	The path for cookies issued by the application. The default value (\) is recommended, because most browsers are case-sensitive and a path case-mismatch could prevent the cookie from being sent with the request.

Authorization Rules

If you make these changes to an application's web.config file and request a page, you'll notice that nothing unusual happens, and the web page is served in the normal way. This is because even though you have enabled forms authentication for your application, you have not restricted anonymous users.

If you created your project in Visual Studio .NET, you'll find the following access control rule in your web.config file.

```
<configuration>
    <system.web>
        <!-- Other settings omitted. -->
        <authorization>
            <allow users="*" />
        </authorization>
    </system.web>
</configuration>
```

The asterisk (*) is a wildcard character that explicitly permits all users to use the application, even those that haven't been authenticated. Even if you delete this line from your application's web.config file, you won't see any change, because the default settings inherited from the machine.config file allow all users. In order to change this behavior, you need to explicitly override the web.config permissions, as shown here.

```
<configuration>
    <system.web>
        <!-- Other settings omitted. -->
        <authorization>
            <deny users="?" />
        </authorization>
    </system.web>
</configuration>
```

The question mark (?) is a wildcard character that includes all anonymous users. By including this rule in your web.config file, you specify that anonymous users are not allowed. Every user must be authenticated, and every user request will require the security cookie. If you request a page in the application directory now, ASP.NET will detect that the request isn't authenticated, and attempt to redirect the request to the login page (which will probably cause an error, unless you've already created this file).

Now consider what happens if you add more than one rule in the authorization section:

```
<authorization>
    <allow users="*" />
    <deny users="?" />
</authorization>
```

When evaluating rules, ASP.NET scans through the list from top to bottom, and then continues with the settings in any .config file inherited from a parent directory, ending with the settings in the base machine.config file. As soon as it finds an applicable rule, it stops its search. Thus, in the previous case, it will determine that the rule <allow users="*"> applies to the current request, and will not evaluate the second line. That means these rules will allow all users, including anonymous users. Reversing the order of these two lines, however, will deny anonymous users (by matching the first rule) and allow all other users (by matching the second rule).

```
<authorization>
    <deny users="?" />
    <allow users="*" />
</authorization>
```

Remember, if the second line is omitted, ASP.NET will search the parent directory, and will ultimately match the <allow users="*"> rule in the machine.config file for all nonanonymous users.

Controlling Access to Specific Directories

A common application design is to place files that require authentication into a separate directory. With ASP.NET configuration files, this approach is easy. Just leave the default <authorization> settings in the normal parent directory, and add a web.config file that specifies stricter settings in the secured directory. This web.config simply needs to deny anonymous users (all other settings and configuration sections can be left out).

```
<configuration>
    <system.web>
        <authorization>
            <deny users="?" />
        </authorization>
    </system.web>
</configuration>
```

NOTE You cannot change the <authentication> tag settings in the web.config file of a subdirectory in your application. Instead, all the directories in the application must use the same authentication system. However, each directory can have its own authorization rules.

Controlling Access to Specific Files

Generally, setting file access permissions by directory is the cleanest and easiest approach. However, you also have the option of restricting specific files by adding <location> tags to your web.config file. This is the technique used in Microsoft's IBuySpy store case study.

The location tags sit outside of the main <system.web> tag and are nested directly in the base <configuration> tag, as shown here.

```
<configuration>
    <system.web>
        <!-- Other settings omitted. -->
        <authorization>
            <allow users="*" />
        </authorization>
    </system.web>

    <location path="SecuredPage.aspx">
        <system.web>
            <authorization>
                <deny users="?" />
            </authorization>
        </system.web>
    </location>

    <location path="AnotherSecuredPage.aspx">
        <system.web>
            <authorization>
                <deny users="?" />
            </authorization>
        </system.web>
    </location>

</configuration>
```

In this example, all files in the application are allowed, except SecuredPage.aspx and AnotherSecuredPage.aspx, which have an additional access rule denying anonymous users.

Controlling Access for Specific Users

The <allow> and <deny> rules don't need to use the asterisk or question mark wildcards. Instead, they can specifically identify a user name or a list of comma-separated user names. For example, the following list specifically restricts access from three users. These users will not be able to access the pages in this directory. All other authenticated users will be allowed.

```
<authorization>
    <deny users="matthew,sarah" />
    <deny users="john" />
    <allow users="*" />
</authorization>
```

The following rules explicitly allow two users. All other user requests will be denied access, even if they are authenticated.

```
<authorization>
    <allow users="matthew,sarah" />
    <deny users="*" />
</authorization>
```

TIP As you'll see in the next section, the user names are assigned by your application. They might correspond to a name or ID in a database. They won't correspond to a Windows user account.

The Login Page

Once you've specified the authentication mode and the authorization rules, you need to build the actual login page, which is an ordinary .aspx page that requests information from the user and decides whether the user should be authenticated.

ASP.NET provides a special FormsAuthentication class in the System.Web.Security namespace, which provides shared methods that help manage the process. The most important methods of this class are described in Table 25-2.

Table 25-2. Members of the FormsAuthentication Class

Method	Description
FormsCookieName	A read-only property that provides the name of the Forms authentication cookie.
FormsCookiePath	A read-only property that provides the path set for the Forms authentication cookie.
Authenticate()	Checks a user name and password against a list of accounts that can be entered in the web.config file.
RedirectFromLoginPage()	Logs the user in to an ASP.NET application by creating the cookie, attaching it to the current response, and redirecting the user to the page that was originally requested.
SignOut()	Logs the user out of the ASP.NET application by removing the current encrypted cookie.
SetAuthCookie()	Logs the user in to an ASP.NET application by creating and attaching the Forms authentication cookie. Unlike the RedirectFromLoginPage() method, it doesn't forward the user back to the initially requested page.
GetRedirectUrl()	Provides the URL of the originally requested page. You could use this with SetAuthCookie() to log a user into an application and make a decision in your code whether to redirect to the requested page or use a more suitable default page.
GetAuthCookie()	Creates the authentication cookie but doesn't attach it to the current response. You can perform additional cookie customization, and then add it manually to the response, as described in Chapter 10.
HashPasswordForStoringInConfigFile()	Encrypts a string of text using the specified algorithm (SHA1 or MD5). This hashed value provides a secure way to store an encrypted password in a file or database.

A simple login page can put these methods to work with very little code. For example, consider the Login.aspx page in Figure 25-6.

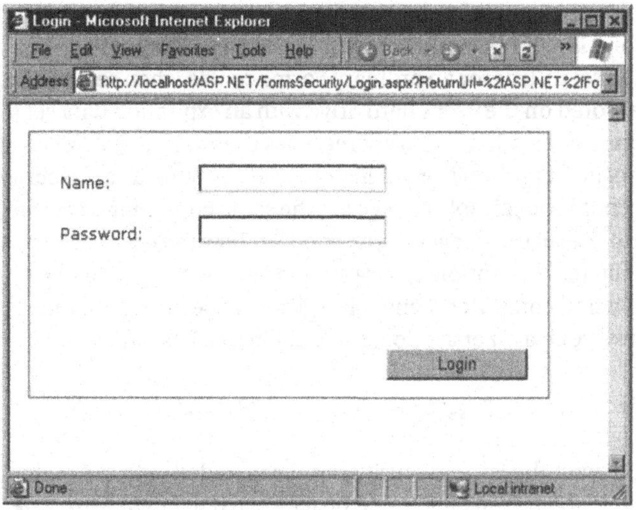

Figure 25-6. A typical login page

This page checks if the user has typed in the password "Secret" and then uses the RedirectFromLoginPage() method to log the user in. Here's the complete page code:

```
Imports System.Web.Security

Public Class Login
  Inherits Page

    Protected txtName As TextBox
    Protected txtPassword As TextBox
    Protected lblStatus As Label
    Protected WithEvents cmdLogin As Button

    Private Sub cmdLogin_Click(sender As Object, e As EventArgs) _
      Handles cmdLogin.Click
        If txtPassword.Text.ToLower() = "secret" Then
            FormsAuthentication.RedirectFromLoginPage( _
              txtName.Text, False)
        Else
            lblStatus.Text = "Try again."
        End If
    End Sub

End Class
```

The RedirectFromLoginPage() method requires two parameters. The first sets the name of the user. The second is a Boolean variable that creates a persistent Forms authentication cookie when set to True, or an ordinary Forms cookie when set to False. A persistent cookie will be stored on the user's hard drive with an expiration data set to 50 years in the future. This is a convenience that's sometimes useful when you're using the Forms authentication login for personalization instead of security. It's also a security risk because another user could conceivably log in from the same computer, acquiring the cookie and the access to the secured pages. If you want to allow the user to create a persistent cookie, you should make it optional, because the user may want to access your site from a public or shared computer. Generally, sites that use this technique include a check box with text such as "Persist Cookie" or "Keep Me Logged In."

```
FormsAuthentication.RedirectFromLoginPage(txtName.Text, chkPersist.Checked)
```

You can test this example with the FormsSecurity sample included with the online code. If you request the SecuredPage.aspx file, you'll be redirected to Login.aspx. After entering the correct password, you'll return to SecuredPage.aspx. As the user is logged in, you can retrieve the identity through the built-in User object, as shown in Figure 25-7.

```
Private Sub Page_Load(sender As Object, e As EventArgs) _
  Handles MyBase.Load

    lblMessage.Text = "You have reached the secured page, "
    lblMessage.Text &= User.Identity.Name & "."

End Sub
```

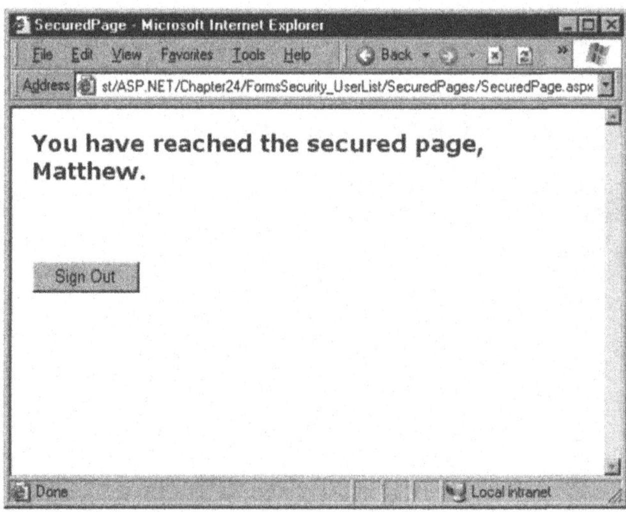

Figure 25-7. Accessing a secured page

Your application should also feature a prominent logout button that destroys the Forms authentication cookie.

```
Private Sub cmdSignOut_Click(sender As Object, e As EventArgs) _
  Handles cmdSignOut.Click

    FormsAuthentication.SignOut()
    Response.Redirect("..\login.aspx")

End Sub
```

User Lists

The sample login page uses a password that's hard-coded in the page code. This is an awkward approach that isn't suitable for most applications. Typically, the code that responds to the Click event of the Login button would look for a user name and password match in a database table (using trivial ADO.NET data access code). Here's an example:

```
Dim ConnectionString As String = "Provider=SQLOLEDB.1;" & _
  "Data Source=localhost;Initial Catalog=pubs;" & _
  "Integrated Security=SSPI"

Dim SQLSelect As String
SQLSelect = "SELECT Name, Password FROM Users Where Name='"
SQLSelect &= txtUser.Name & "' AND Password='"
SQLSelect &= txtPassword.Text & "'"

' Define the ADO.NET objects.
Dim con As New OleDbConnection(ConnectionString)
Dim cmd As New OleDbCommand(SQLSelect, con)
Dim reader As OleDbDataReader

' Try to open database and read information.
Try
    con.Open()
    reader = cmd.ExecuteReader()
    reader.Read()

    ' Verify the returned row for a case-sensitive match.
    If txtPassword.Text = reader("Password") Then
        FormsAuthentication.RedirectFromLoginPage( _
          txtName.Text, False)
    Else
        lblStatus.Text = "No match."
    End If
    reader.Close()
```

```
Catch err As Exception
    lblStatus.Text = "No match."
Finally
    If (Not con Nothing) Then
        con.Close()
    End If
End Try
```

Other approaches are possible. For example, you could use the file or XML access techniques described in Chapters 17 and 18. You could even cache user login information in memory.

ASP.NET also provides a quick and convenient method for storing user account information directly in the web.config file. The disadvantage of this system is that you can't store additional user information (such as a credit card number or shipping address). An advantage is the fact that you can use the Authenticate() method of the FormsAuthentication password to check the supplied user information against the list, without needing to write your own file or database access code. To add a user account, insert a <credentials> subtag to the <forms> tag, and add as many <user> subtags as you need inside the <credentials> tag.

The following example defines two valid users.

```
<configuration>
    <system.web>
        <!-- Other settings omitted. -->
        <authentication mode="Forms">
            <forms name="MyAppCookie"
                   loginUrl="Login.aspx"
                   protection="All"
                   timeout="30" path="/" >
                <credentials passwordFormat="Clear" >
                    <user name="matthew" password="secret" />
                    <user name="sarah" password="opensesame" />
                </credentials>
            </forms>
        </authentication>
    </system.web>
</configuration>
```

Now the login page can use the FormsAuthentication.Authenticate() method, which accepts a user name and password, and returns true if a match can be found in the web.config user list. Note that the password is case-sensitive, but the user name isn't.

```
If FormsAuthentication.Authenticate(txtName.Text, txtPassword.Text) Then
    FormsAuthentication.RedirectFromLoginPage(txtName.Text, False)
Else
    lblStatus.Text = "Try again."
End If
```

Protecting User Passwords with Encryption

In the previous user list example, passwords were stored in a clear format that's visible to anyone who reads the web.config file. This isn't necessarily a serious security risk—remember, web requests for .config files are automatically rejected—but it does expose a potential vulnerability, especially if the server is accessible over a local network. To remedy this problem, you can replace the password in the web.config file with a special hash value. The hash value is a series of bytes that's based on the password, but can't be used to determine the original password (at least not without computation effort that's comparable to brute-force decryption). To authenticate the user, you take the submitted password, and call the Authenticate() method. ASP.NET will then hash the submitted password, and compare it to the hashed value that's stored in the web.config file.

To add the hashed password to the web.config file, you need to create a simple utility page that can encrypt a text string for you. This is trivially easy, thanks to the HashPaswordForStoringInConfigFile() method, which is also provided by the FormsAuthentication class. The page in Figure 25-8 shows an example that encodes the supplied text and places it in another text box so it can be easily copied to the clipboard. Both SHA1 and MD5 algorithms are supported.

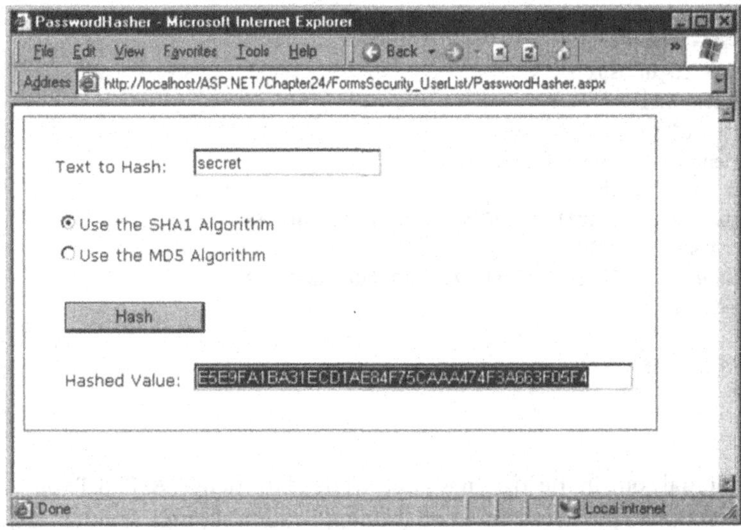

Figure 25-8. Getting the hash value for a password

```
Private Sub cmdHash_Click(sender As Object, e As EventArgs) _
  Handles cmdHash.Click

    Dim Algorithm As String

    If optSHA1.Checked = True Then
        Algorithm = "SHA1"
    Else
        Algorithm = "MD5"
    End If

    txtHash.Text = FormsAuthentication.HashPasswordForStoringInConfigFile(_
                   txtPassword.Text, Algorithm)

End Sub
```

You can now update the web.config file with the hashed values by modifying the passwordFormat attribute of the <credentials> tag.

```
<configuration>
    <system.web>
        <!-- Other settings omitted. -->
        <authentication mode="Forms">
        <forms name="MyAppCookie"
          loginUrl="Login.aspx"
          protection="All"
          timeout="30" path="/" >
            <credentials passwordFormat="SHA1" >
            <user name="matthew"
             password="E5E9FA1BA31ECD1AE84F75CAAA474F3A663F05F4" />
            <user name="sarah"
             password="17618F01A3A21B911C925BCB525A1D21ABD30673" />
            </credentials>
        </forms>
        </authentication>
    </system.web>
</configuration>
```

Note that the actual code in the login page doesn't need to change. ASP.NET will know to hash the supplied password based on your application settings. Incidentally, while the HashPaswordForStoringInConfigFile() is designed for use with user lists in the web.config file, you could also use it when storing user account information in a database. The only difference is that your login page would not use the Authenticate method. Instead, it would call the HashPaswordForStoringInConfigFile() method on the user-supplied password, and compare that to the field in the database.

NOTE You can use various other methods to encrypt passwords for storage in a database or file using the classes provided with .NET. Start by examining the MSDN reference for the System.Security.Cryptography namespace. And keep in mind that no matter what approach you use, you still need to think about encrypting the password information that's sent over the network to hide it from Internet eavesdroppers. As described earlier, the only way to do that is with SSL.

Custom Roles

The authentication strategy you've examined so far provides an all-or-nothing approach that either forbids or allows a user. In many cases, however, an application needs to recognize different levels of users. Some users will be provided with a limited set of capabilities, while other users might be allowed to perform potentially dangerous changes or use the administrative portions of a website.

To allow this type of multitiered access, your code needs to examine the current user identity, and use that information to forbid or allow specific actions. By default, the generic User.Identity object doesn't provide much that can help. Its properties are listed in Table 25-3.

Table 25-3. Identity Properties

Property	Description
Name	The name of the signed-on user (technically, the user name of the account).
IsAuthenticated	True if the user has been authenticated. You could check this property and decide programmatically whether you need to redirect the user to the login page. Note that if the user isn't logged in, the other properties (such as Name) will be empty.
AuthenticationType	A string that represents the type of authentication that was used (such as Forms or Basic).

The User object also provides a method called IsInRole(), which is designed to let you evaluate whether a user is a member of a group. For example, a user who is a member of an Administrators group can be given more access rights.

```
Private Sub Page_Load(sender As Object, e As EventArgs) _
  Handles MyBase.Load

    If User.IsInRole("Administrators")
        ' Do nothing, the page should be accessed as normal because the
        ' user has administrator privileges.
    Else
        ' Don't allow this page. Instead, redirect to the home page.
        Response.Redirect("default.aspx")
    End If

End Sub
```

Unfortunately, with forms authentication there is no way to associate a user account with a role declaratively in the web.config file. However, you can react to the Application_Authenticate event in the global.asax file (which fires when the user logs in) and assign roles to the current user. The process works like this:

- Check if the user is authenticated. The Application_Authenticate event happens several times during request processing. If the user isn't yet authenticated, you can't take any action.
- If the user is authenticated, decide programmatically what role they should have. For example, you might look up the user's name in a database or XML file, and retrieve a list of roles. In your simple example, the logic is hard-coded in the routine.
- Create a new identity using the GenericPrincipal class. You do this by supplying the current (authenticated) identity and adding the appropriate roles as an array of strings.
- Assign the new identity to the user.

The following global.asax code shows this process in action. In order to use it as written, you must have imported the System.Security.Principal namespace.

```
Sub Application_AuthenticateRequest(sender As Object, e As EventArgs)
    If Request.IsAuthenticated Then

        ' Check who the user is.
        If User.Identity.Name.ToLower() = "matthew" Then

            ' Create an array with the names of the appropriate
            ' roles. In our simple example, matthew is an
            ' Administrator and User.
            ' Typically, this information would be retrieved from
            ' another source (like a database).
            Dim Roles() As String = {"Administrator", "User"}
```

```
            ' Assign the new identity.
            ' It's the old identity, with the roles added.
            Context.User = New GenericPrincipal(User.Identity, Roles)
        End If

    End If
End Sub
```

One detail is extremely important in this example. To retrieve the identity, you can use the User property of the Application class (as this example does), or you can use the Context.User property, which is equivalent. However, when assigning the new identity, you need to use the Context.User property. That's because the User property of the Application class is always read-only.

Once you've assigned a role, you can test for it in another page with the User.IsInRole() method, as shown here:

```
Private Sub Page_Load(sender As Object, e As EventArgs) _
  Handles MyBase.Load

    lblMessage.Text = "You have reached the secured page, "
    lblMessage.Text &= User.Identity.Name & "."
    If User.IsInRole("Administrator") Then
        lblMessage.Text &= "<br><br>Congratulations:"
        lblMessage.Text &= "you are an administrator."
    End If

End Sub
```

The result is shown in Figure 25-9.

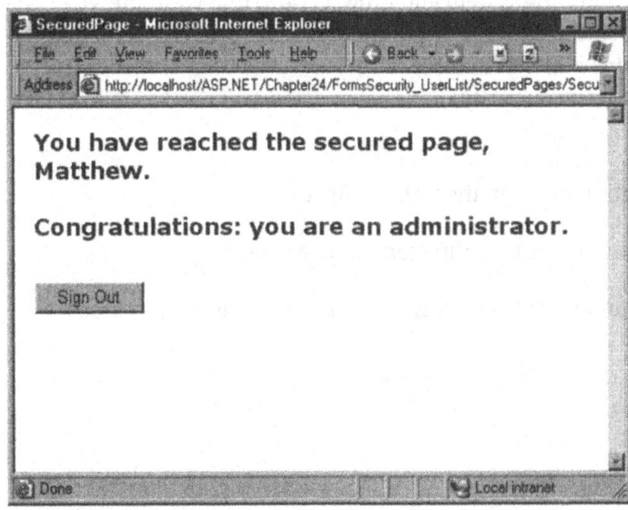

Figure 25-9. Testing role-based security

Passport Authentication Is Another Option

This chapter doesn't cover ASP.NET's Passport authentication, which allows you to authenticate a user using Microsoft's Passport service, which is a part of the My Services initiative. Passport is currently in late beta and scheduled for a yearly user fee based on unique website visitors. Some reference information about enabling the Passport settings is provided in Chapter 29.

Most sites will not need to use Passport authentication. Its main benefit is that it provides a far richer set of user information, which can be drawn from Microsoft's Passport database (the same technology that powers the free Hotmail e-mail site).

Windows Authentication

With Windows authentication, IIS takes care of the authentication process. ASP.NET simply uses the authenticated IIS user, and makes this identity available to your code for your security checks.

If your virtual directory uses the default settings, users will be authenticated under the anonymous IUSER_[ServerName] account. But usually, when programmers refer to Windows authentication for a website, what they mean is configuring IIS so that it forces users to log in before it allows them to access any resources. There are several different options for how the user login information is transmitted, but the end result is that the user is authenticated using a local Windows account. Typically, this makes Windows authentication best suited to intranet scenarios, in which a limited set of known users are already registered on a network server.

The advantage of Windows authentication is that it can be performed transparently (depending on the client's operating system and browser) and that your ASP.NET code can examine all the account information. For example, you can use the User.IsInRole() method to check what groups a user belongs to.

To implement Windows-based security with known users, you need to follow three steps:

1. Set the authentication mode in the web.config file.
2. Disable anonymous access for a directory in IIS Manager.
3. Configure the Windows user accounts on your web server (if they aren't already present).

IIS Settings

To disable anonymous access, start IIS Manager (select Settings ➤ Control Panel ➤ Administrative Tools ➤ Internet Information Services). Then right-click a virtual directory or a subdirectory inside a virtual directory, and choose Properties. Select the Directory Security tab, which is shown in Figure 25-10.

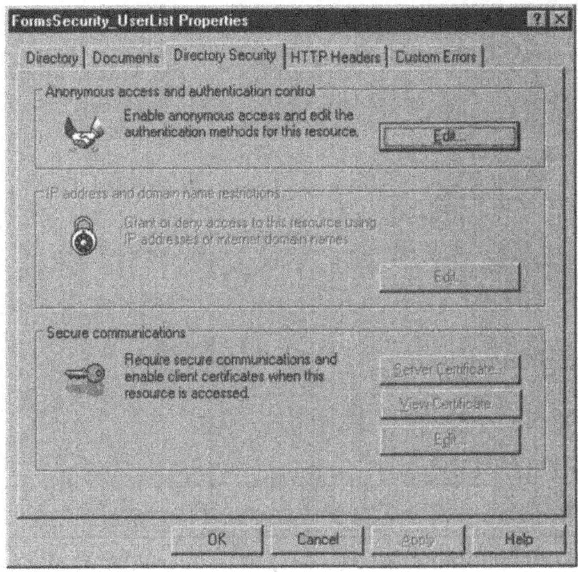

Figure 25-10. Directory security settings

Click the Edit button to modify the directory security settings (see Figure 25-11). In the bottom half of the window, you can enable one of the Windows authentication methods. However, none of these methods will be used unless you explicitly clear the Anonymous access check box. The different authentication methods are described in Table 25-4.

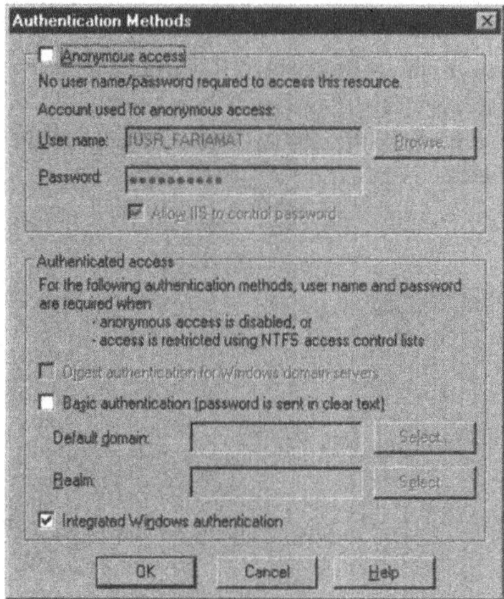

Figure 25-11. Directory authentication methods

Table 25-4. Windows Authentication Methods

Mode	Description
Anonymous	Anonymous authentication is technically not a true authentication method, because the client isn't required to submit any information. Instead, users are given free access to the website under a special user account, IUSR_[ServerName]. Anonymous authentication is the default.
Basic	Basic authentication is a part of the HTTP 1.0 standard, and it's supported by almost all browsers and web servers. When using basic authentication, the browser presents the user with a login box with a user name and password field. This information is then transmitted to IIS, where it's matched with a local Windows user account. The disadvantage of Basic authentication is that the password is transmitted in clear text, and is visible over the Internet (unless you combine it with SSL technology).
Digest	Digest authentication remedies the primary weakness of Basic authentication: sending passwords in plain text. Digest authentication sends a digest (also known as a hash) instead of a password over the network. The primary disadvantage is that Digest authentication is only support by Internet Explorer 5.0 and later. Your web server also needs to use Active Directory or have access to an Active Directory server.

Table 25-4. Windows Authentication Methods (Continued)

Mode	Description
Integrated	Integrated Windows authentication (formerly known as NTLM authentication and Windows NT Challenge/Response authentication) is the best choice for most intranet scenarios. When using Integrated authentication, Internet Explorer can send the required information automatically, using the currently logged-in Windows account on the client, provided it's on a trusted domain. Integrated authentication is only supported on Internet Explorer 2.0 and later, and won't work across proxy servers.

You can enable more than one authentication method. In this case, the client will use the strongest authentication method it supports, as long as anonymous access is *not* enabled. If anonymous access is enabled, the client will automatically access the website anonymously, unless the web application explicitly denies anonymous users with this rule in the web.config file:

```
<deny users="?" />
```

Web.config Settings

Once you've enabled the appropriate virtual directory security settings, you should make sure that your application is configured to use Windows authentication. In a Visual Studio .NET project, this is the default.

```
<configuration>
    <system.web>
        <!-- Other settings omitted. -->
        <authentication mode="Windows" />
    </system.web>
</configuration>
```

Next, you can add <allow> and <deny> elements to specifically allow or restrict users from specific files or directories. You can also restrict certain types of users, provided their accounts are members of the same Windows group, by using the roles attribute.

```
<authorization>
    <deny users="?" />
    <allow roles="Administrator,SuperUser" />
    <deny users="matthew" />
</authorization>
```

In this example, all users who are members of the Administrator or SuperUser group will be automatically authorized to access ASP.NET pages in this directory. Requests from the user named "matthew" will be denied, even if he is a member of the Administrator or SuperUser group. Remember, ASP.NET examines rules in the order they appear, and stops when it finds a match. Reversing these two authorization lines would ensure that the user "matthew" was always denied, regardless of group membership.

If the user accounts are located in a different domain, you should follow the more explicit syntax shown here, which precedes the user name with the name of the domain or server.

```
<allow users="MyDomainName\matthew" />
```

You can also examine a user's group membership programmatically in your code.

```
Private Sub Page_Load(sender As Object, e As EventArgs) _
  Handles MyBase.Load

    If User.IsInRole("MyDomainName\SalesAdministrators") Then
        ' Do nothing, the page should be accessed as normal because
        ' the user has administrator privileges.
    Else
        ' Don't allow this page. Instead, redirect to the home page.
        Response.Redirect("default.aspx")
    End If

End Sub
```

In this example, the code checks for membership in a custom Windows group called SalesAdministrators. If you want to check if a user is a member of one of the built-in groups, you don't need to specify a computer or domain name. Instead, you use this syntax:

```
If User.IsInRole("BUILTIN\Administrators") Then
    ' (Code goes here.)
End If
```

For more information about the <allow> and <deny> rules, and configuring individual files and directories, refer to the discussion under the Authorization Rules section in the "Forms Authentication" section earlier in this chapter.

Note that there is no way to retrieve a list of available groups on the web server (that would violate security), but you can find out the names of the default built-in Windows roles using the System.Security.Principal.WindowsBuiltInRole enumeration. These roles are shown in Table 25-5. Not all will apply to ASP.NET use, although Administrator, Guest, and User probably will.

Table 25-5. Default Windows Roles

Role	Description
AccountOperator	Users with the special responsibility of managing the user accounts on a computer or domain.
Administrator	Users with complete and unrestricted access to the computer or domain.
BackupOperator	Users who can override certain security restrictions only as part of backing up or restore operations.
Guest	Like the User role, but even more restrictive.
PowerUser	Similar to Administrator, but with some restrictions.
PrintOperator	Like a User, but with additional privileges for taking control of a printer.
Replicator	Like a User, but with additional privileges to support file replication in a domain.
SystemOperator	Similar to Administrator, with some restrictions. Generally, system operators manage a computer.
User	Users are prevented from making systemwide changes, and can only run "certified" applications.

A Windows Authentication Test

One of the nice things about Windows authentication is that no login page is required. Once you enable it in IIS, your web application can retrieve information directly from the User object. You can access some additional information by converting the generic Identity object to a WindowsIdentity object (which is defined in the System.Security.Principal namespace).

The following is a sample test page that uses Windows authentication. It's shown in Figure 25-12.

```
Imports System.Security.Principal
Imports System.Web.Security

Public Class SecuredPage
  Inherits Page

    Protected lblMessage As Label

    Private Sub Page_Load(sender As Object, e As EventArgs) _
      Handles MyBase.Load
        lblMessage.Text = "You have reached the secured page, "
        lblMessage.Text &= User.Identity.Name & "."
```

```
        Dim WinIdentity As WindowsIdentity
        WinIdentity = CType(User.Identity, WindowsIdentity)
        lblMessage.Text &= "<br><br>Authentication Type: "
        lblMessage.Text &= WinIdentity.AuthenticationType
        lblMessage.Text &= "<br>Anonymous: "
        lblMessage.Text &= WinIdentity.IsAnonymous
        lblMessage.Text &= "<br>Authenticated: "
        lblMessage.Text &= WinIdentity.IsAuthenticated
        lblMessage.Text &= "<br>Guest: " & WinIdentity.IsGuest
        lblMessage.Text &= "<br>System: " & WinIdentity.IsSystem
    End Sub

End Class
```

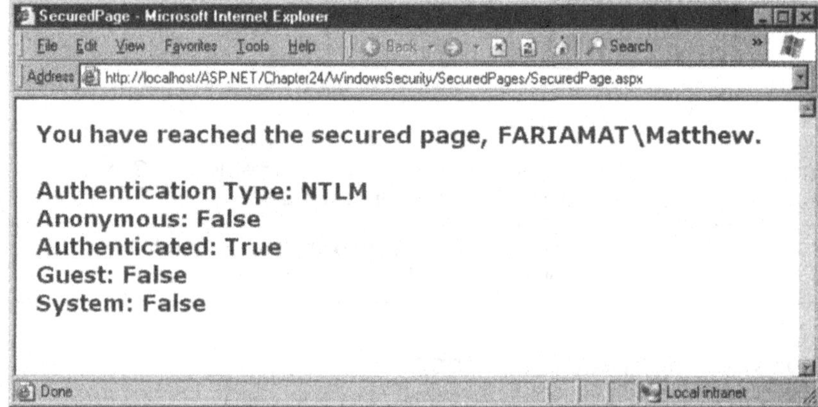

Figure 25-12. Retrieving Windows authentication information

Windows Authentication with a Web Service

Windows authentication works with a web service in much the same way that it works with a web page. The difference is that a web service is executed by another application, not directly by the browser. For that reason, there's no built-in way to prompt the user for a user name and password. Instead, the application that's using the web service needs to supply this information. The application might read this information from a configuration file or database, or might prompt the user for this information before contacting the web service.

For example, consider the following web service, which provides a single TestAuthenticated() method. This method checks if the user is authenticated. If the user is authenticated, it returns the user name (which will be a string in the form [DomainName]\[UserName] or [ComputerName]\[UserName]).

```
Public Class SecuredService
    Inherits System.Web.Services.WebService

    <WebMethod()> _
    Public Function TestAuthenticated() As String
        If User.Identity.IsAuthenticated = False Then
            Return "Not authenticated."
        Else
            Return "Authenticated as: " & User.Identity.Name
        End If
    End Function

End Class
```

In order to submit user credentials to this service, the client needs to modify the NetworkCredential property of the proxy class. You have two options:

- You can create a new NetworkCredential object, and attach this to the NetworkCredential property of the proxy object. When you create the NetworkCredential object, you'll need to specify the user name and password that you want to use. This approach works with all forms of Windows authentication.

- If the web service is using Integrated Windows authentication, you can automatically submit the credentials of the current user by using the shared DefaultCredentials property of the CredentialCache class, and applying that to the NetworkCredential property of the proxy object.

Both the CredentialCache and NetworkCredential classes are found in the System.Net namespace. Thus, before continuing, you should import this namespace:

```
Imports System.Net
```

The following code shows a web page with two buttons. One button performs an unauthenticated call, while the user submits some user credentials. The unauthenticated call will fail if you've disabled anonymous users for the web application. Otherwise, the unauthenticated call will succeed, but the TestAuthenticated() method will return a string informing you that authentication wasn't performed. The authenticated call will always succeed as long as you submit credentials that correspond to a valid user on the web server.

```
Public Class TestSecuredService
  Inherits System.Web.UI.Page

    Protected WithEvents cmdUnauthenticated As System.Web.UI.WebControls.Button
    Protected WithEvents cmdAuthenticated As System.Web.UI.WebControls.Button
    Protected WithEvents lblInfo As System.Web.UI.WebControls.Label

    Private Sub cmdUnauthenticated_Click(sender As Object, e As EventArgs) _
      Handles cmdUnauthenticated.Click
        Dim SecuredService As New localhost.SecuredService()
        lblInfo.Text = SecuredService.TestAuthenticated()
    End Sub

    Private Sub cmdAuthenticated_Click(sender As Object, e As EventArgs) _
      Handles cmdAuthenticated.Click
        Dim SecuredService As New localhost.SecuredService()

        ' Specity some user credentials for the web service.
        ' This example uses the user account "GuestAccount" with the password
        ' "Guest".
        Dim Credentials As New NetworkCredential("GuestAccount", "Guest")
        SecuredService.Credentials = Credentials

        lblInfo.Text = SecuredService.TestAuthenticated()
    End Sub
End Class
```

Figure 25-13 shows what the web page looks like after a successfully authenticated call to the computer fariamat.

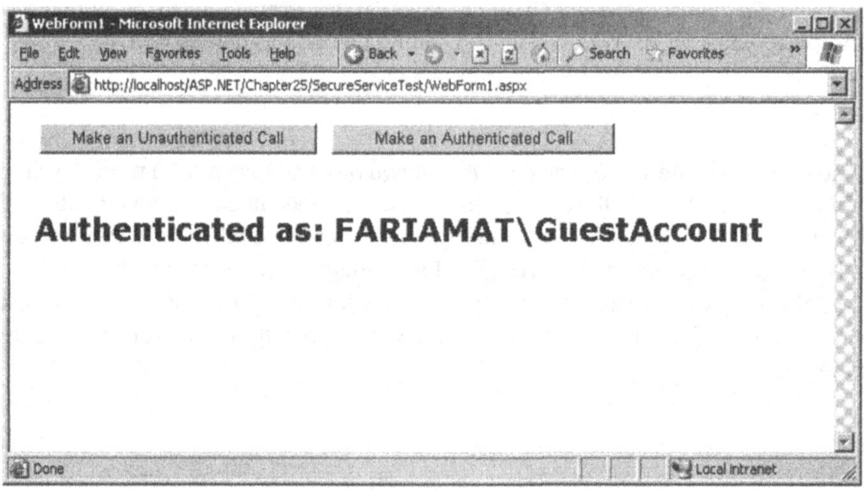

Figure 25-13. Succesful authentication through a web service

If you wanted to use the credentials of the currently logged-in account with Integrated Windows authentication, you would use this code instead:

```
Dim SecuredService As New localhost.SecuredService()
SecuredService.Credentials = CredentialCache.DefaultCredentials
lblInfo.Text = SecuredService.TestAuthenticated()
```

In this example (as in all web pages), the current user account will be the account that ASP.NET is using, not the user account of the remote user who is requesting the web page. If you use the same technique in a Windows application, you'll submit the account information of the user who is running the application.

NOTE Forms authentication won't work with a web service because there's no way for a web service to direct the user to a web page. In fact, the web service might not even be accessed through a browser—it might be used by a Windows application or even an automated Windows service.

Impersonation

Impersonation is an additional option that's available in Windows or forms authentication, although it's most common with Windows users in an intranet scenario. In order for impersonation to work, the authenticated user account must correspond to a Windows account, which isn't guaranteed (or even likely) with forms authentication.

With impersonation, your ASP.NET code interacts with the system under the identity of the authenticated user—not the normal system account. This technique is usually chosen when you don't want to worry about authorization details in your code.

For example, if you have a simple application that displays XML files, you can set specific permissions for each XML file, restricting them from some users and allowing them to others. Unfortunately, your ASP.NET XML viewer utility always executes under the ASPNET or local system account, which probably has authority to view all these files. Thus, any authenticated user can view any file. To remedy this situation, you can specifically add additional user verification checks in your code, and refuse to open files that aren't allowed. However, this will typically result in a lot of extra code. On the other hand, if impersonation is enabled, your ASP.NET code will be prevented from accessing any XML files that the current user isn't allowed to view. Of course, this means your application will encounter an error when you try to read the file—so you'll need to use exception-handling code to deal with the situation gracefully.

To enable impersonation, you simply add an <identity> tag to the web.config file, as shown here:

```
<configuration>
    <system.web>
        <!-- Other settings omitted. -->
        <identity impersonate="true" >
    </system.web>
</configuration>
```

Keep in mind that the user account will require read-write access to the Temporary ASP.NET Files directory where the compiled ASP.NET files are stored, or the user will not be able to access any pages. This directory is located under the path C:\[WinDir]\Microsoft.NET\Framework\[Version]\Temporary ASP.NET Files.

ASP.NET also provides the option to specifically set an account that will be used for running code. This technique is less common, although it can be useful if you want different ASP.NET applications to execute with different, but fixed, permissions. In this case, the user's authenticated identity isn't used by the ASP.NET code.

```
<configuration>
    <system.web>
        <!-- Other settings omitted. -->
        <identity impersonate="true" userName="matthew" password="secret" >
    </system.web>
</configuration>
```

This approach is more flexible than changing the machine.config account setting. The machine.config setting determines the default account that will be used for all web applications on the computer. The impersonation settings, on the other hand, override the machine.config setting for individual websites.

Unfortunately, the password for the impersonated account cannot be encrypted in the web.config file. This may constitute a security risk if other users have access to the computer, and can read the password.

Programmatic Impersonation

Sometimes it's more useful to use impersonation programmatically through the WindowsIdentity.Impersonate() method. This allows you to execute some code in the identity of a specific user (like your file access routine), but allows the rest of your code to run under the local system account, guaranteeing that it won't encounter any problems.

In order to use programmatic impersonation, you need to use Windows authentication by disabling anonymous access for the virtual directory. You also need to make sure that impersonation is disabled for your web application. (In other words, make sure that you do *not* add the <identity> tag to your web.config file.) This way, the standard account defined in the machine.config file will be used by default, but the authenticated Windows identity will be available for you to use when you need it.

The following code shows how your code can use the Impersonate() method to switch identities:

```
If User.GetType() Is WindowsPrincipal
    Dim ID As WindowsIdentity
    ID = CType(User.Identity, WindowsIdentity)
    Dim ImpersonateContext As WindowsImpersonationContext

    ImpersonateContext = ID.Impersonate()
    ' Now perform tasks under the impersonated ID.
    ' This code will not be able to access perform any task
    ' (like reading a file) that the user would not be allowed to do.

    ' Revert to the original ID as shown below.
    ImpersonateContext.Undo()
Else
    ' User isn't Windows authenticated.
    ' Throw an error to or take other steps.
End If
```

The Last Word

In this chapter, you learned about the multilayered security architecture in ASP.NET and IIS, and how you can safeguard your web pages and web services by using a custom login page or Windows authentication. You also learned the basics about certificates and SSL.

Security is an enormous topic. There are entire books dedicated to exploring cryptography and good security practices. Mastering these concepts takes time, and before you deploy any .NET website, it's a good idea to have it reviewed by a security professional.

CHAPTER 26

The IBuySpy Case Studies

OVER THE LAST 25 CHAPTERS, you've learned about the individual features, technologies, and design patterns that you can use in a professional ASP.NET application. The next step is to start combining these ingredients in your own creations.

Making the transition from simple sites to multitier web applications isn't always easy. Building a successful ASP.NET application requires knowledge, planning, and the occasional painful experience. Fortunately, Microsoft provides some invaluable help with the IBuySpy case studies, a pair of full-featured web applications that demonstrate best practices for an e-commerce storefront and a web portal. The IBuySpy case studies generated a great deal of excitement when they first appeared in the early beta days of ASP.NET, but have since been overshadowed by the foggy cloud of .NET hype. They don't ship with Visual Studio .NET or the .NET Framework, aren't mentioned in the online help, and aren't heavily promoted on Microsoft's MSDN site. In fact, the IBuySpy case studies are poised to become one of ASP.NET's best-kept secrets.

In this chapter, you'll learn everything you need to know to install, configure, and find your way around the IBuySpy case studies. You'll learn how the applications are structured, what tricks they use, and where the techniques you've learned—such as data binding, component-based development, security, and user controls—are put to use. Even experienced developers are sure to find a few new insights in the IBuySpy code. Best of all, Microsoft encourages developers to reuse the logic and code from the IBuySpy applications in their own websites.

TIP Before reading this chapter, make sure you've read Chapter 22, which explains how a large-scale application can be divided into layers with separate functions. The IBuySpy case studies make good use of components and layered design. It's also a good idea to be familiar with Chapter 23, because custom user controls are used extensively.

Installing the IBuySpy Applications

The IBuySpy samples aren't included on the Visual Studio .NET setup CDs. You need to visit the `http://www.asp.net/ibuyspy` website (shown in Figure 26-1). On the left are links that allow you to run one of the IBuySpy applications from the Internet, or you can download a setup program that lets you install it on your local computer.

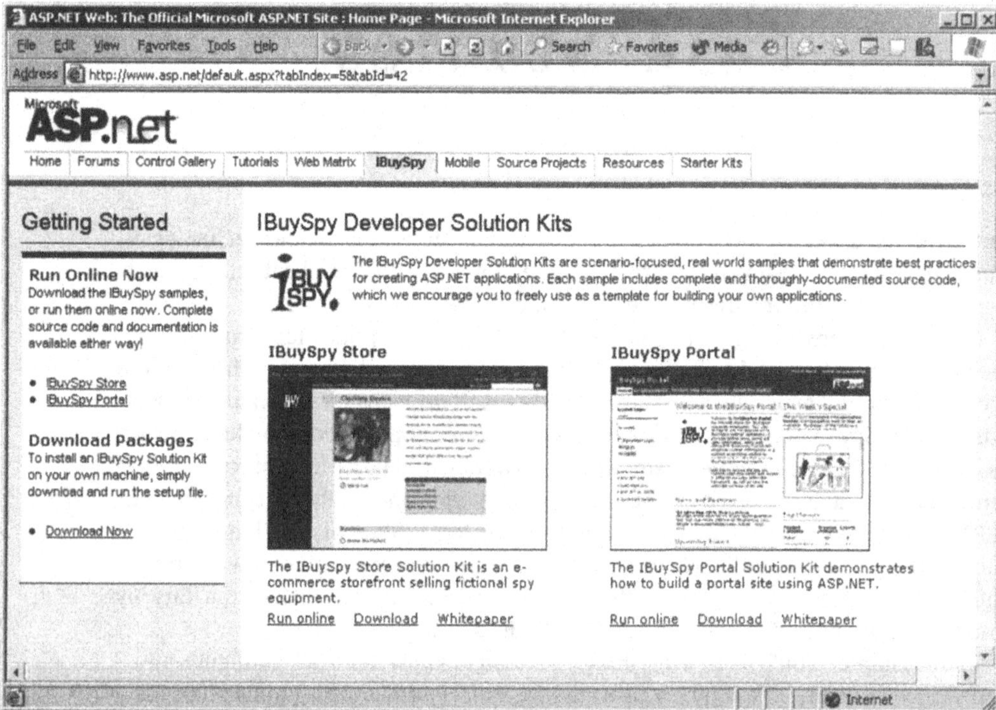

Figure 26-1. The IBuySpy website

TIP The IBuySpy website also provides a browser-based forum, where users can post questions and discussion about the IBuySpy samples.

The best way to work with the case studies is to install them locally, where you can tweak the code and use debugging tools to study how it works. To install the IBuySpy case studies, click any of the Download links. This will bring you to a download page with additional options (see Figure 26-2).

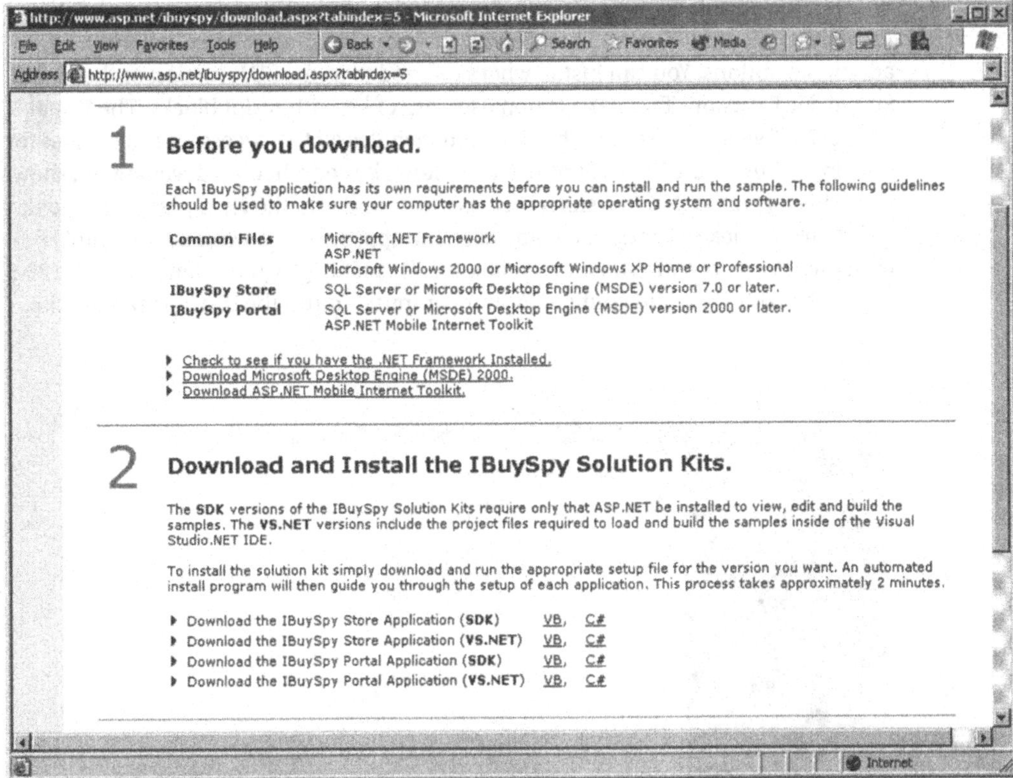

Figure 26-2. The IBuySpy download page

There are two IBuySpy case studies. Both case studies use common ASP.NET features such as ADO.NET data access, server controls, caching, and user controls.

- The IBuySpy store provides a full-featured three-tier e-commerce site. It incorporates a shopping basket, customer account information and login, high-performance data caching, and transactions. There are even web services for order entry and status retrieval.
- The IBuySpy portal provides a configurable web portal for an intranet or the Internet that's built out of custom user controls. By default, it's designed as an employee portal for the fictitious IBuySpy company, but you can easily replace the content to create your own custom portal. Best of all, it includes ASP.NET administration pages that allow you to customize its content and behavior without altering a line of code.

From the download page you can choose to install the VB or C# versions of either IBuySpy application. Once you've determined your language choice, you have two additional options. You can install what's referred to as the SDK version or the Visual Studio .NET version. The SDK version uses .aspx files with script blocks. The Visual Studio .NET version uses code-behind, and includes all the necessary project files for opening the file in the Visual Studio .NET editor. The code-behind development shown in the Visual Studio .NET versions there is most similar to the examples in this book.

When you make your decision and click the appropriate download link, you'll be prompted to save or run a single executable file. This setup program (shown in Figure 26-3) copies the code files, and configures your computer to run the IBuySpy sample site.

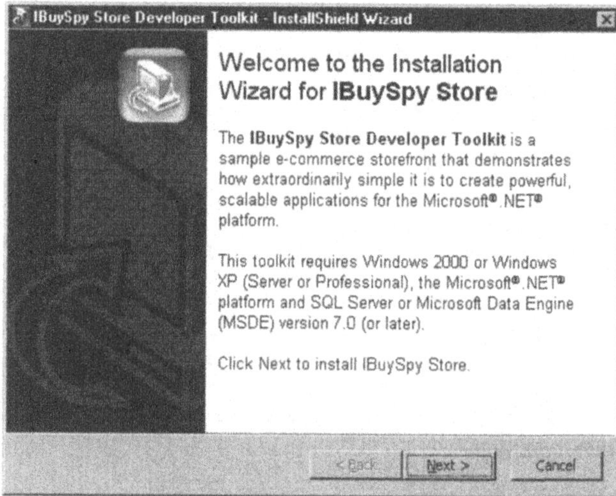

Figure 26-3. An IBuySpy setup

Once the IBuySpy files are copied to your computer, the setup application installs the required database (and some sample data) using the SQL Server or MSDE database engine. Before you can perform this step, you need to enter the appropriate user information for your database (see Figure 26-4).

Select the database server (localhost for the current computer) and click Configure. The setup application will connect using Windows integrated authentication. Once the databases have been created, the virtual directory will be configured. When the process is complete, click Finish to end the setup program.

At this point, you can run the IBuySpy application you installed, or you can load it in Visual Studio .NET. To run the application, simply request the start page from the appropriate virtual directory (such as http://localhost/StoreVBVS/Default.aspx for the IBuySpy store). To load the application in Visual Studio .NET, use the desktop shortcut, or look for the .vbproj file in the appropriate directory (such as C:\StoreVBVS\StoreVBVS.vbproj for the IBuySpy store).

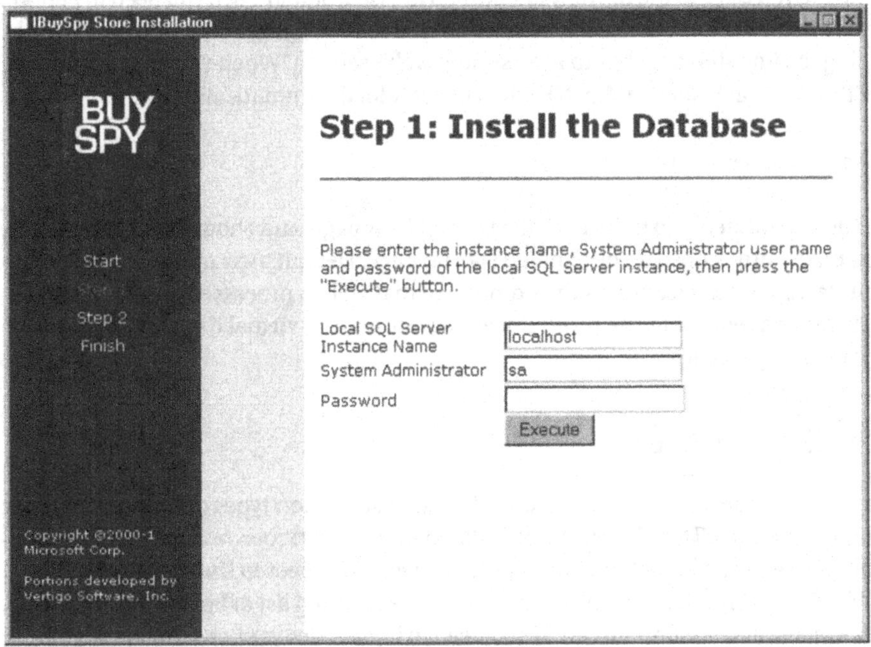

Figure 26-4. Installing the IBuySpy database

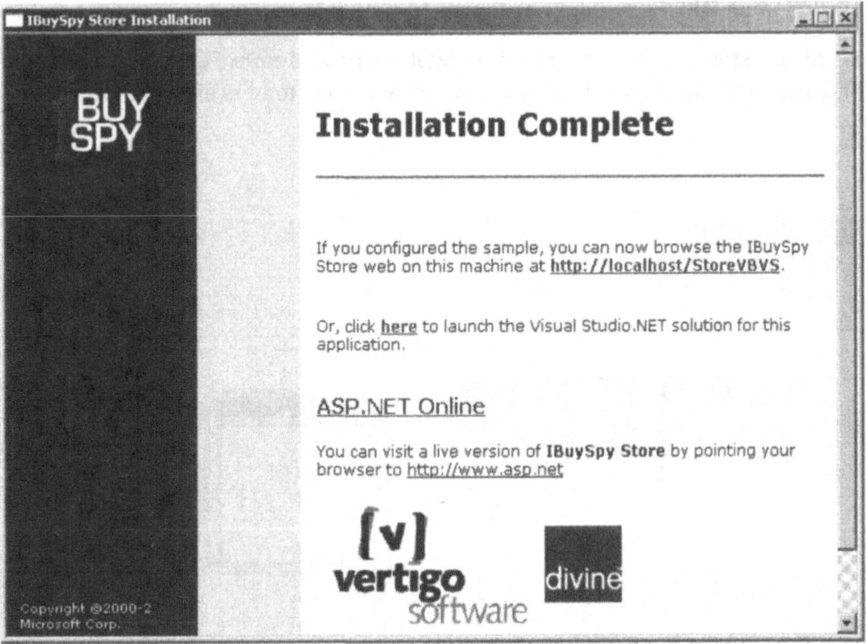

Figure 26-5. The completed IBuySpy store installation

Before you can run the IBuySpy application in Visual Studio .NET, you need to perform two minor modifications. First, you need to enable debugging in the web.config file by adding the line shown below to the <system.web> section. When you create your own .NET projects in Visual Studio .NET, this line is added automatically.

```
<compilation debug="true" />
```

The second step is to right-click the Default.aspx page, and choose Set As Startup. By default, the project has no designated startup page. Default.aspx makes a good choice for a startup page, because it's the home page that will be processed automatically if users make a request to the http://localhost/StoreVBVS virtual directory without specifying a page file.

The IBuySpy Store

The IBuySpy store is an example of one of the most common types of web applications: e-commerce sites. The IBuySpy store is designed for a fictitious retailer that sells high-tech spy gadgets. It includes all the staples you would expect to find from an online retailer, including a searchable product catalog, a featured list of best-selling products, user reviews, and a shopping cart. If you need to implement your own online storefront, you'll find that the IBuySpy example provides you with a well-designed and carefully tested template that can become the basis for your own site.

The Data Layer

The IBuySpy store uses seven tables in a database named *store*. Figure 26-6 shows the part of the database used to store information about customers and their orders.

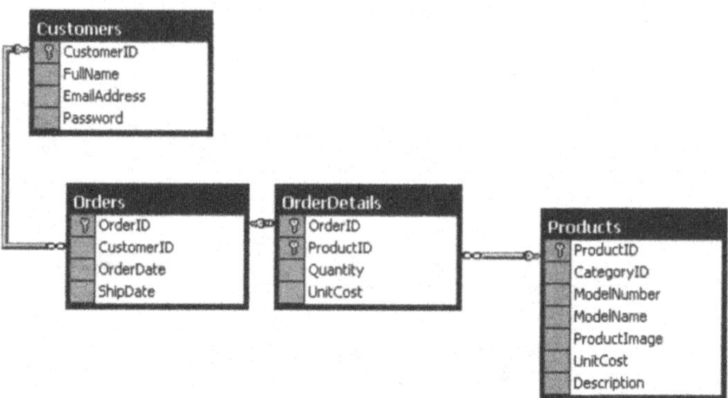

Figure 26-6. Customer and order information

Each customer record can be linked to any number of child order records. The order information is split into two tables, Order and OrderDetails. Each order is represented by a single Order record, which contains multiple line items. Each line item is represented by a separate OrderDetails record. As a bare minimum, the Order record needs to track the date the product was ordered and shipped, and the OrderDetails record needs to indicate the corresponding product, and the cost. The cost in the linked product record is subject to change, and thus cannot be relied upon when calculating the total cost of the order.

Figure 26-7 shows the remainder of the database. (You'll notice that the Products table from Figure 26-6 is repeated with some additional information.)

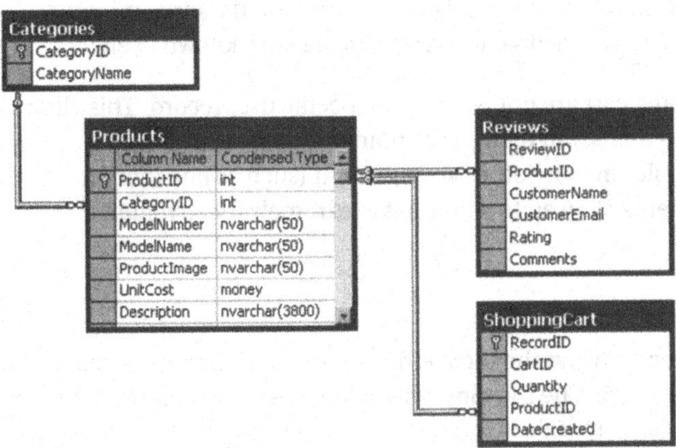

Figure 26-7. Product information

Every product must be assigned inside an existing category (such as General, Tools, or Travel, to name a few). In addition, every product can have an unlimited number of customer reviews. Finally, a ShoppingCart table stores user selections that haven't been ordered. This information could be stored in session state, but using a database table can provide better scalability, and it allows the information to remain for future visits, rather than timing out after a predetermined amount of time. To find all the items in a given user's cart, you would look for all the records with the same CartID.

Some points of interest:

- User passwords are not encrypted in the database. Thus, you should assume that this application would store its information in a carefully guarded SQL Server database that isn't accessible to most users.

- Product images are stored as file names (such as "image.gif"). Your ASP.NET application can use this name as a relative URL with an image control. However, the file must be present in the application directory on the web server. No error checking will be performed to enforce this restriction or alert you about a missing file. Another option would be to store the binary picture information in the database itself. This approach would solve the problem of missing pictures, but it could hamper performance and would make the pictures inaccessible to static HTML pages that might need to use them. You'll notice when running the IBuySpy store locally that a blank sample image is used for every product. If you run IBuySpy online (or configure the Products table on your own), each product will have its own individual image.
- Customer reviews are not linked to the customer records in the Customers table. This is a design decision that allows noncustomers to add their comments. Other websites (such as Amazon.com) restrict reviews to known users.
- Items in the shopping cart are not tied to any specific user record. This allows a user to start picking items and filling a shopping cart before registering with the site. Most users would find any other arrangement (such as one that forced you to register before being allowed to shop) to be extremely inconvenient.

Stored Procedures

Stored procedures are almost always the most efficient way to retrieve information or commit changes to the database. The IBuySpy store takes this philosophy to heart, and performs all of its data access through 23 separate stored procedures. The stored procedures are outlined in Table 26-1.

Table 26-1. Stored Procedures in the IBuySpy Store

Stored Procedure	Description
CustomerAdd	Inserts a new customer into the Customers table.
CustomerDetail	Retrieves information about a specified customer.
CustomerLogin	Looks for a customer record with the corresponding name and password. If no record is found, the login has failed.
CustomerAlsoBought	Uses a complicated stored procedure that accepts a product ID, and selects the five most popular products that were also purchased by users who bought the identified product. This type of query allows the website to provide a hook like "If you like product X, you may also like products Y and Z."
OrdersAdd	Adds a new order at the end of the checkout process by retrieving all the records from the appropriate shopping cart. Uses a transaction to ensure that there is never a partial (inconsistent) update.

Table 26-1. Stored Procedures in the IBuySpy Store (Continued)

Stored Procedure	Description
OrdersDetail	Retrieves information about a specified order. This information is retrieved in several separate pieces.
OrdersList	Retrieves a list of products that have been ordered by a specified customer.
ProductCategoryList	Retrieves a list of product categories.
ProductDetail	Retrieves detailed information about a specified product.
ProductsByCategory	Retrieves a list of products in a specified category.
ProductSearch	Retrieves product records using a text-based search with the SQL Like keyword. The search examines the information in the ModelNumber, ModelName, and Description fields, looking for the user-supplied keywords.
ProductsMostPopular	Retrieves the top five most popular products.
ReviewsAdd	Adds a user review.
ReviewsList	Retrieves a list of all the reviews for a given product.
ShoppingCartAddItem	Adds the specified product to the specified shopping cart by inserting a new ShoppingCart record. If the product already exists in the shopping cart, the quantity field of the current record is updated instead.
ShoppingCartEmpty	Removes all the records with the specified shopping cart ID.
ShoppingCartItemCount	Returns the number of items in the specified shopping cart.
ShoppingCartList	Returns the list of items in the specified shopping cart.
ShoppingCartMigrate	Moves a temporary shopping cart (created for a user who doesn't have an account or isn't logged in) to the final account for the logged-on user. This occurs just before the item is purchased.
ShoppingCartRemoveAbandoned	Deletes shopping carts that have been on the system for more than a day.
ShoppingCartRemoveItem	Removes the specified product from the specified shopping cart.
ShoppingCartTotal	Calculates the total cost of all the items that are in the specified shopping cart.
ShoppingCartUpdate	Modifies the quantity field for the specified product and shopping cart.

The Business Components

The IBuySpy store web pages never access the database directly. Instead, they work through a layer of five components that encapsulate all the database code for the site. This allows the database code to be changed without affecting the page code, and it also provides a more logical interface for you to program with. For example, the page code for working with the shopping cart is extremely intuitive because the underlying database details are handled transparently.

To see the methods that are provided by any one of the IBuySpy component classes, you can use the Solution Explorer, as shown in Figure 26-8.

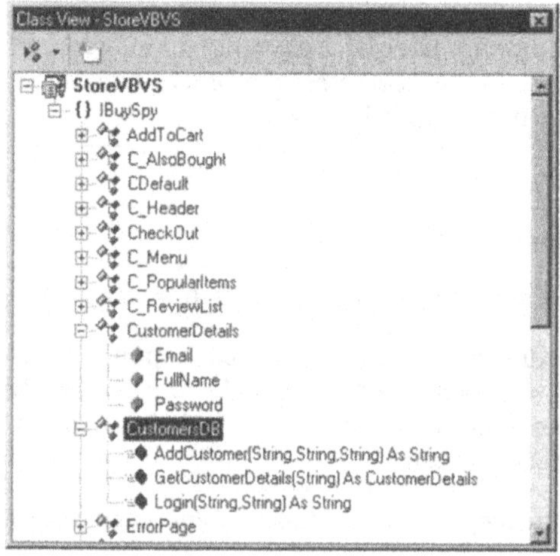

Figure 26-8. The CustomersDB component classes

The code in the IBuySpy store components is straightforward and well commented. You will also find that it's somewhat lengthy, because every stored procedure call requires several parameter objects, each of which must be constructed separately.

For example, the CustomersDB component provides two classes: the utility class CustomersDB, which contains all the database functionality, and the CustomerDetails data class, which encapsulates the information for a single customer record.

```
Public Class CustomerDetails
    Public FullName As String
    Public Email As String
    Public Password As String
End Class
```

The multitiered organization the IBuyStore is shown in Figure 26-9.

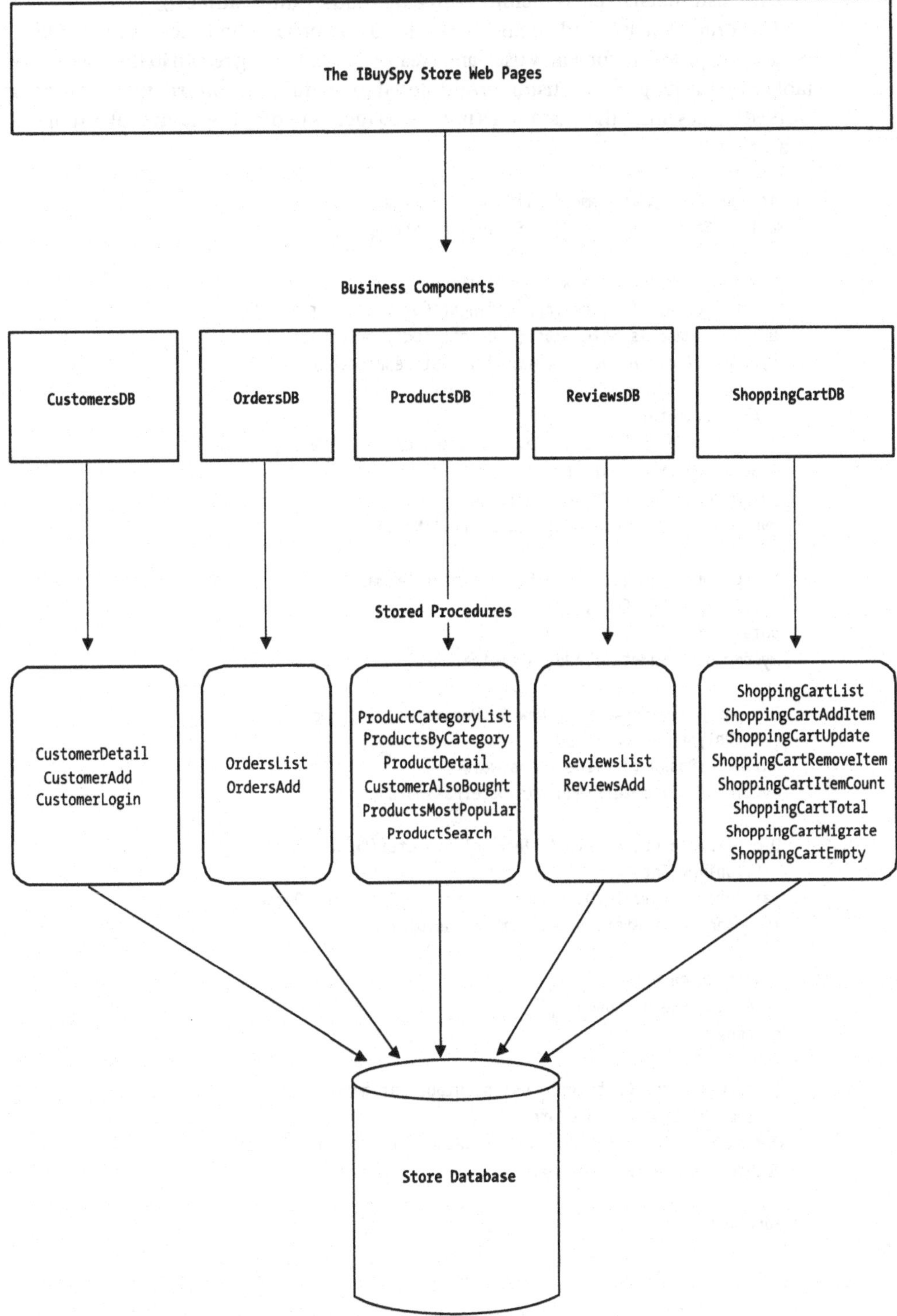

Figure 26-9. The IBuySpy store application design

The CustomersDB class includes three methods: AddCustomer(), GetCustomerDetails(), and Login(). The AddCustomer() method accepts the name, e-mail, and password for a new user, and creates the underlying record in the Customers table with the help of the CustomerAdd stored procedure. To confirm that the process worked successfully, the customer's unique ID (generated by the database) is returned as a string.

```
Public Function AddCustomer(fullName As String, _
  email As String, password As String) As String

    Dim myConnection As New SqlConnection( _
      ConfigurationSettings.AppSettings("ConnectionString"))
    Dim myCommand As SqlCommand("CustomerAdd", myConnection)
    myCommand.CommandType = CommandType.StoredProcedure

    ' Add Parameters
    Dim parameterFullName As New SqlParameter("@FullName", _
      SqlDbType.NVarChar, 50)
    parameterFullName.Value = fullName
    myCommand.Parameters.Add(parameterFullName)

    Dim parameterEmail As New SqlParameter("@Email", _
      SqlDbType.NVarChar, 50)
    parameterEmail.Value = email
    myCommand.Parameters.Add(parameterEmail)

    Dim parameterPassword As New SqlParameter("@Password", _
      SqlDbType.NVarChar, 50)
    parameterPassword.Value = password
    myCommand.Parameters.Add(parameterPassword)

    Dim parameterCustomerID As New SqlParameter("@CustomerID", _
      SqlDbType.Int, 4)
    parameterCustomerID.Direction = ParameterDirection.Output
    myCommand.Parameters.Add(parameterCustomerID)

    myConnection.Open()
    myCommand.ExecuteNonQuery()
    myConnection.Close()

    ' Calculate the CustomerID using output parameter
    ' from the stored procedure.
    Dim customerId As Integer = CInt(parameterCustomerID.Value)
    Return customerId.ToString()

End Function
```

NOTE The IBuySpy examples follow the C# naming convention of starting variables with a lowercase first letter, unless they're publicly visible (like a class property). The IBuySpy examples also don't use variable control prefixes (such as txtName to indicate a text box that contains a user's name).

There's nothing unusual about this example—it's exactly like the database components you considered in Chapter 22. You'll also notice that the connection string is retrieved from the web.config configuration file.

To use this component, the client needs to create an instance of the CustomerDB class and submit the appropriate information. Here's the logic used in the Register.aspx page:

```
' Add New Customer to CustomerDB database
Dim accountSystem As New IBuySpy.CustomersDB()
Dim customerId As String
customerID = accountSystem.AddCustomer(Name.Text, Email.Text, _
                                       Password.Text)

If customerId <> "" Then
    ' The user was created. You can continue with the task at hand.
End If
```

Now consider the GetCustomerDetails() method, which returns information as a CustomerDetails object.

```
Public Function GetCustomerDetails(customerID As String) _

  As CustomerDetails

    Dim myConnection As New SqlConnection( _
      ConfigurationSettings.AppSettings("ConnectionString"))
    Dim myCommand As New SqlCommand("CustomerDetail", myConnection)
    myCommand.CommandType = CommandType.StoredProcedure

    ' Add Parameters to stored procedure.
    Dim parameterCustomerID As New SqlParameter("@CustomerID", _
      SqlDbType.Int, 4)
    parameterCustomerID.Value = CInt(customerID)
    myCommand.Parameters.Add(parameterCustomerID)

    Dim parameterFullName As New SqlParameter("@FullName", _
      SqlDbType.NVarChar, 50)
    parameterFullName.Direction = ParameterDirection.Output
    myCommand.Parameters.Add(parameterFullName)
```

```
        Dim parameterEmail As New SqlParameter("@Email", _
          SqlDbType.NVarChar, 50)
        parameterEmail.Direction = ParameterDirection.Output
        myCommand.Parameters.Add(parameterEmail)

        Dim parameterPassword As New SqlParameter("@Password", _
          SqlDbType.NVarChar, 50)
        parameterPassword.Direction = ParameterDirection.Output
        myCommand.Parameters.Add(parameterPassword)

        myConnection.Open()
        myCommand.ExecuteNonQuery()
        myConnection.Close()

        ' Create CustomerDetails object.
        Dim myCustomerDetails As New CustomerDetails()

        ' Populate CustomerDetails object using output parameters.
        myCustomerDetails.FullName = CStr(parameterFullName.Value)
        myCustomerDetails.Password = CStr(parameterPassword.Value)
        myCustomerDetails.Email = CStr(parameterEmail.Value)
        Return myCustomerDetails

    End Function
```

The Login() method follows similar logic, but throws an exception if a matching user record cannot be found. All of the other components follow the same series of methodical steps—first creating the appropriate parameter objects, then calling the procedure, and finally retrieving the important information from the output parameters to use as a return value if needed. Once you understand this basic organizing principle, it's easy to read through the classes and code to understand what's taking place.

The Web Services

The IBuySpy store web services aren't integrated into the core application. Instead, they provide another approach you can use for ordering a product and checking on its status. However, to make the best use of these web services, you would need to create another client application (such as a desktop Windows program) that uses them.

If you'd like to view the web services using the test page, request the InstantOrder.asmx page. Two web methods are provided: OrderItem() and CheckStatus(). They use the same components used by the web pages in the IBuySpy store application.

The Application Configuration

The web.config file for the IBuySpy store is short and simple. It serves five main purposes:

- It defines the connection string used for the database. The setup program configures this information when you install the IBuySpy store site.

```
<appSettings>
    <add key="ConnectionString"
         value="server=localhost;Trusted_Connection=true;database=Store" />
</appSettings>
```

- It disables session state management for the entire application, ensuring optimum performance. Any data that needs to be retained is kept in view state or the database.

```
<sessionState mode="Off" />
```

- It identifies a custom error page to be used in case of an application error.

```
<customErrors mode="RemoteOnly"
              defaultRedirect="ErrorPage.aspx" />
```

- It enables forms-based security.

```
<authentication mode="Forms">
    <forms name="IBuySpyStoreAuth" loginUrl="login.aspx"
           protection="All" path="/" />
</authentication>
```

- It specifies that certain pages (those used for ordering or checking order item status) require an authenticated user.

```
<location path="Checkout.aspx">
    <system.web>
        <authorization>
            <deny users="?" />
        </authorization>
    </system.web>
</location>
<location path="OrderList.aspx">
    <system.web>
        <authorization>
            <deny users="?" />
        </authorization>
    </system.web>
</location>
<location path="OrderDetails.aspx">
    <system.web>
        <authorization>
            <deny users="?" />
        </authorization>
    </system.web>
</location>
```

The Web Pages

The IBuySpy store includes 13 .aspx pages, 5 .ascx user controls, and 1 .asmx web service. Because so much of the IBuySpy store logic is handled by the business components and stored procedures in the database, the web page code is brief, simple, and easily readable.

The following sections walk through the most important pages. The sections are ordered so that they follow the path a user might take through the IBuySpy website, from the default page to the product catalog, and then to the user registration and the final checkout.

The Default.aspx Page

The initial Default.aspx (shown in the browser in Figure 26-10) has a code-behind class with barely five lines of code. It looks for a cookie called IBuySpy_FullName, and uses it to configure a welcome message.

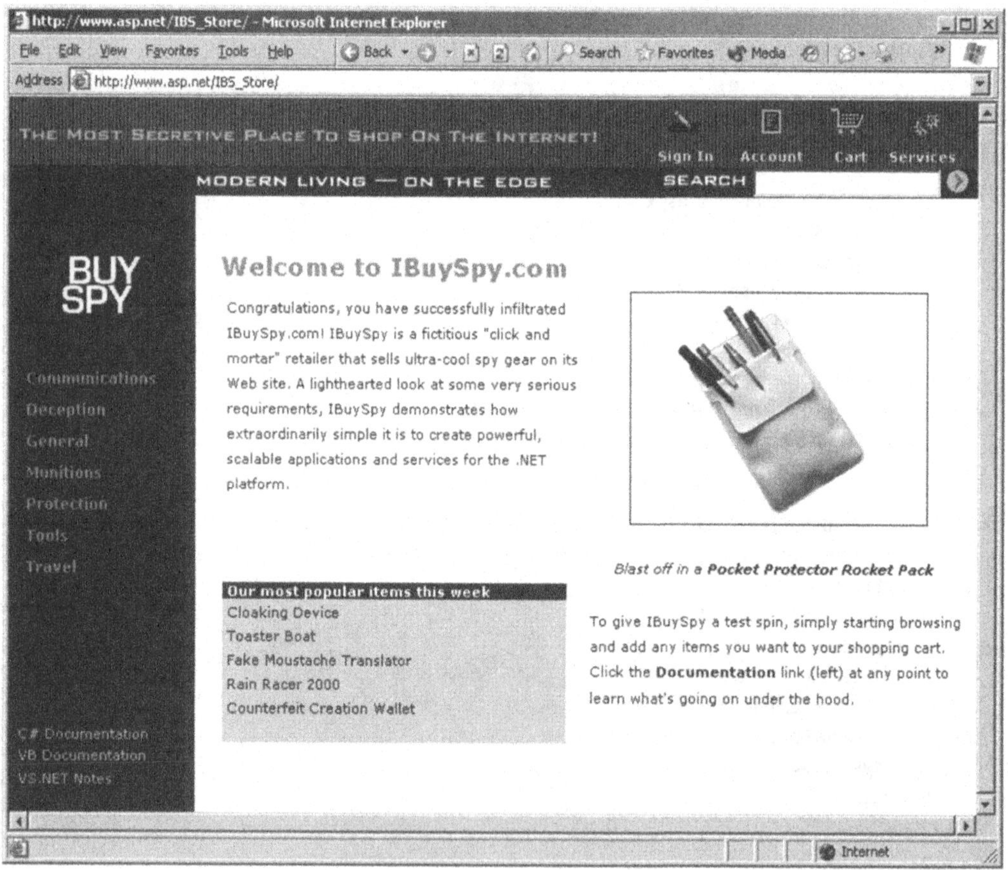

Figure 26-10. The IBuySpy store home page

```
Private Sub Page_Load(sender As Object, e As EventArgs) _
  Handles MyBase.Load

    ' Customize welcome message if personalization cookie is present
    If Not Request.Cookies("IBuySpy_FullName") Is Nothing Then
        WelcomeMsg.Text = "Welcome "
        WelcomeMsg.Text &= Request.Cookies("IBuySpy_FullName").Value
    End If

End Sub
```

The rest of the page processing work is offloaded to several separate user controls (as diagrammed in Figure 26-11).

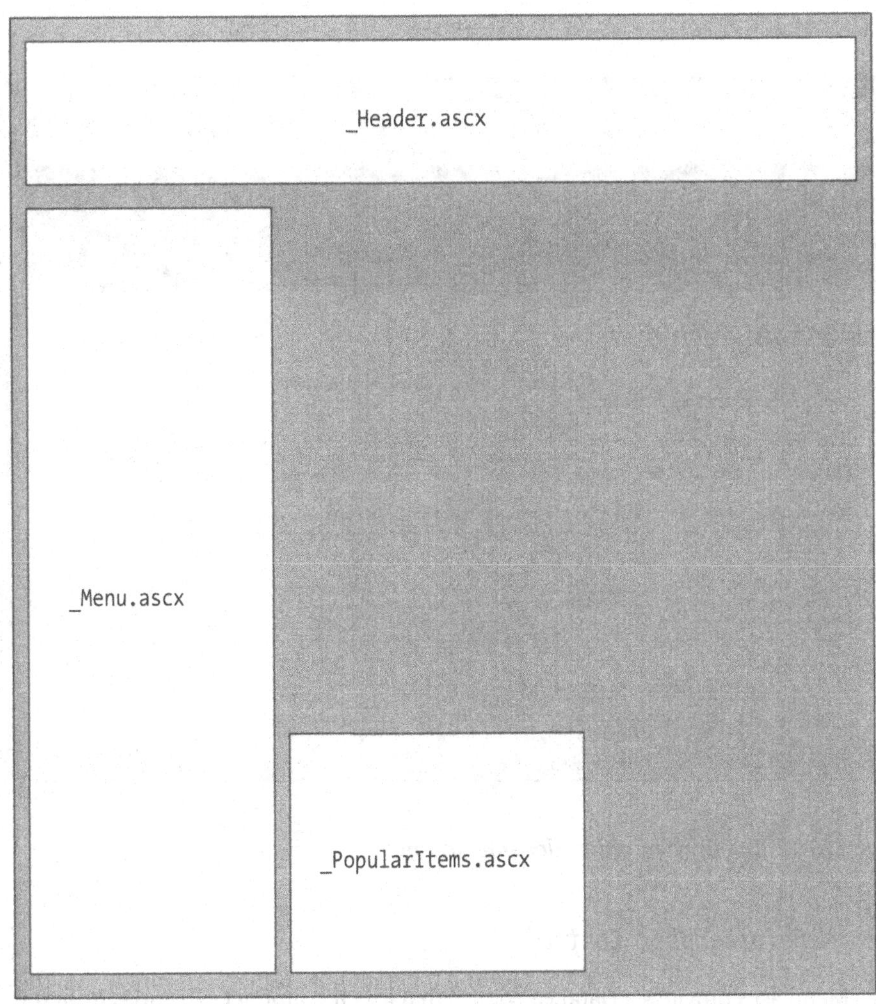

Figure 26-11. User controls on the default.aspx page

- _Header.ascx provides the graphical header at the top of the page. No ASP.NET code is used to create this header, but the user control still centralizes the HTML markup code involved so it doesn't need to be repeated in each page.
- _Menu.ascx provides the menu navigation on the left, which provides a link for every product category in the database through a data-bound DataList control.
- _PopularItems.ascx uses a Repeater control to list the five most popular items, as selected from the database.

The IBuySpy store also includes HTML files that provide a code listing for each file, along with some basic information about the application and its design. To see these files, click the documentation link that appears at the bottom right, under the list of product categories (see Figure 26-12).

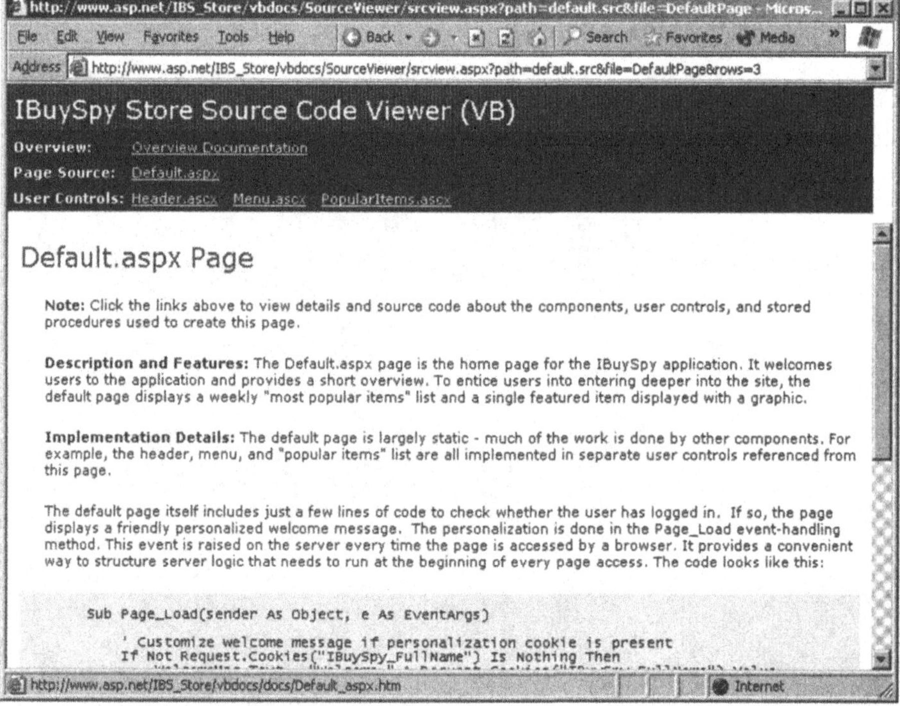

Figure 26-12. The IBuySpy online documentation

The _Menu.ascx User Control

The _Menu.ascx provides a DataList control that lists the product categories from the database. The DataList provides two templates, which format the appearance of the category differently depending on whether it's currently selected. Each template creates the category as a hyperlink, with the text drawn from the CategoryName database field. The hyperlink jumps to the productslist.aspx page, and passes the selected category ID through the query string.

```
<asp:DataList id="MyList" cellpadding="3" cellspacing="0"
     width="145" SelectedItemStyle-BackColor="dimgray"
     EnableViewState="false" runat="server" >

    <ItemTemplate>
        <asp:HyperLink cssclass="MenuUnselected" id="HyperLink1"
         Text='<%# DataBinder.Eval(Container.DataItem,
              "CategoryName") %>'
         NavigateUrl='<%# "productslist.aspx?CategoryID=" &
         DataBinder.Eval(Container.DataItem, "CategoryID") &
         "&selection=" & Container.ItemIndex %>' runat="server" />
    </ItemTemplate>
    <SelectedItemTemplate>
        <asp:HyperLink cssclass="MenuSelected" id="HyperLink2"
         Text='<%# DataBinder.Eval(Container.DataItem,
              "CategoryName") %>'
         NavigateUrl='<%# "productslist.aspx?CategoryID=" &
         DataBinder.Eval(Container.DataItem, "CategoryID") &
         "&selection=" & Container.ItemIndex %>' runat="server" />
    </SelectedItemTemplate>

</asp:DataList>
```

The user control code binds the DataList, with the help of the ProductsDB class. First, however, the code checks if a selection has already been made and sent back in the current query string, in which case it sets the DataList's SelectedIndex property accordingly.

```
Private Sub Page_Load(sender As Object, e As EventArgs) _
  Handles MyBase.Load

    ' Set the current selection of list.
    Dim selectionId As String = Request.Params("selection")

    If Not selectionId Is Nothing Then
        MyList.SelectedIndex = CInt(selectionId)
    End If

    ' Obtain list of menu categories and bind to the list control.
    Dim products As New IBuySpy.ProductsDB()

    MyList.DataSource = products.GetProductCategories()
    MyList.DataBind()

End Sub
```

Lastly, to improve performance the menu user control is cached for one hour, which indicates that product categories aren't expected to change frequently. The VaryByParam attribute indicates that a separate version is required depending on the selection value in the query string. Remember, the currently selected item will be displayed with different formatting, which means that a separate cached version of the control is required for each selected category.

```
<%@ OutputCache Duration="3600" VaryByParam="selection" %>
```

The ProductsList.aspx Page

The ProductsList.aspx page simply retrieves the list of products in the selected category (as indicated in the query string). Once again, the process is made extremely easy through the ProdcutsDB database component. Here's the code that runs when the page loads:

```
Private Sub Page_Load(sender As Object, e As EventArgs)_
  Handles MyBase.Load

    ' Obtain categoryId from QueryString
    Dim categoryId As Integer = CInt(Request.Params("CategoryID"))

    ' Obtain products and databind to an asp:datalist control
    Dim productCatalogue As New IBuySpy.ProductsDB()

    MyList.DataSource = productCatalogue.GetProducts(categoryId)
    MyList.DataBind()

End Sub
```

The DataList uses an attractive layout that displays a picture and an Add to Cart link (see Figure 26-13). It uses a single template (ItemTemplate), and a sophisticated HTML layout that places it as a table nested inside another table. This ensures that the DataList and the required user controls can be organized precisely on the page. Another approach would be to use HTML frames, as discussed in the sidebar at the end of Chapter 9.

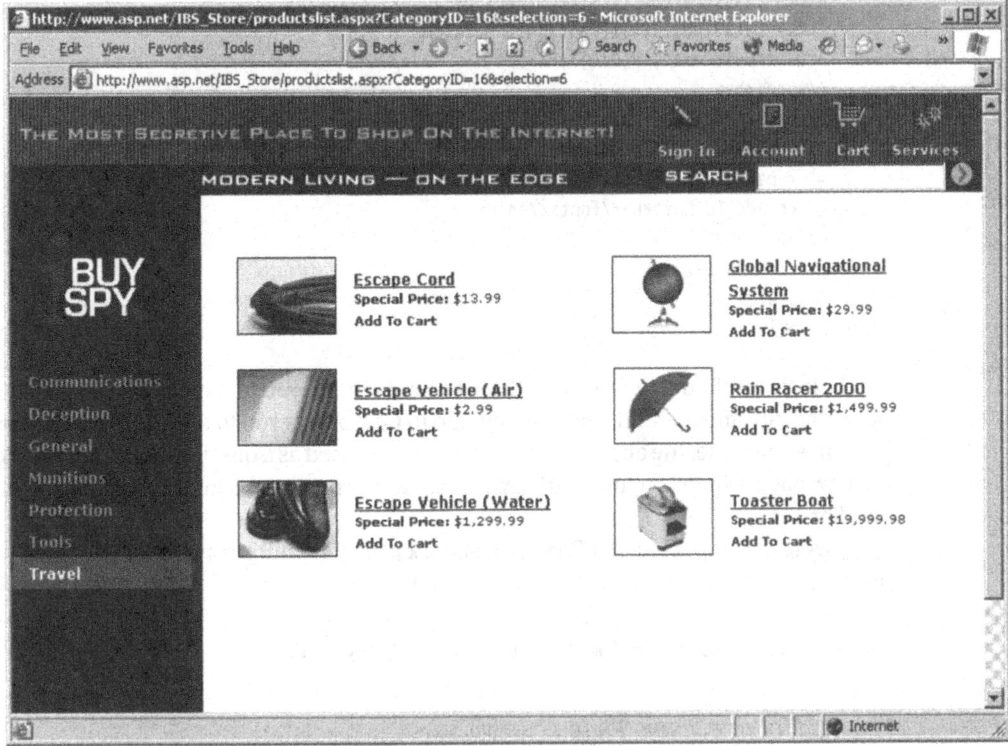

Figure 26-13. The list of products

Here are the templates for the DataList:

```
<asp:DataList id="MyList" RepeatColumns="2" runat="server">
<ItemTemplate>
    <table border="0" width="300"><tr><td width="25"> </td>
    <td width="100" valign="middle" align="right">
      <a href='ProductDetails.aspx?productID=<%#
         DataBinder.Eval(Container.DataItem, "ProductID") %>'>
         <img src='ProductImages/thumbs/
            <%# DataBinder.Eval(Container.DataItem,
                "ProductImage") %>'
            width="100" height="75" border="0">
      </a>
    </td>
    <td width="200" valign="middle">
      <a href='ProductDetails.aspx?productID=<%#
         DataBinder.Eval(Container.DataItem, "ProductID") %>'>
         <span class="ProductListHead">
           <%# DataBinder.Eval(Container.DataItem, "ModelName") %>
         </span><br>
      </a>
```

```
        <span class="ProductListItem"><b>Special Price: </b>
          <%# DataBinder.Eval(Container.DataItem,
              "UnitCost", "{0:c}") %>
        </span><br>
        <a href='AddToCart.aspx?productID=<%#
           DataBinder.Eval(Container.DataItem, "ProductID") %>'>
           <span class="ProductListItem"><font color="#9D0000">
           <b>Add To Cart<b></font></span>
        </a>
    </td></tr></table>
</ItemTemplate>
</asp:DataList>
```

The logic is still straightforward: Clicking an item brings you to the ProductDetails.aspx page for more information, and clicking Add to Cart brings you to the AddoToCart.aspx page. In either case, the appropriate product ID is passed as a query string parameter to the new page, which can then perform the necessary operations in its Page_Load event handler.

As would be expected, the ProductList.aspx page uses output caching. The list of products in a given category is retained for 100 minutes.

```
<%@ OutputCache Duration="6000" VaryByParam="CategoryID" %>
```

The AddToCart.aspx Page

The AddToCart.aspx page actually has no server controls or HTML output. Instead, it performs the processing required for adding the item to the shopping cart, and then it forwards the user to the ShoppingCart.aspx page. This extra step ensures that if the user hits the Refresh button, the item will not be added again (as the AddToCart.aspx page code will not run). Here's the code:

```
Private Sub Page_Load(sender As Object, e As EventArgs) _
  Handles MyBase.Load

    If Not Request.Params("ProductID") Is Nothing Then
        Dim cart As New IBuySpy.ShoppingCartDB()

        ' Obtain current user's shopping cart ID.
        Dim cartId As String = cart.GetShoppingCartId()

        ' Add Product Item to Cart.
        cart.AddItem(cartId, CInt(Request.Params("ProductID")), 1)
    End If

    Response.Redirect("ShoppingCart.aspx")
End Sub
```

The first step when using the ShoppingCartDB component is to call the GetShoppingCartID() method. It returns a unique ID for the shopping cart, which will be one of two things. If the user has already logged in, the shopping cart ID will be his unique ID. If the user is a guest or a customer who has not logged in, a randomly generated GUID will be calculated, ensuring that the shopping cart ID is unique. The shopping cart ID is then stored in a special cookie called IBuySpy_CartID. Calling GetShoppingCartID() at a later point simply retrieves the value from the cookie, ensuring that the same value is used for a user's entire session. This ID is required to use all of the other ShoppingCartDB methods—without it there is no way to find the user's items in the ShoppingCart table.

The code for the ShoppingCartDB() function is shown here:

```
Public Function GetShoppingCartId() As String

    Dim context As HttpContext = HttpContext.Current

    ' If the user is authenticated,
    ' use their customer ID as a shopping cart ID.
    If context.User.Identity.Name <> "" Then
        Return context.User.Identity.Name
    End If

    ' If user isn't authenticated,
    ' either fetch (or issue) a new temporary ID.
    If Not context.Request.Cookies("IBuySpy_CartID") Is Nothing Then
        Return context.Request.Cookies("IBuySpy_CartID").Value
    Else
        ' Generate a new random GUID using System.Guid class.
        Dim tempCartId As Guid = Guid.NewGuid()

        ' Send tempCartId back to client as a cookie
        context.Response.Cookies("IBuySpy_CartID").Value = _
          tempCartId.ToString()
        Return tempCartId.ToString()
    End If

End Function
```

Remember, there is no item in the database that represents a shopping cart. Instead, each record in the ShoppingCart table represents an individual shopping cart item. If there are no items for a given shopping cart ID, there is effectively no shopping cart. At any given time, you would expect to find that the ShoppingCart table has a range of records representing various items from a host of different users, as shown in Figure 26-14.

Data in Table 'ShoppingCart' in 'store' on 'FARIAMAT'

RecordID	CartID	Quantity	ProductID	DateCreated
1	cd0a7589-d1df-4dc6-b02b-cc734f8ecf9c	1	402	2001/12/17 9:25:52 AM
2	20	1	399	2001/12/17 3:55:37 PM
3	20	1	363	2001/12/17 3:57:37 PM
4	20	1	377	2001/12/17 3:57:41 PM
5	20	1	376	2001/12/17 3:57:44 PM
6	d1d3e4c9-d0b6-4ee3-b4e7-974ea4e9f7ab	1	374	2001/12/17 3:57:46 PM
7	20	1	400	2001/12/17 3:57:49 PM
8	20	1	404	2001/12/17 3:58:43 PM
9	d1d3e4c9-d0b6-4ee3-b4e7-974ea4e9f7ab	2	400	2001/12/17 4:00:26 PM
10	15	1	399	2001/12/17 4:00:56 PM
11	cd0a7589-d1df-4dc6-b02b-cc734f8ecf9c	1	363	2001/12/17 4:01:07 PM

Figure 26-14. ShoppingCart data

The ShoppingCart.aspx Pages

After the item has been added to the ShoppingCart table, the user is automatically forwarded to a new page, ShoppingCart.aspx, which provides a list of the currently selected items in a DataGrid control, as shown in Figure 26-15.

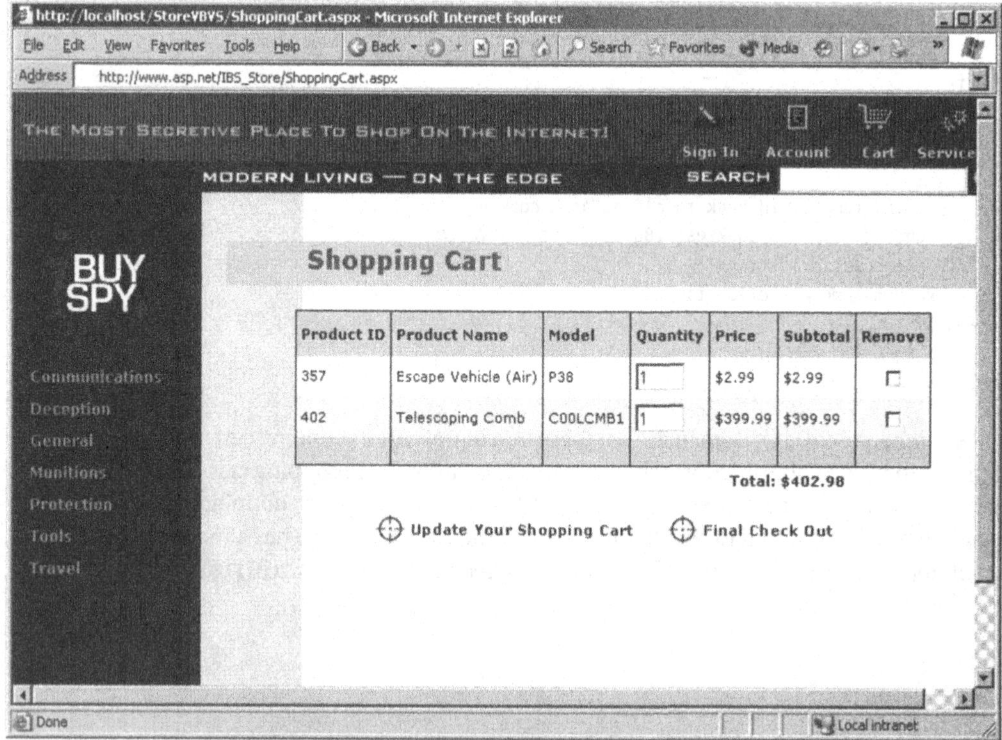

Figure 26-15. The contents of the current shopping cart

The first time the page loads, the code retrieves the user's shopping cart ID, looks up the corresponding items, and binds them to the DataGrid control using a custom subroutine called PopulateShoppingCartList(), which is shown here:

```
Private Sub PopulateShoppingCartList()

    Dim cart As New IBuySpy.ShoppingCartDB()

    ' Obtain current user's shopping cart ID.
    Dim cartId As String = cart.GetShoppingCartId()

    ' If no items, hide details and display message.
    If cart.GetItemCount(cartId) = 0 Then
        DetailsPanel.Visible = False
        MyError.Text = "There are currently no items"
        MyError.Text &= "in your shopping cart."
    Else
        ' Databind Gridcontrol with Shopping Cart Items.
        MyList.DataSource = cart.GetItems(cartId)
        MyList.DataBind()

        ' Update Total Price label.
        lblTotal.Text = String.Format("{0:c}", _
                             cart.GetTotal(cartId))
    End If

End Sub
```

The user can then modify quantities or remove items. The ShoppingCart.aspx file simply calls the appropriate routines in the ShoppingCartDB component.

Users who decide to proceed and purchase items by clicking the Final Checkout ImageButton will be redirected to the Checkout.aspx page. This page is secured by the web.config settings, which means that users who aren't logged in will be redirected to the Login.aspx page.

The Login.aspx and Register.aspx Pages

The Login.aspx page provides the user with two options: sign in with a recognized user ID and password combination, or register as a new user. The Login.aspx page is shown in Figure 26-16.

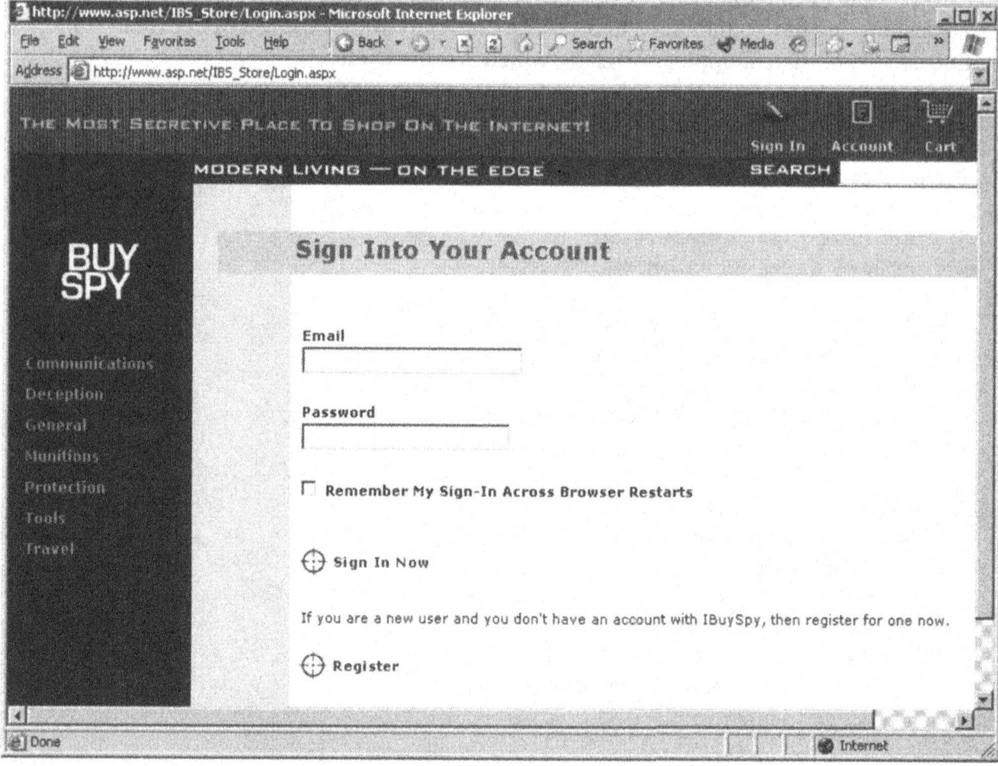

Figure 26-16. The login request

If the user chooses to register, the browser is redirected to the Register.aspx page, where various pieces of user information are collected and inserted in a record in the Customers database. This page uses input control validation to verify all values (as shown in Figure 26-17).

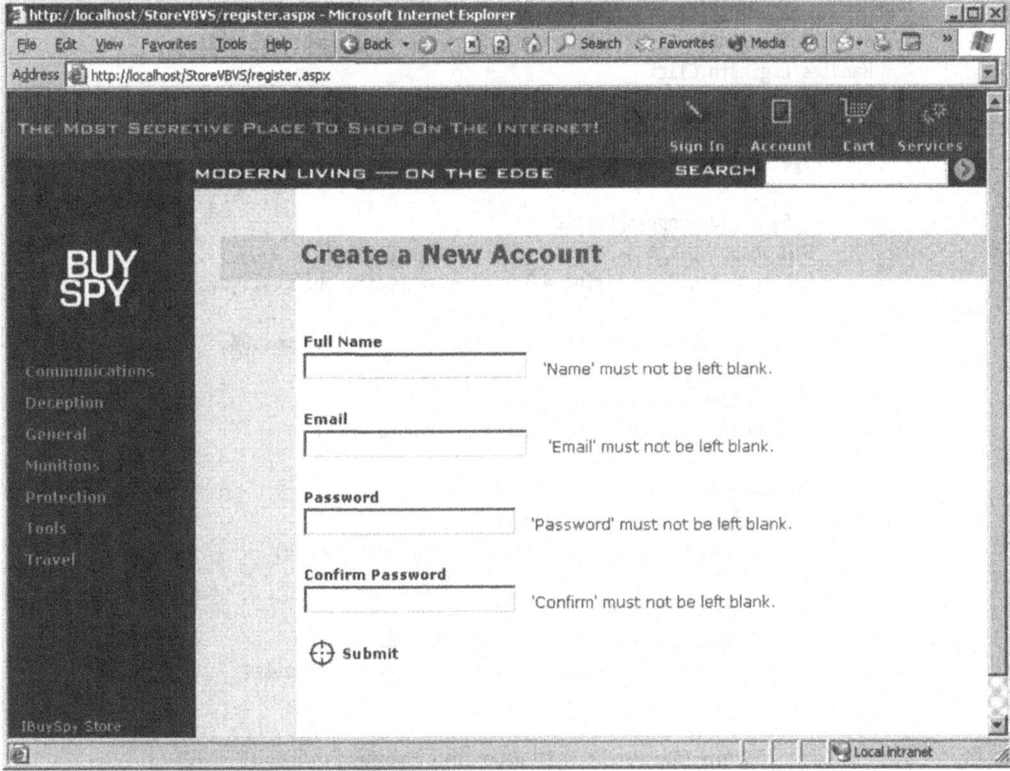

Figure 26-17. Validating the Register.aspx page

If the user chooses to log in, several steps are performed in sequence:

1. The input controls are validated to make sure reasonable values have been entered.

2. The CustomersDB.Login() method is used to authenticate the user.

3. If successful, the user's shopping cart items (which were previously stored with a random GUID) are modified to use the corresponding customer ID. This change is performed through the ShoppingCartDB.MigrateCart() method, which uses the ShoppingCartMigrate stored procedure.

4. The user's name is stored in the IBuySpy_FullName cookie for personalization purposes. If the user has chosen to create a persistent cookie, the cookie is given a one-month expiration date.

5. The user is redirected back to the page that caused the security check. In the example so far, this would be the Checkout.aspx page.

The full code is shown here.

```
Private Sub LoginBtn_Click(sender As Object,  e As ImageClickEventArgs) _
  Handles LoginBtn.Click

    ' Only attempt a login if all form fields on the page are valid.
    If Page.IsValid = True Then

        ' Save old ShoppingCartID.
        Dim shoppingCart As New IBuySpy.ShoppingCartDB()
        Dim tempCartID As String = shoppingCart.GetShoppingCartId()

        ' Attempt to Validate User Credentials using CustomersDB.
        Dim accountSystem As New IBuySpy.CustomersDB()
        Dim customerId As String = _
          accountSystem.Login(email.Text, password.Text)

        If customerId <> "" Then
            ' Migrate existing shopping cart items.
            shoppingCart.MigrateCart(tempCartID, customerId)

            ' Lookup the customer's full account details.
            Dim customerDetails As IBuySpy.CustomerDetails
            customerDetails = accountSystem.GetCustomerDetails( _
                                  customerId)

            ' Store the user's full name in a cookie
            ' for personalization purposes.
            Response.Cookies("IBuySpy_FullName").Value = _
              customerDetails.FullName

            ' Make the cookie persistent only if the user
            ' selects "persistent"
            ' login check box.
            If RememberLogin.Checked = True Then
                Response.Cookies("IBuySpy_FullName").Expires = _
                  DateTime.Now.AddMonths(1)
            End If

            ' Redirect browser back to originating page.
            FormsAuthentication.RedirectFromLoginPage(customerId, _
              RememberLogin.Checked)

        Else
            Message.Text = "Login Failed!"
        End If

    End If

End Sub
```

The Checkout.aspx Page

The final step is the Checkout.aspx page, which requires the user's final confirmation. Information is then shuffled from the ShoppingCart table to the Orders table, using the OrdersDB.PlaceOrder() method, which relies on the OrdersAdd stored procedure to perform all the necessary database operations. The stored procedure also uses a transaction to ensure that the Orders and OrderDetail records are committed or canceled as a whole. This ensures that the IBuySpy code requires the least amount of database logic possible.

```
Private Sub SubmitBtn_Click(sender As Object, e As ImageClickEventArgs) _
  Handles SubmitBtn.Click

    Dim cart As New IBuySpy.ShoppingCartDB()

    Dim cartId As String = cart.GetShoppingCartId()
    Dim customerId As String = User.Identity.Name

    If (Not cartId Is Nothing) And (Not customerId Is Nothing) Then

        ' Place the order.
        Dim ordersDatabase As New IBuySpy.OrdersDB()
        Dim orderId As Integer = _
          ordersDatabase.PlaceOrder(customerId, cartId)

        ' Update labels to reflect the fact that the order
        ' has taken place.
        Header.Text = "Check Out Complete!"
        Message.Text = "<b>Your Order Number Is: </b>"
        Message.Text &= orderId.ToString
        SubmitBtn.Visible = False

    End If

End Sub
```

The page ends with a final confirmation message (see Figure 26-18).

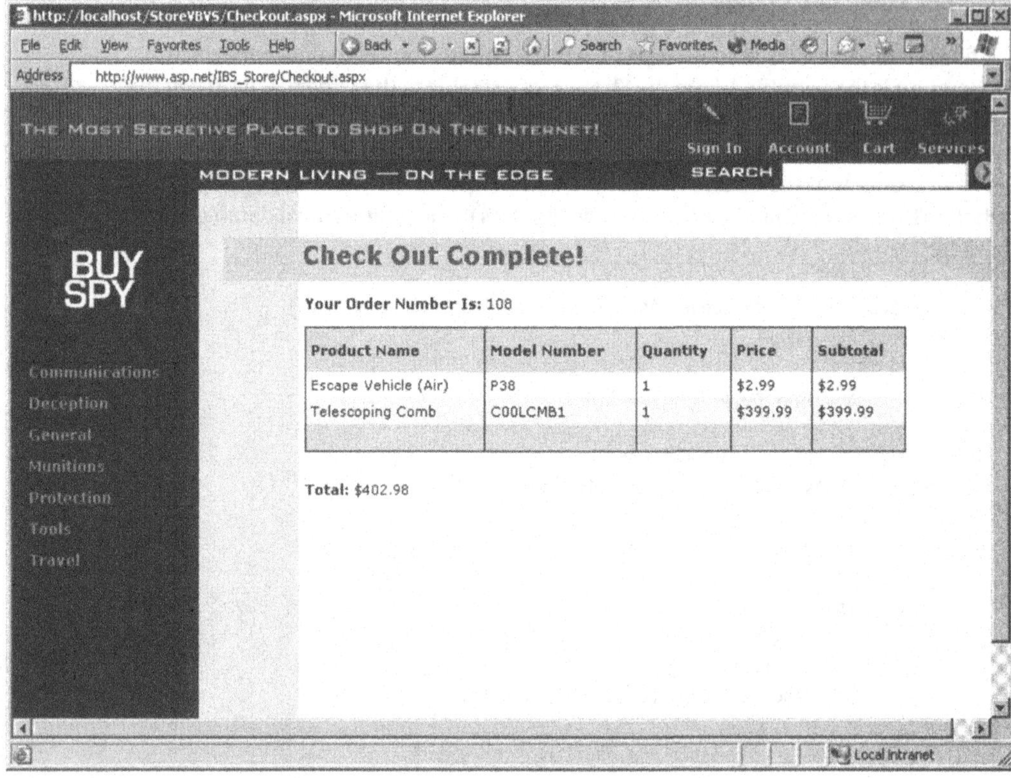

Figure 26-18. A confirmed order

The IBuySpy Store Provides Other Features

This discussion of the IBuySpy store walked you through the process of selecting an item, creating an order, and registering the user. Several other topics, like searching for a specific item, retrieving information about currently ordered items, and adding user comments were not addressed at all. However, there's really nothing more to learn—the application framework follows the exact same pattern you've seen with orders. For example, user comments are added through the ReviewDB components, which relies on the ReviewsAdd and ReviewsList stored procedures. Reviews are themselves displayed in a templated DataList control, which is actually wrapped in a _ReviewList user control.

Perhaps the most important aspect of the IBuySpy store case study is the way it demonstrates how a few simple guidelines can be used throughout a website to make a predictable, well-organized, and easily extensible framework. You'll find that every feature—from reviews to the checkout process—unfolds in the same way, using the same, disciplined approach of stored procedures and database components.

The IBuySpy Portal

A portal is a location on the Web that groups together a cluster of different types of information, usually around a central theme. For example, you might visit a programming website that provides code samples, news, and online discussions. Or you might visit a city-specific site that has information about local entertainment, the weather, and commuter traffic. The defining feature of a portal application is that this information is combined on a single page or a small group of pages. In other words, it provides "one-stop shopping" for a significant amount of information. Many portal sites also allow some level of user customization. The IBuySpy portal doesn't allow user-specific customization, but it does allow an administrator to choose the list of displayed modules, and even select where the modules will appear on the page. In fact, the majority of the complexity of the IBuySpy portal results from the fact that almost every aspect of the portal is configurable and stored in a table in the database.

The IBuySpy portal module is intended to represent a company-specific site that could be hosted on an Intranet or on the Web. For example, you could create a portal for a programming team that uses separate modules to display project deadlines, provide links to code resources, and even display information about upcoming social events.

In the last example you worked from the ground up, starting with the database foundation. This time you'll consider the user interface first, and gradually delve into the lower-level details.

The User Interface

By default, IBuySpy portal presents five tabs. The first tab is shown in Figure 26-20.

This tab is actually made up of seven distinct modules. Each module is contained in a separate control and completely independent from the other (see Figure 26-19).

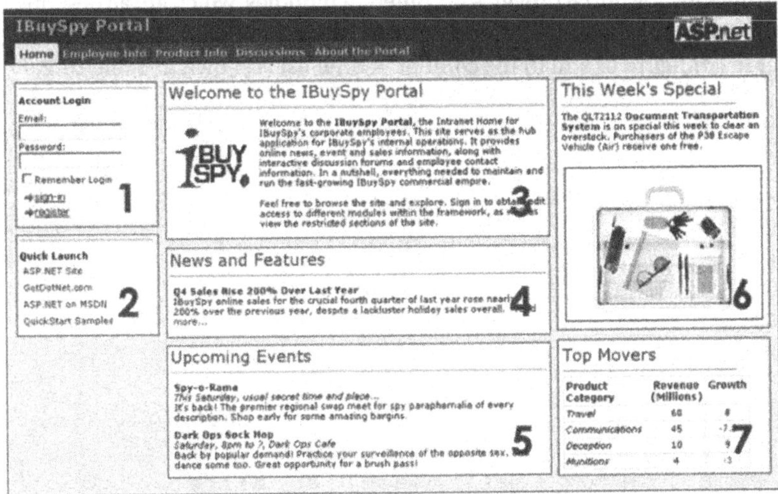

Figure 26-19. The modules in a tab

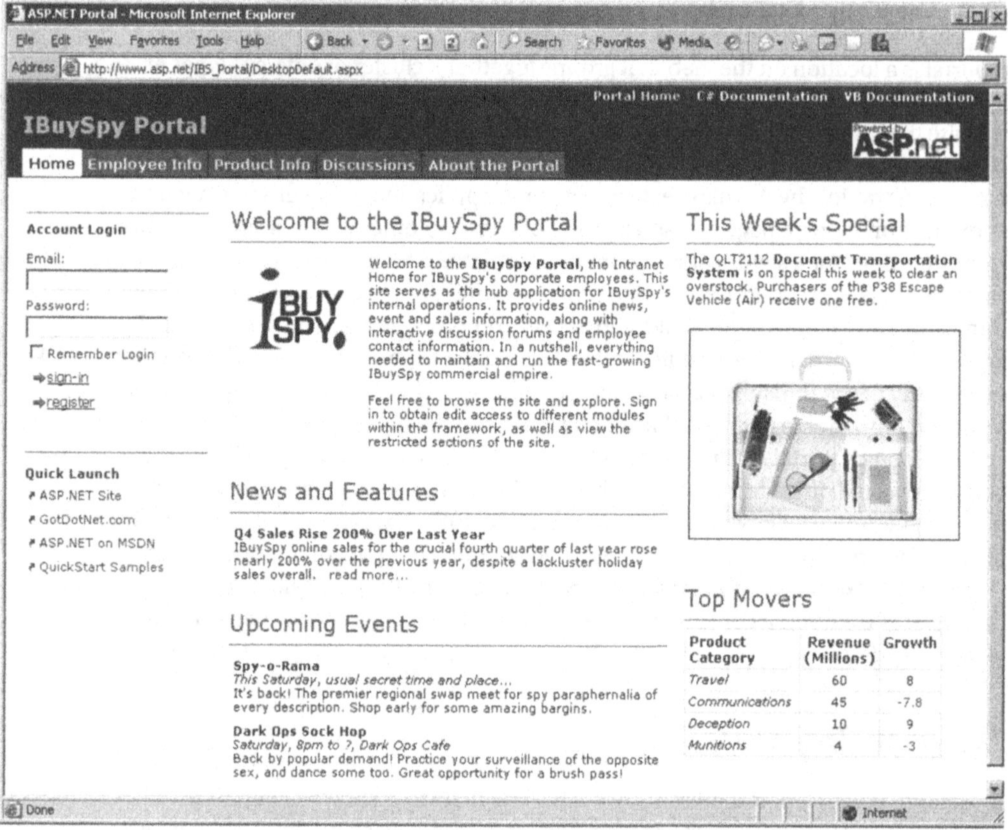

Figure 26-20. A tab in the IBuySpy portal

Altogether, the IBuySpy portal provides ten different modules, which are all described in the documentation for the website. Most of these modules provide Edit links that allow the user to configure or add to the content. A brief list is shown in Table 26-2.

Table 26-2. The IBuySpy Modules

Module*	**Description**
Announcements (4)	Displays a list of recent announcement, each of which includes a title, text, and a "read more" link. Announcements can be set to automatically expire after a particular date.
Contacts	Displays information for a group of people, such as a project team.
Discussion	Displays a group of message threads on a specific topic. Includes a Read/Reply Message page, which allows authorized users to reply to existing messages or add a new message thread.
Documents	Displays a list of documents with links that allow the user to browse the document online or download it. The document itself can be linked by a URL or stored directly in the SQL database.
Events (5)	Displays a list of upcoming events with time and location information. Like announcements, events can be set to automatically expire from the list after a particular date.
Html/Text (3 and 6)	Displays a block of HTML or text drawn from a database.
Image	Renders an image using an HTML <img> tag. The module sets the link to a file name drawn from the database, but it doesn't guarantee that the file exists.
Links	Displays a list of hyperlinks.
QuickLinks (2)	Displays a list of hyperlinks with the Quick Launch title. It's intended to be used as a compact list of global links that can be used for multiple different portal pages.
Sign-In (1)	Provides fields for entering user name and password information. This module is automatically inserted on the first tab if the user isn't authenticated.
Xml/Xsl (7)	Displays the result of an XML/XSL transform. As with the Image control, only the link to XML and XSL file is stored in the database.

* Number in Figure 26-19.

In at least one way, the IBuySpy pages are probably unlike any ASP.NET website you've worked with before. The entire interface is generated dynamically. Every module is supported by a single user control, which is supported by a separate component, which in turn draws information from a table in the database.

The initial page for the application (DesktopDefault.aspx) loads the appropriate tabs and portal modules dynamically. The (abbreviated) code for this task is shown here:

```
Private Sub Page_Init(sender As Object, e As EventArgs) _
  Handles MyBase.Init

    ' Obtain PortalSettings from Current Context.
    Dim _portalSettings As PortalSettings = _
      CType(HttpContext.Current.Items("PortalSettings"), _
      PortalSettings)

    ' Dynamically inject a signin login module into the top left
    ' corner of the home page if the client isn't authenticated.
    If Request.IsAuthenticated = False And _
      _portalSettings.ActiveTab.TabIndex = 0 Then
        LeftPane.Controls.Add( _
          Page.LoadControl("~/DesktopModules/SignIn.ascx"))
        LeftPane.Visible = True
    End If

    If _portalSettings.ActiveTab.Modules.Count > 0 Then

        ' Loop through each entry in the configuration system
        ' for this tab.
        Dim _moduleSettings As ModuleSettings
        For Each _moduleSettings In _
          _portalSettings.ActiveTab.Modules

            Dim parent As Control
            parent = Page.FindControl(_moduleSettings.PaneName)

            ' Create the user control and dynamically
            ' inject it into the page.
            Dim portalModule As PortalModuleControl = _
              CType(Page.LoadControl(_moduleSettings.DesktopSrc), _
              PortalModuleControl)
            portalModule.PortalId = _portalSettings.PortalId
            portalModule.ModuleConfiguration = _moduleSettings
            parent.Controls.Add(portalModule)

            ' Dynamically inject separator break between
            ' portal modules.
            parent.Controls.Add(New LiteralControl("<" + "br" + ">"))
            parent.Visible = True
```

```
        Next _moduleSettings

    End If

End Sub
```

Dissecting the Code . . .

- The foundation of this technique is the Page.LoadControl() method, which retrieves a user control from the .ascx file name and turns it into an object. The user control can then be added to any container control, including a panel, table cell, or server-side <div> tag.
- The code in the IBuySpy portal doesn't make any assumptions about what panels are available on the page. Instead, it retrieves a list of container control names from the PortalSettings.ActiveTab.Modules collection, and uses the Page.FindControl() method to locate the control with the indicated name. The PortalSettings class (provided in the Configuration component) retrieves the list of names from the database.
- The sign-in module is the only module that's hard-coded. You can see that it's retrieved from the DesktopModules/SignIn.ascx file and added to the control named LeftPane.

The IBuySpy Portal Is Completely Customizable

There are several ways that you can configure the IBuySpy portal:

- **Use the built-in administration tool.** Whenever you log in as a user with administrative privileges, an additional Admin tab will be added to end of the tab row. This tab lets you choose modules and assign them to panels on each page.
- **Modify the underlying data in the database.** You can perform this task directly using a database utility like SQL Server's Enterprise Manager, or you can click the Edit link for the appropriate control when it's displayed on the page.
- **Add your own controls.** All you need to do is develop a user control and add a record to the database that identifies its file name and title. Optionally, your user control can make use of additional database tables or a special component, like the default IBuySpy modules do.

The Business Components

The IBuySpy portal follows a multitiered design that's similar to the IBuySpy store. The main difference is that each module is independent and uses its own user control, module, and data. The organization of layers is shown in Figure 26-22 for three of the modules.

This chapter won't delve into the methods exposed by each module, because there are far too many. The basic design is quite similar to the IBuySpy store. For example, the AnnouncementsDB component provides methods such as GetAnnouncements(), GetSingleAnnouncement(), DeleteAnnouncement(), and AddAnnouncement(). For a quick list of all the available methods, look at Visual Studio .NET's Class View window.

In addition, there are some components that are used as part of the portal framework. These are used to retrieve information such as the number of tabs to display and the modules to place on each one. These include Configuration.vb (where most of the dynamic layout information is retrieved) and Security.vb (where users are authenticated and user roles are determined). In addition, the AdminDB tool is used to support the administration pages, which include SecurityRoles.aspx, TabLayout.aspx, ModuleSettings.aspx, and ModuleDefinitions.aspx.

The Data Layer

The IBuySpy portal site stores its information in a database named *portal*. There are three types of tables in the portal database:

- Tables that contain data for a specific module. These include Announcements, Contacts, Discussions, Documents, Events, HtmlText, and Links.
- Tables used for user information like Users, Roles, and UserRoles (see Figure 26-21). The Users table contains the actual user list, while Roles contains different configured-access levels. For example, you could create a special role record called StaffPlanner that defines a type of user that can modify event and announcement information, but no other type of content. Because one user can have multiple roles, and one role can be used for multiple users, a third table (UserRoles) is required to link them together.

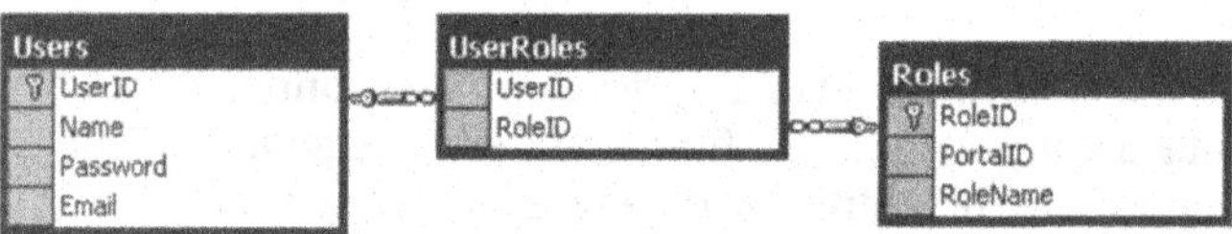

Figure 26-21. Tables with user settings

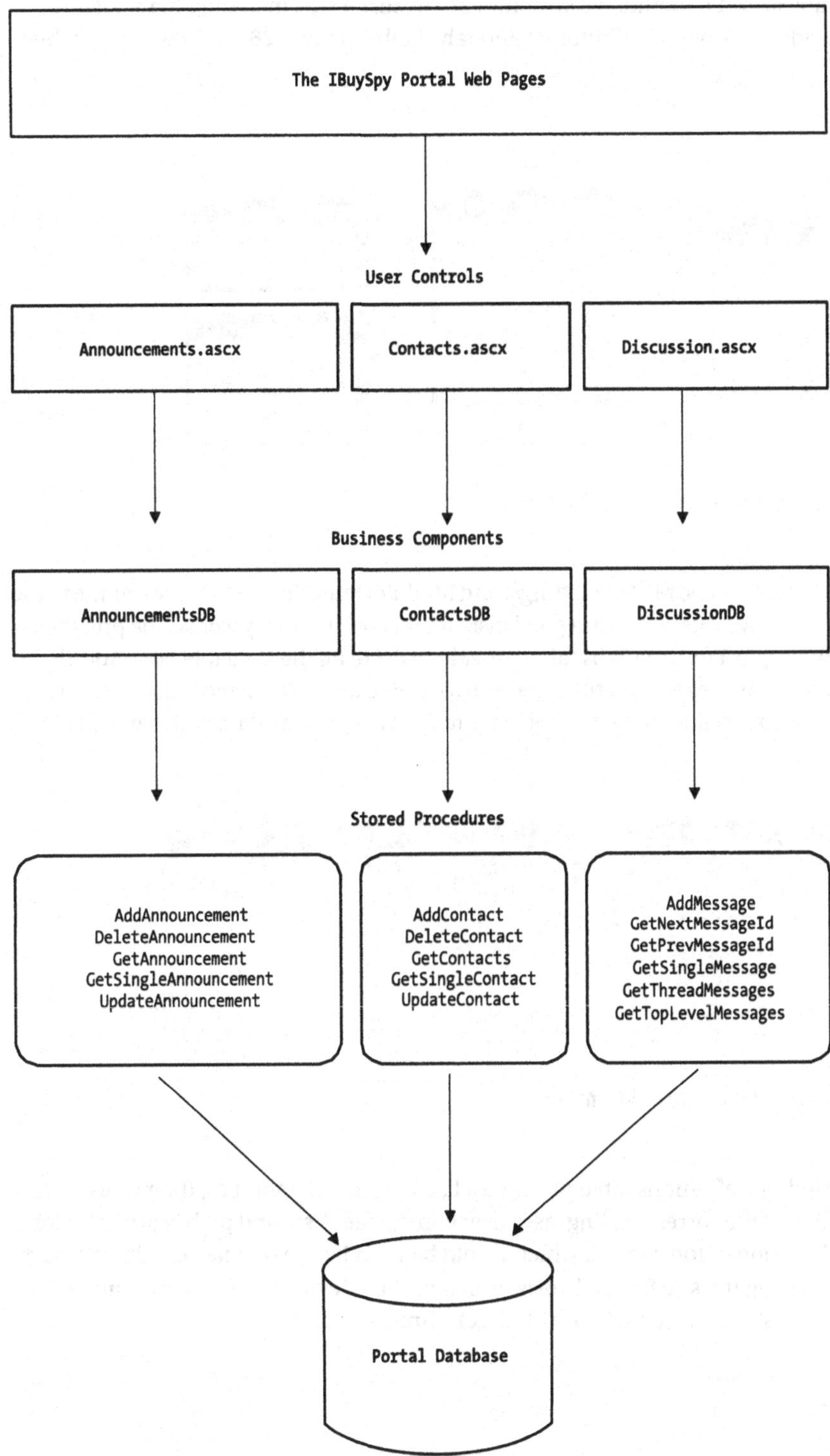

Figure 26-22. The IBuySpy portal architecture

- Tables used to define the structure of the portal site, including the available modules (ModuleDefinitions) and tabs (Tabs). Figure 26-23 shows these tables.

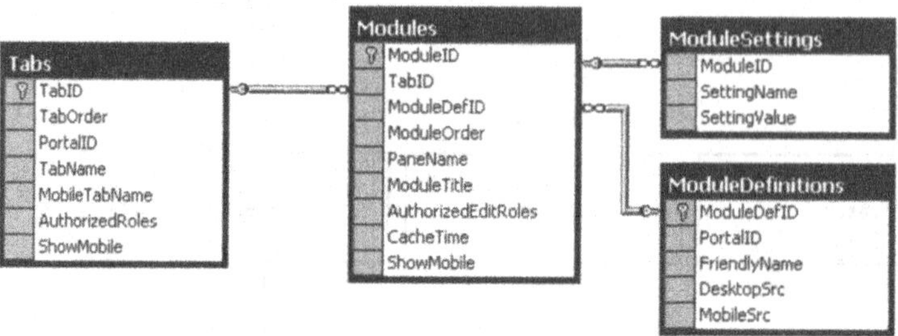

Figure 26-23. Tables with portal settings

The Modules, Tabs, ModuleSettings, and ModuleDefinitions tables are unique to the IBuySpy portal website, and give a good insight into how it actually works. The principle is strikingly simple. First, the Tabs table provides a list of all the available tabs. Additional information specifies the tab title, the relative order, and a semicolon-delimited list of user roles who are able to see this tab. Figure 26-24 shows the data in these tables.

Data in Table 'Tabs' in 'portal' on 'FARIAMAT'

TabID	TabOrder	PortalID	TabName	MobileTabName	AuthorizedRoles	ShowMobile
0	0	-1	Unused Tab	Unused Tab	All Users;	0
1	0	0	Home	Home	All Users;	1
2	1	0	Employee Info	HR	All Users;	1
3	2	0	Product Info	Products	All Users;	1
4	3	0	Discussions	Discussions	All Users;	0
5	4	0	About the Portal	About	All Users;	1
6	5	0	Admin	Admin	Admins;	0

Figure 26-24. Data in the Tabs table

The ModuleDefinitions table provides a list of available modules, their titles, and the location of the corresponding .ascx user control file. A second path is provided for a "mobile" version of the control, which would be used by the MobileDefault.aspx page when accessing the site from a browser on a mobile device such as a cell phone. Figure 26-25 shows the data in the ModuleDefinitions table.

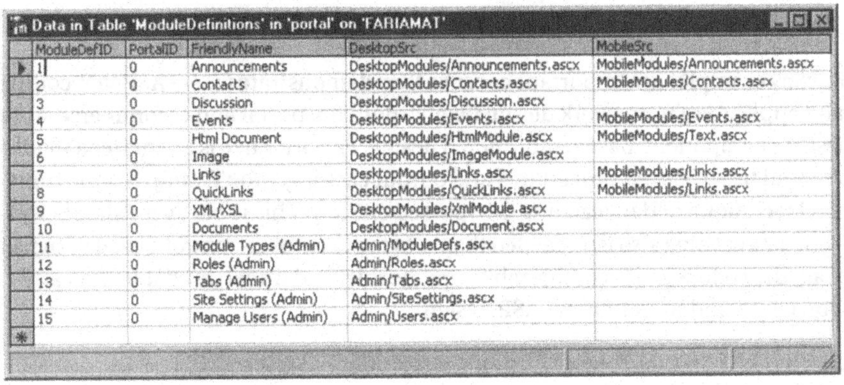

Data in Table 'ModuleDefinitions' in 'portal' on 'FARIAMAT'

ModuleDefID	PortalID	FriendlyName	DesktopSrc	MobileSrc
1	0	Announcements	DesktopModules/Announcements.ascx	MobileModules/Announcements.ascx
2	0	Contacts	DesktopModules/Contacts.ascx	MobileModules/Contacts.ascx
3	0	Discussion	DesktopModules/Discussion.ascx	
4	0	Events	DesktopModules/Events.ascx	MobileModules/Events.ascx
5	0	Html Document	DesktopModules/HtmlModule.ascx	MobileModules/Text.ascx
6	0	Image	DesktopModules/ImageModule.ascx	
7	0	Links	DesktopModules/Links.ascx	MobileModules/Links.ascx
8	0	QuickLinks	DesktopModules/QuickLinks.ascx	MobileModules/Links.ascx
9	0	XML/XSL	DesktopModules/XmlModule.ascx	
10	0	Documents	DesktopModules/Document.ascx	
11	0	Module Types (Admin)	Admin/ModuleDefs.ascx	
12	0	Roles (Admin)	Admin/Roles.ascx	
13	0	Tabs (Admin)	Admin/Tabs.ascx	
14	0	Site Settings (Admin)	Admin/SiteSettings.ascx	
15	0	Manage Users (Admin)	Admin/Users.ascx	

Figure 26-25. Data in the ModuleDefinitions table

Finally, the Modules tab links the ModuleDefinitions and Tabs tables together. It specifies the modules that will appear for each tab, and indicates the appropriate control name where the user control should be added.

The DotNetNuke Project

If you're interested in incorporating the ideas in the IBuySpy portal into your own applications, you should examine a recent offshoot called DotNetNuke.

DotNetNuke is a highly regarded open-source project with a clear goal: to provide an extensible portal framework that developers can use with their own customized modules. With the help of DotNetNuke, other developers can create rich portal websites just by installing the portal framework, plugging in the modules that are most useful for their needs, and customizing the information in the back-end database. The name is based on PHP-Nuke, a similar product that works with Linux and PHP (a server-side scripting language).

For more information about DotNetNuke, and to download the framework and custom modules, visit `http://www.dotnetnuke.com`.

The Last Word

The IBuySpy examples are important because they demonstrate where ASP.NET coding ends and application framework design begins. Both the portal and e-commerce store emphasize a component-based, multitiered design. Performance is guaranteed thanks to the careful use of stored procedures and output caching. (You'll note that the more advanced technique of data caching is bypassed entirely. This is partly for simplicity's sake—but data caching also isn't needed thanks to the clear, user-control-based designs.) Best of all, the code is more configurable, updateable, and understandable than anything you could find in traditional ASP design.

Part Six
ASP.NET Reference

CHAPTER 27

HTML Server Controls

HTML SERVER CONTROLS were introduced in Chapter 6 as a simple way to start programming with ASP.NET's new event-driven web page model. While Chapter 6 is an ideal tutorial for getting started, this chapter provides a more detailed reference that describes the key properties and events for each HTML server control, along with sample control tag declarations.

This chapter *won't* teach you about the ASP.NET server control class hierarchy or how the classes relate to one another. Instead, this reference is designed to be as useful as possible "in the field"—in other words, while you're actually programming ASP.NET code. To get additional background information and ASP.NET insight, you should use the tutorial chapters earlier in this book.

HTML Controls

HTML controls are server controls that map directly to common HTML tags. They provide far fewer features than web controls, but they're more predictable, and easier to use for some migration tasks. HTML server controls give you the ability to manipulate portions of a web page in your code, but they also allow you to retain precise control over how the page will be rendered in the final HTML output sent to the client. You can create an HTML server control by adding a runat="server" attribute to most common HTML elements.

HTML controls share a small set of common properties, as indicated in Table 27-1.

Table 27-1. Common HTML Control Properties

Member	Description
Attributes	Provides a name/value collection of all the attributes in an HTML server control. Many attributes have corresponding control properties, but this collection allows you to use other attributes or add your own proprietary ones.
Style	Provides a name/value collection of all the CSS (cascading style sheet) properties that are applied to the control.
Visible	When False, the control will not be rendered in the final page output and will not be shown to the client.
Disabled	When True, the control will be read-only and will not accept user input.
TagName	A string that indicates the HTML tag name for the server control as a string (for example, "a" for the <a> tag).

Table 27-1. Common HTML Control Properties (Continued)

Member	Description
InnerHtml*	Gets or sets the text found between the opening and closing tags of the control. Special characters are not converted to HTML entities, which means that you can use this property to apply formatting using nested tags such as <b>, <i>, and <h1>.
InnerText*	Gets or sets the text between the opening and closing tags of the specified HTML control. Special characters are automatically converted to HTML entities. For example, the less than character (<) is converted to <.
Name**	The unique identifier for an input control.
Value**	The user content for an input control (for example, the text entered in a text box).
Type**	A string representing the value of the type attribute for an input control (for example, "text" is returned for an HtmlInputText control).

* Only provided for container controls that have both an opening and closing tag and inherit from HtmlContainerControl (includes HtmlTableCell, HtmlTable, HtmlTableRow, HtmlButton, HtmlForm, HtmlAnchor, HtmlGenericControl, HtmlSelect, and HtmlTextArea).

** Only provided for input controls (HtmlInputText, HtmlInputButton, HtmlInputCheckBox, HtmlInputImage, HtmlInputHidden, HtmlInputFile, and HtmlInputRadioButton), which inherit from HtmlInputControl.

HtmlAnchor

HtmlAnchor represents the server-side equivalent of the HTML <a> tag. This tag creates a hyperlink to another page or a bookmark.

```
<a id="MyAnchor"
   href="http:\\www.prosetech.com"
   name="bookmarkname"
   target="_blank"
   title="My Site"
   runat="server" >
Click Here
</a>
```

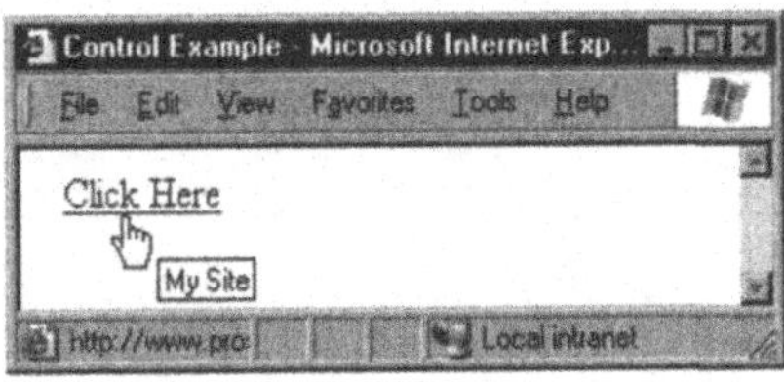

Figure 27-1. The HtmlAnchor control

Table 27-2. HtmlAnchor Members

Member	Description
HRef	The destination URL that the browser will go to when the hyperlink is clicked.
InnerText and InnerHtml	The content that the user must click to follow the link. You can use the InnerHtml property to add formatting tags to the text, or other HTML elements such as images and line breaks.
Name	The bookmark name, which can be used to identify a specific location in a page. You can then link to this location by adding #bookmarkname to the end of the page URL in a request.
Target	The target window or frame where the destination page will be opened. This can name a specific frame, or use a special constant such as _blank (for a new window), _parent (the containing frameset), _self (the current window), or _top (the top-level parent).
ServerClick event	Allows you to react to the link click programmatically. If you code an event handler for this event, you don't need to enter values for HRef and Target.

HtmlButton

HtmlButton represents the server-side equivalent of the <button> tag, which is supported in Internet Explorer 4.0 or higher. It creates a standard push button that can contain any HTML content, including images. In the following example, the button surface combines two pictures, some bolded text, and two horizontal lines:

```
<button id="MyButton"
        runat="server" type="button" >
   <img src="happy.gif" ><hr>
   <b>A Special Button</b><hr>
   <img src="happy.gif" >
</button>
```

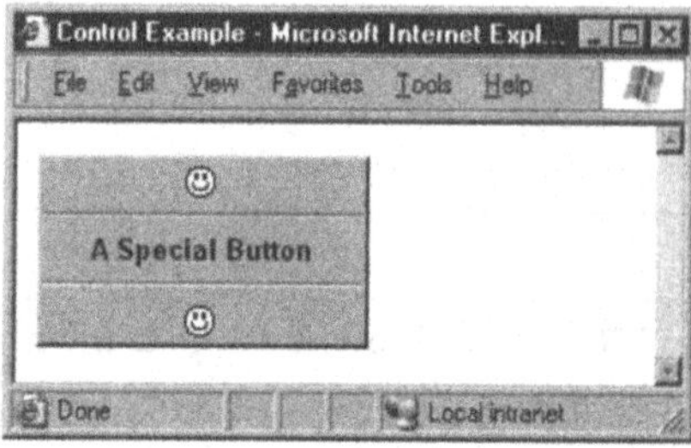

Figure 27-2. The HtmlButton control

Table 27-3. HtmlButton Members

Member	Description
CausesValidation	If set to True (the default), the page will automatically be validated using all the validation controls on the form when the button is clicked. Depending on the browser capabilities, an invalid page may not be posted back (see Chapter 9).
InnerText and InnerHtml	The content on the surface of the button.
ServerClick event	Occurs when the user clicks the button.

HtmlForm

HtmlForm represents the server-side equivalent of the <form> tag. All ASP.NET controls must be contained inside a server-side HtmlForm control for your code to be able to access them. However, you'll rarely need to interact directly with the HtmlForm itself. In fact, by default Visual Studio .NET doesn't even define a variable in code-behind classes for you to access the HtmlForm on a page.

```
<form id="MyForm"
      method="POST"
      runat="server" >
   [Other controls or content goes here.]
</form>
```

Table 27-4. HtmlForm Members

Member	Description
Method	Indicates how the browser sends data to the server.
Enctype	A string specifying the encoding type the browser will use when posting data to the server. The standard encoding is "application/x-www-form-urlencoded" but "multipart/form-data" is required to allow file uploads on pages that use the HtmlInputFile control.

HtmlGenericControl

HtmlGenericControl represents HTML server controls that aren't represented by other dedicated classes, such as <div>, <span>, <body>, <font>, and so on.

```
<span|body|div|font|other>
      id="MyControl"
      runat="server" >
   [Content goes here.]
</span|body|div|font|other>
```

Table 27-5. HtmlGenericControl Members

Member	Description
InnerText and InnerHtml	The text and HTML content contained between the opening and closing tags for the control.
TagName	Similar to the basic TagName property exposed by all HTML controls, but *not* read-only. This allows you to modify the actual tag programmatically (for example, changing a server-based <div> tag to a server-based <span> tag on postback).

HtmlImage

HtmlImage represents the server-side equivalent of the HTML <img> tag, which displays a picture (typically a GIF, JPG, or PNG file).

```
<img id="MyImage"
     alt="The Monkey"
     align="top"
     border="3"
     src="monkey.jpg"
     runat="server" >
```

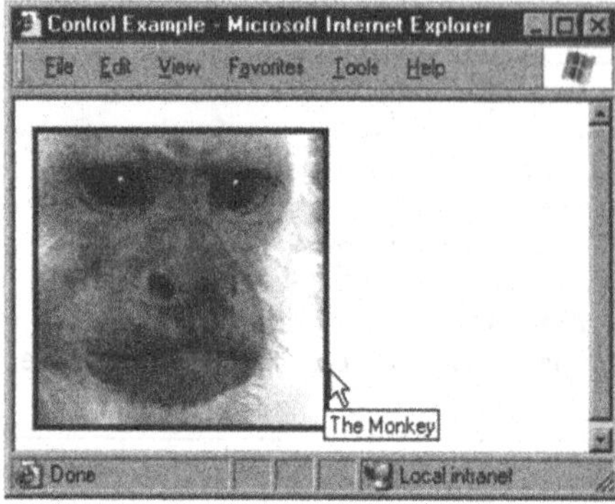

Figure 27-3. The HtmlImage control

Table 27-6. HtmlImage Members

Member	Description
Alt	The text that will be displayed in a browser that doesn't support pictures, and the pop-up tooltip text shown in Internet Explorer when the user hovers over the picture with the mouse.
Align	The alignment of an image relative to the page (left, top, or right) or the contents of the page (top, middle, bottom).
Border	Sets the width of the border in pixels.
Height and Width	Sets the proportions of the image in pixels. To avoid distortion, it's usually easier not to specify these properties, and let the image automatically use its intrinsic size.
Src	The path and file name of the image that will be displayed. This can be an absolute or relative link.

HtmlInputButton

HtmlInputButton represents the server-side equivalent of the HTML <input type="button">, <input type="submit">, and <input type="reset"> tags.

```
<input type="button"
       id="MyButton"
       value="Click Me!"
       runat="server" >
```

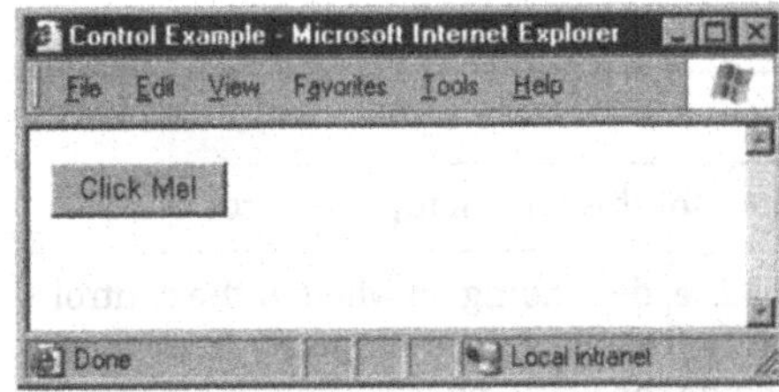

Figure 27-4. The HtmlInputButton control

Table 27-7. HtmlInputButton Members

Member	Description
CausesValidation	If set to True (the default), the page will automatically be validated using all the validation controls on the form when the button is clicked. Depending on the browser capabilities, an invalid page may not be posted back (see Chapter 9).
Type	Identifies the type of button tag (server, submit, or reset).
Value	Sets the button's caption.
ServerClick event	Occurs when the user clicks the button.

HtmlInputCheckBox

HtmlInputCheckBox represents the server-side equivalent of the HTML <input type="checkbox"> tag, which creates a check box that can be checked or unchecked. This control doesn't have any associated caption text. Instead, you need to add content next to the control tag.

```
<input type="checkbox"
       id="MyCheckBox"
       checked runat="server" >
  Keep Me Logged In
```

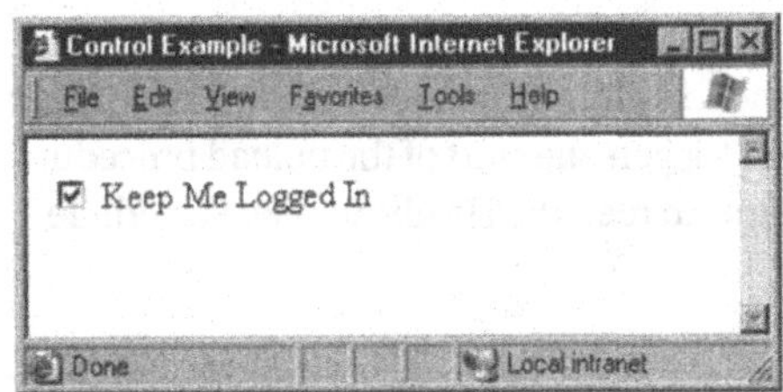

Figure 27-5. The HtmlInputCheckBox control

Table 27-8. HtmlInputCheckBox Members

Member	Description
Type	Returns "check box" for this type of input control.
Checked	Indicates True or False, depending on whether the control is checked. In the control tag, you don't specify True or False. Instead, include the word "checked" on its own to indicate that the initial state of the control is checked.
ServerChange event	Occurs when the check box state changes between checked and unchecked. Your event handler code cannot react to this event immediately. Instead, it will be triggered first with the next postback. For a check box that reacts instantaneously, use the CheckBox web control instead.

HtmlInputFile

HtmlInputFile represents the server-side equivalent of the HTML <input type="file"> tag, which allows the user to upload a file. For a complete example of how to use this control, refer to Chapter 17.

```
<input type="file"
       id="MyFileUploader"
       accept="image/*"
       size="30"
       runat="server" >
```

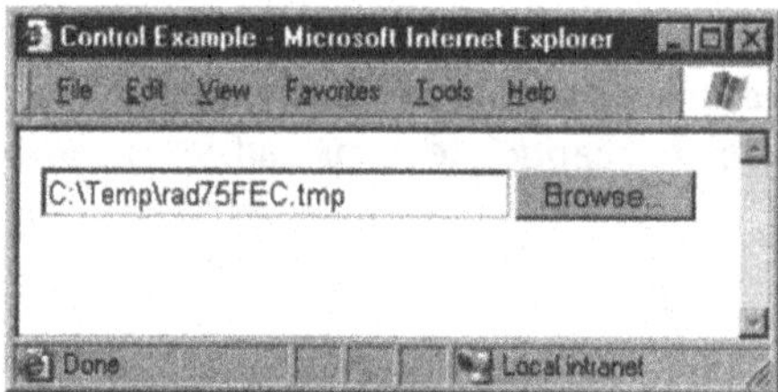

Figure 27-6. The HtmlInputFile control

The browser provides the Browse button functionality automatically. However, to allow uploading you need to add a button control that triggers the start of the upload procedure. The event handler for this button simply attempts to read the HtmlInputFile.PostedFile property.

Table 27-9. HtmlInputFile Members

Member	Description
Type	Returns "file" for this type of input control.
Accept	A comma-separated list of MIME encodings used to constrain the file types the user can select. MIME encodings take the format "application/type" where application represents a class of applications (such as video, image, or text), and type represents a unique MIME type (or asterisk for all).
Size	Set the width of the file-path selection text box in character columns.
MaxLength	Set the maximum number of characters that are allowed for the path.
PostedFile	Allows you to access the posted file as an HttpPostedFile object. Use the PostedFile.SaveAs method to save the file to a location on the server. If the user hasn't chosen a file, this property will be set to Nothing.

HtmlInputHidden

HtmlInputHidden represents the server-side equivalent of the HTML <input type="hidden"> tag, which allows you to store information between postbacks. In ASP.NET coding, it's generally easier to use the Page.ViewState collection instead to store any information you need to retain. This technique is described in Chapter 10.

```
<input type="hidden"
       id="MyHiddenInformation"
       value="[Some Hidden String Data]"
       runat="server"
```

Table 27-10. HtmlInputHidden Members

Member	Description
Type	Returns "hidden" for this type of input control.
Value	Contains the hidden information (as a single string).

HtmlInputRadioButton

HtmlInputRadioButton represents the server-side equivalent of the HTML <input type="radio"> tag. Usually, you'll add radio buttons in a group that allows only one item to be selected at a time. The following example shows two radio buttons in a group called GenderGroup. Note that this control doesn't have any associated caption text. Instead, you need to add content next to the control tag.

```
<input type=radio
      id="Option1"
      name="GenderGroup"
      runat="server" >
   Male<br>
<input type=radio
      id="Option2"
      name="GenderGroup"
      runat="server" >
   Female
```

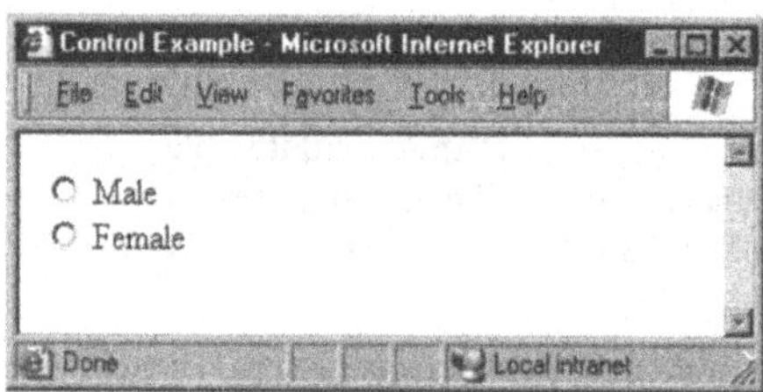

Figure 27-7. The HtmlInputRadioButton control

Table 27-11. HtmlInputRadioButton Members

Member	Description
Type	Returns "radio" for this type of input control.
Name	Identifies the radio button group. Only one radio button can be selected in a group.
Checked	Indicates True or False, depending on whether the radio button is selected. In the control tag, you can include the "checked" attribute on its own to indicate that the radio button is initially selected.
ServerChange event	Occurs when the radio button state changes between selected and unselected. Your event-handler code cannot react to this event immediately. Instead, it will be triggered first with the next postback. For a radio button that reacts instantaneously, use the RadioButton web control instead.

HtmlInputText

HtmlInputText represents the server-side equivalent of the HTML <input type="text"> tag, which allows single-line text box input.

```
<input type="text"
       id="MyText"
       maxlength="20"
       size="40"
       value="Matthew"
       runat="server">
```

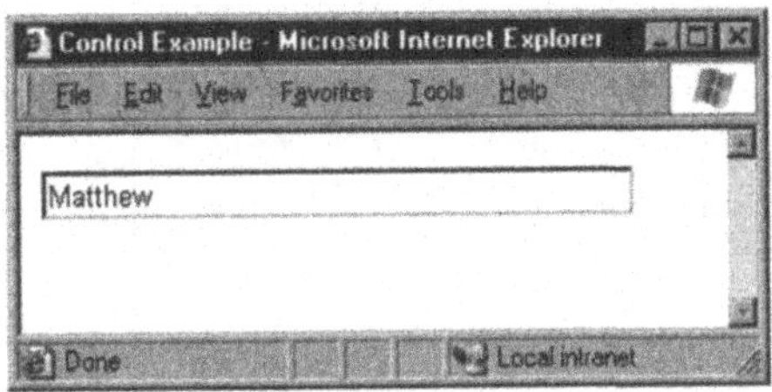

Figure 27-8. The HtmlInputText control

Table 27-12. HtmlInputText Members

Member	Description
Type	Can be the standard "text" or "password," which uses asterisks (*) to mask user input.
MaxLength	The maximum number of characters that the user can type into the text box.
Size	Sets the character width of the text box.
Value	Sets or returns the text in the text box.
ServerChange event	Occurs when the text in the text box is changed. Your event-handler code cannot react to this event immediately. Instead, it will be triggered first with the next postback. For a text box that reacts instantaneously, use the TextBox web control instead.

HtmlSelect

HtmlSelect represents the server-side equivalent of the HTML <select> tag, which is used to create a list of items. This can be a drop-down list that shows one item at a time or a multiline list box. It can also be set to allow single or multiple selection.

```
<select id="MyList"
        size="3"
        runat="server" >
  <option value="1">Option 1</option>
  <option value="2">Option 2</option>
  <option value="3">Option 3</option>
  <option value="4">Option 4</option>
</select>
```

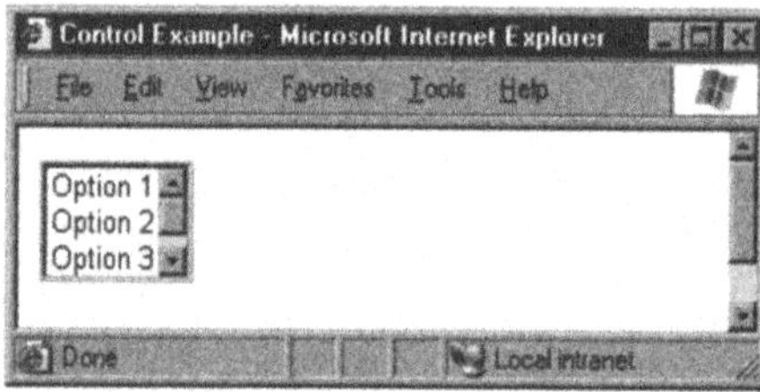

Figure 27-9. The HtmlSelect control

Table 27-13. HtmlSelect Members

Member	**Description**
DataSource, DataTextField, and DataValueField	Allows you to bind the list to any data source. If you're binding to a data source with more than one field, you can bind one field to the option item text, and another field to the hidden value attribute for each option item.
Size	The number of items that will be shown at once. When set to 1, the HtmlSelect control will become a drop-down list.
Multiple	When True, the user can select more than one list item at a time. To specify this in the control declaration, just include the attribute "multiple" on its own. A multiple-select list control will automatically be a list box instead of a drop-down list.
SelectedIndex	A zero-based index number that indicates or sets the currently selected item.
SelectedIndices	An array of selected index numbers that can be used when multiple item selection is enabled.
SelectedValue	Returns the text of the currently selected item.

Table 27-13. HtmlSelect Members (Continued)

Member	Description
Items	Provides a collection of System.Web.UI.WebControls.ListItem objects that represent all the items in the list. You can check each item's Selected property to see if it's currently selected. You can use the Text and Value items to retrieve or set the information in the option item's text or its value attribute.
ServerChange event	Occurs when the selection is changed. Your event-handler code cannot react to this event immediately. Instead, it will be triggered first with the next postback. For a list that reacts instantaneously, use the ListBox or DropDownList web control instead.

HtmlTable

HtmlTable represents the server-side equivalent of the HTML <table> tag, which is used to create a multicolumn table. The basic format of an HtmlTable control tag is as follows:

```
<table id="programmaticID"
       align="left|center|right"
       bgcolor="bgcolor"
       border="borderwidth"
       bordercolor="bordercolor"
       cellpadding="spacing_within_cells"
       cellspacing="spacing_between_cells"
       height="tableheight"
       width="tablewidth"
       runat="server" >
   <tr>
      <td></td>
   </tr>

</table>
```

Table 27-14. HtmlTable Members

Member	Description
Align	The alignment of an table relative to the page (left, top, or right) or the contents of the page (top, middle, bottom).
BgColor	The background color of all the cells in the table.
Border	The width of the border in pixels (the default of –1 means no border).
BorderColor	The color of the border as a color code or friendly name (such as "red").
CellPadding	The space, in pixels, between the border of a cell and its contents.
CellSpacing	The space, in pixels, between cells in the table.
Height and Width	The height and width of the table in pixels. Alternatively, you can specify a percentage by appending a percent sign to the number in the control tag. Percentages are relative to the height or width of the browser window.
Rows	Provides a collection of HtmlTableRow objects that represent the individual <tr> elements in the table. You can use methods such as Add, Insert, and Remove to dynamically configure a table.

The table is composed of HtmlTableRow and HtmlTableCell elements. You can interact with these elements individually to set row-specific or cell-specific properties (such as the text or the formatting).

Table 27-15. HtmlTableRow Members

Member	Description
Align, BgColor, BorderColor	These style properties have the same effect for individual rows as the corresponding HtmlTable properties have for the entire table.
Height	The height of a row in pixels, which may be constrained by the height of the table.
VAlign	The vertical alignment of a row, which can be middle, top, bottom, or baseline.
Cells	Provides a collection of HtmlTableCell objects that represent the individual <td> (table cell) and <th> (table header) elements in the table. You can use methods such as Add, Insert, and Remove to dynamically configure a table row.

Table 27-16. HtmlTableCell Members

Member	Description
Align, BgColor, BorderColor	These style properties have the same effect for individual cells as the corresponding HtmlTable properties have for the entire table.
Height and Width	The height or width of a cell in pixels, which can be constrained by the height of the row.
InnerText and InnerHTML	The text or HTML content inside the table cell.
VAlign	The vertical alignment of a cell, which can be middle, top, bottom, or baseline.
NoWrap	If True, the text in the box will not wrap, but the column will be resized to fit. The default is False.
RowSpan and ColSpan	Specifies how many rows or columns a given cell should span. This setting, which allows one cell to occupy a larger area, isn't supported by all browsers.

A complete table can be created programmatically by adding HtmlTableCell and HtmlTableRow objects at runtime to the HtmlTableRow.Cells and HtmlTable.Rows collections, respectively. (An example of this technique is provided in Chapter 7 with the Table web control.) However, these dynamically created tables will not be persisted in viewstate automatically, and so must be manually re-created after each postback.

Another possibility is to create the table declaratively. Note that tags contained in the HtmlTable tag, such as <tr> and <td>, don't need the runat="server" tag, because this is assumed automatically.

```
<table id="MyTable" cellSpacing="1" cellPadding="1" width="300" border="1"
       runat="server" >
  <tr>
    <td>Cell 1, 1</td>
    <td>Cell 1, 2</td>
    <td>Cell 1, 3</td></tr>
  <tr>
    <td>Cell 2, 1</td>
    <td>Cell 2, 2</td>
    <td>Cell 2, 3</td></tr>
  <tr>
    <td>Cell 3, 1</td>
    <td>Cell 3, 2</td>
    <td>Cell 3, 3</td></tr>
</table>
```

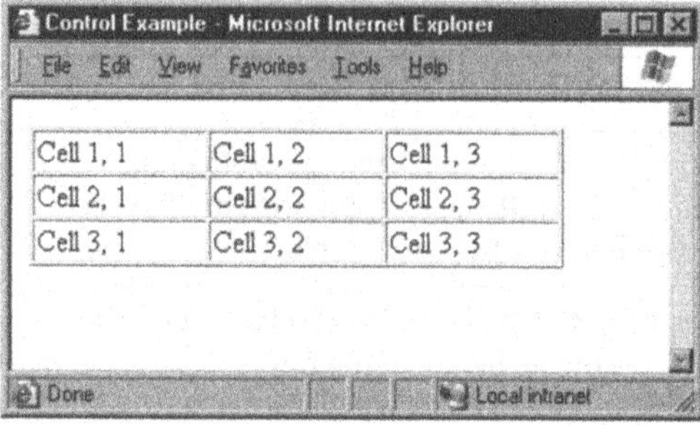

Figure 27-10. The HtmlTable control

HtmlTextArea

The HtmlTextArea class represents a multiline text box and is the server-side equivalent of the HTML <textarea> tag.

```
<textarea id="MyText"
          cols="40"
          rows="5"
          runat="server" >
The Initial Text.
</textarea>
```

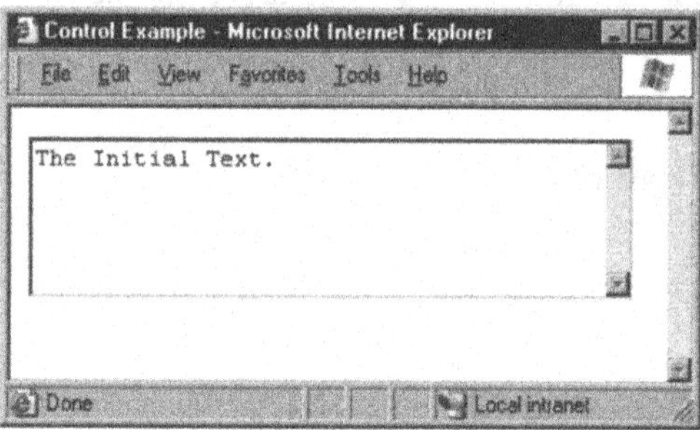

Figure 27-11. The HtmlTextArea control

Table 27-17. HtmlTextArea Members

Member	Description
Cols	The character width of the text area. The default is –1 (not set), in which case the browser will apply a default size.
Rows	The display height of the text area, in characters. The default is –1 (not set), in which case the browser will apply a default size.
Value	Can be used to get or set the text in the text area. You can insert initial text between opening and closing tags, as shown in the example.
ServerChange event	Occurs when the text in the text area is changed. Your event-handler code cannot react to this event immediately. Instead, it will be triggered first with the next postback. For a text box that reacts instantaneously, use the TextBox web control instead.

CHAPTER 28

Web Controls

ASP.NET SERVER CONTROLS were introduced in Chapters 6, 7, and 9, and data controls were featured in Chapter 16. In these chapters, and throughout the book, you'll find a number of complete examples that show you how to use server controls in your web pages. When you're beginning your ASP.NET programming career, these tutorial chapters are the best place to start.

However, as you become more familiar with ASP.NET, it helps to have more detailed, concise information that shows each control at a glance. This chapter provides that service with a thorough reference that highlights the key points about each web control. The controls are organized by type, and each one is shown with a sample control tag declaration and a list of important members.

Basic Web Controls

Some web controls duplicate the functionality of HTML server controls, and others are high-level objects that render themselves with dozens of lines of HTML code. When compared to HTML server controls as a whole, web controls provide a higher-level abstraction, more extensive functionality, and the ability to post back automatically and raise a much richer set of events. You'll also find that web controls are more consistent—mirroring their Windows equivalents with common properties such as Text, ForeColor, and BorderStyle.

Table 28-1. Common Web Server Control Properties

Member	Description
AccessKey	Specifies the keyboard shortcut as one letter. For example, if you set this to "Y," the Alt-Y keyboard combination will automatically change focus to this web control. This feature is only supported on Internet Explorer 4 and higher.
BackColor, BorderColor and ForeColor	Sets the colors used for the background, border, and foreground of the control. Usually, the foreground color is used for text. Colors can be set in the attribute tag using standard HTML color identifiers such as the name of a color (for example, "black" or "red") or an RGB value expressed in hexadecimal format (like #ffffff). You can also set the color in code by assigning a System.Drawing.Color object.
BorderWidth	Specifies the size of the control border in pixels.
BorderStyle	One of the values from the BorderStyle enumeration, such as Dashed, Dotted, Double, Groove, Ridge, Inset, Outset, Solid, or None.

Table 28-1. Common Web Server Control Properties (Continued)

Member	**Description**
Enabled	When set to False, the control will be visible, but will not be able to receive user input or focus.
Font	Specifies the font used to render any text in the control, as a special System.Drawing.Font object. In the control tag, you must specify the Font using the special object walker syntax, as described in Chapter 7.
Height and Width	Specifies the width and height of the control. By default, these numbers will be interpreted as pixel measurements, but you can specify otherwise, as described in Chapter 7. For some controls, these properties will be ignored when used with older browsers.
Style	Provides a name/value collection of all the CSS (cascading style sheet) properties that are applied to the control. This property is generally less used with web controls, in favor of higher-level properties (such as BackColor) that take precedence.
TabIndex	A number that allows you to control the Tab order. The control with a TabIndex of 0 has the focus when the page first loads. Pressing Tab moves the user to the control with the next lowest TabIndex, provided it's enabled. This property is only supported in Internet Explorer 4.0 and higher.
Tool	Displays a text message when the user hovers the mouse over the control. Many older browsers don't support this property.
Visible	When set to False, the control will be hidden and will not be rendered to the final HTML page that is sent to the client.

ASP.NET developers commonly ask what color names are valid to use in the .aspx control tag. To find the complete list, you can refer to the System.Drawing.KnownColor enumeration. You can also retrieve the named colors as Color objects through the properties of the System.Drawing.Color class.

The following is a list of valid color names:

AliceBlue
AntiqueWhite
Aqua
Aquamarine
Azure
Beige
Bisque
Black
BlanchedAlmond
Blue
BlueViolet
Brown
BurlyWood
CadetBlue
Chartreuse
Chocolate
Coral
CornflowerBlue
Cornsilk
Crimson
Cyan
DarkBlue
DarkCyan
DarkGoldenrod
DarkGray
DarkGreen
DarkKhaki
DarkMagenta
DarkOliveGreen
DarkOrange
DarkOrchid
DarkRed
DarkSalmon
DarkSeaGreen
DarkSlateBlue
DarkSlateGray
DarkTurquoise
DarkViolet
DeepPink
DeepSkyBlue
DimGray
DodgerBlue
Firebrick
FloralWhite
ForestGreen
Fuchsia
Gainsboro
GhostWhite
Gold
Goldenrod
Gray
Green
GreenYellow
Honeydew
HotPink
IndianRed
Indigo
Ivory
Khaki
Lavender
LavenderBlush
LawnGreen
LemonChiffon
LightBlue
LightCoral
LightCyan
LightGoldenrodYellow
LightGray
LightGreen
LightPink
LightSalmon
LightSeaGreen
LightSkyBlue
LightSlateGray
LightSteelBlue
LightYellow
Lime
LimeGreen
Linen
Magenta
Maroon
MediumAquamarine
MediumBlue
MediumOrchid
MediumPurple
MediumSeaGreen
MediumSlateBlue
MediumSpringGreen
MediumTurquoise
MediumVioletRed
MidnightBlue
MintCream
MistyRose
Moccasin
NavajoWhite
Navy
OldLace
Olive
OliveDrab
Orange
OrangeRed
Orchid
PaleGoldenrod
PaleGreen
PaleTurquoise
PaleVioletRed
PapayaWhip
PeachPuff
Peru
Pink
Plum
PowderBlue
Purple
Red
RosyBrown
RoyalBlue
SaddleBrown
Salmon
SandyBrown
SeaGreen
SeaShell
Sienna
Silver
SkyBlue
SlateBlue
SlateGray
Snow
SpringGreen
SteelBlue
Tan
Teal
Thistle
Tomato
Transparent
Turquoise
Violet
Wheat
White
WhiteSmoke
Yellow
YellowGreen

Button

This control creates the familiar clickable push button on a web page. Clicking a button automatically posts back the page, and raises the appropriate Click event.

```
<asp:Button id="cmdClickMe"
     Text="Click Me"
     CausesValidation="True"
     runat="server"/>
```

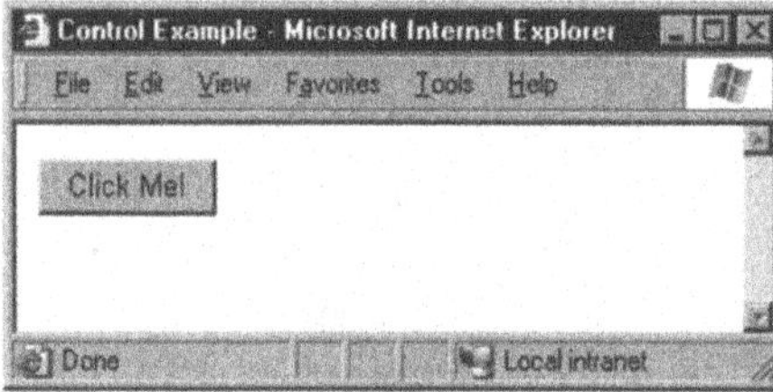

Figure 28-1. The Button control

Table 28-2. Button Members

Member	Description
Text	The button's caption.
CausesValidation	If set to True (the default), the page will automatically be validated using all the validation controls on the form when the button is clicked. Depending on the browser capabilities, an invalid page may not be posted back (see Chapter 9).
Click and Command events	Occur when the button is clicked. The only difference between the two is that the Command event receives extra information, namely the CommandName and CommandArgument properties. The examples in this book don't use the Command event (except in the case of templated data controls). Instead, they rely on .NET's ability to compare and identify control objects.
CommandName and CommandArgument	Extra information provided to the Command event, which can allow you to uniquely identify the button in the case that your event handler is receiving the events from multiple different button controls. The CommandName is a string meant to represent the action (such as "Sort") while CommandArgument stores any additional information (such as the field to sort by).

CheckBox

This control creates a check box that can be checked or unchecked, along with an associated label.

```
<asp:CheckBox id="chkSignUp"
     AutoPostBack="False"
     Text="Keep Me Logged In"
     TextAlign="Right"
     Checked="True"
     runat="server"/>
```

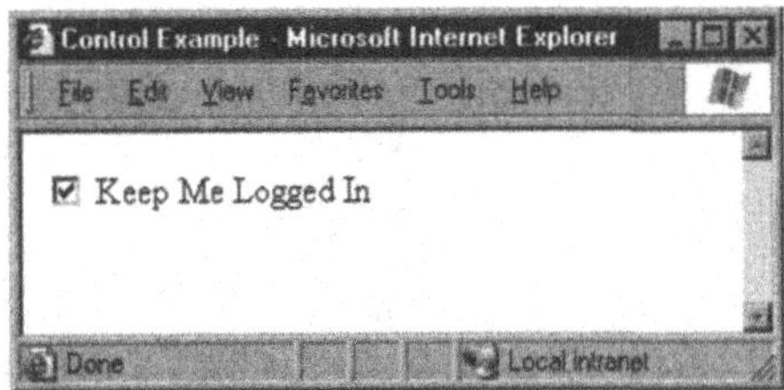

Figure 28-2. The CheckBox control

Table 28-3. CheckBox Members

Member	Description
AutoPostBack	Determines whether the page will be posted back when the check box state is changed. This allows your code to react to the CheckedChanged event immediately.
Text	The label that is displayed next to the check box.
TextAlign	The side of the check box where the text will be displayed. Can be Left or Right.
Checked	Indicates or sets the current state of the check box.
CheckedChanged event	Fires when the check box state changes (for example, when the user clicks to check or uncheck the check box). If AutoPostBack is False, this event will be "delayed" until the next postback.

HyperLink

This control represents a link to another page, either as underlined hyperlink text or as an image. Unlike the anchor tag (and HtmlAnchor control), this control cannot be used to create a bookmark. The HyperLink class doesn't provide any type of Click event—for this type of functionality you need to use the LinkButton web control.

```
<asp:HyperLink id="lnkProseTech"
    NavigateUrl="http:\\www.prosetech.com "
    Text="Click Here"
    Target="_blank"
    ToolTip = "MySite"
    runat="server"/>
```

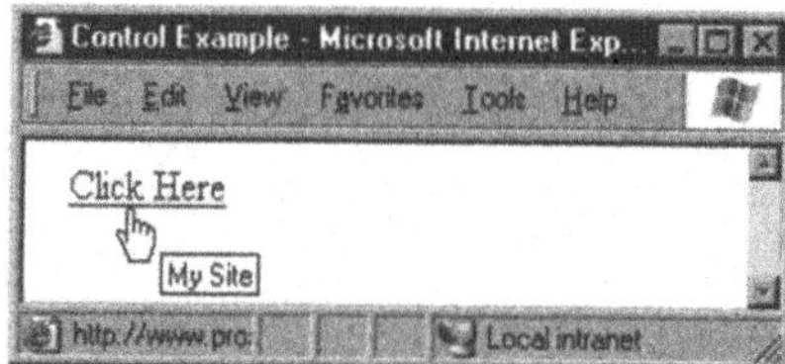

Figure 28-3. The HyperLink control

Table 28-4. HyperLink Members

Member	**Description**
NavigateUrl	The destination URL the browser will go to when the hyperlink is clicked.
Text	The text content that the user must click to follow the link.
ImageUrl	The image that the user must click to follow the link (as a relative or absolute file name). If both ImageUrl and Text are set, the image will take precedence and the text will not be shown, unless there is a problem finding and displaying the image.
Target	The target window or frame where the destination page will be opened. This can name a specific frame, or use a special constant such as _blank (for a new window), _parent (the containing frameset), _self (the current window), or _top (the top-level parent).

Image

This control displays an image (typically a GIF, JPG, or PNG file).

```
<asp:Image id="imgMonkey" runat="server"
    ImageUrl="monkey.jpg"
    AlternateText="The Monkey"
    ImageAlign="top"
    BorderWidth="3"
    runat="server" />
```

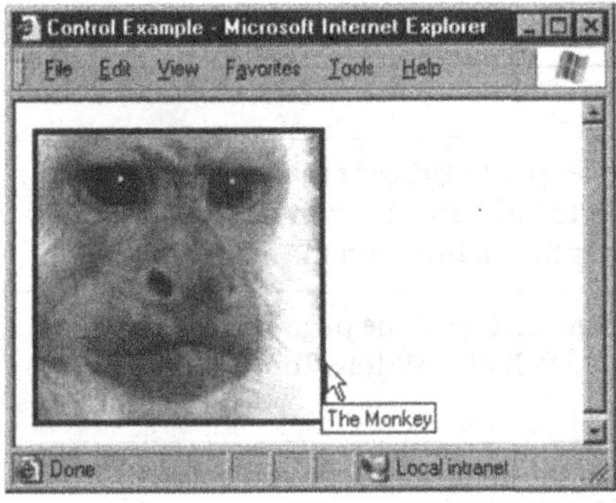

Figure 28-4. The Image control

Table 28-5. Image Members

Member	Description
AlternateText	The text that will be displayed in a browser that doesn't support pictures, and the pop-up tooltip text shown in Internet Explorer when the user hovers over the picture with the mouse.
ImageAlign	The alignment of an image relative to the page and its text (includes values such as Left, Right, Middle, Top, Bottom, and Texttop.
ImageUrl	The path and file name of the image that will be displayed. This can be an absolute or relative URL path.

ImageButton

This control is almost identical to the Image control, with one important difference—it raises a server-side Click event when the user clicks it.

```
<asp:ImageButton id="imgMonkey" runat="server"
    ImageUrl="monkey.jpg"
    AlternateText="The Monkey"
    ImageAlign="top"
    BorderWidth="3"
    runat="server" />
```

Table 28-6. ImageButton Members

Member	Description
AlternateText	The text that will be displayed in a browser that doesn't support pictures, and the pop-up tooltip text shown in Internet Explorer when the user hovers over the picture with the mouse.
ImageAlign	The alignment of an image relative to the page and its text (includes values such as Left, Right, Middle, Top, Bottom, and Texttop.
ImageUrl	The path and file name of the image that will be displayed. This can be an absolute or relative URL path.
CausesValidation	If set to True (the default), the page will automatically be validated using all the validation controls on the form when the image is clicked. Depending on the browser capabilities, an invalid page may not be posted back (see Chapter 9).
Click and Command events	Occur when the image is clicked. The only difference between the two is that the Command event receives extra information, namely the CommandName and CommandArgument properties.
CommandName and CommandArgument	Extra information provided to the Command event, which can allow you to uniquely identify the image in the case that your event handler is receiving the events from multiple different controls. The CommandName is a string meant to represent the action (such as "Sort") while CommandArgument stores any additional information (such as the field to sort by).

Label

This control represents ordinary text on a web page. You can set the Text property as an attribute, as with any other control.

```
<asp:Label id="lblText"
     Text="This is the label text."
     runat="server"/>
```

You can also set the Text property by adding text between separate opening and closing tags.

```
<asp:Label id="lblText"
     runat="server">
  This is the label text.
</asp:Label>
```

This choice is provided by some other web controls, but it's most useful with the Label control, which may require a large amount of static text and embedded HTML elements.

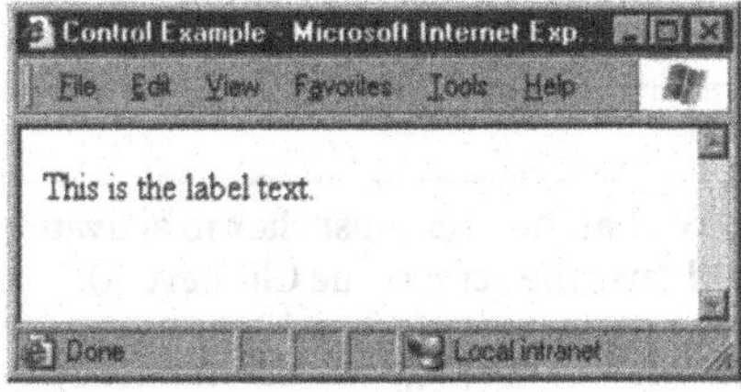

Figure 28-5. The Label control

Table 28-7. Label Members

Member	Description
Text	The text displayed in the label. You can embed HTML tags (such as <b> and) along with the content to further format the text.

LinkButton

The LinkButton control is similar to the HyperLink control (in fact, the appearance is identical). The difference is that while the HyperLink control automatically navigates to the specified URL, the LinkButton control doesn't have any associated URL. Instead, it raises a server-side Click event. One reason you might want to use the LinkButton control is to replace a normal HyperLink with a hyperlink that forces the page to be validated before allowing the user to continue.

```
<asp:LinkButton id="lnkClickMe"
    Text="Click Here"
    Tooltip="My Site"
    CausesValidation="True"
    runat="server"/>
```

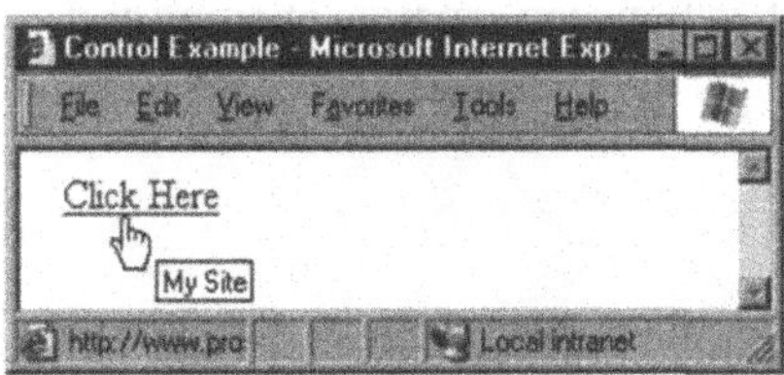

Figure 28-6. The LinkButton control

Table 28-8. LinkButton Members

Member	Description
Text	The underlined text that the user must click to activate the hyperlink (and raise the server-side Click event).
CausesValidation	If set to True (the default), the page will automatically be validated using all the validation controls on the form when the link is clicked. Depending on the browser capabilities, an invalid page may not be posted back (see Chapter 9).
Click and Command events	Occur when the link is clicked. The only difference between the two is that the Command event receives extra information, namely the CommandName and CommandArgument properties.
CommandName and CommandArgument	Extra information provided to the Command event, which can allow you to uniquely identify the link in the case that your event handler is receiving the events from multiple different controls. The CommandName is a string meant to represent the action (such as "Sort") while CommandArgument stores any additional information (such as the field to sort by).

Literal

A Literal control places plain text on a page without any HTML markup (unless you specify it). You can use a Literal control to provide the same functionality provided by the Label control. However, you cannot apply any formatting, styles, or fonts to a Literal control by using the standard WebControl properties.

```
<asp:Literal id="ltrText"
     Text="<i>This</i> is plain literal text."
     runat="server"/>
```

You can also set the Text property by adding text between separate opening and closing tags.

```
<asp:Literal id="ltrText"
     runat="server">
  <i>This</i> is plain literal text.
</asp:Label>
```

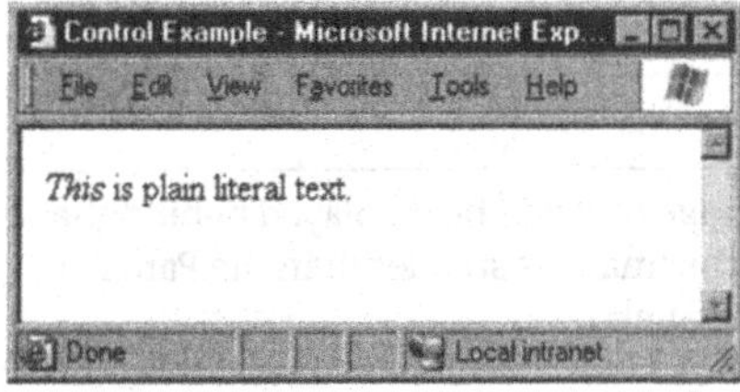

Figure 28-7. The Literal control

The System.Web.UI.WebControls.Literal class shouldn't be confused with the System.Web.LiteralControl class, which is used by ASP.NET to represent static HTML content that doesn't need to be made available on the server side.

Table 28-9. Literal Members

Member	Description
Text	The text displayed on the page. You can embed HTML tags (such as <b> and) along with the content to further format the text.

Panel

The Panel control is used to group other controls. It can be used with or without a border. One of the most useful ways to use a Panel is to hide an entire group of controls, by setting the containing Panel's Visible property to False. This technique allows you to simulate a multipage wizard in one page, by alternately hiding and showing different Panel controls. Panels are always made of both an opening and a closing tag.

```
<asp:Panel id="pnlControls"
     BackImageUrl="url"
     HorizontalAlign="Left"
     Wrap="True"
     runat="server">
  This is the first line....<br>
  This is the second line.
</asp:Panel>
```

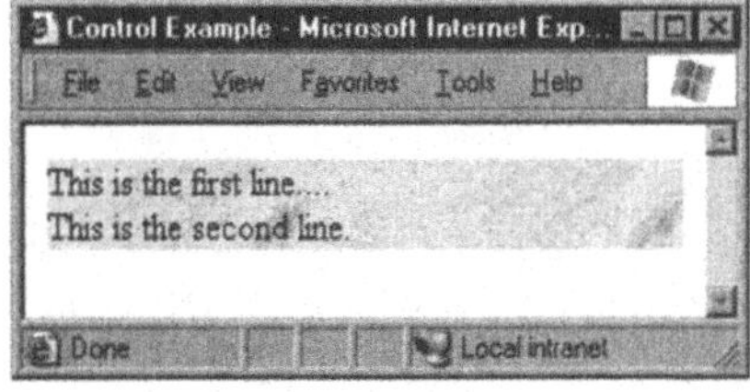

Figure 28-8. The Panel control

Table 28-10. Panel Members

Member	Description
BackImageUrl	This property sets an image that will be displayed behind the content in the Panel. If the image is smaller than the Panel, it will be tiled to fill in the Panel.
HorizontalAlign	Gets or sets the horizontal alignment of the contents within the panel.
Wrap	When set to True, the contents will be wrapped inside the Panel (depending on the Height and Width properties you've set for the Panel). Otherwise the Panel will be automatically sized to fit its contents.

PlaceHolder

The PlaceHolder class can be used as a container for dynamically added controls. The PlaceHolder really has no useful properties of its own. However, you can place a control inside it by adding a control object to its Controls collection.

```
<asp:PlaceHolder id="Holder"
     runat="server"/>
```

RadioButton

This control represents a radio button that, in conjunction with other radio buttons, allows a user to select exactly one choice from a group of options. Every RadioButton control has an associated label that you can use.

```
<asp:RadioButton id="optMale"
     AutoPostBack="False"
     Checked="True"
     GroupName="Gender"
     Text="Male"
     TextAlign="Right"
     runat="server"/>
<br>
<asp:RadioButton id="optFemale"
     AutoPostBack="False"
     GroupName="Gender"
     Text="Female"
     TextAlign="Right"
     runat="server"/>
```

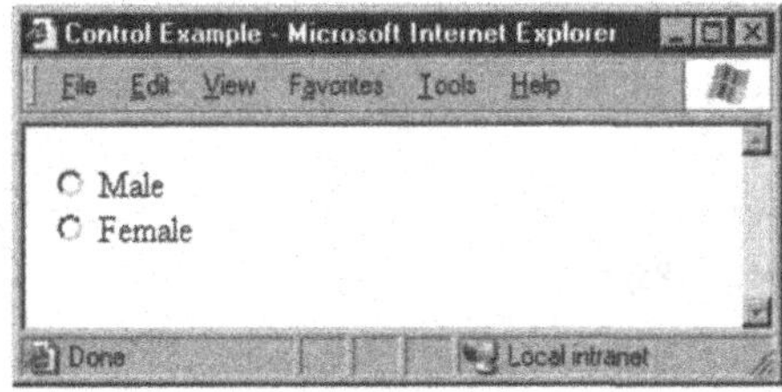

Figure 28-9. The RadioButton control

Table 28-11. RadioButton Members

Member	**Description**
AutoPostBack	Determines whether the page will be posted back when the radio button state is changed. This allows your code to react to the CheckedChanged event immediately.
GroupName	Identifies the radio button group. Only one radio button can be selected in a group.
Text	The label that is displayed next to the radio button.
TextAlign	The side of the radio button where the text will be displayed. Can be Left or Right.
Checked	Indicates or sets the current state of the radio button. When filled in, Checked is True.
CheckedChanged event	Fires when the radio button state changes (for example, when the user clicks a different option in the same group). If AutoPostBack is False, this event will be "delayed" until the next postback.

Table

This control represents a table with rows and columns. Tables are made up of TableRow controls, which in turn are made up of TableCell objects. The format is as follows:

```
<asp:Table id="programmaticID"
     BackImageUrl="url"
     CellPadding="cellpadding"
     CellSpacing="cellspacing"
     GridLines="None|Horizontal|Vertical|Both"
     HorizontalAlign="Center|Justify|Left|NotSet|Right"
     runat="server">

   <asp:TableRow>
      <asp:TableCell>
         Cell text
      </asp:TableCell>
   </asp:TableRow>

</asp:Table>
```

Table 28-12. Table Members

Member	**Description**
BackImageUrl	This property sets an image that will be displayed "behind." The image will be tiled if it's smaller than the table.
CellPadding	The space, in pixels, between the border of a cell and its contents.
CellSpacing	The space, in pixels, between cells in the same table.
GridLines	Specifies the types of gridlines that will be shown in the table (None, Horizontal, Vertical, or Both).
HorizontalAlign	The alignment of the table with the rest of the page.
Rows	Provides a collection of TableRow objects that represent the individual rows in the table. You can use methods such as Add, Insert, and Remove to dynamically configure a table.

The table is composed of TableRow and TableCell objects. You can interact with these elements individually to set row-specific or cell-specific properties (such as the text or the formatting). You can use the standard properties such as BorderStyle and BackColor with any of these objects to fine-tune the appearance of your table. Remember, however, any changes you make programmatically in code will *not* be persisted in the page's view state.

Table 28-13. TableRow Members

Member	Description
HorizontalAlign	The horizontal alignment of a row, which can be Left, Center, Right, or Justify.
VerticalAlign	The vertical alignment of a row, which can be Middle, Top, Bottom, or Baseline.
Cells	Provides a collection of TableCell objects that represent the individual cells in the table. You can use methods such as Add, Insert, and Remove to dynamically configure a table row.

Table 28-14. HtmlTableCell Members

Member	Description
ColumnSpan and RowSpan	Specifies how many rows or columns a given cell should span. This setting, which allows one cell to occupy a larger area, isn't supported by all browsers.
HorizontalAlign and VerticalAlign	The horizontal or vertical alignment of a single cell. These settings work the same as the corresponding TableRow properties.
Text	The actual text in the cell.
Wrap	If False, the text in the box will not wrap, but will extend the cell's border. The default is False.

A complete table can be created programmatically by adding TableCell and TableRow objects at runtime to the TableRow.Cells and Table.Rows collections, respectively. (An example of this technique is provided in Chapter 7.) Another possibility is to create the table declaratively.

```
<asp:Table id="Table1" runat="server"
    CellPadding="10"
    GridLines="Both"
    HorizontalAlign="Center">
    <asp:TableRow>
       <asp:TableCell>
          Row 0, Col 0
       </asp:TableCell>
       <asp:TableCell>
          Row 0, Col 1
       </asp:TableCell>
    </asp:TableRow>
```

```
    <asp:TableRow>
       <asp:TableCell>
          Row 1, Col 0
       </asp:TableCell>
       <asp:TableCell>
          Row 1, Col 1
       </asp:TableCell>
    </asp:TableRow>
</asp:Table>
```

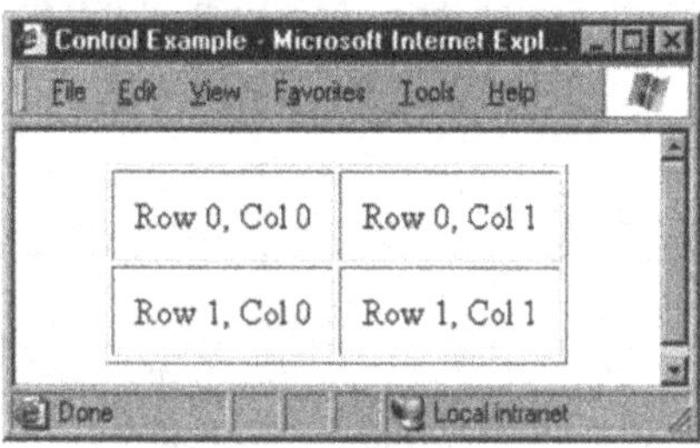

Figure 28-10. The Table control

TextBox

This control represents a text box in which the user can enter information. Depending on the settings you specify, this control may be generated as an HTML <input type="text"> tag, a <textarea> tag, or an <input type="password"> tag.

```
<asp:TextBox id="txtEntry"
     AutoPostBack="False"
     Columns="30"
     MaxLength="100"
     Rows="2"
     Text="Sample Text"
     TextMode="Multiline"
     Wrap="True"
     runat="server"/>
```

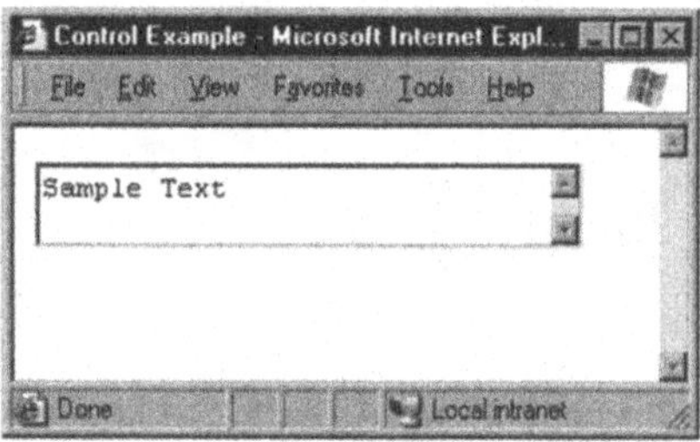

Figure 28-11. The TextBox control

Table 28-15. TextBox Members

Member	Description
AutoPostBack	Determines whether the page will be posted back when the text box is changed and focus changes to another control (for example, when the user presses the Tab key after making a modification). This allows your code to react to the TextChanged event immediately.
Columns	The character width of the text area. The default is –1 (not set), in which case the browser will apply a default size.
MaxLength	The maximum number of characters that can be entered into the text box.
Rows	The display height, in characters, of the text area. The default is –1 (not set), in which case the browser will apply a default size.
Text	Gets or sets the text.
TextMode	Specifies a value from the text mode enumeration, either SingleLine, MultiLine, or Password.
TextChanged event	Occurs when the text in the text area is changed and focus changes to another control.
Wrap	When set to True, the text will automatically wrap at the border. This setting is only applicable when TextMode is set to MultiLine.

List Controls

There are four basic list controls. Each of them inherits its basic functionality from the abstract ListControl class.

Table 28-16. ListControl Members

Member	Description
AutoPostBack	Determines whether the page will be posted back when the list control selection is changed. This allows your code to react to the SelectedIndexChanged event immediately.
DataMember and DataSource	These properties allow the list control to be bound to a data source, as described in Chapter 15. The DataSource property identifies the data source that contains the information. If there is more than one table in the data source (as with a DataSet), DataMember identifies the table to use.

Table 28-16. ListControl Members (Continued)

Member	Description
DataTextField, DataValueField, and DataTextFormattingString	DataTextField indicates the field that will be used to populate the visible portion of the list, and DataTextFormattingString specifies a format string that will be used to format it. DataValueField indicates the field that will be used to assign each item's value. The value is accessible through the ListItem class, but not visible to the user.
Items	Provides all the items in the list as a collection of ListItem objects. You can use the methods (such as Add, Remove, and Insert) to modify the class. These dynamic changes will be automatically persisted in the page's view state.
SelectedIndex	Gets or sets the integer index that identifies the selected item. The list is zero-based (so the first item has index 0) and –1 represents no selection.
SelectedItem	Retrieves the item that is currently selected, as a ListItem object.
DataBind()	This method fills the control with the data from the data source. This method is required to update the list control data and is often performed on postback. You can also call the Page.DataBind() method to bind all data-bound controls at once.
SelectedIndexChanged event	Fires when the selection in the list changes. If AutoPostBack is False, this event will be "delayed" until the next postback.

The items of all web control lists are represented using the ListItem object.

Table 28-17. ListItem Members

Member	Description
Text	Gets or sets the text that is displayed for this item in the list.
Value	Gets or sets the string value that is associated with this item (but not displayed). A typical use of the Value property is to store the unique database ID number for a row.
Selected	True if the item is currently selected.

DropDownList

This control represents a drop-down single-select list. To create a DropDownList, you can add entries in code using the Items collection, or you can nest ListItem tags inside the DropDownList tag, as shown here.

```
<asp:DropDownList id="lstItems"
                  AutoPostBack="False"
                  Width="100"
                  runat="server">
  <asp:ListItem value="1" selected="True" Text="Item 1"/>
  <asp:ListItem value="2" Text="Item 2"/>
  <asp:ListItem value="3" Text="Item 3"/>
</asp:DropDownList>
```

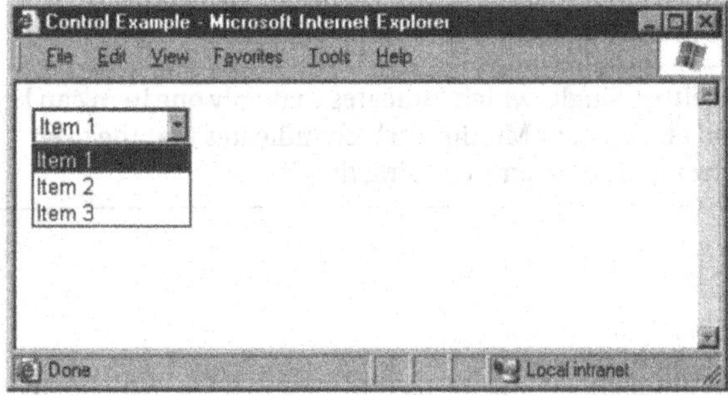

Figure 28-12. The DropDownList control

The DropDownList control doesn't add any new properties, methods, or events on top of the basic ListControl class.

ListBox

This control displays a list of items. The ListBox control can allow single or multiple selection, and can be filled in the control tag or dynamically through code. ListBox item changes will be remembered across postbacks.

```
<asp:ListBox id="lstItems"
             AutoPostBack="False"
             Rows="3"
             SelectionMode="Single"
             Width="100"
             runat="server">
  <asp:ListItem value="1" selected="True" Text="Item 1"/>
  <asp:ListItem value="2" Text="Item 2"/>
  <asp:ListItem value="3" selected="True" Text="Item 3"/>
</asp:ListBox>
```

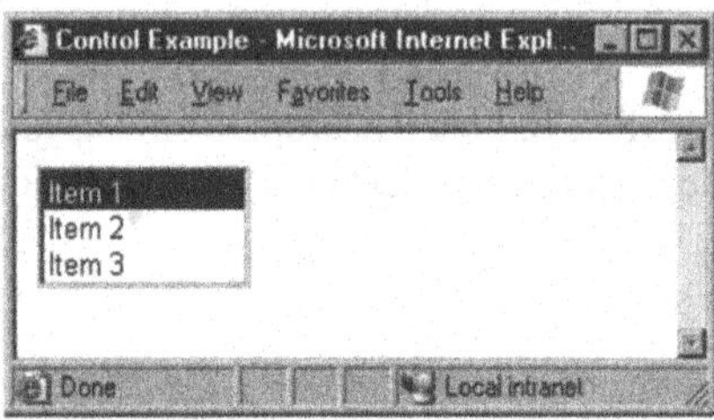

Figure 28-13. The ListBox control

Table 28-18. ListBox Members

Member	Description
Rows	The number of rows that will be visible at once in the list control (from 1 to 2000). The default value is 4.
SelectionMode	Can be either Single, which indicates that only one item can be selected at a time, or Multiple, which indicates that the user can select multiple items by using the Ctrl key.

CheckBoxList

The CheckBoxList is a list of individual check box items grouped in a list, which can be checked or unchecked in any combination. The only difference between using a CheckBoxList control instead of multiple CheckBox controls is convenience, and more data binding options.

```
<asp:CheckBoxList id="lstItems"
                  CellPadding="5"
                  RepeatColumns="2"
                  RepeatDirection="Vertical"
                  RepeatLayout="Table"
                  TextAlign="Right"
                  AutoPostBack="False"
                  Width="200"
                  runat="server">
  <asp:ListItem value="1" selected="True" Text="Item 1"/>
  <asp:ListItem value="2" Text="Item 2"/>
  <asp:ListItem value="3" selected="True" Text="Item 3"/>
  <asp:ListItem value="3" Text="Item 4"/>
</asp:CheckBoxList>
```

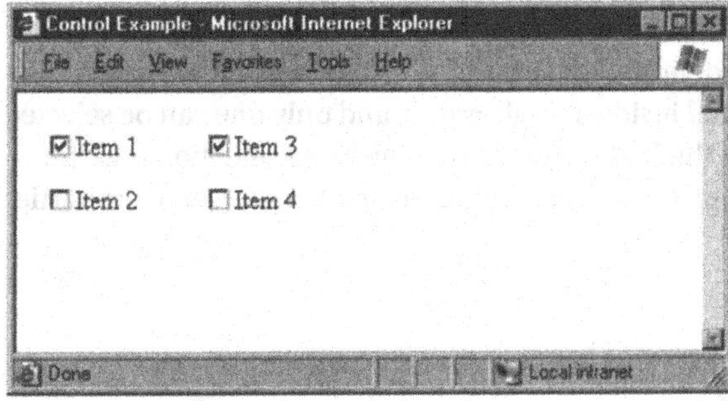

Figure 28-14. The CheckBoxList control

For more examples of how you can use different column ordering with the CheckBoxList, refer to Chapter 7.

Table 28-19. CheckBoxList Members

Member	Description
CellPadding	ASP.NET creates each check box in a separate cell of an invisible table. CellPadding is the space, in pixels, between the border of each cell and its contents.
CellSpacing	The space, in pixels, between cells in the same table.
RepeatColumns	The number of columns that the check box list will use.
RepeatDirection	Defines how ASP.NET fills the check box grid. When set to Vertical, the items in the list are displayed in columns filled from top to bottom, then left to right, until all items are rendered. When set to Horizontal, the items in the list are displayed in rows filled left to right, then top to bottom, until all items are rendered. Remember, the number of columns is always set by the RepeatColumns property.
RepeatLayout	Specifies whether the check boxes are displayed in an invisible table. This property can be either Table (the default) or Flow (in which case no table will be used).
TextAlign	Indicates whether text will be on the right- or left-side of the check box.

RadioButtonList

The RadioButtonList is a list of individual radio buttons grouped in a list. These radio buttons are automatically contained inside a single group, and only one can be selected at a time. Aside from the fact that the RadioButtonList allows one selection and the CheckBoxList allows multiselection, the two controls offer an identical set of properties and events.

```
<asp:RadioButtonList id="lstItems"
                    CellPadding="5"
                    RepeatColumns="2"
                    RepeatDirection="Vertical"
                    RepeatLayout="Table"
                    TextAlign="Right"
                    AutoPostBack="False"
                    Width="200"
                    runat="server">
  <asp:ListItem value="1" Text="Item 1"/>
  <asp:ListItem value="2" Text="Item 2"/>
  <asp:ListItem value="3" selected="True" Text="Item 3"/>
  <asp:ListItem value="3" Text="Item 4"/>
</asp:RadioButtonList>
```

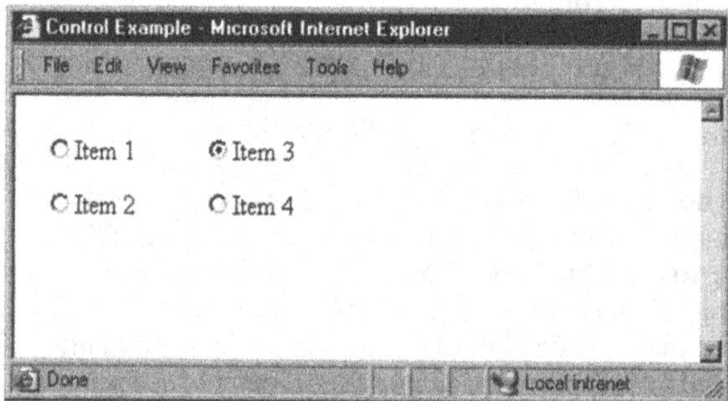

Figure 28-15. The RadioButtonList control

For more examples about how you can use different column ordering with the RadioButtonList, refer to Chapter 7.

Table 28-20. RadioButtonList Members

Member	Description
CellPadding	ASP.NET creates each radio button in a separate cell of an invisible table. CellPadding is the space, in pixels, between the border of each cell and its contents.
CellSpacing	The space, in pixels, between cells in the same table.
RepeatColumns	The number of columns that the list will use.
RepeatDirection	Defines how ASP.NET fills the radio button grid. When set to Vertical, the items in the list are displayed in columns filled from top to bottom, then left to right, until all items are rendered. When set to Horizontal, the items in the list are displayed in rows filled left to right, then top to bottom, until all items are rendered. Remember, the number of columns is always set by the RepeatColumns property.
RepeatLayout	Specifies whether the radio buttons are displayed in an invisible table. This property can be either Table (the default) or Flow (in which case no table will be used).
TextAlign	Indicates whether text will be on the right- or left-side of the radio button.

Rich Controls

The designation "rich controls" is a loose one. Technically, there is no sharp distinction between the controls in this section—the AdRotator, Calendar, and Xml control—and those already explained in this chapter. Generally, however, these controls are separated because they represent a much higher level of abstraction. For example, there is no HTML tag that is at all similar to the Calendar control. Instead, ASP.NET generates dozens of lines of standard HTML code to create the Calendar's output with each postback. If you were to attempt to dynamically write this content to a web page on your own as needed, you would have an enormous, time-consuming task on your hands.

The AdRotator and Calendar controls were first introduced in Chapter 9, and this chapter includes complete examples that best demonstrate how they work in a web page.

AdRotator

The AdRotator displays a randomly selected banner graphic on your page. Using the AdRotator control is a quick and easy way to ensure that a page rotates through a series of different graphics, without having to add this code yourself.

The AdRotator control uses a special XML file that lists all the different available images. This file uses the format shown here (only a single Ad element is shown).

```
<Advertisements>

  <Ad>
    <ImageUrl>prosetech.jpg</ImageUrl>
    <NavigateUrl>http://www.prosetech.com</NavigateUrl>
    <AlternateText>ProseTech Site</AlternateText>
    <Impressions>1</Impressions>
    <Keyword>Computer</Keyword>
  </Ad>

</Advertisements>
```

Table 28-21. Advertisement File Elements

Element	Description
ImageUrl	The image that will be displayed. This can be a relative link (a file in the current directory) or a fully qualified Internet URL.
NavigateUrl	The link that will be followed if the user clicks the banner.
AlternateText	The text that will be displayed instead of the picture if it cannot be displayed. This text will also be used as a tooltip in some newer browsers.
Impressions	A number that sets how often an advertisement will appear. This number is relative to the numbers specified for other ads. For example, a banner with the value 10 will be shown twice as often as the banner with the value 5.
Keyword	A keyword that identifies a group of advertisements. This can be used for filtering. For example, you could create ten advertisements, and give half of them the keyword "Retail" and the other half the keyword "Computer." The web page can then choose to filter the possible advertisements to include only one of these groups.

The AdRotator control provides a smaller set of properties. Its control tag is shown here.

```
<asp:AdRotator
     id="Ads"
     AdvertisementFile="MainAds.xml"
     KeyWordFilter="Computer"
     Target="_blank"
     runat="server"/>
```

Table 28-22. AdRotator Members

Member	Description
AdvertisementFile	The path to the XML advertisement file. This can be a relative or absolute path.
KeywordFilter	If you set the KeywordFilter, when ASP.NET randomly selects an image to display in the AdRotator control it will only consider those entries that have a matching keyword.
Target	The target window or frame where the destination page will be opened. This can name a specific frame, or use a special constant such as _blank (for a new window), _parent (the containing frameset), _self (the current window) or _top (the top-level parent).
AdCreated event	Occurs after the image is chosen but before the page is sent to the client. This event receives a special AdCreatedEventArgs object that describes the entry that was chosen (including its AlternateText, ImageUrl, and NavigateUrl). This allows you to synchronize other portions of your page to match.

Calendar

The Calendar control displays the dates for a single month on a web page, and provides pager controls that allow the user to move from month to month. The Calendar control is the most sophisticated ASP.NET control (aside from the DataGrid), and provides a rich set of events and the ability to restrict or format any individual date.

In order to understand the Calendar control, you need to realize that it's ultimately rendered as an HTML table, with every date box in an individual cell. A template that shows all the Calendar tag options is shown here. As with many ASP.NET, all of these attributes are optional. You can create a default Calendar control on a page simply by specifying the tag <asp:Calendar id="MyCalendar" runat="server" />.

```
<asp:Calendar id="programmaticID"
    CellPadding="pixels"
    CellSpacing="pixels"
    DayNameFormat="FirstLetter|FirstTwoLetters|Full|Short"
    FirstDayOfWeek="Default|Monday|Tuesday|Wednesday|
                Thursday|Friday|Saturday|Sunday"
    NextMonthText="HTML text"
    NextPrevFormat="ShortMonth|FullMonth|CustomText"
    PrevMonthText="HTML text"
    SelectedDate="date"
    SelectionMode="None|Day|DayWeek|DayWeekMonth"
    SelectMonthText="HTML text"
    SelectWeekText="HTML text"
```

```
        ShowDayHeader="True|False"
        ShowGridLines="True|False"
        ShowNextPrevMonth="True|False"
        ShowTitle="True|False"
        TitleFormat="Month|MonthYear"
        TodaysDate="date"
        VisibleDate="date"
        OnVisibleMonthChanged="OnVisibleMonthChangedMethod"
        runat="server">

    <TodayDayStyle />
    <DayHeaderStyle />
    <DayStyle />
    <NextPrevStyle />
    <OtherMonthDayStyle />
    <SelectedDayStyle />
    <SelectorStyle />
    <TitleStyle />
    <TodayDayStyle />
    <WeekendDayStyle />

</asp:Calendar>
```

Table 28-23. Calendar Members

Member	**Description**
CellPadding	ASP.NET creates a date in a separate cell of an invisible table. CellPadding is the space, in pixels, between the border of each cell and its contents.
CellSpacing	The space, in pixels, between cells in the same table.
DayNameFormat	Determines how days are displayed in the calendar header. Valid values are Full (as in Sunday), FirstLetter (S), FirstTwoLetters (Su), and Short (Sun), which is the default.
FirstDayOfWeek	Determines which day is displayed in the first column of the calendar. The values are any day name from the FirstDayOfWeek enumeration (such as Sunday).
NextMonthText and PrevMonthText	Sets the text that the user clicks to move to the next or previous month. These navigation links appear at the top of the calendar, and are the greater than (>) and less than (<) signs by default. This setting is only applied if NextPrevFormat is set to Custom.
NextPrevFormat	Sets the text that the user clicks to move to the next or previous month. This can be FullMonth (for example, December), ShortMonth (Dec), or Custom, in which case the NextMonthText and PrevMonthText properties are used. Custom is the default.

Table 28-23. Calendar Members (Continued)

Member	Description
SelectedDate and SelectedDates	Sets or gets the currently selected date as a DateTime object. You can specify this in the control tag in a format like this: "12:00:00 AM, 12/31/2002" (depending on your computer's regional settings). If you allow multiple date selection, the SelectedDates property will return a collection of DateTime objects, one for each selected date. You can use collection methods such as Add, Remove, and Clear to change the selection.
SelectionMode	Determines how many dates can be selected at once. The default is Day, which allows one date to be selected. Other options include DayWeek (a single date, or an entire week) or DayWeekMonth (a single date, entire week, or entire month). There is no way to allow the user to select multiple noncontiguous dates.
SelectMonthText and SelectWeekText	The text shown for the link that allows the user to select an entire month or week. These properties don't apply if the SelectionMode is Day.
ShowDayHeader, ShowGridLines, ShowNextPrevMonth, and ShowTitle	These Boolean properties allow you to configure whether various parts of the calendar are shown, including the day titles, gridlines between every day, the previous/next month navigation links, and the title section. Note that hiding the title section also hides the next and previous month navigation controls.
TitleFormat	Configures how the month is displayed in the title area. Valid values include Month and MonthYear (the default).
TodaysDate	Sets which day should be recognized as the current date, and formatted with the TodayDayStale. This defaults to the current day on the web server.
VisibleDate	Gets or sets the date that specifies what month will be displayed in the calendar. This allows you to change the calendar display without modifying the current date selection.
DayRender event	Occurs once for each day that is created and added to the currently visible month before the page is rendered. This event gives you the opportunity to apply special formatting, add content, or restriction selection for an individual date cell. For a complete example, refer to Chapter 7.
SelectionChanged event	Occurs when the user selects a day, a week, or an entire month by clicking the date selector controls.
VisibleMonthChanged event	Occurs when the user clicks the next or previous month navigation controls the move to another month.

The Calendar also allows you to fine-tune its appearance by using nested style subtags. Each nested style tag specifies the formatting settings that it wants to override. These can include standard WebControl properties such as Font, BackColor, and ForeColor, or some additional properties inherited from the TableItemStyle class, as described in Table 28-24. Note that more than one style may apply to a given cell.

```
<SelectedDayStyle
    Font="FontName"
    BackColor="HTML Color Name or Code"
    ForeColor="HTML Color Name or Code "
    HorizontalAlign="Center|Justify|Left|NotSet|Right"
    VerticalAlign="Bottom|Middle|Notset|Top"
    Wrap="True|False" />
```

Table 28-24. TableItemStyle Members

Member	Description
HorizontalAlign	Gets or sets the horizontal alignment of the contents within the date cell.
VerticalAlign	Gets or sets the vertical alignment of the contents within the date cell.
Wrap	Specifies whether the contents in the cell will wrap, or whether the cell will be automatically expanded to fit. This property is useful when adding custom content to a day cell.

Table 28-25. Calendar Styles

Member	Description
DayHeaderStyle	The style for the section of the calendar that displays the days of the week (as column headers).
DayStyle	The default style for the dates in the current month.
NextPrevStyle	The style for the navigation controls in the title section that move from month to month.
OtherMonthDayStyle	The style for the dates that aren't in the currently displayed month. These dates are used to "fill in" the calendar grid. For example, the first few cells in the topmost row may display the last few days from the previous month.
SelectedDayStyle	The style for the selected dates on the calendar.
SelectorStyle	The style for the week and month-date selection controls.
TitleStyle	The style for the title section.
TodayDayStyle	The style for the date designated as today (represented by the TodaysDate property of the Calendar).
WeekendDayStyle	The style for dates that fall on the weekend.

A sample Calendar control tag is shown here.

```
<asp:Calendar id=Calendar
    NextMonthText="-->"
    PrevMonthText="<--"
    Width="200"
    Height="180"
    CellPadding="4"
    DayNameFormat="FirstLetter"
    Font-Size="8pt"
    Font-Names="Verdana"
    runat="server" >

   <DayHeaderStyle Font-Size="7pt" Font-Bold="True"
    BackColor="#CCCCCC" />
   <SelectedDayStyle Font-Bold="True" ForeColor="White"
    BackColor="#666666" />
   <TitleStyle Font-Bold="True" BorderColor="Black"
    BackColor="#999999" />
   <WeekendDayStyle BackColor="#FFFFCC" />

</asp:Calendar>
```

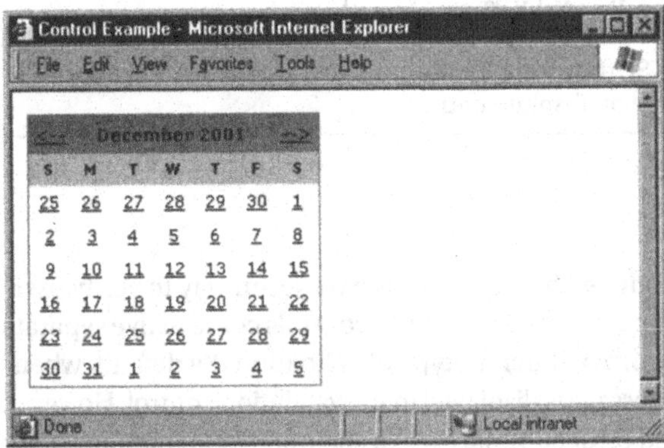

Figure 28-16. The Calendar Control

Xml

The Xml control allows you to display an XML document on a web page. This control doesn't apply any special formatting, and by default it will just render all the embedded text in a continuous string with no spaces or line breaks. To add the appropriate formatting to the XML document, you need to specify an XSL transform to use with the control. The Xml control is shown in a full example in Chapter 18.

```
<asp:Xml id="xmlMyDoc"
     DocumentSource="MyDoc.xml"
     TransformSource="MyDoc.xsl"
     runat="server">
```

This example specifies an XML file by file name. Alternatively, you can specify XML content as a string (using the DocumentContent property) or by supplying an XmlDocument object (using the Document property). At least one of the XML document properties must be set. If more than one XML document property is set, the last property takes effect. The documents in the other properties are ignored.

Table 28-26. Xml Members

Member	Description
Document	The XML content to display as a System.Xml.XmlDocument object.
DocumentContent	The XML content to display as a string.
DocumentSource	The XML file to display. You can use a relative path (which is always relative to the location of the web page file) or an absolute path.
Transform	The XSL transform to apply to the content as a System.Xml.Xsl.XslTransform object.
TransformSource	The XSL transform file to apply to the content. You can use a relative or absolute path.

Validation Controls

The validation controls were introduced in Chapter 9 as a powerful way to verify user input and display custom error messages. The validation controls come in five separate versions, each one tailored to perform a different type of validation. By default, when validation fails, the custom error message is displayed in the validation control. However, you can also display the combined error summaries in a separate ValidationSummary control. For more information about how validation controls work with the Page model, refer to Chapter 9.

All the five validation controls inherit from the BaseValidator class, which defines some basic functionality, as described in Table 28-27. The BaseValidator class inherits the properties of the System.Web.UI.Label control, including formatting properties all web controls share, such as Font and ForeColor. You can also set the Enabled property to False to stop validation.

Table 28-27. BaseValidator Members

Member	Description
ControlToValidate	Identifies the control that this validator will check. Each validator can verify the value in one input control.
Display	The Display property allows you to configure whether this error message will be added dynamically as needed (Dynamic), or whether an appropriate space will be reserved for the message (Static). Static is useful when the validator is in a table, and you don't want the width of the cell to collapse when no message is displayed.
EnableClientScript	If set to True, ASP.NET will add special JavaScript and DHTML code to allow client-side validation on browsers that support it.
ErrorMessage	If validation fails, the validator control will display this error message.
IsValid	After validation is performed, this returns True or False depending on whether it succeeded or failed. If you use automatic validation, you won't need to check this property manually.
PropertiesValid	Returns True if the control specified by ControlToValidate is a valid control.
RenderUplevel	Returns True if ASP.NET has determined that the client browser supports up-level rendering with JavaScript and DHTML code. You don't need to examine this property, because ASP.NET will automatically set the appropriate default for EnableClientScript.

CompareValidator

This control compares the value in one input control with the value in another. The type of comparison depends on the Operator property. For example, you can verify that two values are equal or that one is less than the other.

```
<asp:CompareValidator id="vldRetype"
    ErrorMessage="Your password does not match."
    Operator="Equal"
    Type="String"
    ControlToCompare="txtPassword"
    ControlToValidate="txtRetype"
    runat="server" />
```

Table 28-28. CompareValidator Members

Member	Description
ControlToCompare	The input control that contains the comparison value.
Operator	Specifies the type of comparison. By default, the operator is Equal, and validation succeeds as long as the two values are the same. Other possibilities are specified in the ValidationCompareOperator enumeration, and include GreaterThan (>), GreaterThanEqual (>=), LessThan (<), LessThanEqual (<=), NotEqual (<>), and DataTypeCheck (a comparison of data type only).
Type	The data type of the values that will be compared (such as String, Integer, Double, Date, or Currency). Before the comparison is made, ASP.NET attempts to convert both values to this data type, and throws an exception if it cannot.
ValueToCompare	The comparison value as a constant. You can set this instead of ControlToCompare. If both ValueToCompare and ControlToCompare are set, ControlToCompare takes precedence.

RangeValidator

This control checks whether a given value in an input control matches a set value or falls within a predefined range.

```
<asp:RangeValidator id="vldAge"
    ErrorMessage="The date is incorrect."
    Type="Date"
    MaximumValue="2001/12/01"
    MinimumValue="2002/12/30"
    ControlToValidate="txtDate"
    runat="server" />
```

Table 28-29. RangeValidator Members

Member	Description
MaximumValue	The largest valid value for ControlToCompare.
MinimumValue	The smallest valid value for ControlToCompare. You can set MaximumValue and MinumumValue to the same number, date, or string to validate for a single value.
Type	The data type of the values that will be compared (such as String, Integer, Double, Date, or Currency). Before the comparison is made, ASP.NET attempts to convert both values to this data type, and throws an exception if it cannot.

RegularExpressionValidator

This control checks whether a user-entered value matches a specified regular expression. A quick introduction to regular expression syntax can be found in Chapter 9.

```
<asp:RegularExpressionValidator id="vldEmail"
    ErrorMessage="This email is missing the @ symbol."
    ValidationExpression=".+@.+"
    ControlToValidate="txtEmail"
    runat="server" />
```

Table 28-30. RegularExpressionValidator Members

Member	Description
ValidationExpression	A string that contains the regular expression pattern ASP.NET will use for validation.

RequiredFieldValidator

This control checks whether a user has entered a value in a given control. This validator is often used in conjunction with other validation controls, because all other controls will automatically skip their validation if they find an empty value.

```
<asp:RequiredFieldValidator id="vldPassword"
    ErrorMessage="You must enter a password."
    ControlToValidate="txtPassword"
    runat="server" />
```

Table 28-31. RequiredFieldValidator Members

Member	Description
InitialValue	This is the designated initial value of the associated input control. If the RequiredFieldValidator finds that the current value matches the initial value, validation will fail. Usually, InitialValue is set to an empty string to ensure that a user has entered some content.

CustomValidator

This control allows you to use your own validation algorithm. You perform validation at the server side by responding to the ServerValidate event. In addition, you can specify a client-side validation function that will prevent the page from being posted back when an error is countered.

```
<asp:CustomValidator id="vldCode"
     ErrorMessage="Your entry did not match the secret code."
     ControlToValidate="txtCode"
     runat="server" />
```

Table 28-32. CustomValidator Members

Member	Description
ClientValidationFunction	A string that contains the function name (typically written in JavaScript) that will be used for client-side validation. This property isn't required (and in some cases, such as when you're using a "secret" algorithm, shouldn't be used). Note that even if you do set this property, you must still add analogous ASP.NET code to the ServerValidate event to ensure that validation is performed even on down-level browsers, and even if the user spoofs your page. An example showing how you can write a ClientValidationFunction is shown in Chapter 9.
ServerValidate event	Your code responds to this event to perform the actual validation on the server-side. You receive a ServerValidateEventArgs object that contains the user-entered value (Value) and allows you to specify whether validation succeeded (the Boolean property Valid).

ValidationSummary

This control displays a summary of all error messages for every validation control that failed to validate its content.

```
<asp:ValidationSummary id="vldSummary"
     DisplayMode="BulletList"
     HeaderText="Errors Found:"
     runat="server">
```

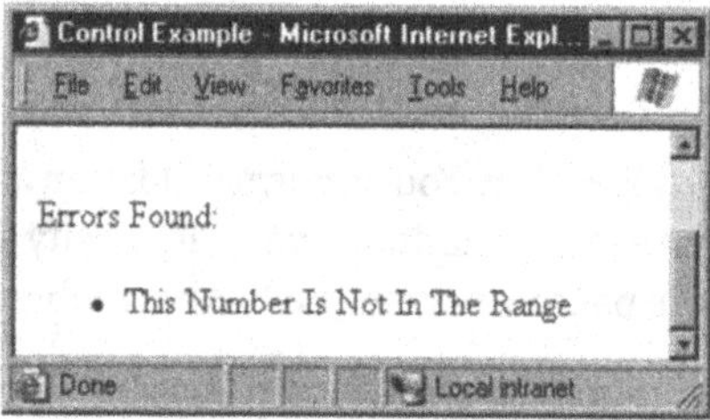

Figure 28-17. The ValidationSummary control

Table 28-33. ValidationSummary Members

Member	Description
DisplayMode	Sets the format for the validation summary text. This can be List, SingleParagraph, or BulletList (the default).
EnableClientScript	If set to True, ASP.NET uses additional client-side scripting code to ensure that the ValidationSummary control is updated dynamically as errors are entered or fixed.
HeaderText	Sets a title that appears at the top of the validation summary control.
ShowMessageBox	When set to True, the validation summary is shown in a message box window that appears as soon as validation fails.
ShowSummary	When set to True, the validation summary is shown inline in the page.

Data Controls

The data controls are often considered ASP.NET's most sophisticated (and complex) controls. They include the DataGrid, DataList, and Repeater, all of which are designed to work with ASP.NET data binding. The basic principle is that you bind a data source such as an array, collection, or DataSet to the data control, and it generates a list with one entry for each item in the data source. All the data controls support templates, which allow you to fine-tune their appearance.

When starting out with these controls, it's absolutely necessary to have a good explanation that describes basics about templates and advanced control features such as sorting, paging, selection, and editing. For these examples, refer to Chapter 16.

The DataList and DataGrid inherit some basic functionality from the BaseDataList class. This includes support for data binding and some table-specific formatting properties. Note that the Repeater control does *not* inherit from BaseDataList, and so doesn't support these members.

Table 28-34. BaseDataList Members

Member	Description
CellPadding	CellPadding is the space, in pixels, between the border of each cell and its contents.
CellSpacing	The space, in pixels, between cells in the same table.
DataMember and DataSource	These properties allow the control to be bound to a data source, as described in Chapters 16 and 17. The DataSource property identifies the data source that contains the information. If there is more than one table in the data source (as with a DataSet), DataMember identifies the table to use.
DataKeyField	Specifies a field from the data source that will automatically be used to assign a unique identifier to each row. This value will not be displayed, but is useful for accessing specific rows.

Table 28-34. BaseDataList Members (Continued)

Member	Description
DataKeys	If the DataKeyField is set, the DataKeys collection automatically provides all the keys for the records in the data list. You cannot use this property to add or remove rows. Instead, you use this collection to look up the data key for a specific row by index number (usually in an event handler).
GridLines	Specifies the types of gridlines that will be shown in the table (None, Horizontal, Vertical, or Both).
HorizontalAlign	Gets or sets the horizontal alignment of the contents within the cell.
DataBind()	This method fills the control with the data from the data source. This method is required to update the data control display and is often performed on postback. You can also call the Page.DataBind() method to bind all data-bound controls at once.
SelectedIndexChanged event	Fires when the selection in the data control changes.

Repeater

Out of all the data controls, the Repeater is the most straightforward. Think of the Repeater as a no-frills way to repeat ASP.NET or HTML elements, once for each item in the data source. The Repeater has no support for additional features such as selection, editing, and sorting, and has no built-in layout. However, these characteristics also make the Repeater extremely flexible—unlike the DataList and DataGrid control, the Repeater doesn't place data inside any sort of table structure unless you explicitly add table tags. The Repeater is also the only control that allows the developers to split HTML tags across templates.

The format for the Repeater control tag is shown here. Note that the content for the Repeater control doesn't appear in the .aspx file. Instead, it's set at runtime through code, using data binding. That makes the Repeater control tag quite simple, with little more than the optional templates where you can specify formatting and HTML elements.

```
<asp:Repeater id="programmaticID"
     runat="server">

   <HeaderTemplate />
   <ItemTemplate />
   <AlternatingItemTemplate />
   <SeparatorTemplate />
   <FooterTemplate />

</asp:Repeater>
```

Table 28-35. Repeater Members

Member	Description
DataMember and DataSource	These properties allow the control to be bound to a data source, as described in Chapters 16 and 17. The DataSource property identifies the data source that contains the information. If there is more than one table in the data source (as with a DataSet), DataMember identifies the table to use.
Items	Allows you to examine all the items in the Repeater control as a collection of RepeaterItem objects. Because the Repeater control is data-bound, you cannot directly modify the Items collection.
DataBind()	This method fills the control with the data from the data source. This method is required to update the Repeater control display and is often performed on postback. You can also call the Page.DataBind() method to bind all data-bound controls at once.
ItemCreated event	Occurs when an item is created and added to the Repeater control. The event arguments provide the relevant item as a RepeaterItem object.
ItemDataBound event	Occurs after an item is data-bound, but before it's rendered on the page. The event arguments provide the relevant item as a RepeaterItem object.
ItemCommand event	Occurs when any button is clicked in the Repeater control. (In order for a button to be present, you must have added it in one of the templates.) The event arguments provide the command name associated with the button (CommandName), a reference to the button (CommandSource), and the RepeaterItem where the button click occurred (Item).

Table 28-36. RepeaterItem Members

Member	Description
DataItem	Provides the data associated with this item.
ItemIndex	Indicates the numeric (zero-based) index of the item in the Repeater control.
ItemType	Returns one of the ListItemType enumerated values identifying what template the item is in (such as Header, Footer, Item, and so on).

The formatting for the Repeater control is completely defined through templates. Every template can contain a mix of HTML elements, ASP.NET server controls, and data-binding expressions bracketed with <%# %> characters. You cannot set any attributes for the template tags. Many example templates are shown in Chapter 16.

Table 28-37. Repeater Templates

Member	**Description**
ItemTemplate	Defines the content and layout of the items in the list. This is the only required template.
AlternatingItemTemplate	If defined, this template is used for the format and layout of every second item. Every odd-numbered item uses the ItemTemplate. If not defined, every item uses ItemTemplate.
SeparatorTemplate	If defined, this is rendered between every item.
HeaderTemplate	If defined, this is rendered once at the beginning of the Repeater control as a heading.
FooterTemplate	If defined, this is rendered once at the end of the Repeater control as a footer.

A sample Repeater tag with three templates is shown here. It creates a table structure to hold data from a bound dataset (which must contain a field named au_fname). This example could be used with the Authors table from the pubs database installed with SQL Server.

```
<asp:Repeater id="repeatAuthor"
              runat="server">

    <HeaderTemplate>
       <h3>The Repeater:</h3>
       <table bgcolor="LightYellow" border="2">
    </HeaderTemplate>
    <ItemTemplate>
       <tr><td><%# Container.DataItem("au_fname") %></td></tr>
    </ItemTemplate>
    <FooterTemplate>
       </table>
    </FooterTemplate>

</asp:Repeater>
```

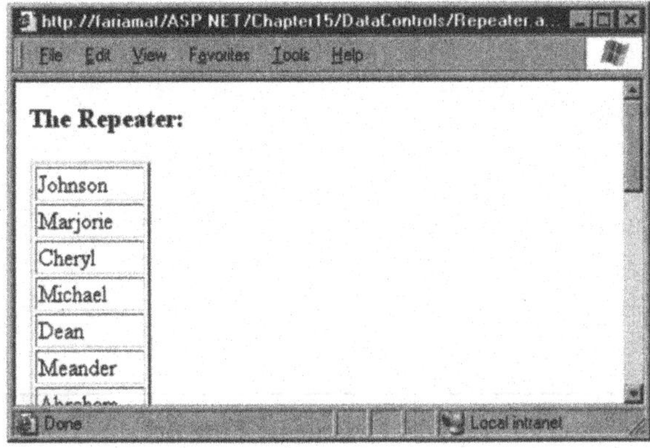

Figure 28-18. The Repeater control

DataList

The DataList displays data in a table with a single cell for each item. The DataList control provides built-in support for selection and editing. Unlike the DataGrid, the DataList doesn't support paging or sorting.

The format for the DataList tag is shown here. Note that the content for the DataList control doesn't appear in the .aspx file. Instead, it's set at runtime using data binding, as with all the data controls. Some of the properties shown in the control tag are inherited from the BaseDataList class, and are described in Table 28-34.

```
<asp:DataList id="programmaticID"
     CellPadding="pixels"
     CellSpacing="pixels"
     GridLines="None|Horizontal|Vertical|Both"
     RepeatColumns="ColumnCount"
     RepeatDirection="Vertical|Horizontal"
     RepeatLayout="Flow|Table"
     ShowFooter="True|False"
     ShowHeader="True|False"
     runat="server">

   <AlternatingItemStyle />
   <EditItemStyle />
   <FooterStyle />
   <HeaderStyle />
   <ItemStyle />
   <PagerStyle />
   <SelectedItemStyle />
```

```
    <HeaderTemplate />
    <ItemTemplate />
    <AlternatingItemTemplate />
    <EditItemTemplate />
    <SelectedItemTemplate />
    <SeparatorTemplate />
    <FooterTemplate />

</asp:DataList>
```

Table 28-38. DataList Members

Member	**Description**
EditItemIndex	Gets or sets the item in the DataList control that is currently being edited. To stop editing, set this value to –1. The index number is zero-based, so the first item is at index 0.
Items	Allows you to examine all the items in the DataList control as a collection of DataListItem objects. Because the DataList control is data-bound, you cannot directly modify the Items collection.
RepeatColumns	The number of columns that the DataList will use. (Each column contains all the information for a single item.) By default, only one column is used.
RepeatDirection	Defines how ASP.NET fills the DataList when you're using more than one column. When set to Vertical, the items are displayed in columns filled from top to bottom, then left to right, until all items are rendered. When set to Horizontal, the items in the list are displayed in rows filled left to right, then top to bottom, until all items are rendered. Remember, the number of columns is always set by the RepeatColumns property.
RepeatLayout	Specifies whether the list items are displayed in an invisible table, with one cell for each item. This property can be either Table (the default) or Flow (in which case no table will be used).
SelectedIndex	Gets or sets the item in the DataList control that is currently selected. To clear the selection, set this value to –1. The index number is zero-based, so the first item is at index 0.
SelectedItem	Provides the currently selected item as DataListItem object.
ShowFooter	If set to True, the footer will be displayed at the bottom of the DataList, provided you have created a FooterTemplate.
ShowHeader	If set to True, the header will be displayed at the top of the DataList, provided you have created a HeaderTemplate.

Table 28-38. DataList Members (Continued)

Member	Description
EditCommand, CancelCommand, UpdateCommand, and DeleteCommand events	These commands occur when the user clicks the corresponding button. You must handle these events to perform the required data source updating, if required. Note also that the DataList doesn't have predefined editing controls. This means that you need to add your own buttons for editing, and set their CommandName properties to Edit, Cancel, Update, or Delete. For more information, refer to Chapter 16.
ItemCreated event	Occurs when an item is created and added to the DataList control. The event arguments provide the relevant item as a DataListItem object.
ItemDataBound event	Occurs after an item is data-bound, but before it's rendered on the page. The event arguments provide the relevant item as a DataListItem object.
ItemCommand event	Occurs when any button is clicked in the DataList control. (In order for a button to be present, you must have added it in one of the templates.) The event arguments provide the command name associated with the button (CommandName), a reference to the button (CommandSource), and the DataListItem where the button click occurred (Item).

Table 28-39. DataListItem Members

Member	Description
DataItem	Provides the data associated with this item.
ItemIndex	Indicates the numeric (zero-based) index of the item in the DataList control.
ItemType	Returns one of the ListItemType enumerated values identifying what template the item is in (such as Header, Footer, Item, SelectedItem, and so on).

Like the Repeater, you configure the content of the DataList using embedded template tags. You can also configure the appearance using style tags. Each nested style tag specifies the formatting settings that it wants to override. These can include standard WebControl properties such as Font, BackColor, and ForeColor, or some additional properties inherited from the TableItemStyle class, as described in Table 28-24. Note that more than one style may apply to a given item. For example, a selected item will be formatted with the normal ItemStyle, and then with the SelectedItemStyle.

Table 28-40. DataList Templates and Styles

Member	Description
ItemTemplate and ItemStyle	Defines the content and layout of the items in the list. This is the only required template.
AlternatingItemTemplate and AlternatingItemStyle	If defined, this template is used for the format and layout of every second item. Every odd-numbered item uses the ItemTemplate (and ItemStyle). If not defined, every item uses ItemTemplate.
SeparatorTemplate and SeparatorStyle	If defined, this is rendered between every item.
HeaderTemplate and HeaderStyle	If defined, this is rendered once at the beginning of the DataList control as a heading.
FooterTemplate and FooterStyle	If defined, this is rendered once at the end of the DataList control as a footer.
SelectedItemTemplate and SelectedItemStyle	If defined, this template is used for the format of the selected item (as determined by the DataList.SelectedIndex).
EditItemTemplate and EditItemStyle	If defined, this template is used for the format of the item that is currently being edited (as determined by the DataList.EditItemIndex).

A sample DataList tag with two templates and three styles is shown here. It binds to a data source that must contain a field named au_fname and au_lname. This example could be used with the Authors table from the pubs database installed with SQL Server.

```
<asp:DataList id="listAuthor"
     BorderColor="#DEBA84"
     CellSpacing="2"
     BackColor="#DEBA84"
     CellPadding="3"
    runat="server" >

    <HeaderStyle Font-Bold="True" ForeColor="White"
     BackColor="#A55129" />
    <ItemStyle Font-Size="Smaller" Font-Names="Verdana"
     ForeColor="#8C4510"
     BackColor="#FFF7E7" />
    <AlternatingItemStyle BackColor="#FFE0C0" />
```

```
    <HeaderTemplate>
        <h2>Author List</h2>
    </HeaderTemplate>
    <ItemTemplate>
        <b><%# Container.DataItem("au_fname") %>
        <%# Container.DataItem("au_lname") %></b>
    </ItemTemplate>

</asp:DataList>
```

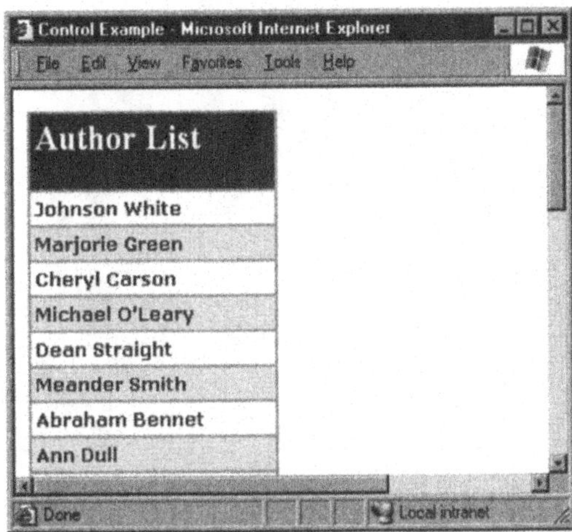

Figure 28-19. The DataList control

DataGrid

The DataGrid displays data in a multicolumn table with a single row for each item. The DataGrid control is the most feature-rich data control, and provides built-in support for selection, editing, paging, and sorting. It's also the only data control that can generate columns automatically without any templates, although you can insert nested Column tags for more precise control.

The format for the DataGrid tag is shown here. Note that the content for the DataGrid control doesn't appear in the .aspx file. Instead, it's set at runtime using data binding, as with all the data controls. Some of the properties shown in the control tag are inherited from the BaseDataList class, and are described in Table 28-34.

```
<asp:DataGrid id="programmaticID"
     AllowPaging="True|False"
     AllowSorting="True|False"
     AutoGenerateColumns="True|False"
     BackImageUrl="url"
     CellPadding="pixels"
     CellSpacing="pixels"
     GridLines="None|Horizontal|Vertical|Both"
     HorizontalAlign="Center|Justify|Left|NotSet|Right"
     PagedDataSource
     PageSize="ItemCount"
     ShowFooter="True|False"
     ShowHeader="True|False"
     runat="server" >

   <AlternatingItemStyle />
   <EditItemStyle />
   <FooterStyle />
   <HeaderStyle />
   <ItemStyle />
   <PagerStyle />
   <SelectedItemStyle />

   <Columns>
      <asp:BoundColumn />
      <asp:ButtonColumn />
      <asp:EditCommandColumn />
      <asp:HyperLinkColumn />
      <asp:TemplateColumn />
   </Columns>

</asp:DataGrid>
```

Table 28-41. DataGrid Members

Member	Description
AllowPaging	If set to True, a subset of the data will be displayed, along with the pager controls. The CurrentPageIndex and PageSize properties determine what data will be displayed.
AllowSorting	If set to True, the column headers will become hyperlinks. When the user clicks one of these hyperlinks, the SortCommand event will occur, and you'll be provided with the SortExpression that has been defined for that column. You must then requery the database and rebind the DataGrid.
AutoGenerateColumns	If set to True, a new BoundColumn will be created for each field in the database when you bind the DataGrid. This will be in addition to any explicitly defined columns defined in the DataGrid tag.

Table 28-41. DataGrid Members (Continued)

Member	Description
BackImageUrl	The location of an image to display "behind" the DataGrid.
Columns	Provides a collection of DataGrid column objects. If the DataGrid columns are generated automatically (by setting the AutoGenerateColumns property to True) this collection will not contain them.
CurrentPageIndex	Gets or sets which page is currently being displayed, if AllowPaging is set to True. The first page has the index 0.
EditItemIndex	Gets or sets the item in the DataGrid control that is currently being edited. To stop editing, set this value to –1. The index number is zero-based, so the first item is at index 0.
Items	Allows you to examine all the items in the DataGrid control as a collection of DataGridItem objects. Because the DataGrid control is data-bound, you cannot directly modify the Items collection.
PageCount	Returns the total number of pages if paging is enabled, based on the PageSize.
PageSize	Gets or sets the number of rows to provide on each page if AllowPaging is True. By default, this value is 10, so a DataSet with 100 rows will require 10 separate page views.
SelectedIndex	Gets or sets the item in the DataGrid control that is currently selected. To clear the selection, set this value to –1. The index number is zero-based, so the first item is at index 0.
SelectedItem	Provides the currently selected item as DataGridItem object.
ShowFooter	If set to True, the footer will be displayed at the bottom of the DataGrid.
ShowHeader	If set to True, the header (column titles) will be displayed at the top of the DataGrid.
EditCommand, CancelCommand, UpdateCommand, and DeleteCommand events	These commands occur when the user clicks the corresponding button. You must handle these events to perform the required data source updating. To allow editing options, you need to have added the appropriate buttons or an EditCommandColumn.
ItemCreated event	Occurs when an item is created and added to the DataList control. The event arguments provide the relevant item as a DataListItem object.
ItemDataBound event	Occurs after an item is data-bound, but before it's rendered on the page. The event arguments provide the relevant item as a DataListItem object.

Table 28-41. DataGrid Members (Continued)

Member	Description
ItemCommand event	Occurs when any button is clicked in the DataList control. (In order for a button to be present, you must have added it in one of the templates.) The event arguments provide the command name associated with the button (CommandName), a reference to the button (CommandSource), and the DataListItem where the button click occurred (Item).
PageIndexChanged event	Occurs when the user clicks one of the pager controls when paging is enabled. You'll receive the NewPageIndex, and you must set the CurrentPageIndex to match and rebind the DataGrid.
SortCommand event	Occurs when the user clicks one of the column hyperlinks when sorting is enabled. You'll receive the column's SortExpression, and you must requery the data source and rebind the DataGrid with the sorted results.

Table 28-42. DataGridItem members

Member	Description
DataItem	Provides the data associated with this item.
ItemIndex	Indicates the numeric (zero-based) index of the item in the DataGrid control.
ItemType	Returns one of the ListItemType enumerated values identifying what template the item is in (such as Header, Footer, Item, SelectedItem, and so on).

You can configure the appearance of the DataGrid using style tags. Each nested style tag specifies the formatting settings that it wants to override. These can include standard WebControl properties such as Font, BackColor, and ForeColor, or some additional properties inherited from the TableItemStyle class, as described in Table 28-24. Note that more than one style may apply to a given item. For example, a selected item will be formatted with the normal ItemStyle and then with the SelectedItemStyle.

Table 28-43. DataGrid Styles

Member	Description
ItemStyle	Defines the formatting for ordinary rows in the grid.
AlternatingItemStyle	If defined, this style is used for the format and layout of every second row. Every odd-numbered row uses the ItemStyle. If not defined, every item uses ItemStyle.
HeaderStyle	Defines the formatting for the header, where the column titles are displayed.
FooterStyle	Defines the formatting of the footer.
SelectedItemStyle	Defines the formatting of the selected item (as determined by the DataGrid.SelectedIndex). If you don't set this style, the user will not be able to distinguish which item is selected.
EditItemStyle	Defines the formatting of the item that is currently being edited (as determined by the DataGrid.EditItemIndex).
PagerStyle	Defines the formatting for the page selection links of the DataGrid control. This is only shown if you're using paging.

If AutoGenerateColumns is True, ASP.NET will automatically create a collection of rows, one for each field in the data source. This default behavior is useful for quick tests, but often isn't suitable for a real application, because it forces you to use default column names, ordering, and sizes, and doesn't allow you the flexibility to add other controls or formatting inside a column.

To define your own columns, add a nested <Column> tag inside the <asp:DataGrid> tag. Then add each column control inside the <Column> tag in the order you want them to appear. You have five column choices, all of which inherit from the DataGrid-Column class described in Table 28-44. Each type of column is described individually.

Table 28-44. DataGridColumn Members

Member	Description
FooterText	A string that defines the text that will be shown in the footer region for this column.
HeaderImageUrl	The location of an image to display in the header region of the column.
HeaderText	A string that defines the text that will be shown in the header region for this column.
SortExpression	The field that will be used for sorting. This field name will be passed to your code through the SortCommand event, at which point you can use it to create a new query.
Visible	Allows you to hide or show the column.

BoundColumn

Each bound column represents a single field from the data source. The data is displayed in ordinary text. If you set the DataGrid to automatically generate its columns, it will create a single BoundColumn for each field in the data source.

```
<asp:BoundColumn
     DataField="DataSourceField"
     DataFormatString="FormatString"
     FooterText="FooterText"
     HeaderImageUrl="url"
     HeaderText="HeaderText"
     ReadOnly="True|False"
     SortExpression ="DataSourceFieldToSortBy"
     Visible="True|False" />
```

Table 28-45. BoundColumn Members

Member	Description
DataField	The name of the field in the data source that will be bound to the column.
DataFormatString	A string that specifies how the data from the field will be formatted. Format strings are particularly useful with numbers, dates, and currency values, and are described in Chapter 15.
ReadOnly	If False, the column will not be converted into a text box for editing, and the user will be able to modify the value. If the DataGrid doesn't contain any edit buttons, this setting will have no effect. The default is False.

ButtonColumn

This displays a column that contains a single button control. One common way to use this column is to add a View or a Details button that automatically navigates to a new window with more information about the selected item.

```
<asp:ButtonColumn
     ButtonType="LinkButton|PushButton"
     Command="CommandName"
     DataTextField="DataSourceField"
     DataTextFormatString="FormatString"
     FooterText="FooterText"
     HeaderImageUrl="url"
     HeaderText="HeaderText"
     Text="ButtonCaption"
     Visible="True|False"/>
```

Table 28-46. ButtonColumn Members

Member	Description
ButtonType	Specifies LinkButton (which looks like a hyperlink) or CommandButton (which looks like a standard button control). The default is CommandButton.
CommandName	A string of text that represents the action that this button performs. Your code can examine the CommandName property, and uses it to distinguish between buttons when one event handler handles several different commands.
DataTextField	This optional property identifies the field in the data source that will be used as a caption for the button.
DataTextFormatString	A string that specifies how the data from the DataTextField will be formatted. Format strings are particularly useful with numbers, dates, and currency values, and are described in Chapter 15.
Text	Specifies the caption for the button. If you set this property, the button for every item in the grid will have the same text. You should set either Text or DataTextField, but not both.

EditCommandColumn

This control displays a column with editing commands. Initially, this column will display a single button with a caption such as "Edit" next to every item. When the user clicks this button, you'll handle the EditCommand event and place the appropriate row in edit mode. At that point, the edited row will display two buttons: a cancel button and an update button.

```
<asp:EditCommandColumn
    ButtonType="LinkButton|PushButton"
    CancelText="CancelButtonCaption"
    EditText="EditButtonCaption"
    FooterText="FooterText"
    HeaderImageUrl="url"
    HeaderText="HeaderText"
    UpdateText="UpdateButtonCaption"
    Visible="True|False"/>
```

Table 28-47. EditCommandColumn Members

Member	Description
ButtonType	Specifies LinkButton (which looks like a hyperlink) or CommandButton (which looks like a standard button control). The default is CommandButton.
CancelText	Specifies the text that appears on the button that cancels editing. This is usually the word "Cancel," but you must set this property, or the cancel button will not be shown.
EditText	Specifies the text that appears on the button that initiates editing. This is usually the word "Edit," but you must set this property, or the edit button will not be shown.
UpdateText	Specifies the text that appears on the button that updates an edited row. This is usually the word "Update," but you must set this property, or the update button will not be shown.

HyperLinkColumn

A hyperlink column allows you to create a hyperlink for each item in the grid. You can create a column that has the same text for every item (such as "View") by setting the Text property, or you can bind the hyperlink column to a field in the data source. You can also bind the URL to a field in the data source. Note that unlike the ButtonColumn, you cannot handle the hyperlink Click event. Instead, the NavigateUrl or DataNavigateUrlField will be used automatically.

```
<asp:HyperLinkColumn
     DataNavigateUrlField="DataSourceField"
     DataNavigateUrlFormatString="FormatExpression"
     DataTextField="DataSourceField"
     DataTextFormatString="FormatExpression"
     FooterText="FooterText"
     HeaderImageUrl="url"
     HeaderText="HeaderText"
     NavigateUrl="url"
     Target="window"
     Text="HyperLinkText"
     Visible="True|False"/>
```

Table 28-48. HyperLinkColumn Members

Member	Description
DataNavigateUrlField	Identifies the field in the data source that will be used as the hyperlink destination. In other words, your data source must provide a field that specifies a web URL. Alternatively, you can set the NavigateUrl property with a constant value.
DataNavigateUrlFormatString	Specifies a format string that will applied to the DataNavigateUrlField.
DataTextField	Identifies the field in the data source that will be used for the text of the link. Alternatively, you can set the Text property with a constant value.
DataTextFormatString	Specifies a format string that will be applied to the DataTextField.
NavigateUrl	The destination URL that the browser will go to when the hyperlink is clicked. If you use this property (instead of DataNavigateUrlField), every item will have the same destination URL.
Target	The target window or frame where the destination page will be opened. This can name a specific frame, or use a special constant such as _blank (for a new window), _parent (the containing frameset), _self (the current window) or _top (the top-level parent).
Text	The text content that the user must click to follow the link. If you use this property (instead of DataTextField), every item will have the same link text.

TemplateColumn

The TemplateColumn is the most flexible type of column, because it allows you to specifically control the appearance of a control (for example, combining more than one field in a column) and the controls that are used to edit it. Using the template column is very similar to using the DataList control: You need to define a separate template for each part of the control. The template contains a mix of data-binding expressions, HTML formatting, and ASP.NET controls.

Note that if you omit the <EditItemTemplate>, the column will be read-only.

```
<asp:TemplateColumn
     FooterText="FooterText"
     HeaderImageUrl="url"
     HeaderText="HeaderText"
     SortExpression="DataSourceFieldToSortBy"
     Visible="True|False">

         <ItemTemplate />
         <HeaderTemplate />
         <FooterTemplate />
         <EditItemTemplate />

</asp:TemplateColumn>
```

Table 28-49. TemplateColumn Templates

Member	**Description**
ItemTemplate	Defines the content and layout of this column for each item in the grid. This is the only required template.
HeaderTemplate	Defines the content of the header portion of this column (the column title). When using this template, you won't set the HeaderText property.
FooterTemplate	Defines the content of the footer portion of this column. When using this template, you won't set the FooterText property.
EditItemTemplate	Defines the content and layout of the column in edit mode. This allows you to specify the controls that will be used by inserting ASP.NET control tags (as shown in Chapter 16).

CHAPTER 29

Configuration Files

CHAPTER 5 INTRODUCED ASP.NET's new configuration system, which revolves around plain-text XML files. This system is a great stride forward from ASP programming—it's easy, multilayered, and supports dynamic updates. Making a modification requires little more than a few minutes with Notepad, and settings come into effect for all new client requests immediately after you make a change. The only ingredient ASP.NET configuration lacks is an attractive graphical tool for configuration—although you'll probably find that the simple text editor approach is refreshingly straightforward.

Chapter 5 provides an overview of ASP.NET's configuration system, and important settings for security, state management, and debugging are discussed throughout the book. This chapter provides a reference and is the best choice when you need one-stop shopping for configuration file information. Every important web.config section is explained concisely and completely.

Configuration Files

ASP.NET has two configuration files. The machine.config file is found in the framework configuration directory C:\[WinDir]\Microsoft.NET\Framework\[Version]\Config, and specifies settings that will be inherited by all the ASP.NET applications hosted by the current computer. This file includes far more information than the standard web.config file, including many options that you won't ever need to inspect or modify. In addition, each web application usually has its own web.config file, which specifies additional settings that override the machine.config defaults.

In fact, an application can use multiple web.config files to configure several layers of configuration. The only rule is that only one web.config file can be used per directory, and every subdirectory inherits the settings from the web.config file of its parent (which, in turn, inherits the machine.config file settings). This multilayered approach means that a web.config can be much shorter and omit unimportant details. Web.config files only need to specify settings that are specific to the application.

More information about the technology behind ASP.NET's configuration files can be found in Chapter 5, along with information about how to add your own custom settings to represent global constants. This chapter focuses exclusively on the standard set of tags.

Configuration File Sections

Both the machine.config and web.config files follow the same format. They use case-sensitive XML, a set of common tags, and camel casing (so section names always begin with a lowercase letter, and use capitals to denote each new word). If you don't want to set a particular setting in a web.config, you can leave out the related tag. However, the structure must always remain constant—if you need to use a subtag, you must also include the parent tag.

The first two levels of a configuration file look like this:

```
<configuration>
   <configSections />
   <system.diagnostics />
   <system.net />
   <system.runtime.remoting />
   <appSettings />
   <system.web />
</configuration>
```

The machine.config file uses <configSections> to specify the section handler classes that will process the configuration files, <system.diagnostics> to configure some low-level debugging options, <system.net> to specify a few network settings, and <system.remoting> to specify options for .NET remoting (a remote object framework used in controlled networks). These sections are never used in a web.config file, don't require any customization, and aren't specific to ASP.NET applications. They aren't described in this chapter.

Out of the other two sections, <appSettings> is only used to create customized, application-specific constants, as described in Chapter 5. An example is shown here. It adds a special global constant that can be used (with the help of the System.Configuration.ConfigurationSettings class) to retrieve the name of an XML file containing product information.

```
<appSettings>
   <add key="ProductCatalog" value="myXmlFileName.xml" />
</appSettings>
```

Using custom settings in this way allows you to create a central repository for application values that could change and shouldn't be embedded directly inside page code. It's similar to using an .ini file or the Windows registry, but it's easier to modify from another computer on the network, and it supports dynamic updates.

The other settings are all located under the <system.web> tag. These include various options that allow you to configure ASP.NET security, tracing, error handling, state management, and much more. Taken together, they represent the heart of ASP.NET configuration.

The following listing shows the hierarchy of <system.web> tags. The rest of the chapter will consider each of these sections, in alphabetical order. For best readability, the following listing doesn't include any of the closing tags, except for the root <configuration> and <system.web> elements. It's meant to provide an at-a-glance overview.

```
<configuration>
   <system.web>

      <authentication>
         <forms>
            <credentials>
         <passport>
      <authorization>
         <allow>
         <deny>
      <browserCaps>
         <result>
         <use>
         <filter>
            <case>
      <compilation>
         <compilers>
            <compiler>
         <assemblies>
            <add>
            <remove>
            <clear>
      <customErrors>
         <error>
      <globalization>
      <httpHandlers>
         <add>
         <remove>
         <clear>
      <httpModules>
         <add>
         <remove>
         <clear>
      <httpRuntime>
      <identity>
      <machineKey>
      <pages>
      <processModel>
      <securityPolicy>
         <trustLevel>
      <sessionState>
      <trace>
```

```
      <trust>
      <webServices>
         <protocols>
            <add>
            <remove>
            <clear>
         <serviceDescriptionFormatExtensionTypes>
            <add>
            <remove>
            <clear>
         <soapExtensionTypes>
            <add>
         <soapExtensionReflectorTypes>
            <add>
         <soapExtensionImporterTypes>
            <add>
         <WsdlHelpGenerator>

   </system.web>
</configuration>
```

<authentication>

This section allows you to configure the type of mechanism used to authenticate a user. Authentication is the process whereby your application verifies that a user is who he or she claims to be. These settings work in conjunction with the <authorization> section settings, which specify the permissions and restrictions for a specific user or user type, and the IIS security settings, which take effect before the request is processed by the ASP.NET application. The interactions between these different layers of security are a common source of confusion for new web developers, and are described in detail in Chapter 25.

```
<authentication mode="Windows|Forms|Passport|None">
   <forms name="name"
          loginUrl="url"
          protection="All|None|Encryption|Validation"
          timeout="30" path="/" >
      <credentials passwordFormat="Clear|SHA1|MD5">
         <user name="username" password="password" />
      </credentials>
   </forms>
   <passport redirectUrl="internal"/>
</authentication>
```

The <authentication> tag identifies the type of authorization. There are four supported options.

Table 29-1. <authentication> Attributes

Attribute Setting	Description
Mode="Windows"	Windows authentication is typically used in one of two ways. You can use it to configure IIS to allow anonymous access to all users. This option is similar to previous ASP applications, and not much different from setting the ASP.NET authentication mode to "None." Alternatively, you can configure IIS to use Basic, Digest, or Integrated Windows authentication (NTLM/Kerberos), or certificates to authenticate each user. This system is typically best in an intranet (network) scenario with a limited set of known users, rather than a public web application.
Mode="Forms"	Forms authentication allows you to use a custom login page with your own authentication code. ASP.NET handles the underlying security management, automatically maintains a cookie that tracks whether the user has been logged in, and automatically reroutes the user to your login page if the cookie isn't present or is expired.
Mode="Passport"	Passport authentication uses Microsoft's Passport authentication service. It's similar to Forms authentication in that the user needs to sign in at a dedicated login page (although newer versions of Windows can perform this step automatically) and is tracked using a cookie. However, you don't handle any aspect of the login process.
Mode="None"	No authentication. All users are allowed, although you could secure specific pages with your own authentication code.

If you're using Forms authentication, the <forms> tag provides several additional customization options.

Table 29-2. <forms> Attributes

Attribute Setting	Description
Name	The name of the HTTP cookie to use for authentication. (By default, the value of name is .ASPXAUTH.) If multiple applications are running on the same web server and each application requires a unique cookie, you must configure the cookie name in each application's web.config file. Otherwise, you can use the default.
loginUrl	Your custom login page, where the user is redirected if no valid authentication cookie is found. The default value is default.aspx.
protection="All"	The application uses both data validation and encryption to protect the forms authentication cookie. This option uses the configured data validation algorithm and Triple-DES or DES for encryption. This is the default (and recommended) value.
protection="None"	Encryption and validation are disabled for the cookie. This is much less secure (but potentially faster) and is typically only used if you use authentication for simple personalization.
protection="Encryption"	The cookie will be encrypted using Triple-DES or DES, but data validation isn't performed on the cookie.
protection="Validation"	Validation is used to verify that the contents of an encrypted cookie haven't been altered in transit.
timeout	An integer that specifies the number of minutes before the cookie expires, if no page requests have been received. ASP.NET will refresh the cookie when it receives a request, as long as half of the cookie's lifetime has expired. The default value is 30.
Path	The path for cookies issued by the application. The default value (\) is recommended, because most browsers are case-sensitive and a path case-mismatch could restrict the cookie from being sent with the request.

The <forms> tag also has a <credentials> subtag used to store the login information for users. You don't need to store user information here. For example, you could use database-based authentication in your custom login page, which would be better suited to handle a large number of users or track additional user information (such as credit card number or home address).

Table 29-3. <credentials> Attributes

Attribute Setting	Description
passwordFormat="Clear"	Passwords aren't encrypted.
passwordFormat="MD5"	Passwords are encrypted using the MD5 hash algorithm.
passwordFormat="SHA1"	Passwords are encrypted using the SHA1 hash algorithm.

Add as many <user> attributes as you need, one for each separate login ID.

Table 29-4. <user> Attributes

Attribute Setting	Description
Name	The account's user name.
password	The account's password.

If you're using Passport authentication, you can configure the <passport> subtag of the <authentication> tag.

Table 29-5. <passport> Attributes

Attribute Setting	Description
redirectUrl	The web page where the user is redirected to if the user requires authentication and hasn't signed on with Microsoft Passport. This could be a specially configured page on your site or the Passport site.
redirectUrl="internal"	Using the word "internal" indicates that you have the Passport service installed on your server, and allows ASP.NET to use it for user authentication automatically. If it hasn't been configured and the user isn't already logged in, an error message will be shown.

<authorization>

The <authorization> group is a list of access rules that either allow or deny a particular type of user. At runtime, ASP.NET searches through the list of <authorization> elements from top to bottom, until it can match the currently authenticated user with a suitable access rule. If there's more than one match, it uses the first one it finds. If it can't find any match, it will allow access to the requested resource, because the default authorization in the machine.config file is set to <allow users="*"/> (unless you modify it). ASP.NET will read this rule last.

```
<authorization>
   <allow users="list of users"
          roles="list of roles"
          verbs="list of verbs" />
   <deny users="list of users"
         roles="list of roles"
         verbs="list of verbs" />
</authorization>
```

The asterisk (*) is a wildcard that means "all users." The question mark (?) is a wildcard that means "all anonymous users." Thus, a simple way to force users to log in with the specified authentication service is to add a single <deny> rule for anonymous users. To allow only a certain type of user, add an <allow> rule followed by <deny users="*" /> to deny all other users. There are also more complicated options to allow or deny certain users; these are discussed in Chapter 25 along with some specific examples.

Table 29-6. <allow> and <deny> Attributes

Attribute Setting	Description
users	A comma-separated list of user names that are allowed/denied access to the resource.
roles	A comma-separated list of roles that are allowed/denied access to the resource.
verbs	A comma-separated list of HTTP transmission methods that are allowed/denied access to the resource. Verbs registered to ASP.NET include GET, HEAD, POST, and DEBUG.

<browserCaps>

This section replaces the browscap.ini file from traditional ASP programming. It specifies the set of default browser capabilities that will be assumed if ASP.NET cannot detect the client browser's capabilities. This is becoming a fairly unusual event, but can still occur for unknown or unsupported types of browsers. These default values will be returned by the HttpBrowserCapabilities class (which is exposed as the Request.Browser property of a web page).

```
<browserCaps>
   <result type="System.Web.HttpBrowserCapabilities, System.Web" />
   <use var="HTTP_USER_AGENT" />
        browser=Unknown
        version=0.0
        majorver=0
        minorver=0
        frames=false
        tables=false
    <filter>
        <case match="[regular expression]"
         with="[regular expression]" >
            browser=Unknown
            version=0.0
            majorver=0
            minorver=0
            frames=false
            tables=false
        </case>
    </filter>
</browserCaps>
```

The <use> subtag identifies the various default settings, which are fairly self-evident. The <result> subtag identifies the ASP.NET class where the resulting information will be stored and made available to your application, and should never need to be changed. In addition, you can use <filter> subtags as an advanced option to try and identify unknown browsers. Each <filter> subtag specifies a regular expression, which ASP.NET will use to interpret the browser's User-Agent string in order to try and "guess" what type of browser sent the request and apply additional settings. This is a tricky and rarely used option.

<compilation>

This section specifies the compile options for ASP.NET applications, and should be configured at the machine.config level, rather than in individual web.config files. These options are less important if you're using Visual Studio .NET, which can set its own command-line options for compilation according to the project settings. Typically, you won't modify this section yourself.

```
<compilation debug="true|false"
             defaultLanguage="language"
             explicit="true|false"
             strict="true|false"
             tempDirectory="directory for temporary files" >
   <compilers>
      <compiler language="language"
                extension="ext"
                type="TypeName"
                warningLevel="number"
                compilerOptions="options" />
   </compilers>
```

```
   <assemblies>
      <add assembly="assembly" />
      <remove assembly="assembly"  />
      <clear />
   </assemblies>
</compilation>
```

The <compilation> tag specifies some basic compilation options. A few low-level settings have been omitted.

Table 29-7. <compilation> Attributes

Attribute Setting	Description
Debug	When set to True, debug symbols will be generated for testing your application in every compilation. The default is False, which is required for respectable performance. Visual Studio .NET, which allows you to test your application with a precompiled code-behind class, circumvents this settings.
DefaultLanguage	The default programming language, which is defined in an appropriate <compiler> subtag. The default is vb, for Visual Basic .NET.
Explicit	Indicates the default setting of Option Explicit in Visual Basic. The default is True, which forces you to declare all variables before using them.
Strict	Indicates the setting of the Option Strict option for Visual Basic, which is False by default. You can override this in your code-behind files with the Option Strict statement and provide enhanced type safety.
TempDirectory	The directory used for temporary file storage during compilation.

The <compilers> tag specifies the individual compilers used for each supported .NET language, what types of files the compiler is responsible for, and what additional options are required. This section is configured at install time and shouldn't need to be changed. However, it's interesting to note that the language compiler is just another .NET class—meaning that the ASP.NET engine can easily handle other .NET-compatible languages, as long as they ship with suitable compiler classes.

In the case of Visual Basic, the Microsoft.VisualBasic.VBCodeProvider class is used.

```
<compiler language="vb;vbs;visualbasic;vbscript"
          extension=".vb"
          type="Microsoft.VisualBasic.VBCodeProvider,
                System, Version=1.0.5000.0,
                Culture=neutral, PublicKeyToken=b77a5c561934e089"/>
```

The <assemblies> tag references assemblies that will be required when compiling an ASP.NET page. You can also precompile your code-behind files, and reference additional assemblies at compilation time as command-line parameters, as explained in Chapter 5.

<customErrors>

This section (described in Chapter 11) allows you to configure how ASP.NET deals with errors. Depending on your settings, ASP.NET may report detailed error information, or it may redirect the user to a web page that contains a custom error message (and any other support information). Possible errors include unhandled application exceptions in your web page code and HTTP server errors. You can supplement these settings by configuring IIS error redirect settings, which will take effect for web server errors that aren't handled by ASP.NET (such as a user request for an .html page that doesn't exist).

```
<customErrors defaultRedirect="url"
              mode="On|Off|RemoteOnly">
   <error statusCode="statuscode"
          redirect="url"/>
</customErrors>
```

The <customErrors> tag configures the error mode and specifies the default behavior for unhandled exceptions.

Table 29-8. <customErrors> Attributes

Attribute Setting	Description
defaultRedirect	Specifies the default web page that will be shown if an error occurs. If defaultRedirect isn't specified, an ASP.NET-generated error page is shown instead.
mode="On"	Custom errors are enabled. If an error occurs, and no defaultRedirect page is specified, users will see a generic error page.
mode="Off"	Custom errors are disabled. If an error occurs, and no defaultRedirect page is specified, users will see a detailed error page with diagnostic information about the code where the problem occurred.
mode="RemoteOnly"	Custom errors are only shown to remote clients. If an error occurs when serving a local request, the rich error page is used. This option, which helps when debugging locally, is the default.

You can also add as many <error> subtags as needed. Each <error> tag specifically identifies an HTTP server error, and a custom error page that will be used if it occurs.

Table 29-9. <error> Attributes

Attribute Setting	Description
statusCode	The HTTP error code that will cause redirection.
redirect	The custom error page that will be used for this HTTP error.

<globalization>

The settings in this section allow you to configure culture and encoding options for multiple client languages. Strictly speaking, these settings don't need to be defined. Without them, the default machine.config file settings will be used, and any property that isn't declared there will be set according to the server's regional settings (check the Regional and Language Options settings in the Control Panel).

```
<globalization requestEncoding="any valid encoding string"
               responseEncoding="any valid encoding string"
               fileEncoding="any valid encoding string"
               culture="any valid culture string"
               uiCulture="any valid culture string" />
```

Fine-tuning globalization settings is beyond the scope of this book. However, if you've programmed multilingual sites before, you'll already be familiar with culture settings and string encodings. The only difference is the location where you configure these settings.

<httpHandlers>

This section allows you to map incoming URL requests to the specific classes that can handle these requests. These settings are similar to the file mapping in IIS, but they take effect later. When IIS receives a request, it first checks it against its list of registered file mappings (which is configured in IIS Manager). If the extension is mapped to aspnet_isapi.dll, IIS passes the request to ASP.NET, which then checks the file type against its list of recognized HttpHandlers.

```
<httpHandlers>
   <add verb="verb list"
        path="path/wildcard"
        type="type,assemblyname"
        validate="" />
   <remove verb="verb list"
          path="path/wildcard" />
   <clear />
</httpHandlers>
```

The machine.config configures several default HttpHandlers. A short list of some of the most important ones is shown here.

```
<httpHandlers>
   <add verb="*" path="trace.axd"
    type="System.Web.Handlers.TraceHandler"/>
   <add verb="*" path="*.aspx"
    type="System.Web.UI.PageHandlerFactory"/>
   <add verb="*" path="*.asmx"
    type="System.Web.Services.Protocols.WebServiceHandlerFactory" />
      <add verb="*" path="*.config"
    type="System.Web.HttpForbiddenHandler"/>
   <add verb="*" path="*.vb"
    type="System.Web.HttpForbiddenHandler"/>
</httpHandlers>
```

As you can see, file types are mapped to .NET classes. (You won't actually see these classes in the class library reference, however, because they're marked private and hidden by default, and because they can't be used in an application.) For example, all .aspx files are processed by the System.Web.UI.PageHandlerFactory, which transforms them into the familiar System.Web.UI.Page classes (a "factory" is object-oriented lingo for a class that produces other classes). Similarly, System.Web.Services.Protocols.WebServiceHandlerFactory handles web service requests, and various forbidden files, such as .config and .vb, are handled by the System.Web.HttpForbiddenHandler, which does little more than refuse the request.

If you want, you can create your own HttpHandler classes by implementing the System.Web.IHttpHandler interface, and use them to create simple CGI-like applications. Custom HttpHandlers are useful in some situations in which you don't need ASP.NET's web page model—for example, if you just need a mechanism to let clients retrieve a dynamically modified binary file. However, for most programmers this effort isn't worthwhile and seems like a giant step backward to the old world of Internet programming.

Table 29-10. <add> and <remove> Attributes

Attribute Setting	Description
verb	Either a comma-separated list of HTTP verbs (for example, "GET, POST") or an asterisk (*) to represent all.
path	Either a single URL path or a simple wildcard string (like "*.aspx").
type	A comma-separated combination of the class followed by the assembly. ASP.NET searches for the assembly DLL first in the application's private \bin directory and then in the system assembly cache. You can use unmanaged DLLs to replicate file-mapping functionality like that in the IIS Manager settings, but it isn't recommended.
validate	If set to False, ASP.NET will not attempt to load the class until it receives a request for the registered file type, which can improve startup time (but may hide possible errors until later).

<httpModules>

This section allows you to configure HttpModules, special classes that will be automatically loaded and made available for each request. ASP.NET uses modules to provide support for security, caching, and session state management.

```
<httpModules>
   <add type="classname,assemblyname" name="modulename" />
   <remove name="modulename" />
   <clear />
</httpModules>
```

The machine.config file defines the basic set of HttpModules.

```
<httpModules>
   <add name="OutputCache"
        type="System.Web.Caching.OutputCacheModule"/>
   <add name="Session"
        type="System.Web.SessionState.SessionStateModule"/>
   <add name="WindowsAuthentication"
        type="System.Web.Security.WindowsAuthenticationModule"/>
   <add name="FormsAuthentication"
        type="System.Web.Security.FormsAuthenticationModule"/>
   <add name="PassportAuthentication"
        type="System.Web.Security.PassportAuthenticationModule"/>
   <add name="UrlAuthorization"
        type="System.Web.Security.UrlAuthorizationModule"/>
   <add name="FileAuthorization"
        type="System.Web.Security.FileAuthorizationModule"/>
</httpModules>
```

You can create your own modules by writing classes that implement the System.Web.IHttpModule interface. This could be a highly advanced technique to create a special security, caching, or authentication service that works at a lower level than a typical ASP.NET application.

Table 29-11. <add> or <remove> Attributes

Attribute Setting	Description
name	Provides a "friendly name" for the module. This is the name that will be used for the event handlers in the global.asax file.
type	A comma-separated combination of the class, followed by the assembly. ASP.NET searches for the assembly DLL first in the application's private \bin directory and then in the system assembly cache.

<httpRuntime>

This section configures some miscellaneous HTTP runtime settings. These are similar to the ASP settings that are configured through IIS Manager (for example, they set the maximum number of requests and request timeout).

Table 29-12. <httpRuntime> Attributes

Attribute Setting	Description
appRequestQueueLimit	Sets the maximum number of requests that ASP.NET will queue at a time. When the limit is reached, incoming requests will be rejected with a "503 – Server Too Busy" error.
executionTimeout	Sets the maximum number of seconds that a request is allowed before ASP.NET shuts it down automatically.
maxRequestLength	Sets the maximum size for uploaded files. This is an important factor when using the HtmlInputFile control (as described in Chapter 17). You shouldn't set this limit too high, however, or it will expose you to possible denial-of-service attacks.
minFreeLocalRequestFreeThreads	The minimum number of free threads ASP.NET reserves (that is, keeps available) for requests from the local computer.
minFreeThreads	ASP.NET will keep this many threads free for current requests that require additional threads to complete their processing.
useFullyQualifiedRedirectUrl	Specifies if URL redirects are fully qualified (which is necessary for some mobile controls). Relative redirects are the default.

<identity>

You can use this section to specify a Windows user account under which your code will run. If you don't enable impersonation, ASP.NET code will automatically run under the account that's configured in the <processModel> section. By default, this will be the special ASPNET account, which has a set of carefully limited privileges.

You have two options with the <identity> section. You can configure all users to run under a set user account, or you can allow all users to authenticate themselves individually, and run under their own user accounts. To take the first approach, set the impersonate attribute to false, and then enter the userName and password for the account. To take the second approach, leave out the userName and password attributes, and set the impersonate attribute to true. In the latter case, you should also configure the IIS virtual directory settings so that users will be forced to authenticate themselves, as described in Chapter 25.

```
<identity impersonate="true|false"
          userName="username"
          password="password"/>
```

Generally, impersonation is enabled so the programmer can avoid dealing with authentication and authorization issues in code. Instead, when impersonation is enabled, the operating system will permit or restrict access to certain resources (such as files) based on the authenticated IIS user account. Note that even when impersonation is enabled, the local system process account will still be used to compile the code and create the cached pages. Only the application code will execute under the impersonated account. However, as a bare minimum, an account requires read-write access to the "Temporary ASP.NET files" directory where the compiled ASP.NET files are stored, or it won't be able to run any pages.

NOTE The <identity> tag is completely separate from the application's trust level (defined in the <trust> tag), which effectively sets the maximum permissions that any user will have in an ASP.NET application.

Table 29-13. <identity> Attributes

Attribute Setting	Description
impersonate	When True, ASP.NET will run under the identity provided by IIS. This could be a user-specific account or a generic anonymous user (typically IUSR_[servername] as in traditional ASP). When set to False, impersonation isn't used, and the typical ASP.NET system account is used to execute requests.
username and password	When impersonate is set to True, you can override the IIS identity by specifying a user name and password.

<machineKey>

ASP.NET uses a machine-specific key to encode some data (such as the forms authentication cookie and view state data) so that it can only be accessed from the server that created it.

```
<machineKey validationKey="autogenerate|value"
            decryptionKey="autogenerate|value"
            validation="SHA1|MD5|3DES" />
```

In general, you can allow ASP.NET to automatically generate these key values. However, this will cause problems in multiserver scenarios (such as a web farm) where one server might handle a request at one moment and another server will handle it later. In this case, you must manually set the same keys on all web severs.

Table 29-14. <machineKey> Attributes

Attribute Setting	Description
validationKey	Specifies the key used to validate data. Can be a hard-coded string of 40-128 hexadecimal characters (the longer the better) or the value AutoGenerate, which indicates that ASP.NET will create it automatically (the default).
decryptionKey	Specifies the key used to encrypt data. Can be a hard-coded string of 40-128 hexadecimal characters (the longer the better) or the value AutoGenerate, which indicates that ASP.NET will create it automatically (the default).
validation="SHA1"	ASP.NET will use SHA1 hashing.
validation="MD5"	ASP.NET will use MD5 hashing.
validation="3DES"	ASP.NET will use Triple-DES (3DES) encryption. When 3DES is selected, forms authentication defaults to SHA1, and view state validation uses 3DES encryption.

<pages>

This section allows you to configure some miscellaneous settings that determine how pages are created and served.

```
<pages buffer="true|false"
       enableSessionState="true|false|ReadOnly"
       enableViewState="true|false"
       enableViewStateMac="true|false"
       autoEventWireup="true|false"
       smartNavigation="true|false"
       pageBaseType="typename, assembly"
       userControlBaseType="typename" />
```

Table 29-15. <pages> Attributes

Attribute Setting	Description
buffer	When a response is buffered, transmission of the page to the client won't be initiated until the page is completely rendered. This is the default.
enableSessionState	Enables or disables session state.
ReadOnly	If True, web pages can read but not modify session state variables.
enableViewState	Enables or disables viewstate, which allows controls to store their state across postbacks using a special hidden field. As a more flexible option, you can allow viewstate (the default) but disable viewstate use for specific controls on a specific web page.

Table 29-15. <pages> Attributes (Continued)

Attribute Setting	Description
pageBaseType	A code-behind class that web forms (.aspx pages) derive from automatically. By default, this is System.Web.UI.Page.
userControlBaseType	A code-behind class that user controls (.ascx files) derive from automatically. By default, this is System.Web.UI.UserControl.
autoEventWireup	When set to True, can connect web page events automatically (without the need for a Handles clause). This can also be configured using a page-level directive, as explained in Chapter 5.

<processModel>

This section stores a number of low-level settings that govern how the ASP.NET service works. Advanced users could use these settings to configure optimum performance for a specific hardware setup, but the default options are usually best. The <processModel> tag settings apply to all ASP.NET web applications on the server, and it's always entered in the machine.config file, not a web.config file.

```
<processModel enable="true|false"
              timeout="mins"
              idleTimeout="mins"
              shutdownTimeout="hrs:mins:secs"
              requestLimit="num"
              requestQueueLimit="Infinite|num"
              restartQueueLimit="Infinite|num"
              memoryLimit="percent"
              cpuMask="num"
              webGarden="true|false"
              userName="username"
              password="password"
              logLevel="All|None|Errors"
              clientConnectedCheck="HH:MM:SS"
              comAuthenticationLevel="Default|None|Connect|Call|
                                      Pkt|PktIntegrity|PktPrivacy"
              comImpersonationLevel="Default|Anonymous|Identify|
                                     Impersonate|Delegate"
              maxWorkerThreads="num"
              maxIoThreads="num" />
```

The most important attributes are userName and password, which set the user account that will be used to run all ASP.NET code. For example, if you set userName to userA (and set the password accordingly), all your web page and web service code will run as though it's logged in under the userA account. Your code will not be able to perform any task that userA would not be allowed to do, such as writing to certain files, accessing the registry, retrieving data from a database, and so on.

ASP.NET also recognizes two special accounts, which are described in Table 29-16.

- **The ASPNET account.** This is a limited account that is created when ASP.NET is installed. It's used by default. To use the ASPNET account, you must set userName to Machine and password to AutoGenerate.
- **The local system account.** This account has a wide range of administrator-level privileges for the local computer. To use the local system account, you must set userName to System and password to AutoGenerate.

Table 29-16. userName Values

userName	Description
Machine	This uses the limited ASPNET account that is created when ASP.NET is installed. It's used by default. To use the ASPNET account, you must set userName to Machine and password to AutoGenerate.
System	This uses the local system account, which has a wide range of administrator-level privileges for the local computer. To use the local system account, you must set userName to System and password to AutoGenerate.

TIP If you're using impersonation (as configured by the <identity> tag), it will override the default account you set in the <processModel> tag. See Chapter 25 for more information.

Most of the other settings are beyond the scope of an ordinary web application. The most important or interesting ones are documented in Table 29-17.

Table 29-17. <processModel> Attributes

Attribute Setting	Description
enable	Determines whether ASP.NET should run in a separate worker process (True, the default) or in-process with IIS (False). When set to False, all other settings are ignored, and your web applications may be slightly faster (although if one crashes, they may all be affected).
timeout	Determines how long the process will run before it's recycled (a new process is created and the old one terminated). The default values is Infinite, although you can specify a time in the format HH:MM:SS.
idleTimeout	Similar to the timeout setting, but takes effect when the ASP.NET worker process is idle. The default is Infinite.

Table 29-17. <processModel> Attributes (Continued)

Attribute Setting	Description
shutDownTimeout	This sets the amount of time the ASP.NET worker process is given to try and shut down gracefully before it's assumed to be "locked up," and the process is terminated. By default, this value is only 5 seconds.
requestLimit	Provides another way to support ASP.NET worker-process recycling. For example, if you notice that the performance of ASP.NET degrades after about 10,000 requests, you can set this value to 10000. After 10,000 requests, a new process will be started to handle the new requests and the old process will be terminated.
requestQueueLimit	This allows the ASP.NET process to be recycled if a certain number of queued requests is detected. This could detect that a thread is blocked or unable to service requests because of an error. The default is a fairly generous 5,000 queued requests.
memoryLimit	This provides automatic memory recycling if too much memory is used. The default value of 60 isn't a value in megabytes, but a percentage of the total system memory. Memory "leaks" are almost impossible with managed .NET code, but could still be a problem if you're using legacy COM components that don't properly clean up after themselves.
userName and Password	Can be used to specify the account that the ASP.NET worker process runs under. This determines the permissions that your web page code will have. The default is the special account ASPNET.
logLevel	Configures how ASP.NET logs events. The default is Errors, which only records information about errors that occur. All entries are written to the Windows event log, which was explained in Chapter 11.
clientConnectedCheck	Allows you to configure how often ASP.NET checks if the client is still connected. For example, during a long running task the client might hit the Refresh button to start a new request, but leave the current request processing. ASP.NET can save some effort by detecting that these requests have been abandoned and then aborting the unneeded work. By default, ASP.NET will check every five seconds.

NOTE If you're using Windows Server 2003, and IIS 6 is set to worker process isolation mode, these settings will not be used. Instead, similar settings can be configured directly in IIS Manager utility.

<securityPolicy>

This section maps named security levels to specific policy files. These definitions can then be used in other sections. For example, the <trust> section specifies the code access security level for your ASP.NET code by referring to one of the defined trust levels in the <securityPolicy> section.

```
<securityPolicy>
   <trustLevel name="value" policyFile="value" />
</securityPolicy>
```

By default the machine.config file defines four levels of authorization, named Full, High, Low, and None. Each option is mapped to a security policy file (except for Full).

```
<securityPolicy>
   <trustLevel name="Full" policyFile="internal"/>
   <trustLevel name="High" policyFile="web_hightrust.config"/>
   <trustLevel name="Low" policyFile="web_lowtrust.config"/>
   <trustLevel name="None" policyFile="web_notrust.config"/>
</securityPolicy>
```

These files provide an extensive set of options and are also found in the Config directory. You can create your own security configuration files and define your own <trustLevel> tags.

Table 29-18. <trustLevel> Attributes

Attribute Setting	Description
name	The name of the security level.
policyFile	The security policy file that contains the settings for this security level.

<sessionState>

This section configures how session state information will be stored. There are typically two reasons for modifying the default values in this section—to provide a longer or shorted session timeout, or to configure a different session state management method in order to support a web farm setup.

```
<sessionState mode="Off|Inproc|StateServer|SQLServer"
              cookieless="true|false"
              timeout="number of minutes"
              stateConnectionString="tcpip=server:port"
              sqlConnectionString="sql connection string" />
```

Session state management is explored in Chapter 10, along with some common-sense advice about how to use it. Note that in order to enable a different type of session management, you may need to perform a few extra steps beyond just modifying the appropriate web.config file. These steps are described in Chapter 10.

Table 29-19. <sessionState> Attributes

Attribute Setting	Description
mode="Off"	Session state isn't enabled.
mode="Inproc"	Session state is stored on the web server in the same process as the ASP.NET worker threads. This provides the best performance by far and is the default setting.
mode="StateServer"	Session state is out-of-process and maintained by a dedicated service. This service can be hosted on any server, which allows multiple servers in a web farm to access the same session collection for a client.
mode="SQLServer"	Session state is stored in a temporary SQL Server database. This also allows multiple servers to access the same session state collection, and allows session state information to persist even if the server is rebooted.
cookieless	When set to False, a cookie is automatically used to track a client session. This is the default. When True, munged URLs are used to encode the session ID in web links.
timeout	The number of minutes a session can be idle before it's abandoned (that is, the maximum amount of time that can be taken between client requests without losing session data). The default is 20 minutes.
stateConnectionString	When StateServer mode is used, this attribute specifies the server name and port where session state is stored (such as "tcpip=127.0.0.1:42424").
sqlConnectionString	When SQLServer mode is used, this attribute specifies the database connection string (such as "data source=127.0.0.1;user id=sa").

<trace>

This section configures tracing, which is useful when debugging and testing an application. When tracing is enabled, a long list of diagnostic information about a web page request is recorded.

```
<trace enabled="true|false"
       localOnly="true|false"
       pageOutput="true|false"
       requestLimit="integer"
       traceMode="SortByTime|SortByCategory" />
```

Tracing can be used in two ways: with output shown on every page or with output available through a special web page. Tracing is explored in Chapter 11.

Table 29-20. <trace> Attributes

Attribute Setting	Description
enabled	Specifies whether tracing is enabled for an application. The default is False.
localOnly	True if tracing information is only available on the host web server (the default). When set to False, you can use remote tracing to debug or profile a deployed application.
pageOutput	True if tracing output is appended to each page. False if tracing information is only available through the trace utility (which is accessed by requesting trace.axd).
requestLimit	The number of trace requests to store on the server at any one time. The default is 10.
traceMode="SortByTime"	Trace information is displayed in the order it's processed. This is the default.
traceMode="SortByCategory"	Trace information is displayed alphabetically by user-defined category.

<trust>

This section configures the code-access security level for a web application. This determines the trust level under which your code will run. For example, if you limit the trust level for your code, certain operations (such as deleting files or interacting with the system) may not be allowed.

```
<trust level="Full|High|Low|None" />
```

By default, application code has Full trust level, and the operations of your code aren't checked against any security policy settings.

Table 29-21. <trust> Attributes

Attribute Setting	Description
level="Full"	The Full level is the only level that doesn't use any security policy file to apply limitations.
level="High|Low|None"	These three options refer to the security levels defined in the <trustLevel> subtag in the <securityPolicy> section. For example, level="High" would apply the security restrictions from the "High" level policy file.

<webServices>

This section configures Web Service settings, such as the type of supported transmission protocols and the classes that provide various pieces of web service functionality. These settings are defined at the machine.config level and shouldn't be modified.

The sole exception is the <WsdlHelpGenerator> subtag, which allows you to specify a custom page to use for the Internet Explorer Web Service test page.

```
<wsdlHelpGenerator href="DefaultWsdlHelpGenerator.aspx"/>
```

To create a custom version of this file, copy the standard DefaultWsdlHelpGenerator.aspx file (which is found in the C:\[WinDir]\Microsoft.NET\Framework\[Version]\Config directory along with the machine.config file), and modify the appropriate settings. For example, you could add a special company logo or header by adding custom HTML elements or ASP.NET controls to this page.

Index

Symbols

A

B

D

E

G

H

I

J

K

L

M

N

O

P

S

T

U

W

X

Y

Z

Printed in the United States
By Bookmasters